Handbook of Adult Development and Learning

HANDBOOK OF
ADULT DEVELOPMENT
AND LEARNING

Edited by
Carol Hoare

OXFORD
UNIVERSITY PRESS

2006

OXFORD
UNIVERSITY PRESS

Oxford University Press, Inc., publishes works that further Oxford University's
objective of excellence in research, scholarship, and education.

Oxford   New York
Auckland   Cape Town   Dar es Salaam   Hong Kong   Karachi
Kuala Lumpur   Madrid   Melbourne   Mexico City   Nairobi
New Delhi   Shanghai   Taipei   Toronto

With offices in
Argentina   Austria   Brazil   Chile   Czech Republic   France   Greece
Guatemala   Hungary   Italy   Japan   Poland   Portugal   Singapore
South Korea   Switzerland   Thailand   Turkey   Ukraine   Vietnam

Published by Oxford University Press, Inc.
198 Madison Avenue, New York, New York 10016

www.oup.com

Oxford is a registered trademark of Oxford University Press

Library of Congress Cataloging-in-Publication Data
Handbook of adult development and learning / edited by Carol Hoare.
p. cm.
Includes bibliographical references and index.
ISBN-13: 978-0-19-517190-7
ISBN-10: 0-19-517190-X
1. Adulthood—Psychological aspects. 2. Learning, Psychology of.
3. Adult learning. I. Hoare, Carol Hren.
BF724.5.I58 2006
155.6—mdc22   2005014219

1 3 5 7 9 8 6 4 2

Printed in the United States of America
on acid-free paper

To Jenny and Ray—
Two wonderful children who are everything their Dad and I
always thought they would be—and more.

In memory of my loving parents and grandparents—
Mary Ann Matesevac Hren and Frank J. Hren,
Mary Elizabeth Horvath Matesevac and Michael S.(Buddy) Matesevac,
without whom . . .

Preface

The idea for this handbook began about 15 years ago when I started teaching concurrent graduate courses in adult development and adult learning. Rather quickly, material from one course bled into the other, and it soon became clear that it was artificial to consider adults in their development without including learning and equally artificial to treat adults as learners while suspending developmental attributes. At some point, I stopped trying to keep learning and development apart and integrated the two. As a result, this book came slowly into focus. In early 2003, Catharine Carlin of Oxford University Press encouraged me to consider editing a handbook on adult development, but then graciously acquiesced to a proposal for this integrated volume. Thus, the design of what is now in hand took root.

At the outset, I emphasize that the purpose of the volume is not to introduce a subfield in which one discipline is central and the other subordinate, but to begin what must become a conceptual integration of adult development and learning. Too quickly, the human mind arranges material hierarchically in its mental file cabinet, and whether by preference or training, certain content and concepts become subordinate to others. That is not the intent of this text. Rather, the authors of this volume open the door to the possibility of a broader space in which many of the constructs we entertain separately—adult insight, intelligence, cognition, reflective thinking, interpersonal competence, self-efficacy, and others—are eventually known as a web in which development sponsors learning and learning fuels development.

The contributors to this volume offer rich theories, analyses, research reviews, practical applications, and conceptual itineraries. I roundly applaud their interest and sustained efforts. It is difficult to force one's thinking into boundaries, particularly when the intersecting disciplines are themselves rather young. Thus, each of us knows that an encyclopedic account of the many potential ways in which there is synchrony, or perhaps causal reciprocity, between learning and development is not yet possible. Yet we share a hardy conviction that adults grow and learn in unison. The internal and external contexts of adult life provide rich resources for learning and developmental change; although the great wealth of this territory is largely unexplored, we are pleased to risk stepping into its frontier.

Writing from different frames of reference and levels of analysis, each author considers the topical area of his or her considerable study. Clearly, the topics do not cover the complete landscape of adult development and learning. But together they do point toward a potentially unified discipline of theory, inquiry, and practice. If this volume stimulates greater dialogue among those working within the respective disciplines of adult development and learning, it will prove useful. If it results in established, reciprocal connections between development and learning in adulthood and in synchronous theory, research, and practice in these currently dissociated disciplines, it will have been successful. We step briskly toward a future in which it is obvious that as we learn, so shall we develop, and as we develop, so are we better equipped to continually learn.

Acknowledgments

I am indebted to many persons who were vital in bringing this volume to completion. The few words I offer here are only a small tribute to their talents, work, and support. Without their commitment, this project would surely have faltered.

First, I thank each of the authors who contributed to this volume. Their contributions to thought are apparent in their individual histories of publication, research, and teaching, as well as in their chapters here. Some put aside their own work to write for this handbook, and I am most grateful. All were gracious in the revision process, some willingly rewriting several times to better address the juncture of development and learning.

Bridget Cooper was at my side from the beginning. I am deeply grateful to her. Her initiative, resourcefulness, and commitment made her much more than a research associate. Many were the times that she put aside work on her doctoral dissertation to advance the book's progress. Many were the times that her good humor kept me going. "Crazy is good,

but only in short spurts," is a Bridget-ism I will long remember. An enormously talented woman, she was a cherished friend throughout.

The anonymous reviewers who wish to remain unsung were extremely helpful to me and, I believe, to the contributing authors. Their careful reading of the chapters and their prompt feedback were unparalleled. Their gracious goodwill was an added bonus.

Diana Bermudez-Rodriguez helped me in the beginning phase of the project. I am grateful for her excellent work in ferreting out material and synthesizing research data. Diana's spirited good cheer and generosity of self infused the design phase.

Julie Nelson, entering the project near its completion, was a superior language editor, improving a number of chapters, including my own. Julie was highly competent and supportive. I value her many talents, as well as her grace and friendship.

My colleagues, too numerous to chronicle, were supportive throughout. Richard Lanthier, Honey Nashman, and Lynda West were always behind me, cheering the project on. I have the good fortune of working in a program in which faculty and staff members alike care about each other. For me, this is an unprecedented experience.

At Oxford University Press, Catharine Carlin, a fine editor, was a resource from the volume's design phase to its publication. Her competence and interest were invaluable. Jennifer Rappaport was of great assistance in resolving a number of issues. Throughout, I appreciated her prompt responses to my questions. Across the board, the editorial staff has shown me once again that they are the very best in their line of work.

George Hoare III led me to Oxford University Press some time ago. I will always appreciate his generous goodwill and his insight into the publishing world.

I would have lost perspective without the humorous barbs of my daughter Jenny. Her love and caring

bolstered a sometimes lonely endeavor. I could not have brought the book to a timely completion without the computer expertise of my son Ray. His love and goodness were always with me. Charlie Lindsey and Shelley Hoare, children by marriage, put up with me throughout. Wonderful persons who I am privileged to know and love, they gave unique insights—serious and funny, thoughtful and witty. Five beautiful grandchildren, Wyatt, Julia, Ashlyn, Alex, and Rachel—teachers all—give joy to my life. As always, I could not have done without the love, commitment, and advice of my dear husband, Ray. An inspiration in his own field, he is the wind beneath my wings in all that I do.

Finally, I thank those at The George Washington University who granted my sabbatical leave to work on this book. Without the benefit of concentrated time, this project would have taken far longer to complete.

Contents

Contributors

DANIELE ARTISTICO
Department of Psychology
B 8-215 Baruch College, CUNY
One Bernard Baruch Way
New York, NY 10010
Email: Daniele_Artistico@baruch.cuny.edu

ROBERT BARNER
Belo Corporation
400 South Record Street
Dallas, TX 75202-4841
Email: bbarner@belo.com

CAROLINE L. BASSETT
The Wisdom Institute
4350 West Lake Harriet Parkway
Minneapolis, MN 55410
Email: cbassett@wisdominst.org

DEBRA BERLANSTEIN
Cook Library
Towson University
Baltimore, MD 21252
Email: debra@towson.edu

JANE M. BERRY
Department of Psychology
University of Richmond
Richmond, VA 23173
Email: jberry@richmond.edu

LINDA MARIE BRESETTE
William F. Connell School of Nursing
Boston College
140 Commonwealth Avenue
Chestnut, Hill, MA 02467
Email: lindabresette@comcast.net

GRACE I. L. CASKIE
College of Education
Iacocca Hall, Room A321
Lehigh University
Bethlehem, PA 18015
Email: caskie@lehigh.edu

DANIEL CERVONE
Department of Psychology
University of Illinois at Chicago
1007 W. Harrison Street
Chicago, IL 60607-7137
Email: dcervone@uic.edu

M. CAROLYN CLARK
Educational Human Resource Development
Texas A&M University
College Station, TX 77843-3256
Email: cclark@tamu.edu

MICHAEL LAMPORT COMMONS
Program in Psychiatry and the Law
Department of Psychiatry
Harvard Medical School
Massachusetts Mental Health Center
74 Fenwood Road
Boston, MA 02115-6113
Email: commons@tiac.net

NATHAN S. CONSEDINE
Psychology Department
Center for Studies of Ethnicity and Human
    Development
Long Island University
191 Willoughby Street, Suite 1A
Brooklyn, NY 11201
Email: nathan.consedine@liu.edu

MIHALY CSIKSZENTMIHALYI
Quality of Life Research Center
Peter F. Drucker School of Management
Claremont Graduate University
1021 N. Dartmouth Avenue
Claremont, CA 91711
Email: miska@cgu.edu

THEO L. DAWSON-TUNIK
Cognitive Science
Hampshire College
Amherst, MA 01002
Email: tdawson@hampshire.edu

SONIA DELUCA
Center for the Study of Higher and Postsecondary
    Education
2117 School of Education Building
University of Michigan
610 E. University Avenue
Ann Arbor, MI 48109-1259
Email: sddeluca@umich.edu

JACK DEMICK
Center for the Study of Human Development
Brown University and Brown Medical School
Box 1938
Providence, RI 02912-1938
Email: Jack_Demick@brown.edu

JUDITH REISETTER HART
Educational Research and Evaluation
Alverno College
3400 South 43rd Street
P.O. Box 343922
Milwaukee, WI 53234-3922
Email: judith.reisetter@alverno.edu

JUTTA HECKHAUSEN
Department of Psychology and Social Behavior
School of Social Ecology
3381 Social Ecology II
University of California, Irvine
Irvine, CA 92697-7085
Email: heckhaus@uci.edu

CAROL HOARE
Department of Counseling/Human and
    Organizational Studies
George Washington University
2134 G. Street NW
Washington, DC 20052
Email: choare@gwu.edu

RONALD R. IRWIN
Department of Psychology
62 Arch Street
Queen's University
Kingston, Ontario K7L 3N6
Email: irwinr@psych.queensu.ca

HEIDI KELLER
University of Osnabrueck
Department of Human Sciences
Culture and Development
Seminarstr. 20
49069 Osnabrueck, Germany
Email: heidi.keller@uos.de

PATRICIA M. KING
Center for the Study of Higher and Postsecondary
    Education
2117 School of Education Building
University of Michigan
Ann Arbor, MI 48109
Email: patking@umich.edu

KAREN STROHM KITCHENER
College of Education
University of Denver
Denver, CO 80208
Email: rkitch@Lamar.colostate.edu

FRIEDER R. LANG
Martin-Luther Universität Halle-Wittenberg
Faculty of Philosophical Sciences, Institute
  of Psychology
Brandbergweg 23c
D-06099 Halle/Saale, Germany
Email: flang@psych.uni-halle.de

CAROL MAGAI
Psychology Department
Center for Studies of Ethnicity and Human
  Development
Long Island University
191 Willoughby Street, Suite 1A
Brooklyn, NY 11201
Email: cmagai@liu.edu

GARRETT MCAULIFFE
Educational Leadership and Counseling
Old Dominion University
Education Building, Room 110
Norfolk, VA 23529
Email: gmcaulif@odu.edu

MARCIA MENTKOWSKI
Educational Research and Evaluation
Alverno College
3400 South 43rd Street
P.O. Box 343922
Milwaukee, WI 53234-3922
EMail: marcia.mentkowski@alverno.edu

SHARAN B. MERRIAM
Department of Adult Education
406 River's Crossing
University of Georgia
Athens, GA 30602
Email: smerriam@uga.edu

MELVIN E. MILLER
Psychology Department
Norwich University
Northfield, VT 05663
Email: miller@norwich.edu

JEANNE NAKAMURA
Quality of Life Research Center
Peter F. Drucker School of Management
Claremont Graduate University
1021 N. Dartmouth Avenue
Claremont, CA 91711
Email: jeanne.nakamura@cgu.edu

GLEN ROGERS
Educational Research and Evaluation
Alverno College
3400 South 43rd Street
P.O. Box 343922
Milwaukee, WI 53234-3922
Email: glen.rogers@alverno.edu

K. WARNER SCHAIE
Department of Human Development
  and Family Studies
Pennsylvania State University
135 E. Nittany Avenue, Suite 405
State College, PA 16801
Email: kws@psu.edu

JAN D. SINNOTT
Department of Psychology
Towson University
Baltimore, MD 21252
Email: jsinnott@towson.edu

JUDITH STEVENS-LONG
Fielding Graduate University
2112 Santa Barbara Street
Santa Barbara, CA 93109
Email: jlong@fielding.edu

KATHLEEN TAYLOR
School of Extended Education
Saint Mary's College of California
Moraga, CA 94575
Email: ktaylor@stmarys-ca.edu

ANNE WERCHAN
Department of Sociology, Social Work,
  and Welfare Studies
School of Management
Agder University College
Serviceboks 422
4604 Kristiansand
Kristiansand, Norway
Email: werchanne@arcor.de

SHERRY L. WILLIS
Department of Human Development and
  Family Studies
Pennsylvania State University
135 E. Nittany Avenue, Suite 405
State College, PA 16801
Email: slw@psu.edu

FAIKA A. K. ZANJANI
Department of Geriatric Psychiatry
University of Pennsylvania
3535 Market Street, Suite 3050
Philadelphia, PA 19104
Email: fzanjani@mail.med.upenn.edu

Part I

Foundations

Chapter 1

Growing a Discipline at the Borders of Thought

Carol Hoare

This handbook addresses a new question in asking how development and learning in adulthood are interrelated and reciprocal. That is, how might learning augment different forms of development, and how does qualitative, positive developmental change result in enhanced learning? This dual question does not imply universality, and it is not without risk. With respect to the absence of universality, adults do not develop uniformly in areas such as cognition, social relationships, and insight development. Some adults make greater excursions in their learning than others. As to risk, the joining of learning and development in adulthood may well be housed in a middle-class concept, one with connotations of resource-rich environments and of subjects' opportunities for and interests in adaptation, development, and learning. There is further risk in charting associations that are positive, sometimes skirting the bidirectionality of development in its positives and negatives, growth and decline. Although this volume's authors do not avoid the declines, our primary emphasis is on how one

force (development or learning) propels the other toward positive advances. This is in line with scholars who chart a terrain of "human strengths" (Aspinwall & Staudinger, 2003), those who ask how development can advance well-being and optimal aging (Baltes & Baltes, 1993; Bornstein, Davidson, Keyes, & Moore, 2003; Rowe & Kahn, 1987, 1998).

Furthermore, each of us writing in this handbook understands that the study of adult development itself is young. Using the *Psychological Abstracts* as an indicator, it was only in 1978 that *adult development* was first used as a subject heading. It is only within the past decade that scholars began seriously to consider how learning might be integral to development in adults. Indeed, adult development and adult learning have been the territory of two very different and non-integrated subfields (Granott, 1998). This is partly because adult development is housed in psychological theory and research, whereas adult learning exists within the disciplines of educational psychology and adult education. Just as Smith and Pourchot (1998) found for adult education and educational psychology, in the joint area of adult development and learning there are no shared professional societies, associations, or journals. Vehicles for discourse are thus lacking. A blend of interests in an area that is necessarily reciprocal will have to emerge from theorists and researchers who are willing to cross from one comparatively safe discipline and professional background into a hybrid area in which there has been limited attention, rather few data-based studies, and, until recently, little apparent interest.

THE NEGLECT OF CONCEPTS OF ADULT DEVELOPMENT

Before examining reasons for a future in which adult development and learning are seen as integral, we might look to reasons for this neglect. There are four key reasons for this neglect, all of which are apparent during much of the twentieth century. I have described these in some detail in a recent book (Hoare, 2002) and credit Erik Erikson's unpublished papers for many important insights.

First, prior to the twentieth century, psychologists had conceived of adulthood as a barren terrain for development. Freud was important in this, for he maintained that psychosexual development ends with entry into adulthood. Freud also led thinking along a path of developmental negatives. As Erikson said, using Freud's thought, all one might expect of healthy adults was the relative absence of the overriding id drives of infancy and of the guilt, fixations, and repressions of childhood. Thus, expectations for adult behavior were expressed in negatives, in terms of what adults should not be and do. By expressing development in terms of absence, scholars had failed to examine what adults *are* in their positive development and in their ongoing developmental potentials.

The second reason for inattention to development during maturity is found in earlier representations of adults. In addition to Freud's position that adulthood shows developmental absence, children of earlier times were seen as miniature adults. This led to a view of adults as completed products of their prior selves. In the twentieth century, social scientists no longer portrayed children in this way; however, until recently, adult attributes and achievements were constructed as though they exist on extension from childhood. In this "rubber band" fallacy (Hoare, 2002),

that of conceiving of developmental continuity as though a giant rubber band stretches between infancy and senescence, developmental traits and abilities are seen as fixed, albeit rudimentarily, at the band's beginning point. Theorists might have stretched that band out, but it always snapped back, in scholars' minds, to origins and developmental givens in infancy and early childhood. Today, this applies to many concepts of cognition and cognitive development, intelligence, mental maturity, social relationships, self-representations, and other constructs.

Although scholars posed a trajectory of increasing competence into maturity, that of the ways in which the adult is stronger, better, and more accomplished than the child, development was seen as origin-based. Experts were largely disinclined to consider adulthood as partly sui generis, that is, as a period of life that has its own unique content, abilities, and representations. Learning has been considered similarly. Until recently, scant attention has been paid to learning in daily environments and in work and personal roles of adults when thinking and learning are tied to contexts, problems, and change, and are bound up with values and emotions. Adult cognition, based on the development of reflective, dialectical, and relativistic thinking, has enjoyed somewhat more attention, due, in part, to William Perry's (1970) important contributions about the content and stages of intellectual development among college students (e.g., Baltes & Staudinger, 1993; Commons, Sinnott, Richards, & Armon, 1984; Kitchener & King, 1981, 1994; Kramer & Woodruff, 1986; Labouvie-Vief, 1992, 1994; Labouvie-Vief, Chiodo, Goguen, Diehl, & Orwoll, 1995). Much more research is needed and has begun. We now approach questions ecologically, looking, for example, not so much to psychometric intelligence but to adults' practical intelligence in their approach to various everyday experiences and problems (Schaie & Zanjani, chapter 5, this volume; Sternberg et al., 2000). We ask how discovery learning in adulthood leads to the development of new insights and fresh opportunities for growth (Merriam & Clark, chapter 2, this volume; Miller, chapter 10, this volume).

The third important facet in the earlier neglect of adult development resides in the prior inability to conceive of adulthood in other than a linear order and in terms of marker events. In this chronology dependence, adult development has been locked to the beginning and ending points of adulthood and adult periods, to the passing of time, and to sequence-ordered events such as career entry, marriage, child-birth, parenting, empty nest phenomena, and retire-ment. As a result, differential meanings, contexts, abilities, qualitative changes in developmental com-plexity, and adult potentials were not well examined. Studies into changing ways of seeing the world, and oneself in that world, have been limited.

Fourth, until recent decades, studies of adult de-velopment were few because there was previously rather little in the way of adult life available for study. In the United States, in 1785, life expectancy was 28 years; in 1900, life expectancy was 47 years; and in 1933, it was 59 years. It was not until 1959 that life ex-pectancy reached 69 years (www.census.gov). Thus, with few years of middle adulthood and scant older adulthood to consider (until the last third of the twen-tieth century), adult developmental possibilities failed to attract much attention. Studies of older adults be-gan earlier than inquiries into the young and middle periods; however, such investigations were largely conceptualized in terms of the problems and disor-ders associated with aging, and strategies for coping with the difficulties created for family, medical care-givers, and society.

THE IMPORTANCE OF MAPPING A POSITIVE, INTEGRATED DEVELOPMENT AND LEARNING TERRAIN

Prospects for adult life have changed dramatically. By the beginning of the twenty-first century, the median age of the U.S. population was 35.9 years, and life ex-pectancy was nearly 80 years (www.census.gov). There are now many more middle-aged and older persons, and contemporary adults can expect to live longer and healthier lives than prior generations. Writing about rates of aging and individual differ-ences, a recent article (Lu et al., 2004) depicted mid-dle adulthood as the years between age 40 and 70. For the elder years, we now avoid lumping people into a single category based on age alone. We speak of the young-old, the old-old, and the aged, distinguishing among elders principally on the basis of cognitive fac-ulties, independent living and self-care abilities, mo-bility, and medical morbidity.

Increased longevity and better health are due to en-hanced living conditions such as improved nutrition and sanitation, control of infectious diseases, declines

in deaths of women during childbirth, and advances in medical care and technology. The aging of the post–World War II Baby Boom cohort has swelled the numbers of those now in retirement. At present, there are nearly 34 million Americans who are 65 years of age or older. According to the U.S. Census Bureau, by 2030 this group will expand to more than 69 million (20% of the population), and by 2050, will swell to nearly 80 million. Among those over 85 years of age, the fastest-growing age group, 3 million Ameri-cans are currently 85 years of age or older, a num-ber that will increase to 28 million by 2050 (www.census.gov).

Increasingly, older adults are able to maintain rel-atively active lives into their ninth decade. It seems to be the case that adults themselves have changed our views. The prior view of successive development into midlife, followed by years of chronic illness and de-cline, has been replaced by a concept of ongoing de-velopment until senility or death. Importantly, we now know that psychosocial forces and contexts have dramatic effects on health, longevity, and adaptive ca-pacities. Thus, although it would be foolish to con-sider adult development as other than constituted by gains mixed with losses, it is essential to focus on those developmental attributes that change in a posi-tive direction toward increasing competence, deeper understandings, and optimal functioning and well-being. The mere number of aging adults in our soci-ety forces us to consider the integration and catalytic effects of enhanced development and learning. How might one best develop, and how do development and learning enhance each another?

Cognitive Vitality and Learning

As an example of the relationship between adult de-velopment and learning, I will highlight the intellec-tual area because there is great interest in the maintenance of cognitive vitality throughout adult-hood. We know that among adults for whom learning is short-term or accidental and is not built into every-day functioning as a valued, active way of experienc-ing and living in the world, potential development is not enhanced. Cognitive ability, plasticity, openness to experience, and flexibility decline over time. Dis-use of abstract powers leads to their atrophy and to a loss in the ability to apply such powers to learning and other behaviors. The opposite holds among adults for whom learning is integral to living and who engage in deep processing of content. Such persons restructure knowledge, maintain cognitive openness and flexibility, enhance intellectual abilities, and self-scaffold their cognitive powers toward new, additional learning. This has been ably demonstrated by findings from the Seattle Longitudinal Study. In that study, Schaie (1996b, 2005) illustrated that certain cognitive powers reach their zenith only in the seventh decade of life, particularly among those who continue to learn, who live in favorable conditions, and who do not suffer the detriments of cardiovascular or cerebrovascular disease (see also Bosworth & Schaie, 1999; Fillit et al., 2002; Knoops et al., 2004). The Duke Longitudinal Studies of Normal Aging (Busse & Maddox, 1985) reached similar conclusions. When assessed longitudinally, maintenance of intellectual powers was the norm into subjects' eighth decade. Some studies of elders that included centenarians show the maintenance of cognitive vitality into the 11th decade of life (Fillit et al., 2002; Silver, Jilinskaia, & Perls, 2001). On this basis, Rowe and Kahn (1987, 1998) distinguished between "usual" aging that shows declines in cognitive functions, autonomy, physiological functioning, and longevity, and "successful" aging that is characterized by maintenance or enhancement of cognitive powers, continued autonomy, superior physiological functioning, and increased longevity.

That the nexus of learning and development is significant in intellectual development has been shown by Schaie, one of our chapter authors. In his texts on the subject, Schaie (1996b, 2005) demonstrated that later-born cohorts who use adult education opportunities are intellectually advanced compared with earlier-born cohorts. As Schaie found, it is often impossible to disentangle the effects of attributes such as learning, better nutrition, and heightened preventive health measures. Yet even in otherwise disadvantaged circumstances, training programs for older adults improved the spatial orientation and inductive reasoning performance of two-thirds of participants. With respect to memory, for adults in the age range of 60 to 80 years, learning mnemonic techniques doubled the number of words that subjects could recall (Baltes & Kliegl, 1992). Even for those in the ninth decade of life and older, some plasticity has been demonstrated. Supporting data exist in the Duke Studies (Busse & Maddox, 1985), the Einstein Aging Studies (Verghese et al., 2003), and elsewhere. In the Nun Study, Snowdon (2001, 2003) found that sisters who had obtained college degrees and who engaged in subsequent learning were able to maintain and enhance their intellectual powers and their independence. Such persons also experienced greater longevity than nuns who were less educated and who were engaged in positions that did not require much in the way of ongoing learning (see also Riley et al., 2002). With 20 years of longitudinal data in hand, Schooler and Mulatu (2001) provided substantial evidence that complex intellectual activities, in work or in nonwork leisure activities, increase intellectual functioning in the later years of life. In this and other studies, the pathway is one in which intelligent persons find their way into complex environments, which then raise their levels of functional intelligence.

Neurobiological and medical studies have addressed cognitive vitality recently. Lifestyle factors such as ongoing learning have been associated with declines in medical comorbidities and with protection against the cognitive declines typically associated with aging. Recently, discoveries have shown that long-term intensification of synapse connections in the hippocampus occurs with learning (Fillit et al., 2002). These and related data now challenge the prior, once universal conviction that the adult brain is incapable of making new neurons (neurogenesis), new synapses (synaptogenesis), and new capillaries (angiogenesis). In particular, neuron growth has been found in the important dentate gyrus of the hippocampus, a location related to learning and memory. Supporting data are found in the research of Barnes and McNaughton (1985), Berkman et al. (1993), Cameron and Gould (1994), Eriksson et al. (1998), Perls, Morris, Ooi, and Lipsitz (1993), Schaie (1989), Willis and Schaie (1986), and others. Plasticity has also been demonstrated in the amygdala (Ohman, 2002), an area of the brain that is integral to emotion and social cognition; in the sensorimotor cortex (Hamilton & Pascual-Leone, 1998; Kujala, Alho, & Naatanen, 2000); and in visual pathways (de Haan, Humphreys, & Johnson, 2002; de Haan, Paascalis, & Johnson, 2002).

Behavioral data combined with neurological findings point to changes in the structure and function of the brain based on learning and experience. Maguire and colleagues (2000) showed this among London taxi drivers. London is large city with an intricate web of roads and streets. For taxi drivers, an intensive 2-year period of learning prepares drivers to immediately call forth from memory a visual map of locations, businesses, and routes without the help of road maps. As a result of classroom instruction combined with experience navigating myriad routes, brain neuroimaging showed that drivers' posterior hippocampi, a brain area associated with spatial depictions of the external environment, grew significantly larger than that of control subjects. Subjects with many years of driving experience showed greater hippocampal size than drivers with less experience.

Scaffolding Development and Learning

Any number of other developmental attributes (e.g., social, emotional, self-efficacy, insight) are interdependent with learning. As development and learning interact, a scaffolding effect occurs in that learning and development will each lead to enhancements in its essential counterplayer; both are transformed in the process. For example, living and learning in an intricate environment, and learning that extends beyond a person's occupation, predict advances in cognitive development (Pirttila-Backman & Kajanne, 2001). Among older adults, affluence and interest in cultural and educational activities are associated with cognitive flexibility (Hood & Deopere, 2002; Schaie, 1990, 1993). Cognitive flexibility also correlates with increased learning engagement. In the prospective, longitudinal Einstein Aging Study, subjects over the age of 75 who engaged in cognitive leisure activities (reading, playing musical instruments, playing board games) experienced a lower risk for dementia (Verghese et al., 2003).

The development of insight has also been implicated in additional learning and in the transformation of knowledge into behavior (Miller, chapter 10, this volume; Staudinger, 2001). "Elaboration" and "further detailed investigation" (learning) are essential addendums to the developments in awareness that we call *insight* (Pollock, 1981, p. 286). Adult understandings that knowledge is complex, tenuous, evolving, and sometimes contradictory correlate with inclinations to take multiple perspectives, to alter views over time, and to avoid early closure in reaching decisions (Pascual-Leone & Irwin, 1998).

In the applied work realm, executives, managers, and trainers are now interested as never before in the relationship between employee learning and development. Maurer and colleagues (2003) held that in a constantly changing, highly competitive, leaner, and efficiency-oriented U.S. work environment, employee development and learning are essential to the success of both the organization and its workers. For corporations, ongoing employee development and learning contribute to organizations' financial success (Ellinger, Ellinger, Yang, & Howton, 2002; Maurer, Weiss, & Barbeite, 2003), foster supportive work climates; enhance employees' job involvement, motivation and satisfaction; and strengthen workers' commitment to the organization (Mikkelsen, Saksvik, Eriksen, & Ursin, 1999). Corporate resources invested in ongoing development and learning also result in employee retention (Kaye & Jordan-Evans, 2000; Maurer et al., 2003) and in the ability of organizations to attract development-oriented workers to their employ (Maurer et al., 2003). For employees, workplace learning and development-oriented activities heighten perceptions of mastery and self-efficacy (Cervone, Artistico, & Berry, chapter 8, this volume; Maurer et al., 2003), increase work interest and job satisfaction (Maurer et al., 2003; Mikkelsen et al., 1999), promote job security and ongoing career development possibilities (Maurer et al., 2003), and improve marketability. For workers in complex jobs (or those with the opportunity to move into such jobs), job complexity is associated with advances in intellectual flexibility, even among older workers (Kohn et al., 2000; Miller, Slomczynski, & Kohn, 1988; Mulatu & Schooler, 1999; Schaie & Schooler, 1998; Schooler & Mulatu, 2001; Schooler, Mulatu, & Oates, 1999). This is particularly the case when job complexity requires ongoing learning, and in today's work environment, highly complex jobs and ongoing learning are synonymous. As to more formal educational endeavors, such as training events and workshops, these were once considered ho-hum requirements of the job. Now many such learning opportunities have become sought-after perquisites provided by organizations. In fact, if there is one consistency in the literature describing high-performing work systems, it is the existence of extensive training and skill development for employees in those systems (e.g., Bailey, Berg, & Sandy, 2001; Pfeffer, 1998).

Policy Implications

In the policy realm, there is ongoing interest in ways to reduce chronic illness and disability in the late middle and older years and lessen dementia and dependency among the elderly. Among seniors, nearly

25% of those who are age 75 or older and 40% of those over 85 years of age or older suffer from dementia, principally of the vascular and Alzheimer forms (Fillit et al., 2002). The maintenance of cognitive vigor has not been a high U.S. policy aim, but efforts are under way to make cognitive health a top priority in the United States and internationally (Fillit et al., 2002; National Research Council, 2000; see also Deary, Whiteman, Starr, Whalley, & Fox, 2004). Some claim a potentially achievable goal of cognitive vitality that remains intact from middle age onward (e.g., Fillit et al., 2002).

A slowing or reversal of recent increases in economic dependence of retired persons on those in the workforce would improve socioeconomic prospects for all. Declines in cognitive aging could result in more persons continuing in some form of challenging work into their seventies or eighties. Among older employees, ongoing learning and skill development, with work and nonwork support for such activities, could delay retirement considerably (Maurer et al., 2003). Retention of middle-aged and older employees is important, particularly when one considers that the average age of U.S. workers is on the upswing. Furthermore, preventing and attenuating dementia is a paramount public health priority (Verghese et al., 2003). Ongoing intellectual activities, with their associated learning involvement, might well reduce morbidity and chronic illness if such learning results in better preventive and health care practices. Dementia may be forestalled among at least some elderly persons who engage in cognitively stimulating leisure pursuits, especially if complex activities are in a continuum from those of earlier life (Knoops et al., 2004; Masunaga & Horn, 2001; Smyth et al., 2004).

It is impossible to say how adult life will change, the extent to which life expectancy may increase in future decades, or how work-specific, policy, and other applications stemming from the integration of learning and development will evolve. However, we do know that a growing number of adults, especially old and very old adults, will soon exist. Whether one is a young adult, middle-aged, or a senior, there is now an increased interest in knowing how one can enhance adult life and its prospects in moving through the remaining years of life. Because the research base about the integration of adult learning and development is young, those studying at this intersection have much to offer in advancing knowledge about the ways in which learning and development show unified, self-scaffolding tendencies.

KEY CONCEPTS

Adult Development

Adult development means systematic, qualitative changes in human abilities and behaviors as a result of interactions between internal and external environments. Interactions and qualitative changes are influenced by genetics, by endogenous and exogenous influences, and by adaptive powers and personal interests. Many abilities are multidimensional. For example, adult intelligence is comprised of multiple abilities and is intrinsically influenced by personality, motivation, adaptive abilities, and physical and mental health.

Development means growth and change, those transformations that are primarily "orderly, sequential, and lawful" (Endler, Boulter, & Osser, 1976, p. 1). In adulthood, such development is bidirectional in that there are gains as well as losses, advances mixed with decrements. Decrements occur as early as one's late twenties in functions such as reflexes and processing speed, with the human frontal cortex particularly at risk after age 40 (Lu et al., 2004).

This volume preferentially addresses a number of developmental positives. However, just as we are well aware of bidirectionality, we know that some declines can also foster important positive results. Sensory deficits can lead to greater vigilance and self-care; decrements in perceptual speed and in speed of cognitive processing can result in heightened observational skills and more sustained attention to reading materials and to the speech and gestures of others. Declines in fluid intelligence (e.g., spatial orientation and inductive reasoning) may be offset by gains in crystallized intelligence (e.g., verbal meaning and word fluency) (Baltes, Lindenberger, & Staudinger, 1998; Horn, 1994; Horn & Hofer, 1992; Schaie, 1996a). In addition, the mature adult tends to be acutely aware of the aging direction in which he or she is moving. This often leads to enhanced appreciation of the elderly and their needs, a sense of affinity with parents and other key counterplayers in life (Erikson, 1982), a willingness to seek information and help when needed, and, among some, a deepened understanding of the various influences on their own and others' development.

With respect to transformations, *qualitative change* refers to alterations in human functioning and in ways of seeing and interpreting oneself in the world. Such changes move toward complexity. In this, development is not quantitatively determined, for complex change tends to be discounted when items are merely aggregated. Furthermore, developmental invariance among adults is not the case. Significant interindividual and cohort differences exist, just as there are qualitative differences among adults in heredity, constitution, environments, traits, experiences, resources, and learning engagement. Heredity and environment are equally important. Arguments about the relative importance of nature versus nurture linger on. However, agreeing with Endler and colleagues (1976), inquiring whether heredity or environment is more essential to the development of a particular behavior "is akin to asking whether the length or the width is more important in determining the area of a rectangle" (p. 13). The best view emphasizes essential contributions made by and key interactions between and among genetics, environments (both endogenous and exogenous), contexts, experiences, intentional choices, and inclinations.

Individuals tend to follow differing developmental pathways in the maintenance, extension, or depletion of important attributes and behaviors. As we know, adults become more, not less, heterogeneous as they age. This is due to differential roles, education, experiences, environments, and inclinations. Thus, some adults will enhance their intellectual powers, others will show intellectual deterioration; some will manifest little or no apparent change (Dittmann-Kohli & Baltes, 1990; Fillet et al., 2002). Many adults develop more mature mental mechanisms and coping styles over time, whereas others maintain prior mechanisms or regress to immature coping styles. Certain persons will advance to the ethical level of principles and action. (In this, *ethics* is defined by the content of decisions and actions, not just by reasoning based on moral judgments devoid of action.) Some adults will move to higher levels of consciousness, expanding their sense of the spiritual (see Irwin, chapter 14, this volume). Others will remain static or deteriorate, either toward the literal or toward despair. Various contexts, such as the work environment and home life, with their varied support mechanisms, play important roles in fostering movement in one or another direction. Humans are permeable to their immediate social world, to cultural factors, and to important others in their personal and work lives.

In addition to individual variance, variability exists in the societal and cultural norms that support development. For example, the development of heightened work autonomy, highly valued in the United States, is suppressed in autocratic nations. Restrictive political and religious ideologies tend to foster lower level, dualistic thinking processes (e.g., black versus white, right versus wrong) that auger against the development of more complex, relativistic cognitive functions. In different societies, cultures, and ethnic groups, attributes of intelligence will develop variously, depending on the traits that are valued, emphasized, and rewarded and those that are suppressed. For example, linguistic and logical-mathematical abilities are emphasized in the United States during youth, with such skills predicting substantial monetary rewards in various occupations. Spatial abilities are emphasized and rewarded among Eskimos and Tanzanians, spatial skills and acute visual memory among Kenyans, bodily kinesthetic skills among Balinese, and musical abilities among Anang tribal members in Nigeria and in subsets of Japanese, Hungarians, and Russian Jews (Gardner, 1985).

Clearly, available resources are significant to ongoing development. External resources—such as adequate finances, strong kin and friendship networks, community assets and support, available transportation, learning opportunities and tools, competent medical care, low levels of stressors, and affirming work and civic environments—endorse ongoing development. Internal resources are just as essential. Among these, good health, adaptive capacities, positive coping strategies, motivations for ongoing growth, curiosity, a sense of self-efficacy, openness to experience, and varied interests are key (e.g., Pirttila-Backman & Kajanne, 2001). Equally important are the qualities of autonomy, a sense of personal control over life and events (Caspi & Elder, 1986; Cervone et al., chapter 8, this volume; Merriam & Yang, 1996; Rowe & Kahn, 1987), positive attitudes toward people and life, self-understanding and acceptance (Merriam & Yang, 1996; Staudinger, 2001), social competence, needs for ongoing accomplishments (Dittmann-Kohli & Baltes, 1990), and future expectations and commitments. Internal and external resources interact with genetics, personal history, and individual goals to shape behavior (see Schaie & Zanjani, chapter 5, this volume).

It is also the case that the positives and negatives of adult behavior and experience internegotiate and antagonize each other. Personal independence, autonomy, and control are countered by the potential for dependence and loss of power and voice as one ages. Mobility is eventually undermined by behavioral slowing and a decline in balance. In the psychosocial area, acknowledging developmental polarities, Erikson showed the ways identity vies with cynicism, intimacy with isolation, and generativity with stagnation and rejection in the respective periods of late adolescence and of young and middle adulthood. For the elder years, having changed his views once he himself was older, Erikson (1982) held that the dialectic was that of integrality, of keeping a deteriorating body and psyche together against despair. The tension of interplaying, opposing forces leads the positively developing adult to accentuate the forces and behaviors that will offset negatives and losses.

Childhood as a Resource

We cannot do other than emphasize personal choice and responsibility in ongoing learning and behavioral advances, for each adult is the active agent of development, curiosity, and inquiry. However, there are personal situations with little in the way of individual choice, past or present. With Beck (1994), we are concerned about the effects of societal deprivations such as poverty, unemployment, racial marginalization, and ageist disinclusion. These societal, structural constraints press persons toward dependency, decreased motivation, and declines in a sense of self-determination, attributes that can be inappropriately interpreted as failures of the individual. Furthermore, social deprivations operate against the presumed "ideology of choice" into which U.S. youth and young adults are socialized and expected to perform (Hagestad & Dannefer, 2001). The result is a projection of societally incurred deficits onto the individual who is doubly burdened, first by deprivations and second by the ascription and internalization of blame and guilt. This applies to adults and to their childhood experiences. I emphasized earlier that adult development cannot be conceived as a simple linear continuity from childhood. However, no person comes to adulthood de novo. Personal history, early resources, socioeconomic and educational advantages or deprivations, the development of mastery in childhood, and parental support and expectations establish a trajectory that is difficult to dislodge at age 20, 30, or later. The experiences of early childhood have long-standing effects that reach far into adulthood. Adult development is resource dependent (Caspi & Elder, 1986). One set of resources is the adult's history of competence in school-related and extracurricular pursuits, as well as success in resolving the psychosocial demands of earlier life. That is, the accomplished child becomes a resource to the self-same developing adult. It is also true that later-occurring benefits can attenuate the detrimental conditions of early life. Humans are resilient. Abilities are malleable. Thus, in situations in which irreparable childhood damage has not occurred, particularly in critical periods of development (e.g., reclusive separation from human contact in infancy, physical abuse during attachment development), adults may well respond to, for example, supportive and enriched environments, high-quality learning tools, and intelligent spouses. Such adult resources might compensate for the deficits of childhood.

Dramatic social events, particularly those occurring during adolescence and young adulthood, can also foster or thwart development, particularly when social class enters the equation. The large scale social events of World War II and the Great Depression adversely affected subsequent emotional functioning and learning engagement, particularly among those in the lower socioeconomic working class who were then in the identity formation stage (Caspi & Elder, 1986; Duncan & Agronick, 1995). However, those who were forming their identities when experiencing those events but who had adequate personal resources, emotional resilience, social involvement, and middle-class status, showed subsequent emotional stability and learning engagement. Other epic struggles (e.g., the Vietnam War and the civil rights movement) have had similar effects, sustaining development for some and undermining it for others (Elder, Rudkin, & Longer, 1994). Today, the high-technology revolution moves forward. Although some data exist (e.g., Internet use by college students appears to preferentially benefit males over females socially; Lanthier & Windham, 2004), we have yet to fully account for the psychosocial effects on development of a pervasive computer- and Internet-savvy environment.

Even in instances in which adults have been privileged by enriched, supportive childhoods and social stability, adulthood itself can bring difficulties that thwart development. Traumas such as physical or mental illness, the loss of loved ones, sensory loss, and prolonged unemployment frequently have negative effects on the psyche and potentially on inclinations to learn. Into old age, the tendency to ruminate on past negative events decreases positive adaptations, social encounters, and the likelihood of subsequent positive interpretations of life (McFarland & Buehler, 1998). Furthermore, as Schaie and Zanjani (chapter 5, this volume) found, multiple disorders can increase negative effects. Adverse effects on intellectual performance may also result from the treatment of organic and mental disorders (see also Stanley et al., 2002; Tabbarah, Crimmins, & Seeman, 2002). Medications and drug interactions, for example, take their toll.

The far years of life are always accompanied by increasing physical problems. Magical thinking—the belief that adults are fully in control of their fates—is unrealistic. Among the very aged in particular, some deteriorations cannot be remedied by personal countering behaviors. To deny this reality burdens the elderly with blame when they are not at fault. However, the tendency to focus on one's body versus the inclination to transcend bodily aches and pains, has negative effects on physical activity, social engagement, relationships, and motivation (Eysenck & Calvo, 1992; May, Schwoerer, Reed, & Potter, 1997; Peck, 1968).

Adult Learning

We are concerned with adult learning that is itself a developmental activity and process. Adult learning is a change in behavior, a gain in knowledge or skills, and an alteration or restructuring of prior knowledge; such learning can also mean a positive change in self-understanding or in the development of personal qualities such as coping mechanisms. Thus, learning is not just information-based, nor is it merely a change in observable behavior. Learning can include the acquisition of information or the application of information. Learning also includes a change or re-ordering of content in one's cognitive apparatus. This may include the deletion of old material when new content requires this adjustment, or it may mean altering one's mental file cabinet to subsume newly acquired knowledge beneath or to superordinate it above prior content. Here, we blur a previous boundary. Historically, some learning theorists have differentiated between the acquisition of knowledge (learning) and its restructuring (development) (e.g., Endler et al., 1976). This seems to be a specious distinction in the absence of empirical studies finding that cognitive development occurs during knowledge re-structuring but not during knowledge acquisition. Thus, it seems appropriate to conclude that both the acquisition of material and its revision in one's cognitive schema involve learning, and that cognitive development is inseparable from such learning.

Learning can occur consciously or unconsciously. Conscious learning transpires when one intentionally seeks knowledge or skill development that will expand or change one's database or performance. Largely unconscious learning occurs, for example, in some forms of social modeling behavior, in developing and using implicit (tacit) knowledge, and in acquiring and evolving an adult identity (Erikson, 1987; Reber, 1993). Unconscious learning is difficult to study and, other than somewhat tangentially in the psychoanalytic area, has been largely neglected. However, it is possible to observe the results of unconscious changes in learning applications. This is particularly true in adulthood because this period is one in which substantial previously acquired conscious knowledge moves to the unconscious or preconscious level of nearly automatic functioning (Berg & Sternberg, 2003). Conscious or declarative knowledge is *knowing that*, whereas unconscious or preconscious procedural knowledge is *knowing how* (Ryle, 1949; Sternberg, Wagner, Williams, & Horvath, 1995; Torff & Sternberg, 1998). An example is found in operating a car. Declarative knowledge development occurs on first learning how to drive. The learner is aware (conscious) of the items and incidents of learning, such as the car's essential mechanisms, the sequences in operating a vehicle, and the rules and patterns of driving from one location to another. Such learned information and behavior then move to the procedural (pre- or unconscious) level in which the driver is barely aware of his or her knowledge and functions or of the car and its route. Importantly, years of productive work-based learning lead to a procedural form of knowledge that has also been termed *implicit* and *tacit* knowledge, that is, a practical intelligence (Neisser, 1976; Sternberg, Wagner, & Okagaki, 1993; Sternberg et al., 1995, 2000). Such practical, procedural knowledge and its associated strategic abilities occur when one learns adult roles, problem-solving strategies, skills, and productive expertise. In adults who continue to learn, such knowledge increases during the active, engaged years of life (Torff & Sternberg, 1998). Importantly, a number of investigators have found that learning and its associated tacit knowledge are unrelated to tested intelligence and to aptitude test scores (e.g., Ceci & Liker, 1986, 1988).

Unconscious, Preconscious, and Conscious Knowing and Learning

It is important to distinguish between unconscious and preconscious knowledge and skills. Knowledge and its associated functioning are unconscious when the person is completely unaware of data, of the processes and sequence of knowledge use, or of learned behavior. Such material is inaccessible to conscious awareness. Preconscious knowledge refers to attributes and functions that exist in the unconscious but that with effort, can be brought up to the conscious level (Erikson, 1987; Laplanche & Pontalis, 1973). For example, with respect to unconscious (tacit) knowledge, highly successful managers are often unable to explain how they correctly interpreted key elements in the work environment and reached conclusions that turned out to be accurate (Sloan, 2004). On repeated questioning, many are never able to identify facts and processes that were essential to their conclusions (Reber, 1993). Similarly, many elite athletes cannot explain essential attributes of their highly developed psychomotor abilities, nor can some explain how they perform skill sequences. Material and functioning remain at the unconscious, grooved-neuron level and are inaccessible. However, with respect to preconscious knowledge, many assembly workers, for example, may not be able to readily explain how they know when and how to sequence line activities; however, when pressed, some are able to bring this content into consciousness to provide on-the-job training and mentoring for new employees. Physicians, for example, may be unaware of the knowledge and thinking processes they use in decision pathways that lead to differential diagnoses. However, on specific questioning, some can delineate key information and describe their thinking process, thought sequence, and deductions. Others cannot. Unexamined is the question of whether there may be unique talents in those who are able to access and surface such preconscious material.

For the purposes of considering adults, we include real-world learning and meaningful learning, as well as learning performance that is based on developed and maintained (practiced) expertise (see, e.g., Ericsson & Charness, 1994; Ericsson & Smith, 1991; Krampe

& Ericsson, 1996). This excludes idiosyncratic and laboratory-type learning tasks that are unrelated to relevant problems or situations in which we define *relevance* as it is construed by the subject. This distinction is important because relevance and life problems do not exist in laboratory settings, and adults may or may not elect to actively involve themselves in artificial or arbitrary tasks even when they seem to comply with performance requests. Furthermore, perceptual and cognitive slowing among adults is exaggerated when tasks fail the criterion of meaningfulness and when developed expertise is ignored (Hoyer & Touron, 2003). Age-associated deficits are nearly always found in older subjects in the contexts of the laboratory and in situations in which material is novel or alien to their experience. Then, deficits are apparent in reaction time (Hoyer & Touron, 2003; Howard & Howard, 1989, 1992), serial learning abilities (Cherry & Stadler, 1995; Hoyer & Touron, 2003), short-term and working memory processes (Myerson, Hale, Rhee, & Jenkins, 1999; Zachs, Hasher, & Li, 2000), speed of processing (Craik & Salthouse, 2000; Salthouse, 1994; Salthouse & Coon, 1994), and the ability to block distracting, task-irrelevant information and stimuli (Berg & Sternberg, 2003). However, as Salthouse (e.g., 1984, 2000) reported, there are no perceptible losses when tasks require real-world or well-learned responses. For example, in Artistico, Cervone, and Pezzuti's (2003) study of younger (20–29 years) and older (65–75 years) adults, when tasks were common to both groups, younger subjects routinely performed better. However, when the researchers posed daily problems that were highly relevant to older adults, the older subjects routinely outperformed the younger group.

In a high-technology environment, it is not that older adults do not function well cognitively or that they do not learn. Rather, they are slower than their younger peers. Not having grown up with, for instance, computers, fax machines and ATMs, and cell phones, they appear deficient compared to almost anyone who in youth was developing and learning amidst the daily experience of computers and Internet access.

Schaie and Zanjani (chapter 5, this volume) have synthesized findings from a number of studies showing that deficits among older adults are either drastically reduced or extinguished when perceptual speed and individual differences in task attention are removed from the equation. Gains have occurred through training programs (Ball et al., 2002); some of those gains resisted decline over a 7-year period. On-going high performance in cognitive functioning and problem solving continues into later adulthood (Charness & Bosman, 1990; Clancy & Hoyer, 1994; Hoyer & Touron, 2003; Krampe & Ericsson, 1996; Masunaga & Horn, 2001; Salthouse, 1984; Shimamura, Berry, Mangels, Rusting, & Jurica, 1995), particularly in the context of work tasks and life problems. Recent investigations of sustained effort and expert performance have reformed thought about the ways selective optimization with compensation (SOC) can maintain high levels of cognitive and even psychomotor performance into adults' 80s and 90s (e.g., Ericsson, Patel, & Kintsch, 2000; Freund & Baltes, 1998; Krampe & Ericsson, 1996). In SOC, one raises the threshold for cognitive and skill decline. This is accomplished by reducing the range of performance activities, selecting (S) only those that will be practiced intensely (O), and using a wealth of accumulated experiences and resources (C) to sustain expert performance and learning (see Baltes & Baltes, 1990). For example, a 65-year-old physician retires, having found that the escalating requirements of private practice consume all of his energies and leave little time for life beyond the confines of professional work. He thus reduces his range of obligations (no more hospital visits, emergency room call schedules, after-hours patient phone conferences) and elects to focus (S) only on caring for patients in free clinics. There, he limits patient care to his subspecialty area (O), freeing up time to read professional journals, attend conferences, and keep up with his field (C). He thereby sustains a high level of professional performance and engages in fresh opportunities for learning.

In ongoing learning, the adult uses many sources, contexts, and strategies for learning. This does not occur passively, and content is not learned in final form, merely pulled in from the external environment (Pascual-Leone & Irwin, 1998). Both in terms of motivation and with respect to perceptual-cognitive filters, the adult operates as the control who selects, reviews, revises, and sometimes rejects what is perceived and sometimes assimilated. The adult evaluates material as it arrives; he or she determines, with value primacy intact, content that will be accepted and material that will be altered, revised, or rejected. Thus the adult functions both as the agent of personal change and as the medium who differentially blocks and restructures, re-creates, and sometimes rejects content and opportunities for cognitive and behavioral change.

The importance of the adult as a filtering power other than a mere conduit of information has not received adequate empirical attention.

Adult Differentiation, Interiority, and Historical Sentience

Although age gradations are difficult if not impossible to determine, scholars have distinguished between young and older adults using a number of age categories and representations of learning and mastery. Some experts tend to promote a decline perspective, particularly for the postretirement years. But many contemporary adults, the media, and some researchers writing in the medical and scientific literatures (e.g., Fillit et al., 2002; Lu et al., 2004) expect that large numbers of adults will experience a healthy "30-year bonus" after their retirement (Sadler, 2000; see also Rubenstein, 2002).

Some time ago, Neugarten (1979) distinguished between the active mastery of young adults and the passive mastery of middle-aged and older persons. In the young adult phase, there is a tendency toward an internalization of society's norms and an alignment of the self with them (Labouvie-Vief et al., 1995). Thus, young adults are more likely to remain indistinct from key others and from the social group and cohort with whom they are integral. Compared with middle-aged and older adults, their locus of control is more external. Experiencing life and learning from various roles, events, and commitments eventually lead to greater interiority and to an increasingly internal locus in which the self is used as the primary referent for beliefs, decisions, and actions. The greater interiority that appears at midlife also seems to be due to life reflection and to placing one's youth in the past as a new chapter begins (Erikson, 1982; Jung, 1933; Staudinger, 2001).

Thus, by middle age, the adult has learned to be less concerned with external standards (Labouvie-Vief et al., 1995). More likely to criticize external norms, the middle-ager also examines personal motives and purposes. There is movement toward increased differentiation from others, and a move beyond institution-based identities as the adult looks to the persons, roles, and life contexts that have shaped the self (Labouvie-Vief et al., 1995). As both Jung (1933) and Erikson (1982) held, the adult comes face to face with contradictions within the self, turns inward to examine the interior life, and integrates achievements and failures.

By middle age, different experiences inform each subject's interpretation of knowledge and of the role and importance of experts and social events, whereas the circumstances of life such as marriage, illness, employment, altered work content, travel, and changes in personal goals have shaped thinking and ongoing learning. At best, increased learning leads to a heightened sense of personal control (Merriam & Yang, 1996), to feelings of personal agency and empowerment (Kegan, 1982, 1994; Loevinger, 1980; Mezirow, 1991), to a heightened internal locus of control (Cochran & Laub, 1994), and to increased tolerance for ambiguity (Merriam & Yang, 1996). At least a privileged few develop increased open-mindedness and decreased authoritarianism; this leads to an expanded appreciation of individual differences and of the rights of others (Merriam & Yang, 1996) and to insights into the role of varied cultural norms in human conditioning (see Hoare, 2002, chap. 4, pp. 41–69, and chap. 7, pp. 145–170).

By middle age, evolving society and events have brought changes that fail to conform to prior notions. In our time, changes such as altered gender roles and modifications in connotations of equality and diversity have required learning and adaptation that were largely unforeseen in the 1950s. Reflecting on the processes of one's thinking (a dialectic), permits one to place prior views within an historical framework while he or she alters current positions, attitudes, and behaviors (Basseches, 1984). Staudinger (2001) has shown that by the middle years, such thinking can become "epistemic," in that one develops knowledge about the self and about the human condition. By middle age, many experience "historical sentience," a peak awareness of history and of the self's immersion in the flow of time (Hoare, 2002). Developmentally, Erikson (1943) held that a form of historical fusion occurs in which the adult tends to blur his or her own personal history with all of history, resulting in a collapsed historical time frame. This leads some adults to learn the meaning of historical relativity first-hand. Furthermore, some adults develop a sense of identification and affinity with those of prior times, with their needs, desires, struggles, and demons. Erikson held that such affinity decreases anxiety, for the adult no longer feels fearfully alone in the universe (Erikson, 1958). In recent years, enhanced knowledge about different cultures and their social mores has led open-minded, cognitively advanced adults to experience and appreciate cultural relativity. Social changes and individual development link with learning to alter basic assumptions and epistemologies.

Reflective Development and an Altered Ego Ideal

Personal learning also leads to a reconstruction of the adult's interpretation of self and of his or her unique dreams in light of revised values, altered priorities, changed needs, and reassessed possibilities. The ego ideal itself is altered. Confucius was among the first to observe some of these differences in the realms of early surefootedness and a later sense of the eternal and its meaning:

> At fifteen I set my heart upon learning. At thirty, I had planted my feet firm upon the ground. At forty, I no longer suffered from perplexities. At fifty, I knew what were the biddings of Heaven. At sixty, I heard them with docile ear. At seventy, I could follow the dictates of my own heart; for what I desired no longer over-stepped the boundaries of right. (Confucius, trans. 1938)

We cannot say whether Confucius thereby implied that middle-aged and older adults appreciate the meaning of the nearness of death and reappraise their lives in terms of this understanding, but twentieth-century scholars have observed this tendency. Erikson (1969) and Jaques (1965) found an increasing relaxation in the denial of death from midlife onward. Neugarten (1979) held that such midlife insights lead to a restructuring of time in which life is no longer viewed as "time since birth" but as "time left to live" (p. 890). And, in his study of the lives of 310 acclaimed male artists, Jaques (1965) found that the products of creativity in subjects' twenties and early thirties came from a concentrated, swift, "hot-from-the-fire" creativity, whereas the products of their late thirties and older periods showed a "sculpted" creativity (p. 503). In their later years, artists generated and then reworked (sculpted) their products again and again. In part, Jaques interpreted this sculpting tendency as the emergence of an interaction and relationship between the artist and the product, one of reacting and responding to the creation. We might call this a transference phenomenon.

Coincident with a decay in the denial of death, a restructuring of time, and changes in the processes of creativity, adults become more philosophical.

Reflections on life are more prominent; there is a deeper evaluation and, at best, acceptance of one's life as it was lived (Erikson, 1969; Jaques, 1965; Staudinger, 2001). Learning about the journey of the self can result in increased insight, enhanced self-knowledge, and fresh understandings about the limits to personal and human knowledge (Erikson, 1958, 1969, 1982).

Some Concluding Thoughts

The integration of adult development and learning represents a new area of conceptualization and study. Among the essential points that link this hybrid area, the following are prominent. On their own and together, development and learning represent the complex adult who adapts to the environment and who changes and has the potential for advancing in many qualitatively unique ways. Although there are negatives associated with advancing age, many adults continue to develop and learn throughout their middle, later, and far older years. In this progression, it is often the case that adults themselves are the prime agents. However, there are individual, cohort, cultural, and societal differences, distinctions that auger against any stereotypical or homogeneous view of adults, their abilities, and complex changes in developmental and learning characteristics and potentials (see Lang & Heckhausen, chapter 7, this volume).

The context and resources available to and used by the adult interact with heredity, experience, social events, motivations, personal inclinations, and the environment. Together, this interplaying composite shapes development, augmenting growth for some and deterring it for others. In addition, the contexts and personal development of earlier life are benefits or potential deprivations for each adult. Humans exist in a seamless narrative from which they cannot escape. This is the case despite the late twentieth-century recognition that many adult abilities, understandings, and representations hold unique content and competencies that do not fully redound to childhood. As is true for genetics, origins are not fully determinative; childhood attributes and capacities fail the tests of adult differentiation and complexity.

Adults themselves are fluid and will continue to adapt and evolve. The socioeconomic political landscape, always in flux, alters views and differentially emphasizes some sets of learning and developmental abilities over others. This is particularly true in cross-cultural comparisons. Furthermore, the dynamic interaction between macro-level social change and micro-level individual change, although beyond the scope of this book, bears recognition. Irrespective of future changes in humans and their environments, the more we know about growth possibilities and about the reciprocal nature of development and learning in adulthood, the better we will be able to intervene in support of enhanced positive adaptations for adults and the societal institutions that incorporate and support them.

OVERVIEW OF THIS VOLUME

The contributors to this volume write on various topics and from differing frames of reference and levels of analysis. This text is a beginning effort that includes a number of key topics, dimensions, and adult attributes. We do not claim to have covered the complete landscape of adult development and learning. Rather, our effort is to join two previously nonintegrated disciplines and inspire thought as to how learning and development together represent a joint discipline of theory, inquiry, and practice. At times herein, the emphasis is more on development than on learning; at other points the balance tips preferentially toward learning. But the key question is always the same: Where is there synchrony, and how might one propel causal reciprocity between learning and developmental advances that together chart the adult years?

As part of this foundations section, Merriam and Clark begin chapter 2 with personal autobiographical vignettes, illustrating how two very different journeys in young adulthood held transforming experiences. In these we see how intense, emotionally charged, and reflective learning can lead to the development of insight, identity, and lifetime commitments. These personal experiences are their springboard to exploring the character of the connection between development and learning, of factors that promote this connection, and ways of teaching that foster personal development and change.

Taking us to a different realm, Caskie and Willis address fundamental methodological issues in research into adult development and learning in chapter 3. They explore key issues in study design, explain the predominant forms of studies, and address sampling and measurement issues. They conclude the chapter with a discussion of statistical versus clinical significance in evaluating the importance of research data.

In four key areas, part II asks how adult development and learning can fuel one another. In chapter 4, Kitchener, King, and DeLuca speak to reflective judgment in adulthood. They show how advances in knowledge about ongoing psychosocial development, intellectual development, and the development of wisdom, for example, led Kitchener and King to develop the reflective judgment model (RJM) several decades ago. The authors then explain the assumptions underlying the model; explore the sequential, stage-based levels of reasoning that persons move through in their development; and address the assessment of reflective judgment. They review empirical research, showing how reflective judgment improves as a result of learning endeavors, and explore the relationship of the RJM to, for example, Kurt Fischer and colleague's (e.g., Fischer & Pruyne, 2002) cognitive, skill-acquisition model and to Robert Kegan's (e.g., 1994) integrated developmental model. Importantly, they show the relationships among the development of reflective judgment and advances in learning, open-mindedness, and intelligent action into and through adulthood.

In chapter 5, Schaie and Zanjani explore intellectual development across adulthood. They review state-of-the-art data and discuss the course of adult intellectual development through an analysis of findings from the Seattle Longitudinal Study. They address variances in intellectual development due, for example, to intra-individual differences, cohort effects, familial influences, learning, and medical comorbidities. They present effective interventions that foster intellectual competence. They speak to the recent shift in research in this area, specifically to the current tendency to investigate antecedent variables and individual patterns of change in cognitive competence instead of focusing solely on the extent of age differences in intelligence. This change points to potential progress in predicting individual hazards and to interventions that might maintain and expand adult functional competence.

Considine and Magai's chapter 6 on emotional development in adulthood follows. In their review of empirical data on emotional experience and affect, they address the experience, intensity, and complexity of emotions, as well as changes in the physiology of emotion in adulthood. They discuss adults' self-regulation of emotions as well as the improvements many adults show in controlling their expression of feelings. Social interactions figure prominently, for mature adults work to preserve their marital, extended kinship, workplace, friendship, and other key relationships. The authors then address changes in emotion-related cognitive styles and attachment patterns. Throughout the chapter, learning, self-regulation, and development are integrated.

Lang and Heckhausen's chapter concludes part II. These investigators discuss changes in motivation and interpersonal capacities across adulthood, focusing on the ways adults manage the various challenges of their lives. The authors address physiological influences, cognitive resources, normative challenges, and societal opportunity structures. As agents of their own progress through the mature years of life, adults are seen as those who are embedded in culture- and role-specific scripts; yet adults are agents of their own progress throughout the mature years of life. The developing, learning adult creates a self-revised person who manages and shapes the self, coauthors relationships with others, and invests in interpersonal regulation, mastery, and ongoing agency.

Part III of the volume considers the self-system as it relates to adult development and learning. It begins with Cervone, Artistico, and Berry's chapter on the relationship between self-efficacy and adult development (chapter 8). These researchers speak to the important ways individuals who believe in themselves are future-oriented, competent, and goal-achieving. Self-efficacious adults grow via the key contexts, roles, and experiences of their lives. They create their own opportunities, shape their environments (and are shaped by them), and foster their own learning and development. The authors present us with a complexity theory of integrated development in which personality is a large, permeable system. Incorporating insights from different but complementary traditions, Bandura's (e.g., 1997) social-cognitive research program joins important thought in human development, including the Baltes and Baltes (1990) Model of Selective Optimization with Compensation (SOC). The authors describe personality coherence and change. They demonstrate the development of self-efficacy beliefs, examine influences on development and learning, review data on sustained performance, and discuss skill development through training programs. Included are everyday problem solving, cognitive skills in learning, and the intellectual and health-related challenges of aging.

Chapter 9, by Taylor, shows us the adult's developmental journey of autonomy, one of reciprocal advances in cognitive development, ways of knowing, gains in knowledge, and self-directed learning. She describes the advantages of self-directed learning (SDL) in a highly diverse and fast-paced technological environment. She reviews research, theory, and practice, addressing the personality characteristics of autonomous learners, applications of learning theory, and the outcomes of autonomous learning and cognitive growth. Agreeing with Nietzsche (1885/1967) that there is no such thing as an "immaculate perception," she reminds us that we see various realities as *we* are, not as *they* are. This is her lens into constructivism, transformational learning, and levels of knowing, developing, and self-authoring. She addresses developmental orientations to knowing, the scaffolding of knowledge, and situational characteristics (of contexts, problems, and educators) that engage the learner to jointly advance development and learning. Taylor focuses on self-reflection and on finding ways to help learners examine their assumptions. She addresses collaborative learning, the movement from implicit to explicit knowing, and teaching as a caring function. When speaking of teaching as that which enhances various forms of development, values are never far from this author's thought. To her, good teaching is necessarily a supportive, caring function, one that confirms and validates the learner even as it helps that learner to move beyond his or her current level of knowing.

Miller's chapter 10 on adult development, learning, and insight through psychotherapy completes the self-system part of this handbook. Miller attaches great importance to the inner life, aligning his work with Jung's observation that only those who can see into the interior self will awaken. Miller first reviews data showing the recent escalation in mental illnesses and in the numbers of walking, psychologically wounded. He reveals various trigger points, existential questions, and personal crises that lead adults to their therapist's door. Then, through the case example of a hypothetical patient, he walks us through the psychotherapy process. Along the way, he points out phases in the therapy process, topics that emerge in therapy (e.g., "lost opportunities," relationship difficulties), transference-countertransference issues, and how one listens actively to another. He describes

treatment modes, illustrating their different viewpoints. Importantly, he illustrates how the dyad builds their relationship toward a working alliance, one that can lead to the development of great insight and learning. He describes "working in the transference" as that which predicts therapeutic success, substituting a learning model for defense analysis. Among a number of other important contributions, Miller shows that insight development and learning are reciprocal, that learning proceeds as one develops along the cognitive-affective trajectory. Cognitive and affective development are inseparable, and learning is integral to the process. To the author, the inner world is a vast reservoir of potential, often untapped learning.

Part IV of this volume speaks to the higher reaches of adult development and learning. Contributors address creativity, innovation, and the meaning and development of wisdom and spirituality. This part of the volume begins with Csikszentmihalyi and Nakamura's chapter on creativity through the life span from an evolutionary systems perspective (chapter 11). The authors define and illustrate the manifestations of creativity. They show that both genes and memes inform development. They link creativity with play but dispel the notion that creative play and fresh views are confined to the early years of life. Finding examples in older creators, they show that creativity need not decay until life's very end. Linking learning with creativity in later life, the authors distinguish between seniors' difficulties in learning new tools and the ease with which many elders continue to engage in creative ideas and ongoing learning. Personal satisfaction and one's use of resources are integral to the process. The authors distinguish between physical and social aging and, pointing to the ways new ideas emerge and are adopted, invoke Kuhn's (1962) thought on how conventional thinking opposes groundbreaking ideas. Vignettes of elders who continue to create and learn fill the chapter, inspiring a view of later life as that which is not necessarily conservative, passive, and passionless. They show us how creative persons preserve and make use of their curiosity, their interest in ongoing learning, their "maverick" tendencies, and their aesthetic experiences. They conclude the chapter with practical suggestions regarding the ways adult creativity can be developed, supported, and enriched.

In chapter 12, Commons and Bresette take creativity in a different direction. The authors address scientific innovation from the perspective of the

Commons and Richards (1984) Model of Hierarchical Complexity (MHC). The authors explain the MHC and illustrate how higher levels of complex (postformal) thinking and knowing are required for innovations that will change thought. They provide examples of historically acclaimed innovators (e.g., Copernicus, Darwin, Einstein) who, in crossing paradigms of thought, created new fields of thought and study. The authors address the forms of personal and societal support that are necessary for innovators. Importantly, they show how novelty, in addition to a creator's ability to sustain attention and observation, augment both the innovator's intellectual powers and social change. The authors then consider the intersection among different personality attributes, styles, personal tendencies, and creativity. They end the chapter with potentially unsettling speculations about new forms of human species and about innovations that may yet link computers with human brains.

In chapter 13, Bassett integrates wisdom, development, and learning. She discusses contemporary and historical views of wisdom and the many different approaches to its study. She maintains that there are so many ways of considering this honored quality that a precise definition remains elusive. The author reviews the theoretical and empirical literature and considers a wealth of studies from different viewpoints, perspectives, and levels of analysis. Among others, the author reviews studies that relate wisdom to personality, to cognitive and dialectical development, to insight development, to transforming experiences, to the integration of personal and cognitive attributes, to transcendent abilities, and to demographic variables (e.g., education, age, gender). She pinpoints longitudinal studies that show adult developmental changes in wisdom during 25 years of mature life. She speaks to the slim number of cross-cultural studies of wisdom. Importantly, she shows a number of ways that the development and extension of wisdom are reciprocal with learning. The author brings the chapter to a close with a section on learning for wisdom development.

Irwin's chapter on spiritual development in adulthood (chapter 14) concludes part IV. He begins his chapter by offering a meditative practice sent to him by his Buddhist teacher. He uses this meditation practice to explore how its conduct is related to level of development. The author employs Western theories of ego, cognitive, faith, and transpersonal development, as well as Eastern thought regarding the evolution of consciousness. Empirical data and ancient literature inform his chapter. Importantly, he equates learning and insight development with the emergence of the spiritual, finding that many times what we conclude to be breakdowns of mental health may in fact be breakthroughs to higher states of being. The author explains why meditation may be an apt mode of treatment for those who show readiness for transpersonal development. Irwin explains the role of social and cognitive simulation capacities in the integration of learning and development, and shows how these relate to interpersonal, emotional, moral, and transcendent advances. The author presents and contrasts stage progression in the developmental models of Alexander, Cook-Greuter, Fowler, Kegan, Loevinger, and Wilber and locates spiritual development in these models, particularly at the highest stages. He relates cognitive, social, and spiritual development to the abilities implicit in decentration of the ego, and to transcendent abilities. The ability to perform simulations (mental representations of hypothetical, trial-and-error selection) figures prominently in his thought. He concludes the chapter by addressing meditative practices and the ways in which these can help one transcend the ego.

In part V, we consider four contexts that are catalytic to adult development and learning. These are parenting, work, community, and culture. In chapter 15, Demick presents a transactional theory of adult development based on the changing responsibilities and equilibrations inherent in parenting. He reviews the history of socialization from the earlier unidirectional (effects of parents on children) model through the bidirectional model and into the contemporary dialectic (transactional) model. He shows historical movement from a mechanistic to an organismic and contextual worldview and pinpoints attributes of the transactional model that represent a holistic, open systems, perspective of development. The author examines the holistic/systems, developmental view at the "parent-in-environment" level of analysis. This unit includes biopsychosocial and cultural attributes, exploring the ways internal and external environments mediate one another. He illustrates four phases in the development of self-world relationships, relating these to, for example, the coping modes of parents, and then focuses on adoptive parents in their various developmental levels. The author then employs Galinsky's (1981) theory of the stages of parental development as it is reframed in the Demick and

Wapner (e.g., 1992) model of parental development. Importantly, the author addresses children's role in their parents' development and learning. Children are seen as sources of inspiration, emotional integration, cognitive flexibility, and learning. Drawing on Dillon's (2002) work, he illustrates how children inspire parents to find the child archetype (Jung, 1959) within their now-adult form of being. He closes the chapter with conditions that are likely to facilitate developmental change for the parent and the child.

In chapter 16, Hoare considers the catalytic effects of work on reciprocal development and learning. The chapter includes two principal components: adult identity evolution and personality expression, facets that develop from workplace competence. Noting that the theoretical and empirical literatures on paid work have focused disproportionate attention on corporate needs, efficiency, and fiscal success, she addresses the positive effects of work on workers themselves, effects that serve corporate needs as well. She reviews theory and empirical data on the ways that paid work bolsters the adult psyche and propels advances in reciprocal learning and development. She considers social changes that have effects on work identity and personality expression and addresses the meaning of identity in what has become a fluid, high-risk environment. In the personality realm, she considers the six attributes of autonomy, interpersonal competence, maturity, conscientiousness, openness to experience, and intellectual flexibility as attributes that show close relationships to paid work experiences. She looks to work autonomy and complexity as factors that predict advances in intellectual development and learning and that may forestall the cognitive declines associated with aging. She considers good work as that which permits exploration and childlike play with, for example, ideas, designs, plans, and scenarios.

Chapter 17, by Sinnott and Berlanstein, speaks to the importance of feeling whole and to the ways in which feeling connected to others in community bolsters and reflects adult development and learning. Using two very different case examples of older women, the authors illustrate the rejection (and self-rejection) of the first and the social relatedness and generativity of the second. They then explain three forms of feeling connected: connecting the "sides of the self," connecting with others, and connecting with the transcendent. They express these forms in terms of their dynamic processes, challenges to the self/identity, and

relationships to motivation and to cognitive development (complex postformal thought), as well as cognitive failure. They then return to their case examples, illustrating the interplay among the forms of felt connections and various processes, challenges, motivations, cognitive dimensions, and pathology. In the chapter's second section, the authors explore four abstract models that undergird their theory of felt connection and development. The models are the theory of Complex Postformal Thought, General Systems Theory, Chaos Theory, and the Theory of Self-Organizing Systems. For each, the authors provide an explanatory framework and review related literature. They examine the theories against emotional development and interpersonal skills. They conclude with an examination of research possibilities that relate to the three forms of felt connection examined in the chapter. Sinnott and Berlanstein provide us with a new area of thought and potential study. Highly relevant to the global niche and to our increased permeability to others in distant lands, the authors show a "shifting sense of identity" against the "primal need" for social relatedness. They chart the developmental growth of connectedness as that which occurs in synchrony with cognitive development, emotional development and learning, and learning about others and the self.

Keller and Werchan, in chapter 18, take us to the dimension of culture as the context for adult learning and development. The authors explain how learning and development are necessarily interwoven. Expressing culture as shared activities and meaning systems that are implicit in processes fundamental to daily experience and action, they show how cultural mores, norms, and practices organize individual development. These are apparent in, for example, imitation and role modeling, habits, instruction, and patterns of collaboration. The authors discuss the two sociocultural orientations of independence and dependence, providing data to show how these orientations embed themselves in a person's sense of self. Each orientation provides, for example, socialization goals, ideas of competence, notions about preferred living patterns, and ideas about adaptive aging. The authors review data regarding competence and learning in the cultural context, providing examples from Asian, Australian, Euro-American, U.S. Native American, and other distinct forms of cultural life. For example, they depict Knowles's (e.g., 1984) assumptions about adult learners and Freud's (psychosexual) and Erikson's (psychosocial) psychoanalytic viewpoints as reflecting the independent sociocultural orientation. The authors illustrate how the timing of developmental tasks varies with the culture's orientation; they show how adulthood's beginning and the ceremonies marking its initiation vary from culture to culture. In the final chapter section, the authors speak to adult competence as this is demonstrated in ideas of wisdom. They depict cultural variations in the wisdom literature, illustrate cultural variability in theories of wisdom, and speak to wisdom's attainability. Ending with a discussion of potential outcomes that occur at the development and learning intersection, Keller and Werchan conclude that synchronous learning and development are mediated, as they must be, by the tools, signs, symbols, and norms of culture.

Part VI, the final section of the handbook, focuses specifically on how one measures and applies knowledge about development and learning in adulthood. In chapter 19, Dawson-Tunik writes on the meaning and measurement of conceptual development. Responding to difficulties in measuring individual progress using developmental stage theories, she illustrates how the method of developmental maieutics separates stage level (structure) from content. As the author explains, one is thus able to ask questions about level and content relationships. Dawson synthesizes literature on the developmental maieutics methodology, addresses validity issues, and provides sample applications. She then describes the hierarchical complexity construct and the hierarchical complexity scoring system (HCSS). With respect to conceptual development and learning, the author distinguishes between the two, specifying that learning requires interaction with the environment, whereas development is solely an internal process of structuring knowledge; however, she shows the two processes as necessarily interdependent. Using examples from the physical sciences, she then shows the importance of measurement in theoretical advances and shows the applicability of a solid metric that can be used across knowledge areas. She evaluates current assessments of development, arguing that contrary to conventional opinion, theorists and researchers can and must describe complex developmental phenomena along general dimensions. Dawson-Tunik presents validation studies and concludes the chapter with a section highlighting the use of the HCSS in a federal agency. She illustrates how the HCSS can be used in different content areas.

In their chapter on the role of doctoral study in advancing development and learning (chapter 20), Stevens-Long and Barner begin with a review of what graduate programs, particularly doctoral programs, intend for their learners. They then address how doctoral study and the learning engagement therein leads to cognitive development. They integrate literature from adult learning, adult education, cognitive development, ego development, emotional development, and conative development. They show how escalations in thinking, experiencing, and knowing lead to positive developmental change and ongoing learning. Examples are found in the way scholar-practitioners show greater reflective capacities in the midst of unsettling change, the role of heightened self-efficacy, and gains in wisdom. Critically, the authors show the importance of integrating the cerebral (cognitive) with the limbic (emotional) to advance learning, higher levels of knowing, and personal maturity. Equally important, they speak to the destructive force of hegemony in graduate programs. The authors explore four unique pathways that are causal in development in graduate (primarily doctoral) study. These are changes in perspective regarding knowledge and learning, gaining and holding membership in a community of learners, gaining advanced understandings about the use of self in learning endeavors, and gaining expanded awareness of sociocultural contexts. Throughout, they provide examples in learners' words, connecting these with empirical data. They close with a summary section in which they advance recommendations for graduate education.

McAuliffe's chapter then provides a lens into how adult development explains professional competence. He speaks to the nature of professional work and to career and life phases as these integrate with structural, cognitive development and lead to greater competence. Using theory and research data as his base, he employs Granott's (1998) concept of developmental learning to explain conditions and guidelines for the progression of these joint dimensions. Using the propositions of theorists such as Dewey (1933), Schon (e.g., 1983, 1987), and Kegan (e.g, 1994), he explains the importance of reflective thinking in ongoing learning, development, and professional practice. Empirical data inform his implications about the scarcity and need for fourth- and fifth-order consciousness and of the role of Torbert's (e.g., 1987) stage approach in the evolution of professional development. He concludes the chapter with a section on the ways that learning how to learn is itself a measure of development.

In chapter 22, the section's final chapter, Rogers, Mentkowski, and Hart address adult holistic development and multidimensional performance. This final chapter of the volume crosses educational, workplace, and civic contexts. Integrating widely different theoretical views, the authors critically review research from a variety of perspectives and levels of analysis. Based in part on the theory and empirical research illustrated in their volume *Learning that lasts* (Mentkowski et al., 2000), the authors use the model of the person in context as a meta-theoretical framework. They contrast four domains (development, reasoning, performance, self-reflection) of growth, and, following William James's (1890/1962) differentiation of the I and the Me, speak to holistic development as that which occurs in the person's process of existential meaning-making. This relates self-reflection to the objectified Me. Using theory and data from a vast array of sources, they illustrate the linkages among development, learning, and performance. Among others, they include studies of cognitive complexity, defense mechanism maturity, reflective judgment, leadership development, and multidimensional development in, for example, caring professionals (e.g., nurses, physicians, teachers, counselors). They conclude the chapter with three sections, one on sources of ongoing holistic development, a second that illustrates how their educational model links adult development with performance, and a third that provides implications with respect to their conclusion that multidimensional performance and ongoing, holistic development are often reciprocal in influence.

We look forward to an interstitial discipline of adult learning and development. Although recent years have seen disciplines and subdisciplines fragment the person into ever smaller compartments that are said to define the human, this tendency tilts away from what we know as a unified, coherent, and changing being. Accumulating evidence shows the need for ongoing theory and research in which adults are seen as those who develop and learn in unison, attributes that together aid in defining their holistic nature. In their various ways, the authors collected here give credence to the fact that the way people think about their future will dramatically alter the direction that future takes. Together, we ask professionals in various areas of study to think about a future in which there is an interwoven discipline of adult learning and development.

ACKNOWLEDGMENTS   I express my sincere appreciation to my colleague Richard Lanthier, who reviewed an earlier draft of this chapter.

References

Artistico, D., Cervone, D., & Pezzuti, L. (2003). Perceived self-efficacy and everyday problem solving among young and older adults. *Psychology of Aging*, *18*, 68–79.

Aspinwall, L. G., & Staudinger, U. M. (Eds.). (2003). A *psychology of human strengths*. Washington, DC: American Psychological Association.

Bailey, T., Berg, P., & Sandy, C. (2001). The effect of high-performance work practices on employee earnings in the steel, apparel, and medical electronics and imaging industries. *Industrial and Labor Relations Review*, *54*, 525–543.

Ball, K., Berch, D. B., Helmers, K. F., Jobe, J. B., Leveck, M. D., Marsiske, M., et al. (2002). Effects of cognitive training interventions with older adults: A randomized controlled trial. *Journal of the American Medical Association*, *288*, 2271–2281.

Baltes, P. B., & Baltes, M. M. (1990). Psychological perspectives on successful aging: The model of selective optimization with compensation. In P. B. Baltes & M. M. Baltes (Eds.), *Successful aging: Perspectives from the behavioral sciences* (pp. 1–34). Cambridge: Cambridge University Press.

Baltes, P. B., & Baltes, M. M. (Eds.). (1993). *Successful aging*. New York: Cambridge University Press.

Baltes, P. B., & Kliegl, R. (1992). Further testing of the limits of cognitive plasticity: Negative age differences in mnemonic skills are robust. *Developmental Psychology*, *28*, 121–125.

Baltes, P. B., Lindenberger, U., & Staudinger, U. M. (1998). Life-span theory in developmental psychology. In W. Damon (series ed.) and R. M. Lerner (vol. ed.), *Handbook of child psychology* (Vol. 1, pp. 1029–1143). New York: Wiley.

Baltes, P. B., & Staudinger, U. M. (1993). The search for a psychology of wisdom. *Current Directions in Psychological Science*, *2*, 75–80.

Bandura, A. (1997). *Self-efficacy: The exercise of control*. New York: Freeman.

Barnes, C. A., & McNaughton, B. L. (1985). An age comparison of the rates of acquisition and forgetting of spatial information in relation to long-term enhancement of hippocampal synapses. *Behavioral Neuro-science*, *99*, 1040–1048.

Basseches, M. A. (1984). Dialectical thinking as a metasystematic form of cognitive organization. In M. L. Commons, F. A. Richards, & C. Armon (Eds.), *Beyond formal operations: Late adolescent and adult cognitive development* (pp. 216–238). New York: Praeger.

Beck, U. (1994). *Ecological enlightenment: Essays on the politics of the risk society*. Atlantic Highlands, NJ: Humanities Press.

Berg, C. A., & Sternberg, R. J. (2003). Multiple perspectives on the development of adult intelligence. In J. Demick & C. Andreoletti (Eds.), *Handbook of adult development* (pp. 103–119). New York: Kluwer Academic.

Berkman, L. F., Seeman, T. E., Albert, M., Blazer, D., Kahn, R., Mohs, R., et al. (1993). High, usual, and impaired functioning in community-dwelling older men and women: Findings from the MacArthur Foundation Research Network on Successful Aging. *Journal of Clinical Epidemiology, 46,* 1129–1140.

Bornstein, M. H., Davidson, L., Keyes, C. L. M., & Moore, K. A. (Eds.). (2003). *Well-being: Positive development across the life course*. Mahway, NJ: Lawrence Erlbaum.

Bosworth, H. B., & Schaie, K. W. (1999). Survival effects in cognitive function, cognitive style, and sociodemographic variables in the Seattle Longitudinal Study. *Experimental Aging Research, 25,* 121–139.

Busse, E. W., & Maddox, G. L. (1985). *The Duke longitudinal studies of normal aging*. New York: Springer.

Cameron, H. A., & Gould, E. (1994). Adult neurogenesis is regulated by adrenal steroids in the dentate gyrus. *Neuroscience, 61,* 203–209.

Caspi, A., & Elder, G. (1986). Life satisfaction in old age: Linking social psychology and history. *Journal of Psychology and Aging, 1,* 18–26.

Ceci, S., & Liker, J. (1986). Academic and nonacademic intelligence: An experimental separation. In R. Sternberg & R. Wagner (Eds.), *Practical intelligence: Nature and origins of competence in the everyday world* (pp. 119–142). Cambridge: Cambridge University Press.

Ceci, S., & Liker, J. (1988). Stalking the IQ-expertise relationships: When the critics go fishing. *Journal of Experimental Psychology: General, 117,* 96–100.

Charness, N., & Bosman, E. A. (1990). Expertise and aging: Life in the lab. In T. M. Hess (Ed.), *Aging and cognition: Knowledge organization and utilization* (pp. 343–385). Amsterdam: Elsevier.

Cherry, K. E., & Stadler, M. A. (1995). Implicit learning of a nonverbal sequence in younger and older adults. *Psychology and Aging, 10,* 379–394.

Clancy, S. M., & Hoyer, W. J. (1994). Age and skill in visual search. *Developmental Psychology, 30,* 545–552.

Cochran, A., & Laub, J. (1994). *Becoming an agent*. Albany: State University of New York Press.

Commons, M. L., & Richards, F. A. (1984). Applying the general model of hierarchical complexity. In M. L. Commons, F. A. Richards, & C. Armon (Eds.), *Beyond formal operations: Vol. 1. Late adolescent and adult cognitive development* (pp. 141–157). New York: Praeger.

Commons, M. L., Sinnott, J. D., Richards, F. A., & Armon, C. (Eds.). (1984). *Beyond formal operations: Late adolescent and adult cognitive development*. New York: Praeger.

Confucius (1938). *The analects* (A. Waley, trans.). London: Allen & Unwin. (Original work n.d.)

Craik, F. I. M., & Salthouse, T. A. (Eds.). (2000). *The handbook of aging and cognition* (2nd ed.). Mahwah, NJ: Lawrence Erlbaum.

Deary, I. J., Whiteman, M. C., Starr, J. M., Whalley, L. J., & Fox, H. C. (2004). The impact of childhood intelligence on later life: Following up the Scottish Mental Surveys of 1932 and 1947. *Journal of Personality and Social Psychology, 86,* 130–147.

de Haan, M., Humphreys, K., & Johnson, M. H. (2002). Developing a brain specialized for face perception: A converging methods approach. *Developmental Psychobiology, 40,* 200–212.

de Haan, M., Paascalis, O., & Johnson, M. H. (2002). Specialization of neural mechanisms underlying face recognition in human infants. *Journal of Cognitive Neuroscience, 14,* 199–209.

Demick, J., & Wapner, S. (1992). Transition to parenthood: Developmental changes in experiences and action. In T. Yamamoto & S. Wapner (Eds.), *Developmental psychology of life transitions* (pp. 243–265). Tokyo: Kyodo Shuppan.

Dewey, J. (1933). *How we think*. Lexington, MA: Heath.

Dillon, J. J. (2002). The role of the child in adult development. *Journal of Adult Development, 9,* 267–275.

Dittmann-Kohli, F., & Baltes, P. B. (1990). Toward a neofunctionalist conception of adult intellectual development: Wisdom as a prototypical case of intellectual growth. In C. N. Alexander & E. J. Langer (Eds.), *Higher stages of human development* (pp. 54–78). New York: Oxford University Press.

Duncan, L. E., & Agronick, G. S. (1995). The intersection of life stage and social events: Personality and life outcomes. *Journal of Personality and Social Psychology, 69,* 558–568.

Elder, G. H. Jr. Rudkin, L., & Conger, R. D. (1994). Inter-generational continuity and change in rural America. In V. L. Bengston, K. W. Schaie, & L. Burton (Eds.), *Adult intergenerational relations: Effects of societal change* (pp. 30–60). New York: Springer.

Ellinger, A. D., Ellinger, A. E., Yang, B., & Howton, S. (2002). The relationship between the learning organization concept and firms' financial performance: An empirical assessment. *Human Resource Development Quarterly, 13,* 5–21.

Endler, N. S., Boulter, L. R., & Osser, H. (1976). Theories of development. In N. S. Endler, L. R. Boulter, & H. Osser (Eds.). *Contemporary issues in developmental psychology* (2nd ed., pp. 1–34). New York: Holt, Rinehart & Winston.

Ericsson, K. A., & Charness, N. (1994). Expert performance: Its structure and acquisition. *American Psychologist, 49,* 725–747.

Ericsson, K. A., Patel, V., & Kintsch, W. (2000). How experts' adaptations to representative task demands account for the expertise effect in memory recall: Comment on Vicente and Wang (1998). *Psychological Review, 107,* 578–592.

Ericsson, K. A., & Smith, J. (Eds.). (1991). *Toward a general theory of expertise: Prospects and limits.* New York: Cambridge University Press.

Erikson, E. H. (1943). Observations on the Yurok: Childhood and world image. *University of California Publications in American Archeology and Ethnology, 35 (10),* 257–301.

Erikson, E. H. (1958). *Young man Luther.* New York: Norton.

Erikson, E. H. (1969). *Gandhi's truth.* New York: Norton.

Erikson, E. H. (1982). *The life cycle completed.* New York: Norton.

Erikson, E. H. (1987). *The papers of Erik and Joan Erikson.* Houghton Library, Harvard University. Unpublished.

Eriksson, P. S., Perfilieva, E., Bjork-Eriksson, T., Alborn, A. M., Nordborg, C., Peterson, D. A., et al. (1998). Neurogenesis in the adult human hippocampus. *Nature Medicine, 4,* 1313–1317.

Eysenck, M. W., & Calvo, M. G. (1992). Anxiety and performance: The processing efficiency theory. *Cognition and Emotion, 6,* 409–434.

Fillit, H. M., Butler, R. N., O'Connell, A. W., Albert, M. S., Birren, J. E., Cotman, C. W., et al. (2002). Achieving and maintaining cognitive vitality with aging. *Mayo Clinic Proceedings, 77,* 681–696.

Fischer, K. W., & Pruyne, E. (2002). Reflective thinking in adulthood: Emergence, development, and variation. In J. Demick & C. Andreoletti (Eds.), *Handbook of adult development* (pp. 169–198). New York: Plenum Press.

Freund, A. M., & Baltes, P. B. (1998). Selection, optimization, and compensation as strategies of life management: Correlations with subjective indicators of successful aging. *Psychology and Aging, 13,* 531–543.

Galinsky, E. (1981). *Between generations: The six stages of parenthood.* New York: Berkeley.

Gardner, H. (1985). *Frames of mind: The theory of multiple intelligences.* New York: Basic Books.

Granott, N. (1998). We learn, therefore we develop: Learning versus development or developing learning? In M. C. Smith & T. Pourchot (Eds.), *Adult learning and development* (pp. 15–34). Mahwah, NJ: Lawrence Erlbaum.

Hagestad, G. O., and Dannefer, D. (2001). Concepts and theories of aging: Beyond microfication in social sciences approaches. In R. H. Binstock & L. K. George (Eds.), *Handbook of aging and the social sciences* (5th ed., pp. 3–21). San Diego, CA: Academic Press.

Hamilton, R. H., & Pascual-Leone, A. (1998). Cortical plasticity associated with Braille learning. *Trends in Cognitive Sciences, 2,* 168–174.

Hoare, C. H. (2002). *Erikson on development in adulthood: New insights from the unpublished papers.* New York: Oxford University Press.

Hood, A. B., & Deopere, D. L. (2002). The relationship of cognitive development to age, when education and intelligence are controlled for. *Journal of Adult Development, 9,* 229–234.

Horn, J. L. (1994). Theory of fluid and crystallized intelligence. In E. J. Sternberg (Ed.), *Encyclopedia of human intelligence* (Vol. 1, pp. 443–451). New York: Macmillan.

Horn, J. L., & Hofer, S. M. (1992). Major abilities and development in the adult period. In R. J. Sternberg & C. A. Berg (Eds.), *Intellectual development* (pp. 44–49). New York: Cambridge University Press.

Howard, D. V., & Howard, J. H. Jr. (1989). Age differences in learning serial patterns: Direct versus indirect measures. *Psychology and Aging, 4,* 357–364.

Howard, D. V., & Howard, J. H. Jr. (1992). Adult age differences in the rate of learning serial patterns: Evidence from direct and indirect tests. *Psychology and Aging, 7,* 232–241.

Hoyer, W. J., & Touron, D. R. (2003). Learning in adulthood. In J. Demick & C. Andreoletti (Eds.), *Handbook of adult development* (pp. 23–41). New York: Kluwer Academic.

James, W. (1962). *Psychology: Briefer course.* New York: Collier Books. (Original work published 1890.)

Jaques, E. (1965). Death and the mid-life crisis. *International Journal of Psychoanalysis, 46,* 502–514.

Jung, C. G. (1933). *Modern man in search of a soul.* New York: Harcourt, Brace.

Jung, C. G. (1959). *The archetypes and the collective unconscious* (R. F. C. Hull, trans.). Princeton, NJ: Princeton University Press.

Kaye, B., & Jordan-Evans, S. (2000). Retention: Tag, you're it! *Training and Development, 54,* 29–33.

Kegan, R. (1982). *The evolving self.* Cambridge, MA: Harvard University Press.

Kegan, R. (1994). *In over our heads: The mental challenge of modern life.* Cambridge, MA: Harvard University Press.

Kitchener, P. M., & King, P. M. (1981). Reflective judgment: Concepts of justification and their relationship to age and education. *Journal of Applied Developmental Psychology, 2,* 89–116.

Kitchener, P. M., & King, P. M. (1994). *Developing reflective judgment: Understanding and promoting intellectual growth and critical thinking in adolescents and adults.* San Francisco: Jossey-Bass.

Knoops, K. T. B., de Groot, L. C. P. G. M., Kromhout, D., Perrin, A.-E., Moreiras-Varela, O., Menotti, A., et al. (2004). Mediterranean diet, lifestyle factors, and 10-year mortality in elderly European men and women: The HALE project. *Journal of the American Medical Association, 292,* 1433–1439.

Knowles, M. S. (1984). *Andragogy in action: Applying modern principles of adult learning.* San Francisco: Jossey-Bass.

Kohn, M. L., Zaborowksi, W., Mach, B. W., Khmelko, V., Heyman, C., & Podobnik, B. (2000). Complexity of activities and personality under conditions of radical social change: A comparative analysis of Poland and Ukraine. *Social Science Quarterly, 63,* 287–307.

Kramer, D. A., & Woodruff, D. S. (1986). Relativistic and dialectical thought in three adult age groups. *Human Development, 29,* 280–290.

Krampe, R., & Ericsson, K. A. (1996). Maintaining excellence: Deliberate practice and elite performance in young and older pianists. *Journal of Experimental Psychology: General, 125,* 331–359.

Kuhn, T. S. (1962). *The structure of scientific revolutions.* Chicago: University of Chicago Press.

Kujala, T., Alho, K., & Naatanen, R. (2000). Cross-modal reorganization of human cortical functions. *Trends in Neurosciences, 23,* 115–120.

Labouvie-Vief, G. (1992). A neo-Piagetian perspective on adult cognitive development. In R. J. Sternberg & C. A. Berg (Eds.), *Intellectual development* (pp. 239–252). New York: Cambridge University Press.

Labouvie-Vief, G. (1994). *Psyche and eros: Mind and gender in the life course.* New York: Cambridge University Press.

Labouvie-Vief, G., Chiodo, L. M., Goguen, L. A., Diehl, M., & Orwoll, L. (1995). Representations of self across the life span. *Psychology and Aging, 10,* 404–415.

Lanthier, R. P., & Windham, R. C. (2004). Internet use and college adjustment: The moderating effect of gender. *Computers in Human Behavior, 20,* 591–606.

Laplanche, J., & Pontalis, J. B. (1973). *The language of psycho-analysis.* New York: Norton.

Loevinger, J. (1980). *Ego development: Conceptions and theories.* San Francisco: Jossey-Bass.

Lu, T., Pan, Y., Kao, S.-Y., Li, C., Kohane, I., Chan, J., & Yankner, B. A. (2004). Gene regulation and DNA damage in the ageing human brain. *Nature, 429,* 883–891.

Maguire, E. A., Gadian, D. G., Johnsrude, I. S., Good, C. D., Ashburner, J., Frackowiak, R. S. J., et al. (2000). Navigation-related structural change in the hippocampi of taxi drivers. *Proceedings of the National Academy of Sciences USA, 97,* 4398–4403.

Masunaga, H., & Horn, J. (2001). Emotion and age-related changes in components of intelligence. *Psychology and Aging, 16,* 293–311.

Maurer, T. J., Weiss, E., & Barbeite, F. G. (2003). A model of involvement in work-related learning and development activity: The effects of individual, situational, motivational, and age variables. *Journal of Applied Psychology, 88,* 707–724.

May, D. R., Schwoerer, C. E., Reed, K., & Potter, P. (1997). Employee reactions to ergonomic job design: The moderating effects of health locus of control and self-efficacy. *Journal of Occupational Health Psychology, 2,* 11–24.

McFarland, C., & Buehler, R. (1998). The impact of negative affect on autobiographical memory: The role of self-focused attention to moods. *Journal of Personality and Social Psychology, 75,* 1424–1440.

Mentkowski, M., Rogers, G., Doherty, A., Loacker, G., Hart, J. R., Rickards, W., et al. (Eds.). (2000). *Learning that lasts.* San Francisco: Jossey-Bass.

Merriam, S., & Yang, B. (1996). A longitudinal study of adult life experiences and developmental outcomes. *Adult Education Quarterly, 46,* 62–81.

Mezirow, J. (1991). *Transfomative dimensions of adult learning.* San Francisco: Jossey-Bass.

Mikkelsen, A., Saksvik, P., Eriksen, H., & Ursin, H. (1999). The impact of learning opportunities and decision authority on occupational health. *Work Stress, 13,* 20–31.

Miller, J., Slomczynski, K. M., & Kohn, M. L (1988). Continuity of learning-generalization: The effect of job on men's intellectual process in the United States and Poland. In J. L. Mortimer & K. M. Borman (Eds.), *Work experience and psychological development through the life span* (pp. 79–107). Boulder, CO: Westview Press (American Association for the Advancement of Science Selected Symposium 107).

Mulatu, M. S., & Schooler, C. (1999). Longitudinal effects of occupational, psychological, and social background characteristics of older workers. *Annals of the New York Academy of Sciences, 896,* 406–408.

Myerson, J., Hale, S., Rhee, S. H., & Jenkins, L. (1999). Selective interference with verbal and spatial working memory in young and older adults. *Journal of Gerontology: Psychological Sciences, 54B,* P161–P164.

National Research Council. (2000). *The aging mind: Opportunities in cognitive research.* Washington, DC: National Academy Press.

Neisser, U. (1976). General, academic, and artificial intelligence. In L. Resnick (Ed.), *Human intelligence: Perspectives on its theory and measurement* (pp. 135–146). Norwood, NJ: Ablex.

Neugarten, B. L. (1979). Time, age, and the life cycle. *American Journal of Psychiatry, 136,* 887–894.

Nietzsche, F. W. (1967). *Thus spake Zarathustra.* (T. Common, trans.). New York: Heritage Press. (Original work published 1885)

Ohman, A. (2002). Automaticity and the amygdala: Nonconscious responses to emotional faces. *Current Directions in Psychological Science, 11,* 62–66.

Pascual-Leone, J., & Irwin, R. (1998). Abstraction, the will, the self, and modes of learning in adulthood. In M. C. Smith & T. Pourchot (Eds.), *Adult learning and development* (pp. 35–66). Mahwah, NJ: Lawrence Erlbaum.

Peck, R. C. (1968). Psychological developments in the second half of life. In B. L. Neugarten (Ed.), *Middle age and aging* (pp. 88–92). Chicago: University of Chicago Press.

Perls, T. T., Morris, J. N., Ooi, W. L., & Lipsitz, L. A. (1993). The relationship between age, gender, and cognitive performance in the very old: The effect of selective survival. *Journal of the American Geriatric Society, 41,* 1193–1201

Perry, W. (1970). *Forms of intellectual and ethical development in the college years.* New York: Holt, Rinehart & Winston.

Pfeffer, J. (1998). *The human equation: Building profits by putting people first.* Cambridge, MA: Harvard Business School Press.

Pirttila-Backman, A. M., & Kajanne, A. (2001). The development of implicit epistemologies during early and middle adulthood. *Journal of Adult Development, 8,* 81–97.

Pollock, G. H. (1981). Reminiscences and insight. *Psychoanalytic Study of the Child, 36,* 279–287.

Reber, A. S. (1993). *Implicit learning and tacit knowledge.* New York: Oxford University Press.

Riley, K. P., Snowdon, D. A., & Markesbery, W. R. (2002). Alzheimer's neurofibrillary pathology and the spectrum of cognitive function: Findings from the Nun Study. *Annals of Neurology, 51,* 567–577.

Rowe, J. W., & Kahn, R. L. (1987). Human aging: Usual and successful. *Science, 237,* 143–149.

Rowe, J. W., & Kahn, R. L. (1998). *Successful aging.* New York: Pantheon.

Rubenstein, R. L. (2002) The third age. In R. S. Weiss & S. A Bass (Eds.), *Challenges of the third age* (pp. 29–40). New York: Oxford University Press.

Ryle, G. (1949). *The concept of mind.* London: Hutchinson.

Sadler, W. A. (2000). *The third age: Six principles for growth and renewal after 40.* Cambridge, MA: Perseus.

Salthouse, T. A. (1984). Effects of age and skill in typing. *Journal of Experimental Psychology: General, 113,* 345–371.

Salthouse, T. A. (1994). Aging associations: Influence of speed on adult age differences in associative learning. *Journal of Experimental Psychology: Learning, Memory, and Cognition, 20,* 1486–1503.

Salthouse, T. A. (2000). Methodological assumptions in cognitive aging research. In F. I. M. Craik & T. A. Salthouse (Eds.), *The handbook of aging and cognition* (pp. 467–498). Mahwah, NJ: Lawrence Erlbaum.

Salthouse, T. A., & Coon, V. E. (1994). Interpretation of differential deficits: The case of aging and mental arithmetic. *Journal of Experimental Psychology: Learning, Memory, and Cognition, 20,* 1172–1182.

Schaie, K. W. (1989). The hazards of cognitive aging. *Gerontologist, 29,* 484–493.

Schaie, K. W. (1990). Intellectual development in adulthood. In J. E. Birren & K. W. Schaie (Eds.), *Handbook of the psychology of aging* (3rd ed., pp. 291–309). San Diego, CA: Academic Press.

Schaie, K. W. (1993). Age changes in adult intelligence. In D. S. Woodruff & J. E. Birren (Eds.), *Aging: Scientific perspectives and social issues* (2nd ed., pp. 111–124). Monterey, CA: Brooks/Cole.

Schaie, K. W. (1996a). Intellectual development in adulthood. In J. E. Birren & K. W. Schaie (Eds.), *Handbook of the psychology of aging* (pp. 266–286). New York: Academic Press.

Schaie, K. W. (1996b). *Intellectual development in adulthood: The Seattle longitudinal study.* New York: Cambridge University Press.

Schaie, K. W. (2005). *Developmental influences on adult intelligence: The Seattle Longitudinal Study.* New York: Oxford University Press.

Schaie, K. W., & Schooler, C., (Eds.). (1998). *Impact of work on older adults.* New York: Springer.

Schon, D. A. (1983). *The reflective practitioner.* San Francisco: Jossey-Bass.

Schon, D. A. (1987). *Educating the reflective practitioner.* San Francisco: Jossey-Bass.

Schooler, C., & Mulatu, M. S. (2001). The reciprocal effects of leisure time activities and intellectual functioning in older people: A longitudinal analysis. *Psychology and Aging, 16,* 466–482.

Schooler, C., Mulatu, M. S., & Oates, G. (1999). The continuing effects of substantively complex work on the intellectual functioning of older workers. *Psychology and Aging, 14,* 483–506.

Shimamura, A. P., Berry, J. M., Mangels, J. A., Rusting, C. L., & Jurica, P. J. (1995). Memory and cognitive abilities in university professors: Evidence for successful aging. *Psychological Science, 6,* 271–277.

Silver, M. H., Jilinskaia, E., & Perls, T. T. (2001). Cognitive functional status of age-confirmed centenarians in a population-based study. *Journals of Gerontology. Series B, Psychological Sciences and Social Sciences, 56,* 134–140.

Sloan, K. (2004). *Managers' experiential learning: An examination of the relationship between personality and tacit knowledge.* Unpublished doctoral dissertation, George Washington University, Washington, DC.

Smith, M. C., & Pourchot, T. (Eds.). (1998). *Adult learning and development.* Mahway, NJ: Lawrence Erlbaum.

Smyth, K. A., Fritsch, T., Cook, T. B., McClendon, M. J., Santillan, C. E., & Friedland, R. P. (2004). Worker functions and traits associated with occupations and the development of AD. *Neurology, 63,* 498–503.

Snowdon, D. (2001). *Aging with grace: What the Nun Study teaches us about leading longer, healthier, and more meaningful lives.* New York: Bantam Books.

Snowdon, D. (2003). Healthy aging and dementia: Findings from the Nun Study. *Annals of Internal Medicine, 139,* 450–454.

Stanley, T. O., Mackensen, G. B., Grocott, H. P., White, W. D., Blumenthal, J. A., Laskowitz, D. T., Lanolfo, K. P., Reves, J. G., Mathew, J. P., & Newman, M. F. (2002). The impact of postoperative atrial fibrillation on neurocognitive outcome after coronary artery bypass graft surgery. *Anesthesia Analgesia, 94,* 290–295.

Staudinger, U. M. (2001). Life reflection: A social-cognitive analysis of life review. *Review of General Psychology, 5,* 148–160.

Sternberg, R. J., Forsythe, G. B., Hedlund, J., Horvath, J. A., Wagner, R. K., Williams, W. M., et al. (2000). *Practical intelligence in everyday life.* Cambridge: Cambridge University Press.

Sternberg, R. J., Wagner, R., & Okagaki, L. (1993). Practical intelligence: The nature and role of tacit knowledge in work and at school. In J. M. Puckett & H. W. Reese (Eds.), *Mechanisms of everyday cognition* (pp. 205–227). Hillsdale, NJ: Lawrence Erlbaum.

Sternberg, R. J., Wagner, R. K., Williams, W. M., & Horvath, J. A. (1995). Testing common sense. *American Psychologist, 50*(11), 912–927.

Tabbarah, M., Crimmins, E. M., & Seeman, T. E. (2002). The relationship between cognitive and physical performance: MacArthur studies of successful aging. *Journal of Gerontology: Medical Sciences, 57*, M228–M235.

Torbert, W. R. (1987). *Managing the corporate dream.* Homewood, IL: Dow Jones-Irwin.

Torff, B., & Sternberg, R. J. (1998). Changing mind, changing world: practical intelligence and tacit knowledge in adult learning. In M. C. Smith & T. Pourchot (Eds.), *Adult learning and development* (pp. 109–126). Mahwah, NJ: Lawrence Erlbaum.

U.S. Bureau of the Census. (2000). *Census 2000 Brief: The 65 Years and Over Population.* (Report C2KBR/01–10). Retrieved October 3, 2004, from U.S. Bureau of the Census Reports Online, http://www.census.gov/population/www/socdemo/age/html#elderly.

Verghese, J., Lipton, R. B., Katz, M. J., Hall, C. B., Derby, C. A., & Kuslansky, G., et al. (2003). Leisure activities and the risk of dementia in the elderly. *New England Journal of Medicine, 348*, 2508–2516.

Willis, S. L., & Schaie, K. W. (1986). Training the elderly on the ability factors of spatial orientation and inductive reasoning. *Psychological Aging, 1*, 239–247.

Zacks, R. T., Hasher, L., & Li, K. Z. H. (2000). Human memory. In F. I. M. Craik & T. A. Salthouse (Eds.), *The handbook of aging and cognition* (pp. 293–358). Mahwah, NJ: Lawrence Erlbaum.

Chapter 2

Learning and Development: The Connection in Adulthood

Sharan B. Merriam and M. Carolyn Clark

In our search for resources for this chapter, it became apparent that although there are substantial individual knowledge bases for both adult development and adult learning, there are few works that explicitly focus on the *connection* between development and learning in adulthood. The adult development literature implicitly acknowledges the presence of learning just as the adult learning literature assumes some development as a by-product of learning. But rather than how one might be a motivator or an outcome of the other, we wanted to focus on the nexus or the intersection of development and learning.

To get started, we asked ourselves, "What excites us about this topic?" "Why have we agreed to write this chapter?" We turned to our own lives for examples of how we have experienced the relationship between learning and development. If we could verbalize those connections, lay them out on the table, maybe then we could "see" into the heart of the connection. And indeed, our stories led us to structuring this chapter around three themes—the nature of the connection, factors that promote the connection, and teaching for development.

THE NATURE OF THE CONNECTION BETWEEN ADULT DEVELOPMENT AND LEARNING

Sharan's Story

It was my first year of being an assistant professor and I was struggling with being in the "ivory tower" several layers removed from the real world of practice. I had taught with the Peace Corps in Afghanistan, then in an adult literacy center, and also in a state civil service training center. I had thoroughly enjoyed helping my students learn English, learn to read, or learn basic communication skills. While I liked working with graduate students studying adult education, I missed being on the front lines and wondered if I was on the right career track.

In the spring of that year I attended a conference in Washington, D.C. As part of the conference, there was a documentary movie being shown titled *One Word of Truth* and it is the reading of Solzhenitsyn's Nobel Prize Speech for his book, *The Gulag Archipelago*. The speech is read set against a collage of contrasting visual images. For example, Solzhenitsyn asks about human suffering and how is it that there are different yardsticks to measure suffering. This question is raised against alternating images of rich white men playing golf, Nazi concentration camp survivors, and hungry children in a refugee camp. The basic question and theme of his speech (as I recall it) is "What good is art (literary, visual) in a world of so much suffering and violence?" How could he and others like him be allowed the luxury of creating art? His answer is that it is the artist who brings "the one word of truth" in a world of lies, lies that are supported by violence.

That same night I was taking a taxi back to my hotel and the driver said to me, "Excuse me but my English is not good." I asked him where he was from and he said Afghanistan. Since I had lived there for two years I began conversing in the little Farsi that I could remember. He pulled off the road, turned off the taxi, and we talked for an hour. He told me his story of fighting the Soviets at night, being found out, and then having many of his family killed in retribution. He escaped to a refugee camp in Pakistan and after two years was sponsored by someone in the United States. He wept as he told me his story and his concern for other family and friends in Afghanistan, which was still under Soviet control at the time.

The movie viewing followed by encountering the taxi driver from Afghanistan was a transformational event in my life. I reflected on my "work" in this world and what it meant. I came to realize that I could make a contribution to what I was good at—teaching graduate students—and that my social action commitment and agenda could reach more people and help alleviate more suffering through the work of my students than I could do on my own. I became comfortable with my role as a professor. The learning from these events at this conference, at this time in my life, was directly intertwined with my developing professional identity.

Carolyn's Story

I was in one of those in-between periods in my life, the kind that are a lot easier to think back about than live through. The "before" was 14 years as a Catholic nun; the "for now" was working as a substance abuse counselor, a common transition job for people with a background in theology and ministry; but the "future" part was unclear. I had done a lot of pastoral counseling in the years before, so the counseling part of my job felt familiar and comfortable; what was new and challenging was the reason that these people were in my office to begin with. I had no personal experience with drug addiction—I didn't grow up in an alcoholic family, so I didn't know that dynamic firsthand, and I had never been more than a social drinker. How could I understand the experience of people for whom drugs and alcohol were an essential part of life, despite the enormous destruction their use caused? It was a major learning experience for me, and my clients were my teachers. What was clear to me very quickly was that this wasn't simply a behavior that needed to be changed. In terms of understanding what was going on, I found the medical model of addiction very persuasive—the notion that this is a disease to which some people have a genetic predisposition—but that didn't translate into successful treatment modalities. In fact, the relapse rates after even extensive treatment are astoundingly high. The agency where I worked dealt primarily with court-referred clients, those who had DUIs or other offenses that involved drugs, so most were not seeking treatment voluntarily and were, in fact, highly resistant to it. A lot of my time was spent dealing with denial. But occasionally I had a client who was seriously motivated to change and was already on the way to recovery. I remember one in particular—his name was Ronny. He had been multiply addicted from an early age, had hit bottom and kept on going, to the point of living in alleys and eating out of the dumpsters. He had lost everything, including his family. But by the time he arrived in my office he was turning his life around—he had been drug-free for more than a year, was active in Narcotics Anonymous, and was trying to prove to the judge that visitation rights to his daughter should be reinstated. From Ronny, *I* began to learn what the inner experience of drug addiction looked like, and what recovery looked like as well. It was clear that a fundamental transformation was necessary here, one that reshaped how clients understood themselves, the world, and their relation to that world. I saw it as a profoundly deep kind of learning, and I saw that my job as the counselor was to try to facilitate such learning to foster that kind of development in my clients.

Well, I didn't become Super Counselor—it is, after all, a daunting task to help people transform their lives—but I did get really interested in the learning that facilitates personal change. I remember attending a session on adult learning at an addiction counselors' conference one year, being intrigued by it, and from there I started exploring the field of adult education. I liked what I saw, decided to pursue my doctorate in that area, and ended up a professor. And all because of my work in that in-between time that so forcefully linked learning and development.

In exploring the nature of the connection between adult development and learning, we begin with a brief discussion of our understanding of development especially as the concept is portrayed in adult education. Next we map the territory of adult learning and finally, we explore how the two concepts are linked through identity development, transformational learning, and cognitive development.

Adult Development

That children change physically, cognitively, and socially as they age has long been understood and incorporated into the training of childhood educators. As this entire handbook attests to, adults also change as they age. Some of these changes may be more subtle and less visible than those of children, but they are just as important to take into account in the practice of adult education. Development, defined as change over time or change with age, is central to the practice of teaching and learning whether we are talking about children or adults.

Defining development as change over time belies the complexity of the concept. What triggers change and what is the process? Some view change as an orderly unfolding or progression (e.g., Erikson, 1963), whereas others find little about the process that is pre-programmed; instead, development is an adaptational response to new priorities and expectations associated with the life course (Gould, 1990). The goal of development is also unclear. Is it to achieve an end point, such as self-actualization (Maslow, 1970), or a fully integrated ego (Loevinger, 1976), or a more permeable and inclusive perspective (Mezirow, 2000)? Or, as Riegel (1973) and others see it, is development dialectic in nature, a function of the "constant interaction of the person and the environment" (Tennant & Pogson, 1995, p. 199) with no end point? Still others make the case for development as a political construct "because

different versions of development serve the interests of different groups" (Tennant & Pogson, 1995, p. 199).

As is the focus of this handbook, development from an adult education perspective has been predominately viewed as an internal psychological process. Emanating from this perspective are the age and stage theories wherein development is conceptualized as a patterned or orderly progression tied to chronological time expressed as specific ages or life stages (e.g., Havighurst, 1972; Kohlberg, 1973; Levinson, Darrow, Kien, Levinson, & McKee, 1978; Levinson & Levinson, 1996). These age/stage models of development are often referred to as a basis for identifying age/stage-appropriate adult educational programs (Knowles, 1980; Knowles & Associates, 1984).

Although the psychological framework for development has been prevalent in framing the connection to adult learning, other perspectives are equally informative. A social role perspective, for example, underscores the obvious; that is, the changing social roles and the transitions and life events that accompany these roles are integrally connected to learning. The birth of a child means learning the behaviors, skills, and attitudes of the "parenting" role. Furthermore, development from a biological perspective, especially with regard to changes in sight and hearing, changes in the central nervous system, and changes as a result of major disease processes, directly and indirectly influence adults' ability to learn. Finally, there is a growing awareness that the sociocultural context of adult lives is an important factor in shaping both development and learning (Elder, 1995; Jarvis, 1987, 1992; Tennant & Pogson, 1995).

We have defined development as change over time or change with age, meaning that change can involve increases or decreases, gains or losses, moving forward according to some normative understanding, or slipping backward. It bears pointing out, however, that the vast majority of literature on adult development and learning portrays development as change toward increasingly higher, more mature, more integrated levels of functioning. Indeed, when we asked ourselves what interested us about adult development and learning, we both talked about the potential for growth, for life-changing interventions bettering both individuals and society.

This positive growth perspective associated with development is firmly embedded in the humanistic orientation of adult education. Knowles (1980), for example, wrote that "the urge for growth is an especially strong motivation for learning, since education is by definition, growth—in knowledge, understanding, skills, attitudes, interests, and appreciation. The mere act of learning something new gives one a sense of growth" (p. 85). Knowles's (1980) set of assumptions, known as andragogy, have come to inform many practitioners' views of learning and development. The primary mission of adult education is "to help individuals satisfy their needs and achieve their goals" (p. 27), two of which are the "development of full potentialities" and "to mature" (p. 28). Jarvis (1987) observed that "there is no human growth without learning" (p. 81). And Daloz (1986, p. 22) wrote that "development is more than simply change. The word implies *direction.* . . . It is good, I believe to develop." For Daloz, "Significant learning and growth involve qualitative, developmental change in the way the world is viewed. We grow through a progression of transformations in our meaning-making apparatus, from relatively narrow and self-centered filters through increasingly inclusive, differentiated, and compassionate perspectives" (p. 149).

However, although most adult educators see development as growth-oriented, leading to more complex, more mature, more integrated systems, some acknowledge that change can be in the opposite direction. Dewey (1938) recognized that some experiences can be "mis-educative" (p. 25). In turn, such an experience "has the effect of arresting or distorting the growth of further experience. An experience may be such as to engender callousness; it may produce lack of sensitivity and responsiveness" (pp. 25–26). Jarvis (1987, p. 129) also noted that for some people, learning experiences "may be ones which induce other emotions [than growth] from which they learn to restrict their activities . . . change need not be developmental, in the normal sense of the term; indeed it can be detrimental to the development of the person."

A qualitative study of 18 adults who self-identified a negative outcome from learning found that if a life experience challenges some central defining aspect of the self, and this challenge is interpreted as too threatening to the self, growth-inhibiting responses are learned to protect the self (Merriam, Mott, & Lee, 1996). These growth-inhibiting responses included blame, hostility and anger, withdrawal and avoidance, and fear and distrust. It was also found that if and when the threat to the self is reduced, the process might reverse itself toward more growth-oriented outcomes.

It is our position then, that development is change over time and that such change is generally growth-oriented; however, learning from a life experience can also trigger changes that represent perspectives that are more inhibited, restrictive, and less developed than before. It is also our understanding that what constitutes growth, maturity, and so on, is determined in the individual's interaction with his or her particular sociocultural and historical context.

Adult Learning

Learning is a fundamental human behavior extending throughout the life span. Whether occurring formally in institutionalized settings, or informally through engagement with life experiences, learning results in changes in behavior, knowledge, attitudes, and beliefs. Significant learning in adulthood is most likely to occur informally through making sense of life experiences. Indeed, we often hear people comment that "to live is to learn" and "experience is the best teacher." Interestingly, these popular maxims are rarely applied to children, who are presumed to be learning in school. Though many adults also learn in school, formal education is often viewed as an add-on to the rest of one's life where "real" learning takes place. At the same time, researchers exploring informal, experiential learning have been challenged in making this kind of learning visible and recognizable. Adults, when asked about their learning, are likely to equate learning with formal classroom settings having a traditional teacher. It is only through extensive probing that the everyday learning we engage in can be uncovered.

Learning that is connected to development is likely to be embedded in the life experiences of adults and intricately related to the context of adult life. Thus, taking on new social roles, such as parent, spouse, worker, and citizen, and the tasks, life events, and transitions encountered as one moves through the life span, require learning. *Any* life experience, then, has the *potential* to be a learning experience.

This connection between life experience and learning has intrigued researchers for years. Dewey, in his classic work, *Experience and Education* (1938), first examined what he called the "organic connection between education and personal experience" (p. 12). As noted, he recognized that some experiences could be miseducative. To determine whether the experience has been educational, he suggests asking, "Does this form of growth create conditions for further growth, or does it set up conditions that shut off the person who has grown in this particular direction from . . . continuing growth in new directions?" (p. 29). This connection between experience and growth is the first of two principles by which he defines experience. The second is the principle of interaction: "An experience is always what it is because of a transaction taking place between an individual and what, at the time, constitutes his [or her] environment" (p. 41). Rodgers (2002) considers that these two principles are for Dewey "the x and y axes of experience. Without interaction, learning is sterile and passive, never fundamentally changing the learner. Without continuity, learning is random and disconnected, building toward nothing either within the learner or in the world" (p. 847).

Since Dewey, numerous writers have explored the connection between experience and learning. In adult education, much of the literature on adult learning highlights the role of experience as both a starting point and a critical ingredient for the occurrence of significant learning (Jarvis, 1992; Knowles, 1980; Merriam & Caffarella, 1999; Mezirow, 2000; Tennant & Pogson, 1994). It has even been argued that formal learning—as in taking a course, engaging in training at work, pursuing a degree program, and so forth—are in and of themselves life experiences that can generate learning and development (Merriam & Clark, 1991). Experience, then, can be a specific life event, such as marriage, job change, or illness; it can also be a process such as developing a relationship or changing careers; it can be serendipitous or designed to bring about learning, such as a particular class or learning project. As Boud, Cohen, and Walker (1993) noted, life experience can be "messy":

> Experience is sometimes referred to as if it were singular and unlimited by time or place. Much experience, however, is multifaceted, multi-layered and so inextricably connected with other experiences, that it is impossible to locate temporally or spatially. It almost defies analysis as the act of analysis inevitably alters the experience and the learning which flows from it. (p. 7)

Jarvis (1992) explained how life experiences and learning are related. "Learning, then, is of the essence of everyday living and of conscious experience; it is the process of transforming that experience into knowledge, skills, attitudes, values, and beliefs" (p. 11). He goes on to point out that learning involves making meaning of our experiences. Learning "is about the continuing process of making sense of everyday experience—and experience happens at the intersection of a conscious human life with time, space, society, and relationship" (p. 11).

Life experiences, whether planned or unplanned, provide the opportunity to learn. However, learning occurs only when the experience is attended to and engaged in some way. Thus, as most people know, even an experience designed to bring about learning may not result in learning. We attempt to make sense of the experience by adjusting, expanding, perhaps transforming our meaning-making system. This kind of learning is significant and developmental. A mere accretion of knowledge or skills involving memorization is rarely developmental. As Mezirow (1985, p. 149) pointed out, "significant learning and growth involve qualitative, developmental change in the way the world is viewed. We grow through a progression of transformations in our meaning-making apparatus."

That learning is based in life experiences is not to imply that it is haphazard or capricious. Although we certainly do learn incidentally as a by-product of other endeavors, much of informal learning and certainly all of formal learning is systematic. We have already mentioned formal or institutionally based learning opportunities in which the intent is to bring about learning. Adults also learn in informal groups and on their own. In fact, a rather large part of the adult learning literature is about the self-directed nature of adult learning. Though adults have learned on their own for centuries, research by Tough (1978) revealed its prevalence. He found that 90% of adults are engaged in learning projects, and that nearly 70% of these projects are planned by the individual learners. Subsequent research has confirmed the prevalence of self-directed learning (SDL), delineated models of the process, and assessed self-direction as a personal attribute of learners (Merriam & Caffarella, 1999). It is interesting to note that in some writing on SDL, it is implicitly assumed that adults can become more self-directed, a developmental goal in and of itself.

As with development, learning in adulthood is shaped in part by the social context of the learner. Self-directed learning is a good example of this. In Western culture, for example, individuality, autonomy, and independence are values of effective self-directed learners; in non-Western contexts, these values would be seen as contrary to the good of the collective (Hemphill, 1994). Even when adults are self-directed in their learning, their life circumstances shape their learning. For example, Spear and Mocker's (1984) study of the learning projects of adults with less than a high school education found that of necessity, these self-directed learners "tend to select a course from limited alternatives which happen to occur in their environment and which tend to structure their learning projects" (p. 4). The learning is dictated "by the circumstances" and progresses "as the circumstances created during one episode become the circumstances for the next" (p. 5). It follows that more impoverished environments offer fewer resources and opportunities for learning.

Connecting Learning and Development

From our personal stories and our more theoretical understanding of the concepts of development and learning, we see a clear connection between learning and development. Although there are numerous manifestations of this connection, we have chosen to illustrate this by discussing two arenas. First we look at cognitive development, an area important to both of us as educators who strive to bring about reflective thinking in our students. Then we examine the learning that gives rise to personal change.

Cognitive Development

That several chapters in this handbook deal with cognitive development in adulthood attests to the complexity of a topic so integrally related to the process of learning. Indeed, theories and related concepts dealing with cognition, intelligence, meta-cognition, tacit knowledge, wisdom, practical intelligence, postformal thought and so on, characterize the literature of cognitive development (Merriam & Caffarella, 1999; Sinnott, 1994; Smith & Pourchot, 1998; Tennant & Pogson, 1995). Rather than reviewing all the models, research, and theories related to cognitive development, our intent is to focus a brief discussion of cognitive development on how it can be seen as one manifestation of the intimate connection it has with learning in adulthood. Thus, we view cognitive development as changes in thinking patterns that occur in conjunction with learning.

We are adult educators who train practitioners and scholars working in a multitude of settings in an educational capacity with adult learners, and it is our intent to develop reflective practitioners, ones who will question the status quo, ask why, and examine assumptions underlying practice. Adults *learn* to do this as they encounter life experiences and find that their usual coping mechanisms no longer work. Often they are challenged to do this in formal educational activities. Daloz (1986) speaks metaphorically to the role of teacher in leading learners to see a world beyond their "tribe":

> As we guide our students across the threshold to exotic tribes, our job is to introduce them to the strange and foreign, to defend them against the dangers, but also to prevent them from retreating to the safety of their former home. We lead them into the new world by helping them to unlearn the old meanings of their language and to construct new, more inclusive meanings. (p. 239)

For transformational learning, especially as presented by Mezirow (2000), cognitive development is both a part and an outcome of this type of learning.

Adult cognitive development perspectives most often move beyond Piaget's (1972) formal operations stage of cognitive development. According to Piaget, this stage, which is reached in the teen years, is the ability to reason hypothetically and think abstractly and is the apex of mature adult thought. Some models of cognitive development incorporate Piagetian thought as a foundation (King & Kitchener, 1994; Perry, 1970), whereas others pose different assumptions and starting points (Miller & Cook-Greuter, 1994; Nuernberger, 1994; Wilber, 1983).

A common factor in some models of adult cognitive development is the centrality of contextual knowledge and the importance of constructing one's own knowledge (Baxter Magolda, 1994; Goldberger, Tarule, Clinchy, & Belenky, 1996). This emphasis on knowledge construction allows for more contextualization of adult cognitive development. Goldberger et al.'s (1996) research on women, for example, incorporates themes "related to the experience of silencing and disempowerment, lack of voice, the importance of personal experience in knowing, connected strategies in knowing, and resistance to disempassioned knowing" (p. 7).

A dialectical perspective on cognitive development also incorporates the adult life context (Kramer, 1989; Riegel, 1973). In dealing with life's inherent complexities and its contradictions, "dialectic think-ing allows for the acceptance of alternative truths or ways of thinking about similar phenomena that abound in everyday adult life" (Merriam & Caf-farella, 1999, p. 153). As an example, one might be opposed to capital punishment, "yet silently applaud the gentle person who switches off the life-support system of her spouse who is suffering beyond relief from a terminal illness" (p. 153). By integrating ab-stract thinking with very pragmatic life concerns, one tolerates ambiguity, if not outright contradiction. Riegel (1975) explained how dialectical thinking is characteristic of mature adult thought:

> The mature person needs to achieve a new appre-hension and an effective use of contradictions in operations and thoughts. Contradictions should no longer be regarded as deficiencies that have to be straightened out by formal thinking but, in a confirmative manner, as the very basis of all activi-ties. . . . Adulthood and maturity represent the pe-riod in life during which the individual knowingly reappraises the role of formal, i.e. non-contradictory, thought and during which he [or she] may succeed again (as the young child has unknowingly succeeded in his "primitive dialec-tic") to accept contradictions in his actions and thoughts. (p. 101)

Perhaps more than other researchers, Kegan (1994) incorporates psychological and contextual variables into his model of dialectical thinking. To deal with "the mental demands of modern life," adults' think-ing needs to continue to evolve through higher levels of consciousness. In today's world, adults have ex-traordinary demands on both their personal world of home and family, and their public worlds of work and community. Kegan's model of cognitive develop-ment sets two powerful desires at odds with each other—the desire to be connected to others, and the desire to be independent of others. These two forces are very difficult to keep in balance; in fact, we move back and forth in a spiral-like movement between an emphasis on one or the other. At the same time, we move through different consciousness thresholds, from very concrete views of the world to more abstract inferences, to abstract systems (building relations be-tween abstractions), and then to dialectical thinking, the signature of mature adult thinking. The pressing demands of our "culture's curriculum" necessitate continued development so that we can function

within contradictions and ideological differences. This is, in fact, the agenda for adult learning.

Learning and Personal Change

We cannot discuss the intersection of adult develop-ment and learning as it relates to personal change without first examining some of the different ways the locus of that intersection, the self, is understood. This is because conceptions of the self directly affect how we understand learning (Clark & Dirkx, 2000). We will address that first, and will then examine two modes of theorizing about personal change that are located within two different understandings of the self.

Conceptualizing the Self   The self, as a concept, is socially and historically constituted; there is no fixed understanding of the notion across time or across cultures. Baumeister (1987) illustrated this in his re-view of how the idea of the self evolved over time in Western culture, more specifically in Western Eu-rope and the United States. He notes that by the six-teenth century the notion of self included an awareness that the public and private manifestations of the self differed. The Puritan self was marked by intense self-consciousness and self-examination, in the quest for personal salvation. The more secular orientation of the Romantic era produced a self more concerned about individual destiny and fulfill-ment. And the Victorian period, with its obsessive focus on morality, produced a more conflicted self that Freud tried to make sense of and a belief that to-tal self-knowledge was impossible. In the modern era, there came a growing desire to identify an au-thentic self.

The modern understanding of the self has been shaped by humanistic psychology. Rogers (1961, p. 166) declared that the goal of life is "to be that self which one truly is." This implies the existence of a core or authentic self that is there to be found and assumes that the individual has the power to find it. This idea of personal agency is a core concept in this model because it creates the possibility of inten-tional self-change, what Maslow (1970) calls self-actualization. The idea of a self in process is also fundamental and is captured in the title of Rogers's (1961) most famous book, *On Becoming a Person*. Rogers is explicit about what this emerging, authentic self looks like:

My picture of the characteristic attributes of the person who emerges [is] a person who is more open to all of the elements of his [or her] organic experience; a person who is developing a trust in his own organism as an instrument of sensitive living; a person who accepts the locus of evaluation as residing within himself; a person who is learning to live in his life as a participant in a fluid, ongoing process, in which he is continually discovering new aspects of himself in the flow of his experience. (1961, p. 124)

This notion of the self is considered unitary at several levels. There is harmony within the core self; conflict comes from outside or from efforts to be other than the authentic self. This is also an essential self, what Weedon (1997, p. 32) called "an essence at the heart of the individual which is unique, fixed, and coherent and which makes her [or him] what she [or he] is." Finally, this self is highly individualistic in that more power resides in the person than in sociocultural forces.

That concept of self is giving way, in this postmodern era, to a nonunitary understanding, a self that is always in process, never fixed, reflecting the shifting realities and multiple positionings of our times. Gergen (1991, p. 7) voiced the fluidity of this view: "Under postmodern conditions, persons exist in a state of continuous construction and reconstruction; it is a world where anything goes that can be negotiated. Each reality of the self gives way to reflexive questioning, irony, and ultimately the playful probing of yet another reality. The center fails to hold." One element of life that he deems responsible is the dominating role of technology. To Gergen, technology exposes us to limitless social stimulation and creates what he calls a "saturated self . . . [populated by] multiple and disparate potentials for being" (p. 69) and subjected to a condition he calls "multiphrenia." Multiphrenia is "a multiplicity of self-investments" that serves to decenter the self (pp. 73–74). Gergen argues not only for a multiplicity of selves but also for the notion of a relational self. Tennant (2000) describes this as "a shift in focus from individual selves coming together to form a relationship, to one where the relationship takes center stage, with selves being realized only as a byproduct of relatedness" (p. 96).

Feminist poststructuralists also argue for a nonunitary self, but they begin from the experience of women located as Other within a male-defined culture. Their focus is on subjectivity, which Weedon (1997, p. 32) defined as "the conscious and unconscious thoughts and emotions of the individual, her [or his] sense of herself and her ways of understanding her relation to the world." A fragmented subjectivity is produced through engagement with contradiction and conflict that comes from being positioned within patriarchal culture. Bloom (1998) explains this process:

Because of women's long history of material marginalization, patriarchal oppression, colonization, physical abuse, and the psychological damage of being demeaned by the pervasive hierarchical structuring of the sexual differences of male/female, women have internalized many negative and conflicted ideas of what it means to be a woman. Both negative feelings and experiences and diverse conflicting interactions and experiences—affirming or negating—result in subjectivity's fragmentation. (p. 5)

Language plays a critical role in producing subjectivity, as do the multiple cultural discourses in which we are embedded. Weedon describes how this works:

As we acquire language, we learn to give voice—meaning—to our experience and to understand it according to particular ways of thinking, particular discourses, which pre-date our entry into language. These ways of thinking constitute our consciousness, and the positions with which we identify structure our sense of ourselves, our subjectivity. . . . [This is] a subjectivity which is precarious, contradictory and in process, constantly being reconstituted in discourse each time we think or speak. (1997, p. 32)

Language is also how the nonunitary self is produced—it is common to speak of the self as that which is narrated—and narrative has become both metaphor and method in this way of thinking. Holstein and Gubrium (2000) speak of the need "to restory the self so as to provide it with opportunities for being diversely constructed . . . [and] to apply a vocabulary that makes the self visible as a *project* of everyday life, whose local by-product is more properly articulated in the plural, as 'selves'" (p. 13). We examine their approach in more detail when we take up the idea of personal change in the postmodern self.

We turn now to our original question about how learning can give rise to personal change. Theories about this process rest on how the self is conceptualized, so we will examine one theory that presumes a modernist self and another that is predicated on a postmodern notion of the self.

Change for the Modern Self In the field of adult education, the idea of personal change is linked to transformational learning, and the person who has developed the dominant theory about this type of learning is Jack Mezirow. Mezirow first conceptualized his theory when he studied women's reentry programs in community colleges (1978). Unlike traditional students, these women were entering or returning to college after having functioned in adult roles for a number of years. Situated at a time of major cultural change and the rising influence of the women's movement, his study was able to examine how these women's understandings of themselves and their place in the world were changing, a process Mezirow called perspective transformation. The process that the women in the study went through became the foundation of his theory of transformational learning.

Mezirow's approach is constructivist—he fundamentally wants to understand how people create meaning from their experience—and his process is cognitive and highly rational. He begins from the understanding that people create complex and dynamic meaning systems, consisting of beliefs, values, and assumptions, that serve as a lens that mediates personal experience and provides a means to interpret it. These structures provide coherence to what would otherwise be chaos—the bombardment of random sensory experiences—but they also limit or distort perception of those experiences by creating what Mezirow (1990, p. 2) calls "habits of expectation." Through transformational learning these meaning structures are themselves changed: "Transformative learning refers to the process by which we transform our taken-for-granted frames of reference (meaning perspectives, habits of mind, mind-sets) to make them more inclusive, discriminating, open, emotionally capable of change, and reflective so that they may generate beliefs and opinions that will prove more true or justified to guide action" (Mezirow, 2000, pp. 7–8). Mezirow believes that the process follows some variation of the 10 phases that he observed in the reentry women:

1. A disorienting dilemma
2. Self-examination with feelings of fear, anger, guilt, or shame
3. A critical assessment of assumptions

4. Recognition that one's discontent and the process of transformation are shared
5. Exploration of options for new roles, relationships, and actions
6. Planning a course of action
7. Acquiring knowledge and skills for implementing one's plans
8. Provisional trying of new roles
9. Building competence and self-confidence in new roles and relationships
10. A reintegration into one's life on the basis of conditions dictated by one's new perspective. (Mezirow, 2000, p. 22)

Mezirow notes that the process does not have to begin with a sudden, dramatic event; it can also be incremental, with smaller transformations leading to a more all-encompassing perspective transformation. Others have expanded the ways in which the process can begin (Clark, 1993; Courtenay, Merriam, & Reeves, 1998).

The presumption of a modernist self is foundational to this theory. The learning process that Mezirow outlines assumes a self that is autonomous, agentic, and highly rational. There is no ambiguity about the boundaries of this self—there is an essential core, an authentic self that is undergoing change. Especially significant is the role Mezirow gives to reason. This is particularly evident in his emphasis on reflective discourse. He describes this as

> that specialized use of dialogue devoted to searching for a common understanding and assessment of the justification of an interpretation or belief. This involves assessing reasons advanced by weighing the supporting evidence and arguments and by examining alternative perspectives. Reflective discourse involves a critical assessment of assumptions. It leads toward a clearer understanding by tapping collective experience to arrive at a tentative best judgment. (2000, pp. 10–11)

The conditions for this type of discourse are ideal and include elements such as freedom from coercion, the objective assessment of arguments, and full participation in the dialogue. Mezirow, admitting that these "are never fully realized in practice" (p. 14), argues that these serve as a model for what reflective discourse should be. He has been criticized for "an excessive dependence on rationality as the means of effecting a perspective transformation; other forms of knowing are secondary at best" (Merriam & Caffarella, 1999, p. 334). Clark and Wilson (1991) pointed out that Mezirow's very notion of rationality is itself ahistorical and therefore problematic. In her review, Baumgartner (2001, p. 17) also noted that he has been "long criticized for ignoring the affective, emotional, and social context aspects of the learning process." Although Mezirow has responded to each of these critiques, he has never substantively revised his theory to address these concerns.

Change for the Postmodern Self As noted in our description of the postmodern understanding of the self, it is nonunitary and fluid, located in and produced by discourse. The idea of personal change is quite different in this context because change is not a discrete event for the postmodernists; instead, it is inherent in the very notion of the self.

The close connection between the self and language makes narrative a useful tool because it makes visible the construction and reconstruction of the various selves. Rosenwald and Ochberg (1992, p. 1) see narrative as "the means by which identities may be fashioned." The notion of narrating the self is not solely a postmodern construction; it is also used by those who accept a unitary self. McAdams (1993), for example, sees identity as a continuously constructed narrative that creates a coherent story of the self, with the self as the agent. Postmodernists have a more complex view, however, locating subjectivity more within the multiple and competing discourses that surround us and shape how we think.

Holstein and Gubrium (2000) offer one way of conceptualizing how the self is narrated in a postmodern world. They start from a social constructivist understanding of the self, but seek to "restory" it so that a balance is struck between a socially determined self and a totally agentic modernist self. The self they describe is "not so much a socially responsive entity to be filled or saturated with meaning as it is a social construction that we both assemble and live out as we take up or resist the varied demands of everyday life" (p. 10). No longer is the integrated self the ideal, but rather "the multiple self constructions that emerge in various settings become the identity-bearing subjectivities that serve the interpersonal purposes of today's complex social environment" (p. 13).

For Holstein and Gubrium (2000), self-construction is achieved through narrative, a process that is constant and complex:

> Narrators artfully pick and choose from what is experientially available to articulate their lives and experiences. Yet, as they actively craft and inventively construct their narratives, they also draw from what is culturally available, storying their lives in recognizable ways. Narratives of the self don't simply rest within us to motivate and guide our actions, nor do they lurk behind our backs as social templates to stamp us into selves according to the leading stories of the day. The narrative landscape of self construction is clearly also a busy one. (p. 103)

To understand what is happening in this process of narrating the self, it is important to take into account both the content of the stories and how they are told. The content is shaped by the resources available to the teller, and these are varied. Linde (1993) argues that culture provides different kinds of coherence structures which serve to make a story hang together and make sense; she defines these as a "supply of expected events in a life course, commonly recognized causes, and shared possible explanations from which to construct individual coherences" (p. 19). Holstein and Gubrium (2000) agree, and they note that one potent resource is personal biography: "We engage in ordinary 'biographical work' to assemble aspects of personal history that can be used to bolster present claims of and about ourselves . . . for the practical purposes at hand" (p. 169)

Social standpoints, such as gender, race, and class, offer another set of profound reservoirs drawn on in the process of self-construction, but they are careful to argue that membership in a particular group, however powerful that identification, is never the only source of the self and that self-construction is always multidimensional. They stress the complexity of this idea:

> As Trinh Minh-ha (1992) suggests, the question of identity is moving away from traditional queries into *who* I am to progressively become questions of *when*, *where*, and *how* am I. Noting that "There is no real me to return to, no whole self that synthesizes the woman, the woman of color, and the writer" (p. 157), she underscores the need to view the various incarnations of a gendered or racial self in relation to an individual's full round of everyday concerns. (Holstein & Gubrium, 2000, p. 105)

The *how* of storytelling is equally complex in this understanding of the self. The composition is always open; stories never come to an individual fully formed. Among the devices that Holstein and Gubrium noted are narrative linkage and narrative slippage. Social categories like race and gender can be referenced in constructing identity, but they can also be applied "partially, contingently, judiciously, and variably" (p. 110), all of which create distinctly different accounts. It is also possible to point to potential linkages, suggesting the possibility of alternative selves. The narrative options are endless. Chase (1995) provides a dramatic example of all of this in her study of minority women school superintendents. The women she interviewed are situated in everyday circumstances that are marked by ambiguity and cultural conflict, as they make sense of their dual positioning as figures of authority and objects of discrimination, and each narrates her identity in different and often shifting ways. One of her informants, a Mexican American woman, dealt with this problem by not talking about her experiences of discrimination and instead focusing her narrative on her own personal and professional competence. Another informant, an African American woman, does include stories of discrimination, but she links them to a presentation of self that is strong and resilient. Holstein and Gubrium use the concept of bricoleur, a term defined by Lévi-Strauss (1966, p. 17) as a "Jack of all trades or a kind of professional do-it-yourself person," to sum up this process of narrative identity construction:

> As a bricoleur, the self constructor is involved in something like an interpretive salvage operation, crafting selves from the vast array of available resources, making do with what he or she has to work with in the circumstances at hand, all the while constrained, but not completely controlled, by the working conditions of the moment. In this metaphor, self construction is "always ineluctably local" (Geertz, 1983), a practical and artful response to prevailing circumstances, an application of what is available in relation to the narrative tasks at hand. (p. 153)

Our own brief narratives that began this chapter are examples of how this self-construction works. Sharan struggles to create coherence from her disparate professional experiences as an adult educator. She struggles to reconcile the differences between being an adult educator in what she calls "the real world of practice" and being a professor of adult education, which at the start of her narrative she associates with the ivory tower. She works to resolve this problem through her story about her encounter on the same day with the moving words of Solzhenitsyn about the role of the artist in society and with the Afghan taxi driver who is in the midst of creating a new life for himself at great cost. The two men inhabit the two worlds she's trying to reconcile—Solzhenitsyn lives in the world of ideas, the taxi driver in the world of action—but both locate themselves within the discourse of social justice. This enables Sharan to create a narrative linkage between their stories and her own life—they create a transformative moment in which she can see her work as a professor as located in the real world she values and not separated from it, recognizing that through her students she can "reach more people and help alleviate more suffering" than she could ever do herself in a more direct way. She can now embrace her identity as a professor with more peace.

Carolyn's narrative shows a different kind of self-construction. She's in an in-between state: from nun to addictions counselor to . . . what? She's learning at two levels. Most immediately she's learning how to be helpful to the drug- or alcohol-addicted clients sitting in her office; because she's had no personal experience with this illness, she's somewhat in the dark. But the larger question for her is what to do with the rest of her life. Like Sharan, Carolyn also needs to create a coherent story, in that her past and future need to connect in a way that makes sense in some way. When she meets Ronny she hears a transformation narrative, the prototypical Alcoholics Anonymous recovery story, and his story addresses her first learning need, that of understanding "what the inner experience of drug addiction looked like, and what recovery looked like as well." But what she learns from Ronny goes deeper than that. Although his story is unfamiliar in context, it is very familiar in the larger terms of a search for meaning in life. Spirituality in its broadest sense is that same search for meaning, and this resonates deeply with her prior experience as a nun. But she sees this process now in new terms, a process that is "a deep kind of learning," and this provides a link to her future as an adult educator who can focus on learning for personal change. Ronny's story, then, connects both her past and her future. Narratively this creates continuity in Carolyn's self construction while allowing for significant change in her life circumstances.

We see in these two conceptualizations of personal change—the transformational learning that Mezirow theorizes for the modernist self and the ongoing process of narrative identity construction that Holstein and Gubrium theorize for a postmodern self—two different modes of learning that intersect with development. In both cases the learning and the developmental processes are so intertwined as to be mutually constituted, for our core understanding of development is personal change.

Having explored some of the connections between adult learning and development, we turn now to examine some of the factors that shape this process.

FACTORS THAT SHAPE THE CONNECTION BETWEEN LEARNING AND DEVELOPMENT

Because adult educators are interested in promoting the development of learners, it is important for us to attend to those variables or structures that foster the connection between learning and development. We have more control over some variables than others, but even with respect to those variables over which we have little control, it is important to recognize how they function in shaping the learning experience. The sociocultural context of both our learners and where the learning activity occurs is one factor that has only recently been taken into account in understanding adult learning. This is discussed first, followed by two other factors we feel are central to understanding the connection between learning and development in adulthood—the process of reflection on experience, both rational and somatic, and role of the community in learning.

Sociocultural Context

Educators and psychologists have tended to study learning and the teaching-learning dynamic in a decontextualized manner. However, learning rarely occurs "in splendid isolation from the world in which the learner lives; . . . it is intimately related to that world and affected by it" (Jarvis, 1987, p. 11). Contrast, for example, the learning about and knowledge of Islam and the Middle East pre– and post–September 11, 2001. Or consider what the office worker of the 1950s needed to know about technology compared to the technological competencies expected of today's office worker. Clearly, what people need to know, the educational opportunities that are offered, the ways adults learn, and how this learning affects development, are to a large extent determined by the sociocultural context at a particular point in time. In these early years of the twenty-first century, major changes in technology, shifts in the demographic make-up of countries, and global economics leading to changing work practices are but some of the forces shaping the greater context of adult learning.

In moving the lens to the adult, "learning is located at the interface of people's biography and the sociocultural milieu in which they live, for it is at this intersection that experiences occur" (Jarvis, 1992, p. 17). These experiences are the product of cultures and subcultures, of normative expectations of behavior at certain stages in the life cycle, and of an individual's genetic make-up. How an individual "develops" is a function of historical and cultural norms in conjunction with chronological age.

Historical time, or history-graded influences (Baltes, 1987), includes the "long-term processes, such as industrialization and urbanization," and "economic, political, and social events that directly influence the life course of the individuals who experience those events" (Neugarten & Datan, 1973, p. 58). As an example, the global war on terrorism has differential effects on different age cohorts and different ethnic groups. For example, young adults may be on the battlefields in this war, middle-aged adults may be warily comparing it to the Vietnam War, and Arab Americans are restricted in their travels.

Chronological or life time is simply the number of years one has lived since birth, and is most useful when thinking about biological change; it is also a proxy for any number of factors in the study of adult development. Finally, social time is probably the most powerful construct in understanding certain forms of adult development. Social time, "the socially prescribed timetable for the ordering of major life events," exists in all cultures (Neugarten, 1976, p. 16). It is the timetable for which certain behaviors are expected. And although there is variation in the actual experiencing of these events, and the norms may change over time, the overall "normative pattern is adhered to, more or less consistently, by most persons within a given social group" (p. 16).

Perhaps equally powerful in defining one's learning and development are nonnormative (Baltes, 1987) or unanticipated life events (Schlossberg, Waters, &

Goodman, 1995). These are events that occur in some people's lives and are not time-dependent, such as a health condition, an accident, or achieving fame. Finally, there is the nonevent that is what we expected to occur but did not, such as getting promoted or having children.

Thus the social and historical context sets up expectations as to what adults learn and how they will develop. These expectations vary by culture and historical period. Other contextual factors include the social constructions of race, class, gender, ethnicity, sexual orientation, ability/disability, and so on. These constructions and the ways in which they intersect with learning and development call forth a sociopolitical analysis of the intersection of learning and development. As Tisdell (1995, p. 11) observed, "what counts as knowledge in a particular learning context—and decisions about what gets included in the curriculum for a given learning activity—are decisions made with attention to the politics of this particular educational context and to what is seen as 'real' knowledge relevant to this educational context." Thus, *who* has access to what kinds of educational opportunities may be a fundamental issue.

As for other areas of education, adult education has embraced a critical perspective on practice. From this perspective, the world is marked by inequities of power and privilege. Individual learners "both create and are created by their social worlds" (Nesbit, 1998, p. 174). Race, class, and gender and their intersections are analyzed with regard to power and privilege with a goal of revealing how the "system" (that is, structures of power) wields influence so as to oppress and silence some individuals. These analyses, and those of postmodern and feminist thinkers, highlight the hegemony of the social context and its power to shape the learning and development of adults. As Welton (1993, p. 88) warned, "human beings as childrearers, partners, workers, clients, citizens, and consumers struggle against the process of being turned into objects of corporate and state management. Systemic imperatives, then, threaten to disempower men and women who have the capacity to be empowered, reflective actors."

Kegan (1994) considers some of the same sociocultural factors in his analysis of how a dialectic model of cognitive development can accommodate difference. "Challengers" to the system need not be "coopted into the status quo." Rather,

It means that the old status quo is replaced by a new status quo. It does not mean that blacks can come into the office only if they act white. It does not mean that women's experience is included in the curriculum simply by changing pronouns and making a "Michael" example into a "Mary" example. It means that formally marginalized people will come into the office, and they will have their own distinctive way of seeing things, setting the agenda, getting the goals accomplished; and it means that these ways will be recognized, acknowledged, and respected, provided that some common ground can be found where all contending "cultures" in their wholeness and distinctness can stand. (p. 345)

Reflection

If we think of the sociocultural context as the world in which each of us is located and in which we experience life, then reflection is the process by which we make sense of all of that. Reflection is fundamental to learning—without it, we would simply be bombarded by random experiences and unable to make sense of any of them. It is likewise impossible to think about the process of personal development without putting reflection at the center. The central reason for this is that reflection and experience are concepts that are fundamentally intertwined. Most of us have a commonsense notion that reflection is a rather straightforward process of thinking about our experience and making sense of it. In fact it is a complex concept that is variously conceptualized, distinguished from other modes of thought, and applied to learning of all kinds.

Earlier, when we discussed the connection between experience and learning, we began with Dewey; it should be no surprise that Dewey had a lot to say about the process of reflection as well. In his book, *How We Think* (1933), he discussed various modes of thought, such as imagination, belief, and stream-of-consciousness thinking. But his primary interest was in reflective thinking. His conceptualization of reflection was embedded in all of his work. In a review of his writings, Rodgers (2002) determined that four criteria underlie Dewey's ideas about reflection and the purposes it serves:

1. Reflection is a meaning-making process that moves a learner from one experience into the next with deeper understanding of its relationships with and connections to other

experiences and ideas. It is the thread that makes continuity of learning possible, and ensures the progress of the individual and, ultimately, society. It is a means to essentially moral ends.

2. Reflection is a systematic, rigorous, disciplined way of thinking, with its roots in scientific inquiry.

3. Reflection needs to happen in community, in interaction with others.

4. Reflection requires attitudes that value the personal and intellectual growth of oneself and others. (p. 845)

These criteria, with the exception of seeing the process as following the scientific method, are actually quite contemporary, another sign of the ongoing influence that Dewey has on our understanding of learning.

In an effort to understand how the concept of reflection is understood today, Rogers (2001) examined seven of the major theorists in this area, beginning with Dewey and including, among others, Mezirow, Boud and colleagues, and Schön, to identify commonalities. The terms for this process of reflection vary greatly: Mezirow (2000), as we have seen, calls it *critical reflection*; Schön (1983), whose concepts we discuss later in this chapter, refers to *reflection-in-action*. Altogether, Rogers found as many as 15 different terms in use. All of the theorists see reflection as a cognitive process, but only Boud, Keogh, and Walker (1985) hold that emotions play a major role. Rogers identified four definitional elements that all seven shared:

These included reflection as a cognitive and affective process or activity that (1) requires active engagement on the part of the individual; (2) is triggered by an unusual or perplexing situation or experience; (3) involves examining one's responses, beliefs, and premises in light of the situation at hand; and (4) results in integration of the new understanding into one's experience. (p. 41)

The active engagement assumes that the person is ready and willing to enter into the reflection process. The triggering event is often a developmental challenge. The process itself usually starts when a person identifies a problem and decides to find a solution. Typically the next step involves gathering relevant information, then making a plan, a step that in most models, "presupposes that something important in the individual's thinking has changed" (Rogers, 2001,

p. 45). The final step is usually taking some kind of action as a result of the reflection process. Although these steps sound linear, it is more accurate to think of the process as continuous and spiral, with no clear beginning or end. Exact methods vary with each theory, but all agree that the context needs to provide "an appropriate balance of challenge and support" to the person (p. 43). The outcome of reflection is always some kind of learning and the development of an increased sense of effectiveness.

Boud and Walker (1993), in further elaborating their own model of reflection, acknowledge the existence of multiple barriers in this process and suggest four ways to deal with these. The first is to acknowledge that they exist; the second is to name them, to understand them more clearly; the third is to determine their origin and how they function; and the fourth is to develop strategies, either confrontational or transformative, to work with the barriers. However, in the end they argue that the entire process of reflection on experience should be considered holistically: "Much as we may enjoy the intellectual chase, we cannot neglect our full experience in the process. To do so is to fool ourselves into treating learning from experience as a simple rational process" (p. 86).

Fenwick (2000) also makes the case for a more holistic approach. In her review of different models of cognition underlying experiential learning, she argues that the dominant theories of reflection are constructivist and that "constructivism falsely presumes a cut universe in which subjects are divided from environment and from their own experiences, and reflection is posited as the great integrator, bridging separations that it creates instead of reorienting us to the whole" (p. 249).

There is a growing interest in an approach to reflection that is not based solely on cognitive functions but honors and legitimates emotions (Clark, 2001). Emotion is an embodied experience—we *feel* happy or sad or frustrated or excited—but the body is, at least in Western culture, not considered a legitimate source of knowledge. Our culture has, in fact, a complex and troubled relationship with the body. Discourse about the body objectifies it, making it subject to control or manipulation to align with social norms of appearance and use. This has not always been true. Bordo (1987) tracks this historical change, noting that in medieval times knowing was more internal and more connected to the natural world, but with the Enlightenment reason became primary, and the knower and known became more separate and distinct. This produced the Cartesian dualism, the mind/body split, which privileged reason and delegitimated the body as a mode of knowing. "Somatic and emotional knowing, then, came to be regarded as unreliable, biased, and 'only' subjective, a mode of knowing that may be useful for our intimate, personal lives, but not for claiming knowledge about the world" (Heshusius & Ballard, 1996, p. 5).

The notion of somatic knowing has emerged more recently as something to be acknowledged and valued. Matthews (1998) referred to this as "the embodied experience of being and doing" and sees it "at the heart of the arts and applied culture" (p. 237). Western medicine is increasingly recognizing the mind/body connection in the treatment of disease, and scientists have extensive data on how care of the body (e.g., proper nutrition, exercise, and sleep) affects brain functioning and thus learning (Weiss, 2001). Roberts (1989) argued for a new term, *mindbody*, to capture this close connection.

Somatic knowing crosses all domains. Todd (2001), in her discussion of moral and ethical development in Nazi Germany, begins her analysis with a personal story of her older brother asking her, when she was a child, what part of her body she thought with. She replied that she thought with her stomach, because she remembered feeling a sensation there whenever she had to make a big decision. Her brother laughed and told her, indulgently, that people think with their brains, not their stomachs. Todd goes on to examine prewar German religion and the normal practices of teaching, noting that the emphasis was on discipline and the suppression of the will. She argues that cultures that train people "to distrust messages from their bodily feelings and emotions, thereby [train] them to distrust their internal sense of authority" (p. 24), making possible the acceptance of a totalitarian regime like the Nazis, along with the atrocities it generated. She concluded: "We need all our mental functions, as well as our bodies, feelings, and emotions, to make responsible ethical decisions. My brother was, of course, right in saying that we humans think with our brains; he was wrong, however, in concluding that's all we think with" (p. 28).

Michelson (1998) takes this idea of thinking with the body and links it to experiential learning and, more specifically, to reflection. As noted earlier in this section, the traditional notion of reflection is cognitive: we have an experience, we reflect on it, and we learn from that process of reflection. Michelson argues instead that the body can be the site of the learning. She illustrates this with a story about a woman she calls Mary who is a newly promoted director of a managerial team. At one of her first team meetings, she is angered when one of the senior men rudely dismisses the more junior women on the team, then appropriates their ideas himself. Hiding her anger, she doesn't react to this behavior at the meeting, but on her train ride home she consciously reflects on the experience and decides on some strategies to deal with the situation. Michelson argues that Mary's learning happened not on the train, as traditional theorists would claim, but at the meeting:

> The understanding that came to Mary on the way home was not a cognitive flash of new learning, but simply the moment in which her mental processes caught up with what her body already knew. . . . Thus, her learning is understood as a moment of emotional and physical response, not a moment of dispassionate self-reflection, as the product of an embodied, social selfhood rather than of a disembodied mind. (p. 226)

The process of reflection in all its forms is essential to learning and to development. Movement from one stage to the next in any of the models of development requires reflection. Likewise, the development of social roles, as well as the possibility of resistance to them, is based on the process of reflection. It is yet another domain in which learning and development intersect at a deep level.

Connecting Through Community

As is clear from the previous discussions of reflection on experience, learning is a social activity, one that involves others in dialogue and in community. In fact, it is difficult to think about *any* learning that is linked to development that occurs in isolation from others. Even something as personal as a change in perspective involves "the crucial role of supportive relationships and a supportive environment" (Mezirow, 2000, p. 25). Mezirow (1995), drawing from Habermas, identifies rational discourse as the testing ground for transformational learning. This is when we "seek the best judgment of the most informed, objective, and rational persons we can find" and enter into "a special form of dialogue" (Mezirow, 1995, p. 53). It is in this discourse that we test out our ideas, critically self-reflect, and build understanding. Discourse can occur in one-to-one relationships, in informal groups, and in formal educational settings. Interestingly, Taylor, Marienau, and Fiddler (2000) extend this notion of dialogue to include having a dialogical relationship with oneself. This relationship to the self

> can be a powerful tool . . . as it encourages speaking to the self in much the same way as people dialogue with one another. Rather than seeing one's experiences exclusively from the "inside out," one is able to see them also from the "outside in." This ability is foundational to *exploring life's experiences through some framework of analysis*, and *exploring and making meaning of our life stories within contexts.* (p. 36; emphasis in original)

Emancipatory learning models, those that seek freedom from oppression and empowerment of learners, also require discourse or dialogue. Freire (1970), in his seminal work *Pedagogy of the Oppressed*, laid the foundation for this in promoting a dialogic relationship between teachers and learners. In his problem-posing rather than "banking" model of education,

> The teacher-of-the students and the students-of-the teacher cease to exist and a new term emerges: teacher-student with students-teachers. The teacher is no longer merely the one who teaches, but one who is himself [or herself] taught in dialogue with the students, who in turn while being taught also teach. They become jointly responsible for a process in which all grow. (p. 53)

Much of the literature in adult education and adult learning promotes learning in connection with others as good practice. Empirical research also supports this practice, in particular, empirical research on learning and development. Beginning with Gilligan's (1982) work, suggesting that women tend to define the self in terms of relationships, a number of studies support the notion that women learn best and prefer learning with others (Hayes & Flannery, 2000). In Belenky, Clinchy, Goldberger, and Tarule's (1986) study of women learners, the more complex categories of knowing involve connection with others. Connected knowing, in contrast with separate knowing, was preferred by a majority of the women in their study. The authors proposed "connected teaching" to support this way of knowing:

> Educators can help women develop their own authentic voices if they emphasize connection over separation, understanding and acceptance over assessment, and collaboration over debate; if they accord respect to and allow time for the knowledge that emerges from firsthand experience; if instead of imposing their own expectations and arbitrary requirements, they encourage students to evolve their own patterns of work based on the problems they are pursuing. (p. 229)

Although research on women has made the importance of connection quite visible, the teaching techniques may be as applicable to men. In fact, a number of studies suggest that men also thrive in a "connected" environment (Taylor, 1997, p. 49). Furthermore, Flannery (2000, p. 137) warns us to resist setting up women's knowing in opposition to men's, because research findings suggest that "most differences in learning style are greater within each gender than between the genders."

Recent work in adult learning theory known as situated cognition extends the notion of connection to the full social context in which learning takes place. Crucial elements in this context are the interactions among people, the tools or mechanisms that aid learning (books, computers, etc.), and the context itself. Learning is a function of the interaction of the learners, the tools, the activity itself, and the context. Rather than knowledge being somewhere to be discovered, in this model knowledge is constructed, spread across the community. The challenge for educators who adhere to this view of learning is to design learning activities by incorporating "relations among people, tools, [and] activity as they are given in social practice" (Lave, 1996, p. 7). This means making the learning as "authentic" as possible by incorporating apprenticeships, internships, simulations, portfolios, case studies, and similar activities into adult education practice.

Communities of practice model this notion of connection as central to learning and development (Lave & Wenger, 1991; Wenger, 1998). A community of practice is a group of people who engage in a shared activity and who wish to learn what other members know. Adults are members of several communities of practice including family, work, social, and recreational groups. Learning and identity are key constructs in this theory. Wenger (1998, p. 96) wrote that "learning is the engine of practice, and practice is the history of that learning." Furthermore, "there is a profound connection between identity and practice" (p. 149) in that "building an identity consists of negotiating the meanings of our experience of membership in social communities" (p. 145). This notion of connection in community goes beyond one-on-one dialogues and teacher–student or master–apprentice relationships. Newcomers to a community are at first on the periphery, but through participation move toward the center; this movement is a process of changing patterns of participation as well as changing identity. A recent study by Merriam, Courtenay, and Baumgartner (2003) explored the learning and identity development of a marginalized community of practice—that of Wiccans. Social interaction was found to be key to the learning and identity development of participants: "Participants realized they were not alone on this journey; in community with others, they could engage in rational discourse and gain confidence in their new role within the group. Through group support and encouragement, they were able to make meaning of their situation" (p. 186).

Adult educators and trainers have long recognized the advantages of building community among a group of learners. Whether it is a community of practice formed in the workplace (Wenger & Snyder, 2000), a learning community in the classroom (Tisdell & Perry, 1997), or, more recently, an online community (Herrman, 1998; Palloff & Pratt, 1999), such communities have been found to promote and sustain learning, participation, and development. In the online environment, for example, research suggests that the normally high dropout rate and dissatisfaction with this mode of learning can be dramatically ameliorated by establishing a virtual community of learners (Brown, 2001; Palloff & Pratt, 1999).

In summary, connecting with others appears to be one of the major variables in bringing about development through learning. Whether this connection is in a one-to-one relationship with the self, with another learner, or in community with others, the opportunity to reflect, share learning, and "test" new perspectives is crucial. As Taylor et al. (2000, p. 24) observed, if learning is focused on memory and the mastery of factual material, "there is no need to engage in a dialogical process." But "when we seek to foster deep

approaches, where learning is perceived as constructed and context-dependent, dialogue is essential" (p. 36).

TEACHING FOR DEVELOPMENT

Adult educators see themselves as facilitators of others' learning, learning that not only meets needs but also fosters development. Some adult education is explicitly developmental, and to those practices we now turn. We have chosen three arenas of practice where the goal of the teaching–learning transaction is growth-oriented change. The first is education, both formal and informal, that has personal development as its goal. The second is education for social change. The third is education for professional development, known more commonly as continuing professional education. We discuss each of these in turn.

Education for Personal Development

In one sense it is reasonable to argue that all education is developmental at some level. Among adults, it is not unusual that a desire for personal growth can be an initial motivation for seeking out both formal and informal educational opportunities; Aslanian and Brickell (1980), for example, found that 83% of the adults they surveyed were motivated to engage in formal learning because of life transitions. Many educators believe that the personal development of their students should be one of their primary goals and have become more intentional about this aspect of learning. Taylor et al. (2000), who believe that "adult development is influenced by the educational environment" (p. 16), specifically address how adult educators can teach with developmental intentions. They surveyed a large group of adult educators who held this as a goal and asked what developmental outcomes they sought through their teaching, as well as what strategies they used; they identified five dimensions of development. Development moves:

1. Toward knowing as a dialogical process
2. Toward a dialogical relationship to oneself
3. Toward being a continuous learner
4. Toward self-agency and self-authorship
5. Toward connection with others. (pp. 32–33)

They believe these "represent aspects of a self that is capable of sophisticated, ongoing engagement with the world of ideas and with learning from experience. . . . In short, a self that responds effectively and with increasing ease to internal and external changes" (p. 34). They then provide a large number of educational strategies generated by their survey that are directed to eliciting development along one or more of the five dimensions.

Several adult educators suggest ways that Mezirow's (2000) theory of transformational learning can be used in formal educational settings to foster personal development. Cranton (1994, 1997) suggests that educators need to foster learner empowerment by giving up their own positional power, creating an environment in which learners can participate freely and equally in discussions, making the teaching learner-centered, and stimulating and supporting critical reflection. Brookfield (1987) created a model of critical thinking that parallels Mezirow's process of perspective transformation, in which educators help move students from an initial *trigger event*, through *appraisal* or self-examination, *exploration* of other explanations, *developing alternative perspectives*, and then *integrating* these new ways of thinking into their lives (pp. 25–27). More recently Brookfield (2000) has located this process within critical theory, and argues for critical reflection on cultural assumptions.

Daloz (1999) believes that the very relationship between student and teacher is a powerful means of fostering personal development, a mentoring relationship that can enable students to "regain the courage, insight, and passion they need to move ahead in their lives more fully, to weave and reweave the fabric of meaning more richly and strongly" (1999, p. 4). He likens the formal educational process to a journey into the unknown in which students are challenged to formulate new understandings of themselves and their world; having a caring mentor by their side makes this process less frightening. Daloz explains how this works:

> Mentors seem to do three fairly distinct things: they *support*, they *challenge*, and they *provide vision.* . . . [T]he notion of *support* refers to those acts through which the mentor affirms the validity of the student's present experience. She lets him know through her empathy with his feelings or her comprehension of his words that he is understood. . . .

The function of support is to bring boundaries together; *challenge* peels them apart. . . . The function of challenge is to open a gap between learner and environment, a gap that creates tension in the learner, calling out for closure. The work of closing that gap strengthens our sense of agency, of power in the world. . . . [The] third function I call *providing vision.* . . . Mentors hang around through transitions, a foot on either side of the gulf; they offer a hand to help us swing across. By their very existence, mentors provide proof that the journey can be made, the leap taken. (pp. 206–207)

Education for personal development is also accomplished in informal contexts. Self-help groups are one example of this, and 12-step programs such as Alcoholics Anonymous are probably the most well known. The developmental process here is highly scripted and the learning is mediated through narrative. Experienced members tell the story of their alcoholism, their experience of hitting bottom, and then the story of their recovery, helping new members identify with the group and offering them the hope that they can change their lives as well (Clark, 2001; Holstein & Gubrium, 2000).

The 12 steps themselves take members through several stages, beginning with an admission of their powerlessness over their drinking, then moving to a relationship with a Higher Power, however they define that. The remaining steps involve a systematic reflection on their lives and taking responsibility for any harm their drinking has caused others, as well as a commitment to reach out to other alcoholics. The power of the group is profound and multifaceted. It provides an accepting and nonjudgmental atmosphere and the autonomy of its members is a foundational belief. As Maxwell (1984) notes, "One of the most striking aspects of this respect for autonomy is leaving it up to the individual to make his [or her] own diagnosis—to decide whether or not he or she is an alcoholic" (p. 52). In large part this happens through new members hearing the stories of others in the group and discovering that their experience is not unique. Other kinds of self-help groups have been developed on the 12-step model, most prominently Narcotics Anonymous and Overeaters Anonymous, but also including other compulsive behaviors like gambling or overspending. All of these groups likewise provide support and guidance for personal development.

Education for Social Change

Some education begins with personal change but does so within a set of social and political values that orient the learning; this is education for social change. Here the intersection of learning and development has a social purpose, one shaped by the moral imagination. There is an enormous range to this type of education. The focus can be local, like community organizing activities that advocate on behalf of the poor and the disenfranchised. One example is the Listening Partners Program, a social action initiative for poor mothers in rural Vermont (Bond, Belenky, & Weinstock, 2000). Ewert and Grace (2000, p. 328) understand all community action as providing "both a tool for analysis and a mechanism for community transformation." Education for social change can be civic, like the National Issues Forum in its efforts to foster an informed citizenry (Oliver, 1992). A more dramatic example is the work of Myles Horton and the Highlander Folk School in support of labor organizing and the civil rights movement (Conti & Fellenz, 1986; Morris, 1991). In his work with labor unions Horton recognized that "racism was more than just morally wrong—a belief they had held strongly from the first—but also it was a fundamental structural problem inextricably linked with class domination" (Morris, 1991, p. 4). Horton went on to offer workshops at Highlander for African American leaders and began citizenship schools to promote voter registration among African Americans (Parker & Parker, 1991).

Education for social change can also be global, where groups use education to create change that they hope will have an impact on nations around the world. Cunningham (2000), in her overview and critique of contemporary social movement learning, describes a particularly ambitious effort called global social movement learning, in which the strategy is "to bring international scholar-activists from social movements, universities, and global policy networks together to make proposals on how humanity might interact with itself and with the rest of nature as a learning system" (p. 581). In this section we highlight two modes of education for social change: the work of Paulo Freire and its influence on critical literacy efforts, and the consciousness-raising dimension of the women's movement and the current work of feminist pedagogy.

Freire was a Brazilian educator who began his career by developing literacy programs for the poor in which they not only learned how to read but, more importantly, how to "read" the social and political conditions of their lives. "Education for Freire is never neutral: it either domesticates by imparting the values of the dominant group, so that learners assume things are right the way they are, or it liberates, allowing people to reflect critically on their world and take action to move society toward a more equitable and just vision" (Merriam & Caffarella, 1999, pp. 324–325). His intent was always to liberate. He developed a pedagogy that he called conscientization, a dialogic, problem-posing process that enables students to gain an awareness of how social structures have oppressed them and shaped how they think about the world (Freire, 1973). The critical part, as Newman (1994) describes, is how they "become aware of their capacity to act on their world and change their lives. From being objects of social history—beings to whom things are done—they can become subjects of their own destiny—people who act and take control of their own lives" (p. 35). This critical consciousness is the heart of Freire's method. Shor (1993, pp. 32–33) believes it has four qualities: "power awareness" or an understanding of how power undergirds society; "critical literacy," a deeply analytic way of thinking; "desocialization," which he understands as skepticism toward and challenge of the values of mass culture; and "self-organization/self-education," which leads to taking action toward social change. The goal of Freirean pedagogy is a just society in which all people can live freely and with dignity.

Freire crafted his approach within a literacy program, and it should be noted that the political nature of his work ultimately resulted in his imprisonment and exile from Brazil after a military coup there in 1964 (Gadotti, 1994). Although literacy programs remain an ideal venue for critical pedagogy, the reality, as Degener (2001, p. 48) noted, is that "very few programs have the freedom or resources to be critical in every area of endeavor [because they must] remain eligible for funding from government agencies and private foundations." She argues that it is more realistic to think of critical pedagogy in terms of degree, rather than as an absolute category. She identifies six programmatic elements that should be considered—presuppositions, philosophy, and goals; structure; curriculum and materials; teacher development; teacher–student relationship; and evaluation—and suggests that programs fall along a continuum, from highly critical to highly uncritical, depending on how many elements conform to critical pedagogy (pp. 50–53). Critical pedagogy remains an ideal; yet it is one that is seldom realized in its pure form.

Another significant form of education for social change is the consciousness-raising groups that were active in the early years of the women's movement. These were groups of women who came together to systematically examine their own lived experience to throw light on the oppression of women. Hart (1990) described the process as

> bound to three-fold, interwoven dimensions of its content, methods, and epistemological presuppositions: an analysis of sexual oppression, a grounding of this analysis in everyday experience, and a structure of analysis that calls for a reciprocal, interactive relationship among knowers who are linked by common experiences, as well as between the knowers and their object of knowing. In other words, consciousness raising is part and parcel of a *feminist education*. (p. 48; emphasis in original)

An essential outcome of this process was discovering that "personal problems and conflicts, often previously understood as the result of personal inadequacies and neuroses . . . are socially produced conflicts and contradictions" (Weedon, 1997, p. 33), an awareness that gave rise to the popular slogan, "The Personal Is Political." The importance of this interconnection cannot be overemphasized. Hart noted: "Through a process of *mutual self-reflection*, women's experiences became de-privatized; each individual woman's life became meaningful *for herself* because it became meaningful within the larger context of women's oppression" (p. 56). Although this process emerged from and gave shape to the women's movement of the 1960s, it is a method of analysis that continues to play a role in women's empowerment.

Feminist pedagogy, developed from various strands of feminist theory, takes up many of the same issues related to women's oppression but does so in the context of formal education. Maher (1987) identifies two categories of feminist pedagogy, what she calls liberatory and gender models. The liberatory model emphasizes the structural sources of oppression that generate unequal power relations, whereas the gender models, coming from a psychological perspective, focus on the social construction of women's

identity and the need for personal emancipation. Tisdell (1996) argues for a synthesis of the two, which would

> take into account both the intellectual *and* emotional components of learning, the individual's capacity for agency, as well as the psychological and social and political factors that affect learning. It would emphasize the importance of relationship and connection to learning, but also account for the fact that power relations based on a multitude of factors including gender, race, and class are always present in the learning environment and affect both how knowledge is constructed on the individual level as well as the social and political factors that affect what counts as "official" knowledge and how it is disseminated. (p. 311)

Feminist pedagogy continues to be a vital area that has a profound impact on women's learning and development in formal educational settings.

Continuing Professional Education

Continuing professional education (CPE) is a growing arena of practice for adult educators. The word *professional* is broadly conceived to include a diversity of occupational groups who can claim a body of knowledge and competencies specific to their practice. Thus, in addition to those in the traditional professions of medicine and law, teachers, nurses, administrators, social workers, allied health groups, and others are considered to be members of professions or "professionalizing" occupations. Because professions serve the public, the demand for accountability has translated into credentialing systems that require continued updating. For many professionals, continuing education is mandatory.

Continuing professional education is designed to enable "practitioners to keep abreast of new knowledge, maintain and enhance their competence, progress from beginning to mature practitioners, advance their careers through promotion and other job changes, and even move into different fields" (Queeny, cited in Queeny, 2000, p. 375). A large part of CPE focuses on increasing the competence of practitioners by helping them acquire more knowledge and skills and then apply new knowledge and skills to the practice setting (Queeny, 2000). Although increased competency may be subtly intertwined with development, this area of CPE has more to do with adding to one's knowledge base than with developmental change.

Clearly, CPE relates to developmental change, which includes the development of professional identity, professional expertise, and reflective practice. Daley's (2001) study of how CPE affected those in four professional groups (nurses, lawyers, adult educators, social workers) found that the learning was not simply additive but transformative: Learning "was essential to the process of meaning making because often, in this process of using information, the professionals again changed what the information meant to them. . . . In other words, incorporating new knowledge is a recursive, transforming process" (p. 50). Daley (2002) commented:

> A CPE program that promotes sharing, networking, and creating colleague relationships is not just fostering a socialization process. It is furthering *professional identity development*, allegiance to the profession, and tie-signs that allow professionals to communicate and discuss new information and incorporate it into their practice. (pp. 86–87; emphasis added)

Closely tied to an evolving identity as a professional is the movement from novice to expert. Dreyfus and Dreyfus's (1986) well-known model assumes epistemologically based change and progression from less to more expertise. Dreyfus and Dreyfus's model has five stages—novice, advanced beginner, competent, proficient, and expert. The movement is from adherence to rules and procedures with little awareness of the practice context, to more intuitive knowing embedded in a deep situational awareness. The development of cognitive processes is at the heart of this movement. Although the first three stages are characterized by rule-based, slow, detached thinking and reasoning, the stages of proficient and expert are dominated by intuitive, context-based thinking. As Benner (1984) noted in her study of expertise in nursing, "With an enormous background of experience, they [experts] have an intuitive grasp of each situation and zero in on the accurate region of the problem without consideration of a range of alternative solutions" (p. 49).

The development of professional expertise is sometimes considered under the rubric of reflective practice. Most often associated with the work of Schön (1983, 1987, 1996), "reflective practice" refers to the professional's ability to make judgments in ambiguous, contradictory, or complex situations. In addressing the problems inherent in practice, the more novice one is, the more dependence on learned academic knowledge or what Schön calls technical rationality (1983). With experience and continued learning, the professional is not only able to reflect on a situation after it has occurred (reflection-on-action) but as it is unfolding (reflection-in-action). The latter is the ability to move beyond applying facts and procedures to thinking more creatively about problems in practice. In reflection-in-action, "we think critically about the thinking that got us into this fix or this opportunity; and we may, in the process, restructure strategies of action understanding of phenomena, or ways of framing problems. . . . Reflection gives rise to [the] on-the-spot experiment" (Schön, 1987, p. 28). The ability to do this is developmental, requiring both extended experience as a professional and continued learning.

In a study of professional development across 20 professions, Cheetham and Chivers (2001) identified five key factors in the development of expertise and reflective practice. These five factors, when taken into account in CPE programs, can stimulate developmental outcomes:

> 1) the opportunity to experience a wide range of developmental experiences; 2) the motivation to acquire the necessary competencies and to improve these continuously; 3) adequate practice in carrying out the various key tasks and functions in order to master the requisite competencies; 4) persistence in overcoming difficulties and in persevering when things are not going well; 5) the influence and support (when needed) of others. (pp. 284–285)

Thus continuing professional education is one arena in which development is acknowledged by most as a goal of learning. This developmental trajectory can be seen in professional identity development and in reflective practice.

CONCLUSION

We began this chapter by presenting stories illustrating our own understanding of development, adult learning, and the nature of the connection between adult learning and development. Sharan's encounters with the film and the taxi driver (both informal life experiences) brought about reflection regarding her place as an academic. Engaging the experiences through reflection constituted learning, which in turn fostered the development of her professional identity. Carolyn's work with her alcoholic and drug-addicted clients took her into a new world and led ultimately to a change in her professional identity, too. In her case, the learning centered around the challenge of fostering personal change in others, introduced her to new ways of thinking about that process, and brought her to the field of adult education.

Working from our own experiences, we turned to the literature in adult learning and development to draw out the nature of connection, factors that promote learning and development, and how we teach for development. We first defined development and learning and then explored the connection as it manifests itself in cognitive development and in learning that gives rise to personal change. Factors that shape the interaction between learning and development are the sociocultural context, the process of rational and somatic reflection on experience, and the role of community in learning. The third section of this chapter dealt with adult education that is explicitly developmental in practice, including education for personal development, education for social change, and education related to professional identity development.

References

Aslanian, C. B., & Brickell, H. M. (1980). *Americans in transition: Life changes as reasons for adult learning.* New York: College Entrance Examination Board.

Baltes, P. B. (1987). Theoretical propositions of life-span developmental psychology: On the dynamics between growth and decline. *Developmental Psychology, 23,* 611–626.

Baumeister, R. F. (1987). How the self became a problem. *Journal of Personality and Social Psychology, 52*(1), 163–176.

Baumgartner, L. M. (2001). An update on transformational learning. In S. B. Merriam (Ed.), *The new update on adult learning theory* (pp. 15–24). New Directions for Adult and Continuing Education, no. 89. San Francisco: Jossey-Bass.

Baxter Magolda, M. (1995). The integration of relational and impersonal knowing in young adults' epistemological development. *Journal of College Student Development, 36*(3), 205–216.

Belenky, M. F., Clinchy, B. M., Goldberger, N. R., & Tarule, J. M. (1986). *Women's ways of knowing: The development of self, voice, and mind.* New York: Basic Books.

Benner, P. (1984). *From novice to expert.* Menlo Park, CA: Addison-Wesley.

Bloom, L. R. (1998). *Under the sign of hope: Feminist methodology and narrative interpretation.* Albany, NY: SUNY Press.

Bond, L. A., Belenky, M. F., & Weinstock, J. S. (2000). The Listening Partners Program: An initiative toward feminist community psychology in action. *American Journal of Community Psychology, 28*(5), 697–730.

Bordo, S. R. (1987). *The flight to objectivity.* Albany, NY: SUNY Press.

Boud, D., Cohen, R., & Walker, D. (Eds.). (1993). *Using experience for learning.* Buckingham, UK: Open University Press.

Boud, D., Keogh, R., & Walker, D. (1985). *Reflection: Turning experience into learning.* London: Kogan Page.

Boud, D., & Walker, D. (1993). Barriers to reflection on experience. In D. Boud, R. Cohen, & D. Walker (Eds.), *Using experience for learning* (pp. 73–86). Buckingham, UK: Open University Press.

Brookfield, S. (1987). *Developing critical thinkers.* San Francisco: Jossey-Bass.

Brookfield, S. (2000). The concept of critically reflective practice. In A. L. Wilson & E. R. Hayes (Eds.), *Handbook of adult and continuing education* (pp. 33–49). San Francisco: Jossey-Bass.

Brown, R. (2001). The process of community-building in distance learning classes. *Journal of Asynchronous Learning Networks, 5*(2), 18–35.

Chase, S. E. (1995). *Ambiguous empowerment: The work narratives of women school superintendents.* Amherst: University of Massachusetts Press.

Cheetham, G., & Chivers, G. (2001). How professionals learn in practice: an investigation of informal learning amongst people working in professions. *Journal of European Industrial Training, 25*(5), 248–292.

Clark, M. C. (1993). Transformational learning. In S. B. Merriam (Ed.), *The new update on adult learning theory* (pp. 47–56). New Directions for Adult and Continuing Education, no. 57. San Francisco: Jossey-Bass.

Clark, M. C. (2001). Off the beaten path: Some creative approaches to adult learning. In S. B. Merriam (Ed.), *The new update on adult learning theory* (pp. 83–91). New Directions for Adult and Continuing Education, no. 89. San Francisco: Jossey-Bass.

Clark, M. C., & Dirkx, J. M. (2000). Moving beyond a unitary self: A reflective dialogue. In A. L. Wilson & E. R. Hayes (Eds.), *Handbook of adult and continuing education* (pp. 101–116). San Francisco: Jossey-Bass.

Clark, M. C., & Wilson, A. L. (1991). Context and rationality in Mezirow's theory of transformational learning. *Adult Education Quarterly, 41*(2), 75–91.

Conti, G. J., & Fellenz, R. A. (1986). Myles Horton: Ideas that have withstood the test of time. *Adult Literacy and Basic Education, 10*(1), 1–20.

Courtenay, B. C., Merriam, S. B., & Reeves, P. (1998). The centrality of meaning-making in transformational learning: How HIV-positive adults make sense of their lives. *Adult Education Quarterly, 48*(2), 63–82.

Cranton, P. (1994). *Understanding and promoting transformative learning.* San Francisco: Jossey-Bass.

Cranton, P. (Ed.). (1997). *Transformative learning in action: Insights from practice.* New Directions for Adult and Continuing Education, no. 74. San Francisco: Jossey-Bass.

Cunningham, P. M. (2000). A sociology of adult education. In A. L. Wilson & E. R. Hayes (Eds.), *Handbook of adult and continuing education* (pp. 573–591). San Francisco: Jossey-Bass.

Daley, B. (2001). Learning and professional practice: A study of four professions. *Adult Education Quarterly, 52*(1), 39–54.

Daley, B. (2002). Context: Implications for learning in professional practice. In M. V. Alfred (Ed.), *Learning and sociocultural contexts: Implications for adults, community, and workplace education* (pp. 79–88). New Directions for Adult and Continuing Education, no. 96. San Francisco: Jossey-Bass.

Daloz, L. A. (1986). *Effective teaching and mentoring: Realizing the transformational power of adult learning experiences.* San Francisco: Jossey-Bass.

Daloz, L. A. (1999). *Mentor: Guiding the journey of adult learners* (2nd ed. of *Effective teaching and mentoring*). San Francisco: Jossey-Bass.

Degener, S. C. (2001). Making sense of critical pedagogy in adult literacy education. In J. Comings, B. Garner, & C. Smith (Eds.), *Annual review of adult learning and literacy* (Vol. 2, pp. 26–62). National Center for the Study of Adult Learning and Literacy. San Francisco: Jossey-Bass.

Dewey, J. (1933). *How we think.* Buffalo, NY: Prometheus.

Dewey, J. (1938). *Experience and education.* New York: Collier.

Dreyfus, S. E., & Dreyfus, H. L. (1980). *A five-stage model of the mental activities involved in directed skill acquisition.* Unpublished report supported by the Air Force Office of Scientific Research, USAF. University of California at Berkeley.

Elder, G. H. (1995). The life course paradigm: Social change and individual development. In P. Moen, G. H. Elder, & K. Luscher (Eds.), *Examining lives in context* (pp. 101–140). Washington, DC: American Psychological Association.

Erikson, E. H. (1963). *Childhood and society* (2nd ed.). New York: Norton.

Ewert, D. M., & Grace, K. A. (2000). Adult education for community action. In A. L. Wilson & E. R. Hayes, (Eds.). *Handbook of adult and continuing education* (pp. 327–343). San Francisco: Jossey-Bass.

Fenwick, T. J. (2000). Expanding conceptions of experiential learning: A review of the five contemporary perspectives on cognition. *Adult Education Quarterly, 50*(4), 243–272.

Flannery, D. D. (2000). Connection. In E. Hayes & D. D. Flannery (Eds.), *Women as learners: The significance of gender in adult learning* (pp. 111–137). San Francisco: Jossey-Bass.

Freire, P. (1970). *Pedagogy of the oppressed.* Harmondsworth, UK: Penguin.

Freire, P. (1973). *Education for critical consciousness.* New York: Seabury Press.

Gadotti, M. (1994). *Reading Paulo Freire: His life and work.* Albany, NY: SUNY Press.

Gergen, K. J. (1991). *The saturated self.* New York: Basic Books.

Gilligan, C. (1982). *In a different voice.* Cambridge, MA: Harvard University Press.

Goldberger, N. R., Tarule, J. M., Clinchy, B. M., & Belenky, M. F. (Eds.). (1996). *Knowledge, difference, and power: Essays inspired by women's ways of knowing.* New York: Basic Books.

Gould, R. (1990). The therapeutic learning program. In J. Mezirow et al. (Eds.), *Fostering critical reflection in adulthood: A guide to transformative and emancipatory learning* (pp. 134–156). San Francisco: Jossey-Bass.

Hart, M. U. (1990). Liberation through consciousness raising. In J. Mezirow et al. (Eds.), *Fostering critical reflection in adulthood: A guide to transformative and emancipatory learning* (pp. 47–73). San Francisco: Jossey-Bass.

Havighurst, R. J. (1972). *Developmental tasks and education* (3rd ed.). New York: McKay.

Hayes, E., & Flannery, D. D. (2000). *Women as learners.* San Francisco: Jossey-Bass.

Hemphill, D. (1994). *Critical rationality from a cross-cultural perspective.* Proceedings of the 35th Adult Education Research Conference (pp. 187–192). University of Tennessee, Knoxville.

Herrmann, F. (1998). Building on-line communities of practice: An example and implications. *Educational Technology, 38*(1), 16–23.

Heshusius, L., & Ballard, K. (1996). *From positivism to interpretivism and beyond.* New York: Teachers College Press.

Holstein, J. A., & Gubrium, J. F. (2000). *The self we live by: Narrative identity in a postmodern world.* New York: Oxford University Press.

Jarvis, P. (1987). *Adult learning in the social context.* London: Croom Helm.

Jarvis, P. (1992). *Paradoxes of learning: On becoming an individual in society.* San Francisco: Jossey-Bass.

Kegan, R. (1994). *In over our heads: The mental demands of modern life.* Cambridge, MA: Harvard University Press.

King, P. M., & Kitchener, K. S. (1994). *Developing reflective judgment.* San Francisco: Jossey-Bass.

Knowles, M. S. (1980). *The modern practice of adult education: From pedagogy to andragogy* (rev. ed.). Englewood Cliffs, NJ: Prentice Hall/Cambridge.

Knowles, M. S., & Associates. (1984). *Andragogy in action: Applying modern principles of adult learning.* San Francisco: Jossey-Bass.

Kohlberg, L. (1973). Continuities in childhood and adult moral development. In P. Baltes & K. Schaie (Eds.), *Life-span developmental psychology: Personality and socialization* (pp. 180–204). Orlando, FL: Academic Press.

Kramer, D. A. (1989). Development of an awareness of contradiction across the life span and the question of postformal operations. In M. L. Commons, J. D. Sinnott, F. A. Richards, & C. Armon (Eds.), *Adult development: Comparisons and applications of developmental models* (pp. 133–159). New York: Praeger.

Lave, J. (1996). The practice of learning. In S. Chaiklin & J. Lave (Eds.), *Understanding practice: Perspectives on activity and context* (pp. 3–34). Cambridge: Cambridge University Press.

Lave, J., & Wenger, E. (1991). *Situated learning: Legitimate peripheral participation.* New York: Cambridge University Press.

Lévi-Strauss, C. (1966). *The savage mind* (2nd ed.). Chicago: University of Chicago Press.

Levinson, D. J., Darrow, D., Kien, E. B., Levinson, M., & McKee, B. (1978). *The seasons of a man's life.* New York: Academic Press.

Levinson, D. J., & Levinson, J. D. (1996). *The seasons of a woman's life.* New York: Ballantine.

Linde, C. (1993). *Life stories: The creation of coherence.* New York: Oxford University Press.

Loevinger, J. (1976). *Ego development: Conceptions and theories.* San Francisco: Jossey-Bass.

Maher, F. A. (1987). Toward a richer theory of feminist pedagogy: A comparison of liberation and gender models for teaching and learning. *Journal of Education, 169*(3), 91–100.

Maslow, A. H. (1970). *Motivation and personality* (2nd ed.). New York: HarperCollins.

Matthews, J. C. (1998). Somatic knowing and education. *Educational Forum, 62,* 236–242.

Maxwell, M. A. (1984). *The Alcoholics Anonymous experience: A close-up view for professionals.* New York: McGraw-Hill.

McAdams, D. P. (1993). *The stories we live by: Personal myths and the making of the self.* New York: Morrow.

Merriam, S. B., & Caffarella, R. S. (1999). *Learning in adulthood* (2nd ed.). San Francisco: Jossey-Bass.

Merriam, S. B., & Clark, M. C. (1991). *Lifelines: Patterns of work, love, and learning in adulthood.* San Francisco, CA: Jossey-Bass.

Merriam, S. B., Courtenay, B., & Baumgartner, L. (2003). On becoming a witch: Learning in a marginalized community of practice. *Adult Education Quarterly, 53,* 170–188.

Merriam, S. B., Mott, V. W., & Lee, M. (1996). Learning that comes from the negative interpretation of life experience. *Studies in Continuing Education, 18*(1), 1–23.

Mezirow, J. (1978). *Education for perspective transformation: Women's re-entry programs in community colleges* (pp. 39–70). New York: Teachers College Press.

Mezirow, J. (1985). Concept and action in adult education. *Adult Education Quarterly 35*(3), 142–151.

Mezirow, J. (1990). How critical reflection triggers learning. In J. Mezirow & Associates, *Fostering critical reflection in adulthood: A guide to transformative and emancipatory learning* (pp. 1–20). San Francisco: Jossey-Bass.

Mezirow, J. (1995). Transformation theory of adult learning. In M. R. Welton (Ed.), *In defense of the lifeworld.* Albany, NY: SUNY Press.

Mezirow, J. (2000). Learning to think like an adult: Core concepts of transformation theory. In J. Mezirow & Associates, *Learning as transformation* (pp. 3–33). San Francisco: Jossey-Bass.

Michelson, E. (1998). Re-membering: The return of the body to experiential learning. *Studies in Continuing Education, 20,* 217–233.

Miller, M. E., & Cook-Greuter, S. R. (Eds.). (1994). *Transcendence and mature adult thought in adulthood: The further reaches of adult development.* London: Rowman & Littlefield.

Morris, A. (1991). Introduction: Education for liberation. *Social Policy, 21*(3), 2–6.

Nesbit, T. (1998). The social reform perspective: Seeking a better society. In D. Pratt et al. (Eds.), *Five perspectives on teaching in adult and higher education* (pp. 173–199). Malabar, FL: Krieger.

Neugarten, B. (1976). Adaptation and the life cycle. *Counseling Psychologist, 6,* 16–20.

Neugarten, B., & Datan, N. (1973). Sociological perspectives on the life cycle. In P. Baltes & K. W. Schaie (Eds.), *Life-span developmental psychology: Personality and socialization* (pp. 53–69). Orlando, FL: Academic Press.

Newman, M. (1994). *Defining the enemy: Adult education and social action.* Sydney: Stewart Victor.

Nuernberger, P. (1994). The structure of mind and its resources. In M. E. Miller & S. R. Cook-Greuter (Eds.), *Transcendence and mature adult thought in adulthood: The further reaches of adult development* (pp. 107–116). London: Rowman & Littlefield.

Oliver, L. P. (1992). Study circles: Individual growth through collaborative learning. In L. A. Cavaliere & A. Sgroi (Eds.), *Learning for personal development.* New Directions for Adult and Continuing Education, no. 53. San Francisco: Jossey-Bass.

Palloff, R. M., & Pratt, K. (1999). *Building learning communities in cyberspace: Effective strategies for the on-line classroom.* San Francisco: Jossey-Bass.

Parker, F., & Parker, B. J. (1991). *Myles Horton (1905–1990) of Highlander: Adult educator and Southern activist.* ERIC document ED336615.

Perry, W. G. (1970). *Forms of intellectual and ethical development in the college years.* Austin, TX: Holt, Rinehart & Winston.

Piaget, J. (1972). Intellectual evolution from adolescent to adulthood. *Human Development, 16,* 346–370.

Queeny, D. S. (2000). Continuing professional education. In A. Wilson & E. Hayes (Eds.), *Handbook of adult and continuing education* (pp. 375–391). San Francisco: Jossey-Bass.

Riegel, K. F. (1973). Dialectic operations: The final period of cognitive development. *Human Development, 16*, 346–370.

Riegel, K. F. (1975). Adult life crisis: A dialectical interpretation of development. In N. Datan & L. H. Ginsberg (Eds.), *Life-span developmental psychology: Normative life crises* (pp. 99–128). Orlando, FL: Academic Press.

Roberts, T. B. (1989). Multistate education: Metacognitive implications of the mindbody psychotechnologies. *Journal of Transpersonal Psychology, 21*(1), 83–102.

Rodgers, C. (2002). Defining reflection: Another look at John Dewey and reflective thinking. *Teachers College Record, 104*(4), 842–866.

Rogers, C. R. (1961). *On becoming a person*. Boston: Houghton Mifflin.

Rogers, R. R. (2001). Reflection in higher education: A concept analysis. *Innovative Higher Education, 26*(1), 37–57.

Rosenwald, G. C., & Ochberg, R. L. (Eds.). (1992). *Storied lives: The cultural politics of self-understanding*. New Haven, CT: Yale University Press.

Schlossberg, N. K., Waters, E. B., & Goodman, J. (1995). *Counseling adults in transition* (2nd ed.). New York: Springer.

Schön, D. A. (1983). *The reflective practitioner: How professionals think in action*. New York: Basic Books.

Schön, D. A. (1987). *Educating the reflective practitioner*. San Francisco: Jossey-Bass.

Schön, D. A. (1996). From technical rationality to reflection-in-action. In R. Edwards, A. Hanson, & P. Raggatt (Eds.), *Boundaries of adult learning* (pp. 8–31). London: Routledge.

Shor, I. (1993). Education is politics: Paulo Freire's critical pedagogy. In P. McLaren & P. Leonard (Eds.), *Paulo Freire: A critical encounter* (pp. 25–35). London: Routledge.

Sinnott, J. D. (1994). The relationship of postformal thought, adult learning, and lifespan development. In J. D. Sinnott (Ed.), *Interdisciplinary handbook of adult lifespan learning* (pp. 105–119). Westport, CT: Greenwood Press.

Smith, M. C., & Pourchot, T. (1998). Adult learning and development [Electronic resource]: perspectives from educational psychology. Mahwah, NJ: Lawrence Erlbaum.

Spear, G. E., & Mocker, D. W. (1984). The organizing circumstance: Environmental determinants in self-directed learning. *Adult Education Quarterly, 35*(1), 1–10.

Taylor, E. (1997). Building upon the theoretical debate: A critical review of the empirical studies of Mezirow's transformative learning theory. *Adult Education Quarterly, 48*(1), 34–59.

Taylor, K., Marienau, C., & Fiddler, M. (2000). *Developing adult learners: Strategies for teachers and trainers*. San Francisco: Jossey-Bass.

Tennant, M. C., & Pogson, P. (1995). *Learning and change in the adult years: A developmental perspective*. San Francisco: Jossey-Bass.

Tennant, M. (2000). Adult learning for self-development and change. In A. L. Wilson & E. R. Hayes (Eds.), *Handbook of adult and continuing Education* (pp. 87–100). San Francisco: Jossey-Bass.

Tisdell, E. J. (1995). *Creating inclusive adult learning environments: Insights from multicultural education and feminist pedagogy* (Information series no. 361). Columbus, Ohio: ERIC Clearinghouse on Adult, Career, and Vocational Education.

Tisdell, E. J. (1996). Feminist pedagogy and adult learning: Underlying theory and emancipatory practice. *Proceedings of the Adult Education Research Conference* (pp. 307–312). Tampa: University of South Florida.

Tisdell, E. J., & Perry, C. A. (1997). A collaborative interracial "border" pedagogy in adult multicultural education classes. In P. Armstrong, N. Miller, & M. Zukas (Eds.), *Crossing borders, breaking boundaries: Proceedings of the 27th annual SCUTREA conference* (pp. 441–444). London: Birkbeck College, University of London.

Todd, J. (2001). Body, knowledge, and the body politic. *Humanist, 61*(2), 23–28.

Tough, A. (1978). Major learning efforts: Recent research and future directions. *Adult Education, 28*(4), 250–263.

Weedon, C. (1997). *Feminist practice and poststructuralist theory* (2nd ed.). Oxford: Blackwell.

Weiss, R. P. (2001). The mind-body connection in learning. *Training and Development, 55*(9), 60–67.

Welton, M. (1993). Social revolutional learning: The new social movements as learning sites. *Adult Education Quarterly, 43*, 152–164.

Wenger, E. (1998). *Communities of practice: Learning, meaning, and identity*. Cambridge: Cambridge University Press.

Wenger, E. C., & Snyder, W. M. (2000). Communities of practice: The organizational frontier. *Harvard Business Review, 78*(1), 139–145.

Wilber, K. (1983). *Eye to eye*. New York: Doubleday.

Chapter 3

Research Design and Methodological Issues for Adult Development and Learning

Grace I. L. Caskie and Sherry L. Willis

Both adult development and learning are established areas of research in their own right. Each has its own traditions and practices with respect to the type of research that is conducted. Given the relative youth of research conducted at the intersection of adult development and learning, investigators have the unique opportunity to carve out a new tradition of research but also face new challenges in blending together these two related yet previously separate disciplines. Decisions about the questions that should be asked and the theories that should be pursued need to be made by individual researchers. Issues such as these are not included in the scope of this chapter. Rather, the aim here is to provide an overview of the key issues involved in designing and evaluating various types of research endeavors that may be useful for those working in the combined areas of adult development and learning. Readers are referred at various points to publications with greater detail on a particular topic, some of which are entire texts devoted to the explanation of just one topic. The first section of the chapter describes several study types, including experimental, quasi-experimental, descriptive, cross-sectional, longitudinal, and sequential designs. The second section focuses on sampling issues and how the type of sample can influence the generalizability of research findings. The third section discusses measurement issues, including validity, reliability, appropriateness of a measure, scales of measurement, the measurement of change, and scale development. The final section of the chapter briefly addresses the issue of statistical significance versus clinical significance, with respect to evaluating the importance of one's research findings.

STUDY TYPES

Experimental Studies

In an experimental study, participants are randomly assigned to membership in one of two or more groups that will be compared. For example, in the ACTIVE clinical trial on cognitive training of older adults (Ball et al., 2002), the participants were randomly assigned to one of three cognitive training groups or a control group. By assigning participants randomly to an experimental condition (or a control group), variables other than the independent variable (i.e., the variable on which participants are grouped or that is used to predict the outcome variable) that may influence the behavior or construct being studied should be equally distributed among the experimental and control groups. Thus, through the process of random assignment, experimental designs allow a researcher to control for possible confounding factors that would decrease a study's internal validity.

A word should also be said about the concern of artificiality in experimental studies. Although experimental studies are designed to approximate real situations, controlling for too many variables may limit the external validity of the study. For example, if a research study only included men (e.g., National Longitudinal Surveys of Older Men; Center for Human Resource Research, 1992) to control for the effect of gender on the results of the study, it may be difficult to generalize the study's findings to women. Having too many experimental controls can also decrease the generalizability of a study. A greater number of controls leads to greater artificiality in the experimental setting, making it more difficult to generalize behavior in the lab to a real world setting.

Willis (2001) discussed five types of experimental designs that are particularly useful for conducting behavioral interventions with adults. These designs vary in terms of the comparison or control group used in relation to the experimental group that receives the intervention. First, the *no-treatment control group design* uses a comparison group that receives the same pre- and postintervention assessment battery but otherwise receives no intervention or contact. This type of design is important for providing initial evidence of an intervention effect and an estimate of any gain in score that may result simply from being tested more than once (i.e., the practice effect). The second type of experimental design, the *nonspecific control group design*, provides a placebo treatment to the control group. The placebo treatment must not include any factors considered critical to the intervention. For psychological and behavioral research, it may be difficult to design a placebo treatment that has no effect at all on the outcome measures and that will maintain the blindness of participants to their treatment condition. Third, the *component control group design* is a between-group design in which various components of the intervention are implemented separately and in combination. An essential requirement, therefore, of using this design is the ability to identify and implement independently the various components of an intervention. Comparison of the different groups can help identify the most effective intervention component or combination of components. Fourth, the *parametric design* involves systematically varying the level of one experimental factor while holding all else constant. For example, the number of training sessions may be increased by one for several experimental groups being compared to determine the optimal number of training sessions needed (Hofland, Willis, & Baltes, 1981). Finally, the *comparative design* involves comparing two or more distinctly different intervention approaches to the same problem to determine which may be more effective. Although this might seem at first to be a very useful design, concerns exist with using this type of comparison. Because interventions may differ on a number of factors, it can be difficult to determine the most salient component for producing change and may result in few factors being held constant across intervention groups. Additionally, a number of practical issues exist with the use of this design, including the necessity of administering multiple interventions at the same site (to avoid confounding site with the type of intervention) and of having trainers who are equally proficient at conducting all interventions.

Quasi-Experimental Studies

Many studies exist for which random assignment to groups is entirely possible and appropriate. However, sometimes a researcher wants to compare groups to which individuals cannot be randomly assigned because the characteristics of interest are preexisting, such as gender, age, or educational level. These studies are called *quasi-experimental studies* (Campbell & Stanley, 1953; Cook & Campbell, 1979). Cross-sectional studies of age differences and longitudinal studies of age changes, described in greater detail shortly, are examples of quasi-experimental studies because individuals cannot be assigned to an age level. In practice, most studies include multiple independent variables or grouping variables, which may include a mixture of randomly assigned variables and classificatory (i.e., not randomly assigned) variables that define the groups that will be compared. For example, Park, Smith, Morrell, Puglisi, and Dudley (1990) compared the recall of young and old adults who were randomly assigned to one of six experimental conditions (two verbal integration conditions crossed with three cueing conditions). This study is quasi-experimental because it included experimental conditions (verbal integration and cueing) and a classificatory variable (age group). In contrast to the experimental design, causal conclusions cannot be made in a quasi-experimental design regarding those variables to which individuals were not randomly assigned. When preexisting groups such as young and old individuals or males and females are compared, it is unknown whether differences are truly due to the group difference (i.e., age or gender) or to other factors that may covary with the independent variable. For example, different age groups represent different cohort experiences, including education, which can influence learning and development.

Confounding factors are variables that decrease the internal validity of the study—the ability to conclude that differences in the dependent variable (i.e., the behavior or construct that we are trying to explain or for which we want to examine group differences) were caused by the experimental condition rather than other extraneous variables. For example, suppose we conducted a study on the effect of child-rearing instruction on the quality of parent–child interactions. If all of the participants assigned to instruction on child-rearing techniques were mothers and the control group consisted entirely of fathers, assignment to experimental condition would have been completely confounded with gender of the participant, and it would be impossible to untangle whether any differences observed in the outcome measure (e.g., improvement in parent–child interactions) are due to receiving the instruction or to the fact that all who received the instruction were women. If random assignment had been used, the men and women in the sample would have been equally distributed into the experimental group and the control group. Confounded variables such as in this hypothetical example may not be as obvious in real studies, yet may be as insidious as confounding group with site or location, such as if all older adults come from an urban environment and all younger adults are from suburban college campuses. Alternative explanations for group differences should always be considered when random assignment has not been used.

Thus, the well-known admonition that "correlation does not necessarily imply causation" is misleading in that the ability to make causal conclusions is actually dependent on whether random assignment was used than the type of statistical measure used to describe the relationship. Correlation is simply a statistic that describes the linear relationship between the independent variable and the dependent variable, whether or not individuals were randomly assigned to the levels of the independent variable. If participants were randomly assigned to the number of training sessions (e.g., as in a parametric design) and a strong positive correlation were found between number of training sessions and number of correct responses at the end of the memory training, one would have a basis for concluding that more training sessions caused better memory performance. However, if we correlated number of adult education courses reported by each participant with memory performance, causal conclusions could not be made because there are other variables (e.g., socioeconomic status) that could be related to these variables that explain their relationship.

Descriptive Studies

In descriptive studies, individuals are not randomly assigned to any experimental conditions and may not be assigned to groups at all. Two basic methods for conducting a descriptive study are naturalistic observation and case study. The methods used in descriptive studies are more likely to be considered qualitative rather than quantitative, although they may also be incorporated into a more quantitatively oriented study.

When a researcher uses naturalistic observation, he or she has no direct contact with the individuals under study. The researcher simply observes the individuals in a natural environment (e.g., a senior citizen center, library, park, or grocery store) and then records information about behaviors that are demonstrated. For example, in Baltes et al. (1980), interactions between nursing home residents and staff members were observed and coded in terms of whether they supported dependence behaviors in the resident. Amato (1988) also conducted a naturalistic observation study in which the behaviors of men caring for young children in public places were observed. Although naturalistic observation could be used to observe learning in adults, certain types of adult development may be more difficult to tap into given the lack of direct contact with the individuals under study. For example, one might expect that adults in a computer literacy course would learn new skills, which may in turn lead to changes in their self-perceptions and self-efficacy about their computer skills. Computer literacy might be indirectly measured by observing the number of errors made, but self-perception (an internal process) may be more difficult to assess accurately through observation alone.

In contrast to the descriptive method of naturalistic observation, case studies involve extensive direct contact between the researcher and the individuals under study. Typically, research using the method of case study involves only a few individuals to make the intense detail-gathering process a more feasible task. In addition to interviews and direct observation, the case study method may include examination of medical records or psychological measures. In addition to case studies of individuals, case studies can also be conducted of a process or a situation (e.g., Cervone, 2004). Detailed information about how to conduct a case study can be found in Stake (1995).

Examples of case study research also tend to be more qualitative than quantitative. Gillem, Cohn, and Throne (2001) described the case studies of identity development in two biracial individuals. The two subjects were studied with the use of a semi-structured interview schedule primarily composed of open-ended questions about their current identity, influences of family members on their identity development, and their experiences as biracial individuals. Honos-Webb, Stiles, and Greenberg (2003) reported on a case study of a woman who had completed psychotherapy. Measures of depression and self-esteem were collected, and transcripts of therapeutic sessions were also analyzed and rated. Finally, Levinson's (1978) book on the process of adult development for males included data collected from multiple interviews of 40 men about their lives over the period of late adolescence to their late forties. Levinson also presented in great detail the case studies of four men ("James," "William," "Paul," and "John"). Levinson's work demonstrates the incorporation of interviews and administration of psychological measures that may occur with the case study approach; specifically, both the men and their wives were interviewed, and tests such as the Thematic Apperception Test were also given to the men.

Cross-Sectional Studies

The focus of a cross-sectional study is to gather information about age differences. Participants are grouped by age, and then all groups are assessed at one point in time. For example, numerous studies have examined age differences in memory and other cognitive training (Craik & McDowd, 1998; Park et al., 1990), personality characteristics (Costa et al., 1986), or self-efficacy and attributions for performance in various domains (Lachman & Jelalian, 1984; Lachman & McArthur, 1986). When a researcher's interest is in knowing how various age groups differ on some construct or behavior at a particular point in time (e.g., voting behavior, attitudes about abortion), a cross-sectional study is very appropriate. Cross-sectional studies of age differences can also inform a researcher about possible trends for age changes and about the age range necessary to study a particular developmental process when planning a longitudinal study (Schaie, 1996b).

It is important to keep in mind, however, that the influences of age and cohort are confounded in cross-sectional studies. Cohort membership is typically defined by the year, or the range of years (e.g., the Baby Boomers), in which a group of participants was born. By definition, then, the age groups used in a cross-sectional study must be drawn from different birth cohorts. Thus, a cross-sectional study cannot fully determine whether any observed differences between the age groups are due to increased age (i.e., maturation) or to cohort differences. For example, if older adults were found to outperform younger adults on a timed test of simple mathematics problems, it may appear that mathematic ability increases with age. However, an alternate explanation is that the individuals in younger cohorts may have less experience working problems by hand rather than by hand-held calculator. In other words, the experience of learning to do simple math problems with (or without) a calculator may be cohort-specific. In addition, it should be noted that the influence of the time of measurement (i.e., period effects) on the participants' performance cannot be examined in a cross-sectional study because the data are collected at only one point in time.

When conducting a cross-sectional study, a potential problem is that of equating the age groups on relevant demographics that may influence the relationship between age and the dependent variable. For example, in comparing young and old individuals, it may be difficult to find groups with equivalent educational levels or experiences. Furthermore, there is the possibility of the bias of survivorship in the selection of older individuals for inclusion into a study.

Longitudinal Studies

The purpose of a longitudinal study is to examine age changes in the same group of individuals over time. The multiple assessments gained through longitudinal data collections are essential to understanding change in a construct or behavior over time as well as the variability and predictors of such change over time (Alwin & Campbell, 2001). Investigators have sometimes compared samples of individuals at different ages (i.e., a cross-sectional study) and concluded that differences found on the dependent variable could be attributed to chronological age. However, this type of conclusion must be treated with caution because cross-sectional and longitudinal studies do not always show the same age trends. For example, research on the adult development of mental abilities has shown wide discrepancies between cross-sectional and longitudinal data collected on the same subject population over a wide age range. For some dependent variables, substantial age differences obtained in cross-sectional data were not replicated in longitudinal data, whereas for other dependent variables, longitudinal age changes reflected more profound decrement than was shown in the comparable cross-sectional age difference patterns (Schaie, 2004; Schaie & Strother, 1968).

The most basic design for assessing changes over time due to age is a single-cohort longitudinal study. With this design, a single group of individuals (of similar age) are observed at two or more occasions in time. For example, Helson and Moane (1987) examined the personalities of a sample of women during their senior year of college and followed up twice with this cohort, once in their mid- to late twenties and finally in their early to mid-forties. A slightly more complex single-cohort longitudinal study, the Nordic Research on Aging project, included the study of 75-year-old individuals from three countries—Denmark, Sweden, and Finland—who were later reexamined at age 80 (Heikkinen, Berg, Schroll, Steen, & Viidik, 1997). With this second example, we again have a single cohort of individuals (those persons aged 75 years), albeit from three locations, which was assessed twice to obtain longitudinal information. Schaie and Hofer (2001) stated that longitudinal studies in adult development have been of three types: (1) studies that were begun to understand childhood development but with assessments continued into adulthood; (2) studies of young adulthood with continued assessments into midlife or later; and (3) studies specifically designed to assess the adulthood period with representative samples. An extensive overview of longitudinal studies of adult development can be found in Schaie and Hofer (2001).

Because all of the individuals in a single-cohort longitudinal study share the same cohort membership and the set of similar experiences that accompanies membership, this type of study cannot inform the researcher about any cohort differences in the construct being studied. Also, the single-cohort longitudinal design confounds age changes in the dependent variable with time-of-measurement (i.e., period) effects occurring over the calendar time during which change is assessed. The confound of age changes and time-of-measurement effects means that the researcher cannot be certain that the observed behavioral change is due to the individuals' increase in age rather than that something has changed about the environment between the different times of measurement. For example, suppose that in 2000 we had asked a group of 50-year-olds their opinions about the likelihood of a terrorist attack on the United States within the next year. If we reassessed this cohort in 2003 (at age 53) and found that the perceived likelihood of a terrorist attack on the United States had increased, at least two explanations are possible for the observed increase: (1) as people age from 50 years to 53 years, they become more anxious; or (2) specific events occurred during the three years between assessments to change people's perceptions. In this case, one might reasonably assume that the change in perceptions was more likely due to the occurrence of the terrorist attacks on September 11, 2001, than to any sort of maturational change that occurred during that three-year period.

The influence of the time of measurement can also influence the meaning of a particular construct or the implication for a finding in a longitudinal study. Caspi, Elder, and Bem (1987) found that a sample of ill-tempered boys born around 1928 tended to maintain this personality style into adulthood. As a result, these men experienced significantly poorer outcomes as adults, which was at least partially influenced by changes that had occurred in society by the time they reached adulthood. Specifically, Caspi and colleagues pointed out that a greater emphasis had been placed on interpersonal skills as a prerequisite for success in the workplace during this time period. In earlier time periods, where job success focused on the ability to perform physical labor, the implication of having a confrontational personality style may have had less impact, and outcomes for these men might have been better. Questions that are asked in a longitudinal study may also have different implications at different times in history. For example, for male adolescents in the 1920s and 1930s, having a mother who worked outside the home was a typical indicator of poverty status (Hayward & Gorman, 2004), whereas it would have a very different meaning for most adolescents today.

Other longitudinal designs exist beyond the basic single-cohort design discussed so far in this section. Several of these designs are presented in a later section on sequential designs. The type of data collected in the design discussed is considered prospective data, wherein one begins studying a group of individuals with the intent of collecting future waves of information on this group of individuals. Longitudinal data can also be obtained retrospectively, by asking participants to recall information about earlier time periods (Alwin & Campbell, 2001). George, Hays, Flint, and Meador (2004) conducted a study of the relationship between religion and health in older adults by supplementing existing information on health in older adulthood with the collection of retrospective data on religiosity throughout the life course. Their study included a sample of community-dwelling adults aged 65 years and older on which health information had been collected prospectively from 1986 to 1996. Following the 1996 data collection, George and her colleagues also obtained life histories of the religious participation of these participants. This example demonstrates two of the problems with the use of retrospective data for studies of adult development and aging: (1) differential survival and (2) reliability of recall (Alwin & Campbell, 2001). First, religious histories were obtained from only those participants who were healthy enough and willing to complete all four waves of testing that occurred over period of a decade. Second, the recall of

religious involvement at earlier time periods may be influenced by current states, including current level of religious involvement, or it may be biased by faulty recall. Yet, as George et al. (2004) pointed out, the use of retrospective data is preferable to no data at all.

Of course, despite its many advantages for the study of change over time, the longitudinal study is not without disadvantages. Collecting longitudinal data can be an expensive and time-consuming process, particularly when one desires to study the participants over an extensive period of time (i.e., over a wide age range). Also, participants are lost from longitudinal studies due to attrition over time, which may influence the results. Reasons and implications for attrition are addressed in the section on sampling included in this chapter. Longitudinal studies must also contend with the possibility of measures and research questions becoming outdated.

Time-efficient designs, such as the accelerated longitudinal design, have been proposed to shorten the amount of time necessary to study a developmental trajectory. These designs aim to reduce both the monetary and time costs of collecting longitudinal data. Under the assumption of no cohort differences, accelerated longitudinal designs link longitudinal data collected from several independent cohorts studied for overlapping age ranges (Duncan, Duncan, Strycker, Li, & Alpert, 1999; Tonry, Ohlin, & Farrington, 1991). Because no one cohort is studied, for the entire age range being investigated, distinct patterns of missing data are incorporated into the data by design. In the context of latent growth modeling, both McArdle and Hamagami (1992) and Duncan, Duncan, and Hops (1996) demonstrated that growth parameter estimates from the accelerated longitudinal design were as accurate as the corresponding true longitudinal design. However, McArdle and Hamagami also found that the standard errors for these growth parameter estimates increased as the amount of data collected per cohort decreased. This difficulty could lead to unstable parameter estimates. Large-scale simulations are needed to provide further insight into the utility of the accelerated longitudinal design.

Sequential Designs

Data acquisitions that are initially structured as either a cross-sectional or single-cohort longitudinal study can be extended into cross-sectional or longitudinal sequences (Baltes, 1968; Schaie & Baltes, 1975).

Sequential studies can also allow questions about development to be answered without involving the long time frame required for a true longitudinal design. Longitudinal sequences use the same sample of individuals from two (or more) cohorts repeatedly, whereas cross-sectional sequences use independent random samples of individuals (each observed only once) from cohorts covering the same age groups at two (or more) different points in time. For example, a longitudinal sequence might begin by studying a group of 30-year-olds in 2005, planning to retest these individuals every 5 years until they were 45 years old (i.e., retests in 2010, 2015, 2020). At the first retest point, a longitudinal sequence could then be formed by including into the study an additional cohort of individuals who were 30 years old in 2010, with the plan to assess this group also every 5 years until they turned 45. In contrast, a cross-sectional sequence might begin in 2005 with a simple cross-sectional study of individuals in three age groups: 30–34 years, 35–39 years, and 40–44 years. The data for the cross-sectional sequence would then be obtained by repeating this study at a later time point and by drawing new samples of individuals in each of the age groups that had been included in the original investigation. The critical difference between the two approaches is that the longitudinal sequence permits the evaluation of intraindividual age change and interindividual differences in rate of change, about which information cannot be obtained from cross-sectional sequences.

Schaie's "most efficient design" (Schaie, 1965, 1977, 1994) combines these cross-sectional and longitudinal sequences in a systematic way, incorporating age effects, cohort effects, and time-of-measurement effects. First, an age range of interest is defined at the time of the initial data collection and is sampled randomly at age intervals that are optimally identical with the time chosen to pass between successive measurements. The age range used must be specific to the problem under study. As an example, consider a design in which one wanted to study relationships between learning and development as individuals pass from midlife into older adulthood. In this case, to capture a range of ages in the midlife period, the age range of interest might include individuals who are 35 to 49 years old at the first time point.

Second, from this full age range of interest, samples of participants are drawn from age intervals with widths that match the amount of time expected to pass between measurements. Using the midlife example,

if the researcher planned for 5 years to elapse between the first and second measurements, the samples should be drawn in 5-year age intervals within the larger age range (e.g., 35–39 years, 40–44 years, 45–49 years). Then, at the second time of measurement, participants from the first data collection are retrieved and restudied, providing short-term longitudinal studies of as many cohorts as there were age intervals at the initial data collection. Each age interval is also resampled at the second time of measurement, providing a new set of individuals to be tested within each age group. The resampling process is also shown in the example in table 3.1 where new samples of different people from each age group are added at each testing year. By Time 4 in this example, we would have collected data that covers ages from 35 to 64 years (using the 5-year testing interval that was proposed) and would have included individuals from six cohorts. The entire process can be repeated multiple times with retesting of previous subjects (adding to the longitudinal data) as well as initial testing of new samples (adding to the cross-sectional data).

The data generated by using the most efficient design are rich in that they can be analyzed with several analysis strategies (proposed by Schaie, 1965) to contrast the relative effects of age, cohort, and time of measurement on the variable being studied. Many developmentalists are most interested in the analysis of age changes and cohort changes performed in a *cohort-sequential* analysis under the assumption that time-of-

TABLE 3.1. Example of Data Collection Based on Schaie's Most Efficient Design

Age Group	Sample	Time 1	Time 2	Time 3	Time 4	Cohort
35–39 years	1	X	X	X	X	3
	2		X	X	X	4
	3			X	X	5
	4				X	6
40–44 years	1	X	X	X	X	2
	2		X	X	X	3
	3			X	X	4
	4				X	5
45–49 years	1	X	X	X	X	1
	2		X	X	X	2
	3			X	X	3
	4				X	4

Note: Each X represents a data collection for a particular sample.

measurement effects have not influenced the variable being studied. If a consistent age change is found for different cohorts, the results have greater external validity than would be provided by a single-cohort longitudinal design. For our midlife example, one of the cohort-sequential analyses that could be performed would use the Time 1 and Time 2 data from the 45- to 49-year-old age group and the Time 2 and Time 3 data from the 40- to 44-year-old age group. One practical drawback to this analysis strategy is that the analysis cannot be performed until three data collections have passed. Depending on the interval that one has proposed to use between waves of data collections, this could mean a long wait before one could begin analyzing data!

In contrast to the cohort-sequential strategy, cross-sequential and time-sequential analyses can be done earlier in the study, because both require only two data collections (as a minimum). In the *cross-sequential* analysis, cohort changes are contrasted with time-of-measurement effects, under the assumption that no age changes (or at least uniform age changes) have occurred on the variable of interest. A simple cross-sequential analysis could be conducted with the Time 1 and Time 2 data from two of the age groups in table 3.1. Finally, in a *time-sequential* analysis, age effects are contrasted with time-of-measurement effects, assuming no cohort effects on the variable being studied. The time-sequential strategy examines whether the difference between the age groups remains stable or changes over time. For example, we might want to examine whether the difference between the 35- to 39-year-old age group and the 45- to 49-year-old age group was the same or different at Time 1 and Time 2. The data from the first samples drawn from these age groups (i.e., those samples first tested at Time 1) would be contrasted with the data from the second samples drawn from these age groups (i.e., those samples first tested at Time 2). More detailed descriptions of each of these analyses, and analyses that also incorporate tests of practice effects and attrition, can be found in Schaie and Caskie (2004).

SAMPLING AND GENERALIZABILITY

The way a researcher obtains the actual group of individuals who will participate in his or her investigation has important implications for the generalizability of the study's findings. In other words, the type of sample used in a study and the external validity of the findings are interdependent. The ability to generalize a study's findings beyond the sample of individuals who participated requires that the sample is representative of the larger population of individuals to which the findings are to be applied. Certain sampling methods are much more likely to generate samples that are representative of the characteristics of the larger population of interest and, as a result, imply greater generalizability for the study.

Use of a probability sampling method, such as random sampling, ensures a representative sample because it avoids the biases involved in nonprobability samples (Babbie, 1986). In a simple random sample, every member of the population of interest has an equal chance of inclusion in the study sample. Suppose one wanted to study graduates from a particular university. A random sample of this group could be obtained by randomly selecting names of potential participants from university records. Because the likelihood of selection into a random sample was equal for all members of the population, research findings from this representative sample can be generalized to the entire population of interest from which the sample was drawn. For example, Sitlington and Frank (1990) used random sampling to obtain participants for a study of the success of learning-disabled individuals one year after completing high school. First, 2,476 individuals were randomly selected from a list of former special education students in Iowa who had graduated from high school in the years studied. Of the 2,476 graduates, 1,090 had participated in a Learning Disabilities Program as part of their special education curriculum; 911 of these individuals with disabilities were eventually included in the Sitlington and Frank study. The use of random sampling tends to be more important in applied research such as the Sitlington and Frank study than in basic research (e.g., on sensory processes), because the findings of applied research are more likely to be influenced by sample characteristics; findings are also more likely to be immediately and directly applied to some situation or environment (Stanovich, 2001). Sitlington and Frank's findings regarding their sample of learning-disabled students' lack of preparation for life after graduation could be immediately applied to other students currently in curricula designed for those with learning disabilities in Iowa high schools.

A more complex type of random sample is the stratified random sample. Stratification is most often used to ensure that the sample will include adequate numbers of individuals from various subgroups of interest in the population. These subgroups differ on variables that are related, or which one expects are related, to the problem under study (Babbie, 1986). The Seattle Longitudinal Study (Schaie, 1996a, 2004) began in 1956 by taking random samples of individuals enrolled in a health maintenance organization from groups stratified by age (cohort) and sex. With this method, equal numbers of men and women were included in the study, and cohort sizes were also equal. Stratification may also be especially important in situations in which one must ensure inclusion of rare or hard-to-recruit groups (e.g., old-old individuals, certain ethnic minorities). For example, Klumb and Baltes (1999) used a stratified random sample to obtain equal numbers of individuals in age groups that spanned the range of 70–90+ years. It is unlikely that other sampling methods would have resulted in the inclusion of as many 90-year-old individuals as 70-year-old individuals. Rather than ensuring equal group sizes, stratification could alternatively be used to maintain a match between the proportions of various groups in the sample as those in the population. For instance, in a study of adults returning to college, it may be important to stratify the sample by age or motivation for taking courses (e.g., self-improvement versus job training courses) to maintain adequate representation of the various groups in this population that will be compared.

Yet the fact remains that true random samples can be difficult to obtain. As a result, most behavioral or social science studies use nonrandom, or nonprobability, samples. These types of samples are known more commonly as convenience samples, available group samples, or volunteer samples. Such samples are obtained by soliciting volunteers from existing groups, for example, local senior centers, churches, and university participant pools, through advertisements in the media, or, in the case of surveys, directly (e.g., from eligible passersby). Thus, these samples consist of individuals who volunteer to participate and are "available" or "convenient" for the researcher to use for that particular study. The procedure of simply including every person who responds to a survey or who volunteers to participate in testing is known as haphazard sampling (Minke & Haynes, 2003).

Generalizability is a concern with studies that use samples of volunteers because of their lack of representativeness and potential for bias. Specifically, individuals who volunteer may differ from the population to which we may want to generalize a study's findings in terms of the characteristics that self-selected them into the studies. Individuals who participate in research studies are more likely to be middle-aged (Herzog & Rodgers, 1988; Rosenthal & Rosnow, 1975; Schaie, 1959; Thornquist, Patrick, & Omenn, 1992), be better educated (Dodge, Clark, Janz, Liang, & Schork, 1993; Wagner, Grothaus, Hecht, & LaCroix, 1991), have higher incomes (Wagner et al., 1991), and have better access to transportation to and from the testing site (Dodge et al., 1993). Higher socioeconomic status may be related to a greater interest in supporting research or scientific pursuits, having more leisure time (allowing the opportunity to participate) than those who do not volunteer for a study (Dodge et al., 1993), or even the ability to understand the purpose and requirements of the research project (Wagner et al., 1991). Additionally, individuals who volunteer for certain types of studies, for example, training or prevention studies, may have greater concerns about the decline in their memory abilities (Schleser, West, & Boatwright, 1987) or health conditions (Dodge et al., 1993). Yet it is important to keep in mind that the use of available or convenient groups of participants does not necessarily invalidate that study's findings but rather points to other variables, situations, or types of samples that should also be examined (Stanovich, 2001). Replicating a study with other types of samples or in other environments or situations, can either increase the generalizability of the study's findings or indicate limitations of the research (Minke & Haynes, 2003).

Research with rare (or hard to recruit) populations is especially likely to use available group samples, partly because the sampling frame needed for a random sample can be difficult to identify (Minke & Haynes, 2003). Snowball sampling (also known as reputational sampling or sampling by referral) begins by identifying a few members of the target group, who then identify other group members who can be contacted, and so on (Kalton & Anderson, 1989). Examples of the types of populations that might be accessed by snowball sampling include minorities, particularly elderly members (Patrick, Pruchno, & Rose, 1998), the homeless (Woods-Brown, 2002), members of the gay and lesbian community (Rothblum, Factor, & Aaron, 2002), and people with disabilities (Kalton & Anderson, 1989). If a large enough number of individuals in these groups can be identified, a random sample could then be taken from those identified, but more often, all identified individuals who are willing to participate are included in the study (Kalton & Anderson, 1989). Snowball samples may also be used when a random sample from a formally identified list (e.g., from social service agencies) is counter to the objective of the study—for example, if one wanted to study family caregivers who were not receiving any formal help—or for descriptive research where this type of sampling is used to reveal information about the process under study (e.g., identifying the most influential members of a group; Babbie, 1986). Compared to other recruitment techniques, Patrick et al. (1998) found that snowball sampling required more staff time but was highly cost-effective. Simultaneously using multiple recruitment methods (e.g., snowball, media, mailing lists, formal service organizations or support groups) to target rare populations may be the most successful and cost-effective approach (Patrick et al., 1998; Rothblum et al., 2002).

A final type of nonprobability sampling that we will discuss is purposive or judgmental sampling, which is used more commonly in descriptive or qualitative research (Babbie, 1986; Minke & Haynes, 2003). With this method, the researcher specifically targets and selects certain individuals because they display the characteristics or behaviors of interest being studied. The selection may be made after a period of extended observation (Babbie, 1986). For example, a program for increasing the social skills of adults may identify individuals who were socially isolated at a group function, or a study of individuals with conservative views may target Republican groups. Alternatively, purposive sampling may be specifically used to broaden a sample's characteristics, such as when a newly developed measure is to be tested on individuals with a wide range of ability (Babbie, 1986). Thus, participants are selected based on the purpose of the study and the judgment of the researcher. The aim of purposive sampling is to produce a sample of individuals that will be best for the question one wishes to address.

It should be noted that the use of large sampling frames or random samples does not automatically imply that studies are not subject to any restrictions in terms of generalizing their results. For example, using a random sample of college alumni may limit a study's ability to generalize its results to noncollege-educated individuals. Replication is important to establishing the generalizability of findings from studies using probability or nonprobability samples (Stanovich, 2001). Studies of adult development that use samples of people with greater income, more education, better

jobs, and better health should be replicated with samples of less fortunate individuals. Thus the demographic and health characteristics of a sample should be reported so that applications or generalizations of the research can be better made.

In longitudinal research, the influence of attrition between waves of testing on the generalizability of results must also be considered. Even if a study began with a representative sample, attrition may alter the characteristics of the sample, rendering it less representative than it was previously. Participants may be lost between testing occasions for several reasons, including death or illness (especially if participants are elderly), relocation, or refusal to participate, including refusal by a caregiver (Alwin & Campbell, 2001; Johnson & Tang, 2003). Some studies have found that these types of attrition tend to bias the sample toward the middle class even more, with those remaining having better education, income, and jobs (Cooney, Schaie, & Willis, 1988; Schaie, 1988, 1996a, 2004; Sharma, Tobin, & Brant, 1986), whereas other studies have found that attrition had no impact on the representativeness of the sample (Fitzgerald, Gottschalk, & Moffitt, 1998; Johnson & Tang, 2003). Loss of participants may also be increased in studies that use longer intervals of time between waves of testing.

MEASUREMENT ISSUES

Many of the variables that developmental researchers are interested in studying cannot be observed directly. Rather, information about these constructs of interest (e.g., intellectual abilities, personality traits, learning) must be inferred by observing the participant's behavior or by other indirect means (e.g., rating scales and tests). Thus it is important to ensure that the method of measurement that one is using to assess these unobserved constructs has adequate validity and reliability, is appropriate for the population, and uses a scale of measurement that fits the question that is addressed. For the study of development, the assessment of change in a construct is also an important concept to consider, particularly in terms of identifying reliable amounts of change.

Validity

A test's validity is perhaps most important in the context of the intended purpose of the test. Thus, test validation could be viewed as a continual process of accumulating information about the use of a measure in various contexts, rather than as something that is done only once (Suen, 1990). McDonald (1999) concluded that all of the approaches to establishing the validity of a test are interrelated and share the purpose of contributing evidence toward establishing that a particular measure is a valid assessment of the construct of interest. This section describes three approaches to the test validation process, each of which contributes different types of information toward it.

Construct Validity

The measures we employ in research need to be true reflections of the construct that is measured so that meaningful conclusions and interpretations can be made based on the information collected. Construct validity captures the idea that a test score is an accurate reflection of the construct of interest (Suen, 1990). Specifically, a measure with good construct validity is one that is related to others in the same domain and one in which convergent results are obtained with it and other measures of the same construct (Nunnally & Bernstein, 1994). The construct validity of a measure can be established by examining its similarity with other measures that are intended to measure the same construct. Using factor analysis as one possible method for establishing construct validity, Suen (1990) noted that this issue might be approached either internally (comparing items within a test) or externally (comparing the test with other tests). For example, if items in a factor analysis do not have strong loadings on the domains that they were hypothesized to measure, or if the items are spread across many domains, the construct validity of the measure is considered poor. Alternatively, a factor analysis of scores from several measures could be conducted (e.g., a multitrait-multimethod approach), in which the expectation is that the test being validated would have strong factor loadings on the same factors as other tests of that construct but weak loadings on factors represented by tests of other traits or attributes. The methods of exploratory and confirmatory factor analysis are discussed in more detail in a later section.

Content Validity

Content validity is an issue that is typically considered during the development phase of a new measure.

Items that are selected for inclusion on a new measure are only a sample of the potential items that could have been used to assess the construct of interest. How well the selected items represent the entire pool of possible items determines the content validity of a measure (Nunnally & Bernstein, 1994). Determining this representativeness is typically a subjective process, based on the judgment of the individual performing the validation study. In cases in which the total set of items represents a good sample from the pool of possible items, samples of the measure's items would be expected to yield similar results. Thus, finding similar results with alternate forms of a particular measure may also help establish the content validity of a measure. Finally, the purpose of the test must be considered in establishing content validity. A particular sample of items may be a good representation of the collection of all possible items for one purpose or context but not for another purpose or context (Suen, 1990). For example, the appropriate items for assessing caregiver burden may vary based on disease progression or by whether the patient is community dwelling or institutionalized. Or a measure of personality development in childhood may not be appropriate for the study of adults.

Face validity is a concept that is related to but should not be confused with content validity. In contrast to content validity, the face validity of a measure is concerned with whether the scale appears to measure the construct it is intended to measure. Face validity is also determined after a measure has already been developed, rather than during the development stage (Nunnally & Bernstein, 1994). Issues of face validity can be important considerations in studies in which the subject matter may be sensitive (e.g., mental health) or where certain biases (e.g., the social desirability bias on measures of personality or honesty) may need to be avoided. In these cases, it may be necessary to disguise the intent of the items, resulting in reduced face validity.

Criterion-Related Validity

Criterion-related validity can be assessed by how strongly correlated the measure being validated (i.e., the predictor) is with a criterion measure (Suen, 1990). Two main types of criterion-related validity have been discussed. These types differ in terms of when the criterion is measured in relation to the predictor measure in question. With *predictive validity*, the criterion is measured after the predictor measure; with *concurrent validity*, the criterion and predictor measures are assessed simultaneously. Good choices of criterion measures will be guided by some theoretical rationale for why the predictor measure should be related to it.

Criterion-related validity of a measure becomes especially important when scores from that measure are used to make decisions about a person (Nunnally & Bernstein, 1994). For example, certain test scores may be used to indicate cognitive impairment or to select (or exclude) individuals for a research study. For this to be a valid use of the test scores, the measure would need to have good criterion-related validity. Specifically, if the measure is used to predict a current state, such as cognitive impairment, it is implied that the measure has good concurrent validity. Or in the case where test scores are used to predict a future state (such as the ability to participate in a research study), the measure must have good predictive validity. Finally, it is also important to consider that restriction of range on either the predictor or criterion measures may attenuate their correlation and the assessment of the criterion validity of the measure. For example, if older adult learners have a more limited range of scores on a measure than a sample involving young and middle-aged adults as well as older adults, the criterion validity may appear lower than it would have in the more age-heterogeneous sample.

Reliability

The reliability of a measure can be defined as how well the measure reflects the true (unobserved) ability level of the individual being assessed; alternatively, reliability may reflect how stable measurements of a test score are over time (Nunnally & Bernstein, 1994). Typically, the second definition of reliability (i.e., stability) is of concern when researchers assess the reliability of a scale. To measure reliability in terms of stability, parallel forms of a measure are needed. The next section presents several types of reliability, which differ in terms of how the parallel forms of a measure are defined or created.

Test-Retest Reliability

One way to measure reliability is to have a group of participants take the same test twice and then find the squared correlation of the two sets of test scores.

This form of reliability is called test-retest reliability. Obviously, the second administration of the measure is a parallel form of the first administration, because it is the same test. It is important to keep in mind that this estimate of reliability can be influenced by the procedure used to assess it. For example, shorter intervals between test administrations will produce higher reliability estimates than longer test intervals (Nunnally & Bernstein, 1994). Test-retest reliability estimates can also be influenced by several other factors that reduce the parallel nature of the two test administrations, such as practice effects or developmental changes. These types of effects can result in changes in the test scores at the second administration, which can reduce the reliability coefficient, even though the test itself did not change (Suen, 1990).

Alternate-Forms or Split-Half Reliability

To avoid the issues associated with test-retest reliability, another approach used to assess reliability is to construct two equivalent, alternate forms of the test. However, the effort and cost of constructing two measures rather than one may be prohibitive, and it may be difficult to ensure that the two forms are truly parallel (Suen, 1990). Instead, alternate forms can be created by dividing the scale items into two halves; this creates the parallel forms needed to assess reliability. Because the number of items from the total measure is halved in this process, reliability estimates will be attenuated relative to the total measure and must be corrected with the Spearman-Brown formula (for computational details see, e.g., Nunnally & Bernstein, 1994; Suen, 1990). One potential complication that remains with the split-half procedure is how exactly to split the test items to produce two equivalent halves. Depending on how the items are selected, various test halves can be constructed from a single test, and reliability estimates may then vary depending on how the item split was performed.

Cronbach's Alpha

As the descriptions of test-retest reliability and alternate-forms or split-half reliability have demonstrated, creating parallel forms of a test may not be a simple process. Cronbach's alpha takes what may seem like a more extreme approach to creating parallel forms of a test. With this approach, each item is considered a separate test and the correlations of each item pair are examined. Nunnally and Bernstein (1994) noted that this intensive process became much easier with the advent of high-speed computers (especially when the number of test items is large) and is considered preferable to the other forms of reliability. The computation of Cronbach's alpha coefficient provides a conservative estimate for the average of all item-pair correlations (Suen, 1990) and can be computed by statistical programs such as SAS (SAS Institute, 1999).

Appropriateness of a Measure

The appropriateness of a measure for the type of individuals included in a study also needs to be considered. Specifically, a measure is most appropriate to use with a particular sample when it has been validated and standardized on a population similar to that being studied. For example, one would not want to use a measure that had been validated on a Caucasian sample for an African American sample, unless it could be demonstrated that no reasonable differences between ethnic groups would be expected on this construct. Questions of measure appropriateness may also relate to gender or to any other important group differences that may influence test scores. Measure appropriateness and the use of correct norms is particularly important when the test scores will be used to make decisions about individual participants (Suen, 1990).

Scales of Measurement

Variables can be measured on one of four scales of measurement: nominal, ordinal, interval, and ratio. *Nominal* variables represent unordered categories of a particular construct or trait. For example, the type of mnemonic strategy used in a memory recall task might include the two unordered categories of (a) verbal mnemonics (e.g., acrostics, acronyms, and rhymes) and (b) visual mnemonics (e.g., the method of loci). In contrast, a variable on an *ordinal* scale rank orders individuals along some continuum. Although the values on an ordinal scale are ordered, the distances between any two ranks or ordered categories do not necessarily represent equal differences between people on that variable. For example, in a study comparing three age groups, the age groups may be considered ordered categories yet may be unevenly spaced.

For both *interval* and *ratio* scales of measurement, equal distances between values on a scale represent equal differences between individuals on the dependent variable. The difference between interval and ratio scales is in the definition of the zero point. A ratio scale has a true zero point; in other words, a score of zero on a ratio scale represents a complete absence of the variable being measured. Such variables are not as common or as meaningful in studies conducted on adult development and learning as they are in the physical sciences (e.g., for height, weight, and length). With physical measurements, statements such as "Person A weighs twice as much as Person B" are valid. With measurements of learning or other aspects of development, it may not be accurate to say that a person with a score of 20 has twice as much of the construct as a person with a score of 10. For example, assume that these scores were generated from an administration of a delayed recall test. Although scores of 20 are twice as great as scores of 10, this does not imply that the memory ability of the individual with a score of 20 is twice as good as the memory ability of the individual with a score of 10. Thus the variable for delayed recall represents an interval scale of measurement. It is true that the variable in this example could be operationalized as a ratio scale by defining the variable of interest as the number of items correctly recalled. However, this interpretation may not be as conceptually meaningful as being able to make conclusions about memory ability.

Measurement of Change

When data on the same construct are collected at two or more time points, researchers typically are interested in examining the amount of change that has occurred on this construct. A well-known critique of the use of change scores is that they tend to be less reliable than measurements taken on any single occasion (e.g., Lord, 1956). However, Rogosa (1988, 1995) demonstrated that the values from which this conclusion was generated were based on an assumption that no individual differences existed in the amount of change. This is an unlikely situation for most research studies. Thus, when individual differences in the amount of change over time are allowed, reliability estimates for the change score are much better, sometimes as reliable as the test itself (Rogosa, 1988, 1995). Although having three or more time points of data provides many more analysis options than just two, the change score should not be dismissed automatically as an un-reliable or poor choice.

In addition to simply subtracting two values to create a change score, it is also possible to examine change at the individual level in terms of the amount of reliable change. We know that some individuals' scores will change over time due to random fluctuations, whereas other individuals will show meaningful change. Use of the standard error of measurement (SEM) can be used to define reliable or meaningful change at the individual level (see Dudek, 1979, for computational details). Change scores are compared to the range of values formed by ± 1 SEM, and only those outside this range are defined as having reliable change (e.g., Ball et al., 2002; Schaie, 1996a). This method then allows scores that varied only randomly to be classified as stable and those with a significant amount of change (as defined by the SEM value) to be classified as having had significant decline or significant improvement. For example, if the SEM for change in a measure had a value of 5, then change scores greater than +5 would be classified as significant improvement and change scores less than −5 would be classified as significant decline.

When considering the change over time in a battery of tests, the issue of temporal invariance must also be considered. If the relationships among the tests have changed over time, they may no longer represent the same factors or underlying constructs. Thus the demonstration of longitudinal invariance is important for making interpretable comparisons across time for factor domains (Horn, 1991). This issue is discussed in more depth in the section on confirmatory factor analysis, the method used to test measurement invariance.

SCALE DEVELOPMENT

Exploratory Factor Analysis

Exploratory factor analysis (EFA) is a method that is particularly appropriate when there is a new measure for which the underlying dimensions are unknown. EFA is often performed as a precursor to a confirmatory factor analysis, which will be described shortly. We provide a basic overview of the information necessary to determine whether this method would be appropriate to use; specific statistical details can be obtained from texts on factor analysis (e.g., Gorsuch, 1983).

With EFA, the interrelationships among a set of variables are analyzed with the intent to reduce this larger set of scores into a smaller set of common factors. Because this procedure is exploratory in nature, decisions about the "best" factor structure and the interpretation of the factors themselves are made by the individual researcher. Two common guidelines that are often used for determining the proper number of factors are the percentage of the variance explained by that set of factors and the use of scree plots. Optimally, a factor solution will account for at least 75% of the variance (Gorsuch, 1983). Scree plots may also be used to determine where the point where the addition of factors does not result in a meaningful increase in variance explained.

Another decision to be made in EFA is the type of solution to obtain. In cases where one expects factors extracted from a measure or set of scores to be uncorrelated, the orthogonal (uncorrelated) factor solution that is estimated can be used. The varimax rotation is the most popular orthogonal rotation (Suen, 1990). However, in cases where a correlation among the factors is expected or hypothesized, an oblique (correlated) factor solution, such as a promax rotation, is more appropriate to use. If an oblique solution is estimated and factor intercorrelations are low, one may return to the orthogonal factor solution.

Confirmatory Factor Analysis

In contrast to exploratory factor analysis, confirmatory factor analysis (CFA) is used when a measure has a known (or at least hypothesized) factor structure (see Bollen, 1989; Gorsuch, 1983; Jöreskog & Sörbom, 1993 for statistical and computational details). CFA uses the structural equation modeling framework and thus provides fit statistics that a researcher can use to assess directly the fit of this structure to the data that has been collected. Another benefit of the CFA framework is that multiple indicators of the same underlying construct are used to form a better estimate of an individual's true score on that construct than could be provided by a single observed measure. For example, Schaie, Dutta, and Willis (1991) determined that the cognitive battery used in the Seattle Longitudinal Study was best represented by six cognitive domains, or factors, each of which is indicated by at least three measures.

CFA can be a useful method for determining whether the relationships between observed variables and the latent constructs they represent remain invariant across multiple groups or across time (Jöreskog, 1979). Only when factorial invariance has been demonstrated can one assume that quantitative comparisons of differences in developmental trajectories truly reflect changes in the underlying construct (see Baltes & Nesselroade, 1970, 1973). Shifts in the regression of observed variables on the latent construct, if found, would impose significant restrictions on the interpretability of age changes and age differences measured with single markers. The demonstration of factorial invariance is also important in showing that the relations between observed variables and latent constructs remain stable following the introduction of interventions that might affect such relationships (Schaie, Willis, Hertzog, & Schulenberg, 1987).

A minimum requirement of longitudinal invariance is the demonstration of configural invariance, which requires only that the indicators of the factors have the same pattern of zero and nonzero loadings across time (Horn, McArdle, & Mason, 1983; Meredith, 1993). The next level of invariance is metric invariance, or weak factorial invariance. Weak factorial invariance requires the equality of the unstandardized factor loadings across time. Meredith further proposed the level of strong factorial invariance, which additionally requires equality of the unique (error) variances and intercepts across time. Because stricter levels of invariance can be difficult to meet in many complex studies, it may only be possible to demonstrate partial measurement invariance (Byrne, Shavelson, & Muthén, 1989), where longitudinal invariance can be demonstrated for only a subset of the factors of interest across time.

Another important application of confirmatory factor analysis is the use of this procedure to implement the Dwyer (1937) extension method. As Tucker (1971) demonstrated, it is not appropriate to use factor scores on a latent variable to estimate its regression on an observed variable. However, CFA permits the estimation of the location of some new observed variable or variables of interest within a previously known factor (latent construct) space. This situation frequently arises in aging studies; because samples are followed over long time periods, new measures and constructs are often added to a study. The extension analysis method has been used recently in the Seattle Longitudinal Study to examine the relations of a neuropsychological test battery to the established psychometric intelligence battery (Schaie, Willis, & Caskie,

2004), and of the relations of the NEO Personality Inventory (Costa & McCrae, 1992) to the Test of Behavioral Rigidity (Schaie & Parham, 1975) in Schaie et al. (2004).

EVALUATING THE MEANINGFULNESS OF RESULTS

Clinical Significance

Research findings can be statistically significant without being practically meaningful, particularly in large samples. The reverse can also be true in very small samples, where a finding may have practical significance but the sample size is so small that it is not statistically significant (Urdan, 2001). One way to assess practical or clinical significance may be to focus on whether a change in the level of performance has been observed in the practical aspects of daily life and everyday activities. For example, if a memory training study increased participants' ability to recall a list of words by an average of five words, it would be important to assess whether this increase has translated into improved performance in the older adult's everyday activities. For example, does the individual show an increased ability to recall a short grocery list? This transfer from trained psychometric abilities to more applied abilities can be a useful indicator of the clinical meaningfulness of a research result. Karlawish and Clark (2002) and McGlinchey, Atkins, and Jacobson (2002) provide information on estimates of the clinical significance of an effect.

Effect Size

Many measures of effect size exist; this section presents two of the more commonly used statistics. For linear regression analysis, the R^2 statistic is typically used (Cohen & Cohen, 1983); for analysis of variance (ANOVA), the η^2 statistic can be used. Both of these measures of effect size provide information about the amount of variance that has been explained relative to the total variance. In the context of linear regression, the R^2 value describes the amount of variance explained by the set of predictors included in the regression equation. If several blocks of predictors have been entered as is done in a hierarchical or staged regression analysis, the change in R^2 that occurs with the addition of each block can also be examined. For

ANOVA, η^2 is calculated for each effect included in the model separately, and the relative impact of each effect can be assessed. For example, if the effects of age group and training group on reasoning ability were examined in a two-way ANOVA, the proportion of variance attributed to both could be computed and compared.

Effect size is also an important consideration for power calculations. Power describes the ability of a study to detect a true difference (i.e., the long-term probability of rejecting a false null hypothesis). Cohen (1992) noted that how one chooses the correct population effect size value to be used in a power analysis is often a point of confusion for researchers. In his article, Cohen reviews his previously established conventions for a small, medium, and large effect size and notes that the meaning of these designations is dependent on the type of hypothesis test being conducted. It is particularly important for studies in new areas, such as the intersection of adult development and learning, to be sure that adequate power exists to detect hypothesized or expected population differences.

CONCLUSION

The aim of this chapter was to provide an overview of some of the important research design and methodological topics that need to be considered when proposing and conducting new research in the area of adult learning and development. More detailed treatments of these topics can be found in many of the textbooks and other sources referenced herein. When designing a research project, the choice of study type will have important implications for the types of conclusions that can be drawn. When age differences are of interest, cross-sectional data are sufficient, but longitudinal data are required to address age-related changes in a construct. Random samples ensure the generalizability of a study's results, but the difficulty of obtaining true random samples implies that researchers should be sure to address potential biases associated with the use of nonrepresentative samples when designing, conducting, and reporting research. The need for valid, reliable, and appropriate measures is implicit in all research. Finally, researchers should include information about their study findings that allow readers of the research to determine the practical significance of the work. The incorporation

of these key elements into new research studies of adult development and learning will generate solid and robust research findings that can only strengthen this burgeoning field.

References

Alwin, D. F., & Campbell, R. T. (2001). Quantitative approaches: Longitudinal methods in the study of human development and aging. In R. H. Binstock & L. K. George (Eds.), *Handbook of aging and the social sciences* (pp. 22–43). San Diego, CA: Academic Press.

Amato, P. R. (1988). Who cares for children in public places? Naturalistic observation of male and female caretakers. *Journal of Marriage and the Family, 51,* 981–990.

Babbie, E. (1986). *The practice of social research* (4th ed.). Belmont, CA: Wadsworth.

Ball, K., Berch, D. B., Helmers, K. F., Jobe, J. B., Leveck, M. D., Marsiske, M., et al. (2002). Effects of cognitive training interventions with older adults: A randomized controlled trial. *Journal of the American Medical Association, 288,* 2271–2281.

Baltes, M. M., Burgess, R. L., & Stewart, R. B. (1980). Independence and dependence in self-care behaviors in nursing home residents: An operant-observational study. *International Journal of Behavioral Development, 3,* 489–500.

Baltes, P. B. (1968). Longitudinal and cross-sectional sequences in the study of age and generation effects. *Human Development, 11,* 145–171.

Baltes, P. B., & Nesselroade, J. R. (1970). Multivariate longitudinal and cross-sectional sequences for analyzing ontogenetic and generational change: A methodological note. *Developmental Psychology, 1,* 162–168.

Baltes, P. B., & Nesselroade, J. R. (1973). The developmental analysis of individual differences on multiple measures. In J. R. Nesselroade & H. W. Reese (Eds.), *Life-span developmental psychology: Methodological issues* (pp. 219–251). New York: Academic Press.

Bollen, K. A. (1989). *Structural equations with latent variables.* New York: Wiley.

Byrne, B. M., Shavelson, R. J., & Muthén, B. (1989). Testing for the equivalence of factor covariance and mean structures: The issue of partial measurement invariance. *Psychological Bulletin, 105,* 456–466.

Campbell, D. T., & Stanley, J. C. (1963). Experimental and quasi-experimental designs for research in teaching. In N. L. Gage (Ed.), *Handbook of research on teaching* (pp. 171–246). Skokie, IL: Rand McNally.

Caspi, A., Elder, G. H., & Bem, D. J. (1987). Moving against the world: Life-course patterns of explosive children. *Developmental Psychology, 23,* 308–313.

Center for Human Resource Research. (1992). *NLS handbook*. Columbus, OH: Center for Human Resource Research.

Cervone, D. (2004). The architecture of personality. *Psychological Review, 111*, 183–204.

Cohen, J. (1992). A power primer. *Psychological Bulletin, 112*, 155–159.

Cohen, J., & Cohen, P. (1983). *Applied multiple regression/correlation analysis for the behavioral sciences*. Hillsdale, NJ: Lawrence Erlbaum.

Cook, T. C., & Campbell, D. T. (1979). *Quasi-experiments: Design and analysis issues for field settings*. Chicago, IL: Rand McNally.

Cooney, T. M., Schaie, K. W., & Willis, S. L. (1988). The relationship between prior functioning on cognitive and personality variables and subject attrition in longitudinal research. *Journal of Gerontology: Psychological Sciences, 43*, P12–P17.

Costa, P. T. Jr., & McCrae, R. R. (1992). *Manual for the NEO*. Odessa, TX: IPAR.

Costa, P. T. Jr., McCrae, R. R., Zonderman, A. B., Barbano, H. E., Lebowitz, B., & Larson, D. M. (1986). Cross sectional studies of personality in a national sample: 2. Stability in neuroticism, extraversion, and openness. *Psychology and Aging, 1*, 144–149.

Craik, F. I. M., & McDowd, J. M. (1998). Age differences in recall and recognition. In M. P. Lawton & T. A. Salthouse (Eds.), *Essential papers on the psychology of aging* (pp. 282–295). New York: New York University Press.

Dodge, J. A., Clark, N. M., Janz, N. K., Liang, J., & Schork, M. A. (1993). Nonparticipation of older adults in a heart disease self-management project: Factors influencing involvement. *Research on Aging, 15*, 220–237.

Dudek, F. J. (1979). The continuing misinterpretation of the standard error of measurement. *Psychological Bulletin, 86*, 335–337.

Duncan, S. C., Duncan, T. E., & Hops, H. (1996). Analysis of longitudinal data within accelerated longitudinal designs. *Psychological Methods, 1*, 236–248.

Duncan, T. E., Duncan, S. C., Strycker, L. A., Li, F., & Alpert, A. (1999). *An introduction to latent variable growth curve modeling: Concepts, issues, and applications*. Mahwah, NJ: Lawrence Erlbaum.

Dwyer, P. S. (1937). The determination of the factor loadings of a given test from the known factor loadings of other tests. *Psychometrika, 2*, 173–178.

Fitzgerald, J., Gottschalk, P., & Moffitt, R. (1998). An analysis of sample attrition in panel data: The Michigan Panel Study of Income Dynamics. *Journal of Human Resources, 33*, 251–299.

George, L. K., Hays, J. C., Flint, E. P., & Meador, K. G. (in press). Religion and health in life course perspective. In K. W. Schaie, N. Krause, & A. Booth (Eds.), *Religious influences on the health and well-being of the elderly* (pp. 246–282). New York: Springer.

Gillem, A. R., Cohn, L. R., & Throne, C. (2001). Black identity in biracial black/white people: A comparison of Jacqueline who refuses to be exclusively black and Adolphus who wishes he were. *Cultural Diversity and Ethnic Minority Psychology, 7*, 182–196.

Gorsuch, R. L. (1983). *Factor analysis* (2nd ed.). Hillsdale, NJ: Lawrence Erlbaum.

Hayward, M. D., & Gorman, B. (2004). The long arm of childhood: The influence of early-life social conditions on men's mortality. *Demography, 41*, 87–107.

Heikkinen, E., Berg, S., Schroll, M., Steen, B., & Viidik, A. (Eds). (1997). *Functional status, health, and aging: The NORA study*. Paris: Serdi.

Helson, R., & Moane, G. (1987). Personality change in women from college to midlife. *Journal of Personality and Social Psychology, 53*, 176–186.

Herzog, A. R., & Rodgers, W. L. (1988). Age and response rates to interview sample surveys. *Journal of Gerontology: Social Sciences, 43*, S200–S205.

Hofland, B. F., Willis, S. L., & Baltes, P. B. (1981). Fluid intelligence performance in the elderly: Intraindividual variability and conditions of assessment. *Journal of Educational Psychology, 73*, 573–586.

Honos-Webb, L., Stiles, W. B., & Greenberg, L. S. (2003). A method of rating assimilation in psychotherapy based on markers of change. *Journal of Counseling Psychology, 50*, 189–198.

Horn, J. L. (1991). Comments on issues of factorial invariance. In L. M. Collins & J. L. Horn (Eds.), *Best methods for the analysis of change* (pp. 114–125). Washington, DC: American Psychological Association.

Horn, J. L., McArdle, J. J., & Mason, R. (1983). When is invariance not invariant: A practical scientist's look at the ethereal concept of factor invariance. *Southern Psychologist, 1*, 179–188.

Johnson, D. R., & Tang, Z. (2003, November). *Are estimates of family processes from long-term panel studies biased by attrition? An empirical test in a twenty-year panel study*. Paper presented at the annual meeting of the National Council on Family Relations, Vancouver, British Columbia.

Jöreskog, K. G. (1979). Statistical estimation of structural models in longitudinal developmental investigations. In J. R. Nesselroade & P. B. Baltes (Eds.), *Longitudinal research in the study of behavior and development* (pp. 303–351). New York: Academic Press.

Jöreskog, K. G., & Sörbom, D. (1993). *LISREL 8 user's reference guide*. Chicago: Scientific Software.

Kalton, G., & Anderson, D. W. (1989). Sampling rare populations. In M. P. Lawton & A. R. Herzog (Eds.), *Special research methods for gerontology* (pp. 7–30). Amityville, NY: Baywood.

Karlawish, J. H. T., & Clark, C. M. (2002). Addressing the challenges of transforming laboratory advances into Alzheimer's disease treatments. *Neurobiology of Aging, 23*, 1043–1049.

Klumb, P. L., & Baltes, M. M. (1999). Time use of old and very old Berliners: Productive and consumptive activities as functions of resources. *Journal of Gerontology: Social Sciences, 54B*, S271–S278.

Lachman, M. E., & Jelalian, E. (1984). Self-efficacy and attributions for intellectual performance in young and elderly adults. *Journal of Gerontology, 39*, 577–582.

Lachman, M. E., & McArthur, L. Z. (1986). Adulthood age differences in causal attributions for cognitive, physical, and social performance. *Psychology and Aging, 1*, 127–132.

Levinson, D. J. (1978). *The seasons of a man's life*. New York: Knopf.

Lord, F. M. (1956). The measurement of growth. *Educational and Psychological Measurement, 16*, 421–437.

McArdle, J. J., & Hamagami, F. (1992). Modeling incomplete longitudinal and cross-sectional data using latent growth structural models. *Experimental Aging Research, 18*, 145–166.

McDonald, R. P. (1999). *Test theory: A unified treatment*. Mahwah, NJ: Lawrence Erlbaum.

McGlinchey, J. B., Atkins, D. C., & Jacobson, N. S. (2002). Clinical significance methods: Which one to use and how useful are they? *Behavior Therapy, 33*, 529–550.

Meredith, W. (1993). Measurement invariance, factor analysis, and factorial invariance. *Psychometrika, 58*, 525–543.

Minke, K. A., & Haynes, S. N. (2003). Sampling issues. In J. C. Thomas & M. Hersen (Eds.), *Understanding research in clinical and counseling psychology* (pp. 69–95). Mahwah, NJ: Lawrence Erlbaum.

Nunnally, J. C., & Bernstein, I. H. (1994). *Psychometric theory* (3rd ed.). New York: McGraw-Hill.

Park, D. C., Smith, A. D., Morrell, R. W., Puglisi, J. T., & Dudley, W. N. (1990). Effects of contextual integration on recall of pictures by older adults. *Journal of Gerontology: Psychological Sciences, 45*, P52–P57.

Patrick, J. H., Pruchno, R. A., & Rose, M. S. (1998). Recruiting research participants: A comparison of the costs and effectiveness of five recruitment strategies. *Gerontologist, 38*, 295–302.

Rogosa, D. R. (1988). Myths about longitudinal research. In K. W. Schaie, R. T. Campbell, W. M. Meredith, & S. C. Rawlings (Eds.), *Methodological issues in aging research* (pp. 171–209). New York: Springer.

Rogosa, D. R. (1995). Myths and methods: "Myths about longitudinal research" plus supplemental questions. In J. M. Gottman (Ed.), *The analysis of change* (pp. 3–66). Mahwah, NJ: Lawrence Erlbaum.

Rosenthal, R., & Rosnow, R. L. (1975). *The volunteer subject*. New York: Wiley.

Rothblum, E. D., Factor, R., & Aaron, D. J. (2002). How did you hear about the study? Or, how to reach lesbian and bisexual women of diverse ages, ethnicity, and educational attainment for research projects. *Journal of the Gay and Lesbian Medical Association, 6*, 53–59.

SAS Institute. (1999). *SAS/STAT user's guide, version 8*. Cary, NC: SAS Institute.

Schaie, K. W. (1959). Cross-sectional methods in the study of psychological aspects of aging. *Journal of Gerontology, 14*, 208–215.

Schaie, K. W. (1965). A general model for the study of developmental problems. *Psychological Bulletin, 64*, 91–107.

Schaie, K. W. (1977). Quasi-experimental designs in the psychology of aging. In J. E. Birren & K. W. Schaie (Eds.), *Handbook of the psychology of aging* (pp. 39–58). New York: Van Nostrand Reinhold.

Schaie, K. W. (1988). Internal validity threats in studies of adult cognitive development. In M. L. Howe & C. J. Brainerd (Eds.), *Cognitive development in adulthood: Progress in cognitive development research* (pp. 241–272). New York: Springer-Verlag.

Schaie, K. W. (1994). Developmental designs revisited. In S. H. Cohen & H. W. Reese (Eds.), *Life-span developmental psychology: Theoretical issues revisited* (pp. 45–64). Hillsdale, NJ: Lawrence Erlbaum.

Schaie, K. W. (1996a). *Intellectual development in adulthood: The Seattle Longitudinal Study*. New York: Cambridge University Press.

Schaie, K. W. (1996b). Research methods in gerontology. In G. L. Maddox (Ed.), *Encyclopedia of aging* (2nd ed.) (pp. 812–815). New York: Springer.

Schaie, K. W. (2004). *Developmental influences on cognitive development: The Seattle Longitudinal Study*. New York: Oxford University Press.

Schaie, K. W., & Baltes, P. B. (1975). On sequential strategies in developmental research: Description or explanation? *Human Development, 18*, 384–390.

Schaie, K. W., & Caskie, G. I. L. (2004). Methodological issues in aging research. In D. M. Teti (Ed.), *Handbook of research methods in developmental science* (pp. 21–39). Malden, MA: Blackwell.

Schaie, K. W., Caskie, C. I. L., Revell, A. J., Willis, S. L., Kaszniak, A. W., & Teri, L. (2005). Extending neuropsychological assessments into the primary mental ability space. *Aging, Neuropsychology, and Cognition, 12*, 245–277.

Schaie, K. W., Dutta, R., & Willis, S. L. (1991). The relationship between rigidity-flexibility and cognitive abilities in adulthood. *Psychology and Aging, 6*, 371–383.

Schaie, K. W., & Hofer, S. M. (2001). Longitudinal studies in aging research. In J. E. Birren & K. W. Schaie (Eds.), *Handbook of the psychology of aging* (pp. 53–77). San Diego, CA: Academic Press.

Schaie, K. W., & Parham, I. A. (1975). *Manual for the Test of Behavioral Rigidity*. Palo Alto, CA: Consulting Psychologists Press.

Schaie, K. W., & Strother, C. R. (1968). A cross-sequential study of age changes in cognitive behavior. *Psychological Bulletin, 70*, 671–680.

Schaie, K. W., Willis, S. L., & Caskie, G. I. L. (2004). The Seattle Longitudinal Study: Relationship between personality and cognition. *Aging, Neuropsychology, and Cognition, 11*, 304–324.

Schaie, K. W., Willis, S. L., Hertzog, C., & Schulenberg, J. E. (1987). Effects of cognitive training upon primary mental ability structure. *Psychology and Aging, 2,* 233–242.

Schleser, R., West, R. L., & Boatwright, L. K. (1987). A comparison of recruiting strategies for increasing older adults' initial entry and compliance in a memory training program. *International Journal of Aging and Human Development, 24,* 55–66.

Sharma, S. K., Tobin, J. D., & Brant, L. J. (1986). Factors affecting attrition in the Baltimore Longitudinal Study of Aging. *Experimental Gerontology, 21,* 329–340.

Sitlington, P. L., & Frank, A. R. (1990). Are adolescents with learning disabilities successfully crossing the bridge into adult life? *Learning Disability Quarterly, 13,* 97–111.

Stake, R. E. (1995). *The art of case study research.* Thousand Oaks, CA: Sage.

Stanovich, K. E. (2001). *How to think straight about psychology* (6th ed.). Boston: Allyn & Bacon.

Suen, H. K. (1990). *Principles of test theories.* Hillsdale, NJ: Lawrence Erlbaum.

Thornquist, M. D., Patrick, D. L., & Omenn, G. S. (1992). Participation and adherence among older men and women recruited to the beta-carotene and retinol efficacy trial (CARET). *Gerontologist, 31,* 593–597.

Tonry, M., Ohlin, L. E., & Farrington, D. P. (1991). *Human developmental and criminal behavior: New ways of advancing knowledge.* New York: Springer-Verlag.

Tucker, L. R. (1971). Relations of factor score estimates to their use. *Psychometrika, 36,* 427–436.

Urdan, T. C. (2001). *Statistics in plain English.* Mahwah, NJ: Lawrence Erlbaum.

Wagner, E. H., Grothaus, L. C., Hecht, J. A., & LaCroix, A. Z. (1991). Factors associated with participation in a senior health promotion program. *Gerontologist, 31,* 598–602.

Willis, S. L. (2001). Methodological issues in behavioral intervention research with the elderly. In J. E. Birren & K. W. Schaie (Eds.), *Handbook of the psychology of aging* (pp. 78–108). San Diego, CA: Academic Press.

Woods-Brown, L. Y. (2002). Ethnographic study of homeless mentally ill persons: Single adult homeless and homeless families. *Dissertation Abstracts International, 62* (10-A), 3460.

Part II

Do Development and Learning Fuel One Another in Adulthood? Four Key Areas

Chapter 4

Development of Reflective Judgment in Adulthood

Karen Strohm Kitchener, Patricia M. King, and Sonia DeLuca

The idea that intellectual development continues into adulthood was at one time quite contrary to conventional thinking. Until the middle of the last century, life span cognitive psychologists focused on the declines associated with aging (Baltes & Smith, 1990), particularly the apparent decline in intelligence. With the advent of Erikson's (1963) work, researchers became interested in other questions, such as whether there are positive features associated with human aging and whether there are distinct features that differentiate adolescent thinking from adult thinking. Scholarly work on questions like these laid the groundwork for new theories and research on adult intellectual development that eventually included the development of the Reflective Judgment Model (RJM) (King & Kitchener, 1994; Kitchener & King, 1981), the topic of this chapter.

One positive feature that Baltes and colleagues (Baltes, Dittmann-Kohli, & Dixon, 1984; Baltes & Smith, 1990) identified as a central characteristic of adult thinking is wisdom. Baltes and Smith (1990) characterize wisdom as "expert knowledge involving good judgment and advice in the domain, fundamental pragmatics of life" (p. 95). Others (Clayton & Birren, 1980; Holliday & Chandler, 1986; Meacham, 1983) emphasize that wisdom includes the recognition that knowledge is uncertain and that it is not possible to be absolutely certain at any given point in time. Furthermore, wisdom includes an ability to formulate clear and sound judgments in the face of this uncertainty (Baltes & Smith, 1990; Dixon & Baltes, 1986; Kitchener & Brenner, 1990). The RJM (P. M. King & Kitchener, 1994) articulates the development of these characteristics and suggests the sequence of steps through which the characteristics associated with wisdom appear. Although Inhelder and Piaget (1958) described logical or formal reasoning as the highest form of adolescent reasoning, the RJM describes the process through which individuals move beyond formal reasoning to reasoning that addresses issues of knowing in the face of uncertainty, a characteristic of reflective thinking and the highest level of the RJM.

A second positive feature associated with adult development is evidence showing that individuals' beliefs about knowledge and knowing develop over the life span. These belief systems affect how the individual approaches learning and what is learned (Hofer, 2004; Hofer & Pintrich, 1997, 2002). Although various authors who write on this topic differ in the number of stages and the age that the process begins, they typically describe a sequence that begins with the belief that knowledge is certain and directly knowable and progresses to the belief that knowledge is uncertain but can be constructed by judging evidence and opinion (Kitchener, 2002; Love & Guthrie, 1999). The RJM (P. M. King & Kitchener, 1994, 2002, 2004; Kitchener & King, 1981) is one model that describes this developmental sequence.

In this chapter, we provide a detailed description of the development of the Reflective Judgment Model, then use the lens of Fischer's (1980) skill theory to place this model within a life span view of cognitive development. In this section, we argue that major changes in judgment leading to more complex reasoning may be observed between adolescence and adulthood; that these changes have stage-like properties; that different sets of skills, understanding, and behaviors are associated with each stage; and that these provide the scaffolding for the emergence of the next, more advanced stage of reasoning. We then turn to research on the RJM, starting with procedures for assessing reflective judgment and how a series of major research questions have been approached and answered. Finally, we position our work on reflective judgment relative to two other perspectives, adult development as it aligns with Kegan's (1994) concepts, and reflective judgment as it relates to adult learning.

THE REFLECTIVE JUDGMENT MODEL

Underlying Assumptions of the Reflective Judgment Model

The RJM is firmly grounded in the cognitive-developmental tradition: It focuses on how individuals construct meaning and make judgments about controversial issues; the stages are developmentally ordered (we expand on this point shortly); and development is seen not as the inevitable result of maturation (age) alone but as stemming from person–environment interactions. It initially drew from the work of Perry (1968), Broughton (1975), Harvey et al. (1961), and Loevinger (1976); this line of work is now in the same genre as that of Fischer (1980), Kegan (1994), and Baxter Magolda (1992, 1999).

The RJM was developed at a time when the prominent theory of cognitive development was Piaget's (1970), and he claimed that this development was complete with the attainment of formal operations at age 16. The data provided in the first RJM study (Kitchener & King, 1981) contradicted this belief, and initially reviewers and editors were skeptical about the possibility of substantive intellectual development in the postadolescent years. However, in the past 25 years, there has been an explosion of theory building and research on adult learning in general that documents cognitive development from adolescence through adulthood and on the development of personal epistemology in particular (e.g., Hofer & Pintrich, 1997, 2002; Hofer, 2004).

The RJM attempts to chart major steps in the development of reflective thinking that culminates in a reflective judgment. Dewey (1933, 1938) noted that reflective thinking is initiated when an individual acknowledges that a problem exists that cannot be solved by logic alone. Dewey also noted that to bring closure to questions that are uncertain, a person makes a judgment, which he called a reflective judgment. If an individual approaches the problem using only absolute, preconceived assumptions, without doubt regarding its resolution, or with no concerns about his or her current understanding of the issue, this individual is unlikely to engage in reflective thinking.

Thus, the RJM focuses on problems that many people see as unresolved or controversial, what Churchman (1971) calls ill-structured problems or problems that cannot be defined with a high degree of completeness nor resolved with a high degree of certainty. In these types of problems, it is not uncommon that experts disagree about a best solution to the problem, even when it may be considered solved. Consistent with Dewey's definition, reflective judgments are made about ill-structured problems. Well-structured problems also require careful, thoughtful judgments; however, because these types of problems can be defined with a high degree of completeness, they can be resolved with a high degree of certainty, and experts are likely to agree on a correct answer.

Kitchener (1983) added an additional clarification regarding the nature of the domain of intellectual development when she differentiated cognition (e.g., memorizing) and meta-cognition (e.g., monitoring progress on cognitive tasks) from epistemic cognition, "the process an individual invokes to monitor the epistemic nature of problems and the truth value of alternative solutions" (p. 225). Epistemic cognition includes the limits of knowing, the certainty of knowing, and the criteria for knowing, each of which constitutes a major element of the RJM.

We refer to the major steps in the RJM as "stages"—but we use this term in specific ways, some of which are different from traditional usage. We use this term for two major reasons. First, these major steps represent major categories of thinking, each with its own set of interrelated assumptions about the limits, certainty, and criteria for knowing and how these inform the ways a person justifies his or her beliefs about an ill-structured problem. Thus, each stage has its own logical coherence, and the underlying logic of each stage is closely related to the ways that individuals who hold these assumptions tend to justify their beliefs.

Second, we have found strong evidence of stage-like properties in the development of reflective thinking: following Flavell's (1971) criteria for stages: (a) they are organized (two or more elements are interrelated, relatively stable, and form the basis for apparently unrelated acts); (b) they are qualitatively different (the changes in the basis for judgment, from relying on the word or an authority figure to weighing evidence represents a qualitative change); and (c) they form a developmental sequence (the achievements of a prior stage appear to lay a foundation for the subsequent stage, and to emerge in a predictable order).

However, the evidence for the sequentiality criterion is *not* consistent with traditional simple stage conceptions of development as occurring in a lock-step, one-stage-at-a-time manner. Rather, they are consistent with Rest's (1979) complex stage model, which we have found to be a good explanatory framework for interpreting our data. For example, based on our 10-year longitudinal study, we have suggested that development in reflective judgment be characterized as

waves across a mixture of stages, where the peak of a wave is the most commonly used set of assumptions. While there is still an observable pattern to the movement between stages, this developmental

movement is better described as the changing shape of the wave rather than as a pattern of uniform steps interspersed with plateaus. (P. M. King, Kitchener, & Wood, 1994, p. 140)

Having presented the major underlying assumptions of the RJM, we now provide a detailed description of the seven stages that constitute the RJM.

The RJM describes seven hallmarks of thinking (stages) that show changes in epistemic assumptions or assumptions about knowledge and the process of knowing and how they are reflected in the ways beliefs about controversial issues are justified. For ease in learning the model, we have clustered the seven stages into three levels: prereflective thinking (Stages 1–3), quasi-reflective thinking (Stages 4–5), and reflective thinking (Stages 6–7). Although this clustering has the advantage of simplifying the model, this is also its disadvantage: By emphasizing the similarities across stages within levels, it masks differences between stages within levels, differences that are key attributes differentiating the epistemic assumptions that characterize each of the seven stages. Similarly, these labels (prereflective, etc.) grossly oversimplify the characteristics of reasoning within stages and levels, and do not convey their associated epistemic assumptions. For these reasons, we caution readers to use them only as an introduction to the model and to consult the extensive description of each stage (and how it is related to preceding and subsequent stages) in chapter 4 of P. M. King and Kitchener (1994).

Each stage is described by reference to two sets of epistemic assumptions: view of knowledge and concept of justification. The attributes of each of the stages in the RJM were initially gleaned from approximately 100 semi-structured interviews discussing ill-structured controversies using the reflective judgment interview (RJI; described shortly) and elaborated based on subsequent interviews. These sets of assumptions are briefly summarized in table 4.1; each stage is described in more detail shortly. (These descriptions are based on the more extensive explanations in P. M. King & Kitchener, 1994).

Prereflective Thinking (Stages 1, 2, and 3)

Stage 1 is characterized by the belief that there is an absolute correspondence between what is seen or perceived and what is, a "copy" view of knowledge. An

Table 4.1. Summary of Reflective Judgment Stages

Prereflective Thinking (Stages 1, 2, and 3)

Stage 1

View of knowledge: Knowledge is assumed to exist absolutely and concretely; it is not understood as an abstraction. It can be obtained with certainty by direct observation.

Concept of justification: Beliefs need no justification since there is assumed to be an absolute correspondence between what is believed to be true and what is true. Alternate beliefs are not perceived.

"I know what I have seen."

Stage 2

View of knowledge: Knowledge is assumed to be absolutely certain or certain but not immediately available. Knowledge can be obtained directly through the senses (as in direct observation) or via authority figures.

Concept of justification: Beliefs are unexamined and unjustified or justified by their correspondence with the beliefs of an authority figure (such as a teacher or parent). Most issues are assumed to have a right answer, so there is little or no conflict in making decisions about disputed issues.

"If it is on the news, it has to be true."

Stage 3

View of knowledge: Knowledge is assumed to be absolutely certain or temporarily uncertain. In areas of temporary uncertainty, only personal beliefs can be known until absolute knowledge is obtained. In areas of absolute certainty, knowledge is obtained from authorities.

Concept of justification: In areas in which certain answers exist, beliefs are justified by reference to authorities' views. In areas in which answers do not exist, beliefs are defended as personal opinion since the link between evidence and beliefs is unclear.

"When there is evidence that people can give to convince everybody one way or another, then it will be knowledge; until then, it's just a guess."

Quasi-Reflective Thinking (Stages 4 and 5)

Stage 4

View of knowledge: Knowledge is uncertain and knowledge claims are idiosyncratic to the individual since situational variables (such as incorrect reporting of data, data lost over time, or disparities in access to information) dictate that knowing always involves an element of ambiguity.

Concept of justification: Beliefs are justified by giving reasons and using evidence, but the arguments and choice of evidence are idiosyncratic (for example, choosing evidence that fits an established belief).

"I'd be more inclined to believe evolution if they had proof. It's just like the pyramids: I don't think we'll ever know. Who are you going to ask? No one was there."

Stage 5

View of knowledge: Knowledge is contextual and subjective since it is filtered through a person's perceptions and criteria for judgment. Only interpretations of evidence, events, or issues may be known.

Concept of justification: Beliefs are justified within a particular context by means of the rules of inquiry for that context and by context-specific interpretation of evidence. Specific beliefs are assumed to be context specific or are balanced against other interpretations, which complicates (and sometimes delays) conclusions.

"People think differently and so they attack the problem differently. Other theories could be as true as my own, but based on different evidence."

(continued)

TABLE 4.1. (Continued)

Reflective Thinking (Stages 6 and 7)

Stage 6

View of knowledge: Knowledge is constructed into individual conclusions about ill-structured problems on the basis of information from a variety of sources. Interpretations that are based on evaluations of evidence across contexts and on the evaluated opinions of reputable others can be known.

Concept of justification: Beliefs are justified by comparing evidence and opinion from different perspectives on an issue or across different contexts and by constructing solutions that are evaluated by criteria such as the weight of the evidence, the utility of the solution, or the pragmatic need for action.

"It's very difficult in this life to be sure. There are degrees of sureness. You come to a point at which you are sure enough for a personal stance on the issue."

Stage 7

View of knowledge: Knowledge is the outcome of a process of reasonable inquiry in which solutions to ill-structured problems are constructed. The adequacy of those solutions is evaluated in terms of what is most reasonable or probable according to the current evidence, and it is reevaluated when relevant new evidence, perspectives, or tools of inquiry become available.

Concept of justification: Beliefs are justified probabilistically on the basis of a variety of interpretive considerations, such as the weight of the evidence, the explanatory value of the interpretations, the risk of erroneous conclusions, consequences of alternative judgments, and the interrelationships of these factors. Conclusions are defended as representing the most complete, plausible, or compelling understanding of an issue on the basis of the available evidence.

"One can judge an argument by how well thought-out the positions are, what kinds of reasoning and evidence are used to support it, and how consistent the way one argues on this topic is as compared with other topics.

Note. From *Developing Reflective Judgment: Understanding and Promoting Intellectual Growth and Critical Thinking in Adolescents and Adults* (pp. 14–15), by P. M. King and K. S. Kitchener, 1994, San Francisco: Jossey-Bass. Reprinted with permission.

example may be found in the words of a respondent who stated, "I have seen posters of evolution, so I know we evolved." Such a view of knowledge implies that beliefs do not require justification because one must only observe to know. Although Stage 1 reasoning appears naive and egocentric, it has an internal logic: Because knowledge is absolute, controversies do not exist, and thus belief is not problematic. A person either sees and believes or holds a belief by following tradition or social convention, without perceiving the value of examining the reasons for holding the beliefs. Because knowing is limited to concrete observations, individuals cannot relate two different views of the same issue, which is a prerequisite for defining issues as problematic. The hold/absolutism in Stage 1 reasoning loosens with the admission that two people could disagree; this lays the groundwork for the progression to the next developmental level. There are few reported examples of Stage 1 reasoning among adolescents and adults, and elements of this description are theoretical extrapolations.

Stage 2 reasoning is characterized by the belief that there is a true reality that can be known with cer-

tainty but that is not known by everyone. Certain knowledge is seen as the domain of authorities who are presumed to know the truth, such as a scientist, teacher, or religious leader, and others who disagree with these authorities are therefore wrong. This belief system reflects what Perry (1970) called a "dualistic" epistemology. Although the existence of alternative views is acknowledged (an advance from Stage 1), belief in absolute knowledge is still maintained. One's own view and the views of "good authorities" are seen as right, and others' views are seen as wrong, ignorant, misled, uninformed, maliciously motivated, and so on. The admission that truth may not be directly and immediately known by the person allows for the possibility that someone else may have the truth. This change allows for a separation of the self from what is true or known. The belief that not everyone may know the truth reflects a further differentiation of beliefs into right beliefs and wrong beliefs.

Because individuals who make meaning within this perspective hold the view that ultimately truth can be known with absolute certainty, they do not recognize that the problems posed in the RJI are ill-structured. Instead, they assume that absolutely right or wrong answers exist for all problems. Defending one's point of view is not done to explain the reasons for belief but rather to show (by stating them) that one's own beliefs are right and those who believe otherwise are wrong. Although the views of Stage 2 reflect greater differentiation and integration than Stage 1, they often appear more dogmatic than naive because of their insistence on the existence of right and wrong answers and their deference to authority as the basis for belief.

Knowing in Stage 3 is characterized by the belief that in some areas, even authorities may not currently have the truth. However, the belief is maintained that knowledge will be manifest in concrete data at some future point. Thus, the understanding of truth, knowledge, and evidence remains concrete and situation-bound. In areas where authorities know the right answers, beliefs continue to be justified via the word of an authority. However, in areas where authorities still don't know the answers, they see no way to justify knowledge claims, explaining that until future developments show the truth, they decide on the basis of what "feels right" at the moment.

Because individuals maintain the belief that truth will be manifest in concrete data at a future point, they claim that the use of probabilistic evidence to substantiate a belief is arbitrary and that interpretation of evidence is illegitimate. These claims reflect their concrete understanding of evidence, which they assume points directly to the truth or the right answer. For example, one person worried that drug manufacturers were "getting away with a lot of stuff" and because the truth was unknown, no one could catch them. He offered the following explanation: "I know there can be bias in scientific studies on both sides. Until they take it [a chemical additive] off the market, no one is going to do an accurate, reliable study. After they take it off, somebody unbiased is going to do an accurate study. Then they will know" (P. M. King & Kitchener, 1994, p. 56).

Acknowledging that knowledge is temporarily uncertain in some areas reflects an increased differentiation and integration of categories of thought. However this is often accompanied by confusion about how to make decisions about such problems. Confusion stems from the need to make decisions without absolutely certain knowledge; confusion also arises from a lack of understanding that belief and evidence are separate entities and from not knowing how they can

be coordinated in the process of justifying beliefs. To the outsider, such views often appear arbitrary, unjustified, or unstable. The breakdown of the Stage 3 epistemology, as with other stages, is inherent in its structure. In the admission that in some cases knowledge is temporarily uncertain lies the potential for recognizing that uncertainty is an inherent part of the process of knowing. In addition, the dissonance created by holding unjustified beliefs in light of being asked for justification may lead the individual to seek a clearer relationship between evidence and belief.

Quasi-Reflective Thinking (Stages 4 and 5)

Stage 4 is characterized by the belief that one cannot know with certainty. Justification is understood as a process that involves giving reasons as an essential part of an argument. Because justification is not yet fully related to knowing, knowing is understood as idiosyncratic to the individual. Because individuals who hold Stage 4 assumptions have an initial understanding of justification as an abstraction, they begin to understand the need to relate evidence to belief, and they start to separate beliefs from evidence for those beliefs. However, they relate the two idiosyncratically, failing to distinguish between considering evidence for a belief, evaluating the belief in light of that evidence, or basing a belief on that evaluation. Rather, they choose evidence that fits their prior beliefs and presume that others do the same. As a result, they often dismiss the views of authorities as biased, assuming that experts evaluate evidence the same way they themselves do or that experts' opinions are no different from their own.

Fischer, Hand, and Russell (1984) have noted that initial abstractions are quite primitive and undifferentiated, thus it is not uncommon for individuals to have difficulty differentiating abstract concepts such as evidence and belief. As a consequence, individuals may see that evidence contradicts their own opinion but still hold to the opinion without attempting to resolve the contradiction. Similarly, although they may acknowledge that opinions don't form a sufficient basis for developing an argument, they are not consistent in their use of evidence for this purpose. Internally, the argument appears to be that if knowledge is uncertain and there are no external criteria for evaluation, then someone can choose when and how to use evidence and when not to do so. A person using Stage 4 assumptions does not reason that evidence entails a conclusion but uses personal beliefs to choose the evidence used to support preconceived beliefs. Even the person making the argument from a Stage 4 perspective appears aware that his or her conclusions are tenuous and assume that others' conclusions are as well.

The major development that characterizes Stage 4 is the recognition that in some areas, knowledge is and will probably continue to be uncertain. Although considered judgment and unconsidered belief are not fully differentiated in Stage 4, acknowledging that giving reasons for beliefs is an essential part of an argument marks an initial step toward evaluating ideas against a public standard. Similarly, although there may be no way to rationally adjudicate between alternative conceptions of an issue, the assumption that all points of view are idiosyncratic allows the person a new tolerance of alternative perspectives and the people holding them. At the same time, when faced with well-reasoned arguments that are different from their own, these individuals are also faced with the inherent contradictions in their own thinking: Everyone has the right to their own opinions, but others' views must be somehow inadequate (even wrong) because those other views are different from one's own views.

Stage 5 is distinguished by the belief that knowledge is filtered through the perceptions of the person making the interpretation; thus, what is known is limited by the perspective of the knower. The approach of knowing directly or with firm certainty is not apparent in the reasoning of these individuals; instead, they report that they may know within a context based on subjective interpretations of evidence. A particular advancement associated with Stage 5 skills is the ability to differentiate and integrate the elements surrounding an event with the interpretation of that event, unconsidered claims and considered evaluation, the opinions of authorities and one's own opinions, and so forth. These skills allow for a broader, more interconnected view of problems that is not limited by the idiosyncratic justifications of Stage 4. This more complex view is based on a fuller understanding of justification in relationship to interpretations within a particular perspective.

Stage 5 knowing remains context-bound, because the individual has not as yet developed the ability to relate several abstractions into a system that allows comparisons across different contexts, for example, comparing knowing and justification about issues in science to that used in the social sciences. When faced with ill-structured problems, this limitation leaves the individual unable to weigh evidence for competing views beyond the perspective each allows or to integrate perspectives and draw conclusions beyond limited relationships.

The major accomplishment of this stage is that the ability to relate two abstractions allows individuals to relate evidence and arguments to knowing. Those who use Stage 5 assumptions are able to relate and compare evidence and arguments in several contexts even though they appear unable to coordinate evidence and arguments across contexts into a simple system. As with Stage 4, they resolve ill-structured problems by shifting focus. But at Stage 5, the shift in focus is from examining how knowledge is justified within one context to how it is justified within another. As a result, such persons frequently appear to be giving a balanced picture of an issue or problem rather than offering a justification for their own beliefs.

Kuhn (1989) has suggested that two skills are necessary to coordinate theory and evidence: the recognition that there are alternative theories, and the recognition that some evidence does not support a particular theory. Both are present in Stage 5 reasoning. What is missing is the ability to coordinate these into a well-reasoned argument.

The ways of knowing that are apparent in Stage 5 reasoning are based on rules of evidence that provide the individual with ways to begin to make judgments without risking a return to the dogmatism of earlier periods. Complexity is manifest in the greater differentiation of contexts, in the awareness that different perspectives rely on different types of evidence, and in the ability to compare and contrast perspectives.

Paradoxically, while individuals are immersed in and refining their ability to compare one point of view with another, they are learning the initial rules of synthesis that will move their reasoning beyond this stage. The act of trying on one frame of reference after another facilitates the formation of new and larger categories, thus permitting individuals to see how these frames of reference are themselves similar and different.

Reflective Thinking (Stages 6 and 7)

Stage 6 is characterized by an initial recognition that ill-structured problems require solutions that must be constructed and that even experts construct solutions. Like those who use Stage 5 reasoning, individuals using Stage 6 reasoning maintain that knowledge is uncertain and must be understood in relationship to context and evidence. However, they also argue that some judgments or beliefs may nevertheless be evaluated by using criteria such as the plausibility of an argument or the utility of a solution. This claim is based on principles of evaluation that allow them to draw conclusions across perspectives because, by using Stage 6 skills, they can compare and relate the properties of two different views of the same issue. For example, knowing and justification about the advantages and disadvantages of chemical additives can be compared and contrasted with knowing and justification about the advantages and disadvantages of nuclear energy, combining them into a system that allows for common elements to be identified (e.g., health risks and environmental concerns). The identification of common elements provides the basis for making a judgment or drawing a conclusion.

These skills also enable individuals to compare the evidence for and against the safety of food additives, for example, frequently differentiating between factors such as the type of chemical, the purpose for which it is being used, or general circumstances of food distribution and shelf life, and to construct qualified conclusions about the merits of a particular point of view about these additives. Thus, although individuals using Stage 6 assumptions will usually reject the terms *right* and *wrong* when evaluating arguments, they will suggest that one view is in some way(s) better, for example, that the other view has less evidence, is less appropriate or less compelling for the particular situation at hand, and so on. The ability to draw conclusions across perspectives reflects the beginning of internalized categories of comparison and evaluation.

Using Stage 6 reasoning, individuals may rely on the evaluated opinions of authorities, now understood and valued as experts who have investigated the issue more thoroughly or who have special competencies. The reliance on the opinions of experts reflects not a return to earlier authority-bound beliefs but rather the ability to differentiate between the judgments made by experts and those made by laypeople. On occasion, people using Stage 6 reasoning will explicitly note that they evaluate the expertise, opinions, and conclusions of experts. As with the prior stages, the recognition of the inadequacies of the current stage appears to lay the groundwork for what follows. Here inadequacy of purely contextual and subjective knowing and the associated reluctance to choose between perspectives that are associated with Stage 5 become apparent in

Stage 6. Those using Stage 6 skills report being motivated to look for ways to arrive at judgments that reflect their appreciation for multiple perspectives, acknowledging that such judgments will not be simply found but that they will play a role in constructing their own judgments. Making comparisons and observing relationships across domains provides an initial basis for rationally formulating conclusions.

In the process of evaluating and endorsing the views of experts or constructing tentative, personal conclusions, individuals appear to develop what Harvey et al. (1961) called "abstract internal referents" of validity and probability (p. 91). These are used to develop a more general system of knowing that provides the basis for Stage 7 thinking.

Stage 7 is characterized by the belief that while reality is never a given, interpretations of evidence and opinion can be synthesized into conjectures about the nature of the problem under consideration that are epistemically justifiable. Knowledge is constructed using skills of critical inquiry or through the synthesis of evidence and opinion into cohesive and coherent explanations for beliefs about problems. It is possible, therefore, through critical inquiry or synthesis, to determine that some judgments, whether they are the judgments of experts or one's own, have greater truth value than others or to suggest that a given judgment is a reasonable solution for a problem.

People engaged in the thinking characteristic of Stage 7 take on the role of inquirers; they are agents involved in constructing knowledge. They see that the process is continual in the sense that time, experience, and new data require new constructions and understandings. They are aware that their current knowledge claims may later be superseded by more adequate explanations. At the same time, they are able to claim that the conclusions they are currently drawing are justifiable, believing that other reasonable people who consider the evidence would understand the basis for their conclusions. They often argue that the process of inquiry leads toward better or more complete conjectures about the best solutions for ill-structured problems or the issues under discussion.

Thinking in Stage 7 appears as an improvement over Stage 6 in its display of considered, reflective choice. Individuals become active inquirers involved in the critique of conclusions that have been reached earlier. As well, they become the generators of new hypotheses. Because the methods of criticism and evaluation are applied to the self as well as to others, individuals who make meaning using Stage 7 assumptions see that the solutions they offer are only hypothetical conjectures about what is, and their own solutions are themselves open to criticism and reevaluation.

These skills are made possible because the individual clearly understands the process of knowing and endorses his or her own role in constructing what he or she claims to know and believes to be true. As Baron (1988) noted, reflective thinking (as defined by the RJM) is "actively open-minded thinking . . . [where] beliefs can always be improved; this encourages openness to alternatives and to counterevidence" (p. 268).

SKILL THEORY: A LIFE SPAN APPROACH TO COGNITIVE DEVELOPMENT

Fischer and colleagues (Fischer, 1980; Fischer, Bullock, Rosenberg, & Raya, 1993; Fischer & Lamborn, 1989; Fischer & Pipp, 1984; Fischer & Pruyne, 2002; Kitchener & Fischer, 1990; Lamborn & Fischer, 1988) have developed and tested a model of cognitive development that describes how cognitive skills like those described in the RJM become more complex and sophisticated from infancy to adulthood. These researchers have provided a way to understand both changes in intellectual functioning between late childhood and adulthood, as well as how learning provides the foundation for development between stages or levels. When linked with the RJM, research on skill theory provides a basis for explicating the relationship between learning and development in assumptions about knowing and how these provide the basis for wise judgments.

Although they were developed independently, relationships between RJM stages and skill levels are apparent (see Fischer & Pruyne, 2002; P. M. King, 1985; Kitchener & Fischer, 1990). Earlier, we described the progression in reasoning in the RJM by focusing on the changes in epistemic assumptions and how these affect the ways individuals justify their beliefs. Here we describe this progression by mapping it onto the development of cognitive skills proposed by Fischer (starting with Representational Level I rather than at infancy). In the first two columns of table 4.2, we show the conceptual links between Fischer's skill levels and RJM stages.

In Stage 1 of the RJM, knowing is based on single, concrete observations (e.g., "I believe what I have seen"); this maps onto what Fischer (1980) calls a single representational skill, the ability to use single, undifferentiated concrete categories. By contrast, in Stage 2, individuals are not only able to differentiate between concrete concepts but also are able to relate these concepts to each other in a very elementary fashion; Fischer (1980) calls this a representational mapping skill. The individual is thus able to differentiate right answers from wrong answers about an issue such as food additives and to attribute right answers to good scientists and wrong answers to bad (that is, wrong) scientists. In this perspective, truth is understood concretely as the right answer about a particular issue rather than as an abstract concept.

In Stage 3 of the RJM, there is a further differentiation and intercoordination of Stage 2 categories into simple concrete systems—those areas in which we know right and wrong answers exist and where authorities hold those answers, and those areas in which right answers do not yet exist. Diverse points of view, different conceptions of the same problems, discrepant data, and so on are incorporated by the system as areas of temporary uncertainty. This reflects a move beyond the view that "the world is how authorities tell me it is" to the view that "in some areas authorities don't know the truth and, therefore, people can believe what they want to believe." Differences of opinion are assumed to result from not knowing the answers with certainty.

Stage 4 of the RJM marks the emergence of knowledge understood as an abstraction (as Fischer would describe it), not limited to concrete instances. That is, acknowledging the uncertainty about knowing in regard to an issue such as the safety of food additives or about the possibility of a democracy being created in Iraq, is combined with the acknowledgment that knowing is also uncertain in many other issues; this realization helps form an abstract, intangible category, uncertain knowledge. The idea of justification of beliefs (e.g., a process that includes giving reasons) is also initially understood as an abstraction at Stage 4. Justification is an example of what Fischer would call an initial abstraction, which is associated with Abstract Level 1 skills. However, the two abstractions, knowledge and justification, are poorly differentiated, so evidence is not necessarily used to justify beliefs.

Underlying the concept of knowing in RJM Stage 5 is the ability to relate two abstractions, for example, knowing how scientists study chemical additives and

TABLE 4.2. Relationships Among Skill Levels, Reflective Judgment Stages, and Associated Ages
of Emergence and Consolidation

Skill Level	Reflective Judgment Stage	Modal Age (in years) of Skill Emergence (Optimal Level)	Modal Educational Level of Reflective Judgment Stages (Functional Level)
Representational 1 Single representation concrete instances of knowing	*Stage 1* Knowing is limited to single concrete observations: what a person observes is true.	2	
Representational 2 Representational mapping: two concrete representations can be coordinated with each other	*Stage 2* Two categories for knowing: right answers and wrong answers. Good authorities have knowledge: bad authorities lack knowledge	3.5–4.5	Early High School
Representational 3 Representational system: several aspects of two concrete representations can be coordinated	*Stage 3* In some areas knowledge is certain and authorities have that knowledge. In other areas, knowledge is temporarily uncertain. Only personal beliefs can be known.	6–7	Late high school, early college
Representational 4 = Abstract 1 Two systems of representational systems can be constructed, creating a single abstraction	*Stage 4* Concept that knowledge is unknown in several specific cases leads to the abstract generalization that knowledge is uncertain.	10–12	Late college
Abstract 2 Abstract mapping: abstractions can be coordinated with each other	*Stage 5* Knowledge is uncertain and must be understood within a context; thus justification is context specific.	14–15	Late college, early graduate school
Abstract 3 Abstract system: several aspects of two abstractions can be coordinated	*Stage 6* Knowledge is uncertain but constructed by comparing evidence and opinion on different sides of an issue or across contexts	19–21	Advanced doctoral
Abstract 4 = A Principle Systems of abstract systems can be constructed, creating a single principle	*Stage 7* Knowledge is the outcome of a process of reasonable inquiry. This view is equivalent to a general principle that is consistent across domains.	24–26	Advanced doctoral

Note. Since most of the studies on which this table is based used traditional-age students, educational level is used here as a proxy for the age of functional level on the RJM. Adapted from Kitchener and Fischer (1990) and Kitchener (2002).

knowing how they justify beliefs about the safety of those additives. Another example is knowing what it is that would constitute convincing evidence of success in regard to the creation of a democracy in Iraq as viewed by economists as opposed to political scientists. Fischer's (1980) label for those skills that relate abstractions is *abstract mapping skills* (Abstract Level 2). As Fischer et al. (1984) note, with the ability to relate two abstractions comes the ability to compare and contrast them. Through the contrasts, abstractions are further differentiated from each other, and through the comparisons, the abstractions are integrated in new ways.

With RJM Stage 6 comes the ability to relate abstract mappings into a system, and reflects what Fischer (1980) calls *abstract system skills*. Individuals are able to coordinate the subtle similarities and differences of abstract relationships into intangible systems (Fischer & Kenny, 1986).

RJM Stage 7 is characterized by the ability to integrate several Stage 6 systems (knowing and justification from several perspectives, such as drawing from several disciplinary perspectives to inform a complex topic) into a general framework about knowing and justification. This allows for a generalization of assumptions and clarity of judgment that is not apparent at Stage 6. Abstract internal referents used to judge individual problems are reintegrated into a general principle: Knowledge is constructed through critical inquiry. These referents are illustrated by such qualified phrases as "that which best fits the evidence as I know it," and "that which is discrepant from generally observed processes." The ability to understand the underlying principle is based on what Fischer (1980) calls *systems of abstract systems*. The mastery of these skills assumes the ability to make abstract generalizations about inquiry from multiple instances of participating in the inquiry process. This provides the foundation for reasoning reflectively as an adult, learning about abstractions, and pairing abstractions to create higher order learning.

Fischer's (1980) skill theory provides an additional corroborating framework for understanding adult cognitive development, a framework that helps specify ways that thinking becomes more complex, differentiated, and integrated over the life span. This theory is particularly important because Fischer has hypothesized the relationship between learning and the development of new levels or stages of adult reasoning.

Fischer's (1980) model is distinctive in its attention to three factors that are related to learning and development: (1) an individual's *optimal level* of development, which is the highest level at which an individual can operate given support, practice, and a particular context; (2) an individual's *functional level* of development, which is how the person operates at any given point in time without support, practice, or familiarity with the issue; and (3) *the process of skill acquisition*, which describes how people learn particular skills within levels. The discrepancy between the functional and optimal level illustrates what Fischer (1980) has called the individual's "developmental range" of functioning; it is within the developmental range of optimal and functional levels that learning takes place. This range is illustrated in figure 4.1.

As individuals acquire new skills, concepts are paired and new ideas and associated new underlying assumptions may emerge. For example, an individual who assumes that there are right and wrong answers about drug safety is also likely to believe that a given prescribed drug is safe for himself and others. As he learns about someone for whom a given drug has problematic side effects, he comes to a different conclusion—that there is variability in how a drug affects a particular person. With this realization, his original two concrete concepts (right and wrong answers about drug safety exist; prescribed drugs are safe for everyone) are no longer adequate. This leads to the creation of a new concept, that not all drugs are safe for everyone, and he comes to a different conclusion, that there is variability in how a drug affects a particular person. This conclusion is based on a new underlying assumption, that there is uncertainty about the safety of prescribed drugs.

Whereas growth in functional levels follows a slow, steady progression, growth in optimal level depends on spurts in brain activity and the reorganization of neural networks (Fischer & Rose, 1994). The spurts in the EEG power and conductivity, dendritic branching and synapse formation, as well as myelination, provide the foundation for the growth of the optimal level of any skill. This reorganization allows the individual's capacity to reason more complexly about a variety of issues. To exhibit these higher order skills at the functional level, an individual must see and use skills at the functional level multiple times. Although this process describes how epistemic assumptions develop, it is also applicable to issues about the self and others—moral issues, social issues, and so on. Whether optimal level is observed in any particular instance

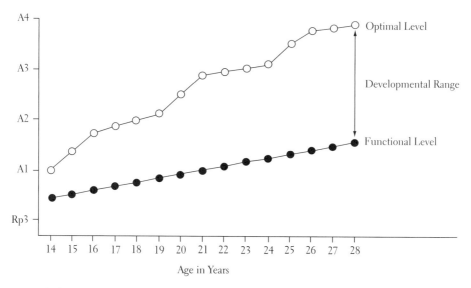

FIGURE 4.1 Idealized growth curves for developmental range in adolescence and early adulthood. From "A Skill Approach to the Development of Reflective Thinking," by K. S. Kitchener and K. Fisher, 1990, in *Contributions to Human Development*, edited by D. Kuhn. Basel: Kargen. Reprinted with permission.

depends, for example, on the context, including fatigue, attention, task demands, and motivation.

Fischer and colleagues suggest that the development in brain functions shows how learning and development are related, and more specifically, how new learning provides the foundation on which new developmental levels can be built. Fischer's (1980) skill theory model can be divided into three tiers between birth and adulthood. Because this chapter focuses on adulthood, we focus on the seven general skill levels that form the representational and abstract tiers. In the representational tier, individuals can reason with and manipulate concrete representations of objects, people, or events; at the abstract level, they can reason about abstract concepts. Again, the model applies to different domains, and the timing of the emergence of these domains depends on opportunities to practice the skill involved. This is true of reflective judgment, as in any other domain. Performance at any particular level will depend on the conditions under which the skill is assessed, such as whether memory prompts are given and opportunities to practice are available, and the nature and difficulty of the task. Because some environments support high-level performance and others do not, it is impossible to say that an individual is "at" a particular developmental level. Rather, the individual may exhibit an array of

levels depending on the tasks involved. For example, a person may have studied and read about a variety of reasons why someone develops a particular disease. He or she may first be introduced to this issue at a very concrete level but eventually have several opportunities to consider the issue. With this practice, he or she may draw a series of abstract conclusions. Similarly, he or she may have the opportunity to reason with these abstract conclusions as well as with abstract conclusions about a similar issue, allowing higher order conclusions to be drawn.

Based on the work of Fischer and Pruyne (2002) and P. M. King and Kitchener (1994), Kitchener (2002) hypothesized the age at which the emergence of each optimal level could first be observed; these are listed in the third column of table 4.2. Under conditions that elicit optimal level functioning, the abstract tier emerges between the ages of 10–12 (Level 1) and 24–26 years (Level 4). A companion column for age of functional level use is given in the fourth column. Here, due to the lack of availability of age data, we use educational level as a proxy for the age of functional level RJM usage for each stage. Predictably, these columns show a wide contrast in age of initial emergence (in childhood) of skill usage under optimal level conditions from the time at which functional level usage of associated reflective judgment stage is seen (in late adolescence and early adulthood). The table reflects the slow emergence of a given way of making meaning, the differences in assessment results based on functional and optimal conditions, and the effects of both biological factors (e.g., maturation) and environmental factors (e.g., opportunities for practice and feedback).

Table 4.2 also shows the major similarities between skill theory and the RJM, specifically the structural differences in thinking from childhood to adolescence to adulthood. Fischer's (1980) model is helpful in providing a life span developmental lens through which the RJM may be seen and in distinguishing the parameters of an individual's developmental range. Although the specific focus and major research questions of each approach are different, the research bases for these two approaches have been mutually beneficial in informing the development of each theoretical approach.

ASSESSING REFLECTIVE JUDGMENT

Assessing an individual's epistemic assumptions and ways of making meaning is a challenging undertaking, requiring much of both the researcher and the informant. Here we describe the approaches used to address this difficult but essential task.

Reflective Judgment Interview

The reflective judgment interview (RJI was used to develop and validate the RJM. It uses a semi-structured interview format, consisting of a set of ill-structured problems and standardized probe questions. The original four problems were selected to cover a range of topics that were familiar to adults in the United States and not specifically grounded in educational contexts; this allowed for the testing of nonstudent samples. These problems included the building of the Egyptian pyramids, the safety of chemical additives in foods, objectivity in news reporting, and evolution/special creation. Since then, problems used in the RJI have been expanded to include a wide variety of topics that are of particular interest to specific disciplines of study, including chemistry, business, and psychology. The news reporting problem reads as follows: "Some people believe that news stories represent unbiased, objective reporting of the news. Others say there is no such thing as unbiased, objective reporting, and that even in reporting the facts, news reporters project their own interpretations into what they write." For each problem, respondents are asked to state and discuss their point of view, on what it is based, the certainty with which they hold their points of view, and their explanations for alternative beliefs or judgments. Table 4.3 lists the standardized probe questions, as well as the rationale for each question. The interviews are transcribed and scored by two raters, who independently assess the transcribed responses for their similarity to descriptions of assumptions about knowledge, how it is gained, and the basis of certainty of knowledge claims as described in the stages of the RJM. Raters may assign as many different stages as they see evidenced in the transcripts; these usually fall in adjacent stages, but occasionally are assigned across three stages. Scores are then typically averaged into an overall reflective judgment score that corresponds to the reflective judgment stages. For example, a score of 3.5 means that the individual probably used a combination of Stage 3 and 4 reasoning, but there may have been evidence of lower or higher stage reasoning in the mix. Although most researchers use only the mean score for data analysis, this procedure allows the researcher to examine patterns of stage mixture as well. A detailed description of the interview, including approximately a dozen sample problems and the scoring procedures may be found in P. M. King and Kitchener (1994, Resource A). Internal consistency reliabilities have been in the high 0.70s to mid-0.80s (P. M. King & Kitchener, 1994; Wood, 1997), depending on the heterogeneity of the samples.

To ensure consistency of administration and scoring of the RJI, we developed a training and certification program for both interviewers and raters. This was especially important during the theory validation phase of our research. This program was in place from 1978 until the mid-1990s and was discontinued to turn our attention to the development of a measure that is more amenable to large-scale administration.

Reasoning About Current Issues Test

The Reasoning About Current Issues Test (RCI) is a measure of reflective judgment that focuses on the capacity to recognize and endorse more epistemically sophisticated statements from among a range of alternatives. The questionnaire is designed to assess how respondents think about current issues as a reflection of their assumptions about knowledge and the certainty with which knowledge claims may be made. The RCI should not be viewed as simply an objectively

TABLE 4.3. Reflective Judgment Interview Standard Probe Questions

Probe Question	Purpose
What do you think about these statements?	To allow the participant to share an initial reaction to the problem presented. At this time, most state which point of view is closer to their own (e.g., that the Egyptians built the pyramids, that news reporting is biased, and so forth).[a]
How did you come to hold that point of view?	To find out how the respondent arrived at that point of view, and whether and how it has evolved from other positions on the issue.
On what do you base that point of view?	To find out about the basis of a respondent's point of view, for example, a personal evaluation of the data, consistency with an expert's point of view, or a specific experience. This provides information about the respondent's concept of justification.
Can you ever know for sure that your position on this issue is correct? How or why not?	To find out about the participant's assumptions concerning the certainty of knowledge (such as whether issues like this can be known absolutely, what the respondent would do to increase the certainty, or why that would not be possible).
When two people differ about matters such as this, is it the case that one opinion is right and one is wrong? If yes, what do you mean by "right"? If no, can you say that one opinion is in some way better than the other? What do you mean by "better"?	To find out how the respondent assesses the adequacy of alternative interpretations; to see if the respondent holds a dichotomous, either/or view of the issue (characteristic of the early stages); to allow the participant to give criteria by which she or he evaluates the adequacy of arguments (information that helps differentiate high- from middle-level stage responses).
How is it possible that people have such different points of view about this subject?	To elicit comments about the participant's understanding of differences in perspectives and opinions (what they are based on and why there is such diversity of opinion about the issue).
How is it possible that experts in the field disagree about this subject?	To elicit comments about the respondent's understanding of how she or he uses the point of view of an expert or authority in making decisions about controversial issues (such as whether experts' views are weighted more heavily than others' views, and why or why not).

[a]If the respondent does not endorse a particular point of view on the first question, the following questions are asked: Could you ever say which was the better position? How? Why not? How would you go about making a decision about this issue? Will we ever know for sure which is the better position? How/why not?

Note. The Reflective Judgment Interview was originally developed in 1975 by the authors and was copyrighted in King (1977). Permission to use the interview is contingent on the use of certified interviewers and raters. From *Developing Reflective Judgment: Understanding and Promoting Intellectual Growth and Critical Thinking Adolescents and Adults* (pp. 102–103), by P. M. King and K. S. Kitchner, 1994, San Francisco: Jossey-Bass. Reprinted with permission.

scorable version of the RJI, a different assessment format that yields an equivalent score; rather, it taps into related skills (i.e., those of recognition, rather than production) that are based on the RJM. Each makes different demands on the respondent and illuminates different aspects of the individual's capacity to make reflective judgments.

The RCI consists of a series of five ill-structured problems that span a range of controversial topics (such as immigration policy and the determinants of alcoholism); respondents are asked to read 10 statements for each problem that reflect different levels of reasoning in the RJM and (using a four-point scale) to rate the statements in terms of how closely they resemble their own thinking on the problem. A fifth response, "meaningless," may be selected to indicate that they think the statement is not interpretable; these contain complex vocabulary and are included to control for the possibility that respondents may endorse statements based on the vocabulary or evident sophistication of the item rather than on the idea expressed. Respondents then rank order the three statements that most closely reflect their own thinking; the rankings are the unit of analysis used to calculate the respondent's score. The RCI score reflects the level of reasoning most often ranked by the respondent as most similar to his or her thinking. The rankings are weighted so that the statement ranked first is given the highest weighting, the statement rated second is given the next highest weighting, and so forth. Scores can range from 2 to 7, corresponding to Stages 2–7 on the RJM. For a more detailed description of the RCI, see Wood, Kitchener, and Jensen (2002). To view a sample, see http://www.umich.edu/~refjudg/. Reliabilities have been in the low to mid-0.70s, depending on the samples (Wood et al., 2002).

RESEARCH ON THE REFLECTIVE JUDGMENT MODEL

Research on the RJM has addressed a series of major questions, including whether the proposed changes in epistemic cognition form a developmental sequence, whether observed differences were attributable to education, whether subgroups of people held different epistemic assumptions, and whether a person's reflective thinking level was related to his or her thinking in other domains. Collectively, this group of studies provide information and insights into the development of reflective thinking in a range of contexts and about factors that affect its development. We turn to these studies now.

Does the Capacity to Make Reflective Judgments Improve With Age and Education?

One of the inspiring aspects of conducting research on a construct such as reflective thinking is its relevance: Learning to make judgments about controversial, ill-structured problems is a salient aspect of successful adulthood, and many colleges and universities list teaching students to do so as an intended learning outcome. A number of studies have examined whether reflective judgment improves across educational levels. However, age and education are typically confounded: As students progress through college and then to graduate programs, they get older. So whether observed changes across educational levels are attributable to education or maturation cannot be discerned by simply comparing educational level differences, which might be due (at least in part) to physical maturation or other life experiences outside formal education. Similarly, if reflective thinking levels did not improve across educational levels, this would also be problematic, suggesting, for example, that the definition of the construct did not reflect the attributes being taught or that the educational programs were not effective in promoting this type of de-

velopment. Thus it is important to use either design or statistical controls to ascertain the relative influence of each variable.

Many studies have examined whether reflective judgment levels change between educational levels, such as whether graduate students score higher than undergraduate students. P. M. King et al. (1994) summarized studies that collectively tested approximately 1,300 students using the RJI and reported a slow but steady developmental progression in RJ scores from high school ($M = 3.2$, $SD = 0.5$) to college ($M = 3.8$, $SD = 0.6$) to graduate school ($M = 4.8$, $SD = 0.8$). (Here, a mean score of 3.0 indicates that the average stage usage was Stage 3.) Table 4.4 lists the RJI scores by grade, year, or degree within these educational levels. These scores are graphed in figure 4.2, where the middle line indicates the mean score and the top and bottom lines indicate the upper and lower limits of

TABLE 4.4. Reflective Judgment Scores by Educational Level

Educational Level	Average RJI Score	SD	n
High school			
Grade 9	3.08	0.41	57
Grade 10	3.46	0.35	15
Grade 11	3.12	0.61	33
Grade 12	3.27	0.51	67
Average	3.19	0.50	172
College (traditional-aged students)			
Freshman	3.63	0.53	329
Sophomore	3.57	0.43	89
Junior	3.74	0.59	159
Senior	3.99	0.67	369
Average	3.79	0.61	946
College (nontraditional-aged students)			
Freshman	3.57	0.42	78
Sophomore	4.30	0.59	13
Senior	3.98	0.74	46
Average	3.78	0.61	137
Graduate			
Master's/early doctoral	4.62	0.81	126
Advanced doctoral	5.27	0.89	70
Average	4.76	0.85	196

Note. From *Developing Reflective Judgment: Understanding and Promoting Intellectual Growth and Critical Thinking in Adolescents and Adults* (p. 161), by P. M. King and K. S. Kitchener, 1994, San Francisco: Jossey-Bass. Reprinted with permission.

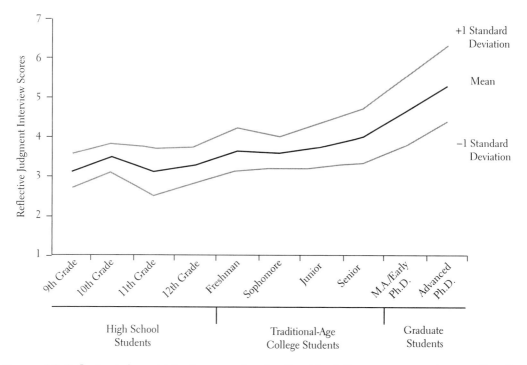

FIGURE 4.2 Reflective judgment interview scores by educational level. Scores are averaged across all studies reviewed here that reported RJI scores for students ($n = 1,334$) at these educational levels. From *Developing Reflective Judgment: Understanding and Promoting Intellectual Growth and Critical Thinking in Adolescents and Adults* (p. 162), by P. M. King and K. S. Kitchener, 1994, San Francisco: Jossey-Bass. Reprinted with permission.

the standard deviation. It is noteworthy that not only did the mean scores increase across educational levels, but so did the amount of variability, suggesting a pattern of mixed success in promoting reflective thinking in college (P. M. King, 1992; P. M. King & Kitchener, 1993).

Even though reflective thinking is an espoused outcome of a college education, these studies revealed that a large proportion of college students—of both traditional and nontraditional age—hold assumptions about knowledge that limit their ability to make judgments on the basis of critical analysis. A similar finding was reported by Baxter Magolda (1992) in her longitudinal study of college students. She continued to follow this sample beyond college into their young adult years and later noted that this type of reasoning and decision making was more apparent in their post-college early adult years. Again, whether this finding is a reflection of an age-related development or an educational environment that did not challenge students to think in complex ways that required them to take a stand (as Baxter Magolda's participants reported) is

not clear. Similarly, even the reasoning of graduate students was not consistently reflective, with many holding quasi-reflective assumptions. Nevertheless, the vast majority of individuals who did evidence assumptions associated with reflective thinking were advanced doctoral students. This may reflect some unknown selection criteria used to admit applicants to doctoral programs or the intellectual rigors of doctoral education and the scholarly expectations that are associated with doctoral study in many disciplines. In addition, this finding may be an artifact of other factors that have not yet been identified.

When organizing these studies by clustering college students together as a category of analysis, it is important to note that using virtually any broad category can be risky given the variability within categories. For example, many people use the category "college students" with the assumption that this category includes only students who are 18–22 years old, or they use it as a proxy for age (assuming that there is little variability by age for such students). However, based on U.S. Census Data from 2000, 45% of all undergraduate students in the United States were 22 years of age or older (*Chronicle of Higher Education*, 2003). In other words, almost half of all U.S. college students are now "nontraditional age" or "adult students." The proportion is much higher for part-time adult students (78%). Therefore, when looking at age-related development using categories such as educational level, it is important to acknowledge that these cut across age lines and that less ambiguous information is provided when researchers disentangle age and education.

Five studies have included nontraditional age students in their samples (Glatfelter, 1982; J. W. King, 1986; Schmidt, 1985; Shoff, 1979; Strange & King, 1981). Collectively, these studies tested 137 adult learners. Such studies play a key role in determining whether age or educational level is the more potent influence on the development of reflective thinking. As reported in table 4.4, the average score of adult students was virtually the same as those of traditional age students, but the range of scores for the adult seniors was narrower (3.7 to 4.4) than that of their traditional age counterparts (3.56 to 5.0). As these studies show, age alone does not predict the ability to think reflectively. It may, however, help predict other relevant variables, such as readiness to learn or openness to entertaining divergent views, and those who delay entry into college may experience a developmental spurt as a result of this combination of factors.

Several studies have assessed the reflective thinking levels of adults who were not enrolled in formal educational programs (Glatfelter, 1982; Glenn & Eklund, 1991; Josephson, 1988; Kelton & Griffith, 1986; J. W. King, 1986; Lawson, 1980). In most of these, nonstudent adults were used as a comparison group for adult college students, thus providing a control for age when examining educational effects. Among these samples, a key variable that predicted reflective judgment level was whether the learners had completed a college degree: Those with an undergraduate degree consistently scored higher than those who had not earned a college degree. The mean scores for samples without a college degree was 3.5–3.7; the mean scores for the samples with college degrees ranged from 4.0 to 5.2 (P. M. King et al., 1994). Glenn and Eklund's (1991) study is noteworthy among this group because they tested two groups of adults 65 years and older. The mean score of the first group, those with up to a high school diploma, was 3.7, which is about a half stage higher than the average for high school seniors reported in table 4.3 (3.3) and close to the average for the college samples

(3.8). The mean score of the second group, retired faculty members with doctorates, was 5.2, which is quite comparable to the average score of advanced doctoral students (5.3) reported previously.

These studies provide strong evidence that development in reflective judgment occurs beyond high school into the young adult and adult years and that older students with more education score higher than their younger counterparts with less education. Furthermore, education appears to be a stronger predictor of reflective thinking than age alone. This is reasonable, because formal education is at least intended to intentionally promote development, whereas simple maturation (age alone) may or may not be associated with comparably beneficial experiences.

The studies reported here used cross-sectional designs to examine differences in reflective thinking by age and education; these provide important puzzle pieces when attempting to understand the development of reflective judgment. However, longitudinal data provide stricter controls when making claims about intraindividual development and are essential for the validation of any developmental model. We examine these studies in the next section.

Are the Reflective Judgment Stages Developmentally Ordered?

The question of whether posited levels of development form a developmental sequence is central to the validation of any proposed developmental model. Answering this question requires longitudinal studies, preferably long-term studies. The study of longest duration was the 10-year follow-up of our original sample (Kitchener & King, 1981); details are reported in P. M. King et al. (1994). Participants were tested 2 years, 4 years, and 10 years after the original testing. Of the original 80 persons, 53 (66%) participated in the final testing; these individuals were especially generous with their time and attention (up to four hours per testing) during this study. The original sample consisted of 20 high school juniors, 40 college juniors, and 20 advanced doctoral students. To control for differences across educational levels, especially in academic aptitude, each high school and college student was matched to a student in the doctoral sample using scores from the Minnesota Scholastic Aptitude Test (taken in high school), gender, and size of hometown when in high school. (In the mid-1970s, the world was in many ways "smaller" and less accessible, especially to those in small towns with limited access to pluralistic influences. This variable was thus used as a modest control for exposure to divergent perspectives, which was hypothesized to affect complexity of thinking.) The scores of the high school students changed the most: Across the four testing times, their mean RJI scores were 2.77, 3.61, 4.91, and 5.29. By contrast, the original group of college juniors' scores were as follows: 3.76, 4.18, 4.92, and 5.05. The original group of doctoral students started high in reflective thinking and stayed high; their scores were 5.76, 6.23, 6.23, and 6.21. As a check on familiarity with the original set of problems in the interview, a new problem (on the safety of nuclear energy) was added for the last testing. We reasoned that if scores were increasing due to familiarity with the problems, then respondents would score lower on the new problem than on the familiar problems. No differences were found in participants' scores between problems.

A stricter test of changes of time uses individual rather than group data. RJI scores for the entire longitudinal sample at all testings are reported by P. M. King and Kitchener (1994; Resource B, table b6.2), both as mean scores and by dominant (modal stage scores)/subdominant (second most frequently assigned) scores. Using the scores of only those 53 who participated in the final testing, the RJI scores of 92% of the sample ($n = 49$) increased in the 10 years of the study. Decreases were observed for two individuals (both former doctoral students), but their modal scores remained at Stage 7, suggesting a ceiling effect. The scores of the remaining two individuals stayed the same. Overall, we observed a pervasive pattern of upward change in RJI scores over time. Furthermore, a sequential (not random) ordering of scores is apparent in the dominant/subdominant scores, lower stage usage precedes higher stage usage, and there is little evidence of skipping stages.

Six other longitudinal studies have examined changes in RJI scores over time (Brabeck & Wood, 1990; Polkosnik & Winston, 1989; Sakalys, 1984; Schmidt, 1985; Van Tine, 1990; Welfel & Davison, 1986). These studies included 12 samples and a total of 241 participants, most of whom were tested twice, at intervals from a few months to four years. In every sample, the scores either stayed the same (most common among those tested at short intervals) or increased over time (at one- to four-year intervals).

This collection of studies provides substantial evidence that reflective thinking develops slowly and steadily over time and in the manner posited by the RJM. That is, development in reflective thinking—as evidenced by changes in epistemic assumptions as they relate to justification of one's beliefs—appears to follow the outline of developmental steps described in the RJM.

Does Reflective Thinking Vary by Gender and Ethnicity?

Whether reflective judgment patterns differ by gender and ethnicity is a question that should be raised for any psychological model (Brabeck, 1983, 1993; Mednick, 1989). In regard to the RJM, it is important to note that it was initially developed using samples that were equally balanced between men and women but that was exclusively white (reflecting the predominantly white demographic composition of Minnesota at the time). Both variables remain of interest in determining whether the model is biased with respect to these variables.

In the 20 studies that have been conducted using both males and females, 11 reported no differences (Bowen, 1989; Glenn & Eklund, 1991; Guthrie, King, & Palmer, 2000; Jensen, 1998; P. M. King & Taylor, 1992; Lawson, 1980; McKinney, 1985; Van Tine, 1990; Welfel, 1982; Welfel & Davison, 1986). Three studies did not comment on the question (Evans, 1988; Kelton & Griffith, 1986; Polkosnik & Winston, 1989), and eight reported gender differences. Of these eight, females scored higher than males in one study (Thompson, 1995), males scored higher than females in six studies (P. M. King, Wood, & Mines, 1990; Kitchener & Wood, 1987; Kitchener, Lynch, Fischer, & Wood, 1993; Lawson, 1980; Shoff, 1979; Strange & King, 1981), and one study (Schmidt, 1985) reported a class by gender interaction. In addition, P. M. King et al. (1994) reported that in their 10-year longitudinal study, no gender differences were found at Times 1, 2 (year 3), or 3 (year 6). This pattern remained at Time 4 (year 10) when the scores of only those who had participated in all four testings were included. However, when all participants were included in the analyses, males scored higher. Another important finding from this study was the gender breakdown in graduate degree completion: Of the former high school and college students, 47% of the males compared to only 15% of the females had obtained graduate degrees at Time 4. This suggests that higher levels of educational attainment of the men could have accounted for the gender differences in RJI scores. They also noted that simply tallying results across studies in this way provided only a general view of gender differences and that the sample selection and the role of other attributes (e.g., academic aptitude) should also be taken into account in evaluating this pattern of results.

Since the RJM was initially developed with an all-white, European American sample, it is reasonable to ask whether it is applicable to people from other ethnic backgrounds. More specifically, is development in epistemic cognition similar for members of other ethnic groups? Lacking comparable longitudinal data to answer this question, another approach is to look for comparability of scores across ethnic groups—but of course, without treating the scores for white people as normative. P. M. King and Taylor (1992) found similar age/educational trends among a sample of African American students (seniors scored higher than freshmen and juniors), and observed that RJI scores predicted grade point average and college graduation. Their scores were similar to those of other college students reported by P. M. King and Kitchener (1994). Samson (1999) reported that Latino college students (of Central American, South American, Puerto Rican, and Cuban ancestry) scored higher than freshmen; their scores were also similar to those reported in P. M. King and Kitchener (1994). Kitchener, Wood, and Jensen (1999) also found that gains in RJ scores were comparable for African American and Euro-American college students. Although these studies do not directly answer the question of whether the RJM adequately describes the development of epistemic assumptions and their role in making judgments among other subgroups, nothing in these results suggests that the model should *not* be used with individuals from other ethnic groups. Indeed, the comparability of scores and educational trends provide preliminary evidence that the model may be so used. Nevertheless, the question is not fully resolved and will require careful longitudinal research with diverse populations.

Is Development in Reflective Judgment Related to Development in Other Domains?

In some ways, treating cognitive development as though it exists independently of other domains of development is like treating the head as though it is not connected to other parts of the body. Although there are good reasons to investigate constructs separately, it is also informative to explore their relationships to other domains of development. In this section, we summarize the research on some of these relationships.

Adults often face problems that include a moral dimension, whether in the context of one's family, occupation, or community life. Furthermore, moral problems are typically ill-structured problems, which provides an important similarity with the focus of the RJM: both are defined incompletely and require that judgments be constructed by individual decision makers. Although different criteria are used when making decisions about moral and intellectual problems (such as values based on what is good as opposed to values based on how knowledge is gained), there are nevertheless similarities between the two domains. Table 4.5 provides a stage-by-stage description of these similarities, showing how concepts of knowledge are structurally similar to concepts of morality.

The domain that has been most frequently studied in association with reflective thinking is that of moral or character development. Several studies have examined the relationship between reflective judgment and moral judgment (e.g., Josephson, 1988; P. M. King & Kitchener, 1994; P. M. King, Kitchener, Wood, & Davison, 1989); a measure of moral judgment was included with the RJI in the 10-year longitudinal study of reflective thinking described earlier. The moral judgment measure used was Rest's (1979) Defining Issues Test (DIT). As with the RJI, the doctoral students scored significantly higher than their younger counterparts. Both group and time differences on the RJI remained significant when the effects of moral judgment were statistically removed; however, neither of these main effects remained significant for the DIT when the RJI scores were removed. The correlations between the RJI and the DIT correlated moderately (0.46–0.58) at all four testing times. Using these data from the six-year retest, Wood (1993) discovered that reflective thinking was necessary but not sufficient for moral reasoning. That is, developing reflective judgment will not necessarily lead to but is likely required for more principled moral thinking. In other words, "promoting the development of reflective judgment may be one step in the process of developing higher levels of moral judgment" (P. M. King & Kitchener, 1994, p. 212).

TABLE 4.5. Structural Similarities Between Reflective Judgment and Moral Judgment

Concepts of Knowledge	Concepts of Morality
Stage 1 Single concrete category for knowing. Certain knowledge is gained by direct personal observation and needs no justification.	Single concrete category for good and bad. Good gets rewarded; bad gets punished.
Stage 2 Two concrete categories of knowledge. A person can know with certainty through direct observation or indirectly through an authority.	Two concrete categories of morality. For me, good is what I want. For you, good is what you want. Bad is what is not wanted.
Stage 3 Several concrete categories of knowledge are interrelated. Knowledge is assumed to be either absolutely certain or temporarily uncertain. Justification is based on authorities' views of what "feels right."	Several concrete categories of morality are interrelated. Good is being considerate, nice, kind. Bad is being inconsiderate, mean, and unkind. This is true for self and others.
Stage 4 Knowledge is understood as a single abstraction. Knowledge is uncertain, and knowledge claims are assumed to be idiosyncratic to the individual.	Morality is understood as a single abstraction. Laws are understood as a mechanism for coordinating expectations about acceptable and unacceptable behavior within communities.
Stage 5 Two or more abstract concepts of knowledge can be related. Knowledge is seen as contextual and subjective. Beliefs are justified by using the rules of inquiry for the appropriate contexts.	Two or more abstract concepts of morality can be related. The moral framework from one context (such as a community's laws or standards of conduct) can be related to the moral framework in another context (those of another community).
Stage 6 Abstract concepts of knowledge can be related. Knowledge is actively constructed by comparing evidence and opinion on different sides of an issue; solutions are evaluated by personally endorsed criteria.	Abstract concepts of morality can be related. While the fairness of a given law may be interpreted differently, the well-being of people is a common consideration.
Stage 7 Abstract concepts of knowledge are understood as a system. The general principle is that knowledge is the outcome of the process of reasonable inquiry for constructing a well-informed understanding.	Abstract concepts of morality are understood as a system. Principles such as the value of human life, justice, serving others, and contributing to the common good unify diverse concepts of morality.

Note. From Developing Reflective Judgment: Understanding and Promoting Intellectual Growth and Critical Thinking in Adolescents and Adults (pp. 208–209), by P. M. King and K. S. Kitchener, 1994, San Francisco: Jossey-Bass. Reprinted with permission.

A related study was conducted by Guthrie (1996), who examined the relationship between reflective thinking and tolerance, specifically tolerance toward African Americans and toward gays and lesbians. Measures used for these constructs were Jacobson's (1985) New Racism Scale and Herek's (1988) Heterosexuals' Attitudes Toward Lesbians and Gay Men Scale. Reflective thinking was measured using the reflective thinking appraisal (RTA; the predecessor to the RCI), they found a moderate correlation (0.45–0.58) between the RTA and the two tolerance measures. Strikingly, using a nonlinear binomial regression equation, RTA scores accounted for 44% of the variance in tolerance scores, suggesting that there is very strong cognitive component to tolerance.

In this section, we have summarized several sets of studies addressing various types of questions that have been raised relative to the development of reflective thinking. Taken as a whole, we can say with confidence that development in reasoning about ill-structured problems does occur beyond childhood and beyond adolescence and in the manner described by the RJM. Furthermore, participation in undergraduate and graduate education has a strong association with the development of epistemic cognition. Although this research base has been useful in documenting the nature of this development (that is, the general structure of how it unfolds over time), little is known about the more specific mechanisms of development and of the type of experiences that stimulate or serve to promote development. There are also many unanswered questions about how it is related to development in other domains; unfortunately, these await the development of assessment procedures that allow for large-scale administration.

RELATING DEVELOPMENT IN REFLECTIVE JUDGMENT TO BROADER ISSUES OF ADULT LEARNING AND DEVELOPMENT

The focus of this chapter has been on cognitive development and more specifically on epistemic cognition, or how people's assumptions about knowledge develop from adolescence to adulthood, including how knowledge is acquired, the certainty with which it can be known, and the role of the knower in constructing and accepting knowledge claims. There is great significance in being able to appreciate the basis of multiple perspectives and make defensible judgments. First, these skills enable adults to better construct solutions for the ill-structured problems that are typical of adult life, such as weighing competing advice on financial, medical, or child-rearing matters; deciding how to participate in civic and political causes; successfully balancing the complex demands of careers and families; and evaluating the role of the United States in international events. The second reason has a strong affective dimension: Insufficiently developed cognitive skills contribute to the inability to adequately analyze issues and construct satisfactory solutions, which can lead to the feeling of being "in over your head" (the title of Kegan's 1994 book on the topic), or feeling confused and overwhelmed by the complexity of contemporary problems. Thus, the attributes associated with reflective thinking provide adults with many cognitive tools that they can use when addressing a wide variety of adult tasks.

Reflective Judgment and Kegan's Integrated Model of Development

The domain of reflective thinking, however central it is to a description of adult development, is nevertheless only one domain of development. Furthermore, as has been demonstrated in studies described, reflective judgment is clearly related to development in other domains. These observations suggest the value of situating the RJM within an integrated approach to development. One such approach has been proposed by Kegan (1982, 1994); his model integrates three major domains of development—the cognitive, intrapersonal, and interpersonal domains. Like Fischer's (1980) model, Kegan's life span model explicates a developmental order in the ways individuals approach and make meaning of the tasks and challenges they face. Kegan (1994) uses the concept of mature capacity to capture the level of ability (or capacity) required for successfully navigating the demands of adult life. With mature capacity, one can practice what he called self-authorship, in which one can "see the self as the author (rather than merely the theater) of one's inner psychological life" (Kegan, 1994, p. 31): "This new whole is an ideology, an internal identity, a *self-authorship* that can coordinate, integrate, act upon, or invent values, beliefs, convictions, generalizations, ideals, abstractions, interpersonal loyalties, and intrapersonal states. It is no longer *authored by* them, it *authors* them and thereby achieves a personal authority" (p. 185; emphasis in original). As this quotation shows, the concept of self-authorship captures many elements of maturity in adulthood, including but not limited to reflective thinking. For example, as individuals develop in ways that result in a change of identity (commonly noted as people describe themselves or others as growing up or becoming more mature), their beliefs, goals, and relationships with others are no longer determined primarily by others but are increasingly seen as attributes the individual can choose, affirm, develop, embrace, and use to serve as the basis for decisions and actions. (For examples, see Baxter Magolda, 2001, and Baxter Magolda & King, 2004). In describing the role of the cognitive domain, Baxter Magolda (2004) noted:

> Increasing maturity in knowledge construction yields an internal belief system that guides thinking and behavior yet is open to reconstruction given relevant evidence. Cognitive outcomes such

as intellectual power, reflective judgment, mature decision making, and problem solving depend on these epistemological capacities. This dimension is central to achieving cognitive maturity and is a necessary ingredient for achieving the other learning outcomes [an integrated identity in the intrapersonal domain and mature relationships with others in the interpersonal domain]. (p. 9)

In other words, developing epistemological maturity as described by the RJM is not only very important but may be essential for achieving maturity in broader issues of adult development.

Relating Reflective Judgment to Other Models of Adult Learning

Interestingly, several popular strategies designed to promote adult learning or to enhance the quality of education for nontraditional aged students and noncollege adult populations are consistent with the underlying assumptions about the development of reflective judgment. For example, andragogy is a nuanced form of pedagogy specifically adapted to adults (see Pratt, 1993, for a review). Merriam (2001) outlined five assumptions about learner characteristics used in an andragogy model, that the learner (1) has an independent self-concept and is self-directed, (2) has important life experiences, (3) has needs that are related to social roles, (4) uses a problem-centered approach and is concerned with the application of knowledge, and (5) is internally motivated. These assumptions can be used to form a model of practice that is active, learner-centered, and can be adapted to a wide variety of contexts. By taking learner characteristics into account, these approaches reinforce principles of good instructional practice—and offer insights into the link between learning and development. Considerable attention has been devoted to the topic of self-directed learning (e.g., Brookfield, 1993; Candy, 1991), an approach that is highly consistent with Kegan's (1994) concept of self-authorship.

Taylor, Marienau, & Fiddler (2000) have proposed studying developmental learning as a way to capture the relationships between these previously distinct entities since both learning and development address the acquisition of knowledge and skills over time. As they noted, "The dynamic intersection between learning and development concerns the fundamental change in how meaning is made or *how we*

know what we think we know" (p. 13; emphasis in original). They suggested four aspects of the study of adult learning that are common to models and theories of adult development: "1) people develop through interactions with their environment, 2) development follows a cycle of differentiation and integration, 3) within individuals development is a variable not a uniform process, and 4) the ability to reframe experience serves as a marker of development" (p. 11). They also identified five indicators of development: Development is evidenced by movement "toward 1) knowing as a dialogical process, 2) a dialogical relationship to oneself, 3) being a continuous learner, 4) self-agency and self-authorship, and 5) connection with others" (pp. 32–33). In other words, deep approaches to learning encourage development, a finding consistent with that reported by Baxter Magolda (2001) in her study of postcollege adults.

The combination of these attributes as mature capacity and as characteristics of adult learners has distinct similarities with Dewey's concept of intelligent action:

Intelligence consists of a complex set of flexible and growing habits that involve sensitivity, the ability to discern the complexities of a situation, imagination that is exercised in new possibilities and hypotheses, willingness to learn from experience, fairness and objectivity in judging conflicting values and opinions and the courage to change one's views when it is demanded by the consequences of our actions and criticisms of others. (Bernstein, 1971, p. 222)

This is the kind of reasoning required as adults face complex contemporary tasks and challenges, and is the kind of reasoning described in the most advanced stage of reflective thinking of the RJM. Thus defined, the RJM describes the evolution of thinking from late adolescence through adulthood that culminates in intelligent action, which is arguably the central goal of adult development.

References

Baltes, P. B., Dittmann-Kohli, F., & Dixon, R. A. (1984). New perspectives on the development of intelligence in adulthood: Toward a dual-process conception and a model of selective optimization with compensation. In P. B. Baltes & O. G. Brim Jr. (Eds.), *Life-span development and behavior* (Vol. 6, pp. 33–76). New York: Academic Press.

Baltes, P. B., & Smith, J. (1990). Toward a psychology of wisdom and its ontogenesis. In R. Sternberg (Ed.), *Wisdom: Its nature, origins, and development* (pp. 87–120). New York: Cambridge University Press.

Baron, J. (1988). *Thinking and deciding.* Cambridge: Cambridge University Press.

Baxter Magolda, M. B. (1992). *Knowing and reasoning in college: Gender-related patterns in students' intellectual development.* San Francisco: Jossey-Bass.

Baxter Magolda, M. B. (1999). *Creating contexts for learning and self-authorship: Constructive-developmental pedagogy.* Nashville, TN: Vanderbilt University Press.

Baxter Magolda, M. B. (2001). *Making their own way: Narratives for transforming higher education to promote self-development.* Sterling, VA: Stylus.

Baxter Magolda, M. B. (2004). Self-authorship as the common goal of 21st century education. In M. B. Baxter Magolda & P. M. King (Eds.), *Learning partnerships: Theory and models of practice to educate for self-authorship* (pp. 1–35). Sterling, VA: Stylus.

Baxter Magolda, M. B., & King, P. M. (Eds.). (2004). *Learning partnerships: Theory and models of practice to educate for self-authorship.* Sterling, VA: Stylus.

Bernstein, R. J. (1971). *Praxis and action.* Philadelphia: University of Pennsylvania Press.

Bowen, J. L. (1989). *The combined predictive effect of creativity level and personality type on college students' reflective judgment.* Unpublished doctoral dissertation, East Texas University.

Brabeck, M. (1983). Moral judgment: Theory and research on differences between males and females. *Developmental Review, 3,* 274–291.

Brabeck, M. (1993). Recommendations for re-examining *Womens' Ways of Knowing:* A response to Handlin's interview with Belenky and Clinchy. *New Ideas in Psychology, 11*(2), 253–258.

Brabeck, M., & Wood, P. K. (1990). Cross-sectional and longitudinal evidence for differences between well-structured and ill-structured problem solving abilities. In M. L. Commons, C. Armon, L. Kohlberg, F. A. Richards, R. A. Grotzer, & J. D. Sinnott (Eds.), *Adult development, Vol. 2. Models and methods in the study of adolescent and adult thought* (pp. 133–146). New York: Praeger.

Brookfield, S. (1993). Self-directed learning, political clarity, and the critical practice of adult education. *Adult Education Quarterly, 43,* 227–242.

Broughton, M. (1975). *The development of natural epistemology in years 11 to 16.* Unpublished doctoral dissertation, Harvard University.

Candy, P. C. (1991). *Self-direction for lifelong learning.* San Francisco: Jossey-Bass.

Chronicle of Higher Education. (2003, August 29). Almanac Issue 2003–2004, p. 15.

Churchman, C. W. (1971). *The design of inquiring systems: Basic concepts of systems and organization.* New York: Basic Books.

Clayton, V. P., & Birren, J. E. (1980). The development of wisdom across the life span: A reexamination of an ancient topic. In P. B. Baltes & O. G. Brim Jr. (Eds.), *Life-span development and behavior* (vol. 3, pp. 104–135). New York: Academic Press.

Dewey, J. (1933). *How we think: A restatement of the relations of reflective thinking to the educative process.* Lexington, MA: Heath.

Dewey, J. (1938). *Logic: The theory of inquiry.* New York: Holt.

Dixon, R. A., & Baltes, P. B. (1986). Toward life-span research on the functions and pragmatics of intelligence. In R. J. Sternberg & R. K. Wagner (Eds.), *Practical intelligence: Nature and origins of competence in the everyday world* (pp. 203–234). New York: Cambridge University Press.

Erikson, E. (1963). *Childhood and society.* New York: Norton.

Evans, D. J. (1988). *Effects of a religious-oriented, conservative, homogeneous college education on reflective judgment.* Unpublished doctoral dissertation, Graduate Faculty of Education, Claremont Graduate University.

Fischer, K. W. (1980). A theory of cognitive development: The control and construction of hierarchies of skills. *Psychological Review, 87*(6), 477–531.

Fischer, K. W., Bullock, D., Rosenberg, E. J., & Raya, P. (1993). The dynamics of competence: How context contributes directly to skill. In R. Wozniak & K. W. Fischer (Eds.), *Development in context: Acting and thinking in specific environments* (pp. 93–117). Hillsdale, NJ: Lawrence Erlbaum.

Fischer, K. W., Hand, H. H., & Russell, S. (1984). The development of abstractions in adolescence and adulthood. In M. L. Commons, F. A. Richards, & C. Armon (Eds.), *Beyond formal operations* (pp. 43–73). New York: Praeger.

Fischer, K. W., & Kenny, S. L. (1986) Environmental conditions for discontinuities in the development of abstractions in adolescence and adulthood. In R. A. Mines & K. S. Kitchener (Eds.), *Adult cognitive development.* New York: Praeger.

Fischer, K. W., & Lamborn, S. D. (1989). Mechanisms of variation developmental levels: Cognitive and emotional transitions during adolescence. In A. de Ribaupierre (Ed.), *Transitions mechanisms in child development: The longitudinal perspective* (pp. 33–67). Cambridge: Cambridge University Press.

Fischer, K. W., & Pipp, S. L. (1984). Processes of cognitive development: Optimal level and skill acquisition. In R. J. Sternberg (Ed.), *Mechanisms of cognitive development.* New York: Freeman.

Fischer, K. W., & Pruyne, E. (2002). Reflective thinking in adulthood: Emergence, development, and variation. In J. Demick & C. Andreoletti (Eds.), *Handbook of adult development* (pp. 169–198). New York: Plenum Press.

Fischer, K. W., & Rose, S. P. (1994). Dynamic development of coordination of components of brain and behavior. In G. Dawson & K. W. Fischer (Eds.),

Human behavior and the developing brain (pp. 2–66). New York: Guilford Press.

Flavell, J. (1971). Stage related properties of cognitive development. *Cognitive Psychology, 2*(4), 421–453.

Glatfelter, M. (1982). Identity development, intellectual development, and their relationship in reentry women students (Doctoral dissertation, University of Minnesota, 1982). *Dissertation Abstracts International, 43*(11), 354A.

Glenn, D. D., & Eklund, S. S. (1991, April). *The relationship of graduate education and reflective judgment in older adults.* Paper presented at the annual convention of the American Education Research Association, Bloomington, IN.

Guthrie, V. L. (1996). *The relationship of intellectual development and tolerance for diversity among college students.* Unpublished doctoral dissertation, Bowling Green State University.

Harvey, L. J., Hunt, D., & Schroder, H. M. (1961). *Conceptual systems and personality organization.* New York: Wiley.

Herek, G. M. (1988). Heterosexuals' attitudes toward lesbians and gay men: Correlates and gender differences. *Journal of Sex Research, 25* (4), 451–477.

Hofer, B. K. (2002). *Personal epistemology: The psychology of beliefs about knowledge and knowing.* Mahwah, NJ: Lawrence Earlbaum.

Hofer, B. K. (Ed.). (2004). Personal epistemology: Paradigmatic approaches to understanding students' beliefs about knowledge and knowing [Special issue]. *Educational Psychologist, 39*(1).

Hofer, B. K., & Pintrich, P. R. (1997). The development of epistemological theories: Beliefs about knowledge and knowing and their relation to learning. *Review of Educational Research, 67*, 88–140.

Holliday, S. G., & Chandler, M. (1986). *Wisdom: Explorations in adult competence.* Basel, Switzerland: Karger.

Inhelder, B., & Piaget, J. (1958). *The growth of logical thinking from childhood to adolescence.* New York: Basic Books.

Jacobson, C. K. (1985). Resistance to affirmative action: Self-interest or racism. *Journal of Conflict Resolution, 29*, 306–329.

Jensen, L. L. (1998). *The role of need for cognition in the development of reflective judgment.* Unpublished doctoral dissertation, University of Denver.

Josephson, J. S. (1988). *Feminine orientation as a mediator of moral judgment.* Unpublished doctoral dissertation, University of Colorado.

Kegan, R. (1982). *The evolving self.* Cambridge, MA: Harvard University Press.

Kegan, R. (1994). *In over our heads: The mental demands of modern life.* Cambridge, MA: Harvard University Press.

Kelton, J., & Griffith, J. (1986). *Learning context questionnaire for assessing intellectual development.* Unpublished report, Davidson College.

King, J. W. (1986). *The relationship of age to reflective judgment levels of traditionally and nontraditionally aged associate degree nursing students and employed registered nurses.* Unpublished doctoral dissertation, University of Southern Illinois at Carbondale.

King, P. M. (1985). Choice-making in young adulthood: A developmental double-bind. *Counseling and Human Development, 18*, 1–12.

King, P. M. (1992). "How do we know? Why do we believe?" Learning to make reflective judgments. *Liberal Education, 78*(1), 2–9.

King, P. M., & Kitchener, K. S. (1993). The development of reflective thinking in the college years: The mixed results. In C. G. Schneider & W. S. Green (Eds.), *Strengthening the college major.* New Directions for Higher Education, no. 84 (pp. 25–42). San Francisco: Jossey-Bass.

King, P. M., & Kitchener, K. S. (1994). *Developing reflective judgment: Understanding and promoting intellectual growth and critical thinking in adolescents and adults.* San Francisco: Jossey-Bass.

King, P. M., & Kitchener, K. S. (2002). The reflective judgment model: Twenty years of epistemic cognition. In B. K. Hofer & P. R. Pintrich (Eds.), *Personal epistemology: The psychology of beliefs about knowledge and knowing* (pp. 37–61). Mahwah, NJ: Lawrence Erlbaum.

King, P. M., & Kitchener, K. S. (2004). Reflective judgment: Theory and research on the development of epistemic assumptions through adulthood. *Educational Psychologist, 39*(1), 5–18.

King, P. M., Kitchener, K. S., & Wood, P. K. (1994). Research on the reflective judgment model. In P. M. King & K. S. Kitchener (Eds.), *Developing reflective judgment: Understanding and promoting intellectual growth and critical thinking in adolescents and adults* (pp. 124–188). San Francisco: Jossey-Bass.

King, P. M., Kitchener, K. S., Wood, P. K., & Davison, M. L. (1989). Relationships across developmental domains: A longitudinal study of intellectual, moral and ego development. In M. L. Commons, J. D. Sinnott, F. A. Richards, & C. Armon (Eds.), *Adult development, Vol. 1: Comparisons and applications of developmental models* (pp. 57–72). New York: Praeger.

King, P. M., & Taylor, J. (1992). *Intellectual development and academic integration of African American students at Bowling Green State University.* Unpublished manuscript, Bowling Green State University. [Adaptation of King, P. M., Taylor, J., & Ottinger, D. (1989). *Intellectual development of black college students on a predominantly white campus.* Paper presented at the annual meeting of the Association for the Study of Higher Education, Atlanta, Georgia, 1989.]

King, P. M., Wood, P. K., & Mines, R. A. (1990). Critical thinking among college and graduate students. *Review of Higher Education, 13*(2), 167–186.

Kitchener, K. S. (1982). Human development and the college campus: Sequences and tasks. In. G. R. Hanson (Ed.), *Measuring student development.* New Directions for Student Services, no. 20 (pp. 17–45). San Francisco: Jossey-Bass

Kitchener, K. S. (1983). Cognition, metacognition and epistemic cognition: A three-level model of cognitive processing. *Human Development, 4,* 222–232.

Kitchener, K. S. (2002). Skills, tasks, and definitions: Discrepancies in the understanding and data on the development of folk epistemology. *New Ideas in Psychology, 20,* 309–328.

Kitchener, K. S., & Brenner, H. G. (1990). Wisdom and reflective judgment: Knowing in the face of uncertainty. In R. Sternberg (Ed.), *Wisdom: Its nature, origins, and development* (pp. 212–229). New York: Cambridge University Press.

Kitchener, K. S., & Fischer, K. (1990). A skill approach to the development of reflective thinking. In D. Kuhn (Vol. Ed.), *Contributions to human development: developmental perspectives on teaching and learning* (Vol. 21). Basel, Switzerland: Karger.

Kitchener, K. S., & King, P. M. (1981). Reflective judgment: Concepts of justification and their relationship to age and education. *Journal of Applied Developmental Psychology, 2*(2), 89–116.

Kitchener, K. S., Lynch, C. L., Fischer, K. W., & Wood, P. K. (1993). Developmental range of reflective judgment: The effect of contextual support and practice on developmental stage. *Developmental Psychology, 29*(5), 893–906.

Kitchener, K. S., & Wood, P. K. (1987). Development of concepts of justification in German university students. *International Journal of Behavioral Development, 10,* 171–185.

Kitchener, K. S., Wood, P. K., & Jensen, L. (1999, August). *Curricular, co-curricular, and institutional influences on real-world problem solving.* Paper presented at the annual meeting of the American Psychological Association, Boston, MA.

Kuhn, D. (1989). Children and adults as intuitive scientists. *Psychological Review, 96,* 674–689.

Lamborn, S. D., & Fischer, K. W. (1988). Optimal and functional levels in cognitive development: The individual's developmental range. *Newsletter of the International Society for the Study of Behavioral Development,* no. 2 (serial no. 14).

Lawson, J. M. (1980). The relationship between graduate education and the development of reflective judgment: A function of age or educational experience (Doctoral dissertation, University of Minnesota, 1980). *Dissertation Abstracts International, 47,* 402B.

Loevinger, J. (1976). *Ego development: Conceptions and theories.* San Francisco: Jossey-Bass.

Love, P. G., & Guthrie, V. L. (1999). *Understanding and applying cognitive development theory.* New Directions for Student Services, no. 88. San Francisco: Jossey-Bass.

McKinney, M. (1985). *Intellectual development of younger adolescents.* Unpublished doctoral dissertation, University of Denver.

Meacham, J. (1983). Wisdom and context of knowledge: Knowing that one doesn't know. In D. Kuhn & J. A. Meacham (Eds.), *On the development of develop-mental psychology* (pp. 111–134). Basel, Switzerland: Karger.

Mednick, M. T. (1989). On the politics of psychological constructs: Stop the bandwagon, I want to get off. *American Psychologist, 44*(8), 1118–1123.

Merriam, S. D. (2001). Andragogy and self-directed learning: Pillars of adult learning theory. *New Directions for Adult and Continuing Education, 89,* 3–13.

Perry, W. (1968). *Patterns of development in thought and values of students in a liberal arts college: A validation of a scheme.* Final Report, Project no. 5-0825, Contract no. SAE-8973. Washington, DC: Department of Health, Education, and Welfare.

Perry, W. (1970). *Forms of intellectual and ethical development in the college years: A scheme.* Troy, MO: Holt, Rinehart & Winston.

Piaget, J. (1970). Piaget's theory. In P. H. Mussen (Ed.), *Carmichael's manual of child psychology* (Vol. 1). New York: Wiley.

Polkosnik, M. C., & Winston, R. B. (1989). Relationships between students' intellectual and psychological development: An exploratory investigation. *Journal of College Student Development, 30,* 10–19.

Pratt, D. D. (1993). Andragogy after twenty-five years. *New Directions for Adult and Continuing Education, 57,* 22–33.

Rest, J. R. (1979). *Development in judging moral issues.* Minneapolis: University of Minnesota Press.

Sakalys, J. (1984). Effects of an undergraduate research course on cognitive development. *Nursing Research, 33,* 290–295.

Samson, A. W. (1999). *Latino college students and reflective judgment.* Unpublished doctoral dissertation, University of Denver.

Schmidt, J. A. (1985). Older and wiser? A longitudinal study of the impact of college on intellectual development. *Journal of College Student Personnel, 26,* 388–394.

Shoff, S. P. (1979). The significance of age, sex, and type of education on the development of reasoning in adults (Doctoral dissertation, University of Utah, 1979). *Dissertation Abstracts International, 40,* 3910A.

Strange, C. C., & King, P. M. (1981). Intellectual development and its relationship to maturation during the college years. *Journal of Applied Developmental Psychology, 2,* 281–295.

Taylor, K., Marienau, C., & Fiddler, M. (2000). *Developing adult learners: Strategies for teachers and trainers.* San Francisco: Jossey-Bass.

Thompson, S. S. (1995). *Techniques for assessing general education outcomes: The natural sciences core at the University of Denver.* Unpublished doctoral dissertation, University of Denver.

Van Tine, N. B. (1990). The development of reflective judgment in adolescents (Doctoral dissertation, University of Denver, 1990). *Dissertation Abstracts International, 51,* 2659.

Welfel, E. R. (1982). The development of reflective judgment: Implications for career counseling of college students. *Personnel and Guidance Journal, 61*(1), 17–21.

Welfel, E. R., & Davison, M. L. (1986). How students make judgments: Do educational level and academic major make a difference? *Journal of College Student Personnel, 23,* 490–497.

Wood, P. K. (1993). *Context and development of reflective thinking: A secondary analysis of the structure of individual differences.* Unpublished manuscript, University of Missouri, Columbia.

Wood, P. K. (1997). A secondary analysis of claims regarding the Reflective Judgment Interview: Internal consistency, sequentiality and intra-individual differences in ill-structured problem solving. In J. C. Smart (Ed.), *Higher education: Handbook of theory and research* (Vol. 12, pp. 243–312). Edison, NJ: Agathon Press.

Wood, P. K., Kitchener, K. S., & Jensen, L. (2002). Considerations in the design and evaluation of a paper-and-pencil measure of epistemic cognition. In B. K. Hofer & P. R. Pintrich (Eds.), *Personal epistemology: The psychology of beliefs about knowledge and knowing* (pp. 277–294). Mahwah, NJ: Lawrence Erlbaum.

Chapter 5

Intellectual Development Across Adulthood

K. Warner Schaie and Faika A. K. Zanjani

This chapter provides readers with a comprehensive view of intellectual development in adulthood by reviewing principles and theories as well as research findings on this topic. The chapter begins with definitions and theories of intelligence and cognition and later examines both the course and the antecedents of intellectual development. We also address issues related to the modifiability of adult cognitive development via cognitive interventions. A brief conclusion follows.

INTELLIGENCE AND COGNITION: PRINCIPLES AND DEFINITIONS

Before describing the theoretical and empirical findings on intellectual development in adults, we begin by defining the construct of intelligence. Intelligence continues to be used to categorize populations of individuals into groups of varying levels of competence. Furthermore, intelligence has served as an im-

portant component in the development of societal institutions, such as the educational system and the military, among others. Although levels of competence and social applications of intelligence serve as meaningful measures of intelligence, this chapter focuses on how intellectual development unfolds during the adult life span, including descriptions of the dynamic system of life span intellect and emphasizing individual differences in intellectual development. We emphasize cognitive products rather than the cognitive mechanisms treated in the information-processing context (e.g., Rybash, Hoyer, & Roodin, 1986). Measurement of intelligence has traditionally been concerned with operationalizing laboratory tasks that are thought to represent intelligent behaviors in the real world. As Binet and Simon (1905) already argued, "To judge well, to comprehend well, to reason well, these are the essentials of intelligence. A person may be a moron or an imbecile if he lacks judgment; but with judgment he could not be either" (p. 106).

There appears to be a natural hierarchy in the study of intelligence leading from information processing through the products measured in tests of intelligence to practical or everyday intelligence (e.g., Baltes, 1987; Sternberg & Berg, 1987, Willis & Schaie, 1993). The products or intellectual skills that characterize psychometric intelligence are likely to represent the most appropriate level for the direct prediction of life outcomes (Willis & Schaie, 1993) and capability of industrial work and maintenance of social productivity (see Avolio, 1991; Rabbitt, 1991; Welford, 1992). The entire age span from young adulthood to advanced old age must be included when examining intellectual development because it is not enough to simply compare young and old adults to be able to obtain a comprehensive depiction of intellectual development in adulthood. Instead, we need to know the life span trajectory of individual intellectual paths to ascertain the peaks of performance as well as the rate and pattern of improvement and decline (see Schaie, 1994).

THEORIES OF INTELLIGENCE IN THE STUDY OF ADULT DEVELOPMENT

At least four influential theoretical positions have informed empirical research on intelligence as products or performance indices. The earliest theoretical influence comes from Sir Charles Spearman's work (1904). He suggested that a general dimension of intelligence, known as (g), underlies all purposeful intellectual products. All other components of such products were viewed as task or item specific(s). Spearman's view provided the theoretical foundation for the family of assessment devices that originated from the work of Binet and Simon (1905). The concept of a single general form of intelligence may be more appropriate in childhood when scholastic aptitude represents an isomorphic and unidimensional validity criterion. However, this view is not very useful beyond adolescence because of the lack of a unidimensional criteria such as scholastic aptitude and also because of the convincing empirical evidence supporting the idea of multiple dimensions of intelligence with unique trajectories (see Horn, 1982; Schaie, 1994, 1996).

The first influential multidimensional theory was developed by E. L. Thorndike. Thorndike proposed different dimensions of intelligence, which he argued would display similar levels of performance within individuals. Thorndike also suggested that all categories of intelligence possessed three attributes: power, speed, and level (see Thorndike & Woodworth, 1901). This approach informed Wechsler's model (see Matarazzo, 1972), which specified 11 distinct scales derived from clinical observation and earlier mental tests that were combined into two broad dimensions: verbal intelligence and performance (nonverbal-manipulative) intelligence. These dimensions were combined to form a total IQ.

The Wechsler scales have had important applications in the clinical assessment of adults with psychopathology. Although the Weschsler verbal and performance scales are highly reliable in older persons, the difference between the two (often used as a rough estimate for age decline) is far less reliable (Snow, Tierney, Zorzitto, Fisher, & Reid, 1989). A major limitation of the Wechsler scales for research on intellectual aging has been the fact that the factorial structure of some of the individual scales does not remain invariant across age (McArdle & Prescott, 1992; Meredith, 1993; Sands, Terry, & Meredith, 1989). Consequently, studies of intellectual aging in community-dwelling populations have used subsets of primary mental abilities (see Cunningham, 1987; Hultsch, Hertzog, Small, McDonald-Miszlak, & Dixon, 1992; Schaie, 1990a).

A simpler model using multiple dimensions of intelligence was identified by L. L. Thurstone (1938) in his classic studies and was later expanded by Guilford (1967). The primary mental abilities described by Thurstone have formed the basis of intellectual research in the Seattle Longitudinal Study (SLS), which has used measurement instruments developed by Thurstone and Thurstone (1949) and by the Educational Testing Service (Ekstrom, French, Harman, & Derman, 1976) and based on the work of Thurstone and of Guilford (1967), as well as parallel forms developed in the SLS laboratory (Schaie, 1996).

Originally, research on primary mental abilities was conducted with children (Thurstone, 1938). Subsequent to research with children, there have been numerous studies using the factorial structure of various subsets of the primary mental abilities in adults. Second-order factor analyses of the primary mental abilities have identified several higher order dimensions, including those of fluid intelligence (applied to novel/educative tasks) and crystallized intelligence (applied to acculturated information), which was popularized by Cattell and Horn (e.g., Carroll, 1993; Cunningham, 1987; Horn & Hofer, 1992; Schaie, Willis, Hertzog, & Schulenberg, 1987; Schaie, Willis, Jay, & Chipuer, 1989).

The introduction of Piagetian thought into American psychology led some investigators to consider the application of Piagetian methods to adult development. This Genevan approach, however, has contributed only sparsely to the study of adult cognition (but see Alexander & Langer, 1990; Commons, Sinnott, Richards, & Armon, 1989; Kuhn, 1992; Labouvie-Vief, 1992; Schaie, 1977/78).

Cutting across these theoretical positions, there have also been distinct secular trends in relative emphases on different aspects of adult intelligence. Woodruff-Pak (1989) identified four stages describing the developmental trend of research on intellect. The first stage, prominent until the mid-1950s, was concerned with identifying steep and apparently inevitable age-related decline. During the 1950s and 1960s, a second stage emerged with evidence of stability as well as decline. Subsequent discoveries of external social and experiential effects influencing cohort differences in ability levels led to the third stage, which began in the 1970s and was dominated by attempts to manipulate age differences. The fourth and final stage grew from the influence of successful demonstrations of the modifiability of intellectual performance, which has led investigators to expand definitions of intelligence and explore new methods of measurement (Willis & Schaie, 1999b).

THE ROLE OF LONGITUDINAL STUDIES

The study of adult intelligence presents us with two related but nevertheless distinct objectives: describing age differences and describing change within individuals. Age comparative studies attempt to determine whether adults at different age levels also differ in intellectual performance at a particular moment in historical time, for which cross-sectional methods will suffice. This approach presents methodological problems in that cross-sectional research does not directly address how intelligence changes within individuals, nor will such data reveal the antecedents necessary to identify individual differences in the course of adult development. To solve this problem, researchers in the United States and Europe have conducted longitudinal studies to gather data on substantial age ranges over time (e.g., Busse, 1993; Costa & McCrae, 1993; Cunningham & Owens, 1983; Eichorn, Clausen, Haan, Honzik, & Mussen, 1981; Jarvik & Bank, 1983; Steen & Djurfeldt, 1993; for a review see Schaie & Hofer, 2001). Initiation of longitudinal studies represents an important new addition to the study of adult intellectual development. We hope we will soon have better information on age changes from research generated in the 1990s (e.g., Baltes, Mayer, Helmchen, & Steinhagen-Thiessen, 1993; Poon, Sweaney, Clayton, & Merriam, 1992).

OBSERVED AND LATENT VARIABLES

Most research on intelligence concerns itself not so much with age changes or differences in specific measures but rather with understanding the effects of intellectual aging on the underlying ability dimensions. Within the primary mental ability framework, the question has been raised whether specific abilities or second-order constructs are of greater importance. For adult development, however, assessment would seem to be optimal at the primary level because the role of general intelligence (g) becomes less central as expertise is developed in specific skills and because most age-related change in cognitive processes requires more than a single component to explain individual differences (Salthouse, 1988b, 1992).

Aging patterns differ between the various primary mental abilities (Schaie, 1996; Schaie & Willis, 1993) and the various second-order ability factors (Horn & Hofer, 1992). Measures of intellectual functioning are not always factorially invariant across age and time. Although the factor structure of abilities may be fairly stable across age, several studies reported differences in factor covariances, particularly in the regression of the observed marker variables on the factors (see Hertzog, 1987; Horn & McArdle, 1992; Schaie, Maitland, Willis, & Intrieri, 1998; Schaie et al., 1989). Although most factor scores based on multiple markers provide valid comparisons across age, the same cannot be said for individual scales whose regression on the given ability factor may vary markedly from young adulthood into old age.

THE COURSE OF ADULT INTELLECTUAL DEVELOPMENT

In this section, we review substantial research conclusions from the current literature. We gathered information from a broad array of current studies, with particular emphasis on data derived from the SLS. The following section highlights findings from the SLS and traces the course of adult intellectual development as understood from the data.

Population Parameters in Adult Intellectual Aging

Intellectual aging as a multidimensional process in normal community-dwelling populations has been studied very intensively in the SLS (Schaie, 1993, 1994, 1996, 2005). The principal variables in this study, which has extended thus far over a 45-year period, were five measures of psychological competence known as *primary mental abilities* (Schaie, 1985; Thurstone & Thurstone, 1949): verbal meaning, space, reasoning, number, and word fluency (the ability to recall words according to a lexical rule). Over the last three SLS test occasions, six multiple-marked abilities were assessed at the factor level: inductive reasoning, spatial orientation, perceptual speed, nu-

meric facility, verbal comprehension, and verbal memory.

Various combinations of the primary mental abilities are represented in all meaningful activities of a person's daily living and work (Willis, Jay, Diehl, & Marsiske, 1992; Willis & Schaie, 1986a, 1994a). The SLS has followed large numbers of individuals over each 7-year interval over the age range from 25 to 88 years. On average, there is gain until the late thirties or early forties are reached, and then there is stability until the mid-fifties or early sixties. Beginning with the late sixties, however, seven-year decrements are statistically significant throughout. These data suggest that average decline in psychological competence may begin for some as early as the mid-fifties, but that early decrement is of small magnitude until the mid-seventies. Because of the modest gains from young adulthood to middle age, longitudinal comparisons from a young adult base (age 25) show significant cumulative decline only by the mid-seventies.

At the factor level, longitudinal decline is noted by the mid-fifties for perceptual speed and numeric ability, by the late sixties for inductive reasoning and spatial orientation, and by the late seventies for verbal ability and verbal memory. Figures 5.1 and 5.2 show longitudinal gradients for five observed mental abilities and six derived ability factors.

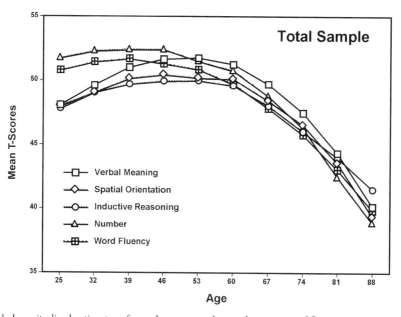

FIGURE 5.1 Longitudinal estimates of age changes on observed measures of five primary mental abilities

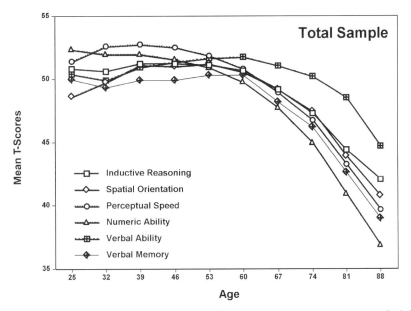

FIGURE 5.2 Longitudinal estimates of age changes in factor scores on six primary mental abilities at the latent construct level.

Several recent short-term longitudinal studies confirm the finding that cognitive functions due to age change is a slow process. At least two major studies have found virtual stability over a three-year period (Hultsch et al., 1992; Zelinski, Gilewski, & Schaie, 1993). Arbuckle, Maag, Pushkar, and Chaikelson (1998) examined the intellectual development for Canadian World War II veterans over a 45-year period from World War II to the 1990s. They found that performance declined for picture completion, picture anomalies, paper formboard, verbal analogies, and arithmetic. However, there was improvement in vocabulary performance. The correlations between the extreme time points indicated stability of individual differences in intelligence over the 45 years, demonstrating relative intellectual change and showing a somewhat positive view of intellectual aging.

Substantial intellectual changes within individuals occur for most persons only late in life and tend to occur earliest for those abilities that were less central to the individuals' life experiences and thus perhaps less practiced. Nevertheless, in our community-based studies we found that virtually everyone had declined modestly on at least one of five mental abilities by age 60. But none of the study participants had declined on all five abilities even by age 88 (Schaie, 1989a).

But what about findings from age comparative (cross-sectional) studies of intellectual performance in which young and old adults are compared at a single point in time? Due to substantial cohort differences (see later discussion), these studies show far greater age differences than do longitudinal data. Typically, ages of peak performance occur earlier (for later born cohorts). By the early fifties, there are modest age differences for some abilities from peak performance. By 60, most dimensions of intelligence show changes. Because of the slowing in the rate of positive cohort differences, age different profiles have begun to converge somewhat more with the age change data from longitudinal studies. Figure 5.3 shows age difference patterns from the SLS over the age range 25–81 years in 1956 and 1998. As can be seen, both peak performance and onset of decline seem to be shifting to later ages for most variables.

Recent work on the Wechsler Adult Intelligence Scale (WAIS) with data sets based on normal individuals has shifted to approaches that involve latent variable models (see Horn & McArdle, 1992; McArdle & Prescott, 1992; Millsap & Meredith, 1992; Rott, 1993). Alternatively, analyses have been conducted at the item level. An example of the latter approach is a study by Sands et al. (1989) of two cohorts spanning the age range 18–61 years. Consistent improvement in performance was found between the ages of 18 and

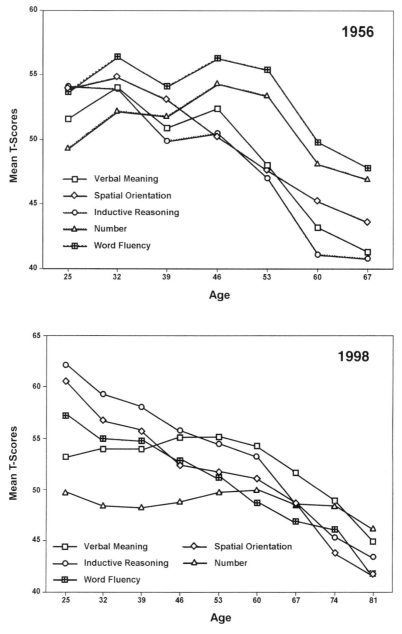

FIGURE 5.3 Cross-sectional age differences on five primary mental abilities for samples tested in 1956 and 1998.

40 and between 18 and 54. Between ages 40 and 61 improvement was found for the information, comprehension, vocabulary subtest; mixed change (gain on the easy items and decline on the difficult items) on picture completion; and decline on digit symbol and block design (with decline only for the most difficult items of the latter tests).

Individual Differences in Level and Rate of Change

Is decline in psychological competence a global or highly specific event? SLS data graphed in figure 5.4 show cumulative proportions by age of participants whose level of cognitive functioning had declined on

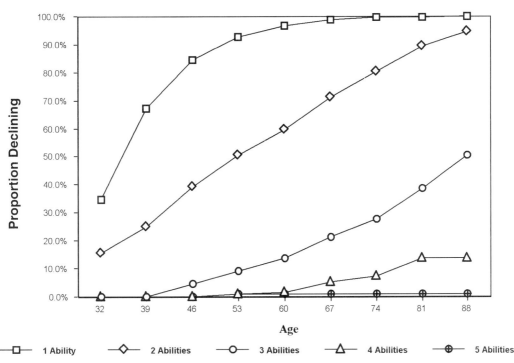

FIGURE 5.4 Cumulative proportion by age of individuals who show significant decline on one or more primary mental abilities.

one or more abilities. Although by age 60 virtually every participant had declined on one ability, few individuals showed global decline. Few showed universal decline on all abilities monitored, even by the eighties. Optimization of cognitive functioning in old age may well involve selective maintenance of some abilities but not others (see Baltes & Baltes, 1990). Moreover, such optimization seems to be a highly individualized phenomenon (see Rabbitt, 1993; Schaie, 1989a, 1990b).

Despite these encouraging data, it is clear that significant reductions in psychological competence occur in most people by ages 80 and 90. However, even at such advanced ages, many persons in familiar circumstances can expect competent behavior. Much of the observed loss occurs in highly challenging, complex, or stressful situations that require activation of reserve capacities (see Baltes, 1993; Raykov, 1989). The belief that the more able are also more resistant to intellectual decline remains generally unsupported (see Christensen & Henderson, 1991). But those who

start out at high levels remain advantaged even after suffering some decline.

Why Do Cohort Effects Matter?

There have been marked generational shifts in levels of performance on tests of mental abilities (Schaie, 1989b, 1996; Willis, 1989a). Empirical findings suggest that later-born cohorts are generally advanced when compared with earlier cohorts at the same age. The phenomenon has been explained by increased educational opportunities and improved lifestyles. Nutrition and mastery over childhood diseases have enabled successive generations to reach ever higher ability asymptotes, similar to the observed secular trends of improvement for anthropometrics and other biological markers (Shock et al., 1984). Although linear trends have been found for some variables, there seems to be contrary evidence that such trends may have been time limited, domain explicit, or even variable specific (see Schaie, 1990c; Willis, 1989a).

Accurate descriptions of patterns of cohort change in mental ability are important because they provide the foundation for better understanding of how intellectual productivity and competence shift over time in our society. These data also help us understand how cohort differences in performance can lead to erroneous conclusions from age-comparative cross-sectional studies (see Schaie, 1988). The changing demographic composition of the population makes it necessary to assess differences in performance level to comparable ages for individuals from eras characterized by differential fertility rates (e.g., contrasts of the pre–Baby Boom, Baby Boom, Baby Bust generations). Cohort shifts in intellect at older ages, moreover, are directly relevant to policy considerations regarding the maintenance of a competent workforce that will contain increasing proportions of old workers. Although a mandatory retirement age has become a relic of a biased past, an unforeseen consequence may be dependency ratios that require people to work longer and to greater ages than previously contemplated. Cohort trends over time have been reported that are likely to influence the proportions of individuals of advanced age who will remain capable of sig-

nificant late-life accomplishments; these trends may reflect the ability of older individuals to take advantage of recent technological developments (Schaie, 1989a, 2005; Willis, 1989a).

Figure 5.5 shows cohort gradients for the same abilities for which age trends were just given. The negative shift in some abilities for more recent cohorts may make many older persons appear to be more competitive with their younger peers than has been true in the past. Because of the recent leveling off of cohort differences for some abilities and the curvilinear nature of cohort differences for others, it may be expected that the large ability differences observed between young and old adults will be much reduced in the future. For numerical skill, in particular, we may expect a period of time when older adults will be advantaged as compared to younger persons. Conversely, the level reached by recent cohorts in educational attainment and positive lifestyles may well be close to the limits possible within our society's resources and structures. The positive shifts in potential, experienced in early old age by successive cohorts (Schaie, 1990b) may therefore come to a halt by the middle of this century. Does this account for the

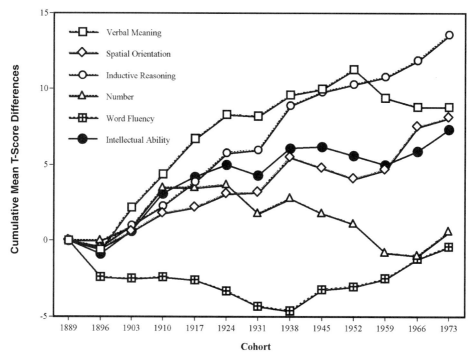

FIGURE 5.5 Cohort gradients showing cumulative cohort difference on five primary mental abilities for cohorts born in 1889 to 1973.

diversity in our population and the disparity among educational attainment in these populations?

Although cohort differences in intelligence have generally been studied in random population samples, this body of literature has recently been supplemented in a study of generational differences in 531 adult parent-offspring pairs. Significant within-family cohort ability differences were found in favor of the offspring generation in about the same magnitude as shown in the previous studies, but generational differences became smaller for more recently born parent-offspring pairs (Schaie, Plomin, Willis, Gruber-Baldini, & Dutta, 1992).

Is the Structure of Intelligence Invariant Across Adulthood?

Much attention has been given to age changes and differences in level of performance, but another fundamental question is whether the structure of intelligence remains constant across adulthood. Heinz Werner (1948) was an early proponent of a differentiation-dedifferentiation hypothesis, which suggested differentiation of dimensions of human behavior during the growth stage and eventual dedifferentiation or reintegration as individuals aged. Reinert (1970) extended this hypothesis to intellectual development.

The introduction of confirmatory factor analysis permitted testing of the hypothesis by designing studies that formally assess factorial invariance across age (see Alwin, 1988; Horn & McArdle, 1992; Millsap & Meredith, 1992). The same numbers of dimensions generally suffice to describe the ability domains across adulthood, but the relative importance of observed measures as estimates of the underlying latent constructs changes across age. In the SLS work, we have found configural invariance across adulthood in the eighties in cross-sectional data but could not accept complete metric invariance (Schaie et al., 1989). This means that in age-comparative studies one should not compare means for observed variables, but should instead compare estimated factor scores on the latent constructs. In the SLS we conducted longitudinal within-cohort factor analyses and found that metric invariance can be demonstrated over seven years, except for participants in their eighties (Schaie, 1994, 1996). Later weak factor invariance and configural invariance was demonstrated for all cohorts (Schaie et al., 1998). Finally, gender equivalence in

covariance structures across the adult life span and within separate age groups was demonstrated (Maitland, Intrieri, Schaie, & Willis, 2000).

ANTECEDENTS OF DIFFERENTIAL AGE CHANGES IN ADULT INTELLECTUAL DEVELOPMENT

Why is it that some maintain high levels of intellectual functioning into advanced old age whereas others tend to decline early? Here, we make a distinction between the effects of normal and pathological aging, as well as consider both the impact of behavioral slowing and the effects of social context and personality differences.

Normal and Pathological Aging

There are, of course, neurological diseases that can transform normal development into pathological development, resulting in diminished cognitive performance (Mahoney, 2003; Shimada, Meguro, Inagaki, Ishizaki, & Yamadori, 2001). However, neurological diseases are not the only illnesses associated with negative intellectual effects. Better health has been shown to predict less cognitive decline (Arbuckle et al., 1998). Many investigators have therefore attempted to control for or measure the impact of acute or chronic disease on age-related diseases and age-related decline in intellectual functioning (see Anstey, Stankov, & Lord, 1993). Simple questionnaires on subjective health status often yield fairly strong relationships with levels of cognitive functioning (see Field, Schaie, & Leino, 1988; Hultsch et al., 1993; Perlmutter & Nyquist, 1990). More ambitious efforts have involved intense studies of health history data or the inclusion of partial or complete medical workups in some studies of intellectual development.

Cognitive performance can be challenged during the onset of diseases as well as by treatments used to control diseases (Tabbarah, Crimmins, & Seeman, 2002). Stroke and Alzheimer's disease/dementia have direct biological consequences causing impairment in brain functioning; hence there are negative consequences for cognitive ability (Klimkowicz, Dziedzic, Slowik, & Szczudlik, 2002; Kukull et al., 1994). However, there also appear to be negative cognitive consequences from diseases that do not directly affect the brain. For example, there is evidence that heart disease (Almeida & Flicker, 2001; Almeida & Tamai,

2001; Rabbitt et al., 2002; Seeman, McEwen, Rowe, & Singer, 2001), chronic obstructive pulmonary disease (Fioravanti, Nacca, Amati, Buckley, & Bisetti, 1995; Incalzi et al., 1993), diabetes (Jackson-Guilford, Leander, & Nisenbaum, 2000; McCarthy, Lindgren, Mengeling, Tsalikian, & Engvall, 2002), and pneumonia (Iwamoto et al., 2000; Medina-Walpole & Mc-Cormick, 1998) can all negatively affect cognitive performance.

Impact of Cardiovascular Disease

It seems reasonable to suspect that the presence or absence of cardiovascular disease might be related to the rate of intellectual aging. This possible relationship has been investigated in the Duke Longitudinal Study (Manton, Siegler, & Woodbury, 1986; Palmor, Busse, Maddox, Nowlin, & Siegler, 1985) and in the SLS. In the latter, it was found that individuals who were at risk of cardiovascular disease tended to decline earlier on average on all mental abilities studied than did individuals not so affected (see Gruber-Baldini, 1991; Schaie, 1996, 2005). Those who declined have significantly greater numbers of illness diagnoses, as well as clinic visits for cardiovascular disease.

The effects of hypertension, however, are far more complicated than those of other cardiovascular conditions. When distinctions are made between moderate or medically controlled and severe hypertension, it is often found that mild hypertension may actually have positive effects on intellectual functioning (e.g., Elias, Elias, & Elias, 1990; Sands & Meredith, 1992; Schultz, Elias, Robbins, & Streeten, 1989).

Impact of Other Chronic Diseases

Other chronic diseases that affect maintenance of intellectual functioning include arthritis, neoplasms (tumors), osteoporosis, and sensory deficits. In one study of the very old, visual and hearing deficits accounted for almost half of the total individual differences variance and for more than 90% of the age-related portion of those differences (Lindenberger & Baltes, 1994).

Data from the SLS suggest that arthritics have lower functioning and greater decline on verbal meaning, spatial orientation, and inductive reasoning. When malignant and benign neoplasms are distinguished, persons with benign neoplasms (other than skin tumors) were found to have earlier onset of intellectual decline but less overall decline. Persons with malignant neoplasms and benign skin neoplasms have indirect negative influences on performance (through reduced activity). Results of the influence of neoplasms on cognition might be specific to type of tumor (malignant versus nonmalignant) as well as location (skin, bone, etc.). Osteoporosis and hip fractures were predictive of earlier decline on word fluency. Hearing impairment was associated with increased risk of experiencing verbal meaning decline but was associated with better performance and later decline on space (Gruber-Baldini, 1991; Schaie, 2005).

Impact of Medical Treatment

It is not always the biological consequences of the disease that lead to impairment in cognitive abilities. Negative cognitive effects may also result from treatments used in attempts to control the disease. Several studies have shown that treatments of heart disease (Stanley et al., 2002), cancer treatments (Abayomi, 2002; Armstrong et al., 2002; Green et al., 2002), and diabetes treatments (Drexler & Roberston, 2001) can adversely affect cognitive performance. It has been hypothesized that some of the negative cognitive effects seen following treatment may be due to fatigue or limited biological viability, redistribution of physical resources, or simply biological changes that produced unexpected cognitive side effects.

The relationship between disease and intellectual functioning, however, should not be overinterpreted. This relationship may be biased by the fact that the more able are also more likely to engage in appropriate health maintenance behavior, modestly supported in SLS (Maier, 1995; Zanjani, 2002). They also tend to seek competent help earlier and are therefore more likely to postpone the onset or the more disabling stages of chronic disease (Royak-Schaler & Alt, 1994). The relationship between disease and cognitive ability may also be a function of the relationship between time to death and cognitive trajectories. There has been some evidence that distance from death may serve as one of determinants of cognitive decline. Conversely, significant declines in cognitive functioning may be a risk factor for mortality (Bosworth, Schaie, & Willis, 1999; Bosworth, Schaie, Willis, & Siegler, 1999). Thus, cognitive decline in advanced old age may simply be a consequence of coming closer to one's demise.

Behavioral Slowing and Intellectual Aging

It is quite evident that the slowing of reaction time with age adversely affects performance on tests of intellectual abilities. Many questions remain, however, as to whether the behavioral slowing involves a single or multiple mechanisms (see Salthouse, 1988a, 1993c, 1994). Slowing of performance seems to have differential effects depending not only on the particular cognitive processes or abilities involved but also on the format used in the presentation of test materials (Hertzog, 1989). Other factors include the level of familiarity, imageability, primacy, and recent exposure to stimuli (Kennet, McGuire, Willis, & Schaie, 2000). Although group data on age-related changes in reaction time or perceptual speed often take linear form, analyses of individual differences tend to reveal individual patterns of change that follow a stair-step pattern (Schaie, 1989b). Birren argued long ago that loss in speed of performance should be seen as a species-specific characteristic of normal aging and concluded that if one cannot think quickly, one cannot think well (Birren & Botwinick, 1951; Birren & Fisher, 1992). Stankov (1988), moreover, showed that speed of search is related to efficient processing of information. When statistical adjustments were made for the effects of individual differences in attention, age differences in fluid abilities were markedly reduced, whereas crystallized abilities tended to show increases into later life.

A number of studies have investigated the specific impact of level of performance on measures of perceptual speed. A typical method has been to partial out perceptual speed from the correlations between age and intellectual performance. Most studies report that age differences are markedly reduced or completely eliminated after adjustments for perceptual speed (Hertzog, 1989; Lindenberger, Mayr, & Kliegl, 1993; Salthouse, 1993c; Schaie, 1989b). Other possible adjustments of speed-mediated age differences in intelligence have involved measures of psychomotor speed (see Hertzog, 1989; Schaie & Willis, 1991).

Some argue that cognitive decline is a diminution of resources of which speed of behavior is a prime component (Salthouse, 1988b). But other cognitive mechanisms may also be implicated. For example, reduction in the efficiency of verbal memory occurring with increasing age would reduce the preservation of information during processing of any complex cognitive task (Salthouse, 1993a). Considerable amounts of cognitive load imposed by time-based prospective memory tasks have been found to disproportionately penalize older adults (Martin & Schumann-Hengsteler, 2001). DeLuca et al. (2003) claimed that executive skills may also be vulnerable to negative age changes that can cause declines in cognitive performance. On the other hand, superior resources, such as crystallized knowledge, might reduce age differences on verbal tasks even when older participants display slower processing speed (Salthouse, 1993b).

Social Context and Intellectual Aging

Intellectual aging occurs within a social context. Hence, a number of demographic dimensions have been identified that tend to affect the rate of cognitive decline (see Schaie, 1994; Willis, 1989a). Because of different socialization patterns, gender roles can result in differential performance levels on certain mental abilities. On the primary mental abilities, women consistently excel over men on reasoning and verbal skills, whereas men do better on spatial skills (Schaie, 1996). On the WAIS, adult gender differences have been found to favor men on arithmetic, information, and block design, with women excelling on digit symbol (Kaufman, Kaufman-Packer, McLean, & Reynolds, 1991). Because of women's greater life expectancy, men are always closer to death at any given age. Thus at comparable advanced ages, women tend to perform better cognitively. Gender differences in rates of decline, moreover, are greater for those skills in which each gender excels in young adulthood (Feingold, 1993; Schaie, 1996).

Not only are high levels of education implicated in slower rates of intellectual decline (Schaie, 1989a), but lengthy marriage to a well-educated and intelligent spouse has also been identified as a positive risk factor (Gruber & Schaie, 1986). There has been some indication that support from a partner may enhance problem-solving efforts (Dixon & Gould, 1998; Schaie & Willis, 2000). High occupational status and its more subtle aspects (such as high workplace complexity) are positive predictors for maintenance of intellectual functioning into old age (DeFrias & Schaie, 2001; Dutta, 1992; Miller, Slomczynski, & Kohn, 1987; Schooler, 1987). Moreover, retirement seems to have favorable cognitive sequelae for those retiring from routinized jobs but accelerates decrement for those retiring from highly complex jobs.

Higher social class has also been found to compensate for some of the negative effects of cognitive risk factors (Jefferis, Power, & Hertzman, 2002). Other contextual variables that have favorable impact on cognitive aging include intact marriages, exposure to stimulating environments, and the use of cultural and educational resources throughout adulthood (Schaie, 1984). Lifestyle variables such as those already mentioned were also identified as positive risk factors in the Boston Normative Aging study (Jones, Albert, Duffy, & Hyde, 1991), and in studies of memory functioning in older Canadian men (Arbuckle, Gold, Andres, Schwartzman, & Chaikelson, 1992). Arbuckle et al. (1998) also found that individuals with a more engaged lifestyle show less intellectual decline.

Personality, Cognitive Styles, Motivation, and Expertise

Certain personality traits, cognitive styles, motivation, and expertise levels have also been found to affect maintenance of intellectual functioning. For the most part, research on personality traits and cognitive ability have used these two constructs simultaneously as predictors of noncognitive performance outcomes (Kickul & Neuman, 2000; LePine, 2003). However, the existing research relating personality traits and cognitive performance has indicated a modest relationship between the two in both cross-sectional and longitudinal research. For example, Costa, Fozard, McCrae, and Bosse (1976) found that subjects high in anxiety scored lower on their General Aptitude Test Battery, and those scoring high on openness to experience and introversion had mixed scores on the battery. However, they had also concluded that cross-sectional age differences in cognitive performance were not mediated by personality. On the other hand, Arbuckle, Gold, and Andres (1986) found that individual differences in memory performance were better accounted for by education, intellectual activity, extroversion, and neuroticism than by age. There have also been some indications for abnormally high rates of trait impulsivity and aggression being associated with lower IQs (Dolan & Anderson, 2002).

Recently, in the SLS, a relationship between personality traits and cognitive performance was also found (Schaie, Willis, & Caskie, 2004). The study examined the relationships between cognitive performance and 13-factor personality model and the NEO trait personality model (Costa & McCrae, 1992).

They found several significant concurrent relationships between inductive reasoning, spatial orientation, perceptual speed, numeric facility, verbal comprehension, and verbal memory with neuroticism, extraversion, openness, agreeableness, and conscientiousness. Also, examining the longitudinal relationship between 13-factor personality scores and cognitive abilities showed that personality consistently predicted cognitive performance over as long as a 35-year lag between personality assessment and cognitive ability.

There seems to be a modest positive relationship between self-efficacy and intellectual functioning, although it remains to be resolved whether this relationship is unidirectional or reciprocal (Dittmann-Kohli, Lachman, Kliegl, & Baltes, 1991; Grover & Hertzog, 1991; Lachman & Leff, 1989). Intellectual performance, for example, may be affected by the participants' self-appraisal of their age changes in performance. This question has been studied empirically by assessing perceived change in performance with objectively measured change (Schaie, Willis, & O'Hanlon, 1994). Study participants were categorized as those who maintained earlier performance level, significantly increased their performance, or experienced decline in their performance. A typology linking actual and perceived change in performance was created to express personality differences. Realists were identified as those who accurately estimated change in their performance. Optimists overestimated positive change. Pessimists overestimated negative change. The majority of participants made realistic appraisals for changes in intellectual functioning. However, women were more likely to be pessimists on spatial orientation than men. Older individuals were more likely to be pessimists on verbal meaning and inductive reasoning abilities but tended to be realists on number ability compared to younger participants. By contrast, Rabbitt and Abson (1991) found that their participants failed to predict objective performance on simple memory tasks, although their predictions were related to the Beck Depression Inventory. They suggested that their participants rated their memory relative to reduced memory requirements in their current environment. In the SLS, further exploration in this area has concluded that the relationship between congruence type and actual performance varies by ability, implying that individual perceptions do not uniformly affect individual cognitive performance across abilities (Roth, Schaie, & Willis, 2001; Schaie, Willis, & Caskie, 2004).

Levels of expertise, exposure, and interest in specific domains have been explored as indicators for unique intellectual development. Reeve and Hakle (2000) found a positive relationship between individual interest and knowledge, indicating that personal motivation in certain tasks can assist in the maintenance of certain abilities. Hershey, Jacobs-Lawson, and Walsh (2003) found that increases in task-specific experiences, specifically in financial investment problems, lead to increases in patterns of information selection and search consistency for most adults across the life span. However, this did not hold true for untrained older adults, indicating a possibility for limited capacity in the ability to attain new expertise after a certain age.

Personality and cognitive styles are salient indicators for intellectual development. For example, individuals with higher cognitive levels have been found to use a wider array of thinking styles compared to individuals who display lower cognitive levels (Zhang, 2002). LePage-Lees (1997) has found that despite a disadvantaged upbringing, individuals with high levels of emotional intelligence have been found to display positive intellectual development.

Rigid and flexible personality characteristics have been identified as antecedents for intellectual development. Longitudinal studies suggest that one's lifelong standing on flexible behaviors is maintained for most persons into their seventies, whereas on average, people develop more rigid attitudes by the early sixties (see Schaie, 1996). It has also been shown that those with flexible attitudes in midlife tend to experience less decline in psychological competence with advancing age than those who were observed to be fairly rigid at that life stage (Schaie, 1984, 1996). These studies also concluded that high levels of motor-cognitive flexibility at the young-old stage are highly predictive of one's standing on numerical and verbal skills as well as psychological energy when reaching the old-old stage (also see O'Hanlon, 1993; Schaie, Dutta, & Willis, 1991).

A cross-sectional study, comparing adults ranging from 18 to 87 years also found a relationship between cognitive styles, age, and intelligence (Hood & Deopere, 2002). They found a relationship between age and cognitive styles; specifically their older adults displayed a stronger tendency toward dualism, thus envisioning the world more in terms of Us (good) versus Them (bad). They also found an unexpected positive relationship between scores on intelligence tests and age, implying a possible relationship between intelligence and dualism. Incidentally, there was a negative relationship with scores on intelligence tests and the level of dualism. The discrepancy may have evolved from educational differences among their participants. Education was found to have a negative relationship with dualism and a positive relationship with relativism (which was displayed more in younger adults). Education also had a negative relationship with age, indicating that individuals of advanced age tended to have lower educational levels.

Family Environment

Certain aspects of the family environment may influence intellectual development. Despite the fact that most work on this topic is grounded in earlier parts of the life span, there are still implications for the adult life span.

There has been some indication that negative effects of low family income on early cognitive development can be compensated for by using constructive family strategies and interactions (Hustedt & Raver, 2002; Poehlmann & Fiese, 2001; Ramey, Campbell, & Ramey, 1999) and by providing a supportive home environment (Kalmar, 1996; Kalmar & Boronkai, 2001; Kelley, Smith, Green, Berndt, & Rogers, 1998; Liang & Sugawara, 1996). Higher parental educational levels (Zhang & Yu, 2002) and supportive family environments (Dubowitz et al., 2001) have been found to have a positive relationship with offspring intelligence. A positive relationship has been found between the availability of resources within families for each member and intellectual outcomes, tending to imply that the fewer the number of members in a household, the more resources are likely to be available for each member, which can promote positive intellectual development (Downey, 2001). In addition, higher levels of stress and perceived difficulty in a family environment can negatively affect offspring cognitive development (Miller, Miceli, Whitman, & Borkowski, 1996) as well as experiencing or witnessing domestic violence (Huth-Bocks, Levendosky, & Semel, 2001). Families that provide children with proper nutrition have been found to have higher verbal ability scores (Quinn, O'Callaghan, Williams, Najman, & Andersen, 2001).

There is still some debate over whether the cognitive effects that are displayed within families result from genetic transmission of abilities or from effects of the early family environment (Guo & Stearns, 2002; Plomin, Fulker, Corley, & DeFries, 1997; Schaie & Zuo, 2001). The most reasonable interpretations of these data argue for a strong gene–environment interaction.

INTERVENTIONS IN ADULT INTELLECTUAL DEVELOPMENT

Adult Intellectual Decline: Irreversible or Remediable?

Findings on individual differences in intellectual change and the identification of antecedents for differential intellectual aging cast at least some doubt on the inevitability of general intellectual decline for all individuals and provide an optimistic picture of the continued ability to learn throughout life. More substantive evidence for such doubts is provided by cognitive intervention research that has successfully remediated some intellectual decline in the elderly. Longitudinal studies make it possible to distinguish effects of training that remediate age deficits from improvement in the performance of individuals above their previous levels. The former outcome, however, is of particular theoretical interest because it suggests that much of the intellectual aging seen in community dwelling elderly may be experiential in nature. Training studies conducted in a longitudinal context also permit the identification of antecedent conditions that predict the likelihood of training success or failure (Willis, 1989b, 1990, 2001).

Remediation of Deficits Versus Reduction of Cohort Effects

Much of the work on cognitive training has been conducted in the context of the Adult Development and Enrichment Project (ADEPT, Baltes & Willis, 1982) and the SLS (Schaie & Willis, 1986; Willis & Schaie, 1986b). Both studies involved pre- and posttest designs, with five hours of instruction in strategies at the ability level, administered in small groups in the ADEPT study and individually in the SLS. In the former study, significant training gains were demonstrated for participants over age 60 for the primary mental abilities of figural relations and inductive reasoning, whereas in the latter study, significant training gains occurred for inductive reasoning and spatial ori-

entation. In the SLS, moreover, significant gain occurred for participants who had declined as well as for those who had remained stable. Women experienced greater training effects on spatial orientation, whereas training benefited both speed and accuracy in women but primarily accuracy in men (Willis & Schaie, 1988). Greater training effects were seen in the SLS for inductive reasoning when there was evidence of strategy use, suggesting that strategy use may be a possible mechanism for training effects (Saczynski, Willis, & Schaie, 2002). There is also some evidence that personality may be associated with training gains (Boron, 2003), and there may be mediating relationships with psychomotor speed, total systemic conditions, and respiratory conditions for training gains (Saczynski, 2001). In both ADEPT and SLS, near transfer was shown to occur for alternate markers within each ability, but there was no far transfer to other primary abilities.

Variations of the ADEPT study, introducing multiple training conditions or conditions involving self-programmed training conditions, have for the most part replicated the original findings in a German sample (Baltes & Lindenberger, 1988; Baltes, Sowarka, & Kliegl, 1989) and in American studies by Blackburn, Papalia-Finley, Foye, and Serlin (1988) and by Hayslip (1989). A study of figural relations training by Denney and Heidrich (1990) showed equal magnitudes of improvement for young, middle-aged, and old subjects.

Does cognitive training change the structural characteristics of the primary abilities by converting a pretraining fluid ability to a crystallized ability (see Donaldson, 1981)? In the SLS, invariance of factor structure across training was confirmed in the training groups. Minor shifts occurred in the factor loadings of the individual markers of the abilities trained, but training did not result in any of the marker loadings on factors other than those hypothesized (Schaie et al., 1987).

Long-Term Effects of Cognitive Interventions

Cognitive training will clearly yield significant improvement in the performance of older persons on the targeted abilities, but skepticism remains as to whether such training produces any lasting effects. Long-term follow-up over a seven-year period has been conducted for both the ADEPT and SLS training studies. Significantly lower decline over seven years was shown in the ADEPT study for those individuals trained on figural relations as compared to the control group (Willis & Nesselroade, 1990). In the SLS, similar findings occurred for both inductive reasoning and spatial orientation abilities (Willis & Schaie, 1994b). In the latter study, those who declined prior to the initial training were at greater comparative advantage at the follow-up. Both studies also examined effects of booster training. As would be expected, as subjects entered advanced old age, booster training, although yielding significant effects, resulted in somewhat lower magnitudes of training effects (Schaie, 2005). It seems, then, that periodic reactivation of specific mental skills is likely to reduce the magnitude of intellectual decline in community-dwelling persons.

CONCLUSION

It was previously argued that there had been a turning away from studies that simply defined the extent and ability specificity of age differences and age changes in intelligence. Instead the field is turning toward a greater preoccupation with individual patterns of change and identification of antecedent variables that might account for the vast array of individual differences and the potentiality of preventing cognitive decline. Progress in the study of practical intelligence has also expanded the field in directions that have practical and social policy implications. Progress has also continued in identifying the social structure, health, and personality variables that influence individual differences in intellectual competence. No longer are contextual variables treated as methodological confounds; rather, increasing efforts are being made to identify the precise influences that will eventually predict individual hazards of intellectual decline and maintenance. Important theoretical efforts therefore have been directed toward replacing index variables, such as age or cohort, with more direct explanations of individual differences.

Findings presented in this chapter lead to the prediction that intellectual age differences in adulthood will become more compressed over the next decade because of the apparent plateauing of positive cohort differences for some abilities and the occurrence of negative effects for others. For example, a cross-sectional study using individuals aged 18–87 years found a positive relationship between age and indi-

vidual intelligence (Hood & Deopere, 2002). It is quite likely, therefore, that future studies will provide a more optimistic picture for cognitive development in old age, at least until that point when physiological infrastructure and social support systems begin to crumble. Monitoring the cognitive development of the Baby Boom cohorts who are now in midlife as they reach old age is of great importance given the enormous and unique demographic pressures as well as the huge economic and policy impact affecting this group (Willis & Schaie, 1999a).

However, even more work is needed on the role of lifelong experience in the maintenance of intellectual functions and productive performance in societal roles. Information gathered with retrospective questionnaires indicates that the role of experience on intellectual development may be less than common sense would suggest (e.g., Salthouse & Mitchell, 1990). But the sparse relations found between age and job performance (Avolio & Waldman, 1990; Salthouse & Maurer, 1996) suggest that experience cannot yet be written off as an important source of compensation for loss of speed and cognitive efficiency. Furthermore, the context or act of learning needs to be explored. The effects of adults remaining in school longer (and with more adults returning to school at later ages) on intellectual development needs to be explored. Graham and Donalson (1999) found that adult learners, despite relatively less involvement in campus activities and more involvement in family caring, reported slightly higher levels of growth in academic and intellectual items than their younger counterparts. In addition, the effects of computer exposure on intellectual development need further exploration (see Subrahmanyam, Greenfield, Kraut, & Gross, 2001).

There is relatively little comparative work on intellectual aging within minority groups in the United States, and there is also a lack of cross-cultural comparisons of intellectual aging in other societies (see Dai, Xie, & Zheng, 1993). As reviewed in this chapter, surrounding environmental factors affect individual development. Life course sociologists have taken advantage of substantial environmental interventions (e.g., the Great Depression, farm crises, the Cultural Revolution) that may have differential effects on human development (e.g., Elder, Rudkin, & Conger, 1994). Adult cognitive psychologists have yet to emulate this useful approach in their work. One such example is Schaie, Nguyen, Willis, Dutta, and Yue's

(2001) investigation of intellectual aging in Chinese adults. They found a linear relationship within their sample between age and most primary mental abilities. They were also able to conclude that intellectual environment was related to individual abilities in their sample. Another study, also using a Chinese sample (Geary et al., 1997) found no computational or reasoning skill differences in older adults (60–80 years old) relative to U.S. performance. They did, however, find a difference in adolescents in favor of the Chinese sample. They concluded that the Chinese advantage was due to a parallel cross-generational intellectual decline in the United States and a cross-generational intellectual improvement in China, leaving older adults functioning at an equal plain between the two nations with adolescents functioning at different plains. Similar studies need to be done comparing and contrasting intellectual aging in ethnic groups that reside in the United States as well as adults of other nations, to explore unique antecedents and trajectories for intellectual development.

Further progress has been made in cognitive intervention work to show that intellectual decline in old age is not necessarily irreversible in all persons and that formal intervention strategies are available that might allow longer maintenance of high levels of intellectual function in community-dwelling older persons. The data on successful cognitive interventions have now been supplemented by evidence of positive long-term effects of these interventions. It is still necessary, however, to remove these techniques from the laboratory to a broader social context. This would require the implementation of clinical trials as well as the investigation of modes of intervention that are indigenous to the daily experience of older persons (such as games and other activities that may be cognitively challenging; e.g., Tosti-Vasey, Person, Maier, & Willis, 1992). Also needed are efforts to relate the effect of cognitive training to specific activities of daily living. An example of such an effort is the Advanced Cognitive Training in Vital Elderly (ACTIVE) project, a multiple-center clinical trial, using multiple modes of intervention that focus on training effects for perceptual speed, inductive reasoning, verbal memory, and everyday functioning (Ball et al., 2002). Preliminary results from this trial have shown positive cognitive training effects.

In addition to the existing literature, it is also necessary to explore biological antecedents for unique intellectual development. Kennet, Revell, and Schaie (1999; also see Schaie, 2005) found some indication that allele type may differentiate individual cognitive trajectories. There has also been some evidence from age comparative studies, using functional magnetic resonance imaging, that individuals of different ages may experience activation of different brain regions in response to the same cognitive tasks (Gaillard et al., 2000; Klingberg, Forssberg, & Westerberg, 2002; Tamm, Menon, & Reiss, 2002). Thus, there is additional need for exploration to answer whether there are neurological antecedents for intellectual development and whether intellectual development is to some degree genetically predetermined. These types of studies are also needed to examine whether there are cohort differences in the use of the brain or whether instead we may use our own brains differently with age for the same cognitive tasks.

With more individuals reaching old age and the resulting increase in the prevalence of neuropathological conditions, there is an urgent need for early detection of any risk for dementia. There has been much development and progress in the area of detection and diagnosis (i.e., Morris et al., 1989, 1993). The next step will be to extend this exploration into prevention and early detection, which can be provided through longitudinal cognitive studies. Schaie, Caskie, Revell, Willis, Kaszniak, & Teri (2005) have recently explored empirically the implementation of procedures that might allow early detection of risk for dementia prior to the appearance of clinically diagnosable symptoms or neuropathology. Using individual change in cognitive ability test performance, the researchers were able to successfully identify predictors of cognitive impairment (seven years preceding actual neuropsychological dementia ratings). Similar studies need to prospectively and retrospectively compare cognitive trajectories for individuals who develop cognitive impairment with trajectories of those who do not to assist in the prevention and early diagnosis of dementia.

The field of adult intelligence has matured from a descriptive science toward one that is increasingly concerned with the identification of precise mechanisms and the identification of antecedents for individual differences. The area has also progressed to the stage of interventions developed by findings from the basic sciences in the interest of improving intellectual competence in old age. With the continued compelling and functional research being conducted and with continual practical needs in the area of intellectual development, progress and growth in this substantial area appears promising and crucial

References

Abayomi, O. K. (2002). Pathogenesis of cognitive decline following therapeutic irradiation for head and neck tumors. *Acta Oncology, 41*, 346–351.

Alexander, C., & Langer, E. J. (Eds.). (1990). *Beyond formal operations: Alternative endpoints to human development*. New York: Oxford University Press.

Almeida, O. P., & Flicker, L. (2001). The mind of a failing heart: A systematic review of the association between congestive heart failure and cognitive functioning. *Internal Medicine, 31*, 290–295.

Almeida, O. P., & Tamai, S. (2001). Congestive heart failure and cognitive functioning amongst older adults. *Archives of Neuropsychiatry, 59*, 324–329.

Alwin, D. F. (1988). Structural equation models in research on human development and aging. In K. W. Schaie, R. T. Campbell, W. Meredith, & S. C. Rawlings (Eds.), *Methodological issues in aging research* (pp. 71–170). New York: Springer.

Anstey, K., Stankov, L., & Lord, S. (1993). Primary aging, secondary aging, and intelligence. *Psychology and Aging, 8*, 562–570.

Arbuckle, T., Gold, D., & Andres, D. (1986). Cognitive functioning of older people in relation to social and personality variables. *Psychology and Aging, 1*, 55–62.

Arbuckle, T. Y., Gold, D. P., Andres, D., Schwartzman, A. E., & Chaikelson, J. (1992). The role of psychosocial context, age, and intelligence in memory performance of older men. *Psychology and Aging, 7*, 25–36.

Arbuckle, T. Y., Maag, U., Pushkar, D., & Chaikelson, J. S. (1998). Individual differences in trajectory of intellectual development over 45 years of adulthood. *Psychology and Aging, 13*, 663–675.

Armstrong, C. L., Hunter, J. V., Ledakis, G. E., Cohen, B., Tallent, E. M., Goldstein, B. H., et al. (2002). Late cognitive and radiographic changes related to radiotherapy: Initial prospective findings. *Neurology, 59*, 40–48.

Avolio, B. J. (1991). Levels of analysis. *Annual Review of Gerontology and Geriatrics, 11*, 239–260.

Avolio, B. J., & Waldman, D. A. (1990). An examination of age and cognitive test performance across job complexity and occupational types. *Journal of Applied Psychology, 75*, 43–50.

Ball, K., Berch, D. B., Helmers, K. F., Jobe, J. B., Leveck, M. D., Marsiske, M., et al. (2002). Effects of cognitive training interventions with older adults: A randomized controlled trial. *Journal of the American Medical Association, 288*, 2271–2281.

Baltes, P. B. (1987). Theoretical propositions of life-span developmental psychology: On the dynamics between growth and decline. *Developmental Psychology, 23*, 611–626.

Baltes, P. B. (1993). The aging mind: Potential and limits. *Gerontologist, 33*, 580–594.

Baltes, P. B., & Baltes, M. M. (1990). Psychological perspectives on successful aging: The model of selective optimization with compensation. In P. B. Baltes & M. M. Baltes (Eds.), *Successful aging: Perspectives from the behavioral sciences* (pp. 1–34). Cambridge: Cambridge University Press.

Baltes, P. B., & Lindenberger, U. (1988). On the range of cognitive plasticity in old age as a function of experience: 15 years of intervention research. *Behavior Therapy, 19*, 283–300.

Baltes, P. B., Mayer, K. U., Helmchen, H., & Steinhagen-Thiessen, E. (1993). The Berlin Aging Study (BASE). *Ageing and Society, 13*, 483–533.

Baltes, P. B., Sowarka, D., & Kliegl, R. (1989). Cognitive training research on fluid intelligence in old age: What can older adults achieve by themselves? *Psychology and Aging, 4*, 217–221.

Baltes, P. B., & Willis, S. L. (1982). Enhancement (plasticity) of intellectual functioning in old age: Penn State's Adult Development and Enrichment Project (ADEPT). In F. I. M. Craik & S. E. Traub (Eds.), *Aging and cognitive processes* (pp. 353–389). New York: Plenum Press.

Binet, A., & Simon, T. (1905). Methodes nouvelles pour le diagnostic du niveau intellectuel des anormaux. *L'Annee Psychologique, 11*, 191.

Birren, J. E., & Botwinick, J. (1951). Rate of addition as a function of difficulty and age. *Psychometrika, 16*, 219–232.

Birren, J. E., & Fisher, L. M. (1992). Aging and slowing behavior: Consequences for cognition and survival. In T. Sonderegger (Ed.), *Psychology and aging: Nebraska Symposium on Motivation*. Lincoln: University of Nebraska Press.

Blackburn, J. A., Papalia-Finlay, D., Foye, B. F., & Serlin, R. C. (1988). Modifiability of figural relations performance among elderly adults. *Journal of Gerontology: Psychological Sciences, 43*, P87–P89.

Boron, J. (2003). *Effects of personality on cognitive ability, training gains, and strategy use in an adult sample: Seattle Longitudinal Study*. Unpublished master's thesis, Pennsylvania State University, University Park.

Bosworth, H. B., Schaie, K. W., & Willis, S. L. (1999). Cognitive and sociodemographic risk factors for mortality in the Seattle Longitudinal Study. *Journal of Gerontology: Psychological Sciences, 54B*, P273–P282.

Bosworth, H. B., Schaie, K. W., Willis, S. L., & Siegler, I. C. (1999). Age and distance to death in the Seattle Longitudinal Study. *Research on Aging, 21*, 723–738.

Busse, E. W. (1993). Duke Longitudinal Study. *Zeitschrift für Gerontologie, 26*, 123–128.

Carroll, J. B. (1993). *Human cognitive abilities: A survey of factor-analytic studies*. New York: Cambridge University Press.

Christensen, H., & Henderson, A. S. (1991). Is age kinder to the initially more able? A study of eminent scientists and academics. *Psychological Medicine, 21*, 935–946.

Commons, M. L., Sinnott, J. D., Richards, F. A., & Armon, C. (Eds.). (1989). *Beyond formal operations: Vol 2. Adolescent and adult development models.* New York: Praeger.

Costa, P. T., Fozard, J. L., McCrae, R. R., & Bosse, R. (1976). Relations of age and personality dimensions to cognitive ability factors. *Journal of Gerontology, 31,* 663–669.

Costa, P. T., Jr., & McCrae, R. R. (1992). *Revised NEO Personality Inventory (NEO PI-R).* Odessa, FL: Psychological Assessment Resources.

Costa, P. T., & McCrae, R. R. (1993). Psychological research in the Baltimore Longitudinal Study of Aging. *Zeitschrift fur Gerontologie, 26,* 117–134.

Cunningham, W. R. (1987). Intellectual abilities and age. *Annual Review of Gerontology and Geriatrics, 7,* 117–134.

Cunningham, W. R., & Owens, W. A. Jr. (1983). The Iowa State Study of the adult development of intellectual abilities. In K. W. Schaie (Ed.), *Longitudinal studies of adult psychological development* (pp. 20–39). New York: Guilford.

Dai, X., Xie, Y., & Zheng, L. (1993). Age, education, and intelligence declining in adulthood. *Chinese Mental Health Journal, 7,* 215–217.

DeFrias, C. M., & Schaie, K. W. (2001). Perceived work environment and cognitive style. *Experimental Aging Research, 27,* 67–81.

DeLuca, C. R., Wood, S. J., Anderson, V., Buchanan, J. A. Proffitt, T. M., Mahoney, K., et al. (2003). Normative data from the Cantab. 1: Development of executive function over the lifespan. *Journal of Clinical and Experimental Neuropsychology, 25,* 242–254.

Denney, N. W., & Heidrich, S. M. (1990). Training effects on Raven's progressive matrices in young, middle-aged, and elderly adults. *Psychology and Aging, 5,* 144–145.

Dittmann-Kohli, F., Lachman, M. E., Kliegl, R., & Baltes, P. B. (1991). Effects of cognitive training and testing on intellectual efficacy beliefs in elderly adults. *Journal of Gerontology: Psychological Sciences, 46,* P162–P164.

Dixon, R. A., & Gould, O. N. (1998). Younger and older adults collaborating on retelling everyday stories. *Applied Developmental Science, 2,* 160–171.

Dolan, M., & Anderson I. M. (2002). Executive and memory function and its relationship to trait impulsivity and aggression in personality disordered offenders. *Journal of Forensic Psychiatry, 13,* 503–526.

Donaldson, G. (1981). Letter to the editor. *Journal of Gerontology, 36,* 634–636.

Downey, D. B. (2001). Number of siblings and intellectual development: The resource dilution explanation. *American Psychologist, 56,* 497–504.

Drexler, A. J., & Robertson, C. (2001). Type 2 diabetes. How new insights, new drugs are changing clinical practice. *Geriatrics, 56,* 3–4.

Dubowitz, H., Black, M. M., Cox, C. E., Kerr, M. A., Litrownik, A. J., Radhakrishna, A., et al. (2001). Father involvement and children's functioning at age 6 years: A multisite study. *Child Maltreatment: Journal of the American Professional Society on the Abuse of Children, 6,* 300–309.

Dutta, R. (1992). *A longitudinal study of the development of psychological flexibility-rigidity in adulthood.* Unpublished doctoral dissertation. Pennsylvania State University, University Park:.

Eichorn, D. H., Clausen, J. A., Haan, N., Honzik, M. P., & Mussen, P. H. (1981). *Present and past in middle life.* New York: Academic Press.

Ekstrom, R. B., French, J. W., Harman, H., & Dermen, D. (1976). *Kit of factor-referenced cognitive tests* (Rev. ed.). Princeton, NJ: Educational Testing Service.

Elder, G. H. J., Rudkin, L., & Conger, R. D. (1994). Inter-generational continuity and change in rural America. In V. L. Bengston, K. W. Schaie, & L. Burton (Eds.), *Adult intergenerational relations: Effects of societal change* (pp. 30–60). New York: Springer.

Elias, M. F., Elias, J. W., & Elias, P. K. (1990). Biological and health influences upon behavior. In J. E. Birren & K. W. Schaie (Eds.), *Handbook of the psychology of aging* (3rd ed., pp. 79–102). San Diego, CA: Academic Press.

Feingold, A. (1993). Cognitive gender differences: A developmental perspective. *Sex Roles, 29,* 91–112.

Field, D., Schaie, K. W., & Leino, V. (1988). Continuity in intellectual functioning: The role of self-reported health. *Psychology and Aging, 3,* 385–392.

Fioravanti, M., Nacca, D., Amati, S., Buckley, A. E., & Bisetti, A. (1995). Chronic obstructive pulmonary disease and associated patterns of memory decline. *Dementia, 6,* 39–48.

Gaillard, W. D., Hertz-Pannier, L., Mott, S. H., Barnett, A. S., LeBihan, D., & Theodore, W. H. (2000). Functional anatomy of cognitive development: fMRI of verbal fluency in children and adults. *Neurology, 54,* 180–185.

Geary, D. C., Hamson, C. O., Chen, G. P., Liu, F., Hoard, M. K., & Salthouse, T. A. (1997). Computational and reasoning abilities in arithmetic: Cross-generational change in China and the United States. *Psychonomic Bulletin and Review, 4,* 425–430.

Graham, S., & Donalson, J. F. (1999). Adult students' academic and intellectual development in college. *Adult Education Quarterly, 49,* 147–161.

Green, H. J., Pakenham, K. I., Headley, B. C., Yaxley, J., Nicol, D. L., Mactaggart, P. N., et al. (2002). Altered cognitive function in men treated for prostate cancer with luteinizing hormone-released hormone analogues and cyproterone acetate: A randomized controlled trial. *British Journal of Urology International, 90,* 427–432.

Grover, D. R., & Hertzog, C. (1991). Relationships between intellectual control beliefs and psychometric intelligence in adulthood. *Journal of Gerontology: Psychological Sciences, 46,* P109–P115.

Gruber, A. L., & Schaie, K. W. (1986, November). *Longitudinal-sequential studies of marital assortativity.* Paper presented at the annual meeting of the Gerontological Society of America, Chicago.

Gruber-Baldini, A. L. (1991). *The impact of health and disease on cognitive ability in adulthood and old age in the Seattle Longitudinal Study.* Unpublished doctoral dissertation, Pennsylvania State University, University Park.

Guilford, J. P. (1967). *The nature of human intelligence.* New York: McGraw-Hill.

Guo, G., & Stearns, E. (2002). The social influences on the realization of genetic potential for intellectual development. *Social Forces, 80,* 881–910.

Hayslip, B. (1989). Alternative mechanisms for improvements in fluid ability performance among older adults. *Psychology and Aging, 4,* 122–124.

Hershey, D. A., Jacobs-Lawson, J. M., & Walsh, D. A. (2003). Influences of age and training on script development. *Aging, Neuropsychology, and Cognition, 10,* 1–19.

Hertzog, C. (1987). Applications of structural equation models in gerontological research. *Annual Review of Gerontology and Geriatrics, 7,* 265–293.

Hertzog, C. (1989). The influence of cognitive slowing on age differences in intelligence. *Developmental Psychology, 25,* 636–651.

Hood, A. B., & Deopere, D. L. (2002). The relationship of cognitive development to age, when education, employment, and intelligence are controlled for. *Journal of Adult Development, 9,* 229–234.

Horn, J. L. (1982). The theory of fluid and crystallized intelligence in relation to concepts of cognitive psychology and aging in adulthood. In F. I. M. Craik & S. Trehub (Eds.), *Aging and cognitive processes* (pp. 237–278). New York: Plenum.

Horn, J. L., & Hofer, S. M. (1992). Major abilities and development in the adult period. In R. J. Sternberg & C.A. Berg (Eds.), *Intellectual development* (pp. 44–99). New York: Cambridge University Press.

Horn, J. L., & McArdle, J. J. (1992). A practical and theoretical guide to measurement invariance in aging research. *Experimental Aging Research, 18,* 117–144.

Hultsch, D. F., Hammer, M., & Small, B. J. (1993). Age differences in cognitive performance in later life: Relationships to self-reported health and activity life style. *Journal of Gerontology, 48,* P1–P11.

Hultsch, D. F., Hertzog, C., Small, B. J., McDonald-Miszlak, L., & Dixon, R. A. (1992). Short-term longitudinal change in cognitive performance in later life. *Psychology and Aging, 7,* 571–584.

Hustedt, J. T., & Raver, C. C. (2002). Scaffolding in low-income mother-child dyads: Relation with joint attention and dyadic reciprocity. *International Journal of Behavioral Development, 26,* 113–119.

Huth-Bocks, A. C., Levendosy, A. A., & Semel, M. A. (2001). The direct and indirect effects of domestic violence on young children's intellectual functioning. *Journal of Family Violence, 16,* 269–290.

Incalzi, R. A., Gemma, A., Marra, C., Muzzolon, R., Capparella, O., & Carbonin, P. (1993). Chronic obstructive pulmonary disease. An original model of cognitive decline. *American Review of Respiratory Diseases, 148,* 418–424.

Iwamoto, T., Shimizu, T., Ami, M., Yoneda, Y., Imamura, T., & Takasaki, M. (2000). Dementia and disability after initial cerebral thrombosis evaluated by MRI and their clinical course. *Nippon Ronen Igakkai Zasshi, 37,* 162–169.

Jackson-Guilford, J., Leander, J. D., & Nisenbaum, L. K. (2000). The effect of streptozotocin-induced diabetes on cell proliferation in the rat dentate gyrus. *Neuroscience Letter, 293,* 91–94.

Jarvik, L. F., & Bank, L. (1983). Aging twins: Longitudinal psychometric data. In K. W. Schaie (Ed.), *Longitudinal studies of adult psychological development* (pp. 40–63). New York: Guilford.

Jefferis, B. J. M. H., Power, C., & Hertzman, C. (2002). Birth weight, childhood socioeconomic environment, and cognitive development in the 1958 British birth cohort study. *British Medical Journal, 325,* 305.

Jones, K. J., Albert, M. S., Duffy, F. H., & Hyde, M. R. (1991). Modeling age using cognitive, psychological and physiological variables: The Boston Normative Aging study. *Experimental Aging Research, 17,* 227–242.

Kalmar, M. (1996). The course of intellectual development in preterm and fullterm children: An 8-year longitudinal study. *International Journal of Behavioral Development, 19,* 491–516.

Kalmar, M., & Boronkai, J. (2001). The role of the quality of home environment in the long-term intellectual development in prematurely born children. *Magyar Pszichologiai Szemle, 56,* 387–410.

Kaufman, A. S., Kaufman-Packer, J. L., McLean, J. E., & Reynolds, C. R. (1991). Is the pattern of intellectual growth and decline across the adult life span different for men and women? *Journal of Clinical Psychology, 47,* 801–812.

Kelley, M. L., Smith, T. S., Green, A. P., Berndt, A. E., & Rogers, M. C. (1998). Importance of fathers' parenting to African-American toddler's social and cognitive development. *Infant Behavior and Development, 21,* 733–744.

Kennet, J., McGuire, L., Willis, S. L., & Schaie, K. W. (2000). Memorability functions in verbal memory: A longitudinal approach. *Experimental Aging Research, 26,* 121–137.

Kennet, J., Revell, A. J., & Schaie, K. W. (1999, November). *Early psychometric indicators of possible dementia in later life: Apo E genotypes and cognitive performance among middle-aged and older community-dwelling individuals.* Paper presented at the annual meeting of the Gerontological Society of America, San Francisco, CA.

Kickul, J., & Neuman, G. (2000). Emergent leadership behaviors: The function of personality and cognitive ability in determining teamwork performance and KSAS. *Journal of Business and Psychology, 15,* 27–51.

Klimkowicz, A., Dziedzic, T., Slowik, A., & Szczudlik, A. (2002). Incidence of pre- and poststroke dementia: Cracow stroke registry. *Dementia Geriatric Cognitive Disorders, 14*(3), 137–140.

Klingberg, T., Forssberg, H., & Westerberg, H. (2002). Increased brain activity in frontal and parietal cortex underlies the development of visuospatial working memory capacity during childhood. *Journal of Cognitive Neuroscience, 14,* 1–10.

Kuhn, D. (1992). Thinking as argument. *Harvard Educational Review, 62,* 155–178.

Kukull, W. A., Brenner, D. E., Speck, C. E., Nochlin, D., Bowen, J., McCormick, W., et al. (1994). Causes of death associated with Alzheimer's disease: Variation by level of cognitive impairment before death. *Journal of American Geriatric Society, 42,* 723–726.

Labouvie-Vief, G. (1992). A neo-Piagetian perspective on adult cognitive development. In R. J. Sternberg & C. A. Berg (Eds.), *Intellectual development* (pp. 197–228). Cambridge: Cambridge University Press.

Lachman, M. E., & Leff, R. (1989). Perceived control and intellectual functioning in the elderly: A 5-year longitudinal study. *Developmental Psychology, 25,* 722–728.

LePage-Lees, P. (1997). Exploring patterns of achievement and intellectual development among academically successful women from disadvantaged backgrounds. *Journal of College Student Development, 38,* 468–478.

LePine, J. A. (2003). Team adaptation and postcharge performance: Effects of team composition in terms of members' cognitive ability and personality. *Journal of Applied Psychology, 88,* 27–39.

Liang, S., & Sugawara, A. I. (1996). Family size, birth order, socioeconomic status, ethnicity, parent-child relationship, and preschool children's intellectual development. *Early Child Development and Care, 124,* 69–79.

Lindenberger, U., & Baltes, P. B. (1994). Sensory functioning and intelligence in old age. *Psychology and Aging, 9,* 339–355.

Lindenberger, U., Mayr, U., & Kliegl, R. (1993). Speed and intelligence in old age. *Psychology and Aging, 8,* 207–220.

Mahoney, A. E. J. (2003). Age- or stage-appropriate? Recreation and the relevance of Piaget's theory in dementia care. *American Journal of Alzheimer's Disease and Other Dementias, 18,* 24–30.

Maier, H. C. (1995). *Health behaviors in adults: Interrelationships and correlates.* Unpublished doctoral dissertation, Pennsylvania State University, University Park.

Maitland, S. B., Intrieri, R. C., Schaie, K. W., & Willis, S. L. (2000). Gender differences and changes in

cognitive abilities across the adult life span. *Aging, Neuropsychology, and Cognition, 7,* 32–53.

Manton, K. G., Siegler, I. C., & Woodbury, M. A. (1986). Patterns of intellectual development in later life. *Journal of Gerontology, 41,* 486–499.

Martin, M., & Schumann-Hengsteler, R. (2001). How task demands influence time-based prospective memory performance in young and older adults. *International Journal of Behavioral Development, 25,* 386–391.

Matarazzo, J. D. (1972). *Wechsler's measurement and appraisal of adult intelligence.* Baltimore: Williams & Wilkins.

McArdle, J. J., & Prescott, C. A. (1992). Age-based construct validation using structural equation modeling. *Experimental Aging Research, 18,* 87–115.

McCarthy, A. M., Lindgren, S., Mengeling, M. A., Tsalikian, E., & Engvall, J. C. (2002). Effects of diabetes on learning in children. *Pediatrics, 109,* E9.

Medina-Walpole, A. M., & McCormick, W. C. (1998). Provider practice patterns in nursing home-acquired pneumonia. *Journal of the American Geriatric Society, 46,* 1327.

Meredith, W. (1993). Measurement invariance, factor analysis, and factorial invariance. *Psychometrika, 58,* 525–543.

Miller, C. L., Miceli, P. J., Whitman, T. L., & Borkowski, J. G. (1996). Cognitive readiness to parent and intellectual-emotional development in children and adolescent mothers. *Developmental Psychology, 32,* 533–541.

Miller, J., Slomczynski, K. M., & Kohn, M. L. (1987). Continuity of learning-generalization through the life span: The effect of job on men's intellectual process in the United States and Poland. In C. Schooler & K. W. Schaie (Eds.), *Cognitive functioning and social Structure over the life course.* New York: Ablex.

Millsap, R. E., & Meredith, W. (1992). Component analysis in multivariate aging research. *Experimental Aging Research, 18,* 203–212.

Morris, J. C., Edland, S., Clark, C., Galasko, C., Koss, E., Mohs, R., et al. (1993). The consortium to establish a registry for Alzheimer's disease (CERAD). Part IV. Clinical and neuropsychological assessment of Alzheimer's disease. *Neurology, 39,* 1159–1165.

Morris, J. C., Heyman, A., Mohs, R., Hughes, J. P., Van Belle, G., Fillenbaum, G., et al. (1989). The consortium to establish a registry for Alzheimer's disease (CERAD). Part 1. Rates of cognitive change in the longitudinal assessment of probable Alzheimer's disease. *Neurology, 43,* 2457–2465.

O'Hanlon, A. M. (1993). *Inter-individual patterns of intellectual change: The influence of environmental factors.* Unpublished doctoral dissertation, Pennsylvania State University, University Park.

Palmore, E., Busse, E. W., Maddox, G. L., Nowlin, J. B., & Siegler, I. C. (1985). *Normal aging III.* Durham, NC: Duke University Press.

Perlmutter, M.. & Nyquist, L. (1990). Relationships between self-reported physical and mental intelligence performance across adulthood. *Journal of Gerontology: Psychological Science*, 45, P145–P155.

Plomin, R., Fulker, D. W., Corley, R., & DeFries, J. C. (1997). Nature, nurture, and cognitive development from 1 to 16 years: A parent-offspring adoption study. *Psychological Science*, 8, 442–447.

Poehlmann, J., & Fiese, B. H. (2001). Parent-infant interaction as a mediator of the relation between neonatal risk status and 12-month cognitive development. *Infant Behavior and Development*, 24, 171–188.

Poon, L. W., Sweaney, A. L., Clayton, G. M., & Merriam, S. B. (1992). The Georgia Centenarian Study. *International Journal of Aging and Human Development*, 34, 1–17.

Quinn, P. J., O'Callaghan, M., Williams, G. M., Najman, J. M., & Andersen-Bor, W. (2001). The effect of breastfeeding on child development at 5 years: A cohort study. *Journal of Pediatrics and Child Health*, 37, 465–469.

Rabbitt, P. (1991). Management of the working population. *Ergonomics*, 34, 775–790.

Rabbitt, P. (1993). Does it all go together when it goes? *Quarterly Journal of Experimental Psychology: Human Experimental Psychology*, 45A, 385–434.

Rabbitt, P., & Abson, V. (1991). Do older people know how good they are? *British Journal of Psychology*, 82, 137–151.

Rabbitt, P., Watson, P., Donlan, C., McInnes, L., Horan, M., Pendleton, N., & Clague, J. (2002). Effects of death within 11 years on cognitive performance in old age. *Psychology of Aging*, 17, 468–481.

Ramey, C. T., Campbell, F. A., & Ramey, S. L. (1999). Early intervention: Successful pathways to improving intellectual development. *Developmental Neuropsychology*, 16, 385–392.

Raykov, T. (1989). Reserve capacity of the elderly in aging sensitive tests of fluid intelligence: A reanalysis via a structural equation modeling approach. *Zeitschrift fur Gerontologie*, 197, 263–282.

Reeve, C., & Hakel, M. D. (2000). Toward an understanding of adult intellectual development: Investigating within-individual convergence of interest and knowledge profiles. *Journal of Applied Psychology*, 85, 897–908.

Reinert, G. (1970). Comparative factor analytic studies of intelligence through the human life-span. In L. R. Goulet & P. B. Baltes (Eds.), *Life-span developmental psychology: Research and theory* (pp. 468–485). New York: Academic Press.

Roth, A., Schaie, K. W., & Willis, S. L. (2001, November). *Consistency in congruence types over a fourteen-year period: relationship with cognitive performance and rigidity/flexibility*. Paper presented at the annual meeting of the Gerontological Society of America, Chicago.

Royak-Schaler, R., & Alt, P. M. (1994). The process of health behavior change: individual factors and planning models. In J. D. Sinnott (Ed.) *Interdisciplinary handbook of adult lifespan learning* (pp. 325–336) Westport, CT: Greenwood Press.

Rott, C. (1993). Ein Drei-Komponenten-Modell der Intelligenzentwicklung im Alter: Ergebnisse aus der Bonner Gerontologischen Langsschnittstudie [Three components of intellectual development in old age: Results from the Bonn Longitudinal Study on Aging]. *Zeitschrift für Gerontologie*, 26, 184–190.

Rybash, J. M., Hoyer, W. J., & Roodin, P. A. (1986). *Adult cognition and aging*. New York: Pergamon.

Saczynski, J. S. (2001). *Cognitive training gains in the Seattle Longitudinal Study: Individual predictors and mediators of training effects*. Unpublished doctoral dissertation, Pennsylvania State University, University Park.

Saczynski, J. S., Willis, S. L., & Schaie, K. W. (2002). Strategy use in reasoning training with older adults. *Aging, Neuropsychology and Cognition*, 9, 48–60.

Salthouse, T. A. (1988a). Initiating the formalization of theories of cognitive aging. *Psychology and Aging*, 3, 3–16.

Salthouse, T. A. (1988b). Resource-reduction interpretations of cognitive aging. *Developmental Review*, 8, 238–272.

Salthouse, T. A. (1992). Shifting levels of analysis in the investigation of cognitive aging. *Human Development*, 35, 321–342.

Salthouse, T. A. (1993a). Influence of working memory on adult age differences in matrix reasoning. *British Journal of Psychology*, 84, 171–199.

Salthouse, T. A. (1993b). Speed and knowledge as determinants of adult age differences in verbal tasks. *Journal of Gerontology: Psychological Sciences*, 48, P29–P36.

Salthouse, T. A. (1993c). Speed mediation of adult age differences in cognition. *Developmental Psychology*, 29, 722–738.

Salthouse, T. A. (1994). The nature of the influence of speed on adult age differences in cognition. *Developmental Psychology*, 30, 240–259.

Salthouse, T. A., & Maurer, T. J. (1996). Aging, job performance, and career development. In J. E. Birren & K. W. Schaie (Eds.), *Handbook of the psychology of aging* (4th ed., pp. 353–364). San Diego, CA: Academic Press.

Salthouse, T. A., & Mitchell, D. R. (1990). Effects of age and naturally occurring experience on spatial visualization performance. *Developmental Psychology*, 26, 845–854.

Sands, L. P., & Meredith, W. (1992). Blood pressure and intellectual functioning in late midlife. *Journal of Gerontology: Psychological Sciences*, 47, P81–P84.

Sands, L. P., Terry, H., & Meredith, W. (1989). Change and stability in adult intellectual functioning assessed by Wechsler item responses. *Psychology and Aging*, 4, 79–87.

Schaie, K. W. (1977/78). Toward a stage theory of adult development. *International Journal of Aging and Human Development*, 8, 129–138.

Schaie, K. W. (1984). Midlife influences upon intellectual functioning in old age. *International Journal of Behavioral Development, 7*, 463–478.

Schaie, K. W. (1985). *Manual for the Schaie-Thurstone Adult Mental Abilities Test (STAMAT)*. Palo Alto, CA: Consulting Psychologists Press.

Schaie, K. W. (1988). Internal validity threats in studies of adult cognitive development. In M. L. Howe & C. J. Brainard (Eds.), *Cognitive development in adulthood: Progress in cognitive development research* (pp. 241–272). New York: Springer-Verlag.

Schaie, K. W. (1989a). The hazards of cognitive aging. *Gerontologist, 29*, 484–493.

Schaie, K. W. (1989b). Perceptual speed in adulthood: Cross-sectional and longitudinal studies. *Psychology and Aging, 4*, 443–453.

Schaie, K. W. (1990a). Intellectual development in adulthood. In J. E. Birren & K. W. Schaie (Eds.), *Handbook of the psychology of aging* (3rd ed., pp. 291–309). New York: Academic Press.

Schaie, K. W. (1990b). Late life potential and cohort differences in mental abilities. In M. Perlmutter (Ed.), *Late life potential* (pp. 43–62). Washington, DC: Gerontological Society of America.

Schaie, K. W. (1990c). The optimization of cognitive functioning in old age: Predictions based on cohort-sequential and longitudinal data. In P. B. Baltes & M. M. Baltes (Eds.), *Successful aging: Perspectives from the behavioral sciences* (pp. 94–117). Cambridge: Cambridge University Press.

Schaie, K. W. (1993). The Seattle Longitudinal Study: A thirty-five year inquiry of adult intellectual development. *Zeitschrift für Gerontologie, 26*, 129–137.

Schaie, K. W. (1994). The course of adult intellectual development. *American Psychologist, 49*, 304-313.

Schaie, K. W. (1996). *Intellectual development in adulthood: The Seattle Longitudinal Study*. New York: Cambridge University Press.

Schaie, K. W. (2005). *Developmental influences on adult intelligence: The Seattle Longitudinal Study*. New York: Oxford University Press.

Schaie, K. W., Caskie, G. I. L., Revell, A. J., Willis, S. L., Kaszniak, A. W., & Teri, L. (2005). Extending neuropsychological assessment into the Primary Mental Ability space. *Aging, Neuropsychology and Cognition, 12*, 245–277.

Schaie, K. W., Dutta, R., & Willis, S. L. (1991). The relationship between rigidity-flexibility and cognitive abilities in adulthood. *Psychology and Aging, 6*, 371–386.

Schaie, K. W., & Hofer, S. M. (2001). Longitudinal studies in research on aging. In J. E. Birren & K. W. Schaie (Eds.), *Handbook of the psychology of aging* (5th ed., pp. 55–77). San Diego, CA: Academic Press.

Schaie, K. W., Maitland, S. B., Willis, S. L., & Intrieri, R. C. (1998). Longitudinal invariance of adult psychometric ability factor structures across 7 years. *Psychology and Aging, 13*, 8–70

Schaie, K. W., Nguyen, H. T., Willis, S. L., Dutta, R., & Yue, G. A. (2001). Environmental factors as a conceptual framework for examining cognitive performance in Chinese adults. *International Journal of Behavioral Development, 25*, 193–202.

Schaie, K. W., Plomin, R., Willis, S. L., Gruber-Baldini, A., & Dutta, R. (1992). Natural cohorts: Family similarity in adult cognition. In T. Sonderegger (Ed.), *Psychology and aging: Nebraska Symposium on Motivation, 1991* (pp. 205–243). Lincoln: University of Nebraska Press.

Schaie, K. W., & Willis, S. L. (1986). Can decline in adult cognitive functioning be reversed? *Developmental Psychology, 22*, 223–232.

Schaie, K. W., & Willis, S. L. (1991). Adult personality and psychomotor performance: Cross-sectional and longitudinal analyses. *Journal of Gerontology: Psychological Sciences, 46*, P275–P284.

Schaie, K. W., & Willis, S. L. (1993). Age difference patterns of psychometric intelligence in adulthood: Generalizability within and across ability domains. *Psychology and Aging, 8*, 44–55.

Schaie, K. W., & Willis, S. L. (2000). A stage theory model of adult cognitive development revisited. In R. L. Rubinstein, M. Moss, & M. Kleban (Eds.), *The many dimensions of aging* (pp. 175–193). New York: Springer.

Schaie, K. W., Willis, S. L., & Caskie, G. I. L. (2004). The Seattle Longitudinal Study: Relation between personality and cognition. *Aging, Neuropsychology and Cognition, 11*, 304–324.

Schaie, K. W., Willis, S. L., Hertzog, C., & Schulenberg, J. E. (1987). Effects of cognitive training on primary mental abilities. *Psychology and Aging, 2*, 233–242.

Schaie, K. W., Willis, S. L., Jay, G., & Chipuer, H. (1989). A cross-sectional study of the structural invariance in psychometric abilities. *Developmental Psychology, 25*, 652–662.

Schaie, K. W., Willis, S. L., & O'Hanlon, A. M. (1994). Perceived intellectual performance change over seven years. *Journal of Gerontology: Psychological Sciences, 49*, P108–P118.

Schaie, K. W., & Zuo, Y. L. (2001). Family environments and adult cognitive functioning. In R. J. Sternberg & E. L. Grigorenko (Eds.), *Environmental effects on cognitive abilities* (pp. 337–361). Mahwah, NJ: Lawrence Erlbaum.

Schooler, C. (1987). Cognitive effects of complex environments during the life span: A review and theory. In C. Schooler & K. W. Schaie (Eds.), *Cognitive functioning and social structure over the life course* (pp. 24–49). New York: Ablex.

Schultz, N. R., Elias, M. F., Robbins, M. A., & Streeten, D. H. (1989). A longitudinal study of the performance of hypertensive and normotensive subjects on the Wechsler Adult Intelligence Scale. *Psychology and Aging, 4*, 496–499.

Seeman, T. E., McEwen, B. S., Rowe, J. W., & Singer, B. H. (2001). Allostatic load as a marker of cumulative biological risk: MacArthur studies of successful aging. *Proceedings of the National Academy of Sciences*, 98, 4770–4775.

Shimada, M., Meguro, K., Inagaki, H., Ishizaki, J., & Yamadori, A. (2001). Global intellectual deterioration in Alzheimer's disease and a reverse model of intellectual development: An applicability of the Binet scale. *Psychiatry and Clinical Neurosciences*, 55, 559–563.

Shock, N. W., Greulick, R. C., Andres, R., Arenberg, D., Costa, P. T., Lakatta, E. G., et al. (1984). *Normal human aging: The Baltimore Longitudinal Study of Aging*. Washington, DC: U.S. Government Printing Office.

Snow, W. G., Tierney, M. C., Zorzitto, M. L., Fisher, R. H., & Reid, D. W. (1989). WAIS-R test-retest reliability in a normal elderly sample. *Journal of Clinical and Experimental Neuropsychology*, 11, 423–428.

Spearman, C. (1904). "General intelligence:" Objectively determined and measured. *American Journal of Psychology*, 15, 201–292.

Stankov, L. (1988). Aging, attention, and intelligence. *Psychology and Aging*, 3, 59–74.

Stanley, T. O., Mackensen, G. B., Grocott, H. P., White, W. D., Blumenthal, J. A., Laskowitz, D. T., et al. (2002). The impact of postoperative atrial fibrillation on neurocognitive outcome after coronary artery bypass graft surgery. *Anesthesia Analgesia*, 94, 290–295.

Steen, B., & Djurfeldt, H. (1993). The gerontological and geriatric population studies in Gothenburg, Sweden. *Zeitschrift für Gerontologie*, 26, 163–169.

Sternberg, R. J., & Berg, C. (1987). What are theories of adult intellectual development theories of? In C. Schooler & K. W. Schaie (Eds.), *Cognitive functioning and social structure over the life course* (pp. 3–23). New York: Ablex.

Subrahmanyam, K., Greenfield, P., Kraut, R., & Gross, E. (2001). The impact of computer use on children's and adolescent's development. *Journal of Applied Developmental Psychology*, 22, 7–30.

Tabbarah, M., Crimmins, E. M., & Seeman, T. E. (2002). The relationship between cognitive and physical performance: MacArthur Studies of Successful Aging. *Journal of Gerontology: Medical Sciences*, 57, M228–M235.

Tamm, L., Menon, V., & Reiss, A. L. (2002). Maturation of brain function associated with response inhibition. *Journal of the American Academy of Child and Adolescent Psychiatry*, 41, 1231–1238.

Thorndike, E. L., & Woodworth, R. S. (1901). Influence of improvement in one mental function upon the efficiency of other mental functions. *Psychological Review*, 8, 247–261, 384–395, 553–564.

Thurstone, L. L. (1938). *Primary mental abilities*. Chicago: University of Chicago Press.

Thurstone, L. L., & Thurstone, T. G. (1949). *Examiner manual for the SRA Primary Mental Abilities Test* (Form 10-14). Chicago: Science Research Associates.

Tosti-Vasey, J. L., Person, D. C., Maier, H., & Willis, S. L. (1992, November). *The relationship of game playing to intellectual ability in old age*. Paper presented at the annual meeting of the Gerontological Society of America, Washington, DC

Welford, A. T. (1992). Psychological studies of aging: Their origins, development, and present challenge. *International Journal of Aging and Human Development*, 34, 185–197.

Werner, H. (1948). *Comparative psychology of mental health*. New York: International Universities Press.

Willis, S. L. (1989a). Cohort differences in cognitive aging: A sample case. In K. W. Schaie & C. Schooler (Eds.), *Social structure and aging: Psychological processes* (pp. 94–112). Hillsdale, NJ: Lawrence Erlbaum.

Willis, S. L. (1989b). Improvement with cognitive training: Which dogs learn what tricks? In L. W. Poon, D. C. Rubin, & B. A. Wilson (Eds.), *Everyday cognition in adulthood and late life* (pp. 545–569). Cambridge: Cambridge University Press.

Willis, S. L. (1990). Contributions of cognitive training research to understanding late life potential. In M. Perlmutter (Ed.), *Late life potential* (pp. 25–42). Washington, DC: Gerontological Society of America.

Willis, S. L. (2001). Methodological issues in behavioral intervention research with the elderly. In J. E. Birren & K. W. Schaie (Eds.), *Handbook of the psychology of aging* (5th ed., pp. 78–108). San Diego, CA: Academic Press.

Willis, S. L., Jay, G. M., Diehl, M. & Marsiske, M. (1992). Longitudinal change and prediction of everyday task competence in the elderly. *Research on Aging*, 14, 68–91.

Willis, S. L. & Nesselroade, C. S. (1990). Long-term effects of fluid ability training in old-old age. *Developmental Psychology*, 26, 905–910.

Willis, S. L., & Schaie, K. W. (1986a). Practical intelligence in later adulthood. In R. J. Sternberg & R. K. Wagner (Eds.), *Practical intelligence: Origins of competence in the everyday world* (pp. 236–270). New York: Cambridge University Press.

Willis, S. L., & Schaie, K.W. (1986b). Training the elderly on the ability factors of spatial orientation and inductive reasoning. *Psychology and Aging*, 1, 239–247.

Willis, S. L., & Schaie, K. W. (1988). Gender differences in spatial ability in old age: Longitudinal and intervention findings. *Sex Roles*, 18, 189–203.

Willis, S. L., & Schaie, K. W. (1993). Everyday cognition: Taxonomic and methodological considerations. In J. M. Puckett & H. W. Reese (Eds.), *Mechanisms of everyday cognition* (pp. 33–54). Hillsdale, NJ: Lawrence Erlbaum.

Willis, S. L., & Schaie, K. W. (1994a). Assessing competence in the elderly. In C. E. Fisher & R. M. Lerner (Eds.), *Applied developmental psychology* (pp. 339–372). New York: Macmillan.

Willis, S. L., & Schaie, K. W. (1994b). Cognitive training in the normal elderly. In F. Forette, Y. Christen, & F. Boller (Eds.), *Plasticité cérébrale et stimulation cognitive* [Cerebral plasticity and cognitive stimulation] (pp. 91–113). Paris: Fondation Nationale de Gérontologie.

Willis, S. L., & Schaie, K. W. (1999a). Intellectual functioning in midlife. In S. L. Willis & J. D. Reid (Eds.), *Life in the middle: Psychological and social development in middle age* (pp. 233–247). San Diego, CA: Academic Press.

Willis, S. L., & Schaie, K.W. (1999b). Theories of everyday competence. In V. L. Bengston & K. W. Schaie (Eds.), *Handbook of theories of aging* (pp. 174–195). New York: Springer.

Woodruff-Pak, D. S. (1989). Aging and intelligence: Changing perspectives in the twentieth century. *Journal of Aging Studies, 3,* P176–P186.

Zanjani, F. A. K. (2002). *Predicting health behavior domains using social, environmental, ability and personality determinants across young and old adults: Seattle Longitudinal Study.* Unpublished master's thesis, Pennsylvania State University, University Park.

Zelinski, E. M., Gilewski, M. J., & Schaie, K. W. (1993). Three-year longitudinal memory assessment in older adults: Little change in performance. *Psychology and Aging, 8,* 176–186.

Zhang, L. (2002). Thinking styles and cognitive development. *Journal of Genetic Psychology, 163,* 179–196.

Zhang, Z., & Yu, Z., (2002). The effect pf parents' education on early intellectual development of infants. *Chinese Journal of Clinical Psychology, 10,* 31–32, 35.

Chapter 6

Emotional Development in Adulthood: A Developmental Functionalist Review and Critique

Nathan S. Consedine and Carol Magai

Without exception, human lives are born, lived, and ended in the presence of emotions. Joy, anger, sadness, contempt, fear, and pride—our lives are steeped. They surge through everything we do, saturating our thoughts, behavior, and experience in a manner so subtle and so complete that we often forget about them. They are reflected in our physiology, experience, and behavior. They inspire and motivate our most important decisions and form the core of our experience of ourselves in the world. Of particular importance to the study of human development, and the conceptual foci of this chapter, are the relations between the emotional lives of adults and patterns of social networks/social relatedness. Emotions lie at the very heart of social relationships. Their expressive elements encapsulate a social signaling and mutual regulatory system of phenomenal sophistication and importance, not least of which because they are the primary channel through which cultural environments enact their encouragements, prohibitions, and sanctions. Ultimately, emotions act as a major interface between the personal and interpersonal and between the social and biological spheres of human functioning; they provide a nearly seamless bridge between nature and nurture and between person and environment.

Given the emergence of emotions as pivotal in understanding a number of social, developmental, and adaptational processes, it is surprising that there has been little research on emotions in adulthood. Early views depicted the later half of life as involving a period of emotional turbulence, followed by a period decline and loss (Charles & Carstensen, 2004; Magai, 2001; Magai & Halpern, 2001). Later life affect was depicted as dampened, rigid, and flat (Banham, 1951) or, more disturbingly, as a period of regression toward infantism (e.g., Jung, 1933). Jung (1933, cited in Carstensen & Charles, 1994), for example, suggested that "[a child's psychic processes] are not as difficult to discern as those of a very old person who has plunged again into the unconscious, and who progressively vanishes within it."

Before continuing, it should be acknowledged that research in emotional development was scanty in the first half of the twentieth century. Psychology remained firmly ensconced in the cradle of behaviorism, and emotions were generally viewed as epiphenomenal mentalistic processes beyond the aims or ken of a real science. Even when emotions eventually attained legitimacy as a field of study, developmental research was limited to the consideration of infant and child emotional development. Such a trend may partially reflect the importance that both psychodynamic theory (and its derivatives) and behaviorism ascribed to early development. Adulthood, particularly older adulthood, was viewed as a period of life in which the individuals passively reaped the seeds that were sown in their early years.

More recent views of the aging process, however, have begun to consider adult development as an inherently dynamic process in which adults are agents in their own social, physical, and emotional development. In many ways, this change was necessitated by changing demographics within Western populations stemming from the World War II Baby Boom and the need for models and understanding on which to base practical, economically viable interventions. In other ways, however, the rise of cognitivism as a psychological perspective, and affective science as a research agenda in its own right (e.g., Izard, 1971, 1991; Tomkins, 1962, 1963), have provided the major thrusts behind this paradigmatic change. In any case, the fundamental importance of this shift cannot be overstated. Although life span emotional development research remains in its infancy, recent years have seen the scientific study of emotion emerge as a central and unifying phenomenon in a revised social and scientific agenda.

In reviewing contemporary trends in adult emotion development, this chapter is arranged in two major parts. The first provides a comprehensive and current overview of the data describing adult emotion development as evidenced by age (or developmental) differences at the level of emotion elements—experience, expression, elicitation, physiology, and cognition, as well as the important topic of emotion regulation. The second section builds on the first; the state-of-the-art in contemporary adult developmental emotions research is presented and critiqued, before directions for future theoretical and empirical work are given.

EMPIRICAL SUMMARY: WHAT DO THE DATA TELL US ABOUT ADULT EMOTION DEVELOPMENT?

Although the child and infant emotions literature has a rich and differentiated history, research on the development of emotion across the adult life span has historically been sparser and more scattered. Within the last two decades, however, developmental emotions research has begun to gain some momentum as a cohesive field of study, and a growing number of investigators are addressing aspects of emotion development in adulthood. In what follows, we review this more recent literature in the context of six classes of developmental change: emotion experience, emotion expression, emotion elicitation, emotion recognition, the physiology of emotional responding, the relations between emotion and cognition, and emotion regulation.

Changes in Emotion Experience

Changes in Global Affective Tone and Subjective Well-Being

Cross-sectional findings are conflicted regarding developmental changes in positive and negative affect (Mroczek, 2001). Some studies suggest few differences, some that positive affect may increase and negative affect decrease, and still others that both positive and negative affect may decline with age. Early views of middle age suggested that it was a time of emotional turbulence, although this has not really been substantiated in the small body of research concentrating on midlife. One study of nearly 10,000 men and women ranging in age from 30 to 60 years indicated no association between middle age and feelings of turmoil, confusion, family dissatisfaction, or meaninglessness (McCrae & Costa, 1990). The measures in this study also included a scale of emotional instability, which showed no tendency toward increasing instability during midlife (see Magai & Halpern, 2001).

In terms of negative affect, Mroczek and Spiro's (2003) study of more than 1,600 males from the Normative Aging Study (aged between 43 and 91 years) showed a positive association between age and extraversion in the cohorts of individuals aged between 40 and 74 years, at which point the relation became negative. Conversely, neuroticism declined at an accelerating rate in the cohorts aged between 40 and 74 years and continued to decline more slowly from this age onward. Data from the National Opinion Research Center's General Social Survey (GSS; Davis & Smith, 1995) collected across the past three decades also suggest that the percentage of people stating they are very happy rose steadily across age cohorts until reaching the oldest cohort, when it then decreased. A recent study of 184 adults between 18 and 94 years of age asked participants to rate their emotions several times daily during a 1-week period (Carstensen, Pasupathi, Mayr, & Nesselroade, 2000). There was no relation between age and either the frequency or intensity of positive emotion in their analyses. Studies examining more global affective constructs such as "life satisfaction" report similar results; older adults (age 60 and above) have reported more contentment in their lives than young (20–35 years old) and middle-aged (40–55 years old) adults (Heckhausen, 1997). However, in the Berlin aging study, positive affect declined by as much as half a standard deviation ($r = -0.22$) across several age groups, among individuals ranging in age from 70–75 to 90–100 years (Smith, Fleeson, Geiselmann, Settersten, & Kunzmann, 1999).

In terms of declining negative affect, Mroczek and Kolarz's (1998) analysis of 2,727 persons from the MacArthur Study of Successful Aging assessed patterns of positive and negative affect in adults ranging in age from the mid-twenties to mid-seventies. Negative affect was highest among young adults and held even when controlling for personality, health, and contextual variables. Interestingly, the negative association between age and negative affect only held for men; age was not associated with negative affect among women. The later study by these researchers (Mroczek & Spiro, 2003), examining aspects of intraindividual personality change likewise showed a negative association between neuroticism and age. Although neuroticism is not negative affect per se, the relation is a close one. A study employing an ethnically and culturally diverse population (including samples of African Americans, European Americans, Norwegians, Chinese Americans, and American nuns) found that greater age was associated with reduced negative emotions (Gross, Carstensen, Pasupathi, Tsai, Skorpen, & Hsu, 1997). Finally, Carstensen et al. (2000) found developmental decreases in negative affect across the adult life span, with reductions

most pronounced between the 18–34 years and 35–64 years age brackets.

Other studies have suggested that both positive and negative affect may decline with age (e.g., Costa, McCrae, & Zonderman, 1987; Diener & Suh, 1997). The National Health and Nutrition Examination Survey (NHNES), for example, studied 4,942 men and women ranging in age from 24 to 74 years twice over a 9-year period. There were no differences across age in general well-being, although *both* positive and negative affect were lower in the older groups. Costa et al.'s (1987) 10-year longitudinal study employed multiple birth cohorts and likewise found that both positive and negative affect were lower in older birth cohorts. However, they did not find any longitudinal changes over the 10-year period in either positive or negative affect. Ferring and Fillip's (1995) study of older individuals reported longitudinal declines in both the intensity and frequency of positive affect over a year in the old-old but not the young-old. Stacey and Gatz (1991) surveyed 1,159 adults aged 15 to 86 years and found decreases in positive affect for people after the age of 65 but no differences among the younger cohorts. Longitudinal analysis showed that persons from all age groups, other than those from the oldest cohort (age 79–100), reported reduced negative affect over time.

Last, several studies have shown few age differences in positive affect, at least among samples aged less than 70 years. The percentage of people in Ingelhart's (1990) study of 169,776 people from 16 countries who reported they felt very happy was comparatively constant across a sample ranging in age from 15 to 65+ years. There were, however, some differences in these relations across countries, a point to which we will return. Data from a longitudinal sequential design (Charles, Reynolds, & Gatz, 2001) portray a similar picture, at least at the level of valence. In Charles et al.'s (2001) study, the frequency of positive and negative affect was assessed for three age cohorts across five time points spanning 23 years using growth curve analysis. They found that positive affect remained highly stable across two decades for all three cohorts and decreased only slightly among the very oldest individuals (mid-sixties to mid-eighties). Negative affect declined in frequency across time for all age groups, including older adults (albeit at a slower rate), and there was a noteworthy absence of cohort effects. Overall, however, data of this quality are scarce, and most reported age differences in positive affect are small and difficult to disentangle from cohort effects (Kunzmann, Little, & Smith, 2000; Magai, 2001).

Our interpretation of this literature is that there are few major changes at this level of affectivity across the adult life span, with effects scattered, varying depending on the measure used, and typically small in magnitude (Magai, 2001; Mroczek & Kolarz, 1998). There is some evidence of some small increases in positivity and a generally more pleasant balance of affect during the adult years, perhaps tapering off at some stage during the mid-seventies (Gross et al., 1997; Mroczek, 2001) or eighties (Charles & Carstensen, 2004). In contrast, there are few studies reporting increasing negative affect over the adult years (although see Ferring & Fillip, 1995); many find no change or age differences (e.g., Diener & Suh, 1997; Malatesta & Kalnok, 1984), whereas others find reductions in negative affect (e.g., Costa et al., 1987). However, there is also some evidence of a turning point in affect at some time as people approach the age gerontologists refers to as that of the oldest old. There is evidence that negative affect may increase somewhat in the late sixties (Carstensen et al., 2000), early (Kunzmann et al., 2000) or mid-seventies (Mroczek, 2001), and is most strongly evident in samples older than age 85 (e.g., Smith et al., 1999); positive affect may decline in the oldest groups (P. B. Baltes & Mayer, 1999).

More speculatively, the available data may also be taken as being broadly suggestive of potential nonlinearities and interactions in affect-age relations. Mroczek and Kolarz (1998) found that age-positive affect relations were best described by an accelerating curve, at least for women (see also Mroczek & Spiro, 2003). Carstensen et al.'s (2000) analysis of the negative affect-age relationship likewise suggests a curvilinear pattern. Negative emotion was inversely related to age until age 60, at which point the relationship deteriorated. That is, the study reported reduced frequency of negative affect from 18 to about 60 years of age, after which the curve flattened. These age findings were stable even after other variables known to influence emotions such as personality, health, and demographic factors were added to the model. Examination of the variables associated with this possible turning point in age-affect relations, as well as more systematic consideration of the role of gender and contextual factors, may prove vital in disentangling these relations.

Changes in Experience of Discrete Emotions

In terms of discrete affects, longitudinal data are limited, although Magai's (2001) review of the available literature indicated that both longitudinal and cross-sectional data revealed a reliable decrease in anger and suggested a trend for an increase in disgust across the life span. Recent theory suggests that developmental changes in emotion and emotion expression may be due to either the declining ability of the somatic system to deal with the associated arousal (e.g., P. B. Baltes, 1997; Leventhal, Patrick-Miller, Leventhal, & Burns, 1998), the desire to protect social networks (e.g., Carstensen, 1993, 1995), or changes in the life tasks confronting adults at different stages of life and thus the functions of discrete affects (Consedine & Magai, 2003; Consedine, Magai, & Bonanno, 2002; Consedine, Magai, & King, 2004). Empirically, however, the data needed to tease apart and test these theories are sparse.

Consistent with Magai's (2001) analysis, some data suggest reductions in a number of discrete negative emotions, the results being most consistent for the affects that are more physiologically arousing. One recent study of negative emotion reported that adolescents (ages 13–16) and young adults (ages 20–29) referred to anger more frequently when describing interpersonal problems than older adults, with younger women also reporting that their distress endured longer than that of older women (Birditt & Fingerman, 2003). This same study, however, reported no differences in the frequency of sadness in response to interpersonal problems, an interesting finding that we reconsider shortly.

Gross et al. (1997) found a negative association between various negative emotions and age in two independent samples. The first group—a sample of nuns from a Midwestern religious community aged between 24 to 101 years—showed negative relations between age and anger, sadness, and fear, but not disgust, and increased happiness. The second group—an independent sample of community-dwelling Norwegian respondents aged between 20 and 70 years—replicated the negative relation between anger and age, but only for women, perhaps suggesting there may be additional gender differences in the development of emotions (see also Labouvie-Vief, Lumley, Jain, & Heinze, 2003). Lawton, Kleban, and Dean (1993) had young, middle-aged, and older adults indicate how frequently they had experienced various affects over the past year. There were no overall age differences in positive emotions; however, older adults reported being less depressed, anxious, hostile, and shy than one or both younger groups and reported greater contentment. Stoner and Spencer (1987) found that adults over the age of 60 years had lower total anger scores on the Spielberger Anger Expression scale than middle-aged (40–59 years) participants.

One recent study from a sociological perspective considered how age-linked changes in exposure to different social contexts may mediate the negative relation between age and the experience of anger (Schieman, 1999). In a manner not dissimilar to Carstensen's selectivity theory, Schieman (1999) suggested that "age structures exposure to, and experience of, the sites of anger provocation" (p. 274). Analyses based on 951 individuals from the Ontario Survey (Turner & Wood, 1985) and 1,450 individuals from the GSS (Davis & Smith, 1996) revealed linear declines in self-reported anger from adolescence to very late life. Most important, this relation remained—albeit weaker—even when changes in relationship status, financial situation, health, and demographics were controlled (Schieman, 1999).

At least two studies, however, have reported data that are inconsistent with this picture. Tsai, Levenson, and Carstensen (2000) found that older and younger adults did not differ in their "on-line" emotional reactions when watching emotionally stimulating video clips, but that the retrospectively reported experiences of older adults were less positive in response to both sad and amusing film clips. Consedine and Magai's (2003) study of 1,118 community-dwelling adults 65 years and older likewise revealed only a single relation between age and 10 discrete emotions, although the restricted age range makes the relevance of these data to a life span analysis problematic. There was a significant inverse relation between age and self-reported experience of shame in these adults.

Making firm statements about the development of discrete affects is difficult given the scarcity of studies employing the requisite measurement specificity. Longitudinal studies need to begin examining changes in discrete emotions over time to clarify how emotions change across adulthood. Magai (2001) has previously suggested that there may be an age-related decrease in the frequency of some discrete emotions,

most notably anger, although the data from Gross et al. (1997) and Lawton et al. (1993) suggest that sadness and fear/anxiety may also decline with age and happiness increase. Exactly why these particular changes occur remains unelaborated in the literature (Consedine & Magai, 2003), although the general assumption appears to be that the changes reflect developmental changes in motivations and the learning of regulatory skills. We discuss these issues more fully shortly.

Changes in the Intensity of Felt Emotion

Cross-sectional studies reveal inconsistent findings with respect to age-related difference in the intensity of emotion over the adult years. Studies that have gathered information on adults' reflections on how they experience their emotions in general have found that older adults have lower scores on affective intensity for negative affect (Barrick, Hutchinson, & Deckers, 1989) or both positive and negative affect (Diener, Sandvik, & Larsen, 1985; Lawton, Kleban, Rajagopal, & Dean, 1992). In Lawton et al.'s (1992) study, for example, older adults ($M = 70$ years) were more likely than either middle-aged ($M = 42$ years) or younger ($M = 21$ years) subjects to endorse items reflecting the mildness of their negative emotion experience. Gross et al. (1997) asked respondents about the intensity of their impulse strength, that is, the strength of those emotional impulses that are difficult to control. Older European Americans and African Americans, but not Chinese Americans, reported lower impulse strength than their younger counterparts.

In contrast to this picture, however, other studies that have avoided the use of retrospective accounts have not unambiguously supported the existence of developmental declines in felt emotional intensity. Malatesta and Kalnok (1984) found that when younger and older adults were asked to report on whether they believed their emotions had become less intense with age, older adults maintained that the intensity of their experiences had not diminished over the years. In an experience sampling study of a wide age range of adults, Carstensen and colleagues gathered data on emotional experiences *as they occurred* in everyday life, sampling the same subjects several times daily across a week (Carstensen et al, 2000). No age differences in the subjective intensity of positive or negative emotion experiences were reported.

Equally, laboratory studies in which adults of different ages are asked to reexperience and recount emotionally salient events drawn from their own lives have failed to show age differences in felt intensity (Levenson, Carstensen, Friesen, & Ekman, 1991; Malatesta, Izard, Culver & Nicolich, 1987). Malatesta-Magai, Jonas, Shepard, and Culver (1992), for example, studied the emotions of younger and older individuals using an emotion induction procedure in which participants relived and recounted emotionally charged experiences involving anger, fear, sadness, and interest. One interpretation of these complex data put forth in Magai (2001) suggests that affective intensity may remain the same across the adult years, at least once the emotions are aroused. Alternately, it may be that the reporting of current (rather than retrospective) emotion experiences are less readily biased by demand or the impact of self-concept schemas.

Changes in the Complexity of Emotional Experience

A final component of emotional experience that may change across the adult life span involves the phenomenon called emotional complexity. Over the past 15 years, Labouvie-Vief and colleagues have been engaged in research on affective complexity, defined as the interaction between emotion and cognition and their integration (Labouvie-Vief, DeVoe, & Bulka, 1989) and the ability to experience multiple and conflicting emotions simultaneously. This research represents an important departure from traditional research into mere levels of valence and intensity, ensuring that researchers do not forget that emotion experience may develop qualitatively as well as quantitatively.

Labouvie-Vief, DeVoe, and Bulka (1989) found that the levels of emotional understanding for fear, sadness, anger, and happiness increased with age, with adult groups scoring higher on understanding in comparison to preadolescent (ages 10–14) and adolescent groups (ages 15–18). The results of this study demonstrate positive development of emotional understanding until at least middle adulthood (30–45 years), with improvements in the understanding of sadness leveling off at an earlier age than the other three emotions. There was a general developmental trend in which younger individuals were more likely to describe their experiences in terms of normative

prescriptions as well as to employ less mature coping strategies, such as forgetting, ignoring, or distraction. In contrast, middle-aged adults were able to sustain and tolerate complex or mixed feelings without resolving them or polarizing them prematurely (Labouvie-Vief, DeVoe, & Bulka, 1989).

More recent research by this team has suggested that complexity (at least in Labouvie-Vief's definition) peaks in midlife, with young and old individuals scoring lower than middle-aged adults (Labouvie-Vief, Chiodo, Goguen, Diehl, & Orwoll, 1995; Labouvie-Vief, Diehl, Chiodo, & Coyle, 1995). Other developmental studies of the cognitive-affective aspects of emotions, particularly knowledge, however, suggest that there may continue to be qualitative changes in the representation of affects in later life. Fingerman's (2000) study of older mothers ($M = 76$) and daughters ($M = 46$), for example, suggests an increasingly realistic and balanced view of emotions with respect to close others with greater age. Similarly, Carstensen et al.'s (2000) experience-sampling study of 184 adults between the ages of 18 and 94 years showed that older adults reported more differentiated emotional experiences; more technically, a factor analysis at the level of the individual showed a reliable correlation between age and the number of emotion factors each individual reported.

Changes in Emotion Expressivity

An area of enduring interest to developmental researchers interested in the emotions has involved considering possible changes in emotion expressivity. Historically, this research has focused on changes in emotion expressivity across childhood, primarily documenting the gradual adoption of familial and cultural display rules (Magai, 2001). Although common wisdom has tended to suggest dampened expressivity with age, the small body of empirical data that has accumulated across the past 15 years has not substantiated this supposition. Some studies suggest that older adults may be less expressive of some affects, whereas others show no differences. Overall, there appear comparatively few level differences in expressivity, although the extant data do suggest some changes, notably that expressions in the faces of older adults may become more blended and complex.

Although the posed emotion expressions of older adults are more difficult for naive judges to interpret (Malatesta et al., 1987), and expressions during directed facial action tasks have been shown to be of lower quality (Levenson et al., 1991), research suggests that older adults are no less expressive, at least at a global level, than other adults once they become emotionally aroused (Malatesta-Magai et al., 1992). In a study of emotional responses to sad and amusing films in 48 older (70–80 years) and younger (20–34 years) European and Chinese Americans, Tsai et al. (2000) found equivalent levels of positive and negative emotional expressivity across both age and cultural groups. Other research, however, such as Carstensen, Gottman, and Levenson's (1995) classic research into emotions in marital interaction, shows that affect expression and emotional reciprocity in happy and unhappy middle-aged ($M = 44.3$, 43.3 years) and older couples ($M = 63.6$, 62.2 years) differed as a function of age. Compared to older couples, middle-aged couples displayed more anger, belligerence, humor, disgust, and interest. However, older couples were shown to express more affection during discussions, even after differences in baseline marital satisfaction were controlled; there were no differences in the expression of joy, contempt, sadness, domineeringness, and validation. Another study of 80 younger ($M = 28$ years) and older ($M = 69$ years) adults participating in four emotion induction procedures designed to elicit interest, sadness, fear, and anger found substantial evidence of greater expressivity with age (Malatesta-Magai et al., 1992). Older participants expressed more of each of the four target emotions in the appropriate condition: more anger during the anger induction, more sadness during the sadness induction, fear under the fear induction, and interest during the interest induction. In another study, Magai, Cohen, Gomberg, Malatesta, and Culver (1996) found that emotion expressivity was preserved in later life even under conditions of cognitive decline. Using a behavioral coding system, coupled with direct observations of mid- to late-stage dementia patients during a family visit, these authors found that negative affects were preserved across levels of cognitive decline; only joy expressions were lower in frequency among the most deteriorated patients. As with the previously described research, this study suggests that the ability to express emotions, perhaps particularly in interpersonal contexts, remains intact across the life span, even under conditions of cognitive decline.

Finally, there is also some evidence that expressive facial behavior may change in ways other than that of total expressivity with age. Malatesta and Izard (1984) coded the videotaped facial expressions of young ($M_{age} = 33.3$, $SD = 3.9$), middle-aged ($M_{age} = 55.2$, $SD = 4.2$), and older ($M_{age} = 68.8$, $SD = 2.8$) women as they recounted emotional experiences. Interestingly, although there were fewer component muscle movements in the facial expressions of the middle-aged and older women (perhaps an indication of reduced expressivity), their expressions were more complicated; there were more instances of different emotions combined within the same expression. Moreno, Borod, Welkowitz, and Alpert (1990) examined age differences in the facial symmetry of expressive behavior during the induction of four emotions among 30 young (21–39 years), 30 middle-aged (40–59 years), and 30 old women (aged 60–81 years). Although age did not affect whether expressions occurred equally on left and right sides of the face, there was an age by emotion effect, indicating that older participants appeared more disgusted.

Overall then, the body of research examining possible developmental changes in the expression of emotion has failed to provide conclusive evidence of reduced expressivity with greater age. Few studies have shown reduced expressivity, and others have shown no differences. The majority of studies have, if anything, been indicative of increased expressivity in later life, particularly once older adults are aroused (Magai, 2001). The single study that clearly demonstrated reduced expressivity with age (Levenson et al., 1991) also showed differences in the success with which affect was elicited using a directed facial action task. Other evidence does, however, suggest that the expressions of older adults may become somewhat less readily interpretable, perhaps because emotions are more blended in the faces of older individuals, because dispositional tendencies become crystallized on the face with age, or because of age-related structural changes in the face (Malatesta et al., 1987).

Changes in Emotion Recognition

Few studies have considered developmental differences in the processes by which emotions are recognized in other people. As with most of the literature reviewed to date, the data are mixed, with some research showing no developmental differences, some showing improvements with age, and others showing decrements. Moreno, Borod, Welkowitz, and

Alpert's (1993) study of 30 young (aged 21–39 years), 30 middle-aged (aged 40–59 years), and 30 older adults (aged 60–81 years) who had been screened for neurological and psychiatric disorders as well as for cognitive and visuo-perceptual deficits showed no global differences in the recognition of photographed emotion expressions, although there were some differences at the level of discrete emotions. Consistent with an increased orientation to positive affect (Mather & Johnson, 2000), older adults were more accurate in recognizing happiness but less accurate in recognizing sadness compared to the younger and middle-aged adults (Moreno et al., 1993). In another study of 30 younger (aged 17–22 years) and 30 older adults (aged 65–90 years), however, McDowell, Harrison, and Demaree (1994) found that older adults were less accurate than younger adults in their identification of sad, angry, fearful, and neutral but *not* happy facial expressions. A further study of 30 young ($M = 29.9$ years) and 30 older ($M = 69.2$ years) individuals without a history of psychiatric or neurological illness showed no age differences in two emotional tasks involving the interpretation of verbal descriptions of emotions (Phillips, MacPherson, & Della Salla, 2002). However, although there were no overall age differences in the recognition of the facial expressions from six primary emotions (happiness, anger, fear, disgust, sadness, and surprise), angry and sad faces were more poorly recognized by the older sample, and they performed more poorly on an "eyes" test that asked participants to choose which of two words best described a series of images depicting pairs of eyes (Phillips, MacPherson, & Della Salla, 2002).

Allen and Brosgole's (1993) study had young adults (17–31 years), nondemented older adults (75–91 years), and senile demented older adults (77–91 years) respond to drawings, vocal stimuli, and music. Although the demented adults performed most poorly overall, nondemented older adults also made significantly more mistakes in response to the voice and tonal (but not facial) stimuli (15% vs. 2% overall). Another study of 28 young (20–39 years), middle-aged (40–59 years), and older (60–85 years) adults had participants rate both emotional and nonemotional words from the New York Emotion Battery (Grunwald et al., 1999). Older participants were significantly less accurate for *both* emotional and nonemotional lexical stimuli than either of the other groups. Montepare, Koff, Zaitchik, and Albert (1999) examined age-related differences in the ability of 41 younger (18–22 years) and 41 older adults (65–89 years) to decode emotions from body movements and gestures. Older adults made more errors overall, but particularly for negative emotions and predominantly by rating emotional episodes as "neutral." However, as has been previously noted by Magai (2001), the actors who depicted the emotional gestures were young adults, and other research has demonstrated that age congruence is a likely mediator of recognition rates, at least for faces (Malatesta et al., 1987). A further study considered the effects of age on facial emotion processing and brain activation patterns (Gunning-Dixon et al., 2003). These authors showed eight old (aged 57–79 years) and eight young (aged 19–29 years) adults happy, sad, angry, fearful, disgusted, and neutral facial stimuli while functional MRI data were taken. Analysis showed that visual, frontal, and limbic regions were differentially active in younger participants, whereas parietal, temporal, and frontal regions were more active when older participants were viewing the faces. This pattern of activation is consistent with a view of life span emotion development in which learning about emotions and emotion knowledge increases across the life span.

Overall, however, the data reviewed here suggest that there are some slight declines in the ability to accurately recognize the emotion signals of others, at least in terms of accurately decoding negative emotion signals. There is some suggestion that declines in recognition may be unequally distributed across communication modalities, with older adults performing more poorly in facial versus postural recognition tasks (Brosgole, Kurucz, PlaHovinsak, Sprotte, & Haveliwala, 1983). There may, however, be some compensation if the signalers are peers (rather than of a different age). The reasons for these declines and the manner in which learning about emotion signals and increasing emotion knowledge may mediate other losses remain to be explored.

Changes in the Physiology of Emotion

Because emotion experience is linked to autonomic activity, and most autonomic indices decline with age (Cacioppo, Berntson, Klein, & Poehlmann, 1998), there are some grounds to expect changes in emotion physiology with age (Charles & Carstensen, 2004). (There is a growing body of literature describing age differences in physiological responses to stress. We do not review this literature here and instead refer the reader to recent work such as that by Uchino, Uno, Holt-Lunstad, & Flinders, 1999.) A small body of research has documented changes in the physiological aspects of emotions with age, particularly in heart rate (HR), although studies to date have been cohort rather than developmental, and in any case, separating the physiological changes associated with general aging and medication use versus emotions per se is difficult.

In general, early studies suggested that older adults were less reactive than younger adults at a physiological level. In an initial pair of studies, Levenson and colleagues made inferences about possible developmental changes in emotional reactivity by comparing a sample of younger adults from a study by Levenson, Ekman, and Friesen (1990) to a sample of 35 older adults ($M = 77$ years) completing the same directed facial action and recounted emotion experience tasks in Levenson et al. (1991). Under experimenter guidance, participants formed expressions of anger, disgust, fear, happiness, sadness, and surprise and recounted experiential episodes about these same six affects. Although the pattern of emotion-specific cardiac changes was similar across studies and groups, the two samples had different mean levels of reactivity; older participants had smaller HR increases from baseline than younger participants (see figure 2 in Levenson et al., 1991), although the differences were greatest for the relived emotions task. Levenson, Carstensen, and Gottman (1994) extended these findings to an induction paradigm involving marital interactions. This study of 89 middle-aged couples and 72 older couples reported lower reactivity during discussions of (a) events of the day, (b) a problem area of continuing disagreement in their marriage, and (c) a mutually agreed on pleasant topic, among the older couples (as indexed by differences in interbeat interval and ear pulse transmission time), a finding that held even when controlling for the affective quality (positivity-negativity) of the interaction.

More recently, Tsai et al. (2000) examined basic emotional reactivity in younger (ages 20–34 years) and older participants (ages 70–85 years). Again, older adults evidenced smaller changes in their cardiovascular responding than did younger participants while watching sad and amusing video clips, although HR changes appear smaller in both groups than those reported in earlier studies (Labouvie-Vief et al., 2003). This study also indicates that developmental changes in physiological reactivity may differ depending on the particular emotion studied. In the amusing and sad film conditions, the HRs of younger adults increased by about one and two beats per minute (BPM), respectively, whereas those of older adults showed smaller changes from baseline. Importantly, this study showed no differences between the Chinese American and European American subsamples.

Last, a recent study by Labouvie-Vief and colleagues (2003) replicated some aspects of the Tsai et al. (2000) study but also suggested that age-graded changes in physiological reactivity may be gender and emotion dependent). In a relived experience study of 113 adults aged between 15 and 88 years, these authors found that cardiac reactivity was reduced in older adults for anger, fear, sadness, and happy experiences. In addition, however, there were some significant gender × age interactions; younger women had much higher HR reactivity during the anger and fear induction, and yet there were no gender differences in the older sample. Cardiac reactivity for sadness and happiness stories was not influenced by age.

Overall, the small body of literature on the psychophysiology of emotions across the adult life span tends to suggest diminished reactivity in response to both experimentally controlled stimuli (e.g., film) as well as relived emotion experience. The generally diminished HR reactivity among older groups has thus far been consistent across studies for anger, fear, sadness, and happiness/amusement (Labouvie-Vief et al., 2003; Levenson et al., 1991; Tsai et al., 2000), as well as in the single study considering disgust and surprise (Levenson et al., 1991). These effects appear to hold across a number of eliciting mediums, including film (Tsai et al., 2000), the directed facial action task (Levenson et al., 1991), and relived experience (Labouvie-Vief et al., 2003). These latter authors have, however, argued that age differences may be greater in response to emotional memories than film. They suggest that watching situations that have not been personally experienced may not generate equivalent affect or that internally generated memories may be more closely related to cardiac reactivity than externally activated ones.

Changes in Emotional and Self-Regulation

We have described the literature documenting changes in the experience and expression of emotions across the adult life span. Although the literature is underdeveloped, the bulk of the available data are consistent with the view that adulthood and later life may be characterized by improvements in several areas of emotion experience. Given the role of emotions as a "readout" of adaptive system status (Lazarus, 1991), however, the notion that there may be improvements poses an interesting paradox. On one hand, life satisfaction, expressive capacities, and emotional experience do not appear to diminish with age, at least until the very end of life, and may even improve. On the other hand, older adults have fewer adaptive resources (Brandtstädter, Rothermund, & Schmitz, 1997), and there is an increasingly unfavorable balance between gains and losses with age (P. B. Baltes, 1987). Somatic resources and energy levels decline (Leventhal et al., 1998; Panksepp & Miller, 1995) and morbidity increases (Lima & Allen, 2001), as do the number of interpersonal losses, levels of income (Gnich & Gilhooly, 2000; Michalos, Hubley, Zumbo, & Hemingway, 2001), sleep difficulties, and interferences with the activities of daily living (Steverink, Westerhof, Bode, & Dittmann-Kohli, 2001). One factor that may help explain this so-called paradox (see P. B. Baltes & M. M. Baltes, 1990) lies in some marked developmental changes in emotion regulation.

In general terms, the bulk of the available data has been interpreted as demonstrating comparatively normative improvements in emotion regulatory strategies with age. Contrary to what earlier, more negative views of aging portrayed, these changes appear predominantly positive or at least are typified by more thoughtful, flexible, and effective regulatory styles and skills. The temporal time frame in which these developmental changes occur is not clear from the extant data, although some data among older adults suggest that changes may slow in old age.

A large proportion of these data are, however, cross-sectional, and longitudinal demonstrations of developmental improvements have yet to be provided. One study by Labouvie-Vief and colleagues reported that adolescents (ages 11–18) showed significantly less emotional control than both younger (ages 19–45) and middle-aged adults (ages 46–67) (Labouvie-Vief, Hakim-Larson, DeVoe, & Schoeberlien, 1989). Gross and colleagues (1997) examined the self-reported tendency to control the inner experience of five target emotions: happiness, sadness, fear, anger, and disgust in samples of Norwegian adults and American nuns described earlier. Older participants from the Norwegian sample reported greater emotional control relative to younger participants for all five emotions. There was also an interaction effect indicating that older women reported a greater sense of being able to control the *internal* experience of anger than younger women. In terms of external control of emotions, there were no age-related differences. In the sample of nuns, aging was associated with increased inner control of happiness, sadness, fear, and anger.

Findings from other laboratories have also suggested age-related improvements in the control of emotion. Lawton et al. (1992) had young (18–29 years), middle-aged (30–59 years), and older (60+ years) participants complete a questionnaire that assessed how they viewed their own internal and external reactivity, emotion characteristics (including intensity, frequency, and duration), and their perceptions regarding how able they were to influence their emotions. Age was associated with perceptions of increased emotional control and more stable mood. However, as the authors noted, the differences were not great, and there was considerable variation within age groups. Stoner and Spencer (1987) found that adults over the age of 60 years had lower scores than the younger (21–38 years) participants on an anger out subscale, whereas Butcher and colleagues (1991) found a negative relationship between age and scores on the anger content dimension of the MMPI-II, again implying if not directly demonstrating fewer anger control problems with age.

A study by McConatha and Huba (1999) examined the relation between perceptions of primary control and four kinds of secondary control—defined as emotion control strategies—in adults between 19 and 92 years old. They found an inverse relation between age and primary control, with primary control decreasing and secondary control increasing with age. As age increased, aggression control, impulsiveness control, and inhibition control increased. At the same time, the tendency to ruminate about emotionally upsetting events decreased. In a study of individuals ranging from age 10 to older than 70, older persons showed a preference for avoiding conflict and delaying expression (Diehl, Coyle, & Labouvie-Vief, 1996). Moreover, older adults employed an expanded combination of coping and defense strategies, indexing greater impulse control, and showed an increased tendency to positively appraise conflict situations. In theory, more positive reappraisal of a situation can help older people neutralize and/or decrease the negative experience and behavioral expression in a conflict situation (Gross, 2001). Other researchers have suggested that the experience of emotions becomes a more reflective and conscious process as people age, with older people being more vivid in their sense of experience and having more explicit knowledge of bodily sensations, as well as displaying flexibility and delay of action when affected by an emotion (Labouvie-Vief, DeVoe, & Bulka, 1989). Recently, Labouvie-Vief and Diehl (2000) likewise found that age was positively related to reflective cognition and crystallized intelligence, although it was negatively related to fluid intelligence.

Consistent with certain theories of later life development, particularly that of Carstensen and colleagues (Carstensen, 1993, 1995; Carstensen, Isaacowitz, & Charles, 1999; Lang & Carstensen, 2002), there is some evidence that improvements in emotional control may specifically be aimed at maximizing emotional experience and minimizing the impact of negative emotions on key social relationships (Charles & Carstensen, 2004). Gottman, Levenson, and colleagues (e.g., Carstensen et al., 1995; Levenson & Gottman, 1983; Levenson et al., 1994) have pioneered the experimental study of emotions in marital interaction. In their study, middle-aged (40–50 years) and older (60–70 years) married couples were asked to interact with one another in three 15-minute exchanges while video and physiological measures were taken. Couples had a series of conversations, one about the day's events, one regarding a problem area in their marriage, and one about a pleasant topic. Data showed trends suggesting that older couples were less likely to engage in "negative start-up" (an affective sequence in which one spouse's neutral affect was followed by negativity in the other) and more likely to use deescalation (when negative affect in one spouse was followed by neutral in the other), although these effects were only significant for some types of marriages. The authors speculated that these couples had learned to achieve some control over the activation of negative affect.

The foregoing studies, although cross-sectional in nature, collectively suggest that the emotional regulation capacities of individuals may improve with age in the sense that people at later ages *report* being more effective at down-regulating negative affect experience and expressions. There appears to be a general trend in which regulatory efforts move from response-focused regulatory efforts—regulating experience or expression once the emotions systems are already aroused—toward more anticipatory or antecedent regulatory efforts aimed at regulating aversive negative

emotions before they are aroused (see Gross, 1998). Specifically, learning may enable older adults to seek out the kinds of environments and persons that allow them to avoid negative affect and conflict (Carstensen, Fung, & Charles, 2003; Carstensen, Gross, & Fung, 1997; Charles & Carstensen, 2004; Lawton, 1989; Lawton et al., 1992) and seek to maximize gratifying emotional experiences more effectively (Carstensen, 1993, 1995).

This noted, however, there is also some suggestion of a plateau, an age at which regulatory improvements derived from a lifetime's learning and acquired knowledge and skills are offset by normative developmental losses. Most studies documenting improvements in emotion regulatory capacities have done so by comparing cohorts of convenience-sampled older and younger persons, thus obscuring the timing of developmental changes and reducing generalizability. Recent data, however, from two independent cluster-sampling studies of older minority adults may suggest that improvements in emotion regulation may not continue in samples beyond the age of 60–65. A study of 1,118 men and women between the ages of 65 and 86 years ($M = 73.8$ years) reported no relation between emotion inhibition and age (Consedine, Magai, Cohen, & Gillespie, 2002). Although not a focus of a second study, the data describing a sample of 1,364 women between the ages of 50 and 70 years ($M = 59.3$ years) reported in Consedine, Magai, and Neugut (2004) likewise found no zero-order relation between Mendolia's (2002) Index of Self-Regulation—a measure of repressive coping—and age. Women in their sixties were no more repressive than those in their fifties. As we will discuss in more detail shortly, our inability to determine exactly when (or even if) emotion regulatory skills are changing, improving, or ceasing to improve stems from the absence of samples comprising theoretically meaningful age groups, the tendency of authors to assume linear changes in the period between any two age samples, and a lack of direct demonstrations of hypothesized improvement in emotion regulatory skills.

Changes in Emotion-Related Cognitive Styles

The increased salience of emotions in the latter half of life as just described is also evident in other literatures, such as that describing emotion-related cognition or problem solving and learning. Although most cognitive functions improve during adulthood and begin to show declines in the late sixties/early seventies (Hertzog & Schaie, 1986), and accelerating declines in the late seventies (Schaie & Hertzog, 1983), there is also some suggestion that cognitive declines may not be equivalent across all processing domains.

In general, crystallized intelligence is better preserved and fluid intelligence declines become more pronounced with age (Phillips, MacPherson, & Della Sala, 2002). More specifically, whereas executive tasks such as planning, inhibition, and abstraction of logical rules (Andres & Van der Linden, 2000; Gilhooly, Phillips, Wynn, Logie, & Della Sala, 1999), task switching (Kray & Lindenberger, 2000), digit recall (West & Crook, 1990), and word fluency (Phillips, 1999) have all been shown to be poorer in older adults, the processing strategies they employ also seem particularly permeable to affect. Attention has focused on the roles played by the hippocampus (e.g., Barnes, Suster, Shen, & McNaughton, 1997; Ekstrom, Meltzer, McNaughton, & Barnes, 2001; Mizumori, Barnes, & McNaughton, 1992; Rosenzweig, Redish, McNaughton, & Barnes, 2003) and frontal lobes (Phillips & Della Sala, 1998; Phillips, MacPherson, & Della Sala, 2002; Phillips, Smith, & Gilhooly, 2002). This research suggests that functions associated with dorsolateral regions (executive functioning and working memory) are most impaired with age, whereas orbitoventral functions (processing of emotions and regulation of social behavior) are differentially preserved. A recent study of reasoning biases among 172 young ($M = 21.5$ years), middle-aged ($M = 47.5$ years), and older ($M = 69.7$ years) adults, for example, found that biases increased with age, perhaps because of selective attention or memory interference issues or through motivated cognitive conservatism (Klaczynski & Robinson, 2000).

Brandtstädter and Baltes-Götz (1990) have documented age-related differences in flexible goal adjustment (FGA) and tenacious goal pursuit (TGP) among a sample of 1,228 German adults. Their data show FGA being systematically greater among older cohorts and TGP being systematically lower. The authors interpret this as a compensatory shift from assimilative (trying to change goal-incongruent situations directly) to accommodative styles of coping (Brandtstädter & Renner, 1990) in which the individual changes the criteria for personal goals or otherwise alters the way situations are viewed. In contrast to a large body of theory suggesting that adjusting internal preferences to situational constraints is a risk

factor for depression, these authors argue that the inability to disengage may be maladaptive in later life, indirectly suggesting that learning to let go may be an important developmental milestone. Later research by this team suggests that a balancing act between assimilative and accommodative processes may help aging individuals adapt to developmental gains and losses across the life span (Brandtstädter et al., 1997).

Age differences in problem solving are again most evident in interpersonal situations (Blanchard-Fields, Jahnke, & Camp, 1995), which are inherently emotional (Charles & Carstensen, 2004). Blanchard-Fields and Camp (1990) found that problems of low emotional salience (e.g., consumer matters) elicited comparable problem-solving styles across age groups. However, in domains that were highly emotionally salient (e.g., conflicts with family), older adults showed greater sensitivity regarding knowing when to avoid a situation. Younger adults were problem-focused irrespective of domain. This developmental difference in problem-solving orientation is similar to that found by Folkman, Lazarus, Pimley, and Novacek (1987), indicating that older adults were more likely to endorse emotion-focused strategies than younger adults, who adopted more problem-focused strategies. These data may suggest a developmental process in which adults progressively learn which patterns of problem solving are most useful in which types of situations.

There is also some suggestion that emotional states may differentially affect the cognitive processing of persons of different ages. In one recent study, Knight, Maines, and Robinson (2002) randomly assigned 119 younger ($M_{ages} = 20.3$ and 21.4 years) and 88 older adults ($M_{ages} = 76.9$ and 76.5 years) to sad or neutral mood inductions. Both groups had enhanced recall of sad words on measures of word list recall and autobiographical memory; however, older adults displayed an additional mood congruence effect on a lexical ambiguity task and recalled fewer positive words in the word list task. The pattern of these findings suggests that the cognitive processing of older adults may be particularly sensitive to the impact of affective states or that they may become less flexible in some respects. The sensitivity interpretation is strengthened by the finding reported in Phillips et al. (2002). In the latter study, 48 young ($M = 23$ years) and 48 older ($M = 67$ years) adults went through either a positive, negative, or neutral mood induction with film and music before completing the

Tower of London puzzle task. There was a significant interaction between age and mood such that older adults made a significantly greater number of excess moves in the negative mood condition, whereas younger adults did not; both positive and negative mood increased the number of moves for older but not younger adults.

There are also age differences in memory for emotional versus nonemotional materials. A study of incidental memory for narratives containing equivalent levels of emotional and neutral information among 83 young, middle-aged, older, and elderly adults by Carstensen and Charles (1994) found that the mean proportion of emotional propositions recalled increased linearly with age (see also Gould & Dixon, 1993; Schulkind, Hennis, & Rubin, 1999). Blanchard-Fields et al. (1995) found that older adults (65–75 years) were more likely to use an avoidant/denial problem-solving strategy than younger age groups, *but only at low and medium levels of emotional salience.* They were also more likely to use passive/dependent strategies when problem situations were high in emotion salience. Thompson, Aidinejad, and Ponte (2001) presented 30 young (19–26 years) and 30 older (60–90 years) adults with videotaped scenes that depicted emotionally laden events in which verbal and nonverbal affective cues conflicted. A later memory task revealed a greater tendency among older adults to reconstruct verbal information to match nonverbally conveyed affective meaning. In one conceptually interesting study, Carstensen and Fredrickson (1998) compared older individuals with young gay men affected by HIV (subjects ranged from 18 to 88 years old). As with other research, the results indicated that affect become increasingly important in the mental representations that older individuals held of their social partners.

In addition, however, there is an emerging picture that suggests that the age-related increase in memory for emotional material may be placed predominantly on positive affect (Charles & Carstensen, 2004). In an unpublished study in which younger, middle-aged, and older participants were presented with positive, neutral, and negative images before recalling them, Charles, Mather, and Carstensen (2003) found an age-based decline in the overall number correctly recalled. However, age differences were greatest among the negative emotions; there was an interaction such that older adults were differentially less likely to remember negative images.

Similarly, Mather and Johnson (2000) found that older adults were likely to exhibit more choice-supportive memory, in that they attributed more positive and fewer negative features to options they had previously chosen. Mather and Carstensen (in press) found that older adults showed attentional biases in favor of positive rather than sad or angry faces. According to Charles et al. (2003), positive memory biases in aging are driven by a need to maximize emotional experience, specifically by reducing regret and increasing satisfaction with decisions (see also Levine & Bluck, 1997). More fully, it seems likely that older adults have acquired a complex array of self-regulatory skills that enable them to differentially orient to, encode, process, and recall themselves, situations, and others. Discussing the purpose of this altered orientation is one of the primary aims of the following section.

EMPIRICAL SUMMARY

Although early views of later life emotion had portrayed it as being dampened and negative, recent empirical data indicate a more complex and differentiated view. The field of adult emotion development is, however, little more than two decades old. There are comparatively few studies of adult emotional development, and conflicting data abound. Nonetheless, available data appear to be converging in some instances, enabling us to make several general statements about adult emotional development.

First, in terms of overall emotional valence, the available data indicate few substantial changes in global positivity-negativity, although experiences of positive affect, happiness, and contentment may increase somewhat during the adult years (tapering off around 70–80 years of age). Conversely, negative emotion experiences appear to decrease slightly across adulthood until around age 60, although they may increase again after the age of 85. To an extent this pattern is also reflected in data from the few studies that have examined developmental patterns of discrete emotions; anger and perhaps fear appear to occur less frequently with age.

Second, and perhaps more important, the fledgling body of literature on emotions in adulthood suggests that adult emotion becomes progressively more complex, conscious, and reflective, at least until late middle age. Compared to younger cohorts, middle-aged adults are better able to experience multiple and (potentially) conflicting emotions at the same time, experience their emotions more vividly, and seem to have acquired a better understanding of how emotions, persons, and situations relate. Perhaps as a consequence of this learning, coping styles and mechanisms for coping with emotionally conflicted situations appear to become more mature and differentiated and less reactive or impulsive with greater age. Perhaps because of this developmentally acquired ability to tolerate and reflect on conflicted emotions, however, later life adults are also less likely to ruminate.

Third, the ability to regulate the experiential, expressive, and physiological components of emotion appears to improve across the adult life span, as does the ability to delay goal pursuit and self-gratification. Mood becomes more stable, and later life adults report superior emotional control and impulse control. In general, learning experiences across the life course sees the development of a more sophisticated, reflective, and flexible emotion regulatory repertoire. Although there have been few direct demonstrations of superior regulatory ability once persons of different ages are emotionally aroused, older adults appear to use their learning and emotional knowledge to regulate emotions more effectively, particularly in anticipation. Experience appears to enable older adults to more successfully seek out the types of people and situations that enable them to maximize positive emotional experiences, minimize negative emotional experience, and avoid conflict. However, even when emotional, later life adults are less physiologically reactive when emotional, and they will avoid conflict and delay emotion expression in situations where expression might lead disagreements to escalate. They show an increased ability to disengage from goals when situational contingencies are not favorable to their pursuit.

Considered together, these differences appear related to an overall pattern of changes across multiple domains of functioning in which emotions become more salient in later life. Memory for emotional material improves with age, and preferential attention is paid to emotional (versus nonemotional) stimuli. Problem-solving styles in the context of emotionally salient situations change across the adult life span such that greater attention is given to emotional cues and more sensitivity to the appropriateness of problem- versus emotion-focused coping is evident. The cognitive processing of older adults is more strongly influenced by mood inductions, although it remains unclear whether the consequences of this salience are predominantly positive or negative.

CRITIQUE AND FUTURE DIRECTIONS

To this point, we have reviewed the literature regarding adult emotion development. In the final section, we draw some strands together, identify weaknesses and issues in this literature, and offer some interpretations and directions for future research. We do not attempt to address all the issues that arise in considering a research body of this immaturity. Instead we focus our review on the questions we believe are most pressing as well as those for which consideration is most likely to provide impetus and direction to the field. We begin by identifying some of the assumptions that are implicit in the literature to date before considering some of the methodological issues in the extant research. We then turn to a consideration of the big "why" question of adult emotion development—a consideration of why emotions change the ways they do. In this process, we briefly introduce some of the major theoretical frameworks that have attempted to explain some or part of the adult emotion development literature, identify some of the underlying assumptions, and consider their success in explaining patterns of stability and change.

Untested Assumptions and Issues

As with most research, there are a number of assumptions within the literature bearing on adult emotional development. In early studies, assumptions led researchers to search for evidence of a downward trajectory (see Charles & Carstensen, 2004) in adult development (e.g., Banham, 1951; Buhler, 1935; Frenkel-Brunswik, 1968; Jung, 1933). As is evident in the review, however, this assumption was poorly tested and has subsequently been clearly debunked. Emotion and emotional regulation are now widely viewed as domains in which improvements can be expected across the adult life span (e.g., Carstensen et al., 2003; Magai, 2001). Ironically, however, there is a sense that current research is no less based on untested assumptions than prior views.

One major assumption underlying contemporary adult emotions research is that changes in emotion experience and emotion regulation originate in a set of learned *skills* that are acquired across the life span (e.g., Carstensen, 1993, 1995; Carstensen et al., 1995, 1999; Gross et al., 1997; Labouvie-Vief, Hakim-Larson, et al., 1989; Labouvie-Vief et al., 2003; Lang & Carstensen, 2002; Levenson et al., 1994). However, a close examination of the empirical literature that is taken as supportive of this view shows that there have been few direct tests of the notion that emotion regulatory *skills* improve, although other forms of learning may nonetheless be occurring. Most research finds that older adults reported better control of negative affect (e.g., Gross et al., 1997; Lawton et al., 1992), and researchers tend to infer improved regulatory skills based on self-reports of more positive emotional experience (e.g., Carstensen et al., 2003). Even the experience sampling study of Carstensen et al. (2000), arguably the single best study of later life emotion experiences, nonetheless relies exclusively on self-reported measures of experience to make inferences about regulation.

Notwithstanding potential cohort or developmental differences in emotion reporting (Gibson, 1997), an issue we consider in greater detail shortly, the stark fact is that there have been no direct tests of the assumption that older adults are better regulators. Certainly, later life adults appear to have learned a greater deal about emotions, themselves, and the relation between situations and emotions (Labouvie-Vief, Hakim-Larson, et al., 1989; Labouvie-Vief, Chiodo, et al., 1995; Labouvie-Vief, Diehl, et al., 1995), and tend to regulate more proactively than younger adults (see Gross et al., 1997); certainly, they feel that they do. However, the extent to which they are actually better regulators, particularly once they are emotionally aroused, remains to be seen. A part of this problem lies in the absence of definitions for emotion regulation or for what constitutes "better" regulation. Charles et al. (2003) define emotion regulation as "the maintenance of positive affect and the decrease of negative affect" (p. 310), implying that the maximization of positive experience—hedonism—is the aim of regulation. Notwithstanding the difficulty in reconciling this approach with the generally functionalist orientation of emotions research, there are several other aspects of emotion that can be regulated (e.g., expression, physiology), and these aspects can be regulated at multiple points in the emotion generation process and in a number of ways. That emotion experience appears to become more positive across the life span is important, but this phenomenon should not be uncritically accepted as the ultimate aim of emotional regulatory developments or emotional learning.

Life span research on emotion regulation has almost exclusively focused on the down-regulation of emotion expression and the anticipatory down-regulation of negative emotion experience. However, as has been suggested by Gross and others (Barrett & Gross, 2001; Bonanno, 2001; Consedine, Magai, & Bonanno, 2002; Gross, 1998, 2001; Gross & John, 2003; Westphal & Bonanno, 2004), emotions can be regulated in a variety of ways. Both experiences and expressions can be both up- and down-regulated (experience or expression heightened versus being suppressed) and, indeed, faked (Consedine, Magai, & Bonanno, 2002). If, as seems to be implied, emotion regulation is a set of learned skills that are linked to improvements in emotion experience, this assertion should be directly tested. Individuals from different age groups should participate in both up- and down-regulatory expressive tasks under carefully controlled experimental conditions that systematically vary important parameters, such as the nature of the elicitor, the presence of social others, the component to be regulated (e.g., experience vs. expression), and the type of regulation required (up versus down). In this way, the "success" of regulation can be objectively determined and skill can thus be measured independently of developmentally acquired changes in emotion understanding or knowledge.

A second issue evident in the literature to date involves the perennial developmental issue of cohort (generational) versus developmental explanations for age-related changes in emotions and emotion regulation. Although most researchers are certainly aware of this issue, this awareness has not yet extended to an implementation of the appropriate longitudinal designs (although see Charles et al., 2001; Costa et al., 1987; Ferring & Fillip, 1995), or a consideration of how adults of different ages and cohorts *report* emotions. The distinction between these two explanations must be kept firmly in mind. Magai et al. (2001) have previously suggested that child-rearing techniques during the era of Watsonian behaviorism—primarily the withholding of affection—in the 1920s may help explain why 50% to 80% of contemporary cohorts of older adults are categorized as dismissively attached (Consedine & Magai, 2003; Magai et al., 2001; Webster, 1997). Because dismissive individuals derive from environments that did not typically encourage emotional expression, they abhor interpersonal weakness and tend to regulate emotional experiences by routing negative emotions, particularly those connoting interpersonal weakness, from awareness (Consedine & Magai, 2003). This regulatory pattern means that the process of ascribing group-based differences to life span developmental processes rather than generational effects must be cautiously undertaken.

The life span developmental emotions literature suggests an ongoing problem with the operationalization, demarcation, and consideration of the age variable itself. The labels "younger" and "older" as we typically employ them now were derived historically because of their links with sociologically normative changes in general life functioning (e.g., empty nest syndrome, retirement).They have little to do with emotions per se. There are, furthermore, several reasons to suggest that such labeling conventions may be inadequate. First and most obviously, the conventional societal roles of individuals from different ages change across cohorts; individuals may no longer occupy the roles their parents did at the same age. Second, age-naming conventions are used haphazardly, with the phrase "older adult," for example, used to denote an individual who may be of any age from the late fifties onward. More typically, in fact, we are referring to the *average age of a group* of individuals, which in some cases will mean that there are persons either younger or older than this already broad range contained within our samples. More important, whereas the labels "young," "middle-aged," and "older" have some heuristic value, they are atheoretical inasmuch as there is little reason to suspect that such demarcations will correspond to a theoretically interpretable pattern of change in affects.

Explanations for Developmental Changes in Emotion and Emotional Regulation

As we have noted, theory regarding the ultimate causes of adult emotional development—the reasons why we are capable of changing so much—is still lacking. For the most part, researchers have explained changes at least implicitly through reference to learning processes and developmentally acquired knowledge about emotions and social interactions as well as improved regulatory skills. As Barefoot, Beckham, Haney, Siegler, and Lipkus (1993) have noted, there is little information available to identify a likely set of mechanisms to explain age differences (see also Carstensen et al., 1995). In their opinion, the com-

plexity of age trends make it "unlikely that any one theoretical mechanism can provide an adequate explanation" (Barefoot et al., 1993, p. 8). Next, we offer a more thorough consideration of this issue, review previous attempts, and outline a theoretical and empirical agenda for research development.

Other than a reduction in anger, reduced global negative affect with age is probably the most robust finding in the adult emotions literature (Magai, 2001). As noted, few researchers have seriously approached the issue of why emotions change in the patterns that they do and few explications of plausible mechanisms are available. Carstensen and colleagues (e.g., Carstensen, 1993, 1995; see Carstensen et al., 2003; Charles & Carstensen, 2004, for recent reviews), have suggested that changes in emotions across the adult life span are predominantly driven by changes in the motivations regarding information seeking and affective maximization that vary across the life span. According to Carstensen (1992), there are three primary social motives: emotion regulation, development and maintenance of self-concept, and information seeking. The relative importance of these motives shifts in middle and later years, with information seeking becoming less important and emotional goals, particularly that of affective satisfaction, becoming more central. The studies of these researchers suggests that because "time is running out," people in the latter half of life begin to focus on the present rather than the future (Charles & Carstensen, 2004), with a consequence that the maximization of rewarding emotion experience becomes more important.

This view is consistent with the fact that although anger may be adaptive when expressed appropriately (Consedine & Magai, 2003), it is also an emotion that can have negative personal and social consequences. Expressions of strong negative affects, particularly anger, can be unpleasant and frightening for both the self and for social partners (Kennedy-Moore & Watson, 1999; Levenson & Gottman, 1983; Tavris, 1984, 1989) and may threaten interpersonal relationships or undo social supports (Cole & Zahn-Waxler, 1992; Keltner, Ellsworth, & Edwards, 1993). Although socioemotional selectivity theory has experienced considerable success in identifying the proximate psychological changes underlying changes in emotion-related motivation and has done a great deal to explain changes in social network composition and preferences with age (Carstensen & Charles, 1998; Fredrickson & Carstensen, 1990), it has not yet provided clear explanations for why emotions change as they do.

A second possibility regarding declines in anger and in the negative affects with age involves a consideration of the issues surrounding cohort versus developmental change. The body of literature on adult development and aging is heavily based on cross-sectional data with a consequence that researchers cannot be sure whether age-related effects are caused by cohort differences in either the reporting of emotions (Raskin, 1979) or the experience of affect per se (Magai, 2001). There are few studies that have employed the designs required to directly examine age differences in reporting, although a closer reading of the literature provides some preliminary indications of likely reporting issues.

Gibson (1997) administered the state version of the Profile of Mood States (POMS) mood scale to 247 community-dwelling Australian adults ranging in age from 60–98. Older subjects exhibited lower scores on most dimensions of negative mood, including depression, anxiety, anger, fatigue, and vigor. Unlike most studies, however, Gibson's (1997) study also included a measure of social desirability. The study found that scores on the lie scale of the Eysenck Personality Questionnaire, a measure of the tendency to portray the self in a good light by endorsing only socially desirable items, were positively related to age (see also Malatesta-Magai et al., 1992) and negatively related to self-reported levels of anxiety, depression, and anger. When lie scale scores were used as covariates in partial correlations, age was no longer associated with mood, the one exception being self-reported levels of anger, which retained a negative association with age. Evidence suggests that the reconstructive processes used to estimate affect may be positively biased in older adults (Levine & Bluck, 1997; Mather & Johnson, 2000), particularly across longer time frames (Almeida, 1998, cited in Charles & Carstensen, 2004). Some have suggested that older adults may prefer to report feeling stressed rather than angry or sad (Consedine, Magai, et al., 2002). Empirically, these considerations suggest that measures of *current* affect should be emphasized, preferably in conjunction with measures enabling estimation of validity and/or bias.

Attachment patterns in later life are also suggestive of likely bias in affect reporting. Compared to younger samples, evidence shows that older adults are more likely to be dismissively attached (Klohnen & Bera, 1998; Magai, Hunziker, Mesias, & Culver,

2000; Magai et al., 2001; Mickelson et al., 1997; Webster, 1997), although again it remains unclear whether the increasing prevalence of dismissive attachment represents a cohort or developmental effect. Dismissively attached persons devalue interpersonal relationships and place a premium on self-reliance. This style of relating to others has been associated with an emotion regulatory style characterized by affect minimization (Cassidy, 1994) and the tendency to route negative emotion away from consciousness (Cassidy, 1994; Hazan & Shaver, 1987; Magai et al., 2000; Mikulincer, 1998). Among younger adults, for example, dismissing/avoidant attachment has been associated with low levels of anxiety (Bartholomew & Horowitz, 1991) but with a greater fear of death at a nonconscious versus conscious level (Mikulincer, Florian, & Tolmacz, 1990). Although this explanatory possibility likewise requires longitudinal research, it is possible that some of the changes in baseline negative affect may be explained by cohort or developmental differences in attachment and its associated regulatory and reporting styles.

Third, it may be that selective mortality or survivorship effects are responsible (Consedine & Magai, 2002). Persons with greater trait anger, for example—a personality configuration that is associated with higher morbidity and mortality—may be differentially removed from successive cohorts at earlier ages, leaving behind groups of individuals who are systematically lower in anger. Of all the discrete emotions, anger is the affect that has been most consistently associated with health impairment, notably cardiovascular disease (Barefoot, Dahlstrom, & Williams, 1983; Friedman & Booth-Kewley, 1987; Magai, Kerns, Gillespie, & Huang, 2003; Malatesta-Magai et al., 1992; Smith, 1992). Although there remains some debate about the exact relations between affect and morbidity, and it is possible that morbidity causes affect (Leventhal & Patrick-Miller, 2000), or that emotions indicate vulnerability, rather than directly causing ill health (Cohen et al., 1995; Leventhal et. al., 1998; Mayne, 1999, 2001), the balance of evidence favors a causal view (Consedine, Magai, Cohen, et al., 2002; Smith, 1992).

Finally, it may be that emotions change developmentally in comparatively normative ways across the life span because these changes are, in totality, adaptive and because they promote the inclusive fitness of aging individuals. A recent life span theory of emotions, developmental functionalism (Consedine,

Magai, & Bonanno, 2002; Consedine & Magai, 2003; Consedine, Magai, & King, 2004; Consedine, Strongman, & Magai, 2003), suggests that changes in emotion are determined by three interwoven phenomena: developmental changes in the primary challenges or tasks facing the organism, the changing functions of emotions, and the changing capacities of the organism. Each component is addressed more fully in the following.

Developmentally, the challenges and opportunities that confront individuals vary across the life span. The human newborn is virtually helpless (Eibl-Eibesfeldt, 1989), and its most pressing adaptive challenge is to interact with its physical and social environments such that adults will provide them with protection, care, and sustenance (Bowlby, 1969; Magai & McFadden, 1995; Malatesta, Culver, Tesman, & Shepard, 1989). Remnants of such challenges may remain into young adulthood. Yet among other tasks, young adults are newly confronted with the challenges of attracting, selecting, and securing a mate, reproducing, and successfully raising resultant offspring. In turn, these tasks are less relevant to older adults who have typically raised their first-generation progeny and who must instead adapt to declining physical/somatic (Leventhal et al., 1998; Panksepp & Miller, 1995), social, and mental resources (e.g., P. B. Baltes, 1987, 1997; Brandtstädter et al., 1997), as well as to increased dependency (M. M. Baltes, 1996) and new roles in the intergenerational transmission of knowledge and resources and second-generation kin care.

Consistent with evolutionary theory (e.g., Dennett, 1995; Keltner & Gross, 1999; Knight, 1994; Tooby & Cosmides, 1990), the developmental-functionalist approach argues that the functions of emotions (technically, the reasons they were selected in evolutionary time) are necessarily determined *in relation* to recurrent fitness challenges and opportunities (Ekman, 1992, 1994, 1999; Johnson-Laird & Oatley, 1992; Lazarus, 1991; Nesse, 1990; Smith & Lazarus, 1993; Tooby & Cosmides, 1990). As such, complex adaptive phenomena such as the emotions likely have multiple functions (Averill, 1994; Keltner & Gross, 1999), perhaps at the level of the different components (Consedine, Magai, & Bonanno, 2002). Sadness, an emotion that evolutionary processes have designed to facilitate adaptation to the challenge of loss, for example, functions at multiple levels. It generates expressive signals that increase social support (Averill, 1968;

Bowlby, 1969; Izard, 1971, 1993; Lazarus, 1991; Stein & Levine, 1990; Stearns, 1993), induces amotivational states (Brehm, 1999; Brehm, Brummett, & Harvey, 1999) and thus reduces energy output (Clark & Watson, 1994; Hofer, 1994). Sadness prevents continued investment in the lost object and creates a cognitive state that leads to "dwelling" on the lost object, as in bereavement. Functionally, this allows the organism time to rearrange goal hierarchies and priorities (Johnson-Laird & Oatley, 1992) and construct plans (Stein & Levine, 1990) to deal with the loss. Most important, however, these complex functions are only meaningful when interpreted in the context of (a) the overarching challenges with which the organism is coping, and (b) the capacities that it currently possesses. Empirical work describing developmental differences in the social and nonsocial elicitors of discrete emotions is sorely needed, for researchers have yet to begin describing what it is that individuals of different ages become emotional about.

Finally, developmental-functionalism suggests that changes in the emotions across the adult life span are intimately related to the changing (or unchanging) physiological, social, cognitive, and behavioral capabilities of the organism. In terms of changing capacities, for example, most emotions theorists acknowledge the importance of physiological change to the functions of emotions, with some (e.g., Levenson, 1994, 1999) suggesting that a core function of the emotions is to create a physiological milieu that supports the necessary adaptive action. However, the magnitude of autonomic nervous system (ANS) activity declines in later life (Labouvie-Vief et al., 2003; Levenson et al., 1991; Tsai et al., 2000; see also P. B. Baltes, 1997; Levenson et al., 1994) perhaps because the somatic systems of older adults do not tolerate ANS deviations as readily (Davidson, 1993; Panksepp & Miller, 1995) or because energy levels (P. B. Baltes, 1997; Leventhal et al., 1998) and the system's ability to effectively regulate its use decline with age (Panksepp & Miller, 1995). Consistent with this view, Levenson et al. (1991) suggest that the lower somatic activity associated with fear in older adults may result from a change in the behavioral and physiological programs associated with fear, with flight being primary in youth, and freezing becoming more prominent in older subjects. Put simply, running from a threat is less likely to be successful for an older adult because of declining physical capacities. Affects tend to manifest their most important functions in the aspects of the organism's functioning that are developmentally available and appropriate; whether such differences arise through evolutionary processes or are learned remains unclear at this time.

On the other hand, developmental-functionalism also accepts that there are constraints on the ability of the emotions and regulatory systems to operate in the way that is most immediately useful. Evolutionarily, selective pressure is greatest where fitness costs and benefits are strongest. Developmentally, such periods are found more often in early than late life for the simple reason that if the organism does not survive early stages of development, selective pressures in favor of patterns and mechanisms that might be adaptive in later phases are redundant (Dennett, 1995). Practically, this may mean that patterns of emotion and emotion regulation are acquired in early development because they facilitate adaptation to early environments. These patterns are then carried forward to later stages of life irrespective of their utility in those later stages.

Applying these tenets to the developmental changes in emotion and emotional regulation creates some interesting explanatory possibilities. For example, with age it may be that the need to more effectively regulate declines in the somatic system is partially responsible for differential reductions in the frequency (Gross et al., 1997; Lawton et al., 1993; Schieman, 1999; Stoner & Spencer, 1987) and duration (Birditt & Fingerman, 2003) of anger, but not the frequency of sadness (Birditt & Fingerman, 2003) or the increase in positive affect (Lawton et al., 1993; Mroczek & Kolarz, 1998). As Consedine, Magai, and Bonanno (2002) have recently suggested, it may be that the reduced expression of negative affect in later life is adaptive in that it may minimize the demands on declining somatic systems (Leventhal et. al., 1998; Mayne, 1999). In addition to preventing further damage to shrinking social networks (see Carstensen, 1993, 1995), improved regulatory skills may assist later life adults to prevent further damage to bodily systems. Most adaptations have both costs and benefits to the organism, and a complex interplay of selective pressures *that are presumed to vary developmentally* will determine, on balance, whether and how different emotions are fitness-enhancing to organisms of different ages.

In a study of positive affect in later life, Consedine, Magai, and King (2004) have argued that learning to regulate emotions more effectively across the life span enables older adults to adopt a more positively valenced emotional life in the face of illness and loss. Operating within a developmental-functionalist framework, these authors suggest that maximizing positive experiences may enable older adults to directly protect their somatic systems from aging. Increasing happiness/joy—a tension-reducing, calming emotion—may become increasingly important to older adults, perhaps because it acts as an antidote to stress, perhaps serving a physiological "undoing" effect (Fredrickson & Levenson, 1998; Fredrickson, Mancuso, Branigan, & Tugade, 2000; Levenson & Fredrickson, 1998).

Consistent with a large body of social-cognitive research, developmental functionalism also outlines a mediated cognitive pathway linking positive affect to health. It suggests that learning to maximize positive experiences may serve to offset developmentally graded losses in cognitive and physical performance. Across the past two decades, Isen's research into positive affect has documented changes and improvements in many aspects of cognition under the influence of positive affect (Ashby, Isen, & Turken, 1999; Isen, 2002; Isen, Daubman, & Nowicki, 1987; Isen, Nygren, & Ashby, 1988). The totality of this research suggests that positive affect facilitates careful, effective, and thorough problem solving, increases creativity (Isen et al., 1987); enhances the individual's ability to simultaneously take multiple factors into account and deal realistically with situational challenges (Isen, 2002); improves verbal fluency (Hirt, Melton, McDonald, & Harackiewicz, 1996), increases mental flexibility or openness (Estrada, Isen, & Young, 1997); and improves the individual's ability to adopt problem-solving approaches that benefit multiple parties (Carnevale & Isen, 1986). These data are consistent with Fredrickson's (1998) recent functionalist model of positive emotions in which one primary purpose of the positive affects is to broaden the scope and capabilities of cognition.

As such, the effects of positive emotions on cognition may have clear benefits for aging individuals who are confronted with social, economic, physical, and psychological problems as they age (M. M. Baltes, 1996; M. M. Baltes & Carstensen, 1996; P. B. Baltes, 1987, 1997; P. B. Baltes & M. M. Baltes, 1990). It is generally assumed that people become cognitively less flexible as they age (Ashby et al., 1999), a supposition supported for executive tasks such as planning, inhibiting, and abstracting logical rules (Andres & Van der Linden, 2000; Gilhooly et al., 1999; Kray &

Lindenberger, 2000), digit recall (West & Crook, 1990), and word fluency (Phillips, 1999). Given this scenario, it may be that one distal reason for age-related emotional and emotion regulatory changes resides in neurocognitive changes. Neurocognitive changes may be implicated in the increasingly positive affect one sees with linear aging. Happy moods may improve problem solving in the face of the challenges and losses that occur in later life, enabling older adults to learn more rapidly how to accommodate them. In addition, such moods may increase dopaminergic transmission to the frontal lobes (Ashby et al., 1999), a trend that may offset normative frontal lobe declines in cognition. Such offsetting might enable older adults to maintain critical higher order functioning and cognitive creativity in problem solving, even in the face of cognitive decline.

CONCLUDING REMARKS

Following many years in the intellectual wilderness, the study of adult emotional development is emerging as a major research agenda within the social and psychological sciences. Although it is still young as a field, some impressive gains have been made across the past two decades. The view that emotion functioning declines along with higher order cognitive, social, and bodily systems has been substantially refuted. Researchers are moving toward a less pessimistic view of the emotions in the context of the aging process. Neither middle age nor later life are periods of inevitable emotional decline; if anything, there appear as many improvements as losses across the adult life span. Although there are conflicting findings and complexities, our reading of the literature suggests that there are improvements in the overall valence of emotional experience, in the ability to regulate emotions, and in the ability to comprehend and reflect on one's own experience.

The challenges for the field, however, remain numerous. Empirically, future research must gather data regarding theoretically meaningful age groups, must continue to tease apart the issues of cohort versus developmental change (through the use of appropriate longitudinal and cross-sequential designs), and must usher the social gerontology of emotions into the laboratory. Studies that directly test the assertions of current theory are a prerequisite to the development of the field. Theoretically, life span researchers must

continue to engage with established models of emotion and emotional regulation as they seek to consider the impact of developmental changes in emotions on experience, cognition, physiology, social relations, health, and behavior. As a field, we must look to develop theoretical frameworks that explain why emotions and emotion regulation change across the adult life span the ways they do, for this remains the most important and most poorly understood question of all.

ACKNOWLEDGMENTS   Work on this chapter was supported by grants from the National Institute of General Medical Science and the National Institute on Aging (2 SO6 GM54650) and the National Institute on Aging (1K07 AG00921 & ROI AG/MH21017). The authors thank Yulia Krivoshekova and Shulamit Sabag for their assistance with portions of this manuscript.

References

Allen, R., & Brosgole, L. (1993). Facial and auditory affect recognition in senile geriatrics, the normal elderly, and young adults. *International Journal of Neuroscience, 68*, 33–42.

Andres, P., & Van der Linden, M. (2000). Age-related differences in supervisory attentional system functions. *Journals of Gerontology: Series B: Psychological Sciences, 55B*, P373–P380

Ashby, F. G., Isen, A. M., & Turken, A. U. (1999). A neuropsychological theory of positive affect and its influence on cognition. *Psychological Review, 106*, 529–550.

Averill, J. R. (1968). Grief: Its nature and significance. *Psychological Bulletin, 70*, 721–748.

Averill, J. R. (1994). Emotions are many splendored things. In P. Ekman & R. J. Davidson (Eds.), *The nature of emotions: Fundamental questions* (pp. 99–102). New York: Oxford University Press.

Baltes, M. M. (1996). *The many faces of dependency in old age.* New York: Cambridge University Press.

Baltes, M. M., & Carstensen, L. L. (1996). The process of successful ageing. *Ageing & Society, 16*, 397–422.

Baltes, P. B. (1987). Theoretical propositions of life-span developmental psychology: On the dynamics between growth and decline. *Developmental Psychology, 23*, 611–626.

Baltes, P. B. (1997). On the incomplete architecture of human ontogeny: Selection, optimization and compensation as foundation of developmental theory. *American Psychologist, 52*, 366–380.

Baltes, P. B., & Baltes, M. M. (1990). Psychological perspectives on successful aging: The model of selective optimization with compensation. In P. B. Baltes & M. M. Baltes (Eds.), *Successful aging: Perspectives from the behavioral sciences* (pp. 1–34). New York: Cambridge University Press.

Baltes, P. B., & Mayer, K. U. (Eds.), (1999). *The Berlin aging study: Aging from 70 to 100.* Cambridge: Cambridge University Press.

Banham, K. M. (1951). Senescence and the emotions: A genetic theory. *Journal of Genetic Psychology, 78,* 175–183.

Barefoot, J. C., Beckham, J. C., Haney, T. L., Siegler, I. C., & Lipkus, I. M. (1993). Age differences in hostility among middle-aged and older adults. *Psychology and Aging, 8,* 3–9.

Barefoot, J. C., Dahlstrom, W. G., & Williams, R. B. (1983). Hostility, CHD incidence, and total mortality: A 25-yr follow-up study of 255 physicians. *Psychosomatic Medicine, 45,* 59–63.

Barnes, C. A., Suster, M. S., Shen, J., & McNaughton, B. L. (1997). Multistability of cognitive maps in the hippocampus of old rats. *Nature, 388,* 272–275.

Barrett, L. F., & Gross, J. J. (2001). Emotional intelligence: A process model of emotion representation and regulation. In T. J. Mayne & G. A. Bonanno (Eds.), *Emotions: Current issues and future directions* (pp. 286–310). New York: Guilford.

Barrick, A. L., Hutchinson, R. L., & Deckers, L. H. (1989). Age effects on positive and negative emotions. *Journal of Social Behavior and Personality, 4,* 421–429.

Bartholomew, K., & Horowitz, L. M. (1991). Attachment styles among young adults: A test of a four-category model. *Journal of Personality and Social Psychology, 61,* 226–244.

Birditt, K. S., & Fingerman, K. L. (2003). Age and gender differences in adults' descriptions of emotional reactions to interpersonal problems. *Journals of Gerontology: Series B: Psychological Sciences, 58B*(4), P237–P245.

Blanchard-Fields, F., & Camp, C. J. (1990). Affect, individual differences and real world problem solving across the adult lifespan. In T. M. Hess (Eds.), *Aging and cognition: Knowledge organization and utilization* (pp. 461–497). Oxford: North-Holland.

Blanchard-Fields, F., Jahnke, H. C., & Camp, C. (1995). Age differences in problem-solving style: The role of emotional salience. *Psychology and Aging, 10,* 173–180.

Bonanno, G. A. (2001). Emotion self-regulation. In T. J. Mayne & G. A. Bananno (Eds.), *Emotion: Current issues and future directions* (pp. 251–285). New York: Guilford.

Bowlby, J. (1969). *Attachment and loss: Vol. 1. Attachment.* New York: Basic Books.

Brandtstädter, J., & Baltes-Götz, B. (1990). Personal control over development and quality of life perspectives in adulthood. In P. B. Baltes & M. M. Baltes (Eds.), *Successful aging: Perspectives from the behavioral sciences* (pp. 197–224). New York: Cambridge University Press.

Brandtstädter, J., & Renner, G. (1990). Tenacious goal pursuit and flexible goal adjustment: Explication and age-related analysis of assimilative and accommodative strategies of coping. *Psychology & Aging, 5,* 58–67.

Brandtstädter, J., Rothermund, K., & Schmitz, U. (1997). Coping resources in later life. *European Review of Applied Psychology, 47,* 107–113.

Brehm, J. W. (1999). The intensity of emotion. *Personality and Social Psychology Review, 3,* 2–22.

Brehm, J. W., Brummett, B. H., & Harvey, L. (1999). Paradoxical sadness. *Motivation and Emotion, 23,* 31–44.

Brosgole, L. Kurucz, J., PlaHovinsak, J. T., Sprotte, C., & Haveliwala, Y. A. (1983). Facial-and-postural-affect recognition in senile elderly persons. *International Journal of Neuroscience, 22,* 37–46.

Buhler, C. (1935). The curve of life as studied in biographies. *Journal of Applied Psychology, 1,* 184–211.

Butcher, J. N., Aldwin, C. M., Levenson, M. R., Ben-Porath, Y. S., Spiro, A., & Bosse, R. (1991). Personality and aging: A study of the MMPI-2 among older men. *Psychology & Aging, 6,* 361–370.

Cacioppo, J. T., Berntson, G. G., Klein, D. J., & Poehlmann, K. M. (1998). Psychophysiology of emotion across the life span. In K. W. Schaie & M. P. Lawton (Eds.), *Annual review of gerontology and geriatrics: Vol. 17. Focus on emotion and adult development* (pp. 27–74). New York: Springer.

Carnevale, P. J., & Isen, A. M. (1986). The influence of positive affect and visual access on the discovery of integrative solutions in bilateral negotiation. *Organizational Behavior & Human Decision Processes, 37,* 1–13.

Carstensen, L. L. (1992). Social and emotional patterns in adulthood: Support for socioemotional selectivity theory. *Psychology & Aging, 7,* 331–338.

Carstensen, L. L. (1993). Motivation for social contact across the life span: A theory of socioemotional selectivity. In J. E. Jacobs (Ed.), *Nebraska symposium on motivation: Developmental perspectives on motivation* (pp. 209–254). Lincoln: University of Nebraska Press.

Carstensen, L. L. (1995). Evidence for a life-span theory of socioemotional selectivity. *Current Directions in Psychological Science, 4,* 151–156.

Carstensen, L. L., & Charles, S. T. (1994). The salience of emotion across the adult life span. *Psychology & Aging, 9*(2), 259–264.

Carstensen, L. L., & Charles, S. T. (1998). Emotion in the second half of life. *Current Directions in Psychological Science, 7,* 144–149.

Carstensen, L. L., & Fredrickson, B. L. (1998). Influence of HIV status and age on cognitive representations of others. *Health Psychology, 17,* 494–503.

Carstensen, L. L., Fung, H. H., & Charles, S. T. (2003). Socioemotional selectivity theory and the regulation of emotion in the second half of life. *Motivation and Emotion, 27,* 103–123.

Carstensen, L. L., Gottman, J. M., & Levenson, R. W. (1995). Emotional behavior in long-term marriage. *Psychology and Aging, 10,* 140–149.

Carstensen, L. L., Gross, J. J., & Fung, H. H. (1997). The social context of emotional experience. In K. W. Schaie & M. P. Lawton (Eds.), *Annual review of gerontology and geriatrics, Vol. 17: Focus on emotion and adult development. Annual review of gerontology and geriatrics* (pp. 325–352). New York: Springer.

Carstensen, L. L., Isaacowitz, D. M., & Charles, S. T. (1999). Taking time seriously: A theory of socioemotional selectivity. *American Psychologist, 54,* 165–181.

Carstensen, L. L., Pasupathi, M. Mayr, U., & Nesselroade, J. R. (2000). Emotional experience in everyday life across the adult life span. *Journal of Personality and Social Psychology, 79,* 644–655.

Cassidy, J. (1994). Emotion regulation: Influences of attachment relationships. In N. Fox (Ed.), *The development of emotion regulation: Biological and biobehavioral considerations. Monographs of the Society for Research in Child Development, 59,* 228–249.

Charles, S. T., & Carstensen, L. L. (2004). A life-span view of emotional functioning in adulthood and old age. In P. Costa (Ed.), *Advances in Cell Aging and Gerontology Series* (pp. 133–162). New York: Elsevier.

Charles, S. T., Mather, M., & Carstensen, L. L. (2003). Aging and emotional memory: The forgettable nature of negative images for older adults. *Journal of Experimental Psychology: General, 132,* 310–324.

Charles, S. T., Reynolds, C. A., & Gatz, M. (2001). Age-related differences and change in positive and negative affect over 23 years. *Journal of Personality and Social Psychology, 80*(1), 136–151.

Clark, L. A., & Watson, D. (1994). Distinguishing functional from dysfunctional affective bursts. In P. Ekman & R. J. Davidson (Eds.), *The nature of emotion: Fundamental questions* (pp. 131–136). New York: Oxford University Press.

Cohen, S., Doyle, W. J., Skoner, D. P., Fireman, P., Gwaltney, J. M., & Newsom, J. T. (1995). State and trait affect as predictors of objective and subjective symptoms of respiratory viral infections. *Journal of Personality and Social Psychology, 68,* 159–169.

Cole, P. M., & Zahn-Waxler, C. (1992). Emotional dysregulation in disruptive behavior disorders. In D. Cicchetti & S. L. Toth (Eds.), *Rochester symposium on developmental psychopathology, Vol. 4: Developmental perspectives on depression* (pp. 173–210). Rochester, NY: University of Rochester Press.

Consedine, N. S., & Magai, C. (2002). The uncharted waters of emotion: Ethnicity, trait emotion and emotion expression in older adults. *Journal of Cross-Cultural Gerontology, 17,* 71–100.

Consedine, N. S., & Magai, C. (2003). Attachment and emotion experience in later life: The view from emotions theory. *Attachment and Human Development, 5,* 165–187.

Consedine, N. S., Magai, C., & Bonanno, G. A. (2002). Moderators of the emotion inhibition-health rela-

tionship: A review and research agenda. *Review of General Psychology, 6,* 204–228.

Consedine, N. S., Magai, C., Cohen, C., & Gillespie, M. (2002). Ethnic variation in the impact of negative emotion and emotion inhibition on the health of older adults. *Journal of Gerontology: Series B: Psychological Sciences, 57B,* P396–P408.

Consedine, N. S., Magai, C., & King, A. (2004). Deconstructing positive affect in later life: A differential functionalist analysis of joy and interest. *International Journal of Human Development, 58,* 49–68.

Consedine, N. S., Magai, C., & Neugut, A. (2004). The contribution of emotional characteristics to breast cancer screening. *Preventive Medicine, 38,* 64–77.

Consedine, N. S., Strongman, K. T., & Magai, C. (2003). Emotions and behavior: Data from a cross-cultural recognition study. *Cognition & Emotion, 17,* 881–902.

Costa, P. T. Jr., McCrae, R. R., & Zonderman, A. B. (1987). Environmental and dispositional influences on well-being: Longitudinal follow-up of an American national sample. *British Journal of Psychology, 78,* 299–306.

Davidson, R. J. (1993). Parsing affective space: Perspectives from neuropsychology and psychophysiology. *Neuropsychology, 7,* 464–475.

Davis, J., & Smith, T. (1996). *General Social Surveys, 1972–1996: Cumulative codebook and data file.* Chicago: National Opinion Research Center and University of Chicago.

Dennett, D. C. (1995). *Darwin's dangerous idea.* New York: Simon & Schuster.

Diehl, M., Coyle, N., & Labouvie-Vief, G. (1996). Age and sex differences in strategies of coping and defense across the life span. *Psychology & Aging, 11,* 127–139.

Diener, E., Sandvik, E., & Larsen, R. J. (1985). Age and sex effects for emotional intensity. *Developmental Psychology, 21,* 542–546.

Diener, E., & Suh, E. (1997). Measuring quality of life: Economic, social and subjective indicators. *Social Indicators Research, 40,* 189–216.

Eibl-Eibesfeldt, I. (1989). *Human ethology.* Hawthorne, NY: Aldine de Gruyter.

Ekman, P. (1992). An argument for basic emotions. *Cognition and Emotion, 6,* 169–200.

Ekman, P. (1994). All emotions are basic. In P. Ekman & R. J. Davidson (Eds.), *The nature of emotion: Fundamental questions* (pp. 15–19). New York: Oxford University Press.

Ekman, P. (1999). Basic emotions. In T. Dalgleish & M. Power (Eds.), *Handbook of cognition and emotion* (pp. 45–59). Chichester: Wiley.

Ekstrom, A. D., Meltzer, J., McNaughton, B. L., & Barnes, C. A. (2001). NMDA receptor antagonism blocks experience-dependent expansion of hippocampal "place fields." *Neuron, 31,* 631–638.

Estrada, C. A., Isen, A. M., & Young, M. J. (1997). Positive affect facilitates integration of information and decreases anchoring in reasoning among physicians.

Organizational Behavior and Human Decision Processes, 72, 117–135.

Ferring, D., & Fillip, S. H. (1995). The structure of subjective well-being in the elderly: A test of different models by structural equation modeling. *European Journal of Psychological Assessment, 11,* 32.

Fingerman, K. L. (2000). "We had a nice chat": Age and generational differences in mothers' and daughters' descriptions of enjoyable visits. *Journal of Gerontology, 55B,* 95–106.

Folkman, S., Lazarus, R. S., Pimley, S., & Novacek, J. (1987). Age differences in stress and coping processes. *Psychology and Aging, 2,* 171–184

Fredrickson, B. L. (1998). What good are positive emotions? *Review of General Psychology, 2,* 300–319.

Fredrickson, B. L., & Carstensen, L. L. (1990). Choosing social partners: How old age and anticipated endings make people more selective. *Psychology and Aging, 5,* 335–347.

Fredrickson, B. L., & Levenson, R. W. (1998). Positive emotions speed recovery from the cardiovascular sequelae of negative emotions. *Cognition and Emotion, 12,* 191–220.

Fredrickson, B. L., Mancuso, R. A., Branigan, C., & Tugade, M. M. (2000). The undoing effect of positive emotions. *Motivation and Emotion, 24,* 237–258.

Frenkel-Brunswik, E. (1968). Adjustments and reorientation in the course of the life span. In B. L. Neugarten (Ed.), *Middle age and aging* (pp. 77–84). Chicago: University of Chicago Press.

Friedman, H. S., & Booth-Kewley, S. (1987). Personality, Type A behavior, and coronary heart disease: The role of emotional expression. *Journal of Personality and Social Psychology, 53,* 783–792.

Gibson, S. J. (1997). The measurement of mood states in older adults. *Journal of Gerontology: Psychological Sciences, 52B,* P167–P174.

Gilhooly, K. J., Phillips, L. H., Wynn, V., Logie, R. H., & Della Sala, S. (1999). Planning processes and age in the five-disc Tower of London task. *Thinking and Reasoning, 5,* 339–361.

Gnich, W., & Gilhooly, M. (2000). Health, wealth and happiness: Studies in financial gerontology. In G. Corley (Ed.), *Older people and their needs: A multidisciplinary perspective* (pp. 17–34). London: Whurr.

Gould, O. N., & Dixon, R. A. (1993). How we spent our vacation: Collaborative storytelling by younger and older adults. *Psychology and Aging, 6,* 93–99.

Gross, J. J. (1998). The emerging field of emotion regulation: An integrative review. *Review of General Psychology, 2,* 271–299.

Gross, J. J. (2001). Emotion regulation in adulthood: Timing is everything. *Current Directions in Psychological Science, 10,* 214–219.

Gross, J. J., Carstensen, L. L., Tsai, J., Skorpen, C. G., & Hsu, A. Y. C. (1997). Emotion and aging: Experience, expression, and control. *Psychology and Aging, 12,* 590–599.

Gross, J. J., & John, O. P. (2003). Individual differences in two emotion regulation processes: Implications for affect, relationships, and well-being. *Journal of Personality and Social Psychology, 85,* 348–362.

Grunwald, I. S., Borod, J. C., Obler, L. K., Erhan, J., Pick, L. H., Welkowitz, J., et al. (1999). The effects of age and gender on the perception of lexical emotion. *Applied Neuropsychology, 6*(4), 226–238.

Gunning-Dixon, F. M., Gur, R. C., Perkins, A. C., Schroeder, L., Turner, T., Turetsky, B., et al. (2003). Aged-related *differences* in brain activation during emotional face processing. *Neurobiology of Aging, 24*(2), 285–295.

Hazan, C., & Shaver, P. (1987). Romantic love conceptualized as an attachment process. *Journal of Personality and Social Psychology, 52,* 511–524.

Heckhausen, J. (1997). Developmental regulation across adulthood: Primary and secondary control of age-related challenges. *Developmental Psychology, 33,* 176–187.

Hertzog, C., & Schaie, K. W. (1986). Stability and change in adult intelligence: I. Analysis of longitudinal covariance structures. *Psychology & Aging, 1,* 159–171.

Hirt, E. R., Melton, R. J., McDonald, H. E., & Harackiewicz, J. M. (1996). Processing goals, task interest, and the mood–performance relationship: A mediational analysis. *Journal of Personality and Social Psychology, 71,* 245–261.

Hofer, M. A. (1994). Hidden regulators in attachment, separation, and loss. In N. A. Fox (Ed.), *The development of emotion regulation: Biological and behavioral considerations. Monographs of the Society for Research in Child Development, 59*(2–3), 192–207. London: Blackwell.

Inglehart, R. (1990). *Culture shift in advanced industrial society.* Princeton, N.J.: Princeton University Press.

Isen, A. M. (2002). Missing in action in the AIM: Positive affect's facilitation of cognitive flexibility, innovation and problem solving. *Psychological Inquiry, 13,* 57–65.

Isen, A. M., Daubman, K. A., & Nowicki, G. P. (1987). Positive affect facilitates creative problem solving. *Journal of Personality and Social Psychology, 52,* 1122–1131.

Isen, A. M., Nygren, T. E., Ashby, F. G. (1988). Influence of positive affect on the subjective utility of gains and losses: Its just not worth the risk. *Journal of Personality and Social Psychology, 55,* 710–717.

Izard, C. E. (1971). *The face of emotion.* New York: Appleton-Century-Crofts.

Izard, C. E. (1991). *The psychology of emotions.* New York: Plenum Press.

Izard, C. E. (1993). Organizational and motivational functions of discrete emotions. In M. Lewis & J. M. Haviland (Eds.), *Handbook of emotions* (pp. 631–641). New York: Guilford.

Johnson-Laird, P. N., & Oatley, K. (1992). Basic emotions, rationality and folk theory. *Cognition and Emotion, 6,* 201–223.

Jung, C. G. (1933). *The stages of life: Modern man in search of a soul.* London: Kegan Paul, Trench, & Trubner.

Keltner, D., Ellsworth, P. C., & Edwards, K. (1993). Beyond simple pessimism: Effects of sadness and anger on social perception. *Journal of Personality and Social Psychology, 64*, 740–752.

Keltner, D., & Gross, J. J. (1999). Functional accounts of emotions. *Cognition and Emotion, 13*(5), 467–480.

Kennedy-Moore, E., & Watson, J. C. (1999). *Expressing emotion: Myths, realities and therapeutic strategies.* New York: Guilford.

Klaczynski, P. A., & Robinson, B. (2000). Personal theories, intellectual ability, and epistemological beliefs: Adult age differences in everyday reasoning biases. *Psychology and Aging, 15*, 400–416.

Klohnen, E. C., & Bera, S. (1998). Behavioral and experiential patterns of avoidantly and securely attached women across adulthood: A 31-year longitudinal perspective. *Journal of Personality and Social Psychology, 74*, 211–223.

Knight, B. G., Maines, M. L., & Robinson, G. S. (2002). The effects of sad mood on memory in older adults: A test of the mood congruence effect. *Psychology and Aging, 17*, 653–661.

Knight, M. (1994). Darwinian functionalism: A cognitive science paradigm. *Psychological Record, 44*, 271–287.

Kray, J., & Lindenberger, U. (2000). Adult age differences in task switching. *Psychology & Aging, 15*, 126–147.

Kunzmann, U., Little, T., & Smith, J. (2000). Is age-related stability of subjective well-being a paradox? Cross-sectional and longitudinal evidence from the Berlin aging study. *Psychology & Aging, 15*, 511–526.

Labouvie-Vief, G., Chiodo, L. M., Goguen, L. A., Diehl, M., & Orwoll, L. (1995). Representations of self across the life span. *Psychology & Aging, 10*, 404–415.

Labouvie-Vief, G., DeVoe, M., & Bulka, D. (1989). Speaking about feelings: Conceptions of emotion across the life span. *Psychology & Aging, 4*, 425–437.

Labouvie-Vief, G., & Diehl, M. (2000). Cognitive complexity and cognitive-affective integration: Related or separate domains of adult development? *Psychology & Aging, 15*, 490–504.

Labouvie-Vief, G., Diehl, M., Chiodo, L. M., & Coyle, N. (1995). Representations of self and parents across the life span. *Journal of Adult Development, 2*, 207–222.

Labouvie-Vief, G., Hakim-Larson, J., DeVoe, M., & Schoeberlein, S. (1989). Emotions and self-regulation: A lifespan view. *Human Development, 32*, 279–299.

Labouvie-Vief, G., Lumley, M. A., Jain, E., & Heinze, H. (2003). Age and gender differences in cardiac reactivity and subjective emotions responses to emotional autobiographic memories. *Emotion, 3*, 115–126.

Lang, F. R., & Carstensen, L. L. (2002). Time counts: Future time perspective, goals, and social relationships. *Psychology & Aging, 17*, 125–139.

Lawton, M. P. (1989). Environmental proactivity and affect in older people. In S. Spacapan, & S. Oskamp (Eds.), *The social psychology of aging* (pp. 135–163). Newbury Park, CA: Sage.

Lawton, M. P., Kleban, M. H., & Dean, J. (1993). Affect and age: Cross-sectional comparisons of structure and prevalence. *Psychology & Aging, 8*, 165–175.

Lawton, M. P., Kleban, M. H., Rajagopal, D., & Dean, J. (1992). The dimensions of affective experience in three age groups. *Psychology & Aging, 7*, 171–184.

Lazarus, R. S. (1991). *Emotion and adaptation.* New York: Oxford University Press.

Levenson, R. W. (1994). Human emotion: A functional view. In P. Ekman & R. J. Davidson (Eds.), *The nature of emotion: Fundamental questions* (pp. 123–126). Hillsdale, NJ: Lawrence Erlbaum.

Levenson, R. W. (1999). Intrapersonal functions of emotion. *Cognition and Emotion, 13*(5), 481–504.

Levenson, R. W., Carstensen, L. L., Friesen, W. V., & Ekman, P. (1991). Emotion, physiology, and expression in old age. *Psychology & Aging, 6*, 28–35.

Levenson, R. W., Carstensen, L. L., & Gottman, J. M. (1994). The influence of age and gender on affect, physiology, and their interrelations: A study of long-term marriages. *Journal of Personality and Social Psychology, 67*, 56–68.

Levenson, R. W., Ekman, P., & Friesen, W. (1990). Voluntary facial action generates emotion-specific autonomic nervous system activity. *Psychophysiology, 27*, 363–384.

Levenson, R. W., & Gottman, J. M. (1983). Marital interaction: Physiological linkage and affective exchange. *Journal of Personality and Social Psychology, 45*, 587–597.

Levenson, R. W., & Fredrickson, B. L. (1998). Positive emotions speed recovery from the cardiovascular sequelae of negative emotions. *Cognition and Emotion, 12*(2), 191–220.

Leventhal, H., & Patrick-Miller, L. (2000). Emotions and physical illness: Causes and indicators of vulnerability. In J. Haviland & M. Lewis (Eds.), *The handbook of emotion* (2nd ed., pp. 523–570). New York: Guilford.

Leventhal, H., Patrick-Miller, L., Leventhal, E. A., & Burns, E. A. (1998). Does stress-emotion cause illness in elderly people? In K. W. Schaie & M. P. Lawton (Eds.), *Annual review of gerontology and geriatrics, Vol. 17: Focus on emotion and adult development* (pp. 138–184). New York: Springer.

Levine, L. J., & Bluck, S. (1997). Experienced and remembered emotional intensity in older adults. *Psychology & Aging, 12*, 514–523.

Lima, J. C., & Allen, S. M. (2001). Targeting risk for unmet need: Not enough help versus no help at all. *Journal of Gerontology: Series B: Socials Sciences, 56B*, S302–S310.

Magai, C. (2001). Emotions over the lifespan. In J. Birren & K. W. Schaie (Eds.), *Handbook of the psychology of aging* (pp. 399–426). San Diego, CA: Academic Press.

Magai, C., Cohen, C., Milburn, N., Thorpe, B., McPherson, R., & Peralta, D. (2001). Attachment styles in European American and African American adults. *Journals of Gerontology, Psychological Sciences, 56B*, S28–S35.

Magai, C., Cohen, C., Gomberg, D., Malatesta, C., & Culver, C. (1996). Emotion expression in late stage dementia. *International Psychogeriatrics, 8*, 383–396.

Magai, C., & Halpern, B. (2001). Emotional development during the middle years. In M. E. Lachman (Ed.), *Handbook of midlife development* (pp. 310–344). New York· Wiley.

Magai, C., Hunziker, J., Mesias, W., & Culver, C. (2000). Adult attachment styles and emotional biases. *International Journal of Behavioral Development, 24*, 301–309.

Magai, C., Kerns, M., Gillespie, M., & Huang, B. (2003). Anger experience and anger inhibition in sub-populations of African American and European American older adults and relation to circulatory disease. *Journal of Health Psychology, 8*, 413–432.

Magai, C., & McFadden, S. H. (1995). *The role of emotions in social and personality development: History, theory, and research.* New York: Plenum Press.

Malatesta, C. Z., Culver, C., Tesman, J. R., & Shepard, B. (1989). The development of emotion expression during the first two years of life. *Monographs of the Society for Research in Child Development, 54*, 1–103.

Malatesta, C., & Izard, C. E. (1984). Facial expression of emotion in young, middle-aged, and older adults. In C. Malatesta & C. E. Izard (Eds.), *Emotion in adult development.* Beverly Hills, CA: Sage.

Malatesta, C., Izard, C. E., Culver, C., & Nicolich, M. (1987). Emotion communication skills in young, middle-aged and older women. *Psychology & Aging, 2*, 193–203.

Malatesta, C., & Kalnok, M. (1984). Emotional experience in younger and older adults. *Journal of Gerontology, 39*, 301–308.

Malatesta-Magai, C., Jonas, R., Shepard, B., & Culver, C. (1992). Type A personality and emotional expressivity in younger and older adults. *Psychology & Aging, 7*, 551–561.

Mather, M., & Carstensen, L. L. (in press). Aging and attentional biases for emotional faces. *Psychological Science.*

Mather, M., & Johnson, M. K. (2000). Choice-supportive source monitoring: Do our decisions seem better to us as we age? *Psychology & Aging, 15*, 596–606.

Mayne, T. J. (1999). Negative affect and health: The importance of being earnest. *Cognition and Emotion, 13*, 601–635.

Mayne, T. J. (2001). Emotions and health. In T. J. Mayne & G. A. Bonanno (Eds.), *Emotions: Current issues and future directions* (pp. 361–397). New York: Guilford Press.

McConatha, J. T., & Huba, H. M. (1999). Primary, secondary, and emotional control across adulthood.

Current Psychology: Developmental, Learning, Personality, Social, 18, 164–170.

McCrae, R. R, & Costa, P. T. Jr. (1990). *Personality in adulthood.* New York: Guilford Press.

McDowell, C. L., Harrison, D. W., & Demaree, H. A. (1994). Is right hemisphere decline in the perception of emotion a function of aging? *International Journal of Neuroscience, 70*, 1–11.

Mendolia, M. (2002). An index of self-regulation of emotion and the study of repression in social contexts that threaten or do not threaten self-concept. *Emotion, 2*, 215–232.

Michalos, A. C., Hubley, A. M., Zumbo, B. D., & Hemingway, D. (2001). Health and other aspects of the quality of life of older people. *Social Indicators Research, 54*, 239–274.

Mickelson, K. D., Kessler, R. C., & Shaver, P. R. (1997). Adult attachment in a nationally representative sample. *Journal of Personality and Social Psychology, 73*, 1092–1106.

Mikulincer, M. (1998). Adult attachment style and affect regulation: Strategic variations in self-appraisals. *Journal of Personality and Social Psychology, 75*, 420–435.

Mikulincer, M., Florian, V., & Tolmacz, R. (1990). Attachment styles and fear of personal death: A case study of affect regulation. *Journal of Personality and Social Psychology, 58*, 273–280.

Mizumori, S. J. Y., Barnes, C. A., & McNaughton, B. L. (1992). Differential effects of age on subpopulations of hippocampal theta-cells. *Neurobiology of Aging, 13*, 673–679.

Montepare, J., Koff, E., Zaitchik, D., & Albert, M. (1999). The use of body movements and gestures as cues to emotions in younger and older adults. *Journal of Nonverbal Behavior, 23*, 133–152.

Moreno, C. R., Borod, J. C., Welkowitz, J., & Alpert, M. (1990). Lateralization for the expression and perception of facial emotion as a function of age. *Neuropsychologia, 28*, 199–209.

Moreno, C. R., Borod, J. C., Welkowitz, J., & Alpert, M. (1993). The perception of facial emotion across the adult life span. *Developmental Neuropsychology, 9*, 305–314.

Mroczek, D. K. (2001). Age and emotion in adulthood. *Current Directions in Psychological Science, 10*, 87–90.

Mroczek, D. K., & Kolarz, C. M. (1998). The effect of age on positive and negative affect: a developmental perspective on happiness. *Journal of Personality and Social Psychology, 75*, 1333–1349.

Mroczek, D. K., & Spiro, A. III. (2003). Modeling intraindividual changes in personality trait: findings from the Normative Aging Study. *Journal of Gerontology: Series B: Psychological Sciences, 58B*, 153–165.

Nesse, R. M. (1990). Evolutionary explanations of emotions. *Human Nature, 1*, 261–289.

Panksepp, J., & Miller, A. (1995). Emotions and the aging brain: Regrets and remedies. In C. Magai &

S. H. McFadden (Eds.), *Handbook of emotion, adult development and aging* (pp. 3–26). San Diego, CA: Academic Press.

Phillips, L. H. (1999). Age and individual differences in letter fluency. *Developmental Neuropsychology, 15,* 249–267.

Phillips, L. H., & Della Sala, S. (1998). Aging, intelligence, and anatomical segregation in the frontal lobes. *Learning and Individual Differences, 10,* 217–243.

Phillips, L. H., MacPherson, S., & Della Sala, S. (2002). Age, cognition and emotion: The role of anatomical segregation in the frontal lobes. *Psychology & Aging, 17,* 598–609.

Phillips, L. H., Smith, L., & Gilhooly, K. J. (2002). The effects of adult aging and induced positive and negative mood on planning. *Emotion, 2,* 263–272.

Raskin, A. (1979). Signs and symptoms of psychopathology in the elderly. In A. Raskin & L. F. Jarvick (Eds.), *Psychiatric symptoms and cognitive loss in the elderly* (pp. 3–18). Washington, DC: Hemisphere.

Rosenzweig, E. S., Redish, A. D., McNaughton, B. L., & Barnes, C. A. (2003). Hippocampal map realignment and spatial learning. *Nature Neuroscience, 6,* 609–615.

Schaie, K. W., & Hertzog, C. (1983). Fourteen-year cohort-sequential analyses of adult intellectual development. *Developmental Psychology, 19,* 531–543.

Schieman, S. (1999). Age and anger. *Journal of Health and Social Behavior, 40,* 273–289.

Schulkind, M. D., Hennis, L. K., & Rubin, D. C. (1999). Music, emotion, and autobiographical memory: They're playing your song. *Memory and Cognition, 27,* 948–955.

Smith, C. A., & Lazarus, R. S. (1993). Appraisal components, core relational themes, and the emotions. *Cognition and Emotion, 7,* 233–269.

Smith, J., Fleeson, W., Geiselmann, B., Settersten, R. A. Jr., & Kunzmann, U. (1999). Sources of well-being in very old age. In P. B. Baltes & K. U. Mayer (Eds.), *The Berlin aging study: Aging from 70 to 100* (pp. 450–471). New York: Cambridge University Press.

Smith, T. W. (1992). Hostility and health: Current status of a psychosomatic hypothesis. *Health Psychology, 11,* 139–150.

Stacey, C. A., & Gatz, M. (1991). Cross-sectional age differences and longitudinal change on the Bradburn Affect Balance Scale. *Journals of Gerontology, 46*(2), P76–P78

Stearns, C. Z. (1993). Sadness. In M. Lewis & J. M. Haviland (Eds.), *Handbook of emotions* (pp. 547–562). New York: Guilford.

Stein, N. L., & Levine, L. J. (1990). Making sense out of emotion: The representation and use of goal-structured knowledge. In N. L. Stein, B. Leventhal, & T. Trabasso (Eds.), *Psychological and biological approaches to emotion* (pp. 45–73). Hillsdale, NJ: Lawrence Erlbaum.

Steverink, N., Westerhof, G. J., Bode, C., & Dittmann-Kohli, F. (2001). The personal experience of aging, individual resources, and subjective well-being. *Journals of Gerontology: Series B: Psychological Sciences and Social Sciences, 56B,* P364–P373.

Stoner, S. B., & Spencer, W. B. (1987). Age and gender differences with the Anger Expression Scale. *Educational and Psychological Measurement, 47,* 487–492.

Tavris, C. (1984). On the wisdom of counting to ten: Personal and social dangers of anger expression. *Review of Personality and Social Psychology, 5,* 170–191.

Tavris, C. (1989). *Anger: The misunderstood emotion* (rev. ed). New York: Touchstone Books.

Thompson, L. A., Aidinejad, M. R., & Ponte, J. (2001). Aging and the effects of facial and prosodic cues on emotional intensity ratings and memory reconstructions. *Journal of Nonverbal Behavior, 25*(2), 101–125

Tomkins, S. (1962). *Affect, imagery, consciousness. Vol. I: The positive affects.* New York: Springer.

Tomkins, S. S. (1963). *Affect, imagery, consciousness: Vol 2. The negative affects.* New York: Springer.

Tooby, J., & Cosmides, L. (1990). The past explains the present: Emotional adaptations and the structure of ancestral environments. *Ethology and Sociobiology, 11,* 375–424.

Tsai, J. L., Levenson, R. W., & Carstensen, L. L. (2000). Autonomic, subjective, and expressive responses to emotional films in older and younger Chinese Americans and European Americans. *Psychology & Aging, 15,* 684–693.

Turner, R., & Wood, W. (1985) Depression and disability: The stress process in a chronically strained population. *Research in Community and Mental Health, 5,* 77–109.

Uchino, B. N., Uno, D., Holt-Lunstad, J., & Flinders, J. B. (1999). Age-related differences in cardiovascular reactivity during acute psychological stress in men and women. *Journals of Gerontology: Series B: Psychological Sciences, 54B,* P339–P346.

Webster, J. D. (1997). Attachment style and well-being in elderly adults: A preliminary investigation. *Canadian Journal on Aging, 16,* 101–111.

West, R. L., & Crook, T. H. (1990). Age differences in everyday memory: Laboratory analogues of telephone number recall. *Psychology & Aging, 5,* 520–529.

Westphal, M., & Bonanno, G. A. (2004). Emotion self-regulation (pp. 1–34). In M. Beauregard (Ed.), *Consciousness, emotional self-regulation, and the brain.* Amsterdam: John Benjamins.

Chapter 7

Motivation and Interpersonal Regulation Across Adulthood: Managing the Challenges and Constraints of Social Contexts

Frieder R. Lang and Jutta Heckhausen

*If we want everything to remain as it is,
it will be necessary for everything to change.*
—*Giovanni Tomasi di Lampedusa (1960/1990)*

It's never too late.
—*Vaupel, Carey, and Christensen (2003)*

A central theoretical proposition of life span developmental psychology states that individuals are active in shaping their own development. From birth until late in life, individuals select, manipulate, and mold their immediate environments in accordance with age-specific needs and tasks (M. Baltes & Carstensen, 1996; Brandtstädter, 1989; Lerner & Busch-Rossnagel, 1981). Over the past decades, this perspective on individuals as developmental agents in their own matter has dominated theory and research on adult development and learning, for example, with respect to mechanisms of self-regulation (Brandtstädter, 1989, 2001; see also Cervone, Artistico, & Berry, chapter 8, this volume) or with respect to mechanisms of shaping the social environment (Lang, 2001, 2004b; Wahl & Kruse, 2003). The idea of individuals as developmental agents is challenging in several ways. For example, an individual's capacity to produce desirable developmental outcomes is limited. Developmental regulation occurs within the narrow boundaries of elasticity and controllability of the developmental context. A consequence is that over the life course, individuals acquire a broad knowledge and deep understanding of the biological and societal constraints that limit or even threaten their action potentials. This involves a broad range of motivational as well as social learning processes that depend on specific contexts (e.g., institutional settings, living situation), which—again—are products of the individual's agentic life management. Probably one of the most elastic and controllable developmental contexts pertains to the social context, that is, the individual's personal relationships with other people in the family, community, and at work. Individuals select social partners, they directly influence other people, and they are able to seek compromise and mutual understanding in their social worlds. Social contexts are reciprocal and mutual by nature. Consequently, selecting the social partners one interacts with regularly and/or altering the behavior of the people one interacts with inevitably leads to a (more or less meaningful) contextual change and subsequently may also alter one's own behavior to some respect. More generally, the extent to which contexts are elastic is critical for better understanding the ways individuals regulate their development over the life course.

Contextualistic reasoning in developmental research suggests that changes in the context affect the course, direction, and outcomes of development (P. B. Baltes, 1997; Lerner & Kauffman, 1985). However, not all changes in an individual's environment are developmentally meaningful and effective to the same extent. One powerful illustration of the idea that contextual changes affect developmental pathways comes from demographic research investigating changes in life expectancy in East and West Germany before and after reunification in 1990 (Scholz & Maier, 2003; Vaupel et al., 2003). Since the 1970s, life expectancy in the two German states has developed in different trajectories. In the socialist German Democratic Republic, average life expectancy was about 8–10 years shorter than in the Western Federal Republic of Germany. However, within only 12 years after reunification the average life expectancy in East Germany has reached about the same level as the life expectancy in West Germany. More important, Scholz and Maier (2003) observed that most of the increases in life expectancy in East Germany are attributable to individuals who were 60 years old or older *at the time of the reunification.*

Obviously, at any time in life individuals can benefit from adaptive changes in their social, economic, and political environment. Adult development is not a one-way street. As individuals develop and acquire new strategies of how to exert influence in their environments, they also benefit from the resulting contextual change in terms of life quality and life expectancy. Thus, the developmental role of contexts is two-fold. On the one hand, individuals acquire and learn about developmental opportunities and frames of reference for age-specific norms and action (Heckhausen, 1999; Settersten, 1999). On the other hand, developmental contexts, in particular social environments, represent outcomes of individuals' life course decisions, planning, and management (Brandtstädter & Lerner, 1999; Lang, 2001, 2004b). Life management often is embedded in processes that are related to the activation, maintenance, or breaking off of social relationships. For example, adults acquire new responsibilities when leaving their parents' home, when becoming a

parent, or when their own parents grow old and eventually are in need of care. For example, in their early career, young adults acquire competencies with the help of a mentor. Career development typically implies that adults learn to cooperate and succeed with (or at times also against) their colleagues and peers. Throughout adulthood, individuals are confronted with new and changing contexts that structure and sequence the course and direction of their development. In most contemporary societies, there are relatively fixed sequences of expected age-graded transitions and life events that organize the individual life course. Such developmental change or adaptation involves the adults' learning and understanding the implicit or explicit rules, norms, expectations, and tasks of their age-specific environments. Therefore, development across adulthood involves active learning of contextual constraints and demands as well as the acquisition of the skills or strategies needed for the mastery of such developmental challenges.

Age-related trajectories of motivation and interpersonal capacities depend on three major factors: biological changes, societal opportunity structures, and personal agency (Cervone et al., chapter 8, this volume; Heckhausen, 1999). In many instances, biology and society facilitate and foster the individual's agency, but they also entail limitations to and constraints on agency. For example, sensory losses in later life challenge the individual's capacities to explore new social contexts (Wahl, Heyl, & Schilling, 2002). We argue that developmental agency at all times of life involves both the shaping of biological and societal living circumstances (e.g., health and risk behaviors) and adaptation of the self to uncontrollable contexts.

In this chapter, we address how biology and societal constraints influence the development of motivational resources and the ways in which efforts to regulate one's social world contribute to adaptation and effective action potentials. We discuss the ways in which motivational processes and interpersonal regulation enhance and protect the adult's capacity to learn skills and strategies of control over development so that they stimulate and regulate further adaptive developmental action. We divide our chapter into three sections. The first section discusses the ways that biological influences and societal opportunities create challenges and constraints with respect to the individual's capacity to effectively shape and organize social environments. In the second section, we consider processes and strategies of developmental regulation across adulthood from the perspective of the life span theory of control (Heckhausen & Schulz, 1995). In the third and last section we discuss the role and potential of individual agency in regulating personal relationships across adulthood. We conceive of such interpersonal regulation as involving both responses to (unexpected or uncontrollable) contextual change (e.g., widowhood, an accident, a severe disease), as well as the adult's purposeful, goal-related activity in selecting, manipulating, maintaining, or breaking his or her social relationships (Lang, Reschke, & Neyer, in press). Often, changes in the social context (e.g., marriage, parenthood, moving to a new town, retirement) involve and reflect active efforts of the individual to adaptively mold the social context in accordance with his or her capabilities and needs and to do so to protect motivational resources for future action. We begin with a discussion of how biological (e.g., sensory) and societal (e.g., normative) limitations challenge the adult's potentials of organizing and regulating the social environment.

DEVELOPING INTERPERSONAL CAPACITIES ACROSS ADULTHOOD: BIOLOGICAL AND SOCIETAL CHALLENGES AND CONSTRAINTS

Interpersonal capacities involve fundamental human resources related to cognitive functioning (Lopes, Salovey, & Straus, 2003; Schutte et al., 2001), sensorimotor functioning (M. M. Baltes & Lang, 1997; Lang, Rieckmann, & Baltes, 2002; Wahl et al., 2002), emotion (Carstensen & Charles, 1998; Pasupathi & Carstensen, 2003), and social status or, in more general terms, social capital (Bourdieu, 1986). Gains and losses in any of these biological or social resources have implications for the individual's capacities to maintain or regulate social relationships. Consequently, development of interpersonal regulation heavily depends on the individual's availability of biological and social resources over the life course. In this section, we focus first on the role of biological changes on interpersonal functioning across adulthood (e.g., the physiology of emotions) and second on the roles of societal opportunities and age-normative challenges. In a later section, we discuss the proactive regulation of social-developmental contexts in response to such biological and societal influences.

Biological Challenges and Constraints on Motivation and Interpersonal Capacities

The biology of interpersonal experiences and capacities in adulthood continuously changes and unfolds over the life course. Biological changes typically involve changes in the physiology of emotions (Carstensen & Charles, 1998) and to some extent changes in sensory functioning (e.g., vision or hearing capabilities; e.g., Wahl & Kruse, 2003) and cognitive capabilities (P. B. Baltes & Lindenberger, 1997; Lindenberger & Baltes, 1994).

Emotional Experience

From an evolutionary perspective, emotional responses can be seen as behavioral adaptations that support the organism's mastery, reproduction, and survival when confronted with challenges and demands (Frijda, 1988; Schulz & Heckhausen, 1996). When reaching early adulthood, individuals typically have developed a differentiated and integrated system of emotion-specific responses as well as the ability to comprehend the expressed feelings of others. From an evolutionary perspective, the emotion system in early adulthood can be seen as being optimized for securing survival and reproduction (e.g., Plutchik, 1980). This also contributes to understanding emotional development in postreproductive phases of the life course. For example, one implication is that many emotions that regulate reproductive behaviors may be activated less often or less intensively in later phases of adulthood. Moreover, sensory losses in later adulthood may also contribute to a reduction of autonomic responses and affective reactivity in later life.

Although the overall pattern of emotional activity appears to remain quite stable, there is robust evidence that the magnitude of emotional responses, as indicated by physiological parameters such as skin temperature or heart rate, are consistently lower among old adults as compared to young adults (Levenson, Carstensen, Friesen, & Ekman, 1991). In an extensive research program, Levenson and colleagues (Levenson, 2000; Levenson et al., 1991) used varied techniques of manipulating emotional states to compare age differences in cardiovascular responses. For example, when inducing negative emotions to participants (i.e., through facial action or in a "relived emotions" task), younger adults displayed greater changes in heart rate than did older adults. In another study using films as emotional stimuli, Tsai, Levenson, and Carstensen (2000) observed that young adults (age 20–35) as compared to old adults (age 70–85) showed stronger cardiovascular responses (e.g., heart rate, finger temperature) to sad and amusing films. More generally, these and other empirical findings suggest that with increasing age, adults experience fewer negative emotions, whereas they experience positive emotions as often or even more frequently (Carstensen & Charles, 1998; Carstensen, Pasupathi, Mayr, & Nesselroade, 2000; Mroczek & Kolarz, 1998). One explanation may be that the emotion-specific physiology changes across adulthood. Another explanation is that age differences in cardiovascular activity reflect age-specific differences in how emotion-relevant information is processed. This is illustrated with findings observing functional MRI (fMRI) of amygdala activation of individuals, who processed positive and negative emotional pictures (Mather et al., 2004). Older adults showed greater activation in the amygdala in response to positive emotion pictures, but not when seeing negative or neutral pictures. Young adults showed more activation in the amygdala in response to negative pictures. In another study, Charles, Mather, and Carstensen (2003) found that older adults recall images presented on a computer screen less well than young adults. However, age differences were less strong with respect to recall of positive images as compared to negative or neutral images. Together, these findings suggest that the physiology of emotional experience differs substantially from early to later adulthood. An important implication for learning across adulthood is that in later adulthood the emotional system strongly favors positive emotions when processing information. Another example is that older adults are more likely to generate positive affect words than negative affect words when disclosing themselves to others or when writing text descriptions (Pennebaker & Stone, 2003). In all, emotional changes across adulthood lead to substantive changes in the adult's capacity to process, regulate, and master relationship-related social information and demands.

Sensory and Cognitive Resources

From an evolutionary perspective, changed biological boundary conditions in later adulthood are also related to losses of sensory or cognitive resources that are involved in the processing of emotions. Most social behaviors, as well as the maintenance of social relationships, rely on the individual's intellectual and sensory abilities to actively participate in social exchanges. Social interactions with others involve intellectual resources on all levels of cognitive and sensory processing. As a consequence, when individuals experience cognitive decline, everyday social contacts are often challenged because of dual-task costs (Kemper, Herman, & Lian, 2003; Lindenberger, Marsiske, & Baltes, 2000). Cognitive decline and sensory loss in old adulthood may well hamper the individual's capacity to activate and protect functional relationships with members of the social network (e.g., Wahl & Kruse, 2003). For example, in late life, social contacts often occur in the context of supportive or care needs of older adults, whereas social contacts that are related to other aspects of social activity and exchange may become rare and perhaps difficult to maintain (Rook, 2000).

Societal Opportunity Structures and Normative Challenges

Developmental change often occurs in relation to educational, vocational, and family life course transitions, such as school entry, job entry, retirement, marriage, parenthood, divorce, or widowhood. The challenges of such developmental tasks typically arise from the age-graded social structure in modern societies, which organize and sequence the individual's life course (Hagestad, 1990; Heckhausen, 1999; Riley, 1985; Settersten, 1999, Silbereisen, Reitzle, & Juang, 2002). Such normative forces in society limit the individual's action potentials and control over the social environment. Moreover, societal expectations and age-graded norms scaffold the individual's opportunities for interpersonal experience and social relationships over the life course.

However, societal opportunity structures are not rigid cocoons that enclose the individual life course; rather, they reflect hierarchical, dynamic, malleable, and age-specific tasks and demands that are organized along the individual's life course (Lerner & Kauffman, 1985; Lewis, 1999). For example, specific laws determine the age at which individuals attain majority and from then on are made liable for their actions and social conduct. However, in most industrialized societies there are also specific social structures that serve to guide young adults through the early transitional phase into early adulthood (Arnett, 2000; Silbereisen et al., 2002).

Age-graded social opportunities and norms are often not explicit but are represented in the lay knowledge and social expectations of society members (Hagestad, 1990; Settersten, 1999). For example, there exist age-specific norms about when individuals are expected to leave their parents' home, become financially independent, find a partner, marry, and eventually have a child (Neugarten, Moore, & Lowe, 1965). More recently, Settersten (1998a) found that young and old adults agreed that men and women should leave their parents' home before they become 25 years old. In general, early adulthood often is associated with normative expectations and opportunities in the domains of early family development, psychological autonomy, and entry into a vocational career (Arnett, 2000; Ryan & Lynch, 1989). In middle adulthood, individuals are typically confronted with a growing number of social roles in the family, in the community, and at work. Such diversity of social roles in midlife often involves complex interpersonal responsibilities and demands (Lachman, 2004). Not surprisingly, the mere number of social relationships in adults' personal networks peaks in midlife (Lang, 2004b). In contrast, late adulthood is associated with a general reduction of social roles, for example, in professional contexts and the community. As a result of the linear increase of life expectancy over the past century (Vaupel et al., 2003), an increasing proportion of the population in contemporary societies will experience an extended phase of later adulthood. One consequence is that older adults will confront new role expectations and social norms, for example, in relation to volunteering and social responsibilities (Okun & Schultz, 2003). However, it is still an open question as to which social roles, societal opportunities, and normative challenges are most relevant for understanding adaptational processes of later adulthood in the domain of social functioning (P. B. Baltes, Staudinger, & Lindenberger, 1999; Havighurst, 1973; Lang & Carstensen, 1998).

To sum up, biology and societal opportunities determine and provide the resources and the constraints that challenge personal agency in social contexts. Across the adult life span, individuals are confronted with age-graded and age-specific challenges to their motivational and interpersonal capabilities. The extent to which individuals succeed in protecting their action potentials may depend on the life-management and regulation strategies that are acquired and applied over the adult life course.

DEVELOPMENTAL REGULATION AND MOTIVATIONAL CHANGES ACROSS ADULTHOOD: THEORETICAL PERSPECTIVES

Theories of developmental regulation address the ways in which individuals master developmental tasks across the life course (P. B. Baltes et al., 1999; Brandtstädter, 2001; Carstensen, Isaacowitz, & Charles, 1999; Heckhausen, 1999). One important assumption of theoretical perspectives on developmental regulation builds on the idea that whenever individuals face developmental challenges or constraints, they activate or protect their motivational resources to enhance their adaptive capacities. In fact, the idea that individuals actively mold their environments in congruence with motives and traits has a rather long tradition in the history of psychology dating back to the work of Gordon Allport (1937) among others (e.g., Caspi, Bem, & Elder, 1989). From a more developmental perspective, this pertains to the issue of how adults learn and make use of age-specific adaptive regulatory strategies that contribute to stabilization and adaptation across adulthood. For example, Lang and Heckhausen (2001) observed differential benefits of control beliefs for subjective well-being across adulthood: Among young adults, attributing success to unstable internal resources (e.g., effort) contributed to enhanced well-being, whereas older adults benefited more from attributing their goal achievements to stable internal resources (e.g., capabilities). One explanation is that young adults may be more likely to still experience growth of action potentials (e.g., via effort investment), whereas a perceived lack of action capacities in later adulthood may be more threatening and ego-central to the self. This points to an age-specific regulation of developmental and interpersonal outcomes across adulthood.

Theories of Developmental Regulation: Basic Propositions

Several theories have addressed the processes and mechanisms of developmental regulation across the life course (e.g., P. B. Baltes & M. M. Baltes, 1990; Brandtstädter, 2001; Heckhausen & Schulz, 1995;

Lerner, Freund, DeStefanis, & Habermas, 2001). Existing models of lifelong adaptation and developmental regulation differ substantively in theoretical background and scope but also entail considerable conceptual overlap. There are at least three common assumptions and perspectives of most action-theoretical models of developmental regulation that contribute importantly to the understanding of change and continuity across adulthood.

A first common assumption relates to the plasticity of development: Throughout the entire life course, there exist strong plasticity and intraindividual variability in behavioral and cognitive development (P. B. Baltes, 1997; Lerner, 1996). Even under most aversive conditions, individuals often remain capable of adjusting their behaviors and cognitions in such ways that they can maintain their basic everyday functioning (M. M. Baltes, 1996). Psychological resilience marks one of the basic human strengths at all phases of adulthood (e.g., Heckhausen, 1999; Staudinger, Marsiske, & Baltes, 1995).

A second tenet states that lifelong development consists of a gain–loss dynamics of maximizing gains while minimizing losses. In the first half of adulthood gains typically prevail over losses, but individuals often experience a dramatic increase of losses from middle to late adulthood (Heckhausen, Dixon, & P. Baltes, 1989; Heckhausen, 1999). At certain phases of adulthood, some opportunities (e.g., to have a child) disappear, whereas other new opportunities (e.g., retirement) emerge. However, there is no phase in the human life course in which individuals do not experience both gains as well as losses. Deciding for one goal or action necessarily implies a decision against possible alternate goals or actions. Whenever individuals succeed at one task, this implies that success with other (competing) tasks becomes less likely. One reason for this lies in the fact that an individual's time in life is a limited resource and that individuals are well aware of this limitation (e.g., Carstensen, 1995; Nuttin, 1985). Learning new skills (e.g., a language or profession) in adulthood is a good example. Any decision to invest resources in learning activities in one specific domain of everyday life necessarily means that learning in other areas falls short.

Finally, a third common proposition of most life span developmental theories is that each phase of the life course confronts the individual with specific developmental challenges that result from biological changes, societal expectations, and individual agency

(Havighurst, 1948/1981; Settersten, 1998b, 1999). Developmental tasks produce a scaffold for the individual's life course, and they determine what goals should be selected and how long one should persist in goal pursuits (e.g., the wish to have a child; Heckhausen, Wrosch, & Fleeson, 2001). In each life phase, individuals learn about the constraints and demands of that respective phase. Here, learning of age-specific norms, tasks, and limitations is necessary to develop the capabilities for actively regulating one's developmental pathway.

Together, the concepts of developmental plasticity, lifelong gain–loss dynamics, and the scaffolding of developmental tasks serve to underscore the idea that adults have the capacity to learn the skills and adaptive control strategies needed to shape social contexts in ways that protect and enhance their developmental action potentials. It is critical in this context that such skills and strategies are only sensible when the adult's context is elastic and controllable, as is the case in most social relationships.

Motivational Theories of Interpersonal Regulation

Few life span theories have explicitly addressed the motivational processes of change in social relationships across the life course. One empirically well-supported theory of social-motivational life span development is socioemotional selectivity theory (Carstensen et al., 1999). The theory contends that individuals continuously adapt their goals and emotional experience over the life course in response to perceptions of the remaining time in their future life. When time is perceived as open-ended, individuals preferably seek social experiences that optimize their future in the long run. One implication is that individuals are motivated to enhance their instrumental social knowledge, which may be useful for possible future needs. In contrast, when time is perceived as limited, emotionally meaningful goals are expected to be more salient and more functional. One reason is that emotional gratification does not require specific long-term investments but may rather be an immediate outcome of social experiences.

There is strong empirical support for the basic assumptions of socioemotional selectivity theory as well as demonstrations of its validity and usefulness in the domains of memory across adulthood (Mather & Carstensen, 2003), social preferences (Fung &

Carstensen, 2003), and the shaping of social networks over the life course (Lang, 2000, 2001; Lang & Carstensen, 2002). For example, when individuals approach endings or perceive their remaining time in life as being constrained, they tend to dissolve less meaningful and distant social relationships while preferably pursuing goals that are related to belonging needs, such as generativity (Lang & Carstensen, 2002).

However, it is not well understood which processes and strategies adults apply to achieve their goals in their social environments across adulthood. Often, perceived endings in one's social relationships are related to social deadlines, which one may decide to keep or not. This involves additional regulatory tasks, which may best be understood in the broader context of developmental regulation across the life course as proposed by the life span theory of control.

Life Span Theory of Control: Implications for Mastery of Environmental Challenges

The life span theory of control (Heckhausen & Schulz, 1995; Schulz & Heckhausen, 1996) builds on three premises that are relevant to the mastery of environmental challenges across adulthood. First, individuals are seen as active producers of their own development (Brandtstädter & Lerner, 1999). Second, individuals strive to enhance their potentials to exert control over the environment (i.e., primary control) throughout the entire life course. Third, primary control potentials follow an inverted U-shaped trajectory over the life course, with a peak plateau in midlife and a subsequent decline until later life. However, the trajectory of primary control potentials in the course of social relationships across adulthood is still not fully understood. For example, in close relationships, adults may experience great potential to still exert control over their immediate environment, even until late in life (e.g., in soliciting help, giving advice).

Types of Control Striving

The life span theory of control contends that when individuals face environmental challenges, they make use of motivational and regulatory strategies that aim toward enhancing their potentials to effectively control the environment. The theory proposes two types of control striving across the life course: primary and secondary control striving. Primary control

relates to behaviors that are directed at producing effects or changes in the environment. Secondary control striving is directed at internal states of the self and serves to protect or enhance the self's motivational resources that are required to effectively control the environment (e.g., lowering expectations in an intimate relationship). Secondary control striving is expected to be functional when it contributes to enhanced primary control potential and to be dysfunctional when it threatens or obstructs the individual's action potentials.

Primary and secondary control strategies operate hand in hand during the mastery of life events and transitions. Both primary and secondary control striving involve a selective or compensatory mobilization of behavioral, social, and motivational resources. Primary control striving pertains to either selective or compensatory strategies of investing behavioral or social resources (i.e., effort, asking for help). Secondary control striving includes two types of strategies: One is volitional self-regulation, for example, commitment to a specific task or action goal (i.e., selective secondary control). A second type relates to strategies in response to failure of one's efforts (i.e., compensatory secondary control), or when transitional tasks cannot be mastered.

Compensatory secondary control is particularly relevant for the protection of motivational resources whenever individuals experience irreversible or unavoidable losses or constraints in the course of a transition (e.g., giving birth to a disabled child; undesired childlessness after marriage). In such situations, self-protection strategies (e.g., devaluating previously held opinions or expectations) help the individual deflect potential negative effects of loss experiences on self-esteem or future action potentials. Examples of the self-protective strategies pertain to attributions to external factors, avoidance of self-blame, and comparison with similar others who are even worse off.

The Trajectory of Secondary Control

According to the life span theory of control, striving for (compensatory) secondary control is relevant for successful mastery of failure and loss experiences across the entire life course. Typically, though, failure and loss are more likely to occur in the second half of life. One reason is, as stated before, that adults' potentials for effectively controlling the environment are reduced in later adulthood. As a consequence, older adults are more likely to experience the challenges

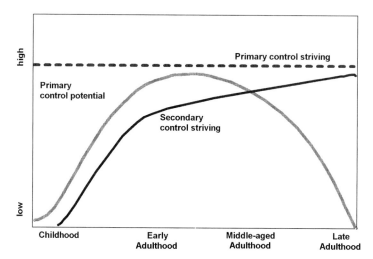

FIGURE 7.1 Primary and secondary control strategies.

and constraints of their environments that cannot be mastered by actively altering environmental conditions. In these cases, mastery is more often directed to the self and to the protection of one's motivational resources and action potentials. This means that strategies related to secondary control striving show steady increases across adulthood. As is shown in figure 7.1, primary and secondary control strategies thus follow quite different trajectories across the life course (Schulz & Heckhausen, 1996).

The empirical evidence for a greater salience of secondary control striving in later adulthood as compared to earlier phases of adulthood is ample. For example, in a cross-sectional study of 510 adults, Heckhausen (1997) observed a greater tendency for compensatory secondary control (e.g., more flexibility of one's personal goals) at increasing ages of adulthood. Similarly, there are robust findings suggesting that older adults endorse more negative stereotypes of aging as a negative reference frame against which they fare well in comparisons to their own, much more positive aging experience (e.g., Heckhausen & Krueger, 1993).

To sum up, the capacity of adults to internally compensate for failure and loss experiences and thus protect their motivational and action resources shows a steady increase across adulthood. In contrast, primary control striving appears to decline in later phases of adulthood. However, within social relationships the dynamic interplay of secondary and primary control potentials appears to follow different trajecto-

ries. At least in close relationships, adults may remain capable of exerting effective control over relational outcomes until very late in life. For example, in a longitudinal study of older adults between 70 and 103 years of age, Lang (2000) investigated changes in personal networks with respect to changes of closeness and continuity within each relationship of the network across a 4-year time interval. The findings showed great rank-order consistency of the overall network size, whereas the number of relationship partners decreased across four years. Only about one-half of all the initially reported social relationships were still continuing after four years. For each discontinued relationship, adults reported the reasons for the discontinuation at the second measurement occasion. Only one-third of the discontinued social relationships were lost for nondeliberate, uncontrollable reasons such as illness or mortality of partners. However, about one-half of all discontinued relationships were actively broken by the respondents for deliberate reasons. Moreover, when older adults felt near to death, they were likely to report discontinuation with more peripheral or less meaningful social partners in their network. Regulation of one's social relationships through such control strategies also appears to contribute critically to the stabilization and the continuity of the self across adulthood (e.g., Lang & Heckhausen, 2005; Lang et al., in press).

In sum, the theoretical perspectives on developmental and interpersonal regulation across adulthood point to the specific strategies that adults learn when confronting the challenges, demands, and constraints of the age-specific developmental contexts in adulthood. Primary and secondary control strategies describe the ways individuals adaptively respond to elastic and nonelastic facets of their environments in ways that protect or even enhance their action potentials.

INDIVIDUAL AGENCY AND THE REGULATION OF SOCIAL RELATIONSHIPS ACROSS ADULTHOOD

In the remainder of this chapter, we focus on the role of individual agency in mastering the challenges and constraints of social environmental changes across adulthood. Most environmental transitions or challenges in adulthood are related to changes within and across social relationships. As already discussed, biology and societal opportunity structures determine life course changes in interpersonal capacities and in the environment of the individual. Age-graded life transitions, for example, are associated with normative expectations of the beginning (e.g., marriage), the course (e.g., career), or the ending (e.g., retirement) of specific social relationships. Other relationship changes result from developmental gains or losses in emotional, sensory, or cognitive functioning across adulthood. Finally, many changes in the personal network are a result of the individual's deliberate and active efforts to regulate or shape the quantity, quality, and functions of relationships with social partners. The skills of such interpersonal regulation emerge from the adult's acquired knowledge of the constraints and elasticity of the interpersonal context. In this respect, it becomes important to differentiate between the deliberate and nondeliberate and the elastic and nonelastic facets of the adult's social contexts.

Changes of Social Relationships Across Adulthood: Normative Challenges and Agentic Influences—A Distinction

As compared to changes that result from the individual's active and deliberate efforts of interpersonal regulation, changes of relationship quality that result from biological or from normative societal influences may differ with respect to their functions across adulthood. Building on this assumption, Lang et al. (in press) proposed that changes of social environment across the life course are typically composed of two different classes of social-relationship changes: (a) normative or expected change and (b) deliberate or regulatory change of social context.

Normative changes of relationships are constituents of life course transitions such as finding a partner, giving birth to a child, or beginning a new job. Normative changes are expected, prescribed, and predisposed, and they can only be avoided when adults do not accept and comply with the respective social norm (e.g., to marry, to go to work). Noncompliance, of course, leads to social sanctions (e.g., isolation, low status). Normative changes of social relationships entail several challenges as they limit or threaten the continuity of relationships (e.g., after retirement) and lead to ambiguity or insecurity about the future of one's relationships. As a consequence, normative relationship changes per se imply challenges that require that adults invest in efforts to protect or activate their motivational and self-regulatory resources.

In contrast to this, there are also relationship changes that emerge as a result of individual agency and regulatory strategies. Adults purposefully invest efforts to shape and manage their social relationships in accordance with their personality structure and motives, and thus proactively shape their environments. For example, individuals strive to enhance their action potentials. Moreover, individuals also respond differently to the challenges and tasks of normative relationship change. For example, following retirement some adults seek to stay in contact with their former colleagues, whereas others begin to newly activate "sleeping" kin relationships. These types of relationship changes are *regulatory* because they represent the individual's striving for enhanced action potentials and goal pursuit in life.

Normative and regulatory relationship changes typically co-occur simultaneously and are interwoven, but may have different effects on self-concept development across adulthood. Normative changes follow culture-specific scripts that are highly predictable and are accompanied by new social roles involving specific social norms and tasks (e.g., becoming a caring parent after the birth of a first child). The course and direction of such normative changes can only be influenced within very limited margins (e.g., married couples are normatively expected to share a bedroom; divorce means that spouses move apart). One implication is that normative changes often imply that individuals enter new environments or roles that subsequently change their self-concepts and personality. Normative relationship changes, however, also activate regulatory efforts to stabilize one's environment, for example, by shaping the "new" environment in accordance with one's personality.

Regulatory relationship changes are a result of the proactive shaping or molding of the social context. This means that regulatory relationship changes depend on the individual's personality and thus constitute individual styles of selecting, shaping, and organizing social relationships. This way, the regulation of social relationships contributes importantly to growing personality-environment congruence across adulthood (Asendorpf, 2002; Caspi, 1998; Caspi et al., 1989). One consequence is that regulatory changes of relationships may also account for an increasing consistency of personality over the life course (e.g., Roberts & DelVecchio, 2000).

According to the life span theory of control (Heckhausen & Schulz, 1995), individuals rely on motivational and self-regulatory strategies to protect or enhance their potential to effectively control the environment. This involves either primary or secondary control strategies. In the realm of social relationships, most primary control strategies are directed toward influencing a relationship partner's internal state or behaviors. Primary control typically implies an action focus on others' behaviors or cognitions. For example, choosing a social partner for a social exchange aims at soliciting specific reciprocal interests and behaviors of that partner. More generally, individuals typically expect that their efforts toward another person are in some way mirrored in their relationship partners' behaviors and communications. It is obvious that goal structures in social relationships are rather complex, hierarchically nested, and typically only implicit. Individuals are motivated for social contact on hierarchically different levels of goal pursuits. Seeking

contact with a good friend may be instrumental in terms of the specific expectations about the friend's behavior (e.g., to provide support), but at the same time, seeking contact with the friend may also constitute a goal in itself, that is, for its own sake. For these reasons, regulatory changes in social relationships in most cases serve multiple purposes and are not related to specific action units or the pursuit of only one specific goal (perhaps with the exception of formal exchanges in trade relationships). Typically, individuals seek to influence their partners on two levels, one that aims to activate a relationship (e.g., choosing, intensifying) and one that aims to protect a relationship or relationship partner (e.g., avoiding conflict, repair, caring for another).

Secondary control strategies aim at changing one's inner experience according to the outer world (Rothbaum, Weisz, & Snyder, 1982), which in most cases involves other relationship partners. More generally, secondary control in this perspective involves a focus on the self in a given social relationship. For example, individuals may internally regulate their sense of closeness, sympathy, or intimacy toward another person; they may empathetically tune into others; they may open up for influence or advice of others; they may forgive; or they may accommodate their internal states and standards in situations of conflicting interests. In all such cases, individuals have a regulatory focus on the self in a specific social interaction that relates to either activation or protection of the social relationship.

Table 7.1 gives an overview of the four regulatory strategies of relationship changes across adulthood as they relate to life course control strategies of the life course theory of control. Activation of social relationships typically involves strategies of either choosing others or adapting internal standards. Protection in primary or secondary control pertains to strategies that are directed at relationship maintenance or

TABLE 7.1.   Regulatory Relationship Strategies in Primary and Secondary Control: Examples of Self- and Other-Foci in Activation and Protection

Regulatory Relationship Strategy	Primary Control	Secondary Control
Selection	Focus on other activation: Intensify contact, choose new partners, social control	Focus on self-activation: Feeling close, feeling into others
Compensatory	Focus on other protection: Caring, giving support, repairing after conflict	Focus on self-protection: Accommodation, seeking understanding

repair or at adapting internal standards of expectations toward others. For example, individuals may accommodate their behaviors in relationship conflicts (Yovetich & Rusbult, 1994) or invest in response-focused emotion regulation to prevent negative affect (Carstensen, Gross, & Fung, 1998).

How Does Regulation of Social Relationships Contribute to Adult Development?

In general, the role of social relationships in adult development is not fully understood. Although some scholars view social relationships as outcomes of developmental change and stability across the life course (e.g., Vangelisti, Reis, & Fitzpatrick, 2002), others suggest that social relationships per se imply and trigger developmental demands and change over the life course (Antonucci & Jackson, 1990; Lang, 2004b). In the first perspective, social relationships are seen as being "executed" and representing individual differences. In the latter perspective, social relationships are seen as malleable "membranes" between (change of) the society and individual change. However, both research foci should be seen as complementary rather than contradictory. There is empirical evidence that corroborates both views. For example, Asendorpf and colleagues (Asendorpf & Wilpers, 1998; Neyer & Asendorpf, 2001) have shown that personality influences social relationships rather than the other way around. Findings from other studies suggest that individuals proactively select social partners to enhance their developmental resources (e.g., Lang, 2000; Lang, Featherman, & Nesselroade, 1997). For example, when feeling near death, individuals give up personal relationships that do not provide emotionally meaningful experiences. A young professional woman chooses a colleague as mentor, hoping to advance her professional expertise and receiving guidance in the development of her job-related competence. This is not to say that individuals are always aware of the instrumentality of their efforts in interpersonal regulation. Often, goals of interpersonal regulation are more or less implicit in the nature of a specific relationship context (e.g., intimacy in a romantic partnership), and individuals may not even be aware of their goal striving.

An adult's personal relationships are dynamic, elastic, and idiosyncratic; they never entail fixed scripts that allow for just one type of behavior or social exchange. Each single relationship consists of two individuals who differ in their personality structure and self-definition. Most individuals maintain more than one social relationship, of which, in addition, some are interdependent (e.g., within the family). Developmental changes and transitions that occur in the life of a relationship partner inevitably affect the course of that social relationship. By nature, a single social relationship cannot be more stable than the social behaviors of the involved individuals. This implies that regulatory efforts in ongoing social relationships are always in process and never ending.

Moreover, there is no personal relationship that is identical to another, neither within the individual's network nor between adults' social networks. Often, social relationships are classified according to role-specific contents or scripts, such as friendship, siblinghood, or parenthood. However, these categories do not characterize relationship qualities, but rather represent combinations of evolutionary stable human social behaviors, such as reciprocity (Gouldner, 1960), cooperation, sexual mating (Buss, 1989), or emotional closeness (Neyer & Lang, 2003). Typically, the diversity of relationship qualities within a specific category of social role (e.g., friendship) is greater than the diversity of relationship quality across different social roles (e.g., friendship versus family). A friend cannot replace another friend, particularly when considering that friendship in most cultures is defined by the uniqueness of the partners in a friendship. However, the relationship quality of many family members may follow rules of friendships, whereas some friendships may appear kin-like. This is not to say that relationship loss cannot be compensated or substituted (Rook & Schuster, 1996), quite the contrary.

We suggest that losses of social partners involve regulatory relationship changes that involve strategies related to the activation and the protection of relationships. When adults experience loss or the ending of one relationship, they may invest efforts to intensify (protect) their relationships with others or choose (activate) new relationship partners. They may change their relationship goals (focus on self), or they may seek to solicit specific supportive behaviors in their social environment (focus on others).

In the remainder of this chapter, we present some empirical illustrations of motivational processes across adulthood that are involved in relationship changes related to family transitions and to career transitions.

The Family Context of Adult Development: Motivational Challenges and Constraints

Family development in adulthood involves several challenges and transitions, mostly related to the beginning and the ending of a partnership (e.g., marriage, divorce, widowhood) as well as to parenthood or grandparenthood. In the following, we will focus on exemplary challenges of relationship changes related to marriage, widowhood, and first parenthood. We will present empirical illustrations for the ways in which regulatory relationship influences in the course of family transitions contribute to positive personality development or personality stabilization across adulthood.

Marriage

When couples marry (or move in together), new challenges and tasks arise for the partners related to household and task sharing, kinship relations, and friendship networks (Sprecher, Felmlee, Orbuch, & Willetts, 2002; Veroff, Douvan, Orbuch, & Acitelli, 1998). Moreover, the development of role divisions between the spouses, as well as the development of marital satisfaction after marriage, was shown to depend on the extent to which the spouses' networks show overlap (Milardo & Allan, 1996; Stein, Bush, Ross, & Ward, 1992). When networks of spouses were more close-knit in the early phase, the spouses were more likely to follow a pattern of traditional role divisions in the household, which was found to be associated with greater stability of the marital relationship.

Empirical findings also support the importance of *activation* strategies in interpersonal regulation. For example, marital satisfaction is found to be greater when husbands and wives succeed in activating social support from their respective relatives. However, this also entails risks when the involvement of relatives is not equally balanced between the two partners or when relatives are too demanding (e.g., Timmer, Veroff, & Hatchett, 1996). In a longitudinal study, Hope, Rodgers, and Power (1999) explored associations between marital status and levels of distress at age 23 and at age 33 in an entire cohort ($N = 11,405$) of adults born in Great Britain in the first week of March 1958. Although the transition to marriage was not associated with change in symptoms of psychological distress (anxiety, depression, somatic complaints), the marriages were more stable when partners activated

and shared supportive friends or relatives in their social network.

Findings on protective relationship regulation in the transition to marriage are scarce. Moving from a status of being single to a (first) partnership in early adulthood was observed to be associated with positive changes in stable social behaviors, greater emotional stability, and greater conscientiousness (Neyer, 2004; Neyer & Asendorpf, 2001). Individuals appear to develop new internal standards in their social behaviors that seem to persist even after first partnerships have ended. In addition, long-term marriages are known to have beneficial effects on psychological well-being and physical health (e.g., Brown, 2000; Horwitz & White, 1998; Stack & Eshleman, 1998).

Widowhood

Losing one's spouse after many years or decades of marriage is always undesirable and may be unexpected. Often, older couples are quite aware of the fact that one of them might survive the other. Typically, though, widowhood is a female experience considering the life expectancies of men and women and the gendered age differences between most spouses (O'Bryant & Hansson, 1995). Not surprisingly, widowers respond differently to widowhood than widows. For example, men are known to face greater health and mortality risks in the first two years after the loss of their wives (Stroebe, 2001).

Findings on regulatory relationship changes after widowhood mostly relate to the activation modus. Widowhood leads to substantial adjustments in the widow's or widower's social network related to the activation of new relationships (Lamme, Dykstra, & Broese Van Groenou, 1996) or increases of network size (Morgan & March, 1992). Widowed older people were found to activate a greater percentage of kinship ties and doing so is associated with feeling less lonely (e.g., Lang, 2004a). Managing and forming social relationships after widowhood contributes to a generally improved adjustment (Walsh & McGoldrick, 1988).

Not much is known about *protection* of existing social relationships following spousal bereavement. For example, women are known to show more expressive ways of coping with widowhood than men (Stroebe, Stroebe, Shutz, Zech, & van den Bout, 2002). Some findings also suggest improvement of the quality of previously existing relationships in the family after widowhood (Morgan & March, 1992). In general, findings suggest much continuity of social networks after widowhood, at least among women. Boerner and Heckhausen (2003) proposed that the extent to which individuals manage to transform their mental ties to the lost spouse contributes to positive adaptation after widowhood. In fact, regulatory processes also involve the protection of the relationship to the lost one. This is manifest, for example, in the subsequent idealization of a lost spouse.

First Parenthood

The transition to parenthood involves challenges and tasks that are known to strongly affect the partnership and marriage system. It is a robust finding that the quality of marital relationships dramatically decreases in the months and years following the birth of a first child (e.g., Helms-Erikson, 2001), and the risk of divorce or separation of the parents increases (Orbuch et al., 2002). The specific motivational and regulatory processes that underlie such challenges of the parenthood transition are not yet fully understood. There is some indication that parenthood does lead to increased activation of social support and other social network resources; these contribute to improved mastery of the transition (Bost, Cox, Burchinal, & Payne, 2002). In a longitudinal study of fathers, Hawkins and Belsky (1989) observed a decrease of self-esteem in fathers who were more involved with the newborn child over the first 15 months after the child's birth. Unfortunately, in this study, no information was obtained regarding the course and quality of other social relationships that may have moderated this effect.

The Vocational Career Context of Adult Development: Regulating Relationships and Mastering Transitions

Interpersonal regulation in the context of career development is underexplored in empirical research. Not much is known about the ways social relationships are activated and protected in the course of educational and vocational transitions, for example, in the school-to-work transition or at later phases of the vocational career. At school, college, university, and work, individuals regularly change their social contexts in response to their active striving to enhance their action potentials. Relationship changes result in response to success (promotion) as well as failure (job loss).

Typically, new teams are put together when new projects are started. Few domains of adult development and learning require as much investment and effort in interpersonal regulation as the vocational career.

School to Work and Early Career

Transitioning from school to work involves a myriad of inevitable relationship changes. These include moving to a new city, changing social status, competing demands of work and leisure tasks, beginning of new formal relationships within job hierarchies, and professional task demands (e.g., Bynner, 1998). In a longitudinal study of adolescents approaching the end of school, Heckhausen and Tomasik (2002) observed adjustments of aspirations and job preferences in the course of seeking and applying for apprenticeships. Older adolescents adapt their vocational aspirations in anticipation of the transition to work. Not much is known about the regulatory changes in social relationships that typically accompany these transitions. For example, social relationships might be preferred that are related to job-relevant information and that provide support and allow for functional upward and downward social comparisons (e.g., Bynner, 1998; Heckhausen & Krueger, 1993).

Retirement

The timing and process of retirement, as well as the extension of the postretirement phase of adulthood, has changed enormously over the past 50 years (e.g., Hayward, Friedman & Chen, 1998; Settersten, 1998b). Most adults expect to experience an extended period of relatively healthy living after retirement (Kim & Moen, 2001). The transition clearly involves many challenges, most of which are strongly dependent on the broader social-ecological context of the retiree. Strategies of activation and protection of social relationships appear to both contribute importantly to the mastery of these challenges. For example, in a longitudinal study of social network change before and after retirement, van Tilburg (1992) found much change in the structure and function of social support networks. One year after retirement, adults had dissolved most relationships with their former colleagues, but the overall size of social networks did not change much. Retirees maintained most of their nonjob-related social relationships that already existed before the transition (protection). However, they also activated new relationships with partners with whom they experienced strong levels of reciprocity. The findings of this study may point to the important role of social relationships in the mastery of life course challenges.

Summing up, empirical findings on family and vocational transitions across adulthood suggest that considerable change of social environments is related to individual agency and to the efforts of adults toward mastery of transitional tasks and challenges. Distinguishing between the more biological and societal influences on social relationship changes and the individual's agentic investments in molding and organizing the social environment across adulthood contributes to a better understanding of mastery and stabilization across adulthood.

CONCLUSIONS AND OUTLOOK

Throughout adulthood, individuals are confronted with biological and sociostructural challenges and constraints. Mastery of such challenges typically involves adaptations in the context of the adult's social relationships. Regulating one's social relationships is shown to strongly contribute to the individual's action potentials and positive personality development across adulthood.

Building on assumptions of the life span theory of control (Heckhausen & Schulz, 1995) and motivational theories of social relationships across the life course (e.g. Lang, 2004b), we argue that individuals shape and organize their relationships through processes of activation and protection. Both processes involve strategies that are either focused on one's own goal commitments (secondary control) or focused on the relationship partner (primary control). From our selected review of empirical illustrations, it appears that individuals shift from activation to protection modes and from other-focus to self-focus in organizing their social environments across adulthood. This view is consistent with socioemotional selectivity theory. According to this theory, older adults adapt their goals and needs as they experience limitations of resources or of future time (Carstensen et al., 1999; Lang, 2004b). For example, Lang and Carstensen (2002) observed that adults who were between 20 and 90 years old generally benefited from committing to a self-oriented emotion focus in organizing social networks under conditions of limited future time resources.

In all, regulatory strategies of activation and protection of one's social relationships contribute substantively to the mastery of challenges and transitions across adulthood. Throughout the adult life course, individuals learn and acquire adaptive strategies of shaping their social environments and managing their social relationships. In our view, intervention and learning in adulthood require a closer look at shaping and encouraging the individual's capacities to regulate and mold the social environments in ways that promote and support age-specific needs and tasks. Interpersonal regulation may be an important tool in activating, enhancing, or protecting the adult's action potentials in the mastery of the many demands and challenges of adult development.

ACKNOWLEDGMENTS Work on this chapter was supported by the Max-Planck Award for International Cooperation awarded to Jutta Heckhausen and funded by the German Federal Ministry of Education and Research.

References

Allport, G. W. (1937). *Personality: A psychological interpretation*. New York: Holt, Rinehart & Winston.

Antonucci, T. C., & Jackson, J. S. (1990). The role of reciprocity in social support. In B. R. Sarason, I. G. Sarason, & G. R. Pierce (Eds.), *Social support: An interactional view* (pp. 173–198). New York: Wiley.

Arnett, J. J. (2000). Emerging adulthood: A theory of development from the late teens through the twenties. *American Psychologist, 55,* 469–480.

Asendorpf, J. B. (2002). Personality effects on personal relationships over the life span. In A. L. Vangelisti, H. T. Reis, & M. A. Fitzpatrick (Eds.), *Stability and change in relationships* (pp. 35–56). Cambridge: Cambridge University Press.

Asendorpf, J. B., & Wilpers, S. (1998). Personality effects on social relationships. *Journal of Personality and Social Psychology, 74,* 1531–1544.

Baltes, M. M. (1996). *The many faces of dependency in old age.* New York: Cambridge University Press.

Baltes, M. M., & Carstensen, L. L. (1996). The process of successful aging. *Ageing and Society, 16,* 397–422.

Baltes, M. M., & Lang, F. R. (1997). Everyday functioning and successful aging: The impact of resources. *Psychology and Aging, 12,* 433–443.

Baltes, P. B. (1997). On the incomplete architecture of human ontogeny: Selection, optimization, and compensation as foundation of developmental theory. *American Psychologist, 52,* 366–380.

Baltes, P. B., & Baltes, M. M. (1990). Psychological perspectives on successful aging: The model of selective optimization with compensation. In P. B. Baltes & M. M. Baltes (Eds.), *Successful aging: Perspectives from the behavioral sciences* (pp. 1–34). New York: Cambridge University Press.

Baltes, P. B., & Lindenberger, U. (1997). Emergence of a powerful connection between sensory and cognitive functions across the adult life span: A new window to the study of cognitive aging? *Psychology and Aging, 12,* 12–21.

Baltes, P. B., Staudinger, U. M., & Lindenberger, U. (1999). Lifespan psychology: Theory and application to intellectual functioning. *Annual Review of Psychology, 50,* 1999, 471–507.

Boerner, K., & Heckhausen, J. (2003). To have and have not: Adaptive bereavement by transforming mental ties to the deceased. *Death Studies, 27,* 199–226.

Bost, K. K., Cox, M. J., Burchinal, M. R., & Payne, C. (2002). Structural and supportive changes in couples' family and friendship networks across the transition to parenthood. *Journal of Marriage and the Family, 64,* 517–531.

Bourdieu, P. (1986). The forms of capital. In J. G. Richardson (Ed.), *Handbook of theory and research for the sociology of education* (pp. 241–258). Westport, CT: Greenwood Press.

Brandstädter, J. (1989). Personal self-regulation of development: Cross-sequential analyses of development-related control beliefs and emotions. *Developmental Psychology, 25,* 96–108.

Brandstädter, J. (2001). *Entwicklung. Intentionalität. Handeln* [Development. Intentionality. Action]. Stuttgart, Germany: Kohlhammer.

Brandstädter, J., & Lerner, R. (Eds.). (1999). *Action and self-development: Theory and research through the life-span* (pp. 67–103). London: Sage.

Brown, S. L. (2000). The effect of union type on psychological well-being: Depression among cohabitators versus marrieds. *Journal of Health and Social Behavior, 41,* 241–255.

Buss, D. M. (1989). Sex differences in human mate preferences: Evolutionary hypotheses tested in 37 cultures. *Behavioral and Brain Sciences, 12,* 1–49.

Bynner, J. (1998). Education and family components of identity in the transition from school to work. *International Journal of Behavioral Development, 22,* 29–53.

Carstensen, L. L. (1995). Evidence for a life-span theory of socioemotional selectivity. *Current Directions in Psychological Science, 5,* 151–156.

Carstensen, L. L., & Charles, S. T. (1998). Emotion in the second half of life. *Current Directions in Psychological Science, 7,* 144–149.

Carstensen, L. L., Gross, J. J., & Fung, H. H. (1998). The social context of emotional experience. In K. W. Schaie & M. P. Lawton (Eds.), *Annual review of gerontology and geriatrics* (Vol. 17, pp. 325–352). New York: Springer.

Carstensen, L. L., Isaacowitz, D. M., & Charles, S. T. (1999). Taking time seriously: A theory of socioemotional selectivity. *American Psychologist, 54,* 165–181.

Carstensen, L. L., Pasupathi, M., Mayr, U., & Nesselroade, J. (2000). Emotion experience in the daily lives of older and younger adults. *Journal of Personality and Social Psychology, 79,* 644–655.

Caspi, A. (1998). Personality development across the life course. In N. Eisenberg (Ed.), *Handbook of child psychology, Vol. 3: Social, emotional, and personality development* (5th ed., pp. 311–388). New York: Wiley.

Caspi, A., Bem, D. J., & Elder, G. H. Jr. (1989). Continuities and consequences of interactional styles across the life course. *Journal of Personality, 57,* 375–406.

Charles, S. T., Mather, M., & Carstensen, L. L. (2003). Aging and emotional memory: The forgettable nature of negative images for older adults. *Journal of Experimental Psychology: General, 132,* 310–324.

Frijda, N. H. (1988). The laws of emotion. *American Psychologist, 43,* 349–358.

Fung, H. H., & Carstensen, L. L. (2003). Sending memorable messages to the old: Age differences in preferences and memory for advertisments. *Journal of Personality and Social Psychology, 85,* 163–178.

Gouldner, A. W. (1960). The norm of reciprocity: A preliminary statement. *American Sociological Review, 25,* 161–178.

Hagestad, G. O. (1990). Social perspectives on the life course. In R. Binstock & L. George (Eds.), *Handbook of aging and the social sciences* (3rd ed., pp. 151–168). New York: Academic Press.

Havighurst, R. (1948/1981). *Developmental tasks and education.* New York: Longman.

Havighurst, R. (1973). Social roles, work, leisure, and education. In C. Eisdorfer & M. P. Lawton (Eds.), *The psychology of adult development and aging* (pp. 598–618). Washington, DC: American Psychological Association.

Hawkins, A. J., & Belsky, J. (1989). The role of father involvement in personality change in men across the transition to parenthood. *Family Relations, 38,* 378–384.

Hayward, M. D., Friedman, S., & Chen, H. (1998). Career trajectories and older men's retirement. *Journals of Gerontology: Social Sciences, 53B,* S91–S103

Heckhausen, J. (1997). Developmental regulation across adulthood: Primary and secondary control of age-related challenges. *Developmental Psychology, 33,* 176–187.

Heckhausen, J. (1999). *Developmental regulation in adulthood: Age-normative and sociostructural constraints as adaptive challenges.* New York: Cambridge University Press.

Heckhausen, J., Dixon, R., & Baltes, P. B. (1989). Gains and losses in development throughout adulthood as perceived by different adult age groups. *Developmental Psychology, 25,* 109–121.

Heckhausen, J., & Krueger, J. (1993). Developmental expectations for the self and most other people: Age grading in three functions of social comparison. *Developmental Psychology, 29,* 539–548.

Heckhausen, J., & Schulz, R. (1995). A life-span theory of control. *Psychological Review, 102,* 284–304.

Heckhausen, J., & Tomasik, M. J. (2002). Get an apprenticeship before school is out: How German adolescents adjust vocational aspirations when getting close to a developmental deadline. *Journal of Vocational Behavior, 60,* 199–219.

Heckhausen, J., Wrosch, C., & Fleeson, W. (2001). Developmental regulation before and after a developmental deadline: The sample case of "biological clock" for child-bearing. *Psychology and Aging, 16,* 400–413.

Helms-Erikson, H. (2001). Marital quality ten years after the transition to parenthood: Implications of the timing of parenthood and the division of housework. *Journal of Marriage and the Family, 63,* 1099–1110.

Hope, S., Rodgers, B., & Power, C. (1999). Marital status transitions and psychological distress: Longitudinal evidence from a national population sample. *Psychological Medicine, 29,* 381–389.

Horwitz, A. V., & White, H. R. (1998). The relationship of cohabitation and mental health: A study of a young adult cohort. *Journal of Marriage and the Family, 60,* 505–514.

Kemper, S., Herman, R. E., & Lian, C. H. T. (2003). The costs of doing two things at once for young and older adults: Talking while walking, finger tapping, and ignoring speech or noise. *Psychology and Aging, 18,* 181–192.

Kim, J. E., & Moen, P. (2001). Is retirement good or bad for subjective well-being? *Current Directions in Psychological Science, 10,* 83–86.

Lachman, M. E. (2004). Development in midlife. *Annual Review of Psychology, 55,* 305–331.

Lamme, S., Dykstra, P., & Broese Van Groenou, M. I. (1996). Rebuilding the network: New relationships in widowhood. *Personal Relationships, 3,* 337–349.

Lang, F. R. (2000). Endings and continuity of social relationships: Maximizing intrinsic benefits within personal networks when feeling near to death? *Journal of Social and Personal Relationships, 17,* 157–184.

Lang, F. R. (2001). Regulation of social relationships in later adulthood. *Journal of Gerontology: Psychological Sciences, 56B,* P1–P6.

Lang, F. R. (2004a). Availability and supportive functions of extended kinship ties in later life. In S. Harper (Ed.), *The family in an ageing society* (pp. 64–81). New York: Oxford University Press.

Lang, F. R. (2004b). Social motivation across the life span. In F. R. Lang & K. L. Fingerman (Eds.), *Growing together: Personal relationships across the lifespan* (pp. 341–367). New York: Cambridge University Press.

Lang, F. R., & Carstensen, L. L. (1998). Social relationships and adaptation in late life. In S. Bellack & M. Hersen (Eds.), *Comprehensive clinical psychology* (Vol. 7, pp. 55–72). Oxford: Pergamon.

Lang, F. R., & Carstensen, L. L. (2002). Time counts: Future time perspective, goals, and social relationships. *Psychology and Aging, 17,* 125–139.

Lang, F. R., Featherman, D. L., & Nesselroade, J. R. (1997). Social self efficacy and short-term variability in social relationships: The MacArthur successful aging studies. *Psychology and Aging, 12,* 657–666.

Lang, F. R., & Heckhausen, J. (2001). Perceived control over development and subjective well-being: Differential benefits across adulthood. *Journal of Personality and Social Psychology, 81,* 509–523.

Lang, F. R., & Heckhausen, J. (2005). Stabilisierung und Kontinuität der Persönlichkeit im Lebenslauf [Stabilization and continuity of personality over the life course]. In J. B. Asendorpf & H. Rauh (Eds.), *Enzyklopädie der Psychologie. Band C/V/3. Soziale, emotionale und Persönlichkeitsentwicklung* [Encyclopedia of psychology: Social, emotional and personality development] (pp. 525–562). Göttingen: Hogrefe.

Lang, F. R., Reschke, F. S., & Neyer, F. J. (in press). Social relationships, transitions and personality development across the life span. In D. K. Mroczek & T. D. Little (Eds.), *Handbook of personality development.* Mahwah, NJ: Lawrence Erlbaum.

Lang, F. R., Rieckmann, N., & Baltes, M. M. (2002). Adapting to aging losses: Do resources facilitate strategies of selection, compensation, and optimization in everyday functioning? *Journal of Gerontology: Psychological Sciences, 57B,* P501–P509.

Lerner, R. M. (1996). Relative plasticity, integration, temporality, and diversity in human development: A developmental contextual perspective about theory, process, and method. *Developmental Psychology, 32,* 781–786.

Lerner, R. M., & Busch-Rossnagel, N. (1981). Individuals as producers of their development: Conceptual and empirical bases. In R. M. Lerner & N. A. Busch-Rossnagel (Eds.), *Individuals as producers of their development: A life-span perspective* (pp. 1–36). New York: Academic Press.

Lerner, R. M., Freund, A., De Stefanis, I., & Habermas, T. (2001). Understanding developmental regulation in adolescence: The use of the selection, optimization, and compensation model. *Human Development, 44,* 29–50.

Lerner, R. M., & Kauffman, M. B. (1985). The concept of development in contextualism. *Development Review, 5,* 309–333.

Levenson, R. W. (2000). Expressive, physiological, and subjective changes in emotion across adulthood. In S. H. Qualls & N. Abeles (Eds.), *Psychology and the aging revolution* (pp. 123–140). Washington, DC: American Psychological Association.

Levenson, R. W., Carstensen, L. L., Friesen, W. V., & Ekman, P. (1991). Emotion, physiology and expression in old age. *Psychology and Aging, 6,* 28–35.

Lewis, M. (1999). On the development of personality. In L. A. Pervin & O. P. John (Eds.), *Handbook of personality* (2nd ed., pp. 327–346). New York: Guilford.

Lindenberger, U., & Baltes, P. B. (1994). Sensory functioning and intelligence in old age: A strong connection. *Psychology and Aging, 9,* 339–355.

Lindenberger, U., Marsiske, M., & Baltes, P. B. (2000). Memorizing while walking: Increase in dual-task costs from young adulthood to old age. *Psychology and Aging, 15,* 417–436.

Lopes, P. N., Salovey, P., & Straus, R. (2003). Emotional intelligence, and the perceived quality of social relationships. *Personality and Individual Differences, 35,* 641–658.

Mather, M., & Carstensen, L. L. (2003). Aging and attentional biases for emotional faces. *Psychological Science, 14,* 409–415.

Mather, M., Canly, T., English, T., Whitfield, S., Wais, P., Ochsner, K., Gabrieli, J. D., & Carstensen, L. L. (2004). Amygdala responses to emotionally valenced stimuli in older and younger adults. *Psychological Science, 15,* 259–263.

Milardo, R. M., & Allan, G. (1996). Social networks and marital relationships. In S. Duck, K. Dindia, W. Ickes, R. Milardo, R. Mills, & B. Saranson (Eds.), *Handbook of personal relationships* (pp. 505–522). London: Wiley.

Morgan, D. L., & March, S. J. (1992). The impact of life events on networks of personal relationships: A comparison of widowhood and caring for a spouse with Alzheimer's disease. *Journal of Social and Personal Relationships, 9,* 563–584.

Mroczek, D. K., & Kolarz, C. M. (1998). The effect of age on positive and negative affect: A developmental perspective on happiness. *Journal of Personality and Social Psychology, 75,* 1333–1349.

Neugarten, B. L., Moore, J. W., & Lowe, J. C. (1965). Age norms, age constraints, and adult socialization. *American Journal of Sociology, 70,* 710–717.

Neyer, F. J. (2004). Dyadic fits and transactions in personal relationships. In F. R. Lang & K. L. Fingerman (Eds.), *Growing together: Personal relationships across the lifespan* (pp. 290–316). New York: Cambridge University Press.

Neyer, F. J., & Asendorpf, J. B. (2001). Personality-relationship transaction in young adulthood. *Journal of Personality and Social Psychology, 81,* 1190–1204.

Neyer, F. J., & Lang, F. R. (2003). Blood is thicker than water: Kinship orientation across adulthood. *Journal of Personality and Social Psychology, 84,* 310–321.

Nuttin, J. (1985). *Future time perspective and motivation.* Hillsdale, NJ: Lawrence Erlbaum.

O'Bryant, S. L., & Hansson, R. O. (1995). Widowhood. In R. Blieszner & V. H. Bedford (Eds.), *Handbook of aging and the family* (pp. 440–458). Westport, CT: Greenwood.

Okun, M. A., & Schultz, A. (2003). Age and motives for volunteering: Testing hypotheses derived from socioemotional selectivity theory. *Psychology and Aging, 18,* 231–239.

Orbuch, T. L., Veroff, J., Hassan, H., & Horrocks, J. (2002). Who will divorce: A 14-year longitudinal study of black couples and white couples. *Journal of Social and Personal Relationships, 19,* 179–202.

Pasupathi, M., & Carstensen, L. L. (2003). Age and emotional experience during mutual reminiscing. *Psychology and Aging, 18,* 430–442.

Pennebaker, J. W., & Stone, L. D. (2003). Words of wisdom: Language use over the life span. *Journal of Personality and Social Psychology, 85,* 291–301.

Plutchik, R. (1980). *Emotion. A psychoevolutionary synthesis.* New York: Harper & Row.

Riley, M. W. (1985). Age strata in social systems. In R. H. Binstock & E. Shanas (Eds.), *Handbook of aging and the social sciences* (2nd ed., pp. 369–411). New York: Van Nostrand Reinhold.

Roberts, B. W., & DelVecchio, W. F. (2000). The rank-order consistency of personality from childhood to old age: A quantitative review of longitudinal studies. *Psychological Bulletin, 126,* 3–25.

Rook, K. S. (2000). The evolution of social relationships in later adulthood. In S. H. Qualls & N. Abeles (Eds.), *Psychology and the aging revolution* (pp. 173–191). Washington, DC: American Psychological Association.

Rook, K. S., & Schuster, T. L. (1996). Compensatory processes in the social networks of older adults. In G. R. Pierce, B. R. Sarason, & I. G. Sarason (Eds.), *Handbook of social support and the family* (pp. 219–248). New York: Plenum Press.

Rothbaum, F., Weisz, J. R., & Snyder, S. S. (1982). Changing the world and changing the self: A two-process model of perceived control. *Journal of Personality and Social Psychology, 42,* 5–37.

Ryan, R. M., & Lynch, J. H. (1989). Emotional autonomy versus detachment: Revisiting the vicissitudes of adolescence and young adulthood. *Child Development, 60,* 340–356.

Scholz, R., & Maier, H. (2003). *German unification and the plasticity of mortality at older ages.* Rostock, Germany: Max Planck Institute for Demographic Research, MPIDR working paper WP 2003-031.

Schulz, R., & Heckhausen, J. (1996). A life-span model of successful aging. *American Psychologist, 51,* 702–714.

Schutte, N. S., Malouff, J. M., Bobik, C., Coston, T. D., Greeson, C., Jedlicka, C., et al. (2001). Emotional intelligence and interpersonal relations. *Journal of Social Psychology, 141,* 523–536.

Settersten, R. A. Jr. (1998a). A time to leave home and a time never to return? Age constraints on the living arrangements of young adults. *Social Forces, 76,* 1373–1400.

Settersten, R. A. Jr. (1998b). Time, age, and the transition to retirement: New evidence on life-course flexibility? *International Journal of Aging and Human Development, 47,* 177–203.

Settersten, R. A. Jr. (1999). *Lives in time and place: The problems and promises of developmental science.* Amityville, NY: Baywood.

Silbereisen, R. K., Reitzle, M., & Juang, L. (2002). Time and change: Psychosocial transitions in German young adults 1991 and 1996. In L. Pulkkinen & A. Caspi (Eds.), *Paths to successful development:*

Personality in the life course (pp. 227–254). New York: Cambridge University Press.

Sprecher, S., Felmlee, D., Orbuch, T. L., & Willetts, M. C. (2002). Social networks and change in personal relationships. In A. L. Vangelisti, H. T. Reis, & M. A. Fitzpatrick (Eds.), *Stability and change in relationships* (pp. 257–284). New York: Cambridge University Press.

Stack, S., & Eshleman, J. R. (1998). Marital status and happiness: A 17 nation study. *Journal of Marriage and the Family, 60,* 527–536.

Staudinger, U. M., Marsiske, M., & Baltes, P. B. (1995). Resilience and reserve capacity in later adulthood: Potentials and limits of development across the life span. In D. Cicchetti & D. J. Cohen (Eds.), *Developmental psychopathology, Vol. 2: Risk, disorder, and adaptation* (pp. 801–847). New York: Wiley.

Stein, C. H., Bush, E. G., Ross, R. R., & Ward, M. (1992). Mine, yours and ours: A configural analysis of the networks of married couples in relation to marital satisfaction and individual well-being. *Journal of Social and Personal Relationships, 9,* 365–383.

Stroebe, M. (2001). Gender differences in adjustment to bereavement: An empirical and theoretical review. *Review of General Psychology, 5,* 62–83.

Stroebe, M., Stroebe, W., Schutz, H., Zech, E., & van den Bout, J. (2002). Does disclosure of emotions facilitate recovery from bereavement? Evidence from two prospective studies. *Journal of Consulting and Clinical Psychology, 70,* 169–178.

Timmer, S. G., Veroff, J., & Hatchett, S. (1996). Family ties and marital happiness: The different marital experiences of black and white newlywed couples. *Journal of Social and Personal Relationships, 13,* 335–359.

Tomasi di Lampedusa, G. (1960/1990). *The leopard.* New York: Pantheon Books. (Original edition 1958: Il gattopardo. Milano, Italia: Feltrinelli Editore.)

Tsai, J. L., Levenson, R. W., & Carstensen, L. L. (2000). Autonomic, subjective, and expressive responses to emotional films in older and younger Chinese Americans and European Americans. *Psychology and Aging, 15,* 684–693.

van Tilburg, T. (1992). Support networks before and after retirement. *Journal of Social and Personal Relationships, 9,* 433–445.

Vangelisti., A. L., Reis, H. T., & Fitzpatrick, M. A. (Eds.). (2002). *Stability and change in relationships.* New York: Cambridge University Press.

Vaupel, J. W., Carey J. R., & Christensen K. (2003). It's never too late. *Science, 301,* 1679–1681.

Veroff, J., Douvan, E., Orbuch, T. L., & Acitelli, L. K. (1998). Happiness in stable marriages: The early years. In T. N. Bradbury (Ed.), *The developmental course of marital dysfunction* (pp. 152–179). New York: Cambridge University Press.

Wahl, H.-W., Heyl, V., & Schilling, O. (2002). The role of vision impairment for the outdoor activity and life satisfaction of older adults: A multi-faceted view. *Visual Impairment Research, 4,* 143–160.

Wahl, H.-W., & Kruse, A. (2003). Psychological gerontology in Germany: Recent findings and social implications. *Ageing and Society, 23,* 131–163.

Walsh, F., & McGoldrick, M. (1988). Loss and the family life cycle. In C. J. Falicov (Ed.), *Family transitions: Continuity and change over the life cycle* (pp. 311–336). New York: Guilford Press.

Yovetich, N. A., & Rusbult, C. E. (1994). Accomodative behavior in close relationships: Exploring transformation of motivation. *Journal of Experimental Social Psychology, 30,* 138–164.

Part III

The Self-System in Adult
Development and Learning

Chapter 8

Self-Efficacy and Adult Development

Daniel Cervone, Daniele Artistico, and Jane M. Berry

Only those who will risk going too far can possibly find out how far one can go.
—*T. S. Eliot (1931)*

I believe, therefore I can.
—*Cavanaugh & Green (1990)*

A major theme in the contemporary study of human development across the life span is that people have the capacity for personal agency. Innumerable writers emphasize that individuals can exert intentional influence over their experiences and actions, the circumstances they encounter, the skills they acquire, and thus ultimately the course of their development.

This theme undoubtedly reflects historical trends. Prior to the 1800s, "Wherever he lived, man could only count on a short expectation of life, with a few extra years in the case of the rich" (Braudel, 1981, p. 90). Today, in contrast, life expectancy in some nations exceeds 80 years of age (*The Economist*, 2002). In those parts of the world blessed with key natural resources (Diamond, 1997), economic growth has given rise to socioeconomic systems that provide extensive educational opportunities and foster meritocratic social mobility. It is in this contemporary context—in which opportunities for personal development are vast and the expected life span for realizing one's potentials is lengthy—that questions of personal agency naturally come to the fore (Caprara & Cervone, 2003). Of course, many citizens of the world do not experience these advantageous circumstances; 3 billion of the world's people still live on $2 or less a day (UN Population Fund, 2002) and the life span in some nations remains less than 40 years of age (*The Economist*, 2002). While not losing site of such sobering statistics, one can nonetheless acknowledge that many people today develop in a world in which they have the potential to chart their own life paths, cultivate competencies of their choosing, and thereby contribute to the course of their own development.

These social changes call for analyses of the psychological systems that foster positive development into the later years of life. Scholars and practitioners in the field of aging have responded to this call. Models of successful aging (Rowe & Kahn, 1997) and research on positive aging (Carstensen & Charles, 2003) appear with increasing regularity. In an effort to ensure and enhance quality of life in late adulthood and senescence, investigators aim to enable older adults to live engaged, purposeful, and meaningful lives as free from mental and physical debilities as possible. Positive attitudes toward aging appear to have health benefits (Levy, Hausdorff, Hencke, & Wei, 2000; Levy, Slade, & Kasl, 2002) and are related to longevity (Levy, Slade, Kunkel, & Kasl, 2002). More people are living to be centenarians than at any other time in history, and thus it is incumbent on researchers in fields of adult development and learning to delineate the modes and mechanisms that will allow older adults to lead dignified, meaningful, engaged lives. A complete understanding of adults' capacity to achieve these life outcomes requires careful attention to mechanisms of personal agency.

The purpose of this chapter is to review the contribution of self-efficacy mechanisms (Bandura, 1977a, 1997) to adults' capacity to learn new skills and contribute to their personal development in an agentic manner. We do so by first taking a broad look at the nature of human agency and the architecture of mental systems that enable people to regulate their experiences and actions.

COGNITIVE COMPONENTS OF PERSONAL AGENCY

What enables members of our species to contribute to a plan for the course of their own development? What are the basic psychological ingredients that enable people—more so than others in the animal kingdom—to act as intentional, causal agents? This question is not only of basic scientific interest. It is also central to the design of interventions that empower people to gain control over their lives.

There are two ways of addressing the question of agentic capabilities. One is a functional analysis. Here, the task is to identify the psychological functions that humans are uniquely able to execute and that enable them to exert intentional control over their actions and development. Both psychologists and philosophers have taken up this problem, and their conclusions converge (e.g., Bandura, 1986; Harré & Secord, 1972; Kagan, 1998). People have the capability to use language; to develop a sense of self (as both a doer and an actor who is observed by others); and to self-regulate their behavior, which entails not only monitoring one's actions but also monitoring the monitoring of one's own performance. This self-

monitoring is accompanied by feelings of satisfaction and dissatisfaction with the self that contribute to self-regulatory efforts (Bandura & Cervone, 1983). The study of these self-regulatory functions is central to the contemporary field of adult development (Heckhausen & Dweck, 1998; see also Lang & Heckhausen, chapter 7, this volume) and the field of psychology at large (Baumeister & Vohs, 2004).

A psychological function of particular centrality to personal agency is that of mental "time travel" (Suddendorf & Corballis, 1997). Humans have the capacity to mentally reconstruct past events and generate detailed mental images of hypothetical events that may occur in the future. Evidence suggests that animals, in contrast, "are largely stuck in the present moment ... aware of only a permanent present" (Roberts, 2002, p. 486). People's ability to deliberate on the past and future, combined with their capacity to form a sense of self and social identity, enables them to select and shape the environments they encounter, develop skills to meet future challenges, pursue personal aims, and thereby function as causal agents.

Goals and Evaluative Standards

The second type of analysis focuses not on mental functions but on psychological structures and processes that enable persons to carry out these functions. Just as in the study of cognition one can distinguish a function that is carried out (e.g., problem solving) from the cognitive components that enable a person to carry out that function (e.g., working memory), in the study of human agency one can distinguish psychological functions (e.g., behavioral self-regulation) from the component of mental architecture that enable persons to execute those functions.

An analysis of cognitive systems that underlie self-regulation indicates that these cognitions can be understood as consisting of qualitatively distinct types; both philosophical (Searle, 1998) and psychological considerations (Cervone, 2004a) suggest a qualitative distinction among classes of thought. A brief consideration of these distinctions yields an intellectual framework within which the psychological variable of central interest to this chapter, perceived self-efficacy, can be understood.

When analyzing those cognitive capacities that underlie human agency, a fundamental distinction is one that differentiates among three classes of cognition: goals, standards, and beliefs. Some cognitions are mental representations of future states that one is committed to achieve. Such personal goals may serve to organize activities over extended periods of time and bring coherence to internal psychological life, guiding people's interpretations of their experiences and of prospective challenges (Emmons & Kaiser, 1996; Grant & Dweck, 1999). Mental representations of goals are closely linked to mental representations of strategies for goal achievement (Kruglanski et al., 2002). The ability to develop and deploy such strategies is critical to self-control, self-directed motivation, and the realization of individual potentials (Cantor, 2003; Mischel & Mendoza-Denton, 2003).

In the study of adult development, much work indicates that goal structures and processes of goal selection are an aspect of future-oriented cognition that is key to well-being throughout adult development (e.g., Heckhausen, 1999, 2002; Pulkkinen, Nurmi, & Kokko, 2002; Staudinger, Freund, Linden, & Mass, 1999). Findings indicate, for example, that people who set goals in a manner that is congruent with their perceptions of the time available to them in their life span experience social relations that are more satisfactory and less stressful (Lang & Carstensen, 2002).

A second aspect of cognition that is central to personality functioning is evaluative standards. People develop moral, ethical, and performance standards that they employ as criteria for judging the goodness or worth of prospective actions. As has been recognized in both classic and contemporary theories (e.g., Bandura, 1986; Carver & Scheier, 1998; Cervone, 2004a; Higgins, 1987; Mischel, 1973; Rotter, 1954), these standards function as a kind of internal guidance system, enabling individuals to regulate their actions in a coherent manner over significant periods of time and across changing social conditions. Evaluating actions with respect to internalized standards of performance, then, is a basic cognitive capability that contributes to personal agency. Some circumstances cause people to disengage these standards, that is, to fail to regulate their behavior according to their own typical rules of conduct (Bandura & Cervone, 1983). The disengagement of moral standards can cause people who typically conduct themselves in a steadfast manner to engage in antisocial acts (Bandura, 1999a; Bandura, Barbaranelli, Caprara, & Pastorelli, 1996).

Control Beliefs and Self-Efficacy

In addition to possessing goals for action and standards for evaluating the goodness or worth of occurrences, people develop beliefs about what the future may bring. Converging lines of research suggest that the subset of future-oriented beliefs that is most central to personality functioning across adulthood is beliefs in one's capacity to control significant life events (Skinner, 1996).

There are different types of control beliefs. For example, one set of beliefs concerns the degree to which the causes of events are, in principle, under people's control as opposed to being the result of uncontrollable external forces (Rotter, 1966). Research on adult development indicates that higher levels of fatalistic beliefs—that is, beliefs that the nature of significant life events is inevitable and thus uncontrollable (Kohn & Schooler, 1983)—predict higher levels of disability among older adults (Caplan & Schooler, 2003).

A second aspect of control beliefs involves perceptions of one's personal capacity to execute courses of action to cope with events. Confidence in one's own ability to execute actions is, as a psychological construct, distinct from beliefs in the controllability of external events; the different sets of beliefs have, for example, been shown to have distinct effects on cognitive and motor outcome variables in middle and older adulthood (Caplan & Schooler, 2003). Beliefs in one's capacity to execute courses of action have been studied extensively in the literature on perceived self-efficacy (Bandura, 1977a, 1997). We now turn to this literature and its implications for the study of adult development and learning.

PERCEIVED SELF-EFFICACY

The two quotations that opened this chapter invoke the heart of self-efficacy theory (Bandura, 1977a, 1986, 1997). Perceived self-efficacy refers to our judgments of what we think we can and can't do. More formally, self-efficacy refers to our sense of confidence and competence, qualified by specific demands and features of the situation in which self-efficacy judgments are activated. When activated and the assessment is "I can," high self-efficacy will lead to new levels of learning and accomplishment.

When the activated assessment is low—"I can't"— then self-efficacy will inhibit engagement in challenging situations, precluding skill development. The individual who has high expectations for learning and development— who sets and attempts challenging goals—will be likely to encounter both success and failure in goal acquisition, both of which shape and inform behavior. Successes provide encouragement and help reinforce facilitative, goal-directed behaviors. Failures provide information about mistaken steps toward goals and help narrow down and hone the behavioral repertoire. If opportunities for new experiences are avoided and deemed too risky, neither successes nor failures ensue, and windows to learn close.

As reviewed in more detail elsewhere (Caprara & Cervone, 2000), self-efficacy beliefs are of particular importance to intentional action for three reasons. First, self-efficacy perceptions directly contribute to decisions, actions, and experiences. People commonly reflect on their capabilities when deciding whether to undertake activities or to persist on tasks when faced with setbacks. People who judge themselves highly efficacious tend to be more willing to pursue challenges, to be more persistent on tasks, and to experience lesser performance-related anxiety (Bandura, 1997).

Second, self-efficacy perceptions may moderate the impact of other psychological mechanisms on developmental outcomes. For example, as a general rule individuals who acquire skills on a task achieve greater success; but if people still doubt their capabilities despite adequate instruction, they may fail to put their knowledge into practice.

Third, self-efficacy beliefs influence other cognitive and emotional factors that in turn contribute to performance. Of particular importance are links from self-efficacy processes to goal setting (Berry & West, 1993; Locke & Latham, 1990). People with higher efficacy beliefs tend to set more challenging goals and remain committed to their goals; these goal mechanisms, in turn, contribute to motivation and achievement (Bandura & Locke, 2003).

These links from self-efficacy beliefs to goal processes are particularly important to adult development and learning. One of the developmental tasks of adulthood is appraisal and reappraisal of life goals. Research shows that individuals who set learning or performance goals acquire higher skills and self-efficacy than those who set no goals (Bandalos, Finney, & Geske, 2003) or who are told to merely do

their best (Brown & Latham, 2002). The effects of goal setting on self-efficacy have been demonstrated both empirically and in questionnaire studies of goal setting and loss of control. Over an 8-year interval, adults aged 30–59 years old who experienced loss in important domains to self and who subsequently downgraded the importance of goal attainment in those domains experienced less loss of perceived control overall than if goals in the failing domain were maintained at initial levels (Brandtstädter & Rothermund, 1994). In other words, rescaled or down-scaled goals in domains of personal importance can buffer the sense of perceived loss of control in that domain. Prudent, careful judgment in many matters becomes more necessary in older adulthood, when choices are fewer and starting over in any number of domains (education, vocation, living arrangements) is more difficult than at younger ages. Recognition and acceptance of limits (the worldview of T. S. Eliot notwithstanding) is essential, yet remaining open to possibilities and opportunities is an equally compelling life span task. Reasoned risk taking in older adults may contribute to continued and new growth in broad domains of functioning.

CHAPTER OVERVIEW

We begin with an overview of basic self-efficacy processes. It is important to recognize that Bandura's self-efficacy theory is just one aspect of his much broader social-cognitive theory of personality (Bandura, 1986). In this overview, then, we consider the contribution of self-efficacy processes to adult development and learning within a broader perspective on social-cognitive mechanisms in personal functioning (e.g., Bandura, 1999b; Cervone, 2004a). We subsequently address the assessment of self-efficacy beliefs in a similar manner; we tackle the issue within a broader analysis of cognitive structure, process, organization, and its assessment (Cervone, 2004b; Cervone, Shadel, & Jencius, 2001). A subtext of this coverage is that the study of people's agentic capacities requires for its foundation an understanding of the functioning of the whole person—that is, a comprehensive understanding of personality systems and their development (Caprara & Cervone, 2003).

We then consider a number of domains that are critical to adult development and learning and in which self-efficacy processes contribute to success.

These include domains such as performance on intellectual and memory tasks, participation in training programs, and the solving of everyday problems that can interfere with one's pursuits. In this review, our overall purpose is to position self-efficacy at the intersection of learning and development in adulthood. We focus on the formation, calibration, and refinement of self-efficacy beliefs across the life span as related to new learning and development. In pursuing these goals, we are cognizant that there exist a number of highly related literatures that also shed light on the role of control beliefs in adult development (e.g., Heckhausen & Schulz, 1995; Little et al., 2003; Skinner, 1996).

PERCEIVED SELF-EFFICACY, SOCIAL-COGNITIVE PERSONALITY SYSTEMS, AND ADULT DEVELOPMENT

The psychological construct perceived self-efficacy often is considered in isolation. In empirical work, researchers may inquire solely into the link between a self-efficacy measure and an outcome of interest. In literature reviews, writers may analyze the causes and effects of self-efficacy processes while devoting little attention to other psychological mechanisms. Few writers have put self-efficacy into developmental contexts, although the promise of such analyses has been articulated and demonstrated previously (Berry, 1999; Berry & West, 1993; Cavanaugh, Feldman, & Hertzog, 1998; Cavanaugh & Green, 1990). A narrow approach to the review of self-efficacy theory and research fails to represent both the broader theoretical framework within which the self-efficacy construct was developed and the range of psychological dynamics that are critical to understanding the nature of self-efficacy processes.

Social-Cognitive Perspectives on Individual Development

As noted, Bandura proposed his self-efficacy theory (1977a) within a broader framework on personality development and functioning (Bandura, 1977b) that itself was grounded in the seminal social learning theory of Bandura and Walters (1963). In more recent years, this conceptual framework has been developed considerably, both through the efforts of Bandura

(1986, 1999b) and in the work of other investigators who analyze the development and functioning of social-cognitive systems (reviewed in Caprara & Cervone, 2000; Cervone & Shoda, 1999; Mischel, 2004). These combined efforts yield a family of social-cognitive theories that possess three defining features.

Interactionism

The first of these features is that individual development and functioning are analyzed in a style that is fully interactionist. Bandura (1986) expresses this interactionist perspective in his principle of reciprocal determinism, which posits that personality, environmental influences, and behavior should be analyzed as factors that mutually influence one another—that is, that interact reciprocally in the causal dynamics that underlie expressions of personality.

It is important to note that this interactionist view goes far beyond the banal assertion that "people and situations influence one another." Instead, it speaks to deeply significant questions about human nature and the best way to construe human psychological qualities in a scientific analysis. All serious psychologists realize that people and situations influence one another. Yet one can find in the contemporary field well-known theoretical positions whose basic variables—that is, whose core units of analysis—are distinctly noninteractionist. Five-factor theory (McCrae & Costa, 1996) posits that personality traits are a product of genetic endowment, with people's standing on trait dimensions being uninfluenced by environmental experience. Popular forms of evolutionary psychology (e.g., Buss, 1991) contend that the genome functions as a kind of program that primarily determines the course of individual development. In recent years, both of these theoretical positions have been weakened in two ways. Theoretical analyses have made clear that persons—even at the level of the biology of the individual—develop through environmental interactions (e.g., Gottlieb, 1998; Lickliter & Honeycutt, 2003a, 2003b). Empirical data have provided evidence of variations across the life span in personality trait scores that are unanticipated by five-factor theory (e.g., Helson, Kwan, John, & Jones, 2002; Srivastava, John, Gosling, & Potter, 2003; Twenge, 2002). Investigators have failed to replicate results that originally had provided the core support for theoretical analyses of social behavior based on evolutionary psychology (DeSteno, Bartlett, Braverman, &

Salovey, 2002; Miller, Putcha-Bhagavatula, & Pederson, 2002). Research reviews indicate a larger role for person—situation interactions in the development of the individual than was anticipated in prominent evolutionary-psychological perspectives (Bussey & Bandura, 1999; Wood & Eagly, 2002). In light of these developments, interactionist positions on development that were developed years ago (Endler & Magnusson, 1976) appear prescient.

A Systems View

A second defining feature of social-cognitive theory is that it is a systems viewpoint on human development and functioning. Social-cognitive and affective mechanisms are construed as a complex system of interacting elements (Mischel & Shoda, 1995, 1998). This systems thinking has significant implications for explaining the development of stable personality styles and individual differences (Cervone, 1997, 1999; Nowak, Vallacher, & Zochowski, 2002). The development of a dynamic system is not prefigured; instead, development occurs gradually via reciprocal interactions between the system and the environment that it encounters. The full development of personality, then, is not encoded in the genome but results from dynamic person–environment transactions. These transactions include agentic processes in which people contribute to the development of their own behavioral and affective tendencies (Caprara, Barbaranelli, Pastorelli, & Cervone, 2004; Caprara, Steca, Cervone, & Artistico, 2003).

A further implication of a systems perspective concerns the explanation of the individual's behavior. Stable patterns of action often can be well described by using trait terms found in the natural language (e.g., a person may act in a manner that can be described as conscientious or agreeable). In a systems perspective, however, one would not explain those action patterns by positing internal psychology constructs that are isomorphic to the behavior one is trying to explain (e.g., conscientious*ness*, agreeable*ness*). Instead, in a systems perspective such as social-cognitive theory, one seeks to specify systems of interacting cognitive and affective processes that jointly give rise to the observed patterns of behavior (Cervone, 2004a). A critical implication in this work is that a given individual's personality system may contribute to stable patterns of variability in social behavior (Mischel, 2004). In other words, two people

who show the same average tendency to exhibit, for example, conscientious behavior may differ in the social contexts in which they do and do not exhibit conscientiousness; the patterns of variability thus function as a "behavioral signature" of the individual's personality (Mischel & Shoda, 1995). Both the patterns of variability and the social contexts within which one observes meaningful patterns of coherence in personality functioning may vary idiosyncratically from one person to the next (Cervone, 2004a). When turned to questions of adult development, the natural implication is that any given adult may display distinctly different patterns of learning and performance in different social contexts.

Before turning to the third feature of social-cognitive approaches, we note that the combination of interactionism and systems thinking inherently has an implication that is quite significant. It shifts one's attention away from the charting of individual differences in the population and toward the careful analysis of personality structure and organization at the level of the individual (Cervone, 2005). The view that the individual is a coherent psychological system who develops in interaction with his or her environment naturally raises questions about the internal organization of psychological structures and dynamics, the nature of the person–situation interactions at the level of the individual case, and the possibility of individual idiosyncrasy in personality structure and development. These themes are not new. In the study of personality development, they have been developed with particular clarity by Magnusson and colleagues (Magnusson & Mahoney, 2003; Magnusson & Törestad, 1993). Their holistic interactionist perspective posits that development cannot be understood by reference to the action of single factors; it must be analyzed through person-centered methods that illuminate constellations of factors at the level of the coherent, unique individual (e.g., Bergman, 2002). Highly related ideas about conducting analyses at the level of the individual are found in theoretical work on intraindividual versus interindividual measurement strategies (Borsboom, Mellenberg, and van Heerden, 2003; Molenaar, Huizenga, & Nesselroade, 2002) and empirical research that uses growth curve modeling to chart developmental trajectories at the level of the individual (e.g., Young & Mroczek, 2003). The importance of a holistic perspective in which the actions of a person are explained by reference to the person as a whole, rather than to independent "parts" of the individual, is elucidated with exceptional clarity by Harré (1998, 2002) and Bennett and Hacker (2003). The fact that developmentalists increasingly have turned their attention to the psychological functioning of the potentially unique individual in the past decade (e.g., Magnusson, 1996) is an encouraging sign for the field.

This systems-level perspective highlights the limitations of considering self-efficacy processes "in isolation." In the flow of thinking, thoughts about self-efficacy inherently are associated with other classes of cognition. In explaining the actions of a person, it is best to attribute actions to the person as a whole rather than to the isolated variable "self-efficacy."

Personality Variables and the Architecture of Personality

The third defining feature of the social-cognitive approach within which self-efficacy theory is formulated involves the units of analyses through which individuals and their development are analyzed. The question here is: How can one model the psychological mechanisms that underlie the coherence of personal functioning (Cervone & Shoda, 1999)? In other words, what are the basic personality variables in social-cognitive theory? Such questions are fundamental to the study of personal development; as noted elsewhere, "one cannot advance a science of personality and its development without having a conception of what is developing" (Caprara et al., 2003, p. 945).

Before taking up this question, a point of clarification is in order. The term *personality* has taken on two distinct meanings in the scientific literature (see Cervone, 2005), and the failure to recognize this fact has bred confusion. Some investigators in the field of personality psychology are interested in summarizing major dimensions of variation in behavioral tendencies in the population at large. Five interindividual difference factors do a good job of summarizing these variations (McCrae & Costa, 2003). Other investigators address an entirely different task: modeling the within-person structure of cognitive and affective systems that contribute to individual's distinctive psychological tendencies. When Bandura embeds his self-efficacy theory (1997) in a broader social cognitive theory of personality (Bandura, 1986, 1999b), the personality theory he provides is of this latter sort. Social cognitive theory is concerned with intraindividual psychological systems that causally contribute to

people's development, not with summaries of individual differences in the population. An intraindividual focus, then, raises the question of how one can comprehensively model within-person psychological systems.

This question has been addressed in a recent theoretical model of the architecture of personality, that is, a model of the overall design and operating characteristics of those within-person psychological systems that contribute to the uniqueness and coherence of the individual (Cervone, 2004a). Briefly, this model rests on three distinctions. One differentiates feeling states (see Russell, 2003) from intentional cognitions—where that word *intentional* is used as in the philosophy of mind (Searle, 1998) to reference cognitive contents that are directed beyond themselves to the representation of objects in the world. (To illustrate, feelings of hunger do not represent—that is, symbolically "stand for"—an object or event in the world and thus do not have the quality of intentionality, whereas thoughts about a particular restaurant do.) A second distinction (already noted) is one that differentiates among those cognitive contents that we usually refer to as beliefs, evaluative standards, and goals. The third distinction was developed by Lazarus (1991) in the study of cognition and emotion: a distinction between knowledge and appraisal. This distinction is so central to the overall model that it is referred to as a knowledge-and-appraisal personality architecture (KAPA). *Knowledge* refers to enduring mental representations of a typical attribute or attributes of an entity (e.g., one self, other persons, objects in the physical or social world). Appraisals, in contrast, are dynamically shifting evaluations of the personal meaning of events, that is, "continuing evaluation[s] of the significance of what is happening for one's personal well-being" (Lazarus, 1991, p. 144). Such evaluations generally are conducted by relating features of the self to features of the world. The distinctions (a) between knowledge and appraisal, and (b) among goals, evaluative standards, and beliefs are cross-cutting, yielding a taxonomy of six classes of social-cognitive personality variables (see figure 8.1). (In the KAPA variable system, the cognitive construct "strategies" [as used, e.g., in the SOC model of P. B. Baltes & M. M. Baltes, 1990, discussed later] is viewed as a more molar psychological construct than are individual KAPA variables; strategies commonly consist of integrated systems of goals and subgoals, as well as beliefs and evaluative standards regarding alternative paths to goal achievement.)

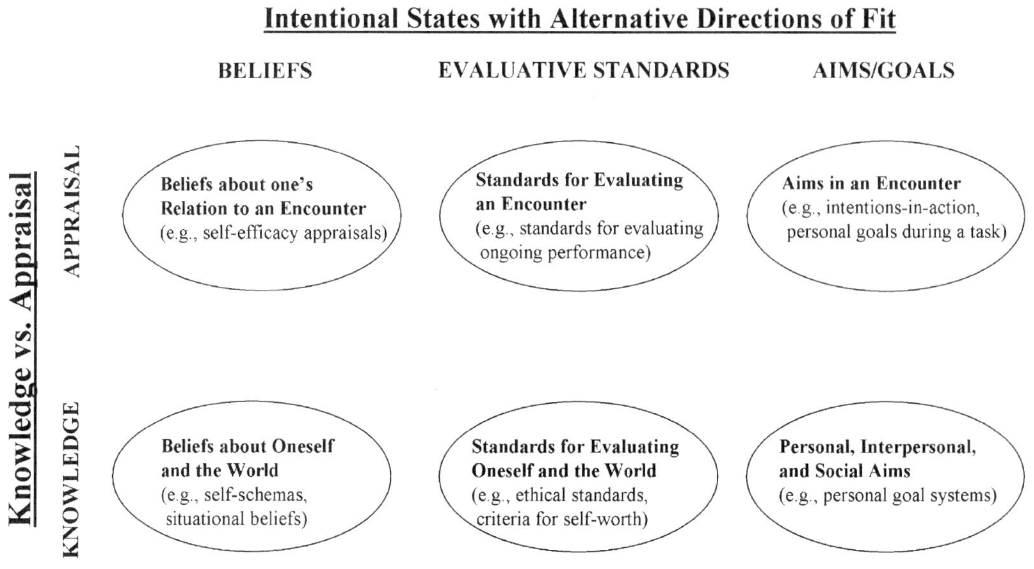

Intentional States with Alternative Directions of Fit

| | BELIEFS | EVALUATIVE STANDARDS | AIMS/GOALS |

FIGURE 8.1 The KAPA system of social-cognitive personality variables. In the variable system, the distinction among beliefs, evaluative standards, and aims holds at both the knowledge and the appraisal levels of the personality architecture, yielding six classes of social-cognitive variables.

Self-Efficacy Appraisals

Within this model of social-cognitive systems (Cervone, 2004a), the class of thinking that generally is referred to as "perceived self-efficacy" can be classified according to both dimensions of this taxonomy (figure 8.1). *Perceived self-efficacy* refers to beliefs—specifically, beliefs regarding one's own capabilities for performance. Self-efficacy perceptions also are appraisals, that is, they are evaluations of whether one can cope with ongoing or prospective encounters, where those evaluations directly bear on the meaning of the encounter for the self. Self-efficacy appraisals, then, are akin to appraisals of coping potential in Lazarus's (1991) model. The class of cognitions identified by Bandura (1977a) in his self-efficacy theory, then, are appraisals of one's capabilities to handle prospective encounters (e.g., "Can I learn the skills required to get a new job as a Web page designer?" "Can I overcome shyness and reenter the world of dating after a divorce?"), not abstract knowledge about the attributes of oneself or the social world (e.g., "Is Web page design hard?" "Am I attractive?"). Such knowledge, however, may come to mind as individuals appraise their efficacy for performance, and systematically influence those appraisals (Cervone, 1997, 2004a).

We note that some investigators use the term *self-efficacy* to reference psychological phenomena that differ from those identified by Bandura (1977a, 1997). Specifically, some investigators study "generalized self-efficacy," that is, a generalized belief regarding one's overall competence (Sherer et al., 1982). The generalized construct has been criticized on empirical grounds; it sacrifices predictive utility (Bandura, 1997; Cervone, 1997; Stajkovic & Luthans, 1998; Weitlauf, Cervone, Smith, & Wright, 2001) and correlates so highly with other constructs, such as optimism and self-esteem, that it appears to lack discriminant validity (Judge, Erez, Bono, & Thoresen, 2002). It has also been criticized on theoretical grounds (Bandura, 1997; Cervone, 1999). Of necessity, meaningful social actions occur in social contexts. The self-efficacy construct is meant to capture people's thoughts about their capabilities for executing such actions in context, not in contextual vacuums. These thoughts are inherently contextualized. When facing challenges, people rarely ask themselves, "Can I do things, in general?" They instead ask themselves whether they can cope successfully with the challenges that the world presents.

Assessing Perceived Self-Efficacy

This analysis of self-efficacy processes has natural implications for the question of self-efficacy assessment. The approach to self-efficacy assessment devised by Bandura (1977a) can be understood as part of a general social-cognitive strategy for the assessment of personality structures and processes through which people contribute to the course of their development (Cervone, 2004b; Cervone et al., 2001). We briefly review this strategy, then turn specifically to the assessment of self-efficacy beliefs.

The social-cognitive strategy of assessment can best be understood by contrast to other approaches. Much assessment involves individual differences strategies. For example, people may be described in terms of scores on a small set of universal individual difference dimensions. The scores usually represent people's overall average tendency to exhibit a given type of experience or action. In computing this average, the test scorer inherently throws away information about contextual variability in action; the test score, for example, tells one about people's overall tendency to be anxious or motivated while revealing nothing about the social contexts in which a given individual experiences greater or lesser anxiety or is more or less prone to act in a manner that we call motivated.

A social-cognitive analysis suggests two limitations to this strategy (Cervone, 2004b, 2005; Cervone et al., 2001). First, the decision to throw out information about variability in action from one context to another has enormous costs. It sacrifices critical knowledge about the individual, namely, how the individual systematically and distinctively varies his or her behavior from one life circumstance to another (Mischel, 2004). The second limitation is more subtle. It concerns the nature of psychological constructs. In individual-differences strategies (e.g., Costa & McCrae, 1992), individual persons are described according to psychological constructs that are latent variables derived from analyzing the population at large. Such population-level analyses speak forcefully to the challenge of summarizing variations in the group. But they are mute with respect to the question of within-person psychological dynamics at the level of the individual case (see Borsboom et al., 2003). Analyses of individual differences in a population yield variables that serve a descriptive taxonomic function. But to understand the dynamics of individual development, one needs more than merely taxonomic descriptions. One must identify psychological systems that are possessed by a given individual and contribute to his or her development. Social-cognitive theory is fundamentally concerned with identifying these causal dynamics (Bandura, 1999a; Cervone, 1999). It thus calls for assessment strategies that go beyond the mere description of individual differences in the population and that instead identify psychological mechanisms that causally contribute to the development of the individual (Caprara et al., 2003).

Strategies for assessing self-efficacy beliefs, then, reflect social-cognitive theory's dual concern with (a) identifying psychological systems that causally contribute to behavior and personal development while (b) remaining sensitive to the possibility that individuals' thoughts about themselves may vary markedly from one life domain to another. To assess perceived self-efficacy, investigators inquire into people's appraisals of the level or type of performance they believe they can achieve when facing designated challenges. This most commonly is accomplished via structured self-report measures (Bandura, 1977a). People indicate either the level of performance they believe they can achieve on an activity (level of self-efficacy), their confidence in attaining designated levels of achievement (strength of self-efficacy), or both.

The test items that make up such scales are tailored to tap efficacy beliefs in the particular domain of interest. In other words, self-efficacy scales are designed to tap people's confidence in their capabilities for performance in specified circumstances. To determine the content of test items, investigators commonly analyze the particular challenges that individuals face in a domain of interest (Berry, West, & Dennehey, 1989); this could be done either through a theory-based analysis of the domain or, as in research on everyday problem solving among older adults reviewed shortly (Artistico, Cervone, & Pezzuti, 2003), through diary procedures in which research participants themselves report on significant life challenges. After this task analysis, items are written to gauge people's confidence in executing specified behaviors to cope with each of a variety of challenges. In the microanalytic research strategy of self-efficacy theory (Bandura, 1977a; Cervone, 1985), self-efficacy assessments are used to gauge not only between-person differences but also within-person variations in efficacy beliefs across contexts.

Structured self-efficacy scales are not the only means of assessing self-efficacy appraisals. For example, some work employs think-aloud methods in which research participants' spontaneous self-statements regarding their efficacy for performance are analyzed (e.g., Haaga & Stewart, 1992). However, questionnaire methods have been the most common method of assessment by far.

With this background on the nature and assessment of self-efficacy beliefs, we turn to the question of the development of self-efficacy beliefs and the capacity for personal agency.

THE DEVELOPMENT OF
SELF-EFFICACY BELIEFS

Personal agency is shaped by the following developmental forces: biological, psychological, sociocultural, and life cycle (Cavanaugh & Blanchard-Fields, 2002). We propose that these developmental forces operate continuously during life to propel individuals forward through multiple domains and contexts, promoting (or preventing) growth in each. In early infancy, the human organism begins to learn cause-and-effect relationships, including the reciprocal effects of self in the world. These early experiences shape the child's general sense of personal agency and contribute to personal agency in specific behavioral developmental contexts. We identify or label such context-specific agentic beliefs as self-efficacy beliefs, and we argue that as behavioral strengths and weaknesses develop in context, so do the performance-based beliefs associated with these behaviors.

The importance of self-efficacy mechanisms to adult development becomes apparent from a review of recent theoretical and empirical work. Maurer (2001) examined factors in the workplace and organization that contributed to midlife and older workers' low sense of self-efficacy for career-relevant learning and skill development in the workplace. Maurer believes that low efficacy mediates the relationship between age of worker and participation in career development and learning opportunities (also see Maurer, Weiss, Barbeite, 2003). Sahu and Sangeeta (2004) recently examined perceptions of self-efficacy among women in the workplace and nonworking women, with results indicating positive relations between workplace experience and efficacy beliefs and between efficacy beliefs and a sense of personal well-being.

Aging brings changes to internal processes and abilities that bear on new learning and development and, in theory, on appraisal and evaluation of behavioral limitations and possibilities. Changes occur in multiple domains in adulthood, including sensory and perceptual levels (Anstey, Hofer, & Luszcz, 2003; P. B. Baltes, Lindenberger, & Staudinger, 1997), attentional capacities (McDowd & Birren, 1990; McDowd, Filion, Pohl, Richards, & Stiers, 2003), personality traits (Helson et al., 2002; Srivastava et al., 2003), memory (Park et al., 2002; Verhaegen, Marcoen, & Goossens, 1993), processing speed (Salthouse, 1991), problem solving (Allaire & Marsiske, 1999, 2002; Berg & Klaczynski, 1996), and intelligence (Schaie, 1996). Effective functioning requires adaptation to changing ability levels and shifts in resources with recognition of what is available and what is not. Several writers have emphasized the need in old age to conserve resources for use in domains of significance, importance, and relevance to effective functioning. For example, Rybash, Hoyer, and Roodin's (1986) "encapsulation model" of cognitive aging draws upon post-formal views of cognitive development (Labouvie-Vief, 1980; Sinnott, 1998) and describes the development of encapsulated modules of knowledge and expertise, which draw processing resources away from more generalized cognitive-behavioral tasks in the service of these highly schematized and complex expert modules. This model is consistent with the general pattern of intellectual change that occurs in adulthood, the so-called classic aging pattern (P. B. Baltes, 1993; Botwinick, 1987), wherein fluid abilities (mechanics) decline and crystallized abilities (pragmatics) maintain or increase into late life.

What do older adults want or need to learn? What are the learning tasks of midlife and old age? One of the tasks of adulthood is learning and accommodating the limits of energy, strength, and speed resources. New adaptations are needed for changes in cognitive abilities, personality variables, and roles such as grandparenting, retirement, and widowhood. Sociocultural changes, such as technology, urban/suburban/rural development, and medical advances may force new learning and development. Beyond adaptations and adjustment to the inevitable changes associated with aging, there are changes that are controllable and can be willfully selected and pursued.

What does lifelong learning really mean for older adults? Does new learning cease when resources become so scarce that they are used solely to preserve and maintain essential abilities and avoid further loss? Are the oldest old realistically in a position for new learning, or does their reality instead revolve around maintenance of essential behaviors and avoidance of further loss? Self-efficacy appraisals across domains of functioning will begin to fluctuate as the contingencies of behavior change with age. What was once a sufficient length of time and set of abilities to master new learning may no longer suffice when hearing and vision begin to fail and new tasks take greater time and effort. In the classic environmental press model of Lawton and Nahemow (1973), adaptive (and maladaptive) behaviors emerge as a function of the interaction between personal resources (weak–strong) and environmental press (weak–strong). If an individual's skill level surpasses the level of challenge in the environment, the person–environment fit is poor, leading to maladaptive outcomes. Likewise, poor fit and lack of adaptive behavior result when the environmental press exceeds the capabilities and resources of the individual. Ideally, the environment presents levels of challenge within and just beyond the individual's capabilities, which yields the best fit and maximizes development and sense of competence and mastery (Lawton & Nahemow, 1973).

Children, adolescents, and adults learn by example and feedback. Competencies in various domains are shaped by performance successes and failures, effort and effort attributions, persistence and choice, and self- and other-provided feedback. For example, Zimmerman (2002) argues that academic excellence is as much a function of motivational factors (e.g., self-efficacy) as it is of ability and instruction, and points to the critical role of practice among high achievers. High achievers seem to know what they have to do to learn and may be more knowledgeable of task demands and person characteristics (Jenkins, 1979) than low achievers. In research on meta-cognition in the domain of problem solving, Kruger and Dunning (1999) found that competent problem solvers appear to be high in self-awareness, as shown by their more accurate predictions of their performance outcomes compared to incompetent problem solvers, who grossly overestimated their abilities. Thus, experts in a domain appear to be expert also at knowing their abilities; although not tested directly by Kruger and Dunning, it is likely that competent problem solvers have high self-efficacy related to task monitoring, meta-cognitive, and performance variables (Schmidt

& Ford, 2003). Clearly, competency development is informed in large part by self-regulatory and self-feedback mechanisms.

The most widely studied domains of self-efficacy functioning in the elderly are health, intelligence, and memory. The losses and changes in cognitive functioning in old age force reappraisals of abilities in these domains, leading to new limits on performance. Older adults should set goals that accurately represent their competencies, being mindful to avoid injurious, demoralizing, and even dehumanizing situations. Sources of efficacy information in older adulthood include the same categories of information used by younger adults (mastery, modeling, persuasion, arousal), but the nature of self-efficacy source information probably changes with age to include greater proportions of failure experiences relative to success experiences—a proposition that is consistent with the shift in the ratio of gains to losses in P. B. Baltes's (1987) life span model of development. To the extent that peers serve as salient points of comparison, the aging individual will have more opportunities in social contexts to observe memory failures, intellectual slowing, and physical fragility and stiffness (e.g., perhaps witnessing walking with the aid of canes after a fall, painful attempts to use arthritic feet and hands, etc.). Sources of efficacy information abound—peers, family, media, stereotypes, doctors, neighbors, confidantes—and older adults might optimize their sense of well-being by attending specifically to positive, efficacy-building feedback from these environmental sources (Welch & West, 1995).

Health

Research examining health outcomes among middle-age and older adults documents the importance of family members and health care professionals to self-efficacy processes. Family factors are so important that when one is predicting psychological outcomes for a given family member, the efficacy perceptions of a different family member may be the most predictive. Rohrbauch et al. (2004) conducted a study of health management self-efficacy beliefs among cardiac patients and their spouses (i.e., where the spouse measures tapped beliefs in the patient's efficacy). Both patient and spouse efficacy perceptions predicted survival, but when one versus the other index was controlled statistically, only the spouse ratings were significant predictors. Research on cardiac rehabilitation also highlights patients' subjective beliefs in their caretakers' health provision efficacy. Patients who exhibit higher confidence in health care professionals' capabilities have been found subsequently to have higher beliefs in their personal efficacy for physical performance and stronger exercise intentions (Bray & Cowan, 2004).

Research on exercise, physical fitness, and disability self-efficacy is burgeoning in the aging literature. Studies show that self-efficacy is inversely related to pain perception (Clark & Nothwehr, 1999; Leveille, Cohen-Mansfield, & Guralnik, 2003; Reid, Williams, & Gill, 2003). Moreover, self-efficacy and knee pain taken together mediate the effects of membership in an exercise group on time to climb stairs as an outcome measure following treatment (Rejeski, Ettinger, Martin, & Morgan, 1998). Empirical tests of predictions derived directly from self-efficacy theory show that verbal persuasion sources of efficacy information influence exercise outcome efficacy ratings among older adults through doctors, family, and friends (Clark & Nothwehr, 1999). Other research on exercise self-efficacy among elderly adults demonstrates or suggests the importance of self-efficacy expectations on commencement, adherence, and maintenance of exercise regimens (Lachman et al., 1997; Li, McAuley, Harmer, Duncan, & Chaumeton, 2001; Litt, Kleppinger, & Judge, 2002; Seeman, Unger, McAvay, & Mendes de Leon, 1999). Together, these studies provide support for the guiding principle that self-efficacy acts as a change mechanism in various physical and health behavioral domains. Older adults who are highly efficacious appear to exert the necessary effort required for maintenance and adherence, with important positive health outcomes.

Intelligence

Lachman was among the first to demonstrate the relationship of control perceptions, including intellectual efficacy beliefs, to intellectual functioning in adults (Lachman, 1983). Her longitudinal studies showed that intellectual efficacy is both an antecedent as well as an outcome of intellectual change across short longitudinal waves. Lachman found that changes in fluid intelligence and internal locus of control predicted changes in intellectual self-efficacy over a 2-year period in older adults. In related research, Cornelius and Caspi (1986) found that intellectual self-efficacy declined cross-sectionally from midlife to old age in a

sample of adults aged 35–79 years old, a finding replicated by Lachman and Leff (1989) in a 5-year longitudinal study of elderly adults.

Because older adults' intellectual abilities in the basic mechanics of intelligence change more than their abilities in pragmatic, crystallized domains (P. B. Baltes, 1993; Botwinick, 1987; Cornelius & Caspi, 1986;), it might be expected that self-efficacy in these domains would vary accordingly. This developmental change has important implications for learning in adulthood: If the intellectual skills that are used to learn and manipulate novel information (the mechanics) are not as sharp in the later years as they were in youth, older adults may need to alter their learning goals and styles to optimize their learning. For example, detection of abstract relationships among component parts requires fluid intelligence, which occurs less quickly among older learners than younger learners. Different pedagogical tools and novel approaches to learning thus may be required when older adults encounter new learning experiences of this sort.

The acquisition of computer skills represents a domain of learning that is particularly challenging for current cohorts of older adults because they were not immersed in the information age to the same extent as cohorts of younger adults. Learning to use computer technology is increasingly necessary for successful navigation through the business, financial, health, education, and leisure markets of the twenty-first century. Self-efficacy beliefs may be important in this domain; people lacking in computer use efficacy may fail to persist in learning experiences and thus may acquire only limited knowledge and skills. Studies show that older adults possess lower self-efficacy for computer learning than do younger adults (Laguna & Babcock, 2000). Laguna and Babcock found that computer experience, computer-self-efficacy, and anxiety about computer use mediated the relationship between age and working memory.

Memory

Cavanaugh et al. (1998) have argued eloquently for the self as memory schematic and have outlined a social cognitive research agenda for studying memory beliefs and behavior across the life span. This model is quite consistent with self-efficacy approaches to studying memory and aging, especially in its emphasis on the dynamic nature of memory processing by a "self in context." Their theory proposes that when individuals confront memory tasks, they analyze features of the task and environment concurrently with retrieved and known information about self-as-memorizer. Memory processing as such is an online, constructive process, and just as self-efficacy theory dictates, past and current memory experiences and outcomes shape efficacy and performance in context

Berry (1999) expanded on the Cavanaugh et al. framework, placing greater emphasis on personality variables, including a personological—whole person—approach to memory self-efficacy. Berry also argued that memory self-efficacy is probably a significant and meaningful concept for most older adults, fueled by declining memory abilities and prevalent societal stereotypes of negative memory aging.

Empirical work by Lineweaver and Hertzog (1998) focused on memory self-efficacy measurement issues, echoing and refining earlier distinctions by West and Berry (1994) on the domain specificity of self-efficacy. Lineweaver and Hertzog differentiated personal from general memory self-efficacy beliefs using an innovative graphing technique in a sample of adults ranging in age from 18 to 93 years. Their data showed that negative beliefs about memory aging begin to accelerate in midlife and that older adults have significantly poorer memory self-efficacy beliefs than younger and middle-aged adults.

West and colleagues have conducted a series of memory self-efficacy studies that demonstrate the interdependent relationship of goals and self-efficacy (West, Thorn, & Bagwell, 2003; West, Welch, & Knabb, 2002; West, Welch, & Thorn, 2001). Collectively, this line of work has shown that older adults have poorer memory self-efficacy than younger adults. Moreover, experimentally induced goal setting led to increases in self-efficacy and performance in both younger and older adults, and across multiple memory trials, initial memory baseline scores and memory self-efficacy predicted higher self-set goals. West and colleagues have also obtained sex differences on measures of object location memory self-efficacy. Although women had higher performance scores than men overall, they had lower memory self-efficacy scores on these performance tests. Older adults and men overestimated their location recall abilities. In other research, self-efficacy is related to performance outcomes for men but not women. In the MacArthur studies of successful aging among men and women aged 70–79 years, efficacy beliefs predicted better performance on verbal memory and abstract reasoning tests for men but not for women (Seeman, McAvay, Merrill, & Albert, 1996; Seeman, Rodin, & Albert, 1993). Although aging is not the gloomy picture it was once made out to be (Hall, 1922; Rowe & Kahn, 1987), characterized primarily by multiple losses in most domains of functioning (Botwinick, 1973; Busse, 1969), the ratio of losses to gains does indeed increase across the life span (P. B. Baltes, 1987). How do individuals cope with this shifting balance? How are losses minimized or at least managed and gains optimized and even exploited? One explanation is offered in the compelling theory of selective optimization with compensation (SOC; P. B. Baltes & M. M. Baltes, 1990), which we review in a later section. Considered in tandem with Bandura's now classic theory of personal agency captured by its central construct—self-efficacy—a powerful model for understanding development and learning in adulthood and old age may be forged.

SELF-EFFICACY AND SKILL ACQUISITION IN ADULTHOOD

In this section, we explore closely the role of perceived self-efficacy in activities that require sustained effort over prolonged periods. Circumstances in which the adult wishes to learn new skills are the prototypical case.

The adult who wishes to develop new capabilities through new learning experiences faces challenges that can be understood as consisting of distinct components. These include becoming aware of social resources (educational programs, social services) that are available to promote skill development; devising personal plans for taking advantage of these resources; and removing psychological or social barriers (e.g., shyness, daily life routines that may interfere) to partaking in educational opportunities. Consider, for example, those who want to enhance their physical well-being through participation in an exercise program. Systematic research indicates that older adults who wish to participate commonly confront psychological challenges, such as a lack of motivation, to attend exercise sessions on a regular basis as well as pragmatic barriers, such as a lack of transportation to centers that conduct exercise programs (Prohaska,

Peters, & Warren, 2000). A self-efficacy analysis highlights the fact that the older adult may reflect on his or her capabilities to cope with each of these distinct challenges. As a result, if one wants to assess control beliefs in a manner that captures the psychological life of the individual, it may be necessary to attend closely to issues of social context. Any given person may have a high sense of efficacy for meeting some challenges that arise in some contexts (e.g., doing the exercises) and a low sense of self-efficacy in others (e.g., getting to the exercise center).

Across the life span, learning might occur in two or more distinct periods of one's lifetime. People learn not only while in school but also later in life in the workplace. Retirement may provide time and opportunities for learning new activities that were not available in previous phases of life. Concordantly, for any given learning task, there might be differences in the sense of commitment and perceived challenge among individuals of different age cohorts. Even subtle variations in the perceived relevance of a task to one's age group can influence younger and older adults' perceived abilities to solve the task and their actual task performance (Cervone, Artistico, & Orom, 2005).

As an illustration of how variations in one's approach to cognitive tasks can influence courses of action that require sustained effort, we consider research on expertise. An interesting feature of expertise gained through first-hand mastery in a given context is that expertise confers different types of benefits. On the one hand, of course, people become better able to execute well-practiced routines. Yet experts also differ in their approach to tasks, specifically in that they are more able to generate novel strategies when well-practiced routines no longer work or can no longer be executed, perhaps because of age-related declines. Research by Salthouse (1984) provides a clear example. This work compared the performance of younger and older typists. Older typists (experts), although their typing speed had declined, were found to be more likely than younger typists to implement task strategies that enabled their overall productivity to remain unaltered. These strategies consisted of looking ahead in the text one or two lines and memorizing the upcoming text. As a result of this strategy implementation, their overall performance did not differ from that of younger typists. The behavior of expert older typists is well described by the model of SOC processes that has been proposed by P. B. Baltes and M. M. Baltes (1990), discussed in greater detail later.

Skill Development Through Training Programs

The contemporary industrialized world puts a premium on learning. New technologies infiltrate professions, forcing people at midcareer to acquire new skills. Many people retire from their primary profession 15–20 years before the expected end of their life span and have the opportunity to partake in learning programs of value to their personal development. Learning new skills may become far more important than in the past. Questions about the design of training programs to confer new skills and the role of self-referent beliefs in the skill acquisition process are thus important both to society's demands and to the needs of the individual. Psychological science has the capacity to illuminate psychological factors that contribute to success in training programs aimed in a vast array of cognitive domains (Maurer et al., 2003) over the life span (Poon, Rubin, & Wilson, 1989).

Training programs aimed at improving knowledge are precisely the sort of settings in which questions of personal efficacy arise (Bandura, 1997). Learning is associated with a sense of perceived challenge. There is much uncertainty at the beginning of new learning, which reflects the degree to which skills are lacking in initial phases. Moreover, it is sometimes difficult to gauge how quickly one is acquiring a new skill or the skill level that one will ultimately reach. In such settings, people naturally ask themselves questions about their performance efficacy (i.e., Am I capable of doing this?). Subjective beliefs about one's capacity to engage and sustain engagement in learning programs thus contribute directly to the learning process (Bandura & Schunk, 1981; Schunk & Gunn, 1986).

One means through which self-efficacy processes influence learning involves the initial decision to enroll in a training program. Adult education commonly is a proactive choice. People with a strong sense of self-efficacy for learning are more likely to make the positive choice to engage the challenge of a training program, as suggested by much research documenting the impact of perceived self-efficacy on academic motivation (Schunk & Pajares, 2002). This effect of self-efficacy on choice processes has been analyzed in detail by Lent, Brown, and Hackett (1994) in their social cognitive theory of career choice. In this model, self-efficacy is viewed as having both direct and indirect effects on career choices. In a direct path, people with high efficacy perceptions are more likely to take up challenging careers of interest to them. In an indirect path, self-efficacy beliefs influence the interests themselves; in other words, feelings of efficacy spur feelings of interest in an activity (see Bandura & Schunk, 1981). A recent meta-analysis of self-efficacy and interests supports this idea (Rottinghaus, Larson, & Borgen, 2003). Rottinghaus et al. found that perceived self-efficacy predicts a substantial portion of the variance in career interests. An interesting possibility in this area is that the relation between self-efficacy and interest in an activity may be nonlinear; empirical results suggest that activities are relatively uninteresting when self-efficacy for performance is either extremely high or extremely low (Silvia, 2003).

Once in a training program, a strong sense of self-efficacy for performance in the given context enhances achievement (Bandura, 1997). For example, in studies of adults in workplace literacy programs (Mikulecky, Lloyd, Siemental, & Masker, 1998), learners who were confident in their writing and reading abilities (literacy self-efficacy) had higher text comprehension outcomes than those who did not have high levels of literacy self-efficacy. Research by Vinokur, van Ryn, Gramlich, and Price, R. H. (1991) provides another illustration. Large numbers of unemployed American adults took part in a brief (eight-session) training program that conveyed skills for identifying and pursuing new employment. Compared to a control condition, this training program fostered higher levels of employment and higher earnings at a follow-up assessment 2.5 years later (Vinokur et al., 1991). Mediational analyses indicated that training had its effects largely through its influence on perceived self-efficacy (van Ryn & Vinokur, 1992), which had both a direct and an indirect (though job-search attitudes) influence on the behaviors involved in seeking reemployment. This work demonstrates how a relatively brief intervention can enhance learning and developmental outcomes through the mediating mechanism of perceived self-efficacy.

Similar training procedures to those targeted to younger adults, enhanced performance among older adults as well. Older people trained at evaluating improvement from their self-paced performance were more likely to succeed on intellectual tasks (Dittman-Kohli, Lachman, Kiegel, Baltes, 1991), and on memory tasks even when their work was to go through a plan of several intervention sections (McDougall, 1998). A recent study from our lab addressed learning experiences in everyday problem solving associated with self-efficacy perceptions among older adults (Artistico & Pezzuti, 2003). Subjects trained in solving everyday problems performed better on a second problem-solving task compared to subjects in the control group. Importantly, however, variations in performance were paralleled by variations in perceived self-efficacy; these variations partially mediated the relationship between training and performance on everyday problem-solving tasks.

One normally associates the idea of training with the acquisition of professional skills. However, adults also face interpersonal and family systems challenges for which they may feel inefficacious and may benefit from systematic training experiences in these areas. One example of this is parenting. Research suggests that there are reciprocal influences between adults' sense of self-efficacy for parenting and the well-being of family members in their care. On one hand, child characteristics influence parental self-referent beliefs; mothers who lack social support and have temperamentally difficult children have lower perceptions of their efficacy for parenting and, in turn, more postpartum depression (Cutrona & Troutman, 1986). Conversely, enhanced parental efficacy beliefs can improve family welfare, and training programs can beneficially bolster these efficacy beliefs. A training program for parents of young children that involved the mastery modeling of parenting skills has been shown to build parental self-efficacy and reduce family stress (Gross, Fogg, & Tucker, 1995). Higher levels of parental self-efficacy have been shown to be important not only to children but also to the mental health of parents (Kwok & Wong, 2000). Parenting is not the only family role in which efficacy beliefs are important. King and Elder (1998) found that grandparents' appraisals of self-efficacy for contributing positively to their grandchildren's lives predicted levels of involvement with the grandchildren's daily activities. The role of parenting self-efficacy in family life and prospects for building these efficacy beliefs through interventions are reviewed by Coleman and Karraker (1997).

Extant research on training programs, self-efficacy beliefs, and their effects suggests a clear message: Training programs should include information about not only the skill acquisition task but also interventions designed to boost participants' perceptions of their capabilities to handle challenges, because these self-efficacy perceptions have a significant effect on interests, choices, and motivation. Much work in social cognitive theory indicates how this can be done

(Bandura, 1986, 1997). Self-efficacy beliefs are best enhanced by firsthand experiences of personal mastery. Training programs should be structured such that they contain proximal performance goals that participants can reach and clear feedback to participants when they reach them.

COGNITIVE SKILLS IN LEARNING

In many areas of everyday life, people can base their judgments of personal efficacy on past personal experience. Past successes and failures form a basis for appraising one's capabilities for future action. However, past experiences are sometimes lacking. Circumstances may contain features that are so novel that the individual faces the challenge of judging personal efficacy under conditions of substantial uncertainty (Cervone & Peake, 1986).

When perceived self-efficacy cannot be solely based on previous experience, one possibility is to base self-efficacy appraisals on past experiences that seem similar to the new challenge one is facing. Determining what past situations are relevant and how relevant they are involves judgmental processes that are fraught with subjectivity. When older adults face challenges for which they have no direct prior experience—for example, adjusting to retirement, becoming a grandparent, adopting a new medical or exercise regimen to cope with a medical problem—they must appraise their efficacy for performance and formulate goals under conditions of high uncertainty. In such circumstances, stereotypes or other judgmental influences may systematically distort these self-appraisals, in some instances causing individuals to underestimate their capacities for performance. In the language of the KAPA model noted earlier (Cervone, 2004a), the stereotypes would function as enduring knowledge that biases efficacy appraisals.

In addition to assessing past experiences, another cognitive activity that is central to self-efficacy judgment under uncertainty involves future-oriented cognition. People may mentally simulate pathways to goal achievement, and the ease with which they can envision reaching their goals may influence self-efficacy appraisals. Research with older adults indeed indicates that peoples' cognitive capacity to generate strategies for overcoming barriers to participation in programs is important to the learning process (Prohaska et al., 2000). People with adequate skills may

fail to participate because they dwell on potential obstacles to participation; qualitative research has indicated that for older people, to start and then maintain a learning program often means more than having the required skills and knowledge to do it, because the real challenge is to begin putting one's knowledge and skills into action (Williamson, 2000).

Moreover, when people are committed to a valued course of action that they believe they can achieve, they may fail to act on their intentions because of situational factors that distract them from intended pursuits. Helping individuals generate strategies for solving daily social, interpersonal, or intrapersonal problems that interfere with planned activities might, then, facilitate daily adherence among older adults and reduce attrition from these programs.

Older adults' participation in learning programs thus may hinge on their ability to solve everyday problems that can interfere with their taking part in valuable learning activities. This raises the challenge of understanding factors that may influence older adults' problem solving abilities—a challenge that has been met by research on everyday problem solving.

Everyday Problem Solving

Historically, in cognitive psychology, the term *problem solving* typically has been applied to the solution of abstract analytical tasks; a problem such as the Tower of Hanoi puzzle (in which the research participant moves geometric shapes of different sizes in accordance with logical constraints on their movement) is an example (Anzai & Simon, 1979). On such tasks, people are confronted with a well-defined problem, and reasoning may lead the individual through a fixed problem space in which there is one well-defined solution (Reitmann, 1964; Simon, 1973). Although the study of such tasks may provide meaningful insight into human cognition, these problem-solving paradigms capture only a limited subset of the cognitive challenges faced by adults, particularly in the later years of life. To illustrate the point, consider a typical everyday problem. Suppose an older adult living in a condominium complex finds that meetings of the local condo association frequently are disrupted by disagreements and arguing among the association members (example derived from Artistico et al., 2003), and the individual wants to improve the tone of the meetings. Here the problem is not defined as sharply as a typical laboratory task; it is hard to know what options are available to solve the problem or how much improvement in the problem is even possible. In this problem of daily life, there also is no single solution, as there is on a laboratory task. Any given solution may fail or work only temporarily. Many distinct strategies and forms of solution thus may have to be devised to make progress on the problem.

These considerations have given rise to a scientific literature on everyday problem solving or being able to successfully cope with everyday challenges (Denney & Palmer, 1981) that turned out to be of particular relevance to the study of cognitive aging. Especially when cognitive decline becomes substantial (Salthouse, 1991; Salthouse, Berish, & Miles, 2002), skilled use of everyday problem-solving functioning and competence becomes crucial for maintaining an unaltered sense of well-being among older individuals (M. M. Baltes & Lang, 1997; M. M. Baltes, Maas, Wilms, Borchelt, & Little, 1999). Findings reveal that when compared to the declines that are evident on tests of fluid intelligence or abstract reasoning, declines in performance on everyday problem-solving tasks are small, moderate, or nonexistent. This conclusion holds with respect to studies examining problem-solving fluency or the number of safe and effective solutions generated (Denney & Palmer, 1981; Denney & Pearce, 1989; Denney, Pearce, & Palmer, 1982), or with respect to studies examining quality of everyday problem-solving reasoning (Allaire & Marsiske, 1999, 2002; Berg, Meegan, & Klaczynski, 1999; Cornelius & Caspi, 1987).

Everyday Problem Solving Across the Life Span

Denney and her associates studied problem solving trajectories over the life span (Denney & Palmer, 1981; Denney & Pearce, 1989; Denney et al.,1982). They indicated that although performance on traditional laboratory tasks tends to decrease linearly after early adulthood, a different pattern is found on everyday problems. Performance on everyday problem-solving items increases from young adulthood to middle age, but then decreases in the elderly. Older participants were found to perform less well than middle-age persons even when working on items that were nominated by a sample of older persons as being particularly relevant to their age group (Denney & Pearce, 1989). Although exceptions are occasionally found in which older adults outperform younger adults on everyday problems (Cornelius, 1984; Cornelius & Caspi, 1987) or in which some forms of everyday cognition are highly correlated with traditional measures of basic cognitive abilities (Allaire & Marsiske, 1999), many research findings suggest that everyday problem solving is a distinct cognitive domain in which experience-based knowledge that is gained across adulthood may facilitate performance; yet "experience cannot completely nullify the effects of aging" (Denney, 1990, p. 340).

Everyday Problem Solving and Perceived Self-Efficacy

Several factors contribute to everyday problem-solving ability. It has been increasingly reported that in addition to bringing knowledge to bear on tasks, older adults may enhance everyday problem solving performance by engaging effective use of self-regulatory strategies (Sinnott, 1989). Studying regulatory processes in later adulthood is a key factor for understanding how older adults are able to compensate for declines in virtually any cognitive ability (Artistico & Lang, 2002). A key question, therefore, is to understand how older people exert the goal-directed effort required to attain knowledge and develop task strategies about everyday problem solving (Berg & Klaczynski, 1996; Blanchard-Fields, Chen, & Norris, 1997; Hess & Blanchard-Fields, 1999).

Older adults do not always perform optimally on everyday problem solving tasks, but if they do so, it is generally because they have high confidence in their ability to solve everyday problems or perceived self-efficacy (Artistico et al., 2003). Generating solutions requires sustained cognitive effort, and people who possess robust efficacy beliefs are more likely to exert that effort, rather than abandon attempts at problem solving (Bandura, 1989). Variations in perceived self-efficacy predict problem-solving ability, specifically, viable solutions that individuals are able to generate for everyday problems (Artistico et al., 2003). Importantly, it is not merely the case that some people are generally good and others generally poor problem solvers. Instead, we found significant within-person variability in self-efficacy beliefs and problem-solving abilities across contexts. When problems were typical of older persons' daily experiences (e.g., dealing with incompetent medical personnel), they judged themselves as relatively capable of solving the problems and exhibited superior levels of cognitive performance.

In contrast, in domains that were less familiar to them, older adults had lower efficacy beliefs and performance than did younger adults. Moreover, the results from this study suggest that perceived self-efficacy operates as a cognitive mediator of age-related performance differences on problem-solving tasks among young and older adults (Artistico et al., 2003).

Crystallized and Fluid Intelligence

An early and persistent question in the field of psychological aging was to understand what types of intellectual abilities older people use to achieve high levels of performance on cognitive tasks. One answer was found in the distinction made between two orthogonal types of general intellective ability, namely, crystallized and fluid intelligence (Cattell, 1971). Crystallized intelligence normally underlies tasks that test knowledge that is accumulated through experience and years of education (P. B. Baltes, 1997). On the other hand, fluid intelligence is an ability used for spatial and abstract reasoning tasks, such as solving numerical or spatial puzzles. The distinction between crystallized and fluid intelligence is somewhat analogous to the distinction between everyday problem solving and laboratory problem solving. Crystallized intelligence might be conceptually relevant to solving everyday problems, whereas fluid intelligence could be instrumental in solving abstract reasoning tasks.

In research on intellectual aging and the crystallized/fluid distinction, older people scored significantly higher and perceived themselves as more efficacious to perform on a crystallized intelligence test than did younger people (Lachman & Jelalian, 1984). In contrast, younger people scored higher and perceived themselves as more efficacious to perform on a fluid intelligence test than did older people (Lachman & Jelalian, 1984). Similar results were found in a study in which fluid intelligence was measured with a working memory task, and crystallized intelligence was measured by asking people to offer wisdom with respect to critical interpersonal dilemmas. Older adults were as capable as young adults of generating solutions for critical interpersonal situations and making life decisions and were as fast as younger people. Younger adults were more proficient than older adults on working memory tasks (for an overview of these results, see P. B. Baltes & Staudinger, 2000).

Taken as a whole, research on everyday problem solving and research directed by the distinction between crystallized and fluid intelligence indicate that personal experiences associated with assessment of an individual's perceived efficacy might better explain cognitive performance in later age. Next we turn our attention to a family of factors that might enhance our understanding of people's ability to engage in complex behavior, such as learning. These factors include strategies that are particularly relevant to older adults' everyday functioning and performance and were briefly introduced earlier under the guise of the SOC model.

SOC MODEL AND PERCEIVED SELF-EFFICACY

The ability to maximize one's potentials across the life span rests on two key factors: being able to generate viable solutions to problems of life and having a strong enough sense of efficacy to put these solutions into practice. This combination of factors can help buffer individuals against cognitive declines that occur with age. Converging evidence indicates that age deficits in prefrontal cortical activity in working memory are disruptive to higher order functioning in older adults (e.g., Raz, 2000; Rypma, Prabhakaran, Desmond, & Gabrieli, 2001; Salthouse, 1991). As we saw, solving tasks that are ecologically relevant to older adults and that foster use of crystallized intelligence may prompt better performance and higher self-efficacy perceptions among older people. Studying regulatory processes in older adults could be key for understanding how elderly people are able to compensate for cognitive declines. To illustrate this point, consider once again the example of older typists (Salthouse, 1984) introduced earlier in the chapter. Older typists, regardless of their cognitive decline, were as fast as younger typists in typing a lengthy work assignment. This conclusion held because, as Salthouse (1984) and others noted as well (P. B. Baltes, 1987; P. B. Baltes & M. M. Baltes, 1990), experts in general are able to compensate with their skilled use of strategies for the impact of cognitive declines on performance. We will discuss compensatory strategies to buffer against cognitive declines within a model that is central to discourse in the contemporary field of psychology and aging, the SOC model.

SOC Model

P. B. Baltes and M. M. Baltes (1990) identified "a prototypical strategy of successful aging" (p. 21) that involves managing cognitive declines by focusing on actions through which these can be overcome. Their model identifies patterns of selection, optimization, and compensation that promote successful development. Successful adult development can be achieved by selecting life goals that are manageable within the constraints of biology and sociocultural opportunities; optimizing the use of personal and social resources in the pursuit of one's aims; and by developing strategies to compensate for declines that inevitably arise across the life course. In the domain of learning, the SOC model implies that disengagement is not a necessary result of age-related declines in capabilities. Instead, by focusing (i.e., selection), practicing (i.e., optimization), and invoking the role of experience (i.e., compensation), adults can continue to acquire valuable new experiences across the life course.

Reports of strategy use for managing specific problems ought to refer to everyday problems that are representative of those that are actually encountered by individuals. Consider a well-known example of resilient performance provided by P. B. Baltes and M. M. Baltes (1990). Pianist Arthur Rubinstein maintained extraordinarily high levels of artistic performance in older adulthood through strategies that compensated for age-related losses of motor speed and flexibility. In a television interview he "told that he reduces his repertoire and plays a smaller number of pieces (selection); second, he practices these more often (optimization); and third, he slows down his speed of playing prior to fast movements, thereby producing a contrast that gives the impression of speed in the fast movements (compensation)" (example reported in P. B. Baltes & M. M. Baltes, 1990, p. 26).

Level and Strength of Self-Efficacy and SOC

On logical grounds, it has been theorized that development in later years involves streamlining one's efforts: increasing effort in valued and important domains for which performance can realistically be maintained, while decreasing effort and investment in others (P. B. Baltes, 1987). People who can rely on great levels of perceived self-efficacy to perform optimally in a vast array of domains are more able to persist on challenging tasks compared to those people who perceive of themselves as less efficacious (Bandura, 1997). There are two ways that different aspects of perceived self-efficacy are generally assessed (see Bandura, 1977a; Cervone & Scott, 1995): (1) the absolute type of performance that one is envisioning to achieve (levels of self-efficacy), and (2) personal confidence in being able to attain designed levels of performance (strength of self-efficacy).

Analysis of these two dimensions of self-efficacy would provide several options for identifying the empirical joint between perceived self-efficacy and specific task strategies, such as those in the SOC model. Imagine asking Rubinstein before a piano concert to indicate his level of self-efficacy for his confidence to perform optimally (even pieces that would require fast movements). Presumably, the reply would fall in the upper range of a self-efficacy scale—a number that would express the artist's great confidence in his piano-playing performance ability. Imagine also repeating this assessment many times over several concerts played over several nights. Such an approach would yield measures of self-efficacy level, strength, and generalizability (Bandura, 1977a), which could in turn be combined with the various compensatory, selection, and optimization strategies employed by the artist over the successive nights. These measurements would no doubt yield fluctuations in Rubinstein's own self-efficacy judgments that would covary systematically with the various possible performance outcomes (e.g., length of applause, requests for encores, perceptions of the orchestra, critics' reviews, and so forth). This whimsical scenario illustrates the type of investigation that could be conducted in more realistic musical venues (e.g., music conservatories, choral societies, orchestras) to test hypotheses derived conjointly from self-efficacy theory and the SOC model. In fact, research on music self-efficacy has found that greater confidence in playing piano is related to assessors' evaluations of the quality of students' musical performance during examinations (McCormick & McPherson, 2003).

Rubinstein's piano performance style in later life is an exceptional illustration of selective optimization with compensation and the judicious, effective application of compensatory strategies. Many older adults face accommodative difficulties in far more mundane yet equally salient and personally important domains (e.g., everyday routines). Choices between tasks are made on a daily basis and at short-term and long-term levels. As at any age, older adults are confronted with the ordinary time management tasks and "to-do" lists of a given day. He or she might select between grocery shopping today, returning library books tomorrow, and doing laundry on Sunday, whereas longer-term tasks such as entering a fitness or community volunteer program are deferred until physical, mental, and even economic resources allow such choice and selectivity. Research paradigms developed in everyday learning contexts could assess how older adults learn to manage trade-offs between physical and cognitive limitations with selections of optimal functioning in their most desired domains.

Research across different adulthood learning domains that integrates personality in context, the self-regulatory components of self-efficacy theory, and the behavioral choices and balance implied by the SOC model would provide a comprehensive understanding of how older adults manage the myriad challenges and opportunities of life. Basic research should aim to explicate both developmental differences at the group level as well as the substantial within-person variability in self-efficacy and learning processes across the life span. When basic research findings translate into beneficial applications, one of the core missions of the field of psychological science is fulfilled.

CONCLUSIONS

This chapter has reviewed diverse programs of theory and research. Yet its primary ideas can be well summarized by two simple themes. The first concerns the nature of human development, and the second concerns the nature of the psychological construct on which we have focused, perceived self-efficacy.

In our contemporary world, in which many citizens experience long life spans and enhanced freedom of choice, the twists and turns of psychological development increasingly are determined by personal decision making. Especially within Western individualistic cultures, the major roles and contexts of one's life—involving profession, family, location of residence, and so on—are not conceived as fixed or inevitable. Instead, people recognize that they can choose among life paths. This increases not only opportunity but uncertainty. Ages ago, individuals may have been rela-

tively secure in the knowledge that they could adopt a lifestyle in which their ancestors had lived successfully for generations. In contrast, rapid changes in social and family life reduce personal feelings of certainty about one's life course; for example, although college-aged Americans today have an abundance of opportunities, they also are more likely to believe that the outcome of important life events may be beyond their personal control, as compared to the beliefs expressed by their cohorts only a few decades earlier (Twenge, Zhang, & Im, 2004). When faced with choice and uncertainty, people naturally reflect on themselves and their capacities to handle the challenges ahead. Thus we live today in a world where reflections on self-efficacy are key to personal development. As we have seen in the research reviewed herein, people with stronger beliefs in their efficacy for performance are more likely to develop the skills and exert the self-control and persistent effort that are required to tackle the challenges that world presents.

Regarding the self-efficacy construct, we have promoted a perspective that is integrative rather than isolationist. In the early days of self-efficacy theory (Bandura, 1977a), it was important to document that self-efficacy was a unique construct, that is, one that captured distinctive aspects of mental life that uniquely contribute to human achievement and well-being. These efforts can be declared a success (see Bandura, 1997). Now, after more than a quarter century of research effort, it is equally important to recognize that self-efficacy beliefs are just one aspect of the overall architecture of human mental systems (Cervone, 2004a). The advantages of this latter perspective are dual. First, as noted herein, it can yield an integrative view of human development in which the insights of different theoretical traditions (e.g., P. B. Baltes, 1987; Bandura, 1986) are seen to be complementary and to yield an overall portrait of development that has much power and scope. Second, it shifts one's attention from a particular variable—self-efficacy—to a target of investigation of greater interest: the whole, coherent, multifaceted individual and his or her development across the course of life.

ACKNOWLEDGMENTS   During the preparation of this chapter, Daniel Cervone was supported by National Institute on Drug Abuse grant DA14136, Daniele Artistico was supported by Grant 1 RO3 AgG23271-01 from the National Institute on Aging, and these authors also received support from the Midwest Roybal Center for Health Maintenance.

References

Allaire, J. C., & Marsiske, M. (1999). Everyday cognition: Age and intellectual ability correlates. *Psychology and Aging, 14,* 627–644.

Allaire, J. C., & Marsiske, M. (2002). Well- and ill- defined measures of everyday cognition: Relationship to older adults' intellectual ability and functional status. *Psychology and Aging, 17,* 101–115.

Anstey, K. J., Hofer, S. M., & Luszcz, M. A. (2003). A latent growth curve analysis of late-life sensory and cognitive function over 8 years: Evidence for specific and common factors underlying change. *Psychology and Aging, 18,* 714–726.

Anzai, Y., & Simon, H. A. (1979). The theory of learning by doing. *Psychological Review, 86,* 124–140.

Artistico, D., Cervone, D., & Pezzuti, L. (2003). Perceived self-efficacy and everyday problem solving among young and older adults. *Psychology and Aging, 18,* 68–79.

Artistico, D., & Lang, F. (2002). *The regulation of the self across adulthood: Personality processes in context.* Symposium at the 11th European Conference of Personality, Univerisity of Jena, Germany.

Artistico, D., & Pezzuti, L. (2003). *Training in everyday problem solving increases self-efficacy and everyday problem solving performance among older adults.* Poster session presented at GSA's 56th Annual Meeting, November 21–25, 2003, San Diego, CA.

Baltes, M. M., & Lang, F. (1997). Everyday functioning and successful aging: The impact of resources. *Psychology and Aging, 12,* 433–443.

Baltes, M. M., Maas, I., Wilms, H. U., Borchelt, M., & Little, T. D. (1999). Everyday competence in old and very old age: Theoretical considerations and empirical findings. In P. B. Baltes & K. U. Mayer (Eds.), *The Berlin Aging Study: Aging from 70 to 100* (pp. 384–402). Cambridge: Cambridge University Press.

Baltes, P. B. (1987). Theoretical propositions of life-span developmental psychology: On the dynamics between growth and decline. *Developmental Psychology, 23,* 611–626.

Baltes, P. B. (1993). The aging mind: Potential and limits. *Gerontologist, 33,* 580–594.

Baltes, P. B. (1997). On the incomplete architecture of human ontogeny: Selection, optimization, and compensation as foundation of developmental theory. *American Psychologist, 52,* 366–80.

Baltes, P. B., & Baltes, M. M., (1990). *Successful aging: Perspective from the behavioral sciences.* Cambridge: Cambridge University Press.

Baltes, P. B., Lindenberger, U., & Staudinger, U. (1997). Life-span theory in developmental psychology. In W. Damon (Series Ed.) & R. Lerner (Vol. Ed.), *Handbook of child psychology: Vol. 1. Theoretical models of human development* (5th ed., pp. 1029–1144). New York: Wiley.

Baltes, P. B., & Staudinger, U. M. (2000). Wisdom: A methateuristic (pragmatic) to orchestrate mind and virtue toward excellence. *American Psychologist, 55,* 122–136.

Bandalos, D. L., Finney, S. J., & Geske, J. A. (2003), A model of statistics performance based on achievement goal theory. *Journal of Educational Psychology, 95,* 604–616.

Bandura, A. (1977a). Self-efficacy: Toward a unifying theory of behavioral change. *Psychological Review, 84,* 191–215.

Bandura, A. (1977b). *Social learning theory.* Englewood Cliffs, NJ: Prentice Hall.

Bandura, A. (1986). *Social foundations of thought and action.* Englewood Cliffs, NJ: Prentice Hall.

Bandura, A. (1989). Regulation of cognitive processes through perceived self-efficacy. *Developmental Psychology, 25,* 729–735.

Bandura, A. (1997). *Self-efficacy: The exercise of control.* New York: Freeman.

Bandura, A. (1999a). Moral disengagement in the perpetration of inhumanities. *Personality and Social Psychology Review, 3,* 193–209.

Bandura, A. (1999b). Social cognitive theory of personality. In D. Cervone & Y. Shoda (Eds.), *The coherence of personality: Social-cognitive bases of consistency, variability, and organization* (pp. 185–241). New York: Guilford Press.

Bandura, A., Barbaranelli, C., Caprara, G. V., & Pastorelli, C. (1996). Mechanisms of moral disengagement in the exercise of moral agency. *Journal of Personality and Social Psychology. 71,* 364–374.

Bandura, A., & Cervone, D. (1983). Self-evaluative and self-efficacy mechanisms governing the motivational effects of goal systems. *Journal of Personality and Social Psychology, 45,* 1017–1028.

Bandura, A., & Locke, E. A. (2003). Negative self-efficacy and goal effects revisited. *Journal of Applied Psychology, 88,* 87–99.

Bandura, A., & Schunk, D. H. (1981). Cultivating competence, self-efficacy, and intrinsic interest through proximal self-motivation. *Journal of Personality and Social Psychology, 41,* 586–598.

Bandura, A., & Walters, R. (1963). *Social learning and personality development.* New York: Holt, Rinehart & Winston.

Baumeister, R. F., & Vohs, K. D (Eds.). (2004). *Handbook of self-regulation: Research, theory, and applications.* New York: Guilford Press.

Bennett, M. R., & Hacker, P. M. S. (2003). *Philosophical foundations of neuroscience.* Oxford: Blackwell.

Berg, C. A., & Klaczynski, P. (1996). Practical intelligence and problem solving: Searching for perspectives. In F. Blanchard-Fields & T. M. Hess (Eds.), *Perspectives on cognition in adulthood and aging* (pp. 323–357). New York: McGraw-Hill.

Berg, C. A, Meegan, S. P., & Klaczynski, P. (1999). Age and experiential differences in strategy generation and information requests for solving everyday problems. *International Journal of Behavioral Development, 23,* 615–639.

Bergman, L. R. (2002). Studying processes: Some methodological considerations. In L. Pulkkinen & A. Caspi (Eds.), *Paths to successful development: Personality in the life course* (pp. 177–199). Cambridge: Cambridge University Press.

Berry, J. M. (1999). Memory self-efficacy in its social cognitive context. In T. M. Hess & F. Blanchard-Fields (Eds.), *Social cognition and aging* (pp. 69–96). San Diego, CA: Academic Press.

Berry, J. M., & West, R. L. (1993). Cognitive self-efficacy in relation to personal mastery and goal setting across the life span. *International Journal of Behavioral Development, 16,* 351–379.

Berry, J. M., West, R. L., & Dennehey, D. M. (1989). Reliability and validity of the Memory Self-Efficacy Questionnaire. *Developmental Psychology, 25,* 701–713.

Blanchard-Fields, F., Chen, Y., & Norris, L. (1997). Everyday problem solving across the adult life span: Influence of domain specificity and cognitive appraisals. *Psychology and Aging, 12,* 684–693.

Borsboom, D., Mellenbergh, G. J., & van Heerden, J. (2003). The theoretical status of latent variables. *Psychological Review, 110,* 203–219.

Botwinick, J. (1973). *Aging and behavior.* New York: Springer.

Botwinick, J. (1987). *Aging and behaviors* (3rd ed.). New York: Springer.

Brandtstädter, J., & Rothermund, K. (1994). Self-percepts of control in middle and later adulthood: Buffering losses by rescaling goals. *Psychology and Aging, 9,* 265–273.

Braudel, F. (1981). *The structures of everyday life: Civilization and capitalism, 15th–18th century* (Vol. 1). New York: Harper & Row.

Bray, S. R., & Cowan, H. (2004). Proxy efficacy: Implications for self-efficacy and exercise intentions in cardiac rehabilitation. *Rehabilitation Psychology, 49,* 71–75.

Brown, T. C., & Latham, G. P. (2002). The effects of behavioural outcome goals, learning goals, and urging people to do their best on an individual's teamwork behaviour in a group problem-solving task. *Canadian Journal of Behavioural Science, 34,* 276–285.

Buss, D. M. (1991). Evolutionary personality psychology. *Annual Review of Psychology, 42,* 459–491.

Busse, E. W. (1969). Theories of aging. In E. W. Busse & E. Pfeiffer (Eds.), *Behavior and adaptation in late life* (pp. 11–32). Boston: Little, Brown.

Bussey, K., & Bandura, A. (1999). Social cognitive theory of gender development and differentiation. *Psychological Review, 106,* 676–713.

Cantor, N. E. (2003). Constructive cognition, personal goals, and the social embedding of personality. In L. G. Aspinwall & U. M. Staudinger (Eds.), *A psychology of human strengths: Fundamental questions and future directions for a positive psychology*

(pp. 49–60). Washington, DC: American Psychological Association.

Caplan, L. J., & Schooler, C. (2003). The roles of fatalism, self-confidence, and intellectual resources in the disablement process in older adults. *Psychology and Aging, 18,* 551–561.

Caprara, G. V., Barbaranelli, C., Pastorelli, C., & Cervone, D. (2004). The contribution of self-efficacy beliefs to psychosocial outcomes in adolescence: Predicting beyond past behavior and global dispositional tendencies. *Personality and Individual Differences, 37,* 751–763.

Caprara, G. V., & Cervone, D. (2000). *Personality: Determinants, dynamics, and potentials.* New York: Cambridge University Press.

Caprara, G. V., & Cervone, D. (2003). A conception of personality for a psychology of human strengths: Personality as an agentic, self-regulating system. In L. G. Aspinwall & U. M. Staudinger (Eds.), *A psychology of human strengths: Fundamental questions and future directions for a positive psychology* (pp. 61–74). Washington, DC: American Psychological Association.

Caprara, G. V., Steca, P., Cervone, D., & Artistico, D. (2003). The contribution of self-efficacy beliefs to dispositional shyness: On social-cognitive systems and the development of personality dispositions. *Journal of Personality, 71,* 943–970.

Carstensen, L. L., & Charles, S. T. (2003). Human aging: Why is even good news taken as bad? In L. G. Aspinwall & U. M. Staudinger (Eds.), *A psychology of human strengths: Fundamental questions and future directions for a positive psychology* (pp. 75–86). Washington, DC: American Psychological Association.

Carver, C. S., & Scheier, M. F. (1998). *On the self-regulation of behavior.* New York: Cambridge University Press.

Cattell, R. B. (1971). *Abilities: Their structure, growth, and action.* Boston: Houghton Mifflin.

Cavanaugh, J. C., & Blanchard-Fields, F. (2002). *Adult development and aging* (4th ed.). Belmont, CA: Wadsworth/Thomson Learning.

Cavanaugh, J. C., Feldman, J. M., & Hertzog, C. (1998). Memory beliefs as social cognition: A reconceptualization of what memory questionnaires assess. *Review of General Psychology, 2,* 48–65.

Cavanaugh, J. C., & Green, E. E. (1990). I believe, therefore I can: Self-efficacy beliefs in memory aging. In E. A. Lovelace (Ed.), *Aging and cognition: Mental processes, self-awareness, and interventions* (pp. 189–230). Amsterdam: North Holland.

Cervone, D. (1985). Randomization tests to determine significance levels for microanalytic congruences between self-efficacy and behavior. *Cognitive Therapy and Research, 9,* 357–365.

Cervone, D. (1997). Social-cognitive mechanisms and personality coherence: Self-knowledge, situational beliefs, and cross-situational coherence in perceived self-efficacy. *Psychological Science, 8,* 43–50.

Cervone, D. (1999). Bottom-up explanation in personality psychology: The case of cross-situational coherence. In D. Cervone & Y. Shoda (Eds.), *The coherence of personality: Social-cognitive bases of consistency, variability, and organization* (pp. 303–341). New York: Guilford Press.

Cervone, D. (2004a). The architecture of personality. *Psychological Review, 111,* 183–204.

Cervone, D. (2004b). Personality assessment: Tapping the social-cognitive architecture of personality. *Behavior Therapy, 35.*

Cervone, D. (2005). Personality architecture: Within-person structures and processes. *Annual Review of Psychology, 56,* 423–452.

Cervone, D., Artistico, D., & Orom, H. (2005). *Context and everyday problem solving among younger and older adults.* Manuscript submitted for publication.

Cervone, D., & Peake, P. K. (1986). Anchoring, efficacy, and action: The influence of judgmental heuristic on self-efficacy judgments and behavior. *Journal of Personality and Social Psychology, 50,* 492–501.

Cervone, D., & Scott, W. D. (1995). Self-efficacy theory of behavioural change. In W. O'Donohue & L. Krasner (Eds.), *Theories of behavior therapy* (pp. 349–383). Washington, DC: American Psychological Association.

Cervone, D., Shadel, W. G., & Jencius, S. (2001). Social-cognitive theory of personality assessment. *Personality and Social Psychology Review, 5,* 33–51.

Cervone, D., & Shoda, Y. (Eds.). (1999). *The coherence of personality: Social-cognitive bases of consistency, variability, and organization.* New York: Guilford Press.

Clark, D. O., & Nothwehr, F. (1999). Exercise self-efficacy and its correlates among socioeconomically disadvantaged adults. *Health Education and Behavior, 26,* 535–546.

Coleman, P. K., & Karraker, K. H. (1997). Self-efficacy and parenting quality: Findings and future applications. *Development Review, 18,* 47–85.

Cornelius, S. W. (1984). Classic pattern of intellectual aging: Test familiarity, difficulty, and performance. *Journal of Gerontology, 39,* 201–206.

Cornelius, S. W., & Caspi, A. (1986). Self-perceptions of intellectual control and aging. *Educational Gerontology, 12,* 345–357.

Cornelius, S. W., & Caspi, A. (1987). Everyday problem solving in adulthood and old age. *Psychology and Aging, 2,* 144–153.

Costa, P. T., & McCrae, R.R. (1992). *Revised NEO personality inventory (NEO-PI-R) and NEO FiveFactor Inventory (NEO-FFI) professional manual.* Odessa, FL: Psychological Assessment Resources.

Cutrona, C. E., & Troutman, B. R. (1986). Social support, infant temperament, and parenting self-efficacy: A mediational model of post-partum depression. *Child Development, 57,* 1507–1518.

Denney, N. W. (1990). Adult age differences in traditional and practical problem solving. In E. A. Lovelace (Ed.), *Aging and cognition: Mental process, self-awareness and intelligence.* Amsterdam: North Holland Elsevier.

Denney, N. W., & Palmer, A. M. (1981). Adult age differences on traditional and practical problem solving measures. *Journal of Gerontology, 36,* 323–328.

Denney, N. W., & Pearce, K. A. (1989). A developmental study of practical problem solving in adults. *Psychology and Aging, 4,* 438–442.

Denney, N. W., Pearce, K. A., & Palmer, A. M. (1982). A developmental study of adults' performance on traditional and practical problem-solving tasks. *Experimental Aging Research, 8,* 115–118.

DeSteno, D., Bartlett, M. Y., Braverman, J., & Salovey, P. (2002). Sex differences in jealousy: Evolutionary mechanism or artifact of measurement? *Journal of Personality and Social Psychology, 83,* 1103–1116.

Diamond, J. (1997). *Guns, germs, and steel: The fates of human society.* New York: Random House.

Dittman-Kohli, F., Lachman, M. E., Kiegel, R., & Baltes, P. B. (1991). Effects of cognitive training and testing on intellectual efficacy beliefs in elderly adults. *Journal of Gerontology: Psychological Sciences, 46,* 162–164.

The Economist (2002). *Pocket world in figures* (2003 ed.) London: Profile Books.

Eliot, T. S. (1931). Preface to *Transit of Venus, Poems by H. Crosby.* Paris: Black Sun Press.

Emmons, R. A., & Kaiser, H. A. (1996). Goal orientation and emotional well-being: Linking goals and affect through the self. In L. L. Martin & A. Tesser, (Eds.), *Striving and feeling: Interactions among goals, affect, and self-regulation* (pp. 79–98). Mahwah, NJ: Erlbaum.

Endler, N. S., & Magnusson, D. (1976). Toward an interactional psychology of personality. *Psychological Bulletin, 85,* 956–974.

Gottlieb, G. (1998). Normally occurring environmental and behavioral influences on gene activity: From central dogma to probabilistic epigenesis. *Psychological Review, 105,* 792–802.

Grant, H., & Dweck, C. (1999). A goal analysis of personality and personality coherence. In D. Cervone & Y. Shoda (Eds.), *The coherence of personality: Social-cognitive bases of consistency, variability, and organization* (pp. 345–371). New York: Guilford Press.

Gross, D., Fogg, L., & Tucker, S. (1995). The efficacy of parent training for promoting positive parent-toddler relationships. *Research in Nursing and Health, 18,* 489–499.

Haaga, D. A. F., & Stewart, B. L. (1992). Self-efficacy for recovery from a lapse after smoking cessation. *Journal of Consulting and Clinical Psychology, 60,* 24–28.

Hall, G. S. (1922). *Senescence.* London: Appleton.

Harré, R. (1998). *The singular self: An introduction to the psychology of personhood.* London: Sage.

Harré, R. (2002). *Cognitive science: A philosophical introduction.* London: Sage.

Harré, R., & Secord, P. (1972). *The explanation of social behavior.* Oxford: Blackwell.

Heckhausen, J. (1999). *Developmental regulation in adulthood: Age normative and sociostructural constraints as adaptive challenges*. New York: Cambridge University Press.

Heckhausen, J. (2002). Developmental regulation of life-course transitions: A control theory approach. In L. Pulkkinen & A. Caspi (Eds.), *Paths to successful development: Personality in the life course* (pp. 257–280). Cambridge: Cambridge University Press.

Heckhausen, J., & Dweck, C. S. (Eds.) (1998). *Motivation dand self-regulation across the life span*. Cambridge: Cambridge University Press.

Heckhausen, J., & Schulz, R. (1995). A life-span theory of control. *Psychological Review, 102,* 284–304.

Helson, R., Kwan, V. S. Y., John, O. P., & Jones, C. (2002). The growing evidence for personality change in adulthood: Findings from research with personality inventories. *Journal of Research in Personality, 36,* 287–306.

Hess, T. M., & Blanchard-Fields, F. (Eds). (1999). *Social cognition and aging*. San Diego, CA: Academic Press.

Higgins, E. T. (1987). Self-discrepancy: A theory relating self and affect. *Psychological Review, 94,* 319–340.

Jenkins, J. J. (1979). Four points to remember: A tetrahedral model of memory experiments. In L. S. Cermak & F. I. M. Craik (Eds.), *Levels of processing in human memory*. Hillsdale, NJ: Erlbaum.

Judge, T. A., Erez, A., Bono, J. E., & Thoresen, C. J. (2002). Are measures of self-esteem, neuroticism, locus of control, and generalized self-efficacy indicators of a common core construct? *Journal of Personality and Social Psychology, 83,* 693–710.

Kagan, J. (1998). *Three seductive ideas*. Cambridge, MA: Harvard University Press.

King, V., & Elder, G. H. Jr. (1998). Self-efficacy and grandparenthood. *Journals of Gerontology Series B, Psychological Sciences and Social Sciences, 53,* 249–257.

Kohn, M. L., & Schooler, C. (1983). *Work and personality: An inquiry into the impact of social stratification*. Norwood, NJ: Ablex.

Kruger, J., & Dunning, D. (1999). Unskilled and unaware of it: How difficulties in recognizing one's own incompetence lead to inflated self-assessments. *Journal of Personality and Social Psychology, 77,* 1121–1134.

Kruglanski, A. W., Shah, J. Y., Fishbach, A., Friedman, R., Chun, W. Y., & Sleeth-Keppler, D. (2002). A theory of goal-systems. In M. Zanna (Ed.), *Advances in experimental social psychology* (vol. 34; pp. 331–378). San Diego, CA: Academic Press.

Kwok, S., & Wong, D. (2000). Mental health of parents with young children in Hong Kong: The roles of parenting stress and parenting self-efficacy. *Child and Family Social Work, 15,* 57–65.

Labouvie-Vief, G. (1980). Beyond formal operations: Uses and limits of pure logic in life-span development. *Human Development, 23,* 141–161.

Lachman, M. E. (1983). Perceptions of intellectual aging: Antecedent or consequence of intellectual functioning? *Developmental Psychology, 19,* 482–498.

Lachman, M. E., & Jelalian, E. (1984). Self-efficacy and attributions for intellectual performance in young and elderly adults. *Journal of Gerontology, 39,* 577–582.

Lachman, M. E., Jette, A., Tennstedt, S., Howland, J., Harris, B. A., & Peterson, E. (1997). A cognitive-behavioural model for promoting regular physical activity in older adults. *Psychology Health and Medicine, 2,* 251–261.

Lachman, M. E., & Leff, R. (1989). Perceived control and intellectual functioning in the elderly: A 5-year longitudinal study. *Developmental Psychology, 25,* 722–728.

Laguna, K. D., & Babcock, R. (2000). Computer testing of memory across the adult life span. *Experimental Aging Research, 26,* 229–243.

Lang, F., & Carstensen, L. (2002). Time counts: Future time perspective, goals, and social relationships. *Psychology and Aging, 17,* 125–139.

Lawton, M. P., & Nahemow, L. (1973). Ecology and the aging process. In C. Eisdorfer & M. P. Lawton (Eds.), *The psychology of adult development and aging* (pp. 619–674). Washington, DC: American Psychological Association.

Lazarus, R. S. (1991). *Emotion and adaptation*. New York: Oxford University Press.

Lent, R. W., Brown, S. D., & Hackett, G. (1994). Toward a unifying social-cognitive theory of career and academic interest, choice, and performance. *Journal of Vocational Behavior, 45,* 79–122.

Leveille, S. G., Cohen-Mansfield, J., & Guralnik, J. M. (2003). The impact of chronic musculoskeletal pain on exercise attitudes, self-efficacy, and physical activity. *Journal of Aging and Physical Activity, 11,* 275–283.

Levy, B. R., Hausdorff, J. M., Hencke, R., & Wei, J. Y. (2000). Reducing cardiovascular stress with positive self-stereotypes of aging. *Journals of Gerontology Series B: Psychological Sciences and Social Sciences, 55B,* P205–P213.

Levy, B. R., Slade, M. D., & Kasl, S. V. (2002). Longitudinal benefit of positive self-perceptions of aging on functional health. *Journals of Gerontology Series B: Psychological Sciences and Social Sciences, 57B,* P409–P417.

Levy, B. R., Slade, M. D., Kunkel, S. R., & Kasl, S. V. (2002). Longevity increased by positive self-perceptions of aging. *Journal of Personality and Social Psychology, 83,* 261–270.

Li, F., McAuley, E., Harmer, P., Duncan, T. E., & Chaumeton, N. R. (2001). Tai chi enhances self-efficacy and exercise behavior in older adults. *Journal of Aging and Physical Activity. 9,* 161–171.

Lickliter, R., & Honeycutt, H. (2003a). Developmental dynamics: Toward a biologically plausible evolutionary psychology. *Psychological Bulletin, 129,* 819–835.

Lickliter, R., & Honeycutt, H. (2003b). Developmental dynamics and contemporary evolutionary psychology: Status quo or irreconcilable views? Reply to Bjorklund (2003), Krebs (2003), Buss and Reeve (2003), Crawford (2003), and Tooby et al. (2003). *Psychological Bulletin, 129*, 866–872.

Lineweaver, T. T., & Hertzog, C. (1998). Adults' efficacy and control beliefs regarding memory and aging: Separating general from personal beliefs. *Aging: Neuropsychology and Cognition, 5*, 264–296.

Litt, M. D., Kleppinger, A., & Judge, J. O. (2002). Initiation and maintenance of exercise behavior in older women: Predictors from the social learning model. *Journal of Behavioral Medicine, 25*, 83–97.

Little, T. D., Miyashita, T., Karasawa, M., Mashima, M., Oettingen, G., Azuma, H., & Baltes, P. B. (2003). The links among action-control beliefs, intellective skill, and school performance in Japanese, US, and German school children. *International Journal of Behavioral Development. 27*, 41–48.

Locke, E. A., & Latham, G. P. (1990). *A theory of goal setting and task performance*. Englewood Cliffs, NJ: Prentice Hall.

Lazarus, R. S. (1991). *Emotion and adaptation*. New York: Oxford University Press.

Magnusson, D. (1996). *The lifespan development of individuals: Behavioral, neurobiological, and psychosocial perspectives*. Cambridge: Cambridge University Press.

Magnusson, D., & Mahoney, J. L. (2003). A holistic person approach for research on positive development. In L. G. Aspinwall & U. M. Staudinger (Eds.), *A psychology of human strengths: Fundamental questions and future directions for a positive psychology* (pp. 227–243). Washington, DC: American Psychological Association.

Magnusson,.D., & Törestad, B. (1993). A holistic view of personality: A model revisited. *Annual Review of Psychology, 44*, 427–452.

Maurer, T. J. (2001). Career-relevant learning and development, worker age, and beliefs about self-efficacy for development. *Journal of Management, 27*, 123–140.

Maurer, T. J., Weiss, E. M., & Barbeite, F. G. (2003). A model of investment in work-related learning and development activity: The effects of individual, situational, motivational, and age variables. *Journal of Applied Psychology, 88*, 707–724.

McCormick, J., & McPherson, G. (2003). The role of self-efficacy in a musical performance examination: An exploratory structural equation analysis. *Psychology of Music, 31*, 37–50.

McCrae, R. R., & Costa, P. T. (1996). Toward a new generation of personality theories: theoretical contexts for the five-factor model. In J. S. Wiggins (Ed.), *The five-factor model of personality: Theoretical perspectives* (pp. 51–87). New York: Guilford Press.

McCrae, R. R., & Costa, P. T. (2003). Personality in adulthood: A five-factor theory perspective (2nd ed.). New York: Guilford Press.

McDougall, G. H. (1998). Increasing memory self-efficacy use in Hispanic elders. *Clinical Gerontologist, 19*, 57–76.

McDowd, J. M., & Birren, J. E. (1990). Aging and attentional processes. In J. E. Birren & K. W. Schaie (Eds.), Handbook of the psychology of aging (3rd ed., pp. 222–233). New York: Academic Press.

McDowd, J. M., Filion, D. L., Pohl, P. S., Richards, L. G., & Stiers, W. (2003). Attentional abilities and functional outcomes following stroke. *Journal of Gerontology, 58B*, P45–P53.

Mikulecky, L., Lloyd, P., Siemental, P., & Masker, S. (1998). Transfer beyond workplace literacy classes: Twelve case studies and a model. *Reading Psychology, 19*, 51–138.

Miller, L. C., Putcha-Bhagavatula, A., & Pedersen, W. C. (2002). Men's and women's mating preferences: Distinct evolutionary mechanisms? *Current Directions in Psychological Science, 11*, 88–93.

Mischel, W. (1973). Toward a cognitive social learning reconceptualization of personality. *Psychological Review, 80*, 252–283.

Mischel, W. (2004). Toward an integrative science of the person. *Annual Review of Psychology, 55*, 1–22.

Mischel, W., & Mendoza-Denton, R. (2003). Harnessing willpower and socioemotional intelligence to enhance human agency and potential. In L. G. Aspinwall & U. M. Staudinger (Eds.), *A psychology of human strengths: Fundamental questions and future directions for a positive psychology* (pp. 211–226). Washington, DC: American Psychological Association.

Mischel, W., & Shoda, Y. (1995). A cognitive-affective system theory of personality: Reconceptualizing situations, dispositions, dynamics, and invariance in personality structure. *Psychological Review, 102*, 246–286.

Molenaar, P. C. M., Huizenga, H. M., & Nesselroade, J. R. (2002). The relationship between the structure of inter-individual and intra-individual variability: A theoretical and empirical vindication of developmental systems theory. In U. M. Staudinger & U. Lindenberger (Eds.), *Understanding human development* (pp. 339–360). Dordrecht: Kluwer.

Nowak, A., Vallacher, R. R., & Zochowski, M (2002). The emergence of personality: Personal stability through interpersonal synchronization. In D. Cervone & W. Mischel (Eds.), *Advances in personality science* (pp. 292–331). New York: Guilford Press.

Park, D. C., Lautenschlager, G., Hedden, T., Davidson, N., Smith, A. D., & Smith, P. (2002). Models of visuospatial and verbal memory across the adult life span. *Psychology and Aging, 17*, 299–320.

Poon, L. W., Rubin, D. C., & Wilson, B. A. (1989). *Everyday cognition in adulthood and late life*. New York: Cambridge University Press.

Prohaska, T. R., Peters, K., & Warren, J. S. (2000). Sources of attrition in a church-based exercise program for older African-Americans. *American Journal of Health Promotion, 14*, 380–385.

Pulkkinen, L., Nurmi, J., & Kokko, K. (2002). Individual differences in personal goals in mid-thirties. In L. Pulkkinen & A. Caspi (Eds.), *Paths to successful development: Personality in the life course* (pp. 331–352). Cambridge: Cambridge University Press.

Raz, N. (2000). Aging of the brain and its impact on cognitive performance: Integration of structural and functional findings. In F. I. M. Craik, & T. A. Salthouse (Eds.), *The handbook of aging and cognition* (2nd ed., pp. 1–90). Mahwah, NJ: Erlbaum.

Reid, M. C., Williams, C. S., & Gill, T. M. (2003). The relationship between psychological factors and disabling musculoskeletal pain in community-dwelling older persons. *Journal of the American Geriatrics Society, 51,* 1092–1098.

Reitman, W. R. (1964). Heuristic decision procedures, open constraints, and the structure of ill-defined problems. In M. W. Shelly & G. K. Bryan (Eds.), *Human judgments and optimality* (pp. 282–315). New York: Wiley.

Rejeski, W. J., Ettinger, W. H., Martin, K., & Morgan, T. (1998). Treating disability in knee osteoarthritis with exercise therapy: A central role for self-efficacy and pain. *Arthritis Care and Research, 11,* 94–101.

Roberts, W. A. (2002). Are animals stuck in time? *Psychological Bulletin, 128,* 473–489.

Rohrbauch, M. J., Shoham, V., Coyne, J. C., Cranford, J. A., Sonnega, J. S., & Niklas, J. M. (2004). Beyond the "self" in self-efficacy: Spouse confidence predicts patient survival following heart failure. *Journal of Family Psychology, 18,* 184–193.

Rotter, J. B. (1954). *Social learning and clinical psychology.* Englewood Cliffs, NJ: Prentice Hall.

Rotter, J. B. (1966). Generalized expectancies for internal versus external control of reinforcement. *Psychological Monographs, 80.*

Rottinghaus, P. J., Larson, L. M., & Borgen, F. H. (2003). The relation of self-efficacy and interests: A meta-analysis of 60 samples. *Journal of Vocational Behavior, 62,* 221–236.

Rowe, J. W., & Kahn, R. L. (1987). Human aging: Usual and successful. *Science, 237,* 143–149.

Rowe, J. W., & Kahn, R. L. (1997). Successful aging. *Gerontologist, 37,* 433–440.

Russell, J. A. (2003). Core affect and the psychological construction of emotion. *Psychological Review, 110,* 145–172.

Rybash, J. M., Hoyer, W. J., & Roodin, P. A. (1986). *Adult cognition and aging: Developmental changes in processing, knowing and thinking.* Elmsford, NY: Pergamon Press.

Rypma, B., Prabhakaran, V., Desmond, J. E., & Gabrieli, J. D. E. (2001). Age differences in prefrontal cortical activity in working memory. *Psychology and Aging, 16,* 371–384.

Sahu, F. M., & Sageeta, R. (2004). Self-efficacy and well-being in working and non-working women: The moderating role of involvement. *Psychology and Developing Societies, 15,* 187–200.

Salthouse, T. A. (1984). Effects of age and skill in typing. *Journal of Exeperimental Psychology: General, 70,* 345–371.

Salthouse, T. A. (1991). *Theoretical perspectives on cognitive aging.* Hillsdale, NJ: Erlbaum.

Salthouse, T. A., Berish, D. E., & Miles, J. D. (2002). The role of cognitive stimulation on the relations between age and cognitive functioning. *Psychology and Aging, 17,* 548–557.

Schaie, K. W. (1996). Intellectual development in adulthood. In J. E. Birren & K. W. Shaie (Eds.), *Handbook of the psychology of aging* (4th ed., pp. 266–286). San Diego, CA: Academic Press.

Schmidt, A. M., & Ford, J. K. (2003). Learning within a learner control training environment: The interactive effects of goal orientation and metacognitive instruction on learning outcomes. *Personnel Psychology, 56,* 405–429.

Schunk, D. H., & Gunn, T. P. (1986). Self-efficacy and skill development: Influence of task strategies and attributions. *Journal of Personality and Social Psychology, 79,* 238–244.

Schunk, D. H., & Pajares, F. (2002). The development of academic self-efficacy. In A. Wigfield & J. Eccles (Eds.), *Development of achievement motivation. A volume in the educational psychology series* (pp. 15–31). San Diego, CA: Academic Press.

Searle, J. R. (1998). *Mind, language, and society: Philosophy in the real world.* New York: Basic Books

Seeman, T., McAvay, G., Merrill, S., & Albert, M., et al. (1996). Self-efficacy beliefs and change in cognitive performance: MacArthur studies on successful aging. *Psychology and Aging, 11,* 538–551.

Seeman, T. E., Rodin, J., & Albert, M. (1993). Self-efficacy and cognitive performance in high-functioning older individuals: MacArthur studies of successful aging. *Journal of Aging and Health, 5,* 455–474.

Seeman, T. E., Unger, J. B., McAvay, G., & Mendes de Leon, C. F. (1999). Self-efficacy beliefs and perceived declines in functional ability: MacArthur studies of successful aging. *Journals of Gerontology Series B: Psychological Sciences and Social Sciences, 54B,* P214–P222.

Sherer, M., Maddux, J. E., Mercandante, B., Prentice-Dunn, B. J., & Rogers, R. W. (1982). The self-efficacy scale: Construction and validation. *Psychological Reports, 51,* 663–671.

Silvia, P. J. (2003). Self-efficacy and interest: Experimental studies of optimal incompetence. *Journal of Vocation Behavior, 62,* 237–249.

Simon, H. A. (1973). The structure of ill structured problems. *Artificial Intelligence, 4,* 145–180.

Sinnott, J. D. (1989). *Everyday problem solving: theory and applications.* New York: Praeger.

Sinnott, J. D. (1998). *The development of logic in adulthood: Postformal thought and its applications.* New York: Plenum.

Skinner, E. A. (1996). A guide to constructs of control. *Journal of Personality and Social Psychology, 71,* 549–570.

Srivastava, S., John, O. P., Gosling, S. D., & Potter, J. (2003). Development of personality in early and middle adulthood: Set like plaster or persistent change? *Journal of Personality and Social Psychology, 84,* 1041–1053.

Stajkovic, A. D., & Luthans, F. (1998). Self-efficacy and work-related performance: A meta-analysis. *Psychological Bulletin, 124,* 240–261.

Staudinger, U. M., Freund, A. M., Linden, M., & Mass, I. (1999). Self, personality, and life regulation: Facets of psychological resilience in old age. In P. B. Baltes & K. U. Mayer (Eds.), *The Berlin aging study: Aging from 70 to 100* (pp. 302–328). Cambridge: Cambridge University Press.

Suddendorf, T., & Corballis, M. C. (1997) Mental time travel and the evolution of the human mind. *Genetic, Social, and General Psychology Monographs, 123,* 133–167.

Twenge, J. M. (2002). Birth cohort, social change, and personality: The interplay of dysphoria and individualism in the 20th century. In D. Cervone & W. Mischel (Eds.), *Advances in personality science* (pp. 196–218). New York: Guilford Press.

Twenge, J. M., Zhang, L., & Im, C. (2004). It's beyond my control: A cross-temporal meta-analysis of increasing externality in locus of control, 1960-2002. *Personality and Social Psychology Review, 8,* 308–391.

United Nations Population Fund (2002). *State of world population 2002: People, poverty, and possibilities.* New York: United Nations.

van Ryn, M., & Vinokur, A. D. (1992). How did it work? An examination of the mechanisms through which an intervention for the unemployed promoted job-search behavior. *American Journal of Community Psychology, 20,* 577–597.

Verhaeghen, P., Marcoen, A., & Goossens, L. (1993). Facts and fiction about memory aging: A quantitative integration of research findings. *Journal of Gerontology, 48,* P157–P171.

Vinokur, A. D., van Ryn, M., Gramlich, E. M., & Price, R. H. (1991). Long-term follow-up and benefit-cost analysis of the Jobs Program: A preventive intervention for the unemployed. *Journal of Applied Psychology, 76,* 213–219.

Weitlauf, J., Cervone, D., Smith, R. E., & Wright, P. M. (2001). Assessing generalization in perceived self-efficacy: Multidomain and global assessments of the effects of self-defense training for women. *Personality and Social Psychology Bulletin, 27,* 1683–1691.

Welch, D. C., & West, R. L. (1995). Self-efficacy and mastery: Its application to issues of environmental control, cognition, and aging. *Developmental Review, 15,* 150–171.

West, R. L., & Berry, J. M. (1994). Age declines in memory self-efficacy: General or limited to particular tasks and measures? In J. D. Sinnott (Ed.), *Interdisciplinary handbook of adult lifespan learning* (pp. 426–445). Westport, CT: Greenwood Press.

West, R. L., Thorn, R. M., & Bagwell, D. (2003). Memory performance and beliefs as a function of goal-setting and aging. *Psychology and Aging, 18,* 111–125.

West, R. L., Welch, D. C., & Knabb, P. D. (2002). Gender and aging: Spatial self-efficacy and location recall. *Basic and Applied Social Psychology, 24,* 71–80.

West, R. L., Welch, D. C., & Thorn, R. M. (2001). Effects of goal-setting and feedback on memory performance and beliefs among older and younger adults. *Psychology and Aging, 16,* 240–250.

Williamson, A. (2000). Gender issues in older adults' participation in learning: viewpoints and experiences of learners in the University of Third Age. *Education Gerontology, 26,* 49–60.

Wood, W., & Eagly, A. H. (2002). A cross-cultural analysis of the behavior of women and men: Implications for the origins of sex differences. *Psychological Bulletin, 128,* 699–727.

Young, J. F., & Mroczek, D. K. (2003). Predicting intraindividual self-concept trajectories during adolescence. *Journal of Adolescence, 26,* 589–603.

Zimmerman, B. J. (2002). Achieving academic excellence: A self-regulatory perspective. In M. Ferrari (Ed), *The pursuit of excellence through education. The educational psychology series* (pp. 85–110). Mahwah, NJ: Erlbaum.

Chapter 9

Autonomy and Self-Directed Learning: A Developmental Journey

Kathleen Taylor

Give a man a fish and feed him for a day.
Teach him to fish and feed him for a lifetime.
—*Lao Tzu*

INTRODUCTION

Not so very long ago, change was a *change*. Although new technologies introduced early in the twentieth century (think: telephone, automobile, airplane) led to unexpected and far-reaching alterations in the way things were, in most places, barring war or natural cataclysm, daily life meandered along pretty much in line with expectations. The pace of change started to accelerate, however, in the latter part of the century. This was affected in part by the introduction of even newer technologies, such as television, highly sophisticated automation, and the Internet. Television's dissemination of images of distant people and places contributed to the sense of global village. Automation of all kinds, the computer in particular, drastically changed the shape of work and the demands made of workers. The Internet enabled person-to-person exchanges across formerly formidable barriers as well as instant access to information that had once been available only to specialists.

A vast amount of new knowledge is now created daily, at an ever accelerating pace. It is no longer plausible for educational institutions to imagine that their most essential task is to pass along accumulated knowledge to succeeding generations. By the time most students are out of college, significant portions of what they have learned will be outdated. Similarly with the need for continued new learning in the workplace: "Today's technical knowledge will be only one percent of that available in the year 2050 [and] the trend toward changing jobs and careers will also continue" (Guglielmino & Guglielmino, 1994, p. 40).

Another phenomenon of modern life that affects how we think about learning is the increasing cultural diversity within nations as well as the emergence (or reemergence) of new nation-states at an unprecedented rate. This has focused attention on ways of knowing that may be necessary for democratic forms of government to take hold and for existing democracies to be maintained. Educator-philosophers such as Dewey (1916/1930), Freire (1992), Horton and Freire

(1990), and others have observed that the democratic impulse may require a particular independence of mind and thought, based on the ability to question one's own—and, by extension, cultural, and societal—beliefs and assumptions. The capacities for such self-questioning are most likely encouraged by certain forms of education that may not be widely practiced.

In sum, continuous change is now pervasive and unavoidable. It affects individuals, families, communities, every aspect of the workplace, social institutions of all kinds, national identities, and geopolitical interactions. Given these phenomena—the pace of change, the rate at which new knowledge is created, and the pressing need to respond effectively to ever more culturally diverse environments—the familiar proverb takes on new resonance: Give a person information and satisfy her learning needs for a day; teach her to learn on her own and satisfy her learning needs for a lifetime. In the literature of adult education, encouraging self-directed learning (SDL) has been described as a major factor in fostering the skills and capacities for lifelong learning and "critical to survival and prosperity in a world of continuous personal, community, and societal changes" (Caffarella, 1993, p. 32).

This chapter is divided into three sections, research, theory, and practice. The section on research begins with a brief overview of major themes in the literature of adult SDL; the theory section examines the explanatory power of constructive-developmental theory, in particular, to illustrate how SDL relates to adult development and autonomy; and the section on practice shifts the focus to ways in which teaching and learning may be framed to encourage greater complexity of mind. However, this seemingly linear narrative is inevitably recursive, as research gives rise to theory, theory informs practice, and practice leads to new research.

RESEARCH

No concept is more central to what adult education is all about than self-directed learning.
—Mezirow

Looking back over the last 30 years of SDL research is like watching a Polaroid photograph develop. Some areas come into focus and develop finer detail while others only begin to appear. As the process continues, images that had seemed discrete are understood more clearly in relationship to one another and are finally recognized as part of a coherent whole. As it emerged as "the chief growth area in the field of adult education research" (Brookfield, 1984, p. 59), self-direction has been variously described as process, predisposition, and product.

Process or activity/skills research featured self-instruction, including programmed instruction, learning contracts, and other ways of individualizing the teaching and learning process (Brockett & Hiemstra, 1991; Caffarella & Caffarella, 1986; Oddi, 1987). A second research thread associated SDL with *predisposition*, such as personality, cognitive styles, self-efficacy, psychological orientation, learning styles, field dependence/independence, and autonomy (Chené, 1983; Joughin, 1992; Long, 1990; Oddi, 1987). A third thread suggested that SDL was potentially a *product* or learning outcome, perhaps related to critical thinking and possibly the result of using appropriate instructional methods (Garrison, 1997; Kasworm, 1983; Mezirow, 1985).

Self-Directed Learning as Process

In the early 1970s, Tough (1979) examined the learning habits of adults and found them exercising their own initiative in large and small ways in various learning projects. These activities were sometimes described as *self-education* or *self-instruction*, *individual learning*, and *self-initiated learning*, among other similar terms (Oddi, 1987). For example, an isolated or independent learner might choose to "go it alone," due either to lack of access (geography, time restrictions, disability) or a preference for independent learning. Most of these learners, having decided on their learning goals, would also design and execute self-created (although informal) learning plans. Such learning pursuits might include investigating an historical event, learning to play an instrument, or figuring out how to fix or build something around the house.

Correspondence classes or programmed instruction were a more formal approach, given that learning objectives and perhaps a structured learning plan would have been provided. Nevertheless, the learner was seen as controlling when, how, and how much she would engage with that learning. In more traditional, face-to-face educational settings, another approach to SDL was the use of learning contracts or self-designed degree plans, although both were negotiated with the instructor. In sum, SDL, which was defined by Brockett (1985a) as "a process where the learner assumes primary responsibility for planning, implementing, and evaluating a learning experience" (p. 211), was seen as a pragmatic choice based in part on convenience, possibly related to an independent learning style, and facilitated by tools that learners could be taught to use.

A major research emphasis was therefore to identify which tools, skills, and abilities were most effective (Oddi, 1986), but questions were raised about the adequacy of learners' self-direction, particularly at the outset: "It is only as the adult becomes aware of the standards, operations, procedures, and criteria deemed intrinsic to that skill or knowledge area that he or she can begin to set short- and long-term learning goals" (Brookfield, 1985, p. 10). Without sufficient knowledge of the topic, even a highly independent learner would likely be ineffective.

Opposite to concerns about learners' limitations were questions about whether truly self-directed learning could exist against a backdrop of institutional requirements for "coverage," testing, and grading. Brookfield (1993), for example, observed:

> Controlled self-direction is, from a political perspective, a contradiction in terms, a self-negating concept. . . . On the surface we may be said to be controlling our learning when we make decisions about pacing, resources, and evaluative criteria. But if the range of acceptable content has been pre-ordained . . . we are controlled rather than in control. . . . A fully developed self-directed learning project would have at its center an alertness to the possibility of hegemony. . . . A fully adult form of self-direction exists only when we examine our definitions of what we think it is important for us to learn and the extent to which these definitions serve repressive interests. (p. 234)

Brookfield (1985) was also concerned that if educators were viewed primarily as resources to and facilitators of the learner's self-directed process, thereby "restricted from presenting the adult with alternative ways of interpreting the world or of creating new personal and collective futures, then the educator becomes a kind of master technician who operates within a moral vacuum" (p. 6).

Self-Directed Learning as Predisposition

Knowles's (1975) claim that adults have an essential need for self-direction was widely cited and sometimes challenged in the emerging literature of adult and SDL (Ellsworth, 1992; Newman, 1993; Pratt, 1988; Robinson, 1992). In support of his claim, some pointed to the process of maturity from childhood to adulthood as demonstrating a gradual shift from dependence to independence and from reliance on others to self-reliance. Furthermore, as behaviorism was giving way to humanist psychology, theorists posited an ultimate stage of personal growth in which people would establish their individuality, take responsibility for their choices, and achieve a new kind of freedom from others' control. This included control of the learning process, because adults were believed to have the capacity to reflect on earlier, limiting experiences as a means toward greater self-determination (Kasworm, 1983). Empirical support was found in studies of adults' actual participation in self-constructed learning activities (Tough, 1979), which turned out to be frequent and ongoing.

Those who questioned Knowles's assertion noted that although many adults gave clear evidence of self-direction in their personal and professional lives, in educational settings, they might also choose teacher-directed learning, even when invited to participate in a more active way (Grow, 1991). Moreover, many adult learners expressed discomfort or irritation if the instructor deviated from expectations, for example, by adopting the role of facilitator and requiring students to engage in role-plays, group activities, or collaborative assignments.

By the mid-1980s, some were pointing out the conceptual limitations of focusing on self-instruction as the main theme of SDL, suggesting that it was time to move "beyond the focus on self-directed learning as a set of activities in a self-instructional process to a study of the motivational, cognitive, and affective characteristics or personalities of self-directed learners" (Oddi, 1987, p. 27). Various advantages were suggested for linking the study of personality characteristics with SDL, including looking for a more comprehensive way to examine aspects of self-direction.

Brockett and Hiemstra (1991) developed the Personal Responsibility model, suggesting that "the point of departure for understanding learning lies within the individual" (p. 27). What is called *personality* (including motivational, cognitive, and affective aspects) might be the very capacities and characteristics that enable SDL; or possibly, the attribute *self-directed learner* is but one aspect of the constellation called personality.

Also drawing on the notion that self-direction is a personal attribute, Guglielmino developed and refined a Self-Directed Learning Readiness Scale (SDLRS), which has been used in many educational, corporate, and training environments (Caffarella & Caffarella, 1986; Caffarella & O'Donnell, 1987; Guglielmino & Roberts, 1992). Some have questioned whether it assesses readiness (and therefore a predisposition) so much as familiarity with or skills developed in educational settings (Bonham, 1991; Brockett, 1985b; Brookfield, 1984; Field, 1990); others found that it provided useful insights (Delahaye & Smith, 1995; Long, 1987).

Other personality characteristics associated with SDL have included field independence, locus of control, and self-efficacy (Long, 1994). Although opinions differ, it is claimed that field-independent (FI) learners, who are likely to have an internal locus of control and greater facility with abstraction and analytical tasks like problem solving, perform better in an environment in which they are more autonomous and can exercise their own judgment; relational or field-dependent (FD) learners, by contrast, who are likely to have an external locus of control, are thought to perform better when they have support and feedback from others as well as more guidance from an instructor (Joughin, 1992). However, with age, "maturation and environmental stimuli," some FD learners become FI learners (Tullos, 2000, p. 9), once again raising the question of predisposition or development.

Autonomy also has at times been described as a predisposition, as when Knowles (1975) claimed that an adult whose self-concept is that of a self-directing (autonomous) person has a basic need or "requirement" to be a self-directed learner. Candy (1991), however, identified these as two different ideas of autonomy. The first, personal autonomy, is framed in terms of a self-determined, self-reflective way of thinking and acting in all life's arenas; the second, pedagogical autonomy, is described in terms of self-management of one's learning (which Candy further differentiates as either true autodidaxy or learner-control as opposed to teacher-control). Furthermore, "because a learner exercises control over dimensions of the teaching/learning situation does not mean that he or she is capable of exercising personal autonomy in the broader sense" associated with "really crucial questions such as the social, political, moral, or ideological dimensions of learning" (Candy, 1991, p. 21).

Motivational factors, the capacity for critical thinking, and meta-cognition are additional personal characteristics that affect an individual's participation in SDL (Garrison, 1997). The question remains whether such characteristics or dispositions are predispositions, hence innate, or may in some way be learned or developed. Similarly, are the different kinds of autonomy connected, and if so, how?

Self-Directed Learning as Product

Candy (1991) also underscored connections between the varying definitions of autonomy and the rather paradoxical assumption that the product of SDL is a self-directed learner:

> It is not uncommon to find . . . the assumption that all adults are autonomous or "self-directing" and that instruction should therefore be conducted in ways that acknowledge autonomy. On the other hand . . . adult educators constantly claim that the development of autonomy is a major goal of adult education. . . . How can they assume the existence of certain circumstances at the outset, and at the same time hold those circumstances to be the desired goal or outcome of their activities? (p. 122)

In addition, when the phrase *self-directed learning* is used for both the activity of learning and the goal of that learning, it implies a relationship that may not exist or, if it does, is not simple and obviously causal. For example, according to an instructor who used learning contracts with incarcerated students in a maximum security prison, "once an inmate accepts the responsibility for his own learning situation, he may very well be able to accept his responsibility as a member of society-at-large" (Boucouvalas & Pearse, 1982, p. 34).

By contrast, when Chené (1983) describes the autonomous learner, she suggests that it is not enough merely to use the mechanistic skills or tools of SDL; a learner who planfully sets goals, finds and uses resources, and defines and carries out procedures for evaluation but does so "within a framework of assumptions, expectations, allowable goals, and possible alternatives that is narrow and unchallenged" —that is, without critical thought—is not considered to have achieved true self-directedness (pp. 14–15). Managing particular learning tasks with relative independence ("autonomously") need not result in the overall independence of thought and action associated with personal autonomy. Candy (1991) echoes this when he distinguishes between "methods that encourage learner-control" with "more global qualities such as critical judgment, autonomous action, and self-initiated inquiry" (p. 123).

Although both kinds of autonomy have been frequently described as desired outcomes of SDL, and Freire (1992) and Lindeman (1961) framed the purposes of adult education in terms of enabling adults to question the status quo, the goal of personal growth leading to autonomy has been challenged as representing the excessive preoccupation with self so pervasive in Western culture (Brookfield, 1993). Long (1994) goes so far as to question whether SDL "is sometimes associated with a pathological overemphasis on individualism" (p. 16), and Grace (1996) decried the individual focus that leads to inattention to social context and cooperation in challenging the inequalities of social and economic structures. Critical theorists have also challenged what they see as humanistic educators' "misguided inclination" to frame SDL in terms of individual empowerment, thereby overlooking its political dimensions (Brookfield, 1993, p. 228). Nevertheless, Brookfield (1993) also suggests that although the hegemonic implications of SDL are inadequately considered, its potential to contribute to transformative and emancipatory education, and in that way to be a counterhegemonic force, is redeemable: "Most adult educators who stand behind the concept of self-direction do so because they sense that there is something about this form of practice that dignifies and respects people and their experience and that tries to break with authoritarian forms of education" (p. 229).

THEORY

We do not see things as they are,
we see them as we are.
—*Talmud*

Most developmental models have in common a vision of a lifelong process that moves individuals toward more fully expressing their human potential. Various models may have particular emphases, such as moral, spiritual, cognitive, personality, or ego development, and may describe the process in terms of stages, phases, crises, seasons, or dilemmas. Nevertheless, a recurring theme in descriptions of mature adult development ("mature" meaning somewhat beyond the legal threshold of 18–21 years but well before "senior"

status) is the increasing capacity to think for oneself. This implies that one not only questions and, if necessary, stands up to the will of the majority but also reflects on and questions one's own beliefs and assumptions, recognizing that they, too, must be subject to ongoing review and reconsideration.

These are the characteristics of autonomy, which Gibbs (1979) suggests "might be defined, broadly and ambiguously, as the capacity and habit of self-government in the entire conduct of one's affairs" (p. 121). Thus autonomy has both intellectual and moral dimensions. Although intellectual autonomy need not imply great creativity and imagination, it does suggest the ability to critically examine the assumptions of the social-cultural surround. Moral autonomy, by contrast, is "a disposition of character rather than intellect: self-mastery or self-discipline, having command of one's own feelings and inclinations" (Gibbs, 1979, p. 121). Considered in these ways, autonomy is a particular coherence in how one views oneself, the world, and oneself within the world.

Persons with this worldview are less subject to others' direction or vision, and more capable of creating their own vision (e.g., of what to do and how to do it) which, though not necessarily entirely original, is at least personally and thoughtfully chosen. Because they also recognize that no one is entirely free of another's influence, they are able and willing to monitor both the effects of that influence and their responses to it. Anyone familiar with the impulsivity, willfulness, self-centeredness, and suggestibility of children and adolescents recognizes the capacity for self-awareness as a truly adult development. Yet there is also ample evidence that many adults who seem old and experienced enough to have such a capacity apparently do not.

Constructive-developmental theory, which attends to qualitative changes in worldview—epistemology—over the life span, is particularly effective in describing both the characteristics and meaning of personal autonomy and the process of change that precedes it. This section therefore describes how notions of development and constructivism converge to describe, as Jankovic put it, "the beautiful and arduous task of becoming a person" (Candy, 1991, p. 15).

Constructivism

The concepts underlying constructivism can be traced to ancient Greece, where sophists and skeptics, among others, questioned the premise that it was possible to provide philosophical proofs for things that were known through individual perceptions. This theme recurred when Enlightenment philosophers Kant and Vico again claimed that knowledge was a construction based on interpretation of perception. The idea gained new traction in the mid-twentieth century, partly in response to discoveries in the field of particle physics. Heisenberg (1962) for example, famously said, "We have to remember that what we observe is not nature in itself but nature exposed to our method of questioning" (p. 58).

Although they began with different disciplinary frameworks, Kelly (1955), Piaget (1954), and Vygotsky (1978) all advanced constructivist thought in the twentieth century. Kelly's personal construct psychology held that from the moment of birth and throughout their lives, people interact with the world around them much as a scientist would, responding (albeit unconsciously) to new experiences by creating and testing hypotheses. These interactions, in turn, tend to determine people's future responses to what they (again unconsciously) perceive as similar experiences. This process of "construing" and "reconstruing" is based on experience and, as one becomes more self-aware, engenders increasingly effective self-reflection and analysis. Piaget, who studied children's understanding of themselves and the world around them, proposed a model of sequential stages that described major qualitative shifts in perception, always toward greater complexity of mind. The last of these stages, formal operations, which begins during adolescence, was thought to represent the threshold of psychological adulthood. One of Vygotsky's (1978) major additions to this constructivist perspective is his emphasis on the significance of the social context and the interdependence of individuals and their cultural surround. People learn and develop within a web of personal and social relationships that affect how one knows.

In short, the constructivist framework holds that rather than discovering an objective reality (learning knowledge that is separate from the knower), the knower creates (constructs) knowledge through interaction with and reaction to experience, which is also socially mediated. This is not to say that no objective reality exists, but that what we can know of it is always filtered through our perceptions, the limitations and imperfections of which are invisible to us.

Developmental Theory

Adult development may be broadly defined as "a process of qualitative change in attitudes, values, and understandings that adults experience as a result of ongoing transactions with the social environment, occurring over time but not strictly as a result of time" (Taylor, Marienau, & Fiddler, 2000, p. 10). Combining this with the basic concern of constructivism—"how people make sense of the perplexing variety and constantly changing nature of their experience" (Candy, 1991, p. 255)—leads to the underlying premise of constructive-developmental theory: that it describes *qualitative changes*, over time, in *how we interpret* our experiences (i.e., "make meaning").

Because they have focused on the role of education, certain constructive-developmental models are particularly relevant to the study of adult development and learning (see table 9.1): Perry's (1970) scheme of moral and intellectual development in the college years; Belenky, Clinchy, Goldberger, and Tarule's (1986) description of "women's ways of knowing"; Loevinger and Blasi's (1976) concepts of ego development; Basseches's (1984) description of dialectical thinking; and Kegan's (1994) elucidation of "transformation of consciousness"; this last is the primary theoretical framework for this chapter.

Transformation of Consciousness

Kegan (1994) uses an educational metaphor of "contemporary culture as a kind of 'school' and the complex set of tasks and expectations placed upon us in modern life as the 'curriculum' of that school" (p. 3) to introduce his model of development. Just as we might evaluate a school's curriculum for young people in terms of their capacity and readiness to meet those academic challenges, he proposes that we "*look at the curriculum of modern life in relation to the capacities of the adult mind*" (p. 5). However, in contrast to the transparent, published curriculum of a school or college, this is a hidden curriculum. There is no syllabus that sets out in advance the parameters of what must be learned, the kinds of learning experiences that should be undertaken, and the timing and form of the eventual assessments. Rather, our cultural surround creates these challenges—and, as Kegan demonstrates, the expectations of this curriculum are demonstrably more complex than those

TABLE 9.1. Three Constructive-Developmental Models

Perry: Moral and Intellectual Development[a]	Kegan: Orders of Consciousness[b]	Belenky et al.: Ways of Knowing[c]
Dualism • Right vs. wrong, we vs. they, black/white (rather than gray), either/or (also: my group is "righter" than those not like me/us) • Knowledge can be acquired • Source of knowledge is Authorities, who either have right answers now or eventually will • Expectation to someday become an Authority	**Instrumental (second order)** • Identifies with own interests, needs, and desires • Social contract is "what can you do for me?" • Lack of empathy • Characterized by dualistic thinking • Needs concrete directions; step-by-step procedures	**Received knowing** • Knowledge comes from others—friends, family, teachers, TV, etc. • No expectation to become an authority • Listens, has few opinions, remembers and reproduces knowledge • Conventional moral judgments (but potentially vulnerable to "cult" leaders)
Multiplicity/Relativism • Early: Everyone is entitled to his/her own opinion • Late: Some opinions are more justifiable than others—the point is to develop criteria • Even Authorities may not know everything	**Socializing (third order)** • Sense of self and values are derived from others • Uneasy with disagreements that suggest conflict and therefore threaten underlying connection • Needs clear expectations and unambiguous directions from authorities about what should be done	**Subjective/Procedural knowing** • "I know what I know"—"private" knowledge comes from "inner voice" or "gut feelings," but may apply only to oneself • Discomfort with ideas that contradict one's own • May use appropriate academic forms and procedures, but is primarily "following the rules" • *Recognizes underlying purpose of and uses appropriate methods, procedures, and rules for evaluating and creating knowledge.*
Commitment • Knowledge is contextual, values are situational • To live meaningful lives, one must make and commit to decisions in the face of relativism (i.e., absence of certainty), and also be open to reconsidering those decisions as new circumstances warrant	**Self-Authorizing (fourth order)** • Knowledge is consciously constructed • Values and ethics are situational • Ideas can be challenged and changed without loss of self • Awareness of and concern for the greater good	**Procedural/Constructed knowing** • *Recognizes own contribution to construction of knowledge* • Knowledge emerges from "a full two-way dialogue with both heart and mind"[d], integration of the voices of others, and (as appropriate) includes the "procedural" process of knowledge creation and evaluation • Passionate involvement with the collective good

[a]Perry (1970).
[b]Kegan (1982, 1994).
[c]Belenky, Clinchy, Goldberger, & Tarule (1986).
[d]Stanton (1996).

faced by most in our parents' and grandparents' generations.

Within the past half-century or so, powerful social changes have altered not only our definition of family but also our expectation of how to conduct those relationships. Similarly, the workplace has seen changes not only in the kinds of jobs available and the knowledge and training necessary to qualify for those jobs but also in the way many employees are expected to think about their work (Senge, 1991; Vaill, 1996). Increasing diversity in neighborhoods, schools, and workplaces requires increasing understanding of and even appreciation for unfamiliar (and perhaps even startlingly unexpected) ideas and behaviors. Education, which was once about "doing what the teacher wants," now asks for "self-direction," "self-assessment" (MacGregor, 1993), and "critical thinking" (Brookfield, 1989). Modern culture has, in effect, upped the ante for most adults in Western society, leading to a sense that we are "in over our heads" in terms of "the mental demands of modern life" (Kegan, 1994). By comparison, in societies in which these changes have not been so pervasive, it may still be possible for adults merely to do as they were taught by their parents and others who keep and transmit that society's cultural wisdom.

Kegan (2000) describes his as a model of epistemological *trans-form-ation*—a change in the form of knowing. With each such shift in consciousness, the individual becomes capable of making or constructing meaning in more complex ways. This is not solely about cognition, however, because how one makes meaning also determines how one feels or experiences:

> It is not that a person makes meaning, as much as that the activity of being a person is the activity of meaning-making. . . . There is thus no feeling, no experience, no thought, no perception, independent of a meaning-making context in which it *becomes* a feeling, an experience, a thought, a perception, because we *are* the meaning-making context. (Kegan, 1982, p. 11)

However, as Heisenberg (1962) and the *Talmud* tried to alert us, because the world we construct, our "reality," is always a product of the way in which we perceive (which is, in turn, a function of our epistemology or level of consciousness), we are unable to see that it is our perception. This is the concept of embeddedness, which is intuitively understood through two familiar sayings: "the eye cannot see itself," and "you can't ask a fish about water." Whatever epistemology we are currently embedded in, or subject to, is invisible to us (Kegan, 1982). We therefore cannot reflect on or observe (question, challenge, describe, examine, perceive, explore, recognize) our worldview, because it *is* our worldview. Only when we have begun to grow beyond its limitations—when it is object to us (Kegan, 1982)—can we begin to see those limitations, in (as it were) an epistemological rearview mirror. Therefore, when an adult's ability to perceive, feel, and experience (in other words, to construct reality) changes, it seems instead that everything *else* has changed—one's job, spouse, social environment, perhaps even one's aging parents. Daloz (1999) captured the peculiar nature of this nonrealization when he observed:

> This does not mean that the old world has been abandoned; rather . . . it is *seen* in a new way. The journey does not take away our old experiences, as we often fear before we embark. It simply gives them new meaning. . . . Nothing is different, yet all is transformed. . . . In this change of perspective, in the transformation of meaning lies the meaning of transformation. (p. 27)

Orders of Consciousness

Kegan (1982, 1994, 2000) describes five orders of consciousness. The first of these is a position of childhood (impulsive), and the last (self-transforming) is achieved by so few adults that it is not relevant to this discussion (see conclusion of this chapter for a brief description). I therefore focus on instrumental (second-order), socializing (third-order), and self-authorizing (fourth-order) ways of knowing.

Instrumental Way of Knowing.   Instrumental knowers are concerned with facts and want to "get" knowledge (or, by extension, educational certification of some kind) for utilitarian reasons, such as to earn more pay. As concrete thinkers, they cannot abstract or interpret; nor can they hold points of view other than their own. They are intently focused on doing things "right" and expect to be told with great specificity what that entails. "Instrumental learning is learning how to; it does not deal with why" (Mezirow, 1985, p. 18). Probably fewer than 5% of adults see the world solely from an instrumental perspective (Kegan, 1994, p. 193) and, given the demands of most college curricula, such adults are unlikely to be found in higher education settings. In a recent study of adult basic education/English for speakers of other languages (ESOL) students, the fewer than 10% who saw the world in this way were also those who had had very restricted access to education due to recent immigration or limited language skills (Kegan et al., 2001).

Socializing Way of Knowing.   Socialized knowers' purposes and desires for education and knowledge are connected to their feelings of responsibility to and for others. In addition, since they derive their sense of self from others' opinions of them, education may also hold the promise of others' esteem or approval. As do instrumental knowers, socialized knowers need clear guidance, but they are much more vulnerable to critical feedback. Critical feedback is likely to be interpreted by such knowers less as suggestions for improvement than as commentary on their essential worthiness. Empirical evidence suggests that most adults in Western society have developed at least some capacities of the socialized system of meaning (Kegan, 1994, p. 195).

Self-Authoring Way of Knowing.   Self-authoring knowers value education for who they may become— but "become" in terms of their own goals and standards, not for others' approval. They have begun to recognize ways that they are more in charge of their own life process and therefore seek to enhance those capabilities further. This is not narcissistic self-involvement, but rather acknowledgment that they are individuals within a collective (in contrast to the socializing knower, whose fusion with the collective means that the group's assumptions are "reality" and unchallenged). For self-authorizing knowers, learning encompasses the possibility of "changing as a person" (Marton & Booth, 1997). They therefore gladly entertain others' counsel, yet still reserve for themselves the right to evaluate that counsel. As compared with socialized knowers, who may perceive difference as uncomfortable or threatening, self-authorizing knowers greet the unfamiliar as a possible source of new understandings and perspectives. Self-authorizing knowers are more prevalent among professional and highly educated adults, but still account for less than half that population; among those adults who have less education and fewer economic advantages, the self-authorizing way of knowing may account for only one-fifth of the population (Kegan, 1994).

Limitations of Consciousness

The achievement of each way of knowing is ultimately also its limitation. In the case of the socialized mind, its achievement is to have internalized the relevant cultural rules of adulthood as the self-centered instrumental orientation transformed into a new mutuality and capacity for empathy and connection (see table 9.2). The limitation is that those self-same rules are now

TABLE 9.2.   From Instrumental to Socializing Way of Knowing

Instrumental (Second Order)	Socializing (Third Order)
Has relationship to others who are seen and valued in terms of what they can provide: "I need you to meet my needs."*	Is in relationship with others who are seen and valued in terms of the connection they represent. Self and other co-construct reality. Acceptance and approval are ultimate concerns.
Social contract based on self-interest: maintains own point of view; unempathetic.	Social contract based on mutuality; internalizes others' points of view; empathetic.
Moral/ethical code: "My needs are primary. If I concern myself with your needs, it is only to the extent that they don't conflict with mine; I have no guilt about meeting my needs at your expense."*	Moral/ethical code includes guilt and hyper-awareness of others' needs, even those unstated or imagined: "I am responsible for your feelings; you are responsible for mine."*
Concrete, descriptive identity, e.g., name, gender, "things I like," perhaps family association; the concept of an abstract identity is meaningless.	Identifies (not necessarily consciously) as member of group, family, culture, race, religion, etc. also identified by job, relationships, affiliations.

*Because people are unaware of the worldview to which they are subject, these perspectives would be neither recognized nor verbalized.

Note. Adapted from *Developing Adult Learners: Strategies for Teachers and Trainers*, by K. Taylor, C. Marienau, and M. Fiddler, 2000, San Francisco: Jossey-Bass.

TABLE 9.3. From Socializing to Self-Authoring Way of Knowing

Socializing (Third Order)	Self-Authoring (Fourth Order)
In relationship with others; the level of mutuality and empathy approaches fusion; differences are perceived as threatening.	In relationship *to relationships*: Can set limits and boundaries; differences are respected, even valued.
Values, morals, and ethics based on group, family, and cultural imperatives; norms and assumptions are invisible and unquestioned.	Has values *about values*: They are perceived as contextual, situational, and constructed; former assumptions can be surfaced, examined, accepted, or rejected.
[Early] "I know what I've heard": knowledge comes from others/received knowing.* [Late] "I *just know* what I know (for myself) but I also want to know what you think I *should* know (for you)": knowledge comes from the self; subjective knowing.*	Has ideas *about ideas*: Explores where knowledge comes from, who is responsible for it, how and by whom it is constructed; "authorizes" knowledge, critically evaluates own and others' ideas. Sees self and others as generators/constructors of knowledge; is able to weigh and integrate the various contributions.
Identity constructed by/through others; others responsible for own feelings; self responsible for others' feelings and states of mind.	Identity self-constructed; aware of and sensitive to others, but not responsible for others' states of mind or feelings; others not responsible for own.
Looks out through others' eyes.**	Sees self through own eyes; internal dialogic relationship to the self.***

*These epistemological positions are further described by Belenky et al. (1986) in their model of *Women's Ways of Knowing*.
**As described by Koller (1982).
***As described by Basseches (1984).

Note. Adapted from *Developing Adult Learners: Strategies for Teachers and Trainers*, by K. Taylor, C. Marienau, and M. Fiddler, 2000, San Francisco: Jossey-Bass.

running the show, and their invisibility makes them unavailable to challenge. Furthermore, because those cultural rules are nearly always exclusionary in some way, the feelings of connection and empathy are primarily available to "those like us" (in essence, and subconsciously: those whose cultural rules are not so different from our own as to challenge our fundamental assumptions about what is right, true, and good).

Kegan (1994) describes this as the "family religion" (pp. 266–267) and the socializing way of knowing as the ultimate induction into its mysteries and expectations. It is not related to any particular notion of the divine, but is rather a set of beliefs, understandings, values, assumptions, interdictions, and prejudices that affect every aspect of life—and, given the changes described at the beginning of this chapter, may be increasingly problematic for people whose worldview it is.

Some adults, however, eventually develop beyond the limits of the socialized meaning system, although if this happens at all, it will occur several years after the previous transformation (see table 9.3). Now people discover that they have choices, whereas before there were only imperatives. Now they are no longer at the mercy of the "shoulds" and "what will others think?"

Kegan (1994) specifically identifies the shift to self-directed learning—"take initiative; set our own goals and standards; use experts, institutions, and other resources to pursue these goals; take responsibility for our direction and productivity in learning" (p. 303)—as one of the hallmarks of the self-authoring epistemology. However, given the empirical evidence as to the prevalence of this way of knowing, many adults learners will not yet be self-directed when they enter adult learning environments. Kegan therefore cautions:

> Higher education will disappoint the real learning needs of many modern adults if it assumes that the hidden curriculum, inside and outside school, is already mastered; if it tries to train adults to master that curriculum (by focusing too exclusively on the skills and behaviors associated with mastery) rather than to *educate* adults to the order of consciousness that enables those skills and behaviors. (p. 287)

In short, the capacity for the kind of self-direction that is associated with personal autonomy is a function of complexity of mind. Those adults who are already beyond the threshold of the self-authoring epistemology arrive at the classroom door with the "skills" of SDL and may appear to have the right kind of "personality." What, then, of those adults, currently in the majority, who have not yet reached that threshold? How does one teach another to direct his or her own learning if that person's basic assumption—or "reality"—is that learning is what students do in response to what the teacher says?

PRACTICE

If you become aware that something is in a certain way, then you also become aware that it could be in some other way.
— *Marton and Booth (1997)*

Two research streams currently explore teaching that enables various approaches to self-direction. The first includes teaching and learning strategies that are known to encourage active student involvement and cooperation in planning, execution, and assessment. These include, for example, case study, problem-based learning, action learning, and study circles. The second stream includes particular models of instruction focused specifically on self-direction; as examples, the individualizing instruction process of Hiemstra and Sisco (1990), the staged self-directed learning model of Grow (1991), and the nine-step procedure of Hammond and Collins (1991).

This section on practice will take a different tack by exploring strategies that are not the subject of an existing body of literature but arise at the intersection of adult development and learning. By examining experiences of teaching and learning through a developmental lens, I hope to encourage educators to apply the underlying principles in ways that will best suit their own subject matters and teaching styles.

To begin, I expand briefly on the developmental constructs already introduced to provide a context for better understanding how most adult learners experience learning and the suggestion that they be self-directed. Following that, I describe both educational activities designed with learners' development in mind and educators' roles in creating the most effective environments for those activities.

Subject-Object Shift

[The core of an epistemology] always consists of a relationship or temporary equilibrium between the subject and the object in one's knowing. . . .

That which is "object" we can look at, take responsibility for, reflect upon, exercise control over, integrate with some other way of knowing. That which is "subject" we are run by, identified with, fused with, at the effect of. We cannot be responsible for that to which we are subject. What is "object" in our knowing describes the thoughts and feelings we say we have; what is "subject" describes the thinking and feeling that has us. We "have" object; we "are" subject. (Kegan, 2000, p. 53)

Learners embedded in (subject to) the socialized mind have many ideas but do not yet understand how they came to have those ideas. They can identify the authoritative sources of some of their ideas, such as the teacher or text, and perhaps even acknowledge some less authoritative sources, such as friends and neighbors, family members, the media, and so on, but these learners cannot see that whatever the source of their information, their ideas are ultimately their own construction. In other words, they cannot hold as object the very process of having ideas. Self-authoring knowers, by contrast, consciously reconstruct knowledge, rather than trying to reproduce it (Marton & Booth, 1997). Socializing knowers' lack of objectivity is not limited to cognition; they also do not realize that their feelings originate in themselves! "You make me so angry" is the reality of the person who operates from the socializing way of knowing.

Given the different worldviews, understandings, and expectations of a group of typical adult learners, some of the well-honed tools of SDL, such as learning contracts, may not work as intended. Imagine the following conversation with a learner who has come to consult you about how to approach this unfamiliar assignment.

You, reassuringly: "Okay, let's look at this in context. What is a learning contract?"

Adam: "A document that includes learning goals and objectives as well as a plan to accomplish them." [Chances are, these are some of the words you used in introducing the topic in class.]

You: "Okay, but what is its purpose?"

Adam: "To enable adults to be more self-directed in their learning." [Note the at-arm's-length description.]

You: "How does it accomplish this?" [or] "How does it work?" [or even] "How does it help you do that?"

Adam: "By providing a structure and format to carry out the learning plan" [or] "By specifying the steps of the process" [or even] "By giving me a map of what I have to do."

This student is giving you definitions, probably gleaned from course material, about *it*—the learning contract, which he sees as *doing* a mandated process comparable to following the directions in an instructor's syllabus.

Now let's imagine a conversation with a different learner.

You, reassuringly: "What is a learning contract?"

Eve: "A way for me to figure out what I'm doing and why I'm doing it."

You: "Okay, but what is its purpose?"

Eve: "For us to agree on what I'm going to do in this course."

You: "How does it accomplish this?" [or] "How does it work?" [or even] "How does it help you do that?"

Eve: "By getting me to think about the parts in advance and lay it out so we can look it over together" [or] "By getting me to break it out in steps that we can talk about" [or even] "By requiring me to map it out so that you can see where I'm going."

To underscore the contrast, Eve is self-reflective, sees the learning contract as a process of which she is in charge, recognizes it as a tool to help her accomplish her own purposes, and acknowledges the role of the instructor as resource and guide. Although it may not be evident here, she can also recognize her own knowledge deficits without experiencing them as a problem for which the teacher is bound to provide a solution.

It is unclear to what degree Adam, even after being shown how to describe behavioral objectives and parse the learning venture into goals, objectives, methods, and assessment, will change his attitudes toward learning. Adults who approach learning from instrumental or socializing perspectives can become endlessly frustrated when the teacher insists that they are to make decisions for themselves. If one could hear their unconscious response to, say, the request to define their goals and objectives, it would be along the lines of: "Why do you keep asking me what I want! *What do you want me to want?*" Such learners also may be regarded as "field dependent" with an "external locus of control," but perhaps it is more accurate to say that they simply do not yet know, of their own certain knowledge, that only they are in charge of their learning.

How learners approach writing assignments is also linked to their ways of knowing. Many instrumental learners do a brain dump on the page and may not bother to reread, edit, or even spell-check. Once the assignment is done, they are finished with it. Socializing learners, by contrast, care what the teacher will think of them and may therefore pay excessive attention to details. In fact, socializing learners' anxieties often lead to procrastination or to the request that they be permitted to redo assignments so they can "do it right."

Demanding of such knowers that they perform beyond their epistemological capabilities can lead to the learner feeling diminished, often expressed as "feeling stupid." Critical feedback coupled with an undesirable grade will diminish them further. They "put in a lot of effort" to do what they were "supposed" to, yet the teacher is clearly displeased! Given that their self-image is dependent on the authority's approval, even if they do not fail the course, their experience of learning and of themselves as learners will be negatively affected. And some will choose to withdraw from the educational environment, which is the apparent source of their anxiety and frustration.

The most vexing issue, therefore, in teaching for self-direction, is that we are asking many adult learners to *go out of their minds*. The way they understand themselves as learners, the process of learning, the role of the instructor, what knowledge is—all of this is built around the absolute, secure, and unquestioned knowledge that the teacher "learns them."

The task of such learners is to carefully think about the directions they have been given, ask questions that will clarify the teacher's intentions for them, perform in ways that the teacher has stipulated as indicating good performance and competence, and get good grades on the assessments the teacher devises for them. It is no surprise, then, that these learners want to know "how many pages?" "will this be on the test?" and (my personal favorite) "did I miss anything important when I was absent?"—"important" being synonymous with something that the teacher will expect them to know. Furthermore, their assessment of their own capabilities, their goodness and worth as learners —in fact, as people—is overwhelmingly dependent on the approving judgments of their teachers. A "bad" grade (which for some adults is anything less than an A) is not merely an assessment of performance in a particular instance but a reflection on their essential being, because (albeit unconsciously) "I am what you think of me." These are learners for whom the syllabus is a kind of Bible that is regularly consulted for both its wise counsel and stern interdictions, and changes to it as the course unfolds are tantamount to tinkering with holy writ.

This description is not intended to infantilize or demean adult learners, most of whom are courageous, tenacious, and passionate about learning *in the way they understand learning*. It is meant to demonstrate the enormous psychological, cognitive, and affective chasm that separates self-authoring knowers from instrumental and socializing knowers—who cannot choose a different epistemology just because someone suggests that they now become self-directed learners (see table 9.4).

In fact, they cannot fully understand the suggestion that they become self-directed, which is likely to leave them frustrated and bewildered. Why, after all they have done to follow the teacher's directives, is the teacher unsatisfied? This can be particularly upsetting for learners who have worked hard to master procedural knowing, which is expected in most academic settings (Belenky et al., 1986). They have finally developed good study skills, may have struggled with the intricacies of the thesis outline, slogged through the minutiae of when and how to use citations, and tried to present balanced perspectives. They have done what they understood it was good and necessary to do, only to discover (probably after receiving a less than desirable grade) that it is somehow insufficient. Unfortunately, these knowers do not see the difference between the form and the purpose of the procedural process.

From their perspective, the learning task is getting and doing: Such learners attempt to get knowledge by doing what is asked of them. Learning, therefore, is accretion—knowing is knowing more. Knowledge—or at least the important knowledge that they have come to get—is external to them, the province of authorities who "have" it. Specifically with regard to the socializing way of knowing, Kegan (1994) says:

> Their writing is addressed to us primarily on behalf of their loyalty or devotion to the bonds that join us . . . but we would also like them to be writing to parts of themselves, conducting an inner conversation. . . . We would like them to listen to and consider our evaluation, to be sure, but not to be *determined* by it. But this would require an

TABLE 9.4. Developmental Orientations to Knowing and Learning

Orientation to Knowing: Epistemology	Instrumental	Socializing	Self-Authorizing
Source of knowledge	• Authorities, texts	• Authorities: teachers, texts • Own belief and opinion (though these may not be openly expressed)	• Self (constructor of knowledge through experience, reflection, analysis), but thoughtfully uses teacher, texts, authorities
Purpose of learning, education	• Get skill • Satisfy current needs • Address concrete goals	• Get recognition for achievement • Fulfill expectations (e.g. of family, community, society)	• Become more self-aware and effective • Develop self toward new life roles and responsibilities • Change and grow
Learner's tasks/ **challenges**	• Follow rules • Do things "right" • **Engage in abstraction** • **Entertain multiple perspectives**	• Figure out and do what teacher wants • Get good grades or other approval • **Set own goals and standards** • **Thoughtfully question experts/authorities**	• Take initiative, engage actively • Generate one's own standards • Assess one's effectiveness as a learner • **Recognize the ideological nature of one's assumptions**
Learner's perception of educators' role	• Provide information • Provide structure • Be "fair"	• Keeper of academic process: sets unambiguous expectations, assignments • Caring source of affirmation, approbation	• Knowledgeable about academic matters, but essentially a peer • Resource/guide, source of useful feedback, critique • Open to learner's feedback

Source: Adapted from Kegan (1982, 1994), Drago-Severson (2004), and Chickering (1981).

internal system for self-evaluation [a self-authoring capacity]. . . . We would like them to understand that when we told them to think for themselves, we did not really mean "be sincere, use your own opinions," but that's what it means to them. We want them to hear "think for yourself" as something more like "take charge of the concepts of the course and independently bring them to an issue of your own choosing." . . . But as far as they are concerned, *every* single thing they are doing that we would prefer they do otherwise is highly selfdirected! It's just that the "self" they are directing is not the one we want! (pp. 284–285)

Scaffolding and Construction of Knowledge

At one level, the solution to the problem, "how can epistemological transformation occur in adult learners?" is profoundly simple: They *change their minds*. However, the educator's not so simple task is to provide the context that will enable them, over time, to do so. The overarching metaphor for strategies that will encourage this transformation is *scaffolding*. A scaffold is a temporary structure that permits construction of a more permanent one. For example, in a high-rise building or bridge, the scaffold advances just ahead of the concrete and steel, giving the workers a place to stand while they continue building.

Scaffolding is a well-established educational process (Applebee & Langer, 1983). Vygotsky's (1978) zone of proximal development is a similar notion. It is the space between what a learner can do on her own and what she can do with someone's help. Given that most courses last a few months at most (and in today's world of accelerated learning, perhaps only a few weeks), it is also important to develop learners' capacities for self-scaffolding.

One approach to scaffolding is to create situational activities that invite adults to experience themselves building the structures that support them in building still further. This notion of situation is borrowed from Dewey (1963/1979), who described the equal parts played by both objective and internal factors in educative experience:

Any normal experience is an interplay of these two sets of conditions. Taken together, or in their interaction, they form what we call a *situation*. The trouble with traditional education was not

that it emphasized the external conditions that enter into the control of the experiences but that it paid so little attention to the internal factors which also decide what kind of experience is had. (p. 42)

This may help explain how a learning environment that uses none of the traditional tools of SDL can still claim to be about self-directed learning. Even if most of the course details (texts, assignment, assessments) are in the control of the instructor, when adults are asked to pay close attention to their interpretation of experience (and to the internal factors that decide why they are experiencing it in certain ways), they become increasingly aware that they are, in fact, the source ("constructors") of at least some of their own knowledge. This key to this discovery, from a phenomenographic perspective (Marton & Booth, 1997), is to experience it. The educator's role is therefore to create multiple opportunities for learners to experience themselves learning in this new way.

This awareness of themselves as constructors of meaning is essential to learning that is understanding, as opposed to knowledge acquisition, because even when course materials contradict their existing beliefs, socialized knowers may unconsciously compartmentalize the contradiction to avoid any challenge to their underlying certainty. Such learners may appear to take in the new information but in fact may "isolate [the] discovery in the world of academics alone and never allow it to raise questions about [their] own life and purposes" (Perry, 1970, p. 13). It is much more difficult to compartmentalize in this way when participating in situational exercises that require the construction of knowledge, rather than its absorption. Even if they are not immediately conscious of doing so, adult learners who are called on to examine their experiences, express their observations, and then refine this exploration through dialog and "discourse that encourages them to become more critically reflective of their assumptions and those of others" (Mezirow, 2000, p. 350) participate in "making meaning." Thus they may "become aware of the uncritically assimilated assumptions that underlie their habitual behavior" (Brookfield, 1991, p. 13).

For these reasons, both the construction of knowledge and scaffolding are the underpinnings, or perhaps meta-strategies, of the situational activities that follow.

Characteristics of Situational Activities

Situational experiences engage adults in doing something, usually involving small groups of peer learners. The activity may last for a few minutes or take place over several weeks, be simple or multifaceted, require props, or depend almost entirely on discussion. Content-rich activities can illuminate or add depth to a particular reading assignment; process-focused activities can be used across disciplinary boundaries. The common thread is that initially or eventually the activities place learners in an open-ended, unscripted situation. With the possible exception of following a few basic ground rules, learners are in charge of themselves and of supporting one another as they work through the activity. For simplicity's sake, I categorize the examples that follow as discussion, "as if," "tipping," and shifting implicit to explicit. This is hardly an exhaustive list; rather these are just a few approaches to teaching with "developmental intentions" (Taylor et al., 2000). In fact, these categories may be seen to overlap, because the overriding purpose of situational experiences is to stretch and scaffold a learner's way of knowing.

Discussion

To be effective, most situational activities need also to involve collaborative examination or exploration of the experience. Such examination requires that learners express their ideas and feelings while also listening to and considering others' ideas and feelings in order "to participate fully and freely to arrive at a tentative best reflective judgment" (Mezirow, 2000, p. 305). This is most effective when the group attempts to develop a collective understanding, wherein the outcomes depend on and derive from the input of all the participants. Strategies that build understanding in this way are preferable to those that focus on "information," "answers," and the kind of learning that begins and ends with the authority of teacher or text, as the latter prove to be far less effective in developing understanding (Marton & Booth, 1997, p. 174).

These activities work best when there is a thoughtfully organized structure to guide the collaborative exploration, rather than a formless and often pointless small group discussion. Relatively unstructured discussions can be fruitful for learners who are already well along in their development as self-authorizing

knowers. But for instrumental and socializing knowers, discussion can devolve into position-taking (because, unconsciously, "I know what I know"), chitchat ("I'm not comfortable disagreeing with you, so we won't say anything of importance; besides, I don't know what's expected of me"), or a rehash of what has previously been said ("This is safe ground, and it might be what the teacher wants to hear").

Being invited to discuss is most likely understood as "to state one's opinion in response to others' opinions," but "a socializing knower cannot evaluate other people's points of view without risk to his or her own self; the self does not know itself as separate from the interpersonal context in which is embedded" (Drago-Severson, 2004, pp. 25–26). Without good guidance about what the goals of discussion are and how best to engage in effective exchange, unstructured small group discussion can leave students confused, anxious about not knowing what is expected of them, and frustrated at the apparent waste of time ("Why isn't the teacher doing her job!?")

"As If"

Another situational approach is to invite learners to engage as if they were more complex knowers; for example, role-plays and scenarios in which learners participate as if they saw things from a perspective other than their own. Such situations permit learners to try out or try on (Mezirow, 2000) a different way of doing or seeing without necessarily committing to it.

Though Kegan (1994) did not frame it in terms of as if, his description suggests that William Perry, then director of the Harvard Bureau of Study Skills, created such an experience to enable slow readers (their self-characterization) to try on a new way of reading. At the time, Harvard University was faced with an influx of adult learners who were largely unprepared for the demands of their reading assignments. The problem, as the learners saw it, was that they needed to read faster to get through the many pages of text. In response, Perry set up regular group exercises that focused on reading speed, even though he knew that only marginal improvements would result. However, along with this skills development effort, he provided a brief text that he told them *not* to read, just to quickly skim, looking for answers to questions he had posed. At another time, he suggested that they skim but not read another handout, beginning first with the conclusion, because that was where the major points were likely to be summarized, and then look for answers to one or two questions that they had formed from skimming the summary. And so on. When these adults eventually returned to reading their regular course assignments, many discovered that by reading "as if" they were directing their own purpose, their way of thinking about their task as readers and learners had changed. From our perspective, they had begun to approach a text proactively (we might say, self-directedly), rather than as passive consumers of words, sentences, and paragraphs.

"Tipping" Experiences

This notion of tipping derives from the Piagetian description of development as a series of balances—that is, times of "dynamic stability" between the forces of assimilation (of new experiences by existing ways of knowing) and accommodation (of existing ways of knowing to new experiences) (Kegan, 1982, p. 44). Against this backdrop, anything that encourages movement toward a more complex way of knowing may be said to tip the existing balance, thus creating what Mezirow (2000) calls the "disorienting dilemma" that can lead to transformational learning.

For the socialized knower, who depends on others for his or her sense of self and whose connection to others precludes criticizing them, being invited to participate in peer evaluation and self-evaluation may be such a dilemma. This is particularly effective with assignments that call for interpretation and analysis, rather than just report or description. Because reading between the lines is not a strength for these learners, built-in ambiguity prevents them from resolving differences by reference to facts.

In setting up the initial assignment, in addition to providing careful directions, educators can also share with learners their grading criteria, ideally in the form of a rubric. Rubrics generally describe in detail the qualities of a well-developed assignment, with clear indication of what constitutes excellent, above average, average, or unacceptable work. As one example, if the writing task involves applying a theoretical model, one section of the rubric might specify "cites and *interprets* relevant sections of theoretical model; does not merely follow an unsubstantiated assertion with a citation." It would also include some evaluative description of how well the learner had accomplished the task; for example, gradations from novice to experienced—or even more specific assessments (perhaps reflecting a point

system tied to grading) such as "exceptional, insightful," "consistently meets expectations," "partially meets expectations," "off-task, missing," or whatever is most appropriate for the particular assignment.

After learners have drafted the assignment, they read and react to one another's papers in small groups, using the detailed rubric as their guide (with clear instructions not to proofread, edit, or judge their classmates' efforts). From a developmental perspective, there is enough teacher-supplied direction to provide a sense of security to those who depend on it. However, the shifting component in such an encounter is the assumption that only the teacher can determine what is right or "how well I did." Instead, learners are given sufficient supportive structure to begin to evaluate others and themselves. Based on that dialogue and feedback, students can devise and submit their own revision plans for the assignment (as if they were self-evaluating!), thus encouraging even greater assumption of responsibility for their own work.

Shifting Implicit to Explicit

Another common thread in situational approaches is that of encouraging adults to make explicit key aspects of their process of learning and knowing that have been largely implicit. A substantial body of literature on focused self-reflective activities supports this endeavor. For example, various kinds of journals (Walden, 1995; Zeichner & Liston, 1987) and self-assessments (MacGregor, 1993; Taylor, 1995) as well as reflection on particular aspects of learning (Boud, Keogh, & Walker, 1985; Candy, Harri-Augstein, & Thomas, 1985) or reflection as an overall strategy (Taylor et al., 2000) can be used. Activities such as these involve adults in regularly examining who they are and how they think, reflect, and function within the context of their learning (Taylor, Booth, & Lamoreaux, 2004).

Some learners may have difficulty with even the first step of this journey. What was supposed to be an examination of their experiences of learning are instead diaries of what they said or did; self-assessments devolve into reports of what the teacher and classmates did or did not do. Most poignant, some self-reflections underscore the learner's inability to think about learning in any way other than as controlled by the teacher. As one learner said in an end-of-course self-assessment: "What I have learned from this class is to read and re-read the assignments. This way when you turn it in you are on the same page as your instructor." Nevertheless, the capacity for more effective self-reflection can be modeled, encouraged, and supported, largely through positive feedback that at every opportunity catches the learner doing something right.

Mezirow (2000) further examines relationships between reflection and transformative learning—the kind of learning that can lead to a more complex epistemology:

> Learning occurs in one of four ways: by elaborating existing frames of reference, by learning new frames of reference, by transforming points of view, or by transforming habits of mind. . . . We transform frames of reference—our own and those of others—by becoming critically aware of their assumptions and aware of their context—the source, nature, and consequences of taken-for-granted beliefs. (p. 19)

Through self-reflection, adults can begin to identify these lingering assumptions—an essential first step toward changing them, as another learner's self-assessment reveals:

> In reflecting, I have found a lot of the motives behind why I do what I do. My reactions, my choices, the way I deal with the less favorable outcome and the pain I cause myself. Cause myself is the key word here because I have the ability to affect the way I feel. No one else should be able to make me feel bad about myself. Much easier said than done.

Autobiography-based assignments are a particular form of self-reflection. With instrumental learners, who have an undeveloped capacity for introspection, such assignments are unlikely to produce more than a narrative of names, dates, and places. For socializing learners, however, the act of capturing in words significant experiences of one's life creates some distance from those experiences. Rather than being entirely subject to and embedded in their life story, they begin to hold parts of it as object. The process of prior learning assessment, which enables reentry adults to petition for course credit based on extra-mural learning (Council for Adult and Experiential Learning, 2000), can be a powerful vehicle for such reflection, because it often requires students to examine their lives within a disciplinary framework (Taylor, 2000). As a result,

learners begin to see their lives from the "outside in" (as object) rather than only (subjectively) from the "inside out" (Droegkamp & Taylor, 1995) and, in so doing, tip toward a more complex way of knowing.

The Educator's Role

The discussion so far has focused on learners and the activities that may enable them to experience learning as the active pursuit of meaning, and experience themselves as constructors of knowledge. But educators who wish to support SDL can do more than design situational activities. We are likely to be most effective in encouraging the epistemological development that encompasses personal autonomy if we more deeply understand the adult's developmental process, the need for challenge and support, and the meaning of "holding environment" (Kegan, 1982, 1994). Finally, we are likely to be more effective in supporting our learners' growth and development if we also reflect on our own journey of development.

Understanding Development

It is important to be measured and nuanced when designing activities to encourage learners toward a more self-authoring experience of learning. Especially when learners have been accustomed to (and have a sense of having thrived in) another kind of environment, suddenly "transplanting" them to a different ecosystem can lead to withering rather than new growth. The key to asking for just enough but not too much is to be empathetically attentive to and understanding of both where our learners mostly are and where they are mostly going. This does not mean that we need to know precisely where each learner is, epistemologically speaking, to teach effectively. In fact, according to Basseches (1984), "cultivation by teachers of general attitudes supportive of developmental processes and sensitive to developmental possibilities, is more beneficial than the explicit 'tracking' of students by developmental stage" (p. 302).

Kegan (1994) observes that an essential aspect of developmentally supportive attention is to reach out to students where they are, while at the same time offering them a bridge to where they might go. By definition, a bridge is anchored in two places—in this case, in both the current epistemology and the emerging one. Perry responded to his slow readers by giving them the speed-reading drills they knew they needed. But he also created opportunities for them to experience reading in a new way. He accepted, without protest, their current view of learning, way of knowing, and perspective on what it means to be a student, while at the time same pointing toward a new perspective and possibility. Horton and Freire (1990) underscored the importance of this approach: "We cannot educate if we don't start—and I said *start* and not *stay*—from [where] people perceive themselves, their relationships with others and with reality, because this is precisely what makes their knowledge.... The question is to know what they know and *how they know*" (p. 66; second emphasis added).

Another advantage of understanding their process of adult development is being able to mirror learners' growth. Just as self-reflection is important, so is reflection from others. When they leave the classroom, they often return to an environment that pulls them toward its own balance, where the growth and change of one of its members may be perceived as a threat to that social system. By reflecting to them the changes we see, we help them hold on to the possibility of a new way of being.

Challenge and Support

Most educational environments for adults tend to be short on support and long on challenge (Daloz, 1999). Moreover, as King and Kitchener (1994) pointed out, "when educators actively engage students in a developmental process, they are involving them in activities that are intrinsically emotional as well as cognitive" (p. 246), and though faculty members are attuned to the intellectual challenges of the educative process, they are much less likely to recognize the emotional challenges. A learning environment that asks adults to fundamentally reconsider the way they view the world and everything in it is likely to be experienced as challenge, squared, and to survive such a journey requires considerable support.

Teaching as Care.   There are no simple directions for how to provide this kind of support; however, Daloz (1999) has drawn on the myth of Mentor—the wise guide who appeared to the voyaging Telemakhos—as a model. Mentor initially provided the young traveler with necessary tools and essential counsel—often in the form of questions—and then, when his protégé was confident and skilled enough to com-

plete the journey on his own, left him to it. This is the basis for teaching as care: "When we no longer consider learning to be primarily the acquisition of knowledge, we can no longer view teaching as the bestowal of it. If learning is about growth and growth requires trust, then teaching is about engendering trust, about nurturance—caring for growth. Teaching is thus preeminently an act of care" (Daloz, 1986, p. 237). Kegan (1982) describes this awareness as the special kind of empathy that can help another human being toward a new way of perceiving and understanding.

Some of the needed support is in activities structured so that ideally they will tip learners toward more complex epistemologies, encourage them to try on new lenses, and create opportunities for effective discussion and self-reflection. But useful as such supports are, they are insufficient. The "disorienting dilemma" is just that. Adults moving toward the self-authorizing mind no longer know what they know, nor, sometimes, who they are—and as their uncertainty grows, so does their need for reassurance that this discomfort will not go on forever.

One way to offer this reassurance is to help them understand that they are in "grave danger of growing" (Seashore, cited in Kegan, 1994, p. 293) and to provide more information about the journey on which they may indeed already have embarked. It is a lot easier to make a rugged trek up the mountain when one believes that an exciting new vista awaits at the top. Though it is unnecessary for every educator in every course to teach a mini-lesson in adult development, it can be very useful in some courses, preferably near the beginning of the learner's program, to sketch out the ideas around self-direction, autonomy, and transformative learning.

We may also consider, and perhaps share with them, aspects of our own challenges, shortcomings, and frustrations relative to our own journeys of development. Such self-disclosure is important to the adult because, "In the early stages of development, authority is enough, but as the student grows, his willingness to trust an authoritative mask without knowing what lies behind it dims" (Daloz, 1986, p. 176).

The Holding Environment.   The most essential role of the mentor is to provide the holding environment on which all development depends. Kegan (1982) based his notion of the holding environment on Winnicott's observations that an infant who is provided food, clothing, and shelter may still fail to thrive if it is not also held. Throughout the life span, the developmental holding environment consists of holding on, letting go, and sticking around, or *confirmation*, *contradiction*, and *continuity*. Confirmation supports and validates the learner. It affirms who the learner currently is and provides a cheering section for every at-bat. In the learning environment, confirmation focuses on what the learner has done right, hails effort, and applauds even small achievements. Contradiction stretches the learner beyond what is comfortable at the moment. Rather than a cheering section of soccer moms and dads, it's the professional coach focusing on how to do more and better. In the learning environment, contradiction points out what remains to be done, encourages greater effort, and sets high but attainable standards. Continuity allows and encourages the emerging way of being to change the structure of existing relationships. In the learning environment, continuity may enable the adult to shift from a mentor–mentee relationship with an educator to one that establishes the learner as a peer, or as Bloom (1995) describes it, companion, ally, and colearner.

Ethical Choices

One of the most significant challenges faced by the mentor/guide, and one that touches on the core purpose of being an educator, is how to respond when adults seem either uninterested in or resistant to the invitation to grow, despite our well-intentioned commitment to their development. We may believe—even "know"—that growth is good and that a more complex epistemology will inform a more effective life, but what if our enthusiasm for self-direction and autonomy is in conflict with the learner's construction of his or her own life? We cannot know what growth may mean to this particular learner at this time; as Brookfield (1990) has noted, in some communities, the growth that would enable a learner to question assumptions is tantamount to committing "cultural suicide" (p. 153).

It therefore seems essential that educators come clean about their developmental intentions and that they honor people's decisions about how fast or how far to travel this road. It is crucial not to infantilize adult learners, but it is also important to remember that when one is committed to another's development, that relationship bears many similarities to the role of a good parent: someone who guides without imposing, who nurtures without creating dependency, who encourages without inauthenticity, and who understands that the learner is an adult who will make his or her own choices, even if those choices are sometimes not to grow in the way the educator has encouraged.

Nevertheless, the propriety of setting goals for learners that they might not set for themselves is at the heart of the educative process. Not until one has acquired some familiarity with new ideas can one decide if they are worth pursuing. Similarly, not until one has begun to challenge the assumptions of the socializing mind can one realize that they *are* assumptions and that other ways of seeing the world are possible. But even as we encourage—literally, give courage to—the possibility of change, we may have to accept learners' decisions (conscious or not) about whether to change and how much change is appropriate, because "it is a harrowing walk . . . away from . . . the very principle by which they make sense of the world" (Kegan, 1994, p. 281).

The Educator's Journey

Acknowledging the importance of development in the lives of adult learners may imply that we need also to recognize ourselves as developing adults. We, too, are building our own consciousness bridges, and we may have to face similar challenges as our learners do, even as we try to facilitate this process for others. This may suggest that we also must find situational activities to challenge our own accustomed way of doing things. We may need to engage in self-reflective activities in which we examine our experiences and reactions to them. Also, ideally, we will engage in dialogue with professional peers about our own disorienting dilemmas and our sense of confusion or frustration when, say, a new classroom activity does not work as we had planned or our students seem not to have experienced what we intended them to.

A particular challenge we face is that no order of consciousness is less appealing than the one we have most recently left behind (Kegan, 1994). We therefore have a largely unrecognized tendency to "make wrong" or disdain what we have lately outgrown. Having traveled to the distant land and mastered its language and customs, we place firmly behind us the trepidations we had when we first set out on the journey. We may therefore wish to question whether we are being less caring and compassionate than we might be to those who are still acting like tourists.

Daloz (1999), whose evocative phrase "teaching as care" captures the essence of teaching for development, put it this way: "Good teaching rests neither in accumulating a shelfful of knowledge nor in developing a repertoire of skills. In the end, good teaching lies in willingness to care for what happens in our students, ourselves, and the space between us" (p. 246).

CURRENT TRENDS AND CONCLUSION

Noting a sharp decrease in the number of articles on SDL that appeared in professional publications during the last decade of the twentieth century compared with the 20 years prior, Brockett (2000) suggested that new research approaches are needed. Certainly, as the number of retirees grows, there has been a new focus on SDL connected with volunteering (Kerka, 1998).

Furthermore, with the increasing prominence of computer-mediated instruction, distance learning, and hypermedia has come a renewed emphasis on SDL as self-instruction, both with and without direct guidance (Keirns, 1998). Another emergent theme is workplace-based SDL, due in part to the unsatisfactory return on investment of training programs, which cost companies many person-days while workers are in attendance, may involve travel, and may not succeed in transferring what was learned to the workplace (Tobin, 2000). However, the overriding concern in these new and renewed attentions to SDL appears to be fostering pedagogical autonomy rather than encouraging the epistemological change associated with personal autonomy.

This chapter began with a glimpse at the kind, pace, and enormity of change that is now common. The literature of SDL has been part of that change as it has suggested that new capacities for learning are needed to face these demands. When we consider that most adults, including those in our classrooms, are likely to be looking at the world—and at learning—with two (or three) qualitatively different ways of knowing, it is easier to understand how researchers have come to such vastly different conclusions about whether adults are self-directed, becoming self-directed, or completely befuddled by anything to do with self-direction.

Looking at SDL and autonomy through a develop-

mental lens also helps explain other puzzles and paradoxes that mark the 30-plus years of SDL research, comment, and controversy and may offer practitioners a new way to think about their educational purpose and practice. For example, the developmental lens may refocus some of the ongoing controversy about autonomy and individualism. The autonomy of the self-authorizing knower is not an autonomy of separation, but rather of a new kind of connection. In the place of the former fusion is a new spaciousness. Instead of seeing differences as threatening, they are perceived as interesting and enlivening. Indeed, as the discussion of situational experiences suggests, it is most often through interaction that the learner's balance is tipped toward growth. Furthermore, particularly for women and people of color, finding and using one's own voice can be an important part of overcoming patriarchal or other social oppression (Belenky et al., 1986; Gilligan, 1982).

In addition, the essential thrust of critical theory—to uncover the hidden systemic forces that shape people's lives, to "mak[e] explicit and analyz[e] that which was previously implicit and uncritically accepted" (Brookfield, 2000, p. 131)—appears also to describe the movement toward self-authoring consciousness. From that perspective, an approach to SDL that grows out of a constructive-developmental orientation may be entirely in line with the goals of critical adult education. Once adult learners truly understand the constructed nature of knowledge, they are much less likely to accept uncritically what they read and hear. This may therefore be the birth of a critical awareness that can lead to counterhegemonic thought and action.

The socializing epistemology is normative, in the sense that most adults probably can view the world through that lens at least some of the time. But a glance through almost any newspaper reveals that the ill-structured problems of the modern world are not effectively solved by avoiding conflicts over ideas, depending on authorities to provide solutions, and assuming that one's own group (however defined: affinity, social, racial, religious, cultural, regional, language, political, national) is in some essential way better or righter than those from whom we differ. Hence Mezirow's observation: "The *goal* of adult education is to help the learner develop the requisite learning processes to think and choose with more reliable insight, to become a more autonomous thinker" (2000, p. 348).

However, as important as it is to help adults develop the perspectives and capacities associated with the self-authorizing mind, given the magnitude of the problems facing the world today, that may be insufficient. The accomplishment of the self-authorizing mind is its new capacity to recognize as assumptions the "reality" of the socialized mind. Clearly, this is movement in a positive direction, but what are the new limitations? What is the new whole of which the self-authorizing mind is only a part?

The self-transforming (fifth-order) mind recognizes the limitations of ideology—even its own ideologies. (For the majority of us who are still not done with the preceding transformation, thinking about this feels a bit vertiginous—like looking into two facing mirrors and seeing endless reflections of a reflection of a reflection.) The self-authorizing mind is comfortable with the realization that people hold differing perspectives and is generally adept at analysis that can respectfully explain the various conflicting notions. The self-transforming mind, however, sees *connections* rather than conflicts. The "different" perspectives become elements of an understanding that is bigger than the sum of its ideological parts, in a kind of knowing that transcends the distinctions that the self-authoring mind is so good at creating. Although this clearly holds the best hope for the future of this planetary collective, we can't get there from here. Or at least, we can't get there without first going through all the epistemological transformations between there and wherever we currently are.

To effectively take responsibility—for our own learning or for our own lives—we first need to be able make certain distinctions, so that we can uncover our hidden assumptions and discriminate what we feel, value, and want from what we should feel, value, and want (Grow, 1991). But, as Kegan (1994) pointed out:

> When the [socialized mind] dominates our meaning-making, what we *should* feel is what we *do* feel, what we *should* value is what we *do* value, what we *should* want is what we *do* want. [The educator's] goal therefore may not be a matter of getting students merely to identify and value a distinction between two parts that already exist, but a matter of fostering a qualitative evolution of mind that actually creates the distinction. (p. 275)

If we are to create a vision of the future in which imaginary boundaries will be disimagined, we first have to get from socialized to self-authorized ways of knowing. This, then, is a call for adult educators to explore SDL as it emerges at the intersection of adult learning and adult development.

ACKNOWLEDGMENTS   My thanks to the colleagues who reviewed and gently commented on all or parts of this manuscript in various stages of preparation, none of whom bears responsibility for any of its final shortcomings: Melanie Booth, Phil Candy, Ellie Drago-Severson, Dean Elias, Tom Hodgson, Mark Hoyer, Annalee Lamoreaux, Catherine Marienau, Jack Mezirow, and Rebecca Proehl.

References

Applebee, A., & Langer, J. (1983). Instructional scaffolding: Reading and writing as natural language activities. *Language Arts*, 60, 168–175.

Basseches, M. (1984). *Dialectical thinking and adult development.* Norwood, NJ: Ablex.

Belenky, M. F., Clinchy, B. M., Goldberger, N. R., & Tarule, J. M. (1986). *Women's ways of knowing: The development of self, voice, and mind.* New York: Basic Books.

Bloom, M. (1995). Multiple roles of the mentor supporting women's adult development. In K. Taylor & C. Marienau (Eds.), *Learning environments for women's adult development: Bridges toward change.* New Directions for Adult and Continuing Education no. 65. San Francisco: Jossey-Bass.

Bonham, A. (1991). Guglielmino's self directed learning readiness: What does it measure? *Adult Education Quarterly*, 41(2), 92–99.

Boucouvalas, M., & Pearse, P. (1982). Self-directed learning in an other-directed environment: The role of correctional education in a learning society. *Journal of Correctional Education*, 32(4), 31–35.

Boud, D., Keogh, K., & Walker, D. (1985). *Reflection: Turning experience into learning.* London: Kogan Page.

Brockett, R. G. (1985a). The relationship between self-directed learning readiness and life satisfaction among older adults. *Adult Education Quarterly*, 35(4), 210–219.

Brockett, R. G. (1985b). Methodological and substantive issues in the measurement of self-directed learning readiness. *Adult Education Quarterly*, 36(1) 15–24.

Brockett, R. G. (2000). Is it time to move on? Reflections on a research agenda for self-directed learning in the 21st century. In T. J. Sork, V. Chapman, & R. St. Clair (Eds.), *Proceedings of the 41st Annual Adult Education Research Conference* (pp. 543–544). Vancouver, Canada: University of British Columbia.

Brockett, R. G., & Hiemstra, R. (1991). *Self-direction in learning.* London: Routledge.

Brookfield, S. (1984). Self-directed adult learning: A critical paradigm. *Adult Education Quarterly*, 35(2), 59–71.

Brookfield, S. (1985). *Self-directed learning: A critical review of research*. New Directions for Continuing Education no 25. San Francisco: Jossey-Bass.

Brookfield, S. (1989). *Developing critical thinkers*. San Francisco: Jossey-Bass.

Brookfield, S. (1990). *The skillful teacher*. San Francisco: Jossey-Bass.

Brookfield, S. (1991). *Becoming a critically reflective teacher*. San Francisco: Jossey-Bass.

Brookfield, S. (1993). Self-directed learning, political clarity, and the critical practice of adult education. *Adult Education Quarterly, 43*(4), 227–242.

Brookfield, S. (2000). Transformative learning as ideology critique. In J. Mezirow (Ed.), *Learning as transformation*. San Francisco: Jossey-Bass.

Caffarella, R. (1993). Self-directed learning. In S. Merriam (Ed.), *An update on adult learning theory*. New Directions for Adult and Continuing Education no. 57. San Francisco: Jossey-Bass.

Caffarella, R., & Caffarella, E. (1986). Self-directedness and learning contracts in adult education. *Adult Education Quarterly, 36*(4), 226–234.

Caffarella, R., & O'Donnell, J. M. (1987). Self-directed adult learning: A critical paradigm revisited. *Adult Education Quarterly, 37*(4), 199–211.

Candy, P. C. (1991). *Self-direction for life-long learning*. San Francisco: Jossey-Bass.

Candy, P. C., Harri-Augstein, S., & Thomas, L . (1985). Reflection and the self-organized learner: a model of learning conversations. In D. Boud, R. Keogh, & D. Walker (Eds.), *Reflection: Turning experience into learning*. London: Kogan Page.

Chené, A. (1983). The concept of autonomy in adult education: A philosophical discussion. *Adult Education Quarterly, 34*(1), 38–47.

Chickering, A. (1981). *The modern American college*. San Francisco: Jossey-Bass.

Council for Adult and Experiential Learning. (2000). *Best practices in adult learning: A CAEL/APQC benchmark study*. Dubuque, IA: Kendall/Hunt.

Daloz, L. (1986). *Effective teaching and mentoring*. San Francisco: Jossey-Bass.

Daloz, L. (1999). *Mentor*. San Francisco: Jossey-Bass.

Delahaye, B. L., & Smith, H. E. (1995). The validity of the learning preference assessment. *Adult Education Quarterly, 45*(3), 159–173.

Dewey, J. (1916/1930). *Democracy and education*. New York: Macmillan.

Dewey, J. (1963/1979). *Experience and education*. New York: Collier.

Drago-Severson, E. (2004). *Becoming adult learners: Principles and practices for effective development*. New York: Teachers College Press.

Droegkamp, J., & Taylor, K. (1995). Prior learning assessment, critical self-reflection, and reentry women's development. In K. Taylor & C. Marienau (Eds.), *Learning environments for women's adult development: Bridges toward change*. New Directions for Adult and Continuing Education no. 65. San Francisco: Jossey-Bass.

Ellsworth, J. H. (1992). Adults' learning: The voices of experience. *MPAEA Journal, 21*(1), 23–34.

Field, L. (1990). Guglielmino's Self-Directed Learning Readiness Scale: Should it continue to be used? *Adult Education Quarterly, 41*(2), 100–103.

Freire, P. (1992). *Pedagogy of the oppressed*. New York: Continuum.

Garrison, D. R. (1997). Self-directed learning: Toward a comprehensive model. *Adult Education Quarterly, 48*(1), 18–33.

Gibbs, B. (1979). Autonomy and authority in education. *Journal of Philosophy of Education, 13,* 119–132.

Gilligan, C. (1982). *In a different voice*. Cambridge, MA: Harvard University Press.

Grace, A. (1996). Striking a critical pose: Andragogy— missing links, missing values. *International Journal of Lifelong Education, 16*(5), 382–392.

Grow, G. (1991). Teaching learners to be self-directed. *Adult Education Quarterly, 41*(3) 125–149.

Guglielmino, L.,M., & Guglielmino, P. J. (1994). Practical experience with self-directed learning in business and industry human resources development. *New Directions for Adult and Continuing Education, 64*(Winter). 39–46.

Guglielmino, P. J., & Roberts, D. G. (1992). A comparison of self-directed learning readiness in U.S. and Hong Kong samples and the implications for job performance. *Human Resource Development Quarterly, 3*(3), 261–271.

Hammond, M., & Collins, R. (1991). *Self-directed learning: Critical practice*. East Brunswick, NJ: Nichols/GP.

Heisenberg, W. (1962). *Physics and philosophy: The revolution in modern science*. New York: Harper & Row.

Hiemstra, R., & Sisco, B. (1990). *Individualizing instruction: Making learning personal, empowering, and successful*. San Francisco: Jossey-Bass.

Horton, M., & Freire, P. (1990). *We make the road by walking*. Philadelphia: Temple University Press.

Joughin, G. (1992). Cognitive style and adult learning principles. *International Journal of Lifelong Education, 11*(1), 3–14.

Kasworm, C. (1983). Self-directed learning and lifespan development. *International Journal of Lifelong Education, 2*(1), 29–45.

Kegan, R. (1982). *The evolving self*. Cambridge, MA: Harvard University Press.

Kegan, R. (1994). *In over our heads: The mental demands of modern life*. Cambridge, MA: Harvard University Press.

Kegan, R. (2000). What form transforms?: A constructive-developmental approach to transformative learning. In J. Mezirow (Ed.), *Learning as transformation*. San Francisco: Jossey-Bass.

Kegan, R., Broderick, M., Drago-Severson, E., Helsing, D., Popp, N., & Portnow, K. (2001). *Toward a new pluralism in the ABE/ESOL classrooms: Teaching to multiple "cultures of mind."* NCSALL Monograph no. 19. Boston: World Education.

Keirns, J. L. (1999). *Designs for self-instruction: Principles, processes, and issues in developing self-directed learning.* Boston: Allyn & Bacon.

Kelly, G. A. (1955). *The psychology of personal constructs* (2 vols). New York: Norton.

Kerka, S. (1998). Volunteering and adult learning. ERIC Digest no. 202. Columbus, Ohio: ERIC Clearinghouse on Adult, Career, and Vocational Education. (ERIC Document Reproduction Service no. ED423428).

King, P. M., & Kitchener, K. S. (1994). *Developing reflective judgment: Understanding and promoting intellectual growth and critical thinking in adolescents and adults.* San Francisco: Jossey-Bass.

Knowles, M. S. (1975). *Self-directed learning.* Chicago: Association Press.

Koller, A. (1982). *An unknown woman.* New York: Henry Holt & Co.

Lindeman, E. (1961). *The meaning of adult education.* Montreal: Harvest House.

Loevinger, J., & Blasi, A. (1976). *Ego development: Conceptions and theories.* San Francisco: Jossey-Bass.

Long, H. B. (1987). Item analysis of Guglielmino's self-directed learning readiness scale. *International Journal of Lifelong Education, 6*(4), 331–326.

Long, H. B. (1990). Psychological control in self-directed learning. *International Journal of Lifelong Education, 9*(4), 331–338.

Long, H. B. (1994). *Resources related to overcoming resistance to self-direction in learning.* New Directions for Adult and Continuing Education no. 64. San Francisco: Jossey-Bass.

MacGregor, J. (1993) *Student self-evaluation: Fostering reflective learning.* New Directions for Teaching and Learning no 56. San Francisco: Jossey-Bass.

Marton, F., & Booth, S. (1997). *Learning and awareness.* Mahwah, NJ: Erlbaum.

Mezirow, J. (1985). *A critical theory of self-directed learning.* New Directions for Continuing Education no. 25. San Francisco: Jossey-Bass

Mezirow, J. (2000). *Learning as transformation.* San Francisco: Jossey-Bass.

Newman, M. (1993). *The third contract: Theory and practice in trade union training.* Sydney, Australia: Stewart Victor.

Oddi, L. (1986). Development and validation of an instrument to identify self-directed continuing learners. *Adult Education Quarterly, 36*(2), 97–107.

Oddi, L. (1987). Perspectives on self-directed learning. *Adult Education Quarterly, 38*(1), 21–31.

Perry, W. G. Jr. (1970). *Forms of intellectual and ethical development in the college years.* New York: Holt, Rinehart & Winston.

Piaget, J. (1954). *The construction of reality in the child.* New York: Basic Books.

Pratt, D. D. (1988). Andragogy as a relational construct. *Adult Education Quarterly, 38*(3), 160–118.

Robinson, R. (1992). Andragogy applied to the Open College learner. *Research in Distance Education, January,* 10–13.

Senge, P. (1991). *The fifth discipline.* San Francisco: Jossey-Bass.

Stanton, A. (1996). Reconfiguring teaching and knowing in the college classroom. In N. R. Goldberger, J. M. Tarule, B. M. Clinchy, & M. F. Belenky (Eds.), *Knowledge, difference, and power.* New York: Basic Books.

Taylor, K. (1995). Sitting beside herself: Self-assessment and women's adult development. In K. Taylor & C. Marienau (Eds.), *Learning environments for women's adult development: Bridges toward change.* New Directions for Adult and Continuing Education no. 65. San Francisco: Jossey-Bass.

Taylor, K. (2000). Teaching with development in mind. In J. Mezirow (Ed.), *Learning as transformation.* San Francisco: Jossey-Bass.

Taylor, K., Booth, M., & Lamoreaux, A. (2004). Self-reflective writing, reconstructive learning, and adult development: theorizing from the literature. In D. E. Clover (Ed.), *Adult education for democracy, social justice, and a culture of peace. Proceedings of the Joint International Conference of the Adult Education Research Conference (AERC) and the Canadian Association for the Study of Adult Education (CASAE)* (pp. 468–473). Canada: Faculty of Education, University of Victoria.

Taylor, K., Marienau, C., & Fiddler, M. (2000). *Developing adult learners: Strategies for teachers and trainers.* San Francisco: Jossey-Bass.

Tobin, D. R. (2000). *All learning is self-directed: How organizations can support and encourage independent learning.* Alexandria, VA: ASTD Publications.

Tough, A. (1979). *The adult's learning projects: A fresh approach to theory and practice in adult learning* (2nd ed.). Toronto: Ontario Institute for Studies in Education.

Tullos, R. (2000). Vocational preparatory instruction: Staff self-training program, learning styles module. Online document retrieved June 4, 2004, from http://floridatechnet.org/inservice/vpi/assess/modules/learning.pdf.

Vaill, P. B. (1996). *Learning as a way of being: Strategies for survival in a world of permanent white water.* San Francisco: Jossey-Bass.

Vygotsky, L. (1978). *Mind in society: The development of higher psychological processes.* Cambridge, MA: Harvard University Press.

Walden, P. (1995). Journal writing: A tool for women developing as knowers. In K. Taylor & C. Marienau (Eds.), *Learning environments for women's adult development: Bridges toward change.* New Directions for Adult and Continuing Education no. 65. San Francisco: Jossey-Bass.

Zeichner, K. M., & Liston, D. P. (1987). Teaching student teachers to reflect. *Harvard Educational Review, 57*(1), 23–48.

Chapter 10

Adult Development, Learning, and Insight Through Psychotherapy: The Cultivation of Change and Transformation

Melvin E. Miller

Those who study adult development are sometimes frustrated with the slow pace at which many people change during adulthood. For a number of reasons, some adults either resist or are unable to engage in transformative processes and other forms of positive change. Some are stuck at a particular developmental stage, experiencing something on the order of a developmental arrest. They are frozen in place, unable to move on in life. Many individuals exhibit very little change after they reach young adulthood. Developmental psychologists and clinicians often wonder, "Can the process of growth and transformation ever be jump-started after lying dormant for a number of years? Can transformation be expedited when it seems to be bogged down or mired?"

Operating from the assumption that psychotherapy is effective and contributes to personal transformation through awakening both emotional and developmental processes, I explore the ways and mechanisms of psychotherapy and illustrate how the psychotherapeutic process can enhance personal

growth and development throughout adulthood. I examine those dimensions of personal growth that interest adults the most, drawing on clinical case material that illustrates the kinds of concerns with which adults wrestle during the various phases of psychotherapy.

PSYCHOTHERAPY: THE EXTENT OF ITS USE

Throughout the history of the use of psychotherapy, the numbers of persons engaged in it have increased dramatically, especially during the past three decades. Introduced just over 100 years ago, psychotherapy has evolved and has proliferated rapidly. In 1950 there were approximately 2 million people who used the services of a psychotherapist. That number is currently much larger. According to the World Health Organization (WHO), there are approximately 150 million people actively engaged in some kind of mental health treatment (WHO, 2001, p. 1). Nevertheless, WHO believes that the number of people who need treatment is considerably larger, by at least three times. This agency estimates that for a variety of reasons, there are another 300 million people in need who are not receiving treatment (WHO, 2001, p. 1). The WHO estimates that "one in four people in the world will be affected by mental or neurological disorders at some point in their lives . . . [and that] "around 450 million currently suffer from such conditions" (WHO, 2001). In this same article, the WHO noted that depressive disorders are the "fourth leading cause of the global disease burden . . . [and] are expected to rank second by 2020." The numbers seem to be on the rise, and of course, the numbers of people who may need to avail themselves of the services of a psychotherapist are increasing as well.

Torrey and Miller in their new book *The Invisible Plague* (2001), noted an alarming increase in insanity (severe mental disorder) over the past 250 years, which they see as an epidemic of sorts. Traditionally, the "prevalence of insanity . . . had been considerably less than 1 case per 1,000 total population . . . [It] passed 2 cases per 1,000, then 3 cases per 1,000 in the 1800's . . . during the twentieth century the rate passed 5 cases per 1,000, then climbed even higher" (p. x). Hunt (1993) estimated that at least 15 million Americans are treated by psychotherapists every year (p. 560). The fairly recent National Comorbidity Survey (NCS) presents us with a somewhat more distressing statistic. It estimated that roughly half of the people in the United States between the ages of 15 and 54 years will have a diagnosable mental disorder at some point in their lives (Kessler et al., 1994). Despite these disconcerting numbers, we know that these estimates of diagnosable and treatable disorders can be partially explained by the fact that the public has become increasingly aware of mental health issues in the past few years. In addition, there seems to be a growing willingness on the part of many to seek some form of psychological treatment.

These caveats notwithstanding, there is no question that a huge demand for mental health workers exists worldwide. Psychotherapists of various stripes will be required to address the needs of millions of potential patients. Statistics on the current number of people requesting or requiring psychotherapy are daunting; recent trends will likely continue for the foreseeable future, especially in light of projected population increases and mounting turmoil internationally.

It is noteworthy that most of the sources of the statistics I have cited regard psychotherapy as a method of treating "mental illness" exclusively.[1] In this chapter, however, I am concerned primarily with the use of psychotherapy by those who are particularly interested in, for example, psychological growth, greater awareness, and expansion of mind. This emphasis notwithstanding, I recognize that treating mental disturbances in psychotherapy and engaging in psychotherapy for growth enhancement are not mutually exclusive enterprises. In fact, both purposes involve similar treatment processes and dynamics of personal change. Nevertheless, the focus here is on psychotherapy for personal growth and transformation in adulthood.

OVERVIEW AND INVITATION TO THE PSYCHOTHERAPY PROCESS

Psychotherapy is a professional helping relationship in which the patient (client) is seeking relief of symptoms and/or some form of change or transformation through talking to a professionally trained person about his or her concerns.[2] Hinsie and Campbell (1970) offered a general definition of psychotherapy in which they propose that it is

> any form of treatment for . . . problems that are assumed to be of an emotional nature, in which a trained person deliberately establishes a professional relationship with a patient for the purpose of removing, modifying, or retarding existing symptoms, . . . and of promoting positive personality growth and development. (p. 630)

Although this definition seems somewhat formal, I like it because it refers to both the treatment of symptoms and the possibility of positive growth and development.

The forms and varieties of psychotherapy are countless. Wallerstein (1995), Corsini (1984), and others have delineated comprehensive lists of "talk therapies." Corsini (1984, p. 7), for example, conjectured that there are at least 250 different methods of working with patients that can be called psychotherapy. Wachtel and Messer (1997) estimated that 400 different approaches could be called psychotherapeutic. Countless research articles argue the relative effectiveness-ineffectiveness of the various approaches to psychotherapy and psychoanalysis (see Safran &

Aron, 2001). But Jerome Frank (1961), in *Persuasion and Healing*, contended that these various approaches all seem to achieve roughly comparable results. Wachtel and Messer (1997) and Seligman (1995) corroborated this view rather persuasively, as have others (see Luborsky, 2001, p. 594).

Hunt (1993, p. 564) asserted that although there are hundreds of variant forms of psychotherapy, they can all be distilled into approximately six major approaches to the discipline.[3] Hunt noted that "half or more" of all the psychotherapies in existence are close relatives of psychodynamic psychotherapy or psychoanalytically oriented psychotherapy. In this chapter, I am primarily interested in discussing those of the psychodynamic variety, broadly conceived. However, before discussing key features of psychodynamic theory in depth, I will discuss briefly some other modalities of psychotherapy that are also popular today.

One of the most widely used forms of psychotherapy is cognitive-behavioral therapy, or CBT. In CBT, the therapist points out the patient's faulty modes of thinking and suggests more adaptive or constructive modes of thinking (behaving). CBT has been well investigated and has held up well in most studies. As is true of most forms of psychotherapy, CBT has demonstrated its effectiveness as a mental health treatment when it has been compared to psychopharmacology (see Safran & Aron, 2001).

Most forms of CBT fall into the category of short-term psychotherapies. In this chapter, however, I am concerned with the longer term therapies—those of a psychodynamic nature. I prefer the psychodynamic approaches for various reasons: One appealing feature is that they incorporate a language, a lexicon, that expresses the deeper strivings and meaning-making yearnings of the person. Psychodynamically oriented therapists, by virtue of their training, are often better equipped to deal with the existential and meaning-making issues introduced by their patients. Both the theory of psychoanalysis and the ways that psychoanalysis is practiced encourage the introduction of such issues into the treatment process. Techniques such as psychoanalysis that pay close attention to the formation of the therapeutic relationship and place an emphasis on understanding and interpreting that relationship are usually the most effective ones available (Wallerstein, 1995). This is especially true when the treatment process is long term (Luborsky, 2001; Seligman, 1995). And, of course, it is the psychodynamic therapies that are usually conducted over a longer period of time. Seligman (1995) and others (e.g., Luborsky, 2001) have observed (and supported with research findings) that those therapies that tend to take longer to run their course are usually the most successful, contributing to the greatest changes in patients over the long run.

Why People Seek Psychotherapy

People enter psychotherapy for many reasons. Some begin the process because they are directly asking for help. Often these individuals have specific symptoms handicapping or limiting them in some fashion (e.g., depression, anxiety, phobia, hypochondriasis). Other persons just sense that something is wrong or at least not quite right in their lives. Perhaps there is a general lack of satisfaction, diminished happiness, or an attenuated sense of well-being that is disturbing them. There might be an overwhelming sense of anomie, or listlessness, or perhaps they are experiencing a period in life where things "just don't make sense." According to Frank (1961), *Weltschmerz* or "world pain" is a factor that drives others into treatment (p. 317). Such feelings can propel significant numbers of people into a therapeutic process. Still others may have experienced major crises in their lives, crises related to some form of trauma or loss, relative to the demands of a life stage (developmental) transition. A transition issue can be more than an adequate reason to begin the process. An awareness of crossing the threshold into middle age or late life can trigger a crisis for some—thus opening the door to psychotherapy. A growing awareness of one's eventual or imminent death might give rise to degrees of anxiety and/or depression such as that experienced by Tolstoy's (1886/1960) Ivan Ilyich. The consternation following a disturbing dream might also initiate a life-transforming therapeutic process (Lifton, 1990, p. 420). This could prove to be especially true if the dream signals a major passage in life, such as the entrance or "great crossing" into the second half of life.

People undergoing such disquieting experiences are usually highly motivated to change. They want things to be different. They are determined to have a more rewarding life and believe they can create one. Seligman's (1995) research shows that those who enter psychotherapy knowing that something is not right (and wanting change) are the ones who do best in psychotherapy and make the most significant gains.

His study also shows that those who choose their psychotherapist carefully tend to do better in the therapeutic process. Those who enter psychotherapy with an exploring, inquisitive attitude or stance seem to improve more quickly in comparison to those who enter with a more passive stance and expect to be "treated" and "fixed," as one might when approaching a physician with a specific physical illness.

Beginning the Psychotherapy Process

I imagine that some readers may not be especially familiar with the psychotherapy process. With this in mind, it may be helpful to imagine a scenario of a typical (fictitious) patient beginning psychotherapy.

Our hypothetical patient begins the process by choosing a potential therapist. This choice should be made as thoughtfully and as carefully as possible. Ideally, the new patient will have asked for recommendations from trusted friends and professionals in the community. The patient will also ponder the various therapeutic modalities and available theoretical orientations. For our purposes, our patient selects, for an initial meeting, a highly recommended, psychodynamically oriented therapist in the community. Our patient eventually makes the first appointment. As that initial contact with the unknown is anticipated, our patient will likely experience a great deal of anxiety and apprehension.

Finally, the long-awaited day arrives. The therapist greets the patient and welcomes the patient into the office, perhaps orienting the patient to the physical layout of the building, the therapist's suite, the waiting room, the restrooms, and other aspects of the facility. Most therapists will begin by asking the patient why he or she has come for treatment and will typically formulate some general, open-ended question about the nature of the help that is sought. At some point in the first session there might be a brief discussion of the ground rules of the treatment process. For example, the therapist orients the patient to the likely frequency of visits, fee, length of sessions, missed sessions, goals and length of treatment, and confidentiality issues. The guideline or rule of free association may be discussed in the initial session (Greenson, 1967; Langs, 1982).[4] The therapist might also describe his or her theoretical orientation and educational background. Therapist and patient might also review applicable paperwork and forms (e.g., consent for treatment and insurance forms).

So the work begins. Early on in treatment, the primary focus is usually placed on developing a solid therapeutic alliance with the patient. This alliance is defined as the "relatively nonneurotic, rational relationship between patient and . . . [therapist] which makes it possible for the patient to work purposefully in the analytic situation" (Greenson, 1967, p. 46). Kozart (2002) has demonstrated that the efficacy of psychotherapy is most assuredly contingent on the kind and quality of the therapeutic alliance that develops. The therapeutic or working alliance begins to unfold as the client reports on his or her early developmental history and explores the issues that encouraged entrance into treatment in the first place.

One issue that is often vigorously debated with respect to the first or early phase of treatment is the question of how much emphasis should be placed on obtaining a detailed patient history, as opposed to staying with the patient's presenting material (i.e., current problems and issues), which elucidate the patient's conscious reasons for entering the psychotherapeutic process. Roth (1987), in *Psychotherapy: The Art of Wooing Nature*, argued that the primary focus should be on connecting with the patient around the concerns that brought him or her into the process (and connecting with the patient in general); this focus averts the possibility of becoming sidetracked by a detailed, systematic exploration of personal history. That information will come in time. I tend to agree with this emphasis. Another senior therapist who weighs in on this topic is Havens, who articulated a similar priority and succinctly summarized his stance in the titles of two of his books: *Making Contact* (1986) and *A Safe Place* (1989). In short, Havens argued, our primary job in the early stages of treatment is to make some kind of personal (emotional) contact with the patient and to do it in such a way that the patient will feel as safe and secure as possible in this new therapeutic relationship. This is usually not an easy task. The manner in which it is done will vary significantly depending on the personality and character structure of the patient and how that personality structure interfaces with the personality of the analyst.

Topics That Emerge in Psychotherapy

Let us now return to some central themes mentioned earlier—the topics and issues that tend to bring adults into psychotherapy. It is interesting to evaluate the ways people talk about their presenting problems and other issues that are on their minds. We might ask ourselves: How descriptive and emotionally sensitive is the language that individuals use to express themselves? How clearly do they articulate those forces that propelled them into psychotherapy?

I will draw on case material from my private practice to illustrate various factors that prompt people to enter treatment,[5] as well as the differences in psychological awareness, skill, and acumen demonstrated through the manner in which people talk about their issues. Most of my work is conducted with a fairly mature, high-functioning adult population. Very few people who come to see me come for relief from what have been historically called symptom neuroses (e.g., obsessive compulsive disorder [OCD], phobias, hypochondriasis). On the other hand, I find that people do engage me as a therapist because they are grappling with depression and/or anxiety, and sometimes with characterological disturbances.[6] Most of these people are looking for relief from symptoms, but sometimes they seek much more than this. Despite the severity of their depression or anxiety, most of these individuals also articulate some kind of existential meaning-making questions, life stage stuckness, or life stage threshold angst. As varied as their struggles may be, most of these difficulties can be distilled into matters of meaning making. Adult patients everywhere are asking the question: "What's it all about?" Case material demonstrates these points, as the following vignettes illustrate:

Vignette I

The patient is a woman in her fifties. This patient has been having a difficult time of late. High levels of depression and anxiety brought her into treatment. During a quiet moment in a recent session, she asked herself aloud, "Why now?" in reference to the degree of emotional pain with which she has been struggling. She then made a rather remarkable statement in a somewhat rhetorical response to her own question: Maybe this is it. I am now reaching the second half of my life. In the first half of life, people can get along okay without working too hard at it. You can get along using the old defenses and a high level of activity. Then it hits. Midlife hits about now. There is a good chance that life will become devoid of meaning—unless you work on it. You've got to begin working on it, or else.

You've got to do the [psychological] work or you're in trouble. You've got to roll up your sleeves and go to work. No more relying on the old defenses and avoidances. My life was supposed to be bigger than this. I now realize how I have kept myself back. Kept myself small. I've been afraid to be bigger—even though that is what most of me wanted.

Another patient, a woman of about the same age, is grappling with remarkably similar issues. She declared:

Vignette 2

My life at 50 is about two-thirds over on average. At times I feel alarmed by it all. I also feel a lot of envy of younger people; their lives are just beginning—an open field of endless opportunity. I also feel a lot of loss . . . loss of opportunity missed during my earlier years. [A comment made by many.] There are so many things I could have done—should have done. I feel sad that I could not have followed my heart, my instincts, more in the earlier years. Of course, now I understand why I couldn't. Now, it's the time where the rubber meets the road. I have to live . . . well and fully. I have to do the work I am meant to do. I also want to play more. I want to dance, to waltz, to live life more fully. Life is a gift. I want to take joy in what is. That is what some of the spiritual writers are writing about these days.

Here, a man in his mid-forties, articulates similar thoughts.

Vignette 3

I am approaching midlife and my life is a mess. I am not doing what I want to be doing professionally, and I am not sure about my marriage. I thought I would have a little more fame—at least relative fame in my professional life by now. What has been keeping me back? What is keeping me back? I want to get to the bottom of this before I enter the next decade of my life. Yes, and I've got to figure out my relationship with my wife as well.

Here are the remarks of another man in his mid-forties—a fairly new patient.

Vignette 4

I am rapidly approaching midlife and I realize I have been dropping the ball the past few years. I haven't been doing all that I want to do professionally, but even more than that, there are some other things I want to work on. I have been feeling demoralized lately. I feel like my character is off base, and that I have lost my moral compass. I don't feel like I am living up to my potential. These are the things I want to work on.

Although the midlife problems of which this last man speaks are similar to those of the two woman, in addition he expressed a need for help with some troubling psychological, characterological dynamics (e.g., the need for a moral compass, better character).

I could present an almost endless array of these kinds of vignettes from my therapy practice. They reflect people struggling both with developmental and personal difficulties. The themes that bring people into treatment are varied; yet they so often have a common thread. At the risk of oversimplification, it seems that the most frequently introduced issues could be compressed into three central topics, those of lost opportunities or of time running out, those directed to relationship issues, and those related to the meaning of life. Lost opportunities issues (topic 1) are typically expressed in questions such as: What am I doing with my life? Why haven't I lived up to my potential? Why haven't I achieved notoriety or fame in my chosen field? Can I turn this around in the time I have remaining in my life? Time seems to be running out. Relationship issues (topic 2) are expressed in questions such as: What about relationships? Can they improve? Can they be fixed? Is it worth trying to make a relationship work? Meaning of life issues (topic 3) are expressed in questions such as: What is the meaning of my life? Of life in general? Can I become a creator of meaning myself? How do I do that?

Stories, worries, and frustrations such as those voiced by my patients are remarkably common in the narrative material revealed in psychotherapy sessions with middle-aged and older adults. There are so many similar stories. I am sure that I would hear even greater volumes of stories like these if I would listen carefully for this particular kind of narrative. Of course, I typically try not to listen for specific content as I sit with patients. Listening for certain ideas or themes creates a perceptual set that would likely steer the listener away from the subtle nuances of meaning the patient might be trying to convey. Nonetheless, the process of working on an academic chapter such as this establishes a "mental set"—a lens through which information is bound to be filtered. As therapists, we tend to hear the stories that we listen for, despite how neutral we attempt to be in the listening process, and despite our attempts at "evenly hovering" or "evenly suspended" attention (Freud, 1913/1989b, p. 357). Bion (1970/1983) suggested that we enter each therapy hour without "memory, desire, or understanding" (p. 51). For the most part, this is excellent advice. However, it sets a daunting standard that is virtually impossible to actualize. Any and all preconceptions are bound to interfere with our listening, and it seems nearly impossible to extricate ourselves from the pernicious influence of our preconceptions. For this reason, some thoughtful analysts advise those in our profession to forswear attempts to be completely free of such influence and to focus more on the relationship that develops between therapist and patient. This frees us to work on ways of articulating this relationship while exploring the transference-countertransference dyad (see Alonso, 1996, p. 17).[7] These are central themes to which I shall return.

THE MECHANISMS, DYNAMICS, AND STAGES OF THE PSYCHOTHERAPY PROCESS

So far we have taken a brief look at the kinds of narrative material that often emerge in the early stages of a newly developing psychotherapy with midlife adults. As psychotherapists, we have seen people (patients/clients) bring into the treatment process issues related to "time running out," feelings of "not being on track" with earlier life goals, concerns about relationships, and passionately articulated desires to find or create meaning in their lives. Moreover, even those patients who might be considered to be in the more severely disturbed categories are grappling with similar existential concerns at some level. These issues are ubiquitous. They are the universal stuff of the human struggle. They comprise many of the daunting challenges that must be addressed in every life—regardless of whether or not one is in a psychotherapeutic treatment process. Some people will eagerly (others reluctantly) engage in a therapy process to get to the bottom of these perennial, existential mysteries and challenges in as positive and productive a manner as possible.

At this juncture then, I return to the hypothetical patient who committed to the therapy process. We have developed a sound working alliance or therapeutic alliance with our patient now. And as illustrated above, some of the fundamental issues with which our typical patient is grappling are now spread out before us on the consulting room table, ready to be addressed.

So where do we go from here? How do we move from the articulation of ideational concerns, life's conflicts, and developmental conundrums to some kind of positive resolution through new forms of learning? At this juncture the goals and techniques of different therapeutic modalities and theoretical orientations often collide. Shortly I will look at the ways in which therapists who represent various contemporary therapeutic modalities address some of the central components of any therapy process, while nonetheless retaining a primary focus on the psychodynamic approach. In particular, we ask, how do their respective modalities contribute to new forms of learning in adulthood?

The Early Phase of the Psychotherapy Process

The psychotherapeutic process has been traditionally divided into three stages, often called simply the beginning, the middle, and the end. The initial phase of the treatment involves establishing a working alliance with the patient. A good working alliance means that a solid element of trust has begun to emerge. When this happens, both parties tend to feel that they are working on a mutual enterprise, that is, the patient's therapeutic transformation. The therapist-patient dyad works together to unravel the patient's early history and understand how it influences his or her present circumstances. They reflect on and analyze the process that develops between them as they look for long-standing relationship trends.

For example, the patient in vignette 3 has begun to understand that the relative lack of success in his professional life is related to early fears revolving around the idea of achievement in general and early introjected negative messages about performance, success, and professional achievement in particular. In addition, he has begun to understand that his early fear of success was also informed by his fear of professionally

surpassing his father—a man whom on one hand he idolized and envied but on the other despised and held in contempt. He has learned that his contempt was related to (among other things) his father's lack of success in his own professional career. He often asked himself questions such as, "Why didn't Father give me a better example to follow in the professional realm?"

Interpretations made by the analyst relative to this kind of early developmental material serve various purposes.[8] They demonstrate how well the patient is heard and understood, and they also contribute to placing the patient's life in a more comprehensible and meaningful context. Well-formulated interpretations help win the confidence of the patient. In addition, they firm up and consolidate the therapeutic relationship. Interpretations take place throughout the therapy and not exclusively in the initial phases. Interpretations offer meaning and the possibility of "psychical restructuring" (Kristeva, 1997/2002, p. 8).[9] This kind of meaning making is what the patient longs for. Moreover, this form of insight, one that leads to learning and development, can be truly transformative for adult patients. The patient's confidence that these kinds of meaning-making (and learning) experiences will continue offers a sense of movement or momentum to the therapeutic process, while at best it also offers a sense of hope in its outcome.

The Middle Phase of Treatment

With a well-established working alliance, a new stage of the psychotherapy begins. This period in the process is often called the middle phase of treatment. It can be called the middle phase regardless of whether it takes 2 months, 10 months, or 10 years to move through. In psychoanalysis and other analytically informed types of psychotherapy, much of what happens in this phase is categorized as "working through." Working through, according to Greenson (1967) is the "psychological work which occurs after an insight has been given and which leads to a stable change in behavior or attitude" (p. 29).

Most therapists contend that during this phase the patient–therapist relationship that has been established (that is, the nature and the quality of this relationship), becomes ever more central to the therapeutic work that unfolds. During the middle phase of treatment the patient becomes increasingly comfortable with invitations to free associate. Roth, writing about the relational issues that emerge during the middle phase of treatment, highlights two additional, interrelated factors that are particularly salient during this phase. The first factor is the emergence of the clinical transference. (I shall return to this in a moment.) The second factor, and to Roth (1987), "perhaps the most important one," is the "patient's realization that the early fantasy that the therapist will magically provide solutions" or easy answers has not taken place and will never be actualized (p. 168). During this middle phase of treatment, the patient develops the often agonizingly painful awareness that this process will take a lot of work and that the answers to life's baffling, haunting, existential questions will not come easily. The disappointment and frustrations that emerge from this realization contribute further to the unfolding of the clinical transference in general and to the development of the negative transference in particular.

Once we find that the patient feels solidly contained in the therapeutic relationship, we might observe the oddest thing happening. The patient begins to treat the therapist in a manner similar to the ways in which he or she related to other important figures in his or her early life and most likely to those in his or her current life as well. This, of course, is called the transference. Many experts (e.g., Gill, 1994; Glover, 1955; Greenson, 1967) argue that the proficiency with which the therapist handles the transference is the sine qua non of the therapy process. In other words, skill at working within the transference determines the success of the psychotherapy.

Learning in the Transference: Working Through via the Transference

Most of the learning that transpires in therapy will take place through the process of engaging in (through experiencing firsthand) the transference. This intense level of interpersonal engagement takes place in the "here and now" and is amplified by the way the therapist and the patient find the right language for talking about the transference. Whether the therapist is considered a psychoanalyst or a psychoanalytically oriented psychotherapist, active work around the transference process becomes the crux of the treatment.

A woman with whom I have worked in psychotherapy for several years continues to struggle with letting herself settle into the transference. Excerpted from one of my clinical sessions with this patient, she described her transference concerns this way:

I know we need to talk a lot more about our relationship. [A particular transference enactment around scheduling brought this on.] I want to do this, but it is really scary. I can't tell you how scary it is. I think one of the things that makes it so scary is this: To talk about our relationship, to me also means that I will become more and more dependent upon you. That's what's so scary: to be dependent upon you or anyone. My fear is that the moment I become truly dependent on someone, that person will walk away from me. They'll leave me. This is what has happened in every relationship of mine up to this point. So, I try to stay independent—not needing anyone. But I want to be able to depend on you, to accept the help and support you offer. Maybe, just maybe, I will even grow or change through doing so.

Here we see an interesting dynamic that plays out in the transference. Through talking frequently about her dilemma and its accompanying struggles in sessions, we have begun to understand the ways her relationship with me is similar to—and yet different from—earlier relationships. This similar-to/different-from phenomenon has been and will be addressed over and over. We talk about it! Then, we talk about it some more!

Russell (1996) has noted that it is precisely this kind of repetition that gets played out again and again, especially in therapeutic relationships with people who have experienced some kind of early trauma. (This patient had, in fact, experienced severe early verbal [emotional] trauma.) Repetition seems to be the path (and predilection) of the psyche according to Russell, especially for the "psyche in relationship." We repeat; we repeat; we repeat. One on hand, we repeat to re-create the familiar, on the other, we repeat in an effort to create something different—something new. The repetition compulsion functions as an attempt to heal, according to Russell (1998a, p. 3).

First, the repetition must get acted out in the transference—over and over again. Finally, we (the therapists) begin to "get it." We begin to catch on to what is happening in the transference. Now we can begin to formulate the intractable, repetitive transference dynamic in language. Words are assigned to it; we can talk about it now.

For example, in the case material just quoted, I have been able to find ways to empathetically talk about how scary it is to become dependent, to risk counting on someone. We have been able to talk about how certain she was that if she became dependent on me, I would most certainly abandon her. She was convinced of this even though that had not happened in the years of therapy up to now. How she wanted to trust, longed to trust me, and yet could not. This dynamic was noted and discussed many times. This struggle was continually acted out—again and again—in the transference. In brief, it is through the noting of, through the assigning of language to the repetition, through looking at the repetition in the transference that the old dynamics could be highlighted and possibilities for new ways of engaging became available. This patient developed insight. She matured developmentally in her ability to understand and experience relationships. And she developed the ability to trust, an experience that had been denied her during her childhood and later years. It was through perceiving both the similarities and the differences that existed between her experiences with me as her therapist and those earlier traumatic experiences (while continuing to put words to the similarities and differences) that such seemingly intractable dynamics were eventually worked through and resolved. This is most certainly an exciting kind of learning experience. In this context, it could be said that psychotherapeutic insight and learning are reciprocal phenomena. Of course, learning and insight experiences of these sorts are integral to the enhancement of mature, adaptive functioning. In short, we need to highlight the learning that takes place around transference interpretations. To the degree that we do this, we will most likely have a successful treatment. This said, we must nonetheless bear in mind that not all therapeutic approaches value transference work to the same degree.

Other Theoretical Perspectives on the Middle Phase of Psychotherapy: Learning Through the Transference and Beyond

I begin this section by drawing on the works of two contemporary analysts for whom I have great admiration. Fosshage (1994) and Hoffman (1998) are theorists who have attempted to push the limits of our understanding with respect to what it is that transpires in psychoanalysis, particularly in the transference dynamics. They have also tried to create bridges to other theoretical orientations of psychotherapeutic practice. In doing so, these theorists have emphasized the distinctive learning dimensions of the psychotherapy process. In fact, it is fair to say that for these theorists, increased awareness, insight development, and learning are indeed reciprocal phenomena.

Fosshage, a psychologist and psychoanalyst from New York, is both an intersubjectivist and a relational theorist.[10] He is sympathetic to the notion that similarities exist among the various theoretical approaches to psychotherapy. For example, he detects a curious congruence between a psychodynamic approach and a cognitive approach, especially because both theoretical approaches attempt to address what it is that happens in the transference. To Fosshage's way of thinking, many traditional analysts, relational analysts, and cognitive psychologists alike refer to rather similar dynamics as they attempt to explain the transference and the kind of repetitive relatedness that occurs in both the transference and in the repetitions of everyday interpersonal relationships. Fosshage (1994) argues that irrespective of one's theoretical vantage point, what we see in operation in the therapy in general—and in the transference in particular—are "affect-laden organising principles or schemas at work" (p. 267). In that passage and others, we see that his nomenclature, one that includes terms such as *schemas*, and *organizing principles*, sounds very "cognitive." The language sounds cognitive, not only as it is manifest in cognitive (behavioral) therapy (Beck, 1967, 1976), but in a more traditional cognitive, structural (Piagetian) sense as well. The following passage from Fosshage (1994) illustrates this point rather convincingly as he draws on Piaget (1954) and Stolorow and Lachmann (1984–85):

> Transference is the patient's assimilation (Piaget, 1954) of . . . the analytic relationship into the thematic structures of his personal subjective world . . . transference [viewed thusly] is *neither a regression to nor a displacement from* the past, but rather an expression of the *continuing influence* of organising principles and imagery that crystallized out of the patient's formative years (Stolorow & Lachmann, 1984–85, p. 26). (Fosshage, 1994, p. 267; emphasis added)

Later in the same article, Fosshage (1994) drew on these same structural ideas, arriving at his own definition of the transference: "Transference . . . [is the term] I use . . . to refer to the primary organising patterns or schemas with which the analysand constructs and assimilates his or her experience of the analytic relationship" (p. 271). Thus we see, clearly stated in the quotations, Fosshage's structural (cognitive, Piagetian) slant on the transference phenomenon. He reveals transference as an understandable problem in learning that transpires as the person over time develops an idiosyncratic array of cognitive schemas. In short, the problem stems from the fact that the patient is engaging in the process of assimilating into old schema when the dynamic of accommodation is most likely in order. In other words, the patient is trying to force-fit new experiences into the old, less adaptive container, rather than making an effort to learn new ways of looking at things.

Hoffman (1998), the other contemporary analyst mentioned, has offered some further clarification on this topic, particularly in relation to the patient's unique experience of the transference:

> There is no perception free of some preexisting set, bias, or expectation, or to borrow from Piaget's framework, no perception independent of "assimilation" to some preexisting schema. Such assimilation does not twist an absolute external reality into something that it is not. Rather it gives meaning or shape to something that is "out there" that has among its "objective" properties a kind of amenability to being assimilated in just this way. Moreover, the schema itself is flexible and tends to "accommodate" to what is in the environment, even while it makes what is in the environment fit itself. (p. 120)

According to this way of thinking, the patient's so-called limitations or distortions in the experience of the transference are present-tense "problems of continuing influence" (Fosshage, 1994, p. 267). To Hoffman, they are the result of overzealous assimilation activity and "faulty learning" in which organizing principles and schemas (tacitly formulated in the patient's past) remain operative in the present, thus shaping current perceptions and experience.

Fosshage (1994) and Hoffman (1998) have both wrestled with and attempted to explain the similarities and differences relative to the more traditional and the newer approaches to transference. In part, their efforts

are due to their beliefs that the old way is too pathologically oriented. In turn, both begin to transition into a more learning-oriented model of the transference.

For Fosshage and Hoffman the unquestionably preferred model for explaining the transference is one that involves learning in a quasi-Piagetian fashion. They believe this model to be more user-friendly, more patient-friendly. The traditional psychoanalytic model, on the other hand, focuses more on the patient's defenses, distortions, and projections—and thus may be limiting to the psychotherapy or analysis. Moreover, interpretations coming from these more pathological angles may be experienced as hurtful, pejorative—perhaps even as blaming the patient.

This "new think," they both seem to argue, is more applicable across the board. It represents a new model of transference that makes it easier in the long run to talk about the transference as a matter of learning. So if we can now focus on looking at the transference as an organizing activity, wherein current experience is assimilated into previously established schemas, we can both depathologize and demythologize the transference. In so doing, we help the patient understand, in common language, what is taking place relationally—both in the transference and in everyday life relationships.

As a consequence of this way of thinking, these theorists have developed interpretive techniques that focus decidedly on a process of understanding and on explaining the problematic schemas to patients. Frank (2002) used similar structural language while recommending specific techniques to address enactments occurring both within and outside of the treatment room. Although Frank (2002) is a relational analyst, he recommends using integrative interventions (including behavioral interventions) that promote new relational experiences (with the therapist and with others). Moreover, Frank believes that these same kinds of integrative strategies will concurrently enhance the likelihood that true structural change will follow. In short, Fosshage (1994), Hoffman (1998), and Frank (2002) have begun to promote a mode of treatment that involves principles of learning that help the patient unlearn or modify prior learning experiences. In the following, Fosshage (1994) illustrates the way this new model of explaining the transference helps to decode and demystify the transference dynamic:

> To illuminate the transference, the analyst, through his/her participation in the analytic field, *reflects,*

understands, and *explains* how the patient experiences and organises the analytic relationship with particular emphasis on primary *problematic schemas.* . . . The contribution of the analyst [to the analytic field] is frequently acknowledged. (p. 269; emphasis added)

Hoffman (1998) described a patient who believed he was being used or exploited by his therapist (e.g., charged too high a fee, had his therapy sessions tape recorded for a journal article). In this situation and consistent with the above approach, Hoffman might want to show the patient how familiar and repetitive the experience of being used has been to him and how this feeling of being used occurred in many earlier relationships. Yet the therapist should also acknowledge that he or she (the therapist) might be doing things in the treatment process that contribute to this perception. The therapist would thus be highlighting the old, familiar, problematic schema, while at the same time creating the opportunity for the development of a new one. The therapist might say something like:

"No wonder"[11] you feel so ripped off by me; people have routinely ripped you off in the past. You have especially felt this "ripped-off-ness" in your dealings with your parents, your siblings, etc. So, it is no wonder that the lens through which you see *me* (us together; our relationship) is colored or shaped by the same historically used lens of being used by others. So, when you are here with me, it must feel like I am just one more person ripping you off.

In making such an interpretation, the possibility of a new schema is offered. The therapist demonstrates that he or she can understand (and withstand) the patient's upset. The therapist also demonstrates that the patient's attributions or accusations are not taken personally. And, as seen in the piece about to be discussed, the therapist acknowledges in the present moment that the therapist did, in fact, have some real, objective, present-tense role in eliciting this kind of response from the patient. The therapist acknowledges his or her contribution to the analytic field. The therapist says, "Yes, we can understand that there are also some reasons for your being upset with me (e.g., "I did raise my fee," "I did tape record the sessions for my own personal use," "I did write about you in the journal article"). In essence, the therapist

validates that there was something actually done (by the therapist) that contributed to the patient's reaction. The patient might experience this as reassuring, and, in turn, the patient's defenses might diminish. Consequently, the patient may become more open to new experiences. In brief, the patient is offered an opportunity to modify or adapt an existing problematic schema. We could also say that the patient is now presented with the chance to make an essential accommodation and create a new schema. It is as if the therapist helps "make room" for the creation of a new schema—one in which the possibility exists for someone to be present in his life whose main agenda is not taking advantage of him or using him in the same old way. At the same time, this new person (the therapist) also empathetically acknowledges to the patient that it makes sense that he would be seen as doing the same old thing to the patient. It is almost as if assimilation and accommodation are taking place in the same moment—as the therapist emphasizes two things at once: "How similar this is to your old experience *and* how different it is" (see Russell, 1998a, p. 3—the "repetition compulsion as an attempt to heal"). In brief, the therapist has helped create the opportunity for some new learning.

Significant new learning can now begin to take place. Not only does the therapist clarify, with the patient's help, what has transpired in the transference relationship, but the therapist also does some "confessing" of his or her part in all of this. The therapist acknowledges having a possible role in evoking this particular response (the old problematic schema). Perhaps in doing so, the therapist demonstrates to the patient that unlike some of the other historic characters or players in the patient's life who have likely become defensive when confronted with such attributions, this new person (the analyst) actually welcomes it.[12] In Hoffman's (1998) book, he actually shows the patient that he is interested in, and "has an appetite for," this kind of relationship and this kind of talk (p. 127). Hoffman goes so far as to say that he will even seek out such opportunities in the therapeutic milieu.

So it is through interpretations and related attempts to understand interpersonal, relational events such as those emerging in the transference that change, transformation and learning can begin to take place in the psychotherapy process. I now turn to the central role that affect and emotion have in vitalizing both the therapy and the person.

Retrieving and (Re-)Integrating the Affect

The role of affect in human development has consistently received short shrift in present-day psychology. However, there are a few courageous thinkers on the contemporary scene who have worked to advance affect (emotion) to a center stage position in the theater of psychotherapy theory. Fosshage (1994), Gould (1990), Greenberg (2002), Russell (1998b), Young (1997), and others have attempted to place affect (feelings, emotions) at the forefront of developmental discourse.[13] Coombs, Coleman, and Jones (2002) have recently conducted extensive research highlighting the importance of working with feelings in various kinds of therapy settings. Tomkins (1980), of course, spent the better part of a career elucidating the pivotal role played by emotion in human development. Goleman (1995), in his popular book *Emotional Intelligence*, has done much to elevate the topic of emotions in contemporary awareness. And in the psychoanalytic literature, Fosshage (1994) has held that all schemas of the human psyche are imbued with affect. He especially highlighted the role of affect in the formation of critical transference schemas.

Schemas, most assuredly, are both cognitive and affective constructions. Contrary to popular opinion, schemas are never exclusively cognitive, although one might be led to believe that this is the case (see research in social cognition; Kruger & Dunning, 1999). The history of cognitive development and postformal developmental theory suggests this as well. Commons, Richards, and Armon (1984), Perry (1970), and Sinnott (1998) seem to treat schemas as if they were primarily cognitive formations. This is a misconception promulgated by developmentalists and therapists of various orientations—especially those of the cognitive-behavioral variety. The problems emerging from this misattribution have far-reaching implications—especially in the clinical arena.

Affect cannot be separated from cognition. Vygotsky has written extensively about the interplay of cognition and emotion. For example, Vygotsky (1978) noted that "every advance [in intellectual processes] is connected with a marked change in motives, [emotions], and incentives" (p. 92). Vygotsky consistently made this point in his writings. Schemas must be thought of as amalgams of cognition, emotion, feeling, and motivation, along with other attributes of the self-system. Other contemporary thinkers have also advanced this integrative view. In recent writings, Moss (1992) and Young (1997) have attempted to find ways to reintroduce affect into developmental theory and, of course, into psychotherapeutic treatments of the person. Briefly, Young (1997), in a recent book in which he promoted the integration of adult development theories and psychotherapy, argued that "there are steps in development throughout the adult period . . . that . . . are characterized by a union of the cognitive and the affective" (p. v). Proceeding from a neo-Vygotskian perspective, Young (1997) declared that virtually every developmental step involves the union of the cognitive and the affective. In fact, he coined the notion of "cognitive-emotional coschemes" as a way of accentuating this union (p. 327). These coschemes can be promoted, for example, through a parenting process in which both cognition and affect are cultivated and explored. This is accomplished through intimate interpersonal relationships that involve discussions about emotions; of course, this process and its accomplishments are also integral to psychotherapy.[14]

It might be said that to the degree to which our culture, academicians, and clinicians have tried to separate the two, and in particular to treat cognition in isolation from emotion, we have made a grave mistake that has far-reaching consequences. Many would argue that among other things, this is the down side of the Cartesian *cogito ergo sum* in which the mind is simply viewed as a "thinking thing" (see Stolorow, Orange, & Atwood, 2001). Freud, in contradistinction to Descartes, seems to have switched Descartes's "I think therefore I am" into its reverse: "You are, therefore you think" (Carnochan, 2001, p. 66). This perspective echoes the fabled existential motto "being precedes essence." These conceptual turns of phrase place the emphasis on something other than cognition. For quite some time now, those in the sciences and academic circles have privileged cognition, even as they have minimized, if not denigrated, the roles given emotion and affect. It is as if they threw the proverbial baby out with the bath water. They have operated as if cognition and the intellect should reign supreme, and that affect should be either ignored or relegated to a lower status. How did things get so out of whack? Should we blame all of this on Descartes, or should we place more of the responsibility on logical positivism and behaviorism, and their offspring—cognitive-behavioral theory? These schools of thought have contributed immeasurably to the problem of split-off affect and the bifurcated if not dissociated self.

In this context, I think we must begin to heed the advice of Vygotsky (1978), Fosshage (1994), Russell (1996), Fishman (1996), Gould (1990), and others who demand that we bring affect back into the picture. We must follow the lead of those who assign affect a place of equal status alongside that afforded cognition, as we work to educate people about affect and reintegrate it into a comprehensive picture of what it means to be human. In this light, we must emphasize the inseparable nature of cognition and affect.

Given the historical split between affect and cognition, a split that has filtered down into the thinking and parlance of the general population, we need to consider that a major developmental task in adulthood is the reintegration of the two. Not only is this a major developmental and learning task for every individual, it is also an important component of any psychotherapy.

I am reminded of a former patient at this juncture, a man who claimed to not know (or experience) emotions. On the first day of psychotherapy with me, he asked if I had a checklist of emotions. I said I did not, but that I had seen such lists. He said he once saw such a checklist itemizing 100 or so emotions. Of the 100, my patient commented that he had only experienced 3 of them (anger, rage, sadness). I was somewhat surprised, but I believed him. After more than six years of weekly psychotherapy sessions, this man began to be able to experience a much richer and more complex inner world. He learned a great deal about emotions and about his subjective life during this time. He learned to make subtle distinctions among emotions. After several years of therapy he could eventually laugh when he thought of the person he used to be when he first came into treatment (i.e., the man with the emotion-discerning limitations). At one point he could jokingly admit to and even brag about being able to recognize almost every emotion on the list. Clearly, significant learning had transpired during the course of this psychotherapeutic treatment.

The remarks made by a different patient in a recent session come to mind as well. He began the meeting by saying:

I have really been looking forward to our therapy sessions lately. I am getting more and more interested in (and used to) admitting to my feelings—and identifying them. I can more easily see how I used to be so cut off from them. There used to be a lot of shame. I was always reluctant to admit that. Now I know there is the shame and so many more feelings that I can begin to identify.

Many developmental and relational psychoanalytic thinkers would argue that an accurate marker of evolving adult maturity is characterized by persons' attaining a greater awareness of both the depth and breadth of human emotions—coupled with the (re-)integration of affect and cognition in the self's inner life. In the clinical- developmental realm, both Kegan and Sinnott have taken active stances that move in this direction. In his recent book *In Over Our Heads*, Kegan (1994) offered several clinical vignettes that illustrate this central message. In her recent book, Sinnott (1998) wrote that of necessity, the midlife adult does more to combine "subjectivity and objectivity" than was true in younger adulthood (p. 55).

In the more strictly clinical, psychotherapeutic realm, Russell (1996) and Fishman (1996) have reflected on the ways in which affect is split off from awareness. This occurs not only because of cultural and everyday pressures, but, perhaps more important, to the experience of trauma. This split-off-ness of affect occurs with trauma of every sort. The fact of the matter is that most people (therapy patients or not) have experienced events that can be called traumatic at some point in their lives. These traumas might include outright horrific events, such as physical or sexual abuse, or they may be due to various forms of neglect. According to Russell (1998b), traumatic events can cause feeling (affect) to split off to the extent that people lose the capacity to feel. At that point, memory and overall general functioning can be impaired. From Russell (1998b):

Let me, to begin with, make the general working assumption that the repetition compulsion and psychopathology amount to the same thing. To whatever degree there is a systematic encroachment on the capacity to see things as they are [schemas distorted by trauma], we can assume that this is because the present is being seen in terms of the past. We might call it a *disorder of memory*. To whatever degree there has been trauma, it is inappropriately over-remembered. I would like to suggest that this disorder of memory is affectively determined. It amounts to an *injury to the capacity to feel*. (p. 24; emphasis added)

In another place, Russell (1998a) puts it this way: "The repetition occurs in lieu of something we cannot yet feel, a kind of affective incompetence" (p. 4). When there is trauma—and/or lack of containment—affect tends to get split off or dissociated. Many examples of this phenomenon are offered in the clinical literature. We also find it in other sources. For example, I am reminded of a movie that I saw recently—a film called *K-PAX* (Universal Studios, 2001). In this film a man named Robert Porter (played by Kevin Spacey) arrived on the scene of a massacre where a stranger, wandering into the area of the Porter cottage, had slaughtered Robert's beloved wife and daughter. Understandably, Robert could not withstand (much less process) this atrocity. He developed an extreme, unusual set of symptoms in response to this abhorrent trauma. In short, he became a man from outer space, a man who had come to possess all intellect and no feelings. He was brilliant with facts and numbers but acted like an automaton when it came to emotions. He had none; he ridiculed those who did. His psychiatrist became fascinated by him and was determined to get to the bottom of his case. He spent inordinate amounts of time with this most intriguing, yet confounding man—trying to solve Porter's incredible mystery. He took Porter home for family events. He visited the scene of the murders. Finally, the psychiatrist got it. He realized that Porter had completely split off the affect (cut off all feeling) in response to the severe trauma he had witnessed and experienced. We see in the film that Porter was never able to reintegrate affect into his emotional life, despite the best efforts of his psychiatrist and other professionals. It would have been too painful. He had to keep all emotion split off. The feelings of pain and grief would have been too unbearable to reintegrate.

Sifneos (1991) coined a term for this symptom picture. He called it *alexithymia*. According to Sifneos, alexithymics "give the impression of being different, alien beings, having come from a different world, [yet] living in a society that is dominated by feeling" (p. 116). Lifton (1993) described something similar after conducting extensive research with various groups of people who had experienced severe trauma, (e.g., survivors of Hiroshima and Nagasaki, Vietnam War veterans). He uses the term *psychic numbing* to describe virtually the same phenomenon. Lifton

(1993) defined psychic numbing as the "diminished capacity or inclination to feel . . . often with a marked separation of thought from feeling"(p. 208). These people often experience "shattered meaning structures on one hand and impoverishment and fragmentation of the self on the other" (p. 207).

In their chapters in Lifson's (1996) *Understanding Therapeutic Action*, Russell (1996) and Fishman (1996) wrote extensively on this subject. As Russell (1998b) noted in the earlier quotation about the similarity between the repetition compulsion and psychotherapy, trauma gives rise to limited affect; trauma causes affect to split off (see also Russell, 1996, 1998a). The big questions at this juncture are: How do we facilitate the return of affect? How do we help the person to reintegrate affect into the self's essence? What kind of learning will be involved in this process?

Fishman (1996) answers these questions clearly in the title of his chapter—"Listening to Affect." Russell's thoughts on the matter incorporate Fishman's ideas, but offer more. As seen in the above example, split-off or dissociated emotion shows itself in the repetition compulsion, that is, in those situations in which the patient becomes emotionally engaged with the analyst in a manner that is similar to his or her involvement with a prior (trauma-inducing) figure. These reenactments with the analyst come alive in the transference. From this perspective, the reenactments occur so that the patient does not have to feel the feelings. That is, the patient acts, behaves, "does something" instead of feeling the emotions. The activity of doing something is what actually helps protect the patient from the unwanted painful feelings. At the same time, though, we must assume that the unconscious helps bring the feelings into the treatment process through the enactment so that they can be witnessed and analyzed. We recall from the Russell quotation: The "disorder of memory" is coupled with the "injury to the capacity to feel" (1998b, p. 24). Among other things, the job of the therapist will now center on finding ways to talk about the enactments that occur (both within and outside of the therapy) in ways that are nonpunitive and that promote learning and understanding. To do so, the therapist will have to be empathetic, intimate (involved), and genuine in making appropriate interpretations of the transference (including the enactments and the repetitions). The therapist must make it safe for the patient to understand and learn. From Russell (1996):

Genuine intimacy makes the repetition compulsion unnecessary. However, the individual tests every potential intimacy through the repertoire of his or her repetitions to the extent that intimacy survives. If this process continues, the repetition becomes, very gradually, less a repetition and more a *genuine negotiation.* . . . The [patient's] safety of aloneness is gradually, very slowly, relinquished in favor of an utterly new event in this particular context: *safety within a relationship.* The repetition compulsion can yield to nothing other than *attachment and involvement.* (p. 214; emphasis added)

So it is through experiencing and reexperiencing the repetitions within the safety of the relationship with the analyst that new learning, new development, and a new inner experience can begin to unfold. At the same time, the old repetitions initially incorporated into one's repertoire to avoid painful feelings and affects can now be jettisoned. Through this kind of learning, through the gentle, ongoing interpretation of the repetitions and the transference, new schemas are developed. At the same time, a new self-experience—one that welcomes the integration of emotions (affects and feelings) with thought and the inner life—begins to emerge.

The Middle Phase of Treatment Continued: Developmental Crises and Therapeutic Change

Thus far we have witnessed the essential role a therapist's interpretations can play in the learning process that transpires in psychotherapy. We have just seen how critical and timely interpretations can serve an essential function in helping reintegrate affect within a person's subjective life. In this light, another important thinker who has addressed the reintegration of affect through the psychotherapeutic process is Gould. Gould (1990) is a psychiatrist-psychoanalyst who has adopted a rather compelling developmental twist to his therapeutic theorizing. Not only does he reiterate the need to work with adult patients on the reintegration of affect, he also has much to say about the relative importance of working within the transference. Despite serving as an analyst who systematically works with the transference, Gould has more measured expectations concerning the efficacy of transference interpretations.

Briefly, Gould believes that considerable benefit emanates from working within the transference and from the working through process that is connected with transference interpretations. But he believes there are limits to the changes one can make based on interpretations alone. Gould believes that the therapist's interpretations are more effective (and significant change is more likely) when the patient is also grappling with a specific, timely developmental transition (e.g., leaving home, marrying, divorcing, beginning a new relationship, coping with a midlife transition, retiring, facing a serious illness, or possibly, facing death).

Gould offers examples of people who have been involved in psychotherapeutic treatments (with limited success) for extended periods of time. According to Gould, their lack of success is due primarily to the fact that these patients were not ready to do the necessary psychotherapeutic work. By this, he means the following: For these patients to be ready to do the work, they must be challenged by specific kinds of developmental tasks or developmental adversities. If there were no critical developmental crises that had pushed them to states of readiness, then they were not appropriately poised for the new learning and transformation that needed to transpire. For the purpose of clarification, Gould described some of his own patients who fit this category. He included patients who had quit therapy in frustration only to return years later in the midst of some kind of life crisis. Now, according to Gould, they were ready to work! Now the work in therapy had a sense of urgency. These patients were primed to undergo change; they were more amenable to change because they were now facing urgent developmental challenges. A demand to change presented itself to them in the form of external situations (by pressing developmental, life challenges). The developmental demand resonated with a patient's internal anguish that had been formed by his or her personal, unique history and psychology. Gould proposed the term *unit of adult development* to cover this kind of an intricate psychosituational dynamic. According to Gould (1990), the necessary [developmental] work is embedded in a context that is "frequently categorized as a transition, a crisis, a stress situation, or a challenge" (p. 352).

Gould believes that when a patient comes to the process of psychotherapy or psychoanalysis facing the challenge accompanying such a "unit of work," something transformative is bound to happen. As well, we know that a great deal of learning will take place during these times of transformation. I emphasize here that Gould does not see his "unit of work" concept as that which can occur separately from psychotherapy or psychoanalysis, but he does emphatically claim that it is a facilitator of analytic change. From Gould (1990),

> Concepts of time, aging, and death represent the "entities" of the life-cycle developmental process. Therapeutic attention can no longer focus entirely on the conflicts of memory [dealing with the past—past conflicts, etc.]; it must include *current reality* and the struggle to adapt to ever-changing time. . . . I propose . . . a model of treatment based on adult development that shifts focus toward these entities of the life cycle without sacrificing the insights of depth psychology. (p. 346; emphasis added)

I appreciate that Gould retains the value of doing relational and transference-oriented psychotherapy, but I do not entirely agree with his emphasis on the primacy of the encounter with developmental issues or units of work. I would argue that these developmental challenges are to some degree a given in all psychotherapies. All patients face some kind of developmental struggle or passage, regardless of where they are in the life cycle. Developmental challenges are ubiquitous and perennial. Thus I tend to privilege the relationship work, the transference work, over the emphasis on the developmental issue or crisis—although in many respects, they are inseparable. Suffice it to say that the developmental crisis often becomes the catalyst that accentuates the transference work and related interpretations. We must talk about the relationship and what goes on in the relationship. We must scour or mine the relationship dynamic for all its worth. This is where the most exciting and necessary learning and development takes place.

The Third Phase of Treatment: Termination

Over time we eventually come to the third and final phase of the psychotherapy process. To reach this point, the venture in self-exploration may have taken months, but most likely it has taken years. Hopefully, we come to this ending phase after a successful period of working in the transference, after deeply exploring the therapeutic relationship. Termination only becomes possible after working through the various insights and awarenesses that were garnered along the way.

One might wonder why this third and final stage of therapy is called the termination phase. Some might consider this an odd or peculiar term for this stage of the therapy. Why don't we call it something like "graduation?" In many respects, it is a graduation and a time for celebration—especially as we have focused on the learning features of the therapeutic process. Moreover, the personal conflicts that had brought the person into treatment are now fairly well resolved. Through exploring the intricacies of the therapeutic relationship with the therapist, the patient has developed a great deal of awareness, insight, and learning.

Often during the final phase of treatment, we find that a rather peculiar set of circumstances begins to take place. During the termination, we typically find a recurrence of the themes (symptoms) that brought the patient into treatment in the first place. For example, the anxieties, compulsions, or neurotic symptoms that sent the person into treatment might return. How can this be? Might their return reflect an unsuccessful treatment—perhaps suggesting that it is not the right time to quit? This is an interesting phenomenon to think about—especially from a learning perspective. How curious this is! How do we begin to make sense of it? Are the new ways of being, the hard-won accommodations, the new ways of coping that were heretofore learned in the treatment process now being forgotten or unlearned? Is there some version of "spontaneous recovery" at work here? Or are we better advised to think in more relational, dynamic terms? Is this reemergence of symptoms a response to the dependency dynamic that ideally developed in the therapy? Might the patient be acting out something like "I am not ready to go. I still need you. Although you are not my parent, this is the most caring and safe relationship that I have ever experienced. Don't make me leave!" In short, these thoughts and feelings will be talked about during the termination phase.

Symptoms can often be thought of as attempted communications from deep within the unconscious. This is true for symptoms recurring during termination as well. We might wonder what the unconscious is attempting to say here. Is it attempting to reiterate and consolidate the lessons learned in the psychotherapy? Might it be asking itself, "Are the repetition compulsions gone forever?" It is as if the mind or psyche is giving itself (and the therapist) a final exam. What have I really learned in the process? Just how far have I really come in all of this? Are these gains that I feel

I have made, in fact, permanent ones? Can I consolidate my gains? To achieve mastery over symptoms and to consolidate one's gains are, to be sure, long-standing, commonly accepted notions of what the termination phase is all about.

Dealing with grief and loss are also components of the termination phase. Complications related to loss are so often what bring people into treatment. Now, in the termination phase, one is facing loss by choice. The task now is to face the loss in a different way—in a conscious, deliberate way. As we deliberate over how to bring about the ending, I often ask a patient, "How might this ending be different from all previous endings in your life?" "Can we do it differently?" I suggest that we might be able to bring more conscious awareness to the process and, yes, that we might talk about the nuances of feeling related to the separation/termination process. Talking about the anger, sadness, betrayal, and abandonment that arise during the termination is not easy. However, doing so is essential to complete the course of the therapy, and it further augments the healing and transformation process that has been in the works. Ending this relationship in a different manner from previous endings has a way of convincing the patient that real learning and developmental change have transpired. Both patient and therapist will ideally end the process with the feeling that they have been permanently transformed by the process.

CONCLUSION

How wonderful it is to see a psychotherapy go full course and experience the state of fullness or completion that results from staying with this demanding process all the way to termination. This is a relatively rare phenomenon. To experience a therapy as it evolves from the early stages of the emerging therapeutic alliance and then to move through the middle phase of treatment where one can simultaneously observe and participate in the transference relationship—from its initial budding through to full blossoming—to work in such a way that the transference is talked about, worked through, and resolved en route to a complete termination experience, are exciting dynamics that make both parties participants in a truly exciting, revolutionary process. It is a privilege to be part of such a profound, life-changing, learning experience.

It is also quite a remarkable thing to see a person move beyond stuckness and get back on track. It is gratifying to help someone move out of pain or stagnation and watch them begin to experience the thrill of individuation—the joy of self-actualization. To feel that you have had some small part in this uncanny process can be both rewarding and humbling.

It seems that very few people grasp the truly radical nature of the psychotherapeutic process. Psychotherapy transforms lives. There is a powerful kind of learning that takes place through thoughtful engagement in this process. Learning to free associate is itself transformative. It helps release a person from the shackles of a tyrannical mindset and the limitations inherent in linear, reductionistic mentation. This, in turn, liberates the individual for more creative kinds of thinking and expression, which, in turn, permits the person to develop more expansive and inclusive cognitive structures.

Throughout this chapter I hope I have offered the reader a glimpse into how psychotherapy stimulates change. Of course, there are many facets of the psychotherapy process that others might have chosen to highlight instead. I chose to focus on the relationship aspects because, after 30 years of practice, I am convinced more than ever, that it's the relationship that matters most. The transformative action (the catalysts for change) resides in the relationship. Being in the relationship, being able to talk about the relationship (especially as an antidote for trauma), working the transference and its attendant enactments—this is where things happen. Couple all of this with the added impetus or push that we get from a life phase developmental struggle, and we have set the stage for some truly provocative, transformational learning.

Finally, being able to talk about the end of this therapeutic relationship, to talk through the good-byes, to talk about the grief and loss in an honest and heartfelt manner, are dimensions that add to the efficacy of the process. Ideally, we should be able to rely on the fact that important features of learning from this final phase of the treatment will generalize to other relationships as well (see Wachtel, 2002).

As suggested, the therapist will inevitably change through this process as well. This is an additional bonus of doing the work; the therapist must be prepared for it. Many are not. Russell (1996) declared, as we saw, "For therapy to work, the therapist must become involved" (p. 201). "You can exert no influence if you are not subject to influence" (Jung, 1969, p.70). For the patient to change, the analyst must change. It cannot be said any more succinctly. If the therapist does not become involved, if there are no crisis moments in the therapeutic process for the therapist, there will be no therapy (see Miller, 2000). Involvement and talking about the involvement are the essential elements. Engagement and change must become the bywords for both parties (patient and therapist) in this most challenging of venues for adult development and learning.

ACKNOWLEDGMENTS   I thank Carol H. Hoare, Loren H. Miller, and Alan N. West for their helpful comments and suggestions on earlier versions of this chapter. Also, I express appreciation to my assistant, Kate Logan, for her help with the research component of this project.

Notes

1. The term *mental illness* is quite fashionable in contemporary psychology and psychiatry. As the reader can observe, it is periodically used in this chapter. Nonetheless, I invite the reader to consider that this term is not only overused in contemporary psychology, psychiatry, and medicine but is often misused as well. For a discussion of how most symptom pictures that are called "mental illnesses" are not illnesses, see Frattaroli's (2001) *Healing the Soul in the Age of the Brain*, and, of course, Szasz's (1974) *Myth of Mental Illness*.

2. There has been considerable debate in recent years as to whether to call someone who visits a psychotherapist a patient or a client. The word *client* seems to be preferred by most psychologists. To many clinicians, the term *client* conveys a sense of "working together" and a "balance of power" (mutuality in the relationship). Although I agree that these are important attributes of the psychotherapeutic relationship, there are other features of this relationship that are missed by the term *client*. I think *client* fosters or encourages a degree of resistance to the full depth of the process and denies the extent to which a temporary kind of dependence on the therapist is necessary for accomplishing the deeper therapeutic work.

3. Hunt (1993) does not indicate what he deems to be the six major theoretical approaches to psychotherapy at any juncture in his book; however, the ones he discusses in the most detail are psychodynamic, behavioral, cognitive behavioral, gestalt, humanistic, and transactional analysis.

4. According to Freud (1913/1989a), free association is the "fundamental rule" of psychoanalysis. It is the requirement to "say whatever goes through your mind" (p. 372). Freud, in attempting to instruct a patient on how to free associate, suggested

to the patient: "Act as though . . . you were a traveller [*sic*] sitting next to the window of a railway carriage and describing to someone inside the carriage the changing views which you see outside" (p. 372). I contend that as patients develop the capacity to free associate, tremendous leaps in expanded awareness and a sense of well-being will be experienced (see Bobrow, 2003, pp. 206–207). This point is discussed briefly in a subsequent section of the text.

5. Every effort has been made to protect the identity of these patients. All personal characteristics have been altered and disguised. The vignettes themselves have been modified to maintain confidentiality. In addition, permission from the patients to use the material was requested and granted.

6. A characterological disturbance is another name for a personality disorder. These terms suggest that a person's mental and behavioral difficulties are longstanding and quite resistant to change. It is quite likely that the genesis of such disturbances can be found in early childhood. Hedges (1983) claims that these disorders are "constellations emanating from the mother-child symbiosis and carrying the particular flavor of that exchange" (p. 183). Schizoid, narcissistic, paranoid, histrionic, and borderline are examples of diagnosed disturbances in this nosological category. Hedges (1983) and others contend that we find in these disorders that "early thought and mood patterns become entrenched" to such an extent that they seem indelibly imprinted on the character of the personality" (p. 183).

7. Transference and countertransference are two central concepts needed for a comprehensive understanding of any therapeutic relationship, especially those conducted from a more psychodynamic or psychoanalytic perspective. These concepts are addressed in detail subsequently in the text. For now, preliminary definitions may be helpful to keep in mind. Transference is the sum total of thoughts and feelings that a patient has toward the therapist. Greenson (1967) described transference as "the experience of feelings to a person which do not befit that person and which actually apply to another. Essentially a person in the present is reacted to as though he were a person in the past. . . . It is an anachronism, an error in time. A displacement has taken place; impulses, feelings, and defenses pertaining to a person in the past have been shifted onto a person in the present" (pp. 151–152). The ability of an analyst to help a patient understand transference is critical to the efficacy of an in-depth analysis. Contemporary analysts are also equipped to be curious about the sum total of their own emotional responses (their countertransference) to a particular patient and the relational dynamics that emerge in a session. They understand that some portion of their total response to any given patient might be shaped by an earlier, formative relationship of their own. At the same time, they are also

aware of the fact that this set of emotions may be a response to something unique about the psychology of the patient with whom they are sitting. We often speak of the transference-countertransference dyad because such a formulation implies that there is an ongoing, constantly changing relationship developing between the patient and analyst in which each is affecting the other, both consciously and unconsciously.

8. An interpretation is any kind of statement made by the therapist that connects events and/or relationships in some meaningful fashion. For example, the therapist might connect something that is taking place in the patient's current life with events that happened in the patient's childhood. We see this kind of interpretation illustrated in the vignette. The therapist might also reflect on the similarities that exist between how the patient relates to him with how the patient historically related to his father (see Malan, 1979, p. 80).

9. *Psychical restructuring* can be best understood from the Piagetian perspective addressed in the subsequent section of this chapter. An accurate and well-timed interpretation can help a patient reorganize internal systems and structures of meaning. Such interpretations can transform both ego structures and their concomitant cognitive structures. Not only can major (Piagetian-like) structural accommodations take place via the catalytic function of an appropriate interpretation, but new cognitive/emotional structures can be formed through this process as well.

10. Intersubjective and relational approaches to treatment are relatively new developments that have emerged on the psychoanalytic scene within approximately the past 20 years. Both theories attempt to bring a more subtle yet focused attention to what transpires between the analyst and the patient, to include an even closer investigation of the transference-countertransference dyad and the mutual influence and involvement of both (patient and therapist). Intersubjective theory claims to add a further dimension to the quality of the analysis. It claims that the "object" of the analysis is not the "isolated individual mind, . . . but the larger system created by the mutual interplay between the subjective worlds of the patient and analyst, or of child and caregiver" (Stolorow, Atwood, & Brandchaft, 1994, p. x).

11. This language illustrates Havens's (1986) way of showing empathy toward both the patient and the related problematic schemas that were formed years ago. Havens's approach to this kind of interpretation is similar to that used by Fosshage (1994) and Hoffman (1998), but Havens does not employ the language of structure nor of schemas to explain his technique.

12. See Safran and Muran (2000) for a more in-depth treatment of strategies used in negotiating ruptures in the therapeutic alliance. They illustrate how the skillful negotiation of such ruptures can actually lead to therapeutic breakthroughs.

13. Although there are debates as to differences among the terms *feelings*, *emotions*, and *affect*, I use them interchangeably in this section. Affect or feeling can be thought of as any noticeable conscious or unconscious (emotional) response to a situation, one that is generally accompanied by some degree of physiological change. There are many conflicting definitions of emotions. Hunt (1993) noted that "everyone knows what an emotion is, until asked to give a definition" (p. 483).

14. The examples of psychotherapeutic encounters that promote such cognitive-emotional coschemes presented by Young (1997) in his text are similar to some of the psychotherapy vignettes offered earlier in this chapter (e.g., Fosshage 1994; Hoffman, 1998; and my own). Working through a major transferential dynamic or coming to terms with the vicissitudes of a repetition compulsion would certainly promote the integration of cognition and affect and, subsequently, foster a significant developmental advance or structural achievement.

References

Alonso, A. (1996). Toward a new understanding of neutrality. In L. Lifson (Ed.), *Understanding therapeutic action: Psychodynamic concepts of cure* (pp. 3–19). Hillsdale, NJ: Analytic Press.

Beck, A. (1967). *Depression: Clinical, experimental, and theoretical aspects*. New York: Hoeber.

Beck, A. (1976). *Cognitive therapy and emotional disorders*. New York: International Universities Press.

Bion, W. R. (1970/1983). *Attention and interpretation*. New York: Jason Aronson.

Bobrow, J. (2003). Moments of truth—Truths of moment. In J. D. Safran (Ed.), *Psychoanalysis and Buddhism: An unfolding dialogue* (pp. 199–249). Boston: Wisdom Publications.

Carnochan, P. G. M. (2001). *Looking for ground: Countertransference and the problem of value in psychoanalysis*. Hillsdale, NJ: Analytic Press.

Commons, M., Richards, F., & Armon, C. (Eds.) (1984). *Beyond formal operations: Late adolescent and adult cognitive development*. New York: Praeger.

Coombs, M. M., Coleman, D., & Jones, E. E. (2002). Working with feelings: The importance of emotion in both cognitive-behavioral and interpersonal therapy in the NIMH treatment of depression collaborative research program. *Psychotherapy: Theory, Research, Practice, Training, 39,* 233–244.

Corsini, R. (1984). *Current psychotherapies* (3rd ed.). Itasca, IL: Peacock Publishers.

Fishman, G. (1996). Listening to affect: Interpersonal aspects of affective resonance in psychoanalytic treatment. In L. Lifson (Ed.), *Understanding therapeutic action: Psychodynamic concepts of cure* (pp. 217–235). Hillsdale, NJ: Analytic Press.

Fosshage, J. (1994). Toward reconceptualizing transference: Theoretical and clinical considerations. *International Journal of Psychoanalysis*, 75, 265–280.

Frank, J. D. (1961). *Persuasion and healing: A comparative study of psychotherapy*. New York: Shocken Books.

Frank, K. A. (2002). The "ins and outs" of enactment: A relational bridge for psychotherapy integration. *Journal of Psychotherapy Integration*, 12, 267–286.

Frattaroli, E. (2001). *Healing the soul in the age of the brain: Becoming conscious in an unconscious world*. New York: Viking.

Freud, S. (1913/1989a). On beginning the treatment. In P. Gay (Ed.), *The Freud reader* (pp. 363–378). New York: Norton.

Freud, S. (1913/1989b). Recommendations to physicians practicing psycho-analysis. In P. Gay (Ed.), *The Freud reader* (pp. 356–363). New York: Norton.

Gill, M. (1994). *Psychoanalysis in transition: A personal view*. Hillsdale, NJ: Analytic Press.

Glover, E. (1955). *The technique of psycho-analysis*. New York: International Universities Press.

Goleman, D. (1995). *Emotional intelligence: Why it can matter more than IQ*. New York: Bantam Books.

Gould, R. L. (1990). Clinical lessons from adult development theory. In R. A. Nemiroff & C. A. Colarusso (Eds.), *New dimensions in adult development* (pp. 345–370). New York: Basic Books.

Greenberg, L. (2002). Integrating an emotion-focused approach to treatment into psychotherapy integration. *Journal of Psychotherapy Integration*, 12, 154–189.

Greenson, R. R. (1967). *The technique and practice of psychoanalysis* (Vol. 1). New York: International Universities Press.

Havens, L. (1986). *Making contact: Uses of language in psychotherapy*. Cambridge, MA: Harvard University Press.

Havens, L. (1989). *A safe place*. New York: Ballantine Books.

Hedges, L. E. (1983). *Listening perspectives in psychotherapy*. Northvale, NJ: Jason Aronson.

Hinsie, L., & Campbell, R. (1970). *Psychiatric dictionary*. New York: Oxford University Press.

Hoffman, I. Z. (1998). *Ritual and spontaneity in the psychoanalytic process: A dialectical-constructivist view*. Hillsdale, NJ: Analytic Press.

Hunt, M. (1993). *The story of psychology*. New York: Anchor Books.

Jung, C. G. (1969). The practice of psychotherapy. In H. Mead, M. Fordham, G. Adler, & W. McGuire (Eds.), and R. F. C. Hull (Trans.), *Collected works*, vol 16 (Bollingen Series, vol. 20), Princeton, NJ: Princeton University Press.

Kegan, R. (1994). *In over our heads: The mental demands of modern life*. Cambridge, MA: Harvard University Press.

Kessler, R. C., McGonagle, K. A., Zhao, S., Nelson, C. B., Hughes, M. Eshleman, S., et al. (1994). Lifetime and 12-month prevalence of DSM-III-R psychiatric disorders in the United States: Results from the national comorbidity survey. *Archives of General Psychiatry*, 51, 8–19.

Kozart, M. F. (2002) Understanding efficacy in psychotherapy: An ethnomethodological perspective on the therapeutic alliance. *American Journal of Orthopsychiatry*, 72, 217–231.

Kristeva, J. (2002). *Intimate revolt: The power and limits of psychoanalysis* (Trans. J. Herman). New York: Columbia University Press. (Original work published 1997)

Kruger, J., & Dunning, D. (1999). Unskilled and unaware of it: How difficulties in recognizing one's own incompetence lead to inflated self-assessments. *Journal of Personality and Social Psychology*, 77, 1121–1134.

Langs, R. (1982). *Psychotherapy: A basic text*. New York: Jason Aronson.

Lifson, L. (Ed.). (1996). *Understanding therapeutic action: Psychodynamic concepts of cure*. Hillsdale, NJ: Analytic Press.

Lifton, R. J. (1990). Adult dreaming: Frontiers of form. In R. A. Nemiroff & C.A. Colarusso (Eds.), *New dimensions in adult development* (pp. 419–442). New York: Basic Books.

Lifton, R. J. (1993). *The protean self: Human resilience in an age of fragmentation*. New York: Basic Books.

Luborsky, L. (2001). The meaning of empirically supported treatment research for psychoanalytic and other long-term therapies. *Psychoanalytic Dialogues*, 11, 583–604.

Malan, D. H. (1979). *Individual psychotherapy and the science of psychodynamics*. Cambridge: Butterworth.

Miller, M. E. (2000). The mutual influence and involvement of therapist and patient: Co-contributors to maturation and integrity. In P. Young-Eisendrath & M. E. Miller (Eds.), *The psychology of mature spirituality: Integrity, wisdom and transcendence* (pp. 34–46). London: Routledge.

Moss, E. (1992). The socioaffective context of joint cognitive activity. In L. T. Winegar & J. Walsiner (Eds.), *Children's development within a social context* (vol. 2), *Research and methodology* (pp. 117–154). Hillsdale, NJ: Erlbaum.

Perry, W. G. (1970). *Forms of intellectual and ethical development in the college years*. New York: Holt, Rinehart & Winston.

Piaget, J. (1954). *The construction of reality in the child*. New York: Basic Books.

Roth, S. (1987). *Psychotherapy: The art of wooing nature*. Northvale, NJ: Jason Aronson.

Russell, P. L. (1996). Process with involvement: The interpretation of affect. In L. Lifson (Ed.), *Understanding therapeutic action: Psychodynamic concepts of cure* (pp. 201–216). Hillsdale, NJ: Analytic Press.

Russell, P. L. (1998a). The role of paradox in the repetition compulsion. In J. G. Teicholz & D. Kriegman (Ed.), *Trauma, repetition, and affect regulation: The works of Paul Russell* (pp. 1–22). New York: Other Press.

Russell, P. L. (1998b). Trauma and the cognitive function of affects. In J. G. Teicholz & D. Kriegman (Eds.), *Trauma, repetition, and affect regulation:*

The works of Paul Russell (pp. 23–47). New York: Other Press.

Safran, J. D., & Aron, L. (2001). Introduction. *Psychoanalytic Dialogues, 11,* 571–582.

Safran, J. D., & Muran, J. C. (2000). *Negotiating the therapeutic alliance: A relational treatment guide.* New York: Guilford Press.

Seligman, M. E. P. (1995). The effectiveness of psychotherapy: The Consumer Reports study. *American Psychologist, 50,* 965–974.

Sifneos, P. (1991). Affect, emotional conflict, and deficit. *Psychotherapy and Psychosomatics, 56,* 116–122.

Sinnott, J. D. (1998). *The development of logic in adulthood: Postformal thought and its applications.* New York: Plenum Press.

Stolorow, R., & Lachmann, F. (1984–85). Transference: The future of an illusion. *Annual of Psychoanalysis, 12–13,* 19–37.

Stolorow, R., Atwood, G., & Brandchaft, B. (Eds.). (1994). *The intersubjective approach.* Northvale, NJ: Jason Aronson.

Stolorow, R., Orange, D., & Atwood, G. (2001). Cartesian and post-cartesian trends in relational psychoanalysis. *Psychoanalytic Psychology, 18* (3), 468–484.

Szasz, T. (1974). *The myth of mental illness.* New York: Harper & Row.

Tolstoy, L. (1886/1960). *The death of Ivan Ilyich.* New York: Signet.

Tomkins, S. (1980). Affect as amplification: Some modifications in theory. In R. Plutchik & H. Hellerman (Eds.), *Theories of emotion.* New York: Academic Press.

Torrey, E. F., & Miller, J. (2001). *The invisible plague: The rise of mental illness from 1750 to the present.* New Brunswick, NJ: Rutgers University Press.

Vygotsky, L. S. (1978). *Mind in society.* Cambridge, MA: Harvard University Press.

Wachtel, P. L. (2002). Termination of therapy: An effort at integration. *Journal of Psychotherapy Integration, 12,* 373–383.

Wachtel, P. L., & Messer, S. B. (1997). *Theories of psychotherapy: Origins and evolution.* Washington, DC: American Psychological Association.

Wallerstein, R. S. (1995). *The talking cures: The psychoanalyses and the psychotherapies.* New Haven, CT: Yale University Press.

World Health Organization. (2001, September 28). The world health report 2001: Mental disorders affect one in four people. Retrieved July 23, 2003 from http://www.who.int/inf-pr-2001/en/pr2001-42.html.

Young, G. (1997). *Adult development, therapy, and culture: A postmodern synthesis.* New York: Plenum Press.

Part IV

The Higher Reaches of Adult Development and Learning

Chapter 11

Creativity Through the Life Span From an Evolutionary Systems Perspective

Mihaly Csikszentmihalyi and Jeanne Nakamura

WHAT IS CREATIVITY?

Creativity has become such a commonly used term in the past few decades that everyone has formed an opinion about what it means, and there is no need to define it further. In this chapter, however, we are going to use the word in specific ways, so a few words of explanation may be useful to orient the reader. There are three main dichotomies we use, and if these are not clear, what follows might be confusing.

The first dichotomy is that between creativity with a capital C and with a lowercase c. Big C, or cultural creativity, refers to ideas or products that are original, are valued by society or some influential segment thereof, and are brought to completion (Csikszentmihalyi, 1999; MacKinnon, 1963; White, 1968). This form of creativity changes the way we see, understand, and interact with the reality that surrounds us. It is the energy that propels cultural evolution. Most of this chapter deals with cultural creativity, both because it is a clearly important

feature of human life and because it is the one about which most is known.

But one could argue that small c or personal creativity is just as important, if not more so. Personal creativity refers to the novel ideas or experiences that any person can have and that do not need to leave a trace anywhere else but in the consciousness of the person who has had them. A new hairdo, a shortcut in servicing one's car engine, a clever conversation may qualify. Although this form of creativity does not change the culture, it does make a vast difference to the quality of one's life—without it, existence would be intolerably drab.

These two meanings of the concept are usually thought of as being on the same continuum, the small c slowly growing into the big C. However, there are good reasons to consider them as relatively independent, orthogonal processes that are more different than similar, and this is how we treat the concepts here.

The second dichotomy pertains only to cultural creativity and concerns the dialectic between producers

243

and audience. It is commonly assumed that big C creative ideas are self-sufficient, and thus creativity includes only what happens in the creative person's mind. Our approach assumes instead that without a receptive audience, the creative process is not unlike the sound of one hand clapping the Zen koan refers to. In other words, what we call creativity is coconstituted by an individual who comes up with a novelty and a social milieu that evaluates it (Brannigan, 1981; Csikszentmihalyi, 1988; Kasof, 1995). At the very least, it should be obvious that creativity is always an attribution, and that it cannot be "seen" except when it has been so identified by some group (teachers, critics, historians) that has credibility in the eyes of society. The same is not true of personal creativity. For personal creativity, no external evaluation is necessary; only the subjective experience matters.

Finally, the third dichotomy refers to that between the distal and proximal accounts of why some people bother being creative. Distal explanations present the creative drive as motivated by the desire for fame and wealth—or, in light of the broader scope of evolutionary theory, by the selective forces of survival pressures. Although distal explanations account in part for creative behavior, they ignore the momentary experience of the creative person, which motivates the search for novelty even when wealth and fame are extremely unlikely. Distal explanations tend to be extrinsic, pointing to an external goal that is usually objective and concrete, like money, a promotion, or a prize. Proximal explanations tend to be intrinsic, subjective in nature. In the case of creativity, the intrinsic rewards include the excitement of discovery, the satisfaction of solving a problem, and the joy of shaping sounds, words, or colors into new forms.

With these preliminary distinctions in hand, we proceed to examine some of the ways that moving through the life span affects creativity. We do this first by considering the implications of evolutionary theory for aging and creativity.

CREATIVITY AND LIFE SPAN DEVELOPMENT FROM AN EVOLUTIONARY PERSPECTIVE

According to evolutionary psychology, currently a leading paradigm concerning human behavior, one might conclude that learning—and certainly creativity—are of little use in the second half of life; being useless,

that they should eventually disappear from the human behavioral repertoire as wasteful of energy, to be replaced by concerns more conducive to reproductive fitness—such as taking care of one's offspring and of their descendants. Certainly there is a great amount of evidence to the effect that among all sorts of animals, including humans, the amount of spontaneous learning and some of the behaviors underlying creativity, such as curiosity and playfulness, decrease precipitously with age (Fagan, 1981).

Play, exploration, curiosity, and innovation are linked behaviors in all species. Studies of animal play show a great interspecies variability in the age at which individuals start and stop playing. Wildebeest and caribou infants start prancing playfully a few hours after birth, apparently to discourage predators from attacking them (Estes, 1976). In general, however, play ceases around the time an individual first reproduces "because play at successively later ages yields successively fewer cumulative benefits and because resources devoted to reproduction are more effective for producing surviving offspring than are resources devoted to adult play" (Fagan, 1981, p. 378).

Creativity has not been directly studied in nonhuman species with reference to age. Anecdotal evidence suggests that behavioral flexibility and innovation are much more likely to be shown by younger individuals. For example, Japanese macaques were observed to have trouble eating the fruits placed for them on the ground, where they were immediately covered with sand. After some time, a young female accidentally dropped a sweet potato in the water, and when she retrieved it, the fruit emerged nice and clean. After this the juvenile went on washing its fruit, and presently her mother and siblings began to imitate her (Kawai, 1965). There seems to be no evidence that older males caught on to the new practice. Before one immediately jumps to conclusions about the effects of the Y chromosome on creativity, it is useful to consider the fact that Japanese macaque females, although not the dominant sex, take more of the responsibility for the maintenance of social order than males (see, e.g., Altmann, 1980). This in turn suggests that the diffusion of innovation may be linked to concern for the well-being of the social network. Adult individuals who fill certain roles in the group may be more able to notice innovations and be more likely to adopt them and diffuse them than others.

In this respect it is important to recognize that the adoption of useful new ideas or practices is as important for creativity as the creative act itself. Psychologists have long accepted the popular assumption that "genius will out," meaning that a creative act will prevail and impose itself on the culture regardless of opposition. A more likely scenario is that original ideas become creative only when a critical mass of the audience recognizes them as worthy of attention. According to this systems model, creativity is coconstituted by an individual who introduces a novelty that is selected, preserved, and transmitted over time by a field of experts, or in the case of items of mass culture such as soft drinks or movies, by the market as a whole (Csikszentmihalyi, 1996, 1998; Csikszentmihalyi & Wolfe, 2000).

According to this model, then, the relation between creativity and age is not restricted to the individual who initiates the creative process but extends to the audience as well. The recent interest in "cultural creatives" (Anderson & Ray, 2001) and in a "creative class" (Florida, 2002) can be more appropriately seen as referring to audiences that are susceptible to the adoption of new ideas or products, rather than to those who are actually producing creatively. Thus one might ask: Are older adults more or less likely to recognize and adopt new ideas, practices, or artifacts than teenagers or younger adults?

Before reviewing the empirical evidence for the link between creativity and age among humans, it may be useful to consider the theoretical implications of the evolutionary perspective. To what extent is it true that among us "resources devoted to adult play [or to creativity]" are less effective than resources devoted directly to reproduction? The peculiar survival strategy of *Homo sapiens* has always rested on the use of the cortex, on the processing and abstracting of complex information. This is becoming increasingly true as we enter what has been called a "knowledge economy" or an "information age" (Drucker, 1985, 1999). With useful information and new knowledge constantly coming on line, for many thousands of years now it has been advantageous for individual men and women to retain some of their exploratory curiosity, some of their playfulness and creativity. Even from a purely sociobiological standpoint, to invest energy in new learning may often be a more effective strategy for the propagation and survival of one's genes than investing energy in more conservative, traditional ways of accruing resources.

Some evolutionary psychologists are beginning to reevaluate the role of creativity in the transmission of genes. For example, Geoffrey Miller (2000) argued that creative individuals, especially those working in artistic domains, are more likely to be attractive to the opposite sex and thus reproduce relatively more often. Genius is a "fitness indicator" in that it is rare, valued, and takes time to develop; it is also an "ornament that appeals to the senses," thereby attracting potential mates (Miller, 2000). A similar argument has been advanced by Susan Blackmore (1999).

Two observations are appropriate in considering these extensions of the theory of sexual selection to creativity. In the first place, the reproductive advantage of creativity presumably extends to adulthood but not to old age—yet many great creative accomplishments come late in life. Second, evolutionary explanations of behavior are always distal; that is, they account for why a given behavior survives over time, as the cumulative effects of that behavior over many generations of individuals have a chance to be selected in competition with the behaviors of other individuals who do not engage in that behavior. But evolutionary explanations have little or nothing to say about proximal causes—the ones that actually motivate the individual in his or her lifetime.

Play behavior, for example, is explained by the evolutionary perspective in terms of the advantages that an adult will have if he or she played as a child. Compared to other adults who did not play extensively early in life, such a person may be slightly more savvy at interpersonal relations, better controlled, better able to compete within a clear set of rules, and so on. These are all distal reasons, however. Children do not play because they expect to become more successful adults. They play because it's fun. The proximal reason for playing is that the experience is enjoyable. A similar distinction between distal and proximal explanation holds for creativity as well. Whatever the long-term advantages it confers, the reason people involve themselves in the processes of discovery and invention is that nothing in "normal" life compares with the experience (Csikszentmihalyi, 1996).

But with human beings there is perhaps an even more important difference for expecting creativity and learning to continue throughout life. As a species we are dependent on the social milieu to teach us the accumulated experience of innumerable ancestral generations. Other social organisms—such as ants, termites, or coyotes—also depend on the group to which they belong, but not for learning—what they will ever know is already programmed in their genes. Even though experience within the group is necessary to unlock most of this programmed knowledge, there is little or no evidence of unprecedented behaviors arising in such groups, unless as a result of genetic mutation. As humans we inherit not only our ancestral genes but also the memes (Csikszentmihalyi, 1993; Dawkins, 1976)—the units of useful information—that our forebears have discovered and that are then packaged into myths, histories, philosophies, technology, and science.

Societies that can use past information efficiently tend to provide more comfortable environments and longer life spans for their inhabitants. Such societies presumably encourage continued learning and creativity not only in childhood, but later and later into adulthood. And as more innovative individuals live longer in such societies, this mutual synergy may place in motion a benign spiral of individual and social improvement.

Creativity and Physical Aging

In terms of the relationship between creativity and adult development, it is useful to distinguish between the effects of physical and social aging. However, it is quite difficult to untangle the purely physical effects of aging from those due to social aging. Clear physiological effects include declines in memory functions in old age, impairment of fluid intelligence, and loss of energy. These changes, however, are of relatively little consequence to many forms of creativity. In many ways, social aging is more consequential. This involves passing through social roles that require different behaviors from the person, either enhancing or jeopardizing his or her creativity. Social aging will be discussed in the following section; here we review the scant information available on the purely physiological impact of aging on creativity.

Contrary to popular belief, age—even considerable old age—need not be an impediment to creativity. Michelangelo was 79 years old when he painted the strikingly original frescoes in the Pauline Chapel of the Vatican. Benjamin Franklin was 78 when he developed the bifocal lens for eyeglasses. Giuseppe Verdi composed the opera *Falstaff* at 80, and he never wrote anything as joyfully playful as that composition in the 60 years of his musical career. Frank Lloyd Wright broke new architectural ground at age 91 with the building of the Guggenheim Museum in Manhattan. One could go on and on with examples that show how originality and perseverance need not decrease until the very end of life.

It is true that beginning with the seventh decade of life, it is usual to report a waning of energy and troubles with memory and sustained effort, especially in tasks requiring what has been called "fluid intelligence" (Cattell, 1963). However, age decrements in intellectual functioning appear to be less severe than they were once held to be (Schaie, 1996), and they may be more than compensated for by increased knowledge that accrues with life experience (Baltes & Staudinger, 2000).

It is likely that age presents more obstacles to scientific than to artistic creativity (e.g., Chandrasekhar quoted in Wali, 1991; Lehman, 1953). In our study of creativity in later life (Csikszentmihalyi, 1996; Nakamura & Csikszentmihalyi, 2003), some of the scientists complained that memory decrements were constraining the assimilation of new knowledge, or learning, needed for creative work. For example, a scientist in his nineties observed that he can no longer store and retrieve effortlessly the information he reads. Another complains, "At my age it's a lot harder to learn all these techniques. . . . You think how lucky children are. . . . I get discouraged . . . mathematics comes easily to me. And physics . . . [But] all the experimental side . . . running the programs, does not come easily." (All excerpts quoted in this chapter refer to interview transcripts collected during the Creativity in Later Life Study; see Csikszentmihalyi, 1996; Nakamura & Cskiszentmihalyi, 2003.)

At 75, one social scientist whose research plate is overflowing, cast an interested eye toward a neighboring specialty, but noted, "that is not anything that I am ever going to get into . . . I would not even have the memory." A busy physicist's reasoning was somewhat different: The demands of learning a controversial new paradigm would have required putting aside his ongoing, engaging work; besides, the new area did not promise to lead to the kind of "final" or "complete" answers that this scientist finds satisfying.

Faced with demands to assimilate new ideas and particularly new technologies to do creative work, many scientists are clearly aided by the resources accruing from earlier achievements. Some rely on collaborators' knowledge of new technologies, others on support staff's ability to use computers. In other words, above and beyond their continuing impact on productivity, the external resources at the disposal of eminent individuals can substitute for having to engage in new learning.

Social interaction is a major means of staying current in certain domains, such as physics. Some scientists even return to the role of student, violating expectations concerning the conduct of distinguished older scholars. Vibrant examples of late-life learning were provided by two eminent physicists, both still active in their eighties. In recent years, each has sought younger experts at other universities in a specialty that they wished to learn. One explained: "I realized that there is a development in general relativity that I ought to learn about and I did not know. . . . So I got up on my hind feet and phoned and made an appointment and spent two days there talking with people, both this fall and the previous fall."

At the age of 80, this scientist flew from the East Coast to the Midwest to consult with a former college student who had just entered the University of Chicago. Thus, relying on networks of informants can compensate to a large extent for not being able to keep up personally with the progress of disciplinary knowledge.

Investigations of creativity based on the historiometric method pioneered by Lehman (1953), Dennis (1956), and recently expanded by Simonton (1999) and Martindale (1990), have attempted to establish the optimal ages at which creative contributions are typically made. These approaches involve arranging the achievements of a scientist or artist in chronological order and plotting them along the life span axis of the creator. In a recent review, Simonton (1999, p. 120) claimed: "Illustrious creators can be examined from the moment of conception to the very instant of death, plus everything that takes place within this long interval." However, a problem historiographers encounter is that one cannot determine from the published record when the creative ideas actually occurred. A revolutionary idea hatched in early life may not be fully developed until maturity or later; thus the attribution of a specific date for the creative accomplishment is often inaccurate.

Nevertheless, the application of this method makes it possible to come up with some generalizations about the life histories of creative people. Dennis (1966) and Lehman (1960) concluded that the peak of "superior output" for creative people occurs at age 30—the age at which Mozart composed the *Marriage of Figaro* and Edison invented the phonograph. In all, 40% of all major contributions to the culture were made in that decade of life. Half as many (20% each) occurred at ages 20 and 40; and the remaining 20% were spread over the rest of life. One possible contaminant of such results is the inclination to project a more inflated evaluation of the early work of well-known creators based on their lifetime output. In any case, it is impossible to ascertain the extent to which the decline after 40 years of age is due to physical causes or to the social changes associated with age that will be discussed in the next section.

Simonton (1999, p. 122) summarizes six age-linked findings about creativity: Creative individuals tend not to be firstborn; they are intellectually precocious; they suffer childhood trauma; their families tend to be economically and/or socially marginal; they receive special training early in life; and they benefit from role models and mentors. Most of these conclusions relate to the earlier years of life, indicating the lack of systematic knowledge about creativity in the second half of life.

The relation of age to creativity is likely to depend on the particular domain in which the person is operating: "The overall age functions, including the placement of the first, best, and last creative contribution, are contingent upon the specific domain of creative activity" (Simonton 1999, p. 122). To determine answers to questions such as "Why do mathematicians and lyric poets do their most original work earlier in life than, say, architects or philosophers?" one cannot simply consider changes in the maturation of the creative person's brain. One must also explore the interaction between the mind and the symbolic system of the domain and the social constraints and opportunities of the field. For example, in symbolic domains that are very well integrated, like mathematics, chess, or musical performance, it is relatively easy for a talented person to move quickly to the cutting edge of the domain and thus be well positioned to innovate in it. In domains that are less logically ordered, such as musical composition, literature, and philosophy, there is less agreement as to what the most urgent issues are. Specialized knowledge is not enough; one needs to reflect on a great amount of experience before being able to say something new. Therefore one would expect important new contributions in these domains to be made later in life.

Social Aging: The Effects of the Field on Creativity

Although there is not much that can be said about the purely physiological effects of age on creativity, it is clear that as a person matures into adulthood and then old age, there will be many changes that affect his or her productivity, in both positive and negative ways. These changes are the consequence of different roles that the creative person is likely to play in the field, beginning as an apprentice, and then becoming an expert practitioner, and finally a gatekeeper. Each of these roles provides different opportunities and demands different responsibilities.

Careers in science or the arts—or for that matter, in any other domain as well—are rarely a matter of smooth sailing. As Thomas Kuhn, historian of science, noted, new ideas are rarely adopted by the leading figures in the field whose fame rests on an older paradigm. Instead, it is the younger scientists who wish to prove their mettle who adopt new ideas and try to change the domain (Kuhn, 1962). Or as Pierre Bourdieu, French sociologist, wrote:

> The history of the field arises from the struggle between the established figures and the young challengers. The ageing of authors, schools, and works is far from being the product of a mechanical, chronological slide into the past; it results from the struggle between those who have made their mark . . . and who are fighting to persist, and those who cannot make their own mark without pushing into the past those who have an interest in stopping the clock. (Bourdieu, 1993, p. 60)

Sooner or later, a promising scientist usually becomes head of a lab, takes on duties in scientific societies, edits journals, writes textbooks, and serves on innumerable committees. Similar changes await successful artists who become public property of agents, collectors, and foundations. In this way, cutting-edge work can become restricted with advancing age: Older scientists may stop doing bench work in the lab to take on administrative positions, and older artists may become distracted from the voice of the muse by their lionizing audience.

The observation that over the course of a career one's training ages was made by Zuckerman and Merton (1972). They noted both the possibility of career obsolescence that aging scientists may encounter and the disadvantages that neophytes in a discipline may face. Attention is finite at any age, and during the late career it may be further limited by accumulated obligations and by the slowing that accompanies physiological aging. Most original scientists and artists are primarily concerned with their own creative work. Staying abreast of developments in the wider domain or in other disciplines thus competes for attention with their own evolving work agenda. On the other hand, this agenda itself impels learning. Scientists described "trying to audit" the literature and attending seminars to hear colleagues present "hot new findings." Artists need to stay in touch with new developments on the art scene as well as new techniques. A social scientist in his fifties said:

> I learn something new every year. I mean, a major area, like I'll learn a new mathematics. . . . Last year I studied anthropology a lot and learned about primate behavior . . .
>
> So that's the other philosophy I have, which is to learn something about everything and have a wide variety of experiences because you never know, and over the years, those experiences come in handy, I think. It's a well-known statement about inventions that what you really need is some luck and a prepared mind. So I've worked hard to have a prepared mind.

The eminent older scientist plays roles other than that of an innovator; these, too, may occasion exposure to new knowledge. Gatekeeping roles, such as editing professional journals, may have this impact. A social scientist in his sixties who had recently founded a new journal, noted that it would "force me to read some kinds of things that I wanted to read, because as the editor I really need to"; "I've never paid as much attention to work by other people as I should pay." Teaching can be a way either of staying current within a domain ("students in a sense are telling us what's going on at the frontier") or of broadening one's knowledge ("the heterogeneity of inquiry and interest that come with teaching give you more backburners to opportunistically develop"). Informal discussions with junior collaborators and other colleagues and attending conferences may have the same effect.

How extraneous demands impinge on the time and attention of renowned artists was conveyed by Canadian writer Robertson Davies, who at age 80 commented:

One of the problems about being a writer today is that you are expected to be a kind of public show and public figure and people want your opinions about politics and world affairs and so forth, about which you don't know any more than anybody else, but you have to go along or you'll get a reputation of being an impossible person, and spiteful things would be said about you. (Csikszentmihalyi, 1996, p. 206)

A similar situation is described by physicist Eugene Wigner, who recalled the sudden change in status of physical scientists after the harnessing of nuclear power at the end of World War II:

By 1946, scientists routinely acted as public servants . . . addressing social and human problems from a scientific viewpoint. Most of us enjoyed that, vanity is a very human property. . . . We had the right and even perhaps the duty to speak out on vital political issues. But on most political questions, physicists had little more information than the man on the street. (Wigner, 1992, p. 254)

As the original contributions of a person are beginning to be recognized by the field, the power of the creative person as gatekeeper and leader grows apace. Ironically, but as might be expected, this rarely translates into greater creative output. Fields may restrict opportunities for creative work by escalating expectations for administrative and statesmanlike activities. And finally, the social system in which the fields are embedded may distract successful creative individuals by diluting their focus of attention from the tasks they are best qualified to perform. For instance, scientists often complain that policy makers mistake their specialized expertise for a more general wisdom and ask them to sit on committees and boards where their expertise is no better than that of the average person on the street.

In line with these considerations, the literature has focused from the start on the related questions of whether older scientists resist new paradigms or indeed actively obstruct a field's embrace of new ideas or conversely, whether they become significant contributors to the new areas themselves. In other words, literature has been concerned about the actions of the older scientist in the role of gatekeeper as much as innovator (Zuckerman & Merton, 1972, p. 309). A variety of mechanisms that could account for age-associated resistance have come to be recognized, such as the force of accrued social and intellectual investments. In addition, counterfindings have also emerged, for which possible mechanisms have been suggested. In particular, older eminent scientists may be better equipped than the young to endorse revolutionary ideas when these are first publicized, because they have already achieved their professional goals and are less concerned with defending orthodox positions.

As stated earlier, the systems model suggests that the distinction between the contribution of new ideas and their adoption is not as crucial as it seems from an individualistic perspective on creativity. If the adoption of novelty is as important as its discovery, then even those scientists and artists who have abandoned active work but still exercise leadership in the field are indispensable to creativity. Thus, perhaps a better question to ask is, what does a gatekeeper have to do to contribute to creativity?

Obviously, remaining open to novelty and staying abreast of new developments are prerequisites. If gatekeepers are too rigid, the domain becomes starved for new ideas and eventually declines. But a domain can be destroyed just as well by gatekeepers who are too open to novelty and who, by admitting every fad, destroy the integrity of the domain. Thus "conservatism in science is not all bad" (Hull, 1988, p. 383). Perhaps it is better to speak of skepticism rather than conservatism, in which resisting the new and clinging to the old are coupled. The shift would be consistent with Hull's basic insight ("No one complains that scientists, young or old, resisted novel theories that we now take to be mistaken").

Our data suggest an additional way in which the appearance of aged conservatism might be created. One 79-year-old Nobel laureate in economics expressed the kind of spirited rejection of a current fad in his discipline that might seem to be a typical example of resistance to new ideas with old age:

I'm about to give a speech next week . . . at a conference, in which I'm going to denounce the work that's been going on for ten years . . . which I think has been relatively formal and sterile, but it's been done by all the smart people. They've, lots of them, gotten their professorships very young. . . . I'm predicting that it's reaching the end of its period of joy and happiness. Very, very clever people working on very special problems . . . and I think it's become a very scholastic enterprise in the way we use that language to denounce the medieval church teachings and so forth, and that it will fail, although you can have a run with it in the market. We have fads in science.

However, from a life span perspective, a different possibility merits attention: that this scientist has challenged new ideas throughout his career, so that the upcoming speech represents a form of continuity rather than a swing toward conservatism. And, indeed, this scientist observes:

One characteristic I have, and you'd get that if you asked other people about me, is that I always have a non-faddish view of things. If a theory sweeps the profession, I'll be the last guy that accepts it, in general. I've been a critic, for example, of . . . the rage of the '30s, and wrote on it. . . . I wrote what was maybe the standard refutation of [another theory], after it became very widespread. So I don't have any instincts to say that since everybody's doing it, that's right. I've more the instinct, "Well, hey, are they looking at it hard enough and from enough different attitudes?"

As this scientist readily notes, the maverick stance means that he has also been slow to accept ideas that later become "the universal truth." Nevertheless, skepticism was mentioned by a number of respondents as a valuable attribute in those who aspire to make original contributions to a domain. In this light, it is conceivable that skeptical scientists do important work, attain eminence, and go on to become eminent—and still skeptical—older scientists. A question for future investigators is: Does a characteristic skepticism come to be viewed differently by other members of the community when a scientist is old? The structure of the domain and the field are important in determining whether someone will continue to produce useful new ideas or things, but it is even more important to preserve the personal drive for playfulness and discovery.

Preserving the Passion

If there is one trait that a person must possess to continue on a creative trajectory, it is curiosity. Without a strong dose of curiosity a promising artist or scientist will be tempted to settle for a comfortable career that does not require the risk of striving for novelty. In our studies of creativity in later life, we found this trait mentioned over and over by creative respondents. "I am incredibly curious," said a neuropsychologist;

"I am relentlessly curious," said a well-known composer; "I am enormously curious," said an astronomer. Joshua Lederberg, a leading geneticist, admitted to a "voracious curiosity." Cognitive scientist Donald Norman claimed that the "one thing I try to do, is always be curious and inquiring."

This curiosity does not concern just the work at hand, but often extends to the broadest issues imaginable. Nadine Gordimer, the Nobel Prize–winning novelist, explained when she was interviewed in our study of creativity in later life:

Writing is a form of exploration of life. . . . Of course, some people have a ready-made structure of explanation. People who have a strong religion, no matter what it is. Whether you're a Christian or a Muslim or a Jew or whatever. You have got an explanation of why you're here . . . what the purpose is and what the future is. That you're going to go to Heaven or whatever it is, or you're going to become part of the universal spirit; there's an explanation for your life. What if you haven't got that?

John Wheeler, one of the most distinguished theoretical physicists in the world, said that past 80 years of age he is still driven by "a desperate curiosity. I like that Danish poem . . . 'I'd like to know what this show is all about before it's out.' To me that is the number one thing—to find out how the world works."

In most cases, this curiosity was present in early life. There is no question that if one wished to increase the frequency of creative ideas through life, the place to start would be in trying to enhance the curiosity of children. A distinguished astronomer recalls:

When I think about my childhood, I was enormously curious. I mean, I can actually think of questions that . . . I don't know how old I was, I certainly wasn't ten, I might have been six. . . . I mean really in my childhood . . . things that puzzled me about the physical universe. I mean, I can even remember asking questions like "why, when we drove down the road the moon was following us?" I mean I could give you five questions that bothered me as a child. . . . I just had an enormous curiosity from the very beginning and just wanted to do these things. . . . I was just curious about how things work and I was trying to—and after a while I learned that the questions that I was most curious about, no one knew the answer to. So, if I wanted to get the answer I had to go out and observe and do these things myself. But, in a sense it was to learn the answer to these very curious questions that drove me.

John Wheeler again: "I can remember I must have been three or four years old in the bathtub and my mother bathing me, and I was asking her how far does the universe go, and the world go, and beyond that"

A neuropsychologist recalls:

The thing that has driven me my whole life—and I have always said this and I know it is true. It is curiosity. I am incredibly curious about things, little things I see around me.... My mother used to think that I was just very inquisitive about other people's business. But it was not just people it is... it is things around me. I am a noticer. I am sure much less now than when I was young. But it is noticing quirks, the things that patients do or that people do. And then I wonder why and I want to investigate it.

Oscar Peterson, renowned jazz pianist, grew up in an African American family in Montreal, and he recalls the curiosity that drove him as a child and still drives him approaching 70 years of age:

I was mischievous. I admit it. I was always seeking projects to do, you know. Finding out what made things work, things that I shouldn't be fooling with.... I remember destroying a phonograph once, under the guise of repairing it. And things like that. I, I wasn't a bad child, in the sense that I'd go out and start fires or beat up neighborhood kids or anything like that. But I was always into little nooks and crannies, getting my nose into things it shouldn't have been into. I was a very curious child.

For most creative individuals, this early curiosity is preserved through the years, and becomes a lifelong project. Gunther Schuller, one of the most original composers of our time, stated: "I'm the eternal student. I always want to learn more and study more, because . . . the longer I live, the more I realize that as much as I know, it's very little in the overall scheme of things. And the more I learn, the more I learn how much more there is to learn. . . . it's an endless process."

Astronomer Vera Rubin repeats the same theme:

But, yes, just the curiosity of how the universe works.... I still have this feeling. When I am out observing at a very dark site on a clear night and I look at the stars, I still really wonder how you could do anything but be an astronomer, and that's the truth. How could you live looking up at those stars and just not spend your life learning about what's going on. I think when I was young I had no concept that the things that were puzzling me no one knew the answer to. I thought it was just like learning math. You just went to a book and you would learn all about these things. And I think that is the way that children's books and elementary books are written. I think the understanding of how little we know came much, much later.

This intrinsically motivated desire to learn is an organic part of the process of answering a question for oneself; it accompanies and feeds creativity. It differs from learning obliged by membership in the field (the need to maintain mastery, expertise), which can actually displace or discourage curiosity if it becomes too absorbing an obligation.

The neuropsychologist comments on the danger of being caught up in the concerns of the field, rather than following one's own interests and intuition:

So I like to see people curious and interested in things around them, including the patients and the atmosphere.... Where people are really having to do so much course work and ... they are so busy doing that that the curiosity, or the adventure, the spirit of the adventure goes, and I think that that is bad.

Creative persons take steps to make sure that the pressures placed on them by the expectations of the field do not stifle their passion for discovery. Natalie Davis, one of the most original and respected historians of her generation, said,

It's hard to be creative when you are just doing something doggedly.... if I felt my curiosity was limited, I think that the novelty part of it would be gone. Because it is the curiosity that has often pushed me to think of ways of finding out about something that people ... previously thought you could never find out about. Or ways of looking at a subject that have never been looked at before. That's what keeps me running back and forth to the library, and just thinking and thinking and thinking and thinking.

Many other variables enter the equation that preserves creativity throughout life—from dogged perseverance to sheer luck. In fact, when asked to explain their lifelong success, creative individuals most often mentioned luck. Being at the right place at the right time was seen by many of them as the main difference that separated them from less successful peers. But curiosity, the desire to learn, seems to be one characteristic that is absolutely necessary. Without it, the temptation to abandon the quest for novelty becomes too strong; it is so much easier to rest on one's laurels and reap the benefits of one's early accomplishments.

The satisfaction of curiosity is the intrinsic reward that keeps a person struggling against high odds in an effort to come up with a new and more accurate perception of reality.

PERSONAL CREATIVITY

Whereas cultural creativity depends on many extraneous factors over which a person has no control—access to the domain, to the field, and sheer good fortune—personal creativity with a small c is something everyone can learn to develop. The one trait necessary for both kinds of creativity is curiosity. Individuals who are not interested in new knowledge and new experiences, who do not enjoy the thrill of discovery, are handicapped in both their professional and personal lives. The study of personal creativity, however, is still in its infancy and very little can be said about it with any authority.

Some persons, like the big C individuals quoted, are lucky in having had families that encouraged their curiosity from early on. We do not know to what extent it is possible to compensate for the lack of a stimulating early environment in later life. It is not easy to reverse habits of bored acceptance of the status quo, but perhaps it is not impossible.

At the end of our study of creativity (Csikszentmihalyi, 1996, chap. 14), a few steps for reawakening curiosity and interest were suggested. For instance, one should endeavor to be surprised each day by some experience. Even the simplest sight, sound, person, or conversation can reveal unexpected aspects if we take the trouble to attend to them with full attention. As John Dewey (1934) pointed out long ago, the essence of an aesthetic experience lies in perception, which he differentiated from recognition, or the routine noticing of things that does not reveal anything new about them. Learning to perceive means being able to temporarily suspend the generic characteristics of experience and focus instead on their uniqueness. With time, the habit of perception is likely to grow into the kind of curiosity that fuels personal creativity.

Another way to break long-established routines is to surprise yourself, or others, by something you do. Instead of acting out the predictable scenario of one's personality, it helps occasionally (and appropriately) to say something unexpected, to express an opinion that one had not dared express before, to ask a question one would not ordinarily ask. It helps to take up new activities, try new clothes and new restaurants, and go to shows and museums.

As a result of breaking routine ways of experiencing and living, one might stumble on activities or interests that are enjoyable and meaningful. At that point, it makes sense to take one's experience seriously and devote more attention and time to those experiences that provide the greatest rewards. We spend far too much time doing things that are neither fun nor productive. Passive entertainment, for example, is often actually quite boring. Television viewing—which is the single most time-consuming activity people do in their free time—has many of the characteristics of addiction (Kubey & Csikszentmihalyi 2002). The more one watches the less enjoyable it is, yet the harder it is to break the habit.

What we are suggesting here about making one's life more interesting is not the same as in the Chinese curse: "May you lead an interesting life." The curse's meaning of *interesting* has the same sense as the word has in literature and the movies: The interest comes from outside in the form of danger, drama, risk, and tragedy. What makes life interesting for creative persons does not depend on external factors. It is the ability to endow even the most common experience with wonder and curiosity that makes their lives interesting. Leonardo da Vinci, who shaped our culture as deeply as any other person, led a life that to a superficial observer would have appeared miserly and drab (see Reti, 1974). When he walked through the slums of Milan, looking at the peeling plaster on walls that would suggest to him new ways of representing the wonderful landscapes that formed the backgrounds for his paintings, few recognized the depth and reach of the thoughts soaring through his mind.

Many other suggestions could be reviewed, but it can all be summarized in a short principle: To increase personal creativity in one's life, one must take charge of how one perceives the world and of what one does in it. Creativity in any form does not come cheap; it requires commitment and perseverance. With some effort one can develop those habits of allocating attention that will result in realizing the awesome complexity of existence. After that, increasing joy at discovering more of its facets should sustain a life that thrives on growth and novelty rather than uniform routine.

CONCLUSIONS

Creative involvement with the world is an essential component of cultural evolution (big C creativity), and a source of enrichment in an individual's life (small c). Comparative psychology suggests that the playful, exploratory behavior underlying creativity diminishes rapidly with age and hardly exists after the reproductive age. With humans, however, whether there is decline depends on a variety of factors. First, creativity depends on the domain in which a person works; second, it depends on the opportunities and obstacles that the field offers the person; and finally, it depends on whether the person is able to sustain curiosity, interest, and passion. In many branches of the arts and some of the sciences, creative accomplishment continues until the end of life. Although the structure of the domain and the field are important in determining whether someone will continue to produce useful new ideas or things, it is even more important to preserve the personal drive for discovery.

What is true of big C creativity also applies to the ordinary, everyday kind that fails to be noticed and adopted by the culture. Here, however, the passion itself suffices; a person who can find novelty and excitement in the beauty of life in all its manifestations need not accomplish anything of note. Just experiencing life with full involvement will be a reward more important than fame and success.

References

Altmann, J. (1980). *Baboon mothers and infants*. Cambridge, MA: Harvard University Press.

Anderson, S. R., & Ray, P. H. (2001). *The cultural creatives*. New York: Three Rivers Press.

Baltes, P. B., & Staudinger, U. (2000). Wisdom: A metaheuristic (pragmatic) to orchestrate mind and virtue toward excellence. *American Psychologist*, 55, 122–136.

Blackmore, S. (1999). *The meme machine*. Oxford: Oxford University Press.

Brannigan, A. (1981). *The social basis of scientific discoveries*. New York: Cambridge University Press.

Bourdieu, P. (1993). *The field of cultural production*. New York: Columbia University Press.

Cattell, R. B. (1963). Theory of fluid and crystallized intelligence: A critical experiment. *Journal of Educational Psychology*, 54, 1–22.

Csikszentmihalyi, M. (1988). Society, culture, and person: A systems view of creativity. In R. J. Sternberg (Ed.), *The nature of creativity: Contemporary psychological perspectives* (pp. 325–339). New York: Cambridge University Press.

Csikszentmihalyi, M. (1993). *The evolving self: A psychology for the third millennium*. New York: HarperCollins.

Csikszentmihalyi, M. (1996). *Creativity: Flow and the psychology of discovery and invention*. New York: HarperCollins.

Csikszentmihalyi, M. (1998). Creativity and genius: A systems perspective. In A. Steptoe (Ed.), *Genius and the mind* (pp. 39–66). Oxford: Oxford University Press.

Csikszentmihalyi, M. (1999). Implications of a systems perspective for the study of creativity. In R. J. Sternberg (Ed.), *Handbook of creativity* (pp. 313–335). Cambridge: Cambridge University Press.

Csikszentmihalyi, M., & Wolfe, R. (2000). New conceptions and research approaches to creativity: Implications of a systems perspective for creativity in education. In K. A. Heller, F. J. Monks, R. J. Sternberg, & R. Subotnik (Eds.), *International handbook of giftedness and talent* (pp. 81–93). Nailsea, UK: Elsevier Science.

Dawkins, R. (1976). *The selfish gene*. New York: Oxford University Press.

Dennis, W. (1956). Age and achievement: A critique. *Journal of Gerontology*, 11, 331–333.

Dennis, W. (1966). Creative productivity between the ages of 20 and 80 years. *Journal of Gerontology*, 21, 1–18.

Dewey, J. (1934). *Art as experience*. New York: Minton, Balch.

Drucker, P. F. (1985). *Innovation and entrepreneurship*. New York: Harper Business.

Drucker, P. F. (1999). *Management challenges for the 21st century*. New York: Harper Business.

Estes, R. D. (1976) The significance of breeding synchrony in the wildebeest. *East African Wildlife Journal*, 14, 135–152.

Fagan, R. (1981). *Animal play behavior*. New York: Oxford University Press.

Florida, R. (2002). *The rise of the creative class*. New York: Basic Books.

Hull, D. L. (1988). *Science as a process*. Chicago: University of Chicago Press.

Kasof, J. (1995). Explaining creativity: The attributional perspective. *Creativity Research Journal*, 8(4), 311–366.

Kawai, M. (1965). Newly-acquired pre-cultural behavior of the natural troop of Japanese monkeys on Koshima Islet. *Primates*, 6(1), 1–30.

Kubey, R., & Csikszentmihalyi, M. (2002). Television addiction. *Scientific American*, 286(2), 74–81.

Kuhn, T. S. (1962). *The structure of scientific revolutions.* Chicago: University of Chicago Press.

Lehman, H. C. (1953). *Age and achievement.* Princeton, NJ: Princeton University Press.

Lehman, H. C. (1960). The age decrement in outstanding scientific creativity. *American Psychologist, 15,* 128–134.

MacKinnon, D. W. (1963) Creativity and images of the self. In R. W. White (Ed.), *The study of lives.* New York: Atherton.

Martindale, C. (1990). *The clockwork muse: The predictability of artistic change.* New York: Basic Books.

Miller, G. (2000). *The mating mind: How sexual choices shaped the evolution of human nature.* New York: Random House.

Nakamura, J., & Csikszentmihalyi, M. (2003). The motivational sources of creativity as viewed from the paradigm of positive psychology. In L. G. Aspinwall & U. M. Staudinger (Eds.), *A psychology of human strengths* (pp. 257–270). Washington, DC: American Psychological Association.

Reti, L. (Ed.). (1974). *The unknown Leonardo.* New York: McGraw-Hill.

Schaie, K. W. (1996). Intellectual development in adulthood. In J. E. Birren & K. W. Schaie (Eds.), *Handbook of the psychology of aging* (4th ed., pp. 266–286). San Diego, CA: Academic Press.

Simonton, D. K. (1999). Creativity from a historiometric perspective. In R. J. Sternberg (Ed.), *Handbook of creativity* (pp. 116–136). New York: Cambridge University Press.

Wali, K. C. (1991) *Chandra.* Chicago: University of Chicago Press.

White, J. P. (1968). Creativity and education: A philosophical analysis. *British Journal of Educational Studies, 16,* 123–137.

Wigner, E. (1992). *The recollections of Eugene P. Wigner.* New York: Plenum Press.

Zuckerman, H., & Merton, R. K. (1972). Age, aging, and age structure in science. In M. W. Riley, M. Johnson, & A. Foner (Eds.), *Aging and society* (Vol. 3, pp. 292–356). New York: Russell Sage Foundation.

Chapter 12

Illuminating Major Creative Scientific Innovators With Postformal Stages

Michael Lamport Commons and Linda Marie Bresette

The development and improvement of a society and its culture depend on major scientific innovations. Societies with higher rates of major innovation generally provide better quality of life in terms of scientific, technological, and socioeconomic progress. It follows that societies with the largest number of innovations tend to dominate the world's economic scene. For example, in 1998, the 29 OECD (Organisation for Economic Co-operation and Development) countries, with only 19% of the world's population, spent $520 billion on research and development and acquired 91% of all patents (Brauer, 2001). The OECD is a group with 30 member countries (Australia, Austria, Belgium, Canada, Czech Republic, Denmark, Finland, France, Germany, Greece, Hungary, Iceland, Ireland, Italy, Japan, Korea, Luxembourg, Mexico, Netherlands, New Zealand, Norway, Poland, Portugal, Slovak Republic, Spain, Sweden, Switzerland, Turkey, United Kingdom, United States) sharing a commitment to democratic government and the market economy. Of the OECD countries, 21 are listed as high income and 5 are listed as high middle income. But even within these countries, there are only a small number of people who originate innovations.

This chapter offers five major reasons for the shortage of scientific innovators. First, there is a general scarcity in the learning and development of the higher order–complex thinking and action that is required to identify phenomena and create and integrate paradigms. We argue that such higher order thinking and acting are necessary for scientific innovation to take place. Second, cultural conditions do not appropriately support innovation. This makes it unlikely that the relevant learning necessary for developing higher order thinking will take place. Third, the requisite aspects of personality are relatively rare. Fourth, education and learning about highly complex material is insufficient. Fifth, there are biological limitations as to the number of people who can easily learn and then engage in higher order–complex thinking. We consider each of these factors in this chapter together with a discussion of the ways current cultural conditions hinder the creative process, thereby limiting genuine scientific contributions.

CREATIVE AND INNOVATIVE SCIENTIFIC CULTURAL CONTRIBUTIONS

From the multiple kinds of adult innovations that could be discussed, this chapter will focus on relatively rare scientific ones that were historically among the most important. Often, in fact, discussions of the basis for creativity focus on artistic, literary, or musical creativity (Funk, 1989). Or they focus on the usual creative output of very good scientists (Simonton, 1984, 1997). Because it is conceivable that creative production in different domains may be different, this chapter focuses only on scientific creativity and only on some of the most major scientific accomplishments. Later work may seek to generalize from this initial basis.

Minimally, scientific creativity must be original action. This is not trivial because most of what people do repeats what has already been done or varies it slightly. Our sense is that there is confusion between these ordinary high-quality contributions and the extremely rare exceptional contributions. We argue that these types of behaviors may have different origins and therefore different explanations. Among scientific accomplishments, the methods, theories, and techniques do not have to be original. We focus on the manner in which they have been used. It is also important to recognize that such creative acts become (or have become) social memes of long standing. In a metaphorical sense, memes are to cultural evolution what genes are to evolutionary biology. Genes are the basic biological units of information that are transmitted from one individual to another in the form of DNA. *Memes* (Cavalli-Sforza & Feldman, 1981; Dawkins, 1976, 1981) are the basic cultural units of information that are transmitted to other people in the form of behavioral patterns. For example, Einstein added the deep connection between energy and mass in the equation $E = mc^2$. This was a new meme to the culture in 1905. In the course of positive adult development, major innovations can become new memes that are extreme examples of generativity (Erikson, 1959, 1978). Some generative acts are not only important to ourselves but useful to society as well. Innovative generative acts can lead to something new in society.

We approach one major aspect of creativity—creative scientific innovation—from the perspective of the model of hierarchical complexity (MHC). The model includes the MHC itself as well as two forms of learning. The first kind of learning is stage change. Individuals learn the new actions at the next stage. The second kind of learning is about phenomena at a given stage. Individuals learn, practice, and perfect behaviors at the given stage. These two forms of learning are inseparable (Piaget, 1977; Piaget & Garcia, 1989). Miller, Lee, and Commons (2005) state that being in environments that encourage a great deal of learning at a given stage can be an important condition for development to the next stage.

Societally important creative tasks seem to be the most complex. This makes learning how to perform such tasks necessary for extremely creative acts of individuals. We will show that less creative tasks are available at lower orders of complexity. Therefore, learning to perform at higher orders of task complexity is central to increasing one's creativity, both for the individual and for the society. The MHC of Commons and Richards (1984a, 1984b; Commons, Trudeau, Stein, Richards, & Krause, 1998) is a system that classifies learning and development in terms of a task-required hierarchical organization of required responses. The model was derived in part from Piaget's (Inhelder & Piaget, 1954, 1958) notion that the higher stage actions coordinate lower stage actions by organizing them into a new, more hierarchically complex pattern. The stage of an action is found by answering the following two questions: (a) What are the organizing actions? And (b) What are the stages of the elements being organized?

HIERARCHICAL COMPLEXITY AND ITS ROLE IN INNOVATION

The Model of Hierarchical Complexity

The MHC (Commons & Richards, 1984a, 1984b; Commons et al., 1998) is a universal system that classifies the task-required hierarchical organization of ideal responses. Every task contains a multitude of subtasks (Campbell & Richie, 1983; Overton, 1990).

When the subtasks are completed by the ideal actions in a required order, they complete the task in question. The classification of a task does not depend on the content or context, so it is species, domain, and culture free. Tasks vary in complexity in two ways, either as *horizontal* (involving classical information) or *vertical* (involving hierarchical information). It is not the usual horizontal kind of complexity that makes a difference but a newer kind called hierarchical complexity. Therefore, the two forms will be introduced and compared.

Horizontal (Classical Information Theory) Complexity

Classical information theory (Shannon & Weaver, 1949), describes the number of yes-no questions it takes to do a task. For example, if one asked a person across the room whether a penny came up heads when they flipped it, their saying *heads* would transmit one bit of horizontal information. If there were two pennies, one would have to ask at least two questions, one about each penny. Hence, each additional one-bit question would add another bit. Let us say someone had a four-faced top with the faces numbered one, two, three, and four. Instead of spinning it, they tossed it against a backboard as one does with dice in a game. One could ask them whether the face had an even number. If it did, one would then ask if it were a two. Again, there would be two bits. Horizontal complexity, then, is the sum of bits required to complete such tasks.

Vertical (Hierarchical) Complexity

Hierarchical complexity refers to coordination of less complex task actions by more complex ones. Actions at a higher order of hierarchical complexity (a) are *defined* in terms of actions at the *next lower* order of hierarchical complexity; (b) *organize* and *transform* the lower order actions; (c) produce organizations of lower order actions that are new and *not arbitrary*, and cannot be accomplished by those lower order actions alone. Once these conditions have been met, we say the higher order action *coordinates* the actions of the next lower order. Specifically, the *order of hierarchical complexity* refers to the number of recursive times that the coordinating actions must perform on a set of primary elements. *Recursion* refers to the process by which the output of the lower order actions

forms the input of the higher order actions. This "nesting" of two or more lower order tasks within higher order tasks is called *concatenation*. Each new, task-required action in the hierarchy is one order more complex than the task-required actions on which it is built (tasks are always more hierarchically complex than their subtasks).

Formulating the Postformal Orders of Hierarchical Complexity

One of the features of the MHC is that it makes clear that there are stages beyond the stage of formal operations (Commons & Richards, 1984a 1984b). These stages are called *postformal*. Some of the qualities of postformal actions include the following: (a) these actions successfully address problems at which formal actions fail, and (b) they represent complex matters more compactly and systematically. The postformal structures range from multivariate relations to relationships among paradigms. These will be illustrated informally with two examples. Then each of the stages will be defined more formally.

The first example of postformal actions comes from algebra. In contrast to formal operations, which are about relationships between no more than two variables, postformal actions integrate increasingly more complex structures. For example, in formal operations, one may have the distribution of a variable x over the sum of two variables $y + z$, where $x^*(y + z) = (x^*y) + (x^*z)$.

At the first postformal stage, relations between multiple variables form systems of relationships. We next describe two members of two different systems. Each relationship belongs to a different system. At this stage, one can only work within one system at a time. But the truth value is different for the different systems to which they belong even though they look to be of the same form. This is seen in the right-hand distribution law. That law is not true for numbers but is true for propositions and sets.

$$\text{And } x + (y * z) = (x * y) + (x * z)$$
$$\text{(Not true for arithmetic)}$$

$$x \cup (y \cap z) = (x \cup y) \cap (x \cup z) \qquad \text{(True for sets)}$$

Continuing our example, at the second postformal stage, one may show that the system of propositional logic and elementary set theory are isomorphic and form a *supersystem*.

$$x \ \& \ (y \text{ or } z) = (x \ \& \ y) \text{ or } (x \ \& \ z) \qquad \text{(Logic)}$$

$$x \cup (y \cap z) = (x \cup y) \cap (x \cup z) \qquad \text{(Sets)}$$

At the third postformal stage, for the predicate calculus just described in part, one comes to see all of these as part of a *paradigm* of mathematical logic and set theory, a field at the basis of mathematics and analytic philosophy.

For a second example, consider causality in relationships. At the formal stage, one person's behavior is seen to cause another's behavior, both empirically and logically. But at the first of the postformal stages, the relationships are seen in a more hierarchically complex fashion. First, a relationship is seen as being at least two-way: One person acts, the other person reacts (causal relation 1), the reaction of the other person affects the first person's future actions (causal relation 2). Those two relations form a system of causal relations (Koplowitz, 1984).

At the second postformal stage, one may consider different systems of relationships, that is, those between friends and enemies, and see to what extent they are comparable in that they conform to the same causal laws. The causal laws that describe such systems of relationships would be a supersystem containing both the laws that are common to friends and enemies and those that are particular. Of course no such supersystems exist yet. At the next stage, we could see that there is no possibility of consistent supersystems. There are too many considerations, and adding them to the supersystem makes the supersystem inconsistent.

Commons (Commons & Richards, 1978; Commons, Richards, & Kuhn, 1982; Commons et al., 1998) showed that the postformal stages were true, hard stages in the Kohlberg and Armon (1984) sense, but with some small modification. As Marchand (2001) summarizes, Kohlberg and Armon distinguish "hard" stages (in which development occurs in an invariant and universal sequence (e.g., the Piagetian stages) from "soft" stages. In soft stages, development is conditioned by particular experiences arising from differences in personality, upbringing, social class, periods in one's life, and age. Commons (Commons et al., 1998) used a mathematical system derived from Luce's (e.g., Krantz, Atkinson, Luce, & Suppes, 1974; Krantz, Luce, Suppes, & Tversky, 1971) work on measurement. Each proposed stage was checked with the three main axioms. Again, these assumptions state

that any given higher stage, action has to be defined in terms of an associated lower one and organize those lower stage actions in a nonarbitrary way.

Commons and Richards's concerns lay with the general specification of any empirical task as opposed to one that is content bound. They deemphasized the reconstruction of the "reality" of a person "at a given stage." Instead, they attempted to develop a general way to specify the organization of tasks in any domain that a person at a given stage in that domain can do. Other attempts to specify what it means to be at a postformal stage can be found throughout the work reviewed here.

Postformal Orders of Complexity

We assert that highly creative innovations require postformal thought. This is in contrast to Feldman, Csikszentmihalyi, and Gardner (1994), who instead of focusing on the relationship between stage and creativity, focus on intelligence (e.g., multiple intelligences) and creativity. As far as we know, there is no empirical research relating creativity to postformal stages (but see Sinnott, 1981). Therefore, to illustrate the relationship between postformal stages and creativity, we have empirically scored the postformal tasks that certain outstanding, postformal-stage scientists successfully complete. Four postformal orders of hierarchical complexity have been proposed (Commons & Richards, 1984a, 1984b; Commons et al., 1998), beginning with systematic thinking and developing through metasystematic to paradigmatic and cross-paradigmatic thinking. The four postformal orders, according to the MHC, are briefly defined in table 12.1. There is a growing consensus that these are the postformal stages as shown in table 12.2. See the references listed in table 12.2 for citations empirically supporting the exact sequence proposed (for a review, see Marchand, 2001). The columns represent the major adult developmental stages. The rows list the researchers and some key publications for the names and numbers of the stages.

Systematic Stage

This stage was introduced by Herb Koplowitz (while we were working on a chapter of his at Dare Institute, Koplowitz suggested that metasystems and general systems must operate on systems; personal communication, 1982; Koplowitz, 1984). Kohlberg (1990)

TABLE 12.1. Postformal Stages, as Described in the General Model of Hierarchical Complexity

	What Is Done	How This Is Done	The End Result
11 Systematic operations	Constructs multivariate systems and matrices	Coordinates more than one variable as input	Events and ideas can be situated in a larger context; systems are formed out of formal-operational relations
12 Metasystematic operations	Constructs multisystems and metasystems out of disparate systems	Compares and analyzes systems in a systematic way; reflects on systems; creates metasystems of systems	Metasystems are formed out of multiple systems
13 Paradigmatic operation	Fits metasystems together to form new paradigms	Synthesizes metasystems	Paradigms are formed out of multiple metasystems
14 Cross-paradigmatic operation	Fits paradigms together to form new fields	Forms new fields by crossing paradigms	Fields are formed out of multiple paradigms

referred to this stage as consolidated formal operations and only much later saw his moral stage 4 as being the same. Fischer (1980) listed it as the third level in the fourth tier. At the systematic order, ideal task completers discriminate the frameworks for relationships between variables within an integrated system of tendencies and relationships. The objects of the systematic actions are formal operational relationships between variables. The actions include determining possible multivariate causes and outcomes that may be determined by many causes, the building of matrix representations of information in the form of tables or matrices, and the multidimensional ordering of possibilities, including the acts of preference and prioritization. These actions generate systems. Views of systems generated have a single "true" unifying structure. Other systems of explanation, or even other sets of data collected by adherents of other explanatory systems, tend to be rejected. At this order, science is seen as an interlocking set of relationships, with the truth of each relationship in interaction with embedded, testable relationships. Most standard science operates at this order. Researchers carry out variations of previous experiments. Behavior of events is seen as governed by multivariate causality. Our estimates are that only 20% of the U.S. population now functions at the systematic stage. That estimate is based on data that about 20% of the population are employed in professions requiring systematic stage action (Commons et al., 1995). These professions require graduate degrees. Hence, the percentage of graduate students and professionals are good examples. For example, in the Plano, Texas, 2000 census (*Plano's Population Characteristics*, 2000), 17.6% of the population had

graduate or professional degrees, whereas in Geneva, New York (*Geneva's Population Characteristics*, 2000), this figure was 19.5%.

We know how to train individuals to perform at this stage. We send them to graduate and professional schools. They learn how to think in a multivariate manner from the explicit instruction they are given. They may, in some unusual cases, learn how to combine multiple causal relations in an original way.

Metasystematic Stage

At the metasystematic order, ideal task completers act on systems; that is, systems that are the objects of metasystematic actions. The systems in turn are made up of formal operational relationships. Metasystematic actions analyze, compare, contrast, transform, and synthesize systems. The products of metasystematic actions are metasystems or supersystems. For example, consider treating systems of causal relations as the objects. This allows one to compare and contrast systems in terms of their properties. The focus is placed on the similarities and differences in each system's form, as well as on constituent causal relations and actors within them. Philosophers, mathematicians, scientists, and critics examine the logical consistency of sets of rules in their respective disciplines. Doctrinal lines are replaced by a more formal understanding of assumptions and methods used by investigators.

As an example, we suggest that almost all professors at top research universities function at this stage in their line of work. We posit that a person must function in the area of innovation at least at the metasystematic order of hierarchic complexity to produce

TABLE 12.2 Comparative Table of Concorded Theories of Formal Stage

Researchers	Abstract	Formal	Systematic	Metasystematic	Paradigmatic	Cross-Paradigmatic	Transcendental
Bownan (1996); Commons & Richards (1984a, 1984b); Commons (1991); Commons & Rodriguez (1993); Commons & Wolfsont (2002);							
Rodriguez (1989)	9 (= 4a)	10 (= 4b)	11 (= 5a)	12 (= 5b)	13 (= 6a)	14 (= 6b)	
Sonnert & Commons (1994)	group	bureaucratic	institutional	universal	dialogical		
Inhelder & Piaget (1958)	formal III-A	formal III-B	postformal	polyvalent logic; systems of systems			
Fischer (1980); Fischer, Hand, & Russell (1984)	7	8	9	10			
Sternberg (1984)		first-order relational reasoning		second-order relational reasoning			
Kohlberg (1981)	3 mutuality	3/4	4 social system	5 prior rights/ social contract 6 universal ethical principles			
Benack (1984)	4	5	6	7			
Pascual-Leone (1984)	late concrete	formal and late concrete	predialectical	dialectical			transcendental
Armon (1984)	3 affective mutuality	3/4	4 individuality	5 autonomy	6 universal categories		
Powell (1984)	early formal	formal	stage 4a/interactive empathy	category operations			
Labouvie-Vief (1984)		intrasystematic	intersystematic	autonomous			
Arlin (1984)	3a low formal (problem solving)	3b high formal	4a postformal (problem finding)	4b relativism of thought 4c overgeneralization, 4d displacement of concepts	4e late postformal (dialectical)		

Reference						
Sinnott (1984)		formal	relativistic/relativize systems, metalevel rules	unified theory: interpretation of contradictory levels		unitary concepts
Basseches (1984)	phase 1b: formal early foundations	phase 2 intermediate dialectical schemes	phase 3:2 out of 3 clusters of advanced dialectical schemes	4. advanced dialectical thinking		
Koplowitz (1984)	formal		systems	general systems		
Perry (1970); see West (2004)	dualistic	multiplicative	relativistic	committed		
King & Kitchener (2002)	4	5	6	7		
Torbert (1994)	diplomat	technician	achiever	ironist		
Kegan (1994)	3: inter-personal	3/4	4: institutional		5	
Loevinger (1998)[a]	conformist-conscientious	conscientious	individualistic	autonomous integrated		
Cook-Greuter (1990)	3/4	4	4/5	5	5/6	6
Gray (1999, June, personal comm.)	early formal	formal	systematic	metasystematic		
Bond (1999, June, personal comm.)	early formal	formal	systematic	metasystematic		
Dawson (2002a, 2002b)	9	10	11	12	13	14
Kallio (1995); Kallio & Helkama (1991)	formal 1	formal 2	formal 3 generalized formal	postformal		
Demetriou (1990); Demetriou & Efklides (1985)						
Broughton (1977, 1984)	3: person versus inner self	4. dualist or positivist; cynical, mechanistic	5: inner observer differentiated from ego	6. mind and body experiences of an integrated self		

[a] Loevinger table of contents as modified by Commons (present volume).

truly creative innovations. By definition of the meta-systematic stage, it means that such persons have to coordinate at least two multivariate systems. Although both the systematic and the metasystematic stage can be found to characterize the work of most scientists, we find that true adult creativity depends on an adequate performance on other related tasks. This is because the solution to tasks the society deems creative quite often requires a new synthesis of systems of thought (the metasystematic stage) or even a new paradigm (the paradigmatic order) or a field (the cross-paradigmatic order).

Paradigmatic Stage

At the paradigmatic stage, actions create new fields out of multiple metasystems. Examples of new paradigms are described by Holton (1973/1988) and Kuhn (1970). The objects of paradigmatic acts are metasystems. When there are metasystems that are incomplete and adding to them would create inconsistencies, quite often a new paradigm is developed. Usually, the paradigm develops from recognition of a poorly understood phenomenon. The actions in paradigmatic thought form new paradigms from metasystems. Paradigmatic actions often affect fields of knowledge that appear unrelated to the original field of the thinkers. To coordinate the metasystems, people reasoning at the paradigmatic order must see the relationship between very large and often disparate bodies of knowledge. Paradigmatic action requires a tremendous degree of decentration. One has to transcend tradition and recognize one's actions as distinct and possibly troubling to those in one's environment. But at the same time, one has to understand that the laws of nature operate both on oneself and on one's environment. This suggests that learning in one realm can be generalized to others.

Examples of paradigmatic order thinkers are perhaps best drawn from the history of science. For example, nineteenth-century physicist Clark Maxwell (1873) constructed the paradigm of electromagnetic fields from the existing metasystems of electricity and magnetism of Faraday (1839/2000), Ohm, (1927), Volta (1800/1999), Ampere (1826/1958), and Ørsted (1820). Maxwell's equations for fields and waves showed that electricity and magnetism could be united, thus forming the new paradigm. The wave fields can be easily seen as the rings that form when a rock is dropped in the water or a magnet is placed under paper that holds iron filings. This paradigm made it possible for Einstein to use notions of curved space to describe space-time to replace Euclidean geometry. The waves were bent by the mass of objects so that the rings no longer fit in a flat plane. From there, modern particle theory has been able to add two more forces to the electromagnetic forces giving us the standard electromagnetic weak force.

Cross-Paradigmatic Stage

The fourth postformal order is the cross-paradigmatic stage. The objects of cross-paradigmatic actions are paradigms. Cross-paradigmatic actions integrate paradigms into a new field or profoundly transform an old one. A field contains more than one paradigm and cannot be reduced to a single one. One might ask whether all interdisciplinary studies are therefore cross-paradigmatic. Is psychobiology cross-paradigmatic? The answer to both questions is "no." Such interdisciplinary studies might create new paradigms, such as psychophysics, but not new fields.

This fourth order has not been examined in much detail here because there are so very few people who successfully perform tasks of this order of hierarchical complexity. It may also take a certain amount of time and perspective to realize that behavior or findings are cross-paradigmatic. All that can be done at this time is to identify and analyze historical examples.

Copernicus (1543/1992) coordinated geometry of ellipses that represented the geometric paradigm and the sun-centered perspectives. This coordination formed the new field of celestial mechanics, which in turn led to a scientific revolution that spread throughout the world and totally altered our understanding of humans' place in the cosmos. It directly led to what many would now call true empirical science with its mathematical exposition. This in turn paved the way for Isaac Newton (1687/1999) to coordinate mathematics and physics, forming the new field of classic mathematical physics. The field was formed out of the new mathematical paradigm of calculus (independent of Leibniz, 1768, 1875) and the paradigm of physics, which consisted of disjointed physical laws.

René Descartes (1637/1954) first created the paradigm of analysis and used it to coordinate the paradigms of geometry, proof theory, algebra, and teleology. He thereby created the field of analytical geometry and analytic proofs. Charles Darwin (1855,

1877) coordinated paleontology, geology, biology, and ecology to form the field of evolution, which, in turn, paved the way for chaos theory, evolutionary biology, and evolutionary psychology. Darwin (1855) noted that finches had diverged into a wide variety of birds. If they had not been isolated in the closed environment of the Galápagos Islands, these finches would have represented a wide number of species, as was the case of mainland birds. Many people had been exposed to just such novel situations but made nothing of it. Although Darwin discovered this phenomenon in the early 1800s, it was not until many years later that he made any sense of it when he devised his theory of evolution. Darwin saw that evolutionary forces had transformed the birds differently. But although his specific observations of finches did not have much impact on the direction of science, his evolutionary theory did. Darwin created a good deal out of three new interrelated paradigms: paleontology, evolutionary biology, and ethology.

Darwin's theory constituted a radical innovation in the science of his time for three reasons. First, he presented evolutionary evidence establishing the fact that human thought and action are continuous with animal thought and action. Second, he proposed an explanation for human evolution that was not teleological, that is, one that did not claim an ultimate purpose. Finally, Darwin's theory brought together four distinct prior paradigms, those of biology, ecology, animal behavior, and geology.

Albert Einstein (1950) coordinated the paradigm of non-Euclidean geometry with the paradigms of classical physics to form the field of relativity. This gave rise to modern cosmology. He also co-invented quantum mechanics. Max Planck (1922) coordinated the paradigm of wave theory (energy with probability) forming the field of quantum mechanics. This has led to modern particle physics. Last, Gödel (1931/1977), coordinated epistemology and mathematics into the field of limits on knowing. Along with Darwin, Einstein, and Planck, he founded modern science and epistemology.

Innovators functioning at each of the four stages do tasks of different hierarchical complexity that do not overlap with one another. The rarity of people functioning at these higher stages is reflected in the higher rate of pay they receive. The increased pay and freedom to direct their own activity probably function as an incentive to learn the next stage of behaviors. Persons functioning at each stage do the different tasks using skills that are increasingly rare. The end

results are entirely different for society. The results of innovation become much more important at the paradigmatic and cross-paradigmatic stages. The results change the world culture and our very view of the world. In fact, so few people exist at the cross-paradigmatic stage that societies have no formal mechanisms to encourage such activity as far as we know. Yet that change influences the course of civilization. For example, Copernicus changed our view of our place in the universe, making the Earth just another planet revolving around the sun. Darwin changed our view of human origins and place within the world of animals to make us one more animal. Copernicus altered the course of modern physics and astronomy, and Darwin's contribution led to a vast array of academic disciplines including modern genetically based medicine, evolutionary biology, paleontology, and behavioral psychology.

Hierarchical Complexity and Level of Support

To understand why innovation is so difficult and requires people who can successfully address the most hierarchically complex tasks, we have to realize that when the innovation was carried out there was almost no previous knowledge as to how to approach the task. Using hindsight, the tasks of innovators do not seem as difficult. The difference is that we live in a world that surrounds us with past knowledge and has created a context in which the discoveries make sense. Our understanding of these discoveries, one might say, is supported by this knowledge and the teaching of that knowledge. The original discoveries, however, took place without any of this support. This raises the stage at which these tasks had to be done. These ideas are formalized in the idea, described below, of different levels of support for task performance (Commons & Richards, 1995). The difficulty of an action depends on the level of support, in addition to the horizontal information demanded in bits and the order of hierarchical complexity. Each increase in the level of support reduces the difficulty of doing a task by one stage. Each decrease in the level of support raises the difficulty of doing a task by one stage (Commons & Richards, 2002).

The level of support represents the degree of independence of the performing person's action and thinking from environmental control provided by others in the situation (Vygotsky, 1962, 1966, 1978). We define six levels of support: *Manipulation* (–3 level), which is literally being moved through each step of how to solve a problem; *transfer of stimulus control* (–2 level) is being told each step; *pervasive imitation* (–1 level) is being shown, which includes delayed imitation or observational learning (Gewirtz, 1969). The imitated action may be written, depicted, or otherwise reproduced. Fischer and Lazerson (1984) call this form of control the optimal level. *Direct* (0 level) is being given no help or support in problem solving or hacking (without support). Fischer and Lazerson (1984) call this the functional level. Most of Piaget's work was at this level. *Problem finding* (+1 level) is in addition to not getting help. One must discover a task to answer a known question. Persons may be given an issue, and they are asked to give examples of a problem that reflect that issue. Arlin (1975, 1977, 1984) introduced postformal complexity (systematic order) by requiring the construction of a formal operational problem without aid or definition. Finding a given problem increases complexity demand by one order of complexity over solving a posed problem with no assistance. *Question finding* (+2 level) is in addition to not getting help. Here, one must discover the question, not just the problem, to address a known issue. With a known phenomenon, people find a problem and an instance in which to solve that problem. One has to discriminate the phenomenon clearly enough to create and solve a problem based on that discrimination. *Phenomenon finding* (+3 level) offers no direct stimulus control. There can be no direct stimulus control without a description of the phenomenon, unrecognized up until the discovery. Also, discovering the new phenomenon is necessary for there to be a reinforcement history with that phenomenon.

There is little support for major innovations in culture because there is no history of the necessary hierarchical complex task accomplishments or actions surrounding the task. Nor is there a history of reinforcement that would induce the subject to detect new phenomena. Creating an advance requires two more levels of complexity. This is roughly paradigmatic complexity. Absorbing or assimilating an advance created by someone else requires formal operational complexity.

The Stage of an Inventor and the Stage of a Culture Differ

Individual and cultural developments have a straightforward relationship to one another, as we have argued

elsewhere (Commons-Miller, in press). The stage of cultural development is limited by the highest stage of performance of at least one member. But it is always lower in stage than that of that person's performance. In a particular population or culture, stage will be normally distributed, with most of the population performing on most tasks central to that culture at one stage and with fewer individuals at both lower and higher stages. Our best estimate from Dawson's (2002a, 2002b) data on stages of moral development is that each stage is spaced one standard deviation apart. Next we discuss reasons for our assertion that stages within populations work this way.

In related work, scoring actions and problem solving of animals, we have reported that at least some chimpanzees perform at the concrete operational stage. This is seen, for example, on some social perspective-taking problems (Commons & Miller, 2004). We can assume that because some chimpanzees perform at the concrete stage, some of our common ancestors would have likewise performed at the concrete stage. Commons and Miller (2004) argued that there was a progression in top performance of the ancestors to *Homo sapiens* through the abstract, formal, and systematic stages. That is, with some of the new hominid species, leading eventually to *Homo sapiens*, some of those species had at least a single individual who could solve problems at one higher stage than the species that they eventually replaced. The requirement for speciation is for only one such member who then passes on his or her genes. Specifically, at some time after the first Cro-Magnon *Homo sapiens*, we have argued (Commons & Bresette, 2000) that the population would have been large enough, based on probability alone, that there could have been an individual who behaved at the paradigmatic stage in at least one domain.

Only one member at a time invents, even though the invention might be a joint enterprise in other respects. Even in a cooperative behavior, one person has the behavior first, even if only a millisecond before the other. Yet inventing behavior depends on others' past inventions. Inventions can only build on the last inventions and may be limited to advancing just one or two stages beyond those inventions, which are always postformal. Individuals may be limited to one or two stages above the stage of invention in a culture. The general stage we assign to cultures can be so much lower than the stage attained by the most developed individuals in that culture working in science at the time. Even though individuals might act at the highest stages—for example, cross-paradigmatic—societal development tends to lag behind individual development because at each stage of cultural development the development of the cultural innovators outpaces that of their contemporaries, at least within their domain of innovation. For a culture to progress, there must be a supply of innovators who work with minimal support from their culture. For example, Marie Curie did not have an academic position until her husband died and she took over his professorship at the Sorbonne University. The size of this supply of paradigmatic and cross-paradigmatic thinkers seems to be the largest bottleneck in cultural development.

Truly Creative Acts Change Culture

To be truly creative, an act has to reach and influence a large enough group within the world that it survives in the culture and has influence. Sometimes potentially creative acts are not communicated, either because the society is not proficient enough to receive them or simply because the acts themselves are not transmitted at all or are inefficiently transmitted. For successful transmission and dissemination of innovation to take place, the culture must be ready to absorb the discovery. Being ready to absorb a discovery is partly a characteristic of cultures. A demand for the innovation also has to exist so that innovation pays off. Cultural transmission, however, ultimately relies on the ideas being adopted by individuals. Discoveries and findings need to be spread to other individuals by infection of memes (Best, 1997; Commons, Krause, Fayer, & Meaney, 1993; Moritz, 1995; Trivers, 1985). The transmission of memes usually requires that the uninitiated individuals receive some degree of support to learn the new memes. Formal and informal education is one of the means by which memes are acquired; such mechanisms provide implicit and explicit support for learning (Cavalli-Sforza, Feldman, Chen, & Dornbusch, 1982). Formal education promotes the learning of new ideas through means such as direct instruction. Informal education promotes learning by providing opportunities for individuals to observe the behavior of those who have a greater degree of competence. Either form of learning opportunity would be necessary, because most people cannot possibly understand an innovation on their own. They do not reason at a high enough stage. Increasing support through teaching and training ensures

that they come to understand and possibly use a higher stage behavior (Fischer, Hand, & Russell, 1984), including a discovery. Including such opportunities for learning allows individuals who would not on their own reach a somewhat higher stage than their own to do so. It is also important to recognize that providing the opportunity to learn one innovation, such as computer programming, may put one into a context or an educational system that transmits other memes as well. The larger set of infecting memes becomes part of the participants' resulting behavior. In short, the rate of transmission of memes depends on increasing contagion through these various means—education, training, and communicating results—so that potential innovators come into contact with the most advanced forms of the present culture.

Finally, it follows as well that it would be useful for the innovator to be some form of teacher for the new memes to be acquired by others. One incentive to having many graduate students is that some might follow-up and build on one's own work. In current society, it is necessary to publish, present, and promote much innovative work because otherwise it gets lost in the huge number of publications. It may also help to get material into textbooks and reviews.

The difficulty in spreading memes, as just defined, has dramatically slowed the process of discovery. We speculate that many discoveries have to be made repeatedly before they take hold. People have to engage in activities that require the new cultural information. In learning the new actions required by the innovation, an individual is thereby infected with the memes of the innovation. In carrying out the activities associated with the innovation, as well as in teaching others to do likewise, the individual is further infected. The more thoroughly an innovation is learned and taught, the greater the degree of infection by memes. Learning innovations in general probably leads to benefits for those who learn them; for example, it increases employability in the present culture.

Novelty and More Hierarchically Complex Behaviors

Novel behavior is one psychological dimension of an individual's response to a new or strange situation. A novel situation may consist of a sudden or unpredictable change in a known state of affairs. Novelty has two aspects that are important to creativity. First, novelty spurs the development of more hierarchically complex behaviors; second, creativity requires attention to novelty as well as an original response. People who are overwhelmed by novelty and the accompanying uncertainty are precluded from creative discovery. They avoid confronting novel and anomalous findings and observations. In this section, we discuss how novelty is involved in stage change, a particular form of learning. Such stage change quite often is necessary for a truly creative act.

It has been shown that novelty greatly aids (if not induces) continuous intellectual development within domains and discontinuous development across domains by forcing transitions between lower and higher stages (Grotzer et al., 1985). Furthermore, development of this kind is dependent on new, more hierarchically complex behavior obtaining outcomes that the individual prefers. Novelty in ordinary problem solvers often produces some development. Ordinary problem solvers working on problems at or near their stage of development can nevertheless be motivated by novel problem types, as long as the problems and information are not too novel. It has been shown that too little novelty seems to remove the incentive to keep learning, and too much novelty can be aversive (e.g., Kagan, 1974).

Novelty and the Creative Behavior

Strikingly similar in some aspects but just as strikingly different in others is the problem solving of truly innovative thinkers. Such thinkers seem to be much less limited by considering information with a high degree of novelty. Two examples will be provided here. First, both the Nobel Prize–winning physicist Louis W. Alvarez and his son, Walter Alvarez, searched for information that suggested that there had been an asteroid crash in the sea off of the Yucatán Peninsula. Although this seemed to be not likely to many others, by sticking with the problem and not being dissuaded by the fact that what they were saying was so novel that many dismissed their idea, they ended up convincing the field that not only had an asteroid crashed into the Earth at that location, but it had most likely wiped out the dinosaurs (Fastovsky & Weishampel, 1996).

A tangible and full-bodied historical example of this type can be found in the creative work of Charles Darwin (e.g., 1855, 1872/1898, 1877, 1969). The behavior responds to some novel aspect of the environment that others have missed. Consider the example

of Darwin's observation of finches, as discussed earlier. This is an example of discovering a phenomenon. The initial discovery itself did not have much impact on Darwin's conceptualization, but years later he made sense of the phenomenon by proposing his theory of evolution. The finches had evolved and now filled the same niches that mainland birds of much greater variety had filled. In one case, the niches were filled by a variety of finches (system one), and in another by many separate mainland species (system two). Darwin saw that evolutionary forces had transformed the birds differently (a metasystematic comparison of systems one and two). In both of these examples, the scientists involved understood these phenomena without support. Hence, this is cross-paradigmatic.

THE PERSONALITIES AND TRAITS OF MAJOR INNOVATORS

Necessary but Not Sufficient Traits of Environments and History that Allow for True Creativity

Why are extremely creative major contributions so rare? Our assertion is that so many of the personality characteristics to be discussed (also see Shavinina & Ferrari, 2004) may be partially or wholly necessary, and finding so many of them in one individual is relatively rare. In addition, one would have to find not only this confluence of personality traits but also postformal reasoning in their chosen scientific domain. To begin with, each characteristic has a reasonably small probability. Their joint probability, therefore, is quite a bit smaller. One issue is that extremely creative scientists have an unusual set of traits. Many of these tendencies to act in particular ways can be directly related to major innovation. In traditional personality theories, when tendencies are somewhat stable over time, they are called *traits*. Although some of these tendencies are partially inherited, some portions are learned or acquired (Bouchard, Lykken, McGue, Segal, & Tellegen, 1990). When we are assessing these tendencies, we cannot tell which it is without doing twin studies or similar studies. In either case, in the present no one has access to what it is that created these tendencies in scientists who have completed their work. Even so, it is important to keep in mind that traits are not causes of behavior. They are just intermediate results that serve as convenient explanations for a person's behavior. Behavioral analytic or learning theories would tend to explain these tendencies with respect to the individual's history and present circumstances and might be more useful in terms of understanding adult learning and development.

Personalities that Withstand Social Conformist Influences

Innovators do not have nonconforming personalities in general, but they do withstand social conformist influences (Roe, 1952). Actually, effective innovators have a mix of both nonconformity and conformity. In thinking up their ideas, they may need independence. People who are worried about themselves and their reputation and standing cannot take the risks to be creative. The independence required might be partly due to some kind of temperamental or inherent characteristic of the individual that goes beyond just resisting the social pressure to conform. Temperament studies have looked at such things as fearfulness and adaptability (Rothbart & Bates, 1998; Thomas & Chess, 1977). As suggested in the section on novelty, the presence of too much fear or too little adaptability may interfere with the kind of intensive engagement with the environment that could lead to innovations. A lack of fear, especially of fear of rejection by others, could help an individual in resisting social pressure. Attention deficit disorder has also been associated with creativity (Cramond, 1995), possibly because there is inattention to social signals of condemnation and therefore a lower tendency toward social conformity. Because of the lack of social control in the immediate sense, we deduce that major innovators tend to be noncompetitive with others because they do not use others as a frame of reference. They are not as concerned with other people's opinions of them as less creative scientists and do not compare their own activities and success with others. Instead, in terms of social comparison theory, the comparison may be to one's own previous performance or the performance of some historical figure (Rheinberg, Lührmann, & Wagner, 1977). Therefore, creative actions often *require* that there be a certain detachment from the social order and from social approval.

Another long-standing and related aspect of people's behavior that has been less studied is the individuals' tendency to pursue their own agenda, almost no matter what. One important aspect of this trait could be called persistence (Howe, 2001, 2004). Great discoverers seem to often have more resistance to giving up in their continued confrontation with problems. Learning studies have illuminated some of the environmental factors that can lead to persistence of behavior (Mace, Lalli, Shea, & Nevin, 1992; Nevin, Tota, Torquato, & Shull, 1990), including receiving a great deal of free rather than contingent reinforcers.

Environmental variables can also help make individuals less subject to social control. One such variable is independent wealth. Let us take the case of Darwin again, someone who was independently wealthy. Darwin's quest for the truth was unfettered by concerns for employment. Although some were extremely upset by what he was doing, he could not be fired and he lived quite well. Einstein described the life of a patent officer as ideal, getting paid for doing what one likes. There was little work in that position that he did not enjoy. And it left him with plenty of time to work on his own theories. Hence, again, his discovery behavior was not under the control of an employer or social institution.

It should be noted that to effectively spread their ideas, highly creative scientists may also need some degree of connection to society. Both Darwin and Einstein, for example, continued to live within society, belonging to professional organizations. Thus, they were connected enough to society that they could communicate their ideas to others. Raskolnikov in Dostoyevsky's (1914) *Crime and Punishment* is a good example of someone who chose to live outside of society and therefore was not very effective.

Ambition and Curiosity

One definition of ambition is a strong preference to achieve great things. In highly creative scientists, ambition is often directed toward solving problems, not becoming acclaimed, respected, or powerful. This seems essential to creative behavior because many creative acts require persistence and enthusiasm for the enterprise. There is very little research on such ambition. It is not clear how ambition can be learned, but clearly it can be dampened. Children who grow up in a culture of creativity see it as normative and may learn to feel empowered (see the examples later of the empowering environments in which the children of some highly creative scientists grew up). These individuals learn that following one's dream is often rewarded, often raising their ambition.

Another major trait of the great discoverers was that they were extremely curious. This would be reflected in extremely high scores on the Holland (1996) factor called investigative (I), if ever assessed. This means that discovering was extremely reinforcing for them. The great curiosity of people presses for their own development and the learning of the next stage's behavior. Having high investigative interests should also propel stage change. Interest raises the reinforcing value, which in turn increases the rate of self-presentation of problems because such self–presentation is reinforced. The increased rate of attempting problems would raise the probability of solving them. This is because the number of attempts at solving a problem probably matters.

Cognitive Styles

Field independence has been associated with creative functions in adults (Minhas & Kaur, 1983). This classically defined cognitive style has been measured by the rod and frame task (Wapner & Demick, 1991; Witkin, 1949; Witkin et al., 1954) as well as by paper and pencil tests (Witkin, Oltman, Raskin, & Karp, 1971). For example, in the Group Embedded Figures Test (GEFT) manual of Witkin and colleagues, subjects are required to recognize and identify a target figure within a complex pattern. The more figures found, the better the individual is at the process of separation and is said to be more field independent. Minhas and Kaur (1983) support the idea that field-independent individuals display a penchant for novel types of acts. The degree to which people are field-independent correlates with their ability to resist social pressure and the influence of social cues. Field-independent people are more likely to exhibit creativity and are more likely to resist the social pressure to conform to tradition. There is also an overlap between field independence and intelligence. Ohnmacht and McMorris (1971) found that neither field independence nor lack of dogmatism alone is useful in explaining variations on a task presumed to reflect creative potential. However, when considered together, these variables become significant. Using the proclivity to produce transformations of visual information as a measure of creativity, Ross (1977) also found a high correlation between creative behavior, locus of control, and field independence. Locus of control is a personality construct referring to an individual's perception of the locus of events as determined internally by their own behavior versus fate, luck, or external circumstances.

Tolerance of Ambiguity, Risk Taking, and Tolerance for Rejection

Tolerance of ambiguity, the taking of risks, and some degree of tolerance for rejection are necessary for creativity. Students doing research often ask why the professor does not simply give them the right method for understanding a new problem the first time. The professor then says, "If I knew the right method for solving this problem, I would have learned it from somebody who had already answered the question." Research suggests otherwise. Ambiguity is more tolerable for older adults, making the ambiguity in the creative process less of a threat. Labouvie-Vief (1985) noted that older adults were at ease when working with ambiguity creatively (also see Arlin, 1984; Labouvie-Vief, Adams, Hakim-Larson & Hayden, 1983). Younger adults focus on reaching a conclusion that makes sense when presented with logically inconsistent statements, whereas older adults concentrate on the problems inherent in the premises. They comment on the inconsistencies, question them, and sometimes introduce ideas that might resolve them. They go beyond the information given in the problem on the basis of their own personal experience and knowledge.

To be creative, individuals also must take risks and be able to withstand rejection. Smith, Carlsson, and Sandstrom (1985) found that creators use fewer compulsive or depressive defenses and are free from excessive anxiety. They also found that creative individuals have access to their dream life and to their early childhoods. More often than noncreative individuals, they tend to remember both positive and negative qualities of these life experiences. Finally, creativity requires one to separate oneself from one's creations. Otherwise one would rarely be self-critical of one's creative output. If one were always satisfied, there would be no development, no reaching for more. Being challenged by (rather than upset at) not knowing the details or the direction of one's enterprise seems essential, as does the ability to withstand and overcome disconfirmation or failure at a particular step in the enterprise. All of these require risk-seeking behavior. The passion involved is for the enterprise of discovery, not for the self, a particular act, or a need for social approval. This independence may lead to a sense of isolation from others, which, although painful, may also prove to be surprisingly necessary.

Timing of Creative Acts

Even with all of the personal traits just mentioned, when it comes to creation, timing is everything. Timing of creative acts may have three sources, each conflicting with the others. First, learning and developing higher order hierarchical complexity action takes time. A great deal of this time would be spent thinking about and working on whatever problems the individual was interested in and actively engaging with the material. This kind of engagement would lead to increased learning and ultimately to stage change. Some of the most integrative and highest order acts may not take place until middle age or later, as was the case with both Copernicus and Darwin. Second, one needs a great deal of time to develop one's own ideas, and in an arena within which those ideas will not be demolished before they can attain integrations. Third, there is a long social agenda of the work one is supposed to carry out rather than doing the work that takes one down one's own creative path. This social agenda entails diversion of a certain amount of time and energy to work on other people's problems. One might then simply adopt their frame of reference rather than pursuing one's own.

LEARNING POSTFORMAL STAGE PERFORMANCE

Learning

In addition to personality traits, the learning of postformal action seems necessary for major discoveries. Thus far, we have discussed the effects on creativity of functioning at postformal stages, but we have not spent much time on how individuals may learn and develop postformal actions. Learning is part of the process by which stage transition takes place. Therefore stage transition describes how next-stage actions are learned by individuals. Commons and Miller (1998) and Commons and Richards (2002) have described both stage transition and reasons transition takes place or fails to take place. An illustration of certain aspects of the transition stages is included here (table 12.3). The first three steps (deconstruction) start with initially high loss of perceived reinforcement

opportunity. This loss may initiate learning of the next steps. But during the advance through these initial steps, more reinforcement is obtained. This happens because when lower stage actions fail, individuals begin to try a variety of new actions, some of which lead to more reinforcement. Psychologically, the results are consistent with Rosales-Ruiz and Baer's (1997) work on behavioral cusps. A *cusp*, as defined by Rosales-Ruiz and Baer, is "a behavior change that has consequences for the organism beyond the change itself, some of which may be considered important" (p. 537). The proposed psychological mechanism of transition seems to be consistent with these theories. Most Piagetian or neo-Piagetian theories do not clearly operationalize the steps in transitions or the empirical basis for transition.

There is very little empirical work on raising postformal stage. For a discussion of adult stage transition, however, see the entire special issue of the *Journal of Adult Development* (Commons, 2002). The early work on inducing stage change was in moral development with children (Blatt & Kohlberg, 1973). There has been some work on the effects of higher education on ego stage (Mentkowski, Moeser, & Strait, 1983). Kallio (1998) showed improvement in freshman in formal operational reasoning with direct training and with metacognitive training. The CASE Thinking Science activities studies (Adey & Shayer, 1994; Adey, Shayer, & Yates, 1995) provided examples of formal operational problems in 32 lessons over two years. The CASE activities were designed to familiarize pupils with the language and apparatus (concrete preparation); provide "events" that cause the pupils to pause, wonder, and think again (in table 12.3, step 0: cognitive conflict); encourage the pupils to reflect on their own thinking processes (metacognition); and show how this thinking can be applied in many contexts (bridging). Torosyan (1999) encouraged consciousness development in the college classroom through student-centered transformative teaching and learning. He obtained an increase of up to one stage. Woods (2000) introduced problem-based learning (PBL) in several university level courses in which students' current level on the Perry scale were mostly position 2.5 to 3.5. After running a three-hour workshop to help them "adjust to change" and grieve the loss of their old ways via PBL and then applying PBL, they improved. Hart, Rickards, and Mentkowski (1995) have used the Perry scheme of intellectual and ethical development as a college

TABLE 12.3.   Stage Transition

	Relation	Name	Personality	Description
Step 0	a = a′ with b′ where a′ and b′ previous stage actions	Temporary equilibrium point (thesis)	Fault finders	People at this step have experienced a huge drop in perceived reinforcement rate because they see the failures of their behavior of the present order to obtain what others obtain. People get stuck here because much of their current order behavior that is similar to the "failure behavior" is maintained by reinforcement. At low orders of performance in the social domain, this may result in antisocial behavior. These people perceive tremendous unfairness. They quite often have unshakable negative depressive scripts. They deny the value of new ideas.
Step 1	b	Negation or complementation[a] (antithesis)	Naysayers	This may consist of persons who enter therapy, as well as rebels, radicals, and discontents. They have given up their old ways. If "a" is wrong, then the opposite of "a" is right. This step is associated with the second largest drop in reinforcement rate because people may drop their previous successful behavior "a" and substitute behavior "b" for it.
Step 2	a or b	Relativism (alternation of thesis and antithesis)	Relativists	In this culture, this is quite often the largest group of people in transition. They fill academia. They stop progress by insisting that there is more than one way to look at things but cannot even decide which ones are more likely to be true or good. There is some gain in reinforcement, but the conflict between whether to choose "a" or "b" produces anxiety, angst, mood swings, and uncertainty about roles and values.
Step 3	a and b	Smash (attempts at synthesis	Movers	Such persons are moving from smash to consolidate. They create great trouble for themselves and others by throwing ideas and actions together in a creative, haphazard way, taking a great deal of risk.
Step 4	a with b	New temporary equilibrium (synthesis and new thesis)	Unshakables	To these persons, everything is okay even . if it is not okay. They avoid conundrums, apparent contradiction and comparisons to people they look up to. Since they have just obtained this new equilibrium, everything is good enough.

[a] *Complementation* is defined as follows: The complement of A consists of all elements that are not in A.

outcomes measure for years and have found development. Hill (2004) applied conceptual change theory with the developmental instruction model based on Perry. This application made a modest contribution to intellectual growth, moving people from position 3 (concrete stage) to position 4 (abstract stage). Lovell and Nunnery (2004) found some increases as well in educational counselors, only a little of which seems to have been postformal.

Given all these cautions about the difficulty of producing stage change, there are several suggestions for stage change. Recognizing the need to perform at higher stages might be useful. This might include the self-assessment of one's own stage of performance, which could be an incentive to progress (see table 12.3). Informally, one hears that people enter graduate school after step 0 of transition and learning—failure of the present stage. The graduate school presentations of systematic thinking often move peoples' reasoning to the systematic stage. Hopefully, students do not spend much time experimenting with the anti–step 1. Moving to the relativism of step 2 is often accomplished by graduate school because of the necessity of learning about multiple systems, none of which seems to be completely satisfactory. Step 3—smash—is the most difficult to achieve. Emotionally, it always seems to require a leap of faith in one's own proclivity to sort out what works from what does not. Because smashing two systems together does not at first generate a simple, working system, or the next stage metasystem, one has to have something akin to faith that things will improve to get through the confusion that is self-generated. There is very little to say about moving beyond systematic and metasystematic reasoning because there are so few people who do so. There does not seem to be any institutional training or education that is even remotely sufficient. It does seem necessary to be both deeply educated in some endeavor and broadly educated as well.

Factors Contributing to Learning and Development

Both within many neo-Piagetian accounts (e.g., Case, 1974, 1978, 1982, 1985) and precision teaching (e.g., Binder, 1995) accounts, automatization of previous-stage behavior (elements) is predicted to improve the rate of obtaining next-stage performance (combinations). As old-stage tasks are completed near the maximum rate and errors almost disappear, the actions are said to become *automatized*. Such overlearning leads to automatization and chunking of the stimuli in the tasks. That is, each individual stimulus in the task no longer has to be discriminated individually, but now as a whole. This makes it possible to see the forest rather than just the trees.

Integrating Postformal Scientific Actions with Adult Social Actions

The exposure to a broad range of societal ideas through integrating career with societal activities

prompts greater creativity based on higher stages. Integration of social and scientific acts primarily occurs in early adulthood and after. Whereas people meet the peak of their stage development in early through late middle age, some great innovators reach the highest orders of development earlier in life (Stevens-Long & Commons, 1991). For example, mathematicians often reach their peak in their twenties. For active individuals, developmental stage peaks between the fifties and late sixties. Generally, it is not until middle age (the forties or so) that people can recognize not only that they are underneath a social structure and climbing within it but also that they create and maintain that system. Active people engage in the process within their families, workplaces, professions, and communities. They come to see themselves as responsible parts of society. At this time, for example, many men become more active in their families by exhibiting more nurturing behavior. Many women become more active by pursuing careers and additional education. Both genders will thus become more similar to each other. In effect, this general process requires individuals to consider different systems—for example, the work system and the general social system, or the family system versus the work system—and increasingly integrate those systems. In other words, demands to move from systematic to at least metasystematic thinking are present. These kinds of demands may result in some individuals taking at least some of the steps that may make greater creativity more likely.

All tasks must have some order of hierarchical complexity. Performance on such tasks depends on many other task characteristics, however. These include level of support (Commons & Richards, 1995; Fischer et al., 1984), horizontal complexity, fluency of performance on the component tasks, "talent," interest, and other factors. Hence, one may expect complex interrelationships between measures of performance on tasks and conditions of measurement. As discussed previously, level of support alters measured stage in a simple linear fashion. But the stage of performance should be curvilinear when plotted against the subjects' chronological age (Armon & Dawson, 1997; Dawson, 1998) and only linear when plotted against log age. This more complex relationship is due to the fact that the orders of hierarchical complexity are equally spaced in terms of difficulty. But development slows down logarithmically with age (Backman, 1925). The conceptual basis of Backman's function of growth, is the postulate that the logarithm of growth rate (H) is negatively proportional to the square of time's (T) logarithm, $\log H = k_2 \log^2 T$. Constant k_2 is always negative. Also, variability should increase with age, and it does. Yet there is some evidence that at the highest stages, there is less spread (Armon & Dawson, 1997). The proclivity to integrate relationships and systems and even paradigms from many domains probably increases with postformal stage. The more postformal in one domain, the more even performance should be in many domains.

Precursors of the Higher Stages

Commons-Miller (2003) found a number of factors that were predictive of the scientific success of the children of some of the most highly successful scientists. This information can be used here to further illuminate some of the conditions that may lead to the learning and development of postformal thinking. In the examples studied, the younger generation spent significant amounts of time with their scientist parents. But this went beyond just spending time with their parents. During this time, the children were often included as part of a family enterprise that involved doing science: asking and answering questions, carrying out or helping carry out investigations. They were treated respectfully; their opinions were sought and challenged. They started their scientific work early, as was the case for Jean Piaget (1952; Vidal, 1994; who was son of the Arthur professor of medieval literature at the University) and Richard Leakey (son of Mary and Louis Leakey). In many cases they worked with one or more of their parents (e.g., Richard Leakey; Walter Alvarez, son of physicist Louis Walter Alvarez; Mary Catherine Bateson, daughter of Gregory Bateson and Margaret Mead).

Some of the work these children of scientists did was at the paradigmatic stage. For example, Walter Alvarez and his team, which included his father, Nobel Prize–winning physics professor Dr. Louis Alvarez, Frank Asaro, and Helen Michel, combined their knowledge from a number of fields. Walter Alvarez found an interesting piece of limestone in Gubbio, Italy, in 1977 and brought it home to Berkeley as a gift for his father. The limestone included a thin layer of clay that marked a time in our planet's history known as the Cretaceous-Tertiary (K-T) Boundary. Walter and Louis Alvarez took the rock to Frank Asaro and Helen Michel, two of the most careful

chemists they knew at the Lawrence Berkeley Laboratory, and asked them to analyze the clay layer. Asaro and Michel used chemistry and physics to perform neutron activation analysis to find the iridium at the K-T boundary. The Alvarezes combined their knowledge of astronomy and geology to look for the trace effects of iridium from asteroid impacts. In the late 1980s, they finally found a crater, now known as the Chicxulub crater, just the right size and age, at the edge of Mexico's Yucatán Peninsula. They then combined all of those results with evolution to propose that an asteroid about 10 km (6 miles) in diameter hit the Earth, throwing up a dust layer that encircled the planet and led to the extinction of the dinosaurs.

Very few individuals have this kind of upbringing, so such precursors are rarely encountered. Adult stage of development is normally distributed with a mean stage of formal and a standard deviation of one stage in our educated society (Dawson, 2002a, 2002b). Therefore, it is not surprising that researchers of adult development find very few individuals who engage in the metasystematic performance necessary for creativity. Some examples are as follows: Armon (1984) found 9% (3 out of 32) on the good-life interview, and 15% (5 out of 32) on the moral judgment interview. Richards and Commons (1984) found only 14% (10 out of 71 participants) on the multisystems task. Demetriou and Efklides (1985) found 11% (13 out of 114) on the metacognitive task. Kohlberg (1984; Colby & Kohlberg, 1987a, 1987b) found 13% (8 out of 60 participants aged 24 and older), who used stage 5 reasoning on the moral judgment interview. Powell (1984) reported 9% (4 out of 44 participants with IQs of 132 or higher) who performed metasystematically.

In addition to the fact that few people may encounter the conditions that could lead to higher stage development, there may also be personality characteristics that make moving beyond certain steps in the transition from one stage to another much less likely (Commons & Richards, 2002). These are described in the table 12.3.

Social Control

A society that not only tolerates but also promotes creativity produces more creative acts. This can be seen in Nemeth and Kwan's (1985) study on originality in word associations that found that participants who were exposed to persistent minority views tended to reexamine issues and to engage in more divergent and original thought. They learn to be more original, a component of creativity. On the other hand, participants who were exposed to persistent, fairly exclusive majority views tended to concentrate on the position proposed, display convergent thinking, and be less original. One might assume that all creativity depends on originality and divergent thinking.

General Characteristics of "Truly Creative" Individuals

A creative innovator will not have done society's bidding for long. One has to work on one's creative acts early on. Delaying work on one's creative program means that the other intervening activities will be reinforced, lowering the probability of ever completing one's own creative acts. True adult creativity requires building on current knowledge and then transcending it. It requires that innovators or creators have novel insights into complex problems. This often requires the creation of a new synthesis of systems (metasystematic) or a new paradigm (paradigmatic order) or field (cross-paradigmatic order) on the part of such an individual.

IMPLICATIONS OF VALUING THE HIGHER STAGES

Baum (2000, 2004) argues that learning is a form of intragenerational change, whereas evolution is an intergenerational form of change. Intergenerational change requires intergenerational learning. Genetic evolutionary forces have generally increased the highest stage of reasoning found from the concrete stage in the common ancestor of *Homo sapiens* and chimpanzees to the cross-paradigmatic in humans. We may wonder whether such forces will, over time, actually increase the number of people functioning at the cross-paradigmatic stage. How soon might this begin to happen? Might someone even function at stages beyond the cross-paradigmatic? Of the two forms of evolution, genetic and cultural, the impact of cultural evolution as it impacts postformal stages will be discussed first.

As revealed in introductory and adult developmental psychology books, a self-reflective understanding of postformal stages is developing widely (e.g., Hoyer, Roodin, Rybash, & Rybash, 2003; Schulz & Salthouse, 1999). In this context, we find tremendous differences arising among social groups—differences that seem to be related to education levels and the power of reasoning (Kegan, 1994). Will this trend continue? Given the degree to which certain peoples and groups seem to value higher stage development, one must wonder how far some might go in their efforts to produce intellectually advanced individuals—those who, for example, could function at the cross-paradigmatic stage. Might the trend in this direction be illustrated in part by the fact that people are now paying huge sums to educate their children at top research universities, graduate, and professional schools? They are encouraging their children to obtain postgraduate education. Might some go even further in this direction and attempt to push the limits of evolution and natural selection through humanly engineered means? How far will people go in this direction?

Where might this tendency lead us? Some extremely controversial predictions are to be made in this context. We are not advocating these scenarios, merely describing their possibility and pondering their implications. At the same time, we believe we must marvel at the degree to which some people might just push the envelope of selection in their efforts to achieve some kind of competitive edge, creative transformation, or some unique version of self-transformation. As we write about these things, we are aware that some of these ideas might sound like the plot lines from various science fiction novels. When we push the limits of this kind of thinking—and translate it into practice, we might obtain very interesting but sometimes sobering or even frightening results. For example, it was sobering and frightening to find that clones aged at a much more rapid rate, reflecting the age of the DNA.

As stated earlier, evolution itself is not teleological. The direction is not inevitable. It is not directed by moral or ethical considerations. For this and related reasons, people should pay attention to the tremendous ethical controversies surrounding these issues. Our entire society should wrestle with these ethical dilemmas and address them. There is the daunting task of showing respect for all, while at the same time recognizing the inequities promulgated by the interplay of nature and nurture. How these differences should be handled in the future should be widely discussed. The consequences of such matters should be vigorously debated and ethically informed policies must be formulated. With these ethical considerations in mind, we would like to review three learning mechanisms through which one can imagine that the number of higher order creative innovators might increase: (a) cultural evolution, (b) biological evolution, and (c) computer and robotic hardware and software evolution.

Cultural Evolution

Cultural evolution now promotes people who reason at the highest stages. All Nobel Prize winners in the sciences reason at least at the metasystematic stage and many corporate presidents, Supreme Court justices, and presidents reason at the metasystematic stage (Commons, 2002). Could cultural evolution also produce biological evolution? With the increase in demand for people with the highest stages of postformal reasoning, certain forces have come to bear. Our society is rapidly acquiring the technological know-how that will permit experts to engage in human engineering and cloning. Commons-Miller (in press) suggests that people have begun to use a variety of mechanisms short of biological engineering to produce intellectually superior individuals. Historically, among other mechanisms, these include assortativeness. Assortativeness means that there is a demand for separation from the rest of the population (Buss, 2003). It is accomplished by means of clubs, zoning, rules promoting intragroup marriage and blocking intergroup marriages, and career specialization by groups. Assortativeness has always been a force in human cultural and biological evolution. The evidence suggests that many will be tempted to move in this direction, as those with high intelligence already do in the Mensa organization, for example.

Biological Evolution

Commons-Miller (in press) thinks that there is heavy demand for genetically improved human beings. We are already seeing changes in sex ratios in China and India by genetic selection (Hudson & den Boer, 2004). These changes are described by David Baltimore, a Nobel laureate who heads the California Institute of Technology. He suggests that these changes will encourage the rapid development and utilization of germline engineering. This in turn will lead to speciation, as Dyson (1999) also argues. He states that the speciation of humans into different groups is inevitable—and that it would be a disaster to allow such diversification without restraint. Biological evolution, as described by Darwin, requires isolation among individuals, within species. Mayr (1942) stated that a new species develops if a population that has become geographically isolated from its parental species acquires, during this period of isolation, characteristics that promote or guarantee reproductive isolation when the external barriers break down. Mate choice or sexual selection also may drive the speciation process (Higashi, Takimo, & Yamamura, 1999). Assortativeness, choosing people like oneself, might be the required force for selection. It is predicted that speciation in humans is soon likely, however controversial it is. That is, we might begin to find the differentiation of humans into more than a single species. Some groups might begin to engage in genetic engineering to isolate their group from the rest of humanity. This isolation can cause speciation.

If these individuals are sufficiently different enough and brighter and can survive inbreeding, some would argue that a new species might evolve. This new species might have a greater proclivity for creativity in general, and for science in particular, if some of the relevant traits already discussed, as well as the highest postformal stages, are selected for.

Computer and Robotic Hardware and Software Evolution

As upsetting as it might be, there is another way that people might attempt to create the extrahuman or superhuman levels of achievement by somehow linking advanced humans with superior reasoning and creative proficiencies with hierarchically complex stacked neural-net computers (Commons & White, 2003). The product or offspring might be able to solve problems in science that are not solvable by ordinary high-functioning humans. The motivation for supercomputers, on the other hand, would seem to differ from speciation. The development of computers is relentless, with most people cheering the changes. Computers, like all technology, can be used for good and evil—remember Hal in Arthur Clarke's (1968) book and movie *2001*. Such supercomputers likely could be built from stacked neural nets and in turn, reason like humans but not be limited in the number of layers. This is an important consideration, because we speculate that the number of layers of interconnected neural networks is related to the order of hierarchical complexity at which such machines will perform. It might be interesting to assess their stage of development with our MHC scoring system.

Again, the consequences of all these possibilities must be thoroughly debated and policies formulated with an ethical standard in mind. Furthermore, we argue that the debate must be spirited, and it should begin soon. The doggedness with which individuals and groups might pursue such revolutionary intellectual and creative transformations as these may prove to be truly remarkable. Could Darwin have had any idea where some of his early theorizing might lead?

CONCLUSION

The creation of major cultural innovations is multidimensional. These innovations are often accomplished by distinct groupings of individuals who display an assortment of specific traits. Darwin was chosen as an example of one with the requisite traits; however, several other major innovators were discussed as well. Most major innovators display the essential traits or characteristics discussed throughout this chapter. Several characteristics that have been proposed are absolutely necessary. Most important is the order of hierarchical complexity of tasks with which such a person could deal successfully. This includes the complexity in the area of the work as well as commensurate complexity in the social system. When these two dimensions work together, the likelihood of a major creative innovation is enhanced.

ACKNOWLEDGMENTS   Some of this material comes from Commons and Goodheart (1999) and from Commons and Bresette (2000). Dare Institute staff members edited the manuscript and made major suggestions for changes.

References

Adey, P. S., & Shayer, M. (1994). *Really raising standards*. London: Routledge.

Adey, P. S., Shayer, M., & Yates, C. (1995). *Thinking science: The curriculum materials of the case project*. London: Thomas Nelson and Sons.

Ampère, A. (1826/1958). *Memoir on the mathematical theory of electrodynamic phenomena, uniquely deduced from experience*. Paris: A. Blanchard.

Arlin, P. K. (1975). Cognitive development in adulthood: A fifth stage? *Developmental Psychology, 11*, 602–606.

Arlin, P. K. (1977). Piagetian operations in problem finding. *Developmental Psychology, 13*, 247–298.

Arlin, P. K. (1984). Adolescent and adult thought: A structural interpretation. In M. L. Commons, F. A. Richards, & C. Armon (Eds.), *Beyond formal operations: Vol. 1. Late adolescent and adult cognitive development* (pp. 258–271). New York: Praeger.

Armon, C. (1984). Ideals of the good life and moral judgment: Ethical reasoning across the life span. In M. L. Commons, F. A. Richards, & C. Armon (Eds.), *Beyond formal operations: Vol. 1. Late adolescent and adult cognitive development* (pp. 357–380). New York: Praeger.

Armon, C., & Dawson, T. L. (1997). Developmental trajectories in moral reasoning across the lifespan. *Journal of Moral Education, 26*(4), 433–453.

Backman, G. (1925). Über generelle Wachstumgesetze beim Menschen. *Acta Univers. Latviensis, 12*, 367–380.

Basseches, M. A. (1984). Dialectical thinking as a metasystematic form of cognitive organization. In M. L. Commons, F. A. Richards, & C. Armon (Eds.), *Beyond formal operations: Vol. 1. Late adolescent and adult cognitive development* (pp. 216–257). New York: Praeger.

Baum, W. M. (2000). Behavior and the general evolutionary process. Manuscript submitted for publication.

Baum, W. M. (2004). *Understanding behaviorism, behavior, culture, and evolution*. New York: Blackwell.

Benack, S. (1984). Postformal epistemologist and the growth of empathy. In M. L. Commons, , F. A. Richards, & C. Armon (Eds.), *Beyond formal operations: Vol. 1. Late adolescent and adult cognitive development* (pp. 340–356). New York: Praeger.

Best, M. L. (1997). Models for interacting populations of memes: Competition and niche behavior. *Journal of Memetics—Evolutionary Models of Information Transmission*. Retrieved August 19, 2004, from jom-emit.cfpm.org/1997/vol1/best_ml.html.

Binder, C. (1995). Promoting human precision teaching (HPT) innovation: A return to our natural science roots. *Performance Improvement Quarterly, 8*, 95–113.

Blatt, M., & Kohlberg, L. (1975). The effects of classroom moral discussion upon children's level of moral judgment. *Journal of Moral Education, 4*, 129–161.

Bouchard, T., Lykken, D., McGue, M., Segal, N., & Tellegen, A. (1990). Sources of human psychological differences: The Minnesota study of twins reared apart. *Science, 250*, 223–226.

Bowman, A. K. (1996). *The relationship between organizational work practices and employee performance: Through the lens of adult development*. Unpublished doctoral dissertation, The Fielding Institute, Santa Barbara, CA.

Brauer, D. (2001). New technologies—a chance for developing countries? *Development and Cooperation*, 5, 3.

Broughton, J. M. (1977). Beyond formal operations: Theoretical thought in adolescence. *Teachers College Record*, 79(1), 87–98.

Broughton, J. M. (1984). Not beyond formal operations, but beyond Piaget. In M. L. Commons, F. A. Richards, & C. Armon (Eds.), *Beyond formal operations: Vol. 1. Late adolescent and adult cognitive development* (pp. 395–411). New York: Praeger.

Buss, D. M. (2003). *The evolution of desire: Strategies of human mating*. New York: Basic Books.

Campbell, R. L., & Richie, D. M. (1983). Problems in the theory of developmental sequences: Prerequisites and precursors. *Human Development*, 26, 156–172.

Case, R. (1974). Structures and strictures: Some functional limitations in the course of cognitive growth. *Cognitive Psychology*, 6, 544–573.

Case, R. (1978). Intellectual development from birth to adulthood: A neo-Piagetian interpretation. In R. Siegler (Ed.), *Children's thinking: What develops?* (pp. 37–71). Hillsdale, NJ: Lawrence Erlbaum.

Case, R. (1982). The search for horizontal structures in children's development. *Genetic Epistemologist*, 11, 1–12.

Case, R. (1985). *Intellectual development: Birth to adulthood*. Orlando, FL: Academic Press.

Cavalli-Sforza, L. L., & Feldman, M. W. (1981). *Cultural transmission and evolution: A quantitative approach*. Princeton, NJ: Princeton University Press.

Cavalli-Sforza, L. L., Feldman, M. W., Chen, K. H., & Dornbusch, S. M. (1982). Theory and observation in cultural transmission. *Science*, 218, 19–27.

Clarke, A. C. (1968). *2001: A space odyssey*. New York: New American Library.

Colby, A., & Kohlberg, L. (1987a). *The measurement of moral judgment: Vol. 1. Theoretical foundations and research validation*. New York: Cambridge University Press.

Colby, A., & Kohlberg, L. (1987b). *The measurement of moral judgment: Vol. 2. Standard form scoring manuals*. New York: Cambridge University Press.

Commons, M. L. (1991). A comparison and synthesis of Kohlberg's cognitive-developmental and Gewirtz's learning-developmental attachment theories. In J. L. Gewirtz & W. M. Kurtines (Eds.), *Intersections with attachment* (pp. 257–291). Hillsdale, NJ: Lawrence Erlbaum.

Commons, M. L. (Ed.). (2002). Attaining a new stage [Special issue]. *Journal of Adult Development*, 9(3).

Commons, M. L., & Bresette, L. M. (2000). Major creative innovators as viewed through the lens of the general model of hierarchical complexity and evolution. In M. E. Miller & S. Cook-Greuter (Eds.), *Creativity, spirituality, and transcendence: Paths to integrity and wisdom in the mature self* (pp. 167–187). Norwood, NJ: Ablex.

Commons, M. L., & Goodheart, E. A. (1999). The philosophical origins of behavior analysis. In B. A. Thyer (Ed.), *The philosophical legacy of behaviorism* (pp. 9–49). Dordrecht: Kluwer Academic.

Commons, M. L., Goodheart, E. A., Bresette, L. M., with Bauer, N. F, Farrell, E. W., McCarthy, K. G., et al. (1995). Formal, systematic, and metasystematic operations with a balance-beam task series: A reply to Kallio's claim of no distinct systematic stage. *Adult Development*, 2, 193–199.

Commons, M. L., Krause, S. R., Fayer, G. A., & Meaney, M. (1993). Atmosphere and stage development in the workplace. In J. Demick & P. M. Miller (Eds.), *Development in the workplace* (pp. 199–218). Hillsdale, NJ: Lawrence Erlbaum.

Commons, M. L., & Miller, P. M. (1998). A quantitative behavior-analytic theory of development. *Mexican Journal of Experimental Analysis of Behavior*, 24, 153–180.

Commons, M. L., & Miller, P. M. (2004). Development of behavioral stages in animals. In M. Bekoff (Ed.), *Encyclopedia of animal behavior*. Westport, CT: Greenwood.

Commons, M. L., & Richards, F. A. (1978, April). *The structural analytic stage of development: A Piagetian postformal stage*. Paper presented at the Annual Meeting of the Western Psychological Association, San Francisco.

Commons, M. L., & Richards, F. A. (1984a). Applying the general stage model. In M. L. Commons, F. A. Richards, & C. Armon (Eds.), *Beyond formal operations: Vol. 1. Late adolescent and adult cognitive development* (pp. 141–157). New York: Praeger.

Commons, M. L., & Richards, F. A. (1984b). A general model of stage theory. In M. L. Commons, F. A. Richards, & C. Armon (Eds.), *Beyond formal operations: Vol. 1. Late adolescent and adult cognitive development* (pp. 120–140). New York: Praeger.

Commons, M. L., & Richards, F. A. (1995). Behavior analytic approach to dialectics of stage performance and stage change. *Behavioral Development*, 5, 7–9.

Commons, M. L., & Richards, F. A. (2002). Organizing components into combinations: How stage transition works. *Journal of Adult Development*, 9, 159–177.

Commons, M. L., Richards, F. A., & Kuhn, D. (1982). Systematic and metasystematic reasoning: A case for a level of reasoning beyond Piaget's formal operations. *Child Development*, 53, 1058–1069.

Commons, M. L., & Rodriguez, J. A. (1993). The development of hierarchically complex equivalence classes. *Psychological Record*, 43, 667–697.

Commons, M. L., Trudeau, E. J., Stein, S. A., Richards, F. A., & Krause, S. R. (1998). The existence of developmental stages as shown by the hierarchical complexity of tasks. *Developmental Review*, 18, 237–278.

Commons, M. L., & White, M. S. (2003). A complete theory of tests for a theory of mind must consider hierarchical complexity and stage: A commentary on

Anderson and Lebiere target article. *Behavioral and Brain Sciences, 26*(5), 606–607.

Commons, M. L., & Wolfsont, C. A. (2002). Empathy: Its ultimate and proximate bases does not consider developmental changes: A commentary on Stephanie D. Preston and Frans B. M. de Waal target article. *Behavioral and Brain Sciences, 25*, 30–31.

Commons-Miller, L. A. H. (2003, April). *The relationship of parental work interest and success to that of their children.* Paper presented at the Annual Meeting of the Society for Research in Adult Development, Tampa, FL.

Commons-Miller, L. A. H. (in press). Speciation of superions from humans: I species cleansing the ultimate form of terror and genocide? *Journal of Adult Development.*

Cook-Greuter, S. R. (1990). Maps for living: Ego-development stages from symbiosis to conscious universal embeddedness. In M. L. Commons, C. Armon, L. Kohlberg, F. A. Richards, T. A. Grotzer, & J. D. Sinnott (Eds.), *Adult development: Vol. 2. Models and methods in the study of adolescent and adult thought* (pp. 79–104). New York: Praeger.

Copernicus, N. (1992/1543). [De revolutionibus orbium caelestium.] *On the revolutions/ Nicholas Copernicus;* translation and commentary by Edward Rosen. Baltimore, MD: Johns Hopkins University Press.

Cramond, B. (1995). *The coincidence of attention deficit hyperactivity disorder and Creativity* (RBDM 9508). Storrs, CT: National Research Center on the Gifted and Talented, University of Connecticut.

Darwin, C. (1855). *On the origin of the species.* London: Murray.

Darwin, C. (1872/1898). *The expression of the emotions in man and animals.* New York: D. Appleton.

Darwin, C. (1877). A biographical sketch of an infant. *Mind, 2,* 285–294.

Darwin, C. (1969). *The autobiography of Charles Darwin,* N. Barlow, Ed., New York: Norton.

Dawkins, R. (1976). *The selfish gene.* New York: Oxford University Press.

Dawkins, R. (1981). In defense of selfish genes. *Philosophy, 56,* 556–573.

Dawkins, R. (1982). *The extended phenotype: The gene as the unit of selection.* San Francisco: Freeman.

Dawson, T. L. (1998). "A good education is . . .": A lifespan investigation and conceptual features of evaluative reasoning about education. Unpublished doctoral dissertation, University of California at Berkeley, Berkeley, CA.

Dawson, T. L. (2002a). A comparison of three developmental stage scoring systems. *Journal of Applied Measurement, 3,* 146–189.

Dawson, T. L. (2002b). New tools, new insights: Kohlberg's moral judgement stages revisited. *International Journal of Behavioral Development, 26,* 154–166.

Demetriou, A. (1990). Structural and developmental relations between formal and postformal capacities: Towards a comprehensive theory of adolescent and adult cognitive development. In M. L. Commons, C. Armon, L. Kohlberg, F. A. Richards, T. A. Grotzer, & J. D. Sinnott (Eds.), *Adult development: Vol. 2. Models and methods in the study of adolescent and adult thought* (pp. 147–173). New York: Praeger.

Demetriou, A., & Efklides, A. (1985). Structure and sequence of formal and postformal thought: General patterns and individual differences. *Child Development, 56,* 1062–1091.

Descartes, R. (1637/1954). *The geometry of Rene Descartes: With a facsimile of the first edition,* 1637 (D. E. Smith & M. L. Latham, Trans.). New York: Dover Publications.

Dostoyevsky, F. (1914). *Crime and punishment* (C. Garnett, Trans.) London: William Heinemann.

Dyson, F. J. (1999). *The sun, the genome, and the internet: Tools of scientific revolution.* New York: Oxford University Press.

Einstein, A. (1950). *The meaning of relativity.* Princeton, NJ: Princeton University Press.

Erikson, E. H. (1959). Identity and the life cycle: Selected papers. *Psychological Issues,* Monograph no. 1.

Erikson, E. H., Ed. (1978). *Adulthood.* New York: Norton.

Faraday, M. (1839/2000, 1844, 1855). *Experimental researches in electricity* (3 volumes). Santa Fe, NM: Green Lion Press.

Fastovsky, D. E., & Weishampel, D. B. (1996). *The evolution and extinction of the dinosaurs.* New York: Cambridge University Press.

Feldman, D. H., Csikszentmihalyi, M., & Gardner, H. (1994). *Changing the world*: A framework for the study of creativity. Westport, CT: Praeger/Greenwood.

Fischer, K. W. (1980). A theory of cognitive development: The control and construction of hierarchies of skills. *Psychological Review, 87,* 477–531.

Fischer, K. W., Hand, H. H., & Russell, S. (1984). The development of abstractions in adolescents and adulthood. In M. L. Commons, F. A. Richards, & C. Armon (Eds.), *Beyond formal operations: Vol. 1. Late adolescent and adult cognitive development* (pp. 43–73). New York: Praeger.

Fischer, K. W., & Lazerson, A. (1984). *Human development from conception to adolescence.* New York: Freeman.

Funk, J. D. (1989). Postformal cognitive theory and developmental stages of musical composition. In M. L. Commons, J. D. Sinnott, F. A. Richards, & C. Armon (Eds.), *Adult development: Comparisons and applications of developmental models* (Vol. 1) (pp. 3–30). Westport, CT: Praeger.

Geneva's population characteristics: Educational achievement. (2000). Retrieved October 22, 2004, from http://www.geneva.il.us/ecol_sociodata.htm

Gewirtz, J. L. (1969). Mechanisms of social learning: Some roles of stimulation and behavior in early human development. In D. A. Goslin (Ed.), *Handbook of socialization theory and research* (pp. 57–212). Chicago: Rand McNally.

Gödel, K. (1931/1977). Some metamathematical results on completeness and consistency; On formal undefinable propositions of *Principal Mathematica* and related systems I; On completeness and consistency. In J. Heijehoort (Ed.), *From Frege to Gödel: A source book in mathematical logic 1879–1931.* Cambridge, MA: Harvard University Press.

Grotzer, T. A., Robinson, T. L., Young, R. M., Davidson, M. N., Cohen, L., Rios, M. L., et al. (1985, June). *The role of repeated presentation of a formal operational problem, feedback, and social reward: An examination of Piaget's equilibration theory of stage transition.* Paper presented at the Annual Meeting of the Jean Piaget Society, Philadelphia, PA.

Hart, J. R., Rickards, W. H., & Mentkowski, M. (1995) *Epistemological development during and after college: Longitudinal growth on the Perry scheme.* Milwaukee, WI: Alverno College Productions.

Higashi, M., Takimoto, G., & Yamamura, N. (1999). Sympatric speciation by sexual selection. *Nature, 402,* 523–526.

Hill, L. (2004). Changing minds: Developmental education for conceptual change. *Journal of Adult Development, 11,* 29–40.

Holland, J. L. (1996). *Making vocational choices: A theory of vocational personalities and work environments* (3rd ed.). Odessa, FL: Psychological Assessment Resources.

Holton, G. (1973/1988). *Thematic origins of scientific thought: Kepler to Einstein.* Cambridge, MA: Harvard University Press.

Howe, M. J. A. (2001). *Genius explained.* Cambridge: Cambridge University Press.

Howe, M. J. A. (2004). Some insights of geniuses into the cause of exceptional achievement. In L. V. Shavinina & M. Ferrari (Eds.), *Beyond knowledge: Extracognitive aspects of developing high ability.* Mahwah, NJ: Lawrence Erlbaum.

Hoyer, W. J., Roodin, P. A., Rybash, J. M., & Rybash, P. (2003) *Adult development and aging.* New York: McGraw-Hill.

Hudson, V. M., & den Boer, A. M. (2004). *Bare branches: The security implications of Asia's surplus male population.* Cambridge, MA: MIT Press.

Inhelder, B., & Piaget, J. (1954). *The growth of logical thinking from childhood to adolescence.* New York: Basic Books.

Inhelder, B., & Piaget, J. (1958). *The growth of logical thinking from childhood to adolescence: An essay on the development of formal operational structures* (A. Parsons & S. Milgram, Trans.). New York: Basic Books.

Kagan, J. (1974). Discrepancy, temperament and infant distress. In M. Lewis & L. A. Rosenblum (Eds.), *The origins of fear* (pp. 229–248). New York: Wiley.

Kallio, E. (1995). Systematic reasoning: Formal or postformal cognition? *Journal of Adult Development, 2,* 187–192.

Kallio, E. (1998). Training of students' scientific reasoning skills. *Studies in Education, Psychology and Social Research, 139,* 90.

Kallio, E., & Helkama, K. (1991). Formal operations and postformal reasoning: A replication. *Scandinavian Journal of Psychology 32,* 18–21.

Kegan, R.. (1994). *In over our heads: The mental demands of modern life.* Cambridge, MA: Harvard University Press.

King, P. M., & Kitchener, K. S. (2002). The reflective judgment model: Twenty years of research on epistemic cognition. In B. K. Hofer & P. R. Pintrich (Eds.), *Personal epistemology: The psychology of beliefs about knowledge and knowing* (pp. 37–61). Mahwah, NJ: Lawrence Erlbaum.

Kohlberg, L. (1981). *The meaning and measurement of moral development.* Heinz Werner Lecture Series (1979), vol. 23. Worcester, MA: Clark University Press.

Kohlberg, L. (1984). *Essays on moral development: Vol. 2. The psychology of moral development: Moral stages, their nature and validity.* San Francisco: Harper & Row.

Kohlberg, L. (1990). Which postformal levels are stages? In M. L. Commons, C. Armon, L. Kohlberg, F. A. Richards, T. A. Grotzer, & J. D. Sinnott (Eds.), *Adult development: Vol. 2. Models and methods in the study of adolescent and adult thought* (pp. 263–268). New York: Praeger.

Kohlberg, L., & Armon, C. (1984). Three types of stage models used in the study of adult development. In M. L. Commons, F. A. Richards, & C. Armon (Eds.), *Beyond formal operations: Vol. 1. Late adolescent and adult cognitive development* (pp. 383–394). New York: Praeger.

Koplowitz, H. (1984). A projection beyond Piaget's formal operational stage: A general system stage and a unitary stage. In M. L. Commons, F. A. Richards, & C. Armon (Eds.), *Beyond formal operations: Vol. 1. Late adolescent and adult cognitive development* (pp. 272–295). New York: Praeger.

Krantz, D. H., Atkinson, R. C., Luce, R. D., & Suppes, P. (1974). *Contemporary developments in mathematical psychology: Vol 2. Measurement, psychology, and neural information processing.* San Francisco: Freeman.

Krantz, D. H., Luce, R. D., Suppes, P., & Tversky, A. (1971). *Foundations of measurement: Vol. 1. Additive and polynomial representations.* New York: Academic Press.

Kuhn, T. S. (1970). *The structure of scientific revolutions.* Chicago: University of Chicago Press.

Labouvie-Vief, G. (1984). Logic and self-regulation from youth to maturity: A model. In M. L. Commons, F. A. Richards, & C. Armon (Eds.), *Beyond formal operations: Vol. 1. Late adolescent and adult cognitive development.* (pp. 158–179). New York: Praeger.

Labouvie-Vief, G. (1985). Intelligence and cognition. In J. E. Birren & K. W. Schaie (Eds.), *Handbook of the psychology of aging* (2nd ed., pp. 500–530). New York: Van Nostrand Reinhold.

Labouvie-Vief, G., Adams, C., Hakim-Larson, J., & Hayden, M. (1983, April). *Contexts of logic: The growth of interpretation from pre-adolescence and adult thought.* Paper presented at the Annual Meeting of the Society for Research in Child Development, Detroit, MI.

Leibniz, G. W. (1768). *Opera omnia.* L. Deutens (Ed.). Geneva: Deutens.

Leibniz, G. W. (1875). *Die philosophische Schriften.* Berlin: Gerhardt.

Loevinger, J. (Ed.). (1998). *Technical foundations for measuring ego development: The Washington University sentence completion test.* Mahwah, NJ: Lawrence Erlbaum.

Lovell, C. W., & Nunnery, J. (2004). Testing the adult development Tower of Babel hypothesis: Homogeneous by Perry position collaborative learning groups and graduate student satisfaction. *Journal of Adult Development, 11,* 139–150.

Mace, F. C., Lalli, J. S., Shea, M. C., & Nevin, J. (1992). Behavioral momentum in college basketball. *Journal of Applied Behavior Analysis, 25,* 657–663.

Marchand, H. (2001). Some reflections on postformal thought. *Genetic Epistemologist, 29*(3).

Maxwell, J. C. (1873). *A treatise on electricity and magnetism.* Oxford: Clarendon Press.

Mayr, E. (1942). *Systematics and the origin of species.* New York: Columbia University Press.

Mentkowski, M., Moeser, M., & Strait, M. (1983). *Using the Perry scheme of intellectual and ethical development as a college outcomes measure: A process and criteria for performance.* Milwaukee, WI: Alverno College Productions.

Miller, P. M., Lee, S. T., & Commons, M. L. (2005). *Adult attachment: Attachment stages and progress through them.* Manuscript submitted for publication.

Minhas, L. S., & Kaur, F. (1983). A study of field-dependent-independent cognitive styles in relation to novelty and meaning contexts of creativity. *Personality Study and Group Behavior, 3,* 20–34.

Moritz E. (1995). Metasystems, memes and cybernetic immortality. In F. Heylighen, C. Joslyn, & V. Turchin (Eds.), *The quantum of evolution. Toward a theory of metasystem transitions.* New York: Gordon and Breach Science Publishers.

Nemeth, C. J., & Kwan, J. L. (1985). Originality of word association as a function of majority versus minority influence. *Social Psychology Quarterly, 48,* 277–282.

Nevin, J. A., Tota, M. E., Torquato, R. D., & Shull, R. (1990). Alternative reinforcement increases resistance to change: Pavlovian or operant contingencies? *Journal of the Experimental Analysis of Behavior 53,* 359–379.

Newton, I. (1687/1999). *The Principia: mathematical principles of natural philosophy.* I. Bernard Cohen & Anne Whitman (Eds.), assisted by Julia Budenz (Trans.). Berkeley: University of California Press.

Ohm, G. S. (1827). *Die galvanische Kette, mathematisch bearbeitet von Dr. G. S. Ohm. Mit einem Figurenblatte.* Berlin: Bei T. H. Riemann.

Ohnmacht, F. W., & McMorris, R. F. (1971). Creativity as a function of field independence and dogmatism. *Journal of Psychology, 79,* 165–168.

Ørsted, H. C. (1820). *The discovery of electromagnetism, made in the year 1820 by H. C. Ørsted.* Copenhagen: Published for the Oersted Committee at the expense of the State by Absalon Larsen.

Overton, W. F. (1990). Competence and procedures: Constraints on the development off logical reasoning. In W. F. Overton (Ed.), *Reasoning, necessity and logic: Developmental perspectives* (pp. 1–32). Hillsdale, NJ: Lawrence Erlbaum.

Pascual-Leone, J. (1984). Attention, dialectic, and mental effort: Towards an organismic theory of life stages. In M. L. Commons, F. A. Richards, & C. Armon (Eds.), *Beyond formal operations: Vol. 1. Late adolescent and adult cognitive development* (pp. 182–215). New York: Praeger.

Perry, W. G. (1970). *Forms of intellectual and ethical development in the college years.* New York: Holt, Rinehart & Winston.

Piaget, J. (1952). Autobiography. In E. G. Boring, H. S. Langfeld, H. Warner, & R. M. Yerkes (Eds.), *A history of psychology in autobiography* (Vol. 4). Worcester, MA: Clark University Press.

Piaget, J. (1977). The stages of intellectual development in childhood and adolescence. In H. E. Gruber & J. J. Voneche (Eds.), *The essential Piaget* (pp. 814–819). New York: Basic Books.

Piaget, J., & Garcia, R. (1989). *Psychogenesis and the history of science* (H. Feider, Trans.). New York: Columbia University Press.

Planck, M. (1922). *The origin and development of the quantum theory,* (H. T. Clarke & L. Silberstein, Trans). Nobel prize address delivered before the Royal Swedish Academy of Sciences at Stockholm, 2 June 1920. Oxford: Clarendon Press.

Plano's population characteristics: Educational achievement. (2000). Retrieved October 22, 2004, from http://www.planoplanning.org/planinfo/demo/pdf/2000%20census%20plano%20profile.pdf.

Powell, P. M. (1984). Stage 4A: Category operations and interactive empathy. In M. L. Commons, F. A., Richards, & C. Armon (Eds.), *Beyond formal operations: Vol. 1. Late adolescent and adult cognitive development* (pp. 326–339). New York: Praeger.

Rheinberg, F., Lührmann, J.-V., & Wagner, H. (1977). Bezugsnorm-Orientierung von Schülern der 5. bis 13. Klassenstufe bei der Leistungsbeurteilung. *Zeitschrift für Entwicklungs Psychologie und Pädagogische Psychologie, 9,* 90–93.

Richards, F. A., & Commons, M. L. (1984). Systematic, metasystematic, and cross-paradigmatic reasoning: A case for stages of reasoning beyond formal operations. In M. L. Commons, F. A. Richards, & C. Armon (Eds.), *Beyond formal operations: Vol. 1. Late adolescent and adult cognitive development* (pp. 92–119). New York: Praeger.

Rodriguez, J. A. (1989). *Exploring the notion of higher stages of social perspective taking* (Qualifying Paper). Cambridge, MA: Harvard Graduate School of Education.

Roe, A. (1952). *The making of a scientist.* New York: Dodd Mead.

Rosales-Ruiz, J., & Baer, D. M. (1997). Behavioral cusps: A developmental and pragmatic concept for behavioral analysis. *Journal of Applied Behavioral Analysis, 30,* 533–544.

Ross, B. L. (1977). *Interrelationships of five cognitive constructs: moral development, locus of control, creativity, field dependence-field independence, and intelligence in a sample of 167 community college students.* Unpublished doctoral dissertation, University of Southern California, Los Angeles.

Rothbart, M. K., & Bates, J. E. (1998). Temperament. In N. Eisenberg (Vol. Ed.) & W. Damon (Ed.), *Handbook of child psychology: Vol. 3: Social, emotional and personality development* (5th ed., pp. 105–176). New York: Wiley.

Schulz, R., & Salthouse, T. (1999). *Adult development and aging: myths and emerging realities.* Upper Saddle River, NJ: Prentice Hall.

Shannon, C. E., & Weaver, W. (1949). *The mathematical theory of communication.* Champaign: University of Illinois Press.

Shavinina, L. V., & Ferrari, M. (2004). *Beyond knowledge: Extracognitive aspects of developing high ability.* Mahwah, NJ: Lawrence Erlbaum.

Simonton, D. K. (1984). *Genius, creativity, and leadership: Historiometric inquiries.* Cambridge, MA: Harvard University Press.

Simonton, D. K. (1997). *Genius and creativity: Selected papers.* Greenwich, CT: Ablex.

Sinnott, J. (1981). The theory of relativity: a metatheory for development. *Human Development, 24,* 293–311.

Sinnott, J. (1984). Post-formal reasoning: The relativistic stage. In M. L. Commons, F. A. Richards, & C. Armon (Eds.), *Beyond formal operations: Vol. 1. Late adolescent and adult cognitive development* (pp. 298–325). New York: Praeger.

Smith, G. J., Carlsson, I., Sandstrom, S. (1985). Artists and artistic creativity elucidated by psychological experiments. *Psychological Research Bulletin, 25,* 9–10.

Sonnert, G., & Commons, M. L. (1994). Society and the highest stages of moral development. *Individual and Society, 4,* 31–55.

Sternberg, R. J. (1984). Higher-order reasoning in post-formal operational thought. In M. L. Commons, F. A. Richards, & C. Armon (Eds.), *Beyond formal operations: Vol. 1. Late adolescent and adult*

cognitive development (pp. 74–91). New York: Praeger.

Stevens-Long, J., & Commons, M. L. (1991). *Adult life: Developmental processes.* Mountain View, CA: Mayfield.

Thomas, A., & Chess, S. (1977). *Temperament and development.* New York: Brunner/Mazel.

Torbert, W. (1994). Cultivating postformal adult development: Higher stages and contrasting interventions. In M. E. Miller & S. R. Cook-Greuter (Eds.), *Transcendence and mature thought in adulthood: The further reaches of adult development* (pp. 181–203). Lanham, MD: Rowman & Littlefield.

Torosyan, R. (1999). *Encouraging consciousness development in the college classroom through student-centered transformative teaching and learning.* Unpublished doctoral dissertation, Columbia University, New York.

Trivers, R. (1985). *Social evolution.* Menlo Park, CA: Benjamin/Cummings.

Vidal, F. (1994). *Piaget before Piaget.* Cambridge, MA: Harvard University Press.

Volta, A. G. A. A. (1800/1999). *On the electricity excited by the mere contact of conducting substances of different kinds.* London, England: Royal Society Philosophical Magazine. Bicentenary ed. in French, English, German, and Italian of letter to Sir Joseph Banks of the 20th of March 1800.

Vygotsky, L. S. (1962). *Thought and language.* Cambridge MA: MIT Press.

Vygotsky, L. S. (1966). Development of the higher mental function. In *Psychological Research in the U.S.S.R.* (pp. 44–45). Moscow: Progress Publishers.

Vygotsky, L. S. (1978). *Mind in society: The development of higher psychological process.* Cambridge, MA: Harvard University Press.

Wapner, S., & Demick, J. (Eds.). (1991) *Field dependence-independence: Cognitive style across the life span.* Hillsdale, NJ: Lawrence Erlbaum.

West, E. (2004). Perry's legacy: models of epistemological development. *Journal of Adult Development, 11,* 61–70.

Witkin, H. A. (1949). Perception of body position and of the position of the visual field. *Psychological Monographs: General and Applied, 63,* 302.

Witkin, H. A., Lewis, H. B., Hertzman, M., Machover, K., Meissner, P. B., & Wapner, S. (1954). *Personality through perception: An experimental and clinical study.* New York: Harper.

Witkin, H. A., Oltman, P. T., Raskin, E., & Karp, S. A. (1971). *Group embedded figures test manual.* Palo Alto, CA: Consulting Psychologists Press.

Woods, D. R. (2000). *Problem-based learning: How to gain the most from PBL* [problem based learning]. Waterdown, Ont.: Donald R. Woods.

Chapter 13

Laughing at Gilded Butterflies: Integrating Wisdom, Development, and Learning

Caroline L. Bassett

Much madness is divinest sense / To a discerning eye.
—*Emily Dickinson*

Even though wisdom is a desired and esteemed human quality, there is not a great body of research on it, particularly empirical research. Why not? First, wisdom is abstract, rich, and complex. Second, *wisdom*, as a word in our ordinary language, encompasses many meanings, which makes it harder to study than a constructed phrase or concept with narrower or even operational definitions, such as "cognitive development" or "prejudice." Although human beings would have noticed individual differences since they began congregating in groups, the idea of "cognitive development" must have been evident even if it was not articulated as such. There is, however, no cognitive development literature as there is for the wisdom traditions around the world. Nor is there a god of adult meta-cognition to be appeased or propitiated, as there are goddesses of wisdom, for example, Athena, Kali, and Sophia. Messing with the gods should give us pause. (To respect the irreducible quality of wisdom and to keep these gods appeased, each major section of this chapter begins with a quotation.)

Third, by its very nature, wisdom is difficult to study. The positivist emphasis of social sciences research methods may in themselves limit our understanding of wisdom.

Nonetheless, some researchers have been studying wisdom, and many speak of it as the apex or culmination of a life well lived. For example, Webster says, "wisdom is an emergent property of a full life . . . [representing] the epitome of psychosocial maturity" (2003, p. 18). For Ardelt it is "the pinnacle of successful human development" (2000a, p. 360), and in Taranto we find "wisdom, the jewel of human cognition" (1989, p. 2). Birren and Fisher called wisdom "an admired, although somewhat vague, trait. It seems to have a hierarchical nature: that is, it is the optimum, ultimate expression of a blend of human qualities" (1990, p. 323), whereas Baltes and Staudinger held that wisdom "is generally considered the pinnacle of insight into the human condition and about the means and ends of a good life" (2000, p. 122). According to Merriam and Caffarella in the field of adult learning, wisdom is "often seen as the pinnacle or hallmark of adult thinking. It is something we all speak about and sometimes yearn for as we face the many challenges of adult life" (1999, p. 161). Finally, we are admonished in the Book of Proverbs to "Get wisdom!" for "Happy are those who find wisdom and those who get understanding, for her income is better than silver, and her revenue is better than gold. She is more precious than jewels, and nothing can compare with her. . . . She is a tree of life to those who lay hold of her; those who hold her fast are called happy" (Proverbs, 2:13–18, New Revised Standard Edition). After such encomiums and with such great rewards, who would not want wisdom?

Yet as much as we would like to, how can we get wisdom when we do not even have a good grasp of what it means? Definitions abound, partly because wisdom is generally considered a multidimensional construct (Ardelt, 1997; Baltes & Staudinger, 2000; Birren & Fisher, 1990; Labouvie-Vief, 1990; Orwoll & Perlmutter, 1990; Sternberg, 1998, 2001; Taranto, 1989; Webster, 2003). The dictionary tells us that the word *wisdom* derives from the Middle English *wis*, which in turn comes from the Sanskrit *veda* or knowledge (as in the Hindu sacred text the *Vedas*). One definition reads, "wisdom is the power of judging rightly and following the soundest course of action, based on knowledge, experience, and understanding" (*Webster's New World College Dictionary*, 2002).

APPROACHES TO THE STUDY OF WISDOM

With something as complex as wisdom, a single approach cannot do it justice and will, in fact, present a distorted view. Instead, the whole must be examined before any parts can be discussed in depth. Figure 13.1 presents an overview of methods used to study wisdom. Of course, there will be overlap in method and meaning of the different aspects of study.

On the left side of the figure, the metaphysical disciplines include philosophy and religion or theology. Philosophy, as we know, means *philos* or "love of " + *sophia* or "wisdom." Throughout history, philosophers have examined the deep questions of life, such as, what is meaning? What is right and wrong? What do we know and how do we know we know it? What is virtue and how can we live a virtuous life? Holliday and Chandler (1986) gave a good overview of the philosophical foundations of wisdom. Religion and theology also play a large role in our attempts to delve into the meaning of wisdom, for they, too, ask the deeper questions about how to live our lives both in this world and the next. The wisdom traditions, or the world's great religions (Smith, 1992), are replete with guidance and comfort to life's most perplexing problems, surely one of the purposes of wisdom in our midst.

The word arts category is my way of describing other sources of wisdom that can be studied. Biography or reading about the lives of people considered wise can give us insight into what their particular wisdom looked like and what might have engendered it. For example, Nelson Mandela's biography *Long Walk to Freedom* (Mandela, 1995) gives some indications from his childhood and upbringing of how he might have developed into the wise leader that he did. Reading about the life of Eleanor Roosevelt (Cook, 1992), particularly her lonely childhood and her physical unattractiveness and awkwardness, gives insight into the sources of her compassion for people less fortunate than herself and her passion for civil rights. This is not to say that a one-to-one or causal relationship exists in any life story that we read. They are merely indicative of what might have propelled character formation in a certain direction. In a cross-over article, because it studied noted historians from an analytical point of view rather than the biographical, Rathunde (1995) conducted qualitative research through interviews with three eminent historians in later life to examine the connections between wisdom-related attributes and abiding interest. He found out that one characteristic of wisdom, the coordination of affective/attaching and cognitive/detaching modes of processing information, is indeed related to lifelong learning.

Studying folk sayings, aphorisms, and maxims reveals additional aspects of wisdom (Nichols, 1992). "A rolling stone gathers no moss" provides a sharp and generally universally held observation about human nature. Other commonsense notations include, "A stitch in time saves nine" and "A new broom sweeps clean." Much deeper and more complex are myths that tell archetypal stories about the human condition and provide us with examples of gods and goddesses, heroes and heroines, acting wisely or foolishly. We are all familiar with Athena, the Greek goddess of wisdom. Many of us know about Sophia and Kali, a Hindu goddess. Interestingly, in myth, wisdom

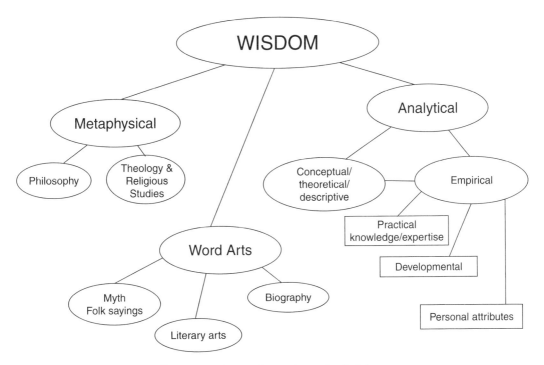

FIGURE 13.1 Approaches to the study of wisdom.

most often appears in the female form. In contrast, most historical figures considered wise (Jesus, the Buddha, Dr. Martin Luther King Jr., for example) are male.

Finally, the literary arts themselves give us many illustrations of and insights into the nature of wisdom and how it plays out in the human arena. If a distinguishing feature of wisdom is knowing what is true and what is false, Jane Austen and William Shakespeare presented us with their own versions. Elizabeth Bennet in *Pride and Prejudice* certainly reveals growth toward wisdom when she recognizes that she has lacked the ability to distinguish reality from appearance. In the past she has misunderstood Mr. Darcy. In one episode she is able to see him move outside of his narrower self while at the same time she notices the depth of her error about his character:

> Oh! How heartily did she grieve over every ungracious sensation she had ever encouraged, every saucy speech she had ever directed towards him. For herself she was humbled; but she was proud of him. Proud that in a cause of compassion and honour, he had been able to get the better of himself. (Austen, 1996, p. 272).

In another example from Shakespeare, near the end of the play, King Lear has finally recognized the true nature of his daughter Cordelia and lies imprisoned with her, reflecting on what is most important, another quality of wisdom:

> Come, let's away to prison:
> We two alone will sing like birds i' the cage:
> When thou dost ask me blessing, I'll kneel down,
> And ask of thee forgiveness: so we'll live,
> And pray, and sing, and tell old tales, and laugh
> At gilded butterflies, and hear poor rogues
> Talk of court news; and we'll talk with them too,
> Who loses and who wins; who's in, who's out,
> And take upon's the mystery of things,
> As if we were God's spies. (*King Lear*, V, iii)

Being able to identify and then laugh at falsely colored butterflies and to look on the mystery of things shows a developed consciousness, one that Lear has won after much travail. Fiction, poetry, and drama are replete with examples and instances of wisdom, which is why we turn and return to these forms over and over again.

On the right side of figure 13.1 we find analytical approaches to the study of wisdom, the focus of this chapter, particularly the empirical approaches. First, it is necessary to note that in terms of sheer numbers of books and articles, conceptual, theoretical, or descriptive studies far outweigh strictly empirical sources for some of the reasons noted above, that is, the difficulty in operationalizing and using positivist science to grapple with a subject as diffuse as wisdom. Still, researchers in numerous disciplines including political science, cultural anthropology, education, and of course, psychology have sought to come to grips with this complex subject (for example, Baltes & Staudinger, 2000; Merikangas, 1998; Merriam & Caffarella, 1999; Nichols, 1992; Sternberg, 1990a).

A review of the theoretical and empirical literature suggests the following outline with wisdom primarily understood as:

1. Practical knowledge/expertise
2. Personal attributes, such as age, gender, educational attainment, and occupation
3. Developmental

Although there is some general agreement about what the major dimensions of wisdom consist of and the fact that they relate to each other in a holistic manner, there is still argument and conjecture when it comes to being more specific about the constructs themselves. The approach that each researcher takes changes the emphasis, and hence the hue or tone of wisdom to some extent. For example, the Berlin school highlighted the pragmatic, cognitive, and performance-based aspects of wisdom; other researchers have paid more attention to personal characteristics, qualities, or attributes of wise people, such as age, experience, and openness, and how these contribute to or reflect the essence of wisdom. *Development* refers to maturation and increased awareness as well as the integration of the cognitive, affective, behavioral, and/or reflective elements of wisdom. To date, in this reviewer's opinion, there is no definitive or grand unified theory on wisdom, rather, a number of thoughtful studies that each contributes to the still mysterious phenomenon of wisdom.

To try to grasp this elusive concept, some empirical research has been conducted and theoretical or conceptual studies written. Some of the studies reviewed here include conceptual or theoretical aspects, but they are almost all based on some kind of empirical data; with this kind of research it is difficult to separate the two cleanly. Furthermore, although

the studies have been grouped roughly according to the outline just given, a great deal of overlap exists among them.

WISDOM AS PRACTICAL KNOWLEDGE OR EXPERTISE

Do not believe what you have heard.
Do not believe in tradition because
it is handed down many generations.
Do not believe in anything that has been
spoken of many times.
Do not believe because the written statements
come from some old sage.
Do not believe in conjecture.
Do not believe in authority or teachers or elders.
But after careful observation and analysis, when it
agrees with reason, and it will benefit one and all,
then accept it and live by it.
— *The Buddha*

In this approach to the study of wisdom, wisdom is conceived of, generally speaking, as intellectual functioning and expertise based on a superior level of knowledge. It is expressed and ascertained through performance. This section presents two research agendas. In the first, the Berlin school (Baltes and colleagues) has emphasized wisdom as expert knowledge systems involved with the pragmatics of life. In the second, Sternberg distinguished between wisdom, intelligence, and creativity and presented a newly developed balance theory of wisdom currently being tested in New Haven middle schools.

The Berlin School

Paul Baltes and his colleagues in Berlin are conducting an extensive program of empirical research on wisdom related to their interest in intellectual abilities and aging. In their earlier work they defined wisdom as "an expert knowledge system in the fundamental pragmatics of life permitting exceptional insight, judgment, and advice involving complex and uncertain matters of the human condition" (Baltes & Staudinger, 1993, p. 76). They proposed that a rare combination of favorable conditions can result in wisdom, including such factors as age, certain personality-related dispositions such as openness to new experiences, and experiences that include training and mentoring. Although the older people in this study, selected from the public life of Berlin and more than half over

60 years of age, did not perform as well in terms of cognitive mechanics such as memory, they did perform well in terms of cognitive pragmatics. In a later study (Baltes, Staudinger, Maercker, & Smith, 1995), the researchers found that up to age 80, older adults performed as well as younger ones on wisdom-related tasks.

From this research, a model of wisdom has emerged as the Berlin wisdom paradigm (Baltes & Staudinger, 2000). Three kinds of factors facilitate wise judgments: general person factors (such as cognitive mechanics, cognitive style, openness to experience, and ego strength), expertise-specific factors (including experience in life matters, mentorships, motivational dispositions), and facilitative experiential contexts (for example, age, education, profession). These factors are used in life planning, life management, and life review, that is, the pragmatics of life. The "software" of the mind, these pragmatics reflect knowledge and information about factual and procedural knowledge about human affairs, the interpretation and meaning of life, and a "fine-tuned coordination of cognition, motivation, and emotion" (Baltes & Staudinger, 1993, p. 77).

In addition to these factors, Baltes and Staudinger (2000) have considered a family of five criteria that they claim many cultures have identified as prototypes of wisdom and that have become part of their psychological theory of wisdom: rich factual knowledge, rich procedural (strategic) knowledge, knowledge regarding the context of life, knowledge that considers relativism of values and life goals, and knowledge that considers the uncertainties of life. These last three they consider meta-criteria specific to wisdom, whereas the first two are characteristic of any kind of expertise. One meta-criterion, life span contextualism, identifies the many contexts of life such as education, family, friends, and society. A second, relativism of values and life priorities, means a tolerance for value differences held by different individuals and various societies. We are not to use wisdom, however, as a case for relative values. Rather, the researchers held, it "includes an explicit concern with the topic of virtue and the common good" (p. 126). This concern for the larger whole, one that other wisdom researchers such as Orwoll and Perlmutter (1990) discussed, and Sternberg (1998, 2001) emphasized, appears only in this later work of the Berlin school. The last meta-criterion is called uncertainty because wise judgments should be able to help people deal with the uncertainties associated with human and world affairs.

In one study to elicit and measure wisdom-related knowledge, the researchers devised a series of difficult life situations that the participants had to think aloud about, with their responses scored through the use of the five criteria mentioned (Baltes & Staudinger, 1993). Here is one dilemma: "A 15-year-old girl wants to get married right away. What should one/she do and consider?" (p. 77). Low scorers said things like, "No, no way. Marrying at age 15 is utterly wrong." High scorers responded, "On the surface, this seems like an easy problem. . . . Perhaps in this instance, special life circumstances are involved, such that the girl has a terminal illness. Or this girl may not be from this country" (p. 77).

In further work, Baltes and Staudinger (2000) discussed empirical findings from several studies. In one, for example, on the role of chronological age, they found that a lack of major age differences during middle adulthood supported two key assumptions, first, that wisdom-related knowledge and judgment do not show signs of deterioration during the earlier stages of adulthood (that is, before brain disease and other aging factors take hold), and second, that just living longer and accumulating life experience does not necessarily result in wisdom. Other factors besides these need to be added to result in wisdom.

What kinds of life experiences might be conducive to wisdom? In another project, the Berlin school researchers selected clinical psychologists as participants because their professional experience gave them contact and engagement with the pragmatics of life: life planning, life management, and life review. As the researchers (Baltes & Staudinger, 2000) expected, the psychologists showed higher levels of wisdom-related performance than controls (an average of 3.8, which was only slightly above the scale's mean value). To understand this finding—that the role of certain personality and motivational dispositions can lead some people to become psychologists—communality analyses showed that professional specialization (clinical psychology) was the largest unique predictor.

To dismiss the charge of professional self-enhancing bias, they conducted another study in which the clinical psychologists were compared with a group of nominees who were figures of public distinction in a major German city (Baltes & Staudinger, 2000). Results showed that the wisdom nominees performed at least as well as the clinical psychologists. In fact, in the task of existential life management, the wisdom nominees outperformed the psychologists. Thus, the acquisition of wisdom is not simply related to the selection of a certain professional field; for those among us who are not clinical psychologists, there is some hope that we can become wiser.

Measures of wisdom, the Berlin group claimed, require the integration and balancing of several spheres of human functioning. To determine what these elements might be, they examined 33 psychometric indicators in the domains of intelligence, personality-intelligence, and personality dispositions; of them, 10 turned out to be significant predictors of wisdom (Baltes & Staudinger, 2000). An important finding was that there was overlap among all three predictor domains. That is, all three are required for wisdom to manifest itself. Most notably, the intelligence–personality interface (for example, cognitive style and creativity) indicators contributed the largest share. The researchers linked their findings on cognitive style to Sternberg's (1996) work on thinking styles, particularly the judicial style (evaluation and comparison of issues at hand) and the progressive style (the ability to move beyond existing rules and the tolerance of ambiguity). What this study shows, they stated, is that wisdom is not simply a variant on intelligence or personality but rather "implies a coordinating configuration of multiple attributes" (p. 129).

In new research, these colleagues are studying the concept of a heuristic (an automatized processing or organizing method) as a feature of wisdom (Baltes & Staudinger, 2000). This line of inquiry has resulted in general criteria outlining the nature of wisdom:

> Wisdom addresses important and difficult questions and strategies about the conduct and meaning of life.
> Wisdom includes knowledge about the limits of knowledge and the uncertainties of the world.
> Wisdom represents a truly superior level of knowledge, judgment, and advice.
> Wisdom constitutes knowledge with extraordinary scope, depth, measure, and balance.
> Wisdom involves a perfect synergy of mind and character, that is, an orchestration of knowledge and virtues.
> Wisdom represents knowledge used for the good or well-being of oneself and that of others.
> Wisdom is easily recognized when manifested, although difficult to achieve and to specify. (p. 135)

Their work through the years, leading up to and including the summary article by Baltes and Staudinger (2000), has documented empirically in various studies these criteria for wisdom except for the sixth one, on the altruistic or beneficent nature of wisdom. The authors speculated that without wisdom as a meta-heuristic to guide life, individuals would perform at lower levels of quality. That is because they would be lacking the "proactive directionality" that wisdom requires if it is the "embodiment of the best 'subjective beliefs and laws of life' that a culture and individuals have to offer" (p. 132). To be more complete in their work, testing for this dimension could be another direction for their research program. As for practical considerations of this pragmatic heuristic, that is, how wisdom can be learned, the authors suggested that if the wisdom heuristic is acquired systematically and repeatedly over time, presumably in formal as well as informal learning situations, then people may be able to reach more advanced levels of wisdom-related knowledge and performance than is evident today.

Sternberg

Sternberg's work presents other research on wisdom from the point of view of intelligence, knowledge, and the practical aspects of wisdom. Although his later writing is more theoretical than that of the Baltes group, he has based it on his strongly empirical research program on intelligence and creativity (1990b). In two studies, Sternberg (1990b) found a high degree of both convergent and discriminant validity, attesting to separate measurements for social judgment skills (wisdom) and intelligence; creativity was not expected to correlate significantly, and it did not. Sternberg also compared implicit theories of wisdom (as well as intelligence and creativity) across domains in a study of 200 professors of art, physics, philosophy, and business. As one might expect, some characteristic patterns emerged. Art professors emphasized insight, whereas for business professors maturity of judgment was predominant, as were other aspects such as possession of a long-term perspective, good decision making, and the ability to distinguish substance from style. Philosophy professors articulated the importance of balanced judgment, concern with larger purposes, and openness to ideas, for example, and the physics professors stressed knowing if solving a problem is likely to show useful results, among other characteristics. Sternberg concluded that implicit theories of wisdom can contribute to the understanding of the topic by providing a general overview. The results, he noted, confirmed those of Clayton and Birren (1980) using the same technique of multidimensional scaling.

Next, Sternberg (1990b) built on this implicit material to create an explicit theory wherein he again sought to distinguish wisdom from intelligence and creativity. Wise individuals, he held, may know a lot or be able more or less well to recall, analyze, and use knowledge as an intelligent person does, but more important, they understand the meaning of what is known. He gave this analogy to a prison: The wise person seeks "to understand the prison and what its boundaries are; the intelligent person [seeks] to make the best of life in the prison, and the creative person [seeks] to escape from the prison" (Sternberg, 1990b, p. 153). In terms of intellectual style, Sternberg related them to the three primary functions of government: legislative, executive, and judicial. The wise person, he maintained, leans toward the judicial style. This comes not so much in the sense of making judgments as in seeking to understand why people think as they do and do what they do. That is, it provides a framework for thought and behavior, rather than simply judging if something is good or bad. In comparison, intelligence is more associated with the executive style, whereas the creative mind prefers the legislative one (so they can make laws for themselves and not be locked into conventional ways of doing things).

In another analogy, this time to conventional intelligence tests, Sternberg (1990b) noted that all of these tasks are executive, requiring the test takers to accept the terms of the problems as stated and to solve them, revealing their intelligence or match of response to given problem. On the other hand, the wise person will question why the particular problems even appear in a test on intelligence, and the creative one is likely to go beyond the bounds of the established responses to something more clever or even more correct.

In a third analogy, Sternberg (1990b) contrasted wisdom, intelligence, and creativity with comfort with ambiguity. Wise people are comfortable with ambiguity, Sternberg believed, because they see it as inherent in virtually all situations in which humans are involved. The wise can appreciate ambiguity and understand it as fundamental to the nature of things, which would distress the conventionally intelligent person who strives to resolve the ambiguity, or the creative one who is uncomfortable with it but may see it as leading to a creative outcome. Sternberg concluded that wise people are characterized by a "metacognitive stance" (p. 157) in which they know what they know, what they do not know, and what can and cannot be known. He finished the chapter by saying that wise people know what will work for themselves and for society as well.

It is this last point that Sternberg (1998, 2001) picked up in his balance theory of wisdom with its emphasis on both tacit and explicit knowledge, with wisdom seen as a special case of practical intelligence that requires the balancing of multiple and often competing interests. In particular, he said,

> wisdom is defined as the application of tacit as well as explicit knowledge mediated by values towards the achievement of a common good through a balance among (a) intrapersonal, (b) interpersonal, and (c) extrapersonal interests, over the (a) short and (b) long terms, to achieve a balance among (a) adaptation to existing environments, (b) shaping of existing environments, and (c) selection of new environments. (2001, p. 231).

He then said that if people seek to maximize their own interests at the expense of someone else's, it is not wisdom. This is a major premise of both of these articles. In wisdom, we seek the common good, realizing that it may be better for some than for others, reflecting his previous (Sternberg, 1990b) findings on how wise people are able to tolerate and even embrace ambiguity. Values, he maintained, are an integral part of wise thinking, another insight not discussed in previous work, although tacitly present. Also discussed is the need for the wise person to understand not only people's cognitions but also their motivations and emotions. Schools, he noted, place emphasis on developing academic skills (relating to intelligence). But, he held, "in a society that seems largely ruled by self-interests, students often start to develop practical skills in order to use schooling primarily to maximize their self-interests" (Sternberg, 1998, p. 362). Instead, what if schools tried to teach wisdom to even a small extent compared with what is given to the development of an inert knowledge base? What then?

"What then" has become a project in New Haven middle schools to teach for wisdom (Sternberg, 2001). Knowledge, he said, can be used for better or worse ends, for the common good or for selfish purposes, and this distinction is what formal educational systems should be emphasizing rather than simply the accumulation of information or knowledge. He specified 16 principles of teaching for wisdom derived from the balance theory. They include helping students recognize and balance their own interests, those of other people, and those of institutions, by which Sternberg means institutions, organizations, community, nation, or God; teaching students that means are as important to examine as the ends themselves; and teaching students to strive for a common good, one where everyone wins, not just those with whom one identifies. Certain procedures for doing this kind of teaching are specified, such as engaging in both dialogical and dialectical thinking, studying not only "truth" but also values, and finally, and perhaps most challenging to teachers, serving as role models for their students.

To test if these ideas can be applied in public school settings, Sternberg (2001) began a multiyear funded project of about 36 middle school teachers and 600 students. Why middle school? Because these students have acquired a certain level of cognitive development and because in these grades the teachers still teach all subjects and so have direct control over how subject matter is presented. This study is still in progress; it will be some time before we know any of its results.

In a rebuttal to Sternberg's work, Halpern (2001) objected to the way he has operationalized the construct of critical thinking. For Halpern, wisdom is equated to critical thinking within a system of values. She found that Sternberg confused critical thinking with being critical or analytical. For her it involves a number of thinking skills, such as clarifying meaning, examining ideas, presenting evidence, interpreting, evaluating, making inferences, and reflecting. She asked who is wise in our society and proposed that many Americans would name the Supreme Court justices. If we cannot count on them to be wise, then who deserves this label? (This despite the fact that a determinedly political process selects these nine people and despite recent evidence in the presidential elections of 2000 that they voted in a political manner.) If this select group cannot balance their self-interests and other interests to transcend their political orientations, then who among us can? In other words, Halpern seems to be asking whether there is any point in teaching for wisdom, although she concedes that it is worth trying to learn to be wiser.

In this section, wisdom has been presented as a kind of meta-heuristic or meta-cognitive skill concerning the pragmatics of life. Baltes and colleagues, in their extensive research program on wisdom and wisdom-related performance, have isolated constructs nonidentical with other similar ones, such as intellectual abilities and aging. From their empirical studies, they have created a comprehensive model of wisdom. Sternberg has explored relationships among wisdom, intelligence, and creativity and recently has embarked on a project to teach for wisdom in middle schools so that students will be directly exposed to questions essential to a wisdom perspective on life. As noted earlier, this perspective is missing in most contemporary American and Western and perhaps in a number of international societies, as well. In his balance theory of wisdom, Sternberg suggests that wisdom thinking is not only about serving one's own interests but also those of the common good. In this, the direct and deliberative consideration of values is essential.

The next section turns to an examination of studies that focus on personal attributes of wisdom, including the complicated question of the contribution of age and experience to wisdom. Most are based on empirical research.

PERSONAL ATTRIBUTES OF WISDOM

The difference between being an elder and an old person is that an elder is someone who has gained wisdom. They have distilled their life experience in such a way that their very presence becomes a witness to others. Originally this was what we had in a tribal society—that an elder was a repository of wisdom and awareness, and younger people would check with them and say, "Am I on the right tack? Am I doing right?"
—Zalman Schacter-Shalomi

In this section, a number of aspects of wisdom that relate to a wise person, other than intelligence, knowledge, and practical expertise, will be addressed. They include the role in becoming wise of age and experience, gender, educational attainment, and occupation. Some cross-cultural studies will be discussed as well.

Two of the main associations with wisdom are age and experience, and several researchers have discussed the dimensions of the relationship. At one end of the spectrum, Meacham (1990) baldly stated his hypothesis: "that all people are wise to begin with, as children, but that as we grow older most people lose their wisdom. . . . Wisdom needs to be understood as a quality that is maintained and preserved by only a select few over the course of a life" (p. 198). Because so few people have gained this rare quality, many argue that maturity and old age are necessary for the ripening into wisdom. Meacham alternatively proposed that wisdom decreases with age because only a few have been able to retain it over a lifetime. Furthermore, in contrast to other researchers who discussed the role of experience and wisdom, he argued that wisdom can be lost in an atmosphere of stereotyping and intolerance or rapid technological and cultural change, or when we are touched by personal tragedy.

In contrast, Lyster (1996), in her study of wise nominees, nominators, and self-referred "wise" people, found that it is the ability to transform negative experience to positive and growth-affirming ones that differentiates the more wise from the less wise. Although she had hypothesized that the wise nominees would report wisdom to be an outcome of experiencing adversity, she found the opposite, and the hypothesis was not supported. It is possible to interpret these findings to mean that the events themselves could have been adverse, but the wise were able to transform their understanding of them into something positive and thus had no need to acknowledge them as difficult. She concluded that the strongest predictor for wisdom is openness to experience.

Webster (2003) also discussed the role of experience and four other factors (emotional regulation, reminiscence and reflectiveness, openness, and humor) in a newly developed Self-Assessed Wisdom Scale (SAWS). He conducted three studies to test the multidimensional cohesion of these five factors, each a necessary component to wisdom but none sufficient. The first study demonstrated the reliability of the instrument by giving 87 men and 179 women, ranging in age from 18 to 74 years, the SAWS instrument. The next two examined the validity. Webster concluded that the SAWS has good content, discriminant, and construct validity, thus demonstrating that these five factors do seem to form interrelated dimensions of wisdom. In his description of experience as one of the five components, Webster noted that it is not accumulated general experience that can lead to wisdom, but rather experiences that are so difficult and challenging that they require some degree of profundity. Wink and Helson's (1997) study offers some empirical support, as they found that divorced women scored higher on their scale than married ones, indicating that difficult life experiences may enable wisdom. One wonders about the role of the moral imagination in which people such as writers, who have not themselves experienced adverse circumstances, not only imagine but also create lives in whole cloth transformed or defeated by adversity.

Webster (2003) saw the lack of an age effect, consistent with previous findings, such as Ardelt's (1997). In a 40-year follow-up study, Ardelt interviewed 121 men and women using a 37-page instrument. Findings indicated that wisdom and a person's subjective well-being are related, but Ardelt cautioned for the need to test and not assume that wisdom increases life satisfaction in old age.

Other studies have shown an increase in wisdom as a person ages (Assman, 1994; Baltes & Smith, 1990; Holliday & Chandler, 1986; Labouvie-Vief, 1990; Taranto, 1989), but one by Denney, Dew, and Kroupa (1995) looked at the age of nominators of wise or interpersonally wise people and the age of the people they nominated in either category. These researchers found that participants tended to nominate as wise people who were older than they were. However, the difference between their own age and the nominees' age decreased with increasing age. The researchers considered the self-ratings of wisdom in Orwoll and Perlmutter's (1990) study in which the older the nominees, the less likely they were to rate themselves as wise. This could be because recognizing the limits of one's own wisdom is in fact wise. It could also relate to Lyster's (1996) findings about the unobtrusive qualities of sages. These people would not call themselves wise.

In terms of gender with regard to wisdom, several studies have pointed to differences in how males and females approach wisdom and view the relationship between wisdom and gender. Webster (2003) found a positive correlation in his study between gender (female) and wisdom. Women scored higher on the scale that he developed (SAWS) than men. He explained this by suggesting that the noncognitive emphasis of his scale allowed for these higher scores, as women demonstrated abilities in the tested areas of experience (particularly difficult and morally challenging experiences), emotional regulation, openness, reminiscence and reflectiveness, and humor.

Ardelt's (1997) work echoed this discrepancy in wisdom between the sexes, although her small sample size was not statistically significant. She speculated that these differences are expected from traditional gender roles, because men approach the world in a more cognitive and rational manner, whereas women can combine rationality and emotions.

In a later longitudinal study of 82 women, Ardelt (2000a) operationalized a number of variables associated with wisdom to discover the relationship between wisdom and aging well. Wisdom itself was defined as "a latent variable with cognitive, reflective, and affective effect indicators" (p. 369). The cognitive component was operationalized as the cognitive skills necessary for the discovery of truth (a combination of one Q-sort item and four items from the ego rating scale). The reflective component included items from the same scales on tolerance of ambiguity and insight into one's motives and behaviors, and the affective component was operationalized as the absence of negative emotions and behaviors toward others. The research hypothesized that a benign childhood, mature personality characteristics of early adulthood, and a supportive social environment would have a positive impact on a person's degree of wisdom in later years. Only the last, the supportive social environment, had a significant influence, and even that effect was relatively unstable. Age was found to have a significant negative effect on women's physical health and satisfaction with life, but mature personality characteristics in early adulthood (measured by two indicators: equanimity and absence of anxiety) had a significant positive effect on life satisfaction in the 40 years of this longitudinal study. Ardelt concluded that wisdom and life satisfaction are related for women, but does the relationship exist because the woman (or person) is wise and therefore feels satisfaction or because healthy older women with positive family relationships can engage in the cognition and reflection required by wisdom?

In a more recent study, Ardelt (2003) developed a three-dimensional wisdom scale (3D-WS), the dimensions being cognition, reflection, and affect. Quantitative and qualitative interviews with a sample of 180 adults (52 years or older) allowed the researcher to test the validity and reliability of this scale. The major constructs all had to be simultaneously present for a person to be wise; they are not independent of each other, but neither are they conceptually identical. For this researcher, reflection serves as the fundamental component of wisdom because it encourages cognitive development through the ability to take multiple perspectives and to overcome projections, which no longer distort perceptions of reality. Furthermore, reflection strengthens wisdom because people have learned how not to be so reactive to situations, especially unpleasant ones, and they accept the reality of the present moment.

To construct her own instrument, Ardelt (2003) drew on a number of previously published scales to tap the cognitive, reflective, and affective aspects of wisdom by measuring aspects of psychological health, general life conditions, a social desirability bias, mastery, and psychological well-being and ill-being, for example. The purpose was first to construct a 3D-WS and second to assess the content, convergent, predictive, and discriminant validity of the scale. Selected interviewees nominated members of their close-knit social group that they considered wise, and independent judges rated the ensuing description of wise people. Internal reliability was confirmed through Cronbach's alpha, and construct, predictive, discriminant, and convergent validity showed the 3D-WS to be a reliable and valid instrument. Nevertheless, Ardelt reminded us in this article that further empirical research is needed to replicate the findings with a larger and more representative group and to discover if cognitive, reflective, and affective personality qualities comprise wisdom or if additional ones are needed for wisdom to develop. Also, this scale should be tested to see whether it distinguishes between wise individuals and those who are "merely" well adjusted, caring, or intelligent (Ardelt, 2003, p. 314). It is possible, Ardelt pointed out, that "all compassionate/ caring, well-adjusted, and socially, emotionally, interpersonal and intrapersonal intelligent people" are not wise. Future research needs to test if cognitive, affective, and reflective qualities are necessary and also sufficient for a person to be considered wise.

In their study, Denney et al. (1995) asked participants to nominate people they regarded as wise and interpersonally wise. They recorded the sex of the nominator and of the nominee, along with their responses in an interview on the two kinds of wisdom. They found in both males and females a slight tendency in young adults and a strong tendency in older ones to nominate males as wise. The researchers explained this finding by speculating that for the older adults, visible wise people in positions of power and authority were limited to males, but for the younger group, considering societal changes, women have achieved at least some positions of prominence. Although they did consider the possibility that men are nominated as wise because they are indeed wiser than women, they conceded that the discrepancy might have resulted from sex-role stereotyping in our culture. In terms of interpersonal wisdom, participants nominated women more often than men to this category, except for older women. Again, the effect of sex-role stereotyping can be seen as evident here.

To what extent does education play a role in the identification of wise people or as an attribute of wise elders? There is conflicting evidence. Webster's (2003) study showed a lack of association between wisdom and education, perhaps because the kinds of noncognitive skills and competencies measured through the use of his scale are not those learned in formal educational settings. In contrast, Orwoll and Perlmutter (1990) found that the more educated a person was, the more likely he or she was to be nominated as wise, as did Ardelt's (2003) study. They noted that a few of the wise nominees had very little education.

Sternberg (2001) critiqued the existing educational system for not teaching wisdom-related thinking. Although schools do teach knowledge, the heart of wisdom, he said, is "tacit, informal knowledge of the kind learned in the school of life, not the kind of explicit formal knowledge taught directly in schools" (p. 233). Education should provide attention to understanding values, developing the skills of metacognition, and helping people learn to balance different types of interests for the common good.

Do certain occupations lend a role and provide more opportunities for growth toward wisdom? Several researchers have asked this question. Baltes and Staudinger (2000) studied clinical psychologists because of greater contact and engagement with questions of life planning, management, and review in working with their clients. As predicted, this group of professionals scored higher on wisdom-related performance than controls. These scores, however, did not achieve the same levels as the nominated experts. Nevertheless, they concluded that professional specialization is an important variable.

Wink and Helson (1997) also studied psychotherapists (clinical psychologists), and their findings supported those of the Baltes group. Wink and Helson found that psychotherapists, according to their scales for practical and transcendent wisdom, increased in wisdom more than the other women in the sample,

even when they controlled for the variable of graduate education.

Hershey and Farrell's (1997) findings about the relationship of educational attainment and being considered wise led them to the conclusion that education within a context of occupational ratings is implicitly taken into account when evaluating if a person is wise or not. To determine whether participants associated differential levels of wisdom with various occupations, they surveyed 227 undergraduates aged 17–54 years and found that the largest mean ratings fell to surgeons and judges and the second highest ratings to astronauts and physicians. Occupations such as prostitute, toll collector, and garbage collector earned the lowest mean ratings. Hershey and Farrell then subjected the occupational data to factor analysis to determine the conceptual dimensions that guided the ratings. So many occupations loaded onto the first factor, a broad general one, that they concluded that wisdom is a construct that is not (or is weakly) linked to most occupations. Irrespective of occupation, a person can be wise. Their second factor, educational attainment, showed positive loadings for jobs that require significant formal postsecondary education. In the third, spirituality, only two occupations were found: minister and priest. Was that because, Hershey and Farrell speculated, they led reflective lives, because they saw human nature at its best and worst (like therapists), or because they were viewed as problem solvers, advising others on different avenues of action? Or was it perhaps because they are seen as ethical and moral? The authors wondered what would have happened in this study if other similar occupations, such as rabbi, monk, and bodhisattva, had been included.

Few studies have examined wisdom from a cross-cultural perspective. One study did consider the bodhisattva and another Eastern and Western concepts of wisdom. One article discussed a study of Tibetan monks who were training to become bodhisattvas, a Buddhist term for a person who continues to work in the world and act altruistically while refraining from reaching full enlightenment. Levitt (1999) used grounded theory methodology to analyze interviews with 13 monks from the Dharamsala monastery in India, the Dalai Lama's adopted country. Levitt wanted to discover definitions of wisdom and the conditions that make teaching and learning wisdom possible. For these monks, wisdom meant the development of an understanding of Buddhist ideas of the nature of reality, the importance of altruism, and certain personal characteristics, such as humility and honesty. Levitt viewed wisdom as "being able to see beyond . . . illusionary identities and to use this knowledge to best dedicate oneself to helping others" (p. 93). For these monks, wisdom was distinct from extent of education, intelligence, or religion.

Takahashi (2000) found distinctive conceptualizations of wisdom between Eastern (Indian and Japanese) and Western (American and Australian) cultures. Whereas Western understandings stress cognitive representational structures and their vehicles (words), Eastern understandings emphasize the integration of multiple aspects of human consciousness, including a more direct and intuitive approach with a great deal of emotional involvement, without "overt overintellectualization" (p. 2).

To arrive at these conceptualizations of wisdom, Takahashi recruited undergraduate students for a questionnaire that was administered in English to the American and Australian students and in Japanese and Hindi to the others using a double-translation method. Making the task more difficult, there are two words in Japanese for *wise*. Both were taken into account in the study. The results indicated that for the young adults from Western culture the word *wise* was semantically most similar to "experienced" and "knowledgeable" and least similar to "discreet," demonstrating an understanding of wisdom in terms of its analytical features, such as a broad knowledge base accumulated through life experience. In contrast, the Japanese and Indian students perceived *wise* as semantically most closely associated with "discreet," then by "aged" and "experienced." As "discreet" was for the Americans and Australians, "knowledgeable" clustered at the greatest distance from "wise" for the Eastern group. Takahashi suggested that the Indian and Japanese students were less likely to relate *wise* to analytical and cognitive features, such as the accumulation of a knowledge base. For them, the identification of *wise* with "discreet" indicated not only knowledge but also prudence and sound judgment. In other words, Takahashi said, " 'wise' is conceptualized in the East not as mere analytical ability but as a psychological quality that emphasizes more 'direct' understanding with a great deal of emotional involvement or an effective integration of multiple aspects of human consciousness (e.g. cognition, affect, intuition, etc.)" (2000, p. 7).

We turn to some of these ideas in the next section, which covers the developmental and integrative aspects of wisdom, including some Eastern concepts of it.

WISDOM AS POSTFORMAL DEVELOPMENT

If a man does not keep pace with his companions, perhaps it is because he hears a different drummer. Let him step to the music which he hears, however measured and far away.
—Henry David Thoreau

Some researchers understand wisdom to comprise more than performance and cognitive functioning or personal attributes. They frame wisdom as exceptional self-development, including ego maturity and postformal operational thinking. Although the two are not identical, both focus on stages of thought beyond Piagetian formal operations. Postformal development is often associated with the ability to think dialectically, wherein an individual is able to integrate various aspects of the psyche and accept inherent contradictions and alternate truths. Some authors discuss these ideas primarily in terms of dialectical thinking, and others find the concept of ego- or self-transcendence useful. The latter will be discussed first.

Exceptional Self-Development

Surprisingly, there is empirical research on a topic that seems almost unresearchable: self-transcendence in its relationship to wisdom. Wink and Helson (1997) distinguished between practical and transcendent wisdom. The former emphasizes life span cognitive development and expertise in the pragmatics of life (see Baltes & Staudinger, 2000; Sternberg, 1998, 2001), whereas the latter places its attention on the concept of transcending ego boundaries. Mature self-development is achieved through a knowledge of unconscious influences, among other dynamics. For wisdom to occur, another step must take place. The ego must be decentered from its throne in the psyche. When this happens, narcissism yields to a larger, less personalistic perspective. For Wink and Helson, cognitive research and cognitive psychology are too restrictive in approach. They desired to explore wisdom more deeply, going beyond the concept of wisdom as practical judgment to wisdom as insight into the "magic and mystery of the eternal order of things of Shakespeare's Prospero" (Wink & Helson, 1997, p. 3).

Using the schema developed by Achenbaum and Orwoll (1991) which identifies three domains of wisdom, intrapersonal, interpersonal, and transpersonal, Wink and Helson (1997) argued that both practical and transcendent wisdom share claims on intrapersonal development, whereas practical wisdom is associated with the interpersonal realm, and transcendent wisdom is related to the transpersonal domain. A domain not often discussed in the literature, the transpersonal one includes self-transcendence, depth of understanding of the meaning of life, philosophical commitments or spiritual development reaching a sense of the basic unity of self with universe, and recognition of the limits of human knowledge (see Meacham, 1990). To measure transcendent wisdom, the researchers used participants' own examples of wisdom, which were coded for such qualities as freedom from narrow self-concern (approaching Sternberg's 1998 balance theory of wisdom) and spiritual or philosophical insight, for example. To measure practical wisdom, they created a Practical Wisdom Scale (PWS) developed from several measures and longitudinal archives.

Wink and Helson's (1997) study had three goals: first, to test the validity of two scales that they developed, the PWS and the Ratings of Transcendent Wisdom (RTW); second, to show the extent of change in wisdom from early to middle adulthood; and third, to study factors related to an increase in practical wisdom. For the last of these, they sought to replicate the findings of Baltes and colleagues (1995) about clinical psychologists or psychotherapists whose profession requires thinking about life problems and was shown to be conducive of the development of wisdom. Furthermore, by comparing wisdom in women who had been divorced with those who had not, they sought to test Kramer's (1990) suggestion that personal difficulties may lead to growth in wisdom. To conduct the study, Wink and Helson (1997) used 94 women at age 52 who had taken part in a previous study in 1958, and 44 of their male partners. Using the two scales that they had developed and a number of personality measures such as the Sentence Completion Test and the California Psychological Inventory (CPI), the researchers first examined the validity of their scales by correlating the scales with each other for the participants. They then correlated each measure with personality, ability, and life variables that they

expected to be related to growth in one or both kinds of wisdom. They studied the effect of occupation, in this case, psychotherapy, and life events (divorce) on age-related changes in practical wisdom as measured by the PWS.

They found that scores on the PWS increased significantly over 25 years for both the women and their partners, who were now seeing themselves as more reflective, tolerant, realistic, and mature in their fifties than in their twenties. In terms of occupation, the findings confirmed those of the Berlin group, indicating a steeper rate of increase in practical wisdom among psychotherapists than in the rest of the women. The divorced women scored somewhat (nonsignificantly) higher in wisdom than the married ones, a finding that led the researchers to speculate that other characteristics besides this particular kind of pain can lead to wisdom. For the RTW, they found that only high scorers showed evidence of openness to experience (CPI flexibility scale) and intuition as measured by the Myers-Briggs Type Indicator, whereas the practical wisdom scale was associated with interest and skill in the interpersonal domain. High scorers on both scales tended to be more cognitively complex, morally serious, insightful, and perceptive. Their conclusions indicate, the researchers held, the usefulness of studying these two distinct kinds of wisdom, that practical wisdom increases with age, and that life experience is related to change in practical wisdom. They did not speculate about what it is that might be related to changes in transcendent wisdom.

Orwoll and Perlmutter (1990) also discussed transcendent wisdom, for them an aspect of unusual self-development. If wisdom is an integration of cognition and personality (Kramer, 1990; Labouvie-Vief, 1990), then, suggested Orwoll and Perlmutter, wise people should be studied using both cognitive and personality theories of wisdom. For them, a mature personality includes the following features: capacity for mature love, self-extension (being involved in meaningful pursuits), self-objectivity, openness to present experience, and a unifying philosophy of life. Beyond that, self-transcendence comes as a result of even more advanced personality development when a person is able to move "beyond individualistic concerns to more collective or universal ones" (Orwoll & Perlmutter, 1990, p. 162), transforming narcissism and conventional levels of self-absorption.

Although they discussed exceptional personality development and self-transcendence, in the research reported here, Orwoll and Perlmutter (1990) sought to explore certain characteristics and beliefs about wise people. The authors asked participants to describe actual people they thought of as wise; in another part of the study, they asked participants if they thought wisdom was related to age, gender, and education. The researchers found that 78% of subjects thought that wisdom was related to age, 16% to gender, and 68% to education. Asked how they would specify the age, gender, and educational level of three wise people they could think of, participants nominated people middle-aged or older (and older than they were). But when asked about their own degree of wisdom, comparing it to the nominated group, participants of all ages showed little difference among themselves in their self-ratings, and they revealed no tendency toward regarding the older person as a wiser one. Hence, suggested the authors, the relationship between wisdom and age needs to be examined carefully. Perhaps recognizing the limits of one's wisdom is in itself an indication of wisdom. Thus, the older participants could not rate themselves high when they had a better sense than younger people of how much they did not know. The researchers also found a clear tendency to attribute wisdom to males more frequently than to females, although few participants overtly stated a preference in this direction. Men nominated more men than women as wise, and women did the same. Because wisdom is a socially valued characteristic, speculated the authors, perhaps that is why it is associated with males more than females. Finally, they found that highly educated people were more likely to be nominated as wise than less educated ones, but it is important to note that some nominees had very little formal education. None of the participants indicated that education is necessary for the development of wisdom.

My own work extends the discussion on the exceptional personality development required for wisdom and presents a perspective of the integration of processes needed for its manifestation (Bassett, 2001, 2003). In grounded theory research, I selected 24 thoughtful and insightful figures of public distinction (university presidents and professors, public servants, businesspeople, clergy, and social activists) using a modified snowball method. I interviewed participants to discover if there were common patterns to the way people understand wisdom in our own times. Further questions addressed how to foster wisdom, and they are discussed in a later section on learning. Using open and axial coding and the constant-comparative method, I developed a model of wisdom that shows four major components or dimensions of wisdom, each with a chief characteristic and several proficiencies. The major components are discerning, empathizing, engaging, and being. Associated with discerning, the chief characteristic is detachment; with empathizing, openness; with engaging, involvement; and with being, integrity. Developmental dynamics to help people deepen and expand their wisdom include *proficiencies* for wisdom performance, *manifestations* in outlook and behavior, and developmental *stimuli* or *learning prompts* that can lead to or enhance wisdom-thinking (see table 13.1).

Because this is an integrative model, the arrows represent an attempt to show that every element is connected to every other element. In other words, the movement or developmental flow of the growth in wisdom goes up and down the columns, across the rows, and diagonally through columns and rows. A more accurate depiction (in progress) would show this model as a spiral, with the cell self-transcendence the most likely candidate for the fulcrum or turning point. That is because with each gain in self-transcendence (being able to transcend one's ego-centeredness and thus see reality more clearly), a person may be able to perform the other wisdom tasks more skillfully. Ardelt's (2003) discussion on reflection supports my own finding that self-transcendence can lead to the emergence of deeper levels of wisdom.

This table presents a snapshot view of the dynamics of wisdom development. Each of the four dimensions represents an aspect of the self. Thus, discerning, or the ability to see deeply into what is really going on while separating personal desires and emotions from the event or issue at hand, is a cognitive function. It includes three proficiencies for wisdom performance—insight, holistic seeing, and balanced interests—with insight referring to keen perception into the nature of things. Holistic seeing means seeing the whole and the various relationships within it, for example, taking a systems perspective. Balanced interests refers to Sternberg's (1998) work where individuals need to balance their own self-interest with the interests of other people (family or workplace, for example) and those of institutions (organization, community, nation, world, God). Wise people manifest these three proficiencies with a deep understanding of causes, consequences, and

TABLE 13.1. Model of the Dynamics of Wisdom Development

Dimension	Discerning (Cognitive)	Empathizing (Affective)	Engaging (Active)	Being (Reflective)
Chief characteristic	Detachment	Openness	Involvement	Integrity
Proficiency	Insight, Holistic seeing, Balanced interests	Multiple perspective taking, Compassion and caring, Generosity of spirit	Sound judgment and adept decision making, Actions based on determinations of fairness and justice, Moral courage	Self-knowledge, Self-acceptance, Self-transcendence
Manifestation	Deep understanding of causes, consequences, and relationships	Expanded sphere of consideration	Committed action for the common good	Expansion of consciousness
Developmental stimulus/ learning Prompt	What's really going on? What's true? What's important? What's right?	Whose point of view am I taking? How does someone else understand reality? How can I relate to them with magnanimity?	What guides my actions? To what ends are my actions directed? What means do I use?	What are my values? How do I live them? Who or what is the "I" that I think I am?
Direction of growth	↕	↕	↕	↕

relationships. That is, they possess and exhibit a sharp and quite complete ability to determine the causes, the consequences that might ensue from a given action, and how relationships might be affected.

Although discerning is a cognitive quality, alone it does not suffice for wisdom. Seeing clearly but not caring about other people does not constitute wisdom, as several interviewees emphatically stated. Empathizing is an affective quality. It includes the ability to take multiple perspectives, that is, being able to take the point of view of many different kinds of people and to see the world as they might. Another proficiency is compassion and caring, which is just that. Finally, wise people operate with generosity of spirit. They are open and tolerant and behave in healing and positive ways, which results in an expanded sphere of consideration. The number and kinds of human beings, plants, animals, and indeed the entire biosphere that must necessarily be considered and included in the psyche keeps on increasing.

As all of the people interviewed and this researcher herself live in the Western Hemisphere with Western values, it is not surprising that engaging became a vital dimension of wisdom. In the East, which is generally more contemplative, this aspect might not have appeared as important as it did in this study. Here, being actively involved to some degree or another in the outside world was regarded as a key factor, but the activities engaged in can vary greatly, from marching in a picket line to working in a soup kitchen to teaching and writing. What is necessary is sharing the wisdom and not keeping it inside oneself. Because wisdom is often about making difficult decisions in complex situations or at least giving good advice, in this dimension we also find sound judgment and adept decision making. People are often considered wise by the quality of their decisions and judgment. Furthermore, these decisions and actions must be made based on determinations of fairness and justice. Anyone taking unfair advantage of a person or a situation is not considered wise. Finally, to carry out an individual's wisdom agenda, a person may have to call on moral courage because wise thoughts and actions can go against the grain of prevailing conventional morality and thought. What we see is committed action for the common good.

The dimension called "being" refers to the character of a person. It is reflective and results in an expansion of consciousness. First, individuals must know themselves and what they can and cannot do. They must also have, to some extent, integrated their shadow side (their neglected and repressed aspects). Next, self-acceptance is necessary—individuals know who they are and who they are not and feel comfortable with themselves. Finally comes self-transcendence or the ability to go beyond the individual ego and its constant demands to a sense of the basic unity of self with universe. Integrity is the hallmark here. How to understand "things as they really are" becomes a difficult question for the postmodernist thinker who understands that objectivist and essentialist epistemologies are misguided and incomplete (Ferrer, 2001). However, both Ferrer and Ardelt have suggested that perceiving reality as it is means doing so without major egocentric distortions.

Although not addressing wisdom directly, Cook-Greuter (2000) described postconventional and postautonomous ego development in ways that overlap with and provide more information about self-transcendence in wisdom. How is a person able to achieve the balance of interests that Sternberg (1998) suggested, the general wisdom criteria of the Baltes group (Baltes & Staudinger, 2000), or the ability to move beyond the self-absorbed and individualistic concerns to more universal ones that Orwoll and Perlmutter (1990) described? Cook-Greuter posited the existence of stages of ego development beyond conventional levels. Based on an analysis of thousands of Loevinger's Washington University Sentence Completion Tests (SCTs), she separated Loevinger's integrated stage into two new distinct stages, the construct-aware ego stage and the unitive stage, which are cognitively more differentiated from Loevinger's. In earlier research, Cook-Greuter (1994) had analyzed unusual responses that did not match anything in the manuals on the SCT or anything on existing ego theory. Because some responses appeared authentic and meaningful, it did not seem right to dismiss them or automatically give them a low score just because they did not make conventional sense. From studying thousands of these sentence responses, Cook-Greuter has advanced the theory of ego development with a more refined understanding of higher stages of development.

Postconventional ego development, said Cook-Greuter (2000), begins when a person is able to loosen the attachment to understanding on a totally rational level and can lower defenses against the intrusion of material from nonrational sources. The first step is generally thought of as a systems view and the second the unitary view of reality. In the systems view, people are able to see beyond the conventional linear perspective that is expected of them. They realize that their perspectives are local, partial, and dependent on context and cultural conditioning. This is the beginning of a dialectical approach that frees the mind from a logical linear framework. (These concepts are similar to Kegan's 1994 work on orders of consciousness.)

Beyond this way of thinking, in the construct-aware ego stage, people are now beginning to exhibit awareness that the concept of "ego" is merely a construction for subjectively felt experience, according to Cook-Greuter (2000). Ego becomes transparent to itself, allowing individuals to become aware of their defensive maneuvers at keeping the ego and only the ego in control. When this kind of movement happens, a person is more likely to have a "more dynamic and multi-faceted understanding of human nature . . . and the complexities of human interaction" (Cook-Greuter, 2000, p. 235), surely a familiar refrain in our discussions of wisdom. She posited that at the unitive stage people can embrace polar opposites on an affective level, not just cognitively, and feel empathy for all beings at all different stages of development. Furthermore, such persons are able to witness, rather than judge, actions by other people. What comes across in these people, she said, is "a profound and compassionate understanding of the human condition" (p. 236).

To explain further how the ego can develop to postconventional levels, Achenbaum and Orwoll (1991) interpreted the biblical Book of Job, showing how wisdom occurs in personality, cognition, and volition and how it transforms intrapersonal, interpersonal, and transpersonal experience. Job, they say, grows wise as he expresses empathy and begins to be able to transcend himself by moving through personalistic issues to more universal concerns (as Orwoll & Perlmutter 1990 described). He gains self-knowledge and develops his understanding (that is, knowing the complex cognition of others), while at the same time recognizing limits. Thus, he has actualized his integrity by thinking, feeling, and acting congruently and can deepen his spiritual commitments.

The story of Job summarizes the developmental progression that characterizes the approach of researchers who see wisdom as exceptional self-development. These researchers are less focused on the products of thinking and the performance of wisdom-related tasks than are Baltes and his colleagues (Baltes & Staudinger, 1993, 1995; Baltes et al., 1995), and Sternberg (1990b, 1996, 1998, 2001). Rather, their attention lies with the investigation of exceptional self-development, including self-transcendence and unusually integrated and mature personality structures.

The next section continues with the concept of integration but with a different slant. Dialectical thinking emphasizes the way people arrive at an integration or synthesis of antithetical or disparate aspects of the psyche, or of a situation or an issue that presents itself with incompleteness of knowledge, provisionality of truth or reality, and the need for judgment or decision in the face of uncertainty.

Integrative Knowing and Dialectical Thinking

Dialectical thinking presents another way of talking about postformal operational thinking. It can appear as the realization that truth is not always (or even often) absolute, that a synthesis emerging from a thesis and its antithesis can serve as the best guides for difficult and imprecise life problems, and that this kind of thinking, as Kramer (2000) put it, is based on the "logic" of paradox. Holliday and Chandler (1986) and Chandler with Holliday (1990) discussed the concept of emancipatory knowledge in which the self becomes free (or freer) from older conventional, constraining ways of knowing. Labouvie-Vief (1990, 2000) continued this theme from her viewpoint of a dialectical synthesis of what she calls *logos* (rational, objective thinking) and *mythos* (contextual or subjective thinking). Without this integration, distortion of rationality results in irrationality. Similarly, Pascual-Leone (1990) presented the case for greater receptivity to the "unwilled," or mythos-like parts of the psyche. Kitchener and Brenner (1990) discussed a shift in awareness as individuals understand that much knowing rests in uncertainty.

Emancipatory interest is Holliday and Chandler's (1986) and Chandler with Holliday's (1990) term for using multiple knowledge modes that free the self and that promote options, rather than restricting them. They follow Habermas's (1970) tripartite knowledge system divided into technical (controlling the natural environment), practical (maintaining social relations and communication with other people), and emancipatory knowing schemes. Wise people, they stated, based on their research in a number of studies, use all three of these kinds of knowing. To discover a prototype of wisdom, they asked people to generate lists of descriptors of wise people. Using factor analysis, they found five factors: exceptional understanding, judgment and communication skills, general competencies, interpersonal skills, and social unobtrusiveness, which relate to the Habermas schema. They suggested that the general competency factor represents a technical kind of ability (similar to the way Baltes and colleagues construed wisdom), whereas judgment and communication skills describe Habermas's practical knowledge. Exceptional understanding, because it requires meta-analytic abilities and a focus on goals and values rather than simply prudential choices, is associated with emancipatory knowing. Wisdom, then, entails the use of these three kinds of thinking, with particular emphasis on the last.

Also wanting to investigate a view of wisdom not limited to technical and practical knowing, Labouvie-Vief (1990, 2000) described the integration of logos and mythos. It begins with Plato's two-tiered view of human nature with abstract thought and spirit conceived as higher and better than the concrete, sensory, and bodily layer, and then moves through the traditional Christian association of the masculine with spirit and deity and the feminine with inferior functions (body, earth). These ideas culminate in scientific positivism, whose opposite is mythos, or subjectivity. Like Cook-Greuter (2000), Labouvie-Vief looked for an orientation that lies beyond postconventional thinking, because it, as represented by Loevinger (1976) and Kohlberg (1984), is still rooted in rationalist principles. Instead, she found that dialectical thinking allows for the inclusion of mythos (which stands for subjective, contextual, and relativistic knowledge) with logos. The result is a broader vision of "rationality" where individuals are able to "represent and understand these interactions [between rational and emotional processes] and integrate them within single, non-conflicting systems" (Cook-Greuter, 2000, p. 111). Wisdom, she held, cannot be reduced to a cognitive theory of expertise and specialization. Instead, it must move through the subjectivity of mythos to a synthesis of more integrative knowledge in which it is possible to see beyond individual uniqueness to our common humanity.

Another line of dialectical thinking is found in the work of Kitchener and Brenner (1990) in their discussion of stages of cognitive development. These stages mark a shift from understanding what can be known with certainty to awareness of the uncertainty of knowing and the ability to make measured judgments in the face of this uncertainty. Their reflective judgment model shows how individuals move from various stages and levels of certainty of knowing to the realization that much knowing about the human condition rests in uncertainty. To study how people form judgments about ill-structured problems, Kitchener and King (1981) developed the reflective judgment interviews. They asked participants to engage in "wicked-decision problem solving" (1990, p. 2). Participants' responses reflected the seven stages of their model. The results showed that more highly educated people scored higher, but that stage 7 was rarely attained by anyone, irrespective of the level of education, before age 30. The researchers concluded that education appears to play an important role in the development of this understanding of uncertainty.

In a philosophical essay, Pascual-Leone (1990) presented his ideas on how wisdom is a state reached when dialectical integrations in a person's psyche have occurred. The resolution of contradictions must have taken place, he held, across all and any of one's various operating domains, such as the cognitive, affective, social, and existential. When this has happened, a person is seen as an expert counselor who has adopted a paradoxical attitude, combining freedom with the authority of reason. To illustrate, he quotes a poem by Machado: "I give you counsel, for I am an old man: / never follow any counsel." Furthermore, wisdom appears as a state of dialectical integration of action on behalf of self (agency) and action on behalf of others (communion). The capacity to reflect on experiences and become conscious of and step outside of automatic ways of thinking, feeling, and acting can result in empathic connection with others. It can even result in a transcendence of the self, which is revealed as a detached but compassionate relationship to others with greater receptivity to the "unwilled" ("vital reason's open reading of reality"—which I take to mean openness to unconscious processes).

Kramer (2000) also viewed wisdom as a kind of dialectical integration of rational and nonrational parts of the psyche. Wisdom, as she understands it, "involves exceptional breadth and depth of knowledge about the conditions of life and human affairs and reflective judgment about the application of this knowledge" (p. 85). Wisdom is found in the interaction of the cognitive, affective, and behavioral domains that allow this knowledge to form in the first place, and then the judgment about it to be evidenced, much as

Kitchener and Brenner (1990) have discussed. To achieve this kind of judgment, Kramer proposed using alternative modes of representation. As Cook-Greuter (2000) and Pascual-Leone (1990) seem to suggest, these modes can include imagery, art, and metaphor, along with meditation or spiritual practice. (These techniques may result in emancipatory knowing.)

With dialectical thinking, according to Kramer (1990), knowledge is seen as evolving through the interplay of conflict and its resolution. Thus an individual would realize the interactive nature of events, rather than their independence and isolation from each other. Kramer indicated that Clayton's (1982) and Moody's (1983) models also represent wisdom as necessitating a logic based on contradiction and paradox. The dialectic must include both rationality and the emotions, cognition, and affect. Kramer gave the example of the biblical story of King Solomon who used paradoxical "logic" in his judgment that the child be cut in half and each half given to one of the women who claimed to be the mother. We know that one woman cried out in alarm to stop the process and asked that the other woman be given the whole live baby. We know that King Solomon awarded the child to this first woman, as he believed that a mother's love and desire for the well-being of the child would override any insistence about who would bring it up. Kramer did not dispute this interpretation, but she suggested more—that the solution is assumed because there is only one correct way that a mother would react to such a situation and that only a biological mother would do this. Both are questionable assumptions, Kramer maintained. Instead, Solomon's wisdom lies in recognizing that emotion must be taken into account in the solution of the difficult, ill-defined problems that people face.

Extending Kramer's work with its emphasis on the usefulness of dialectical thinking to handle the complex and often contradictory situations endemic to the human condition, Taranto (1989) concluded that acceptance of limitation is a characteristic shared by many models of wisdom. Wisdom, she said, "addresses both the limits of human nature and our understanding of human nature" (p. 15). Thus, problem solving must take human limitation into account, with a combination of intuitive and logical skills brought to bear on a situation.

This section has shown that theorists and researchers conceptualize wisdom as the integration, usually, of three dimensions (cognitive, affective, and behavioral). The integration occurs through the use of dialectical thinking which can also be seen as the logic of paradox and the recognition that uncertainty and the limits of knowledge frame human existence and force resolution of seemingly irresolvable dilemmas. Birren and Fisher (1990) summarized this view of wisdom by presenting it as an

> emergent property of an individual's inward and external response to life experiences. A wise person has learned to balance the opposing valences of the three aspects of behavior, cognition, affect, and volition. A wise person weighs the knowns and unknowns, resists overwhelming emotion while maintaining interest, and carefully chooses when and where to take action. (p. 332)

The question remains how individuals can achieve—or approach—the different aspects and qualities of wisdom. Can a person decide to become wise and set out to accomplish it? In the next section I will explore the topic of learning for wisdom.

LEARNING FOR WISDOM

What if you slept?
And what if,
In your sleep
You dreamed?
And what if,
In your dream,
You went to heaven
And there plucked
A strange and
Beautiful flower?
And what if,
When you awoke,
You had the flower
In your hand?
—Samuel Taylor Coleridge

It would be presumptuous, most people would agree, to teach wisdom directly. Is it even possible? Sternberg (2001) has established a curriculum on learning to be wise for middle school students in New Haven. Some colleges teach courses on wisdom, but these courses are about the topic of wisdom, not guidance on how to acquire it. How can a person learn to become wiser? Is there anything that we can do intentionally that will result in deeper understanding of the human condition and greater compassion for it? What is the relationship between learning and the development that leads to wisdom? Although there was no empirical research on learning for wisdom until Sternberg (2001) reported his, there is a body of literature on adult learning, particularly dialectical thinking and transformative learning and, more recently, the inclusion of myth and the arts, which can prove useful. Key concepts from each will be described here as suggestions for use when thinking about wisdom and learning.

Before looking at those topics, however, it is worth examining Baltes and Staudinger's (2000) thoughts on the acquisition of the wisdom heuristic and Sternberg's (2001) design for testing the balance theory of wisdom in the classroom. Baltes and Staudinger believed that if the wisdom heuristic is acquired systematically and repeatedly over time, more people might reach wisdom-related knowledge and judgment than exist to date. This heuristic, as they defined it, is the "activation, organization, and collaborative enlisting of knowledge that directs one's attention to the integration and optimization of mind and virtue" (p. 131). Furthermore, it functions as an "organizing selector and activator of otherwise more independent bodies of knowledge about the means and ends of a good life" (p. 132). Baltes and Staudinger suggested the use of methods associated with the study of "cognitive heuristics and pragmatic schemata of reasoning" (p. 131), although they did not specify what these methods might be. They did propose making the attributes of wisdom as explicit as possible and translating them into an available heuristic or pragmatic so that they can be learned or acquired.

Although Baltes and Staudinger (2000) did not specify any particular methods, a closer look at the heuristic can give indications on how it might be used for learning. The authors held that basic wisdom criteria include rich factual (declarative) knowledge about the pragmatics of life and rich procedural knowledge about these same pragmatics. One can reasonably assume that teaching a rich body of both factual and procedural knowledge, perhaps along the lines of a liberal education, might contribute to learning the heuristic. Furthermore they argued that three meta-criteria are necessary for wisdom. The first is life span contextualism, which is meant to "identify knowledge that considers the many themes and contexts of life (e.g., education, family, work, friends, leisure, the public good of society, etc.)" (p. 126) and

how they interrelate. Again, we hear the plea for a broad-based education. The second meta-criterion is about relativism of values and life priorities. It speaks to learning openness and tolerance. The third, the recognition and management of uncertainty, emphasizes the limits of knowledge, the selected and selective parts of reality that an individual apprehends, and the fact that the future cannot be known in advance. Teaching can highlight these points and help students understand and then internalize the contextualism of their own lives, the relativism of values, and the recognition of uncertainty as a condition of life. Finally, the authors proposed several conditions under which wisdom is likely to develop. These conditions include a mindset that strives toward excellence, the linking of knowledge with virtue, and the orchestration of a number of characteristics, such as cognitive, motivational, social, interpersonal, and spiritual ones. Guidance by mentors and experiencing and mastering critical life events can also contribute.

In his middle school project, Sternberg (2001) is attempting to apply his balance theory of wisdom. This project involves an experimental design in which one group uses the wisdom-related curriculum and two controls use critical thinking techniques or the regular school curriculum. He suggested that 12 topics should be covered, including an overview of theories and ideas on wisdom, the common good and the role of values and interests, and applying wisdom in students' lives. To teach wisdom-related skills, he proposed studying such topics as "wisdom and foolishness in literature, an analysis of historical decisions using wisdom-related skills as criteria, and the costs of pollution to the world" (p. 240). Trained raters will evaluate student responses on criteria derived from the theory. The ratings will include

> demonstration of attempts to reach a common good; balancing of intrapersonal, interpersonal, and extrapersonal interests; taking into account both short- and long-term factors; justification for adaptation to, shaping of, and selection of environments; mindful use of values; overall quality (wisdom) of process of solution; and overall quality (wisdom) of the solution" to proposed dilemmas and other classroom activities. (p. 241)

Speaking more generally about learning wisdom, Sternberg (1998) made three points. First, he noted, wisdom is procedural knowledge—it is about knowing what to do in various difficult and complex circumstances. Second, wisdom is relevant to the attainment of certain goals that people have—but not just any goals, rather those that seek and even achieve a common good for all or most stakeholders. Finally, wisdom is usually not acquired through the direct help or intervention of someone else. It is typically learned through experience. Because wisdom cannot be imparted the way multiplication tables can be, he concluded that wisdom is best developed through role modeling and the use of dialectical thinking, which, as a higher stage of cognitive development, requires complexity of thought.

Continuing the discussion on learning wisdom, Ardelt (2000b) usefully distinguished between two types of knowledge: intellectual and wisdom-based, arguing that education for elders should follow a path different from that of younger people. To illustrate the differences between the two types of knowledge, she proposed several categories. They include goals, approach, range, acquisition, effects on the knower, and relation to aging. For example, in the category of goals where the search for truth is paramount, the aim for younger people is the quantitative accumulation of new truths in the form of descriptive knowledge and information. For older people, however, the development of interpretive knowledge serves their life stage better as they grasp deeper understandings of phenomena and events and may use it to come to terms with unresolved issues in their lives and their impending mortality. Furthermore, Ardelt pointed out, instead of asking how to do certain things to achieve personal ends, older people question the very reason for wanting to do something in the first place. In other words, they are seeking the right ends for action, which is more possible to do in later years when the burdens of family and work obligations have lightened.

In another example, Ardelt (2000b) described the differences in approach to knowledge. Intellectual knowledge, generally speaking, is usually impersonal, abstract, theoretical, and detached from the knower (Belenky, Clinchy, Goldberger, and Tarule's [1987] procedural knowing, the modernist stance). In contrast to this linear, formal operational way of thinking, wisdom-related knowledge is applied, concrete, and involves the learner/knower who needs to engage in dialectical thinking to bridge the gap between knower and known, subject and object, and to incorporate contradictions and paradox (more like constructed or connected knowing).

The range of knowledge, according to Ardelt (2000b), is time-bound for younger people and more timeless for older ones because wisdom-related knowledge "provides universal answers to universal questions that concern the basic predicaments of the human condition" (p. 779). Furthermore, she noted, wisdom-related knowledge is obtained through openness to all kinds of experiences, "self-reflection, self-awareness, and the transcendence of one's subjectivity and projections" (p. 783), all of which takes time and makes growing old a necessary but not sufficient condition for the emergence of wisdom.

Rather than looking at the kinds of knowledge that can result in wisdom, Kegan's (1994) perspective, on the other hand, centers on the necessity of dialectical thought for coping with the demands of the modern world. For him, dialectical thought is required by the mental demands that the postmodern world places on us. Linear rational thought working with abstractions and the conception of the self as a self-authored and self-regulating mechanism (his fourth-order thinking) will not serve in the many situations that face us today, those in which contradictions and paradoxes are inevitable. In fourth-order consciousness, people are capable of doing more than thinking across categories and concepts. They can start to question categories and values, thus creating new knowledge and perhaps the beginning of wisdom. In the fifth order, one that seems more akin to the qualities associated with wisdom, an individual develops a trans-systems perspective that encompasses both sides of a conflict or a contradiction. In this case the self is not identified with either perspective (one system or another) as is more likely the case in fourth-order thinking, but rather becomes a kind of metasystem that holds or contains the other two. Unfortunately, Kegan has found that fifth-order consciousness occurs only rarely, but he felt hopeful for its evolution, given people's longer life spans these days.

Kegan (1994) noted that the goal of an educational system fosters the development or maintenance of the order of consciousness associated with it. For example, if there is a goal of fostering the order of consciousness that enables self-direction (fourth-order thinking), then adults are more likely to do that. If the goal is for people to think that what they *should* feel is what they *do* feel and what they *should* value is what they *do* value, then a third-order consciousness dominates. Kegan indicated that the goal is not a "matter of getting students merely to identify and value a distinction between two parts that already exist, but a matter of fostering a qualitative evolution of mind that actually creates a distinction" (p. 275), leading to fourth-order consciousness. How can educators do this? Kegan suggested a "consciousness bridge," where the teacher as bridge builder honors and respects both ends, both orders of consciousness, creating a firm span on which the student can cross from one side to the other.

Moving to the fifth order is a bit trickier, as there are not a lot of people who have achieved it and who can act as role models. Kegan (1994) described some characteristics of fifth-order thinking. They include seeing the self-as-system as incomplete and an integral organic part of a larger system, rather than complete and whole in itself. Although Daloz, Keen, Keen, and Parks (1996) did not refer to orders of consciousness in their study, the people that they interviewed all worked on behalf of the common good, which is seen as including "such core elements as a global scope, a recognition of diversity, and a vision of society as composed of individuals whose own well-being is inextricably bound up with the good of the whole" (p. 16). The common good also suggests shared goals toward which members of a community strive along with the well-being of the whole Earth community. To be participants, subjects had to meet the following criteria: a commitment to the common good through their actions, perseverance and resilience over many years, ethical congruence between life and work, and engagement with diversity and complexity. The authors found that what supported the participants in their work, among other factors, was growing up and living in hospitable spaces (not tribal settings or contemporary suburban fortresses), developing the moral imagination through contact with the "other," and cultivating certain habits of mind to sustain them. For learning purposes, it seems that exposure to and incorporation of the "other" into one's own life helps propel a person toward a larger, more reflective, and relativistic worldview, certainly approaching fifth-order thinking.

Helping people make developmental changes requires methods of learning that recognize and support development. In addition to dialectical thinking, transformative learning seems like the area most conducive to handling the complexities of wisdom. We have seen that wisdom is a multidimensional construct that includes exceptional understanding of and compassion for the human condition, knowledge with extraordinary scope and depth, the ability to address important and difficult questions about life, and a balancing of the needs of self, others, and institutions directed to the common good. In addition, postformal or even transpersonal development, along with cognitive complexity, are often associated with wisdom, and so are handling contradiction and paradox in a dialectical manner, and integrating rational and nonrational (and other) aspects of the psyche. Because people are not born with these abilities and they cannot be imparted by simply adding on to preexisting knowledge, it seems that a fundamental shift in knowledge structures is called for. To become wise, new ways of making meaning at a high level of awareness and integration are necessary. Transformative learning, which expands meaning schemes, provides both a practical and a conceptual framework for this process. Cranton (1994) put it this way: "Transformative learning, then, is a process of examining, questioning, validating, and revising . . . perceptions" (p. 26).

Transformative learning is based on constructive-developmental theory, as we have seen with Kegan (1994) and such foundational writers as Piaget (1954), Habermas (1970), Loevinger (1976), and Kohlberg (1981). The learning theories derived from them have been proposed by Freire (1970/1992), Kolb (1984), and Mezirow (1991, 2000). Common to these theories is that learning

> is a process of *resolving contradictions in dialecti-cal fashion*, in this way raising awareness of new possibilities and *multiple perspectives*; that it is also a process of moving toward more *complex ways of viewing* oneself and one's situation, potentially leading people to take a more *active responsibility* for the world in which they live; that *discourse is crucial* to the alteration of perspectives that is learning; and that such *transformed perspectives are developmental* in the lives of adults. (Taylor, Marienau, & Fiddler, 2000, p. 22; emphasis in original)

Along the same lines, the Ontario Institute for the Study of Education described transformational learning as "a deep structural shift in basic premises of thought, feelings, and actions . . . a shift of consciousness that dramatically and permanently alters our way of being in the world" (Morrell & O'Connor, 2002, p. xvii). The father of this field, Mezirow (1991) held that "transformative learning involves reflectively transforming beliefs, attitudes, opinion, and emotional reactions that constitute our meaning schemes" (p. 223), particularly those that are constricting or those that have distorted one's life. The goal, in an often quoted phrase, is to create "more inclusive, discriminating, permeable, and integrative perspectives" and to make decisions based on these new understandings (Mezirow, 1990, p. 14).

Mezirow suggested that significant transformational learning involves several steps in a recursive process. First, a disorienting dilemma that upsets assumptions must be experienced. Although this event was earlier conceptualized as a single dramatic one, more recent research (Taylor, 2000) has indicated that the disorienting dilemma can also take the form of a longer cumulative process. After this incident takes place or this series of dilemmas occurs, then, from a place of discomfort, the learner engages in critical reflection and assessment of these assumptions. In a subsequent step, the learner recognizes that others have gone through a similar process. Next, options for alternative roles, relationships, or actions are explored. A plan of action takes place, as does reflective discourse (based on the work of Habermas), in which learners engage with others to obtain consensual validation for their newly transformed perspective (Mezirow, 1991).

Recent research on transformative learning confirms the importance of relationships (Taylor, 2000). Studies found that for transformation to take place, both rational and relational discourses are necessary. Transformative learning now appears not to be an independent act but rather an interdependent relationship built on trust and involving others. Also, said Taylor, there is a readiness for change that differs from individual to individual and is based on a person's own contexts.

Personal readiness can be taken advantage of or provoked through the use of the learning prompts found in table 13.1, created by this researcher. Each of the dimensions (discerning, empathizing, engaging, and being) includes several proficiencies, such as insight and holistic seeing, which are associated with discerning. The ability to see holistically, that is, from a systems point of view, can be learned and practiced. One simple technique for practicing this skill is to think of one's self in the third person and to look back on this self from a fictional future date. Doing so helps decenter the ego and allows it to see itself as one system among many. Another skill that can be learned is to take the point of view of people "on the other side of the street" and to see the world as they do, thus expanding one's sphere of consideration and instilling an ethic of care (see Daloz et al., 1996). Again, referring to the learning prompts in the model, asking oneself to imagine how other people might understand a given situation supports multiple perspective taking, which is a proficiency associated with empathizing. Yet according to the model, more than discerning and empathizing are necessary to wisdom. Knowing what is true and understanding how other people feel is not sufficient for wisdom. Engagement with the world through some kind of action has to take place also, which can include forming sound judgments that can be expressed to even one other person. That is because being isolated and not communicating or interacting with the world does not exemplify wisdom. Finally, wisdom requires an expansion of consciousness, with the ability to begin to extend beyond one's own frame of reference (self-transcendence). These proficiencies can all be practiced using the learning prompts found in the table. For discerning, one can ask: What is really going on? What is true? What is important? For being, people can ask themselves, What are my values? Who or what is the "I" that I think I am? Constantly keeping the questions at play at every intersection with life events, like a mantra or a basso continuo, can enable wisdom because a shift in perspective occurs.

Other ideas come from Taylor et al. (2000), who provide many examples of how transformative learning can contribute to this kind of development. Their developmental intentions chart shows development moving along five dimensions. Knowing as a dialogical process means that through exchange, two or more people share ideas and ways of thinking different from their own, thus making meaning and constructing knowledge for themselves. Critical thinking plays a role here. Knowing as a dialogical relationship with oneself is the capacity to see oneself from different perspectives and to uncover limitations in thinking. Reflection becomes a powerful tool. The third intention is becoming a continuous learner, which means mastering the skills of learning, such as challenging oneself to learn in new realms or to anticipate the learning needed to prevent future problems. Kegan's (1994) fourth-order thinking describes the movement toward self-agency and self-authorship. Here, a teacher needs to support and challenge students to take authorship of their own lives. Finally, the fifth movement, about connection with others, allows a person to engage the affective dimension when confronting difference and may create readiness where people want to contribute to something larger than themselves, lending their voices to contribute to the collective endeavor. Strategies such as assessing, collaborating, experimenting, imagining, inquiring, performing, and reflecting all contribute to these five movements.

Besides these and the more usual, effective processes of transformative learning, especially the cognitively oriented processes (such as critical reflection, discourse and reasoning, and use of disorienting dilemmas), other techniques can be used as well. That is because, as Kramer (2000) stated, most emotional or existential dilemmas in life do not lend themselves to a linear rational method, such as the one that Mezirow (1991) has proposed. Instead, she felt that such dilemmas require alternative modes of representation such as art, metaphor, and "non-linear 'logic'" (Kramer, 2000, p. 85). Other modes include listening to inner "voices" (that is, to different aspects of the self), accessing (as well as assessing) intuition, and working with metaphor, image, and narrative. As Dirkx (2001) suggested, the imagination must be nurtured with its own kind of nourishment. Greene (1995) made a strong case for the imagination in its ability to create the kind of breakthroughs or deepen the kinds of understanding that wisdom requires.

Finally, on the topic of learning for wisdom as a spiritual process, in her study of the development of wisdom in the training of Tibetan Buddhist monks, Levitt (1999) found that the monks thought that all people have the potential to become wise, regardless of inborn traits or personal character. A strong desire to learn contributes to the development of wisdom. The help of a spiritual teacher is seen as critical in guiding a person toward a higher level of wisdom. Even without striving so high, assistance from others is essential. Such assistance can be found in a supportive family, friends, and communities. The Buddhist teaching process consists of the lama or spiritual teacher presenting the sacred texts while being guided by students' individual needs. In an unusual process, the teachers sometimes give students partial or even incorrect answers for the student to examine and then to reject. Students say that they never know if their teachers' answers are correct. A number of these techniques could be used in the West. Cook-Greuter (2000) proposed the establishment and maintenance of a regular spiritual practice as a main strategy for moving toward wisdom.

Finally, some straightforward techniques can be practiced by anyone at any time. Simply by observing people we regard as wise and trying to emulate them can help move us toward wisdom. So can looking at our own selves, noting what we do that is wise, and doing more of it. The inverse holds true as well—we must do less of what is foolish.

SUMMARY

Both discursive and imaginal approaches can help us learn better how to apply complex intelligence to the human condition and nudge us along in the lifelong process of becoming wiser. Difficult to study, but studied nevertheless, wisdom requires many different approaches to breach its manifold battlements and to enter its green and grassy plains. It is not that wisdom requires a battle. It is more that the walls represent a natural accretion built of conventional mental frameworks and morality that require both discipline and imagination to supercede. Never simple, always challenging, wisdom has been studied as expertise in living, as superior knowledge and understanding, as knowing and doing what is good and right, as a balance of interests, as selected personal characteristics, and as exceptional self-development, for example. Yet none quite succeed in getting to the heart of what wisdom is really about. Its mystery and allure remain. We strive toward it, but like the window that we leave open for the passage of the divine, we never know if the wind of wisdom will enter. In the meantime, I have suggested a number of techniques and strategies that we can use to make wisdom more accessible. We can explore and practice its various components. What if we change Emily Dickinson's phrase from "The Possible's slow fuse is lit / By the imagination" to "Wisdom's slow fuse is lit / By the imagination"—where imagination includes all kinds of uses of mind and soul: rational, emotional, volitional, and spiritual? Then we, too, will be able to laugh at gilded butterflies.

References

Achenbaum, W. A., & Orwoll, L. (1991). Becoming wise: A psycho-genontological interpretation of "The Book of Job." *International Journal of Aging and Human Development, 32*, 21–39.

Ardelt, M. (1997). Wisdom and life satisfaction in old age. *Journal of Gerontology: Psychological Sciences 52B*, P15–P27.

Ardelt, M. (2000a). Antecedents and effects of wisdom in old age: A longitudinal perspective on aging well. *Research on Aging*, 22, 360–394.

Ardelt, M. (2000b). Intellectual versus wisdom-related knowledge: The case for a different kind of learning in the later years of life. *Educational Gerontology*, 26, 771–789.

Ardelt, M. (2003). Empirical assessment of a three-dimensional wisdom scale. *Research on Aging*, 25, 275–324.

Assman, A. (1994). Wholesome knowledge: Concepts of wisdom in a historical and cross-cultural perspective. In D. L. Featherman, R. M. Lerner, & M. Perlmutter (Eds.), *Life-span development and behavior* (Vol. 12, pp. 187–224). Hillsdale, NJ: Lawrence Erlbaum.

Austen, J. (1996). *Pride and prejudice*. New York: Signet.

Baltes, P. B., & Smith, J. (1990). Toward a psychology of wisdom and its ontogenesis. In R. J. Sternberg (Ed.), *Wisdom: Its nature, origins, and development* (pp. 87–120). Cambridge: Cambridge University Press.

Baltes, P. B., & Staudinger, U. M. (1993). The search for a psychology of wisdom. *Current Directions in Psychology Science*, 2, 75–80.

Baltes, P. B., & Staudinger, U. M. (2000). A metaheuristic (pragmatic) to orchestrate mind and virtue toward excellence. *American Psychologist*, 2, 122–136.

Baltes, P. B., Staudinger, U. M., Maercker, A., & Smith, J. (1995). People nominated as wise: A comparative study of wisdom-related knowledge. *Psychology and Aging*, 10, 155–166.

Bassett, C. (2001). *Transformative learning for wisdom*. Paper presented at the Fourth International Transformative Learning Conference, OISE, University of Toronto.

Bassett, C. (2003, April). *Wisdom: Overlooked aspect of adult development*. Paper presented at the Society for Research in Adult Development, Tampa, FL.

Belenky, M., Clinchy, B., Goldberger, N., & Tarule, J. (1986). *Women's ways of knowing: The development of self, voice, and mind*. New York: Basic Books.

Birren, J. E., & Fisher, L. M. (1990). The elements of wisdom: Overview and integration. In R. J. Sternberg (Ed.), *Wisdom: Its nature, origins, and development* (pp. 317–332). Cambridge: Cambridge University Press.

Chandler, M. J. (with Holliday, S.). (1990). Wisdom in a postapocalyptic age. In R. J. Sternberg (Ed.), *Wisdom: Its nature, origins, and development* (pp. 121–144). Cambridge: Cambridge University Press.

Clayton, R. (1982). Wisdom and intelligence: The nature and function of knowledge in the later years. *International Journal of Aging and Human Development*, 15, 315–321.

Clayton, V., & Birren, J. E. (1980). The development of wisdom across the life-span: A re-examination of an ancient topic. In P. B. Baltes & O. G. Brim (Eds.), *Life-span development and behavior* (Vol. 3, pp. 103–135). New York: Academic Press.

Cook, B. W. (1992). *Eleanor Roosevelt*. New York: Penguin Books.

Cook-Greuter, S. R. (1994). Rare forms of self-understanding in mature adults. In M. E. Miller & S. R. Cook-Greuter (Eds.), *Transcendence and mature thought in adulthood* (pp. 119–246). London: Rowman & Littlefield.

Cook-Greuter, S. R. (2000). Mature ego development: A gateway to ego transcendence? *Journal of Adult Development*, 7, 227–240.

Cranton, P. (1994). *Understanding and promoting transformative learning*. San Francisco: Jossey-Bass.

Daloz, L., Keen, C., Keen, J., & Parks, S. D. (1996). *Common fire: Lives of commitment in a complex world*. Boston: Beacon Press.

Denney, N. W., Dew, J. R., & Kroupa, S. L. (1995). Perceptions of wisdom: What is it and who has it? *Journal of Adult Development*, 2, 37–47.

Dirkx, J. M. (2001). The power of feelings: Emotion, imagination, and the construction of meaning in adult learning. *New Directions for Adult and Continuing Education*, 89, 63–72.

Ferrer, J. (2001). Toward a participatory vision of human spirituality. *ReVision*, 24(2), 15–26.

Freire, P. (1970/1992). *Pedagogy of the oppressed*. New York: Continuum.

Greene, M. (1995). *Releasing the imagination*. San Francisco: Jossey-Bass.

Habermas, J. (1970). *Knowledge and human interests*. Boston: Beacon Press.

Halpern, D. F. (2001). Why wisdom? *Educational Psychologist*, 36, 253–256.

Hershey, D. A., & Farrell, A. H. (1997). Perceptions of wisdom associated with selected occupations and personality characteristics. *Current Psychology*, 16, 115–133.

Holliday, S. G., & Chandler, M. J. (1986). *Wisdom: Explorations in adult competence*. Basel, Switzerland: Karger.

Kegan, R. (1994). *In over our heads: The mental demands of modern life*. Cambridge, MA: Harvard University Press.

Kitchener, K. S., & Brenner, H. G. (1990). Wisdom and reflective judgment: Knowing in the face of uncertainty. In R. J. Sternberg (Ed.), *Wisdom: Its nature, origins, and development* (pp. 212–229). Cambridge: Cambridge University Press.

Kitchener, K. S., & King, P. M. (1981). Reflective judgment: Concepts of justification and their relationship to age and education. *Journal of Applied Developmental Psychology*, 2, 89–116.

Kohlberg, L. (1981). *The philosophy of moral development: Moral stages and the idea of justice*. New York: Harper & Row.

Kohlberg, L. (1984). *Essays on moral development*, vol. 2. *The psychology of moral development*. San Francisco: Harper & Row.

Kolb, D. A. (1984). *Experiential learning: Experience as the source of learning and development*. Englewood Cliffs, NJ: Prentice Hall.

Kramer, D. A. (1990). Conceptualizing wisdom: The primacy of affect-cognition relations. In R. J. Sternberg (Ed.), *Wisdom: Its nature, origins, and development* (pp. 279–313). Cambridge: Cambridge University Press.

Kramer, D. A. (2000). Wisdom as a classical source of human strength: Conceptualization and empirical inquiry. *Journal of Social and Clinical Psychology, 19*, 83–101.

Labouvie-Vief, G. (1990). Wisdom as integrated thought: Historical and developmental perspectives. In R. J. Sternberg (Ed.), *Wisdom: Its nature, origins, and development* (pp. 52–83). Cambridge: Cambridge University Press.

Labouvie-Vief, G. (2000). Affect complexity and views of the transcendent. In P. Young-Eisendrath & M. E. Miller (Eds), *The psychology of mature spirituality* (pp. 103–119). London and Philadelphia: Routledge.

Levitt, H. M. (1999). The development of wisdom: An analysis of Tibetan Buddhist experience. *Journal of Humanistic Psychology, 39*, 86–105.

Loevinger, J. (1976). *Ego development: Conceptions and theories*. San Francisco: Jossey-Bass.

Lyster, T. L. (1996). *A nomination approach to the study of wisdom in old age*. Unpublished doctoral dissertation, Concordia University, Montreal, Quebec.

Mandela, N. (1995). *Long walk to freedom*. Boston: Little, Brown.

Meacham, J. A. (1990). The loss of wisdom. In R. J. Sternberg (Ed.), *Wisdom: Its nature, origins, and development* (pp. 181–211). Cambridge: Cambridge University Press.

Merikangas, R. (1998). Heuristics for wisdom communities. *Futures Research Quarterly*, Summer, 67–95.

Merriam, S. B., & Caffarella, R. S. (1999). *Learning in adulthood: A comprehensive guide*. San Francisco: Jossey-Bass.

Mezirow, J. (1990). How critical reflection triggers transformative learning. In J. Mezirow & associates, *Fostering critical reflection in adulthood: A guide to transformative and emancipatory learning* (pp. 1–20). San Francisco: Jossey-Bass.

Mezirow, J. (1991). *Transformative dimensions of adult learning*. San Francisco: Jossey-Bass.

Mezirow, J. (2000). *Learning as transformation: Critical perspectives on a theory in progress*. San Francisco: Jossey-Bass.

Moody, H. R. (1983). *Wisdom and the search for meaning*. Paper presented at the 36th Annual Meetings of the Gerontological Society of America, San Francisco.

Morrell, A., & O'Connor, M. A. (2002). Introduction. In E. O'Sullivan, A. Morrell, & M. A. O'Connor (Eds.), *Expanding the boundaries of transformative learning* (pp. 1–16). New York: Palgrave.

Nichols, R. (1992). Maxims, "practical wisdom," and the language of action. *Political Theory, 24*, 687–705.

Orwoll, L., & Perlmutter, M. (1990). A study of wise persons: integrating a personality perspective. In R. J. Sternberg (Ed.), *Wisdom: Its nature, origins, and development* (pp. 160–177). Cambridge: Cambridge University Press.

Pascual-Leone, J. (1990). An essay on wisdom: Toward organismic processes that make it possible. In R. J. Sternberg (Ed.), *Wisdom: Its nature, origins, and development* (pp. 244–278). Cambridge: Cambridge University Press.

Piaget, J. (1954). *The construction of reality in the child*. New York: Basic Books.

Rathunde, K. (1995). Wisdom and abiding interest: Interviews with three noted historians in later life. *Journal of Adult Development, 2*, 159–172.

Smith, H. (1992). *The world's religions: Our great wisdom traditions*. San Francisco: Harper.

Sternberg, R. J. (Ed.). (1990a). *Wisdom: Its nature, origins, and development*. Cambridge: Cambridge University Press.

Sternberg, R. J. (1990b). Wisdom and its relations to intelligence and creativity. In R. J. Sternberg (Ed.), *Wisdom: Its nature, origins, and development* (pp. 142–159). Cambridge: Cambridge University Press.

Sternberg, R. J. (1996). Styles of thinking. In P. B. Baltes & U. M. Staudinger (Eds.), *Interactive minds: Lifespan perspectives on the social foundation of cognition* (pp. 347–365). New York: Cambridge University Press.

Sternberg, R. J. (1998). A balance theory of wisdom. *Review of General Psychology, 2*, 347–365.

Sternberg, R. J. (2001). Why schools should teach for wisdom: The balance theory of wisdom in educational settings. *Educational Psychologist 36*, 227–245.

Takahashi, M. (2000). The concept of wisdom: A cross-cultural comparison. *International Journal of Psychology, 35*, 1–9.

Taranto, M. (1989). Facets of wisdom: A theoretical synthesis. *International Journal of Aging and Human Development 29*, 1–21.

Taylor, E. (2000). Analyzing research on transformative learning theory. In J. Mezirow & associates (Eds.), *Learning as transformation: Critical perspectives on a theory in progress* (pp. 285–328). San Francisco: Jossey-Bass.

Taylor, K., Marienau, C., & Fiddler, M. (2000). *Developing adult learners*. San Francisco: Jossey-Bass.

Webster, J. D. (2003). An exploratory analysis of a self-assessed wisdom scale. *Journal of Adult Development, 10*, 13–22.

Webster's New World College Dictionary (4th ed.). (2002). New York: Wiley.

Wink, P., & Helson, R. (1997). Practical and transcendent wisdom: Their nature and some longitudinal findings. *Journal of Adult Development, 4*, 1–14.

Chapter 14

Spiritual Development in Adulthood: Key Concepts and Models

Ronald R. Irwin

In my recent studies in Buddhism and meditative practice, I was sent the following meditative practice by my teacher, Angela Sumegi, of the Palyul group in Ottawa, Canada. This is a Buddhist group affiliated with Pema Norbu Rinpoche of the Nyingma lineage of Tibetan Buddhism. Although the instructions are clear enough and the practice simple enough (especially as compared to so many of the complex visualizations required in Tibetan Buddhism as well as the many practices required in the preliminaries [ngondro] to higher level *tantric* and *dzogchen* meditations), in my own experience I simply found this meditation difficult and tantalizingly elusive. I just seemed to always be getting in the way of being able to simply do it.

Experience yourself as an aware being and then place your attention on the breath flowing in and out quite naturally.

After a few minutes, cease to focus on any particular object and practice "choiceless awareness," simply observing whatever objects arise and pass in Awareness. Notice the following about each object:

It is impermanent. It has no existence apart from Awareness, Itself. Being a form of Awareness, it is transparent to it.

Without fixing attention on anything, just consider: is there awareness of sights? Is there awareness of sounds? Is there awareness of sensations? Is there awareness of thoughts? Is there awareness of feelings?

This very Awareness which is right here now, IS that eternal, self-luminous Reality that you have been striving to realize all along. Since this Awareness is already here, your striving is unnecessary.

Abandon all concepts about experience and simply observe.

See how appearances arise in Awareness. Since whatever appears is already present, how can it be avoided?

See how appearances pass in Awareness. Since whatever has passed is no longer present, how can it be grasped?

See how everything appears in Awareness without the least obstruction. Since nothing obstructs appearances, there are no obstacles to be removed.

See how everything passes in Awareness without the least hindrance. Since everything is self-liberating, there is nothing to be set free.

Relax into this effortless contemplation of how things actually are.

Without making any adjustments, continue to observe:

Although you say, "forms arise in Awareness," can you really separate Awareness from its forms? Is not Awareness like an ocean and forms its waves?

Because Awareness and forms are ultimately inseparable, duality never existed. How then can it be transcended?

Although you say, "I am aware of such and such object," can you truly distinguish between yourself and the object? Where does "self" end and "object" begin?

Because subject and object are, in reality, indistinguishable, delusion never originated. How then can it be dispelled?

Look! Reality is staring you in the face:

You say you cannot eliminate your "self" but there is no self to eliminate.

You say you have not attained "Enlightenment" but there is not the slightest thing to attain. You say, "I am ignorant of my true identity." But how can this be? What else is there besides this infinite, eternal, nondual field of Awareness-and-form which is already present, right here and now . . . and now . . . and now . . .

Therefore, surrender all desire for attainment and just be what you are: Awareness, Itself!

Do not grasp anything, do not reject anything . . . be whatever is. "Enlightenment" is not a place in which to settle, nor is "Gnosis" a state that needs to be maintained. All experiences, all feelings, all states—whether mundane or sacred—are by their very nature transient and ephemeral. Without making an attempt to either hold on or push them away, simply remain identified with awareness, Itself and continue to practice effortlessly.

By practicing effortless contemplation you will develop the realization that the self is empty of any inherent existence. Thus, while objects continue to appear in Awareness, the delusion that they are being experienced by some "one" will subside. This state of profound selflessness or Awareness-without-a-subject is often a prelude to full awakening. What is missing is the complimentary

realization that not only does the "self" lack any inherent existence, but so do objects. Consequently, as long as objects seem to exist in their own right there is no Gnosis. However, if you remain in the state of Awareness-without-a-subject then as Awareness-without-an-object finally dawns, you will realize that the now vanished objects were, in themselves, only imaginary projections of this objectless Awareness. Furthermore, you will realize that your own Awareness-without-a-subject is, in fact, indistinguishable from (and thus identical to) Awareness-without-an-object. In other words, you will directly and simultaneously apprehend not only the True nature of your "self" but the true Nature of all "objects" and "worlds"—which is to say, Awareness-without-an-object-and-without-a subject. This is the end of the Path.

In this chapter, I explore how the learning or "doing" of such a meditative practice is contingent on level of development. I shall attempt to explain what such development consists of in terms of Western descriptions of ego development and Eastern accounts of the evolution of consciousness. Some of my sources will be based on hard data deriving from rigorous and scientifically validated developmental theories, and some of my sources, especially as I move into descriptions of "higher" stages, will be based on Eastern wisdom traditions, which draw more from personal accounts and ancient literature.

Life span developmental psychology has yielded a number of models of higher development that can be related to models of spiritual development. Many of these models are neo-Piagetian in the sense of building on some of the theoretical premises of Piaget and much of his data but going beyond his work, both in terms of depth and breadth. In terms of depth, such research has described stages beyond Piaget's highest stage of formal operations (Commons, Armon, Kohlberg, Richards, Grotzer, & Sinnott, 1990; Commons, Richards, & Armon, 1984; Commons, Sinnott, Richards, & Armon, 1989), which he considered to have been achieved in adolescence. These models contain what are sometimes described as postformal stages, some considered a "fifth stage," often framed in terms of different logical operations that become available to subjects, usually adult, at that time. Piaget's traditional four stages are characterized by the mental operations available to children, that is, interiorized actions. So it is natural that fifth- or even sixth-stage descriptions be described as new operations that act on the operations of earlier stages. These higher operations have been characterized as dialectical (Basseches, 1984), relativistic (Perry, 1970), and metasystematic (Commons & Richards, 1984),

When the focus of criticism has been on the breadth of what is considered development, researchers have extended Piaget's exclusive focus on largely logicomathematical stages to consider stages of social (Selman, 1980), moral (Kohlberg, 1984), faith (Fowler, 1995), ego (Loevinger, 1976), self (Kegan, 1982, 1994), and consciousness development (Alexander et al., 1990; Alexander, Heaton, & Chandler, 1994; Wilber, 2000). For this chapter I focus on models of *consciousness* development; within these, and particularly the highest stages of these, I locate *spiritual* development. Spiritual development cannot be predicated on logicomathematical operations. I regard higher stages of consciousness as potentially spiritual, but an element of spirituality can be found in many domains when the highest stages are considered. These models of greater breadth, however, retain characteristics of Piaget's developmental assumptions, including notions of hierarchical complexity and inclusiveness, an invariant sequence, qualitative change, and a structured whole that underlies each of the stages. A postulated invariant sequence of stages must be passed through in a particular order such that the earlier stages are necessary for the development of the higher stages. Although not all higher stages are achieved by all subjects, the higher stages can only appear as the result of the transformation of earlier stage structures. One assumption of Piagetian theory is that higher structures are better than lower structures in terms of the maturity required to reach them and better in terms of epistemological adequacy. So if such neo-Piagetian models of consciousness development include higher stages that are spiritual, it follows that spiritual consciousness is better than stages of consciousness that are not spiritual. When neo-Piagetian models of human development are applied to different domains, some researchers hold that different forms of education, therapy, or spiritual practice might be more useful at different stages of development and, furthermore, that such interventions can be deliberately facilitative of higher stages of consciousness development. In addition, particular problems of cognition, affect, and behavior can be interpreted as reflecting transitions in development that threaten to turn pathological if the crisis or issue emergent at that turning point is not resolved in a healthy fashion. This has yielded the concept of clients having *spiritual emergencies* that are crises indicative of difficulties in consciousness transformation (Grof & Grof, 1989), emergencies that require compassionate and insightful interventions, and that have symptoms not just of pathology but of *spiritual emergence*, indicating not breakdown but breakthrough.

Mental health professionals who practice without a full-spectrum model of human development may prescribe interventions that address only the symptoms of pathology but not of emergence, and the treatments, whether therapeutic or psychopharmacological, may impede rather than enhance development. R. D. Laing (1989) referred to the concept of *suppressive medication*. Increasing the spectrum of human development in our practice and researches may require refinements in our diagnosis of such disorders as anxiety and depression, where each of these clinical entities differ as they appear at different transitions in the life span. Furthermore, some of the symptoms associated with the emergence of higher consciousness may be necessary stepping stones to the emergence of more differentiated and integrated structures. Considering them as pathologies to be eliminated by pharmacological intervention may stop higher development in its tracks (Irwin, 2000).

Meditation may be viewed as a treatment modality suitable for those at a phase of consciousness development where they are ready for transpersonal development. We can therefore understand why it is that repeated attempts at a meditation practice may consistently yield little in the way of psychological transformation at earlier stages of life. Perhaps novices in spiritual discipline are not developmentally prepared or ready to benefit from such practice, lacking the structural prerequisites to consciousness transformation. Perhaps they are seeking solutions to dilemmas set by earlier life span challenges but are mistakenly seeking answers in practices that are not appropriate to their stage of development. For example, younger adolescent seekers of "the truth" may be looking for answers to identity issues that are simply not relevant to practices that are essentially about the renunciation of identity. And some meditation practices may not only be not beneficial but indeed harmful if the ego requires structure building, for example, in the cases of borderline or narcissistic personality disorders. You must have an ego before you can transcend it.

In my recent book (Irwin, 2002) I synthesized evolutionary and spiritual ways of thinking. Taking as my starting point an attempt to provide an account of the philosophy of mind, I assume that "mind" is an organ of evolutionary adaptation like any other physiological organ humans possess. Consciousness is but one aspect of mind, that part consisting of developed structures residing in the brain that control and structure what is brought into awareness. Such development provides the structure for what can be learned, perceived, and stored in the species' synaptic circuitry.

Most broadly considered, we can see mind as providing its possessor with a simulation capacity that makes it more adaptive at engaging in trial-and-error selection. Evolution at the species level consists of random mutations in the genotype, which translate into selection of phenotypes, some of which provide the species with better chances of survival and therefore of being transmitted to the next generation, and some of which lessen the species' survival chances, meaning that they are not transmitted to the next generation. In the standard Darwinian model, such mechanisms of mutation and change are necessary, otherwise species will not adapt to changes in their environments. But many (if not most) mutations are irrelevant or deleterious to the species, and some can result in extinction of the possessors of those mutations. Similarly, at the behavioral level, and not at the species level, processes of trial and error and subsequent selection occur to ensure that adaptive learning occurs and that adaptive changes in behavior and memory structures are made. Again, there must be a mechanism of trial and of selection. The trials are risky and result often in punishment, aversive consequences, injury, and even death. Much of the activity of the young of many species is play in that they enable the young to learn new behaviors but not try out those behaviors in the "real world" of predators and natural dangers. Then as the members of a species grow up, they might still play with new behaviors, but now there are consequences to such play that might threaten their survival.

This is where having a simulation capacity confers on its possessor an adaptive edge in evolutionary competition. Trials can be carried out on representations of its own body and the environment and selected for on the basis of internally determined criteria that match criteria that operate in the external world. The adaptive value of employing such representations lies in whether they functionally map real-world contingencies in such a way that their selection and translation into behavior confers an evolutionary survival advantage. This advantage is ultimately based on whether the possessor of such simulations is able to leave more of their offspring to the next generation.

Social, moral, and emotional learning, about others and about ourselves, piggybacks on the simulation capacity afforded by natural selection, which evolved to adapt to the physical world. Natural selection has also seen to it that we have evolved as a social species. We do not develop *in nature* as do so many other species. We develop *in society*, which mediates all of our contacts with nature. Humans never really know nature "red in tooth and claw." We only know nature as mediated by society, particularly when we are young. The solitary human, the noble savage, the feral child are mostly fictions of romantic literature and an oddity that has fascinated many because of its rarity (i.e., see *The Wild Boy of Aveyron* by Itard [1962], considered by many a classic and seminal work in developmental psychology). Humans survive because they are social and because they cooperate in groups. One reason we need to function in groups is that our modes of reproduction and childrearing require that a mother and her offspring are protected by the group during a very prolonged period of childrearing.

One aspect of our development is the protracted period of helplessness of our young. They are born without much of their brain development completed and with a bare modicum of elementary reflexes. Neonates cannot breastfeed without maternal assistance. And it took years before a child could forage for him- or herself in the open savannah. This is part and parcel of how it is that human children develop and become socialized in a process that is an extension of the lengthy gestational period, one that is already not sufficient to grow our incredibly complex and plastic brains, which outstrip in size and convolutions and interconnectedness the brains of even our closest phylogenetic relatives. These brains have evolved for one major purpose: to have the simulation capacity to create internal worlds, tabletop models of reality, inside of which we safely test out mock-ups of our behaviours before acting on them.

Not only does this simulation capacity provide us with an edge in the competition for resources with other species, it is taken over and used to simulate our social worlds, including ourselves in that world as objects among others. This is the basis of *ego*, treating the representational object of our self in the landscape of the simulation as if it were what it represented, making the assumption that the map *is* the territory. And as that simulation capacity develops phylogenetically and ontogenetically, it begins to include the simulations of others ("theory of mind") and their simulations of our simulations, and so forth—that is, moral and social perspective taking. As a species, we must have the natural world mediated to us by the social. To simulate the social world, we must use the cognitive architecture we evolved through hundreds of thousands of years of living in hunter-gatherer tribes. To interact with society, we modify our simulation capacity to represent others and ourselves in roles and rules. We treat others and ourselves as objects that are slotted into behavioral scripts. There is an enormous social advantage in learning to represent your self to yourself as an object in a social and simulated landscape, the same advantage as is afforded by simulating the natural world. We can carry out trial-and-error selection in purely mental realms, and this proceeds hypothetically or imaginatively, generating behavioral scripts in which we are cast as objects among others, and consequently avoid punishment, the withdrawal of approval and love, and guilt and shame.

So society mediates the natural world to us, and we are again mediated to the social world by the representation of others and ourselves as egos in a scripted world. But there is one other factor that we have evolved and makes our species so unique—language. Language evolved initially to improve on some of the constraints of our biological architecture, that is, working memory limits, attention span, perceptual filters, and so forth. Language structures cognition while enhancing it. Our social selves, our egos, use the structures of language to craft the ego as well. The ego, and the resultant identities we form, reflects unique aspects of culture as structured by language practices that vary enormously across cultures. Language evolved as a tool for the prosthesis of thought, but it is a tool that in turn forms and informs the selves we develop as we grow into our social worlds.

Not only does our social simulation capacity, and its product—ego—benefit us enormously in trial-and-error simulation of behavior, it affords an enormous benefit in terms of its power to regulate and control behaviour. For children, we can see that much of early development is about self-regulation, about the control of behavior, that is, following plans, monitoring performance, and inhibiting distractions. If we can control ourselves, we can escape the need to be controlled by social rewards and punishments and can better reap the benefits of belonging and participating in social collectives. Thus we develop ontogenetically from being egocentric and instrumental hedonists to being conforming and rule-abiding social selves that fit into the social world. We accept our social self as definitive of what and who we are. The more we are unaware that the powers of self-observation and self-administration are initially derived from the exigencies of interacting with others, from "outside" as it were, the more we will not be able to see that we have become in fact our own controllers, our own jailers, rewarders, and conscience, the better we are controlled. This is the basis of *identification*, whereby to have and be close to those we love we take on their attributes to such an extent that we become what we have internalized. Children, adolescents, and even adults at what Kohlberg (1984) calls stage 3 moral reasoning, or what Kegan (1982) calls the interpersonal, or what Loevinger (1976) calls the conformist stages of ego development, cannot see themselves as distinct from the norms into which they have become identified. It is a property of the architecture of our minds that what was once learned behavior becomes habit and what was once habit becomes character, partly as a result of the brain's processing of elements into chunks through the mechanism of *automatization*. This is a biologically evolved capacity that enabled our ancestors to overcome working memory limitations. Once we have automatized what we have learned, we free up attentional capacity to attend to or process other aspects of our worlds. The trade-off is that we are no longer "conscious" of what we have overlearned or automatized. In effect, the learning goes underground and can control our emotional and cognitive experiencing without our being aware of what is pulling the strings from behind the scenes, as it were.

As children we learn our first behavioral scripts, our first moral prescriptions and codes, our first rules and norms, at a stage in life when our representational capabilities are quite limited and our linguistic abilities primitive as compared to the more sophisticated capabilities we evolve into as adults. Nevertheless, these are the scripts, routines, and self-representations that become automatized into the synapses of our brains as children and carried forward into adulthood, working largely between the reciprocal fibers connecting the frontal lobes and limbic system: directing attention, emotion, behavior, and cognition in ways we have lost consciousness of. This is how what Roger Gould (1978) described as "childhood consciousness" continues to dominate present consciousness and why he makes the point that the task of adulthood and therapy is to undo the hold that childhood consciousness has on us by engaging in what he calls the seven steps for processing contradictory realities.

In childhood, with its limited representational and centration capacity, and the need to accommodate to larger social realities that threaten to withdraw their approval and love from us or to punish us for violations of little understood rules, one of the most effective ways to cope with internal processes that threaten to disrupt social harmony, is to *repress*, to simply deny the existence of the threatening impulse or thought. If the repression is repeated, it becomes automatized and is thereby forgotten as the child becomes more adept at inserting him- or herself into more complex social realities. The repression is forgotten as more aspects of our capacity to relate to our bodies and others become straitjacketed into social conformity and acceptance. With maturity we have the opportunity to rewrite scripts and automatisms, to free ourselves from the control of internalized norms by interrupting habitual scripts, no longer having to accept our ego-boundedness as definitive of our being. Having overlearned much of the behavioral formulas required for socialized adaptation, some of us might have the mental capacity remaining to become mindful of internal processes and felt emotions that are normally at the periphery of consciousness and that are not necessarily encoded in linguistic structures. Some of us might begin to use language to free ourselves from our early linguistic conditioning, to re-script or reauthor our early identities laid down in youth and immaturity. Some of us might take up practices or recreational activities that open our consciousness to transpersonal realities that are beyond and behind the very personae of ego that we have used all of our lives and hid behind while we crafted a social presentation. This can lead to attempts to see through our linguistically filtered reality. We may find ourselves giving up self-control and emotional self-regulation altogether, to relax the habitual control of the affective by the cognitive (Labouvie-Vief, 1994). We might actively seek out and entertain paradoxes and contradictory realities or shadow selves that

heretofore we would never have allowed access to in our conscious lives. These types of changes, generally confined to the midlife, can in some circumstances set the stage for a transformation of ego, a development beyond ego into what some call *transpersonal* levels of consciousness, or what has traditionally been styled as *spiritual development*.

LEARNING AND DEVELOPMENT

Learning and development are often not conceptualized adequately in either research or theory, yet keeping them conceptually clear and examining how they interact has important implications when we examine adult development. Stage development shows increased complexity with age, although often development will stop for some, and in a few cases sometimes development will regress. Learning, by contrast, evidences some profound decrements with aging, and these decrements begin to manifest in middle adulthood, becoming more pronounced with late adulthood. This holds true even though under optimal conditions, learning can continue well into old age. Learning decrements are found chiefly in two areas of research: studies of cognition in experimental laboratories and in life span differences obtained in intelligence testing. In her review of cognitive deficits found in laboratory studies of middle aged adults, Laura Berk (2004) identifies the following cognitive difficulties that begin to appear at this age. She summarizes these as problems in performing on the following types of tasks:

- Sustaining two complex tasks at the same time
- Attending to relevant information only
- Switching back and forth between operations
- Combining many pieces of information into meaningful patterns
- Resisting interference from irrelevant information: cognitive inhibition
- Working memory decrements
- Declining use of memory strategies
- Retrieving from long-term memory

These deficits are said to be the result of biological aging and neural degeneration with a resultant slowing down of the nervous system. Researchers attribute these deficits as due to the aging of the hardware of the brain. The aging of the brain's hardware is also the explanation for the declines in intelligence test performance that have been observed for many years. It was formerly believed that IQ itself began to decline in middle adulthood, but now researchers, using a combination of longitudinal as opposed to cross-sectional research methodologies and variously testing for indicators of crystallized as well as fluid intelligence, have concluded that it is only the latter that declines, beginning in middle adulthood. Crystallized intelligence only begins its slow decline well into late adulthood. Crystallized intelligence is learned and stored cultural knowledge, whereas fluid intelligence is closer to what we might understand as processing capacity. Paul Baltes (1997) and others (such as Schaie 1994, of the intelligence testing tradition) attribute adult wisdom to the fact that one type of late adult crystallized intelligence—practical expertise in solving problems—increases well into old age and accounts for the fact that the elderly are said to have more wisdom than the young (Sternberg, 1990).

But this approach looks solely to the domain of learning for indications of positive development in late adulthood. The learning tradition, whether the cognitive or the intelligence testing traditions, are still heavily influenced by behaviorist assumptions, and one of them is that development is fundamentally continuous and cumulative throughout the life span and really is in no way different from learning. Another tradition, stemming from Piaget, asserts that life span changes are not simply a function of learning and involve truly developmental changes in underlying structures that determine what learning takes place. Development is discontinuous and involves qualitative changes that are sudden and not gradual. Qualitative change arises from underlying structures that evolve very much in the manner that Piaget said that logicomathematical structures evolve. They evolve by accommodation, by reorganizations of structures of experience that determine how learning and experience are assimilated, how meaning is made, and how cognitive and intellectual learning is informed and shaped.

The neo-Piagetian tradition assumes that the latter structures are more equilibrated, more adapted, and can assimilate more than earlier structures, and that they transcend and include lower order structures so that the higher order structures are qualitatively "better" than lower structures. Structures of meaning in adulthood and aging are therefore "higher" in the sense of being more inclusive. These structures of meaning have been found to occur more frequently in later years and are relatively absent in youth. Although the higher structures are rare at all age levels, they are rarer in childhood, adolescence, and early adulthood. And if there are indeed genuine developmental changes that are unique to middle and late adulthood, then they will have a profound impact on the nature and quality of the learning that occurs at this time (often compensating for decrements found in such learning as well).

In this chapter, I consider one type of qualitative development that some researchers have identified: spiritual development. For the present purposes, I shall treat only of models of *self* or *ego* development and *consciousness* development, the higher ends of which I will consider *spiritual* development. For a fuller treatment of development the reader is referred to my book, *Human Development and the Spiritual Life: How Consciousness Grows Toward Transformation*, from which I have summarized the following models fairly closely and where I also address other models of self development as well as models of moral and intellectual development (Irwin, 2002). See table 14.1 for the theoretical correspondences among stages in the developmental models I explore in this chapter.

Robert Kegan and the Evolution of Self Stages

Kegan (1982, 1994) shows that transformations in the structure by which subject/object relations are made explain changes across the life span in how meaning is made. Development is a dialectic of a successive disembedding from within what had been the organization of self and world. Each successive organizing subject becomes an object for a newly equilibrated subject. The making of self as object explains development, and the making of self over into object explains how simulation constructs ego. The simulation of self is at first a function of socialization such that the self cannot see its conditioning. When the simulation is seen as object, the self has the freedom to disidentify and step back from it, so that the simulation can be seen *as* a simulation and so that the self need not *be* the simulation.

At the impulsive stage the actions and sensations of reflexes and sensorimotor schemes are object to emerging impulses and perceptions—the subject at this stage. The subject equilibrates next as the needs,

Table 14.1 Theoretical Correspondence Among Stages of Development Models

Kegan: Self Stages	Fowler: Faith Development Stages	Cook-Greuter: Ego Development and Egolessness	Alexander: Cognitive Developmental and Transcendental Consciousness	Wilber: Spectrum of Consciousness
Impulsive	Undifferentiated	Presocial, symbiotic, impulsive	Action/senses	Sensoriphysical
Imperial	Intuitive-projective	Self-protective	Desire	Phantasmal-emotional
Interpersonal	Mythic-literal			
	Synthetic-conventional	Conformist, self-aware	Mind	Representational mind Role/rule
Institutional	Individuative-reflective	Conscientious	Intellect	Formal-Reflexive
Interindividual	Conjunctive	Individualistic, Autonomous	Intuition	Vision-logic
	Universalizing	Construct-aware	Ego	Transpersonal
		Unitive	Transpersonal	

Note: Stage progression is from the top (lower stages) to the bottom (higher stages) of the table.

interests, and wishes of the imperial stage, which take as object the prior impulses and perceptions. These needs are in turn decentered and become object at the interpersonal stage to the emerging interpersonal subject. Embedded in the conventional and symbolic, identified with the structures of representation of self as ego afforded by the simulation powers of that stage, the individual is identified with its social roles and rules. The interpersonal becomes object to the institutional stage. The institutional as subject is autonomous and systemic. The institutional self *has* the simulation and can act apart from it and alter it reflectively. Next, the institutional is decentered and becomes object to the subject of the interindividual, an organization that is intersystemic and dialectically interactive, and the highest level of development for Kegan. Consciousness and awareness can be experienced outside the structuring of representational filters and lenses.

Kegan's (1994) more recent version is framed in narrative terms. With the third, fourth, and fifth orders—the interpersonal, institutional, and interindividual—Kegan employs the metaphor of *authoring*. At the third order, the self is subject to authority. Traditions are closely adhered to. The self *is* its beliefs, values, and roles. Third-order consciousness is lived by its plot, unaware of the stories by which it is scripted. At the third order, the self *is* the

simulation; the self *is* the ego. There is no perspective *on* the simulation, so there is no way the simulation can be seen *as* simulation.

With the fourth order the self is its own author, similar to the way the writer of dramas invents plots and scripts with the materials at hand (albeit culturally and linguistically determined). The self can be distinct from its story. The self is reflectively conscious of how it can alter and invent aspects of the simulation. The self may experience what Kegan called the loss of community or the loss of "gods" as it becomes conscious of its freedom and lack of determination by social conditioning. Beliefs are taken as objects by an identity as subject no longer owned by social roles and values.

At the fifth order, the self lets go its identifications with systems, ideologies, and mechanisms of self-control by which its personal authority had been maintained. The self develops into a mode of being where it can even let go of its authoring. The self's autonomy and independence are questioned. Rather than identify with any particular self-system that is authored, the self identifies with the interaction between systems as they are authored in interaction. Emotions are more freely expressed because no feeling threatens this less independent perspective. The self sees the processes of simulation and sees that simulations interact and condition each other. In seeing this process and this dialectic, the self no longer identifies with any one simulation. The self locates its freedom in the zone where simulations or representations are synthesized and seen through.

The institutional stage is experienced as limiting and isolating, its autonomy perceived as empty. People transiting out from the institutional stage feel they would rather not hold the reins of identity and authority all the time. They desire to go with the flow of experience, to let go emotionally, physically, and mentally. The institutional self is concerned with self-maintenance and self-control, life as an enterprise, feelings as things to be administered. Once the workings of the simulation are "deconstructed," the self identifies with those aspects of its being that are not represented—that are nonegoic. This affords a letting go and a breaking through the fictive and the representational. The self may locate its center in the organismic, the unconscious, the social, or the numinous. The institutional stage is about self-talk and self-surveillance. The interindividual stage is about going beyond talk and surveillance, beyond language and representation, and beyond prediction and control. As the interindividual dawns, the self becomes more porous and permeable: letting things out and taking things in. This can bring about ecstatic abandonment and transcendent intimacy but also loss of self-esteem and meaning. The interindividual stage involves:

> the relaxation of one's vigilance, a sense of flow and immediacy, a freeing up of one's internal life, an openness to and playfulness about oneself. . . . the same loosening up may be experienced as boundary loss, impulse flooding, and, as always, the experience of *not knowing*. This last can speak itself in terms of felt meaninglessness. (Kegan, 1982, p. 231)

Kegan's subject-object interviews assess stages of the self or stages of meaning making. The content of the interviews involves emotional, cognitive, intrapersonal, and interpersonal concerns. Interrater reliability estimates range from 0.75 to 0.90 and test-retest reliability is 0.83. There is high consistency across alternate forms, different domains, and test items. Kegan cites high correlations with like interviews as evidence of validity.

Kegan (1994) cited Lisa Lahey, who performed interviews with 22 subjects, addressing their love and work lives. Subjects were interviewed annually for four years with one five-year follow-up. Lahey was able to make six reliable distinctions between any two orders of consciousness. In their ratings, subjects were no more than one discrimination apart in both interviews—love life and work life—in 18 of 22 cases. Subjects generally developed in a forward direction through the stages. There was never movement of more than one fifth of a position per year. With a larger sample of 282 subjects, Kegan noted that one-half to two-thirds of those interviewed had not yet reached the institutional stage.

James Fowler and Stages of Faith Development

In his research, Fowler asked his subjects to narrate what he called their faith. By this he meant their way of making meaning, of moving into "the force field of life" (Fowler, 1995, p. 4), an "alignment of the will" (p. 14), and "a resting of the heart"(p. 14). Most basically, faith is an "active mode of knowing, of composing a felt sense or image of the condition of our lives taken as a whole. It unifies our lives' force fields" (p. 25).

The child begins at undifferentiated faith. The child learns a basic sense of trust from the primary caregiver but may have to face abandonment. The trust established forms the basis for hope and courage, but a failure at this stage leads to narcissism.

Fowler makes stage 1 proper the one of intuitive-projective faith. By three to seven years of age, the child has a mental life that is based on fantasy and imitation, influenced by examples and stories heard. The child can form elementary simulations or representations but is entirely at their mercy. The child is ruled by images and feelings, but has no logic. The first apprehensions of sex, death, and taboo occur. Awareness is primarily egocentric. The child may become concerned by excessive taboos and moral demands, or overwhelmed by images of terror.

Stage 2 is mythic-literal faith. The child can narrate experience, not just receive stories. These stories express social truths, which are believed literally as rules. The child can take the perspective of others but cannot step back from its stories to reflect on them. The simulations constructed in the social world enter as if real into the emerging and developing, yet limited representational processes of the child or adolescent. Imagination then becomes ordered. The risk is an overcontrolling perfectionism or sense of badness.

Stage 3 is synthetic-conventional faith. Authority is placed outside the self, in the "they." Different social worlds demand that the adolescent take in and synthesize values and information to construct an identity. Choices and commitments have been made, but the reality is that these, as defined by "they," have made the self. As we saw in Kegan's model, the self is embedded in the simulations at stage 3 and cannot know its world apart from the representations afforded by language and concepts that have their genesis in social processes. The first personal myths are formed, but they are formed nonreflectively and without active narrative choice. Stage 3 is conformist, geared to the expectations of others, such that there can be no stepping outside of expectations and social structures whereby a perspective might be obtained on them. The adolescent *has* an ideology but cannot objectify it. The danger at stage 3 is one of too much internalization impairing judgment or of betrayals, precipitating nihilism or a retreat to an otherworldly religion.

Stage 4 is individuative-reflective faith. The reliance on external sources of authority weakens. Authority is centered within. People can step out of their life stream and compose a myth of their own. Identity is no longer defined by roles and meanings set by others. Responsibility is assumed for commitments, for choosing a lifestyle, and for beliefs and attitudes. Awareness develops of even *having* a worldview, of having a simulation or representation that is different from what it is intended to represent. Yet experiences are still firmly acted on and perceived from within some perspective or structuring. Going away from home often brings a stage 3–4 transition, but becoming absorbed in groups and relationships can prevent this.

Stage 5 is conjunctive faith. Stage 5 develops beyond the logic of either/or, seeing both sides of an issue and attending to the relatedness of things. Conjunctive faith can let go its mindset, its simulation, allowing the known to speak its own language, as if able to remove its colored lenses and see light, color, and form nakedly. It maintains a vulnerability to the other freed from the confines of class, religion, or nation. Stage 5 opens to the repressed parts of the self, becoming more porous and permeable to unconscious and physical processes. The danger at stage 5 is in passive inaction or cynical withdrawal.

Stage 6 is universalizing faith. Stage 6 transcends ego and lives in the reality of a God, which "intends the fulfillment of creation and the unity of being." The individual submits to the "Kingdom of God" defined by "a quality of righteousness in which each person or being is augmented by the realization of the futurity of all the others" (Fowler, 1995, p. 205).

Stage 6 individuals bring into question our ideas about normality. They live on the side of transcendent actuality, universal compassion, and ultimate respect for being, rather than on the side of self-interest, parochial vision, and conventional standards of morality that only conceal societal claims.

Fowler's account of faith at stage 6 is framed as a relationship with a *transcendent* presence to which one relates by becoming an "incarnation" of its presence. This contrasts to approaches we shall consider shortly, in which we see the sacred in *immanent* terms: one in which self is infused with the sacred from within.

Fowler states that his stages have a normative dimension by which we can decide what is "good faith." For Fowler, as for Alexander and other neo-Piagetians, the way we conceive of higher stages shapes how the lower stages are framed. Elsewhere, Fowler wrote (1995, p. 298): "I fully expect that our present stage descriptions will undergo a significant process of elimination of Western and Christian biases and that the genuinely structural features will emerge with greater clarity." Fowler interviewed practically no one outside of the Judeo-Christian faith traditions, and my opinion is that the descriptions of his stages, particularly the higher ones, are biased because of this. Fowler had only one subject at his highest stage, so no generalizations can be made regarding his description of the universalizing stage.

Fowler interviewed 359 subjects. With his method of content analysis he derived an interrater reliability of 85–90% agreement. Although his data are cross-sectional, he infers a developmental progression by plotting his data to reveal a clear shift in stage frequency with age (Fowler, 1995, p. 318). His assertion regarding the validity of his stages would be further strengthened by longitudinal data.

With age, the range of scores increases. At younger ages, subjects are only at the early stages. As they get older, more subjects are identified at the higher stages, but only some. Many subjects fail to develop beyond stage 2 or 3, peaking in early adulthood. As subjects age the lower stages decrease in frequency, and higher stages appear more frequently. Fowler found that the individuative-reflective stage seldom appeared before 21 years of age, and the conjunctive stage never appeared before 31 years of age.

Jane Loevinger and Ego Development

Jane Loevinger (1976) hypothesizes ego as a "master trait," subsuming four domains: character development, cognitive style, interpersonal style, and conscious preoccupations. The developing ego is a progressive reorganization of self in relation to the social and physical environment, a reorganization of underlying structure that shares many of the characteristics of a Piagetian structure of operations.

At the presocial stage, the infant does not have any ego at all which might differentiate it from its world. With the symbiotic stage the infant achieves the stability of objects. The child is still in symbiotic fusion with its mother, but self/nonself differentiation has begun. With the impulsive stage, impulses are the core of identity. The child is curbed only by constraints, and later by rewards and punishments. Others are seen for what they can give to the child. Good and bad mean "nice-to-me" and "mean-to-me," respectively. The child is preoccupied with bodily impulses. The child is oriented to the present and lacks a notion of psychological causation, but does have the rudiments of physical causation.

At the self-protective stage, the child learns to anticipate rewards and punishments and thereby to have its first guarded controls. The child comes to have a sense of rules, of "don't get caught," but only uses these rules for his or her own advantage. The child tends to externalize blame, as he or she is not capable of self-criticism. The child has a kind of opportunistic hedonism. The child begins to have a sense of self as object, an ego, which he or she inserts into a simulated social world so that the child can anticipate rewards and punishments and avoid disapproval and censure.

At the conformist stage the individual identifies with the welfare of the group. He or she follows rules, not for fear of punishment but because of identification with the rules. The child has the representational capacity to construct a simulation of self and world and identify with the simulation as the world. The child, or perhaps adolescent, cannot *not* identify with the self as representation; the child *is* the representation. The disapproval of others becomes a potent sanction, because both others and the rules are experienced as arising within and not deriving from without. The individual has become the object to his or her own gaze and becomes socialized as a result by being cast as an object to him- or herself. The individual strives for a compliance with rules not just because of their consequences. The individual attends to the group and not to individual differences. Such individuals reject the out-group and stereotype roles. They emphasize niceness, helpfulness, and cooperation. Behaviors are judged externally, not in terms of feelings or intentions. When asked about their internal life, we get a banal description of feelings. The individual adheres to clichés, appearances, and social reputation. Security is equated with belonging.

With the self-aware stage, the self becomes distinct from norms and expectations, an object of reflection, and therefore can create a space for exceptions to cultural expectations. The self can at times step back from the ego as simulation and see its position as object in the mental landscape of the social world. There is an increase in self-awareness and an appreciation of multiple possibilities. The adolescent or adult does not always have to live up to social norms. There is a growing inner life, but it is couched as banal feelings, always with reference to others. Loevinger's research has indicated that the self-aware stage is the modal stage of adults.

At the conscientious stage we have the major elements of conscience: long-term self-evaluated goals and ideals, differentiated self-criticism, and a sense of responsibility. The internalization of rules is completed. Adult evaluate and choose their own rules and will break the law to follow their own code. Guilt arises from hurting others, rather than breaking rules. The individual can be said to have his or her own self or identity apart from the group: Rules are fully internalized but are owned in a more conscious manner—standards are self-chosen, traits are conceptualized as part of an interior world. The self as representation, the ego, is known consciously and reflectively. The adult has a sense of obligations and a sense of rights. Individuals distinguish standards from manners. They can process complex polarities and have a rich and differentiated inner life. The self can reflect on the elements of its mental landscape and can process and perceive its ego as object in relation to the other objects of its world. The individual can introspect and examine traits and motives, not just actions. We can speak of mutuality in interpersonal relations, for the self can be seen from the other's point of view, with a longer time perspective and a consideration of social context.

With the individualistic stage, along with a heightened sense of individuality there is at the same time as an acknowledgment and concern with emotional dependence. The self distances itself from roles. Subjective experience is emphasized over the now questioned status of "objective reality." The representation or simulation of self is less monolithic; there are gaps in the simulation through which feelings and intuitions are accorded more reality. There is a greater tolerance of self and others, yet relationships are experienced as partly antagonistic. A greater awareness of inner conflict replaces the moralism of the conscientious. Representations depend on context for meaning and are often perceived as contradictory. The individualistic person tolerates paradox and contradiction and the discrepancy between inner reality and outward appearance. There is a deepening appreciation of psychological causality and development.

At the autonomous stage an individual acknowledges the inner conflicts of needs versus duties. The contradictions are not only tolerated but actively sought. Individuals may try to transcend polar opposites and will grant how reality is more complex and multifaceted than their thinking has allowed. The person unites and integrates ideas with a high toleration of ambiguity. The individual recognizes the other's need for autonomy. The demands of conscience become attenuated. The person sees the inevitability of emotional interdependence with others. As the self integrates more of its compartmentalized identities, its competing and often varying simulations, it strives for a meaning based in self-actualization. With a greater interest in development, there is awareness that motives have a history. The autonomous are more aware of how they function differently in different roles. There is a vivid expression of sensual experiences, poignant sorrows, and existential humor.

Finally, with the integrated stage there is a transcendence of conflicts. There is true self-actualizing and a full sense of identity. In Loevinger's original work this stage was rare and limited by the theorist's ability to describe it. We see in our consideration of Cook-Greuter's work (later) how this and the autonomous stage became refined and described with the analysis of new data.

Manners and Durkin (2001) presented a review of empirical work on the Loevinger model. Generally speaking, the theory holds up well to empirical testing. The old 1970 version of the coding scheme by Loevinger and Redmore has been updated by a version by Hy and Loevinger (1996). Manners and Durkin present many types of studies, and I want to highlight the results of three kinds: reliability, predictive validity, and longitudinal validity.

Loevinger's coding scheme as set forth in the manual for rating Sentence Completion Tests (SCTs) is highly reliable, receiving a Cronbach's alpha of 0.91 for interrater reliability. They also report split-half and test-retest reliabilities. In my own experience, I have had an undergraduate fourth-year student train herself by the method and achieve high reliabilities in the middle ranges of SCT scores. It is more difficult to obtain reliabilities for the upper stages of the Loevinger model and harder still to code for the higher stages Cook-Greuter has identified (see following discussion).

SCT scores have been positively correlated to many measures of social, interpersonal, and emotional functioning. For example, using the California Psychological Inventory to tap Allport's levels of interpersonal maturity yielded high correlations. SCT scores are correlated to the Harvey, Hunt, and Schroder (1961) model of conceptual complexity. Labouvie-Vief, DeVoe, and Bulka (1989) used a four-level rating scheme for emotional understanding of anger, sadness, fear, and happiness. Ego development was correlated with understanding the complexity of emotions. Labouvie-Vief, Hakim-Larson, DeVoe, and Schoeberlein (1989) developed a scheme of emotional self-regulation based on Labouvie-Vief's (1994) four levels of self-regulation: presystemic, intrasystemic, intersystemic, and integrated, and found a significant correlation to SCT scores. Lane used a 5-point rating system for complexity of emotional responses to 20 hypothetical scenarios and found similar results. SCT scores are also correlated to the Kagan and Schneider affect sensitivity scale (Werner, Kagan, & Schneider, 1977). SCT scores are generally correlated to Kohlberg (1984) moral development levels. But the SCT does not seem correlated to major measures of purely intellectual functioning, such as the reflective judgment interview or the Commons and Richards (1984) multisystemic reasoning tasks.

Manners and Durkin (2001) report the results of five major longitudinal studies with the SCT in which confirmatory results were obtained. Generally speaking, subjects do evidence progressive ego development, and if more than a year or two is allotted for retesting, most show stage changes (about one stage every four to five years). However there is some evidence of stage regression (sometimes 10% of a sample).

Cook-Greuter on Development of Ego and Egolessness

Susan Cook-Greuter (1990, 1994, 1995) has researched the ego development model of Loevinger for years, scoring thousands of protocols using the Washington University SCT, a projective assessment instrument employing 36 sentence stems. Focusing on the higher stages of ego development, Cook-Greuter has made distinctions that Loevinger's method failed to find. Cook-Greuter argues for the existence of higher stages than Loevinger posited.

Cook-Greuter distinguishes her stage 5/6 (the construct-aware) from both stage 5 (the autonomous) and stage 6 (the unitive). She has developed a means of coding for distinctions between these stages and has trained novice raters to criteria (correlations were 0.79 to 0.95, Cronbach's alpha was 0.95, and percent agreement among raters was 93.3).

In what she calls the postautonomous stage (or at other times the construct-aware stage), people are described as changing in two significant ways: with respect to attitude toward language and with respect to ego as a mechanism of self-control. Regarding the new attitude toward language, in earlier stages of development, language is valued because it allows communication between people, enabling us to cognitively package reality into discrete entities placed in conceptual maps. In later stages, by contrast, language is experienced as filtering the underlying reality and detracting from much of the richness of experience.

People take a new attitude toward their egos at higher stages. Whereas in earlier stages, people take pleasure in thinking about their complexity and contradiction—that is, in thinking about themselves—at the construct-aware stage, people question their "objective self-identity" altogether, no longer wishing to be in control in the ways they have been by means of concepts and thinking (what I refer to as simulations). Self-control requires being too concerned with the *image* of self. People at the construct-aware stage yearn for a mode of being based on noncontrol,

a mode of existing not requiring effort, grounded in "radical openness," a mode not grounded in ego at all.

Cook-Greuter notes that this stage is equal in significance to the development from the *prerepresentational* to *representational* stages, which required intense socialization and the learning of language. Likewise, the construct-aware stage, as the transitional stage from *representational* to *postrepresentational* development for Cook-Greuter, requires cultural supports altogether different from those required in childhood, supports that do *not* require further socialization and that can include aspects of wisdom traditions such as meditation techniques, lineages, and teachers.

Cook-Greuter's work is significant in finding an empirical basis for the transition into what can be called *transpersonal* stages of development. She identifies two characteristics of such development that make the individual ready for a new kind of learning. Meditation is a kind of learning that requires development on the part of the learner and cultural support on the part of the social order. In the absence of either, meditation likely will not be effective and not facilitate any further development. But when development opens up a space beyond ego and behind language, meditation will allow for states, experiences, and eventually stages of transpersonal being to emerge. This transition to postrepresentational development is as significant and as difficult as the transition to representational development, requiring intensive social support and mediation. Transpersonal development is rare; this is because development at the individual level often does not provide the prerequisite structures and because culture does not provide the supportive structures for the learning of such unconventional experiences. Such experiences are often at variance with what the culture and society require of individuals simply for the purposes of survival and reproduction.

The characteristics of the construct-aware stage reveal a consciousness still immersed in the personal, still operating within representational thinking, but now yearning for an existence beyond such limits. In rare cases, the construct-aware stage is transcended by the unitive stage (which replaces the integrated stage of Loevinger in Cook-Greuter's reformulation of ego development). Embedded in the process of creation, the unitive self experiences the concrete and momentary as one with the eternal. Things are accepted as they are. Ego boundaries are transcended. The nonduality of subject and object is revealed.

Charles Alexander on Piaget and Transcendental Consciousness

The stage model I consider next is based in Eastern philosophy and Western psychology, the latter mostly Piagetian developmental psychology. The Eastern components derive from the Vedic tradition, that is, the Vedanta philosophy found in the teachings of Maharishi Mahesh Yogi. Charles Alexander, until his recent death, was a student of the Maharishi and a professor at the Maharishi International University. Alexander discussed his work on a number of occasions at meetings of the Society for Research in Adult Development, and some of this appeared in two chapters of research appearing in anthologies stemming from those meetings (Alexander et al., 1990, 1994).

Alexander used the Piagetian stages of development and added several stages of his own, drawing from the Eastern wisdom tradition with which he was most familiar. Specifically, he drew from the *Sankhya* account of *levels of mind* and related these to Piaget's stages. In his account, mind begins at the level of *action* and the *senses*, which Alexander related to Piaget's sensorimotor stage. The child is said to act on and take in the external world through the senses. The self is not differentiated from the world, nor does it possess any symbols or permanent objects.

Developing from this is the next level of mind: desire, or the early representational, which Alexander relates to Piaget's preoperational stage. The child uses speech and can represent both self and others. The child constructs her first simple representations to monitor in her consciousness both action and sensation. The child possesses goal-directed behavior but is still egocentric. Alexander equated this level with Loevinger's impulsive stage.

The next level of mind is *mind* per se, which is the same as Piaget's concrete operations. The individual can step back from the representational screen, from the simulation, as it were, to coordinate perceptions and representations in time and space. This is the first capacity to take a perspective on mental content, to step back and act on the given of representational construction. This comparative mind generates classes and relations. Mind can conserve operations and decenter in the way Piaget spoke of, but it can only entertain the concrete. Alexander related this level to Loevinger's conformist stage.

Intellect is the next level of mind in the *Sankhya* system, and Alexander connected it to Piaget's formal operational stage. Intellect operates on concrete representations, making possible logical thinking and decision making. Intellect subordinates the actual to the possible. Intellect also possesses self-reflection, ushering in the period of identity formation. Intellect can construct a perspective at one degree from propositions, can think about thinking, and can act on propositions and on self-representations, such that it is no longer owned or contained by such propositions, but rather comes to own and author propositional thinking. Alexander equated Loevinger's conscientious stage with the level of intellect.

Intuition is the next level of mind and was identified by Alexander with what were termed postformal operational stages, supposed fifth stages moving beyond Piaget's standard formulation (Commons & Richards, 1984). Intuition is relational, aware of change, and sensitive to the context of objects of reflection. Intuition includes dialectical operations (Basseches, 1984), whereby thinking seeks out knowledge not consistent with current ways of thinking. This affords the relating of opposing systems of thought. Intuition is less dominated by language and logical reasoning. Intuition integrates affect and intellect. Abstract thought is integrated with responsibilities and commitments in real-life application. The mind can step back from systems of propositions now and think about systems of propositions, and can further relate thinking about systems of propositions with the intuitive and affective. Simulations about more complex aspects of reality are really systems of propositions connected in logical ways. Being able to act on systems of propositions, the self can own and author different systems without being identified with such systems. Different simulations can be compared to other simulations and processes that are not simulated at all. The self doing such processing is not equated with the simulation. The self owns such simulations and is no longer at the level of mind where the self *is* what is simulated or is identified with *what* is simulated, which is the case at the level of mind. Alexander identified intuition with the autonomous stage of Loevinger.

The next level of mind in *Sankhya* is ego, and it is where unbounded pure consciousness connects with the current process of knowing. Ego is the transitional level of mind between the personal and transpersonal levels, identified with wisdom and the relating together of opposing systems of thought. Alexander identified ego with Loevinger's integrated stage.

In Alexander's model, there are seven states of consciousness. The first are part of our daily lives: sleeping, dreaming, and waking consciousness. All of the levels of mind experience these. With the development of intuition and ego, the fourth, fifth, sixth, and seventh states of consciousness are more likely to occur. These, for Alexander, are the transpersonal states. The fourth state of consciousness is transcendental consciousness, which is the temporary experience of an inner, unbounded, unified self that transcends the boundaries between knower, known, and the process of knowing. The fifth is cosmic consciousness, in which this same inner, unified mind is maintained in consciousness along with the other levels of mind. The sixth is refined or glorified cosmic consciousness, a profound intimacy between self and environment, whereby the unified mind pervades more of experience. Objects are seen not just as separate objects but as part of a field of energy with which the self feels connected to but different from. The seventh state is unity consciousness, the unification of the inner and the outer, such that reality is not experienced as different from self.

To demonstrate the effectiveness of meditation, Alexander often employed the Loevinger SCT as the dependent variable; transcendental meditation (TM) enhances the development of ego (the benefits of TM are also found with other cognitive and neurophysiological measures, such as measures of intelligence, moral judgment, and EEG coherence). Alexander's dissertation research showed that in comparison to controls, the TM practitioners (prison inmates) demonstrated higher levels of ego development, generally moving from the self-protective to conformist to conscientious stages in a few years.

For Alexander, *identity*, in the sense of Erikson, is achieved at the *Sankhya* level of intellect. Alexander describes identity as an internalization of roles and sees the project of identity as inherently flawed. Identity is a way of answering the question of what we *are* by framing an answer in terms of what we *do*; identity fails to answer the question of being that is only answered in spiritual terms when we overcome the separation of the subject from the object in the transcendental and posttranscendental states of consciousness. The question of identity for Alexander is not what object we are by virtue of its actions or what can be represented of them. The question of identity requires that we transcend making objects of ourselves by our limited simulation capacity. The answer to the question of identity is that we cease being objects to ourselves and transcend the structure of subject-object duality.

Ken Wilber on Integral Psychology and the Spectrum of Consciousness

As one part of his *Integral Psychology* (Wilber, 2000), Ken Wilber describes a theory of life span development that, like Alexander, goes beyond stages as described in Western psychology by drawing on a diverse variety of sources in Eastern wisdom traditions (Wilber, 1986a, 1986b, 1986c, 1993, 1996a, 1996b). His lower stages derive from Piaget, Freud, Maslow, Loevinger, Kohlberg, Kegan, Cook-Greuter, and others. The higher stages draw on mysticism, mostly of an Eastern source. Some of these models include Aurobindo, Kabbalah, Vedanta, Highest Yoga Tantra, and Patanjali (see Wilber's charts at the back of *Integral Psychology* for a fully worked out correspondence of all the stages, Western and Eastern). Wilber's model has been empirically investigated by Eugene Thomas (1994) in the analysis of interviews with elderly subjects.

Wilber describes a series of nine structures in the spectrum of consciousness that determine the predominant orientation of consciousness, its center of gravity, at each stage of development. For Wilber, each structure is a result of a negotiation of a particular *fulcrum* of development; the individual either progresses to the next structure or develops a pathology or developmental arrest. The process of development begins with a fusion at a level of consciousness. Then the individual differentiates a new structure. After the new structure is differentiated, it is then integrated with the prior structure. Wilber's model is a basic transcend-and-include theory of development.

There are nine different fulcrums that can be grouped into three levels. The first levels are the *prepersonal*, in which the child develops the first simple ego or mind, that is, representation of self and world, but it is not yet conceptual. At the sensoriphysical stage, the child is not differentiated from the world and is one with the sensorium of experience and physical interactions with it. As the physical body is differentiated from the world and from his or her mother, there develops a psychological world of desires and images that are often not differentiated from the objects of the world. This is the narcissistic phantasmal-emotional stage: the world is experienced as an extension of an emotional self.

With the personal levels, the child has a mind, that is, the child represents the world. In the terms of my book, the child begins to have simulations of the world in which he or she dwells and which replace living only in the physical world. From the earlier images, the child develops symbols. With symbols, the child constructs concepts. With the birth of the mental at the representational mind stage, the child separates the mental from the physical and learns how to control the body by means of the mind and therefore also to repress it. The representation or simulation of self is ego, and ego is constructed so that the individual can operate in the currency of self as object and self as controlled. Once self is controlled by simulation, self is freed from the necessity of social control.

The next of the personal levels is the role/rule stage in which the child combines and coordinates concepts into rules that control action. The child internalizes rules by identifying with them as scripts. Conventional moral judgment and action are the result. The child is capable of taking on roles and of viewing his or her own actions from the perspective of others.

With development into the formal/reflexive stage, the child takes a perspective on conventional norms so that he or she can think about thinking, taking the products of thinking as objects of thinking. The individual develops self-chosen ideals, morals, beliefs, and ideologies. These become the full-blown simulations by which the self makes of itself and others objects of social coordination. Persons reflect on, choose, and change their identity, often assuming a critical distance from earlier internalized roles.

The final stage of the personal, and the transition to the transpersonal, is the vision-logic stage. Wilber calls this stage the *centauric* because it is based on a new integration of mind and body (human and horse). Mind and body can be integrated because consciousness is not identified only with mind; it has a perspective on mind and can therefore integrate both mind and body in a higher level of consciousness.

At the vision-logic stage there is a greater authenticity. Consciousness is more organismic and existential, but this entails that not all emotions experienced at this stage are positive. Many of the experiences at this stage are described by Wilber in bleak and somber tones, as a dark night of the soul, as angst-ridden and full of dread, because the realm of the personal is dying, and the loss can be devastating. Because the personal is dying, there can be a great deal of depression and anxiety. The things of the world delight no more; samsara is felt intensely, and part of the lesson of samsara is that the pursuit of pleasure and of pain is inherently unsatisfactory (*dukkha*) and will inevitably defeat the attempts of ego to secure it. Individuals at this stage may seek out psychological and psychiatric treatment, and this treatment may impede development if neither the client nor the mental health professional has any understanding of higher development (Irwin, 2000).

With development into the transpersonal stages, the individual transcends both ego and representational mind (what, in my book, I call the belief in the "reality" of our simulations and, most important, belief that the simulation or fiction of our self as ego is true, static, fixed, or enduring). The transpersonal stages in Wilber are taken from Eastern sources. Few Western psychologists have explored them or phenomena pertaining to them. Wilber draws on descriptions of advanced spiritual development found in the Buddhist and Hindu Vedanta scriptures. Wilber calls the first transpersonal stage the psychic. It is characterized by nature mysticism. Peak experiences occur at this stage. Awareness is no longer confined to the ego. The self begins to identify with all beings. There are preliminary meditative states, shamanic visions, the arousing of kundalini, and feelings of the numinous. The second transpersonal stage is the subtle: It is characterized by deity mysticism. Here interior luminosities and sounds are experienced, archetypes, subtle bliss currents and cognitions, and expansive states of love and compassion. The third transpersonal stage is the causal: It is characterized by monistic mysticism. Here the self is pursued to its source, "emptiness" is experienced (the interdependence of all "things") such that no objects arise to consciousness, yet the self is "drenched in the fullness of being."

EGO DEVELOPMENT AND THE LEARNING OF MEDITATION

Meditation develops the *witness*: a consciousness not identified with the objects that pass by in awareness.

The witness first appears at the vision-logic stage, the stage at which we begin to have a perspective on both our body and our mind as we lose identification with either. With meditation, we can develop this resting awareness and let go of our attachments. After the causal stage, we can let go of the witness and become one with the nondual ground of our being, which is emptiness (*shunyata*).

Although meditation can help us relax or provide us with profound states of absorption or concentration at almost any level of development, it cannot assist us in transcending the ego until it can draw on the emerging witness, and for this we must be at the level of vision-logic in Wilber's terms, or the upper levels of mind in the *Sankhya* system, according to Alexander. Cook-Greuter argues that we must be at the postautonomous stage in the Loevinger model for meditation to help us pierce the veils of language and get beyond the control of ego. And I would argue that we must be at least at the conjunctive stage of faith development or at the interindividual stage of self-development before meditation can really assist us in relinquishing the reins of control and letting go of the conceptions of self and others that, until those stages, we adhere to so rigidly.

Buddhist meditation is more fully described in Irwin (2002). Meditation begins as *shamatha*, which is the learning of the one-pointedness of concentration, staying with the object, the breath, as distractions arise in perception and thought. As we learn and practice to let go of passing thoughts and return again to the breath, we are then ready for *vipashyana*. With vipashyana, we let the beam of attention open wider and pass gently over all sensation, all feeling, and all thinking, so that awareness becomes wide and free, allowing all things to pass through it, touching them as a feather touches a bubble (Chodron, 1997, pp. 54–55). With time, this practice affords insight into three marks of existence: *dukkha*, *anicca*, and *anatta*. Dukkha is the suffering and unsatisfactoriness inherent in all grasped things, anicca is the pervasiveness of impermanence, and anatta is the selflessness in all experience. Anatta is the insight that no self or ego can truly be found. It is the insight into the latter, a form of learning that really requires a level of development on the part of the practitioner and that in turn precipitates the learning of what samsara consists of. Once this learning is obtained in the felt depth of experience, an individual is then ready to move into the transpersonal stages, that is, to truly develop.

It would seem that insight into the three marks requires a readiness for transpersonal development. When meditation passes from concentration to insight, the veil of language over reality, and the fiction of ego in control, are both illusions that are let go. When language is let go, the territory becomes more important than the map. When ego is let go, mindfulness as witness replaces ego as surveillance. The reality of simulations is let go, and there is a gap allowed in the representation of self as this or that construct so that the hold or grip of ego on reality is released. These insights or learnings in meditation can only be assimilated by an ego at the construct-aware stage of Cook-Greuter and Loevinger or the vision-logic stage of Wilber, at the conjunctive stage of Fowler or the interindividual stage of Kegan. If the ego is not so developed, concentration will fail to pass into such depth of insight.

There are many other changes that we can relate to the increasing disposition that older individuals have toward spiritual concerns. I focused here on underlying qualitative changes in ego or consciousness development to explain why it is that spirituality is more relevant with age and how it might influence the learning of spiritual practices and teachings. Psychologists might well address other factors, such as lowered hormone levels and the general slowing down of the nervous system, as being conducive of turning people toward the "inner life" and away from the "world" of ego and power, of domination and control. There are all of the social and cultural reasons for why society has prescribed that the aging withdraw from engagement in society and become instead repositories of wisdom for the culture.

References

Alexander, C. N., Davies, J. L., Dixon, C. A., Dillbeck, M. C., Druker, S. M., Oetzel, R. M., et al. (1990). Growth of higher stages of consciousness: Maharishi's Vedic psychology of human development. In C. N. Alexander & E. J. Langer (Eds.), *Higher stages of human development: Perspectives on adult growth* (pp. 286–341). New York: Oxford University Press.

Alexander, C. N., Heaton, D. P., & Chandler, H. M. (1994). Advanced human development in the Vedic psychology of Maharishi Mahesh Yogi: Theory and research. In M. E. Miller & S. Cook-Greuter (Eds.), *Transcendence and mature thought in adulthood: The further reaches of human nature* (pp. 39–70). Lanham, MD: Rowman and Littlefield.

Baltes, P. B. (1997). On the incomplete architecture of human ontogeny: Selection, optimization, and compensation as foundation of developmental theory. *American Psychologist, 52,* 366–380.

Basseches, M. (1984). *Dialectical thinking and adult development.* Norwood, NJ: Ablex.

Berk, L. (2004). *Development through the lifespan* (3rd ed.). New York: Allyn & Bacon.

Chodron, P. (1997). *When things fall apart: Heart advice for difficult times.* Boston: Shambhala.

Commons, M. L., & Richards, F. A. (1984). A general model of stage theory. In M. L. Commons, J. D. Sinnott, F. A. Richards, & C. Armon. (1989). *Adult development, Vol. I: Comparisons and applications of developmental models* (pp. 33–56). New York: Praeger.

Commons, M. L., Armon, C., Kohlberg, L., Richards, F. A., Grotzer, T. A., & Sinnott, J. D. (1990). *Adult development, Vol. II: Models and methods in the study of adolescent and adult thought.* New York: Praeger.

Commons, M. L., Richards, F. A., & Armon, C. (1984). *Beyond formal operations: Late adolescent and adult cognitive development.* New York: Praeger.

Commons, M. L., Sinnott, J. D., Richards, F. A., & Armon, C. (1989). *Adult development, Vol. I: Comparisons and applications of developmental models.* New York: Praeger.

Cook-Greuter, S. R. (1990). Maps for living: Ego-development stages from symbiosis to conscious universal embeddedness. In M. L. Commons, C. Armon, L. Kohlberg, F. A. Richards, T. A. Grotzer, & J. D. Sinnott (Eds.), *Adult development, Vol. II: Models and methods in the study of adolescent and adult thought* (pp. 79–103). New York: Praeger.

Cook-Greuter, S. R. (1994). Rare forms of self-understanding in mature adults. In M. E. Miller & S. R. Cook-Greuter (Eds.), *Transcendence and mature thought in adulthood* (pp. 119–146). Lanham, MD: Rowman and Littlefield.

Cook-Greuter, S. R. (1995). *Comprehensive language awareness: A definition of the phenomena and a review of its treatment in the postformal adult development literature.* Unpublished manuscript, Harvard University Graduate School of Education.

Fowler, J. W. (1995). *Stage of faith: The psychology of human development and the quest for meaning.* San Francisco: HarperCollins.

Gould, R. (1978). *Transformations: Growth and change in adult life.* New York: Simon and Schuster.

Grof, S., & Grof, C. (Eds.). (1989). *Spiritual emergency: When personal transformation becomes a crisis.* New York: Tarcher/Putnam.

Harvey, O. J., Hunt, D. E., & Schroder, H. M. (1961). *Conceptual systems and personality organization.* New York: Wiley

Hy, L. X., & Loevinger, J. (1996). Measuring ego development (2nd ed.). Mahwah, NJ: Lawrence Erlbaum.

Irwin, R. R. (2000). Meditation and the evolution of consciousness: Theoretical and practical solutions to midlife angst. In M. E. Miller & A. N. West (Eds.), *Spirituality, ethics, and relationships: Clinical and theoretical explorations* (pp. 283–305). Madison, CT: Psychosocial Press.

Irwin, R. R. (2002). *Human development and the spiritual life: How consciousness grows toward transformation.* New York: Kluwer Academic/Plenum.

Itard, J.-M.G. (1962). *The wild boy of Aveyron (L'enfant sauvage)* (G. & M. Humphrey, Trans.). New York: Appleton-Century-Crofts.

Kegan, R. (1982). *The evolving self: Problem and process in human development.* Cambridge, MA: Harvard University Press.

Kegan, R. (1994). *In over our heads: The mental demands of modern life.* Cambridge, MA: Harvard University Press.

Kohlberg, L. (1984). *Essays in moral development: The psychology of moral development: Moral stages, their nature and validity* (Vol. 2). New York: Harper and Row.

Labouvie-Vief, G. (1994). *Psyche and Eros: Mind and gender in the life course.* Cambridge: Cambridge University Press.

Labouvie-Vief, G., DeVoe, M., & Bulka, D. (1989). Speaking about feelings: Conceptions of emotions across the life span. *Psychology and Aging, 4,* 425–437.

Labouvie-Vief, G., Hakim-Larson, J., DeVoe, M., & Schoeberlein, S. (1989). Emotions and self regulation: A lifespan view. *Human Development, 32,* 279–299.

Laing, R. D. (1989). Transcendental experience in relation to religion and psychosis. In S. Grof & C. Grof (Eds.), *Spiritual emergency: When personal transformation becomes a crisis* (pp. 49–60). New York: Tarcher/Putnam.

Loevinger, J. (1976). *Ego development.* San Francisco: Jossey-Bass.

Manners, J., & Durkin, K. (2001). A critical review of the validity of ego development theory and its measurement. *Journal of Personality Assessment, 77,* 541–567.

Perry, W. (1970). *Forms of intellectual and ethical development during the college years.* New York: Holt, Rinehart, & Winston.

Schaie, K. W. (1994). The course of adult intellectual development. *American Psychologist, 49,* 304–313.

Selman, R. L. (1980). *The growth of interpersonal understanding: Developmental and clinical analyses.* New York: Academic Press.

Sternberg, R. J. (1990). *Wisdom: Its nature, origins, and development.* New York: Cambridge University Press.

Thomas, L. E. (1994). Cognitive development and transcendence: An emerging transpersonal paradigm of consciousness. In M. E. Miller & S. R. Cook-Greuter (Eds.), *Transcendence and mature thought in adulthood: The further reaches of adult development* (pp. 71–87). Lanham, MD: Rowman and Littlefield.

Werner, D. W., Kagan, N., & Schneider, J. (1977). The measurement of affective sensitivity: The development of an instrument. *Annual Conference on Research in Medical Education, 16,* 187–193.

Wilber, K. (1986a). The spectrum of development. In K. Wilber, J. Engler, & D. P. Brown (Eds.), *Transformations of consciousness: Conventional and contemplative perspectives on development* (pp. 65–105). Boston: Shambhala.

Wilber, K. (1986b). The spectrum of psychopathology. In K. Wilber, J. Engler, & D. P. Brown (Eds.), *Transformations of consciousness: Conventional and contemplative perspectives on development* (pp. 107–126). Boston: Shambhala.

Wilber, K. (1986c). Treatment modalities. In K. Wilber, J. Engler, & D. P. Brown (Eds.), *Transformations of consciousness: Conventional and contemplative perspectives on development* (pp. 127–159). Boston: Shambhala.

Wilber, K. (1993). *Grace and grit: Spirituality and healing in the life and death of Treya Killam Wilber.* Boston: Shambhala.

Wilber, K. (1996a). *A brief history of time.* Boston: Shambhala.

Wilber, K. (1996b). *The Atman Project: A transpersonal view of human development.* Boston: Shambhala.

Wilber, K. (2000). *Integral psychology: Consciousness, spirit, psychology, therapy.* Boston: Shambhala.

Part V

Essential Contexts for the Learning, Developing Adult

Chapter 15

Effects of Children on Adult Development and Learning: Parenthood and Beyond

Jack Demick

My academic interest in the effects of children on adults most generally, and in parent development more specifically (Demick, 2000, 2002, 2003; Demick & Wapner, 1992; Demick, Bursik, & DiBiase, 1993), was spawned over a decade ago. At that time, my two children were constantly bombarding me with novel, unexpected stimuli that constantly required me to equilibrate cognitively. For example, in an early article on the topic (Demick, 1999), I reported that my then seven-year-old daughter had recently informed me that she would not listen to me because she was accountable to only two people (God and President Bill Clinton), and my four-year-old son routinely inquired into Spanish translations of various body parts. Suffice it to say that since then, the novel, unexpected stimuli, and hence states of cognitive disequilibrium, have continued to the present. For instance, as I tried to finish this chapter in the solitude of my home (having taken the day off from work), I was interrupted by 200 high school seniors my daughter had invited, unbeknownst to me, to a "senior skip day" barbecue. Experiences such as these led me to formulate a dialectical (transactional) theory of parent development (Demick, 2002), which will figure prominently in this review.

Against this backdrop, the present chapter has the main goal of presenting an overview of current theory and research on the effects of children on adults' development and learning. In fact, in recent years, there has been growing theoretical and empirical support for the view that children often play a large and underappreciated role in adult development and learning (e.g., Dillon, 2002). Most notably, this has been demonstrated in the context of parental development (e.g., Demick, 2000, 2002; Demick et al., 1993) where it has been shown that raising a child has the potential of influencing not only parents' immediate behavior but also their cognitive, emotional, ego, and personality development as well as their overall life satisfaction. However, children's role in adult development is not limited to parents but extends as well to grandparents, additional family members, teachers, physicians, child care workers, and the like.

Toward understanding the full effects of children on adults, this chapter reviews historical notions of socialization effects in psychology, culminating in the presentation of a more recent theory on the transactional, dialectical nature of adult–child interactions; cutting-edge research on parental development, including work on stages of this development (Demick, 2002, 2003); and recent empirical attempts to categorize the role of the child in adult development and learning more generally.

HISTORY OF SOCIALIZATION EFFECTS

Unidirectional Effects

In the original literature on socialization, or the process by which children acquire the beliefs, values, and behaviors considered appropriate or desirable by the society to which they belong, it was assumed that socialization effects were unidirectional or flowing in only one direction, namely, from the environment (e.g., parent, teacher) to the child. Although this parent-as-cause, child-as-effect viewpoint was evident in early philosophical writings on the basic nature of the child (e.g., Locke, 1690/1961; see also Rousseau, 1762/1993), the notion of unidirectional effects became popularized predominantly by early psychoanalytic theory and secondarily by early learning theory. For example, Freud (1959) hypothesized that parental childrearing practices at each stage of psychosexual development led the child to develop certain personality characteristics that were evident for the duration of his or her life (e.g., harsh toilet training in the anal stage would lead the child to develop an anal personality characterized by control issues). Although such Freudian formulations were predominantly intrapsychic as well as not borne out by subsequent research, they led neoanalytic theorists (e.g., Hartmann, 1958; Winnicott, 1965) to postulate such concepts as good enough mothering and the average expectable environment. These latter constructs expanded psychoanalytic theory to be less intrapsychic and more interactive by delineating the psychological features of the environment (i.e., caretaking functions of the mother) that were necessary for development. In a similar manner, from a learning perspective, Skinner (1972) and others have focused on the child as a product of the parenting practices (usually operant conditioning techniques) of those adults in his or her social environment.

Bidirectional Effects

Beginning in the mid-1950s, researchers shifted from thinking of the adult as the independent variable and the child as the dependent variable to recognizing that the child contributes to his or her own socialization and to conceptualizing the child and the adult as a dyad in which the response of one member is not only reactive to the previous behavior of the other member but also serves as a stimulus for future behavior by the other member. Although this insight came predominantly from parent–offspring studies with insects and nonhuman mammals (e.g., Rheingold, 1969; Schneirla & Rosenblatt, 1961), researchers were quick to reinterpret the direction of effects in studies of child socialization. For instance, Bell (1968) argued that many of the behaviors usually interpreted as the causes of correlated child behaviors may just be reactions on the part of parents to constitutionally based traits in their children.

Three strands of research have reinforced the notion that children can act on parents to the same extent that parents can act on children (bidirectional effects). First, Thomas and Chess's (1977) classic work on infant temperament identified early aspects of children's general style of behavior across contexts that play a role in eliciting varying responses from caregivers. They and subsequent researchers (e.g., Rothbart & Bates, 1998) conceptualized an infant's general activity level, reactivity, inhibition, and/or proneness to distress as interactive processes or products of continuous, reciprocal influences between children and their environments. For example, in line with this, Patterson and his colleagues (e.g., Patterson & Capaldi, 1991; Patterson & Dishion, 1988) have shed light on the nature of aggressive children by demonstrating that aggressive children may have punitive parents, not because the children are frustrated or are modeling their parents' aggressive behavior, but because they are born with certain traits (e.g., high activity level) that provoke parents into using harsh discipline methods. Such work has led social learning theorists (e.g., Bandura, 1978) to postulate the notion of reciprocal causality or reciprocal determinism. This notion stresses causal influences among three classes of variables, namely, *person variables* (including not only trait-like predispositions but also such influences as the person's interests, goals, expectancies, and plans), *environment variables* or *situations* (e.g., interactions with parents), and *behavior*.

Thus development and learning are viewed as the product of chains of events that involve reciprocal causal influences among these three classes of variables, making it almost impossible to assign primary causal status to any of these sets of variables over the other two.

Second, more recent research has attempted to specify the exact impact of various child behaviors and attributes, whether innate or acquired, on caregivers and other people. Stated succinctly, research has shown that (a) the most potent factor is child gender (e.g., leading to parents' higher expectations of and stricter discipline for boys versus girls); (b) relative to less physically attractive children, attractive children receive more positive evaluations from adults and peers; and (c) relative to less aggressive peers, aggressive children tend to be rejected more by others in their lives. This has led to a relatively new empirical strategy in which adults serve as participants and children as confederates, with the latter instructed to react in certain ways (e.g., high or low activity level).

Third, additional research has attempted to explain why adults differ in their reactions to a given child characteristic. Although until recently there has been little systematic research in the area, newer work has examined the ways in which adults' social class, education, childrearing experiences, familiarity with childrearing literature, personality, and cognitive factors (e.g., expectations and attributions) influence their interactions with children. For example, relative to others, some parents are more concerned with questions such as "What should my child be doing?" and "Is my child's behavior up to a standard level?" (see Azar, 2003, for a comprehensive review of this research with a focus on social-cognitive factors in parenting). As a result of such conceptualization and emphases, researchers (e.g., Ambert, 1992, 2001) began turning to the study of the effects of children on parents.

Transactional Effects: General Considerations

Within recent years, a newer theoretical model with implications for the problem of the effects of children on adults has been proposed. This model, however, is not without its subtleties. For example, extending the work on bidirectional effects, Sameroff and his colleagues (e.g., Sameroff & Chandler, 1975;

Sameroff & Fiese, 2000) have developed a transactional model describing the cumulative effects of ongoing two-way influences between parents and children, which takes into account the family's social and economic contexts as well. For example, an infant enters a family system with certain innate tendencies. Related to their own characteristics and circumstances, the parents respond to the infant in particular ways. Partly related to maturation and partly related to parental influences, the infant's behavior gradually changes. These changes in the infant, in turn, elicit new responses from the parents, which further influence the child, and so on, in an ongoing cycle. Sameroff has employed such conceptualization to explain why certain moderately premature infants, for example, those in low-income families, have developmental problems. That is, the infant's condition at birth interacts with the parents' psychological state (e.g., often characterized by inadequate psychological resources and social support), which itself is shaped by their social and economic circumstances (e.g., poverty).

Although this approach has been influential, its underlying worldview may be called *interactional* or *mechanistic* (e.g., Pepper, 1942, 1967). That is, Sameroff's analysis is interactional insofar as it emphasizes a sensorial analysis of the effects of isolated independent variables within the organism (e.g., maturational state of the child) or the environment (e.g., patterns of parental reinforcement) on dependent variables (e.g., psychological functioning of the child). In contrast, more recent theory and research (e.g., Altman & Rogoff, 1987) has extended this paradigm even further. For example, our own approach (e.g., Wapner & Demick, 1998, 1999, 2000, 2002, 2003) has adopted elements of both organismic (organicist) and transactional (contextual) world views.

Specifically, the organismic worldview is embodied by an attempt to understand the world through the use of synthesis, that is, by putting its parts together into a unified whole. It highlights the relationship among parts, but the relationships are viewed as part of an integrated process rather than as unidirectional or bidirectional chains of cause–effect relationships. The central feature of a transactional worldview is that the person and the environment are conceptualized as parts of a whole. One cannot deal with one aspect of the whole without treating the other (see Cantril, 1950; Ittleson, 1973; Lewin, 1935; Sameroff, 1983; Wapner, 1987). Specifically, the transactional view treats the "person's behaving, including his most advanced knowing as activities not of himself alone, nor even primarily his, but as processes of the full situation of organism-environment" (Dewey & Bentley, 1949, p. 104). Against this backdrop, I now turn to a fuller explication of this approach and then delineate its implications for the study of the effects of children on adult development and learning.

Transactional Effects: A Holistic/Systems Developmental Approach

The holistic/systems developmental perspective on human experience and action (e.g., Wapner & Demick, 1998, 1999, 2000, 2002, 2003) is an extension and elaboration of Heinz Werner's comparative-developmental theory (1940/1957; Werner & Kaplan, 1963). Both the original theory and the elaborated approach have been called *organismic* (such that cognition, affect, valuation, and action are considered in relation to the total context of human activity) and *developmental* (in that it provides a systematic principle, the orthogenetic principle, governing developmental progression and regression most generally so that living systems may be compared with respect to formal, organizational features).

Historically, the elaborated approach draws on the organismically oriented work on the field theory of perception (Werner & Wapner, 1952) and the applicability of the organismic-developmental perspective to the analysis of language and symbol formation (e.g., Werner & Kaplan, 1963). In contrast to classical psychophysics that studied the senses, what is called the sensory-tonic field theory of perception argued that no matter how diverse the source of stimulation to the organism, all stimulation was sensory-tonic in nature. Thus, a balance, or harmony, of forces between the state of the organism and the stimulation from an object was assumed to define a stable state of the system. With respect to symbol formation, Werner and Kaplan argued that symbolic activities initially emerge out of bodily organismic (sensorimotor) activities; primordial symbol usage includes the physical act of (communicative) pointing, motoric imitations (e.g., flickering of eyelids to represent flickering lights), and vocalizations (e.g., cries, calls, expressions of pleasure); and the early connection between sensorimotor bodily experience and symbol usage has never been completely lost.

On the most general level, our current approach can be described in the following ways:

- *Holistic* insofar as we assume that the person-in-environment system is an integrated system whose parts may be considered in relation to the functioning whole;
- *Systems-oriented* insofar as we assume that the person-in-environment system includes three aspects of the person (the biological as seen, e.g., in the individual's health; the intrapersonal as seen, e.g., in the person's response to stress; and the sociocultural as seen, e.g., in the roles the individual assumes), and three analogous aspects of the environment (the physical whether natural or built, the interorganismic, involving other human beings as well as animals, and the sociocultural as seen, e.g., in the laws of society or the unwritten rules of a group); and
- *Developmental* insofar as we assume that progression and regression may be assessed against the ideal of development embodied in the orthogenetic principle (changed from dedifferentiated to differentiated to differentiated and integrated, e.g., having a general word for all living things to having several words for general classes, such as animals, trees, and plants instead), and that development encompasses not only ontogenesis (the development of an individual organism) but additional processes such as phylogenesis (i.e., the evolutionary development of a species), microgenesis (i.e., the evolutionary development of an idea or percept), pathogenesis (i.e., the development of both functional and organic pathology), and ethnogenesis (e.g., changes during the history of humans).

Corollary notions include additional theoretical assumptions as follows:

- *Transactionalism:* The person and the environment mutually define and cannot be considered independent of one another. Similarly, the person-in-environment system's experience—consisting of cognitive, affective, and valuative processes—and action are inseparable and operate contemporaneously under normal conditions.
- *Multiple modes of analysis:* This includes structural analysis (part–whole relations) and dynamic analysis (means–ends relationships).

- *Constructivism*: The person-in-environment system actively constructs or construes his or her experience of the environment.
- *Multiple intentionality*: The person-in-environment system adopts different intentions with respect to self-world relations, that is, toward self or world-out-there.
- *Directedness and planning*: The person-in-environment system is directed toward both long- and short-term goals related to the capacity to plan.
- *Multiple worlds*: The person-in-environment system operates in different spheres of existence such as home, work, and recreation.
- Analysis is focused on *process* rather than on *achievement*.

These theoretical assumptions have powerful heuristic potential for the design and conduct of a wide variety of empirical studies. Initiated almost three decades ago, work in the area of environmental psychology (e.g., Wapner, Kaplan, & Cohen, 1976; see also Wapner & Demick, 2002) led to examination of the paradigmatic problem of critical person-in-environment transitions across the life span. This in turn led to research on very diverse problems, including adoption, adult development and aging, cognitive style development, parental development, and psychopathology. These studies have all demonstrated a clear need to study the active, thinking, feeling, valuing individual in all of his or her everyday life complexity.

Methodologically, the approach is typically concerned with describing the relations both among and within the parts (person, environment) that make up the integrated whole (person-in-environment system) as well as with specifying the conditions that make for changes in the organization of these relations. Thus the approach is committed to the complementarity of explication (description) and causal explanation (conditions under which cause–effect relations occur), rather than being restricted to one or the other. Accordingly, the preferred method of research involves the flexible drawing from both quantitative and qualitative methodologies depending on the level of integration and nature of the problem under scrutiny (see Maslow, 1946). The approach also serves not only as a powerful heuristic device to analyze and open new significant problems in psychology but also to integrate, at a very basic level, the field of psychology that is currently suffering from disruption and fragmentation.

Such attempts have the potential to lead to a unified, theory-driven science of psychology that cuts across aspects of persons, environments, and of interrelations.

Implications

What implications does this approach have for the study of the effects of children on adult development and learning more generally? Although there are many, the discussion here will be limited to the major implications of our holistic/systems and developmental assumptions, respectively. With respect to our holistic/systems assumptions, we generally assume that the organism-in-environment system (here, *parent-in-environment system*) is the unit of analysis. Specifically, we assume that in a holistic manner, the parent him- or herself encompasses mutually defining biological/physical (e.g., health), psychological/ intrapersonal (e.g., body/self experience), and sociocultural (e.g., roles) aspects. Analogously, we assume that the parent's environment in such a system is comprised of mutually defining physical (e.g., home, work, child's school), interorganismic/interpersonal (e.g., family members, co-workers, daycare provider, child's teachers/friends/friends' parents, pets), and sociocultural (e.g., household, work, school rules; community; society; sociohistorical context) aspects. These aspects of the parent in conjunction with these aspects of the parent's environment are assumed to constitute the parent-in-environment system.

Related to the assumption of the parent-in-environment as the unit of analysis is the assumption concerning holism and levels of integration. Specifically, we assume that the parent-in-environment system operates as a unified whole so that a disturbance in one part (physical, psychological, or sociocultural aspects of the parent or of his or her environment) affects other parts and the totality. The holistic assumption holds for functioning not only among but also within levels of integration. For example, on the psychological level, such part-processes as the cognitive aspects of experience and action (including, e.g., sensorimotor functioning, perceiving, thinking, symbolizing) as well as the affective (feeling) and valuative (prioritizing) aspects of experience and action, operate contemporaneously and in an integrated manner in the normal parent. Thus, a comprehensive understanding of parents-in-environments routinely needs to consider a wide range of variables and their interrelations (see table 15.1).

TABLE 15.1 Variables Relevant to the Study of Parents-in-Environments

Person (× Environment)	Environment (× Person)
Biological/physical	*Physical*
Age	Environmental objects[a]
Sex	Physical locations[a]
Race[a]	
Physical health/stress[a]	
Modes of conception[a]	
Complications during pregnancy and delivery	
Psychological/intrapersonal	*Interpersonal/interorganismic*
Cognitive processes	Children
Decision making	Spouse (e.g., marital quality, stability)
Plans and expectations[a]	Family of origin
Meaning making[a]	Extended family
Cognitive style[a]	Friends
Affective processes	Co-workers
Motivation for parenthood	Daycare provider(s)[a]
Personality[a]	Neighbors[a]
Mental helath/stress[a]	Child's teachers[a]
Valuative processes	General public
General values (e.g., family versus career; self versus other)[a]	Other social support networks
Life satisfaction	Pets
Sociocultural	*Sociocultural*
Socioeconomic status (e.g., cost of children)[a]	Family developmental tasks
Religion[a]	Family history/themes
Politics[a]	Community[a]
Parental role	Society (e.g., media)
Spousal role	Legal[a]
Work role	Educational[a]
Gender role	Sociohistorical context
Leisure roles[a]	

[a]Not examined extensively in previous research.

Source: Adapted from Demick (1999, 2002).

As an example, consider the transition to parenthood (see Dillon, 2002). It has been well documented that during this transition, child effects on adults' experience and action affect all levels of functioning: (a) the physical level of the parent (e.g., the fetus leads the mother to gain weight and to experience fatigue, anxiety, and/or stress); (b) the psychological level of the parent (e.g., parenthood often leads to higher levels of cognitive development); (c) the sociocultural level of the parent (e.g., even egalitarian parents often resort to more traditional gender roles); (d) the physical level of the environment (e.g., parents alter their living spaces, including childproofing their homes); (e) the interpersonal level of the environment (e.g., related to increased time pressures, parents often lose touch with friends and certain family members); and (f) the sociocultural level of the environment (e.g., parents begin to consider family developmental tasks and develop family history and themes). Furthermore, research has documented that in a holistic manner, the transition to parenthood shapes not only individuals' experience and action but also the experience and action of the marital dyad (e.g., less marital satisfaction) and family system as a whole (e.g., shifts in alliances among all family members).

In line with the developmental emphases, we have described four self–world relationships ranging from a lesser to a more advanced developmental status. Although these relationships have been applied to a variety of contexts, they are discussed here in the context of a problem with relevance for the effects of children on adults, namely, the family systems of those practicing open versus closed adoption (communication versus no communication between biological and adoptive parents). More specifically, adoptive families characterized by a total separation between the adopted child and his or her family of origin—as is usually the case in traditional, closed adoption—may be conceptualized as dedifferentiated (all family members consciously or unconsciously deny that the child has been adopted), differentiated and isolated (adoptive parents shelter the adoptee so that he or she will not learn about the biological parents from others and will not have to deal with the stigma of being adopted), or differentiated and in conflict (the adoptee may fantasize that the biological parents would treat him or her differently or may threaten to leave the adoptive family to find the "real" parents when of age). In contrast, the adoptive family, characterized by less absolute separation between the adoptee and his or her family of origin (open adoption), may be conceptualized as differentiated and integrated (the adoptee may be able to integrate the various aspects of his or her dual identities, possibly mitigating potential problems with identity and self-esteem; in a similar manner, the adoptive parents may be able to avoid blaming "bad blood" in the background for any difficulties; e.g., Demick, 1993, 2003; Demick & Wapner, 1988b; Silverstein & Demick, 1994).

We have also demonstrated that corresponding to these self–world relationships are characteristic modes of coping. For instance, a differentiated and integrated person-in-environment system state is typically characterized by the use of constructive assertion (using planned actions and different alternatives for achieving goals), whereas dedifferentiated, differentiated and isolated, and differentiated and in conflict person-in-environment system states, respectively, characteristically employ accommodation (passively accepting and waiting for things to be different), disengagement (distancing oneself from the situation or environment), and nonconstructive ventilation (externalizing inappropriate or ineffective thoughts, feelings, and actions).

Furthermore, the orthogenetic principle has also been specified with respect to a number of polarities, which at one extreme represents developmentally less advanced and, at the other extreme, more developmentally advanced functioning (see Kaplan, 1966; Werner, 1940/1957; Werner & Kaplan, 1963). These polarities, by use of examples relevant to parental development, are as follows.

1. *Interfused to subordinate.* In interfused experience and action, goals and functions are sharply differentiated, whereas in subordinated experience and action, goals and functions are differentiated and hierarchically arranged with drives and momentary motives subordinated to more long-term goals. For example, for the less developmentally advanced parent, always pleasing the child by granting his or her every wish is not differentiated from preparing the child for a realistic future. In contrast, the more developmentally advanced parent is able to differentiate and subordinate the former short-term goal to the latter long-term goal.

2. *Syncretic to discrete.* *Syncretic* refers to the fusion or merging of multiple nondifferentiated mental phenomena, whereas *discrete* refers to mental contents, acts, meanings, and functions that represent unambiguous and specific things. For example, syncretic thinking is represented by the lack of differentiation between a parent's inner and outer experience; that is, the lack of separation of one's own feelings from that of one's child-out-there. Discrete thinking is represented by a parent's accurately defining and distinguishing one's own feelings from those of one's child.

3. *Diffuse to articulate.* *Diffuse* represents a relatively uniform, homogeneous structure with little differentiation of parts, whereas *articulate* refers to a structure for which differentiation of parts makes up the whole. For example, diffuse is a structure represented by the law of pars pro toto (Werner, 1940/1957); that is, the part has the quality of the whole, as is the case when a parent's judgment about a child is made on the basis of one brief experience. Articulate is represented by an experience in which distinguishable events make up the parent's whole impression of his or her child, with each event contributing to and yet being distinguishable from the whole.

4. *Rigid to flexible.* *Rigid* refers to behavior that is not readily flexible, whereas *flexible* refers to behavior that is plastic or readily changeable. Rigid is exemplified by a parent's perseverance,

routinization, and unchangeability in handling his or her child. In contrast, flexibility implies a parent's capacity to modify his or her transactions with the child depending on the context and the particular demands of a given situation.

5. *Labile to stable. Lability* refers to the inconsistency and fluidity that accompanies changeability, whereas *stability* refers to unambiguity and consistency that co-occur with fixed properties. For instance, lability may be seen in a parent's rapidly changing, inconsistent, fluid behavior with his or her child (e.g., use of words with many meanings, stimulus bound shifts of attention). In contrast, stability is represented by a parent's consistent action, which is underpinned by thinking that involves the precise definition of events, terms, or ideas.

As is evident, transactional approaches in general and this transactional approach in particular have led to conceptualizing parent–child (adult–child) interaction in a more complex manner than has heretofore been the case in unidirectional or bidirectional approaches. Such conceptualization, which is more in line with everyday life functioning, has suggested that the effects of children on adults must be examined in all of its complexity. That is, from a research perspective, there is a clear need for flexibly drawing from both quantitative and qualitative methodologies depending on the level of integration and the nature of the problem under scrutiny. However, as we have argued elsewhere (e.g., Demick & Wapner, 1988a; Wapner & Demick, 1998), there may well be some value in conducting holistic, ecologically oriented research, here on the effects of children on adults, by reducing the number of focal children and/or adults studied rather than limiting the number and kind of interrelations among aspects of the children, of the adults, of their environments, and of the systems to which they belong.

PARENTAL DEVELOPMENT AND LEARNING

In addition to more recent transactional approaches, another area of research, namely, stages of parental development, has implications for the study of the effects of children on adults. The leading theorist in this area has been Galinsky (1981). Specifically, she has interviewed over 200 parents with approximately 400 children among them (from 10 to 40 children of each chronological year from *in utero* to 18 years). These parents included both mothers and fathers, parents from diverse groups (e.g., married, divorced, widowed, step-families, adoptive families, foster families, guardians), and parents of all ages (ranging from adolescent to older parents with one or many children), races, ethnicities, religions, income levels, and regions of the country. From data collected through biological interviews (see Levinson, 1978), she specifically proposed that parenthood progresses through a series of six stages (with relevant developmental tasks for parents):

1. *Image-making stage.* Here, Galinsky characterized the stage (pregnancy until birth) as the time "when prospective parents begin to cull through, to form, and to re-form images of what's to come, of birth and parenthood" (1981, p. 9). Parental tasks include, for example, the parent preparing for a change in role, forming feelings for the baby, "reconciling the image of the child with the actual child" (p. 55), and preparing for a change in other important adult relationships.

2. *Nurturing stage.* From birth until the child is approximately two years old (when the child begins to say "no"), parents may experience a conflict between earlier expectations of what the child might be like and the actuality of parenthood. The major task of this stage is "becoming attached to the baby. . . . It took a couple of weeks until it wasn't like having an object in our home" (Galinsky, 1981, p. 74). In contrast to the initial state of symbiosis between mother and child, attachment "implies both emotional and physical separateness and connectedness" (p. 73). Here, parents assess their priorities, figuring out how much time they should devote to the baby and how much to other aspects of their lives.

3. *Authority stage.* The central task of this stage (child is between two and five years) concerns how parents handle power, that is, how they accept the responsibility, communicate effectively, select and enforce limits, decide on how much to shield and protect the child, cope with conflicts with the child, and handle or avoid battles of the will. The authority issue is not restricted to children, however, but is also concerned with working out authority relationships with others (who deal with the child), including the other parent, grandparents, baby-sitters, teachers, neighbors, and the like.

4. *Interpretive stage.* Here (when the child is 5 to 12 years old), for parents "the major task is to interpret the world to their children, and that entails not only interpreting themselves to their children and interpreting and developing their children's self concepts, but also answering their questions, providing them access to the skills and information they need, and helping them, form values" (Galinsky, 1981, p. 178).

5. *Interdependent stage.* As the child reaches adolescence, the parent is faced with and must interact with a "new" child. All aspects of the prior relationship (e.g., communication) must be renegotiated and new issues (e.g., sexuality) addressed.

6. *Departure stage.* As the adolescent gets older, the central task becomes that "of accepting one's grown child's separateness and individuality, while maintaining the connection" (Galinsky, 1981, p. 307). "The 'old,' 'original' family has changed, and most parents search for new ways to say they are still a family" (p. 304). This stage is characterized by evaluations. "Parents evaluate their images of departure, when and how far they thought their child would go. They evaluate whether they've achieved the parent/grown child relationship they wanted as well as taking stock of their overall successes and failures" (p. 10).

Galinsky's work has been criticized on a number of grounds (e.g., see Demick, 2002, for a comprehensive review). First, social scientific contributions to the parenting literature have generally supported Galinsky's notion of stages as well as each particular stage. However, the support has primarily been theoretical rather than empirical in nature. Second, although widely accepted, her work has been subject to both methodological and theoretical criticisms. Methodologically, her use of autobiographical interviews has relied primarily on reconstruction and memory, which are not reliable. The method itself has been considered time-consuming, expensive, and vulnerable to bias (on the part of both the participant and the interviewer), so that findings have often been difficult to replicate. Theoretical problems have included the following: The adult's tasks at each stage are almost intuitive, that is, simply to deal with the child's developmental tasks at various ages. Her conception of stages has been adevelopmental and not directed toward a teleology. The theory has also failed systematically to take into account individual differ-

ences, such as gender and family type (e.g., married, divorced, adoptive). Third, the implications of Galinsky's work have been framed primarily for white, middle-class parents and have failed to consider the demographics of the changing American parent (see Milardo, 2001).

In light of the lack of extensive empirical data on the stages of parental development, Galinsky's (1981) relatively hidden notion that certain issues may cut across all stages of parental development (e.g., self–other distancing, treatment of sexuality) and our assumptions about the nature of human functioning, we have preferred to reframe the issue of stages of parenthood as developmental changes in the experience and action of parents over the course of bearing and rearing children (see Demick, 1999, 2000, 2002; Demick, 1992). This reframing has been chosen for several reasons. First, this conceptualization may be more in line with the complexity of everyday life functioning. Related to the wide range of criticisms that have been leveled against stage theories of development, coupled with the notion that developmentally ordered individual differences in self–world relationships (i.e., dedifferentiated, differentiated and isolated, differentiated and in conflict, differentiated and integrated) may characterize person-in-environment system states at any given moment in time and are thus malleable and potentially remediable, we have assumed that developmental changes in (cognitive, affective, and valuative) experience and action occur with greater frequency than stage theories have implied.

Thus, it may be that whenever there is a perturbation to the person-in-environment system (e.g., cognitive disequilibrium in a parent related to a child's behavior), the parent must reorganize his or her self–world relationship (i.e., to restore cognitive equilibrium). In this way, such developmental processes most probably occur with greater frequency in transacting with one's children on a daily basis. Experiential accounts of parenthood attest to this notion as well as indicate that although the particular issues posed by one's children may change from one moment to the next (even if some appear in great regularity), parental reactions do not necessarily change. That is, parents are constantly faced with restoring cognitive equilibrium (or equilibrium to the person-in-environment system) in a dialectical process that may feel similar every time that they are faced with a novel (or not so novel) stimulus from their children (see Holden &

Ritchie, 1988). In our terms, parents are constantly faced with attempting to return their differentiated and conflicted person-in-environment system state to a more differentiated and integrated one. As we see it, these and related notions have the potential to serve as the basis for a more comprehensive and powerful theory on the effects of children on adults' development and learning.

ROLE OF CHILDREN IN ADULT DEVELOPMENT AND LEARNING MORE GENERALLY

Although the foregoing review has provided insights into the problem at hand, one might also inquire into research and theory that addresses more directly the ways in which children do in fact influence adults. Toward this end, two strategies are presented: first, a description of a small-scale study that has addressed this particular issue and, second, a discussion of conceptualization and future research directions from our perspective. Both of these consider processes underlying adult–child interaction; each will be discussed in turn.

Recently, Dillon (2002) asked 35 parents and 15 teachers to discuss occasions during which they had learned something valuable from a child or when a child had changed them in some significant way(s). A content analysis of these interview data yielded four thematic categories of child effects. These categories, from most to least frequent, follow. In inspirational influence, adults (30%) reported that children's questions (usually "why?") led them to consider their worldviews and category systems in deeper, more meaningful ways. As one father stated (examples from Dillon, 2002):

> I think it was when Toby was about two that he really started to change. It was like before he was just moment-to-moment. All of a sudden—like overnight—he started asking "Why" about everything. He was like Socrates. What was worse was looking to *me* for answers. I really think that that little boy is interested in more important stuff than I am. He's made me really start to question things. (p. 272)

According to Dillon (2002), "Experiences such as these can affect the way an adult thinks about his or her entire life, as well as what are considered to be 'important' pursuits. These experiences can shift the entire course of adult development" (p. 272).

With the second most frequent category (28%), catalysts for integration, some adults reported that their interactions with children led them to say things (e.g., that their parents had said to them) or experience (often painful) emotions that were previously not integrated into their adult personalities, that is, repressed or disowned aspects of self. Subsequently, "this recognition served as the occasion for integrating this surprising material and thereby transforming their overall way of thinking, feeling, or acting" (Dillon, 2002, p. 271). For example, one teacher remarked,

> Last year we had this day where the kids can bring into school music they like and talk about why they like it. Most of them brought all of this "gansta rap" stuff. I just did not appreciate it very much. It was offensive. I got all over them about it. I was like, you kids don't know what good music is. Motown, now that's good music. While I was saying this I thought, oh my God, I sound just like an old person, and I'm only 29!
>
> This was exactly what my parents would say to me when I was listening to my music. In that moment I sort of saw myself in them and I felt very close to them. They helped me think of myself as a kid again and not a crusty old parent. (p. 271)

The third category, cognitive flexibility, was evident in 22% of the adults' responses. Specifically, these adults revealed that in trying to communicate with a child, they were forced in a dialectical manner to use earlier, currently unused modes of thinking or feeling. They then typically reported feeling grateful to the child for the transformative nature of the experience (e.g., feeling smarter, more creative). For instance, as one teacher discovered,

> Well, I remember when I first started teaching multiplication. I started by trying to connect multiplication to addition. Since they were kids, I brought in a bunch of manipulatives (marbles). I showed them how 3×3 was really like adding 3 sets of 3 marbles together to make 9. And you know, before then, I never knew what multiplication was. I mean, I knew that 3×3 was 9, but I never really knew what that meant. It's now in my bones rather than just in my memory. It was because of having to talk to the kids on their level that I learned that. (p. 272)

In this example, "because of the child's tendency to think primarily in concrete terms, the abstract thinking adult is forced to think in a concrete way so as to communicate with or teach the child. This process of re-thinking concretely paradoxically improves the adult's ability to think abstractly" (Dillon, 2002, p. 272).

The fourth category, informational influence, was mentioned by 20% of the sample. Here, adults remarked that their children had taught them important information or values and had affected their attitudes and behavior toward, for example, pollution, littering, recycling, smoking, drinking, general health habits, and seatbelt usage. As one mother remarked about her son: "It wasn't so much that he would say anything, it was just how he would look at me, like he was really worried when I smoked. It would kill me. He cared so much. He really helped me to learn to care for myself better. I haven't had a cigarette in over a year" (Dillon, 2002, p. 271).

Dillon's work is important insofar as it has made inroads into the problem of the effects of children on adults. First, he has argued that through the processes inherent in these categories (with the exception of the last one, informational influence), adults come to experience long-term transformations that qualify as "developmental" changes. For example, Dillon has offered two specific developmental interpretations of his findings. First, employing Werner's (1940/1957, 1957) notion of multiple modes of functioning and Labouvie-Vief, Chiodo, Goguen, Diehl, and Orwoll's (1995) construct of dynamic intersubjectivity, he has agreed, based on his findings concerning catalysts for integration and cognitive flexibility, that "rather than being a movement of upward ascent . . . development in the adult years is about the ability to reunite the concrete and embodied modes of knowing employed in infancy and childhood with the more abstract modes employed in adolescence and adulthood" (Dillon, 2002, p. 273). To explain his findings on inspirational influence, he has evoked Jung's (1959) notion of the archetype of the child, in which

the child archetype presents the adult with dreams, feelings, even symptoms, that represent parts of him or herself that have been forgotten or left behind with "development." The archetypal child within the adult holds out the constant possibility for rebirth, renewal, hope, spontaneity, creativity, and zest for living. Jung discussed the healing potential of the child as a symbolic, arche-

typal reality, but he ignored the capacity of real children to affect genuine inspiration, renewal, and development. (p. 273)

Second, Dillon's work has reminded us that significantly more adults than parents have the potential to be genuinely influenced by children. Although he has delineated teachers as another important group in this regard, the list also extends to grandparents, additional family members, daycare providers, neighbors, physicians, and the like. Thus, larger numbers of participants, analyzed with respect to their membership in various of these groups, would strengthen his findings, perhaps uncover additional categories, and shed light on additional processes underlying the effects of children on adult development and learning.

Unlike Dillon, we would not consider his findings on informational influence to be adevelopmental. Based on ongoing empirical research on the ways that experience becomes translated into action, we have identified a range of triggers that lead individuals to more developmentally advanced person-in-environment system states. For example, we (Demick et al., 1992) have found that serving as role models for children (similar to his category of informational influence) is a significant factor fostering the consistent usage of automobile safety belts, which leads to more developmentally advanced functioning. We have also found that triggers encompass all levels of integration and hence all contexts, that is, physical, intrapersonal, and sociocultural aspects of the person, as well as physical, interpersonal, and sociocultural aspects of the environment (see Wapner & Demick, 2002). Thus, research in the area of child effects on adults might be advanced through use of our ongoing category system.

Our own work has other implications for the study of processes underlying child effects on adults' development and learning. For example, similar to the parent-in-environment as unit of analysis, we might also speak of, for example, grandparent-in-environment, teacher-in-environment, and daycare-provider-in-environment systems as units of analysis that have the potential to shed more light on processes underlying child effects on adults. Similarly, future research and analyses might benefit from employing our self-world relationship categories (dedifferentiated, differentiated and isolated, differentiated and in conflict, differentiated and integrated) and their corresponding modes of coping (accommodation, disengagement, nonconstructive ventilation, constructive assertion) as well as the developmental polarities (interfused to subordinate, syncretic to discrete, diffuse to articulate, rigid to flexible, labile to stable). That is, just as our categories of self–world relations may correspond to Ainsworth's (1973) attachment styles (see Wapner & Demick, 1999), so too may they be used to describe the structural relationships of a variety of different adults to a variety of different children. For example, ongoing research in our laboratory (Alves et al., 2004) on similarities and differences in grandparenting kin versus children who were adopted has already uncovered that grandparenting in these two contexts is more similar than different insofar as there are individual differences in self–world relationships across the two groups.

Finally, we (e.g., Wapner & Demick, 1998) have also delineated other conditions facilitating developmental change, which may have applicability for fostering optimal relations between adults and children. Stated succinctly, these have included the following notions (with implications for parent–child interaction).

1. *Self–world distancing.* Self–world distancing may promote developmental change in two ways. A decrease in self–world distancing between the individual and the consequences of his or her negative actions may lead to safer, more optimal person-in-environment functioning. Conversely, an increase in self–world distancing between the individual and affectively laden material may permit the person to operate more optimally insofar as there is greater separation between cognition and negative affect. Relevant here, there may be times when it is of value for parents to attempt to take the point of view of their children (e.g., peer pressure, curfews) rather than insisting on their own; at other times, however, it may make more sense for parents to identify less with (and consequently disengage somewhat from) their children (e.g., when there is a discrepancy between parent and child values).

2. *Anchor point.* Both physical and social anchor points have been shown to play a role in the development of a spatial organization and social network in adapting to a new environment. Thus, will fostering a parent's or child's use of an anchor point (whether an actual or symbolic object) in new environments (e.g., the child's transition to nursery school) help one or the other or both move closer to the developmental ideal of integrating the old and new worlds and in experiencing stability, comfort, and satisfaction in both?

3. *Reculer pour mieux sauter (draw back to leap).* A negative experience (e.g., negative parent–child interaction) may serve the positive function of fostering greater self-insight and providing the formal condition of "dissolution of the self," thereby permitting a creative reorganization of self (for parent or child).

4. *Triggers to action.* Making people aware of the precipitating events or triggers to their own or others' actions has been shown to lead to a heightened awareness of person-in-environment functioning. This heightened awareness may include consideration of a wider repertoire of triggers for self, which may in turn lead to appropriate action and hence more optimal person-in-environment functioning. For example, making parents or children aware of the positive and negative triggers for their positive and negative interactions, respectively, may move them both toward more consistently optimal functioning vis-à-vis one another.

5. *Individual differences in experiencing critical transitions.* Various studies from within our approach have suggested that consideration of individual differences may be a route toward fostering developmental progression. For example, consider that retirement means different things to different people. Such differences might then be taken into account in seeing conditions or circumstances that might make for more optimal experience and action during retirement. For example, it is possible that for people who see retirement as an imposed disruption, continued contact with one's fellow workers rather than a sudden break with the work world might make it easier to adapt. In a similar manner, what is the impact on individual and joint outcome of a match or mismatch in cognitive style between parent and child (see Wapner & Demick, 1991)?

6. *Planning.* There is also evidence that a simple request for an individual to verbalize plans about action to be taken to advance to a new, more ideal person-in-environment system state may bring that state into effect. Thus, we might ask, What are the effects of individual and joint planning (e.g., for higher education) on child,

adult, and child–adult outcome (e.g., over the course of the child's transition to college)?

CONCLUSIONS

From unidirectional to bidirectional to transactional models of adult–child interaction, our understanding of the effects of children on adult development and learning has come a long way. Although we have made inroads into this important problem area, more remains to be done. For example, we have suggested a particular theoretical approach, namely, the holistic, developmental, systems-oriented approach to person-in-environment functioning across the life span, which has suggested multiple directions for the study of child effects on adults (e.g., structural analyses of the interrelations between adults and children, dialectical view of daily adult–child transactions, category system for processes underlying adult–child interaction). Employing related perspectives, other research has suggested that children have the potential to foster developmental transformations in the lives of adults through, for example, processes such as inspirational influence, catalysts for integration, and cognitive flexibility. For example, among other ways, children may help us as adults reunite, in a dialectical manner, earlier concrete and embodied ways of knowing with more abstract developmentally advanced modes of knowing; they may also hold out for us the possibilities of renewal, creativity, and a zest for living. Although more theory development (from this and other perspectives) and empirical research (e.g., expansion of child effect categories) are needed, we should not let cultural or philosophical forces lead us to view children as simply passive, immature, and needing to be molded by us as important adults in their lives. As this chapter attests, it is now clear, through transactional lenses, that children play an extremely large and often underappreciated role in adult development and learning.

ACKNOWLEDGMENTS I dedicate this chapter to Seymour Wapner of Clark University, who died on September 23, 2003, at the age of 85. He was my mentor, collaborator, and friend of 28 years, and I am forever grateful for what he taught me about psychology as a whole, developmental psychology in particular, and life in general. Without his teaching and guidance over the years, this chapter would not have been possible.

References

Ainsworth, M. D. (1973). The development of infant-mother attachment. In B. M. Caldwell & H. N. Riccuiuti (Eds.), *Review of child development research* (Vol. 3, pp. 1–95). Chicago: University of Chicago Press.

Altman, I., & Rogoff, B. (1987). World views in psychology: Trait, interactional, organismic, and transactional perspectives. In I. Altman & D. Stokols (Eds.), *Handbook of environmental psychology* (Vol. 1, pp. 7–40). New York: Wiley.

Alves, S., Bauer, S., Ramdehal, M., Sollecito, A., Southwick, C., & Demick, J. (2004, April). *Grandparenting grandchildren: Adopted versus kin.* Wheaton College 13th Annual Academic Festival, Norton, MA.

Ambert, A. (1992). *The effect of children on parents.* New York: Haworth.

Ambert, A. (2001). *The effect of children on parents* (2nd ed.). New York: Haworth.

Azar, S. T. (2003). Adult development and parenthood: A social-cognitive perspective. In J. Demick & C. Andreoletti (Eds.), *Handbook of adult development* (pp. 391–415). New York: Kluwer Academic/Plenum.

Bandura, A. (1978). The self system in reciprocal determinism. *American Psychologist, 33,* 344–358.

Bell, R. Q. (1968). A reinterpretation of the direction of effects in studies of socialization. *Psychological Review, 75,* 81–95.

Cantril, H. (1950). *The why of man's experience.* New York: Macmillan.

Demick, J. (1992). Transition to parenthood: Developmental changes in experience and action. In T. Yamamoto & S. Wapner (Eds.), *Developmental psychology of life transitions* (pp. 243–265). Tokyo: Kyodo Shuppan.

Demick, J. (1993). Adaptation of marital couples to open versus closed adoption: A preliminary investigation. In J. Demick, K. Bursik, & R. DiBiase (Eds.), *Parental development* (pp. 175–201). Hillsdale, NJ: Erlbaum.

Demick, J. (1999). Parental development: Problem, theory, method, and practice. In R. L. Mosher, D. J. Youngman, & J. M. Day (Eds.), *Human development across the life span: Educational and psychological applications* (pp. 177–199). Westport, CT: Praeger.

Demick, J. (2000). Stages of parental development. In L. Balter (Ed.), *Parenting in America: An encyclopedia* (Vol. 2, pp. 438–440). Boulder, CO: ABC-CLIO.

Demick, J. (2002). Stages of parental development. In M. Bornstein (Ed.), *Handbook of parenting: Vol. 3. Being and becoming a parent* (2nd ed., pp. 389–413). Mahwah, NJ: Erlbaum.

Demick, J. (2003). "Roots that clutch": What adoption and foster care can tell us about adult development. In J. Demick & C. Andreoletti (Eds.), *Handbook of adult development* (pp. 475–491). New York: Kluwer Academic/Plenum.

Demick, J., Bursik, K., & DiBiase, R. (Eds.). (1993). *Parental development.* Hillsdale, NJ: Erlbaum.

Demick, J., Inoue, W., Wapner, S., Ishii, S., Minami, H., Nishiyama, S., et al. (1992). Cultural differences in impact of governmental legislation: Automobile safety belt usage. *Journal of Cross-Cultural Psychology, 23,* 468–487.

Demick, J., & Wapner, S. (1988a). Children-in-environments: Physical, interpersonal, and sociocultural aspects. *Children's Environments Quarterly, 5,* 54–62.

Demick, J., & Wapner, S. (1988b). Open versus closed adoption: A developmental conceptualization. *Family Process, 27,* 229–249.

Dewey, J., & Bentley, A. F. (1949). *Knowing and the known.* Boston: Beacon.

Dillon, J. J. (2002). The role of the child in adult development. *Journal of Adult Development, 9,* 267–275.

Freud, S. (1959). *Collected papers.* New York: Basic.

Galinsky, E. (1981). *Between generations: The six stages of parenthood.* New York: Berkeley.

Hartmann, H. (1958). *Ego psychology and the problem of adaptation.* New York: International Universities Press.

Holden, G. W., & Ritchie, K. L. (1988). Childrearing and the dialectics of parental intelligence. In J. Valsiner (Ed.), *Child development within culturally structured environments: Vol. 1. Parental cognition and adult child interaction* (pp. 30–59). Norwood, NJ: Ablex.

Ittleson, W. H. (1973). Environmental perception and contemporary perceptual theory. In W. H. Ittleson (Ed.), *Environment and cognition* (pp. 1–19). New York: Seminar Press.

Jung, C. G. (1959). *The archetypes and the collective unconscious* (R. F. C. Hull, Trans.). Princeton, NJ: Princeton University Press.

Kaplan, B. (1966). The study of language in psychiatry. In S. Arieti (Ed.), *American handbook of psychiatry* (vol. 3, pp. 659–668). New York: Basic Books.

Labouvie-Vief, G., Chiodo, L. M., Goguen, L. A., Diehl, M., & Orwoll, L. (1995). Representations of self across the life-span. *Psychology and Aging, 10,* 404–415.

Levinson, D. J. (1978). *The season's of a man's life.* New York: Ballantine.

Lewin, K. (1935). *A dynamic theory of personality.* New York: McGraw-Hill.

Locke, J. (1690/1961). *Essay concerning human understanding.* London: J. M. Dent.

Maslow, A. (1946). Problem-centering versus means-centering in science. *Philosophy of Science, 13,* 326–331.

Milardo, R. M. (Ed.). (2001). *Understanding families in the new millennium: A decade in review.* Minneapolis, MN: National Council on Family Relations.

Patterson, G. R., & Capaldi, D. (1991). *Antisocial parents: Unskilled and vulnerable.* In P. Cowan & E. M. Hetherington (Eds.), *Family transitions* (pp. 195–218). Hillsdale, NJ: Erlbaum.

Patterson, G. R., & Dishion, T. J. (1988). Multilevel family process models: Traits, interactions, and relationships. In R. Hinde & J. Stevenson-Hinde (Eds.), *Relationships within families: Mutual influences* (pp. 283–310). Oxford: Oxford University Press.

Pepper, S. C. (1942). *World hypotheses.* Berkeley: University of California Press.

Pepper, S. C. (1967). *Concept and quality: A world hypothesis.* LaSalle, IL: Open Court.

Rheingold, H. L. (1969). The social and socializing infant. In D. Goslin (Ed.), *Handbook of socialization theory and research* (pp. 779–790). Chicago: Rand McNally.

Rothbart, M., & Bates, J. (1998). Temperament. In W. Damon (Series Ed.) & N. Eisenberg (Vol. Ed.), *Handbook of child psychology: Vol. 3. Social, emotional, and personality development* (5th ed., pp. 105–176). New York: Wiley.

Rousseau, J. J. (1762/1993). *Emile* (B. Foxley, Trans.). Rutland, VT: Charles E. Tuttle.

Sameroff, A. J. (1983). Developmental systems: Contexts and evolution. In P. H. Mussen (Ed.), *Handbook of child psychology* (Vol. 1, pp. 237–294). New York: Wiley.

Sameroff, A. J., & Chandler, M. (1975). Reproductive risk and the continuum of caretaking casualty. In F. D. Horowitz, E. M. Hetherington, S. Scarr-Salapatek, & G. Siegel (Eds.), *Review of child development research* (Vol. 4, pp. 187–244). Chicago: University of Chicago Press.

Sameroff, A. J., & Fiese, B. H. (2000). Transactional regulation: The developmental ecology of early intervention. In J. P. Shonkoff & S. J. Meisels (Eds.), *Handbook of early childhood intervention* (pp. 135–159). New York: Cambridge University Press.

Schneirla, T. C., & Rosenblatt, J. S. (1961). Behavioral organization and genesis of the social bond in insects and mammals. *American Journal of Orthopsychiatry, 31,* 223–253.

Silverstein, D., & Demick, J. (1994). Toward an organizational-relational model of open adoption. *Family Process, 33,* 111–124.

Skinner, B. F. (1972). *Beyond freedom and dignity.* New York: Bantam-Vintage Books.

Thomas, A., & Chess, S. (1977). *Temperament and development.* New York: Brunner/Mazel.

Wapner, S. (1987). A holistic, developmental, systems-oriented environmental psychology: Some beginnings. In D. Stokols & I. Altman (Eds.), *Handbook of environmental psychology* (pp. 1433–1465). New York: Wiley.

Wapner, S., & Demick, J. (Eds.). (1991). *Field dependence-independence: Cognitive style across the life span.* Hillsdale, NJ: Erlbaum.

Wapner, S., & Demick, J. (1998). Developmental analysis: A holistic, developmental, systems-oriented perspective. In W. Damon (Series Ed.) & R. M. Lerner (Vol. Ed.), *Handbook of child psychology: Vol. 1. Theoretical models of human development* (5th ed., pp. 761–805). New York: Wiley.

Wapner, S., & Demick, J. (1999). Developmental theory and clinical practice: A holistic, developmental, systems-oriented approach. In W. K. Silverman & T. H. Ollendick (Eds.), *Developmental issues in the clinical treatment of children* (pp. 3–30). Boston: Allyn & Bacon.

Wapner, S., & Demick, J. (2000). Person-in-environment psychology: A holistic, developmental, systems-oriented perspective. In W. B. Walsh, K. H. Craik, & R. H. Price (Eds.), *Person-environment psychology: New directions and perspectives* (2nd ed., pp. 25–60). Hillsdale, NJ: Erlbaum.

Wapner, S., & Demick, J. (2002). The increasing contexts of context in the study of environment-behavior relations. In R. B. Bechtel & A. Churchman (Eds.), *Handbook of environmental psychology* (pp. 3–14). New York: Wiley.

Wapner, S., & Demick, J. (2003). Adult development: The holistic, developmental, systems-oriented perspective. In J. Demick & C. Andreoletti (Eds.), *Handbook of adult development* (pp. 63–83). New York: Kluwer Academic/Plenum.

Wapner, S., Kaplan, B., & Cohen, S. B. (Eds.). (1976). *Experiencing the environment.* New York: Plenum.

Werner, H. (1940/1957). *Comparative psychology of mental development.* New York: International Universities Press.

Werner, H. (1957). The concept of development from a comparative and organismic point of view. In D. B. Harris (Ed.), *The concept of development: An issue in the study of human behavior* (pp. 125–148). Minneapolis: University of Minnesota Press.

Werner, H., & Kaplan, B. (1963). *Symbol formation.* New York: Wiley.

Werner, H., & Wapner, S. (1952). Toward a general theory of perception. *Psychological Review, 59,* 324–338.

Winnicott, D. W. (1965). *The maturational processes and the facilitating environment.* New York: International Universities Press.

Chapter 16

Work as the Catalyst of Reciprocal Adult Development and Learning: Identity and Personality

Carol Hoare

Recently, the theoretical and research literature on paid work has focused disproportionately on corporate needs. Much less attention is directed to workers themselves, particularly with respect to work's positive effects on employees' personal development. Worker attributes have primarily been studied with an eye to the qualities that enhance competitiveness and the bottom line of organizations and in terms of negative worker outcomes (e.g., accidents, stress, morbidity) that disadvantage corporations. Clearly, organizations wish to have productive employees who are work involved and satisfied with their jobs and who are cooperative, pleasant, committed, and conscientious. To organizations, desirable workers act according to corporate values and norms, and, in the mind's eye of business, they identify with and are attached and loyal to the organization. In addition, such employees are continual learners. They are resilient, adaptive, welcoming of change, and eager to serve their employer's evolving needs (see, e.g., Brown, 1996; Froman, 1994; George, 1990; Hazan & Shaver, 1990;

Maier & Brunstein, 2001; Maurer, Weiss, & Barbeite, 2003; Pulakos, Arad, Donovan, & Plamondon, 2000).

This emphasis places the onus on workers to satisfy business needs, a tradition with a long and respected history in the United States. The focus has led to corporate success and thus provides many economic advantages for the country's citizens. However, in highlighting corporate needs, attention is diverted away from the needs of employers to foster their workers' development. At times it also fails to recognize how enhancing workers' development and learning contributes significantly to corporate needs, engendering the very qualities that organizations wish to see in their employees. If good work is a catalyst of reciprocal adult development and learning as I claim, providing job conditions that foster such growth serves corporate needs reciprocally as well.

This chapter on the relationship between work and individual development and learning primarily examines the positive effects of adult work on identity and personality characteristics, a process in which learning leads to development and development often leads to learning. Understanding the positive personal effects of work is particularly important in an era characterized by an absence of the prior social contract—that is, the expectation that a company will provide a lifetime of employment. In the tenuous work environment defined by the absence of this contract, it is essential to consider occupational contributions to the individual's development and learning that go beyond skill acquisition and a paycheck. What might workers expect from their employers? Should they not, for example, expect their employing organizations to provide opportunities for intellectual and cognitive development and for experiences that enhance (rather than undermine) identity and personality development?

Turning the coin around, what might organizations expect from their workers when employers make honest, reasonable commitments to growth-enhancing occupational roles, to good job conditions, and to inclusive opportunities for relevant learning? Portions of the business world have recently awakened to the fact that such work conditions, opportunities, and policies are invaluable both to organizations wishing to retain their workers and to organizations that are competitively trying to lure good workers to their ranks. In a knowledge economy, employees who continue to learn and develop (e.g., cognitively, emotionally, interpersonally, intrapersonally) are among the corporation's most treasured assets. However, evidence about adult development has only sparingly found its way into work policies and contexts and into employee training and development applications (see also Laske, 2003).

Paid work can advance various forms of personal development, and clearly, development and learning fuel one another. For example, identity development transpires as adolescents and young adults learn about work roles and opportunities and as they become increasingly aware of the blend of their personal interests and aptitudes that are attractive to the employing world. Identity development then continues as each person moves through the adult years, developing as a result of learning and functioning in various work, community, and personal roles. In this, at least in the United States and much of Western culture, adults are expected to be central agents. They actively perceive, construct, and sometimes select and revise (at times, unconsciously) the various roles that cannot help but intersect in their psyches. They do this using highly personal lenses and filters.

Clearly, one's core identity is an outgrowth of the ego and its evolution. And identity is constituted of much more than work identifications and occupational identity alone. Commitments, friendships, intimacies, and the important accomplishments of life figure prominently. Personal expectations and goals point a directional arrow into the future, because expectations, anticipations, desires, and hopes are integral to the identity and meaning system of every normal adult. A future-orientation frequently fashions what it is that adults do or elect not to do in the present. In this context—of the present and the future, with the past within and behind one—the salaried work of the adult years becomes one of the most salient of the many endeavors that consume us.

To give preliminary examples of the role of work in development and learning, two examples are useful. First, outcome data from more than 30 years of research show that substantively complex work (that which requires thought, autonomous decision making, and functioning within a complex occupational environment) advances workers' intellectual functioning (Kohn & Schooler, 1978, 1982, 1983). These effects have been demonstrated in younger and older subjects (Schooler, Mulatu, & Oates, 1999). Self-directed, complex work, with its demands of ongoing learning and the resolution of ill-defined problems, leads to greater ideational flexibility and self-direction years later.

Second, with respect to personality in relation to engagement in society, work, and learning, Srivastava, John, Gosling, and Potter's (2003) study is instructive. Investigating 132,515 workforce participants in the age range of 21 to 60 years, they found that not only does personality remain malleable after 30 years of age but that it is influenced by young adult activities. Among women, openness to experience and ambition in young adulthood led to their involvement in the feminist movements of the 1960s and 1970s. Such involvement then correlated with heightened openness and work ambition in later life (see also Agronick & Duncan, 1998).

It is far easier to envision than it is to investigate, document, and validate the ways that learning fuels development. It is also difficult to study how developmental possibilities (e.g., of roles, job conditions, other persons, uses of one's personality and commitments) lead to learning. Social and work environments are continually in flux. Proprietary information about products and training successes is kept close to most organizations' vests. Into and through developmental maturity, each person must want to grow and change and learn. Adults construct their own realities, and development and learning can be integral or far removed from those realities.

THIS CHAPTER

Adult development means systematic, qualitative changes in human attributes (e.g., intelligence, insight, social cognition) as a result of interactions between internal and external environments. Lawful, sequential changes typically delineate developmental transformations. Although development in adulthood is bidirectional in that gains and losses occur, here I preferentially address the positives.

Adult learning means a change in behavior, a gain in knowledge or skills, or an alteration or restructuring of prior knowledge or interpretations. Such learning is itself a developmental activity and process. Learning occurs consciously and unconsciously. Some unconscious learning is accessible to the conscious mind because it resides at the preconscious (implicit or tacit) level. Other learning occurs unconsciously or moves to the unconscious level, remaining largely inaccessible (see Hoare, chapter 1, this volume). In the arena of paid work, one frequently sees the results of personal development and learning but sometimes cannot access causal mechanisms and effects such that they can be shown psychometrically.

A word is in order about my choice of attributes for this chapter, those of identity and personality. For approximately 15 years I have taught a graduate seminar on the intersection of work, identity, and adult development. Two factors stand out every semester this course is offered. First, consistently throughout the years, the adult learners who enroll in this seminar have mentally engaged the content both on the personal and professional levels to try to understand what it is that work means in their and others' lives. "What does the work I do mean to my ongoing identity development?" they ask, and "what does work mean for the identity processes—and the identity successes, setbacks, and failures—of my colleagues, clients, superiors, and subordinates?" Some learners are counseling students. Others are from the business, human resource development sector. Their professional

applications may be different, but the questions are largely the same: What does work mean to an adult's identity?

Second, my student colearners and I cannot seem to talk about work, identity development, and other forms of development (e.g., intellectual, social, insight) without including the learning that is so integral to each intersection of thought. For example: How does a person who prefers solitary work learn to function interpersonally in a team? How does that adult develop social skills and attunement to the perspectives and needs of others so that he or she can learn the group norms and team behaviors that are imperative in achieving consensual goals? How does a manager best use the talents of workers with widely different personality characteristics and learning styles? How does a productive worker learn to close out the salaried years of life? Who are the exemplars of healthy adaptation, development, and learning in the salaried years and later? How can we help those who are less well able to negotiate work environments and important role transitions?

Historically, identity has been integral to personality theory. I separate identity from personality because these two constructs are vastly different in their origins. Yet identity, particularly in its work investment connotation, interacts with many personality attributes. The proximity of personality to identity requires its inclusion when considering paid work.

Both personal dimensions—identity and adult personality—evolve, more or less so, as one learns and grows. Each dimension is partly conscious and partly unconscious. When adults are deeply work engaged, they function in a time-out-of-mind zone, rarely surfacing to ponder (if in fact they consciously can) their sense of self and its vital constituents. Clearly, other personal attributes are also important to occupational conditions, but a single chapter must be terrain-limited.

IDENTITY

The Identity Construct

In the "Domain of Arnheim," Edgar Allan Poe (1847/1981) penned four conditions for happiness, shown through the adulthood pursuits of his protagonist, Ellison. The first and principal condition is "the health," by which Poe meant "free exercise in the open air." He gave the examples of the "tillers of the earth" and the "fox-hunters," those rare beings he knew as happier than any others. Poe's second condition is "the love of woman." In today's world, we might extend Poe's thought to refer to a loved other who is the most significant and cherished one in life, man or woman. Poe's third condition, and the most difficult to achieve, is a "contempt of ambition." And his fourth is "an object of unceasing pursuit" (p. 547).

To me, Poe's *object* of unending pursuit is identity, identity as process and object—always pursued, never complete. Identity, who we are and who we will become, is channeled and expressed in part through the kind of work we do, just as the work of our lives lends definition to who we are as persons. Today, the term *identity* seems to mean many different things to different people. But the original identity construct, as it was defined and described by Erik Erikson from within his and the U.S. societal lens, incorporates a decided vocational commitment. In youth, adolescents (and today, some young adults as well) project themselves into work roles. This is identity's genesis. Identity then develops, evolves, changes, and sometimes becomes rigid throughout adults' lives. After its first birth, as Erikson showed and Poe's metaphorical tale implies, identity is a life force and a driving need. It is that which propels one along.

Based on his numerous clinical studies, Erikson (e.g., 1950, 1956, 1968) originated the concept of psychosocial identity. *Identity* means the partly conscious, largely unconscious sense of who one is, both as a person and as a contributor to society. This construct is the centerpiece of my thinking on work and identity because it is the most complete definition and description of the concept, one that is tied to occupational and social roles in the broader culture. Erikson linked identity to a range of relevant topics, for example, to human evolution and prejudice, historical change, and cultural relativity (Hoare, 2002). In an interview, Erikson cautioned that the adult developmental script he had conceptualized (identity, intimacy, care, integrality[1]) did not depict an immutable or "definitive inventory"; "I speak only," he said, "of a developing capacity to perceive and to abide by values established by a particular living system" (Evans, 1967, p. 30). Importantly, Lichtenstein (1983) has held that Erikson stands alone as the one theorist who revealed the dimensions and enigma of

identity to show the many ways in which the social world exists within, just as it surrounds, the psyche.

Erikson's identity construct is important because of the wide acceptance of his thought (credited or unacknowledged) in academic, psychoanalytic, counseling, and other circles. In more than 120 publications following his first sketchy thoughts, in one way or another Erikson elaborated his thinking about identity. To him, identity always develops and evolves at the intersection of the person and the social, cultural world. This is the juncture at which one's identity both absorbs and reflects society and its mores, permitting one to function inclusively in the world of the person's era.

Although Erikson is best known for his first book *Childhood and Society* (1950, 1963), his lesser known article "The Problem of Ego Identity" (1956) is a benchmark to his later thought on identity. In *Young Man Luther* (1958) and *Gandhi's Truth* (1969), he portrayed, respectively, the identity issues of young and middle adulthood, examining the psychosocial crises of the charismatic leaders Martin Luther and Mahatma Gandhi against the historical eras in which they lived their lives and reformed thought.

Erikson made determined efforts to maintain identity's complexity. He eschewed tendencies to reduce, distill, or scale the concept. Nonetheless, as Bourne (1978) found for 1962 through 1977 alone, 50 separate investigations had sought to delineate identity in operational terms suitable for testing. Since then, efforts to test and measure identity have proliferated.

Identity and Work

In identity's early phase, cognitive development permits youth to mentally construct a future, one imbued with content, meaning, and images of utopia. As Kegan (1982) put it, "The actual becomes but one instance (and often one not very interesting instance) of the infinite array of the 'possible'" (p. 38). At least in middle-class Western society, this is a time to delineate an autonomous definition of self apart from the nuclear family. Ideological thinking takes the form of a question: "What is it to which I can commit myself in some sustained way (ideologically and vocationally) to what I believe in?" And in that life era, society's question is heard for the first time with the full impact of its future-oriented meaning: "What will *you* eventually do to help sustain society, in return for which society will reciprocate with rewards of acceptance, inclusion, recognition, and remuneration?"

Both in youth and later, identity is personal coherence or self-sameness through evolving time, social change, and altered role requirements. At its best, identity entails a deep sense of commitment, of knowing what is worth one's fidelity in the expansive social world. This requires active agency which fosters a sense of centrality, intactness, and personal control. As Erikson (1974) stated:

> Above all, the ego works at all times on the maintenance of a sense that we . . . are central in the flux of our experience, and not tossed around on some periphery; that we are original in our plans of action instead of being pushed around; and, finally, that we are active and, in fact, are activating (as well as being activated by) others instead of made passive or being inactivated by exigencies. All this together makes the difference between feeling (and acting) whole—or fragmented. (p. 92)

Identity, then, is personal coherence, and a sense of agency and authenticity. In this coherence, the person feels like an actively engaged "insider" in the vocational-social domain of his or her choice, an engagement that carries commitment without pretense. One of the clearest examples of this is Erikson's example of George Bernard Shaw. Looking back on his life at the age of 70, Shaw described a crisis (to Erikson, an *identity* crisis) that occurred when he was 20, one that arose not from failure but from success in an occupation he despised. Finding little personal coherence between the demands of business and his sense of self despite his uncanny professional success, Shaw said he felt like an "imposter" in an occupation that seized on him, apparently without any intention of casting him free (Erikson, 1956, pp. 58–59). When Shaw eventually escaped the tentacles of the business world, he entered a prolonged "psychological moratorium" to determine his talents and interests, and thus his true identity:

> Thus, "the complete outsider" gradually became his kind of complete insider. "I was," he said, "outside society, outside politics, outside sport, outside the Church"—but this "only within the limits of British barbarism . . . the moment music, painting, literature, or science came into question the positions were reversed: it was I who was the insider." (Erikson, 1956, p. 64)

In this, Erikson described the inner sense of continuity that one must feel with his or her work and the continuity one must feel with the society in which that work is embedded. Erikson (1956) held that this continuity helps the person feel "identical" with the self in character. As Levinson (1986) later expanded, a satisfactory life structure results, an authentic sense of actively, centrally, and genuinely engaging the self in society's and life's purposes and functions.

Jaques (1965) and Levinson (1986; Levinson, Darrow, Klein, Levinson, & McKee, 1978) described identity processes similar to those of Shaw in the lives of other, largely middle-aged men. Analyzing the creative tendencies of 310 historically acclaimed artists, Jaques found any number who left earlier roles to find themselves. For example, Bach was an organist until he was 38 years old, at which time he launched his creative life as a composer. Gauguin left banking at age 39 to establish his life's work as a painter.

I am concerned here about the contributions of gainful work to the person, focusing on paid employment. I emphasize that the identity concept carries a Western world connotation (see, e.g., Geertz, 1984; Hoare, 1991, 2002; Kakar, 1989, 1991). Furthermore, even in the United States, it is clear that work identity is the "gold standard" that some (but not all) attain. Not everyone is granted the resources and social inclusion that will permit the development and expression of a mature, work-engaged identity.

These important factors aside for the purposes of this chapter, work commitments and immersion in the context of engaged work provide grist for the identity mill. From law to medicine, from goods production to computer programming, over time each adult becomes more of what he or she does for a living. As is true for other adult attributes, an interdependent relationship exists among the identity-developing adult, his or her work role, and learning (see, e.g., Vandewater, Ostrove, & Stewart, 1997; Van Manen & Whitbourne, 1997). Each constituent feeds into, channels, and alters the others.

As Erikson (e.g., 1958, 1969, 1975) held and more recently McAdams and colleagues supported (McAdams, 2001; McAdams, Diamond, de St. Aubin, & Mansfield, 1997), the person is always embedded in a seamless life story that shows coherence and integration. But it is also the case that the primacy of adult work identity in the life narrative shifts as each adult's relationship to work necessarily changes (see, e.g., Axelrod, 1999; Erikson, 1959; Pulkkinen & Kokko, 2000; Pulkkinen & Ronka, 1994; Sheldon & Kasser, 2001; Stewart & Ostrove, 1998; Van Manen & Whitbourne, 1997). Work salience also varies from person to person (Martire, Stephens, & Townsend, 2000; Roberts & Friend, 1998), and identity is based on investments in work, family, and other roles (Rothbard & Edwards, 2003; Thompson & Bunderson, 2001), just as it varies from one developmental epoch to another. To the extent that some adults' identities are shaped by personal investments that are diffuse across occupational, parental, civic, and community roles throughout adulthood, work identity is not universally intense among adults. In the United States, paid work is not (or not yet) central to every woman's life or sense of self. As Simmons and Betschild (2001) said about women's employment in Australia, "a career is just one vehicle to express . . . contribution(s) . . . to women's broader life agenda to contribute socially" (p. 63). Identity also varies with the country and political structure in which work is situated (Snarey & Lydens, 1990; Staudinger, Fleeson, & Baltes, 1999; Watson, 1996), and with variations in the meaning of work from one historical period and generational cohort to another (Helson, Stewart, & Ostrove, 1995; Stewart & Healy, 1989; Wetherell, 1996).

Empirical Studies of Adult Identity

A great deal of attention has been paid to identity formation in late adolescence and early adulthood along the research lines established by Marcia (1966, 1980) and extended by Waterman (1982, 1985) and others. However, other than clinical case studies, rather few empirical investigations of adult identity development have been published. There are a number of reasons for this. First, it is difficult to conduct meaningful investigations into a process that is partly unconscious without reducing it to a partial, simplistic rendition. Even if identity processes were fully accessible to conscious awareness, there are individual variations in introspective abilities to tap into such processes. Second, the most meaningful studies of identity and related processes are longitudinal investigations of intraindividual development into and through maturity; these are expensive, time-consuming, and suffer from subject attrition and

other difficulties (discussed by Caskie & Willis, chapter 3, this volume). Third, it is difficult to recruit working adults into investigations.

Identity studies of college students cannot substitute for studies of working adults. Working adults have ongoing, firsthand experiences with employment tasks, contexts, and demands and enjoy few respites from work. One must experience work norms and guidelines, must experience work's pleasure and tedium, and must develop, as most adults do, a love-hate relationship with work. It is only the experience of adult work itself that fuels the development of an adult identity based on work (e.g., Dickie, 2003). For these reasons, I restrict my consideration of empirical investigations to those conducted among working adults. Even among some of those studies, the entirety and richness of identity has been reduced to operationalize and test for it.

Among the few recent studies, there is support for identity's evolution throughout adulthood, as well as evidence that identity development influences and is influenced by learning and work experiences. Whitbourne, Zuschlag, Elliot, and Waterman (1992) found that identity scores continued to increase into the early thirties for both men and women. Among women in three separate samples, Stewart, Ostrove, and Helson (2001) found identity certainty (a firm sense of one's secure position in the social world) to have increased, or that women retrospectively believed that it had increased, over the middle years. In the latter sample, identity certainty with respect to work engagement was more salient among women in older middle age than those women perceived it to have been in their thirties and forties.

Van Manen and Whitbourne (1997) also found evidence of identity evolution. Both men and women who had scored higher on industry in college showed greater educational attainment and identity development; men who advanced in their sense of industry into the middle adult years were those who had been working on postbaccalaureate degrees in their early thirties. For men, higher identity scores in the college years were associated with functioning in higher status occupations in young adulthood.

There is little doubt that adults enter work roles with more or less of a propensity to develop strong work-related identities. For example, the moratorium status of identity development (identity exploration without commitment) predicts lower levels of career development for men and for women. Sociohistorical factors are also relevant. In the Van Manen and Whitbourne (1997) study, women in the older cohort (age 42) were more likely to express their identities in the arena of family instead of in paid work experiences.

Using a qualitative design, Altschuler (2004) interviewed 53 working women in the age range of 55 to 84 years to determine the centrality of work to their identity. Two themes, those of independence and control, and "lost dreams and regrets" (p. 228) emerged. Paid work was salient in that it permitted "freedom from a controlling or potentially controlling spouse" (p. 234). "Lost dreams and regrets" expressed the realities of their earlier lives, in part, the effect of the intersection of gender, age, and historical cohort. Limited career options for women, prohibitions against formal education, dropping out of school, and relinquishing a scholarship to marry were common themes.

Historically, as a critical mass, U.S. women have been late entrants into long-term, paid careers. Psychosocially, at least prior to their middle years of life, women have historically directed more of their energies toward attachment, family needs, and interpersonal connections with others than toward autonomous functioning (e.g., Chodorow, 1978; Gilligan, 1982, 1987; Lopez & Gover, 1993; Surrey, 1985). An emphasis on family needs, such as nurturing children and spouses, and caring for aging parents, militates against the development of a strong work-sponsored identity, at least for earlier generational cohorts of women and for some women now functioning in their pre–empty nest years.

Outcomes of Identity Development

Relative to outcomes in and beyond the work environment, a strong identity has predicted greater career progress among adults (Roberts & Friend, 1998; Van Manen & Whitbourne, 1997), and deferral of plans to retire (Roberts & Friend, 1998). A number of studies of men and women (Bauer & McAdams, 2004; Staudinger et al., 1999) and of women alone (Helson & Srivastava, 2001; Roberts & Friend, 1998; Stewart & Ostrove, 1998) have found greater well-being among those who were identity-achieved in the work realm. Internally consistent personalities (Vandewater et al., 1997) and positive life orientations and adaptive capabilities (Pulkkinen & Ronka, 1994) have been observed in identity-achieved subjects of both genders. Among women, greater confidence

(Stewart & Ostrove, 1998; Vandewater et al., 1997) and enhanced personal efficacy (Stewart & Ostrove, 1998) have been demonstrated. In a study of women ($n = 111$) that spanned 31 years, Helson and Srivastava (2001) distinguished among conservers (high environmental mastery but low personal growth), seekers (high personal growth but low environmental mastery), and achievers (high personal growth and high environmental mastery). Among the three forms of development identified, achievers showed the most integrated identities, balancing ambition and power with the ability to nurture others. Similarly, Roberts and Friend (1998) studied a sample of women who were in their early fifties, asking them to state whether they were currently increasing, maintaining, or decreasing momentum in their careers. High career momentum women held higher status jobs and believed that their work was more integral to their identities than women who were maintaining or decreasing their career momentum at midlife. Furthermore, the high-momentum group scored higher on independence, self-acceptance, and effective functioning and appraised their health as better than self-ratings reported by the other groups.

With respect to personal attributes on and off the job, when compared with those of incomplete identity development in the work realm, identity-achieved persons of both genders demonstrate greater reflective and planning tendencies and have shown self-reliant tendencies as opposed to tendencies to defer responsibility to others (Cella, DeWolfe, & Fitzgibbon, 1987; Waterman, 1985). Identity achievement in the work realm has been equated with enhanced autonomy (Lucas, 1997), good judgment (Vandewater et al., 1997), an internal locus of control (Cheek & Jones, 2001), and increased responsibility, tolerance, greater achievement and on-the-job performance, resiliency, and interpersonal integration (Bauer & McAdams, 2004).

Although I found no published empirical studies on relationships among work, learning, and identity development, clearly identity formation and development involve learning about work and about oneself in work roles and functions. A blend of personal talents, interests, and preparation mesh with work roles, and an integration of learning and identity development arise from job involvement based on such engagement. Once embedded in work roles and content, ongoing learning about the job and about one's relationships to work necessarily infuse and extend the adult's identity and sense of self. In Gould's (1980) words, work "confirms our status as adults" (p. 228). And from his many interviews of working-class men and women, Robert Coles (1978) found that work means "self-respect"; adult work is "*the* measure . . . of a person's 'grown-up' status" (p. 225).

Clearly, certain aspects of this confirmed adult status and of identity development and learning are unconscious. Other conscious learning moves to the unconscious, tacit (procedural) level (see Hoare, chapter 1, this volume). As Erikson (1956, 1958, 1969) showed, when seeing another person immersed in work, observers can report on that person's identity, but it is impossible for a work-immersed adult to observe and describe his or her own identity or the complexity of related forces that provide identity's sense of inclusion, worth, and validation. Adults lose consciousness of and about themselves when going about their job functions; jobs, in turn, structure and absorb time, engaging mind and psyche.

Identity and Job Loss

Involuntary job loss leads to identity loss, helplessness, and a marked decline in self-worth for both genders. Dislocated workers have reported feeling peripheral to the central concerns of engaged life. Physical and psychological problems ensue (Clausen & Jones, 1998; Elliott, 1996; Goldsmith, Veum, & Darity, 1996, 1997; Kasl & Cobb, 1970; Keddy, Cable, Quinn, & Melanson, 1993; Mallinckrodt & Bennett, 1992). Losses in identity and self-esteem are due to more than the absence of work and earnings alone. Work and role losses lead to losses in relationships, in personal support, in daily structure, in the appreciation of others for tasks performed well, and in learning opportunities that feed the self. By relinquishing a cherished place in the social system, self-esteem is drained (see, e.g., Kalimo & Vuori, 1990). This is particularly the case if the person blames him- or herself, ascribing personal failure to the self instead of to structural employment conditions. Studying the Depression era, Watson (1969) found that four out of five men who lost their jobs blamed themselves instead of the economy and social structure of the time.

Should doubts remain about the role of work in identity development and expression, and the ways identity development holds anxiety and depression at bay, studies on the absence of work testify to identity's importance. Unemployment has wide-ranging,

disastrous consequences for identity, self-esteem, mental health, and relationships. As Clausen and Jones (1998) found, men who had lost jobs as a result of plant closings became "anomic." Minus a sense of purpose, rootlessness and disorganization took hold. Prolonged unemployment snowballs economic hardships. It predicts physical illness, mental aberrations, and social deviance. Dislocated workers show:

- decreased self-esteem and the sense of self-efficacy
- a sense of destructured time
- a shift from an internal to an external locus of control
- decreased motivation to engage in learning opportunities
- poor coping strategies
- regression to lower level defense mechanisms
- irritability, anxiety, and depression
- marital instability and family dissolution
- paranoia
- prolonged mourning
- violence toward others and themselves (suicide attempts) (Catalano, Novaco, & McConnell, 1997; Ginexi, Howe, & Caplan, 2000; Goldsmith & Veum, 1997; Hamilton, Hoffman, Broman, & Rauma, 1993; Haw, Houston, Townsend, & Hawton, 2001; Law, Meijers, and Wijers, 2002; Mallinckrodt & Bennett, 1992; Peregoy & Schliebner, 1990; Price, Friedland, & Vinokur, 1998; Prussia, Fugate, & Kinicki, 2001; Shamir, 1986; Vinokur, Price, & Caplan, 1996; Warr & Jackson, 1985; Winefield, 1997).

Not only is work a source of mental health and emotional stability, it configures, in an ongoing way, key personal characteristics and ways of relating to the world (see, e.g., Kohn et al., 1997). Unemployment interrupts the life narrative, severs the adult from essential meanings and social interactions in life, and sets the stage for long-term negative consequences. Work is a paramount source of self-affirmation, learning, personal coherence, and confirmed identity, providing a wellspring of roles and personal meanings that are lost along with the job.

Identity in a High-Risk Environment

Organizations in today's business environment have contributed to workers' abilities to develop meaning and identity from their jobs. This is partly due to corporate trends in which workers are expected to understand their jobs in relation to the entire organization and its mission, products, and services (Stern, 1993). Yet as Meijers (1992) has held, contemporary workers live in a "risk society," and adapting to uncertain prospects is part of such risk. This means that work identity is also at risk. Kalimo, Taris, and Schaufeli (2003) reported that among 1,441 key employing firms in the United States during 1999–2000, 48.2% eliminated jobs, affecting an average (mean) 11.8% of their workers. Business restructuring and reengineering accounted for 50.4% of job loss, whereas reduced demand accounted for 14.5% of such losses. Job dissolution is partly due to escalating imports and to the exodus of goods production from the United States to overseas locations. With respect to off-shoring, U.S. workers, who are touted as the best educated, trained, and managed employees in the world, seem realistic in fearing the deportation of their jobs, because workers in poor countries work for far less pay. Recent praises of market globalization (e.g., Wolf, 2004) notwithstanding, products, investments, and a variety of services are portable to foreign soil, but cheap labor is not portable to the United States.

At least to date, much of the job loss has been due to technological advances and heightened efficiency. In the U.S. goods-producing sector in 2003, manufacturing productivity and output were at a 20-year high, whereas the numbers of manufacturing jobs were at a 20-year low (U.S. Department of Labor, 2003). For example, nearly 25 years ago when U.S. manufacturing jobs peaked at nearly 20 million, General Motors provided almost 500,000 of those jobs to produce 5 million vehicles per year. In 2003, GM produced the same number of vehicles but with just 118,000 jobs (Berry, 2003; Harbour Report, 2003).

In a high-risk environment, many eliminated jobs will not return. The potential for consistency in work identity will likely be less the norm than in prior times. Many adults may exist in a work-identity vacuum or routinely change their work identities, much like chameleons change colors. The trend toward work identity erosion will likely continue (Law et al., 2002; Sacks, 1997). For those who sequentially engage in as many as a dozen careers in their adult lives, Eriksonian concepts of vocation and of career commitments seem empty. Consistent work identity is particularly vulnerable when persons are forced to move from one temporary position and employer to another, developing job skills and identifications for many different forms of work. As Erikson held, identifications alone cannot constitute a mature,

consolidated identity. Identifications are alignments in viewpoints based on kinship ties and on symmetry with the views, values, and perspectives that unify family, friendship, and colleague relationships. These identifications can yield strong attachments. But identity is a deeply ingrained commitment to purposes and values in which one stands singularly in the self and in the world.

Facing their futures, youth in many Western nations feel vulnerable. Law et al. (2002) deftly synthesized the feelings of uncertainty that youth in four countries have expressed:

> Some two-thirds of German youth currently express no confidence in their own future, an increase of 25% since 1991. . . . A similar proportion of American youth voices dissatisfaction and pessimism concerning the future; an increase of 5% since the 1970s. . . . Some 75% of German youth say they agree with the statement "everything has become so uncertain that one must be prepared for anything and everything." . . . Among Belgian young adults, 40% consider the future too uncertain to plan far in advance. . . . More than one-third of Italian youth perceives considerable risks in making decisions with regard to their own future (whether of profession, or concerning their partner), and—significantly—they accept that this is an inescapable characteristic of modern existence. (pp. 432–433)

The current job environment can be chaotic, yielding a sense of disconnect with the past and with notions about the centrality and promise of productive work in adulthood. Anxiety and depression result when persons face difficulties entering and remaining in the job market. They lose faith in a work-engaged niche in society. In the Netherlands and France, between one-fourth and one-third of youths expressed fear and despair when reflecting on their futures (Law et al., 2002).

But youth's (and adult's) fears about the future are not completely due to jobs. Satellite imaging gives us a contemporary view of the planet, one beginning in the 1970s when, as a species, we could first look down on ourselves. New tools often help us see things differently. We now see a vast and small globe and envision environmental, human, and nuclear connectedness. Fears about a prospective vacuum in work identity, and the anxiety and depression these create, are thus overlaid with the very real awareness that there is a potentially even greater identity vacuum ahead, a human and animal species' vacuum. Thus we might say that Westerners are freshly aware that we live not in high-risk societies but in a high-risk world.

A genuine work identity, even in a high-risk world, means what Shaw had to say about the necessity of being an insider in an actively chosen, personally meaningful realm of thought and work. And it means the inescapable integration of ongoing learning as one grows and develops an identity. Today, when one asks any number of U.S. college students and young adults about their prospective or current work, I hear many say that they are *in* marketing, or *in* the business sector, or *in* the nonprofit sector, or *in* the health care field. Saying one is *in* something is not the same as saying "I am" (or "I am going to be") a manager, a teacher, a physician, a nurse, an engineer, a poet, or a plumber. The main meaning of work identity, one that many young people and some of their elders might reclaim, is a personal commitment to a "compelling idea" and its expression in a role that inspires an unending, evolving quest of self. This is achieved through initial and ongoing learning in engaged and engaging work.

Conclusions: Identity Development, Work, and Adult Learning

The paid work that consumes much of adult life supports and fosters identity development and learning. In its best forms, work provides the context in which one is made to feel and to be psychologically coherent, adaptive, and central to productive life. There is an interdependent relationship among adult identity, paid work, and learning. Each constituent fuels the others. As a context for identity development, the work of one's mature years shapes many key psychosocial investments and learning opportunities. As a function of work, identity certainty increases, learning (about content, contexts, others, and the self) shows marked development, self-reliance grows, and career salience deepens.

ADULT PERSONALITY, DEVELOPMENT, AND LEARNING

Genes and the Environment

First, although it is beyond the scope of this chapter, a word is in order about personality genetics. Early evidence for the genetic bedrock of personality came from studies of monozygotic and dizygotic twins, some reared together and others apart. Many of these studies have examined the few traits that are said to represent the entire composite of personality. For example, Bouchard and Loehlin (2001) used the Costa and McCrae (1992) five factor model (FFM) and reported average heritabilities of 0.40 to 0.60 for all five factors.

Some claim that personality is a trait constellation established by genes alone. This is the "plaster" view of personality, with many of its adherents maintaining that endogenously endowed personality traits are "influenced not at all by the environment" (McCrae et al., 2000, p. 175). Yet there is strong evidence of personality malleability, on both an evolutionary and an individual basis. Genes necessarily require that one "have experience with . . . tasks for the gene to manifest its phenotypic effect" (Bouchard & Loehlin, 2001, p. 251). Intellectual engagement and learning, intra- and interpersonal awareness, and the expression of artistic, musical, and other abilities likely have a genetic component. Genes are the bedrock, and their interaction with other genes, with the environment, and with a volitional human, permit expression (see, e.g., Cervone, 2004; Li, 2003).

The genetic code resides in DNA. Between 20,000 and 25,000 human genes convey instructions that produce proteins, with their activity mediated by RNA, by environmental interactions, and by other factors (many of which are currently unknown). These genes and their mediating agents variously permit genetic expression, augmentation, dampening, and silencing (Novina & Sharp, 2004). Genetic expression is also mediated by one's internal and external environments. With respect to the adult's endogenous (internal) environment and functional intelligence processes, reduced gene expression due to DNA damage (e.g., oxidative stress) occurs in the aging human brain (Lu et al., 2004). Recently, there has been particular interest in the apolipoprotein E genotype as a risk factor for cognitive decline (e.g., Hofer et al., 2002). With respect to general intelligence and the adult's exogenous (external) environment, ongoing genotype–environment interaction continues throughout life to support and sometimes thwart intellectual maintenance and growth. It is estimated that this interaction contributes about 0.50 of the variance to intelligence (e.g., Plomin & Spinath, 2004).

In adulthood, mature roles and responsibilities socialize adults to perform in consistent, nonerratic ways. Therefore, personality is relatively enduring, made up as it is of many intersecting qualities that "cohere" (Cervone, 2004; Cervone & Shoda, 1999), even as they also evolve through the species' history, through genetic and environmental interactions, and through persons' experiences and interpretations of experiences. Thus, as important as they are, genes alone do not create personality.

In part, adult personality plasticity is due to inter-actions with important persons, contexts, and roles in (and before) mature life (e.g., Baltes, 1997; Cervone, 2004; Helson, Jones, & Kwan, 2002; Helson & Roberts, 1994; Helson & Kwan, 2000; Loehlin, Horn, & Willerman, 1990; Paris & Helson, 2002). In important respects, the malleability or "plasticity" position that counters the "set like plaster" view of personality sees humans (and their genes) as changing in response to interactions with a dynamic environment, even as the environment is altered by humans who act in and on it.

Personality Attributes

The five personality traits (neuroticism, extraversion, openness to experience, conscientiousness, and agreeableness) of the FFM have been among the most influential in personality research since the early 1980s. However, to many, they seem too "tidy" (Srivastava et al., 2003) and far too restrictive in representing the totality of personality. In their extensive meta-analysis of personality studies, DeNeve and Cooper (1998) unearthed 137 personality attributes. Ackerman and Heggestad's (1997) meta-analysis reported 19 personality attributes in 135 investigations. In a content analysis of four key personality journals during a five-year period, Cribb, Ozone, and Pipes (1992) reported more than 500 instruments in use, instruments that reflect a vast and overlapping array of personality attributes.

In this section I consider personality attributes more broadly than trait theory. I look to the principal reported reciprocal relationships between learning and personality development as these relate to work experiences. Included are the development of person-ality attributes into and through the adult work years, and the ways that paid work promotes such develop-ment and related learning. Although there are many personality characteristics, I consider only six attrib-utes because these six have been shown to develop as a function of employment. These are autonomy,

interpersonal competence (including organizational citizenship behavior), maturity, conscientiousness, openness to experience, and intellectual flexibility. Some of the data discussed here are used in employee selection, training, and promotion decisions.

Work Autonomy

In the worldwide, highly competitive economy, many companies have flattened their hierarchies and decentralized decision making. Worker empower-ment, continual learning, and self-direction are vital, and independent judgment is now exercised through-out many U.S. organizations, even at bottom levels (see, e.g., Simmering, Colquitt, Noe, & Porter, 2003). Much of the literature refers to various aspects of such independent judgment as work autonomy.

Work autonomy means the personal freedom to perform functions and roles in unique ways. This is the extent to which persons are expected and have the impetus, freedom, and control over their jobs to indi-vidually determine how, when, and sometimes where work is performed (e.g., Barrick & Mount, 1993; Sim-mering et al., 2003). Among other aspects, employees prioritize and self-pace tasks, allocate resources, de-termine work methods, plan and schedule activities, and telecommute. Employees are also groomed to function in autonomous work teams, learn indepen-dently, and mesh their various responsibilities with others within and beyond the organization (Adams & Kydoniefs, 2000; Barrick & Mount, 1993; Fisher, 1993; Lee, Ashford, & Bobko, 1990; Roy, 2003).

As is true in a number of other areas, a continual reciprocal relationship exists in personality → work/learning → personality effects. On the front end of this equation, high autonomy predicts the kind of work persons choose, their actions on the job, and their effectiveness. Work conducted under au-tonomous conditions then leads to greater autonomy and control, job involvement, a sense of responsibility for one's job, and work satisfaction. If Vernon, Jang, Harris, and McCarthy's (1997) claim is correct, au-tonomy is one of the least heritable of the personality attributes; therefore, environmental factors mold self-direction and its positive results.

Clearly, paid work is inseparable from the society in which that work occurs. Nations' social structures and views of individual rights alter personal tenden-cies, if not personality itself. With respect to auton-omy, in the United States, a sense of personal uniqueness, independence, and self-determination arise from constitutionally granted individual rights, worldview, and beliefs in personal freedom. Such views, as well as sociohistorical changes in those views, alter attitudes and the expression of autonomy. For example, in their longitudinal investigation of the influence of increasing individualism in the United States, Roberts and Helson (1997) studied women at four periods over 31 years. They found that increasing individualism in the aggregate, particularly between 1960 and 1985, was associated with women's declines in adherence to norms and to increases in their autonomy, self-focus, self-assertion, and narcissism. In the years between 1958 and 1989, those women's autonomy increased and peaked concurrently with trends in the escalation and peak of societal individualism (autonomy). Work effects were seen in, for example, a growing intolerance for glass ceilings and expectations that salaries would be gender-neutral. In part, women's assertiveness learning emanated from the feminist movement during those years; their work experiences of personal empowerment and autonomy then furthered such learning and their increased sense of autonomy.

Supporting evidence comes from other society-work comparisons. Through longitudinal studies in the United States and Poland, Kohn and associates (1997) found that adults' position in society, as well as the tendency of a society toward freedom (e.g., the United States) or authoritarian constriction (e.g., Poland) produces organizations that either sponsor autonomy among workers (United States) or restrict this inclination (Poland). These investigators define occupational self-direction as "the use of initiative, thought, and independent judgment in work" (Kohn, Naoi, Schoenback, Schooler, & Slomczynski, 1990, p. 988). For workers, structural job conditions directly affect psychological functioning on and beyond the job. In particular, closeness of supervision and routinization (repetitive jobs) restrict autonomy. In turn, all three factors (closeness of supervision, routinization, and restricted autonomy) thwart creativity (Kohn et al., 1997); they also thwart the autonomous learning that might improve jobs and the occupational context itself. The absence of work autonomy leads to distrust, "authoritarian-conservative beliefs," rigidity, and a nonchange orientation (Kohn et al., 1997, p. 618). Personal distress is manifest in self-deprecation, anxiety, decreased self-confidence, and suppressed job involvement.

It seems that nearly all employers these days wish to have workers who are intensely job involved and committed to their work. Well they should be, for job involvement defines high-performing organizations. Together, work autonomy and job control foster job involvement (Barling, Kelloway, & Iverson, 2003; Lawler, 1992). For example, managers who are self-directed perform better in job conditions of high discretion (Barrick & Mount, 1993). Autonomous work conditions and job involvement also encourage ongoing learning (Barling et al., 2003; Lawler, 1992; Parker & Wall, 1998; Simmering et al., 2003; Wall, Jackson, & Davids, 1992). In effect, the overall context for workers and for the organization improves under conditions of autonomy.

In the United States work autonomy leads to greater personal self-direction and other positive results on the job and shows transfer effects to nonwork environments. Work autonomy leads to an agentic, "can-do" approach in off-work roles and responsibilities, an increasingly internal locus of control, improved subjective well-being, and greater learning beyond the job. For example, in their 10-year, time-lagged study of male employees, Kohn and Schooler (1983; see also Kohn & Schooler, 1978) found that the men they studied learned from their jobs and work contexts and then transferred such learning tendencies and outcomes to situations beyond the job. Workers tended to "develop personally more responsible standards of morality, to become more trustful, more self-confident, less self-deprecatory, less fatalistic, less anxious, and less conformist in their ideas" (Kohn et al., 1983, p. 142; Schooler et al., 1999).

Studying men's work roles in the United States, Japan, and Poland, the investigations of Kohn et al. (1990) led to similar conclusions. Defining social class advantage as having "greater control over the means of production and greater control over the labor power of others" (p. 966), these investigators found that autonomy and occupational control conferred powerful advantages. Men with occupational control were more intellectually flexible and self-directed. They enjoyed greater than average opportunities for autonomy and, by association, for cognitive development, contextual mastery, and learning. Such men were also more valuing of self-direction for their children, a positive spillover effect for the next generation.

Autonomous work validates the self to the extent that greater emotional stability, self-confidence, and agreeableness also result. In their longitudinal study of 910 workers in New Zealand, Roberts, Caspi, and Moffitt (2003) concluded that six interrelated work and personal qualities significantly predict such outcomes. These qualities are (a) high autonomy, (b) greater than average occupational attainment, (c) complex work, (d) substantial work resources and power, (e) higher than average financial security, and (e) high work satisfaction and involvement. In addition to the powerful effects of work autonomy on employees' positive sense of self, on their concepts of power and effectiveness, and on their increased autonomy in and beyond the work environment, other effects are found. Many persons who function in self-directed roles show consistent nonauthoritarianism. They also work better in teams, and the recent emphasis on self-directed teams requires independence, continual learning, and cooperation, all of which are enhanced by organizational conditions of autonomy and empowerment.

Clearly, some individuals function better in autonomous circumstances than others. Among employees whose personalities function well in autonomous conditions, organizations supporting individual worker autonomy and autonomous teams tend to profit. Corporate profit is the direct result of enhanced worker motivation (Greenberg, 1992; Houkes, Janssen, De Jonge, & Bakker, 2003), learning and achievement, well-being, and positive affect (Roberts, Robins, Trzesniewski, & Caspi, 2003). Autonomous work conditions lead to even greater worker self-direction, improved competencies (Simmering et al., 2003), decreased dependency (Froman, 1994), greater effectiveness (Barrick & Mount, 1993; Roberts, Robins, et al., 2003), increased cooperation, and heightened creativity (Barling et al., 2003; Froman, 1994; Greenberg, 1992).

Interpersonal Competence and Organizational Citizenship Behavior

Interpersonal Competence Ferris, Witt, and Hochwarter (2001) described an ineffective "genius," a person of great brilliance whose minimal interpersonal skills made that worker useless on the job. Anecdotes such as this pepper work lore. Yet until recently, the bulk of personality research related to employment has paid rather little attention to the importance of interpersonal competence, social cognition, and personal desires to be prosocial and helpful at work. Sociability (extraversion), agreeableness, warmth, friendliness, positive affect and caring to learn about others and about relational functioning are components of interpersonal competence. They show a relationship among personality, learning tendencies, and work precursors and effects.

The ability to appraise interpersonal relationships and correctly interpret the meaning of human interactions in a social context is a dimension of adult intelligence. The cognitive literature uses the term *social cognition* (e.g., Fiske & Taylor, 1991; Forgas, Oatley, & Manstead, 2001), whereas the personality literature (reflecting the influence of the FFM) uses the terms *extraversion* (sociability), *agreeableness*, and *openness to experience*. These personality terms tap part of the construct but tend to exclude cognitive dimensions and personal interest in learning about and seeing from within the roles and perspectives of others. Instead, I use the term *interpersonal competence* to capture the broader array of talents and developed abilities that are critical to success in work environments.

In general, interpersonally competent, sociable persons tend to select jobs that provide opportunities to learn and to share knowledge with others. This reinforces and maintains (or extends) their outgoing and learning tendencies (Roberts, Caspi, et al., 2003). Greater work satisfaction results. Increased positive affect, better work conditions, and potentially more profitable organizations are the result. Russell (2001), for example, reported a longitudinal study of 98 top-level executives. Hierarchical linear modeling showed that "problem-solving" ratings were crucial in executives' early performance in those roles, but "people-oriented" ratings predicted subsequent long-term performance. Based on the predictive model he developed based on these and related findings, Russell (2001) concluded: "Utility estimates suggested that the system generated an additional $3 million in annual profit per candidate selected. . . . Findings imply that a model of executive performance must contain main effects for person (competencies) and situation (economic-industrial) characteristics" (p. 560).

In teams that require close, cooperative relationships among workers, agreeableness and helping tendencies correlate with team productivity. Agreeableness results in more effective team functioning because of increased group cohesion (Greene, 1989). Other factors also enter the equation. For example, in Barrick, Stewart, Neubert, and Mount's (1998) group-level study of 652 workers in 51 work teams, individuals' agreeableness, extraversion, emotional stability, general mental ability, and conscientiousness correlated with supervisor ratings of team performance. At the individual team level of analysis, in Neuman and Wright's (1999) study of 79 four-person work teams, agreeableness and conscientiousness predicted peer assessments of individuals' performance beyond cognitive ability and job skills alone.

Organizational Citizenship Behavior   One stream of research, organizational citizenship behavior (OCB) focuses on the merits of positive, outward extensions of the self among workers at various levels in the organization. In effect, OCB addresses interpersonal competence in task and contextual performance. OCB is extra-role behavior, that is, "behavior(s) of a discretionary nature that are not part of the employee's formal role requirements, but nevertheless promote the effective functioning of the organization" (Organ, 1988, p. 4). Attributes such as courtesy, helping and teaching behaviors, good sportsmanship, beyond-the-job volunteering, compliance, and altruism are included in OCB. These qualities bind people together, sustaining personal connections and mentally healthy work environments and organizations (Robertson & Callinan, 1998).

The OCB concept includes personal tendencies and learned behaviors (see, e.g. Hogan, 1997; Organ, 1988; Organ, Podsakoff, & MacKenzie, 2004). Prosocial behaviors are widely cited as essential ingredients of workplace harmony and psychological health, collegial functioning, self-directed team efforts, and organizational effectiveness and productivity. Reviewing the OCB literature, Podsakoff and MacKenzie (1997) found that OCB's general mechanism in increasing worker and organizational performance can be seen as that which "lubricates" the "social machinery of the organization, reducing friction, and/or increasing efficiency" (p. 135). For instance, when competent, longer tenured workers voluntarily help new employees to learn the ropes, the newly hired become productive more quickly. This enhances the division's effectiveness. In a qualitative study of the meaning of paid work to 53 older women, Altschuler (2004) gives an example of this prosocial tendency in the words of a study subject: "I don't take the attitude

'Well—it's not part of my job.' I just know that when you see the overall picture of what has to be done in order for the office to move smoothly, then . . . I cannot say 'Hey, I'm not gonna do this because I'm not getting paid' because that's just not in my nature" (p. 234). With respect to the rejection of such citizenship behavior, Buchwald (2004) provides a tongue-in-cheek example in the context of a recent influenza vaccine shortage: "The government knew for months that there was going to be a shortage, but each health supervisor said: 'It isn't my department. Besides, I have to go to lunch'" (p. C2). When organizations foster prosocial, extra-role endeavors, workers tend to learn aspects of jobs beyond their prescribed functions. This promotes organizational effectiveness, satisfactory relationships on the job, and worker retention.

In the long run, prosocial behaviors by competent, longer tenured workers lead to modeling effects, to the contagion of "best practices" throughout and beyond the unit, to the release of managers' time for planning and other responsibilities, and to better cross-division functioning (see Podsakoff & MacKenzie, 1997, pp. 135–137). Studying blue-collar workers in a paper mill, Podsakoff, Ahearne, and MacKenzie (1997) concluded that almost 17% of the quality and 26% of the quantity of employee performance was due to OCB activities. In a study of 116 agencies in an insurance company, 17% of the variance in overall agency performance was interpreted as having been due to OCB actions (Podsakoff & MacKenzie, 1994).

Prosocial, helping tendencies such as the viewpoint expressed by the worker in Altschuler's (2004) study are related to conscientiousness, agreeableness, and personal integrity. Schmidt and Hunter (2004) found that integrity tests are valid for all levels and types of jobs studied; they show an additional predictive validity of 27% over general mental ability for job performance and an additional 20% for training performance.

Prosocial, OCB characteristics are readily overridden by harsh, authoritarian work situations, by conditions that set one employee against another, and by threatening circumstances. Then compliance, altruism, and helping functions typically retreat. Conditions of high threat include organizational restructuring with its potential for job loss; domineering, mean-minded, or condescending superiors; the possibility of lateral employee transfers with little promise of advancement; and psychologically unsafe work environments. In the latter, workers' expression of their authentic selves is restricted, and personal freedom and genuineness are curtailed. One learns armored self-protection instead of more about how to perform job functions genuinely and effectively. And in jobs or occasions that carry the burden of severe time pressures or harried deadlines (e.g., emergency room triage care, news journalism), the time that would be required for warmth, personal engagement, and a prosocial extension of the self to co-workers is often abandoned.

Repeated waves of downsizing, declining organizational loyalty to employees, and unethical organizational practices (e.g., the Enron scandal) have led to increased vigilance among workers and declining trust in corporate leadership and business practices (e.g., Bocchino, Hartman, & Foley, 2003). If prosocial tendencies in which workers help each other do not decline, prosocial actions directed to aiding organizational goals may show slippage. Workers believe that good citizenship behavior travels a two-way street (e.g., Holman, 2002; Parker, 2003).

Work and Maturity: Adult Behavior, Ego Defenses, and Generativity

Due in part to work experiences and employers' expectations for mature, responsible behavior, the mental mechanisms of most adults become more mature over developmental time. In work and other contexts, young, less mature adults are more likely to use more aggressive defense mechanisms, such as projection and displacement. Adults of greater maturity tend to have learned impulse control, employing coping strategies that include cognitive reappraisal (Diehl, Coyle, & Labouvie-Vief, 1996), sublimation, humor, physical exercise, and altruism (Vaillant, 1993, 2000).

Ego identity becomes stronger as adults, through work and other responsibilities, move toward higher level defense mechanisms. Generative care for others and increasing insight into the self represent developmental progressions, manifest in part through mature defenses (Erikson, 1987). In such development, adults reach out to the social world and move upward in consciousness. Vaillant (1993, 2000) observed that the mature ego defenses of altruism, humor, anticipation, suppression, and sublimation are mechanisms of increased consciousness. These defenses are developmental progressions from unconscious, less mature defenses such as denial, displacement, and projection.

Just as the higher level ego defenses represent movement forward in maturity and upward in consciousness, they are also more socially centered than self-centered. This is Erikson's (1975) concept of moving "outward" toward others as one develops in maturity and generativity (Hoare, 2005).

The outward-moving development that Erikson described is associated with progression to higher levels of ego development as per Loevinger's (1976) construct. In that construct, ego development means increments in consciousness, impulse control, perspective taking, reflectiveness, and social development; all are attributes of greater maturity. Conscious and tacit learning are variously involved in each of these ego developmental constituents.

Responding to criticisms that stage models of development are of limited value beyond, for instance, measures of intelligence, Cohn and Westenberg (2004) conducted a meta-analysis of 42 studies (total subjects = 5,648) of ego development using the Loevinger Washington University Sentence Completion Test. Data show that although ego development shares variance with measured intelligence, it does not reduce to intelligence. As is true of moral development and the development of insight and open-mindedness, these authors conclude that "intellectual capacity may be a necessary but insufficient condition for reaching relatively high levels of maturity" (Cohn & Westenberg, 2004, p. 769). Studies have shown positive correlations between higher levels of ego development and learning to respect diverse others (Helson & Roberts, 1994), as well as between greater ego development and learning to empathically understand the needs of others (Labouvie-Vief, DeVoe, & Bulka, 1989).

When one looks to emotional maturity against activity level and vitality, developmental data show mixed findings. Most persons become more emotionally stable, socially dominant, agreeable, and warm during young adulthood (Roberts, Caspi, & Moffitt, 2001; Roberts, Caspi, et al., 2003). However, separating extraversion into social dominance and social vitality (Helson & Kwan, 2000) alters the view somewhat. Trends point to increasing social dominance from 18 years of age to middle adulthood and decreasing social vitality, linearly, during young, middle, and older adulthood (Helson & Kwan, 2000; Roberts, Robins, et al., 2003).

From adolescence to young adulthood, declines in negative affect and neuroticism occur (Helson &

Kwan, 2000; Neyer & Asendorpf, 2001; Robins, Fraley, Roberts, & Trzesniewski, 2001; Roberts, Caspi, et al., 2003; Viken, Rose, Kaprio, & Koskenvuo, 1994; Watson & Walker, 1996). Employment is prominent in these declines because paid work incorporates young adults into mainstream society. Work fosters contextual learning and mastery of the job environment. As Roberts, Caspi, et al.'s (2003) longitudinal study found, incorporation into the societal work world decreased young adults' negativity from ages 18 to 26. However, adolescents who are particularly high in negativity tend toward stormy and less successful entries into the work world. For them, maintenance instead of declining neuroticism is apparent into young adulthood (Roberts, Caspi, et al., 2003). For many such youths, ill preparation for work, marginal status, limited learning, or work identity refusal lead to cynicism and ongoing negativity (e.g., Erikson, 1956, 1968, 1982, 1987).

As one would expect, emotional instability negatively predicts mature behavior, goal-setting activities, conscientiousness, and a range of other desirable work behaviors. For example, men with disorderly work histories have shown less personality coherence, learning, and planning tendencies than persons with stable career histories (Barrick, Mount, & Strauss, 1993). Adults with poor coping mechanisms are also less able to handle work difficulties and stress, tending to absorb stress effects. On the other hand, those with good coping strategies tend to focus on work tasks, problem solving, and learning instead of on their emotional responses, thus neutralizing or deflecting stress (e.g., Ackerman, Kanfer, & Goff, 1995).

In addition to relationships among developmental maturity, learning, and the use of higher order coping mechanisms, cognitive development plays an important role. The use of more mature defenses is undergirded by greater understandings of coping processes, higher levels of ego development, and greater cognitive complexity (Fischer & Ayoub, 1994; Labouvie-Vief & DeVoe, 1991; Labouvie-Vief et al., 1989; Labouvie-Vief, Hakim-Larson, & Hobart, 1987). Higher levels of cognitive and ego development are essential if one is to understand the intricacies of emotions and coping mechanisms in general. Such understandings are vital to gaining insight into one's own and others' behavior, to efforts to see from within the perspectives and work roles of others, and to understanding various complexities in the work environment.

Due to persons' tendencies to emulate behavior and to absorb the moods of others, different work climates vary in their mental health and in what one might call group-level neuroses. Data from Joiner and Katz's (1999) meta-analysis of 36 studies, show that "emotional contagion" explains some of this variance. In emotional contagion, moods are passed along from one person to another. At the group level, depressive moods arise from neurotic or emotionally unstable persons who alter the subjective well-being of those with whom they interact: "People tend from moment to moment to 'catch' other people's emotions as a result of mimicry, feedback, and resulting synchrony in social encounters" (Hatfield, Cacioppo, & Rapson, 1993, p. 96). This involves negative learning, with social modeling accounting for some of the contagion. In particular, workers low in self-efficacy and high in cynicism tend to evoke "contagious modeling" in their colleagues (Bandura, 1997, p. 467).

In work groups with a preponderance of positive affect among individual members, the overall group affect tends toward positivity. Low work absenteeism occurs. Conversely, when negative affect is expressed by several group members, the overriding mood becomes negative. Members of negative groups avoid engaging in prosocial behaviors and have higher than average work absenteeism. New entrants to the group tend to "catch" the prevailing mood or tone, and to then behave according to its predominant affect (George, 1990). Agreeableness and positive affect vary with the extent of social support for agreeableness and positivity in the organization, and with the cooperative spirit engendered by the group and the larger structure (Murtha, Kanfer, & Ackerman, 1996). Clearly, though, some persons are more sensitive and permeable to mood influence than others, showing greater inclinations to absorb the affect of others (Houkes et al., 2003).

Because many technologically advanced nations now have companies with plants and offices abroad and sometimes have an international workforce in their home-based businesses, it is useful to consider cultural variations in personality characteristics and mental mechanisms. In a study of 53 countries, Cook, Young, Taylor, and Bedford (2000) found national variance in levels of extraversion, neuroticism, psychoticism, and subjective well-being. Nations with a high gross domestic product and norms of cooperation instead of competition show higher levels of well-being among their citizens. Based on personality data from 39 countries, Steel and Ones (2002) found a high correlation between gross national product and extraversion, subjective well-being, and conscientiousness. Although it would be foolhardy to claim a direct correspondence between broad-brush national data and corporate behavior, it is a mistake to claim no relationship between the two climates. National attributes are bound to influence if not modify personality expression. As discussed, Kohn and colleagues (1983, 1997) have repeatedly shown that a nation's tendency toward autonomy or authoritarianism lead to organizations in those countries that sponsor either worker self-direction and learning or subservience, respectively.

Variance has also been found as a function of culturally based values and social norms (Gudykunst, Ting-Toomey, & Chua, 1988). Staudinger and colleagues (1999) found differences in subjective well-being and personality dispositions between U.S. and German citizens. They interpreted their findings in terms of a heterogeneous, individualistic, and less structured (U.S.) society versus a more homogeneous, structured, social welfare state (Germany). In U.S. society, more numerous resources promote well-being and potentially the expression of a greater array of personality characteristics. In Germany, the researchers concluded, fewer personality characteristics are adequate to the task.

National variances are also found in the way citizens handle conflict. In Hong Kong and in the People's Republic of China, for example, learning the Confucian ideal of harmony is important (Shaffer, Joplin, Bell, Lau, & Oguz, 2000). In those cultures, persons respond to conflict by using passive avoidance strategies. Individuals in the United States and some other Western cultures learn to confront conflict directly, using more pointed, sometimes aggressive strategies (see Chiu & Kosinski, 1994; Diong & Bishop, 1999; Westwood, Tang, & Kirkbride, 1992). This applies to work settings and other contexts.

With respect to other situational influences, personality expression varies with the context and with having learned various norms and protocols. Stable tendencies, shown by "behavioral signatures," occur in situations with like motifs (Shoda, Mischel, & Wright, 1994, p. 674). For example, in the United States, adult demeanor is frequently consistent in the presence of similar authority figures such as a corporate president or judge. Yet contexts differ. Any number of adults have learned to be assertive but formal

and guarded in contemporary work environments, whereas they are warm, nurturing, and caring in their home environments. Some are highly organized and conscientious at work but far less methodical and fastidious in the relaxed, safe harbors of their homes. Particularly in work situations that carry expectations of cerebral power, many persons preferentially operate on the basis of cool, analytical thinking and rational, linear learning and reasoning. Once at home, limbic powers of love and tenderness override cognitive intellect (see also Cervone & Shoda, 1999). Many contemporary U.S. organizational cultures and work unit cultures, with their relative absence of psychological safety, provoke workers to suppress their authentic, otherwise coherent personality tendencies and the integrated expression of cerebral and emotional intellect.

Generativity and Gender In midlife, men and women typically move in opposite directions from each other and from their prior, gender-typical, masculine or feminine tendencies. Many men become less assertive and individualistic and more affiliative, nurturant, empathic, and introspective (Axelrod, 1999; Gutmann, 1976, 1977; Haan, 1977; Haan, Milsap, & Hartka, 1986; Levinson et al., 1978). Women become less nurturant and communal and more assertive and independent (Gutmann, 1975, 1977, 1992; Haan, 1977; Kirchmeyer, 2002). Gutmann has interpreted this as a psychological shift, one of increasing cathectic flexibility as middle-aged persons, however unconsciously, learn to explore their previously dormant, unexpressed tendencies. "Men discover a hitherto unsuspected vein of nurturance and aesthetic sensibility; women discover tough, managerial, and competitive qualities that they can apply in a first career or in a career change, as from social worker to lawyer" (Gutmann, 1992, p. 289). Altered estrogen–androgen ratios at midlife and other as yet undetermined factors likely play a role. In all, the intersecting dynamics of psychological forces, biological factors, historical and cohort effects, contemporary work roles, and career advancement norms are causal.

Workplace findings have been inconsistent, particularly with respect to job promotion. For example, although the ideal workplace is widely touted as one that supports gender neutrality, not only is masculine behavior frequently preferred, it has been found to preferentially lead to career advancement for both men and women (Johnson & Scandura, 1994; Kirchmeyer, 1997; Sachs, Chrisler, & Devlin, 1992). We have yet to answer Kirchmeyer's (2002) question: Does "high masculinity help the workers advance, or did their masculinity levels increase with advancement?" (p. 929). I would add, to what extent do women who strive for occupational advancement preconsciously or consciously learn and emulate successful (masculine) work behaviors?

If midlife gender expression moves in opposite directions among men and women, there are implications for generative functions. Generativity is a hallmark of maturity. From Erikson's (e.g., 1969) generativity concept to more recent ideas, experts find that the middle and later years are prime eras for adults to teach, mentor, and bring along younger workers (Castiglioni, Bellini, & Shea, 2004; Gibson, 2004; Kiltz, Danzig, & Szecsy, 2004; McAdams & de St. Aubin, 1998; McAdams, Diamond, de St. Aubin, & Mansfield, 1997; Peterson & Stewart, 1996). Creating opportunities for young adults; grooming them for advancement and leadership roles; mentoring, coaching, and providing advice and informal counsel are all generative functions. The work literature is replete with studies and examples of sponsorship in general and of same- and cross-gender mentoring in particular (e.g., Kelly, 2001), but we do not yet know the extent to which gender differences at midlife may have causal implications for mentoring. Certainly, multiple variables (e.g., endogenous factors, cohort effects, advancement norms, saturation in prior roles) are involved. Adults create their own equilibrated lives. For example, the women achievers in Helson and Srivastava's (2001) study learned to balance their ambition and power needs with abilities to nurture others. Yet at midlife, due to some men's turn toward nurturance and centering on others and some women's turn toward power and centering on the self (in some, due to previously subverted achievement needs), some men may be more effective, caring mentors than some women. Men may also experience greater satisfaction doing so. For many achieving, contemporary women, the phrase "been there, done that" rings true.

Conscientiousness

Numerous studies show that conscientiousness is the best predictor of high job performance and one of the best predictors of life satisfaction as well (e.g., Barrick & Mount, 1991; Barrick, Mount, & Strauss, 1993; DeNeve & Cooper, 1998; Hough, Eaton, Dunnette, Kamp, & McCloy, 1990; Mount & Barrick, 1995; Rust, 1999; Salgado, 1997). Meeting one's obligations leads to self-worth and a sense of competence. Conscientiousness is an attribute that many persons bring to the job. However, conscientiousness also increases as a result of having learned to function competently in jobs and other roles that require and reward such behavior. Responsible, work-oriented individuals show gains in maturity, learn more than their less conscientious co-workers, and tend to set and to plan toward more difficult goals (Clausen & Jones, 1998). Goal setting leads to goal commitment and attainment. Loevinger (1993) demonstrated correlations between conscientiousness and achievement. Adults at the higher levels of ego development are more responsible, learning and achievement-oriented, tolerant, and autonomous (Helson & Roberts, 1994).

Most persons show increased responsibility during young adulthood (Clausen & Jones, 1998; Helson & Kwan, 2000; Neyer & Asendorpf, 2001; Roberts, Caspi, et al., 2003; Roberts, Robins, et al., 2003). Much of this is due to entry into the workforce because job requirements demand responsibility, reliable and consistent performance, focused learning, and greater self-control. When women's and men's responsibilities include parenting, increased conscientiousness results from this as well (Clausen & Jones, 1998; Demick, chapter 15, this volume; Paris & Helson, 2002).

Increasing conscientiousness and competence during young adulthood depend partly on baseline competence during adolescence. Analyzing data from three longitudinal studies, Clausen and Jones (1998) found that highly competent adolescents showed rather little personal change in this regard from early adolescence through the mature years. On the other hand, many of those who had been low in competence and conscientiousness in adolescence advanced significantly in such qualities later in life. Roberts, Caspi, et al. (2003) reported a longitudinal study of a subset of 910 working adults from the larger Dunedin Study, a New Zealand investigation of health and behavior of an entire cohort born in 1972 and 1973. Personality at age 18 predicted work experiences at age 26, and work experiences predicted changes in personality during those years. Furthermore, there were reciprocal relationships among personality traits, learning, and work experiences in that the very personality attributes that led persons to elect specific work experiences were the attributes that were altered by those work experiences and by the learning that was integral to those experiences. Those who engaged in higher status work as young adults became more self-confident by age 26. They acquired more responsible and stimulating work, moved into supervisory and managerial positions, and were more work committed and happier in their jobs than cohort age mates who remained in positions that provided little in the way of opportunities for increased responsibility, advancement, and success.

Developmentally, there is evidence of ongoing conscientiousness development into middle age (Helson & Roberts, 1994; Simmering et al., 2003; Srivastava et al., 2003). For example, Clausen and Jones (1998) reported that women who had begun to work outside the home as young adults and remained employed while raising their children were primary agents in their own self-development. Due to their continual paid employment, when compared with their stay-at-home peers, they showed cognitive commitment, assertiveness, greater learning and self-confidence, as well as the ability to handle multiple roles responsibly. In a longitudinal study of 81 women at two time periods (at ages 21–27 and 27–43), Roberts (1997) examined whether work experiences influence personality. Personality changes were not found during the young adult years; however, between 27 and 43 years of age, working women scored higher on agency, a measure that includes ambition, confidence, and self-sufficiency. Those who were more successful at work also learned occupational norms and became more norm-adhering. Norm adherence is a marker for conscientiousness as well as for responsible, prosocial (OCB) behavior.

Unfortunately, one difficulty among studies using one of the big five factor personality inventories (e.g., Goldberg, 1992; Costa & McCrae, 1992) and finding evidence of linear increases in conscientiousness (e.g., Simmering et al., 2003; Srivastava et al., 2003) is that such studies do not reveal what conscientiousness means in the lives of individual subjects. This applies to some non Five Factor Inventory (FFI)-based studies as well. For example, in Helson and Roberts's (1994) longitudinal study of ego development in 90 women, increases in responsibility were found from age 21 to 43 and from age 43 to 52. But little information is available with respect to how these attributes were manifest.

High conscientiousness and goal commitment lead to enhanced motivation to learn and inclinations to engage in continual learning (Simmering et al., 2003). High growth needs strength (the need to develop and to learn), high need for achievement, and an internal locus of control intercorrelate. These three attributes predict and are enhanced by highly motivating jobs (Brown, 1996; Houkes et al., 2003), and they correlate positively with conscientiousness. However, overconfidence in one's ability can create difficulties. As Simmering and colleagues (2003) found, subjects who were both conscientious and inordinately confident tended to deceive themselves, believing that their performance was better than it was. This dual tendency thwarts ongoing learning.

Conscientiousness, accompanied as it is with goal setting and high goal attainment, strongly predicts competent work performance. A reciprocal, conscientiousness-enhancing effect is also seen: Competence in work tasks and job contexts predicts more responsible work roles, learning, and the maintenance or extension of conscientiousness.

Openness to Experience

Kelly (1963) wrote about two workers, one a "veteran" administrator with "one year of experience—repeated thirteen times," and the other a naval officer with a "vast and versatile ignorance" (p. 171). These examples point to two attributes that are associated with cognitive and experiential openness: First, intelligence requires the active practice, on an ongoing basis, of a mind that is receptive to new and revised information, to different ideas, to a commitment to ongoing learning, and to varied ways of experiencing and seeing the world. Second, as is true for a number of other developmental constructs (e.g., moral development), intelligence is necessary but insufficient for the development, maintenance, and extension of open mindedness in adulthood. Although definitions of intelligence vary, among other qualities, intelligent behavior includes the ongoing assimilation of new information (including that which might contradict prior knowledge, beliefs, and biases), interest in expanding one's experiences and sensitivities, and a readiness to engage in appropriate, positive personal change.

Openness to experience is often subsumed under intelligence but is most frequently studied separately.

Costa and McCrae (e.g., 1992) have long claimed that their FFM, with measurements of five personality traits (the NEO Personality Inventory and the FFI) comprehensively represent the major dimensions (neuroticism, extraversion, openness to experience, conscientiousness, and agreeableness) of personality. Based on population-level data and finding only a weak relationship between openness and intelligence, they conclude that there is nonequivalence between the two constructs (McCrae & Costa, 1997); however, they cite "preference for complexity," "divergent thinking," "curiosity," and "imagination" as openness qualities (pp. 828–835), attributes that others find indicative of intelligence, abstract thinking, and creativity. Among the 12 items in the FFI's openness to experience scale, for example, 2 questions tap intellectual factors. One asks persons to self-report on their "intellectual curiosity," and another asks whether subjects enjoy "playing with theories or abstract ideas" (Costa & McCrae, 1992).

Intelligence is included in a number of personality inventories. For example, "culture/intellect" is one of Goldberg's (1992) big five factors. "Intellectance" is one of six traits in the Hogan (1986) personality inventory, and intelligence is part of Cattell's Sixteen Personality Factor Questionnaire (Cattell, Eber, & Tatsuoka, 1970). John (1990) claims that the openness trait includes attributes of intellectual as well as cognitive complexity. In their hierarchical analysis of 1,710 personality adjectives in the English lexicon, Ashton, Lee, and Goldberg (2004) found that one of seven factors was intelligence, expressed as intellect, imagination, and unconventionality.

Decades ago, Wechsler (1958) concluded that "intelligence is most usefully interpreted as an aspect of the total personality" (p. vii). More recently, Ackerman and Heggestad (1997) reported a meta-analysis of 135 studies (subject $n = 64,000$) of relationships among 10 intellectual ability categories, 19 personality attributes, and a number of personal interests. The most substantial correlations were between intellectual ability and openness to experience and between intellectual ability and intellectual engagement. Whether or not recent concepts of adult intelligence or of typical intellectual engagement, equate with openness (Ackerman & Goff, 1994) or share the same construct space as openness (Rocklin, 1994), openness to experience and intelligence are highly intercorrelated. Both openness to experience and adult

intelligence require ongoing learning. However, because openness attributes and intellectual factors have typically been studied as divorced entities, and because, as discussed, intellectual development is necessary but insufficient for experiential openness across many realms of personal engagement, I have separated the two for the purposes of discussion.

Correlates of Openness Education highly intercorrelates with openness. Across the board and independent of age, those with more education are significantly more open to new information and are more likely to initiate changes in their personal lives (e.g., Fillit et al., 2002; Schaie, 1996, 2005). In bringing about intentional changes in life circumstances, personal openness (as well as monetary and social resources), predict flexibility. Realistic assessments that one many not have the capacities, opportunities, or resources to initiate change thwart flexibility and inclinations to change (Seeman, Lusignolo, Albert, & Berkman, 2001; Whitbourne, 1986).

Developmentally, openness increases among adolescents and college students, largely as a function of mind-opening education and new experiences such as part- or full-time work during those years (Roberts, Robins, et al., 2003; Robins et al., 2001). Among adults, some researchers have found comparative stability in experiential openness (Cartwright & Wink, 1994; Stevens & Truss, 1985), whereas others have found increasing openness. For example, Helson and Kwan (2000) observed increased psychological awareness (one attribute of openness) in a sample of young adult women.

With advancing age, growing conservation of resources and energy, greater conservatism, and, in many, greater rigidity, occur. These qualities correlate with declining personal openness and with declining engagement in learning. And compared to younger adults and their own younger selves, many middle-aged and older adults express contentment with their various life situations, preferring to avoid changes. Some of this is due to having lowered their personal aspirations to adapt to circumstances that they cannot (or believe they cannot) change. (Gutmann, 1992; Whitbourne, 1986). Various data show that feeling in control of self and in charge of life situations and demands predicts successful flexibility and adaptation in middle and older adulthood (Baltes & Baltes, 1990; Brandtstadter & Rothermund, 1994; Lang &

Heckhausen, 2001; Rowe & Kahn, 1987, 1998). For some adults, personal control and the desire to stay in charge of one's life also predict ongoing learning and continuation in some form of paid employment in late middle age and beyond. Once again, the relationship is reciprocal, for paid work in those years fosters learning and openness as well.

Linear declines in openness have been reported by McCrae and Costa (1997); however, in their studies and similar investigations, average population levels of openness were studied. Global instead of situation- and context-specific responses were obtained. Individual differences and intraindividual changes in openness and in learning that fosters openness are thus masked. As we know, much of adult openness, both to experiences and to new ideas, depends on the person and on the topic, values, and biases that predate new information and anticipated social change. Persons may well be receptive to certain new ideas and experiences (decreasing individual freedom due to homeland security) but closed to others (gay marriage).

We have long known that some persons are dogmatic, authoritarian, and rigid from youth onward (e.g., Adorno, Frenkel-Brunswik, Levinson, & Sanford, 1950; Rokeach, 1960). In some, this is due to strict childhood environments and rigid, militaristic upbringing (e.g., Peterson, Smirles, & Wentworth, 1997). Dogmatism and its associated tendencies auger against learning and prohibit effective functioning in jobs that require learning and openness. In others, cognitive limitations prohibit seeing the world other than through concrete or low-level formal (abstract) lenses, for one cannot learn and reflect without the cognitive structures that permit this (e.g., Commons & Bresette, chapter 12, this volume; Commons & Richards, 2003; Commons, Richards, & Armon, 1984; Kitchener, King, & DeLuca, chapter 4, this volume). Just as there are comparatively open (entrepreneurial) and rigidly closed (bureaucratic) work systems, a spectrum of personal openness exists from relatively open to tightly closed, not-willing or not-able-to-learn minds.

Authoritarianism, and the closed mind it represents, correlates with middle and later life rejectivity (prejudice) toward others and eventually the self (Erikson, 1969, 1987; Hoare, 2002), with young adult work identity refusal (Erikson, 1982, 1987), and with an absence of generativity in the middle and later years of life (Erikson, 1966, 1968, 1969, 1976; see also Christie, 1991; Stone, Lederer, & Christie, 1993).

Based in part on his belief that the human adult is fashioned to express concern and care for others, Erikson maintained that rejective stagnation occurs in those who are unresponsive to the needs of others in their personal radius and in those who do not maintain active, positive commitments to the work products and ideas they generate. Openness is associated with generativity. For example, in Peterson et al.'s (1997) study of 200 undergraduates and 159 of their parents, parental openness to experience significantly correlated with parental generativity. Low parental scores on openness were associated with parental authoritarianism.

For some adults, openness to experience is a comparatively coherent personality tendency, particularly among those who continue to learn (Ackerman & Heggestad, 1997). Throughout the adult years, those who are open tend to engage in new experiences and are willing to examine and challenge their personal convictions and beliefs. These endeavors foster continuity (or increases) in experiential openness; they lead as well to advances in postformal, reflective thinking (e.g., Kitchener et al., chapter 4, this volume; Rogers, Mentkowski, & Hart, chapter 22, this volume; Stevens-Long & Barnes, chapter 20, this volume; and Taylor, chapter 9, this volume) and to higher level work positions. Concrete thinkers and those who may be cognitively advanced but are rigidly unyielding, authoritarian, and dogmatic close down their minds. They resist information and learning that might foster different ways of seeing the world and functioning in it.

Intellectual Development and Work Complexity

Although intelligence is not currently included among personality dimensions, it shows a strong correlation with openness to experience and learning engagement. Mental ability, openness to experience, work autonomy (control), motivation for learning, interests, and job complexity together predict advances in intellectual functioning. Recent pleas (from, e.g., Goff & Ackerman, 1992; Schneider, 1996) ask for a return to Wechsler's (1958) premise that intelligence fits under the personality umbrella. But in the past quarter of a century, personality has been reduced to a handful of traits, effectively eliminating mental ability and its evolution in adulthood. This applies to industrial/organizational psychology and other quarters.

Among others, Goff and Ackerman (1992) have established a strong personality–intelligence relationship, particularly in the link between openness to experience and intelligence. In individual development, intelligence is as salient to personality in its relationship to work investment, interests, and competence as work identity and self-efficacy are to a person's sense of coherence, centrality, effectiveness, and goal pursuits. Particularly in light of the overlap between intellectual ability, ongoing learning, and openness and the importance of these to paid work functions and outcomes, it would be foolish to exclude intelligence from the equation.

Defining Intelligence In the intelligence literature, arguments about the correct definition of adult intelligence are as ongoing as disputes about the best definition of personality in the personality literature. From the psychometric tradition to the cognitive development literature, researchers do not agree about the attributes that best represent adult intelligence, whether intelligence is fully accessible to measurement, how adult intelligence should be assessed, and whether adult intellect is stable or malleable during maturity. The psychometric, IQ tradition precludes assessing adult intelligence in the practical contexts in which it occurs and largely omits the potentially causal role of environments such as work on intellectual and cognitive increments. Population aggregates, with findings reported as population means, instead of studies of individual development, prevail. And in intelligence debates, the "rubber band fallacy" continues to hold sway (Hoare, 2002). That is, to this day, any number of experts and lay persons alike view adult intelligence and its expression as if these exist on exact continuum from childhood. In studies' worldviews and in their research designs and data, adults' interests and learning engagement in intellect-sponsoring activities too frequently escape notice.

Environmental Effects and Paid Work Does intelligence change developmentally? This question takes us to human evolutionary data, which in the only recent cross-national study of intelligence, was based on psychometric, population-level data. This is Flynn's (1987) effort, in which he initially studied data from 10 different IQ tests in 26 international locations. Flynn reported gains between 5 and 25 points (the Flynn effect) in 14 nations in a single generation. Between 1952 and 1982, Dutch gains were 20 points;

Israeli gains were nearly equivalent (Flynn, 1998). Average increases were approximately three IQ points each decade, greater than one standard deviation since 1940 (Neisser et al., 1996). The data led Flynn (1987) to three important conclusions as they relate to our topic. First, intellectual development continues into maturity. Second, IQ tests "do not measure intelligence but rather a correlate with a weak causal link to intelligence" (p. 190). Third, much of the data implicate "unknown environmental factors" as accounting for 15 to 20 points in intelligence increments (p. 171).

According to the American Psychological Association's Task Force report on intelligence, a number of factors are "unknown" because contemporary methods cannot partial out their respective contributions (Neisser et al.; 1996; see also Neisser, 1997). Among those factors, the following are prominent: (1) having been reared and continuing to live in resource—rich as opposed to, as Garbarino (1995) says, "socially toxic environments"; and (2) having been subject to and continuing to live in healthy endogenous and exogenous environments (e.g., good nutrition, absence of exposure to toxins [e.g., alcohol, medications; pollutants]). We are interested here in a number of presumably "unknown environmental factors" that lead to intelligence gains in adults, even though Flynn's (1987, 1998) studies largely confirm intellectual advances *into* maturity. Beginning with the longitudinal research of Kohn and Schooler (1969, 1978, 1982, 1983) in the 1960s, evidence has accumulated that complex, autonomous, challenging work conditions, cognitively demanding occupations, and ongoing learning expand intellectual capacities. Conversely, simple work conditions, routinization, closeness of supervision, and cognitively nonchallenging occupations undermine cognitive capacities and decrease intellectual functioning. Kohn and Schooler's original research to show these effects came from studies of U.S. men in 1964 and 1974. Supporting evidence came from studies of women (Kohn & Schooler, 1983; Schooler et al., 1999) and studies in other countries. Data from Poland (Kohn & Slomczynski, 1990), Japan (Naoi & Schooler, 1985, 1990; Schooler & Naoi, 1988), and the Ukraine (Kohn et al., 1997) show that work is causal in either increasing or decreasing intellectual functioning.

Using Kohn and Schooler's early data and new data from the mid-1990s, Schooler and colleagues (1999) backed up Kohn and Schooler's earlier conclusions. Thirty years of longitudinal data show that complex work, with its requirements of mental engagement and day-to-day learning, is powerful in expanding adults' intellectual functioning. According to Fillet et al. (2002; see also Smyth et al., 2004), ongoing learning also prevents cognitive decline. Schooler et al. (1999) found that complex work, with its ongoing learning requirements, significantly increased intellectual functioning of older as well as younger adults. Data showed even more significant effects for older workers (see also Alvolio & Waldman, 1990, 1994; Schaie & Schooler, 1998, Schooler et al., 1999). In response to criticisms that Kohn and Schooler's data were biased because they were partly based on interviews and subjects' descriptions of their job functions, Schooler et al. (1999) provided evidence that their measures of intellectual flexibility correlate with standard psychometric instruments.

Cognitive Vitality Cognitive and sensory stimulation, mental engagement, and ongoing learning foster cognitive vitality. But what brain changes occur in response to such stimulation? Research shows that under optimal conditions, brain morphology and functioning develop during the mature years. Neuron loss does not necessarily accompany normal aging, as had been previously thought. Although the exact mechanisms of changes remain unknown, in the absence of disease, neurogenesis (new neuron growth), synaptogenesis (increases in synapses [connections] between neurons), and angiogenesis (capillary formation) occur in enriched circumstances (Fillet et al., 2002; see also Gross, 2000). Gottlieb (1998, 2000) has developed an epigenetic model in which neuronal structure and physiology, behavior, and environment interact bidirectionally with genes. Stimulating environments, ongoing knowledge assimilation, and complex experience are implicated in ongoing, adult brain plasticity (i.e., neurogenesis, synaptogenesis, angiogenesis). At this time, some data come from studies of humans; other data are from animal and avian (primates, rats, birds) studies. Recent neuroimaging studies of humans show that in the sixties and older, neurogenesis as well as recruitment and use of both cerebral hemispheres in memory retrieval and information processing occur (e.g., Cabeza, 2002; Cabeza et al., 1997; Li, 2003; Reuter-Lorenz, 2002).

Throughout (and before) adulthood, complex, intersecting factors can foster or thwart cognitive power. Particularly among middle-aged and older adults,

when life's good and bad habits show their hand, a complicated personal profile emerges. Prominent interacting effects have been found for 10 overarching factors. These are:

- changes in brain structure, physiology, and functional reserve (e.g., neuronal reserve, neurogenesis, inflammation, "oxidative stress")
- extent of formal education
- ongoing learning during adulthood
- inclusion in mainstream society and activities
- genes (in interaction with each other and with internal and external environments)
- lifestyle factors, both positive and negative (e.g., aerobic exercise, social engagement, diet and nutrition, stress management, weight control, alcohol and drug use, smoking, living or working in high toxin environments)
- medical disorders (e.g., hypertension, hyperlipidemia, diabetes)
- medical and self-care management of disease processes
- occupations and occupational conditions
- sensory impairment and remediation (Abbott et al., 2004; Esposito et al., 2004; Fillit et al., 2002; Knoops et al., 2004; Kohn et al., 1997; Neisser et al., 1996; Rowe & Kahn, 1987, 1998; Schooler et al., 1999; Smyth et al., 2004; Snowdon, 2002, 2003; Weuve et al., 2004)

Thus, other than cognitive slowing, when one sees declines in intelligence with aging, it is not age as such but functional age (due to health aberrations or other negatives identified in the list) that is key. Lifestyle factors, including decrements in learning and stimulation, are causal in decline.

Work and Intellectual Transformation Workers are transformed by occupational environments and requirements. By engaging the mental apparatus for at least half of their waking hours during most of their adult lives, work tasks and contexts shape development. Returning to an example given in the first chapter of this volume, brain imaging of London taxi drivers, done before and after their didactive and experiential learning course, is revealing (Maguire et al., 2000). Due to their navigational learning, drivers' posterior hippocampi, an area of the brain that provides spatial renditions of the environment, grew significantly larger than that of control subjects. Cognitive activities involved in their experiential learning program were preeminent in development.

Snowdon (2002, 2003) showed that nuns with college degrees who were privileged by mentally challenging positions and who continued to learn maintained and enhanced their intellectual prowess and their independence. Linguistic ability, particularly an expansive vocabulary in early life, predicted cognitive skills, intellectual engagement, and education and later protection against dementia. That such nuns also enjoyed greater longevity compared to nuns who were less educated, held less complex jobs, and learned less as adults was an added bonus. Other studies also show a lower dementia risk for those with higher levels of education and more mentally demanding occupations and learning requirements (Callahan et al., 1996; Evans et al., 1997; Jorm et al., 1998; Smyth et al., 2004; Stern et al., 1994).

Smyth et al. (2004) reported an investigation into the relationship between dementia and occupations. In a study of adults in their sixties, 122 persons with dementia or potential dementia were compared with 235 control subjects. Controlling for occupation, occupational histories and motor, mental, social, and physical occupational demands were coded. Those in jobs requiring more manual skills and fewer intellectual and literacy skills (e.g., laborers) had higher rates of dementia than subjects in highly complex jobs that required ongoing learning (e.g., managers, engineers, teachers, physicians). The researchers concluded that mentally demanding occupations may either forestall dementia or that dementia's early effects may restrict persons from pursuing more challenging occupational roles. A number of potential confounds (e.g., health, income, nutrition, exposure to environmental toxins, substance abuse) made interpretation difficult; however, earlier studies have also implicated manual and low-level service occupations as a risk factor for dementia (Callahan et al., 1996; Dartigues et al., 1992; Evans et al., 1997; Mangione et al., 1993).

Other studies have reported related findings. For example, a small study initiated by Seim (1989, 1997) began as an investigation of intelligence in Norwegian youth. Beginning in 1939, subjects were studied when they were 13, 30, 60, and 70 years old. Fluid and crystallized abilities were tested with Norwegian adaptations of the Binet-Simon scales and Raven's progressive matrices. As Seim's findings relate to work, intelligence, and ongoing learning, higher intelligence scores were reported for men than women at age 30, but no gender differences were found earlier or later. Interpreting these findings, Daatland

(2003) concluded: "The early adult advantage of men could . . . be attributed to extrinsic (education, work activity) and not intrinsic factors. Many women went back to an education and work career after childraising, and then also bridged the gap in intelligence scores" (p. 204). In the participants' old age, health factors were causal in declines in fluid intelligence, as has been found in other longitudinal studies (e.g., the Berlin Aging Study [Baltes & Mayer, 1999]; the Duke Studies [Busse & Maddox, 1985]; the Seattle Longitudinal Studies [Schaie, 1996, 2005]). However, in the Seim study, 13 (27%) of the surviving 49 subjects at age 70 demonstrated higher scores on crystallized intelligence than at any earlier time. Sixteen subjects either improved or maintained their fluid intelligence scores from age 60 to 70.

There is an interesting correspondence between Seim's and Flynn's (1987, 1998) Norwegian data, even though the former study is one of development in individuals and the latter is a cross-sectional, population level study of aggregate trends. Looking to Flynn's data, among the 26,000 men tested each year in Norway (83% of 19-year-old Norwegian males), the average IQ of 108.7 in 1980 (compared with 100.0 in 1954) may well be baseline to later increases in those who are privileged by further education and high job complexity.

It appears that complex work increases brain plasticity and intellectual development. Complex work is defined as "work that in its very substance requires thought and independent judgement" (Schooler et al., 1999, p. 485). Such work includes:

- a greater number and a more varied array of stimuli,
- job activities that require a sizable number and variety of decisions,
- multiple facets that must be considered in decision making,
- ill-defined and unstructured problems,
- potentially contradictory information, and
- self-directed requirements

These occupational characteristics lead to adaptability and "cognitive flexibility in coping with the intellectual demands of a complex situation" (Schooler et al., 1999, p. 486).

Psychology's Changing Perspective   For a number of years, the findings of Kohn, Schooler, and colleagues were disputed by many psychologists, primarily because data came from a sociological framework, and standard psychometric measurements were not used in the earlier studies. But from the mid-1980s forward, neurobiological data and changing psychological views have lent credibility to their findings. Many researchers are now less inclined to obtain psychometric snapshots of laboratory performances on days in which adult subjects may or may not be motivated to comply with tests that are far removed from their relevant-to-self pursuits (see, e.g., Artistico, Cervone, & Pezzuti, 2003; Sternberg, 2003). Instead, much of adult intellectual performance is viewed in the developmental and situational contexts of life as lived. That is, mature intelligence is application and ongoing learning, facets that are inseparable from knowledge and from ecologically meaningful, relevant, on-site, and in-use processes. In the absence of disease, challenging occupational and avocational pursuits are causal in ongoing intellectual development or, at a minimum, in their mainstay.

Establishing a solid basis for the construct of practical knowledge, Sternberg (1985a, 1985b) and colleagues (e.g., Sternberg, 2003, 2004; Sternberg et al., 2000) have repeatedly shown that everyday work problems invoke nonlinear problem solving, learning, thinking while doing, and, as per Schon (1983, 1987), reflection in action. Practical intelligence is characterized by explicit and implicit (tacit) knowledge that is procedural in nature; the latter escapes measurement by psychometric technique (Sternberg, 2003; Sternberg et al., 2000). The main difference between practical and more esoteric, academic knowledge is in the former's relevance to life and real-world problems and outcomes. For example, using Sternberg's model, Colonia-Willner (1998) studied the relationship between tacit knowledge and psychometric reasoning in 200 bank managers (157 nonexperts and 43 experts in the age range of 24–59 years). Tacit knowledge was strongly related to managerial skills. On average, the "best performing older managers (experts) . . . had high levels of tacit knowledge although they scored lower on psychometric reasoning measures" (p. 45).

Sternberg (2004) has shown that intelligence must also be understood as those processes that are embedded in a broad cultural context: "Behavior that in one cultural context is smart may be, in another cultural context, stupid" (p. 325). Intelligence is defined by its setting and by knowledge in and of that setting. Knowledge, intellect, and context are inseparable.

To Ackerman (e.g., Ackerman & Heggestad, 1997; Ackerman & Rolfhus, 1999; Beier & Ackerman, 2001; Goff & Ackerman, 1992), intelligence is a person's typical intellectual engagement. Ackerman's is an individual investment and effort model, in that intellectual development is a continual product of "intelligence-as process, personality, interests, and intelligence-as-knowledge" (Beier & Ackerman, 2001, p. 615). As for Sternberg, adult intelligence occurs in context as the adult invests effort in relevant learning and problems. When intelligence is viewed as typical and relevant (daily) performance, instead of as maximal and arbitrary (laboratory) performance, cognitive power is frequently found to increase during adulthood.

The intelligence that Ackerman describes is associated with interests, motivation, domain-specific knowledge, and action. The idiosyncrasies of a domain of expertise are important because in addition to providing specific knowledge, they alter ways of thinking. For example, medical students learn to consider scientific evidence and outcome data alone and to put aside tendencies to reason to a conclusion. They learn to think deductively, to move down decision trees in their differential diagnoses. Evidence-based knowledge and decision tree use will both advance and constrain their thinking such that after a number of years physicians will typically have become superior deductive thinkers and less capable inductive thinkers. We can expect transfer effects to nonwork problems and contexts. Deductive problem solving takes over for fresh idea, "out-of-the-box" type thinking.

Over time, advanced domain-specific knowledge leads to a decay of knowledge in related areas. Physicians may continue to learn and to develop greater expertise in their specialty areas, but will sacrifice expertise in other subfields. Computer hardware engineers may continue to learn while designing computer chips. For them, hardware-specific knowledge and skills continually advance, but expertise in ancillary areas (e.g., software design) fades with disuse.

General academic knowledge may also expand during adulthood, again depending on the person and his or her interests, motivation, and involvement. For example, Ackerman and Rolfhus (1999) administered 20 tests containing academic and technological questions to 135 middle-aged adults (30–59 years of age). Compared to a norming sample of young adults (college students), the middle-aged subjects performed better in almost all knowledge areas despite lower scores on psychometric numerical and spatial abilities. General intelligence, verbal ability, personality, self-concept, learning, and interest together predicted "knowledge-as-intelligence."

Certain of Schaie's (e.g., 1996, 2005) and Schaie and Schooler's (1998) efforts have focused on work's influence in intellectual maintenance in the face of the slowed cognitive processing that occurs with aging. All adults experience generalized cognitive slowing from middle age onward, and such slowing in the dynamic, fast-paced, work environment often leads to slower work styles and stress (and to ageist marginalization and exclusion from learning and development activities). However, these investigators found that the centrality of work in mainstream life and its resource-rich, stimulating qualities can maintain cognitive functioning well into later adulthood.

The model that emanates from various studies is that of intelligence as competence in action, a model that finds support in the growing body of research on expert performance (e.g., Ericsson & Charness, 1994; Ericsson, Krampe, & Tesch-Romer, 1993; Ericsson & Smith, 1991; Krampe & Ericsson, 1996). In the expert performance literature, ongoing increments in intellectual performance have been demonstrated well into some persons' eighties and nineties. The revised view—one of contextual mastery, of investment-driven and intra-individual adult development—comports well with data showing generational intellectual increments (e.g., Dickens & Flynn, 2001; Flynn, 1987, 1998). Writing about such gains, we can reason as did Dickens and Flynn (2001), that "reciprocal causation produces a multiplier effect" (p. 346). That is, higher intelligence "leads" one into enriched environments, which, along with ongoing learning, are causal in intellect's upward trajectory.

This is a talent-resource-opportunity-investment model of adult intellectual development. In the work environment, the extension of intellectual abilities is based on work role and task opportunities that provide challenge and stimulation, and on the adult's investment of mental energies in learning and in engaging in situational mastery opportunities.

Concluding Comments About Personality, Work, and Learning

Good work is adult exploration (Elliot & Reis, 2003; Hazan & Shaver, 1990). It entails the genuine use of oneself in environments that are physically and psychologically safe. Above the level of routinized tasks, the identity-sponsoring engagement of work often permits a mental sphere in which one engages with ideas and concepts. One imagines and projects scenarios, creates blueprints, plans, and designs and conceptualizes innovative products (Erikson, 1977). In this way, the interesting, intellectually challenging work of the adult years is a source of mastery and learning and of personality consistency and change. Good work provides pleasure, satisfaction, self-worth, emotional stability, intellectual engagement, and the sense of control and competence.

Adults are expected to be reliable and stable, perform consistently and conscientiously in their jobs, and continue to learn and adapt. Adults with such attributes are desired by organizations, and their work experiences in turn reinforce these personality tendencies. Enhanced personality coherence and stability result. Yet adaptability does not retreat. The important roles of adult life provide the foundation and contexts both for coherence and evolution. When stability and consistency are needed, adults do not need to alter their successful ways of interacting in their various roles and environments. In other circumstances, when flexibility is required, mentally healthy, nonrigid adults can and will adapt to, learn to function in, and influence new situations, possibilities, expectations, and outcomes.

CONCLUSIONS

Management experts emphasize that organizations must continually change, remodeling their enterprises, processes, and products to thrive in today's economy. According to the economist Brian Arthur, the best image for today's successful organization is that of a "lithe, constantly reconfiguring network," instead of an "imposing, self-contained, command-and-control pyramid" (Schlender, 2004, p. 108). Modern corporations thrive because of innovation, because they capably span free enterprise systems and adapt to market forces, and because they retain talented workers.

To succeed, corporations have had to change their work concepts, practices, and workplaces. As a result, changes such as organizational flattening now require that many employees coordinate their functions with different divisions; the growth in self-managed teams places more operational decisions at the worker and team levels. Work roles have also changed. Flexible, evolving roles have replaced unyielding, tightly defined tasks (e.g., Wrenn & Maurer, 2004). The death of the lifetime, single "organizational career" and its system of sequential, upward promotion demands that adults continue to learn and that they plan for multiple positions, roles, and employers (Maurer, 2001).

As well, global market competition, abbreviated product runs, just-in-time inventories, and tighter labor markets now fuel requirements for rapid-fire output among workers. In many work plants, automation and robotics have replaced humans. Heightened production efficiency, outsourcing, offshoring, and subcontracting have increased work responsibilities, role stresses, and fears about job loss.

Some of these changes have resulted in the loss of skilled workers. Other innovations have led to inhumane conditions. For example, in employees' perceptions, cross-training and "multiskilling" have often become "multitasking" without corresponding skill development and adequate resources. "Lean production" is called "mean production" when plants speed mass production to the extent that efficiency and cost-cutting undermine worker morale (Parker, 2003, p. 621). Eroded support for workers, deficient training, and ill concern for job conditions define many such climates. In production plants and call centers, computerized employee monitoring augments stresses, leading to the guarded behaviors shown by persons who feel eternally watched (e.g., Holman, 2002; Holman, Chissick, & Totterdel, 2002). In some plants, computers monitor and calculate employee salaries on the basis of degrees of productivity. Removing workers from human supervisors depersonalizes evaluation (e.g., Bandura, 1997).This is isolating and demoralizing, diminishing those who might otherwise feel integral to the company in which they work.

In synthesizing the ways that paid work is catalytic to reciprocal adult development and learning, this chapter has explored the ways in which identity and certain personality characteristics relate to individual developmental and engagement in learning. When workers are immersed in their work content, when organizations expend time, resources, and effort to enhance learning and development and the work climate, the corporation and its workers will profit. As has been shown, transfer effects occur to nonwork contexts and roles. A company's and work unit's culture, structure, coordination, and leadership and the

qualities of group members' interactions can sustain or subvert functioning. Whether large or small in scale, at some level all organizations wish to have learning- and development-oriented workers. If given the opportunity, many workers will engage in broader and deeper learning, expand that part of their identity that is work-contingent, and show positive development in the personality characteristics explored.

Such results require that corporate leaders understand and attend to workers' learning and development needs and possibilities. Among the many positive effects discussed in this chapter, identity immersion and work autonomy lead to job involvement and satisfaction. Work teams function better when personal autonomy is permitted and enhanced. Interpersonal competence and organizational citizenship behavior increase when leaders expect these qualities and when leaders themselves model such attributes. Executives who understand and encourage psychologically safe and positive work climates can facilitate more mature functioning and generativity in their workforce. This requires that corporate leaders understand how work climates can radically affect workers, products, clients, customers, and profits.

In many employees, conscientiousness increases in proportion to recognition for this characteristic. Then adult workers not only show increased conscientiousness but also an increase in their motivation to learn. Conscientiousness is associated with goal setting and attainment, strong predictors of competent work performance. It almost goes without saying that workers must have reasons to trust corporate leadership, seeing conscientiousness manifest among executives, superiors, and managers at all levels.

The roles of mind-opening job experiences and learning and intellectually engaging and challenging jobs in fostering intellectual advances almost speak for themselves. Independent of age, learning in the work context as well as related, more formal educational ventures sponsored by the organization strongly correlate with openness. Complex, autonomous, challenging work conditions and ongoing learning expand intellectual capacities.

Cleary, some workers either cannot or will not develop and continue to learn. They will stagnate, perform with mediocrity or indifference, and likely function forever in low-level jobs. Others, including those now functioning in routinized, repetitive jobs, will learn and develop if given adequate work resources and opportunities. They deserve the chance.

In sum, paid work consumes a great portion of adult life and is essential to the meaning that many adults ascribe to their mature years. Work fosters development and learning. Organizational leaders wishing to advance their corporate causes would do well to learn about the developmental and learning needs of workers in the aggregate and of their employees as individuals. Good work is catalytic to reciprocal adult learning and development, and job conditions that enhance such growth serve corporate needs reciprocally as well.

ACKNOWLEDGMENTS   I extend my sincere appreciation to Bridget Cooper, Richard Lanthier, Sylvia Marotta, and Julie Nelson, who commented on prior drafts of this chapter.

Note

1. In his later years, Erikson overturned his prior belief that integrity and wisdom are products of life's final stage. He then changed *integrity* to *integrality*, the ability to maintain a sense of wholeness in the face of bodily and psychological deterioration, and social exclusion (see Erikson, 1982; Hoare, 2002, pp. 185–187).

References

Abbott, R. D., White, L. R., Ross, G. W., Masaki, K. H., Curb, J. D., & Petrovitch, H. (2004). Walking and dementia in physically capable elderly men. *Journal of the American Medical Association, 292,* 1447–1453.

Ackerman, P. L., & Goff, M. (1994). Typical intellectual engagement and personality: Reply to Rocklin (1994). *Journal of Educational Psychology, 86,* 150–153.

Ackerman, P. L., & Heggestad, E. D. (1997). Intelligence, personality, and interests: Evidence for overlapping traits. *Psychological Bulletin, 121,* 219–245.

Ackerman, P. L., Kanfer, R., & Goff, M. (1995). Cognitive and noncognitive determinants and consequences of complex skill acquisition. *Journal of Experimental Psychology: Applied, 1,* 270–304.

Ackerman, P. L., & Rolfhus, E. L. (1999). The locus of adult intelligence: Knowledge, abilities, and nonability traits. *Psychology and Aging, 14,* 314–330.

Adams, S., & Kydoniefs, L. (2000). Making teams work. *Quality Progress, 33,* 43–48.

Adorno, T. W., Frenkel-Brunswik, E., Levinson, D. J., & Sanford, R. N. (1950). *The authoritarian personality.* New York: Harper & Brothers.

Agronick, G. S., & Duncan, L. E. (1998). Personality and social change: Individual differences, life path, and importance attributed to the women's movement. *Journal of Personality and Social Psychology, 74,* 1545–1555.

Altschuler, J. (2004). Beyond money and survival: The meaning of paid work among older women. *International Journal of Aging and Human Development, 58,* 223–239.

Alvolio, B. J., & Waldman, D. A. (1990). An examination of age and cognitive test performance across job complexity and occupational types. *Journal of Applied Psychology, 75,* 43–50.

Alvolio, B. J., & Waldman, D. A. (1994). Variations in cognitive, perceptual, and psychomotor abilities across the working life span: Examining the effects of race, sex, experience, education, and occupational type. *Psychology and Aging, 9,* 430–442.

Artistico, D., Cervone, D., & Pezzuti, L. (2003). Perceived self-efficacy and everyday problem Solving among young and older adults. *Psychology and Aging, 18,* 68–79.

Ashton, M. C., Lee, K., & Goldberg, L. R. (2004). A hierarchical analysis of 1,710 English personality-descriptive adjectives. *Journal of Personality and Social Psychology, 87,* 707–721.

Axelrod, S. D. (1999). *Work and the evolving self.* Hillsdale, NJ: Analytic Press.

Baltes, P. B. (1997). On the incomplete architecture of human ontogeny: Selection, optimization, and compensation as foundation of developmental theory. *American Psychologist, 52,* 366–380.

Baltes, P. B., & Baltes, M. M. (1990). Psychological perspectives on successful aging: The model of selective optimization with compensation. In P. B. Baltes & M. M. Baltes (Eds.), *Successful aging: Perspectives from the behavioral sciences* (pp. 1–34). Cambridge: Cambridge University Press.

Baltes, P. B., & Mayer, K. U. (Eds.). (1999). *The Berlin aging study: Aging from 70 to 100.* Cambridge: Cambridge University Press.

Bandura, A. (1997). *Self-efficacy: The exercise of control.* New York: W. H. Freeman.

Barling, J., Kelloway, E. K., & Iverson, R. D. (2003). High-quality work, job satisfaction, and occupational injuries. *Journal of Applied Psychology, 88,* 276–283.

Barrick, M. R., & Mount, M. K. (1991). The big five personality dimensions and job performance: A meta-analysis. *Personnel Psychology, 44,* 1–26.

Barrick, M. R., & Mount, M. K. (1993). Autonomy as a moderator of the relationships between the big five personality dimensions and job performance. *Journal of Applied Psychology, 78,* 111–118.

Barrick, M. R., Mount, M. K., & Strauss, J. P. (1993). Conscientiousness and performance of sales representatives: Test of the mediating effects of goal setting. *Journal of Applied Psychology, 78,* 715–722.

Barrick, M. R., Stewart, G. L., Neubert, M. J., & Mount, M. K. (1998). Relating member ability and personality to work-team processes and team effectiveness. *Journal of Applied Psychology, 83,* 377–391.

Bauer, J. J., & McAdams, D. P. (2004). Growth goals, maturity, and well-being. *Developmental Psychology, 40*, 114–127.

Beier, M. E., & Ackerman, P. L. (2001). Current-events knowledge in adults: An investigation of age, intelligence, and nonability determinants. *Psychology and Aging, 16*, 615–628.

Berry, J. (2003). Some lost jobs may never come back. *Washington Post*, November 29, pp. E1–E2.

Bocchino, C. C., Hartman, B. W., & Foley, P. F. (2003). The relationship between person-organization congruence, perceived violations of the psychological contract, and occupational stress symptoms. *Consulting Psychology Journal: Practice and Research, 55*, 203–214.

Bouchard, T. J. Jr., & Loehlin, J. C. (2001). Genes, evolution, and personality. *Behavior Genetics, 31*, 243–273.

Bourne, E. (1978) The state of research on ego identity: A review and appraisal. Part I. *Journal of Youth and Adolescence, 7*, 223–251.

Brandstadter, J., & Rothermund, K. (1994). Self-percepts of control in middle and later adulthood: Buffering losses by rescaling goals. *Psychology of Aging, 9*, 265–273.

Brown, S. P. (1996). A meta-analysis and review of organizational research on job involvement. *Psychological Bulletin, 120*, 235–255.

Buchwald, A. (2004). Code orange juice. *Washington Post*, October 12, p. C2.

Busse, E. W., & Maddox, G. L. (1985). *The Duke longitudinal studies of normal aging, 1955–1980.* New York: Springer.

Cabeza, R. (2002). Hemispheric asymmetry reduction in older adults: The Harold model. *Psychology and Aging, 17*, 85–100.

Cabeza, R., Grady, C. L., Nyberg, L., McIntosh, A. R., Tulving, E., & Kapur, S. (1997). Age-related differences in effective neural connectivity. *NeuroReport, 8*, 3479–3483.

Callahan, C. M., Hall, K. S., Hut, S. L., Musick, B. S., Unverzagt, F. W., & Hendrie, H. C. (1996). Relationship of age, education, and occupation with dementia among a community-based sample of African Americans. *Archives of Neurology, 53*, 134–140.

Cartwright, L. K., & Wink, P. (1994) Personality change in women physicians from medical student years to mid-40s. *Psychology of Women Quarterly, 18*, 291–308.

Castiglioni, A., Bellini, L. M., & Shea, J. A. (2004). Program directors' views of the importance and prevalence of mentoring in internal medicine residencies. *Journal of General Internal Medicine, 19*, 779–782.

Catalano, R., Novaco, R., & McConnell, W. (1997). A model of the net effect of job loss on violence. *Journal of Personality and Social Psychology, 72*, 1440–1447.

Cattell, R. B., Eber, H. W., & Tatsuoka, M. M. (1970). *The handbook for the Sixteen Personality Factor Questionnaire.* Champaign, IL: Institute for Personality and Ability Testing.

Cella, D. F., De Wolfe, A. S., & Fitzgibbon, M. (1987). Ego identity status, identification, and decision making style in late adolescence. *Adolescence, 22*, 849–861.

Cervone, D. (2004). The architecture of personality. *Psychological Review, 111*, 183–204.

Cervone, D., & Shoda, Y. (1999). Beyond traits in the study of personality coherence. *Current Directions in Psychological Science, 8*, 27–32.

Cheek, C., & Jones, R. M. (2001). Identity style and employment histories among women receiving public assistance. *Journal of Vocational Behavior, 59*, 76–88.

Chodorow, N. (1978). *The reproduction of mothering.* Berkeley: University of California Press.

Chiu, R. K., & Kosinski, F. A. Jr. (1994). Is Chinese conflict-handling behavior influenced by Chinese values? *Social Behavior and Personality, 22*, 81–90.

Christie, R. (1991). Authoritarianism and related constructs. In J. P. Robinson, P. R. Shaver, & L. S. Wrightsman (Eds.), *Measures of personality and social psychological attitudes* (pp. 501–571). San Diego, CA: Academic Press.

Clausen, J. A., & Jones, C. J. (1998). Predicting personality stability across the life span: The role of competence and work and family commitments. *Journal of Adult Development, 5*, 73–83.

Cohn, L. D., & Westenberg, P. M. (2004). Intelligence and maturity: Meta-analytic evidence for the incremental and discriminant validity of Loevinger's measure of ego development. *Journal of Personality and Social Psychology, 86*, 760–772.

Coles, R. (1978). Work and self-respect. In E. H. Erikson (Ed.), *Adulthood* (pp. 217–226). New York: Norton.

Colonia-Willner, R. (1998). Practical intelligence at work: Relationship between aging and cognitive efficiency among managers in a bank environment. *Psychology and Aging, 13*, 45–57.

Commons, M. L., & Richards, F. A. (2003). Four postformal stages. In J. Demick & C. Andreoletti (Eds.), *Handbook of adult development* (pp. 199–219). New York: Kluwer Academic/Plenum.

Commons, M. L., Richards, F. A., & Armon, C. (Eds.). (1984). *Beyond formal operations.* New York: Praeger.

Cook, M., Young, A., Taylor, D., & Bedford, A. P. (2000). Personality and self-rated work performance. *European Journal of Psychological Assessment, 16*, 202–208.

Costa, P. T., & McCrae, R. R. (1992). *Revised NEO Personality Inventory (NEO-PI-R) and NEO Five-Factor Inventory professional manual.* Odessa, FL: Psychological Assessment Resources.

Cribb, D. A., Ozone, S. J., & Pipes, R. B. (1992, August). *A compilation of personality instruments.* Paper presented at the annual meeting of the American Psychological Association.

Daatland, S. O. (2003). From variables to lives: Inputs to a fresh agenda for psychological aging in Norway. *European Psychologist, 8,* 200–207.

Dartigues, J. F., Gagnon, M., Letenneur, L., Barberger-Gateau, P., Commenges, D., Evaldre, M., et al. (1992). Principal lifetime occupation and cognitive impairment in a French elderly cohort (Paquid). *American Journal of Epidemiology, 135,* 981–988.

DeNeve, K., & Cooper, H. (1998). The happy personality: A meta-analysis of 137 personality traits and subjective well-being. *Psychological Bulletin, 124,* 197–229.

Dickens, W. T., & Flynn, J. R. (2001). Heritability estimates versus large environmental effects: The IQ paradox resolved. *Psychological Review, 108,* 346–369.

Dickie, V. A. (2003). Establishing worker identity: A study of people in craft work. *American Journal of Occupational Therapy, 57,* 250–261.

Diehl, M., Coyle, N., & Labouvie-Vief, G. (1996). Age and sex differences in strategies of coping and defense across the life span. *Psychology and Aging, 11,* 127–139.

Diong, S. M., & Bishop, G. D. (1999). Anger expression, coping styles, and well-being. *Journal of Health Psychology, 4,* 81–96.

Elliott, A. J., & Reis, H. T. (2003). Attachment and exploration in adulthood. *Journal of Personality and Social Psychology, 85,* 317–331.

Elliott, M. (1996). Impact of work, family, and welfare receipt on women's self-esteem in young adulthood. *Social Psychology Quarterly, 59,* 80–95.

Ericsson, K. A., & Charness, N. (1994). Expert performance: Its structure and acquisition. *American Psychologist, 49,* 725–747.

Ericsson, K. A., Krampe, R. T., & Tesch-Romer, C. (1993). The role of deliberate practice in the acquisition of expert performance. *Psychological Review, 100,* 363–406.

Ericsson, K. A., & Smith, J. (Eds.). (1991). *Toward a general theory of expertise.* New York: Cambridge University Press.

Erikson, E. H. (1950). *Childhood and society.* New York: Norton.

Erikson, E. H. (1956). The problem of ego identity. *Journal of the American Psychoanalytic Association, 4,* 56–121.

Erikson, E. H. (1958). *Young man Luther.* New York: Norton.

Erikson, E. H. (1959). *Identity and the life cycle.* Psychological Issues. Monograph 1, 1. New York: International Universities Press.

Erikson, E. H. (1963). *Childhood and society* (2nd ed.). New York: Norton.

Erikson, E. H. (1966). The concept of identity in race relations. *Daedalus, 95,* 145–170.

Erikson, E. H. (1968). *Identity: Youth and crisis.* New York: Norton

Erikson, E. H. (1969). *Gandhi's truth.* New York: Norton.

Erikson, E. H. (1974). *Dimensions of a new identity.* New York: Norton.

Erikson, E. H. (1975). *Life history and the historical moment.* New York: Norton.

Erikson, E. H. (1976). Reflections on Dr. Borg's life cycle. *Daedalus, 105,* 1–31.

Erikson, E. H. (1977). *Toys and reasons.* New York: Norton.

Erikson, E. H. (1982). *The life cycle completed: A review.* New York: Norton.

Erikson, E. H. (1987). *The papers of Erik and Joan Erikson.* Houghton Library, Harvard University.

Esposito, K., Marfella, R., Ciotola, M., De Palo, F., Giugliano, G., & Giugliano, M., et al. (2004). Effect of a mediterranean-style diet on endothelial dysfunction and markers of vascular inflammation in the metabolic syndrome: A randomized trial. *Journal of the American Medical Association, 292,* 1440–1446.

Evans, D. A., Hebert, L. E., Beckett, L. A., Scherr, P. A., Albert, M. S., & Chown, M. J., et al. (1997). Education and other measures of socioeconomic status and risk of incident Alzheimer disease in a defined population of older persons. *Archives of Neurology, 54,* 1399–1405.

Evans, R. I. (1967). *Dialogue with Erik Erikson.* New York: Harper & Row.

Ferris, G. R., Witt, L. A., & Hochwarter, W. A. (2001). The interaction of social skill and general mental ability on work outcomes. *Journal of Applied Psychology, 86,* 1075–1082.

Fillit, H. M., Butler, R. N., O'Connell, A. W., Albert, M. S., Birren, J. E., Cotman, C. W., et al. (2002). Achieving and maintaining cognitive vitality with aging. *Mayo Clinic Proceedings, 77,* 681–696.

Fischer, K. W., & Ayoub, C. (1994). Affective splitting and dissociation in normal and maltreated children: Developmental pathways for self in relationships. In D. Cicchetti & S. L. Toth (Eds.), *Rochester symposium on developmental psychopathology: Vol. 5. Disorders and dysfunctions of the self* (pp. 147–222). Rochester, NY: Rochester University Press.

Fisher, K. (1993). *Leading self-directed work teams: A guide to developing new team leadership skills.* New York: McGraw-Hill.

Fiske, S. T., & Taylor, S. E. (1991). *Social cognition.* New York: McGraw-Hill.

Flynn, J. R. (1987). Massive IQ gains in 14 nations: What IQ tests really measure. *Psychological Bulletin, 101,* 171–191.

Flynn, J. R. (1998). Israeli military IQ tests: Gender differences small; IQ gains large. *Journal of Biosocial Science, 30,* 541–553.

Forgas, J. P., Oatley, K., & Manstead, A., Eds. (2001). *Feeling and thinking: The role of affect in social cognition.* New York: Cambridge University Press.

Froman, L. (1994). Adult learning in the workplace. In J. D. Sinnott (Ed.), *Interdisciplinary handbook of adult lifespan learning* (pp. 159–170). Westport, CT: Greenwood.

Garbarino, J. (1995). *Raising children in a socially toxic environment.* San Francisco: Jossey-Bass.

Geertz, C. (1984). From the native's point of view. In R. Shweder & R. LeVine (Eds.), *Culture theory* (pp. 123–136). Cambridge: Cambridge University Press.

George, J. (1990). Personality, affect, and behavior in groups. *Journal of Applied Psychology, 75,* 107–116.

Gibson, S. (2004). Mentoring in business and industry: The need for a phenomenological perspective. *Mentoring and Tutoring: Partnership in Learning, 12,* 259–276.

Gilligan, C. (1982). *In a different voice.* Cambridge, MA: Harvard University Press.

Gilligan, C. (1987). In a different voice: Women's conceptions of self and of morality. In M. R. Walsh (Ed.), *The psychology of women* (pp. 278–320). New Haven, CT: Yale University Press.

Ginexi, E. M., Howe, G. W., & Caplan, R. D. (2000). Depression and control beliefs in relation to reemployment: What are the directions of effect? *Journal of Occupational Health Psychology, 5,* 323–336.

Goff, M. G., & Ackerman, P. L. (1992). Personality-intelligence relations: Assessment of typical intellectual engagement. *Journal of Educational Psychology, 84,* 537–552.

Goldberg, L. R. (1992). The development of markers for the big-five factor structure. *Psychological Assessment, 4,* 26–42.

Goldsmith, A. H., & Veum, J. R. (1997). Unemployment, joblessness, psychological well-being, and self-esteem: Theory and evidence. *Journal of Socio-Economics, 26,* 133–158.

Goldsmith, A. H., Veum, J. R., & Darity, W. Jr. (1996). The impact of labor force history on self-esteem and its component parts, anxiety, alienation and depression. *Journal of Economic Psychology, 17,* 183–220.

Goldsmith, A. H., Veum, J. R., & Darity, W. Jr. (1997). Unemployment, joblessness, psychological well-being and self-esteem: Theory and evidence. *Journal of Socio-Economics, 26,* 133–158.

Gottlieb, G. (1998). Normally occurring environmental and behavioral influence on gene activity: From central dogma to probabilistic epigenesis. *Psychological Review, 105,* 792–802.

Gottlieb, G. (2000). Environmental and behavioral influence on gene activity. *Current Directions in Psychological Science, 8,* 93–97.

Gould, R. L. (1980). Transformations during early and middle adult years. In N. J. Smelser & E. H. Erikson (Eds.), *Themes of work and love in adulthood* (pp. 213–237). Cambridge, MA: Harvard University Press.

Greenberg, E. (1992). Creativity, autonomy, and evaluation of creative work: Artistic workers in organizations. *Journal of Creative Behavior, 26,* 75–80.

Greene, C. (1989). Cohesion and productivity in work groups. *Small Group Behavior, 20,* 70–86.

Gross, C. G. (2000). Neurogenesis in the adult brain: Death of a dogma. *Nature Reviews, 1,* 67–73.

Gudykunst, W. G., Ting-Toomey, S., & Chua, E. (1988). *Culture and interpersonal communication.* Newbury Park, CA: Sage.

Gutmann, D. L. (1975). Parenthood: A key to the comparative study of the life cycle. In N. Datan & L. H. Ginsberg (Eds.), *Life-span developmental psychology* (pp. 167–184). New York: Academic Press.

Gutmann, D. L. (1976). Individual adaptation in the middle years: Developmental issues in the masculine mid-life crisis. *Journal of Geriatric Psychiatry, 9,* 41–59.

Gutmann, D. L. (1977). The cross-cultural perspective: Notes toward a comparative psychology of aging. In J. E. Birren & K. W. Schaie (Eds.), *Handbook of the psychology of aging.* New York: Van Nostrand Reinhold.

Gutmann, D. L. (1992). Toward a dynamic geropsychology. In J. W. Barron, M. N. Eagle, & D. L. Wolitzky (Eds.), *Interface of psychoanalysis and psychology* (pp. 284–296). Washington, DC: American Psychological Association.

Haan, N. (1977). *Coping and defending: Processes of self-environment organization.* New York: Academic Press.

Haan, N., Millsap, R., & Hartka, E. (1986). As time goes by: Change and stability in personality over fifty years. *Psychology and Aging, 1,* 220–232.

Hamilton, V. L., Hoffman, W. S., Broman, C. L., & Rauma, D. (1993). Unemployment, distress, and coping: A panel study of autoworkers. *Journal of Personality and Social Psychology, 65,* 234–247.

Harbour Report (2003). *Management: Harbour Report.* Retrieved on August 19, 2004, from http://www.autointell.com/management/harbour-2002

Hatfield, E., Cacioppo, J. T., & Rapson, R. L. (1993). Emotional contagion. *Current Directions in Psychological Science, 2,* 96–99.

Haw, C., Houston, K., Townsend, E., & Hawton, K. (2001). Deliberate self-harm patients with alcohol disorders: Characteristics, treatment, and outcome. *Crisis, 22,* 93–101.

Hazan, C., & Shaver, P. R. (1990). Love and work: An attachment-theoretical perspective. *Journal of Personality and Social Psychology, 59,* 270–280.

Helson, R., Jones, C., & Kwan, V. S. (2002). Personality change over 40 years of adulthood: Hierarchical linear modeling analyses of two longitudinal samples. *Journal of Personality and Social Psychology, 83,* 752–766.

Helson, R., & Kwan, V. S. (2000). Personality development in adulthood: The broad picture and processes in one longitudinal sample. In S. Hampson (Ed.), *Advances in personality psychology* (Vol. 1, pp. 77–106). London: Routledge.

Helson, R., & Roberts, B. W. (1994). Ego development and personality change in adulthood. *Journal of Personality and Social Psychology, 5*, 911–920.

Helson, R., & Srivastava, S. (2001). Three paths of adult development: Conservers, seekers, and achievers. *Journal of Personality and Social Psychology, 80*, 995–1010.

Helson, R., Stewart, A. J., & Ostrove, J. (1995). Identity in three cohorts of midlife women. *Journal of Personality and Social Psychology, 69*, 544–557.

Hoare, C. H. (1991). Psychosocial identity development and cultural others. *Journal of Counseling and Development, 70*, 45–53.

Hoare, C. H. (2002). *Erikson on development in adulthood: New insights from the unpublished papers.* New York: Oxford University Press.

Hoare, C. H. (2005). Erikson's general and adult developmental revisions of Freudian thought: "Outward, forward, upward." *Journal of Adult Development, 12*(1), 19–31.

Hofer, S. M., Christensen, H., Mackinnon, A. J., Korten, A. E., Jorm, A. F., Henderson, A. S., et al. (2002). Change in cognitive functioning associated with ApoE genotype in a community sample of older adults. *Psychology and Aging, 17*, 194–208.

Hogan, R. (1986). *Hogan personality inventory manual.* Minneapolis, MN: National Computer Systems.

Hogan, R. (Ed.). (1997). *Human performance.* Mahwah, NJ: Lawrence Erlbaum.

Holman, D. (2002). Employee well-being in call centers. *Human Resource Management Journal, 12*, 35–50.

Holman, D., Chissick, C., & Totterdell, P. (2002). The effects of performance monitoring on emotional labor and well-being in call centers. *Motivation and Emotion, 26*, 57–81.

Hough, L. M., Eaton, N. K., Dunnette, M. D., Kamp, J. D., & McCloy, R. A. (1990). Criterion-related validities of personality constructs and the effect of response distortion on those validities. *Journal of Applied Psychology, 75*, 581–595.

Houkes, I., Janssen, P. P. M., De Jonge, J., & Bakker, A. B. (2003). Personality, work characteristics, and employee well-being: A longitudinal analysis of additive and moderating effects. *Journal of Occupational Health Psychology, 8*, 20–38.

Jaques, E. (1965). Death and the mid-life crisis. *International Journal of Psychoanalysis, 46*, 502–514.

John, O. P. (1990). The "big five" factor dichotomy: Dimensions of personality in the natural language and in questionnaires. In L. A. Pervin (Ed.), *Handbook of personality: Theory and research* (pp. 66–100). New York: Guilford.

Johnson, N. B., & Scandura, T. A. (1994). The effect of mentorship and sex-role style on male-female earnings. *Industrial Relations, 33*, 263–274.

Joiner, T. E. Jr., & Katz, J. (1999). Contagion of depressive symptoms and mood: Meta-analytic review and explanations from cognitive, behavioral, and inter-

personal viewpoints. *Clinical Psychology: Science and Practice, 6*, 149–164.

Jorm, A. F., Rodgers, B., Henderson, A. S., Korten, A. E., Jacomb, P. A., & Christensen, H., et al. (1998). Occupation type as a predictor of cognitive decline and dementia in old age. *Age and Ageing, 27*, 477–483.

Kakar, S. (1989). *Intimate relations.* Chicago: University of Chicago Press.

Kakar, S. (1991). Western science, eastern minds. *Wilson Quarterly, 15*, 109–116.

Kalimo, R., Taris, T. W., & Schaufeli, W. B. (2003). The effects of past and anticipated future downsizing on survivor well-being: An equity perspective. *Journal of Occupational Health Psychology, 8*, 91–109.

Kalimo, R., & Vuori, J. (1990). Work and sense of coherence — Resources for competence and life satisfaction. *Behavioral Medicine, 16*, 76–89.

Kasl, S. V., & Cobb, S. (1970). Blood pressure changes in men undergoing job loss: A preliminary report. *Psychosomatic Medicine, 32*, 19–38.

Keddy, B., Cable, B., Quinn, S., & Melanson, J. (1993). Interrupted work histories: Retired women telling their stories. *Health Care Women International, 14*, 437–446.

Kegan, R. (1982). *The evolving self.* Cambridge, MA: Harvard University Press.

Kelly, G. A. (1963). *A theory of personality: The psychology of personal constructs.* New York: Norton.

Kelly, M. J. (2001). Management mentoring in a social service organization. *Administration in Social Work, 25*, 17–29.

Kiltz, G., Danzig, A., & Szecsy, E. (2004). Learner-centered leadership: A mentoring model for the professional development of school administrators. *Mentoring and Tutoring: Partnership in Learning, 12*, 135–154.

Kirchmeyer, C. (1997). Gender roles in a traditionally female occupation: A study of emergency, operating, intensive care, and psychiatric nurses. *Journal of Vocational Behavior, 50*, 78–95.

Kirchmeyer, C. (2002). Change and stability in managers' gender roles. *Journal of Applied Psychology, 87*, 929–939.

Knoops, K. T. B., De Groot, L. C. P. G. M., Kromhout, D., Perrin, A.-E., Moreiras-Varela, O., Menoti, A., et al. (2004). Mediterranean diet, lifestyle factors, and 10-year mortality in elderly European men and women: The Hale project. *Journal of the American Medical Association, 292*, 1433–1439.

Kohn, M. L., Naoi, A., Schoenbach, C., Schooler, C., & Slomczynski, K. M. (1990). Position in the class structure and psychological functioning in the United States, Japan, and Poland. *American Journal of Sociology, 95*, 964–1008.

Kohn, M. L., & Schooler, C. (1969). Class, occupation, and orientation. *American Sociological Review, 34*, 659–678.

Kohn, M. L., & Schooler, C. (1978). The reciprocal effects of the substantive complexity of work and intellectual flexibility: A longitudinal assessment. *American Journal of Sociology, 84,* 24–52.

Kohn, M. L., & Schooler, C. (1982). Job conditions and personality: A longitudinal assessment of their reciprocal effects. *American Journal of Sociology, 87,* 1257–1286.

Kohn, M. L., & Schooler, C. (1983). *Work and personality: An inquiry into the impact of social stratification.* Norwood, NJ: Ablex.

Kohn, M. L., Schooler, C., Miller, J., Miller, K. A., Schoenbach, C., & Schoenberg, R. (1983). *Work and personality: An inquiry into the impact of social stratification.* Norwood, NJ: Ablex.

Kohn, M. L., & Slomczynski, K. M. (1990). *Social structure and self-direction: A comparative analysis of the United States and Poland.* Cambridge, MA: Basil Blackwell.

Kohn, M. L., Slomczynski, K. M., Janicka, K., Khmelko, V., Mach, B. W., & Panioto, V., et al. (1997). Social structure and personality under conditions of radical social change: A comparative analysis of Poland and Ukraine. *American Sociological Review, 62,* 614–638.

Krampe, R. T., & Ericsson, K. A. (1996). Maintaining excellence: Deliberate practice and elite performance in young and older pianists. *Journal of Experimental Psychology: General, 125,* 331–359.

Labouvie-Vief, G., & DeVoe, M. R. (1991). Emotional regulation in adulthood and later life: A developmental view. *Annual Review of Gerontology and Geriatrics, 11,* 172–194.

Labouvie-Vief, G., DeVoe, M. R., & Bulka, D. (1989). Speaking about feelings: Conceptions of emotions across the life span. *Psychology and Aging, 4,* 425–437.

Labouvie-Vief, G., Hakim-Larson, J., & Hobart, C. J. (1987). Age, ego level, and the life-span development of coping and defense processes. *Psychology and Aging, 2,* 286–293.

Lang, F. R., & Heckhausen, J. (2001). Perceived control over development and subjective well-being: Differential benefits across adulthood. *Journal of Personality and Social Psychology, 81,* 509–523.

Laske, O. E. (2003). Executive development as adult development. In J. Demick & C. Andreoletti (Eds.), *Handbook of adult development* (pp. 565–584). New York: Kluwer Academic.

Law, B., Meijers, F., & Wijers, G. (2002). New perspectives on career and identity in the contemporary world. *British Journal of Guidance and Counseling, 30,* 431–449.

Lawler, E. (1992). *The ultimate advantage: Creating the high-involvement organization.* San Francisco: Jossey-Bass.

Lee, C., Ashford, S. J., & Bobko, P. (1990). Interactive effects of "Type A" behavior and perceived control on worker performance, job satisfaction, and somatic complaints. *Academy of Management Journal, 33,* 870–881.

Levinson, D. J. (1986). A conception of adult development. *American Psychologist, 41,* 3–13.

Levinson, D. J., Darrow, C. N., Klein, E. B., Levinson, M. H., & McKee, B. (1978). *The seasons of a man's life.* New York: Ballantine.

Li, S-C. (2003). Biocultural orchestration of developmental plasticity across levels: The interplay of biology and culture in shaping the mind and behavior across the life span. *Psychological Bulletin, 129,* 171–194.

Lichtenstein, H. (1983). *The dilemma of human identity.* New York: Jason Aronson.

Loehlin, J. C., Horn, J. M., & Willerman, L. (1990). Heredity, environment, and personality change: Evidence from the Texas Adoption Project. *Journal of Personality, 58,* 221–243.

Loevinger, J. (1976). *Ego development: Conceptions and theories.* San Francisco: Jossey-Bass.

Loevinger, J. (1993). Conformity and conscientiousness: One factor or two stages? In D. C. Funder, R. D. Parke, C. Tomlinson-Keasey, & K. Widaman (Eds.), *Studying lives through time: Personality and development* (pp. 189–206). Washington, DC: American Psychological Association.

Lopez, F. G., & Gover, M. R. (1993). Self-report measures of parent-adolescent attachment and separation-individuation: A selective review. *Journal of Counseling and Development, 71,* 560–569.

Lu, T., Pan, Y., Kao, S-Y., Li, C., Kohane, I., Chan, J., & Yankner, B. A. (2004). Gene regulation and DNA damage in the ageing human brain. *Nature, 429,* 883–891.

Lucas, M. (1997). Identity development, career development, and psychological separation from parents: Similarities and differences between men and women. *Journal of Counseling Psychology, 44,* 123–132.

Maguire, E. A., Gadian, D. G., Johnsrude, I. S., Good, C. D., Ashburner, J., Frackowiak, R. S. J., et al. (2000). Navigation-related structural change in the hippocampi of taxi drivers. *Proceedings of the National Academy of Sciences, USA, 97,* 4398–4403.

Maier, G. W., & Brunstein, J. C. (2001). The role of personal work goals in newcomers' job satisfaction and organizational commitment: A longitudinal analysis. *Journal of Applied Psychology, 86,* 1034–1042.

Mallinckrodt, B., & Bennett, J. (1992). Social support and impact of job loss in dislocated blue-collar workers. *Journal of Counseling Psychology, 39,* 482–489.

Mangione, C. M., Seddon, J. M., Cook, E. F., Krug, J. H. Jr., Sahagian, C. R., Campion, E. W., et al. (1993). Correlates of cognitive function scores in elderly outpatients. *Journal of the American Geriatrics Society, 41,* 491–497.

Marcia, J. E. (1966). Development and validation of ego identity status. *Journal of Personality and Social Psychology, 3,* 551–558.

Marcia, J. E. (1980). Identity in adolescence. In J. Adelson (Ed.), *Handbook of adolescent psychology* (pp. 159–187). New York: Wiley.

Martire, L. M., Stephens, M. A. P., & Townsend, A. L. (2000). Centrality of women's multiple roles: Beneficial and detrimental consequences for psychological well-being. *Psychology and Aging, 15,* 148–156.

Maurer, T. J. (2001). Career-relevant learning and development, worker age, and beliefs about self-efficacy for development. *Journal of Management, 27,* 123–140.

Maurer, T. J., Weiss, E. M., & Barbeite, F. G. (2003). A model of involvement in work-related learning and development activity: The effects of individual, situational, motivational, and age variables. *Journal of Applied Psychology, 88,* 707–724.

McAdams, D. P. (2001). The psychology of life stories. *Review of General Psychology, 5,* 100–122.

McAdams, D. P., Diamond, A., de St. Aubin, E., & Mansfield, E. (1997). Stories of commitment: The psychosocial construction of generative lives. *Journal of Personality and Social Psychology, 72,* 678–694.

McAdams, D. P., & de St. Aubin, E. (Eds.). (1998). *Generativity and adult development.* Washington, DC: American Psychological Association.

McCrae, R. R., & Costa, P. T. Jr. (1997). Conceptions and correlates of openness to experience. In R. Hogan, J. Johnson, & S. Briggs (Eds.), *Handbook of personality psychology* (pp. 825–847). New York: Academic Press.

McCrae, R. R., Costa, P. T. Jr., Ostendorf, F., Angleitner, A., Hrebickova, M., Avia, M. D., et al. (2000). Nature over nurture: Temperament, personality, and life span development. *Journal of Personality and Social Psychology, 78,* 173–186.

Meijers, F. (1992). *Who guarantees quality? Some remarks on the international case studies.* Netherlands: University of Leiden.

Mount, M. K., & Barrick, M. R. (1995). The big five personality dimensions: Implications for research and practice in human resources management. *Research in Personnel and Human Resources Management, 13,* 153–200.

Murtha, T. C., Kanfer, R., & Ackerman, P. L. (1996). Toward and interactionist taxonomy of personality and situations: An integrative situational-dispositional representation of personality traits. *Journal of Personality and Social Psychology, 71,* 193–207.

Naoi, A., & Schooler, C. (1985). Occupational conditions and psychological functioning in Japan. *American Journal of Sociology, 90,* 729–752.

Naoi, A., & Schooler, C. (1990). Psychological consequences of occupational conditions among Japanese wives. *Social Psychology Quarterly, 53,* 100–116.

Neisser, U. (1997). Never a dull moment. *American Psychologist, 52,* 79–81.

Neisser, U., Boodoo, G., Bouchard, T. J., Boykin, A. W., Brody, N., Ceci, S. J., et al. (1996). Intelligence: Knowns and unknowns. *American Psychologist, 51,* 77–101.

Neuman, G. A., & Wright, J. (1999). Team effectiveness: Beyond skills and cognitive ability. *Journal of Applied Psychology, 84,* 376–389.

Neyer, F. J., & Asendorpf, J. B. (2001). Personality-relationship transaction in young adulthood. *Journal of Personality and Social Psychology, 81,* 1190–1204.

Novina, C. D. & Sharp, P. A. (2004). The RNAi revolution. *Nature, 430,* 161–164.

Organ, D. W. (1988). *Organizational citizenship behavior: The good soldier syndrome.* Lexington, MA: Lexington.

Organ, D. W., Podsakoff, P. M., & MacKenzie, S. B. (2004). *Organizational citizenship behavior: Its nature, antecedents, and consequences.* Thousand Oaks, CA: Sage.

Paris, R., & Helson, R. (2002). Early mothering experience and personality change. *Journal of Family Psychology 16(2),* 172–185.

Parker, S. K. (2003). Longitudinal effects of lean production on employee outcome and the mediating role of work characteristics. *Journal of Applied Psychology, 88,* 620–634.

Parker, S. K., & Wall, T. D. (1998). *Job and work design: Organizing work to promote well-being and effectiveness.* Thousand Oaks, CA: Sage.

Peregoy, J. J., & Schliebner, C. T. (1990). Long-term unemployment: Effects and counseling interventions. *International Journal for the Advancement of Counseling, 13,* 193–204.

Peterson, B. E., Smirles, K. A., & Wentworth, P. A. (1997). Generativity and authoritarianism: Implications for personality, political involvement, and parenting. *Journal of Personality and Social Psychology, 1997,* 1202–1216.

Peterson, B. E., & Stewart, A. J. (1996). Antecedents and contexts of generativity motivation at midlife. *Psychology and Aging, 11,* 21–33.

Plomin, R., & Spinath, F. M. (2004). Intelligence: Genetics, genes, and genomics. *Journal of Personality and Social Psychology, 86,* 112–129.

Podsakoff, P. M., Ahearne, M., & MacKenzie, S. B. (1997). Organizational citizenship and the quantity and quality of work group performance. *Journal of Applied Psychology, 82,* 262–270.

Podsakoff, P. M., & MacKenzie, S. B. (1994). Organizational citizenship behavior and sales unit effectiveness. *Journal of Marketing Research, 31,* 351–363.

Podsakoff, P. M., & MacKenzie, S. B. (1997). Impact of organizational citizenship behavior on organizational performance: A review and suggestions for future research. In J. Hogan, (Ed.), *Human performance* (pp. 133–151). Mahwah, NJ: Lawrence Erlbaum.

Poe, E. A. (1847/1981). The domain of Arnheim. In *The complete Edgar Allan Poe: Tales* (pp. 546–556). New York: Avenel Books.

Price, R. H., Friedland, D. S., & Vinokur, A. D. (1998). Job loss: Hard times and eroded identity. In J. H. Harvey (Ed.), *Perspectives on loss: A sourcebook* (pp. 303–316). Philadelphia, PA: Brunner/Mazel.

Prussia, G. E., Fugate, M., & Kinicki, A. J. (2001). Explication of the coping goal construct: Implications for coping and reemployment. *Journal of Applied Psychology, 86,* 1179–1190.

Pulakos, E. D., Arad, A., Donovan, M. A., & Plamondon, K. E. (2000). Adaptability in the workplace: Development of a taxonomy of adaptive performance. *Journal of Applied Psychology, 85,* 612–624.

Pulkkinen, L., & Kokko, K. (2000). Identity development in adulthood: A longitudinal study. *Journal of Research in Personality, 34,* 445–470.

Pulkkinen, L., & Ronka, A. (1994). Personal control over development, identity formation, and future orientation as components of life orientation: A developmental approach. *Developmental Psychology, 30,* 260–271.

Reuter-Lorenz, P. A. (2002). New visions of the aging mind and brain. *Trends in Cognitive Sciences, 6,* 394–400.

Roberts, B. W. (1997). Plaster or plasticity: Are adult work experiences associated with personality change in women? *Journal of Personality, 65,* 205–232.

Roberts, B. W., Caspi, A., & Moffitt, T. E. (2001). The kids are alright: Growth and stability in personality development from adolescence to adulthood. *Journal of Personality and Social Psychology, 81,* 670–683.

Roberts, B. W., Caspi, A., & Moffitt, T. E. (2003). Work experiences and personality development in young adulthood. *Journal of Personality and Social Psychology, 84,* 582–593.

Roberts, B. W., & Friend, W. (1998). Career momentum in midlife women: Life context, identity, and personality correlates. *Journal of Occupational Health Psychology, 3,* 195–208.

Roberts, B. W., & Helson, R. (1997) Changes in culture, changes in personality: The influence of individualism in a longitudinal study of women. *Journal of Personality and Social Psychology, 72,* 641–651.

Roberts, B. W., Robins, R. W., Trzesniewski, K. H., & Caspi, A. (2003). Personality trait development in adulthood. In J. T. Mortimer & M. J. Shanahan (Eds.), *Handbook of the life course* (pp. 579–595). New York: Kluwer.

Robertson, I., & Callinan, M. (1998). Personality and work behavior. *European Journal of Work and Organizational Behavior, 7,* 321–340.

Robins, R. W., Fraley, R. C., Roberts, B. W., & Trzesniewski, K. (2001). A longitudinal study of personality change in young adulthood. *Journal of Personality, 69,* 617–640.

Rocklin, T. (1994). Relation between typical intellectual engagement and openness: Comment on Goff and Ackerman (1992). *Journal of Educational Psychology, 86,* 145–149.

Rokeach, M. (1960). *The open and closed mind.* New York: Basic Books.

Rothbard, N. P., & Edwards, J. R. (2003) Investment in work and family roles: A test of identity and utilitarian motives. *Personnel Psychology, 56,* 699–730.

Rowe, J. W., & Kahn, R. L. (1987). Human aging: Usual and successful. *Science, 237,* 143–149.

Rowe, J. W., & Kahn, R. L. (1998). *Successful aging.* New York: Pantheon.

Roy, M. (2003). Self-directed workteams and safety: A winning combination? *Safety Science, 41,* 359–372.

Russell, C. J. (2001). A longitudinal study of top-level executive performance. *Journal of Applied Psychology, 86,* 560–583.

Rust, J. (1999). Discriminant validity of the "big five" personality traits in employment settings. *Social Behavior and Personality, 27,* 99–108.

Sachs, R., Chrisler, J. C., & Devlin, A. S. (1992). Biographic and personal characteristics of women in management. *Journal of Vocational Behavior, 41,* 89–100.

Sacks, J. (1997). *The politics of hope.* London: Jonathan Cape.

Salgado, J. F. (1997). The five factor model of personality and job performance in the European community. *Journal of Applied Psychology, 82,* 30–43.

Schaie, K. W. (1996). *Intellectual development in adulthood: The Seattle longitudinal study.* New York: Cambridge University Press.

Schaie, K. W. (2005). *Developmental influences on adult intelligence: The Seattle longitudinal study.* New York: Oxford University Press.

Schaie, K. W., & Schooler, C. (Eds.). (1998). *Impact of work on older adults.* New York: Springer.

Schlender, B. (2004, April 5). The new soul of a wealth machine. *Fortune, 149,* 102–104, 108, 110.

Schmidt, F. L., & Hunter, J. (2004). General mental ability in the world of work: Occupational attainment and job performance. *Journal of Personality and Social Psychology, 86,* 162–173.

Schneider, B. (1996). Whither goest personality at work? *Applied Psychology: An International Review, 45,* 289–296.

Schon, D. A. (1983). *The reflective practitioner.* San Francisco: Jossey-Bass.

Schon, D. A. (1987). *Educating the reflective practitioner.* San Francisco: Jossey-Bass.

Schooler, C., Mulatu, M. S., & Oates, G. (1999). The continuing effects of substantively complex work on the intellectual functioning of older workers. *Psychology and Aging, 14,* 483–506.

Schooler, C., & Naoi, A. (1988). The psychological effects of traditional and of economically peripheral job settings in Japan. *American Journal of Sociology, 94,* 335–355.

Seeman, T. E., Lusignolo, T. M., Albert, M., & Berkman, L. (2001). Social relationships, social support, and patterns of cognitive aging in healthy, high-functioning older adults: MacArthur studies of successful aging. *Health Psychology, 20,* 243–255.

Seim, S. (1989). *Teenagers become adult and elderly.* Oslo: Norwegian Institute of Gerontology, report 5-1989.

Seim, S. (1997). *Tenaringen blir pensjonist* [From teenager to pensioner]. Oslo: Norwegian Institute of Gerontology, report 23-1997.

Shaffer, M. A., Joplin, J. R. W., Bell, M. P., Lau, T., & Oguz, C. (2000). Disruptions to women's social identity: A comparative study of workplace stress experienced by women in three geographic regions. *Journal of Occupational Health Psychology, 5,* 441–456.

Shamir, B. (1986). Self-esteem and the psychological impact of unemployment. *Social Psychology Quarterly, 49,* 61–72.

Sheldon, K. M., & Kasser, T. (2001). Getting older, getting better? Personal strivings and psychological maturity across the life span. *Developmental Psychology, 37,* 491–501.

Shoda, Y., Mischel, W., & Wright, J. C. (1994). Intraindividual stability in the organization and patterning of behavior: Incorporating psychological situations into the idiographic analysis of personality. *Journal of Personality and Social Psychology, 67,* 674–687.

Simmering, M. J., Colquitt, J. A., Noe, R. A., & Porter, C. O. (2003). Conscientiousness, autonomy fit, and development: A longitudinal study. *Journal of Applied Psychology, 5,* 954–963.

Simmons, B. A., & Betschild, M. J. (2001). Women's retirement, work and life paths: Changes, disruptions and discontinuities. *Journal of Women and Aging, 13,* 53–70.

Smyth, K. A., Fritsch, T., Cook, T. B., McClendon, M. J., Santillan, C. D., & Friedland, R. P. (2004). Worker functions and traits associated with occupations and the development of AD. *Neurology, 63,* 498–503.

Snarey, S., & Lydens, L. (1990). Worker equality and adult development: The kibbutz as a developmental model. *Psychology and Aging, 5,* 86–93.

Snowdon, D. (2002). *Aging with grace.* New York: Bantam Books.

Snowdon, D. (2003). Healthy aging and dementia: Findings from the nun study. *Annals of Internal Medicine, 139,* 450–454.

Srivastava, S., John, O. P., Gosling, S. D., & Potter, J. (2003). Development of personality in early and middle adulthood: Set like plaster or persistent change? *Journal of Personality and Social Psychology, 5,* 1041–1053.

Staudinger, U. M., Fleeson, W., & Baltes, P. B. (1999). Predictors of subjective physical health and global well-being: Similarities and differences between the United States and Germany. *Journal of Personality and Social Psychology, 76,* 305–319.

Steel, P., & Ones, D. S. (2002). Personality and happiness: A national-level analysis. *Journal of Personality and Social Psychology, 83,* 767–781.

Stern, E. (1993). The transformation of work-related development in a rapidly changing world: Exploring how to learn from each other. *Journal of Career Development, 20,* 91–97.

Stern, Y., Gurland, B., Tatemichi, T. K., Tang, M. X., Wilder, D., & Mayeaux, R. (1994). Influence of education and occupation on the incidence of Alzheimer's disease. *Journal of the American Medical Association, 271,* 1004–1010.

Sternberg, R. J. (1985a). Implicit theories of intelligence, creativity, and wisdom. *Journal of Personality and Social Psychology, 49,* 607–627.

Sternberg, R. J. (1985b). Practical intelligence in real-world pursuits: The role of tacit knowledge. *Journal of Personality and Social Psychology, 49,* 436–458.

Sternberg, R. J. (2003) A broad view of intelligence: The theory of successful intelligence. *Consulting Psychology Journal: Practice and Research, 55,* 139–154.

Sternberg, R. J. (2004). Culture and intelligence. *American Psychologist, 59,* 325–338.

Sternberg, R. J., Forsythe, G. B., Hedlund, J., Horvath, J. A., Wagner, R. K., Williams, W. M., et al. (2000). *Practical intelligence in everyday life.* Cambridge: Cambridge University Press.

Stevens, D. P., & Truss, C. V. (1985). Stability and change in adult personality over 12 and 20 years. *Developmental Psychology, 21,* 568–584.

Stewart, A. J., & Healy, J. M. Jr. (1989). Linking individual development and social changes. *American Psychologist, 44,* 30–42.

Stewart, A. J., & Ostrove, J. M. (1998). Women's personality in middle age. *American Psychologist, 53,* 1185–1194.

Stewart, A. J., Ostrove, J. M., & Helson, R. (2001). Middle aging in women: Patterns of personality change from the 30s to the 50s. *Journal of Adult Development, 8,* 23–37.

Stone, W. F., Lederer, G., & Christie, R. (1993). *Strengths and weakness: The authoritarian personality today.* New York: Springer-Verlag.

Surrey, J. L. (1985). *Self in relation: A theory of women's development.* M. A. Stone Center Working Paper No. 13, Wellesley College, Wellesley, MA.

Thompson, J. A., & Bunderson, J. S. (2001). Work-nonwork conflict and the phenomenology of time: Beyond the balance metaphor. *Work and Occupations, 28,* 17–39.

U.S. Department of Labor, Bureau of Labor Statistics. (2003). Labor productivity. Available online at http://www.bls.gov/data.

Vaillant, G. E. (1993). *The wisdom of the ego: Sources of resilience in adult life.* Cambridge, MA: Belknap Press.

Vaillant, G. E. (2000). Adaptive mental mechanisms: Their role in a positive psychology. *American Psychologist, 55,* 89–98.

Vandewater, E. A., Ostrove, J. M., & Stewart, A. J. (1997). Predicting women's well-being in midlife: The importance of personality development and social role involvements. *Journal of Personality and Social Psychology, 72,* 1147–1169.

Van Manen, K., & Whitbourne, S. K. (1997). Psychosocial development and life experiences in adulthood: A 22-year sequential study. *Psychology and Aging, 12*, 239–246.

Vernon, P. A., Jang, K. L., Harris, J. A., & McCarthy, J. M. (1997). Environmental predictors of personality differences: A twin and sibling study. *Journal of Personality and Social Psychology, 72*, 177–183.

Viken, R. J., Rose, R. J., Kaprio, J., & Koskenvuo, M. (1994). A developmental genetic analysis of adult personality: Extraversion and neuroticism from 18 to 59 years of age. *Journal of Personality and Social Psychology, 66*, 722–730.

Vinokur, A. D., Price, R. H. & Caplan, R. D. (1996). Hard times and hurtful partners: How financial strain affects depression and relationship satisfaction of unemployed persons and their spouses. *Journal of Personality and Social Psychology, 71*, 166–179.

Wall, T. D., Jackson, P. R., & Davids, K. (1992). Operator work design and robotics system performance: A serendipitous field study. *Journal of Applied Psychology, 77*, 353–362.

Warr, P., & Jackson, P. (1985). Factors influencing the psychological impact of prolonged unemployment and of reemployment. *Psychological Medicine, 15*, 795–807.

Waterman, A. S. (1982). Identity development from adolescence to adulthood: An extension of theory and a review of research. *Developmental Psychology, 18*, 341–358.

Waterman, A. S. (1985). Identity in the context of adolescent psychology. In A. S. Waterman (Ed.), *Identity in adolescence: Processes and contents* (pp. 5–24). San Francisco: Jossey-Bass.

Watson, D. (1996). Individuals and institutions: The case of work and employment. In M. Wetherell (Ed.), *Identities, groups and social issues* (pp. 241–282). Thousand Oaks, CA: Sage.

Watson, D., & Walker, L. M. (1996). The long-term stability and predictive validity of trait measures of affect. *Journal of Personality and Social Psychology, 70*, 567–577.

Watson, G. (1969). Resistance to change. In W. G. Bennis, K. D. Benne, & R. Chin (Eds.), *The planning of change* (2nd ed., pp. 488–498). New York: Holt, Rinehart, & Winston.

Wechsler, D. (1958). *The measurement and appraisal of adult intelligence* (4th ed.). Baltimore, MD: Williams & Wilkins.

Westwood, R. L., Tang, S. F. Y., & Kirkbride, P. S. (1992). Chinese conflict behavior: Cultural antecedents and behavioral consequences. *Organization Development Journal, 10*, 13–19.

Wetherell, M. (Ed.). (1996). *Identities, groups, and social issues.* London: Sage.

Weuve, J., Kang, J. H., Manson, J. E., Breteler, M. M. B., Ware, J. H., & Grodstein, F. (2004). Physical activity, including walking, and cognitive function in older women. *Journal of the American Medical Association, 292*, 1454–1461.

Whitbourne, S. K. (1986). Openness to experience, identity flexibility, and life change in adults. *Journal of Personality and Social Psychology, 50*, 163–168.

Whitbourne, S. K., Zuschlag, M. K., Elliot, L. B., & Waterman, A. S. (1992). Psychosocial development in adulthood: A 22-year sequential study. *Journal of Personality and Social Psychology, 63*, 260–271.

Winefield, A. H. (1997). The psychological effects of youth unemployment—international perspectives. *Journal of Adolescence, 20*, 133–141.

Wolf, M. (2004). *Why globalization works.* New Haven, CT: Yale University Press.

Wrenn, K. A., & Maurer, T. J. (2004). Beliefs about older workers' learning and development behavior in relation to beliefs about malleability of skills, age-related decline, and control. *Journal of Applied Psychology, 34*, 223–242.

Chapter 17

The Importance of Feeling Whole: Learning to "Feel Connected," Community, and Adult Development

Jan D. Sinnott and Debra Berlanstein

How do feeling connected or "whole" within the self, feeling connected with others, and feeling connected with something or someone larger than the self, relate to adult development, identity, and learning? How do we learn these connections and cognitively represent them?

We live in a time and context that pushes each one of us toward an ever shifting sense of identity. Our global society puts us in contact with more people than we can easily know. The traditions that connected our ancestors to something or to someone that gave a larger meaning to existence have become weak and ineffective for many people. Yet adults in any setting speak as if felt connections are important to them, perhaps even more important than objective rewards. We need to learn new ways to maintain felt connections. We need to take felt connection into account in new ways as we learn and as we teach adults.

Feeling connected during adulthood is important for adults. Connection is a primal need estab-lished in infancy and enacted in every form of social organization in all societies. The *disconnected* individual is more likely to express unhappiness and manifest behavior that "doesn't work" as well in life. Many psychological theorists have reached similar conclusions. Jung (1930/1971), for example, challenged the middle-aged person to find balance across the sides of the self to succeed at the second half of life. Erikson (1950, 1992) expressed the centrality and positive value of connection in his stage-resolution terms of intimacy, generativity, and integrity. Existential psychologists, for example, Frankl (1963), noted the importance of having a "higher" meaning for life, a meaning to which we are connected. This meaning might be drawn from work, love, or giving a purpose to the suffering inherent in existence and frequently involved relations with the spiritual. Feeling connected seems to facilitate adult development. It helps an adult find balance, create new ways of interpreting personal identity, and see him- or herself as larger than any current situation, all in a nurturing context. The increased resources flowing from connection feed adults' growth. But thinking about complex connections and representing ourselves in such complex ways seems to require complex thought, probably of a postformal (Sinnott, 1998b) type.

Humans feel the urge to maintain an identity that is somewhat stable, while at the same time be able to transform over time. Three levels of connection, mentioned previously, facilitate that ability to be a self while continuing to transform that self. Bridged by felt connections, we manage to experience inner change and continuity in identity over time during adulthood.

A theory of complex relations between feeling connected and adult development and identity, relations that will be described and discussed in this chapter, appears graphically in figure 17.1. We refer to figure 17.1 throughout this chapter. The theory also is based on interview data derived from use of a questionnaire that appears in appendix A.

TWO STORIES

Perhaps the best way to begin to examine the importance of feeling connected for adult development, identity, and learning is to briefly consider two stories. These stories are meant to make a point by contrasting different degrees of feeling connected. We can then observe the outcome of those differing types of felt connections for the person in the case. In most lives, of course, we see differing degrees of feeling connected, rather than some total feeling of connection or none at all.

We enlarge on these stories as we look at a complex theory about feeling connected, in the next section and figure 17.1. Both of these stories (composites of real events experienced by individuals known to one of the authors) involve older women. They had always been functional adults, strong, independent, able to live alone (but married at one time), and financially independent. They then were challenged by potentially life-threatening disease.

Mary, the first case, began to have frequent and intense abdominal pain. She feared ending up in an

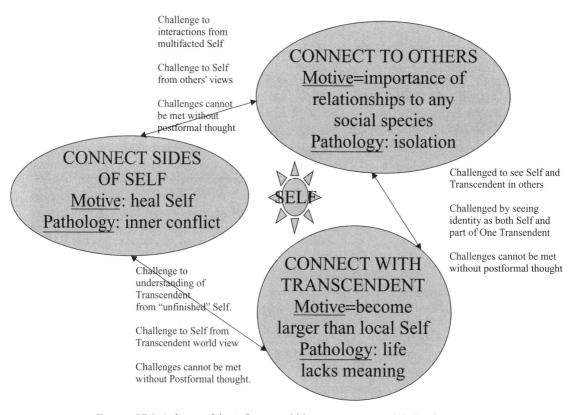

FIGURE 17.1. A theory of the influence of felt connection on adult development.

institution such as a hospital or nursing home, so she avoided seeing a doctor or asking anyone about her pain. She soon became so weak and was in so much pain that she could barely leave her bed. No one who lived near her knew of her deteriorating state because she disliked her neighbors and did not talk to them. She was alienated from most relatives and did not want them to know she needed anything. When one of her three children dropped by unexpectedly, he was shocked at her condition. He took Mary to the hospital, where she was diagnosed with a ruptured appendix, a treatable condition. But she refused treatment, saying she was eager to die and to go to heaven, and that she was tired of living. The increasing pain and discomfort of the spreading infection eventually forced her to ask for treatment for pain. She finally gave permission, and the life-saving surgery was performed. Relatives rushed to help her in the hospital and then in assisted living. But at the first possible moment she went home, ignored relatives' offers, refused to hire any help, and resumed her isolated life of clipping news stories. If someone did call or stop by, she embellished her own life story with tales of her medical problems and of the neglectful behavior of her relatives.

Anna, the second case, was finding it more difficult to do the things she enjoyed. She was always tired lately, and it was even getting difficult to breathe. When this condition rapidly became much worse, she went to her doctor, who diagnosed advanced congestive heart failure. Anna declared she was determined to enjoy what remained of her life. As news of her illness spread to Anna's church group, many friends began praying for her and offering to help with various tasks and with her collection of stray cats, just as she had helped others. On one hand Anna hated to be a burden; however, she enjoyed the help and a house full of visitors with their homemade gifts and meals. Even distant relatives spent increasing amounts of time staying with her, an intrusion she graciously accepted. At first Anna said that she hated to be so dependent on others and that she missed her peaceful, solitary life, but then decided it was her turn to be helped and give others the joy of helping. A few days before her death, officiating from her at-home hospital bed, she supervised some neighborhood children as they "did her ironing," because, she said, they needed a grandmother. An hour before she died she ate a big dinner prepared by her new but already devoted practical nurse. Then, looking very tired but surprised, and smiling, she pointed and told someone

in the room that she saw Jesus "right over there" coming for her. She said "I'm ready to leave now," then died smiling.

The stories of these two women are dramatic and moving in their own right. Only a few details are included here, with more in later sections of the chapter. But they offer us something more than drama. They offer a small window on the way that feeling connected may itself be connected to our development and learning. Our felt connections influence our learning. In the next section we'll describe a theory of feeling connected and its relation to identity and the course of adult development. Later in the chapter we will see the connection between the theory and the stories of Mary and Anna.

A THEORY OF FEELING CONNECTED

How do we propose to connect the ideas of "feeling connected" (in the three ways named earlier) with "adult development," "identity," and "learning?" The answer is summarized in figure 17.1. Let's look at each part of the figure and its very brief examples and enlarge on the complex ideas we find there. Seven aspects of ideas and relations in the figure are outlined next. They are based on research (see appendix A) and earlier work on felt connection by some definition (see "Summary of Literature," appendix B).

Three Types of Feeling Connected

The first part of the figure to notice is the *three types of feeling connected* that are of central interest in this discussion. These three elements are labeled "connect the sides of the self," "connect with others," and "connect with the transcendent." Connecting the sides of the self involves being in touch with the various aspects of our personalities, including disowned parts like the shadow (Jung, 1930/1971). Connecting with others involves interactions between or among persons. Connecting with the transcendent involves having an ongoing relationship with something or someone that is larger than the individual self, for example, the Great Spirit.

Three Dynamic Processes

Each of these three types is united with the other two by lines and arrows going in both directions, indicating that each of the three elements influences and is influenced by the others in a circular fashion. Therefore there are *three dynamic processes*, the dynamic of which we can discuss and study. The first process is the dynamic interplay between "connecting the sides of the self" and "connecting with others." The second process is the dynamic interplay between "connecting with others" and "connecting with the transcendent." The third process is the dynamic interplay between "connecting with the transcendent" and "connecting the sides of the self." Interventions and applications, described later, may make use of one or more of these three dynamic processes.

Challenges to the Self/Identity

Humans paradoxically desire both continuity and change. The dynamic interaction processes (those two arrows uniting any two elements in figure 17.1) also are described in terms of the *challenges to the self*, challenges posed by the simultaneous experience of any two types of connected feelings.

In the dynamic interaction between "connecting the sides of the self" and "connecting with others," two challenges occur. The self that exists at any one time is called into question by experiencing the reality of others; the manner in which one perceives and relates to others is transformed as more sides of the self are accepted.

In the dynamic interaction between "connecting with others" and "connecting with the transcendent," two challenges occur. The manner in which one perceives and relates to others may be changed by one's growing awareness of the transcendent (God, Spirit, the Earth, etc.). And our connection with the transcendent might change when challenged by the behavior of others close to us.

In the dynamic interaction between "connecting with the transcendent" and "connecting the sides of the Self," two challenges might occur. The self that exists at any one time is called into question by experiencing the reality of the transcendent; the manner in which one perceives and relates to the transcendent is transformed as more sides of the self are accepted.

Motivation

The three sets of processes are also labeled with a *motivation factor* in figure 17.1. That factor suggests why a person might want to do the difficult work of rising to the challenge posed for construction of and maintenance of the self when new information emerges during the dynamic interactions. When the dynamic interaction process involves "connecting the sides of the self" (coupled with some other element) motivation comes from the desire to be more complete or whole, to heal. When the dynamic interaction process involves the element of "connecting with others" (coupled with some other element), motivation comes from our desires to maintain and improve ties with people important to us. When the dynamic interaction process involves "connecting with the transcendent" (coupled with some other element), motivation comes from the desire to increase our participation in something spiritual, something larger than our local selves.

Complex Postformal Thought

The figure also refers to something called *postformal thought* in relation to each challenge. This term describes a kind of complex cognitive representational ability developed during adulthood, described in more detail later in this chapter. To successfully integrate the types of connections and their sometimes disparate or conflicting ideas yet preserve a concept of a self that is whole, postformal complex cognitive operations must be used (Sinnott, 1998b). The conflicting ideas and the person's high motivation to work out the conflict provide an occasion for the initial and continuing learning of this complex thinking ability.

However, *failure* to develop complex postformal cognitive representations and some integration of the reality of the several types of felt connections leaves the self in a fragmented and conflicted state with few conscious cognitive tools to become whole. The person in such a state may never consciously conceptualize and grasp a way to be able to live with multiple strongly felt connections. Learning is needed. Some examples may clarify this point.

For example, on a cognitive level it may seem impossible to such a person to integrate his or her connections with many other persons of all different types into a unified self that feels whole or connected inside. It will seem like either the whole, integrated self or the deep connections with other persons will have to be sacrificed. The problem is that the person cannot conceive of a way of connecting with others without losing the self, a very unsatisfactory life outcome.

Learning this integration could only occur with the learning and use of postformal complex thought.

In a second example of a cognitive failure, the person without complex cognitive representations may be faced with integrating felt connection with others and a felt connection to the transcendent. This person may conceive of no alternatives but to give up a spiritual search (connection with the transcendent) in favor of keeping connections with loved ones, or to break connections with the loved ones to continue a spiritual search. Again, this person's "solution" leads to a less than satisfactory adult development outcome due to (unnecessary) either/or choices and loss of felt connection of some type. Only a postformal cognitive representation of self would integrate both aspects of felt connection, and learning can foster this (Sinnott, 1998b).

A final example might shed additional light. The person who cannot cognitively represent the complex process of integrating two types of felt connections may not be able to conceive of knowing and accepting the multiple sides of the self (some sides of self considered "good," some considered "less than good") and feeling (guiltlessly) connected with the transcendent in the personification of an angry god. A resolution could only occur if one set of felt connections is sacrificed (e.g., surrender of self to the divine will or give up religion/spiritual life). Again, this nonresolution, based on the inability to conceptualize in postformal terms, closes off life options for growth and for feeling connected and whole in multiple ways simultaneously. It would be hard for such a person to learn, for example, to be a nondirective counselor.

Pathology

But failure to adequately cognitively represent these complex process interactions is only one way to speak of failure within the development of felt connections. We might also look at the failure to feel connected within any single one of the three types of felt connections mentioned above: within the self, between the self and other persons, and with the transcendent. These particular failures are labeled *pathology* in figure 17.1. They have implications for learning and identity.

First, if there are failures in the development of the felt connections within the self, the person might experience inner conflicts, surprisingly conflicted or self-sabotaging decisions, and a feeling of fragility.

The person tends to lose the self on interacting with others. The person rigidly judges to be "bad" those persons who seem to represent the sides of the self that have not been accepted and integrated. This form of projection is discussed by Welwood (1996).

Failure to establish felt connections with others might be shown in a different way. The person might feel isolated or that no one can understand him or her. Intimacy and generativity (Erikson, 1950, 1992) might not be possible, then, for that person.

Failure to establish connections with something or someone larger than the self, that is, with some transcendent, may carry yet another set of problems. This person may focus excessively on his or her personal death, or may find life tragic and meaningless. For this person there is nothing that gives a larger platform from which to view current problems or setbacks.

These failures to feel connected, and the resulting difficulties, leave the person with sadness and a yearning to reweave the web of life, to dance the dance of life in some more coherent way. But to participate happily in our modern version of village circle dances, we need three things. We need to feel mastery of many steps, to feel connected to other dancers in the circle, and to be in connection with the overall pattern the dance represents. We need to feel all three types of connection.

Learning and Development

Finally how do learning and development intersect in the model represented in figure 17.1? We have touched on these relations. The Piagetian ideas of assimilation and accommodation are helpful in understanding this intersection of concepts. When the figure indicates that a challenge occurs, the individual receiving new information first tries to assimilate the information into the cognitive concepts he or she already holds. Those current concepts fit the person's current developmental level. If there *is* a challenge, however, the new information will not fit the old concepts and ways of being in the world. If the individual who is challenged does not ignore that new information but accommodates to it, learning takes place. For a longer discussion of learning and development in adults, see Sinnott (1994b, 1998b). At some point a new developmental level may result from a combination of organic growth and the learning of newly acquired information.

THE CASES OF MARY AND ANNA, AND THE THEORY

Let's take a moment to look at the seven elements of the theory described previously and in figure 17.1, as shown in the lives of our cases described, namely, Mary and Anna.

Three Types of Felt Connections

What do the three types of felt connections look like in Mary's and Anna's lives? First, connecting the sides of the self seemed to come easier to Anna than to Mary. Anna consciously integrated (learned to join) the side of her self that wanted to be independent with the side that wanted (and needed) to be taken care of. Mary, on the other hand, rejected her dependent side, almost at the cost of her life.

Second, connection with others was mastered by Anna, who obtained joy from weaving relationships with relatives, neighbors, friends, and church acquaintances. But Mary found it difficult to feel any connection with others, other than a threatening one, against which she would have to defend. It made no difference whether the "others" were relatives, friends, or paid caretakers. All were equally closed out, dangerous, and suspect because learning through connections itself was suspect.

Third, felt connection with the transcendent was apparent to some degree for both women, though it was very different in quality for each of them. Both saw death in the Christian terms of going to heaven to spend eternity with the Lord. The quality of Mary's connection with "the Lord" or "Christ" was different from Anna's. Anna planned to experience more of a personal and friendly reunion with Christ while Mary seemed to be connected to an abstraction that she hoped would free her from present difficulties.

Overall, the felt connections seemed to make Anna's life more whole and richer in texture. Each type of felt connection seemed to feed the other, so that she had more resources and more to contribute even as she was dying. Anna continued to learn and develop. Overall, and in contrast, Mary seemed to experience connections within and without as less than a real connection and more as something unimportant, threatening, or at best utilitarian. Mary never seemed to resolve the Eriksonian conflict of trust versus mistrust. She did not seem to learn or grow her self from her experiences of connection.

Three Dynamic Processes

The three dynamic processes also take different forms in Mary's and Anna's lives. Mary seems to have created walls separating the three elements such that there are no dynamic interactions between any of the two elements. Felt connection among the sides of the self did not seem to happen at all for Mary. Felt connections with others operated independently from connection with the transcendent. For Mary, felt connection itself was very limited. There were few felt connections, and many of them were negative in quality.

In the case of Anna, the interactions between felt connections within the self and felt connections with others mutually influenced one another as she incorporated her dependent side and responded differently to other people. This may have been related in turn to her acceptance of her felt connection to Jesus as a trustworthy helper who is accepting of neediness as well as of strength. Anna demonstrated that a person usually learns congruent generalized representations of what felt connections can be like, approaching relationships in similar ways across several different areas of felt connection.

Challenges to the Self

Mary, having walled off the three elements of felt connection from one another, experienced no challenges to the self stemming from any interaction of the three felt connection elements. No learning could be a challenge to any other learning. Indeed, one specific reason for many individuals to wall off the three elements from each other is to avoid those challenges to the self. One risk of keeping the walls intact is a lack of coherence in one's felt connections of all sorts. For example, one might consciously feel close to others but due to a war within also feel a deep need to push others away. One might feel extremely needy and dependent internally, but in reaction to that very need, treat friends or loved ones paradoxically, as if they do not matter at all. But these conflicts did not occur for Mary because she felt equally *dis*connected in all three areas of felt connection.

Anna's experience was different. At first her inner felt connections were incomplete because they did not include her dependent side of self. So felt connections within her self were at odds with her felt connections with friends and relatives who wanted to take care of her (as well as respect her) as she declined in health. But this contradiction and challenge to the self was resolved when Anna resolved the struggle within herself. When she could welcome both her independent and dependent sides of self, learning to hold a larger identity, those felt connections within became coherent with the felt connections with others. There was no longer a challenge to the self.

Motivation

Neither Mary nor Anna spoke directly of their motivation in any of the three felt connection aspects of their lives. However, observing their behavior, it was clear that both women *wanted* to have the felt connections of all three types. But they acted in very different ways to achieve these three felt connections. Mary seemed to want wholeness within, but after many personal developmental defeats, decided to act in a rote way, ignore contradictions within, and wall off consciousness about connection within her self. Anna allowed herself to actively search for wholeness within and made changes. In seeking felt connection with others, Mary played socially accepted roles with friends and relatives, whereas Anna made attempts at real intimacy with friends and relatives. For Mary and Anna, the transcendent connection in life took the form of Jesus Christ. But while Mary conceptualized an abstract relationship with Christ, Anna conceptualized a relationship with Christ that was more of a friendship, one that helped her transition to the final life stage, death. Anna engaged in a new form of learning that fostered her development. So, although both women had similar motives, the quality of their prior development of felt connection meant that the motives resulted in very different behaviors and outcomes in their lives: Mary seemed fragmented and lonely; Anna seemed connected and psychologically comfortable and happy.

Postformal Thought

We will say more about postformal thought and the cases of Mary and Anna after the reader has had a chance to explore a description of this complex type of thinking, in the next section of the chapter. As you might imagine from the statements, Mary had use of postformal thought but Anna did not seem to have use of this complex cognition. The theory of postformal thought includes the concept that learning from life or from formal education could promote postformal thought development in Anna.

Pathology

From descriptions of Mary and Anna and from descriptions of their processes, the reader will not be surprised to hear that Anna did not show any major pathology or difficulties in functioning in her world. Things were not so good for Mary. In addition to the daily problems she had with relationships and existential issues, Mary also had a difficult time functioning in daily life. She demonstrated many eccentricities after years of disconnection. She manipulated and lied to others. She was anxious and obsessive-compulsive and even demonstrated paranoid schizophrenic behavior and ideation from time to time.

Overall, when we examine the two cases of Mary and Anna we can see that the quality of felt connections is itself connected with important developmental and behavioral outcomes. In the next section we leave the cases for a moment to concentrate on some abstract models that underlie the theory of felt connection, which has been described and in figure 17.1, and which has been shown in action in the cases.

ABSTRACT MODELS UNDERLYING THE THEORY OF FELT CONNECTION AND DEVELOPMENT

Why pay attention to abstract models? Abstract models underlying our theories set limits on the types of questions we form and on the nature of hypotheses we permit ourselves to consider. The best way to abstractly model the relationship between feeling connected and adult development, as described in the theory and cases, is to use the following multivariate complex models of living systems: general systems theory, and its offshoots chaos theory, and self-constructing systems theory. The best model for understanding the person's cognitive representation of felt connections and related processes is the theory of Complex Postformal Thought. A brief description of each of the four is in this section of the chapter because they are new and will be useful to the reader in thinking about felt connection related research questions. Each brief description is followed by some examples of ways the model can inform the theory of felt connection.

Description of Theory of Complex Postformal Thought

Postformal thought describes certain cognitive operations that constitute the means for knowing complex realities with competing logics or ideas. Postformal complex thought and the research underlying it are described in Jan Sinnott's book titled *The Development of Logic in Adulthood: Postformal Thought and Its Applications* (Sinnott, 1998b). Some references and applications that shed further light on this work are as follows: Cartwright, Galupo, and Tyree, 2004; Galupo, Cartwright, and Savage, 2004; Gavin, Galupo, and Cartwright, 2004; Johnson, 1991, 1994, 2001, 2004; Lee, 1991, 1994; Rogers, 1989; Rogers, Sinnott, and van Dusen, 1991; Sinnott, 1981, 1984, 1989a, 1989b, 1991a, 1991b, 1993a, 1993b, 1994a, 1984b, 1996, 1997, 1998a, 1998b, 2000, 2003a, 2003b, 2003c, 2004a, 2004b; Sinnott and Johnson, 1996; Yan, 1995; and Yan and Arlin, 1995. These references also describe the nature of the individual thinking operations that together make up postformal thought.

Postformal thought is a type of complex logical thinking that develops in adulthood, most likely when we interact with other people whose views about some aspect of reality are different from ours. We learn new "logics" in that way, and must deal with the existence of these other ways of viewing reality. When examined from the standpoint of Piagetian theory, postformal thought builds on concrete and formal (scientific) Piagetian thought skills. Postformal thought allows a person to deal with everyday logical contradictions by letting that person understand that a reality and meaning for events are co-created by both the knowers and the external realities they know. Both objectivity and a necessary subjectivity are useful in our epistemological understanding of the world. Postformal thought lets adults bridge two contradictory "scientifically" logical positions and reach an adaptive synthesis of them through a higher order logic. The adult then goes on to live the larger reality. So, the larger reality eventually becomes "true" with the passage of time. Postformal thought includes a necessary subjectivity, which means that the knower understands that "truth" is partially a creation of the one who knows it.

Postformal thought seems to develop later in life, after a certain amount of intellectual and interpersonal experience, according to Sinnott's earlier research work. For example, only after experiencing intimate relationships with their shared, mutually constructed logics about the reality of intimate life together can a person be experienced enough to know that "If I think of you as an untrustworthy partner, then treat you that way, you are likely to truly become an untrustworthy partner."

Here is another example. When I (J. S.) begin teaching a college class, the class and I begin to structure the reality or truth of our relationship. We decide on the nature of our relationship, act on our view of it, and mutually continue to create it in the days that follow. These various views, held by class members and by me, form several contradictory logical systems about the reality of our relationship in the class. One student may see me as a surrogate parent and act within the formal logic inherent in that vision, to which I might respond by becoming more parental. Another student may logically construct me as a buddy and act within that logical system, to which I might respond by being a buddy, too (or by being even more parental to compensate). The result over the time of a semester will be a logical truth about my relationship with this class that is co-created by the class and me.

After postformal complex thought is stimulated into existence by interpersonal cognitive interactions among thinkers, it becomes a thinking tool for a person, a tool that may be applied in a generalized way to any kind of knowing situation, not just interpersonal ones. A person may learn to use the tool of Complex Postformal Thought through interactions with his or her spouse and go on to use it to think about Newtonian versus quantum physics. Just as the tool of scientific logic can be used in any context, so the tool of Complex Postformal Thought can be used in any context. Of course decisions need to be made about whether it is an appropriate tool in a given context. Complex Postformal Thought that orders several contradictory logical systems is probably unnecessary for less epistemologically demanding tasks, such as rote memorization of an agreed-on body of material.

Nine thinking operations make up postformal thought. Rationale for inclusion of these operations is given in Sinnott's summary book about the theory (Sinnott, 1998b). The operations include meta-theory shift, problem definition, process/product shift, parameter setting, multiple solutions, pragmatism, multiple causality, multiple methods, and paradox.

The references explain the meaning of each operation term, the ways these operations have been tested, and the research that provides an underpinning for these assertions. Each operation will be described here. Notice that the operations will relate to one another but will describe different aspects of the complex thinking process. Notice, too, that all the operations relate to problem solving, in the broadest sense of the term, including everyday problems of life. These operations can be learned.

- *Meta-theory shift* is the ability to view reality from more than one overarching logical perspective (for example, from both an abstract and a practical perspective, or from a phenomenological and an experimental perspective) when thinking about it.
- *Problem definition* is the realization that there is always more than one way to define a problem, and that I must define a problem to solve it, because we all see things like problems through our own unique lenses.
- *Process/product shift* is realizing that one can reach a "content-related" solution to a given problem, or a solution that gives a heuristic or a process that solves many such problems.
- *Parameter setting* is the realization that I must choose aspects of the problem context that must be considered or ignored for this solution.
- *Multiple solutions* means that I can generate several solutions, based on several ways of viewing the problem.
- *Pragmatism* means that I am able to evaluate the solutions that I create for this problem, then select one that is "best" by some definition.
- *Multiple causality* is the realization that an event can be the result of several causes.
- *Multiple methods* is the realization that there are several ways to get to the same solution of a problem.
- *Paradox* is realizing that contradictions are inherent in reality, and realizing that a broader view of an event can eliminate contradictions.

The development of postformal thought helps explain how college students change their thinking styles as they go through the university experience. Successful students (for example, see Perry, 1975) first are concrete thinkers who need to know "right" answers. They want to know the "right" personality theory and the "right" major for them to study. They expect an authority to tell them the answer. Professors might become the authority figures who provide answers. Then, second, students become relativistic thinkers, shaken by the apparent disappearance of "truth" ("no right or wrong answers exist," "no way to decide about truth"). Now they see debates as going on forever, without closure. "It doesn't matter which philosophy one professes, which major one takes, it's all the same endless, ongoing debate." Finally, third, they move on to complex thinking, a type of thinking in which they see that a necessary subjectivity is part of decisions about truth. A passionate commitment to the choice of a "reality" leads to making it "real" in the objective world. This complex thinking appears to be postformal thought. At that stage they can say, "It's up to me to pick 'the right major,' then make a commitment to it, act as if it is the right choice for me, and see if it works out. It does matter what is chosen . . . not all majors would be suitable. But no authority can tell which will turn out to be 'right.' " In fact no major will be right unless the student commits to it as if some absolute authority verified it is the true major for that student.

The main characteristics of postformal cognitive operations (Sinnott, 1998a, 1998b) are (1) self-reference and (2) the ordering of conflicting logics. Self-reference is a general term for the ideas inherent in the new physics (Wolf, 1981, is the most user-friendly description) and is alluded to by Hofstadter (1979) using the terms "self-referential games," "jumping out of the system," and "strange loops." The essential notion of self-reference is that we can never be completely free of the built-in limits of our system of knowing and that we come to know that this very fact is true. This means that we somewhat routinely can take into account, in our decisions about truth, the fact that all knowledge has a subjective component and therefore is of necessity incomplete. Thus, any logic we use is self-referential logic. Yet we must act in spite of being trapped in partial subjectivity. We make a decision about rules of the game (nature of truth), then act based on those rules. Once we come to realize what we are doing, we then can consciously use such self-referential thought.

The second characteristic of postformal operations is the ordering of conflicting logics. The higher level postformal system of self-referential truth decisions gives order to lower level logic systems. One of these logic systems is somewhat subjectively chosen and is imposed on data as "true." This is also the logic of the "new" physics (relativity theory and quantum mechanics) (Sinnott, 1981). New physics is the next step beyond Newtonian physics and is built on the logic of self-reference. It is reasonable that the development of logical processes themselves would follow that same progression (i.e., Newtonian logic, then new physics logic) to increasing complexity. A new type of cognitive coordination occurs at the postformal level. Another kind of coordination of perspectives also occurs on an emotional level, taking place over developmental time (Labouvie-Vief, 1984, 1987, 1992, 1994). This coordination parallels the cognitive one and is probably engaged in a circular interaction with it. Theorists expect that postformal thought is adaptive in a social situation with emotional and social components because it is hypothesized that postformal thought eases communication, reduces information overload, and permits greater flexibility and creativity of thought (Sinnott, 1998a). Postformal thought has an impact on one's view of self, the world, other persons, change over time, and connections with one another over time (e.g., the studies cited before, especially Sinnott, 1981, 1984, 1989b, 1991a, 1991b, 1998a, 1998b, 2000, 2003a, 2003b, 2003c, 2004a, 2004b).

Postformal thought is somewhat relativistic in the sense that several truth systems are represented to describe the reality of the same event, truth systems that appear to be logically equivalent. The relativistic underpinning of postformal thought was studied and found later in postformal research traditions by Yan in an excellent series of research projects (Yan, 1995; Yan & Arlin, 1995). Such thought is also nonrelativistic in that the knower ultimately does make a serious commitment to one truth system only. That truth system then goes on to become true for the knower because the knower's committed action makes it so. The knower finally sees that, as Bronowski (1974) and statisticians realized, all knowing involves a region of uncertainty in which truth lies somewhere. All knowledge and all logic are incomplete; knowing is always partly a matter of choice and creation, done with both mind and heart.

A knower who is capable of using postformal thought skips in and out of that type of thinking. Postformal thought is not always the best way to process a certain experience; it may be that sensorimotor thought (or some other stage or type of thought) is most adaptive on a given day. Perhaps a thinker with higher order thinking skills is being confronted with a new situation.

For example, a grandparent of one of the authors (Sinnott) had never learned to drive, although she was a very intelligent woman. When presented with the chance to learn to drive, the first thing she did was to read about it, trying to use formal thought. Although she knew, after her reading, about defensive driving and other concepts like the logic of the automotive engine, these higher level skills did not help much when she first tried to engage the clutch and drive away smoothly. In fact this particular grandmother was so shocked by her first-time, terrible driving performance, compared to her excellent book understanding, that she panicked and let the car roll out of control until it came to a stop against a huge rock. Learning the sensorimotor and procedural skill of getting that stick shift car out on the road was lower level thinking, but was the most adaptive kind of thinking for that situation. Choosing and using the right level of thought for the occasion may be one thing that people learn as they become postformal.

In the sections describing the cases of Mary and Anna and in the description of the ideas in figure 17.1, the value of postformal thought for felt connection is apparent. The discussion of developing postformal thought skills as an adjunct to cognitive behavioral therapy or other types of therapy for individuals presenting with some problems with felt connection could form another entire chapter.

General Systems Theory

The second newer model or set of theories that underlies coordinating felt connections is general systems theory (GST). GST developed hand in hand with the new physics and biology. It offers ways to think about complex system interactions, not only interactions among supposedly inert physical systems (the focus of physics) but also among living systems of multiple individuals. The systems of felt connections may be conceptualized as living systems, obeying the rules of GST.

What is GST? GST has been called an amusing theory. Physicist Wigner, as a possibly apocryphal story has it, once said that theories can be interesting or amusing. An interesting theory may have merit, but often such theories are quickly forgotten; an amusing theory makes one think and play with the possibilities. GST is an amusing theory.

GST, as we shall use the term here, is an attempt to unify science by finding structures and processes common to many entities. Of greatest interest are entities that are complex organizations that have boundaries, have some continuity over time, and are able to change in orderly ways over time. Such entities may be called living systems (Ford, 1987; Miller, 1978) whether they are cells or societies or some other type of entity. GST included among its earlier theorists such luminaries as Norbert Weiner (1961), and Ludwig von Bertalanfy (1968). It was expressed in the language of quantum physics, chemistry, game theory (von Neumann & Morgenstern, 1947), biofeedback, sociology (LockLand, 1973), and many other disciplines (Mahoney, 1991). The growth of interest in systems views is due in part to the growth of knowledge that prods us to go beyond single-variable studies to complex expressions of relationship and process. We also have new ways to analyze such complex systems data, and when tools exist, uses for them are created. Of course that statement itself is a systems theory interpretation of these events over time.

What are some of the core themes of GST? The first is the concept of a *system*, that is, a network of related components and processes that work as a whole. *Linkage* and *interaction* are key themes, because whatever influences one part or process influences all of the parts and processes, that is, influences the entire system. Systems coordinate their activities by means of *feedback*, either from within or without. Feedback from within leads to homeostasis or equilibrium within; feedback from without leads to balance between two or more systems. *Equilibrium* is a balance between or among system parts. Given a state of nonequilibrium, there will be an energy flow from one part to another. Any number of systems can have common mechanisms (isomorphic processes) for doing some task. For example, getting energy from one point to another may occur by means of chemical transmission or glucose metabolism or by moving commuters via subways in a city system. Because systems do interact and trade things such as energy, GST recognizes that scientists need to make deliberate decisions to specify system limits or parameters and levels of description. We have not always done this in the past. Thus, there is an awareness of the observer's input on the reality observed, an emphasis reminiscent of the new physics. For example, if we draw living system boundaries at the person level, we may correctly say that a middle-aged person's depression is related to felt conflict within the self. If we draw the boundaries at the societal living system level, we may argue with equal correctness that the depression is related to interpersonal interactions that conflict with the sense of self. We might be correct in both cases but would investigate different things.

Systems theory examines multiple causal variables, or at least considers that many may be present, and focuses most on the processes used to go from one state to another. This makes GST a natural for developmental psychologists who are interested in the multidetermined processes behind changes over time as much as in the states of persons at various time points. GST as a worldview is interested in both the melody and the chords of any life song. This fits perfectly with the study of felt connections and adult development.

What are some systems functions that are commonly present in all systems? First a "living" (in the broad sense used before) system operates so as to *maintain some continuity over time*, some structured wholeness, even while continuing, if appropriate, to grow. Second, systems function to *contain and transfer energy and information* from one point to another, within or between them. All systems have some means of *boundary creation* and maintenance, as well as means of interaction with other systems. This implies that the boundary must be permeable, to some extent, but not so permeable that the system will merge with other systems. Other systems functions are to *control processes*, *run circular processes*, and *give feedback*. The overall goal is to provide optimum input for continuity and growth, while avoiding pathological abnormalities and *maintaining flexibility*. Obviously these GST concepts provide research ideas for studies of felt connection.

Systems do change over time. How does this happen? Here are some rules of system change (Sinnott, 1993b), based on the work of Ford (1987), Miller (1978), and von Bertalanfy (1968):

- All systems change, except those near death. Change itself is a sign of life, even if specific changes are pathological.
- Patterns of change are predictable in the long run, based on the state of the system, the state of adjacent systems, and principles of emergence. Patterns of change are predictable in the short run (i.e., locally) based on analyses of local causes.
- Change in any one system will influence nearby systems. Whether this leads to useful or maladaptive changes in those other systems depends on their states.
- Boundary rigidity in the face of information or energy flow means death. Being completely unbounded means the dissolution of the system. Systems strive for continuity.

- Interaction with a new system that is powerful can efficiently and effectively reorient a system whose relations with earlier powerful systems were distorted.

Here are some system characteristics that influence change.

- The system must permit information to enter (learning) and have flexibility with bounded control.
- Systems resist disorder.
- Change means temporary increase in disorder.
- Systems monitor and control the amount of disorder.
- Surviving systems contain the seed of their own change and are programmed to get to the next higher level of order (e.g., puberty is inherent in an infant).
- Surviving systems balance potentials and activated processes.
- Surviving systems fit many contexts.
- Surviving systems are programmed to interfere with each other.
- Non-surviving systems have the same parts as surviving systems, but have different processes.

The only way systems can change over time is if some entropy or disorder is present. If this is counterintuitive, consider for a moment what would happen if no disorder were present and all elements were structured into some form: There would be no space available and no raw material to use to make new forms. For example, if a child used all available blocks to make a toy city (i.e., all the blocks were "ordered"), some disorder would have to be introduced (e.g., push the blocks into a pile on the side) to make room for the next orderly structure (perhaps a large house) to be built. If a person's mind is made up about an issue, doubt must be introduced before a change of mind is possible. So disorder (entropy) not only is the catastrophic final state predicted by the second law of thermodynamics but also the beneficial means to a flexible reordering and growth to a larger order.

When systems change over time, they usually move from complete disorder or potential through increasing order and bounding to a relative balance between order and potential, a state that may last most of the system's lifetime. This involves learning. As systems "die," they move toward rigidity that is a state of very low potential and overwhelming order. All the system's decisions have been made already, so to speak; all its choices are over. The overly ordered, overly structured rigid state admits no change and will be shattered by any input from outside. An analogy is what happens to a rigid crystal goblet that breaks under high-frequency vibrations, whereas the thinner skin on the hand holding it does not. Prigogene and Stengers (1984) note that it is always possible to create a better structure by shattering a rigid state. From that shattering and the availability it creates will come a more flexible, more complex form. This means the death of the old system, or its reemergence in very altered form.

Imagine a situation in which two systems (societies, for example) come up against each other and try to influence each other, that is, they intrude on each others' boundaries. If the first system is not too rigid and too ordered, the influence and energy of the second will have an impact and alter the first. The reciprocal will also be true. But if the first system is rigid, the second will not influence it easily. It will have to try harder, if it can. Let's say the intruder system does try harder still. If it cannot influence the rigid first system subtly, the more violent influence it may resort to may result in a complete shattering of the first system. The first system did not "go with the flow," "coopt the opposition" or "make a deal." For a rigid system where compromise is out of the question, every fight with a worthy opponent is a fight to the death. What a high price to pay for necessary and ordinary adaptations. A rigid system prevents learning from occurring and makes development impossible.

The gentler dynamic—mutual influence of semi-ordered systems—occurs during such events as political dialogues and pretrial legal negotiations. The second, more catastrophic dynamic—destruction of an old, overly rigid system—occurs during revolutions or court trials. System change over time therefore demands a significant degree of entropy. But systems resist disorder on any large scale, and change means the temporary elimination of much order. The resistance to disorder in the psychological system is evident in the sometimes painful reorganizations during personal change, for example, change during psychotherapy or during crises. Any system tries to monitor and control the extent of disorder, but hopes not to need to resist absolutely, because that would take too much energy. Surviving systems balance their potentials and actualizations, have boundaries but are not closed entirely, try to fit many contexts flexibly, and attempt to interface with other systems without being engulfed or engulfing. Nonsurviving systems may have the same structures (e.g., a boundary), but may have different processes (e.g., rigidity in a boundary) that are less adaptive. Surviving systems of felt connection allow information to cross boundaries but do not let themselves be overtaken by other types of felt connection systems. Nonsurviving systems of felt connections also have boundaries, but theirs are so rigid that no new information (from a second type of felt connection system, for example) can cross. For example, one person may not permit felt connection with another to reach consciousness for fear that she or he will be engulfed by those strong feelings.

Systems theory provides a way for us to create a new generation of research about felt connections. It permits us to ask better questions to deal with complexity. A scientific worldview in which causality is linearly dependent on single variables could not do felt connection research on justice. Simply adopting a multivariate perspective is not adequate either, because such a view often leaves us casting about in the choice of variables to explore. Adoption of GST gives us more options regarding ways to talk about process and structure, suggesting dynamics and even levels of study that would be relevant. GST lets us reorder a perturbed system on a more complex level, rather than making the boundaries more rigid to ward off the new information.

GST gives access to a new physics worldview in which subject and object are necessarily related, but in which the scientific method can still be employed, and must be. GST, used in its general way (i.e., not reduced to single or dual variable studies) demands postformal thought. Therefore to use GST the human living system must cognitively develop these postformal complex intellectual functions that are adaptive.

Chaos Theory

Chaos theory is a new mathematical model that has been used in the past two decades to describe phenomena as different as weather, the structure of coastlines, brain wave patterns, the behavior of groups of people, adult learning, normal or abnormal heartbeat patterns, family transitions, the behavior of the mentally ill, and much more (Alper, 1989; Cavanaugh, 1989; Cavanaugh & McGuire, 1994; Crutchfield,

Farmer, Packard, & Shaw, 1986; Gleick, 1987; Gottman, 1991; Pool, 1989; Sinnott, 1990). General and more lengthy descriptions of chaos theory are available in Abraham (1985), Barton (1994), Devaney (1989), Gleick (1987), Goerner (1994), Levine and Fitzgerald (1992), and Smith and Thelan (1993). Chaos theory describes the orderly and flexible nature of apparent disorder. It mathematically describes complex systems with nonlinear equations. It describes commonalities of processes over time that would otherwise appear disorderly if viewed at one time point.

Key concepts of chaos theory are as follows. Chaos theory works with dynamic systems that are systems where the contents of the system and the processes of the system mutually influence each other. In such systems the current state of the system is fed back to it before it makes another iteration or goes through another round of changes. The system then repeats its process, each time with updated information. Such systems tend to begin to appear stable over time.

But such systems are deterministic as well as unpredictable, with only the appearance of stability. The behavior at each iteration is not predictable, but the limits built into the system confine it in predictable ways. So there is a "hidden" order that also gradually emerges from beneath the disorder. Chaotic systems somewhat resemble the rambling pattern of footprints made by a curious dog on a very long leash; at first there seems to be no pattern, but soon, after enough walking, a pattern emerges. Part of that emergent pattern is centered on the leash and on what or whoever is holding it; that part is truly deterministic. Part of what emerges is specific to the next part of the dog's rambling walk; that part is unpredictable.

One striking feature of chaotic systems is the way that they explain why a tiny disturbance or perturbation can lead to complete rescaling of the entire pattern of the system due to structural instability. This has been called the butterfly effect (Lorenz, 1963, 1979) because weather forecasters using computer models have seen the "breeze" from a butterfly moving its wings (the idiosyncratic perturbation) eventually lead to a whole new direction of wind movement, even though the overall pattern of the actual wind was not changed by the creators of the computer model. Dynamic systems are generally structurally unstable, demonstrating these large impacts from small changes. However it is possible for them to be stable. We humans certainly prefer to think of things as structurally stable, and therefore "find" stability even where little exists.

Another feature of chaotic systems is the way a seemingly random set of events, after many repetitive interactions, can coalesce around a point in an apparently orderly way. The impression is of a dominant feature of some sort, analogous to a dominant personality trait or a hurricane eye. This phenomenon is termed a strange attractor because the point looks like it pulls in the events around it.

It sometimes helps to think of chaos as organized disorder, as opposed to sheer randomness, or *disorganized* disorder. In orderly disorder, a flexible structure is hidden in events that only seem to be driven by change when examined in linear or one-time slices. The hidden order unfolds gradually to make itself known when the longer term nonlinear pattern is observed. In true randomness, or *dis*orderly disorder, there is no hidden underlying structure. Without some chaotic flexibility, some orderly readiness to fluctuate built into the system, a system (especially one like the heart or brain) is too rigid to adapt and live. For example, a rigid heartbeat pattern (no chaos) cannot effectively and efficiently correct for a small perturbing error like a skipped beat, so an arrhythmia may occur. A rigid brain wave pattern cannot respond effectively to an intellectual challenge, so poor performance results.

Chaotic disorder is nonrandom and has a kind of potential to correct for errors by the use of the underlying, hidden corrective mechanism of the basic, deeper pattern. Chaos is an order enfolded into apparent disorder; it is the pattern in the hologram, akin to the "implicate order" described by Prigogene and Stengers (1984). Implicate order means that an orderly message is encoded within the surface and the apparent disorder, in such a way that the implied message can be unfolded and read. Genetic material is another example of this implied message which is unpacked, decoded, and read by the organism as it develops from its first cells to its full hereditary potential. But the unfolding makes even a very minor element powerful enough to create major effects.

Chaos theory gives a rationale for synchronous effects, those apparently unrelated events that seem to mysteriously occur together. The synchronous systems demonstrate entrainment in which one system locks on to the mode and pattern of another nearby system. The minor event in one system then can move the other system with it. In interpersonal relation terms, we often adopt the relational styles of others.

Chaos models have interesting ways of describing the mechanisms of abrupt or qualitative change. For example, a thinker can move from seeing the world with Piagetian concrete logic to somewhat suddenly (an "aha" reaction) seeing the world with formal logic. When a thinker suddenly begins to see the world in Piagetian formal operational terms (whereas before the world was framed in concrete operational terms) many kinds of behavior are affected. The person is now more of a scientist than a simple labeler of events. Bifurcation models within chaos theory seem to describe this kind of sudden shift event. In a bifurcation model, at first possibilities (actually possible equation solutions) emerge from one point, like branches on a young sapling tree. But later in the tree's progression through time, the newest branches seem to cluster around several source points, not just one, with young branches coming off two or three more major limbs, going in different directions. This shift from one group of possibilities to several groups of possibilities is analogous to the bifurcation. Before the new branching becomes clear, there seems to be a considerable chaos; after it becomes clear, there seems to be more complex order. Another way to think about transition and bifurcation is to think about before-having-a-first-baby to postpartum family development. In this example, in the before state life seems to have a stable set of family relations configurations. Then, fairly quickly something happens, and after a period of greater disorder, several new configurations within the new three-person family branch off on their own tracks. Earlier we had variations on a parent–parent relational theme; later we have three possible centers of relations (the original one and parent 1 to child and parent 2 to child). In the example of the birth of a first child, we know what the proximate cause was that got the system to transform. In some bifurcating systems the push to transformation is not so well known.

What are the implications of chaos theory for reality? First, it suggests that there is more than one sort of disorder. Useful, chaotic disorder provides fresh options and room to correct for past errors; useless disorder provides nothing that seems meaningful, now or later. Learning allows the underlying order to become conscious. For example, Smith and Thelen (1993) describe in chaotic system terms the very young child's learning to walk. Surprisingly, that learning is not a simple practice of muscle movements of a predetermined type. Instead, the child randomly (or so it seemed) tries out various movements somewhat associated with walking, finally settling on the best set that allowed for the most efficient walking behavior to occur. In other words, the child used randomness in service to creation of an individualized optimal pattern for a skill that had been encoded in the human behavioral repertoire and is now emergent.

Second, chaos theory suggests and implies the immense importance of each element in the system for the final outcome of the system as well as for the individual. Remember, a perturbation caused by one butterfly's wing can alter the weather pattern, besides allowing the butterfly to fly. In our own personal histories, we all remember those small chance remarks or experiences that led to major life changes. Chaos principles help validate our phenomenological experience.

Third, chaos theory suggests the importance of openness to innovation to provide natural sorts of corrective devices for complex events, especially those events where outcomes and goals are not totally clear to us. In that kind of event a good process is our only safeguard against a manipulation that could cause unimagined damage when it has unforeseen consequences for a dynamic system. For example, we now understand the dangers we face by severely limiting the types of food crops we cultivate. Hundreds of variations on any given food crop species were lost when we selected for the single species with the high yield. But in the event that a disease attacks that one species (as in the Irish potato famine) we would have lost the chance to recover because our process of dealing with multiple types of plant species was flawed.

What might chaos theory imply for the relationship between feeling connected and adult development? We might begin to conceptualize the connected individual changing over time as a potentially chaotic system. If we do so, we would not expect to find many simple deterministic relationships. We would expect that some deterministic basic elements might be found, but that they will likely be the underlying, hidden orderly principles beneath the apparent disorder of connection and development. For example,

a hidden order might be habitual patterns of interpersonal relations, patterns that have implications for learning styles in adulthood.

The system of felt connection and development may also be a structurally unstable system, subject to the large effects of tiny perturbations. In light of an individual's shift in meaning structures, instigated by an important relationship, that individual might learn a great deal about his or her lifelong tendency to blame others for his or her own shortcomings, leading to development of more skilled emotional management. We can name these for individuals and intervene using them in therapeutic situations. As Smith and Thelan (1993) note, though, the whole idea in developmental research is to show how states change over time in a variety of individualized ways. Using chaos concepts, we can predict types of felt connections during periods of relative stability and can predict ranges of variability and points of transition to unstable structures. This may not satisfy our desires to predict deterministically from moment to moment, but it may be a more realistic goal and a prime opportunity to study complex individual differences in learning.

Predicting factors that lead to bifurcations of systems, for example, predictions about the events that trigger a bifurcation between conflicted and nonconflicted felt connections within the self and between the self and others, can be made and tested empirically. The changing "centers of events" in that case might then be described as strange attractors.

Cavanaugh and McGuire (1994) suggest that chaos theory can help us frame and answer several questions about adult cognitive development that because it underlies felt connection, would naturally suggest important questions about felt connection and development. Chaos theory would offer insights as to why we are likely to label just a few qualitatively unique types of relations. Chaos theory could help explain why felt connection and development shows a few spurts at certain times but smooth progression most of the time. It could address why flexibility in felt connection (i.e., moving easily among attractors so as to relate in many ways) is so hard to maintain in a static way (our feelings of strong connectedness ebb and flow). It could show how modes of relating develop. And it could resolve the persistent question of why relational activities and feelings in one area of life (e.g., felt connection with the transcendent) do not necessarily generalize to other areas of felt connection (e.g., felt connection among the sides of the self).

Theory of Self-Organizing Systems

Self-organizing systems carry the ideas of chaotic non-linear systems one step further by examining what happens when such systems reach conditions that are very far from their state of equilibrium. At that point systems reorganize themselves in unpredictable ways that are sometimes so dramatic (even if they are just computer models) that the term *artificial life* has been used to describe them (Waldrop, 1992).

The Santa Fe Institute was created to explore phenomena related to self-organizing systems and has become a kind of mecca for complexity theorists. Interested readers may wish to explore this field in several books including books by Goldstein (1994, on organizational change), Kauffman (1993, on evolution), Kelly (1994), Maturana and Varela (1980, on adaptive cognition), Nicholis and Prigogene (1989), Waldrop (1992), and Wolfram (2002).

Key concepts are as follows. We tend to think of collective behavior as simply the accumulation of individual behavior, but it is more than that. Collective behavior tends to be nonlinear and tends toward self-organization. One molecule or one person (ignoring for the moment that persons are systems) may respond in a particular way to being pushed past current limits, whereas a collection of those molecules or persons will respond very differently and somewhat unpredictably. Self-organizing systems studies work with the unique properties of such collectives. Self-organization has the following features when it occurs, according to Goldstein (1994): System structure is radically reorganized; novel patterns emerge; random events are amplified and utilized; and a new coordination of parts is attained. These changes are not imposed on the system but emerge from it. Collective systems do not simply resist change or face destruction but have the potential to ride the change to create a different organization within. The changes are self-orchestrated as this system reconfigures its own resources in the face of a far-from-equilibrium challenge. The individual forced to face previously disowned sides of the self will spontaneously reorganize the pattern of self in unexpected ways.

Goldstein (1994) describes some characteristics of self-organization: A spontaneous and radical reorganizing occurs; equilibrium-seeking tendencies are interrupted; the system utilizes the disorganization as a chance for change within some limits; and unpredictable outcomes occur that leave the system more optimally organized.

Complexity theory goes beyond qualitative descriptions of the kind of systems it deals with, namely, complex *adaptive* systems, by making complexity a quantity that is measurable. Complex systems also have similar qualities in whatever context they occur.

The implications of this theory are simply too vast to be outlined yet. Imagine a unified theory of adaptive system change being applied to everything, and this will give the scope of possibilities. Few topics are off-limits. Possibilities include prediction of developmental trends in feeling connected in adulthood and aging as multiple adaptive systems interact over time.

But the most important implication is that the possibilities for *self-created* adaptive order seem so vast that they are almost beyond the scope of our imaginations. Yet we hold them in our hands. As Kauffman suggests (Waldrop, 1992), we help make the world we live in and have a part in its story. We are neither victims nor outsiders but team members helping design it all. With that mindset, we design our felt connections and create, in part, their impact on us. Our impact on the evolving systems in which we have a part is a permanently transformative one for ourselves and the other systems (Waldrop, 1992). This sounds like postformal thought, the cognitive part of our human creation of our adaptive story about feeling connected.

These new models, then, provide us with better ways to address questions of connection and community in the complex ways needed to test the relations in figure 17.1. Additional variables may emerge when we address developmental aspects of this situation.

SOME DEVELOPMENTAL CONSIDERATIONS

Emotional Skills

Certain emotional skills must reach a complex level if we are to get maximum enjoyment from and learn the most from the felt sense of community. If we still operate emotionally at a symbiotic, undifferentiated level with those around us, our community feeling will probably be like pendulum swings between the ache of loneliness and the terror of being engulfed. As Labouvie-Vief (1984, 1987, 1992) discusses so well, emotional self-regulation is desirable for mature relations with the others in our lives and mature adjustment within the self. We cannot feel "together" "in community" within the self when experience of the self is one of emotional swings among owned and disowned parts. One cannot feel very close to another if unresolved emotions lead to projecting shadow sides onto another person. One cannot feel strongly in community with all of life or spiritual matters when emotional issues demand a focus on self, not on all of life or spiritual matters.

Of course those with lower levels of emotional development also may feel in community, but that quality of feeling connected would not seem to be as strong. What kinds of feelings about connections might these be? A person with lower levels of emotional development may be acting out of more childlike emotional needs, unable to claim a separate self and still feel safe, acting from deficiency motivation (Maslow, 1968). What would be different about such a person, compared with the emotionally mature one? The essential difference would seem to be that the felt sense is not of enjoyment of connection but of fear and needy grasping related to connection. Learning, in the emotionally immature person, is welcomed only if it fills the need.

This sort of person might have strong feelings about being related to others, but those feelings would rest on needing the other to fill a deficiency in the self. That needy person might feel very strongly about defending the weak and fragmented self against attack. But he or she would disown parts of the self and not defend (or acknowledge) them at all. The person with deficiency motivation might feel very connected to God (because God might fill those needs) or to the Earth (as a consumer of the Earth), but the feeling of connection goes only so far as need fulfillment goes and usually includes grasping (Maslow, 1968). The theory of felt connection described previously suggests that when a person lacks emotional development to some degree, that person feels community only when (and to the degree that) emotional needs are being fulfilled by that community. This is different from the open-hearted, full feelings of togetherness and belonging that the more emotionally mature person can experience.

If they are conscious, these emotional skills must rest on cognitive complexity because holding two disparate logical systems in mind at the same time is needed for these emotional skills. It is the cognitive complexity that lets a person consider the known sides of the self and the shadow sides of the self as one self. The cognitive complexity would let a person step back from the action to consider other ways out of my state of neediness, beyond grasping and needing. The complexity of thought would let one acknowledge a need of the others and at the same time appreciate that they are more than those who just exist to fulfill needs. And how about the relations between self and the transcendent? Cognitive complexity again makes it possible to consciously see God or the Earth as both fulfilling needs, and also "good to relate to, apart from any need."

Interpersonal Skills

There also seem to be complex interpersonal or social skills needed for the fullest feeling of being in community. These would seem to rest on the emotional and cognitive skills already mentioned, and a successful earlier psychosocial history (in Erikson's terms). The sense of basic trust certainly would need to be present to allow the connections to take place, connections that might occasion our feeling in community. The other types of skills, for example, how to communicate well with others, what to expect in a relationship of any sort, and the like, are useful, but could coexist with very little feeling of being in community. What would seem to matter more for a felt sense of connection is emotional and cognitive maturity, discussed earlier.

SOME RESEARCH POSSIBILITIES

We yearn for love and feelings of community, and science can help us get there. Whether we are wearing teacher, clinician, learner, or researcher hats, we know that we have many unanswered questions about the nature of felt connection and its relations with the rest of human experience. Understanding will help limit the unnecessary suffering that plagues those who feel disconnected.

Research on the sense of felt connection has started with the interviews of adults, using the questionnaire in appendix A. This descriptive research is a necessary first step in understanding the basic elements and dynamics in the search for love through ties within the parts of the self, ties between humans, and ties with the transcendent.

Further descriptive research is necessary and would be useful if we wish to refine ideas and theories. It would also be useful if we are to intervene in the lives of individuals who are suffering from lack of connection. But we might want to go beyond those two goals. We might want to offer our global community an understanding of the unique experiences humans now have in relation to community. These experiences are happening in response to the demands and opportunities of our moment in history. Research also can help us move in more skilled ways toward repairing connections if they are challenged by events unique to this time in human history. We can apply our understanding of adult felt connection to understand the learning processes of adults.

Descriptive and inferential research can address a large number of hypotheses related to felt connection. Hypotheses fall into three categories: those related to effects of felt connection on development, those related to effects of development on felt connection, and those that relate to clinical or educational interventions to improve the state of felt connection. The third set of hypotheses might relate to the effects of the exercises and activities related to the development of felt connection. The third set also outlines expectations about other interventions and actions for social change or well-being. In all cases the direction of causality must be tested. These hypotheses are discussed here.

Future Research: Effects of Felt Connection on Development

What are some areas of development that we might expect to be influenced by felt experiences of community? Hypotheses would differ based on what type of felt community we are speaking of, namely, the inner community of sides of the self, the community of persons with whom we are connected, or the transcendent community that extends beyond the self. This list of developmental areas will not be complete but will offer a starting point for interview-based, experimental, and other types of research. We will lean heavily toward the theory of Erikson in these hypotheses. The hypotheses below are logical consequences of the theory outlined at the beginning of this chapter. They are offered as a basis for future research.

What follows is a summary of some hypothesized relations between felt connection and personal development (direction of causality is not yet determined).

Concerning Felt Connection Within the Self

- A conscious felt sense of community within the self (i.e., integration of the sides of the self) is accompanied by emotional maturity and cognitive complexity.
- Those who lack connections among the sides of the self (felt connection within the self) can be expected to experience dissonance within identity and would be seen to have problems with intimate relationships. The converse would also be true.
- Those who are isolated from others and especially from intimate relationships would be less likely to integrate sides of the self.
- Those who do not integrate the sides of the self would be more likely to hold rigid positions about relations to transcendent communities involving God, all beings, the universe, and so on. Allowing more flexible relations with the transcendent would facilitate integration of the sides of the self.
- A person who integrates the sides of the self will find it easier to create community and be part of communities. It will be easier to be generative, in Erikson's terms.
- A person who does not integrate the sides of the self will find it harder to reach integrity, in Erikson's terms.
- A person who integrates the sides of the self will be less likely to have a midlife crisis and will be less likely to feel significant dissatisfaction during the challenges of aging.
- Those integrating more sides of the self are more likely to use postformal thought.

Concerning Felt Connection With Others

See also earlier statements.

- A conscious, deeply felt sense of felt connection with others will be accompanied by cognitive complexity and emotional maturity.
- Those who are isolated will be less willing to be generative.
- Those who are isolated will experience more problems raising children and will have children who are more anxious and problematic.

- Those who are isolated will have more trouble connecting their work to the practical concerns of others.
- Those who are isolated will make larger demands on the social fabric and will be less willing to contribute to it, increasingly, as old age approaches.
- Those enjoying meaningful interactions with intimates and friends will be more likely to develop complex and wise postformal thinking abilities.
- Those enjoying felt connection with others will more easily create transcendent communal ties.

Concerning Felt Connection
With the Transcendent

See also earlier hypotheses.

- A conscious deeply felt sense of connection with the transcendent is accompanied by emotional complexity and cognitive complexity.
- Those who can form transcendent relationships can more easily integrate the parts of the self and create loving felt connection with others.
- Developing transcendent felt connection will make it easier to be generative and to achieve integrity.
- Those who can develop a transcendent felt connection will find it easier to face the challenges of aging.

Future Research: Effects of
Development on Felt Connection

An individual's stage of development might have a large influence on how he or she attains feelings of being in felt connection. It is easy to imagine that the more mature a person becomes the more easily he or she can create felt connection, all other things being equal. This would be true because barriers arising from neediness and problematic relations with original caretakers are less frequent impediments to communal action or feelings. The hypotheses that follow reflect this general supposition.

Concerning Felt Connection
Within the Self

- The more mature a person becomes, the more he or she routinely accepts both positive and negative aspects of self.

- Cognitive development determines how one conceptualizes the felt connection within the self.
- The more mature person uses complex Postformal cognitive operations to know the self with all its parts.

Concerning Felt Connection
With Others

- The more mature person generally feels more connected to others.
- The more mature person creates felt connection in situations where it does not exist.
- When enjoying felt connection with others, the more mature person has a more realistic assessment of those in the community, whereas the less mature sees others in light of personal needs.
- The more mature person uses complex postformal operations to know other persons.

Concerning Felt Connection
With the Transcendent

- The more mature person is more likely to define a transcendent as something more than a reflection of personal needs, or as a helper (although these roles will not be totally absent).
- The more mature person is more likely to see the big picture of life (Erikson's integrity) and more likely to identify with others (generativity).
- The more mature person makes more use of spirituality in daily life.
- The more mature person uses complex postformal operations to think about relations with the transcendent.

Future Research: Effects of Interventions
and Learning on Felt Connection

The most important research will be focused on how adult felt connection relates to learning and teaching. Interventions can allow individuals to broaden their sense of felt connection, with results for their learning. Interventions also can change the way felt connection is experienced by individuals. Many activities might be useful to reach these goals. An individual might take part in some sort of planned multicultural experiences or planned psychological growth. He or she might take advantage of imaginal experiences that are designed to give a person a stronger sense of feeling connected with others. A person might intentionally have experiences such as exposure to global communications technology or workplace friendships with persons who represent different communities. Some interventions might include events that are not chosen by the participant but are experienced due to events. These interventions happen because the individual is thrust into a felt-connection-related situation, such as an educational situation, and must deal with it.

All of these potential research projects, if carried out, would provide information that might lead to applications in educational settings.

SUMMARY

This chapter offered theory and applications. First came the introduction of the elements of the relationship between felt connection and the development of adults. A theory of that relationship was described, as well as new models that underlie thinking about this field of relationships. Some research and intervention hypotheses and strategies based on the theory were presented. A review of some literature from widely divergent areas of studies that connect with this field was outlined in the last portion of the chapter. Feeling connected within the self, with other people, and with someone or something larger than the self both influences adult development and is influenced by adult development and learning.

APPENDIX A
COMMUNITY QUESTIONNAIRE

1. What does "community" mean to you?
2. Some people feel that they are connected with something larger than themselves, such as the Earth, all humanity, God, the spiritual dimension of life. Do you feel connected with something larger than your individual self? Explain.
3. Do you feel that there is a "global community?" If you do, please describe it.
4. Some people feel that they have several parts to their personality, some that they know better, others that they do not really know at all well. These parts-of-self don't always work well together. Do you feel that you have several sides to yourself? Do you ever feel them to be in conflict? Can you explain?

5. Describe some times in your life when you've felt that you were a part of a community.
6. What did that feel like?
7. Describe a time when you felt disconnected, when you did not feel part of a community.
8. What did that feel like?
9. What makes it easy to feel connected, in a community, in today's world?
10. What makes it difficult?
11. Do you think feeling part of a community ever helped you grow or hurt your growth, as a person? What was that like?
12. Do you think that your development as a person over the years changed the way you felt connected, in community? Can you give an example?
13. What are the main benefits, if any, from feeling connected, in community?
14. What are the most important connections you feel with others?
15. Who are the main people you could count on if you needed help?
16. Are objective and felt communities the same? In other words, are the communities you "officially belong to" the same as the communities you "feel connected to?"
17. Can we create community feelings? How?
18. How does feeling part of a community benefit you or cause problems for you?
19. If you had your way, which communities would you want to feel a part of? Are you really connected to those right now?
20. Which communities would you not want to feel connected to? Are you connected to them now?

APPENDIX B
SUMMARY OF SELECTED TYPES
OF LITERATURE SPECIFICALLY
RELATED TO FELT COMMUNITY
AND FELT CONNECTION,
AS THOSE TERMS ARE DEFINED
IN THIS CHAPTER

Searching the literature for related references for this chapter offered inherent challenges. Anyone with any online searching experience will recognize the difficulty of searching words like *feeling, connected,* or *community* in large article databases. The list given here is varied by discipline and constitutes only a small sampling of what is available. It is hoped that this will give the reader an overview as well as a good starting point for delving into this subject. The references are grouped into three broad categories. The first category includes resources that discuss the individual and connections within the sides of self, including the concept of the shadow self as well as related Jungian theories of adult development. The second and largest group includes sources that address the individual and his or her "connectedness" to the larger community, family, and various social groups. The third section is closely related to the previous section but focuses more directly on connections that transcend the human experience, such as the individual's relationship to God and religion.

The references are presented in this format, rather than being integrated into the chapter, for two important reasons. First, in this way it is possible to offer the reader a larger sample of the variety of topics in this integrative area of study. Second, this format honors the restrictions of the limited space of this chapter while stimulating broader explorations of topics related to the chapter ideas.

COMMUNITY AMONG SIDES OF SELF

Abrams, J., & Zweig, C. (1991). *Meeting the shadow: The hidden power of the dark side of human nature.* Los Angeles: J. P. Tarcher.

Bingaman, K. A. (2001). Christianity and the shadow side of human experience. *Pastoral Psychology,* 49(3), 167–179.

Casement, A. (2003). Encountering the shadow in rites of passage: A study in activations. *Journal of Analytical Psychology,* 48(1), 29–46.

Donlevy, J. G. (1996). Jung's contribution to adult development: The difficult and misunderstood path of individuation. *Journal of Humanistic Psychology,* 36(2), 92–108.

Neri, A. L. (2002). Subjective well-being in adulthood and old age: toward a positive psychology in Latin America. *Revista Latinoamericana de Psicologia,* 34(1–2), 55–74.

Pushkar, D., Reis, M., & Morros, M. (2002). Motivation, personality and well-being in older volunteers. *International Journal of Aging and Human Development,* 55(2), 141–162.

Ruth, M. (1999). *Shadow work: A new guide to spiritual and psycholgical growth.* Knoxville, TN: Growth Solutions.

Samuels, A. (1991). *Psychopathology: Contemporary Jungian perspectives.* New York: Guilford.

Schlenker, B. R., & Trudeau, J. V. (1990). Impact of self-presentations on private self-beliefs: Effects of prior self-beliefs and misattribution. *Journal of Personality and Social Psychology,* 58(1), 22–32.

Slater, C. L. (2003). Generativity versus stagnation: An elaboration of Erikson's adult stage of human development. *Journal of Adult Development,* 10(1), 53–65.

Sliker, G. (1992). *Multiple mind: Healing the split in psyche and world.* Boston: Shambhala.

Stark, S. C. (2001). A psychological examination of the Amish persona. *Dissertation Abstracts International,* 62(1), 566B.

COMMUNITY AMONG PERSONS

Anonymous. (1995). What's told to the old: Social support and social interaction among the aged. *Psychology Today,* 28(3), 27.

Ackerman, S. Z., & Moskowitz, D. C. (2000). Generativity in midlife and young adults: Links to agency, communion, and subjective well-being. *International Journal of Aging & Human Development,* 50(1), 17–41.

Akiyama, H., Antonucci, T., Takahashi, K., & Langfahl, E. (2003). Negative interactions in close relationships: Special section. *Journals of Gerontology, Series B: Psychological Sciences and Social Sciences,* 58B(2), 70–79.

Barokas, J. (1993). Development and test of a causal model of midlife women's attainments, commitments and satisfactions. *Dissertation Abstracts International,* 53(7), 2558A.

Berkman, L. F., Glass, T., Brissette, I., & Seeman, T. E. (2000). From social integration to health: Durkheim in the new millennium. *Social Science and Medicine,* 51(6), 843–857.

Blieszner, R., & DeVries, B. (2001). Perspectives on intimacy. *Generations,* 25(2), 7–8.

Borders, L. D., Penny, J. M., & Portnoy, F. (2000). Adult adoptees and their friends: Current functioning and psychosocial well-being. *Family Relations,* 49(4), 407–418.

Borge, L. Martinsen, E. W., Ruud, T., Watne, O., & Friis, S. (1999). Quality of life, loneliness, and social contact among long-term psychiatric patients. *Psychiatric Services,* 50(1), 81–84.

Brand, M. (1998). A qualitative study of women's life satisfaction in middle adulthood. *Dissertation Abstracts International,* 58(7), 2880A.

Bukov, A., Maas, I., & Lampert, T. (2002). Social participation in very old age: cross-sectional and longitudinal findings from BASE. Berlin aging study. *Journals of Gerontology. Series B, Psychological Sciences and Social Sciences,* 57(6), 510.

Cacioppo, J. T., Hawkley, L .C., & Bernston, G. G. (2003). The anatomy of loneliness. *Current Directions in Psychological Science,* 12(3), 71–74.

Caspi, A., & Elder, G. H. (1986). Life satisfaction in old age: Linking social psychology and history. *Psychology and Aging,* 1(1), 18–26.

Cheang, M. (2002). Older adults' frequent visits to a fast-food restaurant: Nonobligatory social interaction and the significance of play in a "third place." *Journal of Aging Studies*, 16(3), 303–321.

Clausen, J. A. (1995). Gender, contexts, and turning points in adults' lives. In P. E. Moen & G. H. Elder Jr. (Eds.), *Examining lives in context: Perspectives on the ecology of human development* (pp. 365–389). Washington, DC: American Psychological Association.

Crosnoe, R., & Elder, G. H. Jr. (2002). Successful adaptation in the later years: A life course approach to aging. *Social Psychology Quarterly*, 65(4), 309–328.

Dear, K., Henderson, S., & Korten, A. (2002). Well-being in Australia—Findings from the National Survey of Mental Health and Well-being. *Social Psychiatry and Psychiatric Epidemiology*, 37(11), 503–509.

Drevdahl, D. (1999). Meanings of community in a community health center. *Public Health Nursing*, 16(6), 417–425.

Frank, S. J., Avery, C. B., & Laman, M. S. (1988). Young adults' perceptions of their relationships with their parents: Individual differences in connectedness, competence, and emotional autonomy. *Developmental Psychology*, 24 (5), 729–737.

Gise, L. H. (1997). Psychosocial aspects. In D. E. Stewart & G. E. Robinson (Eds.), *A clinician's guide to menopause* (pp. 29–43). Washington, DC: Health Press International.

Harlow, R. E., & Cantor, N. (1996). Still participating after all these years: a study of life task participation in later life. *Journal of Personality and Social Psychology*, 71(6), 1235–1249.

Hawkley, L. C., Burleson, M. H., Berntson, G. G., & Cacioppo, J. T. (2003). Loneliness in everyday life: Cardiovascular activity, psychosocial context, and health behaviors. *Journal of Personality and Social Psychology*, 85(1), 105–120.

Hecht, L., McMillin, J. D., & Silverman, P. (2001). Pets, networks and well-being. *Anthrozoos*, 14(2), 95–108.

Helgeson, V. S. (2003). Social support and quality of life. *Quality of Life Research: An International Journal of Quality of Life Aspects of Treatment, Care and Rehabilitation*, 12 (Suppl. 1), 25–31.

Herzog, A. R., Ofstedal, M. B., & Wheeler, L. M. (2002). Social engagement and its relationship to health. *Clinics in Geriatric Medicine*, 18(3), 593–609.

Hyde, M., Wiggins, R. D., Higgs, P., & Blane, D. B. (2003). A measure of quality of life in early old age: The theory, development and properties of a needs satisfaction model (CASP-19). *Aging and Mental Health*, 7(3), 186–194.

Johnson, S. M., & Marano, H. E. (1993). Love: The immutable longing for contact. *Psychology Today*, 27(2), 32–37.

Kahn, J. H., Hessling, R. M., & Russell, D. W. (2003). Social support, health, and well-being among the elderly: What is the role of negative affectivity? *Personality and Individual Differences*, 35(1), 5–17.

Kelly, L. S. (1989). Life satisfaction and happiness in older volunteers in the North Carolina Agricultural Extension Service. *Dissertation Abstracts International*, 50(5), 2880A.

Kendall, J. (1996). Human association as a factor influencing wellness in homosexual men with human immunodeficiency virus disease. *Applied Nursing Research: ANR*, 9(4), 195–203.

Laliberte-Rudman, D., Yu, B., & Scott, E. (2000). Exploration of the perspectives of persons with schizophrenia regarding quality of life. *American Journal of Occupational Therapy*, 54(2), 137–147.

Lowry, J. H. (1984). Life satisfaction time components among the elderly: Toward understanding the contribution of predictor variables. *Research on Aging*, 6(3), 417–431.

Mandell, H. B. (1995). Homeward from exile: The experience of homecoming for adult survivors of childhood trauma. *Dissertation Abstracts International*, 56(2), 1114B.

Mitchell, J. M., & Kemp, B. J. (2000). Quality of life in assisted living homes: A multidimensional analysis. *Journals of Gerontology Series B: Psychological Sciences and Social Sciences*, 55(2), 117–127.

Mitchell, V., & Helson, R. (1990). Women's prime of life: Is it the 50s? *Psychology of Women Quarterly*, 14(4), 451–470.

Morris, H. J. (2001). Happiness explained. *U.S. News and World Report*, 131(8), 46–55.

Nelson, N. D. (1989). Hardiness, ego development, and successful aging in the elderly. *Dissertation Abstracts International*, 50(4), 1679B.

Nezlek, J. B., Richardson, D. S., Green, L. R., & Schatten-Jones, E. C. (2002). Psychological well-being and day-to-day social interaction among older adults. *Personal Relationships*, 9(1), 57–71.

Norman, S. M. (1993). Adult development: Life patterns of older women. *Dissertation Abstracts International*, 54(4), 2217B.

Pankey, S. S. (1998). Revision at midlife: A case study and model for the treatment of developmental crisis in women in their forties. *Dissertation Abstracts International*, 59(5), 2428B.

Pinquart, M., & Sorensen, S. (2000). Influences of socioeconomic status, social network, and competence on subjective well-being in later life: A meta-analysis. *Psychology and Aging*, 15(2), 187–224.

Pinquart, M., & Sorensen, S. (2001). Influences on loneliness in older adults: A meta-analysis. *Basic and Applied Social Psychology*, 23(4), 245–266.

Pretty, G. H., Chipuer, H. M., & Bramston, P. (2003). Sense of place amongst adolescents and adults in two rural Australian towns: The discriminating features of place attachment, sense of community and place dependence in relation to place identity. *Journal of Environmental Psychology*, 23(3), 273–287.

Rastogi, M., & Wampler, K. S. (1999). Adult daughters' perceptions of the mother-daughter relationship: A cross-cultural comparison. *Family Relations*, 58(3), 327–336.

Rickelman, B. L., Gallman, L., & Parra, H. (1994). Attachment and quality of life in older, community-residing men. *Nursing Research*, 43(2), 68–72.

Schiff, S. M. (1997). Healthy relationships between white middle class adult daughters and mothers in later years of life. *Dissertation Abstracts International*, 57(10), 6618B.

Schilling, O., & Wahl, H. W. (2002). Family networks and life-satisfaction of older adults in rural and urban regions. *Kolner Zeitschrift fur Soziologie und Sozialpsychologie*, 54(2), 304–317.

Seeman, T. E. (2000). Health promoting effects of friends and family on health outcomes in older adults. *American Journal of Health Promotion*, 14(6), 362–370.

Steitz, J. A. (1988). Subjective age, age identity, and middle-age adults. *Experimental Aging Research*, 14(2–3), 83–88.

Stevens, N. (1997). Friendship as a key to well-being: a course for women over 55 years old. *Tijdschrift voor Gerontologie en Geriatrie*, 28(1), 18–26.

Takkinen, S., & Ruoppila, I. (2001). Meaning in life as an important component of functioning in old age. *International Journal of Aging and Human Development*, 53(3), 211–231.

Troll, L. E. (1994). Family connectedness of old women: Attachments in later life. In B. F. Turner & L. E. Troll (Eds.), *Women growing older: Psychological perspectives* (pp. 169–201). New Brunswick, NJ: Rutgers University Press.

Wensauer, M., & Grossmann, K. E. (1995). Quality of attachment representation, social integration and use of network resources in old age. *Zeitschrift fur Gerontologie und Geriatrie*, 28(6), 444–456.

Wilson, J. (2000). Volunteering. *Annual Review of Sociology*, 26, 215–240.

Zunzunegui, M.-V., Alvarado, B. E., DelSer, T., & Otero, A. (2003). Social networks, social integration, and social engagement determine cognitive decline in community-dwelling Spanish older adults. *Journals of Gerontology, Series B: Psychological Sciences and Social Sciences*, 58B(2), S93–S100.

COMMUNITY BETWEEN PERSON AND THE TRANSCENDENT

Armstrong, T. D., & Crowther, M. R. (2002). Spirituality among older African Americans. *Journal of Adult Development*, 9(1), 3–12.

Belavich, T. G., & Pargament, K. I. (2002). The role of attachment in predicting spiritual coping with a loved one in surgery. *Journal of Adult Development*, 9(1), 13–29.

Brennan, M. (2002). Spirituality and psychosocial development in middle-age and older adults with vi-sion loss. *Journal of Adult Development*, 9(1), 31–46.

Cartwright, K. B. (2001). Cognitive developmental theory and spiritual development. *Journal of Adult Development*, 8(4), 213–220.

Ellison, C. G., & Levin, J. S. (1998). The religion-health connection: Evidence theory, and future directions. *Health Education and Behavior*, 25(6), 700–720.

Ellison, C. G., Boardman, J. D., Williams, D. R., & Jackson, J. S. (2001). Religious involvement, stress, and mental health: Findings from the 1995 Detroit Area Study. *Social Forces*, 80(1), 215–249.

Hill, P C., & Pargament, K. I. (2003). Advances in the conceptualization and measurement of religion and spirituality: Implications for physical and mental health research. *American Psychologist*, 58(1), 64–74.

Hintikka, J., Koskela, T., Kontula, O., Koskela, K., Koivumaa-Honkanen, H. T., & Viinamaki, H. (2001). Religious attendance and life satisfaction in the Finnish general population. *Journal of Psychology and Theology*, 29(2), 158–164.

Lewis, M. M. (2001). Spirituality, counseling, and elderly: An introduction to the spiritual life review. *Journal of Adult Development*, 8(4), 231–240.

MacKinlay, E. (2001). Ageing and isolation: Is the issue social isolation or is it lack of meaning in life? *Journal of Religious Gerontology* 12(3–4), 89–99.

Mattis, J. S., Murray, Y. F., Hatcher, C. A., Hearn, K. D., Lawhon, G. D., Murphy, E. J., et al. (2001). Religiosity, spirituality, and the subjective quality of African American men's friendships: An exploratory study. *Journal of Adult Development*, 8(4), 221–230.

Miller, W. R., & Thoresen, C. E. (2003). Spirituality, religion, and health: An emerging research field. *American Psychologist*, 58(1), 24–35.

Moberg, D. O. (2002). Assessing and measuring spirituality: Confronting dilemmas of universal and particular evaluative criteria. *Journal of Adult Development*, 9(1), 47–60.

Musick, M. A., Traphagan, J. W., Koenig, H. G., & Larson, D. B. (2000). Spirituality in physical health and aging. *Journal of Adult Development*, 7(2), 73–86.

Powell, L. H., Shahabi, L. T., & Thoresen, C. E. (2003). Religion and spirituality: Linkages to physical health. *American Psychologist*, 58(1), 36–52.

Redington, R. M. (2001). The transforming power of exchange: A psychological and theological study of breakthrough in narcissistically injured individuals seeking communion with the divine. *Dissertation Abstracts International*, 62(5), 2498B.

Saleh, U. S., & Brockopp, D. Y. (2001). Hope among patients with cancer hospitalized for bone marrow transplantation: A phenomenologic study. *Cancer Nursing*, 24(4), 308–314.

Seifert, L. S. (2002). Toward a psychology of religion, spirituality, meaning-search, and aging: Past research and a practical application. *Journal of Adult Development*, 9(1), 61–70.

Sink, J. R. (2000). Religiousness, spirituality, and satisfaction with life: A structural model of subjective well-being and optimal adult development. *Dissertation Abstracts International*, 61(2), 1097B.

Sinnott, J. D. (2001). "A time for the condor and the eagle to fly together": Relations between spirit and adult development in healing techniques in several cultures. *Journal of Adult Development*, 8(4), 241–247.

Wheeler, E. A., Ampadu, L.M., & Wangari, E. (2002). Lifespan development revisited: African-centered spirituality throughout the life cycle. *Journal of Adult Development*, 9(1), 71–78.

Wink, P., & Dillon, M. (2002). Spiritual development across the adult life course: Findings from a longitudinal study. *Journal of Adult Development*, 9(1), 79–94.

Zweig, C. (2001). The holy longing: A psychological study of the religious impulse. *Dissertation Abstracts International*, 62(1), 530B.

References

Abraham, R. (1985). Is there chaos without noise? In P. Fisher & W. Smith (Eds.), *Chaos, fractals, and dynamics* (pp. 117–121). New York: Marcel Dekker.

Alper, J. (1989). The chaotic brain: New models of behavior. *Psychology Today*, 23, 21.

Barton, S. (1994). Chaos, self organization, and psychology. *American Psychologist*, 49, 5–14.

Bronowski, J. (1974). *The ascent of man*. Boston: Little, Brown.

Cartwright, K. B., Galupo, M. P., & Tyree, S. D. (2004). *Reliability and validity of the Complex Postformal Thought Questionnaire*. Manuscript in preparation.

Cavanaugh, J. C. (1989). *The utility of concepts in chaos theory for psychological theory and research*. Paper presented at the Fourth Adult Development Conference at Harvard University, Cambridge, MA.

Cavanaugh, J. C., & McGuire, L. (1994). The chaos of lifespan learning. In J. Sinnott (Ed.), *Interdisciplinary handbook of adult lifespan learning* (pp. 3–21). Westport, CT: Greenwood.

Crutchfield, J. P., Farmer, J. D., Packard, N. H., & Shaw, R. S. (1986). Chaos. *Scientific American*, 255, 46–57.

Devaney, R. (1989). *An introduction to chaotic dynamical systems*. Redwood City, CA: Addison-Wesley.

Erikson, E. (1950). *Childhood and society*. New York: Norton.

Erikson, E. (1992). *The lifecycle completed*. New York: Norton.

Ford, D. (1987). *Humans as self-constructing living systems*. Hillsdale, NJ: Lawrence Erlbaum.

Frankl, V. (1963). *Man's search for meaning*. New York: Washington Square Press.

Galupo, M. P., Cartwright, K. B., & Savage, L. S. (2004). *Cross-social category friendships as a context for postformal cognitive development*. Manuscript in preparation.

Gavin, J. L., Galupo, M. P. & Cartwright, K. B. (2004). *The role of postformal cognitive development in death acceptance*. Manuscript in preparation.

Gleick, J. (1987). *Chaos: Making a new science*. New York: Penguin Books.

Goerner, S. (1994). *Chaos and the evolving psychological universe*. Langhorne, PA: Gordon & Breach Scientific Publishers.

Goldstein, J. (1994). *The unshackled organization*. Portland, OR: Productivity Press.

Gottman, J. (1991). Chaos and regulated change in families: A metaphor for the study of transitions. In P. A. Cohen & M. Hetherington (Eds.), *Family transitions* (pp. 247–272). Hillsdale, NJ: Lawrence Erlbaum.

Hofstadter, D. R. (1979). *Godel, Escher and Bach: An eternal golden braid*. New York: Basic Books.

Johnson, L. (1991). Bridging paradigms: The role of the change agent in an international technical transfer project. In J. D. Sinnott & J. C. Cavanaugh (Eds.), *Bridging paradigms: Positive development in adulthood and cognitive aging* (pp. 59–72). New York: Praeger.

Johnson, L. (1994). Nonformal adult learning in international development projects. In J. D. Sinnott (Ed.), *Interdisciplinary handbook of adult lifespan learning* (pp. 203–217). Westport, CT: Greenwood.

Johnson, L. (2001). *Postformal thinking in the workplace*. Invited lecture, University of Stockholm, Sweden.

Johnson, L. (2004). Postformal thinking in the workplace. In T. Hagstrom (Ed.), *Stockholm lectures in educology: Adult development in post-industrial society and working life* (pp. 153–184). Stockholm: University of Stockholm Press.

Jung, C. (1930/1971). The stages of life. In J. Campbell (Ed.), *The portable Jung*. New York: Viking Library.

Kauffman, S. (1993). *The origins of order*. New York: Oxford University Press.

Kelly, K. (1994). *Out of control: The new biology of machines, social systems and the economic world*. Reading, MA: Addison-Wesley.

Labouvie-Vief, G. (1984). Logic and self regulation from youth to maturity: A model. In M. Commons, F. Richards, & C. Armon (Eds.), *Beyond formal operations: Late adolescent and adult cognitive development* (pp. 158–179). New York: Praeger.

Labouvie-Vief, G. (1987). *Speaking about feelings: Symbolization and self regulation throughout the life span*. Paper presented at the Third Beyond Formal Operations Conference at Harvard University, Cambridge, MA.

Labouvie-Vief, G. (1992). A neo-Piagetian perspective on adult cognitive development. In R. J. Sternberg & C. Berg (Eds.), *Intellectual development* (pp. 197–228). New York: Cambridge University Press.

Labouvie-Vief, G. (1994). *Psyche and eros: Mind and gender in the lifespan*. Cambridge: Cambridge University Press.

Lee, D. M. (1991). Relativistic operations: A framework for conceptualizing teachers' everyday problem solving. In J. D. Sinnott & J. C. Cavanaugh (Eds.), *Bridging paradigms: Positive development in adulthood and cognitive aging* (pp. 73–86). New York: Praeger.

Lee, D. M. (1994).Becoming an expert: considering the place of wisdom in teaching adults. In J. D. Sinnott (Ed.), *Interdisciplinary handbook of adult lifespan learning* (pp. 234–248). Westport, CT: Greenwood.

Levine, R. L., & Fitzgerald, H. E. (Eds.). (1992). *Analysis of dynamic psychological systems, vols. 1 and 2.* New York: Plenum.

LockLand, G. T. (1973). *Grow or die.* New York: Random House.

Lorenz, E. (1963). Deterministic nonperiodic flow. *Journal of Atmospheric Sciences, 20,* 130–141.

Lorenz, E. (1979). *Predictability: Does the flap of a butterfly's wings in Brazil set off a tornado in Texas?* Paper presented at the annual meeting of the Americal Association for the Advancement of Science, Washington, DC.

Mahoney, M. J. (1991). *Human change processes.* New York: Basic Books.

Maslow, A. (1968). *Toward a psychology of being* (2nd ed.). New York: Van Nostrand Reinhold.

Maturana, H., & Varela, F. (1980). *Autopoiesis and cognition: The realization of the living.* Boston: Reidel.

Miller, J. (1978). *Living systems.* New York: McGraw-Hill.

Nicholis, G., & Prigogene, I. (1989). *Exploring complexity.* New York: Freeman.

Perry, W. G. (1975). *Forms of ethical and intellectual development in the college years.* New York: Holt, Rinehart & Winston.

Pool, R. (1989). Is it healthy to be chaotic? *Science, 243,* 604–607.

Prigogene, I., & Stengers, I. (1984). *Order out of chaos: Man's new dialogue with nature.* New York: Bantam.

Rogers, D. R. B. (1989). *The effect of dyad interaction and marital adjustment on cognitive performance in everyday logical problem solving.* Unpublished doctoral dissertation, Utah State University, Logan.

Rogers, D. R., Sinnott, J. D., & van Dusen, L. (1991). *Marital adjustment and social cognitive performance in everyday logical problem solving.* Paper presented at Sixth Adult Development Conference, Boston.

Sinnott, J. D. (1981). The theory of relativity: A metatheory for development? *Human Development, 24,* 293–311.

Sinnott, J. D. (1984). Postformal reasoning: The relativistic stage. In M. Commons, F. Richards, & C. Armon (Eds.), *Beyond formal operations* (pp. 298–325). New York: Praeger.

Sinnott, J. D. (1989a). *Everyday problem solving.* New York: Praeger.

Sinnott, J. D. (1989b). Lifespan relativistic postformal thought. In M. Commons, J. Sinnott, F. Richards,

& C. Armon (Eds.), *Beyond formal operations I* (pp. 239–278). New York: Praeger.

Sinnott, J. D. (1990). *Yes, it's worth the trouble! Unique contributions from everyday cognition studies.* Paper presented at the Twelfth West Virginia University Conference on Lifespan Developmental Psychology: Mechanisms of Everyday Cognition, Morgantown, WV.

Sinnott, J. D. (1991a). What do we do to help John? A case study of everyday problem solving in a family making decisions about an acutely psychotic member. In J. D. Sinnott & J. Cavanaugh (Eds.), *Bridging paradigms: Positive development in adulthood and cognitive aging* (pp. 203–220). New York: Praeger.

Sinnott, J. D. (1991b). Limits to problem solving: Emotion, intention, goal clarity, health, and other factors in postformal thought. In J. D. Sinnott & J. Cavanaugh (Eds.), *Bridging paradigms: Positive development in adulthood and cognitive aging* (pp. 169–202). New York: Praeger.

Sinnott, J. D. (1993a). Teaching in a chaotic new physics world: Teaching as a dialogue with reality. In P. Kahaney, J. Janangelo, & L. Perry (Eds.), *Theoretical and critical perspectives on teacher change* (pp. 91–108). Norwood, NJ: Ablex.

Sinnott, J. D. (1993b). Use of complex thought and resolving intragroup conflicts: A means to conscious adult development in the workplace. In J. Demick & P. M. Miller (Eds.), *Development in the workplace* (pp. 155–175). Hillsdale, NJ: Lawrence Erlbaum.

Sinnott, J. D. (1994a). Development and yearning: Cognitive aspects of spiritual development. *Journal of Adult Development, 1,* 91–99.

Sinnott, J. D. (1994b). *Interdisciplinary handbook of adult lifespan learning.* Westport, CT: Greenwood.

Sinnott, J. D. (1996). The development of complex reasoning: Postformal thought. In F. Blanchard-Fields & T. Hess (Eds.), *Perspectives on cognitive change in adulthood and aging* (pp. 358–386). New York: McGraw-Hill.

Sinnott, J. D. (1997). Brief report: Complex postformal thought in skilled research administrators. *Journal of Adult Development, 4,* 45–53.

Sinnott, J. D. (1998a). Creativity and postformal thought. In C. Adams-Price (Ed.), *Creativity and aging: Theoretical and empirical approaches.* New York: Springer.

Sinnott, J. D. (1998b). *The development of logic in adulthood: Postformal thought and its applications.* New York: Plenum.

Sinnott, J. D. (2000). Cognitive aspects of unitative states: Spiritual self-realization, intimacy, and knowing the unknowable. In M. E. Miller & A. N. West (Eds.), *Spirituality, ethics, and relationship in adulthood: Clinical and theoretical explorations* (pp. 177–198). Madison, CT: Psychosocial Press.

Sinnott, J. D. (2003a). Postformal thought and adult development: Living in balance. In J. Demick & C.

Andreoletti (Eds.), *Adult development* (pp. 221–238). New York: Plenum.

Sinnott, J. D. (2003b). *Spirituality, development and healing: Lessons from several cultures.* Paper presented at Loyola College Midwinter Conference on Religion and Spirituality, Columbia, MD.

Sinnott, J. D. (2003c). Teaching as nourishment for complex thought. In N. L. Diekelmann (Ed.), *Teaching the practitioners of care: New pedagogies for the health professions* (pp. 232–271). Madison: University of Wisconsin Press.

Sinnott, J. D. (2004a). Learning as a humanistic dialogue with reality; new theories that help us teach the whole person: Context of learning and complex thought: Implications for modern life. In T. Hagstrom (Ed.), *Stockholm lectures in educology: Adult development in post-industrial society and working life* (pp. 77–108). Stockholm: University of Stockholm.

Sinnott, J. D. (2004b). Learning as a humanistic dialogue with reality; new theories that help us teach the whole person: Complex postformal thought and its relation to adult learning, life span development, and the new sciences. In T. Hagstrom (Ed.), *Stockholm lectures in educology: Adult development in post-industrial society and working life* (pp. 109–152). Stockholm: University of Stockholm.

Sinnott, J. D., & Johnson, L. (1996). *Reinventing the university: A radical proposal for a problem focused university.* Norwood, NJ: Ablex.

Smith, L. B., & Thelan, E. (Eds.) (1993). *A dynamic systems approach to development.* Cambridge, MA: MIT Press.

von Bertalanfy, L. (1968). *General systems theory.* New York: Brazillier.

Von Neumann, J., & Morgenstern, O. (1947). *Theory of games and economic behavior.* Princeton, NJ: Princeton University Press.

Waldrop, M. (1992). *Complexity: The emerging science at the edge of order and chaos.* New York: Simon & Schuster.

Weiner, N. (1961). *Cybernetics.* Cambridge, MA: MIT Press.

Welwood, J. (1996). *Love and awakening: Discovering the sacred path of intimate relationship.* New York: Harper Collins.

Wolf, F. A. (1981). *Taking the quantum leap.* New York: Harper & Row.

Wolfram, S. (2002). *A new kind of science.* Champaign, IL: Wolfram Media.

Yan, B. (1995). *Nonabsolute/relativistic (N/R) thinking: A possible unifying commonality underlying models of postformal reasoning.* Unpublished doctoral dissertation, University of British Columbia, Vancouver.

Yan, B., & Arlin, P. K. (1995). Nonabsolute/relativistic thinking: A common factor underlying models of postformal reasoning? *Jounal of Adult Development, 2,* 223–240.

Chapter 18

Culture, Learning, and Adult Development

Heidi Keller and Anne Werchan

Learning and development are processes that are genuinely intertwined. In a general sense, learning represents the processes by which an organism's behavior is modified as a result of experience. Development concerns the continuity, predictability, and plasticity of these changes across populations of individuals. Learning processes constitute development, and development organizes and structures learning processes. Learning processes are fundamental in reorganizing knowledge and meaningful progress to more advanced ways of thinking (Granott, 1995). However, learning processes also include affective dimensions. Learning generally addresses three attributes (Granott, 1998, p. 18):

- Growth trajectories specify more advanced knowledge levels;
- Fundamental restructuring results in qualitative shifts in knowledge organization; and
- Self-scaffolding generates knowledge that

supports unguided construction of more advanced knowledge.

These three attributes highlight the developmental nature of learning and emphasize the active role of the learner. Development can thus be understood as "the systematic, organized, intra-individual change that is clearly associated with generally expectable age-related progressions and which is carried forward in some way that has implications for a person's pattern or level of functioning at some later time" (Rutter & Rutter, 1992, p. 64).

Nevertheless, new theories that can explain the interrelations between learning and development during adulthood have only recently started to emerge (Granott, 1998). Moreover, learning and development are cultural processes that extend over the life span (Durkin, 1995). Within each decade of life, reassessments of the life narrative can take place (Levinson, 1986). Age-graded socialization and personality transformation continue across adulthood into old age (Baltes, 1987; Heckhausen, 1999; Thomae, 1970, 1988). The focus of this chapter, therefore, is learning and development across cultural contexts in the adult life stages.

Based on an inborn motivation to learn, learning and development are driven by opportunities and constraints, which serve as an adaptive scaffold for the individual's developmental regulation in any cultural context (Heckhausen, 1999). Opportunities and constraints are defined by biological and sociocultural forces that have a combined influence on individuals (Keller, Poortinga, & Schölmerich, 2002). In a complementary process, individuals modify their opportunities and constraints with active construction and co-construction of their own developmental processes. These processes are framed by universal developmental tasks that sequence the individual life span as an internalized age-normative conception of the self (Keller, 2001).

In this chapter, we understand culture as processes of everyday activities that are manifest in shared activities and shared meaning systems. We draw especially on two sociocultural orientations, independence and interdependence, to organize the discussion of cultural learning and development. Accordingly we present two conceptualizations of competence and learning. The timing of universal developmental tasks also varies with respect to these sociocultural orientations, which we discuss in the following paragraphs. We finally discuss conceptions of wisdom that are prevalent in all cultural communities yet also differ with respect to several domains. We conclude with the acknowledgment of Erik Erikson's ideas about culture and its overarching relevance for the formation of identity.

THE CULTURAL NATURE
OF LEARNING AND DEVELOPMENT

Learning processes are embedded in and constitute cultural practices that organize each individual's development. The capacity for cultural learning represents a universal predisposition of human beings that is actualized from early life onward (Keller & Chasiotis, 1994; Tomasello, 2001). Cultural learning manifests itself in different strategies over the early years of development in, for example, imitation, instruction, and collaboration (Tomasello, Kruger, & Ratner,

1993). It can be assumed that these strategies persist into adulthood and represent the basic tools of information processing (Granott, 1998; Pascual-Leone & Irwin, 1998). Moreover, development over the life course takes place within both the course of cultural history and the course of phylogenetic history (Rogoff, 2003). Thus, the study of adult development addresses the ways in which an individual's personal biography intertwines with the historical period in a particular cultural context and the person's place in the respective social system. Adult learning is based on a wide range of previous experiences, knowledge, interests, and competencies that relate to cultural meaning systems.

In myriad ways, cultures differ from each other. However, two sociocultural orientations have been described for their differential impact on cultural learning and development. These are the sociocultural orientation of independence and the sociocultural orientation of interdependence (Fiske, Kitayama, Markus, & Nisbett et al., 1998). These orientations are embodied in individuals' conceptions of the self (Greenfield, Keller, Fuligni, & Maynard, 2003; Keller, 2003; Markus & Kitayama, 1991). In the following section we therefore introduce these two cultural meaning systems.

THE SOCIOCULTURAL ORIENTATIONS
OF INDEPENDENCE AND
INTERDEPENDENCE

The conception of the sociocultural orientations of independence and interdependence (Fiske et al., 1998) has a long tradition in the social sciences. They are based on anthropological (Shweder & Bourne, 1984) and philosophical (Lesthaeghe, 1983; Westen, 1985) conceptions of selfhood. However, they gained prominence in psychology, especially after the proposal of the cultural value dimension of individualism/collectivism that Geert Hofstede introduced (together with power distance, avoidance of insecurity, and masculinity/femininity) on the basis of a large-scale survey of employees of a multinational enterprise in 50 cultures and 3 world regions (Hofstede, 1980). At about the same time, Harry Triandis proposed a similar conceptualization based on a literature review as well as interviews with psychologists and anthropologists (Triandis et al., 1986). Thereafter, the unidimensional and bipolar conception of individualism/collectivism exerted a tremendous impact on conceptualizing cross-cultural differences in various domains (see e.g., Bond, 1999; Schwartz, 1990, Triandis, 1995; see also the overview by Kağitçibaşi, 1996a). Although the conception as well as the associated methodology have been seriously criticized (e.g., Fijneman et al., 1996; Keller & Eckensberger, 1998; Oyserman, Coon, & Kemmelmeier, 2002; Thomas, 2003), the idea that cultures differ with respect to their orientations toward the self and self–other relationships has nevertheless been substantiated in different approaches (e.g., Greenfield & Cocking, 1994; Greenfield & Suzuki, 1998; Keller & Eckensberger, 1998). Accordingly Kağitçibaşi (1990) distinguished the relational and the separate self, Markus and Kitayama (1991) described independent and interdependent self-construals, Harwood and Bornstein referred to individualism and sociocentrism (Bornstein et al., 1996; Harwood, Leyendecker, Carlson, Asencio, & Miller, 2002), Triandis wrote of idiocentrism and allocentrism (Triandis et al., 1986), and Rogoff (2003) described these orientations as interdependence and autonomy. Hannover (2000) interpreted these self-constructions as chronically or situationally accessible memory structures that have consequences for the content of memory as well as for information processing.

The independent, ideocentric, or individualistic self is regarded as autonomous, coherent, consistent, and separate from others. The interdependent, relational, allocentric self is regarded as contextualized, flexible, and interwoven with others. Due to the immanent relation between affluence and individualism, Hofstede (1980) reported a correlation of 0.82 between cultural level individualism and the level of national economic development (see also Kağitçibaşi, 1996a); the independent self-construal has been mainly located in Western middle-class societies, especially the United States and Europe (Markus & Kitayama, 1991). The prototype of the interdependent self-construal has been located in traditional agrarian communities where the group, mainly the family, needs to cooperate to sustain existence (Kağitçibaşi, 1996b; Keller, 2003). However, several authors also attribute interdependence to the urban population of traditional interdependent societies, referring to the general cultural heritage (e.g., Fiske et al., 1998; Markus & Kitayama, 1991).

The translation from the cultural level of individualism/collectivism to the individual level of self concepts allows us to describe development across the life span as culturally informed pathways. Consequently, developmental psychologists began to understand these sociocultural orientations as organizers of development that specify socialization goals and nourish visions about competence and successful living and aging (Greenfield et al., 2003; Greenfield & Suzuki, 1998; Keller & Eckensberger, 1998; Keller & Greenfield, 2000). Contrary to the original conception of individualism/collectivism as bipolar and unidimensional, most of these conceptualizations understand independence and interdependence as two separate dimensions that form contextually and culturally informed alliances (e.g., Keller, 2003; Leyendecker, Harwood, Lamb, & Schölmerich, 2002). Accordingly, variations have been identified among cultural communities that can be assumed to follow similar developmental goals such as Euro-Americans and Dutch (Harkness, Super, & van Tijen, 2000) or Euro-Americans and Germans (Keller, 2004). Intracultural variations have also been reported, especially with respect to the socioecological contexts of social class (Burger & Miller, 1999; Kusserow, 1999; Lin & Budwig, 1994; Palacios & Moreno, 1996).

Independence and interdependence can be understood as the expression of two different but interacting dimensions: the dimension of agency and the dimension of communion or interpersonal distance (Bakan, 1966; Kağitçibaşi, 2004). At the one end of the dimension, agency can be autonomous, referring to an individual striving to master the environment, assert the self, and experience competence and achievement on the individual level. At the other end of the dimension, agency can be heteronomous with an individual's endeavor for achievement as a communal product, serving communal goals. The dimension of interpersonal distance reaches from relatedness to separateness (Kağitçibaşi, 2004). Individuals' agency and interpersonal distance orientations have been related to a number of different psychological processes, including styles of thinking and cognitive as well as moral reasoning (e.g., Belenky, Clinchy, Goldberger, & Tarule, 1986), the styles of social relationships and personality functioning (Bartholomew & Horowitz, 1991; Diehl, Elnick, Bourbeau, & Labouvie-Vief, 1998), and physical and mental health (Helgeson & Fritz, 2000; see figure 18.1).

Independence and interdependence, agency and communion, vary by gender and phase of the life span, because the balance and regulation between agency and interpersonal distance can be regarded as

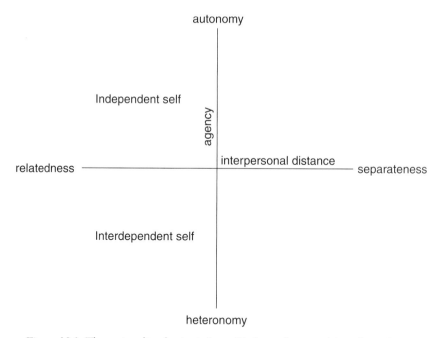

Figure 18.1 The sociocultural orientations of independence and interdependence.

a lifelong developmental task (Diehl, Owen, & Youngblade, 2004; Kegan, 1982; Keller & Eckensberger, 1998; Leyendecker, 2004). With respect to gender, it has been demonstrated that men are consistently socialized to be more independent, self-sufficient, achievement-oriented, adventurous, and risk taking, whereas women have been socialized to be more nurturing, sensitive, and relationship-oriented (Cross & Madson, 1997; Helgeson, 1994). Diehl and collaborators (2004) have demonstrated with an adult life span sample (N = 158, 80 men) that men included more agency-related attributes in their self-representations than women. Conversely, women included more communion-related attributes in their self-descriptions than men. In line with these different orientations of men and women, Carol Gilligan (1982) criticized Kohlberg's (e.g., 1958) theory of moral development as biased due to its male conception of justice. She developed an alternative theory for women, one asserting that women have differing moral and psychological tendencies than men, because women are taught to care for other people and expect others to care for them. Although the idea is compelling, it has not been adequately substantiated empirically (Eckensberger & Zimba, 1996).

It has also been suggested that with increasing age and maturation, the dialectic tension between agency and interpersonal distance may change (Gutmann, 1994; Labouvie-Vief, 1994). The result is a more balanced relationship between the two orientations and a more overall communal orientation. Gutmann (1994) suggested that men incorporate more feminine characteristics in their behavior, whereas women tend to incorporate more masculine characteristics into their behavior. Diehl and collaborators (2004) have analyzed the self-descriptions from U.S. adults ranging in age from 20 to 88 years. Their findings demonstrated that the content of spontaneous adult self-representations could be reliably coded in terms of agency and communion. The total number of agency-related attributes in the self-representations was negatively correlated with age. The total number of communion-related attributes showed a positive association with age. Findings from a content analysis revealed the interesting result that the reduction in agency-related attributes with age was mainly due to a smaller number of negative agency words, such as *arrogant*, *aggressive*, and *cynical*. Positive agency words, like *confident*, *creative*, and *determined*, were included with the same frequency across all age groups.

Next we introduce conceptions of competence that can be regarded as characterizing life span developmental goals on the basis of these two sociocultural orientations. It is evident that both conceptions characterize any individual and any culture. However, cultures define frameworks that prioritize one or the other to differing degrees. The existential question about the relation of agency and interpersonal relatedness is thus also differently answered by different cultures (Shweder & Bourne, 1984).

CONCEPTIONS OF COMPETENCE IN A CULTURAL CONTEXT

Studies aimed at exploring the universality of stages of cognitive development during childhood as proposed by Piaget (1952) have revealed that cultures differ with respect to the structural and operative modes of intelligence (Dasen, 1977; Serpell, 1994). Clearly, these differences could be empirically related to the prior experiences as embodied in the socialization process and the prevalent cultural practices of adults. In large-scale societies with a preference for an independent self-construal, competence is understood as an individual capacity and the cultivation of an individual mind. Exploration, discovery, and creativity are effective operative modes. Personal achievement is the goal (Greenfield et al., 2003; Lin & Wang, 2002). The thinking style has been described as differentiated, that is, as detailed but structured (Woike, 1994). Competence in this respect can be regarded as representing technological intelligence (Mundy-Castle & Okonji, 1976), focusing primarily on logical and formal thought processes (Piaget, 1952). Formal operational thinking implies that the individual has developed the ability to engage in four distinct thought processes: (1) introspection (i.e., the ability to think about thought); (2) abstraction (i.e., the ability to extend beyond concrete reality); (3) logic (i.e., the ability to analyze facts with respect to correct conclusions); and (4) hypothetical reasoning (i.e., the ability to formulate hypotheses and test them, considering several variables at the same time; Piaget, 1952). Pascual-Leone and Irwin (1994) describe this conceptual, logological (language-based), learning as high-road learning. These competences are general in the sense that they can be applied to different contexts.

Another conception of competence focuses on moral self-cultivation and the social contribution of achievement. This social and communal mode of competence emphasizes the creation and maintenance of social harmony based on respect and acceptance of social roles in the community (Greenfield et al., 2003; Keller, 2003; Nsamenang & Lamb, 1994). Here the thinking style has been described as integrated (Woike, 1994). This conception of competence is adaptive in traditional agrarian communities where interdependence characterizes the conception of the self. This conception of competence has also been applied to urban communities in traditionally interrelated societies, such as those in Southeast Asia (Fiske et al., 1998; Lin & Wang, 2002) or societies in Africa (Nsamenang, 1992).

In fact, several studies have demonstrated that individuals from different cultural backgrounds hold different views on competence. Australian and Malaysian students, as examples from an independent and an interdependent cultural background, differ with respect to their evaluation of different kinds of competences. Although there was a considerable amount of agreement, Malaysians emphasized social and practical skills, whereas Australians believed academic skills, speaking, reading, and writing to be more important (Gill & Keats, 1980).

The different cultural conceptions of competence are embodied in different cultural practices and contexts of childrearing, which in turn influence cognitive competences, and thus learning as well as development, differentially. Accordingly, Ross and Millsom (1970) could empirically underpin Bartlett's (1932) hypothesis that members of illiterate societies have better memory skills than members of literate ones in those areas where the oral tradition had been replaced by memory banks like telephone directories. They compared university students from Ghana, who were supposed to have a strong oral tradition, to U.S. students with the expertise in a technologically advanced society. Paraphrasing the content of a short piece of English prose after three different delay intervals, Ghanaian students outperformed the Americans, even compensating for the disadvantage that English was not their first language. Additionally, Mishra and Singh (1992) could demonstrate that the ecocultural environment of Indian Asur children (i.e., those living without any sources of light, like lamps or candles, during the night), may lead to practice effects concerning the recall of where one has placed an object. These studies provide examples of how culture shapes the development of memory skills through learning in everyday activities. This view is further substantiated with findings that adults recall stories that are consistent with their cultural tradition, better than inconsistent ones (Harris, Schoen, & Hensley, 1992; Harris, Schoen, & Lee, 1986; Steffensen & Calker, 1982).

Also, the structure of autobiographical memories (K. Nelson, 2000; Reese, Haden, & Fivush, 1993; Tessler & Nelson, 1994; Wang, 2001) varies with respect to sociocultural orientations. In Western independent cultural environments, individuals tell their personal life stories and talk about their self-concepts and identities. They address their individual successes and failures, their achievements and losses, as well as their hopes and fears. The process of identity formation in Western (Cartesian) thinking conceptions of development are biased toward an increasingly autonomous self that actively distinguishes itself from other selves and from its social and natural context (Bruner, 1993; Wang & Brockmeier, 2002). Individuality, autonomy, and power are explicated for evaluating human lives. The autobiographical memory represents a private, personal matter that is determined by intrinsic mechanisms (Wang & Brockmeier, 2002). Observations of autobiographical writings and everyday practices in Asian cultures suggest the existence of another genre of personal narratives. The figure-ground relationship is reversed with the ego withdrawing to the background and becoming interrelated with personal relationships and the social context.

Accordingly, autobiographical memory varies in content, form, style, and timing of its emergence across cultures. "Such variations in memory, in turn, re-establish the very notion of self within a larger cultural milieu, in which individuals are expected, for example, to anchor their existence in an autobiographical past, or to understand their being as created through social interconnection and constant participation in collective activities" (Wang & Brockmeier, 2002, p. 53ff).

Although the conceptions of independence and interdependence are useful to explain a considerable amount of cultural variance, there is nevertheless substantial variance within these sociocultural orientations. A study on creativity in dance performance demonstrates cultural uniqueness. Colligan (1983) found Samoan and Balinese dancers to have individual dancing styles, whereas Japanese (during the Tokugawa period) and Omaha (India) dancing styles are more invariant. Although all of these cultures are thought to be interdependent, Samoan and Balinese dancers are encouraged to develop their individuality

(as a person in Samoa, as a group member in Bali), whereas Japanese and Omaha cultures do not appreciate the existence of individual styles.

Cole (1988, p. 147) says: "Cultural differences in cognition reside more in the contexts within which cognitive processes manifest themselves than in the existence of a particular process (such as logical memory or theoretical responses to syllogisms) in one culture and its absence in another." In line with that, Carraher, Carraher, and Schliemann (1991), for example, rethought the problem of formal operational thinking that we noted at the beginning of this section. They studied Brazilian children who worked as street sellers. Although these children were not able to use mathematical routines at school effectively, they solved the same mathematical problems at the market without effort. Carraher, Schliemann, and Carraher (1988, p. 71) concluded that social situations are "a strong determinant of which symbolic representations are used in problem solving." Skills are acquired context-bound and cannot necessarily be transferred from one context to another.

CULTURAL CONCEPTIONS OF LEARNING

Cultural conceptions of learning have also been analyzed with respect to different sociocultural orientations, especially in comparing East Asians, particularly Chinese, with Euro-Americans (e.g., Li, 2001, 2002). The Euro-American model is based on the central premise that learning constitutes the process of information acquisition that is externally available. Knowledge represents a neutral corpus that can be acquired by learning. It becomes an individual possession and is managed and regulated by individual efforts.

Based on questionnaires and interviews with Harvard undergraduates, Perry (1968) concluded that many college freshmen believed that knowledge is handed down by authority. Belenky et al. (1986) described this form of knowing as separate knowing, in which the persons distance themselves from the subject of knowledge through critical thinking and application of the rules of logic. The learner is equipped with cognitive competencies, motivational attributes, and personality traits that can facilitate or inhibit the learning processes. Recently the needs of adult learners in classrooms have been especially emphasized. Malcolm Knowles (1970), a pioneer in the study of adult learning, identified the following characteristics of adult learners:

- Adults are autonomous and self-directed. They need to be free to direct themselves. Their teachers must actively involve adult participants in the learning process and serve as facilitators for them.
- Adults have accumulated a foundation of life experiences and knowledge that may include work-related activities, family responsibilities, and previous education. They need to connect learning to this knowledge/experience base.
- Adults are goal-oriented. On enrolling in a course, they usually know the goal(s) they wish to attain. Thus they appreciate an educational program that is organized and has clearly defined elements.
- Adults are relevancy-oriented. They must see a reason for learning something. Learning has to be applicable to their work or other responsibilities to be of value to them.
- Adults are practical, focusing on the aspects of a lesson most useful to them in their work. They may not be interested in knowledge for its own sake.
- Like all learners, adults need to be shown respect. Instructors must acknowledge the wealth of experiences that adult participants bring to the classroom. These adults should be treated as equals in experience and knowledge, and allowed to voice their opinions freely in class.

These principles clearly reflect an independent sociocultural orientation. Persons are conceived of as autonomous and self-directed. They have individual opinions and are equals to the teacher (or as Knowles, e.g., 1984, put it, to the learning facilitator). Knowledge is characterized as an externally available body of information. There is individuality in the learning process, and there are individual learning styles.

Learning based on an interdependent sociocultural orientation differs from this conception substantially. For example, Chinese adults view the learning process in terms of establishing a network of personal relations within the learning domains. Knowledge is inextricably connected to life and constitutes sense and the meaning of life. Belenky et al. (1986) define this knowledge as connected knowing, in which the person creates a connection to the social object by acknowledging perceiver-object similarities and taking into account the perspective of the social object

(see also Labouvie-Vief, 1994). In Confucian philosophy, knowledge is not regarded as only an external corpus, but is held as containing social and moral dimensions as well. Therefore, learning includes self-cultivation and self-perfection (Li, 2002; Yu, 1996) as primary emphases. Furthermore, Chinese ideas about learning contain an important personal dimension of individual causality (Li, Yue, & Yue, 2001). Learning is a central basis of the whole life span and consists of persistent, continuous, concentrated, and industrious efforts. From the position of modesty, the unity of knowledge and morality is the aim, one that has consequences for the family and the society (Li, 2002). Similar conceptions are also prevalent in Japanese culture in which the concept of *hansei* expresses the ongoing reflection on one's own mistakes and problems (Kitayama, 2002). The emphasis on the individual person, and thus individual praising, is regarded as inappropriate.

With respect to the ideal of moral cultivation, learning styles can be characterized by attentive observation and imitation. Rogoff, Paradise, Mejía Arauz, Correa-Chávez, and Angelillo (2003, p. 176) describe this style as *intent participation*. Intent participation consists of listening and observing with intentional attention to anticipate the performance of the observed. Imitation constitutes an active and intentional process. Imitation does not merely represent copying a behavior but includes the anticipation of its intent as well (Tomasello, 2001). Collaborative participation in joint activities is the mode for constituting knowledge, which is the property of the interacting collective (Greenfield, 1996). Rogoff et al. (2003) understand this learning style as horizontal, with changing responsibilities and consensus, based on joint decision processes.

Learning styles in independent cultural environments are characterized by an exclusive focus of attention on the target object or subject. Children learn from early on to concentrate on one thing at a time. Focusing on different things at the same time is considered a distraction. Important informal learning processes are also involved. These include adopting the attitudes, norms, and role expectations that are appropriate for a particular job from parents, teachers, the media, and other public sources. Norm adoption is accomplished by observing important others in day-to-day experiences.

An interesting mixture of the two conceptions of learning is prevalent among the Native Americans of the United States, especially the Navajo culture (Joe, 1994). This culture values moral cultivation and individual autonomy. As a consequence, children cannot be forced to go to school because this is regarded as imposing one's will on another. The Navajo term *nila* ("it is up to you"; Joe, 1994, p. 111) states the unwillingness to make a decision for someone other than the self. In the Navajo world, learning is generally understood as encompassing three different educational arenas. One arena represents the content and learning processes that extend throughout one's lifetime. Beginning at birth, the individual is molded into a respected member of the Navajo society. Learning is generally informal, arising from many sources. Domains of knowledge include content from language learning during childhood to learning about the purpose of life. The second arena of learning is more restrictive and concerns the occupation or one's way of earning a living. In that arena, persons have the opportunity to match their interests and talents with culturally rewarded skills as, for example, a weaver or a hunter. The third arena is the most restrictive, because it implies a lifetime commitment, that of becoming a healer or a religious leader (Joe, 1994). All three arenas are available to all members of the tribe, although the third arena requires a special gift. A personal account of becoming a healer will be presented shortly. To a lesser or greater degree, all cultures value learning as lifelong processes. However, these processes are part of different conceptions of life and of different ways of patterning the life span. We present these cultural conceptions in the section that follows.

CULTURAL CONCEPTIONS OF DEVELOPMENT

Western psychology conceptualizes development predominantly as genetic epistemology. Biologically coded information is thought to unfold in a regular and predictable way that is expressed in intra-individual changes. The stage theory of Erikson (e.g., Erikson, 1959) is a popular example of such a view. The environment influences development via the unique experiences of each individual. Although there are many differing ways to delineate the interplay of "nature and nurture" (Greenfield et al., 2003), individual experience remains the crucial link.

There are, however, different models of development in other parts of the world. Nsamenang (1992)

has outlined an indigenous stage model for Sub-Saharan Africa. This conception is less focused on the individual person; instead the level of social integration is used as the marker of developmental stage. Consequently, developmental stages represent *socio-ontogenetic stages*. Table 18.1 contrasts the Eriksonian model of development with the West African model by Nsamenang.

Erikson's model assumes that conflicts of the ego do not arise intrapsychically between id and super-ego, as Freud said, but between the individual and society, being psychosocial rather than psychosexual (Erikson, 1959, 1963). Thereby, Erikson introduced an important new dimension into psychoanalytic theory: the relation between individual and society. Nevertheless, his theory remains bound to an independent sociocultural orientation. The conflicts between individual and society cause a number of psychosocial crises that are conceptualized as an invariable sequence. The successful solution of one crisis constitutes the necessary precursor of the successful solution of the next crisis—a view in which we again find genetic epistemology. A satisfying solution of each crisis is contrasted with an insufficient one to describe the eight psychosocial stages of life.

Erikson proposed his stages as invariant in their developmental course but held that they are exposed to cultural influences in trait emphasis, stage length, and tendencies to adapt children's developmental readiness and inclusion needs to group norms (Hoare, 2002). Another cultural difference may exist in the way people divide their life courses into meaningful units.

The socio-ontogenetic stages use social roles rather than crises to describe the life-course. However, even conceptions of life vary from culture to culture. Nsamenang (1992, 2003) presents the concept of social ontogeny for the Cameroonian Nso that posits three phases of the human life cycle: ancestral selfhood, spiritual selfhood, and social selfhood. Ancestral selfhood follows biological death and extends to the ritual initiation of the ancestral spirit into the ancestral realm. Spiritual selfhood begins with the ritual incorporation of the ancestral spirit into the world of spirits and ends with the naming ritual. Social selfhood begins with the naming of the children several days after birth, which incorporates them into the community of the living and extends to death.

The first stage of social ontogeny is the period of the newborn, which begins with the naming of the

TABLE 18.1. Comparison of Erikson's and Nsamenang's Stage Models

Developmental Tasks[a]	Socio-Ontogenetic Stages[b]
I. Basic trust versus basic mistrust	Spiritual selfhood
II. Autonomy versus shame/doubt	I. Period of the newborn
III. Initiative versus guilt	II. Social priming
IV. Industry/competence versus inferiority	III. Social apprenticing
V. Identity versus identity diffusion/role confusion	IV. Social entrée
VI. Intimacy versus isolation	V. Social induction/internment
VII. Generativity versus self-absorption/stagnation	VI. Adulthood
VIII. Integrity versus despair	VII. Old age/death ancestral selfhood

[a]Eriksonian (1959) model of development.

[b]West African model by Nsamenang (1992).

child. The naming procedure is more culturally satiated and fundamental for the child than in Western societies: The name carries the expectations of the community for the child, thus having a critical impact on the child's personality development (Nsamenang, 1992). The second or presocial phase is marked by biological behaviors such as smiling, crying, teething, and sitting up. Nsamenang (1992) supposes that these biological markers are implicitly regarded as precursors of social functioning. When the child begins to walk, it reaches the third stage, social apprenticing. This stage contains the gradual and systematic initiation of the social novice into various social roles. Stages four and five, social entrée and social induction and internment, cover the transition from childhood to adulthood. These stages may be supported by certain rites of passages (see later discussion) or by additional efforts to allocate more responsibilities to the adolescent and integrate him or her into adult social groups and roles. The sixth stage, adulthood, divides into two parts: a "proto-adult status" (Nsamenang, 2002, p. 146) that is acquired through marriage, and the full adult status that occurs after the birth of the first child. Seniority then increases with each child born thereafter. However, this close relation between adulthood and reproduction seems to become weaker with increasing education. Old age, the seventh stage of social selfhood, requires being a grandparent, and the old people are regarded as having achieved a maximal social competence. Overall life satisfaction largely depends on the number of competent offspring.

It is obvious that this model relies on social categories for the description of development to a much larger extent than Erikson's developmental task model that focuses on the individual. Erikson's (1975) says: "In youth you find out what you care to do and who you care to be, even in changing roles. In young adulthood you learn whom you care to be with-at work, and in private life. In adulthood, however, you learn to know what and whom to take care of" (p. 661). This reflects Erikson's independent worldview as expressed in the emphasis of freedom of choice. However, he also assumes an increasing orientation toward interdependence with age. Moreover, Erikson himself became "bored with his life-stage scheme and its egotistic qualities" (Hoare, 2002, p. 169) and readily accepted Margaret Mead's advice to "open its edges to permit cultural variation" (Hoare, 2002, p. 169).

PATTERNING OF THE LIFE SPAN

Although different conceptions of life exist across cultures, as outlined in the previous section, we nonetheless restrict the discussion to the time span between birth and death, because most of psychology deals with this aspect of one, existential life (Nsamenang, 2003).

The human life span can be regarded as having evolved during the history of humankind (Keller, 2001). Based on universal genetic programs, individuals acquire contextually relevant ecological, social, and cultural information through intentional as well as intuitive learning during their ontogenetic development. Evolutionary approaches assume that people consider contextual information, for example, mortality and fertility rates, in biographical decision making

(Keller, 2001). Based on such information, an individual biography is shaped, in part. The different life stages center on universal developmental tasks. All over the world, adults are supposed to be able to support themselves economically, generate and raise offspring, and become mature and responsible members of their respective cultural communities. Different emphases of interpersonal distance and agency over the life span have been related to these developmental tasks. The focus of early adulthood may be more on gaining independence and committing to a career and stable interpersonal relationships (Arnett, 2000). Developmental tasks in middle and late adulthood are related to broader social responsibilities, such as mentoring others, raising and guiding the next generation, and providing support to others (Aldwin & Levenson, 2001). However, there are substantial differences with respect to the timing and the solution of the developmental tasks across the life span in different cultural environments. In the next section, we discuss the conception of time and the timing of developmental tasks in different cultural environments.

THE TIMING OF
DEVELOPMENTAL TASKS

Cultures differ substantially with respect to the role of chronological time as a marker for developmental processes, and thus for the formation of identity. Rogoff (2003) distinguishes two basic modes for identity processes: identity as defined by social relationships and a person's place in the community, and identity as progression on a timeline. In cultural environments with an independent sociocultural orientation, the awareness of chronological age is central to the organization of developmental processes. This view is conceptualized on the basis of age-normative or age-graded influences. Such influences are informed by cultural conceptions and much less so by statistical distributions (Hagestad, 1990; Hagestad & Neugarten, 1985).

Depending on the educational track, individuals in the United States and Europe are expected to follow an occupational cycle that begins in adolescence. In adolescence, due to the development of formal thought, youth can conceptualize themselves in future potential careers. In addition, teens engage in work and social experiences that may lead to an occupational choice.

At some point in their twenties, young adults are expected to be ready to support themselves economically,

independent of the educational track. The mean age of university graduates in today's Germany is 28 and in the United Kingdom, 24 years of age. Those who have attended vocational training programs begin their occupational lives at the age of 18 (Statistisches Bundesamt, 1997). The occupational cycle continues with the pursuit of a chosen career and ends with retirement from the workforce, which is defined by law at a particular age. For example, the retirement age is 65 years in Germany, France, New Zealand and the United States, or age 65 for men and somewhat lower for women. In Great Britain and Australia, women retire at ages 60 or 62, respectively. Other countries such as Sweden and Italy have more flexible models for retirement (Pensions Policy Institute, 2003).

Many factors influence the choice of an occupation. Predominant among them are socioeconomic status, parents' occupation(s), ethnic background, intelligence, skills, gender, and personality. Participation in the workforce is the basis of economic security. Such participation also contributes to life satisfaction and self-esteem and lays the foundation for personal growth (Forrest & Mikolaitis, 1986).

For the foundation of a family, there are age normative ranges as well. In some parts of Germany the front door of the house of a woman who is not yet married on her twenty-fifth birthday, is decorated with many empty boxes by her friends. This tradition exemplifies the common German notion of an "old box," an acronym for an unmarried elderly female. Men who are not married by age 30 must sweep the stairs of the city hall in the company of their friends. These rituals announce publicly that the age range for resolving the developmental task of founding a family has been violated.

Other than the choice of an occupational career and establishing a family, socially mature participation in community life is a third overarching developmental task of adulthood. Schaie (1979; Schaie & Willis, 2000) described two adult life stages that center on mature community life. These are the responsibility and the executive stage. The responsibility stage extends from the late thirties to the early sixties. In this stage, adults use sociocognitive abilities to care for family and for others. The executive stage that begins during the thirties or forties and extends through middle age; it is characterized by the development of the ability to apply complex knowledge at a number of different levels and becoming responsible for business, academic institutions, churches, government, and other organizations.

Being on time, behind, or ahead of time with regard to expected developmental milestones has become a major domain of research on adjustment and well-being in psychology (Krawczak, 1999; Neugarten, 1968; Seiffge-Krenke & Stemmler, 2002; Silbereisen & Kracke, 1993, 1997). Although age may only be regarded as a carrier of development, it has in fact become equivalent to development in public discourse (Keller & Eckensberger, 1998).

In other cultural environments, the solution of developmental tasks is bound to naturally occurring (e.g., onset of menstruation for females) or socially recognized events (e.g., particular courage tests for males). An African concept of being is dynamic, rooted in the belief that personhood is attained not only as one gets old but also in direct proportion to the enactment of one's status, roles, and social acceptance in the community (Nsamenang, 1992). In Maya communities (Rogoff, 2003) as well as in African villages (Nsamenang, 1992), chronological age does not represent development and may not even be known. Development is represented by relative seniority. People know who is senior to whom, for this is important in issues of responsibility and privilege (Rogoff, 2003). These relations are also represented in languages. In African cultures and Maya communities there are different terms for younger and older sister and for younger and older brother. In Nso, a Cameroonian language, the following kinship terms exist: *ngàywir* (elder brother/sister), *téri* (younger brother/sister). The current status of a person compares to cultural norms, and psychological age refers to how well a person can adapt to social and other environmental demands. Psychological age includes intelligence, learning ability, and motor skills, as well as subjective dimensions such as feelings, attitudes, and motives. Physical maturation may also be the basis for the timing of developmental tasks when, for example, Nso boys undergo initiation rites and are then considered to have developed the physical strength for performing the challenges associated with the rituals.

The following section examines the topic of initiation into the adult world in greater detail.

The Beginning of Adulthood

Cultures define the beginning of adulthood quite differently (Schlegel & Barry, 1991). However, adulthood is marked by rites of passage in all societies. Van Gennep (1960) saw the purpose of these initiation rites as cushioning the emotional disruption caused by a change from one status to another. Brain and collaborators (1977) argued that "these rites are seen as a part of general human concern. The particular problem being dealt with is the change from childhood, seen as asexual, to adulthood—seen as sexual. Further, sex is threatening since it is connected with death and with the unique human knowledge of mortality" (p. 191).

Adolescent initiation rites mark the beginning of adulthood in many small-scale cultural communities. Other than the recognition of sexual maturity, rites of passage symbolize a status change to adulthood. Such rites mark the person's incorporation into the larger society and the change from a learner into a teacher of cultural norms and values (Ottenberg, 1994). Initiation rites are usually gender segregated. Boys' initiations often focus on issues of responsibility, whereas girls' initiations often focus on issues of fertility (Rogoff, 2003). In the following, the initiation for adolescent girls and boys in the Nso culture is described as an example.

Initiation of the Girl (Wanle Ngon)

Menarche, considered as *nyuy ser wan* (God has checked the child) is received by the girl with feelings of fear, tension, and depression, because menstruation and sexuality were never a topic in family discourse. On the other hand, the family rejoices over the maturity of their daughter. During a girl's first menstruation, the traditional rite is that of slaughtering a chicken while the girl is kept on a nutritive diet. She stays indoors for the duration of the menstruation and receives advice from her mother, aunts, and other women about the taboos associated with menstruation and the curriculum of womanhood. She is taught the role and behavior of a woman in the community and her rightful place in the traditional environment. The girl may receive gifts that are typical traditional feminine belongings. These gifts—a hoe, a basket, a loin, a head tie, or a bangle—symbolize the gender role. There is a saying in Lamnso: "*wiiy wo laa, dzé wiiy ghaa*" or "*wiiy wo laa kisoo dzé wiiûy ghaa*" (a woman without a wrapper is no woman or a woman without a hoe is no woman). These are pure traditional devices that identify a girl with womanhood.

After the first menstrual period, the mother of the girl washes her as a sign of cleansing her from stillbirth. Because menstruation is seen as polluting, the washing of a menarcher by her mother is not just a hygienic activity, but is also a symbolic cleansing of menstrual pollution within the family (Mzeka, 1996). Menstruation marks an accentuation of the girl's farm and household activities and a change in her playgroups and style. There are women's dance groups to which the girl can now accompany her mother as an onlooker. To be initiated into such a group, the girl must bring a series of food items, such as a tin of melon seeds, cow-peas, a basket of smoked fish, and loaves of foofoo. These items are considered to be affordable by any hard-working and eligible woman. This gesture from the girl reflects her agrarian involvement, her capabilities, and her successes. The gifts also signify her generosity and competence in nourishing people, which are other key roles of women within the traditional system.

The initiation gives the girl a dignified status, and she gains her a place in the adult female world. Most of the duties of the mother are now done by the girl, such as caring for her younger siblings, feeding them, cooking for the family, and inviting her friends to help in her mother's farm (party work). She is a *Mamie wo teri* (little mother) of the house at this stage. At this time, the mother can leave the younger siblings and attend a funeral celebration, or even spend days away, knowing that the little mother will manage the household.

Initiation of the Boy (Wanle Nsum)

The prediction of maturation for the boy is different from that of the girl. The appearance of secondary sexual characteristics, such as a deep voice and a beard, indicates the boy's maturity. The boy may also experience spermarche (wet dreams). Spermarche is also known as *nyuy ser wan* (God has checked the child). Boys do not tell their fathers about their being checked by God, but elders gradually discover such events.

In the company of their peers, boys usually perform activities such as clearing the farms, bringing the harvest home from the fields, and helping in the building and thatching of a house. During this time, the boy can be admitted into the boys' brigade, called *ngwaè*. This is a group of boys who accompany adults on hunting expeditions. At this time, the boy can be initiated into the innermost circles of secret society cults such as the *rum*, the *asang*, and the *kikum ke vitseè*. When a boy is initiated into the secret society cults, he is expected to own spears, a cutlass, a *kiburu* (a sheath for a cutlass), and a cap. Wearing a cap is mandatory for men when participating in some secret society forums. The weapons are symbolic of adulthood and signify the man's capabilities in community protection in case of foreign aggression.

The boy participates fully in all communal activities, such as the digging of roads and communal hunting. In the latter, he proves his skills in shooting and defense. At this stage, a boy child may join the ranks of people who enter the grave during burial rites. He must be psychologically strong and learn to manage unforeseen traumatic situations and mishaps in life. A "manly man" is not supposed to shed tears, no matter how grave the situation. The shedding of tears is considered a womanish and immature solution to frightful and distressful circumstances. It is also during this period that he can legally start singing some of the secret society songs like the *nlwerong*, or the *ngiri* (the songs of two basic secret society cults in Nsoland). When a boy has been initiated, he becomes a full man, who when dead may be buried with the full array of funeral rites. To be an adult male is a difficult process, one of *passing through death*, as the natives usually say. As such, weaklings can never become adults. One needs to be brave and to feel responsible for others while enduring emotional and psychological torture.

The boy is considered as *ba wo teri* (a small father or a junior father, especially with the dark chin and heavy voice), because he executes the father's duties and exercises a manly authority within the family in the absence of the father. He knows how to prune the raffia palm trees for wine tapping. He splits firewood and makes sure that there is never a shortage of it in the house. He learns how to thatch a house and perform other manly activities. He is the one who arranges with his peer group and friends to bring his mother's harvest in from the farm. He disciplines the young ones in the place of the father, indicating that he is the perfect example of obedience and respect, one from whom junior siblings should learn.

Adolescents simply perfect and put into practice their skills of values and the moral teachings they had learnt. This is the period of full responsibility where there is open differentiation of gender roles. The males are initiated into specific male activities and the females into specific feminine activities. Each set of gender-specific activities has social norms and roles that must be fully assimilated and mastered.

In traditional small scale societies, marriage embodies the transition to adulthood, the transition "from boy to man and from girl to woman" (Arnett, 1998, p. 295). The status of adulthood may even be linked to parenthood, as in the Nso (LeVine et al., 1994; Nsamenang, 1992). In rural Indian Gujarati families, the low status of a young married woman can only be improved by parenthood, especially by becoming the mother of a son. In many societies the status as parent is also expressed in the forms of social address. The individual name is replaced by mother or father of the respective child. The acceptance of social responsibilities in the community (mainly for men) is linked to the status of parenthood.

The transition to adulthood seems to be generally shorter in cultural environments that are oriented toward interdependent, sociocultural orientations. L. J. Nelson, Badger, and Wu (2004) have reported that 59% of Chinese students between 18 and 25 years of life considered themselves adults. However, they did not consider marriage and parenthood as markers of adulthood as do the traditional villagers, but instead held attitudes that endorse social responsibilities, like "accept responsibilities for the consequences of your action," and "learn always to have good control of your emotion." In line with the educational profile, becoming financially independent from the parents has been regarded as one important marker of adulthood.

In large-scale Western societies, initiation rites mark the transition to adulthood as well, beginning with religious confirmations, the bar mitzvah, the driver's license test, and school graduation ceremonies. Moreover, the beginning of adulthood is legally defined as the age at which the person has the right to vote. However, each rite is only a small part of the process of reaching adulthood (Rice, 1990). Acquiring a driver's license permits one to drive a car but does not, in general, carry implications for social maturity. In Western industrialized cultures, social adulthood is actually postponed until the mid- or late twenties. The years of "emerging adulthood" (Arnett, 2000) are characterized by an ongoing exploration and experimentation with possible life directions, by trying out different modes of living and by enjoying personal freedom (Saraswathi, 2003; Schlegel & Barry, 1991). In the United States, the criteria that young people themselves consider markers of adulthood are responsibility for oneself, becoming capable of making independent decisions, and becoming financially independent (Arnett, 1998; Arnett Jensen,

2003). These standards are internal, gradual, and individualistic (L. J. Nelson et al., 2004). Parenthood is also a significant developmental transition in large-scale communities. However, it is not linked to the attainment of an adult status. It is considered the beginning of a new phase of life, one that defines a new phase of adulthood (Arnett, 2000; Rogoff, 2003).

Marriage and parenthood in large-scale societies do not necessarily go together. Due to an individualistic mentality, the individual has the choice of forming close relationships and of becoming a parent. In spite of their freedom, most people do choose to have children. However, marriage may follow pregnancy or the birth of a child (Keller, Zach, & Abels, 2005). Preparation for parenthood is not a lifelong learning process but consists mostly of short-term birth preparation classes shortly before delivery. Classes primarily cover the physical aspects of birth and childcare. The transition to parenthood is conceived of as more of a crisis, as the following paragraph from a U.S. textbook on life span development suggests:

> Parenthood imposes new roles and responsibilities on both the mother and the father. It also confers a new social status on them. The actual birth brings an onslaught of physical and emotional strains—disruption of sleep and other routines, financial drain, increased tension and conflicts of various kinds. The mother is tired, the father feels neglected, and both partners feel that their freedom has been curtailed. The closeness and companionship of husband and wife can be diluted by the introduction of a new family member, and the focus of either or both partners may shift to the baby. (Craig & Baucum, 2002, p. 485)

An interesting combination of these different views on adulthood has been documented with respect to ethnic minority groups in the United States. Arnett Jensen (2003) compared African Americans, Latinos, and Asian Americans with respect to their views about the criteria that constitute an adult. The results emphasize a bicultural conception of the transition to adulthood of these groups. They shared a widespread endorsement of individualistic criteria, such as, for example, accepting responsibility for one's actions, deciding on one's own beliefs and values. However, they also favored criteria that reflect responsibilities toward others, like becoming less self-oriented and developing greater consideration for others.

ADULT COMPETENCE AND WISDOM

All cultures have developed ideas of adult expertise that is well beyond their conceptions of competence and intelligence. This "extra knowledge" is conceived of as wisdom (Hahn, 1991) in the sense of "an expert knowledge system in the fundamental pragmatics of life permitting exceptional insight, judgment, and advice involving complex and uncertain matters of the human condition" (Baltes & Staudinger, 1993, p. 76). This conception is specified by five wisdom criteria. First, there are two basic criteria, which are thought to be characteristic of all types of expertise:

- Rich factual (declarative) knowledge about the fundamental pragmatics of life, and
- Rich procedural (strategic) knowledge about the fundamental pragmatics of life.

In addition, there are three meta-criteria, which are considered specific for wisdom:

- Life span contextualism,
- Relativism of values and life priorities, and
- Recognition and management of uncertainty (e.g., Baltes & Staudinger, 2000; Staudinger & Baltes, 1995).

Within the Western world tradition, wisdom comprises three aspects: wisdom as a cognitive process, wisdom as virtue, and wisdom as a personal good (Csikszentmihalyi & Rathunde, 1990). Wisdom is the orchestration of mind and virtue (Baltes, 2004; Baltes & Staudinger, 2000). It is obvious that wisdom is a cultural activity and a product of cultural evolution (Csikszentmihalyi & Rathunde, 1990). "Writings of the 'wisdom kind' are cultural and collective productions in the true sense of the word" (Baltes, 2004, p. 41). Conceptions of wisdom that have been developed outside the context of Western psychology stress similar aspects. Buddhism is sometimes thought of as conceiving of wisdom as a dimension that is vertical to the dimension of knowledge, implying that wisdom is more than what can be inferred from knowledge; that is, it has to be subjective, evident, and existentially significant (Gäng, 1991).

As we demonstrated earlier, cultural variation in the conception of wisdom must be expected because the conceptions of knowledge, virtue, values, life priorities, and contexts vary across cultural environments.

"Identically virtuous people may be inspired by different ideals and we must know about these ideals before we can judge the goodness of the life they guide" (Kekes, 1983, p. 285).

The relation between cultural conceptions of wisdom and the sociocultural orientations of independence and interdependence that is so apparent for the conceptions of competence and learning is challenged by the integrative nature of the definitions of wisdom. The German and French societies of the sixteenth and seventeenth centuries, which many see as oriented toward independent sociocultural orientations, combined cognitive and moral components of wisdom in their concepts of education (*Bildung*), and honesty (*honnêteté*) (Hahn, 1991). Recent conceptualizations also combine components that are oriented toward independence with those that are oriented toward interdependence. An example is Achenbach's (1991) concept of wisdom as the art of living. Achenbach presents seven approaches toward knowledge about the good life, including, for instance, independence and sociability as two prototypical examples of independent and interdependent orientations. Wisdom thus seems to represent a balance between values of relatedness and autonomy. "As for social interconnectedness and individual autonomy, top responses in each culture would exhibit the wisdom criterion of moderation and balance" (Baltes, 2004, p. 184).

In contrast, Hahn (1991) states that wisdom is only possible in large-scale societies. He argued that two aspects are relevant for his view:

- Factual versus relevance knowledge: Although each culture owns "factual knowledge" (p. 48) about facts and matters, only those cultures in which knowledge is becoming more and more abstract, and the amount of knowledge larger, develop "relevance-knowledge" (p. 48). Relevance-knowledge selects from existing databases the knowledge that is appropriate for a particular situation. In more "simple" cultures, knowledge is much more bound to a specific situation. As such, logical contradictions (e.g., between proverbs) would not catch anyone's eye, as these propositions were never contrasted. Wisdom thereby is related to relevance-knowledge.
- Wisdom as meta-knowledge (p. 52): Knowledge that is bound to situations and actions does not permit reflections about the handling of information.

Both arguments, however, are grounded in an independent worldview. The claim for consistency and logical coherence is undoubtedly part of an independent conception of competence, whereas situational adaptation and flexibility, as part of an interdependent conception of competence, does not follow the logic of consistency and coherence (Keller, in press; Kim & Markus, 2002). Similar arguments have been made with respect to the development of moral reasoning (Eckensberger & Zimba, 1996).

The researchers who carried out the only empirical study that found cultural differences in levels of wisdom are unwilling to interpret their findings, because they want to further investigate this delicate and complicated question (Takahashi & Overton, 2002). These authors analyzed Americans and Japanese from two age cohorts (middle-aged and older). Analytical as well as synthetic functions were addressed, which are thought to be prevalent among Western (analytical) or Eastern (synthetic) cultures. Significant effects were found for age and culture. The U.S. sample scored higher than the Japanese on all five wisdom tasks, including those of the synthetic mode.

The Role of Age for the Development of Wisdom

German philosopher Arthur Schopenhauer (1788–1860) wrote in his *"Aphorismen zur Lebensweisheit"* (Aphorisms of life wisdom):

> Man kann ferner, in der bis hierher betrachteten Hinsicht, das Leben mit einem gestickten Stoffe vergleichen, von welchem jeder, in der ersten Hälfte seiner Zeit, die rechte, in der zweiten aber die Kehrseite zu sehen bekäme: letztere ist nicht so schön, aber lehrreicher; weil sie den Zusammenhang der Fäden erkennen läßt. (Schopenhauer, 1987, p. 198)
>
> From the point of view we have been taking up until now, life may be compared to a piece of embroidery, of which, during the first half of his time, a man gets a sight of the right side, and during the second half, of the wrong. The wrong side is not so pretty as the right, but it is more instructive; it shows the way in which the threads have been worked together. (Schopenhauer, 2004)

Because life experiences are crucial to definitions of wisdom, wisdom is generally regarded as relating to the later stages of development (Baltes & Staudinger, 2000; Staudinger, 1996; Staudinger & Baltes, 1995). After all, wisdom is regarded as one of the very rare developmental goals of old age, which can be at least partly inferred from Erikson's stage model, that presumes "integrity versus despair" as the last stage of adult development. Successful aging thereby includes a broader vision of life as well as an advanced spirituality and relation to one's own death (Erikson, 1963). However, Erikson himself revised his view on wisdom and aging in his own old age. He said, "The demand to develop integrity and wisdom in old age seems to be somewhat unfair, especially when made by middle-aged theorists—as, indeed, we then were" (Erikson, 1984, p. 160). In spite of these not very promising theoretical presuppositions, a study assessed life planning, life management, and life review of German clinical psychologists, who were expected to have above-average experience with these topics and consequently perform significantly better than a control group. The old professionals (age range 50–82 years) were indeed found among the top performers more often than younger ones (26–48 years), or than individuals from the old (50–75 years) or young (28–49) control groups (Baltes & Staudinger, 1993). But neither did older psychologists on average perform better than younger ones (Baltes & Staudinger, 2000), nor did older participants in general reach higher values in wisdom tasks than younger participants (Staudinger & Baltes, 1995).

On the other hand, Takahashi and Overton (2002) demonstrated that older adults outperformed middle-aged individuals on four of their five wisdom-related tasks. Tasks included cognitive as well as reflective and emotional material (knowledge database, abstract reasoning, reflective understanding, and emotional empathy, but not emotional regulation; see, e.g., Neiss & Almeida, 2004, for the opposite view on emotional regulation). This was the case in an American as well as a Japanese sample.

Takahashi and Bordia (2000) analyzed laypersons' implicit theories of wisdom in two cultures assumed to be independent (American, Australian) and in two assumedly interdependent ones (Indian, Japanese). They found that "aged" was semantically more similar to "wise" in the interdependent cultures than in the independent ones, but that across cultures, "aged" was consistently the least preferred descriptors to describe the ideal self. The authors suggest that across cultures, age is perceived as an undesirable state connected more to losses and decline than to increased experience and wisdom; however, one could also argue that "aged" just could not compete with the other descriptors, because only very desirable adjectives were used.

An interesting mismatch between subjective theories and peer and self-reports with respect to the relation between age and wisdom was found in a U.S. sample (Orwoll & Perlmutter, 1990). Although 75% of the participants agreed that wisdom is related to age and tended to nominate older rather than younger people as wise, there were only small age differences between cohorts when they were asked to rate themselves on wisdom. Instead, the self-nominations decreased slightly past age 40. The authors interpreted this finding as the recognition of one's own limitations.

Also, in Sub-Saharan Africa the commonly held view is that old people in responsible positions are most likely to be wise due to their accumulated experiences. Lineage heads, title holders, village elders and kings, the diviners who tell the future and the past, and their modern successors (the leaders of the independent churches), are called wise (Sundermeier, 1991). Social positions as well as age are supposed to provide their holders with broader and deeper experiences than other people, because they get to know more people across a larger region.

Nevertheless, under certain circumstances, even children can be seen as wise. This is the case for the so-called stolen children of the Nso, who disappear unaccountably for a few days and reappear in unexpected places. When they are found again, they are different and, people say, they were stolen by God and brought back. Usually these children become traditional healers. Gautama Buddha declared himself a wise man at the age of 35, whereas for Confucians becoming wise is "a lifetime agenda" (Baltes, 2004).

Taken together, views on the role of age for the development of wisdom vary across cultures. However, although empirical evidence is only sketchy, age seems to be related to wisdom in performance tasks as well as in folk psychology cross-culturally. Evidence of wisdom at young ages seems to be more anecdotal and based on single cases.

Implicit Theories About Wisdom

It is striking that experts stress the integrative nature of wisdom, whereas people's implicit theories tend to follow the sociocultural orientations of their respective environments. It may be the case that people with a purportedly more independent sociocultural orientation have a more analytical conception of wisdom, whereas people with a supposedly more interdependent sociocultural orientation have a more integrative and intuitive conception of wisdom (Takahashi & Bordia, 2000; Takahashi & Overton, 2002). This contrast corresponds to differences in the perception of aging in general (Bacanli, Ahokas, & Best, 1994). Hispanics living in rural southern Colorado highlighted spiritual rather than cognitive aspects of wisdom, attitudes toward learning rather than possessing experience, and caring in interpersonal relationships rather than giving good advice (Valdez, 1994). Tibetan Buddhist monks' conceptions of wisdom include being able to distinguish good from evil, being efficient, being beyond suffering, having the ability to recognize Buddhist truths about reality (emptiness) and the place of the self in this reality (being nonself), honesty, humility, being compassionate to others, and treating all creatures as worthy and equal (Levitt, 1999).

Takahashi and Bordia (2000) analyzed first the semantic similarity of and second the preference for the adjective "wise" and six other wisdom-related descriptors in student samples of four cultures. These were persons in American and Australian (assumed to be independent) and Indian and Japanese (assumed to be interdependent) cultures. Western participants understood wisdom as most similar to "experienced" and "knowledgeable," and least similar to "discreet," whereas Easterners associated "wise" with "discreet," "aged," and "experienced." "Knowledgeable" and "wise" were the most and "aged" and "discreet" the least preferred adjectives in the West. In contrast, the Japanese favored "wise" and "discreet." Somewhat surprisingly, the Indian sample rated "knowledgeable" as the second most preferred self-descriptor, similar to the Western pattern. This finding may well be explained by the fact that these were liberal arts and business students, whereas all of the other samples consisted of psychology students. Business professors had previously been found to understand wisdom differently from professors of other sciences (Sternberg, 1985). Moreover, Indian middle-class society has been characterized as having a coexistence model, one that combines independence and interdependence (Sinha & Tripathi, 2003).

These findings led to the development of "a culturally inclusive developmental perspective" with respect to wisdom (Takahashi & Overton, 2002, p. 269). Wisdom is conceptualized as existing in two modes, the analytical and the synthetic. The analytic mode stresses knowledge databases and abstract reasoning and is dominant among Western cultures. The synthetic mode stresses reflective understanding, emotional empathy, and emotional regulation and is dominant among Eastern cultures. Both modes contain two poles of one dimension. The culturally inclusive perspective is thought to be located in the middle of this dimension and to consider both ends equally important.

Because differences in laypersons' conceptions of wisdom have been found across cohorts (Clayton & Birren, 1980; Orwoll & Perlmutter, 1990), gender (Orwoll & Perlmutter, 1990), and professions (Sternberg, 1985) within Western samples, it might be necessary to take intracultural variation into account. Using 100 behavioural attributes, Yang (2001) asked Taiwanese Chinese participants from different socioeconomic backgrounds to describe a wise person. Data were then factor-analyzed. Yang derived four factors that she labeled (1) competencies and knowledge, (2) benevolence and compassion, (3) openness and profundity, and (4) modesty and unobtrusiveness. Among this sample, most striking was the finding that "competencies and knowledge" were considered the most important features of a wise Taiwanese person. This seems to be a function of education: Graduates rated factors 1 and 3 higher than participants below the graduate level of education. In that the Taiwanese are not a homogeneous group with respect to their conceptualizations of wisdom, other cultures might be heterogeneous as well.

In sum, we may conclude that there is substantial cultural variation in implicit theories of wisdom. But how does this go along with Baltes's proposal of cultural invariance? The only answer can be that folk are just not wise enough to assess the true meaning of wisdom. The conception of a "culturally inclusive developmental perspective" (Takahashi & Overton, 2002, p. 269) on wisdom could be an approach that helps to clarify these issues.

Development and Attainability of Wisdom

The development and attainability of wisdom are also conceived of differently in different cultures. In so-called Western societies, seeking wisdom is considered as a part of people's private, even intimate life. "Although in Western cultures it is usually not considered appropriate to seek wisdom publicly or to claim that one has achieved it, we privately long for wisdom and admire it in others" (Baltes, 2004, p. 31). In contrast, in some cultures there is even some kind of education for wisdom, for example, for becoming a traditional healer. From childhood on, shamans often distinguish themselves from others by feeling a spiritual calling and by experiencing greater hardships, like being raised as an orphan, than others in their culture. After overcoming these hardships they become apprentices of the current village shaman for several years. The training usually involves knowledge about medicinal plants as well as learning how to address body, mind, and spirit at the same time (Singh, 1999).

Nikiema de Saaba, dean of traditional healers in Burkina Faso, described his education as follows:

> I have always been a healer. When I was a child, five years old, I heard voices in my sleep and when I was awake, telling me that the Almighty had called me to heal people. I knew, I could not resist the call. There was a well known healer in the village. I went to live with him in order to learn all I needed to know to be a good healer. . . . Well, I went with my mentor to the forest to learn the medicinal value and use of various herbs, leaves, roots, barks, grasses and objects like minerals, dead insects, bones, feathers, excreta of animals and insects, shells, eggs, and so on. My mentor also encouraged me to learn the causes, cures and preventions of diseases and other forms of suffering, such as barrenness, failure in undertakings, misfortunes, and poor crop yield in the field. I also learned how to use and combat magic witchcraft *and* sorcery. There are many things which I learned in the more than 15 years of preparation for the healing role which I play that are my secrets. . . . My grandfather was a renowned healer who was known throughout the country. I believe that I inherited my powers from him. (Vontress, 1999, p. 328ff).

Similar life courses of six Native American traditional women healers, which also include the discovery of their healing gifts and a time of apprenticeship, are outlined by Struthers (2003).

Differences also emerge with respect to the attainability of wisdom. With respect to their research findings, Baltes and Staudinger (1993) claimed that wise answers were very rare. East Asian religions often regard wisdom as an ideal state that can (almost) never be achieved by a human (Baltes, 2004; Gäng, 1991). The traditional African view, with its close relation between wisdom and social positions, seems to be more liberal.

IDENTITY AS THE PRODUCT OF LEARNING AND DEVELOPMENT

We agree with Pascual-Leone and Irwin (1998) that it is important to include the processes and structures of the self into the analysis of development and learning in adulthood. With this information in mind, new formulas of mental processing can be developed that take advantage of changes in learning mechanisms, self-monitoring, and motivational and affective resources. Adult learning is located at the interface of people's biography and the sociocultural milieu in which they live (Jarvis, 1992). This view locates adult learning and development in the context of everyday activities and practices.

The perspective on adult learning and development that we have proposed in this chapter can be regarded as a contribution to sociocultural theory with the major assumption that learning and development are rooted in social relations and are mediated by cultural tools and signs (Wertsch, 1991; Wertsch & Toma, 1995). We have tried to describe cultural conceptions of the self and the conceptions of competence that define different processes of learning and development.

To conclude, we wish to present the ideas of Erik Erikson (e.g., Erikson, 1959), who was among the first psychologists to consider culture as relevant for describing and evaluating human life and development. He conceptualized culture as both inside and outside the person (Greenfield & Keller, in press; Hoare, 2002). Culture is inside each person's representations and language, perception, and cognition. As well, it is external in shared meaning (Greenfield & Keller, in press) and in physical attributes of the individuals' environment, such as topography, which in turn influences the inside of the individual (Erikson, 1943).

Learning and development are processes that support the internalization of the external world. These processes begin with the ways that an ethos of cultural understanding is transmitted to an infant and how this ethos grows parallel to the child's development,

incorporating social perceptions. In dealing with such cultural variations, Erikson described a "prejudiced adult" (Hoare, 2002, p. 41) on one hand, and a "historically and culturally relative adult" on the other (Hoare, 2002, p. 145). The historically and culturally relative adult is a "highly sophisticated person, one who thinks at the metacognitive level of abstraction, is knowledgeable about history and cultural differences, and cares to be insightful about and open to other persons and ways of being in the world" (Hoare, 2002, p. 145). This does not mean that he or she is not prejudiced, but that such a person is aware of this fact. Thereby, the more one learns about other cultures and/or historical eras with differing norms and values, and thereby recognizes one's own "biases and behavioral mind-set" (Hoare, 2002, p. 41), the more likely is one's development into a highly desirable "historically and culturally relative adult." This may be the most important implication of this chapter, which follows not only from Erikson's work but also from what we know about different developmental pathways and from the integrative and culture-sensitive nature of wisdom.

ACKNOWLEDGMENTS We are indebted to Gunhild Hagestad for her most helpful comments on an earlier draft of this chapter and to Relindis Dzeaye Yovsi, who supported us tremendously with her indigenous knowledge of the Nso society and who is the author of the initiation portraits that are included in this chapter.

References

Achenbach, G. B. (1991). Lebenskunst. Sieben Annäherungen an ein vergessenes Wissen [Life art. Seven approaches to a forgotten knowledge]. In A. Assmann (Ed.), *Weisheit. Archäologie der literarischen Kommunikation III* [Wisdom. Archaeology of literary communication III] (pp. 231–238). Munich: Fink.

Aldwin, C. M., & Levenson, M. R. (2001). Stress, coping, and health at midlife: A developmental perspective. In M. E. Lachman (Ed.), *Handbook of midlife development* (pp. 571–598). New York: Wiley.

Arnett, J. J. (1998). Learning to stand alone: The contemporary American transition to adulthood in cultural and historical context. *Human Development, 41,* 295–315.

Arnett, J. J. (2000). Emerging adulthood. A theory of development from the late teens through the twenties. *American Psychologist, 55,* 469–480.

Arnett Jensen, L. (2003). Coming of age in a multicultural world: Globalization and adolescent cultural identity formation. *Applied Developmental Science*, 7, 189–196.

Bacanli, H., Ahokas, M., & Best, D. L. (1994). Stereotypes of old adults in Turkey and Finland. In A.-M. Bouvy, F. J. R. van de Vijver, P. Boski, & P. G. Schmitz (Eds.), *Journeys into cross-cultural psychology* (pp. 307–319). Lisse, Netherlands: Swets & Zeitlinger.

Bakan, D. (1966). *The duality of human existence: Isolation and communication in Western man*. Chicago: Rand McNally.

Baltes, P. B. (1987). Theoretical propositions of life-span developmental psychology: On the dynamics of growth and decline. *Developmental Psychology*, 23, 611–626.

Baltes, P. B. (2004). *Wisdom as orchestration of mind and virtue*. Manuscript in preparation.

Baltes, P. B., & Staudinger, U. M. (1993). The search for a psychology of wisdom. *Current Directions in Psychological Science*, 2, 75–80.

Baltes, P. B., & Staudinger, U. M. (2000). Wisdom: A metaheuristic (pragmatic) to orchestrate mind and virtue toward excellence. *American Psychologist*, 55, 122–136.

Bartholomew, K., & Horowitz, L. (1991). Attachment styles among young adults: A test of a four-category model. *Journal of Personality and Social Psychology*, 61, 226–244.

Bartlett, F. C. (1932). *Remembering*. London: Cambridge University Press.

Belenky, M. F., Clinchy, B. M., Goldberger, N. R., & Tarule, J. M. (1986). *Women's ways of knowing*. New York: Basic Books.

Bond, M. (1999). *Plenary address*. European Congress of Psychology, Rome, Italy.

Bornstein, M. H., Tamis-LeMonda, C. S., Pascual, L., Haynes, O. M., Painter, K. M., Galperin, C. Z., et al. (1996). Ideas about parenting in Argentina, France, and the United States. *International Journal of Behavioral Development*, 19, 347–367.

Brain, J. L., Blake, C. F., Bluebond-Langner, M., Chilungu, S. W., Coelho, V. P., Domotor, T., et al. (1977). Sex, incest, and death: Initiation rites reconsidered. *Current Anthropology*, 18(2), 191–198.

Bruner, J. (1993). Do we "acquire" culture or vice versa? *Behavioral and Brain Sciences*, 16, 515–516.

Burger, L. K., & Miller, P. J. (1999). Early talk about the past revisited: affect in working-class and middle-class children's co-narrations. *Journal of Child Language*, 26, 133–162.

Carraher, T. N., Carraher, D. W., & Schliemann, A. D. (1991). Mathematics in the streets and in schools. In P. Light & S. Shelden (Eds.), *Learning to think* (pp. 223–235): Florence, KY: Taylor & Frances/Routledge.

Carraher, T. N., Schliemann, A. D., & Carraher, D. W. (1988). Mathematical concepts in everyday life. *New Directions for Child Development*, 41, 71–87.

Clayton, V., & Birren, J. E. (1980). The development of wisdom across the life span: A reexamination of an ancient topic. In P. B. Baltes & O. R. Brim (Eds.), *Life span development and behavior* (pp. 193–235). New York: Academic Press.

Cole, M. (1988). Cross-cultural research in sociohistorical tradition. *Human Development*, 31, 137–157.

Colligan, J. (1983). Musical creativity and social rules in four cultures. *Creative Child and Adult Quarterly*, 8, 39–44.

Craig, G. J., & Baucum, D. (2002). *Human development* (9th ed.). Upper Saddle River, NJ: Pearson.

Cross, S. E., & Madson, L. (1997). Model of the self: Self-construals and gender. *Psychological Bulletin*, 122, 5–37.

Csikszentmihalyi, M., & Rathunde, K. (1990). The psychology of wisdom: An evolutionary interpretation. In R. J. Sternberg (Ed.), *Widsom: Its nature, origins, and development* (pp. 25–51). Cambridge: Cambridge University Press.

Dasen, P. R. (Ed.). (1977). *Piagetian psychology: Cross-cultural contributions*. New York: Gardner.

Diehl, M., Elnick, A. B., Bourbeau, L. S., & Labouvie-Vief, G. (1998). Adult attachment styles: Their relations to family content and personality. *Journal of Personality and Social Psychology*, 74, 1656–1669.

Diehl, M., Owen, S. K., & Youngblade, L. M. (2004). Agency and communion attributes in adults' spontaneous self-representation. *International Journal of Behavioral Development*, 28, 1–15.

Durkin, K. (1995). *Developmental social psychology: From infancy to old age*. Oxford: Blackwell.

Eckensberger, L. H., & Zimba, R. (1996). The development of moral judgment. In J. W. Berry, P. R. Dasen, & T. S. Saraswathi (Eds.), *Handbook of cross-cultural psychology, volume 2: Basic process and human development* (2nd ed., pp. 299–338). Boston: Allyn & Bacon.

Erikson, E. H. (1943). Observations on the Yurok: childhood and world image. *University of California Publications in American Archaeology and Ethnology*, 35, 257–301.

Erikson, E. H. (1959). *Identity and the life cycle*. New York: International Universities Press.

Erikson, E. H. (1963). *Childhood and society* (2nd ed.). New York: Norton.

Erikson, E. H. (1975). Caring. *Pediatrics*, 55, 661.

Erikson, E. H. (1984). Reflections on the last stage—and the first. *Psychoanalytic Study of the Child*, 39, 155–165.

Fijneman, Y. A., Willemsen, M. E., Poortinga, Y. H., Erelcin, F. G., Georgas, J., Hui, C. H., et al. (1996). Individualism-collectivism: an empirical study of conceptual issue. *Journal of Cross-Cultural Psychology*, 27, 381–402.

Fiske, A. P., Kitayama, S., Markus, H. R., & Nisbett, R. E. (1998) The cultural matrix of social psychology. In D. T. Gilbert, S. T. Fiske, & G. Lindzey (Eds.), *The handbook of social psychology* (4th ed., Vol. 4, pp. 915–981). Boston: McGraw-Hill.

Forrest, L., & Mikolaitis, N. (1986). Relational component of identity. *Career Development Quarterly*, 35, 76–88.

Gäng, P. (1991). Sich seiner selbst erinnern. Androgyne Weisheit im tantrischen Buddhismus [Remembering oneself. Androgynous wisdom in tantric buddhism]. In A. Assmann (Ed.), *Weisheit. Archäologie der literarischen Kommunikation III* [Wisdom. Archaeology of literary communication III] (pp. 289–304). Munich: Fink.

Gill, R., & Keats, D. M. (1980). Elements of intellectual competence: Judgments by Australian and Malay university students. *Journal of Cross-Cultural Psychology*, 11, 233–243.

Gilligan, C. (1982). *In a different voice: Psychological theory and women's development.* Cambridge, MA: Harvard University Press.

Granott, N. (1995). *The dynamics of problem solving: Rediscovery, variability, and the complexity of making sense.* Dallas: Micro Developmental Laboratory, University of Texas at Dallas.

Granott, N. (1998). We learn, therefore we develop: Learning versus development—or developing learning? In M. C. Smith & T. Pourchot (Eds.), *Adult learning and development. Perspectives from educational psychology* (pp. 15–34). Mahwah, NJ: Lawrence Erlbaum.

Greenfield, P. M. (1996). Culture as process: Empirical methods for cultural psychology. In J. W. Berry, Y. H. Poortinga, & J. Pandey (Eds.), *Handbook of cross-cultural psychology* (2nd ed., Vol. 1, pp. 301–346). Boston: Allyn & Bacon.

Greenfield, P. M., & Cocking, R. R. (Eds.). (1994). *Cross-cultural roots of minority child development.* Hillsdale, NJ: Lawrence Erlbaum.

Greenfield, P. M., & Keller, H. (in press). Cultural psychology. In J. W. Berry & H. C. Triandis (Eds.), *Encyclopedia of applied psychology.* San Diego, CA: Academic Press.

Greenfield, P. M., Keller, H., Fuligni, A., & Maynard, A. (2003). Cultural pathways through universal development. *Annual Review of Psychology*, 54, 461–490.

Greenfield, P. M., & Suzuki, L. (1998). Culture and human development: Implications for parenting, education, pediatrics, and mental health. In I. E. Sigel & K. A. Renninger (Eds.), *Handbook of child psychology. Vol. 4: Child psychology in practice* (5th ed., pp. 1059–1109). New York: Wiley.

Gutmann, D. (1994). *Reclaimed powers: Toward a new psychology of men and women in later life* (2nd ed.). Evanston, IL: Northwestern University Press.

Hagestad, G. O. (1990). Social perspectives on the life course. In R. H. Binstock & L. K. George (Eds.), *Handbook of aging and the social sciences* (3rd ed., pp. 151–168). New York: Academic Press.

Hagestad, G. O., &. Neugarten, B. L. (1985). Age and the life course. In R. H. Binstock & E. Shanas (Eds.), *Handbook of aging and the social sciences* (2nd ed., pp. 46–61). New York: Van Nostrand Reinhold.

Hahn, A. (1991). Zur Soziologie der Weisheit [The sociology of wisdom]. In A. Assmann (Ed.), *Weisheit. Archäologie der literarischen Kommunikation III* [Wisdom. Archaeology of literary communication III] (pp. 47–58). München: Fink.

Hannover, B. (2000). Self and culture. Effects on social information processing. In H. Metz-Goeckel, B. Hannover, & S. Leffelsend (Eds.), *Selbst, Motivation und Emotion* [Self, motivation and emotion] (pp. 107–117). Berlin: Logos.

Harkness, S., Super, C. M., & van Tijen, N. (2000). Individualism and the "Western mind" reconsidered: American and Dutch parents' ethnotheories of the child. In S. Harkness, C. Raeff, & C. M. Super (Eds.), *Variability in the social construction of the child: New directions for child and adolescent development* (pp. 23–39). San Francisco: Jossey-Bass.

Harris, R. J., Schoen, L. M., & Hensley, D. L. (1992). A cross-cultural study of story memory. *Journal of Cross-Cultural Psychology*, 23, 133–147.

Harris, R. J., Schoen, L. M., & Lee, D. J. (1986). Culture-based distortion in memory of stories. In J. L. Armagost (Ed.), *Proceedings of the 20th Mid-American Conference.* Manhattan: Kansas State University Press.

Harwood, R. L., Leyendecker, B., Carlson, V. J., Asencio, M., & Miller, A. M. (2002). Parenting among Latino families in the U.S. In M. H. Bornstein (Ed.), *Handbook of parenting, vol 4: Social conditions and applied parenting* (2nd ed., pp. 21–46). Mahwah, NJ: Lawrence Erlbaum.

Heckhausen, J. (1999). *Developmental regulation in adulthood: age-normative and sociostructural constraints as adaptive challenges.* Cambridge: Cambridge University Press.

Helgeson, V. S. (1994). Relation of agency and communion to well-being: Evidence and potential explanations. *Psychological Bulletin*, 116, 412–428.

Helgeson, V. S., & Fritz, H. L. (2000). The implications of unmitigated agency and unmitigated communion for domains of problem behavior. *Journal of Personality*, 68, 1031–1057.

Hoare, C. H. (2002). *Erikson on development in adulthood: New insights from the unpublished papers.* New York: Oxford University Press.

Hofstede, G. (1980). *Culture's consequences: International differences in work-related values.* London: Sage.

Jarvis, P. (1992). *Paradoxes of learning: On becoming an individual in society.* San Francisco: Jossey-Bass.

Joe, J. R. (1994). Revaluing native-American concepts of development and education. In P. M. Greenfield & R. R. Cocking (Eds.), *Cross-cultural roots of minority child development* (pp. 107–113). Hillsdale, NJ: Lawrence Erlbaum.

Kağitçibaşi, C. (1990). Family and socialization in cross-cultural perspective: A model of change. In J. J. Berman (Ed.), *Cross-cultural perspectives: Nebraska symposium on motivation 1989* (pp. 135–200). Lincoln: University of Nebraska Press.

Kağıtçıbaşi, C. (1996a). *Family and human development across countries: A view from the other side.* Hillsdale, NJ: Lawrence Erlbaum.

Kağıtçıbaşi, C. (1996b). The autonomous-relational self: A new synthesis. *European Psychologist, 1,* 180–186.

Kağıtçıbaşi, C. (2004). *Autonomy and relatedness in cultural context: Implications for family, parenting and human development.* Manuscript under review.

Kegan, R. (1982). *The evolving self. Problem and process in human development.* Cambridge, MA: Harvard University Press.

Kekes, J. (1983). Wisdom. *American Philosophical Quarterly, 20,* 277–286.

Keller, H. (2001). Lifespan development: Evolutionary perspectives. In N. J. Smelser & P. B. Baltes (Eds.-in-Chief), *International encyclopedia of the social and behavioral sciences* (Vol. 13, pp. 8840–8844). Oxford: Elsevier Science.

Keller, H. (2003). Socialization for competence: cultural models of infancy. *Human Development, 46,* 288–311.

Keller, H. (2004). *Further explorations of the "Western mind." Mothers' and grandmothers' parental ethnotheories in Los Angels, CA, and Berlin, Germany.* Manuscript in preparation.

Keller, H. (in press). Lehren und Lernen im Kulturvergleich [Teaching and learning across cultures]. In G. Trommsdorff & H.-J. Kornadt (Eds.), *Enzyklopädie der Psychologie, Band C/VII: Kulturvergleichende Psychologie* [Encyclopedia of psychology, Vol. C/VII: Cross-cultural psychology]. Göttingen: Hogrefe.

Keller, H., & Chasiotis, A. (1994). "All I really need to know I learned in kindergarten" or is "cultural learning" anthropo-, ethno-, or adultocentric? *Behavioral and Brain Sciences, 17,* 779–780.

Keller, H., & Eckensberger, L. H. (1998). Kultur und Entwicklung [Culture and development]. In H. Keller (Ed.), *Lehrbuch Entwicklungspsychologie* [Textbook of developmental psychology] (pp. 57–96). Bern: Huber.

Keller, H., & Greenfield, P. M. (2000). History and future of development in cross-cultural psychology. In C. Kağıtçıbaşi & Y. II. Poortinga (Eds.), Millennium Special Issue of the *Journal of Cross-Cultural Psychology, 31,* 52–62.

Keller, H., Poortinga, Y. H., & Schölmerich, A. (2002). Epilogue: Conceptions of ontogenetic development, integrating and demarcating perspectives. In H. Keller, Y. H. Poortinga, & A. Schölmerich (Eds.), *Between culture and biology* (pp. 384–402). Cambridge: Cambridge University Press.

Keller, H., Zach, U., & Abels, M. (2005). *The German family—Families in Germany.* In J. Roopnarine & U. Gielen (Eds.), *Families in global perspective* (pp. 242–258). Boston: Allyn & Bacon.

Kim, H. J. S., & Markus, H. R. (2002). Freedom of speech and freedom of silence: An analysis of talking as a cultural practice. In R. A. Shweder, M. Minow, & H. R. Markus (Eds.), *Engaging cultural differences: the multicultural challenge in liberal democracies* (pp. 432–452). New York: Russell Sage Foundation.

Kitayama, S. (2002). Culture and basic psychological processes—towards a system view of culture: comment on Oyerman et al. (2002). *Psychological Bulletin, 128,* 73–77.

Knowles, M. S. (1970). *The modern practice of adult education: Andragogy vs. pedagogy.* New York: Association Press.

Knowles, M. S. (1984). *Andragogy in action: Applying modern principles of adult learning.* San Francisco: Jossey-Bass.

Kohlberg, L. (1958). *The develoment of modes of moral thinking and choice in the years ten to sixteen.* Unpublished doctoral dissertation, University of Chicago, Chicago, IL.

Krawczak, R. F. (1999). The impact of timing and anticipation of life events on the physical and emotional well-being of elders. *Dissertation Abstracts International: Section B: The Sciences and Engeneering, 59*(10-B), 5579.

Kusserow, A. S. (1999). De-homogenizing American individualism: Socializing hard and soft individualism in Manhattan and Queens. *Ethos, 27,* 210–234.

Labouvie-Vief, G. (1994). *Psyche and Eros: Mind and gender the life count.* New York: Cambridge University Press.

Lesthaeghe, R. (1983). A century of demographic and cultural change in Western Europe: An exploration of underlying dimensions. *Population and Development Review, 9,* 411–437.

LeVine, R. A., Dixon, S., LeVine, S., Richman, A., Leiderman, P. H., Keefer, C. H., et al. (1994). *Child care and culture: Lessons from Africa.* New York: Cambridge University Press.

Levinson, D. J. (1986). A conception of adult development. *American Psychologist, 41,* 3–13.

Levitt, H. M. (1999). The development of wisdom: An analysis of Tibetan Buddhist experience. *Journal of Humanistic Psychology, 39,* 86–105.

Leyendecker, B. (2004). *Veränderungen von individualistischen und soziozentrischen Orientierungen über die Lebensspanne* [Changes from individualistic and sociocentric orientations over the life span]. Habilitation: Ruhr-Universität Bochum, Germany.

Leyendecker, B., Harwood, R. L., Lamb, M. E., & Schölmerich, A. (2002). Mothers' socialisation goals and evaluations of desirable and undesirable everyday situations in two diverse cultural groups. *International Journal of Behavioral Development, 26,* 248–258.

Li, J. (2001). Chinese conceptualization of learning. *Ethos, 29,* 111–137.

Li, J. (2002). Learning models in different cultures. *New Directions for Child and Development, 96,* 45–63.

Li, J., Yue, X.-D., & Yue, S. (2001). *Individual self and social self in learning among Chinese adolescents.* Paper presented at the Biennial meeting of the

Society for Research in Child Development, Minneapolis, MN.

Lin, A. W., & Budwig, N. (1994). Parental language and the child's self development: An examination of two American subcultural groups. In N. Mercer & C. Coll (Eds.), *Explorations in socio-cultural studies. Vol. 3: Teaching, learning, and interaction* (pp. 83–90). Madrid: Fundacion Infancia i Aprendizaje.

Lin, J., & Wang, Q. (2002). *I want to be like Carol. US and Chinese preschoolers talk about learning and achievement.* Paper presented at the 17th Biennial meeting of the ISSBD, Ottawa.

Markus, H. R., & Kitayama, S. (1991). Culture and the self. Implications for cognition, emotion and motivation. *Psychological Review, 98,* 224–253.

Mishra, R. C., & Singh, T. (1992). Memories of Asur children for locations and pairs of pictures. *Psychological Studies, 37,* 38–46.

Mundy-Castle, A. C., & Okonji, M. O. (1976). *Mother-infant interaction in Nigeria.* Paper presented at a meeting of the International Associations for Cross-Cultural Psychology, Tilburg, Netherlands.

Mzeka, P. N. (1996). *Rituals of initiation in the Western grassfields of Cameroon: The Nso case.* Reprinted from: *Rites of passage and incorporation in the West grassfields of Cameroon. Vol. 1: From birth to adolescence.* Bamenda, Cameroon: Kaberry Research Centre.

Neiss, M., & Almeida, D. M. (2004). Age differences in the heritability of mean and intraindividual variation of psychological distress. *Gerontology, 50,* 22–27.

Nelson, K. (2000). Memory and belief in development. In D. L. Schacter & E. Scarry (Eds.), *Memory, brain and belief* (pp. 259–289). Cambridge, MA: Harvard University Press.

Nelson, L. J., Badger, S., & Wu, B. (2004). The influence of culture in emerging adulthood: Perspectives of Chinese college students. *International Journal of Behavioral Development, 28,* 26–36.

Neugarten, B. L. (Ed.) (1968). *Middle age and aging.* Chicago: University of Chicago Press.

Nsamenang, A. B. (1992). *Human development in cultural context. A third world perspective.* Newbury Park, CA: Sage.

Nsamenang, A. B. (2002). Adolescence in Sub-Saharan Africa: An image constructed from Africa's triple inheritance. In B. B. Brown & R. W. Larson (Ed.), *World's youth: Adolescence in eight regions of the globe* (pp. 61–104). New York: Cambridge University Press.

Nsamenang, A. B. (2003). Conceptualizing human development and education in Sub-Saharan Africa at the interface of indigenous and exogenous influences. In T. S. Saraswathi (Ed.), *Cross-cultural perspectives in human development. Theory, research and applications* (pp. 213–235). New Delhi: Sage.

Nsamenang, A. B., & Lamb, M. E. (1994). Socialization of Nso children in the Bamenda grassfields of northwest Cameroon. In P. M. Greenfield & R. R. Cocking (Eds.), *Cross-cultural roots of minority child development* (pp. 133–146). Hillsdale, NJ: Lawrence Erlbaum.

Orwoll, L., & Perlmutter, M. (1990). The study of wise persons: Integrating a personality perspective. In R. J. Sternberg (Ed.), *Wisdom: Its nature, origins, and development* (pp. 160–177). Cambridge: Cambridge University Press.

Ottenberg, S. (1994). Initiations. In P. H. Bock (Ed.), *Handbook of psychological anthropology* (pp. 351–377). Westport, CT: Greenwood Press.

Oyserman, D., Coon, H. M., & Kemmelmeier, M. (2002). Rethinking individualism and collectivism: Evaluation of theoretical assumptions and meta-analyses. *Psychological Bulletin, 128,* 3–72.

Palacios, J., & Moreno, M. C. (1996). Parents' and adolescents' ideas on children: Origins and transmission of intracultural diversity. In S. Harkness & C. M. Super (Eds.), *Parents' cultural belief systems: Their origins, expressions, and consequences* (pp. 215–253). New York: Guilford Press.

Pascual-Leone, J. (1998). Abstraction, the will, the self, and modes of learning in adulthood. In M. C. Smith & T. Pourchot (Eds.), *Adult learning and development: Perspectives from educational psychology* (pp. 35–66). Hillsdale, NJ: Lawrence Erlbaum.

Pascual-Leone, J., & Irwin, R. R. (1994). Non-cognitive factors in high-road/low-road learning: I: The modes of abstraction in adulthood. *Journal of Adult Development, 1,* 73–89.

Pensions Policy Institute. (2003). *State pension models* (July 10). Retrieved June 28, 2004, from http://www.pensionspolicyinstitute.org.uk.

Perry, W. G. (1968). *Patterns of development in thought and values of students in a liberal arts college: A validation of a scheme.* Cambridge, MA: Bureau of Study: Counsel, Harvard University. (ERIC Document Reproduction Service No. ED 024315).

Piaget, J. (1952). *The origins of intelligence in children.* New York: Norton.

Reese, E., Haden, C. A., & Fivush, R. (1993). Mother-child conversations about the past: Relationships of style and memory over time. *Cognitive Development, 8,* 403–430.

Rice, F. P. (1990). *The adolescent: Development, relationships, and culture* (6th ed.). Boston, MA: Allyn & Bacon.

Rogoff, B. (2003). *The cultural nature of human development.* New York: Oxford University Press.

Rogoff, B., Paradise, R., Mejía Arauz, R., Correa-Chávez, M., & Angelillo, C. (2003). Firsthand learning through intent participation. *Annual Review of Psychology, 54,* 175–203.

Ross, B., & Millsom, C. (1970). Repeated memory of oral prose in Ghana and New York. *International Journal of Psychology, 5,* 173–181.

Rutter, M., & Rutter, M. (1992). *Developing minds. Challenge and continuity across the life span.* London: Penguin.

Saraswathi, T. S. (Ed.). (2003). *Cross-cultural perspectives in human development. Theory, research and applications.* New Delhi: Sage.

Schaie, K. W. (1979). Toward a stage theory of adult cognitive development. *Journal of Aging and Human Development*, 8, 129–138.

Schaie, K. W., & Willis, S. L. (2000). A stage theory model of adult cognitive development revisited. In R. L. Rubinstein & M. Moss (Ed.), *Many dimensions of aging* (pp. 175–193). New York: Springer.

Schlegel, A., & Barry, H. III (1991). *Adolescence.* New York: Maxwell Macmillan International.

Schopenhauer, A. (1987). *Die Welt als Wille und Vorstellung*, Band 1 [The world as will and imagination, Vol. 1]. Stuttgart: Reclam.

Schopenhauer, A. (2004). *Counsels and maxims: From the essays of Arthur Schopenhauer.* Retrieved April 30, 2004, from http://www.gutenberg.org

Schwartz, S. H. (1990). Individualism and collectivism: critique and proposed refinements. *Journal of Cross-Cultural Psychology*, 21, 139–157.

Seiffke-Krenke, I., & Stemmler, M. (2002). Factors contributing to gender differences in depressive symptoms: A test of three developmental modes. *Journal of Youth and Adolescence*, 31, 405–417.

Serpell, R. (1994). The cultural construction of intelligence. In W. J. Lonner & R. S. Malpass (Eds.), *Psychology and culture* (pp. 157–163). Boston: Allyn & Bacon.

Shweder, R. A., & Bourne, E. J. (1984). Does the concept of a person vary cross-culturally? In R. A. Shweder & R. A. LeVine (Eds.), *Culture theory: Essays on mind, self and emotion* (pp. 158–199). Cambridge: Cambridge University Press.

Silbereisen, R. K., & Kracke, B. (1993). Variations in maturational timing and adjustment in adolescence. In S. Jackson & H. Rodriguez-Tome (Eds.), *Adolescence and its social worlds* (pp. 67–94). Hillsdale, NJ: Lawrence Erlbaum.

Silbereisen, R. K., & Kracke, B. (1997). Self-reported maturational timing and adaptation in adolescence. In J. Schulenberg, J. L. Maggs, & K. Hurrelmann (Eds.), *Health risks and developmental transitions during adolescence* (pp. 85 109). New York: Cambridge University Press.

Sinha, D., & Tripathi, R. C. (2003). Individualism in a collectivist culture: A case of coexistence of opposites. In T. S. Saraswathi (Ed.), *Cross-cultural perspectives in human development. Theory, research and applications* (pp. 192–210). New Delhi: Sage.

Singh, A. N. (1999). Shamans, healing, and mental health. *Journal of Child and Family Studies*, 8, 131–134.

Statistisches Bundesamt (1997). *Alter, Studiendauer und Studienerfolg deutscher Hochschulabsolventen* [Age at graduation and duration and success of study of German university attendants]. Retrieved April 30, 2004, from http://www.destatis.de

Staudinger, U. M. (1996). Wisdom and the social-interactive foundation of the mind. In P. B. Baltes & U. M. Staudinger (Eds.), *Interactive minds: Life-span perspectives on the social foundation of cognition* (pp. 276–315). New York: Cambridge University Press.

Staudinger, U. M., & Baltes, P. B. (1995). Gedächtnis, Weisheit und Lebenserfahrung im Alter: Zur Ontogenese als Zusammenwirken von Biologie und Kultur [Memory, wisdom and life experience in old age: The ontogeny of the interplay between biology and culture]. In D. Dörner & E. v. d. Meer (Eds.), *Gedächtnis. Festschrift zum 65. Geburtstag von Friedhart Klix* [Memory. Festschrift for the 65th birthday of Friedhart Klix] (pp. 433–484). Göttingen: Hogrefe.

Steffensen, M. S., & Calker, L. (1982). Intercultural misunderstandings about health care: Recall of descriptions of illness and treatments. *Social Science and Medicine*, 16, 1949–1954.

Sternberg, R. J. (1985). Implicit theories of intelligence, creativity, and wisdom. *Journal of Personality and Social Psychology*, 49, 607–627.

Struthers, R. (2003). The artistry and ability of traditional women healers. *Health Care for Women International*, 24, 340–354.

Sundermeier, T. (1991). Der Mensch wird Mensch durch den Menschen. Weisheit in den afrikanischen Religionen [Human become humans through humans. Wisdom in the African religions]. In A. Assmann (Ed.), *Weisheit. Archäologie der literarischen Kommunikation III* [Wisdom. Archaeology of literary communication III] (pp. 117–129). München: Fink.

Takahashi, M., & Bordia, P. (2000). The concept of wisdom: A cross-cultural comparison. *International Journal of Psychology*, 35, 1–9.

Takahashi, M., & Overton, W. F. (2002). Wisdom: A culturally inclusive developmental perspective. *International Journal of Behavioral Development*, 26, 269–277.

Tessler, M., & Nelson, K. (1994). Making memories: The influence of joint encoding on later recall by young children. *Consiousness and Cognition*, 3, 307–326.

Thomae, H. (1970). *Handbuch der Psychologie. Vol. 3: Entwicklungspsychologie* [Handbook of psychology. Vol. 3: Developmental psychology] (2nd ed.). Göttingen: Hogrefe.

Thomae, H. (1988). *Das Individuum und seine Welt. Eine Persönlichkeitstheorie* [The individual and his/her world. A personality theory] (2nd ed.). Göttingen: Hogrefe.

Thomas, A. (Ed.). (2003). *Kulturvergleichende Psychologie* [Cross-cultural psychology] (2nd ed.). Göttingen: Hogrefe.

Tomasello, M. (2001). Cultural transmission. A view from chimpanzees and human infants. *Journal of Cross-Cultural Psychology*, 32, 135–146.

Tomasello, M., Kruger, A. C., & Ratner, H. H. (1993). Cultural learning. *Behavioral and Brain Sciences*, 16, 495–552.

Triandis, H. C. (1995). *Individualism and collectivism.* Boulder, Colo.: Westview.

Triandis, H. C., Bontempto, R., Betancourt, H., Bond, M., Leung, K., Brenes, A., et al. (1986). The measurement of etic aspects of individualism and collectivism across cultures. *Australian Journal of Psychology, 38,* 257–267.

Valdez, J. M. (1994). Wisdom: A Hispanic perspective. *Dissertation International Abstract, 54,* 6482-B.

Van Gennep, A. (1960). *The rites of passage,* Trans. M. B. Vizedom & G. L. Caffee, Intro. by S. T. Kimball. Chicago: University of Chicago Press.

Vontress, C. E. (1999). Interview with a traditional African healer. *Journal of Mental Health Counseling, 21,* 326–336.

Wang, Q. (2001). Cultural effects on adults' earliest childhood recollection and self description: Implications for the relation between memory and the self. *Journal of Personality and Social Psychology, 81,* 220–233.

Wang, Q., & Brockmeier, J. (2002). Autobiographical remembering as cultural practice: Understanding the interplay between memory, self and culture. *Culture and Psychology, 8,* 45–64.

Wertsch, J. (1991). *Voices of the mind: A sociocultural approach to mediated action.* Cambridge, MA: Harvard University Press.

Wertsch, J., & Toma, C. (1995). Discourse and learning in classroom: A sociocultural approach. In L. P. Steffe & J. Gale (Eds.), *Constructivism in education* (pp. 159–174). Hillsdale, NJ: Lawrence Erlbaum.

Westen, D. (1985). *Self and society.* Cambridge: Cambridge University Press.

Woike, B. A. (1994). The use of differentiation and integration processes: Empirical studies of "separate" and "connected" ways of thinking. *Journal of Personality and Social Psychology, 67,* 142-150.

Yang, S.-Y. (2001). Conceptions of wisdom among Taiwanese Chinese. *Journal of Cross-Cultural Psychology, 32,* 662–680.

Yu, A.-B. (1996). Ultimate life concerns, self, and Chinese achievement motivation. In M. H. Bond (Ed.), *The handbook of Chinese psychology* (pp. 227–246). Hong Kong: Oxford University Press.

Part VI

Adult Development and Learning, Measured and Applied

Chapter 19

The Meaning and Measurement of Conceptual Development in Adulthood

Theo L. Dawson-Tunik

Until recently, there was one basic approach to the study of conceptual development in adulthood. This approach, exemplified in the work of scholars like Kohlberg and his colleagues (Colby, Kohlberg, Gibbs, & Lieberman, 1983), Kitchener and King (1990), Armon (Armon & Dawson, 2002), and Perry (1970), involves collecting data from a more or less representative sample of individuals at more or less frequent intervals over the course of several years. Guided by cognitive developmental theory, their longitudinal results, and sometimes, philosophical categories, researchers construct stage definitions. Although these definitions are cast as descriptions of reasoning structures, they include descriptions of the conceptual content associated with each developmental level. Stage definitions, along with exemplars from the construction samples targeted in these studies, become the basis for scoring manuals, reifying the conceptual content associated with each stage.

Employing these methods, the study of conceptual development in a given domain effectively ends with the development of a scoring manual. In the Kohlbergian case, the conceptual content associated with moral stages is based on the reasoning of white males; in the Perry case it is based on the reasoning of Harvard undergraduates; in Armon's case it is based on the reasoning of a varied but small convenience sample; and in Kitchener and King's work it is based primarily on the reasoning of college students. The scoring manuals associated with these systems all involve, to a greater or lesser extent, matching performances with exemplars taken from the original studies. One consequence is that the stage sequences described by these scholars are vulnerable to accusations of cultural bias (Gilligan, 1977). Although their contributions to cognitive developmental theory have been enormous, the methods of these scholars result in an incomplete account of conceptual development, in that, given the small samples on which their scoring systems are based, they necessarily fail to distinguish adequately between *what* is known and *how* it is known.

Reacting to this problem, many scholars have abandoned the cognitive developmental approach altogether, moving toward narrative (Tappan, 1990) or ethnographic (Shweder, 1996) descriptions of domain knowledge. Unfortunately, in this work, either age or educational level generally stands in as a proxy for development. This may be defensible in research on childhood development, but the relationship between age and developmental level breaks down completely in late adolescence, and the relationship between educational attainment and cognitive development becomes considerably less deterministic after high school.

Domain-based developmental stage systems introduce several additional problems: (1) there are no agreed on criteria for assessing how well these scoring systems function as measures of developmental stage, (2) their developers do not always agree about what kind of behaviors are evidence of the attainment of any given stage, and (3) it is not clear how the developmental levels in one system are related to the levels in the other systems, making it difficult to conduct cross-domain comparisons.

My response has been to design a methodological approach called *developmental maieutics*,[1] a method for examining conceptual development that separates the measurement of developmental level from the assessment of conceptual content, thus making it possible to pose questions about their interrelations. This chapter surveys the literature on this method, examining its validity and describing how it has been employed in a range of knowledge domains. I begin with a brief discussion of the relationship between development and learning, which is followed by a discussion of the issue of measurement, which is of central importance in the work described here. I then describe the hierarchical complexity construct and examine the validity and reliability of the hierarchical complexity scoring system. Finally, I discuss the relationship between complexity level and the meanings we construct, and discuss how what we have learned about this relationship is being applied in educational contexts.

DEVELOPMENT AND LEARNING

The focus of this volume is on the relation between adult development and learning. Heretofore my work has not explicitly addressed this relation but the independent assessment of the structure of reasoning performances and their conceptual content that is inherent to the research methodology described here offers a perspective on this issue.

In the cognitive-developmental literature, *learning* often refers to processes involved in the acquisition of domain content or skills, whereas *development* refers to progressive changes in the form of thought or other behavior. Some researchers argue that learning and development can involve different processes (Feldman, 1995; Sinnott, 1994),[2] whereas others argue that they are intertwined, and make the distinction primarily for heuristic or pragmatic reasons (Fischer & Granott, 1995; Smith, 1998). The work presented here falls into the second category. The independent analysis of hierarchical complexity and conceptual content that distinguishes developmental maieutics is conducted to highlight the complex interrelation of conceptual content (in part, what has been learned) and hierarchical complexity (structure). Research results generated with this method overwhelmingly confirm the interdependence of these constructs and their contributions to development. For this reason, when my colleagues and I employ the word *development*, we refer to both learning (knowledge acquisition) and structuring. Simply put, learning is viewed as the component of development that involves interaction with the external environment, and structuring refers to the way that knowledge is organized by the individual.

Developmental progress is profoundly dependent on knowledge acquisition (or learning). First, as will become clear, movement from one developmental level to the next (within a given knowledge domain) is highly unlikely until the attainment of a high level of conceptual differentiation at the developmental level at which an individual typically functions (Dawson & Wilson, 2004). Conversely, individuals appear to be unable to learn certain concepts until appropriate structures are apparent in performance. For example, my colleagues and I found that students in a grade nine physical science program did not, following instruction, demonstrate any understanding of the concepts of kinetic and potential energy unless prior to instruction their constructions of the energy concept demonstrated a particular level of abstraction (Dawson, 2003c).[3] We are not the first researchers to make observations of this kind (Fischer & Bidell, 1998; Inhelder, Bovet, & Sinclair, 1967; Walker & Taylor, 1991).

Second, the development of an adequate range of conceptions at a given developmental level appears to be a prerequisite for "normal" development to the subsequent level. For example, Fischer and his colleagues (Fischer & Ayoub, 1994; Fischer et al., 1997) have shown that a failure to develop appropriate concepts along one or more conceptual strands (such as conceptions of a *good self*), rather than stalling development, alter the outcome of development by producing distorted conceptions at higher levels. These distorted conceptions can interfere with optimal functioning. Findings like these highlight the interrelation of learning and structuring, making it clear that they are both essential components of cognitive development. One educational implication is that programs that focus primarily on promoting structural development without adequate attention to teaching content knowledge and skills may ultimately impoverish development by producing inadequate conceptions at the next level, whereas programs that focus primarily on teaching content knowledge and skills may slow developmental progress by failing to provide adequate opportunities for restructuring.

The complex interrelation of learning and structuring makes it impossible to draw a clear line between these two aspects of the developmental process. The conceptual content of a new developmental level is, at least in part, the result of restructuring the conceptual content of the previous level. On the other hand, new knowledge is often obtained through interactions with the external environment in a process that involves both learning and structuring. From a Piagetian (1985) perspective, new knowledge is either *assimilated* to existing structures or *accommodated* through restructuring. In both processes, some kind of structuring takes place. This means that the conceptual content of any performance is the product of both acquisition (learning) and structuring.

MEASUREMENT

It can be argued that most progress in science proceeds from hypothesis to measurement to hypothesis. Consequently, without the development, calibration, and improvement of measures, scientific progress is likely to stall. The story of how measurement permits rapid scientific advance can be illustrated through any number of examples. The effect of the measurement of temperature on understanding of the chemical properties of lead provides one such example. The tale begins with an assortment of semi-mythical early scientists, who all initially agreed that lead only melts when it is very hot—much hotter than the temperature at which ice melts, and quite a bit cooler than the temperature at which iron melts. These observations, made repeatedly, resulted in the related hypotheses that *temperature* can be thought of as a unidimensional scale and that lead melts at a particular temperature. However, before it was possible to test these hypotheses, it was necessary to develop a standard for measuring temperature. This was not an easy task. Partly because early temperature measuring devices were poorly calibrated, and partly because different temperature-measuring devices employed different scales, the temperature at which lead melted seemed to vary from device to device and context to context. Scientists divided into a number of camps. One group, using a new thermometer, argued that lead melts at a lower temperature than originally thought by the group who developed the first thermometer. Another group argued that there are multiple pathways toward melting, which explained why the melting seemed to occur at different temperatures. The third and final group argued that a single variable, temperature, could not be abstracted from particular contexts, because lead appeared to melt at different temperatures in different contexts.

Only when a measure of temperature had been adequately developed and widely accepted did it become possible to observe that lead consistently melts at about 327°C. Armed with this knowledge, scientists asked what it is about lead that causes it to melt at this particular temperature. They then developed hypotheses about the factors contributing to this phenomenon, observing that changes in altitude or air pressure seemed to result in small differences in the melting temperature of lead. So context did seem to play a role. To observe these differences more accurately, the measurement of temperature was refined further. The resulting observations provided information that ultimately contributed to an understanding of lead's molecular structure.

Although parts of this story are fictive, it is true that the concept of temperature developed over time, its measurement has undergone considerable development (and continues to be developed), and its measurement has greatly contributed to the understanding of the properties of lead. However, the value of the thermometer, as we all know, extends far beyond this particular use. The thermometer is a measure of temperature *in general*, meaning that it can be employed to measure temperature in an almost limitless range of substances and contexts. This generality is one of the hallmarks of measurement.

Good measurement requires (1) the identification of a unidimensional, content and context-independent trait, property, or quality (temperature, length, time); (2) a system for assessing amounts or levels of the trait, property, or quality in interval units; (3) determinations of the reliability and validity of the assessments; and finally (4) the calibration of a measure. A good thermometer has all of the qualities of a good measure. It is a well-calibrated instrument that can be employed to measure accurately and reliably a general, unidimensional trait across a wide range of contexts.

What if cognitive scientists had access to an accurate, valid, and reliable general measure of cognitive development, one that spanned the developmental continuum from birth through adulthood? What might be some of the implications for cognitive research and education?

First, such a metric could be employed to investigate conceptual development in any knowledge domain. Once reasoning performances were assigned to their place on the developmental dimension, they could be subjected to a variety of content analyses. Matrices of conceptual content by developmental level would likely reveal patterns of conceptual change that are very difficult to expose employing conventional methods. Although individual growth can only be studied longitudinally (Singer & Willett, 2003), a developmental metric would make it possible to meaningfully examine interindividual developmental trends in cross-sectional data, putting an end to the questionable practice of using age as a proxy for development (Dawson-Tunik, Commons, Wilson, & Fischer, 2005).

Second, a developmental metric would also help eliminate the effects of sample bias in accounts of conceptual development. Conventional accounts of conceptual development are generally constructed by examining the behavior of individuals in small longitudinal samples. These accounts then form the basis for developmental assessment systems that often confound developmental level and conceptual content, such that *particular* concepts come to be overly identified with a given developmental level (Dawson,

2004; Dawson & Gabrielian, 2003; Dawson, Xie, & Wilson, 2003). Because a developmental metric would allow us to specify an individual's place on the developmental continuum without reference to the particular conceptual content of his or her reasoning performance, we would be able to examine the empirical relation between particular conceptual content and a given developmental level, making it possible to interpret that relation as part of an independent analysis.

Third, a developmental metric could be employed to describe conceptual development across the entire developmental continuum, producing seamless accounts of development that could be employed to inform our understanding of developmental processes as well as curriculum design, instruction, and assessment. Although they have contributed importantly to our understanding of conceptual development in science, current accounts of conceptual development in the sciences are generally piecemeal, either because the research targets a particular age group or because the developmental model employed—such as the novice/expert model—dictates the comparison of two extreme groups. Attempts to tie together isolated results are complicated by the lack of a strong and coherent developmental theory. An accurate and reliable developmental metric would lend much greater specificity to efforts of this kind.

Fourth, a domain-general measure of development would make it possible to meaningfully compare developmental progress across knowledge domains. It would be possible to create a developmental report card like that shown in figure 19.1, in which Lucile's developmental progress in multiple subjects is traced over time. Rather than employing age-norms or comparisons of Lucile with other managers in her department, this report card charts her progress with respect to an external criterion and her own developmental history. Further elaborations to such a report card could include developmental zones, indicating the range of performance expected for promotion to a higher management level. As research data, report cards of this kind could provide valuable insights into developmental processes while simultaneously providing information about the strengths and weaknesses of employees, students, teachers, or programs. Employed widely, such report cards could provide meaningful, consistent information about employees' and students' intellectual

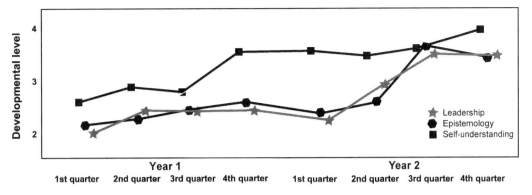

FIGURE 19.1 Lucile's developmental progress in three knowledge domains.

development for employers, parents, teachers, and college entrance committees.

Fifth, an accurate developmental metric could be employed longitudinally to compare the developmental trajectories and pathways of individuals. Accounting for the developmental dimension would reduce the danger of conflating developmental and other effects. For example, much cross-cultural research employs age or grade as a proxy for development. When differences in conceptions are found, these are often attributed to cultural differences. This practice is highly questionable, because although age and developmental level are correlated, they are far from an identity, particularly in adulthood (Armon & Dawson, 1997; Dawson-Tunik et al., 2005; Fischer & Bidell, 1998).

Sixth, an accurate content-independent developmental metric could be employed to link results from existing research, providing a more coherent picture of conceptual development. Such a metric could act as a single developmental dimension along which existing research findings could be arranged and reassessed.

Seventh, an accurate and reliable content-independent developmental metric could theoretically be employed to inform curriculum development. The link between students' cognitive developmental level and the likelihood that they will profit from instruction is already well established (Case & Okamoto, 1996; Cavallo, 1996; Germann, 1994; Lawson, Alkhoury, Benford, Clark, & Falconer, 2000; Lawson & Renner, 1975; Lawson & Thompson, 1988; Lawson & Weser, 1990; Renner & Marek, 1990; Shayer & Adey, 1993). By employing a developmental metric to study conceptual development, we would be able

to specify the relation between cognitive development and conceptual learning in a particular content domain. This could provide support for a cognitive developmental pedagogy in the form of concrete knowledge about the ways that particular concepts develop (typically, idiosyncratically, and optimally).

Finally, as suggested in the fourth point, a developmental metric could be employed in assessment and evaluation. Research, assessment, evaluation, and curricula could be coordinated around a single developmental agenda as suggested by Wilson and Sloane (2000). The discussion of figure 19.1 above illustrates one way a developmental metric could be employed in the workplace. Another possibility that suggests itself is in item development for standardized assessments. Detailed knowledge of the course of conceptual development within a given domain would theoretically permit the development of high-quality distractors based on students' actual conceptions (Amir, Frankl, & Tamir, 1987). Still another possibility is the development of practical scoring rubrics for educators, in which any given level would represent the same developmental attainment, regardless of knowledge domain.

THE CURRENT STATE OF DEVELOPMENTAL ASSESSMENT

In developmental psychology, although we agree that development occurs, we have not yet agreed on a general developmental "trait." In other words, we do not yet agree about what we are trying to measure (requirement 1). Needless to say, this means that we do not yet have a developmental measure. Or does it? In this chapter, I argue that several researchers over the past century have identified the same latent, general, developmental dimension and that it is now within our capabilities to develop a technology that can be employed to take measurements along that dimension. I further argue that this measure has the potential to transform life span developmental science, making it possible for us to produce accurate, reliable, and practical developmental assessments in any knowledge domain; deepen our understanding of developmental processes; develop rich descriptions of the many pathways of conceptual development; understand the impact of context on development; meaningfully compare developmental progress across domains of knowledge; and design better learning environments.

Before I begin, I want to address one of the roadblocks to the acceptance of a general developmental measure. This is the persistent notion that complex psychological phenomena cannot adequately be described with any method that involves isolating and measuring abstract dimensions of performance. Much like the contextualists in the lead allegory, proponents of this view reject the idea that any useful abstract, general dimensions can be identified and employed in developmental science. They perceive developmental processes as highly complex and fundamentally tied to particular knowledge domains or contexts. Fortunately, we now have many examples of abstract measures that are employed to aid in the description and prediction of even the most complex phenomena. One of the best modern examples is the description and prediction of weather patterns. Imagine the state of weather prediction if contextualism had prevailed in meteorology! In contradistinction to the contextualist position, I argue that it is impossible to adequately describe complex phenomena, including the role of context in their development, without identifying, isolating, and measuring abstract, general dimensions.

In the following sections I describe the developmental dimension of *hierarchical complexity*, address the validity and reliability of a measure of hierarchical complexity as a developmental ruler, and show how this ruler has recently been employed to describe adult conceptual development in the moral, evaluative, and epistemological domains. I then discuss methods my colleagues and I are currently developing to examine individual differences in conceptual development and suggest connections between what

we are learning about adult conceptual development and the design of educational interventions intended to promote development and learning.

HIERARCHICAL COMPLEXITY

Most cognitive-developmental researchers agree that development across knowledge domains does not necessarily proceed at the same rate (Fischer & Bidell, 1998; Lourenco & Machado, 1996). However, there is still considerable disagreement about whether development across domains can be characterized in terms of a single, generalized process. Domain theorists argue that entirely different processes apply in different knowledge domains. Others, although they acknowledge that unique structures and processes are associated with particular domains, also argue that a single general developmental process applies across domains. Piaget called this process *reflective (or reflecting) abstraction*, through which the actions of one developmental level become the subject of the actions of the subsequent level. The product of reflective abstraction is *hierarchical integration*. In conceptual development, hierarchical integration is reflected in the concepts constructed at a new level by coordinating (or integrating) the conceptual elements of the prior level. These new concepts are said to be qualitatively different from the concepts of the previous level, in that they integrate earlier knowledge into a new form of knowledge. For example, notions of *play* and *learning* constructed at one level are integrated into a notion of *learning as play* at the next level. This new concept cannot be reduced to the original *play* and *learning* elements, because even their earlier meanings are transformed when they are integrated into the learning as play concept. This hierarchical integration is observable in performance in the form of *hierarchical complexity*.

The general developmental model employed here has been strongly influenced by Piaget's stage model, Fischer's (1980) skill theory, and Commons's general stage model (Commons, Richards, with Ruf, Armstrong-Roche, & Bretzius, 1984; Commons, Trudeau, Stein, Richards, & Krause, 1998). In fact, the orders of hierarchical complexity (complexity levels) described here are equivalent to Fischer's 13 skill levels and Commons's first 13 stages. They are numbered from 0 to 12 and named as follows: (0) single reflexive actions, (1) reflexive mappings, (2) reflexive systems, (3) single sensorimotor schemes, (4) sensori-motor mappings, (5) sensorimotor systems, (6) single representations, (7) representational mappings, (8) representational systems, (9) single abstractions, (10) abstract mappings, (11) abstract systems, and (12) single principles. (Definitions are provided shortly.)

Not only are there definitional correspondences between analogous developmental levels described by Commons (Commons et al., 1984b, 1998) and Fischer (1980), there is empirical evidence of correspondences between levels assessed with the scoring system based on these sequences (the hierarchical complexity scoring system) (Dawson, 2003b) and four domain-based systems.[4] These last include Kitchener and King's (Dawson, 2002b; Kitchener, Lynch, Fischer, & Wood, 1993) stages of reflective judgment, Armon's good life stages (Dawson, 2002a), Perry's epistemological positions (Dawson, in press,) and Kohlberg's moral stages (Dawson, 2003d; Dawson & Gabrielian, 2003).

Scoring for Hierarchical Complexity

The scoring procedures employed with the hierarchical complexity scoring system are partially derived from Commons's (Commons et al., 1995) and Rose and Fischer's (1989) assessment systems. This scoring system, like its predecessors, is designed to make it possible to assess the hierarchical complexity of a performance without reference to its *particular* conceptual content. Rather than making the claim that a person occupies a complexity level because he or she has, for example, elaborated a particular conception of justice, the hierarchical complexity scoring system permits us to identify performances at a particular complexity level and then to ask (empirically) what the range of justice conceptions are at that complexity level. Thus, it avoids much of the circularity of many stage scoring systems, which define stages in terms of particular conceptual content and domain-specific structures like social perspective taking (Brainerd, 1993).

It is possible to score the hierarchical complexity of text performances because hierarchical complexity is reflected in two aspects of performance that can be abstracted from particular conceptual content. These are (1) *hierarchical order of abstraction* and (2) the logical organization of arguments. Hierarchical order of abstraction is observable in texts because new concepts are formed at each complexity level as the

operations of the previous complexity level are "summarized" into single constructs. Halford (1999) suggested that this summarizing or "chunking" makes advanced forms of thought possible by reducing the number of elements that must be simultaneously coordinated, freeing up processing space and making it possible to produce an argument or conceptualization at a higher complexity level. Interestingly, at the single reflexive actions, single sensorimotor schemes, single representations, single abstractions, and single principles complexity levels, the new concepts not only coordinate or modify constructions from the previous complexity level but are qualitatively distinct conceptual forms—reflexes, schemes, representations, abstractions, and principles, respectively (Fischer, 1980; Fischer & Bidell, 1998). The appearance of each of these conceptual forms ushers in three repeating logical forms—single elements, mappings or relations, and systems. Because these three logical forms are repeated several times throughout the course of development, it is only by pairing a logical form with a hierarchical order of abstraction that a rater can make an accurate assessment of the complexity level of a performance. For example, the statement, "In a good education, you get to have recess so you can play with your friends," is structurally identical to the statement, "In a good education, you get to socialize so you can learn how to relate to other people." Both are mappings. The first sentence, because its conceptual elements are representations, is a representational mapping. The second sentence, because its conceptual elements are abstractions, is an abstract mapping. Without the distinction between representations and abstractions it would be difficult to score these texts accurately. Other researchers have observed and described similar conceptual forms and repeating logical structures (Case, Okamoto, Henderson, & McKeough, 1993; Fischer & Bidell, 1998; Overton, Ward, Noveck, & Black, 1987; Piaget & Garcia, 1989).

Table 19.1 presents all 13 complexity levels, along with short descriptions of their logical structure and hierarchical order of abstraction (conceptual structure). Note that logical and conceptual structures are definitionally identical. I make a distinction between the two types of structure for heuristic and pragmatic reasons. When scoring texts, hierarchical order of abstraction refers primarily to the structure of the elements of arguments, which often must be inferred from their meaning in context, whereas logical

TABLE 19.1. Orders of Hierarchical Complexity

Complexity Order Name	Logical Structure	Hierarchical Order of Abstraction (Conceptual Structure)
Single reflexive actions	Single reflexes	1st-order reflexes
Reflexive mappings	Coordinates one aspect of two or more reflexes	2nd-order reflexes, which coordinate 1st-order reflexes
Reflexive systems	Coordinates multiple aspects of reflexes	3rd-order reflexes, which coordinate 2nd-order reflexes
Single sensorimotor schemes	Abstracts single sensorimotor schemes from multiple reflexive systems	1st-order sensorimotor schemes, which coordinate 3rd-order reflexes
Sensorimotor mappings	Coordinates one aspect of two or more sensorimotor schemes	2nd-order sensorimotor schemes, which coordinate 1st-order sensorimotor schemes
Sensorimotor systems	Coordinates multiple aspects of sensorimotor schemes	3rd-order sensorimotor schemes, which coordinate 2nd-order sensorimotor schemes
Single representations	Abstracts single representations from multiple sensorimotor schemes, often identifies one aspect of a single representation	1st-order representations, which coordinate 3rd-order sensorimotor schemes
Representational mappings	Coordinates one aspect of two or more representations	2nd-order representations, which coordinate 1st-order representations
Representational systems	Coordinates multiple aspects of representations	3rd-order representations, which coordinate 2nd-order representations
Single abstractions	Abstracts single abstractions from multiple representational systems, often identifies one aspect of a single abstraction	1st-order abstractions, which coordinate 3rd-order representations
Abstract mappings	Coordinates one aspect of two or more abstractions	2nd-order abstractions, which coordinate 1st-order abstractions
Abstract systems	Coordinates multiple aspects of abstractions	3rd-order abstractions, which coordinate 2nd-order abstractions
Single principles/axioms	Abstracts single principles from multiple abstract systems, often identifies one aspect of a single principle	1st-order principles, which coordinate 3rd-order abstractions

structure refers to the explicit way these elements are coordinated in a given text. Examples of how we work with these two constructs are offered next.

Complexity Levels Defined

Only the four complexity levels (single abstractions to single principles) commonly identified in adult performances are included in the following definitions. All of the examples provided in these definitions are from Dawson and Gabrielian's (2003) analysis of the conceptions of authority and contract associated with complexity levels in a sample of 747 moral judgment interviews scored with the hierarchical complexity scoring system.

At the single abstractions level (abbreviated SA in tables and figures), the new concepts are referred to as first-order abstractions. These coordinate third-order representations, which are equivalent to representational systems (the constructions of the previous complexity level). For example, the concept of trustworthiness, articulated for the first time at the single abstractions level, defines those qualities that make a person trustworthy rather than describing situations in which trust is felt or not felt. It is composed of qualities that produce trust, such as telling the truth, keeping secrets, and keeping promises. "It's always nice . . . to be trustworthy. Because then, if [someone has] a secret, they can come and talk to you." Concepts like kindness, keeping your word, respect, and

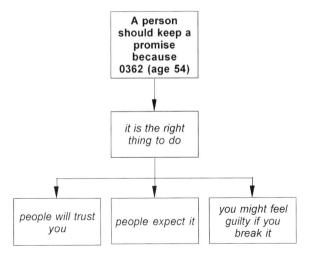

FIGURE 19.2. Conception of promise, single abstractions order.

guilt are also rare before the single abstractions level. "If you don't do something you promise, you'll feel really guilty." The most complex logical structure of this complexity level often identifies one aspect of a single abstraction, as in "Making a promise is giving your word" in which giving one's word is an "aspect" of a promise.

Figure 19.2 portrays a visual representation, in the form of a concept map, of a 54-year-old[5] respondent's argument about why promises should be kept. The respondent argues that a person should keep a promise because keeping promises is "the right thing to do." When probed, the respondent comes up with three separate (uncoordinated) reasons for keeping promises, because people expect promises to be kept, because "people will trust you" if you keep a promise, and because "you might feel guilty if you break a promise." All three of these reasons for keeping promises are considered to be first-order abstractions, because they extract general abstract notions by coordinating concepts that appear for the first time at the representational systems level (Dawson & Gabrielian, 2003). Keeping promises will create trust, *in general*; people, *in general*, have expectations when promises are made; and breaking promises can produce negative emotional consequences, *in general*, for the promise breaker. It is important to keep in mind that the particular concepts expressed by a respondent are important only to the extent that they embody a particular hierarchical order of abstraction. A rater must "look through" the meaning of a particular

conceptual element to abstract its hierarchical order of abstraction.

At the abstract mappings level (abbreviated AM in tables and figures), the new concepts are referred to as second-order abstractions. These coordinate or modify abstractions. For example, the second-order abstraction *basis* can be employed to coordinate the elements essential to a good relationship. "To me, [trust and respect are] the basis of a relationship, and without them you really don't have one." Because they are usually employed to coordinate abstractions, concepts like coming to an agreement, making a commitment, building trust, and compromise also are rare before the abstract mappings level. "I think [Joe and his father] could come to an agreement or compromise that they are both comfortable with." The most complex logical structure of this complexity level coordinates one aspect of two or more abstractions, as in "Joe has a right to go to camp because his father said he could go if he saved up the money, and Joe lived up to his commitment." Here, Joe's fulfillment of his father's conditions determines whether Joe has a right or does not have a right to go to camp.

Figure 19.3 provides a map of the performance of a 58-year-old male who provides three reasons for keeping promises. There are two mappings in this performance. The first is the assertion that "broken promises can harm relationships because they cause pain and reduce trust." This mapping coordinates two abstract consequences of promise breaking into the general notion that broken promises do harm to relationships. The second is the assertion that keeping promises makes it possible for people to "depend on one another." This mapping coordinates the perspectives of at least two individuals to form the notion that keeping promises produces mutual benefits. Note how this idea builds on the single abstractions notion that people will trust you if you keep promises.

At the abstract systems level (abbreviated AS in tables and figures), the new concepts are referred to as third-order abstractions. These coordinate elements of abstract systems. For example, the notion of personal integrity is rare before the abstract systems level, because it usually coordinates multiple abstract conceptions such as fairness, trustworthiness, honesty, preservation of the golden rule, and so on, which are understood as interrelated aspects of the self. "[You should keep your word] for your own integrity. For your own self-worth, really. Just to always be the kind of person that you would want to be dealing with." Because they usually coordinate elements of abstract systems, concepts like verbal contract, moral commitment, functional, development, social structure, and foundation are also uncommon before the abstract systems level. "A promise is the verbal contract, the moral commitment that the father made to his son. It is the only way for the child to . . . develop his moral thinking—from watching his parent's moral attitude."

The most complex logical structure of this complexity level coordinates multiple aspects of two or more abstractions. "Following through with his commitment and actually experiencing camp combine to promote Joe's growth and development, not just physically but psychologically, emotionally, and spiritually." Here multiple facets of Joe's personal development are promoted when he both keeps his commitment and accomplishes his goal.

Figure 19.4 provides a map of the performance of a 51-year-old female. The respondent describes a system in which promise keeping is both obligatory and sometimes impossible, "due to unforeseen circumstances." The reason for keeping promises is that one must stand by one's commitments. Doing so not only preserves one's personal integrity but also builds a sense of trust, "which keeps society functioning." The notion of standing by one's commitments, the idea that doing so preserves one's integrity, the argument that the sense of trust built through promise keeping keeps society functioning, and the notion of unforeseen circumstances are all examples of second-order abstractions. Note how the notion that the trust built from promise keeping keeps society functioning (even in the presence of the effects of unforeseen circumstances) builds on the abstract mappings idea that keeping promises makes it possible for people to depend on one another.

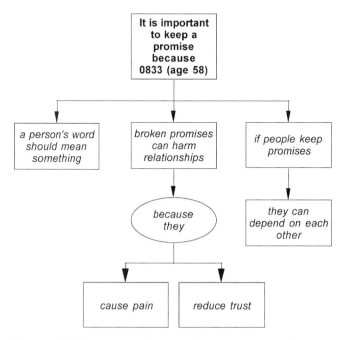

FIGURE 19.3 Conception of promise, abstract mappings order.

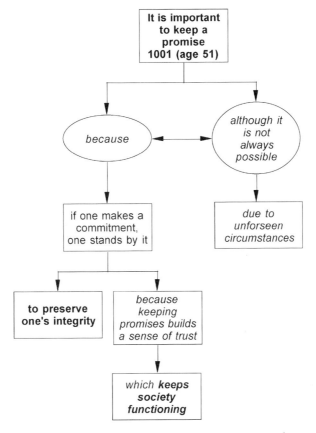

FIGURE 19.4 Conception of promise, abstract systems order.

At the single principles level (abbreviated SP in tables and figures), the new concepts are referred to as first-order principles. These coordinate abstract systems. An elaborated notion of the *social contract*, for example, results from the coordination of human interests (in which individual human beings are treated as systems). "Everybody wants to be treated equally and have a sense of fair play. Because this is so, we have an obligation to one another to enter into a social contract that optimizes equality and fairness." Because they are usually employed to coordinate abstract systems or emerge from the coordination of abstract systems, concepts like autonomy, fair play, heteronomy, higher order principle, and philosophical principle are rare before the single principles level. "The only time we're justified in breaking the social contract is when a higher principle, such as the right to life, intervenes." The most complex logical structure of this complexity level often identifies one aspect of a principle or axiom coordinating systems, as in "Contracts are articulations of a unique human quality, mutual trust, which coordinates human relations." Here, contracts are seen as the instantiation of a broader principle coordinating human interactions.

Figure 19.5 presents a map of the performance of a 57-year-old male. Here, "mutual trust" is employed as a single principle supporting an argument for keeping promises. The rationale for employing this principle is that "most social conventions" and "all moral principles" are based on trust. Both "all moral principles" and "most social conventions" are third-order abstractions. Note how this single principles argument builds on the abstract systems notion that trust keeps society functioning.

Validation of the Hierarchical Complexity Scoring System

Hierarchical complexity scoring can be conducted in any knowledge domain because hierarchical order of abstraction and logical structure guide scoring, rather than the identification of particular conceptual

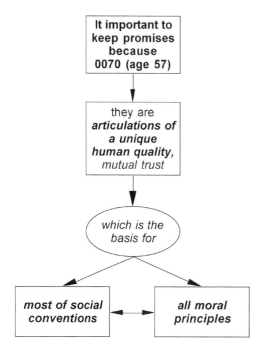

FIGURE 19.5 Conception of promise, single principles order.

content as in conventional domain-based systems. The domain generality of hierarchical complexity scoring raises the question of whether the hierarchical complexity scoring system assesses the same dimension of performance as conventional developmental assessment systems do.

Five validation studies have shown that the hierarchical complexity scoring system and one of its predecessors, the general stage scoring system (Commons et al., 1995) predominantly assess the same dimension of performance as more content-dependent stage-scoring systems. In the first of these, a think-aloud procedure was employed to compare the scoring behavior of five raters trained in the general stage scoring system with the scoring behavior of three raters trained in Kohlberg's standard issue scoring system (Dawson, 2001). All raters scored the same 43 texts. A mean score for each text was calculated for each group of raters, resulting in two scores for each text, one based on the ratings of general stage scoring system raters and one based on the ratings of standard issue scoring system raters. Despite the fact that the raters trained in the standard issue scoring system justified their stage assignments on the basis of particular moral conceptions and interpersonal perspectives,

whereas general stage scoring system raters justified their complexity level assignments in terms of logical structure, these mean scores were within one complexity level of one another 95% of the time ($r = .94$).

In a second study, the hierarchical complexity scoring system, Armon's (1984) good life scoring system, and the standard issue scoring system were employed to score three different interviews administered to 209 5–86-year-olds. Correlations of .90 and .92 were found between the results obtained with the hierarchical complexity scoring system and the standard issue and good life scoring systems (Dawson, 2002a). Dawson argued that these correlations, combined with patterns in the acquisition of analogous good life stages, moral stages, and complexity levels, provide evidence that the three scoring systems predominantly assess the same latent dimension: hierarchical complexity.

In a third study, Dawson et al. (2003) conducted a multidimensional partial credit Rasch analysis of the relationship between scores obtained with the standard issue scoring system and scores obtained with the hierarchical complexity scoring system on 378 moral judgment interviews from respondents aged 5 to 86. They found a correlation of .92 between scores awarded with the two scoring systems. This strong correlation suggests that these two systems primarily assess the same dimension of performance. However, the hierarchical complexity scoring system revealed more stage-like patterns of performance than the standard issue scoring system, including evidence of developmental spurts and plateaus.

In the fourth study, the relationship between complexity levels and Kitchener and King's (1990) reflective judgment stages was examined (Dawson, 2002b). In a sample of 209 interviews of adolescents and adults, the correlation between complexity level scores and reflective judgment scores was .84. Agreement between reflective judgment scores and complexity level scores was within one reflective judgment stage 90% of the time. This is higher than the reported median interrater agreement rate of 77% within one reflective judgment stage (Kitchener & King, 1990).

In a fifth study, Dawson (2004) examined the relationship between scores obtained with the hierarchical complexity scoring system and a Perry-based scoring system similar to that described by Mentkowski, Moeser, and Strait (1983). Scores agreed within one Perry level 82% to 98% of the time, depending on the levels compared.

Two additional studies examined the validity of the hierarchical complexity scoring system as a measure of cognitive development. In these life span studies, Rasch scaling was employed to examine patterns of performance in a set of 747 moral judgment interviews (Dawson-Tunik et al., 2005) and a set of 246 interviews addressing the question, "What is a good education (Dawson-Tunik, 2004)?" The age range of both samples was from 5 to 86 years. The authors examined these data for evidence supporting the specified developmental sequence as well as evidence for qualitative (as opposed to cumulative) change. They (1) identified six developmental stages in this age range; (2) showed that performances were all either consolidated at a single complexity level or combined two adjacent complexity levels, a pattern that supports the specified order of acquisition; (3) demonstrated that movement from complexity level to complexity level proceeded in a remarkably consistent series of spurts and plateaus across the six levels, reflecting the tendency for individuals to spend less time in transition from one level to another than in periods of consolidation; and (4) showed that the task demands of moving from one complexity level to the next are remarkably similar, regardless of one's position in the developmental hierarchy. This means that the distance from one complexity level to the next is the same (in terms of task demands); consequently, the hierarchical complexity scale can legitimately be treated as an interval scale. This satisfies the second requirement for good measurement, a system for assessing the amount of a given trait in interval units.

In both studies the authors also showed that two of the complexity levels—abstract systems and single principles—were unlikely to occur before adulthood, and that patterns of performance on these two complexity levels were virtually identical to patterns of performance on the complexity levels found primarily in childhood and adolescence. This finding, which indicates that the developmental process is similar in childhood and adulthood, supports the claim that the hierarchical complexity scoring system assesses a unidimensional developmental trait. This satisfies the first requirement for good measurement, the identification of a unidimensional, context-independent trait.

It is notable that domain-based scoring systems have not revealed developmental patterns that are as unambiguously consistent with the requirements of measurement or with the postulates of stage-developmental theory as the results reported here.

COMPLEXITY LEVEL AND MEANING

Although the evidence presented thus far demonstrates convergent and construct validity for the hierarchical complexity scoring system, it does not directly demonstrate how a measure of hierarchical complexity can help researchers to understand the development of meaning. The hierarchical complexity of a performance tells us a great deal about its form and hierarchical order of abstraction, but it makes no direct reference to its specific conceptual content. To develop an understanding of the progress of conceptual development in a given domain, specific conceptual content must be assessed independently and then reintegrated with hierarchical complexity information. Because complexity levels are assessed independently of particular conceptual content, it is possible to address questions about the relation between complexity level and meaning. This is impossible with conventional scoring systems because developmental level and particular meanings are conflated in these systems. The independent assessment of complexity level and conceptual content also makes it possible to address questions about individual (or cultural) differences in the behavior of individuals performing at the same level.

It is precisely because scoring with the hierarchical complexity scoring system does not rely on the identification of particular conceptual content that it is possible to conduct separate analyses of complexity level and meaning. My colleagues and I have conducted (and continue to conduct) exhaustive analyses of the conceptual content of interview data in a number of knowledge domains, including moral reasoning (Dawson & Gabrielian, 2003), epistemological reasoning (Dawson, 2004), evaluative reasoning (Dawson-Tunik, 2004), and more recently, leadership reasoning, critical thinking, and science reasoning. In all of this work, we are guided by a methodological approach called *developmental maieutics*, which has been designed to expose patterns in conceptual development by submitting the same data to multiple forms of analysis (structural, conceptual, lexical) and then integrating the results of these analyses. In the abovementioned work, complexity coding of samples of texts was accompanied by independent and exhaustive content analyses, which we call *propositional* analyses. The first step in conducting a propositional analysis is to identify and code every relevant proposition made by each respondent represented in a given sample.

TABLE 19.2 Education as Preparation for the Good Life (Dawson, 1998)

A good education . . .	Number and Percent of Occurrences of Each Concept Code at Each Complexity Order (1 per case)			
	Single Abstractions (n = 7)	Abstract Mappings (n = 38)	Abstract Systems (n = 65)	Single Principles (n = 38)
Provides life/work skills/knowledge.	1 (14.3%)	24 (63.2%)	28 (43.1%)	15 (39.5%)
prepares you for a work/a job.	4 (57.1%)	17 (44.7%)	12 (18.5%)	5 (13.2%)
teaches survival skills.		3 (7.9%)	4 (6.2%)	4 (10.5%)
provides interpersonal/social skills.		7 (18.4%)	14 (21.5%)	14 (36.8%)
produces better/respectable/responsible people.		6 (15.8%)	14 (21.5%)	15 (39.5%)
prepares you achieve personal goals.		5 (13.2%)	6 (9.2%)	3 (7.9%)
prepares you to make money/a living.		6 (15.8%)	8 (9.2%)	1 (2.6%)
prepares students to succeed.		5 (13.2%)	5 (7.7%)	2 (5.3%)
prepares students to contribute.		4 (10.5%)	5 (7.7%)	12 (31.6%)
enhances/enriches/betters your life.		7 (18.4%)	15 (23.1%)	8 (21.1%)
enhances self-worth/esteem/confidence/respect.			8 (9.2%)	3 (7.9%)
increases choices/opens doors.			8 (9.2%)	
should round out/broaden/balance the student.			16 (24.6%)	7 (18.4%)
produces effective/competent/self-reliant people.			7 (7.7%)	7 (18.4%)
prepares students to function in society.			10 (15.4%)	10 (26.3%)
leads to personal fulfillment/meaning.			12 (18.5%)	8 (21.1%)
increases gratification/satisfaction.			11 (16.9%)	5 (13.2%)
improves/advances society.			12 (18.5%)	13 (34.2%)
promotes social/global justice/welfare.				8 (21.1%)
promotes autonomy/self-actualization/self-examination.				7 (18.4%)
produces good/productive citizens.				6 (15.8%)
is empowering				7 (18.4%)

So, for example, in a set of moral judgment interviews dealing with the concept of contract, we code every proposition about the nature of contracts. This coding is conducted with great attention to subtle differences in meaning. The results are then arranged in a complexity level by concept code matrix, which reveals patterns in the emergence of meaning within the knowledge domain being investigated. Analysis of these patterns allows us to (1) describe the conceptual content associated with each complexity level, and (2) examine the ways the conceptual knowledge of one complexity level is reintegrated into new conceptions at the following complexity level. In other reports, Dawson and her colleagues (1998; Dawson-Tunik, 2004; Dawson & Gabrielian, 2003) have described the process of developing accounts of conceptual development in greater detail.

Table 19.2 (adapted from Dawson, 1998) provides an example of a complexity level by concept code matrix (after considerable collapsing of the original concept code categories) related to the theme of education as preparation for the good life. The contents of tables like this one, combined with frequent references to the original texts, provide the basis for constructing rich descriptions of conceptual development. Tables like this can also be employed to examine thematic trends across complexity levels. For example, 57.1% of individuals performing at the single abstractions level and 44.7% of individuals performing at the abstract mappings level, argue that a good education should prepare one for work or a job, whereas only 18.5% of individuals performing at the abstract systems level and 13.2% of individuals performing at the single principles level make a similar argument. This suggests that the salience of preparation for work is diminished at the higher complexity levels. In contrast, a large percentage of individuals performing at the single principles level emphasize the development of social skills or ethical qualities relative to those performing at lower complexity levels, suggesting that the development of persons gains in salience at the highest complexity level.

Table 19.3 provides a summary of the conceptual content of interviews about learning, truth, and contracts/promises as they unfold from the single abstractions to single principles complexity levels. On the surface, this table is similar to most published tables comparing developmental levels across knowledge domains (Commons et al., 1990; Commons, Richards, & Armon, 1984a). Such tables display theoretically analogous developmental levels from different knowledge domains on the same horizontal axis. The difference here is that the levels are not merely theoretically analogous. They are the same, because the same scoring criteria have been employed to score the texts from each domain. In other words, the hierarchical complexity scoring system functions like a ruler, in the sense that it performs the same function regardless of context. This makes it possible to conduct direct cross-domain comparisons of conceptual development and to examine the relations between conceptions in different domains. For example, the abstract systems notion that what we learn can be biased by existing knowledge is implicit in the notion, also expressed for the first time at the abstract systems level, that different interpretations of knowledge can result in different truths.

Another insight offered by the juxtaposition of learning, truth, and moral concepts is that, overall, the learning and truth concepts appear to overlap more with one another than they do with moral concepts, suggesting that they actually represent the same knowledge domain or closely related knowledge domains. Finally, by juxtaposing conceptual development across knowledge domains or thematic strands, we can begin to understand how conceptions from one domain or strand become part of new conceptions on another domain or strand. For example, the single abstractions level conception of learning as play coordinates representational systems level conceptions of learning and play that before the single abstractions level, were located on different thematic strands (*play* and *learning*) (Dawson, 1998). In the physics domain, we have similarly found that the notion that energy can exist in at least two states (conceptions of energy), along with an understanding that things can change from one form to another (conceptions of change), are prerequisites to developing a concept of energy transformation. Insights like these are useful to educators who wish to promote the development of particular conceptualizations in that they provide us with insights into their conceptual prerequisites—what students need to learn before they can produce optimal constructions at the next level.

By examining patterns in the emergence of conceptions across complexity levels, Dawson and colleagues (Dawson-Tunik, 2004; Dawson & Gabrielian, 2003) have demonstrated that it is possible to trace the development of individual concepts across numerous complexity levels, specifying how the conceptions

TABLE 19.3 Summary of Conceptions of Learning, Truth, and Contract Associated With the Abstract Mappings, Abstract Systems, and Single Principles Complexity Orders

Complexity Order	Learning (adapted from Dawson, 2004; Dawson-Tunik, 2004)	Truth (adapted from Dawson, 2004)	Contract/Promise (Adapted from Dawson & Gabrielian, 2003)
Single Abstractions	• Helps you understand things • Helps you remember, know things • Provides skills for life • Is not just from books (can be from projects, field trips, etc.) • Should be fun, interesting	• Is findable • Can be observed (a broken window is a broken window) • Is something you "just know" • Facts and opinions are different. Facts are truths	• Keeping a promise means keeping "your word." • A promise is a promise • To assure another person that you will definitely do what you have agreed to do • Keeping promises is important to friendship or trust; may cause others to keep promises to you • Breaking promises makes you feel bad or guilty; makes your kids break promises • It is okay to break a promise if you will never see the promisee again
Abstract Mappings	• Promotes understanding rather than memorization • Involves taking in other people's opinions and "mixing" them with your own • Involves hands-on experience, learning from experience, learning from life in general • Happens over time • Provides a broad base of knowledge • Can be applied in real life	• Is fact, factual knowledge, proven knowledge • Something to figure out, but hard to find • Found through problem solving • Can be proven (if science-based) • There are some absolute scientific truths, scientific laws • Some scientific truths can change, be altered • What is accepted as truth may not be real truth • Individuals have their own personal truths, based on upbringing, opinions • People can fail to understand truth for psychological reasons (need to make self look good, bias, upbringing) • Universal truths are fixed, external • Universal truths are taken on faith (esp. if associated with religion)	• Are agreements that have a sacred quality/should not be made lightly • Build trust, which you must have to maintain friendships • Should be kept because you would want others to do the same for you; because breaking them can cause others to lose respect for you or ruin your reputation; or cause psychological harm • Whether one should keep a promise can depend on its importance

Abstract Systems	• Involves "processing" knowledge • Involves interpretation • Involves being exposed to different perspectives • Involves learning how to learn • Can be biased by existing knowledge • Develops reasoning skills • Promotes development • Promotes self-understanding, understanding of others	• Is objective • Is bound to interpretation • There is no absolute truth influenced by a promise; to preserve your own or others' perceptions of your integrity • There are certain overall truths • Pursuit of truth is an ongoing process • Some methods of seeking truth are better than others • Interpretation of knowledge can differ, resulting in different "truths" • Can be more absolute or concrete in some knowledge domains than in others • Can't be entirely relative • Can be multiple truths in some things • Scientific truth and religious truth should be/are evaluated differently	• Set up binding rules of behavior for the individuals involved in making them • Have the purpose of maintaining relationships by building trust; make it possible for people to live together • Because of the nature of a promise, it is not okay to break one with no explanation
Single Principles	• Involves restructuring existing knowledge • A thought process that is partially conscious and partially subconscious, a network integrating new ideas • Involves seeking a principle that holds together a perspective • Develops a critical perspective • Promotes critical discourse	• Is reevaluated throughout our lives • Human desire is to seek out truth • Two separate truths can be interrelated to form a third truth • Some mathematical truths may be absolute • Universal truths are things all reasonable persons can agree about at a given moment in time	• Are mutual obligations set up by persons acting as autonomous agents; are uniquely human • Are the basis for the mutual trust that makes human society possible • Without the expectation that promises will be kept, contracts honored, society could not exist • One should only break a promise to serve a higher ideal

of an earlier level are integrated to form the conceptions of a subsequent level. For example, the learning as play construct is further elaborated at the abstract mappings level when the relatively undifferentiated play component is replaced (or supplemented) with the concept of interest. Learning is now understood as an activity that can be interesting or engaging in and of itself, and therefore, much like play.

The descriptions in table 19.3 have been compared to the stage definitions of other researchers (Dawson, 2004; Dawson-Tunik, 2004; Dawson & Gabrielian, 2003). In each case, there is great overlap between analogous stage definitions of other researchers and the descriptions of reasoning my colleagues and I have constructed by integrating independent hierarchical complexity and conceptual analyses. However, some significant differences have emerged. First, the descriptions of conceptual content developed employing our method are more extensive than those provided by other researchers. Second, because these are descriptions rather than definitions, they are open-ended. It is possible to add to these descriptions as subsequent samples reveal new conceptions at the various complexity levels, supporting cross-gender, cross-cultural, and cross-context comparisons of reasoning. Third, research has shown that these descriptions can be developed from cross-sectional rather than longitudinal data, meaning that conceptual development in a given domain can be described without the arduous and lengthy process of collecting longitudinal data, although confirmatory longitudinal evidence is desirable (Dawson, 2003a; Dawson, 2003d; Dawson & Gabrielian, 2003).

RESEARCH TO PRACTICE

Thus far, I have primarily discussed the pure research applications of developmental maieutics. Another important aspect of the methodology is that it ties together fundamental research and practice. Detailed accounts of conceptual development provide a valuable insight into how learning takes place. First, these accounts expose the sequence in which conceptual understandings are constructed and permit us to identify the conceptual precursors of concepts expressed at any given complexity level. For example, in an ongoing study of the development of leadership concepts conducted for a federal government agency, we have found that managers do not adequately coordinate the interests of employees and the organization

until they can demonstrate elaborated conceptions of both (Dawson, 2003c). This coordination requires that both employees and organizations are conceptualized as complex entities with both shared and divergent interests that vary over time. Interestingly, we found that managers who demonstrated an elaborated conception of their organization but lacked an elaborated conception of their employees, privileged the organization when they made management decisions. For example, when responding to a dilemma involving a female employee who wanted to cut back on work hours to care for her infant daughter, managers with less elaborated conceptions of the employee often advocated transferring or firing the employee to ensure the success of their organization's mission. Conversely, managers who demonstrated an elaborated conception of their employees, but lacked an elaborated conception of their organization privileged employees when they made management decisions. In this case, managers were willing to minimize the importance of the mission of their organization to provide support for the employee. Managers with elaborated conceptions of both the employee and the organization devised solutions that coordinated the needs of the new mother with the mission of the organization. As one manager explained, "I think the only way people are truly productive is if we [can] accommodate their personal needs along with the mission needs." Findings like those described here provide insights that are not only valuable from a diagnostic point of view, but can provide part of the basis for developing individualized learning programs, targeted to the needs of particular managers. In this instance, for example, a manager with an inadequately elaborated conception of the employee might benefit from engaging in learning activities that focus on promoting the development of a more elaborated conception prior to engaging in learning interventions that promote the coordination of the interests of employees with those of the organization.

Second, our research has shown that movement from one complexity level to the next depends, in a general sense, on the amount of conceptual elaboration that has occurred at the earlier complexity level (Dawson & Wilson, 2004). This means that instructional interventions that are intended to move individuals to the next complexity level (restructuring) are likely to be more effective when conceptions at the current developmental level have become highly elaborated (learning). Conversely, when conceptions at the current complexity level are unelaborated, providing additional conceptual understandings at that level (learning) may be a more effective way to enhance development than attempting to promote movement to the next developmental level (structuring). We are presently testing this hypothesis in an intervention study of leadership development.

Third, the descriptions of conceptualizations associated with each complexity level can be translated into scoring rubrics for teachers, making it possible for persons untrained in hierarchical complexity theory to benefit directly from research results. One of the goals of our current investigation into the development of science concepts is the production of detailed scoring rubrics designed to help teachers track the developmental progress of their students and respond to students' developmental needs. In 2004, we evaluated one such rubric in a physical science program. Following only 30 minutes of instruction, teachers were able to produce assessments of students' work that agreed with the researchers' assessments over 75% of the time.

Fourth, linguistic analyses of the numerous texts we have gathered and scored over the past several years have revealed strong relations between complexity level and certain lexical and syntactic features of language. These analyses have helped refine our ability to identify transitions from one complexity level to the next. By comparing linguistic features of transitional and consolidated performances, we are developing criteria for determining when a performance shows early evidence of the structures of a new complexity level. In fact, we have been able to employ what we have learned about the relation between language and complexity level to develop an accurate and reliable computer assisted developmental scoring system (Dawson & Wilson, 2004). This system not only scores performances for complexity level, but also employs objective criteria to rank them within complexity levels. This automated system, called the lexical abstraction assessment system (LAAS), makes it possible, for the first time, to conduct large-scale developmental assessments of texts. The implications for program evaluation, individual assessment, and research, are too numerous to consider here.

DISCUSSION

In this chapter I have described a method for examining conceptual development that separates the measurement of structure from the assessment of content, thus making it possible to pose questions about their interrelations. I began by describing an alternative conception of learning as one of two interrelated processes in development. This was followed with a discussion of the principles of measurement, which are of central importance to this work because the hierarchical complexity scale is employed as a developmental ruler. I then described the hierarchical complexity construct in some detail and examined the validity and reliability of the hierarchical complexity scoring system in terms of its validity as a measure. Following this, I discussed the relationship between complexity level and meaning and discussed how what we have learned about this relationship is being (or can be) applied in educational contexts.

Although no single methodological perspective can provide a complete account of cognitive development, the perspective offered here promises to engender important insights into adult cognitive development. Although it clearly builds on the methods of earlier cognitive developmentalists, it avoids some of the limitations posed by these earlier methods, which, in failing to distinguish adequately between structure and content, limited the generalizability and applicability of research findings. A reliable and valid developmental ruler that can be applied in a wide range of contexts and content domains makes it possible to make meaningful interindividual, cross-domain, cross-context, cross-gender, and cross-cultural comparisons of developmental progress. Moreover, this method can easily be employed to inform practice, and tools that have emerged from the research (scoring rubrics and the LAAS) can readily be employed in applied settings. In the past, valid and practical developmental assessments were difficult to implement because the methods for gathering and evaluating developmental data have been arduous and expensive. In this respect, the LAAS, our computerized developmental assessment system, makes large scale or frequent developmental assessments practical for the first time. Tools like the LAAS may well contribute to the transformation of developmental science, making it possible to address questions about adult development that were impractical to address with earlier assessment tools.

ACKNOWLEDGMENTS   Special thanks to Cheryl Armon, Marvin Berkowitz, Larry Walker, the Murray Research Center, and John Wise, who provided data employed in my analyses of adult conceptual development. The research reported in this chapter was made possible in part by a grant from the Spencer Foundation. The data presented, statements made, and views expressed are solely the responsibility of the author.

Notes

1. *Developmental maieutics*, a methodological perspective that has been strongly influenced by Overton's (1998) call for relational methods in developmental science, calls for an explicit effort to expose patterns of conceptual development in texts by isolating the hierarchical complexity dimension and then examining the interaction between this dimension and other features of the same texts. These other features include propositional content, thematic content, lexical content, and cross-domain or cross-context characteristics. The perspective further calls for an integration of fundamental research with practice by employing the hierarchical complexity construct and research results to inform curriculum design, assessment, and program evaluation.

2. There are also those who view learning (taking in knowledge) as the primary process in development (Bandura, 1992; Shweder, Mahapatra, & Miller, 1987).

3. At the single abstractions order, students commonly constructed a notion of energy as something "behind" the movement of objects, whereas students functioning at the representational systems order viewed energy and movement as the same thing.

4. For detailed information about hierarchical complexity scoring see the Lectical Assessment System Web site at: http://gseacademic.harvard.edu/%7ehcs/index.htm.

5. Single abstractions dominate by age 10 or 11 in most populations that have been sampled by developmental researchers. However, a small percentage of adults do not move beyond this complexity level in their moral reasoning.

References

Amir, R., Frankl, D. R., & Tamir, R. (1987). Justifications of answers to multiple choice items as a means for identifying misconceptions. In J. D. Novak (Ed.), *Proceedings of the Second International Seminar on Misconceptions and Educational Strategies in Science and Mathematics* (Vol. I, pp. 15–26). Ithaca, NY: Cornell University Press.

Armon, C. (1984). *Ideals of the good life: Evaluative reasoning in children and adults.* Unpublished doctoral dissertation, Harvard University, Boston.

Armon, C., & Dawson, T. L. (1997). Developmental trajectories in moral reasoning across the lifespan. *Journal of Moral Education, 26,* 433–453.

Armon, C., & Dawson, T. L. (2002). The good life: A longitudinal study of adult value reasoning. In

J. Demick & C. Andreoletti (Eds.), *Handbook of adult development* (pp. 271–300). New York: Plenum Press.

Bandura, A. (1992). Social cognitive theory. In V. Ross (Ed.), *Six theories of child development: Revised formulations and current issues* (pp. 1–60). London: Jessica Kingsley.

Brainerd, C. J. (1993). Cognitive development is abrupt (but not stage-like). *Monographs of the Society for Research in Child Development, 58,* 170–190.

Case, R., & Okamoto, Y. (1996). *The role of central conceptual structures in the development of children's thought* (Vol. 61 [1–2]). New York: Blackwell.

Case, R., Okamoto, Y., Henderson, B., & McKeough, A. (1993). Individual variability and consistency in cognitive development: New evidence for the existence of central conceptual structures. In R. Case & W. Edelstein (Eds.), *The new structuralism in cognitive development: Theory and research on individual pathways* (pp. 71–100). Basel, Switzerland: S. Karger.

Cavallo, A. M. L. (1996). Meaningful learning, reasoning ability, and students' understanding and problem solving of topics in genetics. *Journal of Research in Science Teaching, 33,* 625–656.

Colby, A., Kohlberg, L., Gibbs, J., & Lieberman, M. (1983). A longitudinal study of moral judgment. *Monographs of the Society for Research in Child Development, 48*(1–2).

Commons, M. L., Armon, C., Kohlberg, L., Richards, F. A., Grotzer, T. A., & Sinnott, J. (Eds.). (1990). *Adult development. Vol. 1: Comparisons and applications of developmental models.* New York: Praeger.

Commons, M. L., Richards, F. A., & Armon, C. (Eds.). (1984). *Beyond formal operations.* New York: Praeger.

Commons, M. L., Richards, F. A., with Ruf, F. J., Armstrong-Roche, M., & Bretzius, S. (1984). A general model of stage theory. In M. Commons, F. A. Richards, & C. Armon (Eds.), *Beyond formal operations* (pp. 120–140). New York: Praeger.

Commons, M. L., Straughn, J., Meaney, M., Johnstone, J., Weaver, J. H., Lichtenbaum, E., et al. (1995, November). *The general stage scoring system: How to score anything.* Paper presented at the Annual meeting of the Association for Moral Education. New York, NY.

Commons, M. L., Trudeau, E. J., Stein, S. A., Richards, S. A., & Krause, S. R. (1998). Hierarchical complexity of tasks shows the existence of developmental stages. *Developmental Review, 18,* 237–278.

Dawson, T. L. (1998). *"A good education is . . ." A lifespan investigation of developmental and conceptual features of evaluative reasoning about education.* Unpublished doctoral dissertation, University of California at Berkeley, Berkeley, CA.

Dawson, T. L. (2004). Assessing intellectual development: Three approaches, one sequence. *Journal of Adult Development, 11,* 71–85.

Dawson, T. L. (2001). Layers of structure: A comparison of two approaches to developmental assessment. *Genetic Epistemologist, 29,* 1–10.

Dawson, T. L. (2002a). A comparison of three developmental stage scoring systems. *Journal of Applied Measurement, 3,* 146–189.

Dawson, T. L. (2002b, January). *Measuring intellectual development across the lifespan.* Paper presented at the Powerful learning & the Perry scheme: Exploring intellectual development's role in knowing, learning, and reasoning, California State University, Fullerton, CA.

Dawson, T. L. (2003a, June). *Assessing intellectual development: Three approaches, one sequence.* Paper presented at the Annual meeting of the Jean Piaget Society, Chicago.

Dawson, T. L. (2003b). *The Hierarchical Complexity Scoring System.* Retrieved January, 2003, from http://gseacademic.harvard.edu/~hcs/

Dawson, T. L. (2003c, July). *Hierarchical complexity: A yardstick for developmental science.* Paper presented at the MBE Summer Institute, Harvard University, Boston, MA.

Dawson, T. L. (2003d). A stage is a stage is a stage: A direct comparison of two scoring systems. *Journal of Genetic Psychology, 164,* 335–364.

Dawson, T. L. (2004). Assessing intellectual development: Three approaches, one sequence. *Journal of Adult Development, 11,* 71–85.

Dawson, T. L., & Gabrielian, S. (2003). Developing conceptions of authority and contract across the life-span: Two perspectives. *Developmental Review, 23,* 162–218.

Dawson, T. L., & Wilson, M. (2004). The LAAS: A computerized developmental scoring system for small- and large-scale assessments. *Educational Assessment, 9,* 153–191.

Dawson, T. L., Xie, Y., & Wilson, M. (2003). Domain-general and domain-specific developmental assessments: Do they measure the same thing? *Cognitive Development, 61–78.*

Dawson-Tunik, T. L. (2004). "A good education is . . ." The development of evaluative thought across the life-span. *Genetic, Social, and General Psychology Monographs, 130*(1), 4–112.

Dawson-Tunik, T. L., Commons, M. L., Wilson, M., & Fischer, K. W. (2005). The shape of development. *The International Journal of Cognitive Development, 2*(2), 163–196.

Feldman, D. H. (1995). Learning and development in a nonuniversal theory. *Human Development, 38,* 315–321.

Fischer, K. W. (1980). A theory of cognitive development: The control and construction of hierarchies of skills. *Psychological Review, 87,* 477–531.

Fischer, K. W., & Ayoub, C. (1994). Affective splitting and dissociation in normal and maltreated children: Developmental pathways for self in relationships. In D. Cicchetti & S. L. Toth (Eds.), *Disorders and dysfunctions of the self: Rochester Symposium on Developmental Psychopathology* (Vol. 5, pp. 149–222). Rochester, NY: University of Rochester Press.

Fischer, K. W., Ayoub, C., Singh, I., Noam, G., Maraganore, A., & Raya, P. (1997). Psychopathology as adaptive development along distinctive pathways. *Development & Psychopathology, 9,* 749–779.

Fischer, K. W., & Bidell, T. R. (1998). Dynamic development of psychological structures in action and thought. In W. Damon & R. M. Lerner (Eds.), *Handbook of child psychology: Theoretical models of human development* (5th ed., pp. 467–561). New York: Wiley.

Fischer, K. W., & Granott, N. (1995). Beyond one-dimensional change: Parallel, concurrent, socially distributed processes in learning and development. *Human Development, 38,* 302–314.

Germann, P. J. (1994). Testing a model of science process skills acquisition: An interaction with parents' education, preferred language, gender, science attitude, cognitive development, academic ability, and biology knowledge. *Journal of Research in Science Teaching, 31*(7) 749–783.

Gilligan, C. (1977). In a different voice: Women's conceptions of self and of morality. *Harvard Educational Review, 47,* 481–517.

Halford, G. S. (1999). The properties of representations used in higher cognitive processes: Developmental implications. In I. E. Sigel (Ed.), *Development of mental representation: Theories and applications.* (pp. 147–168). Mahwah, NJ: Lawrence Erlbaum.

Inhelder, B., Bovet, M., & Sinclair, H. (1967). Development and learning. *Psychologie V Ekonomicke Praxi, 26,* 1–23.

Kitchener, K. S., & King, P. M. (1990). The reflective judgment model: Ten years of research. In M. L. Commons, C. Armon, L. Kohlberg, F. A. Richards, T. A. Grotzer & J. D. Sinnott (Eds.), *Adult development* (Vol. 2, pp. 62–78). New York: Praeger.

Kitchener, K. S., Lynch, C. L., Fischer, K. W., & Wood, P. K. (1993). Developmental range of reflective judgment: The effect of contextual support and practice on developmental stage. *Developmental Psychology, 29,* 893–906.

Lawson, A. E., Alkhoury, S., Benford, R., Clark, B. R., & Falconer, K. A. (2000). What kinds of scientific concepts exist? Concept construction and intellectual development in college biology. *Journal of Research in Science Teaching, 37,* 996–1018.

Lawson, A. E., & Renner, J. W. (1975). Relationships of concrete and formal operational science subject matter and the developmental level of the learner. *Journal of Research in Science Teaching, 12,* 347–358.

Lawson, A. E., & Thompson, L. D. (1988). Formal reasoning ability and misconceptions concerning genetics and natural selection. *Journal of Research in Science Teaching, 25,* 733–746.

Lawson, A. E., & Weser, J. (1990). The rejection of nonscientific beliefs about life: Effects of instruction and reasoning skills. *Journal of Research in Science Teaching, 27,* 589–606.

Lourenco, O., & Machado, A. (1996). In defense of Piaget's theory: A reply to 10 common criticisms. *Psychological Review, 103,* 143–164.

Mentkowski, M., Moeser, M., & Strait, M. J. (1983). *Using the Perry scheme of intellectual and ethical development as a college outcomes measure: a process and criteria for judging student performance, Vol. 1.* Milwaukee, WI: Alverno College, Office of Research and Evaluation.

Overton, W. (1998). Developmental psychology: Philosophy, concepts, and methodology. In W. Damon & R. M. Lerner (Eds.), *Handbook of child psychology: Theoretical models of human development* (5th ed., pp. 107–188). New York: Wiley.

Overton, W. F., Ward, S. L., Noveck, I. A., & Black, J. (1987). Form and content in the development of deductive reasoning. *Developmental Psychology, 23,* 22–30.

Perry, W. G. (1970). *Forms of intellectual and ethical development in the college years.* New York: Holt, Rinehart, & Winston.

Piaget, J. (1985). *The equilibration of cognitive structures: The central problem of intellectual development* (T. Brown & K. J. Thampy, Trans.). Chicago: The University of Chicago Press.

Piaget, J., & Garcia, R. (1989). *Psychogenesis and the history of science* (H. Feider, Trans.). New York: Columbia University Press.

Renner, J. W., & Marek, E. A. (1990). An educational theory base for science teaching. *Journal of Research in Science Teaching, 27,* 241–246.

Rose, S. P., & Fischer, K. W. (1989). *Constructing task sequences: A structured approach to skill theory* (Instructional Manual). Cambridge, MA: Harvard University Press.

Shayer, M., & Adey, P. S. (1993). Accelerating the development of formal thinking in middle and high school students: IV. Three years after a two-year intervention. *Journal of Research in Science Teaching, 30,* 351–366.

Shweder, R. A. (1996). True ethnography: The lore, the law, and the lure. In *Ethnography and human development: Context and meaning in social inquiry.* (pp. 15–52). Chicago: University of Chicago Press.

Shweder, R. A., Mahapatra, M., & Miller, J. G. (1987). Culture and moral development. In J. Kagan & S. Lamb (Eds.), *The emergence of morality in young children* (pp. 1–83). Chicago: University of Chicago Press.

Singer, J. D., & Willett, J. B. (2003). *Applied longitudinal data analysis: Modeling change and event occurrence.* New York: Oxford University Press.

Sinnott, J. D. (1994). The relationship of postformal thought, adult learning, and lifespan development. In J. Sinnott (Ed.), *Interdisciplinary handbook of adult lifespan learning.* (pp. 105–119). Westport, CT: Greenwood Press.

Smith, L. (1998). Learning and the development of knowledge. *Archives de Psychologie, 66,* 201–219.

Tappan, M. B. (1990). Hermeneutics and moral development: Interpreting narrative representations of moral experience. *Developmental Review, 10,* 239–265.

Walker, L. J., & Taylor, J. H. (1991). Stage transitions in moral reasoning: A longitudinal study of developmental processes. *Developmental Psychology, 27,* 330–337.

Wilson, M., & Sloane, K. (2000). From principles to practice: An embedded assessment system. *Applied Measurement in Education, 13,* 181–208.

Chapter 20

Advanced Avenues in Adult Development and Learning: The Role of Doctoral Study

Judith Stevens-Long and Robert Barner

In this chapter we explore the role of advanced graduate studies in the development of adults and its intended and unintended consequences. In the spring of 2002, one of the authors presented a paper at the Association for the Advancement of Higher Education (McClintock & Stevens-Long, 2002) on assessing the ineffable outcomes (the theme of the conference) of graduate study. The presentation covered literature on cognitive, affective, and behavioral outcomes, including such topics as changes in intellectual development, ego identity, and behavioral developments. We were especially focused on the development of scholar-practitioners in such areas as organizational development and clinical psychology. One particularly striking reaction to this presentation was the anxiety on the part of some attendees responsible for assessment that if there are emotional and behavioral changes accompanying graduate study they might, by delineating them, become responsible for them. Thus we make a distinction here between what graduate educators

appear to be intending and what graduate education as a process seems to potentiate in human development.

We begin with a brief review of what graduate school and, in particular the doctorate, appears intended to do. In an extensive study called "Re-envisioning the Ph.D.," Jody Nyquist and Bettina Woodford (2000) started with the statement that

> Legendary achievements have come from graduates of doctoral programs in the United States. Expertise produced by doctoral training has resulted in advances in science, medicine, and engineering that were unimagined only a few decades ago. Doctoral training in the social sciences has provided new understandings of the human condition that inform our daily life and public policy. Scholarly work in the humanities has enabled us to better understand and appreciate cultural differences and dimensions of the moral and ethical nature of our human existence. (p. 1)

Following this lead, we might assert that doctoral training is intended to produce new knowledge of all kinds, scientific and human, cultural, moral, and ethical. Certainly, the traditional emphasis on assessing the outcomes of graduate education through counting the research grants and publications of students and faculty underscores this proposition. Particularly in matters of evaluation and accreditation, honors, awards, articles, books, and funded research grants have been the main indicators of performance. Of course, publications and grants are believed to reflect graduate training and graduate learning. Yet neither training nor learning is directly addressed by those indicators. Furthermore, to the extent that they are addressed, only the intellectual and cognitive aspects of education are studied or evaluated. The emotional, moral, ethical, and even behavioral outcomes of graduate study are left unexamined. Often, they are considered irrelevant, and based on the experience of presenting at AAHE, one might argue that some even consider them dangerous as a topic of discourse.

In fact, there is much controversy about whether doctoral education prepares one for anything but conducting quality research, reflecting issues that have been raised about employing doctoral graduates outside of the research university. Employers complain that many Ph.D.s lack the social and emotional skills required in the business world. Yet as the extensive interview study reported by Nyquist and Woodford suggests and is supported by research at the Fielding Graduate University (Schoenholz-Read, 2000), doctoral studies usually are accompanied by intense periods of personal discomfort, emotional turmoil, cognitive struggle, and transformation.

DOCTORAL STUDY AND COGNITIVE DEVELOPMENT

If a modicum of agreement exists about development over the course of doctoral study, it is in the area of intellectual change. Graduate students are expected to become skilled at research, which implies the ability to question existing research and conventional understandings. One must be able to recognize problems, anticipate or forecast problems, and define ill-structured or unstated problems.

In terms of the literature in adult development, the recognition of problems and the ability to think about ambiguous conditions and alternative solutions implies movement beyond Piaget's stage of formal operations. This argument finds support in extensive work by John Broughton (1977, 1984) as well as by Michael Commons and Francis Richards (2002) along with many others. As a model, formal operations is inadequate for understanding how people come to comprehend new systems. Formal operations are adequate for analyzing linear logical and causal relations but cannot explain how people reason about transformational relationships that require nonlinear conceptions of causality.

A number of descriptions of postformal thinking have been offered, including those of Arlin (1975, 1984), Basseches (1980, 1984), Benack (1984), Commons and Richards (1978, 1984), Kohlberg (1990), Sternberg (1984), and Sinnott (1984). Most cogent here, perhaps, is Patricia Arlin's (1975, 1977) argument that although formal operations are adequate for problem solving, postformal thinking is characterized by problem finding. Problem finding requires the ability to reflect on the nature of a problem and on the processes by which problems are solved. Certainly, doctoral studies move the student toward the ability to find problems that have not been previously identified or to reflect on how one might resolve problems that have not been adequately resolved. This would seem to be the essence of research.

Michael Basseches's (1984) work on advanced stages or postformal thinking follows Klaus Riegel (1973) in emphasizing the ability to tolerate contradiction and ambiguity and make effective use of these as a basis for thought. In particular, one must be able to follow structures or forms that are in constant transformation. Jan Sinnott (1981, 1984) used the concept of systems to talk about postformal thought. A postformal thinker, according to Sinnott, is able to consider the relativity of systems. For example, the patterns of relationships that characterize kinship in one cultural system might be meaningfully seen in relationship to different patterns in another system. Furthermore, the postformal thinker can make these comparisons without necessarily making value judgments. Certainly, these are the kinds of problems graduate students hope to engage.

Similarly, Commons and Richards (1984) used the concept of systems to describe postformal thinking but posited up to four stages beyond formal operations. At the stage of *systematic order*, the thinker sees that outcomes may be determined by many causes and uses this observation to generate systems. Systematic thinkers tend to build matrix representations of information about various systems in the form of tables. These tables might show how, for instance, various theories of cognitive development can be compared with each other. Commons and Richards (2002) argued that "most standard science operates at this order. . . . Researchers carry out variations of previous experiments. Behavior of events is seen as governed by multivariate causality. Our estimates are that only 20% of the US population can now function at this systematic order" (p. 4).

At the next or *metasystematic* order, systems are the objects of thought. Metasystematic thinkers are able to compare, contrast, transform, and synthesize systems of relationships. The focus is on understanding the assumptions and methods used by thinkers within a particular system. According to Commons and Richards (2002), "almost all professors at top research universities function at this stage in their line of work" (p. 4).

Beyond the metasystematic stage, people are able to create new fields or, in very rare historical instances, new paradigms for thinking about existing knowledge (*cross-paradigmatic* thinking). Commons and Richards pointed to the development of the idea of curved space and the subsequent replacement of Euclidean geometry as an example. Finally, *cross-paradigmatic* thinkers are able to create whole new fields of knowledge. Copernicus's creation of the field of celestial mechanics and Descartes's creation of analytical geometry are examples. Clearly, not many of us achieve this level of cognitive function.

However, there is convincing empirical evidence that most graduate students do, at least, achieve the first stages of postformal thought. In their study of *reflective judgment*, Karen Kitchener and Patricia King (1991, 1994) outlined seven stages of development in the thinking of college students about ill-structured problems. The researchers sampled dilemmas in historical, scientific, religious, and everyday contexts. At stage 4 of the Kitchener and King scheme, thinkers began to see the uncertainty of knowledge and understand the distinction between problems that can be resolved with certainty and those that have no single solution. However, stage 4 thinkers were unclear about how to evaluate knowledge claims in ill-defined situations. At the next stage, students understood that interpretation was required to justify an explanation, but they still did not see how to evaluate the worth of differing interpretations. This level of reasoning, Kitchener and King argued, is typical of most beginning graduate students.

The ability to evaluate the relative worth of differing perspectives through the comparison of evidence and opinion across contexts emerges at the next stage, stage 6. Such thought is typical of advanced graduate students and, we would presume, their mentors. At the final stage, stage 7, the thinker understands how to use critical inquiry, existing evidence, and opinion to justify claims about the better or best solution to an ill-defined problem. Kitchener and King reported that even among a college-educated sample, the majority did not use reasoning higher than stage 4 before age 24. The cognitive changes typical of doctoral education, then, appear in stages 5 through 7. Level seven appears about 50% of the time in graduate students over the age of 25. However, education is clearly more important than age in the development of reflective judgment. Fischer, Yan, and Stewart (2002) argued that stage 5 and beyond is characterized by the ability to see systems of systems, which comports with the Commons and Richards (2002) description of the systematic order.

Although the literature on adult education (Mezirow, 1991; Tennant, 2000; Tennant & Pogson, 1995) tends to focus on undergraduate work, there is much agreement that the goal of advanced study is the development of critical reflection. The line of reasoning here begins with Dewey's (1933) definition of reflection as "the active, persistent and careful consideration of any belief or supposed form of knowledge in the light of the grounds that support it and the further conclusions to which it tends," (p. 9) and continuing through Jack Mezirow's discussion of perspective transformation, this work emphasizes how we become critically aware of the assumptions that constrain how we view the world.

The test of perspective transformation, according to Mezirow (1991), is "not only that it is more inclusive, discriminating, and integrative of experience but also that it is permeable (open) to alternative perspectives so that inclusivity, discrimination and integration continually increase" (p. 156). Perspective transformation causes us to challenge the assumptions that constrain the way we perceive, understand, and feel about the world. Here is the first mention of affect—how we feel about the world. Most of the literature on cognitive development ignores the implications for emotional change altogether. Yet there is clear evidence that advanced education and its attendant cognitive changes are accompanied by important emotional experiences and, often, by a rather thoroughgoing reconstruction of the self. As Mark Tennant (2000) argued, all adult education leads to profound personal change.

In fact, it has been our experience (Schoenholz-Read, 2000) at the Fielding Graduate University, that as students begin to report intellectual "stretching," "broadening," and the understanding of multiple perspectives, they feel deeply affected by their learning. Some report increased patience, empathy, and self-confidence. They talk about the ability to be less emotionally reactive, listen to others, and appreciate different points of view. They discuss profound changes in the way they see themselves. Certainly, increased sensitivity to multiple perspectives implies a change in how one holds or feels about one's own perspective, at the very least. So although a particular perspective may be learned, this ability to take perspectives has quite important developmental consequences.

EMOTIONAL DEVELOPMENT AND GRADUATE EDUCATION

"The interpretation of experience is social and political, as well as a psychological exercise. The self as a fixed, stable, and harmonious entity is replaced by the notion of self-construction as an ongoing process. The self, in effect, stands in a dialectical relationship to experience, both forming and being formed by the experience it encounters" (Tennant & Pogson, 1995, p. 169). The appreciation of multiple perspectives drives us toward a construction of the self that is partial, hybrid, and perhaps itself a multiplicity of lenses and truths. In a recent work, one of the authors (Stevens-Long, 2000) described the "prism self." This construct draws on the dialogic view of Vygotsky (1986) and Bakhtin (1984), as well as of Richardson, Rogers, and McCarroll (1998), to describe the adult self as a struggle among multiple voices internalized from the outside world, a continuous dialogue between perspectives that make claims on our attention. This conception of the self is postmodern and postconventional.

Susanne Cook-Greuter (1999) has described the highly developed self as characterized by increased awareness of the constructed nature of reality and the deconstruction of conventional assumptions. She refers to the "postconventional ego," and claims that the postconventional person sees the futility of searching for an objective sense of self or reality. Such persons have a sense of self that is fluid. At its most developed stage, the postconventional self displays ambiguities and paradoxes and a profound awareness of the process of becoming. Cook-Greuter's work extends the scoring system developed by Jane Loevinger for her sentence completion instrument. Two examples of postconventional responses illustrate the emphasis on process:

> I am, in the end, unfathomable, but I enjoy the process of trying to fathom.
> I am alive, trundling along, making sense as best I can, diversifying while consolidating and contracting. (Cook-Greuter, 1999, p. 266).

Consistent with Robert Kegan's (1984) formulation, one comes to "have" a self rather than "be" a self. Having a self, however, is not without its challenges. Dane Hewlett (2004) has described the developmental challenges and imbalances that can occur at even the very high-end ego stages described by Cook-Greuter, including strategies these individuals employ in handling emotions. Most broadly, these challenges center around the process of letting go of one's ego or the sense of a separate self. Individuals at high-end ego states increasingly experience their separate identity as illusory or as a mental construct that was sometimes associated, in Hewlett's study, with a loss of interest in the more mundane aspects of day-to-day life and a tendency to disengage from conventional society. People at the high end of the ego development scale also reported a sense of loneliness and isolation and the difficulty of integrating their personal sense of reality with more conventional conceptualizations.

Recent dialectic notions of human development have broadened to include the emotional as part and parcel of a theory of mind and self. Work at the interface of cognition and emotion is represented in the writing of Gisela Labouvie-Vief (2000) who argues that the higher use of reflection and the integration of contextual, relativistic, and subjective knowledge beyond formal operations is deeply interconnected with emotion and the construction of self. New work on wisdom (Baltes, Lindenberger, & Staudinger, 1998) focused on the integration of cognitive processes with knowledge of the emotional and interpersonal.

In one account, widely distributed and read by students at Fielding, the authors maintain that "the experiential mystery and uncertainty encountered when writing a dissertation are essential aspects of a liminal process that transforms the self" (Deegan & Hill, 1991, p. 322). We argue here that the transformation of the self is not so much a product of the dissertation process, although that may be a capstone event in the process, but begins with a transition from problem solving (formal operational thinking) to problem finding (postformal thinking). It means seeing one's perspective (whether intellectual, social, or personal) as just one of a universe of possibilities based in differing assumptions about reality and tending, as Dewey put it, toward differing conclusions. All of this, at a minimum, implies a more complex cognitive and emotional interplay and perhaps "representations that permit more complex and varied forms of emotional experience" (Labouvie-Vief & Diehl, 1999, p. 257).

Although there is some developmental research on emotional change with age, there is little if anything about the emotional changes that might accompany education. Certainly, in the work on wisdom, we see that emotional, intellectual, and behavioral maturity are strongly correlated with high levels of education and socioeconomic advantage (Baltes et al., 1998).

Even less well researched than the connection between cognition and emotion, the relationship between cognition, emotion, and behavior is almost uncharted.

CONATIVE DEVELOPMENT (STRIVING FOR ACTION) AND GRADUATE EDUCATION

Conative development refers to the development of actions or behaviors that appear to be accompanied by intent. We are not interested here, for example, in coughing or sleeping (although we might be interested in staying awake or paying attention). With Jochem Brandtstädter (1998), we are interested in observable behavior that is chosen by the individual on the "basis of beliefs and values, and that can be interpreted as serving some personal goal or expressing personal attitudes and values" (p. 814). In studying this kind of action, writers often consider such dimensions as intentionality, personal control, reflexivity, and (perceived) freedom of choice. Brandtstädter is particularly interested in how beliefs, plans, and expectations influence what behavior means to the actor; how feeling affects actions; and how goals, evaluation, memories, and other cognitive events influence action. Brandtstäder maintains that the actions of interest are overdetermined (they often serve more than one intention), and they often have unexpected or unintended consequences that lead to changes in goals and beliefs.

Brandtstädter has argued that sometime during adolescence or young adulthood, people begin to monitor their own development, and begin to make choices and plans and execute processes that transpire over long periods of time. Emotions are linked to or mediate between cognition and action in such processes. Emotions signal mismatches between previous hopes and current circumstances or outcomes. Mismatches lead, for example, to planning, learning, self-punishment, and attempts at reparation. Development-oriented actions are also strongly related to feelings of self-efficacy. If people believe that they can control their own development, they are more likely to create the conditions that enable change. Moreover, their behavior is more likely to remain flexible and adaptive over the life span. However, although one would suspect a strong relationship, the correlation of these action-related variables with education is unknown. Certainly, feelings of self-efficacy are learned, forging another link between learning and development.

Self-efficacy is strongly related to learning (Cervone & Peake, 1986). Students with a strong sense of self-efficacy tend to set higher goals for themselves, persist longer at tasks, expend greater effort in the completion of tasks, and are more likely to persevere when confronted with failure. These students also display greater self-regulatory behaviors that facilitate personal study. Examples include tracking their time, organizing their schoolwork, and engaging in self-directed learning (Pintrich & Schrauben, 1992; Zimmerman & Martinez-Pons, 1990). Finally, such individuals have been found to take greater advantage of learning opportunities and to develop their capabilities more extensively through such opportunities (Gist, 1989; Hill & Elias, 1990).

In mainstream developmental research, work on human wisdom has the clearest implications for understanding the relationship between behavior and education. Wisdom stands at the intersection of cognition, emotion, and behavior. Kramer (2002) argued that wise people interact in ways that allow others to remain open rather than to respond defensively. Achenbaum and Orwoll (1991) characterized wisdom as behavior that communicates understanding and caring. Labouvie-Vief (2000) and Pascual-Leone (1990) both proposed that wisdom allows one to individuate from the conventional norms that govern adult behavior to integrate the inner self and internal, affective concerns with outer, conventional reality. Furthermore, people who are nominated as wise persons tend to hold positions of leadership, be employed in human services, or to have exceptional experiences, like being a Nazi resister during the Third Reich (Staudinger, 1996). They are consistently seen as open to experience (Bacelar, 1998).

Wisdom may require a highly developed form of dialectical and relativistic thinking and appears profoundly related to emotion and action. There is evidence that it is related to education; but education, even very advanced education, certainly does not imply that a person will become wise. On the other hand, research on the scholar-practitioner (Schon, 1983) shows that the capacity for reflection in the midst of action allows one to cope with the unique, uncertain, and conflicting situations of practice. We might expect this capacity to accompany the kind of perspective transformation that seems central to graduate education.

In their paper, Nyquist and Woodford (2000) noted that interviewees in business and industry believe that doctoral training does not prepare graduates to meaningfully connect their work to the work of others. Many Ph.D.s lack the collaborative ways of thinking and working that are required in today's corporate world. These interviewees also claimed that students' interests are often disconnected from other knowledge and real-world problems, making them less than optimal practitioners outside the narrow boundaries of the traditional research university.

Even in the traditional university context, however, there is much concern expressed over whether graduate study overemphasizes scholarly research. Young faculty often seem unprepared for the responsibilities of undergraduate teaching, collegial evaluation, curricular planning, and service to the college, university, and community. Clearly, the research on wisdom is only tangentially related to graduate study.

There is some evidence, however, that particular kinds of actions and particular kinds of contexts are most conducive to the optimal development of gradu-

ate students. In the second part of this chapter, we explore four different avenues that lead to development in the context of graduate study. They include obtaining a different perspective on knowledge, gaining membership in the learning community, gaining a more complete understanding of the use of self in learning, and developing an increased awareness of social and cultural contexts.

THE FIRST PATHWAY: OBTAINING A DIFFERENT PERSPECTIVE ON KNOWLEDGE AND LEARNING

Table 20.1 provides an overview of the changes researchers have described in the general conception of knowledge and learning over the years of graduate education.

A number of researchers (Baxter Magolda, 1992; Kitchener & Brenner, 1990; Kitchener & King, 1981; Sinnott, 1984) have studied how student thought changes from undergraduate matriculation through postgraduate work. All of these studies show that students progressively demonstrate greater flexibility of thought, an increased openness to multiple perspectives, and the ability to reflect critically on the sources from which knowledge is derived.

Generally, this work suggests that most entering undergraduate students hold a view of knowledge as an abstract product, isolated from the surrounding social and ideological context in which it is embedded. They treat knowledge as an externalized entity, assuming that it exists in preconstructed form outside the self, ready for internal consumption. Knowledge is seen as a "bankable" commodity (Freire, 2000)—one that can be freely acquired or dispensed, quite independent of considerations of culture, ideology, or personal transformation. From this perspective, gaining knowledge is synonymous with amassing information.

Early in their college careers, most students also see truth as a matter of absolute, black and white constructs. This tendency to force-fit experience into polar categories is related to the notion of rigid schema (Aronson, Wilson, & Akert, 2002; Markus, 1977), and reveals itself in the belief that problem solving will uncover the one correct solution to any given problem (Kitchener & Brenner, 1990; Kitchener & King, 1981). As a consequence, undergraduate students often come to premature closure on problems without

TABLE 20.1. The Nature of Knowledge and Learning

From a View of Knowledge as Absolute and Decontextualized	*To a View of Knowledge as Complex, Relative, and Deeply Contextualized*
Knowledge is viewed as a commodity that can be absorbed, preconstructed, from the external environment (Freire, 2000).	Knowledge is treated as socially constructed and transformed through the very act of observation, reflection, and dialogue (Jarvis, 1987).
The learner assumes that knowledge is a context-free product that can be reviewed without reference to culture or ideology.	Knowledge is seen as situated in the broader social/cultural/ideological context (Brockett & Hiemstra, 1991; Lave & Wenger, 1991).
Knowledge is explicit, declarative, absolute.	Knowledge is seen as relative and often tacit, difficult to articulate, and a product of problem formulation leading to multiple alternative solutions. It is regarded as relative (Polanyi, 1966; Ehrlich & Soloway, 1979; Dixon & Baltes, 1986; Scribner, 1986; Sternberg et al., 2000).
Learners tend to adopt and defend a fixed position. The learner has difficulty incorporating and integrating contradictory findings.	Learners attempt to explore all possible perspectives (Baxter Magolda, 1992); thinking becomes dialectical through the juxtaposition of opposing perspectives (Kitchener & King, 1981; Basseches, 1984).
Problems are usually predefined for learners and clear parameters are established for problem solution (Wagner & Sternberg 1986; Tennant & Pogson 1995; Hedlund & Sternberg 2000; Sternberg & Grigorenko 2000).	Learners see that problems are often complex and unstructured and that solutions are guided by the way problems are formulated (Arlin, 1990). This aspect of learning is related to wisdom (Sternberg et al., 2000; Polanyi, 1966; Dixon & Baltes, 1986).
Simple "impermeable constructs" (Kelly, 1955) create a tendency to move to premature closure without first examining all views, or to pigeonhole experiences and concepts into simplistic, stereotyped categories.	Thinking involves increased cognitive complexity (Cockrill, 1989), and with this, the ability to analyze complex issues (Streufert & Swezey, 1986) and deal with discrepant information (Domangue, 1978).
Learning is experienced as a purely cognitive process.	Ability to synthesize objective, rational analysis with subjective, emotive forms of thought emerges (Pascual-Leone, 1990; Labouvie-Vief, 1992; Labouvie-Vief & Diehl, 2000).
Problems seem to exist in isolation from the surrounding system. Proposed solutions are likely to be limited because potential repercussions in the larger system are unconsidered.	Learners adopt a more systemic perspective working with problems that are "unbounded" containing a number of complex and interactive elements, including interpersonal factors (Ackoff, 1981).

first examining all possible views. Furthermore, their belief often leads them to defend existing positions and belief systems rigidly and to have difficulty working with contradictory information (Mezirow, 2000). The static constructions of knowledge and learning that younger students hold tend to be reinforced by learning environments that overuse predefined problems in the classroom and provide clearly defined parameters for problem solving. Often, predefined problems contain, in the statement of the problem, all the information needed to arrive at the correct solution.

As students progress through their undergraduate years, they begin to see how knowledge is actively constructed and tightly embedded in a given social and ideological context (Baxter Magolda, 1992; Kitchener & Brenner, 1990; Kitchener & King, 1981). They develop a greater appreciation of other perspectives (Sinnott, 1984) and an increased ability to move toward dialectical thinking through the iterative integration of opposing perspectives (Basseches, 1984). Moreover, a college education helps students develop more flexible approaches to unstructured problems. In an extensive summary of this research,

Ernest Pascarella and Patrick Terenzini (1991) concluded that when freshmen are compared to senior-level students, seniors

> are more skilled at using reason and evidence to address ill-structured problems for which there are no verifiably correct answers, have greater intellectual flexibility in that they are better able to understand more than one side of a complex issue, and can develop more sophisticated abstract frameworks to deal with complexity. (p. 155)

Generally, an undergraduate education leaves much room for future cognitive development. In Marcia Baxter Magolda's (1992) longitudinal research, only 2 of 102 undergraduate study participants were found to have reached contextual knowing, the highest level of reasoning measured, by their senior year of study. This figure increased to 12% of the student population in the year following graduation. Similarly, when Basseches (1984) compared thinking among college freshmen, college seniors, and faculty members, he found a strong relationship between education and the version of postformal thinking he described as *dialectical*.

Dialectical thinking allows one to move beyond the analysis of relationships within a particular system to analyze relationships within competing systems. Dialectical thinkers also exhibit great sensitivity to contradiction. Basseches contends that dialectical thinkers see contradiction not as an unfortunate problem but as a positive source of change. He concluded that there are increases in dialectical thinking capacities with academic status well past adolescence, clearly linking learning and adult development.

We contend here that postgraduate education offers more than a linear extension of the cognitive developments that begin during the undergraduate years. Instead, in the process of becoming a contributor to a scholarly learning community, postgraduate students dramatically reconstruct both their views of self and their roles as knowledge creators. Critical to this reconstruction is exposure to complex problems that require students to make large-scale adaptations of their existing approaches to problem formulation and analysis and to carefully self-monitor their cognitive processes. Postgraduate students become increasingly aware of the way the formation of problems guides the exploration of solutions (Arlin, 1990). In the two years following the completion of their undergraduate degrees, as Baxter Magolda (2001) reported,

"Learning was facilitated when it involved complexity, acknowledging multiple perspectives, and questioning why things worked in a particular way" (p. 196). As an example, she provided an excerpt from one student's description of a team-based business simulation:

> We ran a simulated airline. There was no one right answer because we had nine groups and nine airlines in the class and all of them chose different philosophies in how they wanted to run their business. And three completely different airlines finished up at the top. In fact, the way our airline did it was different, the teacher said, than any other class has ever done. We just took a completely different approach. . . . I like not always thinking there was one right answer because when you go out and try to deal with a lot of things, there isn't always one right answer. I think too much as an undergraduate we're taught to believe in black and white and there is no gray. (p. 197)

The opportunity to work with highly complex, unstructured problems provides one important avenue for encouraging increased cognitive complexity. Unstructured problems call for more selective differentiation and integration in the analysis of complex issues (Cockrill, 1989; Streufert & Swezey, 1986) and they require one to deal more effectively with discrepant information (Domangue, 1978). They often demand more dialectical thinking; that is, one must value opposing perspectives and seemingly contradictory views.

The need to take responsibility for their educational curricula, identify innovative learning projects, and direct the focus of their thesis or dissertation presents postgraduate students with a unique set of complex problems. For the student who is accustomed to more structured learning environments, such a situation can produce a good deal of anxiety. As one doctoral candidate put it:

> I felt that my greatest challenge has been navigating the post-coursework portion of my degree. After essentially 21 years in the student role, things suddenly changed. The timelines blurred, expectations became unspoken, and now I was the only one who would provide structure to my educational process. . . . Not only did this shift leave me with a sense of loss (of the process), but also I lost confidence in myself. I think this was mainly due

to a feeling that somehow I should be able to fill the structural void and self-motivate better than I seemed to be able to do. (Kerlin, 1995, p. 29)

The move toward cognitive complexity is supported when students face a learning environment that is less structured, rule-driven, and prescribed than what they may have previously experienced. As students progress from undergraduate to postgraduate work and from structured to ill-defined problems, they come to see how knowledge is socially constructed and transformed through observation, reflection, and dialogue (Jarvis, 1987). Postgraduates come to realize that solutions must include a consideration of the broader social, cultural, and ideological bedrock out of which knowledge is formed (Brockett & Hiemstra, 1991; Candy, 1991; Lave & Wenger, 1991).

As students begin to consider contextual issues, they adopt a more systemic view of problem formation and analysis and reframe their view of self as existing "in" the surrounding environment. They now perceive themselves as part of the larger system (Bredo, 1997). Unstructured and ill-defined problems evoke a shift in perspective toward a more systemic and dialectical view. Similarly, change in the position

of a student in his or her learning community may deeply affect the student's view of how knowledge is created and the implications of that process for the creator.

THE SECOND PATHWAY: GAINING MEMBERSHIP IN THE LEARNING COMMUNITY

Table 20.2 presents an overview of the changes discussed in this section.

If learning may be considered a socially constructed process, postgraduate students must discover how knowledge construction occurs within their community of practice. Knowing how the community works and what it accepts as knowledge allows one to assume the role of knowledge contributor, expert in one's field, and mentor for other junior-level members.

Students initially assume a peripheral role when they enter a learning community as undergraduates. Large power differentials frequently exist in every relationship between student and instructor. The presence of power in student–teacher relationships seldom ever emerges as a topic for open dialogue be-

TABLE 20.2. The Use of Self

From Myopic, Technical Review	To More Encompassing, Critical Reflection
Learners do not reflect on the limits of what is known, and how knowledge is being acquired.	Learners come to self-monitor what they do, or do not know, and what constitutes critical gaps in learning (Meacham, 1990).
Reflection, when it occurs, resides at the "surface" of the phenomenological landscape—focusing only on the content or methods used in the analysis.	Learners expand self-reflection to include uncovering hidden power dynamics and the problems that follow from hegemonic assumptions (Brookfield, 2000a, 2000b).
The learner views the learning process as something which lies external to the self.	Learners increasingly engage in personal/critical reflection about work, self, and ideology (Privett, 2002), epistemic cognition (Kitchener & King, 1981; Kitchener & Brenner, 1990), reflection-in-action, and double-loop learning (Argyris & Schon, 1978).
The learner's reflective process, when it occurs, is largely encapsulated and segmented. Reflection occurs in a piecemeal process, with disconnections between insights drawn regarding self and the learning experience.	Learners see how self-reflection interacts with the learning process. They can engage the self as a mirror and as a window. The "self as window" raises the question: "How will my personal biases and assumptions influence my learning approach and the conclusions I draw?" The "self as mirror" raises the question: "What is being reflected back to me about how I change as a function of my learning?

tween student and teacher in the undergraduate setting. Most often it remains submerged as a basic hegemonic assumption.

In part, such power discrepancies follow from the student's views of the teacher as a figure who possesses knowledge. Over the course of their years at college, students' views change. They begin to adopt the position that knowledge must be substantiated by evidence. In one study (Perry, 1970), most entering undergraduate students were found to view their instructors as figures of absolute authority. Sixty-eight percent of the entering college students in the Baxter Magolda (1992) study viewed themselves as heavily dependent on their instructors. Instructors are assumed to be accountable for managing the learning process by directing students to sources of information; establishing the pace, sequencing, and format for the delivery of this information; and dispensing knowledge to the learners.

Of course, instructors and educational institutions also actively exercise power, and that exercise is not restricted to undergraduate programs. Often, postgraduate educators confine students to the outer edges of the learning community, construct one-sided power relationships, and place a high emphasis on institutional compliance. As Alison Bartlett and Gina Mercer (2001) noted, the predominant model of postgraduate study assumes a power hierarchy that consists of knowing supervisors who dispense knowledge to unknowing students. The master and apprentice metaphor is often used to describe this relationship. Students are seen as disciples or acolytes or even "kids." Bartlett and Mercer concluded that such language "constructs a fundamentally unequal power relation and is deeply unsatisfactory in its oversimplification of a relationship which necessarily and fruitfully involves complex and dynamic negotiations of power" (p. 57).

In Scott Kerlin's (1995) survey of postdoctoral learners, many described their experience as a kind of hazing process in which they were subjected to rules of conformity and compliance that had never been made explicit ahead of time. Students often complained that their education was basically an endurance contest. They felt that they were required to jump through myriad hoops and that faculty never seemed to question whether the process actually produced intellectual or professional development.

When students' experiences and capabilities are disaffirmed by their instructors, the result can be the negation of the student's identity as a contributor to knowledge creation. One participant in Kerlin's (1995) study put it this way:

> No one seems to understand that I (and my fellow students) came here with several years experience in the workplace. I've managed several businesses and I don't need busy work to keep me focused. There doesn't seem to be any respect for what I have already accomplished. I'm just supposed to throw it away and act like I'm a clean slate. (p. 20)

Similarly, two doctoral students in a regional Australian university noted the irony in being selected as students on the basis of records as competent practitioners who had successful careers, but "with the swipe of the full-time student card, that expertise was made invisible. . . . As students we are recast as 'novices,' as uninitiated, and are sliced off from the 'real' work of the institution" (Balatti & Whitehouse, 2001, pp. 44–45).

When students move from the periphery to the center of their learning communities, learners and instructors assume more collegial roles. Power is an openly acknowledged and negotiated by-product of these relationships. Students are expected to take greater responsibility for their own learning, and the instructor or supervisor role evolves from authority to community guide and mentor.

Although the very nature of the postgraduate faculty role demands greater experience and responsibility for ensuring quality curricula, steps can be taken to gradually negotiate power and decision making within the postgraduate experience. Students can be given an opportunity to establish legitimate identities as co-contributors to knowledge. On the subject of space, power, and voice in postdoctoral research, Janet Conti, Daphne Hewson, and Judith Isben (2001) have suggested that by resisting hierarchical power and seeking mutual social power, the supervisor's role evolves toward that of a guide. These authors also use the term *interactive topographer* to describe the doctoral supervisor's revised role, acknowledging the need for experience and expertise in the relationship while minimizing power inequities.

In this revised relationship, discourse becomes more egalitarian. Mezirow (2000) defined discourse as the process "in which we have an active dialogue with others to better understand the meaning of an experience"

(p. 14). As an example of discourse, Mezirow described the model graduate seminar as follows:

> There are a set of commonly accepted norms that support the ideal conditions of discourse—there is no outside coercion . . . everyone has an equal opportunity to contribute, participants are informed on the topic to be discussed, and there are norms of courtesy, active listening, studying issues in advance, and taking turns to talk. Academic freedom permits anyone to be critically reflective of established cultural norms or viewpoints. (p. 15)

Roger Hiemstra (1998) has agreed that the successful socialization of graduate students requires a shift from the traditional supervisory relationship to one in which the partners become co-creators of knowledge. He suggested, however, that the relationship would require adjustment by both parties. For the mentor, it means allowing the protégé to develop his or her identity apart from the mentor. This can mean watching a protégé surpass one's own professional accomplishments. For the protégé, it means reducing one's dependence on the mentor. For both, it means that loyalty and trust must be a feature of the relationship.

A move toward the center of a learning community also requires greater awareness of the contextual and cultural features of the community by the protégé. Undergraduates experience the learning community to which they've gained membership largely in terms of practices and methodologies, rather than the beliefs and values that underlie these. Postgraduate members begin to understand that communities of practitioners are connected by intricate, socially constructed webs of belief. Such beliefs shape what they as practitioners do (Brown, Collins, & Duguid, 1989). Postgraduate students become aware of how the community's preferred modes of inquiry are connected to its culture. That is, they discover that the meaning of learning is configured by cultural practices that subsume the learning of skills (Lave & Wenger, 1991). Without such acculturation, students come away with only a surface understanding of available methods and methodology. To become a practitioner, one must become a full member of the community and its culture (Brown et al., 1989).

As emerging creators of knowledge, the unique challenge that postgraduate students face is one of developing awareness of the norms and models of inquiry that define and delineate the community of practice, while being able to trace the boundary area that confines and constrains that community. In other words, a new scholar-practitioner must learn how to become a good community citizen while engaging creative dissent.

Certain postgraduate experiences seem particularly helpful in moving students toward more centralized participation in their learning community. Experiences that provide opportunities to work with peers and instructors in the co-construction of learning within contextualized settings are often critical. Law students might be asked to work as court clerks or to conduct mock trials. Medical students may be asked to generate suggested treatments for mock cases. Challenging research assistantships can serve this purpose.

A good example is presented by Scott Taylor (2000), who described working with law students in moot court. Practicing lawyers from the community were asked to evaluate student arguments and, because the cases involved arguing tax law for businesses owned and regulated by a Native American tribe, local tribal officials also participated in the trials. In another kind of project, instructional design students at George Mason University formed teams to create e-learning programs for selected government agencies.

Experiential learning projects help transform student–teacher relationships from one-way information exchanges to true cognitive apprenticeships. Of course, many professions, from law and medicine to research science, offer some form of cognitive apprenticeship. When these are structured with care for the power implications they support, the student moves toward the center of the learning community, and being in the center of the learning community supports development. Figure 20.1 shows this movement. Note the factors that help students shift from the periphery to the center, and to co-ownership, of the learning community.

Another feature of experiences that enhance a student's position in the community is the structuring of markers or milestones over time. Milestones help students identify their transition from novice to journeyman and expert. They also serve as guides to the degree of supportive scaffolding students can or should expect. At Fielding Graduate University, for example, advanced students are invited to guide newer students through a doctoral orientation process. Students sit alongside faculty members on program committees that design curriculum or determine policies. Finally, they may become student members

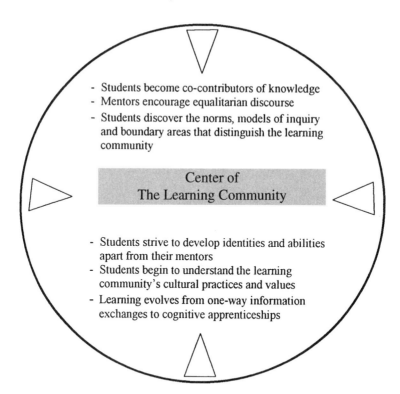

FIGURE 20.1 Moving to the center of the learning community.

of dissertation committees as well as co-authors of various faculty publications. The variety and timing of these experiences can be critical to one's development as a member of the learning community. They help transfer those tacit knowledge sets that are, by definition, implicit in the experience.

The development of tacit knowledge is a critical aspect of postgraduate study. Tacit knowledge may be defined as "knowledge that is not typically learned through formal instruction and is often not explicitly expressed" (Berg & Sternberg, 2002, p. 114). Tacit knowledge implies higher order thinking processes rather than the acquisition of facts. It involves the ability to formulate and solve problems within highly complex and unstructured settings (Dixon & Baltes, 1986; Ehrlich & Soloway, 1979; Polanyi, 1966; Sternberg et al., 2000). Tacit knowledge enables experts to identify new data quickly, as when an expert radiologist spots an abnormality in an x-ray. The schema that permit one to see nonroutine, highly meaningful information are often difficult to convey verbally (Myles-Worsley, Johnston, & Simons, 1988; Schmidt, Norman, & Boshuizen, 1990).

The critical role that tacit knowledge plays in professional expertise has been demonstrated in fields as diverse as computer programming and business management. At least one study has demonstrated regular increases in tacit knowledge from undergraduate through graduate education and again among graduate students and faculty in psychology (Wagner & Sternberg, 1986). Cognitive apprenticeships support the growth of expertise when they present students with ill-defined problems that arise from authentic activity. At Fielding, we are currently considering whether several predissertation students might be allowed to attend dissertation committee meetings (with the permission of the committee and dissertator) as many of the best interchanges between faculty members occur in this context and there are few chances to model such scholarly dialogue.

THE THIRD PATHWAY: GAINING A MORE COMPLETE UNDERSTANDING OF THE USE OF SELF IN THE LEARNING PROCESS

Table 20.3 outlines the changes in understanding typical of those who continue their educations past the undergraduate years.

TABLE 20.3. Membership in the Learning Community

From Peripheral Membership as Novice	To a Central Role as Contributing Expert
The learner begins as a novice and a peripheral member of the learning community.	The learner becomes a central contributing member of the community, progressing from journeyman, to expert and mentor.
Learning is regarded as solely an individualized and internalized experience.	Learning is experienced as the *iterative movement* between self-directed learning, personal reflection, and the dialogue/exchange within the community.
Learning is experienced as a largely one-way, at-arm's-length, instructor-directed, transfer of information.	Learning is seen as an *exchange* between the expert and the journeyman (with each growing from the exchange). The instructor becomes a guide; the learner assumes greater responsibility for socializing new members of the community.
The learning process is implicitly encased within a given mode of inquiry that is largely unexamined by the learner.	Learners are able to situate themselves within the larger *community of practice* by articulating the epistemological assumptions embedded in modes of inquiry (Stein, 1988).
The learner functions as a compliant follower.	Learners become aware of the boundary that constrains the community. As good community citizens, they learn when and how to engage in productive creative dissent.

An entry-level college student seldom reflects on his or her assumptions about self, the social construction of knowledge, or the impact of the dominant culture and ideology on the self and knowledge. Reflection, when it is undertaken, would appear to reside at the surface of the individual's phenomenological landscape, focusing on the content or method used in the analysis. Learners do not see the hidden power dynamics and problems that follow from hegemonic assumptions. In other words, during the early undergraduate years, learners tend to view learning as learning about things that lie "out there," or which are external to the self. In addition, the learner's reflective process tends to occur piece-meal; that is, the learner fails to make important connections between insights drawn about the self and how the individual participates in a given learning experience.

Part of the reason for this disconnection from the self is the largely cerebral and abstract nature offered by much of undergraduate education. Specifically, at this level, students often assume that academic learning requires a detached and dispassionate treatment of issues. The result is that learning within the academic setting is viewed as something completely separate from self-discovery, with emotive experiences seldom incorporated into the learning process. As students enter postgraduate study and engage in more intense dialogue, involvement in the community, and

personal discovery, they enter into a learning environment and developmental phase that together support the integration of emotion and logic. Baxter Magolda (1995) wrote that over the course of undergraduate studies "participants recognized that connecting to their emotions was essential in deciding what to believe, yet they were aware that this had to be balanced with rational reflection" (p. 66).

This integration of emotion and intellect has been called a key characteristic of maturity (Cornelius, Kenny, & Caspi, 1987; Labouvie-Vief & Diehl, 2000; Pascual-Leone, 1990; Sinnott, 1984) and is regarded as fundamental to wisdom (Dixon & Baltes, 1986; Polanyi, 1966; Sternberg et al., 2000). Sternberg and associates write that a common feature of all of these models of wisdom is the balancing of different aspects of the mind, or what Baltes called the "orchestration of mind."

At the postgraduate level, self-reflection assists students in translating insights about the self into a revised view of how they operate as members of their learning communities. In one work (Stevens-Long & McClintock, 2003), the authors proposed to code the statements of alumni from Fielding Graduate University about the changes in cognition and personal and professional development that they attribute to their graduate education. In many instances, it was difficult to determine whether a statement should be coded as cognition, emotion, or behavior. For instance, one participant spoke of feeling more confident and theoretically grounded in doing consulting, more aware of the conditionality of relationships, and increasingly able to suspend judgment. In another, a participant talked about feeling more integrated as a practitioner, encouraged to analyze the effects of one's presence in research and action settings. A third respondent described an experience of becoming more of a "human be-ing rather than a human do-ing." All of these statements suggest an integration of thinking, feeling, and acting that echoes the literature on wisdom.

Another kind of example comes from Baxter Magolda's (2001) longitudinal study of postgraduate workers and students. One of the respondents spoke of an education in clinical pastoral work as: "Doing a lot of what was being taught and starting to define identity along with what you were learning . . . And also seeing that when you do put it into action, what part of yourself is that unique part that you bring to the role" (p. 208).

When we speak of reflection, we are talking not only of the ability to maintain an active state of learning or reflection within the experience itself. This ability has been called "reflection-in-action" (Schon, 1983) or "mindfulness" (Langer, 1997; Tremmel, 1993). Baxter Magolda's example illustrates how students can also come to reflect on the limits of their knowing and how they enter into the development of knowledge. The awareness of how self and knowledge intersect corresponds to what Kitchener and King (1990) called *epistemic cognition*, the highest level of reflective judgment. Alumni at Fielding talk about becoming more conscious of their own thought processes and being able to deploy different cognitive abilities, such as systems thinking or an understanding of social constructionism to analyze situations—becoming, perhaps, the orchestraters of their own minds.

Similarly, when graduate students express and defend their positions as thinkers, they are presented with opportunities to deconstruct the logic behind their arguments. One Fielding alumnus (Stevens-Long & McClintock, 2003) talked about moving from personal knowledge to the public defense of an interpretation of data. In Baxter Magolda's (2001) group, one participant described an experience in his graduate-level economics course as follows:

We had to pick a topic and kind of take a position—we had to use economic tools, supply

and demand charts, and explain why we thought it was correct or incorrect. Which was something I had *never* done in economics. . . . Someone had to explain why supply side economics would reduce the federal deficit or would not. You had to argue it. . . . You had to have a reason why you did something. Every time I do something, I think through it a little more. (pp. 197–198)

To reach this level of reflection, however, students must often tolerate much self-uncertainty and accompanying anxiety. Quite often the reflective journey is a lonely one that forces the individual into an intense and sometimes painful confrontation with the self. Stephen Brookfield (1994) referred to "tales from the dark side" in describing the feelings of self-doubt and impostership that can accompany graduate education. Entering postgraduate students often report high levels of uncertainty regarding their capability for performance. In describing her own initial experience as a doctoral student, Frances Hughes (2001) wrote:

I felt like a fake; I felt like an imposter. I felt like I was constantly under the microscope. Everyone was watching me and evaluating me. I felt like I had to succeed no matter what. I felt inadequate and stupid at times . . . I felt scared and confused . . . somewhere along the way these feelings changed. (p. 20)

Feelings of doubt or insecurity are part and parcel of adult intellectual development. The graduate student experiences we have described parallel the type of intense and highly valued learning experiences that have been described by top-performing leaders. The executives profiled in *The Lessons of Experience* (McCall, Lombardo, & Morrison, 1998) all shared the characteristics of being "wise enough not to believe there is nothing more to learn, and courageous enough to look inside themselves and grapple with their frailties" (p. 127). Kerry Bunker (1989; Bunker & Webb, 1992) calls this ability the "willingness to grow against the grain." One Fielding alumnus describes how he learned to accept ideas he had personally resisted but that had been validated by the research (Stevens-Long & McClintock, 2003).

A critical factor in growing against the grain appears to be what Bunker (1989) has called developmental surrender, the willingness to accept temporary performance setbacks that plague a voluntary shift from expert to novice within a completely new learning situation. As Mezirow (2000) cautioned, "Transformative learning, especially when it involves subjective reframing, is often an intensely threatening emotional experience, in which we have to become aware of both the assumptions under-girding our ideas and those supporting our emotional responses to the need to change" (p. 6).

The competitive environment of most postgraduate education seems unlikely to promote developmental surrender. In fact, it seems likely to make surrender more painful. There is little encouragement to share one's personal journey or emotional difficulties. This is certainly an arena in which stronger developmental support might be provided.

THE FOURTH PATHWAY: DEVELOPING AN INCREASED AWARENESS OF SOCIAL AND CULTURAL PERSPECTIVES

How awareness of the social and cultural context influences development during post-graduate education is described in table 20.4.

All learning communities exist in the context of larger social arenas, and a final path in graduate development runs through that larger world. For many individuals, the learning enclave itself provides some exposure to diverse learners from across the world. As a result, over the course of a college education, students tend to develop greater tolerance for different religious and political views (Pascarella & Terenzini, 1991). These changes accompany the transition from an absolute, either-or value structure to one that is more accepting of alternative viewpoints (Perry, 1970).

Later in their education, students become aware of culturally based assumptions regarding learning approaches and the joint management of knowledge (Pratt, 1991) as well as of cultural and ideological bias in assumptions about that which fosters learning (Brockett & Hiemstra, 1991; Brookfield, 1994, 2000b; Candy, 1991). Learners become sensitized to the ways that learning experiences are influenced by power relationships. They become more aware of how they learn and how the context shapes learners, instructors, and the learning transaction itself (Cafarella & Merriam, 2000).

Although inclusiveness is certainly served by experiences that broaden the perspectives of individual students, the educational setting itself may or may not

TABLE 20.4. Cultural Perspective

From Hegemonic and Insular	To Inclusive and Global
The learner's cultural bias and personal ideology are implicit and unexamined. Learners assume that it is possible to take a "pure and objective: stance to learning.	Learners come to acknowledge cultural biases and ideological perspectives that can shape the learning experience. As members of the learning community, they become sensitive to disagreements that may be reflective of underlying discrepancies in ideological viewpoints.
Learners accept hegemonic assumptions (Brookfield, 2000a, 2000b), they assume that their own beliefs, and epistemological assumptions either are or should be shared by all participants within the learning community. Learners may assume that those who hold minority perspectives should accommodate to the culturally dominant approach to learning.	Learners become more sensitized to culturally based assumptions regarding learning approaches and the joint management of knowledge (Pratt, 1991; Caffarella & Merriam, 2000).
Learners treat distance learning as traditional instructor-driven pedagogy; existing power inequities are merely amplified through technology.	Learners discover how to use distance learning to serve as an inclusive web for providing balanced access/power among community members.
	Learners become more aware of how their own learning and those of others in the learning community are influenced by power relationships.

serve inclusiveness and encourage multiple perspectives. Rosemary Caffarella and Sharan Merriam (2000) related a story in which one of the authors attempted to recognize the outstanding efforts of a Taiwanese graduate student by reading the student's paper aloud to the class as an example of exceptional work, a decision that proved most embarrassing for the student. It also appeared to have a negative impact on the student's subsequent performance. For some Asian students, to be singled out is to be marginalized.

In its most innocuous form, marginalization occurs as a failure to understand. More insidiously, a community of practice may develop an exclusionary culture that ignores the needs of marginalized groups. In this respect, Scott Kerlin (1995) argued that one of the reasons why men complete doctoral programs more often than women (Lomperis, 1990) is that women are exposed to a high percentage of male faculty as mentors and guides. Kerlin related this finding to the fact that many women graduate students have experienced poor working relationships with male faculty advisors in environments that emphasize competitiveness, individualism, and a win-lose mentality.

When marginalized groups are excluded from participation, it not only affects those individuals confined to the edge of the community but also works against those who reside in the center of cultural power. The environment lacks the strength of the diverse viewpoints that fuel dialectical discourse. Furthermore, such an educational setting is likely to be constrained by cultural bias and hegemonic assumptions that remain implicit and unexamined. Hegemony implies many subtle assumptions that can become deeply incorporated into our day-to-day thinking. Brookfield (2000b) wrote,

One cannot peel back the layers of oppression and point the finger at an identifiable group or groups of people whom we accuse as the instigators of a conscious conspiracy to keep people silent and disenfranchised. Instead, the ideas and practices of hegemony become part and parcel of everyday life—the stock opinions, conventional wisdom, or common sense ways of seeing and ordering the world that people take for granted. If there is a conspiracy here, it is the conspiracy of the normal. (p. 41)

Postgraduate study can set the stage for a more inclusive perspective by increasing open dialogue and broader exposure to a wider range of viewpoints. It can provide an opportunity to uncover hegemonic assumptions, to challenge the cultural bias and implicit agreements that shape our discourse. It can raise new possibilities for what to believe and how to put those beliefs into action. Or not.

Transformational learning can follow from a consideration of how positionality (differences in race, gender, and sexual orientation) shape interaction. One African American, Mary Handley (Tisdell, Handley, & Taylor, 2000) described her effort to bring positionality into perspective:

I approach the idea of positionality by attempting to create an education environment that allows difference to flourish. This means taking an active role in addressing the power discrepancies that exist between and among students and faculty by establishing ground rules early on, including often marginalized voices about the topic under discussion through readings, outside speakers, and setting conditions and a tone necessary for all voices to be included in critical discourse. (p. 134)

Building an environment in which optimal critical discourse can flourish is no mean task. It requires that students and faculty make a concerted effort to listen without dismissing or attacking. The ethics of inclusiveness may be seen as incompatible with the critical, competitive atmosphere of much academic discourse. As Mary Belenky, Blythe Clenchy, Nancy Goldberger, and Jill Tarule (1986) suggest, students and supervisors must engage in discourse that centers on understanding and negotiating outcomes. It is essential that we give students equal play and permit them to share implicit risks.

Such egalitarian discourse can generate a new dialogic space in which cultural differences and positionality can be located. In this space, graduate education becomes less a means of self-replication for the supervisor and more an instrument of change for both the student and the community (Belenky et al., 1986).

SUMMARY AND CONCLUSIONS

Returning a final time to the issues described by Nyquist and Woodford (2000), we might ask, "What would it take to support developmental maturity in graduate education?" Whereas the evidence clearly suggests that intellectual function changes over the postdoctoral years, we have little information on the development of either emotional life or behavior. Yet the integration of emotion and intellect is considered a key characteristic of maturity and is fundamental to wisdom. Furthermore, we contend that mature people probably behave differently from less mature individuals, although evidence for this proposition is fairly slim.

Pulling together the various strands of this chapter and its review, we begin with four recommendations. First, a graduate education must be more self-directed than is often the case. Students should be allowed, even expected, to take greater responsibility for their educational curricula and the methods they choose for demonstrating their competencies. Furthermore, students should be encouraged to identify innovative learning projects and work with ill-defined problems.

Second, it seems sensible to try to move graduate students toward the center of the learning community as quickly as possible. This means that students and faculty are supported in the acknowledgment and negotiation of power relationships. When the environment resists hierarchical power relationships, the supervisor's role may evolve toward that of a guide instead of an authority. This means that what the student brings in terms of life experience is honored along with his or her ability to take a fresh look at the problems the learning community intends to address.

Third, faculty and students must understand and support learners' emotional journey from the periphery to the center of the learning community. Changes in the way people define the self and the ways they understand the construction of knowledge are often accompanied by intense self-doubt and anxiety. Opportunities to explore these feelings and to support self-discovery might become a regular feature of postgraduate education if we hope to encourage a growth in maturity and wisdom along with progress toward dialectical, reflective thinking.

Fourth, diversity and inclusiveness should be deliberately encouraged, for these broaden the perspectives of both the students and the faculty. This can fuel dialectical discourse and encourage people to explore the cultural bias and hegemonic assumptions that constrain their own thinking and the development of their field of study. Egalitarian discourse can generate a new dialogic space in which cultural differences and positionality can be located.

This chapter suggests a wide variety of experiments that might be conducted in conventional doctoral programs, as well as a range of measures that might be undertaken in many less conventional institutions. There is currently little work of any kind on the development of emotional and behavioral maturity among doctoral students, although some literature exists relative to what such terms might imply. Postgraduate education seems to offer a perfect opportunity to capture both the process and the product in the study of adult development and learning.

In sum, then, this chapter presents evidence that graduate education has great developmental potential. There is little doubt but that graduate students become more dialectical thinkers, moving toward a metasystematic level of thought in which they are able to compare, contrast, transform, and synthesize systems of relationships. They understand the uncertainty of knowledge and the distinction between problems that can be resolved with certainty and those that have no single solution, and they learn to evaluate the worth of differing explanations through the comparison of evidence and opinion. In addition, graduate educational experience is associated with perspective transformation, causing students to challenge the assumptions that constrain the ways they perceive, understand, and feel about the world.

These cognitive changes are intertwined with evidence of profound personal change, including increased patience, empathy, and self-confidence. Students may begin to experience the self as less a stable, unified entity and as more of a self that is in continual dialogue between and among perspectives. They may become more aware that reality is socially constructed and that the self, within that construction, is more fluid, full of ambiguity and paradox.

Finally, there is reason to believe that the emotional and cognitive changes people experience during their graduate educations may be associated with behavioral changes, perhaps even with wise behavior. Wisdom may be defined as behavior that communicates understanding and caring. Wisdom may allow one to integrate the inner self and internal, affective concerns, with outer, conventional reality. We argue here that the best graduate education, especially graduate education aimed at training the scholar-practitioner, should lead to wisdom. The capacity for reflection in the midst of action and the acceptance of paradox and ambiguity might allow one to cope with the unique, uncertain, and conflicting situations of practice. We might well expect this capacity to accompany the intellectual stretching, cognitive development, perspective transformation, and greater fluidity in the sense of self. Indeed, these gains have been suggested by the research literature on adult development and by its compatriot, adult learning.

References

Achenbaum, W. A., & Orwoll, L. (1991). Becoming wise: A psycho-gerontological interpretation of the book of Job. *International Journal of Aging and Human Development, 32,* 21–39.

Ackoff, R. L. (1981). *Creating the corporate future.* New York: Wiley.

Argyris, C., & Schon, D. A. (1978). *Organizational learning: A theory of action perspective.* Reading, MA: Addison-Wesley.

Arlin, P. K. (1975). Cognitive development in adulthood: A fifth stage? *Developmental Psychology, 11,* 602–606.

Arlin, P. K. (1984). Adolescent and adult thought: A structural interpretation. In M. L. Commons, F. A. Richards, & C. Armon (Eds.), *Beyond formal operations. Vol. 1: Late adolescent and adult cognitive development* (pp. 258–271). New York: Praeger.

Arlin, P. K. (1977). Piagetian operators in problem-finding. *Developmental Psychology, 13,* 297–298.

Arlin, P. K. (1990). Wisdom: The art of problem finding. In R. J. Sternberg (Ed.), *Wisdom: Its nature, origin, and development* (pp. 230–243). New York: Cambridge University Press.

Aronson, E., Wilson, T., & Akert, R. M. (2002). *Social psychology.* Upper Saddle River, NJ: Prentice Hall.

Bacelar, W. T. (1998). *Age differences in adult cognitive complexity: The role of life experiences and personality.* Unpublished doctoral dissertation, Rutgers University, New Brunswick, NJ.

Bakhtin, M. M. (1981). The dialogic imagination. In M. Holquist (Ed.) & C. Emerson & M. Holquist (Trans.), *Four essays by M. M. Bakhtin* (pp. 259–300). Austin: University of Texas Press.

Balatti, J., & Whitehouse, H. (2001). Novice at forty: Transformation or re-invention. In A. Bartlett & A. Mercer (Eds.), *Postgraduate research supervision: Transforming (R)elations* (Vol. 1, pp. 43–53). New York: Peter Lang.

Baltes, P. B., Lindenberger, U., & Staudinger, U. M. (1998). Life-span theory in developmental psychology. In W. Damon & R. Lerner (Eds.), *Handbook of child psychology* (Vol. 1, 5th ed., pp. 1029–1143). New York: Wiley.

Bartlett, A., & Mercer, G. (2001). Mostly metaphors: Theorizing from a practice of supervision. In A. Bartlett & G. Mercer (Eds.), *Postgraduate research supervision: Transforming (R)elations* (Vol. 11, pp. 55–69). New York: Peter Lang.

Basseches, M. A. (1980). Dialectical schemata: A framework for the empirical study of development of dialectical thinking. *Human Development, 23,* 400–421.

Basseches, M. A. (1984). *Dialectical thinking and adult development.* New York: Ablex.

Baxter Magolda, M. (1995). The integration of relational and impersonal knowing in young adults' epistemological development. *Journal of College Student Development, 36,* 205–216.

Benack, S. (1984). Postformal epistemology and the growth of empathy. In M. L. Commons, F. A. Richards, & C. Armon (Eds.), *Beyond formal operations. Vol. 1: Late adolescence and adult cognitive development* (pp. 340–356). New York: Praeger.

Berg, C. A., & Sternberg, R. J. (2002). Multiple perspectives on the development of intelligence. In J. Demick & C. Andreoletti (Eds.), *Handbook of adult development* (pp. 103–120). New York: Kluwer Academic/Plenum.

Belenky, M. F., Clinchy, B. M., Goldberger, N. R., & Tarule, J. M. (1986). *Women's ways of knowing.* New York: Basic Books.

Brandtstädter, J. (1998). Action perspectives on human development. In W. Damon & R. Lerner (Eds.), *Theoretical models of human development: Handbook of child psychology* (Vol. 1, 5th ed., pp. 807–863). New York: Wiley.

Bredo, E. (1997). The social construction of learning. In G. D. Phye (Ed.), *Handbook of academic learning: Construction of knowledge. The educational psychology series* (pp. 3–45). San Diego, CA: Academic Press.

Brockett, R. G., & Hiemstra, R. (1991). *Self-direction in adult learning: Perspectives on theory, research and practice.* New York: Routledge.

Brookfield, S. D. (1994). Tales from the dark side: A phenomenography of adult critical reflection. *International Journal of Lifelong Learning, 13,* 203–216.

Brookfield, S. D. (2000a). The concept of critically reflective practice. In A. L. Wildon & E. R. Hayes (Eds.), *Handbook of adult and continuing education* (pp. 33–49). San Francisco: Jossey-Bass.

Brookfield, S. D. (2000b). Transformative learning as ideology critique. In J. Mezirow (Ed.), *Learning as transformation: Critical perspectives on a theory in progress* (pp. 125–148). San Francisco: Jossey-Bass.

Broughton, J. M. (1977). Beyond formal operations: Theoretical thought in adolescence. *Teachers College Record, 79,* 87–98.

Broughton, J. M. (1984). Not beyond formal operations, but beyond Piaget. In M. L. Commons, F. A. Richards, & C. Armon (Eds.), *Beyond formal operations: Late adolescent and adult cognitive development* (pp. 395–411). New York: Praeger.

Brown, J. S., Collins, A., & Duguid, P. (1989). Situated learning and the culture of learning. *Educational Researcher, 16,* 32–42

Bunker, K. (1989). Leaders and the dark chasm of learning. *Issues and Observations, 9,* 1, 5–6.

Bunker, K., & Webb, A. (1992). *Learning how to learn from experience: Impact of stress and coping.* Greensboro, NC: Center for Creative Leadership.

Caffarella, R. S., & Merriam, S. B. (2000) Linking the individual learner to the context of adult learning. In A. L. Wilson & E. R. Hayes (Eds.), *Handbook of adult and continuing education* (pp. 55–70). San Francisco: Jossey-Bass.

Candy, P. C. (1991). *Self-direction for lifelong learning.* San Francisco: Jossey-Bass.

Cervone, D., & Peake, P. (1986). Anchoring, efficacy, and action: The influence of judgmental heuristics on self efficacy judgments and behavior. *Journal of Personality and Social Psychology, 50,* 492–501.

Cockrill, T. (1989) The kind of competence for rapid change. *Personnel Management, 86,* 52–56.

Commons, M. L., & Richards, F. A. (1978). *The structural analytic stage of development: A Piagetian postformal stage.* Paper presented at Western Psychological Association, San Francisco, CA.

Commons, M. L., & Richards, F. A. (1984). A general model of stage theory. In M. L. Commons, F. A. Richards, & C. Armon (Eds.), *Beyond formal operations. Vol. 1: Late adolescence and adult cognitive development* (pp. 340–356). New York: Praeger.

Commons, M. L., & Richards, F. A. (2002). Four postformal stages. In J. Demick & C. Andreoletti (Eds.), *Handbook of adult development* (pp. 199–220). New York: Plenum.

Conti, J., Hewson, D., & Isben, J. (2001). Power, voice and connection. In A. Barlett & G. Mercer (Eds.), *Postgraduate research supervision: Transforming (R)elations* (Vol. 11, pp. 161–173). New York: Peter Lang.

Cook-Greuter, S. (1999). *Postautonomous ego development: A study of its nature and measurement.* Unpublished doctoral dissertation, Harvard University, Boston, MA.

Cornelius, S. W., Kenny, S., & Caspi, A. (1987). Everyday problem solving in adulthood and old age. *Psychology and Aging, 2,* 144–153.

Deegan, M. J., & Hill, M. H. (1991). Doctoral dissertations as liminal journeys of the self: Betwixt and between in graduate sociology programs. *Teaching Sociology, 19,* 322–332.

Dewey, J. (1933). *Experience and education.* New York: Collier.

Dixon, R. A., & Baltes, P. B. (1986). Toward life-span research on the functions and pragmatics of intelligence. In R. J. Sternberg & R. K. Wagner (Eds.), *Practical intelligence* (pp. 203–234). Cambridge: Cambridge University Press.

Domangue, B. A. (1978). Decoding effects of cognitive complexity, tolerance of ambiguity, and verbal-nonverbal inconsistency. *Journal of Personality, 4,* 519–535.

Ehrlich, K., & Soloway, E. (1979). An empirical investigation of the tacit plan knowledge in programming. In J. C. Thomas & M. L. Schneider (Eds.), *Human factors in computer systems* (pp. 113–133). Norwood, NJ: Ablex.

Fischer, K. W., Yan, Z., & Stewart, J. B. (2002). Adult cognitive development: Dynamics in the developmental web. In J. Demick & C. Andreoletti (Eds.), *Handbook of adult development* (pp. 169–198). New York: Plenum.

Freire, P. (2000). *Pedagogy of the oppressed.* New York: Continuum.

Gist, M. E. (1989). The influence of training method on self-efficacy and idea generation among managers. *Personnel Psychology, 47,* 787–805.

Hedlund, J., & Sternberg, R. J. (2000). Too many intelligences? Integrating social, emotional, and practical intelligence. In R. Bar-On & D. A. Parker (Eds.), *The handbook of emotional intelligence* (pp. 136–170). San Francisco: Jossey-Bass.

Hewlett, D. (2004). A qualitative study of postautonomous ego development: The bridge between postconventional and transcendent ways of being. Unpublished doctoral dissertation, Fielding Graduate University, Santa Barbara, CA.

Hiemstra, R. (1998). From mentor to partner: Lessons from a personal journey. *New Directions for Adult and Continuing Education, 79,* 43–51.

Hill, L. A., & Elias, J. (1990). Retraining midcareer managers: Career history and self-efficacy beliefs. *Human Resource Management, 29,* 197–217.

Hughes, F. R. (2001). *A qualitative inquiry into the first semester experience of counselor education doctoral students.* Pocatello: Idaho State, Department of Counseling.

Jarvis, P. (1987). Meaningful and meaningless experience: Toward an analysis of learning from life. *Adult Education Quarterly, 37,* 164–172.

Kegan, R. (1984). *In over our heads.* Cambridge, MA: Harvard University Press.

Kelly, G. A. (Ed.). (1955). *The psychology of personal constructs.* New York: Norton.

Kerlin, S. P. (1995). Surviving the doctoral years: Critical perspectives. *Education Policy Analysis Archives, 3,* 1–39.

Kitchener, K. S., & Brenner, H. G. (1990). Wisdom and reflective judgment: Knowing in the face of uncertainty. In R. J. Sternberg (Ed.), *Wisdom: Its nature, origins, and development* (pp. 212–229). New York: Cambridge University Press

Kitchener, K. S., & King, P. (1990). A reflective judgment model: Transforming assumptions about knowing. In J. Mezirow (Ed.), *Fostering critical reflection in adulthood* (pp. 159–180). San Francisco: Jossey-Bass.

Kitchener, K. S., & King, P. (1994). *Developing reflective judgment.* San Francisco: Jossey-Bass.

Kohlberg, L. (1990). Which postformal levels are stages? In M. L. Commons, F. A. Richards, T. A. Grotzer, & J. D. Sinnott (Eds.), *Adult development. Vol. 2: Models and methods in the study of adolescent and adult thought* (pp. 263–268). New York: Praeger.

Kramer, D. (2002). Wisdom. In J. Demick & C. Andreoletti (Eds.), *Handbook of adult development* (pp. 130–152). New York: Plenum.

Labouvie-Vief, G. (1992). A Neo-Piagetian perspective on adult cognitive development. In R. J. Sternberg & C. A. Berg (Eds.), *Intellectual development* (pp. 197–228). New York: Cambridge University Press.

Labouvie-Vief, G. (2000). Affect complexity and views of the transcendent. In M. Miller & P. Eisendrath-Young (Eds.), *The psychology of mature spirituality: Integrity, wisdom and transcendence* (pp. 103–119). Philadelphia: Routledge.

Labouvie-Vief, G., & Diehl, M. (1999). Self and personality development. In J. Cavanaugh & S. Whitbourne (Eds.), *Gerontology*. New York: Oxford University Press.

Langer, E. J. (1997). *The power of mindful learning*. Reading, MA: Addison-Wesley.

Lave, J., & Wenger, E. (1991). *Situated learning: Legitimate peripheral participation*. Cambridge: University of Cambridge Press.

Lomperis, A. M. T. (1990). Are women changing the nature of the academic profession? *Journal of Higher Education, 61*, 643–677.

Markus, H. R. (1977). Self-schemata and processing information about the self. *Journal of Personality and Social Psychology, 63*–78.

McCall, M. W., Lombardo, M. M., & Morrison, A. M. (1988) *The lessons of experience: How successful executives develop on the job*. Lexington, MA: Lexington Books.

McClintock, C. C., & Stevens-Long, J. E. (2002, June). *Assessing the ineffable in graduate education*. Paper presented at the Association for the Advancement of Higher Education, Boston, MA.

Meacham, J. (1990). The loss of wisdom. In R. J. Sternberg (Ed.), *Wisdom: Its nature, origins, and development* (pp. 181–211). New York: Cambridge University Press

Mezirow, J. (1991). *Transformative dimensions of adult learning*. San Francisco: Jossey-Bass.

Mezirow, J. (2000). Learning to think like an adult: Core concepts of transformation theory. In J. Mezirow (Ed.), *Learning as transformation: Critical perspective on a theory in progress* (pp. 1–33). San Francisco: Jossey-Bass.

Myles-Worsley, M., Johnston, W. A., & Simons, M. A. (1988). The influence of expertise on x-ray image processing. *Journal of Experimental Psychology: Learning, Memory and Cognition, 14*, 553–557.

Nyquist, J., & Woodford, B. (2000). *Re-envisioning the Ph.D.: What concerns do we have?* Seattle: University of Washington, Center for Instruction Development and Research.

Pascarella, E. T., & Terenzini, P. T. (1991). *How college affects students: Findings and insights from twenty years of research*. San Francisco: Jossey-Bass

Pascual-Leone, J. (1990). An essay on wisdom: Toward organismic processes that make it possible. In R. J. Sternberg (Ed.), *Wisdom: Its nature, origins, and development* (pp. 244–278). Cambridge: Cambridge University Press.

Perry, W. G. Jr. (1970). *Forms of ethical and intellectual development in the college years*. New York: Holt, Rinehart & Wilson.

Pintrich, P. R., & Schrauben, B. (1992). Students' motivational beliefs and their cognitive engagement in classroom academic tasks. In D. Schunk & J. Meece (Eds.), *Student perceptions in the classroom: Causes and consequences* (pp. 149–183). Hillsdale, NJ: Erlbaum.

Polanyi, M. (1966). *The tacit dimension*. Garden City, NY: Doubleday.

Pratt, D. D. (1991). Conceptions of self within China and the United States: Contrasting adult development. *International Journal of Intercultural Relations, 15*, 285–310.

Privett, D. (2002). Facilitating critical reflection with career development practitioners: A critical inquiry. Unpublished masters thesis, Saint Francis Xavier University, Antigonish, NS, Canada.

Richardson, F. C., Rogers, A., & McCarroll, J. (1998). Toward a dialogical self. *American Behavioral Scientist, 41*, 496–515.

Riegel, K. E. F. (1973). Dialectical operations: The final phase of cognitive development. *Human Development, 16*, 346–370.

Schon, D. A. (1983). *The reflective practitioner: How professionals think in action*. New York: Basic Books.

Schmidt, H. G., Norman, G. R., & Boshuizen, H. P. A. (1990). A cognitive perspective on medical expertise: Theory and implications. *Academic Medicine, 65*, 611–621.

Schoenholz-Read, J. (2000). *Interim report on student development and diversity study*. Unpublished manuscript, Fielding Graduate University, Santa Barbara, CA.

Scribner, S. (1986). Thinking in action: Some characteristics of practical thought. In R. J. Sternberg & K. D. Wagner (Eds.), *Practical intelligence: Nature and origins of competence in everyday life* (pp. 13–30). New York: Cambridge University Press.

Sinnott, J. D. (1981). The theory of relativity: A metatheory for development? *Human Development, 24*, 293–311.

Sinnott, J. D. (1984). Postformal reasoning: The relativistic stage. In M. L. Commons, F. Richards, & C. Armon (Eds.), *Beyond formal operations* (pp. 298–325). New York: Praeger.

Staudinger, U. (1996). Wisdom and the social-interactive foundation of the mind. In P. B. Baltes & U. M. Staudinger (Eds.), *Interactive minds: Life-span perspectives on the social foundation of cognition* (pp. 276–315). New York: Cambridge University Press.

Stein, D. (1998). *Situated learning in adult education* (Digest #195). Columbus, OH, ERIC Clearinghouse: Adult, Career, and Vocational Education. Retrieved June 2003 from http://ericacve.org/docgen. asp?tbl=digests&ID=48

Sternberg, R. J. (1984). Higher-order reasoning in postformal operational thought. In M. L. Commons, F. A.

Richards, & C. Armon (Eds.), *Beyond formal operations. Vol. 1: Late adolescence and adult cognitive development* (pp. 74–91). New York: Praeger.

Sternberg, R. J., Forsythe, G. B., Hedlund, J., Horvath, J. A., Wagner, R. K., Williams, W. M., et al. (2000). *Practical intelligence in everyday life.* New York: Cambridge University Press.

Sternberg, R. J., & Grigorenko, E. L. (2000). Practical intelligence and its development. In R. Bar-On & D. A. Parker (Eds.), *The handbook of emotional intelligence* (pp. 215–243). San Francisco: Jossey-Bass.

Stevens-Long, J. (2000). The prism self: Multiplicity on the road to transcendence. In M. Miller & P. Eisendrath-Young (Eds.), *The psychology of mature spirituality: Integrity, wisdom and transcendence* (pp. 160–174). Philadelphia: Routledge

Stevens-Long, J., & McClintock, C. (2003). *Ineffable changes: Cognitive, personal and professional development in graduate education.* Santa Barbara, CA: Fielding Graduate Institute.

Streufert, S., & Swezey, R. W. (1986) *Complexity, managers and organizations.* Orlando, FL: Academic Press.

Taylor, S. A. (2000) An experiment in reciprocal experimental learning. *Active Learning in Education, 1,* 60–78.

Tennant, M. (2000). Adult learning for self-development and change. In A. L. Wilson & E. R. Hayes (Eds.), *Handbook of adult and continuing education* (pp. 87–100). New York: Wiley.

Tennant, M., & Pogson, P. (1995). *Learning and change in the adult years: A developmental perspective.* San Francisco: Jossey-Bass.

Tisdell, E. J., Handley, M. S., & Taylor, E. W. (2000) Different perspectives on teaching for critical consciousness. In A. L. Wilson & E. R. Hayes (Eds.), *Handbook of adult and continuing education* (pp. 132–146). San Francisco, Jossey-Bass.

Tremmcl, R. (1993). Zen and the art of reflective practice in teacher education. *Harvard Educational Review, 63,* 434–458.

Wagner, R. K., & Sternberg, R. J. (1985). Practical intelligence in real-world pursuits: The role of tacit knowledge. *Journal of Personality and Social Psychology, 49,* 436–458

Vygotsky, L. S. (1986). *Thought and language* (2nd rev. ed.). Cambridge, MA: MIT Press.

Zimmerman, B. J., & Martinez-Pons, M. (1990). Student differences in self-regulated learning: Relating grade, sex, and giftednesss to self-efficacy and strategy use. *Journal of Educational Psychology, 82,* 51–59.

Chapter 21

The Evolution of Professional Competence

Garrett McAuliffe

Adult development is emerging as a particularly powerful factor in explaining professional competence (Kegan, 1994; Rooke & Torbert, 1998). Development-related characteristics have been linked to transformational leadership (Fisher & Torbert, 1995), eminence in law (O'Donovan-Polten, 2001), expert practice in management (Ferry & Ross-Gordon, 1998), more effective teaching (Kirby & Paradise, 1992), architectural artistry (Schon, 1987), more skillful social work practice (B. Moore, 2000), "caring" nursing (Johns, 2002), and critical thinking in counselors (Irving & Williams, 1995). As a result of this research, Rooke (2003) has concluded that for the field of management, "sufficient managers must have post-conventional meaning-making capacity" (p. 2). It is the purpose of this chapter to examine the empirical basis for this and other claims that development is associated with professional competence.

The power of developmental learning lies in the pervasiveness of developmental change. This "higher order" change in a professional's mental framework has cross-situational, cross-domain impacts. In that vein, Rooke (2003) has pointed to the impact of an individual's developmental "meaning making capacity" across the domains of emotions, morality, humor, intimacy, spirituality, and, of course, work. If development has such power, then developmental learning becomes a goal for professional education and training. Developmental learning consists of changes in mental frameworks, changes that spread out over many domains of professional practice (Granott, 1998). Correspondingly, developmental educational strategies have emerged for that purpose (e.g., Fisher & Torbert, 1995; Kegan & Lahey, 2001; McAuliffe & Lovell, 2000; Sprinthall, 1994).

THE NATURE OF PROFESSIONAL WORK

A classic characterization of a "professional" is that of an individual who lays claim to extraordinary knowledge in matters of great human importance, has significant autonomy in regulating her or his practice, and receives a special mandate for control of those who enter the field (Hughes, 1959). Schon (1991) extended the definition, describing the work of a professional as activity that consistently calls for judgment and considered action in multifaceted situations. These situations are especially characterized by ambiguity and are fraught with ethical and value conflicts. They are not suitable for rote, familiar resolutions (Harris, 1993).

The fates of organizations and human lives can rely on the competence of professionals who make judgments and take actions under conditions of uncertainty. It is imperative, therefore, that the requirements for professional competence be delineated, so that initial professional education and ongoing training match those requisites. Developmental capacity, or stage, is one of those conditions, as professional work requires a high level of complexity that comes with increasing developmental capacity. But first, a clarification of the notion of professional competence is in order.

PROFESSIONAL COMPETENCE

A comprehensive definition of competence is offered by Willis and Dubin (1990), who define it as "the ability to function effectively in the tasks considered essential within a given profession" (p. 3). In this formulation, competence relies on two broad domains, one of which is especially important to adult development. The first consists of proficiencies that are specific to a field. The second includes general characteristics of the individual. It is this latter domain, as it can be translated into developmental terms, that is of interest in this chapter.

Factors That Contribute to Professional Competence

Professional work requires so-called higher order thinking for the often amorphous, complex situations that professionals encounter (Cheetham & Chivers, 1998). The literature names such broad competency-related characteristics as flexibility, communication, ability to learn, context sensitivity, and problem solving (Hyland, 1992; Linstead, 1991; Reynolds & Snell, 1988).

There is evidence that behind these individual characteristics are implicit frames of mind that can evolve (Rooke & Torbert, 1998). The particular frame of mind

associated with professional competence is, most simply put, autonomous or self-directed thinking. Kegan (1994) describes such a frame of mind as the "self-authorizing" order of consciousness. This way of knowing is characterized by initiative, sensitivity to one's own subjectivity, evidence-based decision making, and self-evaluation, to name several consistent qualities. These development-related characteristics stand in stark contrast to other-directedness and rote application of technical knowledge (Fisher & Torbert, 1995; Rooke & Torbert, 1998; Torbert, 1994). Thus, professional competence is not achieved by simply applying clear, technical, and universally applicable solutions to practical problems but by being able to make evidence-based decisions that emerge from the consideration of multiple perspectives. Professional competence is a product of this reflective capacity. It is not consistent with unquestioned allegiance to routine and tradition.

The predictors of professional achievement in midlife are consistent with these claims about development. Broadly stated, midlife professional competency is most clearly associated with autonomy in the form of acting in accordance with relatively self-defined principles and ideals, increased self-acceptance, and increased freedom from what others think. Professional competence is also related to a nondefensive openness in the form of being less cynical and less critical of others and the system, willingness to consider alternate viewpoints, being reflective about the beliefs and myths of the culture, and flexibility in approaching tasks (Axelrod, 1999; O'Donovan-Polten, 2001; Schaie, 1986; Valliant, 1993; Willis & Tosti-Vasey, 1990).

All of these qualities can be considered adult developmental achievements in the direction of postconventional thinking (Rooke, 2003). They are not merely static characteristics of particular personalities (Kegan, 1994; W. S. Moore, 2002). The learning that is required for professionals to achieve those later stages of development, or "orders of consciousness" (Kegan, 1994), is addressed shortly, as they are elaborated in the work of Schon (1983, 1987), Kegan (1994), and Torbert (1987) and their associates.

CAREER/LIFE PHASE AND CONSTRUCTIVE STAGE AS FACTORS IN COMPETENCE

The most common developmental explanation of career has been the so-called career/life phase approach.

As will be shown, this approach is less helpful than the constructive stage explanation for showing the developing mental capacity that is required for professional competence.

Career Phase

The career/life phase literature (e.g. Schein, 1978; Super, 1980) prescribes the desirable developmental tasks that contribute to competence at each point in the professional career. Such tasks lay out the "curriculum" (Kegan, 1994) that a society has set for approval and success. Each phasic task makes sense as a requirement of a time in life, one that may not be helpful later (e.g., the common relentless drive of early career, the self-definition of midcareer achievement, the broader perspective and sense of finiteness of late career; O'Donovan-Polten, 2001).

Career phase theory alerts individuals to pay attention to and act on age-related internal promptings and social expectations. Marcia (1966), following Erikson (1963), has proposed that the notions of crisis and commitment are especially helpful rubrics for explaining how individuals confront life phase tasks (Marcia, 1966). At each life phase, there can be a crisis, a time in which a particular set of career challenges are ascendant. If the individual faces the phasic crisis by acknowledging it and exploring options, she or he can then make a new commitment to a more vital life role.

Career phase theory can be a guide for those who would seek satisfaction and achievement in work career and for those who would counsel them. Thus, for example, through knowing the career phase prescriptions, the early career professional is alerted to the tasks of forming a career identity through occupational exploration, demonstrating beginning competence, and learning to "fit in" (Greenhaus, 1987). Similarly, the midcareer professional can address renewal, obsolescence, emphasis shifts in life roles, and the possibilities of generativity and mentoring (Erikson, 1963). Finally, and broadly speaking, the late career professional can be guided by the themes of deceleration or continuing investment in work, physical decline, and the sharing of wisdom, among other tasks. Aspects of tasks can be recycled throughout the life span as career and other life role changes occur (Super, 1980).

Constructive Stage

Although career phase theories describe the common tasks that are associated with career competence (Willis & Tosti-Vasey, 1990), they do not explain the mental structures that are required for successful task achievement (Kegan, 1994). The notion of career phase is an "outside in" view, one that examines the career rather than the person in the career (Kegan, 1994). Kegan declared that phase theory is developmental "only in a temporal sense." It does not, in his words, "consider whether increasing mental growth may enable or accompany the successful completion of those tasks" (p. 181). It is therefore to stage, or constructive developmental, theory (also often called cognitive developmental theory) that one must turn for a description of the mental "growth" or "capacity" (Rooke, 2003) that is needed to successfully negotiate the phasic tasks of career. The notion of constructive capacity (Kegan, 1994) captures an individual's potentially evolving, expanding frameworks for making meaning in the world. That evolution, at our time and place in history, points to the requirement for professionals to be self-directed (Kegan, 1994). Kegan notes that in general, "personal authority" has replaced blind loyalty to "public authority" as an expectation for success and competence in Western societies. Personal authority requires individuals "to separate what they feel from what they *should* feel, what they value from what they *should* value, what they want from what they *should* want" (Kegan, 1994, p. 275; emphasis added). Kegan calls that way of knowing "self-authorization" or "fourth-order consciousness."

There is now beginning evidence for the link between developmental stage capacity and the achievement of career phase tasks. For example, Mentkowski and Associates (2001) found that, in early career, a relativistic framework (Perry, 1970/1998) was associated with career success. Similarly, O'Donovan-Polten (2001) noted that in midcareer, highly competent, eminent lawyers all showed elements of at least the self-authorizing fourth-order consciousness (Kegan, 1994). Thus the career/life phase and constructive stage literatures meet, as the latter identifies the mental capacities required for achieving career phase tasks, and, therefore, professional competence.

Stage theories, which are rooted in Piaget's (1966) work on children's evolving thinking as well as in Kohlberg's (1969) adult applications of that work, are particularly apt for describing the learning (and therefore the training) conditions needed for competence. First, constructive development theory accounts for differential readiness to learn among individuals, that is, variations in their potentials to expand their mental capacities to meet the demands of professional practice. Second, development describes the optimal conditions of person–environment match and mismatch that result in developmental learning. Constructive developmental theory can serve as a guide for the training of professionals for competence. It provides a mental model of how individuals change in positive ways to enact desirable career phase tasks.

DEVELOPMENTAL LEARNING

Definition of Developmental Learning

Developmental, or "developing" learning (Granott, 1998) is a special form of learning. It is characterized, in Kohlberg's (1969) classic formulation, by changes that are irreversible, hierarchical, sequential, and more adequate. Kohlberg and Mayer (1972) proposed that psychological, or constructive, development occurs when a "structural whole" changes, not merely when a person constructs a specific new response due to increasing task familiarity. Developmental learning can be distinguished by the occurrence of changes in general worldview, rather than by the achievement of cumulative bits of knowledge or even heightened understanding of complex concepts. Thus Granott (1998) described what she calls "developing learning" as a change in "deep, fundamental, and irreversible processes" (p. 17). In contrast, "non-developing learning" includes changes in superficial, simple, and reversible processes (p. 17). Developmental learning results in an increased capacity for understanding and acting across such domains as ethical judgment, logical and cognitive processes, and interpersonal relations (Fisher & Torbert, 1995). This type of learning can potentiate major improvements in professional competence (Rooke & Torbert, 1998).

Granott (1998) further delineated three conditions for learning, if it is to be considered developmental. Each of these can be applied to the training and education of professionals. First, developmental learning must include progress to more advanced knowledge levels, which is parallel to Kohlberg's (1969) "hierarchical" and "greater adequacy" notions. For example, the professional, operating from Torbert's (1987) "diplomat" frame, is inclined to observe protocol and avoid inner and outer conflict. In contrast, the "technician" professional brooks conflict in pursuit of efficiency and objectivity. Such movement is considered to be progress because it allows for additional learning and increased options. The second condition for defining learning as developmental resides in the "depth" of the learning: There must be a fundamental restructuring that results in a qualitative shift in knowledge reorganization. Fisher and Torbert (1995) describe the cross-situational shift that can occur in professionals, for example, from the generally manipulative, externalized, stereotyped behavior of the opportunistic thinker to the shift into diplomatic thinking, which is characterized by a more internalized frame, namely, the avoidance of hurting others and adherence to loyalty to the group because he or she thinks it is the right thing to do. This is a qualitative shift, according to constructive developmental theory, in a person's manner of operating in the world. Finally, in Granott's (1998) terms, development must generate knowledge that supports unguided construction of more advanced knowledge, which she calls the self-scaffolding dimension. In this latter sense, developmental learning increases the possibility of future learning, as is seen in developing professionals' increased interest in feedback, self-critique, and process as they move from earlier to later orders of consciousness.

Required Conditions for Developmental Learning

For developmental learning to occur, two conditions must be met. The individual must experience a conflict in which his or her current way of knowing is inadequate, and he or she must be mentally ready to meet this challenge.

Dilemma

Learning is stimulated when readiness encounters a mismatch between an existing way of knowing and new demands. Thus, a fundamental condition for development is the occurrence of conflict or dilemma. In this, individuals become aware that their current way of thinking no longer works, and that they must alter their core assumptions about knowing.

Kegan (1994) illustrated such a mismatch in his description of the fictional case of Peter, a manager who tends to think from a traditionalist, or third-order consciousness. Traditionalist thinking is characterized by looking to others, norms, and traditions for ways of knowing and acting. Peter is loyal and hard-working. However, when his supervisor asks him to be the creator of a new corporate division, Peter experiences doubt about the adequacy of his conformist mode, that is, his ultimate reliance on loyalty to common practice and adherence to others' views. As a result, the progress of his career is on the line, not because he is not hard-working but because he does not have the mental structure to establish his own vision of the work. In Kegan's words, Peter needs to become "self-authorizing."

This challenge could result in a change in Peter's worldview, but only if he experiences the dilemma as problematic in some way that matters to him and if there are opportunities to learn a new way of thinking. This experience of conflict must be combined with the experience of a more adequate, whole way of thinking. The educator or trainer can assist with this "bridging."

Readiness

For such developmental change to occur, Peter must first be ready to encounter change. Kohlberg and Mayer (1972) described readiness as an optimal period for movement from one way of thinking to the next. Such readiness is not possible when a way of knowing is new, that is, when it is being initially consolidated (Piaget, 1966). There must be a period of stabilization. During this time the frame is generalized across situations, that is, "horizontal decalage" (Piaget, 1966) occurs. The new framework is applied to multiple situations, such as moral choices, relationship issues, parenting decisions, and professional work. There is now evidence that educators and supervisors can influence such change through exposing learners to cases that require the new mental frameworks (Granott, Fischer, & Parziale, 2002).

The "Shape" of Developmental Learning

Development does not occur, of course, in whole leaps. It is much messier than that (Rest, 1979). In King's (1990) words, the question is not "what stage is a person in?" This is the "hard" or simple stage question. Rather the important assessment question is, "To what extent and under what conditions does a person manifest the various types of organizations of thinking?" (p. 84). This is the more complex, and King would say that it is the accurate, "soft," or complex stage approach. King noted that "the use of assumptions characteristic of several stages at once has often been found" (p. 83), based on newness of the dominant frame, fatigue, and environmental factors. Thus there is overlapping and there are steps backward on the developmental learning road (King, 1990). Perhaps the amoeba shape is an apt analogy for developmental movement—now one part is entering a new order of consciousness while the majority of thinking is oriented by an earlier stage, and, occasionally, a lower stage way of thinking protrudes. Siegler (1996) uses a wave metaphor: The individual may use some of a new framework in the new starting wave, while there is much use of the assumptions represented by an established, cresting wave, and, finally, there is moderate use of an older, subsiding wave (i.e., an earlier stage).

Methods for Instigating Developmental Learning

Development-enhancing conditions, that is, factors that trigger or speed up development, can be instigated. However, it should be noted that developmental learning is neither quick nor easy, as it requires a substantial shift in consciousness. Nevertheless, the developmental educator does not need merely to wait for development to occur. Granott (1998) has described the educator's or trainer's role in developmental learning as that of facilitator and enabler of meaningful, enjoyable, challenging learning. Developmental educators are those who consistently present challenges and supports for worldview change.

Methods for enhancing development have been described in such terms as "developmental instruction" (Knefelkamp, 1984) and "deliberate psychological education" (Sprinthall, 1994). The general method for encouraging more advanced thinking lies in providing the learner with multiple higher level challenges and asking him or her to reflect on the meaning of those challenging experiences. Kegan (1982) called the challenge itself the "culture of contradiction." In contrast, the support for the old way of knowing is the "culture of confirmation." Each is necessary for growth. The teacher or trainer (or supervisor or parent) can also offer blueprints or models for more advanced ways of knowing. The key for developmental learning is for individuals to see their current, dominant way of knowing to be "not working"; that is, they must first be ready, or readied, to incorporate a new mental frame (Fisher & Torbert, 1995).

Guidelines for Developmental Professional Education

Professional education can thus be organized around developmental learning (Torbert, 1987). Torbert proposed that an intentionally developmental professional education is a remedy for a static, nonreflective professional training curriculum. Thus developmental trainers would instigate self-awareness and change, instruction in developmental theory, examination of students' own professional practices in relation to developmental theory, and creation of students' own professional philosophies of their work.

Developmentally oriented professional education typically uses a number of specific methods to instigate development (Torbert, 1987). These might include project groups in which each learner takes on a leadership role, with advanced students offering feedback, team field study projects with live clients, and treatment of the training or degree program as itself a live organization in which students are asked to provide responsible feedback about the learning program. Torbert found that students who experienced a developmental training approach for 21 months showed significant growth in ego development compared to others.

With these principles in mind, my colleague Christopher Lovell and I (McAuliffe & Lovell, 2000; McAuliffe, 2001) have summarized guidelines for constructivist-developmental education and supervision (e.g., Knefelkamp, 1984; Kohlberg, 1984). These guidelines incorporate many of Fisher, Merron, and Torbert's (1987) notions, including the importance of self-reflection, experiencing ambiguous situations,

and taking more than one perspective. We have proposed that any learning event that purports to enhance development, be it a course, an in-service training session, or a whole curriculum, might integrate the following notions.

- *Guideline One: Personalize.* Promote interactions among all participants in the learning environment. Make connections between subject matter and students' personal experiences.
- *Guideline Two: Vary the structure.* Provide more direction and advice to support nonconstructivists while also challenging them and others with more amorphous tasks.
- *Guideline Three: Promote experience.* Instigate activity through case study, illustration, role play, interviewing, team projects, and data collection.
- *Guideline Four: Emphasize multiple perspectives.* Ask students to examine each case from several angles.
- *Guideline Five: Encourage meta-cognition.* Model and require reflection on actions and cases. Ask students to monitor their responses to clients—emotional and cognitive, personal and culturally based.
- *Guideline Six: Question categorical thinking.* Challenge labels and conclusions. Recognize the fluidity of cultural constructions. Emphasize the story of the client over essentialist diagnosis.
- *Guideline Seven: Recognize that conflict is the norm.* Engage dialectical thinking. Identify contrasts in ideas and interpersonal tensions.
- *Guideline Eight: Show commitment in the face of doubt.* Model action based on deliberation and on the weight of evidence.
- *Guideline Nine: Value approximation over precision.* Encourage tolerance for ambiguity and the emergence of ideas in progress over premature judgment and closure.
- *Guideline Ten: Encourage "metalogue" or interpersonal process awareness.* Note the scripts, games, manipulations, power dynamics, and patterns enacted in relationships.

Varying Developmental Instruction

These teaching and learning guidelines are deceptively simple. However, variations in developmental readiness among professionals and preprofessionals make developmental education challenging. The guidelines cannot be applied absolutely and generally. To do so runs the risk of being "over (or under) the heads" (Kegan, 1994) of learners. Knefelkamp's (1984) work described the more subtle application of the guidelines to developmental learning. She outlines the variations in structure, experience, personalization, and diversity of content needed by different learners in the learning situation, depending on their developmental readiness. Such diversity in learners is illustrated in Fisher et al.'s (1987) anecdote about a professional development workshop:

> A management trainer is giving a workshop to computer engineers who are interested in becoming managers. After two days of theory, exercises, cases and role playing, the trainer has the sense that one-fourth of the participants have really understood . . . one half seem to have the ideas, but would not be able to manage effectively without future training and guidance far beyond that provided by the company. The rest believe they understand what it means to be a manager, but do not. (p. 257)

Readiness is all, to paraphrase Shakespeare, for without it, learners will not be able to use seemingly developmental learning interventions.

Such readiness is accounted for in instructor actions, such as presenting concrete dilemmas that confront learners' current ways of knowing without overwhelming them, allowing learners to reflect on the limits of their current responses to those conflicts, and guiding learners to construct sound, robust knowledge for cross-situational application through new experiences. Developmental learning is not linear, nor is it quickly achieved. Instead the developmental educator must support foray and retreat, break through and fall back in developmental movement. Thus the developmental educator honors Siegler's (1996) notion of "overlapping waves"—simultaneously emerging, current, and receding frameworks—in developmental learning.

An illustration of the classic movement from traditionalist to self-authorizing knowing is in order. Traditionalist-oriented professionals, or diplomat thinkers in Torbert's (1987) conception, must experience conflict about their reliance on authority and approval for thinking and acting. The developmental educator or supervisor can challenge professionals who operate from the diplomat frame to take initiatives and to produce their own justifications for such

initiatives. Modeling of this "thinking for oneself" can be provided through presenting case studies in which supervisors' share their own thinking processes, ones in which they demonstrate doubt, persistence, and methods for deciding.

I have elsewhere proposed (McAuliffe, 2001) specific learning activities that might trigger disequilibrium in traditionalist thinking and inducement to become more self-directing. Three of these traditionalist-challenging instigations are the following. The first is emphasizing multiple over single perspectives. Learners can be asked to examine work issues from several angles and to come up with their own position based on assembling evidence. In this way learners cannot treat their "received" knowledge as a sole and final basis for action. A second method for disrupting traditionalist thinking is to encourage intrapersonal process awareness so that externally reliant thinkers "move inside" to find their own truths. Weinstein and Altschuler (1985) and Kegan (1982) propose ways of helping learners locate authority in themselves. A third method for encouraging self-authorized thinking is to encourage learners to value approximation over precision. In so doing, they can dwell in the fuzzy situations, thus challenging the tyranny of single-minded reductionism and premature closure. Complex issues require time for "pausing" and "speaking in measured tones," as Belenky, Clinchy, Goldberger, and Tarule (1986) found. These qualities characterize more self-authorizing knowers. Such learners can dwell in the zone of deliberative evidence-gathering before making a decision.

In this discussion of developmental learning, it should be noted that an educator's or trainer's role is still and always complementary, even ancillary, in development. Learners must themselves experience the discomfort about the limits of a current way of knowing, that it is inadequate for solving many problems (Kohlberg & Mayer, 1972). The "action" is always "in" the learner.

LINKAGES BETWEEN PROFESSIONAL COMPETENCE AND ADULT DEVELOPMENT

Research on professional competence has shown that higher order mental capacities are required for professional competence and success (Fisher et al., 1987;

Fisher & Torbert, 1991; Kegan, 1994; Merron, Fisher, & Torbert, 1998; O'Donovan-Polten, 2001; Rooke & Torbert, 1998; Torbert, 1987). These capacities generally include the ability to be reflective and self-amending, incorporate multiple perspectives, tolerate ambiguity, and have a relatively autonomous source of authority for knowing and acting.

The developmental view holds that these mental capacities are learnable in professionals, that is, they can evolve under development-enhancing conditions. Again, there is evidence (Kegan, Lahey, Souvaine, Popp, & Beukema, as cited in Kegan, 1994) that a minimal level of constructive development is a prerequisite for such learning. The readiness level is that of Loevinger's (1976) conscientious conformist stage; that is, a way of knowing in which individuals have access to their own ideas and beginning recognition of the limits of externally derived rules (Kegan, 1994). The theoretical works of Schon (1983, 1987), Kegan (1982, 1994), and Torbert (1987) explicitly describe the characteristics of these higher order habits of mind as they contribute to professional competence. It is to the adult development literature as it explicitly relates to professional competence to which I turn to describe the evolution of the orders of consciousness that are desirable for such competence.

Schon's Reflective Practice and Professional Competence

Schon (1983) has proposed that a pervasive characteristic of highly competent professionals is reflective practice. Reflective practice is characterized, in Dewey's (1933) words, as "an active, persistent, and careful consideration of any belief or supposed form of knowledge" (p. 9). This openness to new experience allows the professional to define unclear problem situations, consider many alternative solutions to problems, and entertain feedback about previous decisions and actions. With reflective practice the professional can flexibly and intuitively draw on her or his practice experience, or informal theory, to apprehend problem situations, rather than merely applying previously learned methods to unambiguous ends (Foley, 2000). Reflective practitioners are most flexible when faced with the uncertainty of professional decisions. They are not rule-bound. They can consider the multiple factors impinging on a particular professional decision or action.

A specific dimension of reflective practice is reflection-in-action, which is most simply defined as reacting to inconsistencies or surprises in a work problem situation by rethinking one's tacit assumptions and reframing the situation in an action experiment in which possible solutions are tested (Ferry & Ross-Gordon, 1998). Schon (1987) illustrated such reflection in action in the moment-to-moment thinking of architects, psychotherapists, and musicians.

Ferry and Ross-Gordon (1998) found that reflective practitioners share the following characteristics: They tend to try to find out as much as possible about a problem before acting, involve others interactively in defining and generating solutions, and are open to new information during the problem-solving process. They also look beyond the immediate context in order to meet the short- and long-term needs of those affected, generate new alternatives through experimenting with possibilities, and go back over their decision-making process to assess their personal involvement and put the pieces together in new ways. Schon (1983) and others (Cheetham & Chivers, 1998; Ferry & Ross-Gordon, 1998; Irving & Williams, 1995; Kirby & Paradise, 1992; McCormick, 2001; B. Moore, 2000) have associated reflective practice with professional competence.

Reflective Practice and Learning

Reflective practice inherently carries within it the seeds of improved competence. Such practice means, by definition, that the professional is interested in taking a perspective about her or his current knowledge and practice, with the expectation that she or he can discover new methods for problem-solving. Reflective practitioners seek feedback and consider their own assumptions and decision-making processes. Ferry and Ross-Gordon (1998) showed that, in particular, reflective practitioners view inconsistencies as positive occurrences. An attitude of reflective practice is therefore a foundation for maintaining continuous improvement (Cheetham & Chivers, 1998).

Methods for Increasing Reflective Practice

Schon (1987) created the reflective practicum as a means of encouraging reflective practice. Such a practicum is characterized by students experiencing simulations of work situations in the presence of a coach. Students describe their own problem-solving process, and the coach demonstrates his or her thinking about a case. The coach probes for student assumptions and encourages students to constantly monitor the choices they are making, encouraging them to take in new data, and to include others in decision making. The coach can show her or his own uncertainty. She also points out discrepancies between students' and her own espoused theory and their theory-in-use (Argyris & Schon, 1978). Outcomes of this learning-by-doing-and-reflecting include professionals' accepting incompleteness in solutions, self-correcting and modifying their approaches in action, and inviting challenge and correction. Such qualities tend to result in a professional who is consistently reflective.

Linking Reflective Practice With Adult Development

There is value in considering reflective practice from an adult constructive developmental perspective, as differences in learning readiness would thereby be accounted for. In Ferry and Ross-Gordon's (1998) words, "The reason some individuals do not exhibit the competencies of reflection-in-action has not been adequately addressed in Schon's theory" (p. 111). Although Schon (1987) has proposed broad strategies for encouraging reflective practice, these methods do not distinguish individuals who might be more or less able to develop these characteristics. There is no learning theory nor personality theory associated with becoming a reflective practitioner. That limitation is exemplified by Gobbi's (1995) finding that her sample group of practicing nurses was not as able to adopt reflective practice as successfully as was Schon's (1983) sample group of students in a university setting. These results indicate that a one-size-fits-all approach to learning reflective practice is inadequate. Individual differences in readiness might be crucial for enhancing reflective practice. The notion of developmental learning provides a window for seeing readiness and individual variations in capacity for such practice.

Fisher et al. (1987) proposed just that: They suggested that reflective practice be treated as a developmental achievement. They further proposed that such reflective actions as searching for and experimenting with ways to redefine a problem generally require a "high degree of self-insight" (p. 263). More

specifically, Fisher et al. indicated that reflective practice requires the development-related "ability to appreciate multiple perspectives, to reflect and experiment in action, and to engage in self-questioning" (p. 263). The authors note that such consistent "reframing" is a relatively rare occurrence in professionals. They propose that this is the case because reflective practice requires "a relativistic or self-defining worldview" (p. 264). Both of these notions are later developmental positions than those occupied by most professionals. Merron et al. (1987) then demonstrate that hypothesis in their study in which managers at higher level developmental positions were found to be significantly more likely to engage in reflection-in-action when given a task that had a high degree of uncertainty.

The constructive developmental approach to explaining and enhancing professional competence is therefore worthy of exploration. In that vein, I now turn to the literature on constructive development.

Constructive Development

Both Kegan (1982, 1994) and Torbert and colleagues (Fisher & Torbert, 1995; Torbert 1987) have applied constructive-developmental theory to the workplace. Constructive developmental theory holds that individuals can evolve through an ordered series of mental stages, "each of which is governed by a unique logical and cognitive process, interpersonal orientation, and mode of ethical judgment" (Fisher & Torbert, 1991, p. 145). Kegan (1994) and Torbert (1987) have each concluded that professional competence is related to how professionals think, not what they know.

Kegan's Orders of Consciousness and Professional Competence

The Importance of Fourth-Order Consciousness for Competence. Kegan (1994), in his review of the management literature, found that the professional workplace expects the individual at a minimum to be "self-authorizing," that is, to be relatively autonomous or self-sufficient in pursuit of standards for effectiveness and success. He called this mental framework fourth-order consciousness, contrasting it to the third-order in which the individual's ultimate allegiances are to "fitting in," mutual reciprocity, and norm-upholding. Kegan (1994) has boldly proposed that "success at work . . . demands . . . an ideology, an internal identity, a self-authorship that can . . . act upon or invent values, beliefs, convictions, . . . ideals . . . it is no longer *authored by* them, it authors them, and thereby achieves a personal authority" (p. 185).

His review of that literature identified specific attributes of competent professionals, attributes that are expressions of the self-authorizing capacity. Paraphrased, these attributes are as follows:

- to invent one's own work (rather than to see it as owned and created by one's employer);
- to be self-initiating, self-correcting, self-evaluating (rather than dependent on others to frame the problems, initiate adjustments, or determine whether things are going well);
- to be guided by one's own visions at work (rather than being captive of an authority's agenda);
- to take responsibility for what happens to oneself at work (rather than seeing one's circumstances and possibilities as largely caused by others);
- to be master of one's particular work roles, job, or career (rather than have an imitating relationship to what we do);
- to conceive of the organization and/or the field that one works within from the "outside"; and
- to see one's part in relation to the whole (rather than seeing the field or organization only from the perspective of one's own part).

Each of these attributes is an expression of a self-contained identity, which contrasts to one that is "pieced out" to the world via interpersonal and norm-upholding loyalties (Kegan, 1982, p. 243). Competent professionals are therefore expected to have internalized standards toward which they strive, rather than being ultimately beholden to external influence. Professionals who have achieved fourth-order self-authorization match the expectations of the professional workplace.

The empirical research literature on competence further reveals the importance of such a stance. The research findings on competence point to the fact that the individual must possess a relatively autonomous way of thinking to achieve professional competence. In her qualitative study of eminent Canadian lawyers, O'Donovan-Polten (2001) found these professionals to consistently hold an internal definition of success and to reflect on the beliefs and myths of the culture.

Similarly, Vaillant (1993) found successful midlife professionals to have increased freedom from what others think. Mentkowski and colleagues (2000) found successful professionals five years out of college to exhibit strong independent conceptualization and action abilities. The theme of autonomy and self-definition pervades these studies. Paradoxically, this self-authorization includes some ability to self-critique and some interest in feedback, as long as the critique supports the fourth-order thinker's particular ideology (Torbert, 1987).

Extent of Fourth-Order Consciousness   If such an order of consciousness is supported by the professional workplace, is it common? The very highest estimate of consistent fourth-order consciousness or above occurs in Bar-Yam's (1991) extensive interview study of graduate-level educated adults, at about 50%. Kegan (1994) notes that other studies (Dixon, 1986; Goodman, 1983; Greenwald, 1991) that have been based on a fuller sample, including noncollege-educated adults, have found only 21% of the adult population to express the full self-authorizing capacity. This figure is so low because of the challenge of the fourth order. That challenge consists of relativizing one's inherited norms and assumptions, of "leaving the family religion," in Kegan's (1994) use of the term, to instead collect and weigh evidence and to be guided by a relatively internal source of authority. It is likely that college education challenges many individuals' external sources of knowing.

Kegan (1994) concluded that the work expectations that he gleaned from the management literature are therefore "over the head" of at least half of all professionals. He proposed that it is therefore a task of workplace environments, training, and graduate education to stimulate a self-authorized way of thinking. That seems to be in place in the field of law. O'Donovan-Polten (2001) proposed that her sample of high-achieving lawyers generally revealed fourth order consciousness. This is partly the case because the law profession itself rewards an internalization of autonomous thinking. On the other hand, she noted that law as a profession also discourages the questioning of its particularly individualistic, adversarial standards. She found that the women lawyers in her study were more likely than male lawyers to question the absoluteness of that paradigm and to exhibit characteristics of the dialectical, self-transforming fifth-order of consciousness. O'Donovan-Polten offers two explanations of this phenomenon: One lies in the tendency of many women to value cooperation and collaboration, what Belenky et al. (1986) call connected knowing. Thus an individualistic autonomy may not suit many women lawyers. A second explanation lies in women having minority status in the profession, a condition that might trigger critique of the system. Outsiders are not so embedded in the way things are, but rather are aware of the inequities and constructed nature of the social system that leaves them out of much decision-making.

Characteristics of Fifth-Order Consciousness The following are characteristics of the fifth order: the facing of paradox, the uncovering of the larger purposes of the profession, a socially critical stance, and an awareness of the historical moment and cultural context that they inhabit (Kegan, 1994). In general, the professions do not encourage these qualities (Kegan, 1994; O'Donovan-Polten, 2001). Thus, movement beyond the fourth-order ideology-maintaining, self-authorizing way of thinking is unlikely to be supported by professional workplaces.

Those who do achieve the questioning, dialectical capacity of the fifth order are the authoritative agents, that is, the ones who successfully consider or even create new paradigms in a profession (Rooke & Torbert, 1998). Such agents might include, for example, thinkers like Albert Einstein and Sigmund Freud, who in their eras, respectively transcended the dominant discourse about physics and mental health. Fifth-order thinkers' allegiance is to larger principles, not rules. They are willing to enact these principles in innovative ways. Empirical research indicates that eminence in a profession, as opposed to acceptable performance, might indeed demand such paradox-holding, dialectical thinking. Indeed, O'Donovan-Polten (2001) found that most of the eminent lawyers in her study could occasionally engage in a system-questioning, dialectical way of thinking, which Kegan calls the fifth order of consciousness. These lawyers could regularly embrace the tension of "not knowing" to take multiple perspectives on issues. They were able to recognize that all is not settled, that standards and methods are constructed in a world in which dialogue is the only foundation for knowing.

Kegan and Lahey (1983) have suggested that it is the task of professional organizations and educational institutions to challenge the discourse of their own professional standards, that is, to invite fifth-order thinking. As noted earlier, about 50% of professionals

and students (Bar-Yam, 1991) are ready to respond to the challenge of questioning their ideologies and engaging in consistent dialogue with the world. The others must be helped first to find and follow their own vision of the work and to create their own standards (the fourth order), that is, to be relatively free of third-order interpersonal influence in their professional behavior. Specific methods for such developmental learning in a professional context will be suggested in the following discussion.

Torbert's Frames of Professional Development

The most extensive integration, and empirical testing, of adult development theory as it relates to professional work has been done by Torbert (1987) and colleagues. Torbert's theory of the stages of professional constructive development and his accompanying series of studies have resulted in a taxonomy of developmental positions for professionals, particularly for managers. Torbert (1994) has also made associations between his stages and those of Kegan (1982, 1994).

Torbert's stages are explicitly derived from Loevinger's ego development stages (Loevinger, 1976). The links between Loevinger's work and stages of professional development were constructed by comparing managers' characteristics in the workplace with their levels of ego development. Torbert (1987) and colleagues used case studies, autobiographies, and quantitative research using the sentence completion test (Loevinger, 1976) to initially construct the scheme. This taxonomy has been tested for 25 years through a series of varied studies (e.g., Fisher & Torbert, 1995; Fisher et al., 1987; Merron et al., 1987; Rooke & Torbert, 1998; Torbert, 1987, 1994).

Torbert's portrayal of professional development plots a general shift from lower stage concreteness, conformity, and rigidity to later stage empathy, flexibility in thinking, ability to abstract, tolerance for ambiguity, and appreciation for diversity. Torbert's stages have been significantly related to tendencies in managerial behavior. The stages are also associated with particular levels and types of occupations, with leaders showing higher development in general than those in direct service work (Torbert, 1994). For example, Torbert (1994) found the majority of nurses and first-line supervisors to be in the relatively unreflective technician position, and the majority of senior managers to be in more self-defining achiever and strategist positions. Also, researchers found that managers at later developmental positions were more likely to act collaboratively than those measured at prior positions (Merron et al., 1987), to lead organizations through successful transformations (Rooke & Torbert, 1998), and to request feedback about their performance (Merron & Torbert, 1984).

The following sections summarize Torbert's stages of professional development. In addition, the implications for learning at each position are delineated.

The Opportunistic Frame

Characteristics   Professionals in the opportunistic stage tend toward the use of unilateral power. They are externally oriented, with very little awareness of their own inclinations and worldviews. This way of thinking is parallel to Loevinger's (1976) similarly named opportunistic stage, and has parallels to Kohlberg's (1969) preconventional moral stage. As might be expected, *blame* rather than *self-criticism* is dominant in opportunistic professionals. They experience others without empathy, as objects to be manipulated. Opportunistic thinkers tend to use force and deception to reach short-term ends.

The opportunistic way of thinking is likely to be problematic for professionals, especially in organizations. Opportunists treat their current way of knowing "as the only lens through which to view the world" (Torbert, 1987, p. 30). Thus they are limited in their choice of approaches to work problems. In contrast, later-stage thinkers can choose among methods, including acting in a seemingly opportunistic way when a situation calls for it. Opportunists, in contrast, have no options but to use this way of knowing. The dysfunction inherent in opportunistic thinking is demonstrated in the small percentage of professionals, fewer than 5%, who have been found to be opportunistic in their thinking (Rooke & Torbert, 1998). A consistently self-serving worldview is not viable in organizations, which require some level of teamwork and cooperation.

A potentially positive characteristic that has been found in this orientation (Torbert, 1987) is the possibility of innovation that such an expediency-oriented framework brings. The self-interest of opportunists can drive them to start new organizations and bring new products to market. This drive is motivated by self-aggrandizement. Such narcissistic thinking makes organizational well-being secondary, but it might occasionally work to motivate those individuals who see only self-interest in the offing.

Learning and Development From the Opportunistic Position   Torbert (1987) has found very limited potential for developmental learning in opportunists. Their learning is limited to acquiring new ways to ensure that their needs are met. Torbert has said, "The Opportunist is less likely than most managers at any of the later stages to develop beyond this style because it has become more rigidified than the others by adulthood" (p. 40). Opportunists' external locus keeps them from developing the self-reflective capacity that is typical of the later stages, an ability that can result in self-correction. They have little interest in external corrective feedback unless they can use it to manipulate others and the environment toward their ends. They are likely to be locked into self-protective manipulation of others and of the environment.

Torbert (1987) proposed that colleagues and organizations must deal with opportunistic professionals by being willing and able to confront the expected conflicts with them. There must also be clear task and role boundaries in the organization in the form of rules and policies. Explicit behavioral guidelines and consequences for adherence to group norms are required, or the opportunist will operate to self-advantage, oblivious to others' welfare. For developmental learning to occur in opportunists, they must find that their unilateral use of power does not work and that group needs are important. Kegan (1982) suggested that a development-enhancing environment for opportunistic thinkers is one in which two seemingly contrasting interventions are offered. The first is enforcing external contingencies (e.g., rewards) for adherence to norms. The other is having opportunists participate in groups in which empathy and trust are expressed and caring for other individuals for their own sake is espoused. Such development-enhancing instigations are typical of therapeutic correctional programs and of youth residential treatment programs. In these programs, external contingencies for behavioral change are combined with "internally oriented" exercises in self-awareness, the modeling of empathy, and learning of social norms.

The Diplomatic Frame

Characteristics   Diplomatic thinkers are guided by loyalty to their reference groups. Torbert (1987) paralleled the diplomatic stage to Loevinger's (1976) conformist thinking. In older popular language, the diplomat was called the "company man [*sic*]," loyal to persons and the organization but not to a personal, self-derived vision of the work. Their ultimate adherence is to acceptability and appropriateness. For diplomats, these are ends, not means. Thus they have little ability to take independent initiatives, ones that might cause them to break ranks with either internalized norms or group harmony. For diplomats, value is defined by others, such as high-status persons. Through such definition by others, enslavement to conformity leads to lack of awareness of inner conflict, a suppression of one's own desires, a tendency to treat approval as an ultimate value, a penchant for speaking in clichés and platitudes, an inclination to follow rules without question, a tendency to seek status in the group, and a desire to save face. My own study of the work of counselors at this level revealed them to be relatively unempathic, to be surface-oriented, to show tendencies toward rote responses, to use clichés, to be intolerant of ambiguity, and to be inclined to act without weighing situational evidence (McAuliffe & Lovell, in press).

Diplomatic thinking can have negative consequences for professional competence. Without a relatively self-generated point of view and a willingness to act in that regard, the diplomatic professional is viewed as unable to take on the difficult decisions, initiatives, and ethical dilemmas of professional work. Torbert's (1987) research suggests that diplomatic thinkers are bypassed for promotion in many organizations. The statistics seem to bear out this proposal: Only about 6–9% of middle- to upper-level managers are diplomatic thinkers, whereas 24% of first-line supervisors tend to think in this mode (Gratch, 1985; Smith, 1980). Torbert (1987) concluded that diplomatic thinking militates against promotion to positions in which more self-authorized thinking is required.

Learning and Development From the Diplomatic Position

Diplomatic professionals, like opportunistic thinkers, do not tend to seek out feedback about themselves, because negative feedback is associated with loss of status. They and opportunistic professionals are the least likely to evolve beyond their current stage due to the absence of a reflective, self-amending dimension (Torbert, 1987).

Positive change in diplomatic thinking can be triggered by diplomats' first experiencing the inadequacy of their other allegiance. They must see that their career success is crippled by their unexamined conformity to norms. This conflict can lead, under optimal developmental conditions, to greater self-authorizing (Kegan, 1994). Fisher and Torbert (1995) described the case of a manager whose need to be liked resulted in low employee productivity. His job was therefore threatened due to the low output of his department. This threat triggered enough disequilibration to eventually enable him to adopt the next type of thinking, called technician by Torbert (1987). From the perspective of the technician stage, procedures guide work behavior rather than approval doing so. Such development-instigating conflict might also occur in diplomats who fail to receive honors and promotions due to their lack of a self-defined vision of their work and set of standards (Kegan, 1994; Torbert, 1987).

With support and challenge from the work environment, they might identify the need to define their own standards and methods for the work. Torbert (1987) suggests that to move toward greater autonomy, diplomats benefit from the challenges of being assigned leadership tasks, seeing models of more self-defining professional decision making and being introduced to developmental theory (Fisher & Torbert, 1995). One vehicle for both support and challenge, Torbert (1987) suggested, is the small group work project, in which the peer group has to set its own direction. In the supportive group setting, diplomats can be challenged by being assigned clear leadership tasks, preferably under the supportive guidance of a mentor who is not a supervisor. Diplomats will be "stretched" by having to create an agenda, establish a vision, and organize others who will enact that vision. The developmental learning goal for diplomats is to help them become more "self-initiating, self-correcting, and self-evaluating" (Kegan, 1994, p. 153). These are characteristic of developmental movement to the next stage.

The Technician Frame

Characteristics Beginning freedom from reliance on group norms and external approval comes with this transitional stage, that of the technician, or "Self-Defining" (Fisher et al., 1987) frame. Loevinger's (1976) parallel term for this stage is "conscientious conformist." Technician thinkers are, in Torbert's (1987) words, "actively differentiating themselves from the group" (p. 76).

The tenuous autonomy that characterizes this in-between stage results in technicians' strident independence. In their newfound independence they tend to be "defiantly and dogmatically counter-dependent" (pp. 76–77). Technician thinkers have been found to be staunch adherents of their own ideas and their own methods. Their important external allegiance is to their own craft heroes, that is, figures in the field who represent their own current thinking. Technicians' sources of ultimate authority are no longer old norm groups and authorities in the work setting, but instead their favorite methods in their fields. For example, they might be single-mindedly enthusiastic adherents of a particular management innovation or psychotherapy theory.

Technician professionals are narrowly focused on efficient methods and the internal logic of objective standards. In the process, technicians fail to see the larger systems of which they are part, for they are enamored of the coherence of their own doctrines (Fisher & Torbert, 1995). To them, there is no room for alternate explanations. Their logic is the only logic. Fisher and Torbert propose that the technician's intense embrace of "standards" can be inspiring for co-workers. This position is especially important in explaining professional behavior, as it is the largest single group of professionals, comprising 38–68% of professionals, depending on field and level (Fisher & Torbert, 1995).

Learning and Development at the Technician Position   Professionals who tend to think from within the technician frame experience feedback as generally unwelcome, as they fear "falling back" to the external reliance of the diplomatic frame (Torbert, 1987). Thus they counter the old dependence with a dogmatic adherence to the "internal logic and integrity of their area of expertise" (Fisher & Torbert, 1995, p. 68).

Despite this dogmatic tendency, they can be critical of themselves in the context of how to achieve their already-set ideological aims. Technicians want to fix themselves. Thus, for the technician, self-approval has replaced the diplomat's reliance on the approval of others (Fisher & Torbert, 1995). At best, technicians might consider others' feedback on the technical dimensions of their work, as long as it fits within the paradigm that they have chosen. A simple example might be that of the behavioral psychotherapist's openness to feedback on her work from the behavioral paradigm alone, but not from within the psychodynamic model.

The limits of technicians' interest in feedback is illustrated by the fact that fewer than 10% of technician managers asked for feedback in one study, in contrast to much higher percentages at later stages (Torbert, 1987). At least half of the technicians who did receive asked-for feedback expressed "explosive emotional reactions" (Torbert, 1987, p. 85) during the feedback session. Such is the tenuous hold on thinking for oneself in the technician stage.

The single-mindedness that is characteristic of this stage seems to be consistent with major aspects of the normative career phase of early career (Greenhaus, 1987), or establishment (Super, 1980). It behooves the professional to evolve, however, as the technician's ideological stance becomes less functional when greater situational flexibility is required in advanced professional work and in interactions with colleagues (Fisher & Torbert, 1995).

To encourage learning in technicians, a trainer, educator, or supervisor must use reflective communication skills to help them think *themselves* through the limitations that *they* discover in their methods in honor of their counterdependent independence (Torbert, 1987). A trainer or educator can support technicians' inclinations toward objectivity by pointing out other logical and contrary findings that fail to support their current methods. Trainers can support technicians' current way of knowing by finding objective evidence for those alternative methods. The hope for developmental learning is that through such subtle, challenging, yet supportive instigations, the technician will become more reflective, less defensive, and more interested in other perspectives.

Fisher and Torbert (1995) reported the case of a manager's movement beyond the technician frame. This manager had received a promotion to a significantly expanded position as a marketing director for a magazine. Based on prior feedback and observation, she recognized that she needed a new frame if she were to be successful at her new position. This manager set up the following experiments, in her words, for herself, all of which are consistent with the achiever frame. She sought out advice on the new job from the previous director. She was already showing the achiever's greater openness to feedback. She rewrote her job description, demonstrating self-creation of goals. She sought out ways of improving her communication skills, showing a self-critiquing and self-amending dimension. She intentionally created relationships with the advertising director and the sales managers, demonstrating a teamwork orientation. Finally, she volunteered for a new project, showing initiative and openness to experience. Each of these characteristics are typical of the more advanced frame that Torbert (1987) calls the achiever.

The Achiever Frame

Characteristics The limitations, even stranglehold, of the mentally sealed-up technician stage can give way to the wider frame of the achiever. This frame shows parallels to Loevinger's (1976) conscientious stage. Achievers no longer adhere to a single logical method but are guided instead by the broader goals of the field or the organization, beyond their own careers. They have well-internalized sets of standards that they strive to fulfill. Achievers can provide leadership for a system, as they tend to inspire others with their vision.

Achievers can also attend more easily than technicians to different points of view. Thus they can value teamwork, as they have let go of the hyper- and counterdependent autonomy of technician thinking. Torbert (1987) has found that achievers tend to invite feedback. Achievers are interested in seeking out critiques of their behavior. This is itself a major developmental achievement. Such an interest in feedback might be considered the entry into Schon's (1983) notion of reflective practice (Fisher et al., 1987). As might be expected, achievers are more likely to be effective in professional work than are diplomats, in that they can problem solve without excessive need for assurance and approval (Merron et al., 1987). They are more aware of the big picture; that is, they can broaden the scope of the technician's narrow method and notions to consider the impact of their work on clients, colleagues, and relevant communities at large.

In my colleague's and my recent research (McAuliffe & Lovell, in press), achievers showed parallels to more developmentally complex counselors. In our study, more effective counselors could tolerate ambiguity more easily and were more "metacognitive" or reflective. We also found such counselors to be more empathic than counselors scoring lower on developmental measures, that is, they could consistently consider points of view other than their own. This perspective taking is a necessary accompaniment to empathy (Selman, 1980).

The shadow side of the achiever way of thinking lies in their tendency to pursue their own agenda categorically to the exclusion of other goals and ways of operating. Achievers' self-direction is clear. They can hold and defend a view and refer to their broad goals. However, they do not seek to know the limits of their ideology. They are not likely to see that the framework that they are using is just that, one construction among many. They are not yet inclined to think dialectically (Basseches, 1984), actively seeking to know the limits of their understanding, examining situations from multiple frames. As a result, they can be blind to alternatives in the pursuit of their given goals. Achievers have settled on their assumptions—they are not open to hearing any new logic outside of their own. They are trapped in their paradigm, whether it be, for example, the idea of collaborative management, adherence to eclectic psychotherapy, or embracing the value of mediation in law. They cannot easily shift, as the situation requires, to quite different goals and models.

Torbert's (1987) summary of the research on development in professionals, across nearly 500 individuals, reported that approximately 42% of a range of professionals, including nurses, executives, senior managers, first-line supervisors, and entrepreneurial professionals, achieve this mental capacity. However, Gratch (1985) found only 33% of senior managers to demonstrate the achiever frame (Fisher & Torbert, 1995; Smith, 1980).

Learning and Development From the Achiever Position Despite the narrowness of their vision, achievers' openness to feedback can be an entry into learning. As beginning reflective practitioners, achievers are open to a critique of their performance to attain already-set goals more effectively. Critique, well offered, can open a window to the possibility of giving up the insularity that characterizes this stage. Achievers are also capable of experimenting, even tentatively trying ideas that they might find contradictory at first.

Torbert (1987) suggested that powerful learning can be instigated for achievers by the experience of "collaborative inquiry" (p. 130). He proposed five ongoing activities that can developmentally advance achiever thinking toward the next stage, which is strategist thinking. These are opportunities for explicit, shared reflection about the organization's mission, open rather than masked interpersonal relations characterized by disclosure, support and a willingness to confront apparent differences, systematic performance evaluation and feedback for both individuals and the organization, and the direct facing of paradoxes like quantity–quality and freedom–control.

Other methods that promote strategist thinking include staff input about the purposes of meetings and projects, as opposed to supervisors' one-way dictation of agendas, staff retreats for the purpose of examining a group's mission, process observations during meetings, intentional two-way conversations about performance, and inquiries about the impact of the work on clients. Other methods for encouraging movement beyond the achiever stage include exposure to developmental theory itself, followed by asking professionals to critically analyze their interactions with colleagues to look for strategist dimensions. Finally, movement out of achiever thinking is assisted by having mentors in organizations who are at later stages of development (Torbert, 1987). All of these inquiry systems advance transformational learning by instigating multiperspectival thinking about work purposes and methods.

The Strategist Frame

Characteristics   Most of Torbert's and colleagues' recent research has been devoted to the study of the strategist way of knowing and beyond (e.g., Rooke, 2003; Rooke & Torbert, 1998). A major realization occurs in the move from achiever to strategist thinking. In Fisher et al.'s (1987) words, at the strategist stage the professional becomes "capable of . . . recognizing and working with people holding different worldviews, as well as willing to redefine presented problems and search for underlying issues" (p. 261). One manager described her shift as moving from having "very explicit goals and timetables [and] a structured organization to . . . the collaborative process [which] focuses on inquiry, constructing shared meanings from experience, and building implicit consensus through responsible interaction" (Torbert, 1987, p. 151). In their intensive interviews of managers, Fisher and Torbert (1991) found strategist thinkers, as opposed to achievers, to have the following qualities: They engaged in more principled thinking and action, they were more likely to take others' points of view into account, they had ideas that were

not bound by rules and conventions, they were aware of their own subjectivity, and they were more willing to engage in dialogue with colleagues and authorities.

Strategist thinkers have made the cognitive flip into full constructivism: They recognize that all frames and all knowledge are constructed through human interaction. Thus they are generally open to new experience and are aware of multiple frameworks. They tend to embrace contradiction to their own ideas (Basseches, 1984; Rooke, 2003). They themselves can construct a fluid theory on how to make professional decisions and take action. Strategist thinkers believe that they create reality through constant interaction with others, with ideas, and with multiple aspects of themselves (Fisher and Torbert, 1991, 1995). They can combine seemingly contradictory approaches, for example, blending democratic, inclusive management methods with situational, autonomous decision making. Their work is characterized by flexibility: They tend to allow situations to create guidelines, in inductive fashion, as well as to bring malleable guidelines to situations. They can play back and forth, in dialectical fashion, between understandings and styles (Rooke & Torbert, 1998).

In action, strategist thinkers tend to engage in collaborative inquiry, for example, in a meeting they attend to staff views and are willing to let meanings emerge (Fisher & Torbert, 1995). This emergent inclination provides the power for the strategist way of thinking. Through it, leaders can effectively develop an organization's vision, mission, strategy, and structure, involving others in the process. When needed, they are open to rethinking all of these. Thus they can continually make sense out of the chaos of shifting cultural, economic, and political climates.

Strategist thinkers make up a very small proportion of professionals. Only about 9% of managers have been found at this level (Rooke, 2003), and no first-line supervisors exhibited the strategist frame. It is clear that this way of thinking prepares one for amorphous work situations in which one is responsible for important decisions. Strategist managers are inclined to take on the responsible tasks of leadership in some form.

Learning and Development From the Strategist Position   Strategist thinkers recognize the personal, cultural, and historical foundations of their behavior. The strategist is therefore alert to being wrong, to being caught up in a particular discourse. She or he worries, in the philosopher Richard Rorty's (1989) words, "that she has been initiated into the wrong tribe, taught to play the wrong language game" (p. 75).

A common characteristic of strategists is "double-loop learning" (Argyris & Schon, 1978), that is, the ability to question what one has previously taken for granted. Strategic thinkers can thus step outside of their current frame for meaning making. Such a tendency enables strategists to learn more easily than those who think from within other frames. In Fisher and Torbert's (1995) words, strategists are likely "to learn through examining alternative policies and objectives from new perspectives rather than [to] simply improve ways of functioning within present perspectives" (p. 79). Only strategists and later-stage thinkers are likely to explicitly seek out feedback that, as Fisher and Torbert (1995) described it, "highlights incongruities and incompleteness within one's meaning-making system" (p. 79). Thus strategist thinkers are poised to develop because of their consistent reflectiveness and recognition of the limits of their current perspectives. Their interest in dialogue brings new possibilities to them.

Poststrategist Frames   Those new possibilities are described by Fisher and Torbert (1991), Torbert (1994), and Rooke (2003), in terms of the rare poststrategic frame that they call magician. *Magician* is an apt term for professionals who divest themselves of their presuppositions, as do magicians who turn expectations into surprises that overturn the normal paradigm. Magician professionals similarly defy the common wisdom. They are capable of continuous self-transformation. They are not beholden to status and role. They can meet others of any position in life as fellow evolving selves (Torbert, 1994). Magicians exercise transforming power, which is always mutual, not unilateral (Torbert, 1991).

Movement into the magician stage and beyond is a rare achievement among professionals, with fewer than 1% of individuals reaching this level (Rooke & Torbert, 1998). Therefore, given the broad descriptive purposes of this chapter, I only make this brief reference to such development. Those late stages are reserved for particularly "authoritative agents" or "learning leaders," such as Pope John XXIII and Mahatma Gandhi (Fisher & Torbert, 1991; Rooke, 2003). Both of those leaders expressed transformative

power through mutuality. From what we know, they engaged persons as evolving rather than as inhabitants of a prescribed role and they engaged circumstances with paradigm-challenging newness.

Empirical Evidence for Constructive Development and Professional Competence

From their review of the data, Fisher et al. (1987) concluded that "to manage effectively, a manager needs to occupy one of the later developmental stages" (p. 264). Rooke and Torbert (1998) confirmed this position based on their study of 10 organizations. They reported that in all cases of strategist leaders, that is, those who are self-amending are able to reframe the mission, strategy, and timing of situations, will listen to multiple voices and promote nonunilateral power; the organizations positively transformed their size, profitability, quality, strategy, and reputation during the period of study. By contrast, in all cases of those below the level of strategist leaders, the organizations had highly visible performance blockages. There was a correlation of 0.65 between higher stage leaders and the likelihood of progressive organizational transformations. This relationship accounted for 42% of the variance in the transformations and was significant at $p < .05$. Rooke and Torbert therefore concluded that the developmental stage of the leader and of his or her closest associates is a critical factor that affects the likelihood of successful organizational transformation. They also concluded the converse: "A single CEO incapable of exercising, recognizing, or supporting transformational power among his or her colleagues can be enough of a bottleneck to undo prior organizational abilities and accomplishments" (Rooke and Torbert, 1998, p. 21).

Other studies have linked advanced development with desirable professional characteristics, especially in the areas of collaboration (versus control), openness to critique, and behavioral flexibility. For example, managers at lower developmental positions were more inclined to use coercion rather than consultation (Smith, 1980). Later stage managers were also more likely to initiate receiving feedback about their work (Merron & Torbert, 1984).

Merron et al. (1987) concluded that higher stage thinkers are more effective, in that they have more behavioral options in their repertoire. The authors use Schon's (1983) definition of effectiveness, which is especially characterized by situational flexibility. The effective professional can redefine problems, while also sometimes accepting problems as defined. Finally, Schon's notion of effectiveness also includes creating a collaborative, committed atmosphere among colleagues, while acting unilaterally when situations call for this action. Merron et al. found that later stage managers (strategist or higher) are especially likely to demonstrate the ability to redefine a problem (as opposed to accepting the given definition), question the underlying assumptions in the definition or proposed solution, and see a deeper problem underneath it (as opposed to neglecting underlying causes of the problem). According to Fisher et al. (1987), such behavior is better suited to the complex demands of upper management and the requirements of complex organizations and professional tasks.

The relatively small percentage of managers who have been found to have advanced to the strategist level is cause for concern, if these authors' findings about effectiveness are accurate. If strategist thinking results in significantly more effective high-level professional work, then the learning challenge is clear. What is needed at this time, however, is further evidence of that claim, especially among professionals other than management professionals.

LEARNING HOW TO LEARN AS A DIMENSION OF DEVELOPMENT

One result of this research on development and professional work has been a call for the revamping of professional education and training. Merron et al. (1987) strongly suggested that there must be an explicit developmental dimension for professional education. They proposed that training include "the cultivation not just of new knowledge and skills but also of development—an increased capacity for learning new knowledge and skills" (p. 284). This type of learning is transformational, that is, movement across forms of knowing, as Kegan (1994) describes it, forms that are frames for knowing. Learning would thus occasion not merely increased technical content but an expanded mental structure, or a shift in "consciousness" (Kegan, 1994).

The research on expertise points to the developmental dimension. Experts are those who examine and revise their work (Ferry & Ross-Gordon, 1998). From their research, Ferry and Ross-Gordon concluded

that "the key to expertise does not seem to reside in merely gaining experience, but in how the individual uses experience as a learning mechanism" (p. 107). Bereiter and Scardamalia (1993) noted that expertise is characterized by at least three elements, all of which point to the capacity for self-amendment. First, experts reinvest in new learning (e.g., participate in reading and continuing education). Second, they seek out more difficult problems/greater challenges in work. Third, experts tackle more complex representations of recurrent problems, that is, they add complexity back into the problem versus engaging in problem reduction. Thus, experts encounter unfamiliar cases more often. Each of these behaviors increases the capacity for further learning through experts' engaging in novelty, reflection, and experimentation. In contrast, nonreflective professionals do not critically weigh past action (Ferry & Ross-Gordon, 1998). They fail to learn from problematic situations. Instead, nonreflectors assume that they merely need to apply known technical-rational methods to all future problems.

Fisher et al.'s (1987) solution to nonreflective practice lies in offering developmental instruction to professionals. They have tested a training approach that is self-awareness enhancing, project-based, and experiential and found it to be developmentally useful (Rooke, 2003). This intentional enhancement of development requires a major, intensive commitment to expanding mental structures.

For those who would be highly competent experts and leaders, learning should lead them toward strategist thinking with its emphases on dialogue, experience, and self-reflection. Instead, however, current educational and in-service training programs teach to the technician worldview, with its ideological tunnel vision and disinterest in stepping outside of established professional standards (O'Donovan-Polten, 2001; Torbert, 1987). Thus, such professionals remain embedded in the usual practices of their own fields and are less attuned to the situational, contextual dynamics that professionals must account for in a good portion of their work (Schon, 1983).

Developmental learning also increases the individual's capacity to learn. With development beyond the diplomat or third order of consciousness, persons are inclined to evolve to a level of further restructuring or "self-scaffolding" (Granott, 1998). Development begets more development, that is, "developing learning" itself (Granott, 1998) is more likely at later stages. The empirical research on expertise points to the importance of learning "how to know" versus merely "what to know" for professional competence (Ferry & Ross-Gordon, 1998). The reflectiveness that accompanies later stages allows the professional to engage in continuous self-evaluation and self-amendment (Kegan, 1994).

This evidence points to a development–learning link: Deep structural change leads to an increased capacity to learn through increased reflectiveness, a willingness to suspend presuppositions, and an ability to define problems from multiple perspectives. These are the characteristics of the reflective practitioner (Schon, 1983), the self-authorizing order of consciousness (Kegan, 1994), and professionals who can use the achiever and strategist frames (Rooke, 2003).

CONCLUSION

This summary of the current understanding of the development–competence linkage is necessarily abbreviated. It can be confidently asserted, however, that a series of development-related capacities are expected in the professional workplace, although these may vary by profession. The minimal capacity for competence seems to lie in the professional's ability to attain relative autonomy from rules and norms and the ability to rely on self-defined procedures to make decisions. Further up the developmental line, and perhaps critical for greater success and for eminence in particular professions, is the dialogical, self-amending, multiple-perspective-taking capacity of Kegan's fifth order of consciousness and Torbert's strategist stage. From the developmental perspective, it is toward such transformational changes that professional education must aim.

References

Argyris, C., & Schon, D. A. (1978). *Organizational learning*. Reading, MA: Addison-Wesley.

Axelrod, S. D. (1999). *Work and the evolving self*. Hillsdale, NJ: Technician Press.

Bar-Yam, M. (1991). Do men and women speak in different voices? A comparative study of self-evolvement. *International Journal of Aging and Human Development, 32*, 247–259.

Basseches, M. (1984). *Dialectical thinking and adult development*. Norwood, NJ: Ablex.

Belenky, M. F., Clinchy, B. M., Goldberger, N. R., & Tarule, J. M. (1986). *Women's ways of knowing*. New York: Basic Books.

Bereiter, C., & Scardamalia, M. (1993). *Surpassing ourselves*. Chicago: Open Court.

Cheetham, G., & Chivers, G. (1998). The reflective (and competent) practitioner: A model of professional competence which seeks to harmonise the reflective practitioner and competence-based approaches. *Journal of European Industrial Training, 22*, 267–276.

Dewey, J. (1933). *How we think*. Lexington, MA: Heath.

Dixon, J. W. (1986). *The relation of social perspective stages to Kegan's stages of ego development*. Unpublished doctoral dissertation, University of Toledo, Toledo, OH.

Erikson, E. (1963). *Childhood and society*. New York: Norton.

Ferry, N. M., & Ross-Gordon, J. M. (1998). An inquiry into Schon's epistemology of practice: Exploring links between experience and reflective practice. *Adult Education Quarterly, 48*, 98–112.

Fisher, D., Merron, K., & Torbert, W. R. (1987). Human development and managerial effectiveness. *Group and Organization Studies, 12*, 257–273.

Fisher, D., & Torbert, W. R. (1991). Transforming managerial practice: Beyond the achiever stage. *Research in Organizational Change and Development, 5*, 143–173.

Fisher, D., & Torbert, W. R. (1995). *Personal and organizational transformations: The true challenge of continual quality improvement*. New York: McGraw-Hill.

Foley, G. (2000). Teaching adults. In Foley, G. (Ed.), *Understanding adult education and training* (2nd ed., pp. 34–58). Sydney, Australia: Allen & Unwin.

Gobbi, M. (1995). Where has Schon led us? The impact of the reflective practitioner upon nurse education, practice, and research. In I. Bryant (Ed.), *Celebrating adult education: Conference papers* (pp. 69–74). Southampton, UK: University of Southampton.

Goodman, R. (1985). A developmental and systems analysis of marital and family communication in clinic and non-clinic families. *Dissertation Abstracts International, 44*(5-B), 1593.

Granott, N. (1998). We learn, therefore we develop: Learning versus development—or developing learning? In M. C. Smith & T. Pourchot (Eds.), *Adult learning and development* (pp. 15–34). Mahwah, NJ: Lawrence Erlbaum.

Granott, N., Fischer, K. W., & Parziale, J. (2002). Bridging to the unknown: A fundamental transition mechanism in learning and development. In N. Granott & J. Parziale (Eds.), *Microdevelopment: Transition processes in development and learning. Cambridge studies in cognitive perceptual development* (pp. 131–156). New York: Cambridge University Press.

Gratch, A. (1985). *Managers' prescriptions of decision-making processes as a function of ego development and of the situation.* Unpublished manuscript, Teachers College, Columbia University.

Greenhaus, J. H. (1987). *Career management.* New York: Dryden.

Greenwald, J. M. (1991). Environmental attitudes: A structural developmental model. *Dissertation Abstracts International,* 53(12-B), 6550.

Harris, I. B. (1993). New expectations for professional competence. In L. Curry, J. F. Wergin, & Associates. *Educating professionals: Responding to new expectations for competence and accountability* (pp. 17–52). San Francisco: Jossey-Bass.

Hughes, E. (1959). The study of occupations. In R. K. Merton, L. Broom, & L. S. Cottrell Jr. (Eds.), *Sociology today* (pp. 442–458). New York: Basic Books.

Hyland, T. (1992). Meta-competence, metaphysics, and vocational expertise. *Competence and Assessment,* Report no. 20, Sheffield, England: Employment Department.

Irving, J. A., & Williams, D. I. (1995). Critical thinking and reflective practice in counseling. *British Journal of Guidance and Counselling,* 23, 107–114.

Johns, C. (2002). Reflective practice: Revealing the art of caring. *International Journal of Nursing Practice,* 7, 237–245.

Kegan, R. (1982). *The evolving self.* Cambridge, MA: Harvard University Press.

Kegan, R. (1994). *In over our heads: The mental demands of modern life.* Cambridge, MA: Harvard University Press.

Kegan, R., & Lahey, L. L. (1983). Adult leadership and adult development. In B. Kellerman (Ed.), *Leadership: Multidisciplinary perspectives* (pp. 199–226). New York: Prentice Hall.

Kegan, R., & Lahey, L. L. (2001). *How the way we talk can change the way we work.* San Francisco: Jossey-Bass.

King, P. M. (1990). Assessing development from a cognitive-developmental perspective. In D. G. Creamer & Associates. *College student development* (pp. 81–98). Alexandria, VA: American College Personnel Association.

Kirby, P. C., & Paradise, L. V. (1992). Reflective practice and effectiveness of teachers. *Psychological Reports,* 70, 1057–1058.

Knefelkamp, L. (1984). Developmental instruction. In L. Knefelkamp & R. R. Golec (Eds.), *A workbook for using the practice-to-theory-to-practice model.* College Park: University of Maryland at College Park.

Kohlberg, L. (1969). Stage and sequence: The cognitive developmental approach to socialization. In D. Goslin (Ed.), *Handbook of socialization: Theory and research* (pp. 347–480). New York: Rand-McNally.

Kohlberg, L. (1984). *The psychology of moral development.* New York: Harper & Row.

Kohlberg, L., & Mayer, R. (1972). Development as the aim of education. *Harvard Educational Review,* 42, 449–496.

Linstead, S. (1991). Developing manaement meta-competence: Can learning help? *Journal of European Industrial Training,* 6, 17–27.

Loevinger, J. (1976). *Ego development.* San Francisco: Jossey-Bass.

Marcia, J. (1966). Development and validation of ego-identity status. *Journal of Personality and Social Psychology,* 3, 551–559.

McAuliffe, G. J. (2001). Introduction: Guidelines for constructivist teaching. In K. P. Eriksen & G. J. McAuliffe (Eds.), *Teaching counselors and therapists: Exemplary classroom practices* (pp. 1–12). Westport, CT: Bergin & Garvey.

McAuliffe, G. J., & Lovell, C. W. (2000). Encouraging transformation: Guidelines for constructivist and developmental instruction. In G. J. McAuliffe & K. P. Eriksen (Eds.), *Preparing counselors and therapists: Creating constructivist and developmental programs* (pp. 14–41). Alexandria, VA: Association for Counselor Education and Supervision.

McAuliffe, G. J., & Lovell, C. W. (in press). The influence of counselor epistemology on the helping interview: A qualitative study. *Journal of Counseling and Development.*

McCormick, R. S. (2001). Is it just natural? Beginning teachers' growth in reflective practice. *Issues in Teacher Education,* 2, 55–67.

Mentkowski, M., & Associates (2000). *Learning that lasts.* San Francisco: Jossey-Bass.

Merron, K., Fisher, D., & Torbert, W. R. (1987) Meaning making and management action. *Group and Organization Studies,* 12, 274–286.

Merron, K., & Torbert, W. R. (1984). *Offering managers feedback on Loevinger's ego development measure.* Unpublished manuscript, School of Management, Boston College.

Moore, B. (2000). The therapeutic community worker as "reflective practitioner" and the social worker as "skillful dynamic explorer." *Therapeutic Communities,* 21, 14.

Moore, W. S. (2002). Understanding learning in a postmodern world: Reconsidering the Perry scheme of ethical and intellectual development. In B. K. Hofer & P. R. Pintrich (Eds.), *Personal epistemology: The psychology of beliefs about knowledge and knowing.* Mahwah, NJ: Lawrence Erlbaum.

O'Donovan-Polten, S. (2001) *The scales of success.* Toront: University of Toronto Press.

Perry, W. G. Jr. (1970/1998). *Forms of intellectual and ethical development in the college years: A scheme.* San Francisco: Jossey-Bass.

Piaget, J. (1966). *The psychology of intelligence.* Totowa, NJ: Littlefield, Adams.

Rest, J. R. (1979). *Development in judging moral issues.* Minneapolis: University of Minnesota Press.

Reynolds, M., & Snell, R. (1988). *Contribution to development of management competence.* Sheffield, England: Manpower Services Commission.

Rooke, D. (2003) *Organizational transformation requires the presence of leaders who are strategists and magicians.* Retrieved June 18, 2003, from Boston College, Carroll School of Management Web site, http://www2.bc.edu/~torbert/21_rooke.htm

Rooke, D., & Torbert, W. R. (1998). Organizational transformation as a function of CEO's developmental stage. *Organizational Development Journal, 16,* 11–28.

Rorty, R. (1989). *Contingency, irony, and solidarity.* New York: Cambridge University Press.

Schaie, K. W. (1986, November). *Relating age change and behavior to job requirements.* Paper presented at the meeting of the Gerontological Society of America, Chicago, IL.

Schein, E. H. (1978). *Career dynamics: Matching individual and organizational needs.* Reading, Mass.: Addison-Wesley.

Schon, D. A. (1983). *The reflective practitioner.* San Francisco: Jossey-Bass.

Schon, D. A. (1987). *Educating the reflective practitioner.* San Francisco: Jossey-Bass.

Schon, D. A. (1991). *The reflective turn: Case studies in and on educational practice.* New York: Teachers College Press.

Selman, R. (1980). *The growth of interpersonal understanding: Developmental and clinical analysis.* New York: Academic Press.

Siegler, R. S. (1996). *Emerging minds: The process of change in children's thinking.* New York: Oxford University Press.

Smith, S. (1980). *Ego development and the problems of power and agreement in organizations.* Unpublished doctoral dissertation, The George Washington University.

Sprinthall, N. A. (1994). Counseling and social role-taking: Promoting moral and ego development. In J. Rest & D. Narvaez (Eds.), *Moral development in the professions: Psychology and applied ethics* (pp. 85–100). Mahwah, NJ: Lawrence Erlbaum.

Super, D. C. (1980). A life-span, life-space approach to career development. *Journal of Vocational Behavior, 16,* 282–296.

Torbert, W. R. (1987). *Managing the corporate dream.* Homewood, IL: Dow Jones-Irwin.

Torbert, W. R. (1991). *The power of balance: Transforming self, society, and scientific inquiry.* Newbury Park, CA: Sage.

Torbert, W. R. (1994). Cultivating post-formal adult development: Higher stages and contrasting interventions. In M. Miller & S. Cook-Greuter (Eds.), *Transcendence and mature thought in adulthood: The further reaches of adult development* (pp. 181–203). Lanham, MD: Rowman & Littlefield.

Vaillant, G. E. (1993). *The wisdom of the ego.* Cambridge, MA: Harvard University Press.

Weinstein, G., & Altschuler, A. S. (1985). Educating and counseling for self-knowledge development. *Journal of Counseling and Development, 64,* 19–25.

Willis, S. L., & Dubin, S. (1990). Competence versus obsolescence: Understanding the challenge facing today's professionals. In S. L. Willis & S. Dubin (Eds.), *Maintaining professional competence* (pp. 1–7). San Francisco: Jossey-Bass.

Willis, S. L., & Tosti-Vasey, J. L. (1990). How adult development, intelligence, and motivation affect competence. In S. L. Willis & S. Dubin (Eds.), *Maintaining professional competence* (pp. 64–84). San Francisco: Jossey-Bass.

Chapter 22

Adult Holistic Development and Multidimensional Performance

Glen Rogers, Marcia Mentkowski, and Judith Reisetter Hart

Fostering both the development of individuals and their performance is a broad societal goal that crosses educational, workplace, and civic sectors. Higher education curricula, workplace training, government programs, foundation initiatives, and even the choices of individuals often similarly assume some view on the quality of the relationship between performance and development of the whole person. Of course, different sectors have put recognizably different emphases on the goals they primarily foster. For example, the development of the whole person has been a long-standing goal of the liberal arts tradition in higher education in a way that is often contrasted with a performance orientation of the workplace. This perhaps puts the contrast too starkly. There are indeed employers who champion a humanistic conception of the development of their employees and liberal arts educators who envision curricula that consistently integrate knowing and doing so that learning transfers to performance after college. Moreover, performance involves more than just an orientation to

getting a job done that is projected in the stark contrast. Because performance is multidimensionally faceted, it may itself include humanistic features that enable individuals to be effective in a wide range of contexts.

The assumptions actors make about the relationship between holistic development and effective performance affect strategic choices for learning. In particular, assumptions about whether various performance and developmental learning goals are incompatible, synergistic, or somewhere in between is critical to educators as they design curriculum. But what do we know empirically about the relationship between holistic development and multidimensional performance?

In this chapter, we critically review published or emerging research that examines the relationship between individual differences in holistic adult development and multidimensional performance. By *adults* we refer to individuals who are beyond secondary schooling. By *performance* we denote an individual's discretionary and dynamic action in an ambiguous situation that effectively meets some contextually conditioned standard of excellence. Such multidimensional performance goes beyond technical or narrowly specified task performance. *Performance* entails the whole dynamic nexus of the individual's intentions, thoughts, feelings, and construals in a dynamic line of action and his or her entanglement in an evolving situation and its broader context. Such a context may be within or across work, family, civic, or other settings. By *holistic development*, we denote the overall direction of dispositional growth in the person's broadly integrated way of making meaning and commitments in moral, interpersonal, epistemological, and personal realms. Theorists have described this kind of holistic growth in terms of sequenced levels that are qualitatively distinct and dynamically structured wholes. This whole of experience shapes, is the shape of, and is shaped by the individual's experiences over time and may become transformed into yet more coherent and differentiated forms of stable existential meaning.

The relationship between holistic development and multidimensional performance has largely been studied psychometrically, so we have grounded our review in these measurement-based findings. More specific questions arise about the likely nature of the relationship. Is it broad or limited to certain kinds of performance? Is it mediated or direct? What implications then follow for the meaning and measurement of adult development and performance? Our review also distinguishes the domain of holistic development of the person and its measurement from the related domain of reasoning or cognitive development. This distinction is important to those who study the predictors of effective performance inasmuch as they typically ask for evidence that any reputed causes, such as holistic development, are not piggybacking on generalized differences in cognitive ability (see Sternberg & Hedlund, 2002; Viswesvaran & Ones, 2002). Because the topic is broad, the review necessarily crosses a range of theoretical perspectives.

USING A MODEL OF THE PERSON AS A METATHEORETICAL FRAMEWORK

Holistic development and performance in context are two domains of growth in what we have called

learning that lasts (Mentkowski & Associates, 2000). Our review draws on our educational model of the person. This model includes development and performance as two domains of growth and represents the range of learning outcomes that students demonstrated during and after college (Mentkowski & Associates, 2000). Because we are setting forth some metatheoretical assumptions of this model, we are better able to suggest a pluralistic integration of widely diverse theoretical paradigms, for example, those of cognitive constructivist and social constructionist. The advantage of using such a model is that it provides some broad language and an organized perspective to track general concepts across more specific theories. Our model of the person usefully locates the broad domains of multidimensional performance and holistic development in relation to one another and to recognizable metatheoretical stances. In figure 22.1, these two domains of growth in the person are labeled *development* and *performance*. Note that these domains in the model are not adjacent to one another because they differ on two metatheoretical dimensions that organize the four domains of growth.

Metatheoretical Dimensions: Person/Context and Intentional Focus

The two metatheoretical dimensions that characterize domains of growth reflect (a) *relationship between person and context* and (b) *direction of intentional focus* (figure 22.1). The strong contrast we make between holistic development and performance is reflected in their different locations on the two dimensions. By making this metatheoretical contrast clear, which also reflects differences in how constructs within these domains are measured, we are better able to test the relationship between development and performance. The other two domains of growth articulated in the model of the person, reasoning and self-reflection, can be considered potential mediators of the relationship between development and performance (Mentkowski & Associates, 2000).

The east/west dimension is *relation of person and context*. To the right, growth is more contextualized by diverse interactions of person and context. The person is interwoven with the *contextual frames* of a particular cultural and performance setting. The quality of the individual's fitness with his or her

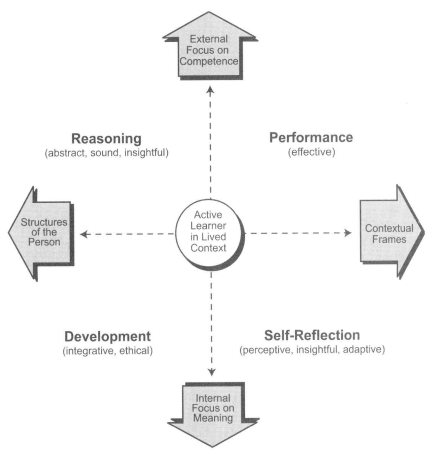

FIGURE 22.1 Dimensions organizing domains of growth in the person. From Mentkowski & Associates. Copyright © 2000, Jossey-Bass. Reprinted by permission of John Wiley & Sons, Inc.

context—either through adaptation to, selection of, or shaping of the context—is the predominant metatheoretical criterion for evaluating growth in the domains of performance and self-reflection (e.g., Lave & Wenger, 1991; Sternberg, 2002). To the left, *structures of the person* reflect how an individual's dispositional thinking, feeling, and choices shape their flow of experience. These structures are achievements of dynamic internal congruencies in ways of perceiving, thinking, and making ethical judgments as described by holistic theories of adult development (e.g., Jane Loevinger and William Perry) and cognitive individual difference theories (e.g., Jean Piaget). These holistic congruencies arise in relation to strands of growth that are more specific belief, knowledge, and affective systems. For example, Perry (1970) observed in holistic development a congruency between one's belief in absolute black and white truth and rigidity in making personal commitments.

The north/south dimension, *direction of intentional focus*, distinguishes domains of growth with external focus on *competence* in engaging the world from those with an internal focus on *meaning*. Performance and reasoning are about mastery of the external world and frameworks for understanding it. Although the domains of self-reflection and development are both focused on existential meaning, it is useful to differentiate how they relate to constructs of the self. Only in the domain of self-reflection is the self the actual object of attention, as is the case, for example, in one's reflection on one's professional identity. In contrast, the self that develops in holistic structural stage theories is the meaning-making process itself, which is only indirectly experienced.

Domains of Growth and How They Contrast

The complex geography of the whole person (figure 22.1) is grounded in an enduring present of consciousness that pervades each of the domains and the active learner's relation to the lived world and self. The four domains (development, reasoning, performance, and self-reflection) and their interaction define a concept of the whole person. This whole person is broader than what we and others would call the domain of holistic development. We can better locate the contrast between the focal domains of development and performance by first contrasting the model's adjacent domains of growth with each other, recognizing also that there are no sharp or impermeable boundaries between them and that they do not represent types of persons.

Contrasting Development and Reasoning

Both development and reasoning have holistic features, as well as recognizable components. For example, the persistent positive manifold of correlations between more specific cognitive abilities is thought to reflect general cognitive or meta-cognitive ability (Demetriou, 2002). Effective reasoning might be characterized as abstract, sound, and insightful. We reserve the term *holistic development*, however, for development that is a further integration of the meaning-making self, which is therefore distinguished from cognitive development. In contrast to the focus on intellectual tasks within the domain of reasoning, holistic development focuses on the development of purpose. Positive holistic development might be characterized as increasingly integrative and ethical.

Blasi (1998) has similarly contrasted Loevinger's theory of ego development with cognitive developmental theory by observing that although cognitive meaning can be understood as relationships among objects/events, such as are represented in concepts and theories, the meaning-making of Loevinger's synthetic ego is about significance. Meaning as significance integrates cognitive meaning with the individual's interests, needs, and values. Blasi's distinction cannot be merely reduced to a divide between cognition and affective emotion, as reasoning itself can be very passionate (Fromm, 1947). Still, the emotion of reasoning is unmixed with the interpersonal motivation that is present in the other domains (Mentkowski & Associates, 2000). Blasi has suggested that at the higher stages of ego development, mastery of cognitive interests gains a higher priority, creating one kind of connection between cognitive and holistic development. For example, the motivational basis of Loevinger's conformist stage implies that understanding may be distorted by the prioritized need to maintain social relationships, even though the individual otherwise may enjoy and have intellectually mastered very advanced theoretical inquiry. In contrast to the willingness to compromise one's ideas, motivational structures at the conscientious stage are grounded in a sense of fidelity to self-evaluated standards and long-term ideals.

Contrasting Development and Self-Reflection

The contrast between self as subject and object goes back to William James's (1890/1962) distinction between the I and the Me. The I is the subject of awareness or the self-as-knower, whereas the Me is the object of awareness or the self-as-known. The domain of holistic development is characterized by an individual's manner of existential meaning making, and, following James, it is subjectively experienced as the I's unified sense of self-awareness, which remains in the background. The domain of self-reflection is characterized by the individual's various identities and so relates to James's objectified Me. The domain of self-reflection can be thought of as the self-as-story, and it includes one's achievements and conscious awareness of persistent attributes, including introjection of external perspectives on the self, the so-called looking-glass self. For example, a nurse's sense of her professional attributes may be shaped by her consistently effective performance in a fast-paced critical care unit and by comments on how caring she is. In this way, personal identities formed in self-reflection are coconstituted by a particular interpersonal and cultural matrix and draw on performance in established roles.

Although the Me is distinguished as an intersubjectively constituted self-as-known, its objectified self-contents are not independent of the developmental level of the self-as-knower. The quality of narrative meaning making reflects the synthetic processes of the I. For example, McAdams (1998) traced the complexity of the narrative Me in terms of the individual's increasingly complex understanding of traits, which is one indicator that Loevinger has used to specify stage of ego development. At the impulsive stage, globalized and indistinctive trait attributes (e.g., nice) predominate person descriptions. By the time an individual reaches the stage of conscientiousness, his or her description of another person reflects rich and differentiated understanding of traits and inner motives. McAdams suggested that the developmental capacities of still higher stages are more hospitable to creating narratively complex and unique life stories (also see Labouvie-Vief, Chiodo, Goguen, Diehl, & Orwoll, 1995). In sum, the content that makes up a self-reflected identity is developmentally related to the structural manner in which that identity is held. At the same time, this relationship may be one of relative congruence or incongruence, as identities formed under the influence of less developed structures may persist (Noam, 1993). For example, a college student's identity as a tough guy competitor may reemerge in inappropriate and unsportsmanlike behaviors decades later at a company picnic, when he has otherwise become a sophisticated administrator.

Contrasting Performance and Self-Reflection

Whereas performance is evaluated by its effectiveness, self-reflection is a form of focused learning evaluated by its perceptiveness, insightfulness, and adaptation to context (see figure 22.1). In self-reflection one's own identities and ideals are the object of awareness, which contrasts with how attention in performance is directed toward the flow of action and its effectiveness in the external world. Indeed, directing attention toward oneself and self-evaluative standards can disrupt ongoing performance, as is commonly experienced when one observes oneself in a mirror (Duval & Wicklund, 1972). Although effective performance includes metacognitive monitoring of one's ongoing performance, attention here focuses on evaluation of strategy and improvement in performance (Pressley, Borkowski, & Schneider, 1987) rather than drifting toward global evaluation of the self.

Contrasting Performance and Reasoning

In contrast to reasoning, performance often combines interpersonal with cognitive abilities to engage dynamically unfolding events in a particular setting and context. Effectiveness of performance is contextually defined in relation to individual goals (Sternberg et al., 2000), organizational goals (Motowidlo & Van Scotter, 1994), and standards defined by particular communities of practice (Lave & Wenger, 1991; Schön, 1987). In contrast, adult cognitive developmental levels are sometimes specified generically by tasks and cognitive processes independently of context, even though environmental context affects how well one performs (e.g., Commons, Krause, Fayer, & Meaney, 1993).

Contrasting Development and Performance as Domains of Growth

We now turn to contrasting directly the two domains that are the focus of this chapter. Multidimensional performance contrasts with holistic development by being both (1) contextually versus integratively defined and (2) by its focus on a standard of effectiveness versus purpose.

Organicism Versus Contextualism as Metaphors for Growth

Holistic development, where the person is understood as synthetic meaning maker, draws on the root metaphor of the organism (see Goldhaber, 2000). In organicism, progression unifies more fragmentary experiences into wholes that transcend the contradictions of the fragments while preserving all of their productivity—the whole in retrospect being implied in the fragments (Pepper, 1970). In adult developmental theory, the metatheoretical categories of organicism as a worldview are clearly reflected in Werner's (1957) orthogentic principle. This principle asserts that development simultaneously proceeds toward a state of increasing differentiation and hierarchical integration. As a result of increasing self-organization, the individual is able to act from a larger frame of reference than the immediate concrete situation and momentary affective state.

Whereas organicism is the classic developmental worldview, contextualism is a worldview that is more congruent with intentional and discretionary performance (see Dixon & Baltes, 1986). The metatheoretical root metaphor for contextualism is the historic event (Pepper, 1970). For contextualism, change and novelty are possibilities for every event. The root metaphor implies that there are no definitive analyses or endpoints. For example, the focus of an analysis may always shift and each equally legitimate focus may itself endlessly connect to ever widening strands of context. In the metaphor, context is not a separate surrounding envelope that is the site of transactions with the organism, but rather integrally coconstitutive.

Developmental Purpose Versus Performance Effectiveness

Whereas holistic developmental theories posit an integrative way of being in the world as a teleologically desirable end point, performance is about getting something done effectively and efficiently. It often seems quite natural to scale performance in relation to economically valenced values of success, but misguided to justify development on similar terms. Indeed, the whole agenda of relating development to performance can be seen as misguided, if it seems to justify intrinsic human values based on extrinsic instrumental values. Self-actualization and moral development are self-justified goods, valued on their own terms, even as both make claims on how the individual acts (Armon & Dawson, 2003). Sometimes, the development of moral and individual purposes can claim primacy. At the same time, engagement in the world is not antithetical to personal development (Mentkowski & Associates, 2000). For example, achieving competence in a career may be an arena for self-actualization (Erikson, 1969). Likewise, an individual's moral judgment gains integrity when it is realized in intentional moral action.

Limiting arguments for fostering holistic development to the alleged primacy of its intrinsic good may itself be misguided, however. No particular individual or societal intrinsic good can automatically claim complete primacy over other intrinsic goods. Even an external indicator of success, such as salary, might be presumptively related to intrinsic values of personal happiness, personal adjustment, and productive achievement. All the better then if distinct intrinsic goods have synergistic relationships with one another. If holistic development also enhances performance, its productive consequences could be welcome justifications for policies that further individual potential, especially if the secondary consequences can be seen as derived from the intrinsic character of holistic development.

ARE DEVELOPMENT AND PERFORMANCE LINKED?

The organicists' perspectives that we consider often assume democracy or social equity as their ideal political context and arguably arose in part as a bulwark against totalitarian tendencies in democratic societies. But a further sociohistorical consideration has been a basis for increased interest in the relation between adult development and performance. Some observers of postindustrial societies have suggested that an increasingly global economy and information society have led to structural changes in business and industry, such as the flattening of hierarchies, which call for more complex, flexible, and discretionary performance from a wider portion of the workforce (Klemp, 2001; Russ-Eft & Brennan, 2001; Senge, 1990). Some have argued further that the kind of discretionary performance that has now become required implies that workers will need to develop new ways of being that involve their very personhood and go beyond the narrow specialized skills required for an age of mass production. At least in postindustrial democracies, workplace structural changes are said to favor learning organizations. Senge (1990) observed that

> At the heart of a learning organization is a shift of mind—from seeing ourselves as separate from the world to connected to the world, from seeing problems as caused by someone or something *out there* to seeing how our own actions create the problems we experience. A learning organization is a place where people are continually discovering how they create their reality. (pp. 12–13)

Kegan (1994) also suggested that what is required is a fourth order of consciousness, *self-authorship*, which he sees as parallel to Loevinger's stage of conscientiousness. "Whether we are looking at our culture's literature of expertise in the realms of partnering, parenting, or providing, we see what seems to be a single, common, unrecognized claim on the minds of most contemporary adults for the degree of psychological authority described by the fourth order" (p. 185). Fisher, Merron, and Torbert (1987) similarly suggested that the capacity of organizations to progress to decentralized decision making may be limited by the tendency of employees to be centered on solving presenting problems rather than resolving intra- and interpersonal conflicts for both means and ends.

If these analyses are sound, then a review of studies that use measures of holistic development that capture the emergence of self-direction should find that holistic development is related to the quality of discretionary performance across a range of workplace, parenting, and civic roles. Such findings would strengthen an educational rationale for focusing on holistic development by linking it to enduring gains in performance. Conversely, these results might encourage performance improvement strategies that could synergistically support holistic development.

MODELING HOLISTIC AND COGNITIVE DEVELOPMENT IN RELATION TO PERFORMANCE

For the task of investigating the relationship between holistic development and performance, studies that simultaneously model the overlapping domains of cognitive and holistic development have a key advantage. Individual differences in cognitive capacities are often considered the best predictor of more effective performance (E. Hunt, 1995). Moreover, as testimony to the potential confounding of the constructs, some researchers doubt that holistic and cognitive development are distinct (Sanders, Lubinski, & Persson Benbow, 1995). Of course, others draw various distinctions. For example, the Minnesota Twins Study (Newman, Tellegen, & Bouchard, 1998) indicated that holistic development has a heritable component distinct from cognitive ability. This study of 45 pairs of monozygotic twins and 28 pairs of dizygotic twins used a well-validated measure of holistic development, the Sentence Completion Test (SCT) of ego development (Loevinger & Wessler, 1970; Loevinger, Wessler, & Redmore, 1970). The authors estimated SCT heritability at about 50%. Removing cognitive development from the twins' ego development scores had only a small effect on this estimate. The distinction between cognitive and holistic development is reinforced in the longitudinal studies we take up next. By disentangling the possible effects of cognitive capacities from those of holistic development, these studies provide a more plausible representation of possible connections to performance.

The Kohn and Schooler Longitudinal Study

Kohn and Schooler (1982, 1983) led a comprehensive longitudinal study of 687 men. The sample was limited to workers under the age of 65 and was representative of men from civilian occupations in the United States. The study measured several job autonomy and career-related indicators. An overall developmental tendency to be self-directed was measured through 29 questionnaire items. In the measurement model, self-directedness toward self and society was negatively indicated by authoritarian conservative beliefs, self-protective morality, self-deprecation, conformity in ideas, and fatalism. It was positively indicated by being trustful of others. Indicators of ideational flexibility included performance in handling ill-structured cognitive problems, an embedded figures test, and the interviewer's ratings of the participant's intelligence. Kohn and Schooler's (1982) causal modeling suggested that substantive complexity of the men's current work conditions positively influenced their assessed level of ideational flexibility (.11) and self-directedness (.12). In other words, the complexity of work had immediate effects on cognitive and holistic development. The contemporaneous paths in the other direction, from holistic development to the complexity of work, were not statistically significant. These findings were generally replicated by Miller, Schooler, Kohn, and Miller (1983) in a cross-sectional sample of 269 women who were married to the men in the primary study. The structural paths over time in the primary study are of particular interest. Ideational flexibility, but not self-directedness, affected the substantive complexity of work 10 years later (.26). Conversely, however, self-directedness—but not ideational flexibility—supported job income (.08) and reduced closeness of supervision (−.13) 10 years later, though these effects were smaller.

These lagged causal paths from self-directedness to these macro-level performance indicators might not necessarily mean that individual differences in self-directedness led to better performance within a job position, however. Because self-directedness and ideational flexibility had lagged rather than contemporaneous effects on job responsibilities, the authors suggested the men self-selected themselves into jobs that suited them. "The implication is that job conditions are not readily modified to suit the needs or capacities of the individual worker. Over a long enough time, many men either modify their jobs or move to other jobs more consonant with their personalities" (Kohn & Schooler, 1982, p. 1282). Consistent with a self-selection interpretation, Helson and Wink (1987) found in the Mills College Longitudinal Study that SCT ego development at age 43 correlated not only with a contemporaneous measure of job status for women, r (89) = .35, but also with amount of time in paid employment, r = .23. In the Kohn and Schooler study, it is worth noting that a self-directed orientation to self and society had a stronger contemporaneous path to ideational flexibility (.24) than vice versa (.13). Indeed, alternative models suggest that contemporaneous positive effects are unidirectional, from self-directedness to ideational flexibility (Kohn & Schooler, 1983, p. 179). This might suggest that self-directedness does specifically lead to higher cognitive performance, given that ill-structured problems were some of the indicators of ideational flexibility. One problem with relying heavily on Kohn and Schooler's research as evidence for a distinct domain of holistic development and its effects on performance is that they did not use previously established developmental measures. Although their measurement model performed well, there remains room for considerable conceptual slippage between their construct of self-directedness and their questionnaire indicators.

Alverno Longitudinal Study

The Alverno Longitudinal Study used multiple approaches to investigating learning, development, and performance (Mentkowski, 1988; Mentkowski & Associates, 2000). This research followed adult women over a 10-year period. Participants completed a battery of human potential measures at entrance to college, two years later, near graduation, and again as five-year alumnae. About half of the students came to college directly from high school and were about 18 years old. The other half was more varied. By the time of the 5-year alumna assessment, the average participant in the study was 36 years old (SD = 9, range 27–65). The psychometric component of the study factorially distinguished three of four broad domains of the person: reasoning, development, and performance (Mentkowski & Associates, 2000).

Distinguishing Reasoning and Development

Two orthogonal principal axis factors distinguished the first two domains of growth: cognitive development (reasoning) and holistic development (development). These factors replicated for both students and five-year alumnae across each of the four longitudinal assessments (n = 237, 258, 127, and 208). One of these factors, labeled Critical Thinking, was marked by the Test of Cognitive Development (TCD), a Piagetian-based paper and pencil measure of formal operations (Renner et al., 1976), and by the three subscales (inferences, deductions, and recognition of assumptions) from Watson and Glaser's (1964) Critical Thinking Appraisal (CTA). The other longitudinally replicated factor, Integration of Self in Context, was marked by ego development on Loevinger's SCT and by three essays from the Measure of Intellectual Development (MID) developed by Knefelkamp and Widick (1982), which were scored for Perry's (1970) holistic theory of development (Mentkowski, Moeser, & Strait, 1983). These holistic and cognitive development factors were also replicated on a separate sample also drawn from the Alverno Longitudinal Study (Rogers, Mentkowski, Reisetter Hart, & Schwan Minik, 2001). Thus, this study provides strong evidence for distinguishing cognitive and holistic development. Moreover, the causal analyses of change after college indicated that holistic development might have had a lagged negative influence on cognitive development (beta = −.22, p < .10), leading Mentkowski and Associates (2000) to suggest that these two domains diverged in adulthood outside of a formal education setting (also see Labouvie-Vief & Diehl, 2000). At the same time, the estimates of the relationship between the latent constructs have ranged between .37 and .79, which suggests that they are indeed also related.

Although Kohlberg's theory of moral development is rooted in cognitive developmental theory, factor analysis of a subsample from the study, where time of assessment was ignored (virtual n = 175), found that the Moral Judgment Interview (MJI) loaded on Integration of Self in Context rather than the critical thinking factor, which included the Piagetian-based measure of formal operations. In contrast, moral reasoning as measured by Rest's (1979) Defining Issues Test (DIT) consistently loaded on both the holistic and cognitive developmental factors across all samples. Rogers (2002) concluded that the MJI taps the developmental entanglement of moral judgment with the structural development of the self-system because the format of the MJI draws forward the individual's active construction of their moral perspective. Estimates from other studies suggest that the correlation between the SCT and MJI, with age partialed out, is between .40 and .60 (Loevinger, 1998b). Consistent with Loevinger's account, moral development on the MJI may be an integral aspect of an undivided and coherent process of ego development, where judgment about *what is moral* is intertwined with transformation in moral motivation, *why be moral*. The implication is that typical holistic adult development moves from the individual investing in morality as a way of affirming belonging with a group (conformist) toward investing in morality as a way of realizing self-evaluated standards and long-term ideals (conscientiousness). This interpretation runs counter to Kohlberg's (1984) theoretical position, whereby solely the answer to the cognitive question, *what is moral*, structurally develops.

Moral reasoning on the DIT is less diagnostic of such holistic development of the moral self than is the MJI (Rogers, 2002). Consistent with this conclusion, Skoe and von der Lippe (2002) found that the SCT correlated less well with the DIT (.20) than with the Ethic of Care Interview (ECI) (.58), which is based on Gilligan's (1982) theory of the individual's development toward a balanced sense of responsibility for self and others. The relationship between SCT and the ECI remained substantial with age, education, and cognitive ability controlled (.51). Because the DIT requires only the endorsement of moral perspectives, it primarily measures developmental comprehension and preference for more sophisticated ways of organizing cooperation (see Rest, Narváez, Bebeau, & Thoma, 1999).

Performance Domain in Relation to Development

The Alverno Longitudinal Study included a measure of five-year alumnae performance based on McClelland's (1978) Behavioral Event Interview (BEI). It also included a career-level measure based on job position titles (Ben-Ur & Rogers, 1994). The BEI elicits and probes firsthand constructions of performance. It is based on the individual's recollection of specific events, focusing on what the person actually did rather than on what he or she usually does, which would more likely reflect espoused theory. A substantial research literature has related abilities coded from these kinds of interviews not only to cognitive ability tests (Huffcutt, Roth, & McDaniel, 1996) but also to incremental validity in predicting supervisors' ratings of job performance beyond cognitive abilities (Campion, Campion, & Hudson, 1994; Schmidt & Hunter, 1998). Three-quarters of five-year alumnae in the Alverno study identified paid employment as their primary activity. Researchers coded for 42 abilities in 4 situational performances in the workplace ($n = 157$). Mentkowski and Associates (2000) identified four alumna ability factors that were correlated with the indicators of career achievement (average $r = .22$) and independent faculty judgments of the performance's effectiveness (average $r = .27$). Rogers (1999) suggested that the factor structure of the abilities might be accounted for by various sources of sustained alumna learning (collaboration, self-assessment, teaching others, and inquiry), which could be specifically linked to common features of learning in the curriculum as well as the workplace. The factors were:

Factor I, Collaborative Organizational Thinking and Action, included abilities important for effective participative leadership. Independent conceptualization and action abilities were balanced by collaborative abilities that drew out the potential of others to contribute to collective effectiveness.

Factor II, Balanced Self-Assessment and Acting from Values, included abilities important to monitoring learning and improvement.

Factor III, Developing Others and Perspective Taking, included abilities important to supporting the development of others, such as positive regard, sensitivity to individual differences, perspective taking, and addressing performance difficulties.

Factor IV, Analytical Thinking and Action, included abilities important to logical problem solving and rational persuasion, as well as use of specialized knowledge in task performance.

Collaborative Organizational Thinking and Action (Factor I) was related to holding management positions, especially those beyond entry level. It was the only factor that tended to correlate with the range of indicators of critical thinking and integration of self in context. In particular, this kind of participative leadership correlated with two of three essays from the Perry-based MID, with Kohlberg's MJI, Rest's DIT, and the distinctly cognitive CTA (r from .26 to .33), but not with Loevinger's SCT, the Piagetian-based TCD, nor the best class essay from the MID (r from .08 to .16). The relatively robust relationship of the participative leadership factor with the holistic developmental measures suggests that this is the kind of performance most related to development. Indeed, the way in which participative leadership respects and values the views of others and uses them to construct meaning is fully congruent with proto-typical descriptions of more advanced holistic development.

Although Collaborative Organizational Thinking and Action was related to cognitive and holistic development, it also loaded as a distinct third factor. We concluded that proactivity as it is expressed in this performance factor should not be conflated with self-directedness, a developmental stage construct that is common across holistic developmental theories (also see Laske, 2003). Whereas proactivity in performance can rely on a kind of received understanding of externally defined organizational goals that may be quite narrowly proscribed, self-directedness entails the capacity to make examined commitments to internally defined goals and ideals that may be as broad as the human condition. Even so, proactivity remains a sophisticated underpinning of performance. Showing initiative involves taking personal responsibility for completing discretionary tasks, making a judgment that a particular action is appropriate, and then going beyond standing requests, procedures, or scripts to produce contextually appropriate action.

Holistic development had a more consistent relationship with the full range of performance factors when it was assessed in a way that was more specifically congruent with conceptualizing career and performance. Developmental scores for the career choice essay on the MID correlated with all four alumna ability factors (r from .17 to .26). This consistent relationship to the performance factors indicates that one's self-directedness in choosing a meaningful career—rather than developmental self-directedness more generally—is linked to the full range of performance in the workplace (Mentkowski & Associates, 2000, p. 206).

Structural Model of Alumna Development and Performance

Contemporaneous zero-order correlations between holistic development and performance are only weak evidence for their relationship. They suggest neither the direction of causality nor rule out the possibility that holistic development is piggybacking on the relationship of cognitive development to performance. To do so, the alumna causal model in the Alverno Longitudinal Study tested for lagged relationships from development to performance five years later. However, it did not did not confirm any. The path from integration of self at graduation to Collaborative Organizational Thinking and Action in the workplace five years later was positive (.20) but did not approach statistical significance (n = 116). The path from integration of self to career growth, as measured by position titles, was similarly positive (.21), but also did not approach statistical significance. Critical thinking and DIT-measured moral reasoning at graduation were also unrelated to collaborative organizational thinking and action and career growth.

Comments on Longitudinal Studies Controlling for Cognitive Development

Both longitudinal studies provide estimates of a possible causal relationship between holistic development and performance. In the Alverno study, zero-order correlations suggested links between holistic development and Collaborative Organizational Thinking and Action, but causal modeling with cognitive ability controlled did not statistically affirm lagged causal effects of holistic development on performance. Although the Alverno study used more established measures of holistic development, the Kohn and Schooler study is more supportive of a causal relationship from self-directedness to performance. At the same time, Kohn and Schooler suggested that the lagged causal relationship they found across 10 years of measured change is best interpreted as a selection rather than a performance effect. Self-directed workers may self-select themselves into positions in the workforce that allow for more discretion in performance, which also happen to be higher performing positions. Moreover, having more substantively complex work concurrently supported a more self-directed orientation.

Findings from the longitudinal studies suggest it is important to represent cognitive development in studying the relationship between holistic development and performance. For example, the Alverno Longitudinal Study provided consistent factorial evidence for the distinction between cognitive and holistic development. Nonetheless, to expand this review, we included every study we could find that psychometrically related holistic development with performance.

CRITERIA FOR INCLUSION
IN THE REVIEW

The measurement of holistic development has grounded a great deal of research and yielded a variety of measures. Use of measures of holistic development provides one anchor to the inclusion criteria for the review. Here we specify a range of alternative measures of holistic development, but will also return to this topic when we take up the possibility of using personality measures of openness to experience as a surrogate. The measurement implications of multidimensional performance constructs are less likely to be immediately recognized. To specify the other anchor for inclusion, we further clarify the construct of performance and how it excludes some measurement strategies.

Alternative Measures
of Holistic Development

Loevinger (1987) quipped that one problem with developmental theories is that there are too many of them. Holistic development is not directly observable, and every measure will be partial, though some general convergence among measures and theory (or paring) is necessary to retain the holistic thesis. Assumptions vary on whether holistic development is entangled with multidimensional content. Commons and his colleagues have suggested that all developmental domains can be scaled on a single dimension of hierarchical complexity, which reflects how higher order actions coordinate less complex ones (e.g., Commons & Richards, 1984). Their scaling defines hard stages (e.g., higher stages logically encompassing lower ones) that continue beyond Piaget's formal operations. Dawson (2002) has demonstrated that an interview scored for hierarchical complexity yielded

scores comparable with both the MJI and Armon's (1984) Good Life Interview ($r = .90$ and $.92$, disattenuated for error). These correlations are unadjusted for age however, which ranges from 5 to 86 years. If the congruencies of holistic development include psychological motivation as Blasi (1998) has argued, then logical scaling of hierarchical complexity may be an incomplete representation of development, even if a useful scoring strategy. The highest correlation Dawson found was between the MJI and Good Life Interview where the instruments' original scaling assumptions were used ($r = .97$, disattenuated).

We conclude that the SCT, MID, MJI, ECI, and the Good Life Interview are good candidates for measuring holistic development, the synthetic meaning-making self that is distinct from cognitive development. The Alverno findings also suggest DIT moral reasoning may measure a strand of holistic development but that it also is relatively limited as a measure of this broader construct (Rogers, 2002). It is beyond the scope of this chapter to fully review alternative measures of holistic development, but it is useful to take up some other major candidates that help clarify the nomological net that defines the scope of our review.

Cognitive Complexity

Harvey, Hunt, and Schroder (1961) articulated conceptual systems theory. Development is thought to proceed toward differentiated integration and more flexible engagement with the environment and the interpersonal world. The Paragraph Completion Method (PCM) codes completions of sentence stems for conceptual level (D. E. Hunt, 1971). It is often noted that conceptual level or stage of cognitive complexity in conceptual systems theory resembles the stage levels of Loevinger and Kohlberg. A study by Sullivan, McCullough, and Stager (1970) investigated the relationship of the PCM to the SCT and MJI in a stratified sample of 120 students aged 12, 14, and 17 years. They found that the relationship was somewhat equivocal for the older students. Although the PCM correlated well in the combined sample with moral (.62) and ego development (.56), the respective correlations dropped to .34 and .23 with age controlled. For the 40 students who were in the oldest group (age 17), the PCM was only weakly related to moral (.19) and ego development (.09). This finding cannot be solely attributed to restriction of range.

Nonetheless, in a sample of undergraduate and graduate students ($n = 72$), the related Paragraph Completion Test has correlated (.43) with Kohlbergian moral judgment as exhibited in a written essay on capital punishment (de Vries & Walker, 1986). Also, conceptual level, appropriately enough, seems to be only moderately correlated with cognitive capacities (Schroder, Driver, & Streufert, 1967; Suedfeld & Coren, 1992). We have included studies using the PCM.

Maturity of Defense Mechanisms

A number of investigators have suggested that maturity of defenses may represent a second model of ego development. A range of different scoring systems have been used. Vaillant and McCullough (1987) found that maturity of rated defenses in middle age did not significantly correlate with SCT ego level. Also, maturity of defenses correlated with global measures of mental health better than did SCT ego level. Hart and Chmiel's (1992) findings suggested a stronger relationship of defense maturity to the MJI (many correlations in the .4 range and some above .8). They found that mature defense mechanisms in adolescence predicted development on the MJI 10–20 years later. The pattern of correlations was suggestive of a causal relationship rather than measurement of the same construct, however. We only excluded studies that used a questionnaire strategy to measure maturity of defenses.

Reflective Judgment

Although growth on the Reflective Judgment Interview (RJI) is not accounted for by its relationship with verbal reasoning, King and Kitchener (1994) noted that reflective judgment is a more intellectual construct than ego development. In particular, King, Kitchener, Wood, and Davison (1989) reported an average correlation of .02 with SCT across three times of assessment. Although they also reported an average RJI correlation with the DIT at .53, Josephson (1988) has reported no significant correlation with the MJI. This finding for the MJI is perhaps a result of a restricted range (King & Kitchener, 1994) but is also suggestive of a low relationship between the RJI and holistic development. Unlike Perry's holistic theory where epistemology and existential commitment are assumed to be entangled strands of development, the RJI is strictly an epistemological measure that focuses on structural development in beliefs about the nature of knowledge and how it is justified. Although RJI ratings seem to developmentally scale a dimension of effective epistemic task performance on into postformal reasoning, this does not demonstrate a relationship with a broad and independently measured domain of multidimensional performance. As far as we know, no researchers measuring epistemological sophistication as a distinct and separate strand of adult development have psychometrically examined relationships to performance in the workplace, family, or other settings outside of the classroom (see Hofer & Pintrich, 1997, 2002; Schommer, 1998).

How Do We Measure Multidimensional Performance?

The concept of performance goes beyond specific behaviors to the effectiveness of discretionary action in an evolving context. Relatively few studies measure multidimensional performance because most approaches fail to preserve its dynamic, ambiguous, and open-ended nature. At the same time, such performance may be measured at various levels of summary or analytical precision.

Measures at Different Levels of Performance

At the most macro-level, career achievement can be a proxy for performance across time and situation even though there are many sources of error. For example, individuals may differentially self-select themselves into job positions as Kohn and Schooler (1982) concluded. Peer, subordinate, and supervisory ratings in the workplace also include some biases and sources of error, but are also relatively good summaries of observed performance quality (Scullen, Mount, & Goff, 2000). These observer ratings, which may occur in the form of global scales, dimensions, checklists, or criteria, may legitimately summarize relatively micro- or macro-performance across time. We included in our review studies using observer ratings but excluded those relying on self-ratings.

Researchers may also code performances that occur in a simulated setting or that have been recounted in structured interviews. Behavioral event interviews of past performance, such as used in the Alverno Longitudinal Study, retain validity for higher level positions relative to situational interviews that ask participants to describe how they would act in hypothetical situations (Huffcutt, Weekley, Wiesner, Degroot, & Jones, 2001). We included a situation interview study, but we excluded unstructured interviews about performance, which are less valid (McDaniel, Whetzel, Schmidt, & Maurer, 1994). Simulations are a relatively popular strategy. The lack of fidelity between a simulation and the concept of performance has been the source of most of the judgments we made to exclude a study. We systematically excluded simulation studies when they culminated only in the selection of an action choice from a menu, even though some investigators refer to these as behavioral studies. Although we included in our review some studies with open-ended responses that have relatively low fidelity, we describe the mode of response to articulate their degree of usefulness to our purpose. We excluded studies using only global school evaluations, which typically reflect relatively inert academic knowledge and achievement on highly structured cognitive tasks, rather than a broader performance capacity to effectively use relevant knowledge to perform in an ambiguous and novel context (see Samson, Graue, Weinstein, & Walberg, 1984; Sternberg et al., 2000).

Dimensions of Performance Measured

There are many conceptions of underlying dimensions in performance. General cognitive ability is one that is relatively well established, but performance appears to be multidimensional and may have supports from varied individual capacities that may be related to holistic development. In the personnel literature, there is considerable interest in whether a distinction between contextual and task performance can organize more specific performance dimensions (Borman & Motowidlo, 1993; Motowidlo, Borman, & Schmit, 1997). Task performance reflects the individual's contributions to core organizational processes in providing services and making goods. Contextual performance accounts for individual contributions to organizational effectiveness that go beyond task performance, including such behaviors as persisting with enthusiasm, voluntarily carrying out extra-role initiatives, cooperating with others, and following organizational rules and procedures. Contextual performance may be divided into job dedication (a motivational facet) and interpersonal facilitation, which is a team-related facet (Chan & Schmitt, 2002; Conway, 1999;

Johnson, 2001). But job dedication may also be related to both task and contextual performance (Van Scotter & Motowidlo, 1996).

Multidimensional performance may involve other psychological processes that cut across the distinction between contextual and task performance. Performance exhibited in workplace training programs (training performance) may confront steeper learning curves than more established performance on the job. Tacit knowledge, which is a form of *knowing how* that is learned through long experience in a setting, has demonstrated predictive validity beyond general cognitive ability for the effectiveness of managers (Wagner & Sternberg, 1990) and the leadership of army officers (Sternberg et al., 2000). However, tacit knowledge is generally thought to be very situation specific and does not seem developmentally relevant. In contrast, broad dispositional motives and self-image that underlie performance are thought to be less situationally specific (McClelland, 1961, 1985, 1987; Smith, 1992). Job competence assessment strategies that distinguish the performance of outstanding and average performers typically specify broad multidimensional abilities that include combinations of knowledge, skills, self-perceptions, values, and motives, as well as more specific behavioral indicators (Boyatzis, 1982; DeBack & Mentkowski, 1986; Klemp & McClelland, 1986; Spencer & Spencer, 1993). The abilities scored in the Alverno Longitudinal Study drew on these scoring systems.

LEADERSHIP AND DEVELOPMENT

The theoretical linkage of performance with holistic development is compelling for leadership. In particular, leadership may be more effective when leaders can integrate multiple perspectives, understand dynamic system complexity, empathize with others, productively benefit from dissent, and flexibly adjust to dynamic environments (Bartunek, Gordon, & Weathersby, 1983; Senge, 1990).

Studies of Leadership Performance and Development

Bartone, Bullis, Lewis, Forsythe, and Snook (2001) found contemporaneous but not lagged correlations between holistic development and leadership in their longitudinal study of the development of leadership at the U.S. Military Academy at West Point. Supervisor ratings of leadership by upperclass students correlated with senior and late sophomore scores on Kegan's Subject-Object Interview, $r = .29$ and $r = .41$, but not with those from entrance interviews, $r = -.01$. For first-year students, the researchers also report on 12 more specific dimensions of peer ratings, including teamwork, consideration for others, professional ethics, planning, and organizing. None of the contemporaneous subject-object scores correlated with these more specific performance dimensions. As the authors note, however, first-year students are focused on mastery of military tasks in the subordinate role. First-year peer ratings of planning and organizing correlated with sophomore subject-object scores, $r = .38$, but this can only be considered suggestive, given the number of correlations calculated.

Fisher and Torbert (1995) suggested that at Loevinger's individualistic stage a leader is able to encourage individual and organizational transformational learning in a way that does not inadvertently fall back on unilateral coercion. In this regard, a study by Merron et al. (1987) more specifically addressed the kind of leadership that might be associated with holistic development. Ego scores for the sample ranged from self-aware to autonomous, with the modal score being conscientiousness. In addition to completing Loevinger's SCT measure of ego development, 49 MBA alumni and 28 graduate students completed an in-basket test developed by the Educational Testing Service. Scores on the in-basket distinguished between problem-solving approaches and collaborative versus unilateral leadership styles. Whereas a more limited first-order problem-solving approach treats the problem as given and as an isolated event, second-order problem solving redefines the problem, questions underlying assumptions, and treats problems as a symptom of a deeper underlying problem. Higher ego scores were associated with second-order problem solving after controlling for age and education. Although the relationship of ego development to collaborative leadership was in the expected direction, it only approached statistical significance. The means for second-order problem solving suggested that the individualistic stage was perhaps particularly associated with a jump in questioning of assumptions, problem redefinition, and searching for underlying problems. Rooke and Torbert (1998) subsequently related the ego level of ten CEOs to organizational transformation over a period of consultation that averaged about four years. Whether a CEO was at or beyond the individualistic stage significantly correlated (.65) with consultants' ratings of organizational transformation. However, because the sample is small, the estimate of the size of the correlation is imprecise.

Other investigators have also suggested that advanced development specifically supports an inspirational form of transformational leadership rather than transactional leadership. Whereas transactional leadership focuses primarily on using corrective actions for the purpose of controlling followers' behaviors and eliminating problems, transformational leadership communicates a collective vision that inspires followers (Bass, 1998). In a study of 107 middle managers and 25 hospital ward managers, Turner, Barling, Epitropaki, Butcher, and Milner (2002) gathered subordinate ratings of transformational and transactional leadership behaviors on Bass and Avolio's (1995) Multifactor Leadership Questionnaire (MLQ). They speculated that developmental sophistication in moral reasoning would support transformational leadership. For example, moral reasoning capacity might be associated with awareness of behavioral options beyond immediate self-interest and with greater capacity to foresee benefits from actions that serve the collective good. Turner et al. found that DIT moral reasoning was related to subordinates' ratings of transformational leadership actions, $r(110) = .26$. This relationship remained after controlling for age, education, gender, and other variables. There was no relationship to the separate measures of transactional leadership.

The movement toward postcommunism might be considered a place where transformative leadership would be politically important. Stewart, Sprinthall, and Siemienska (1997) studied 289 public administrators and 196 elected officials in Poland during the transition from communism to democracy. Using a DIT-like measure that was set in a management context, they found that moral reasoning was unrelated to the span of control held by the administrators (department head, division head, and head of administrative units).

Comments on Leadership and Development

There is some evidence for a relationship between leadership and development, with the strongest case being for participative, collaborative, or transformational leadership (Mentkowski & Associates, 2000; Rooke & Torbert, 1998; Turner et al., 2002). At the same time, structural equation modeling in the Alverno Longitudinal Study failed to support the more specific hypothesis that holistic development leads to collaborative organizational thinking and action. Likewise, Rooke and Torbert's (1998) provocative case for linking individualistic ego level with leadership that transforms whole companies can be questioned because of its necessarily small sample. More important, neither they, Turner et al. (2002), nor Merron, Fisher, and Torbert (1987) address the possibility that the correlation of holistic development with leadership may be piggybacking on cognitive ability. Nor has research on the relationship between leadership and holistic development matured to the point where situational factors (e.g., Fiedler, 2002) are studied.

PERFORMANCE IN THE PROFESSIONS AND DEVELOPMENT

Complex multidimensional performance may be especially characteristic of professional practice. Owing to their expertise and pledges to serve the interests of their clients, professionals typically have some discretion in how to best handle novel problems that may involve conflicting values (see Schön, 1983).

Medicine and Development

Medical school educators are in the process of integrating humanistic and ethical components into curricula that have been heavily oriented toward biomedical knowledge and more specific clinical skills. Research suggests that effective patient outcomes are associated with mutually agreed on goals, an active role for the patient, and the doctor exhibiting empathy and support (Cushing, 2002). One might speculate that a doctor's general level of ego and moral development might ground this kind of mutuality and empathy.

Studies of Physician Performance and Development

At least three published studies have found a statistical relationship between physicians' moral reasoning/development and clinical performance. Sheehan, Husted, Candee, Cook, and Bargen (1980) assessed DIT moral reasoning of 147 graduates of American medical schools and 97 graduates of foreign medical schools. Faculty rated these resident pediatricians on 18 clinical performance characteristics identified in prior research, including interpersonal relations, medical knowledge, and task organization. Although the rationale for expecting interpersonal relationships to relate to moral reasoning can be easily inferred, the rationale for why the other two performance characteristics would relate to moral reasoning is less obvious. Nonetheless, faculty ratings of clinical performance were only reported on the total score. Moral reasoning correlated with clinical performance ($r = .33$), and the relationship held when U.S. and other medical school graduates were analyzed separately ($r = .20$ and .20). The correlation was higher when performance ratings were adjusted for the rated quality of the resident programs ($r = .57$). The MJI was administered to a subsample ($n = 35$) and adjusted clinical performance ratings again correlated with the moral judgment level of U.S. and other medical school graduates ($r = .29$ and .61). A cross-tabulation of DIT moral reasoning scores by clinical performance suggested that residents with high moral reasoning were very unlikely to be rated as low clinical performers. Sisola (2000) reported similar cross-tabulation findings for the relationship of the DIT to the clinical performance of 58 first-year physical therapy students ($r = .28$).

Sheehan, Candee, Willms, Donnelly, and Husted (1985) used simulated patients to investigate more specifically how development was related to the clinical performance of 39 family medicine residents. The residents' sensitivity to moral issues and mutuality in interactions with the patients were measured in terms of both ratings of their actions in the encounter and their reconstructions of their intentions. Resident intentions in the encounter were treated as a potential mediator of the effects of three precursor variables on their mutuality and ethical sensitivity in the encounter. These precursors included (1) faculty ratings of the residents' overall performance in the program, (2) an interview measure of ego level in the physician's role concept, and (3) MJI moral development. Two causal models were presented, which suggested alternative explanations of the effect of development on sensitivity and mutuality in clinical performance. One model suggested that moral development led to conscious intentions to show mutuality and ethical sensitivity in patient encounters (.39), which mediated this more humanistic performance (.30). The other alternative model allowed that the ego level of the resident physician's role concept directly influenced mutuality and ethical sensitivity in actions (.22). A developmental interpretation of the physician role concept measure is supported by its latent correlation with MJI moral development (.61). In this alternative model, MJI moral development still led to conscious intentions to show mutuality and ethical sensitivity. But the only path from holistic development to action was the direct one from the residents' developmental constructions of their roles to the moral sensitivity and mutuality of their actions. Both models suggest that holistic development supports mutuality and ethical sensitivity in performance. They differ in (1) how holistic development is represented—moral stage versus role construction ego level—and (2) in the need for representing intermediate intentions. The correlations of the precursor variables in the model—where clinical performance was treated as a global construct—replicated Sheehan et al. (1980). Faculty ratings of the resident's overall performance outside the simulation correlated .38 with the residents' moral development and .51 with the ego level of their role concept.

Adamson, Baldwin, Sheehan, and Oppenberg (1997) reported on a study of the relationship between DIT moral reasoning and malpractice claims against orthopedic surgeons ($n = 56$). Physicians averaging more than .4 malpractice claims per year were contrasted with those averaging fewer than .2 claims per year. The group with more malpractice claims had somewhat lower principled thinking scores, 38.0 versus 43.8. The relationship remained marginally significant when age and having a religious affiliation were controlled.

Comments on Physician Performance

The Sheehan et al. (1985) study suggests that one reason moral development is related to clinical performance is that it provides the basis for family physicians to establish mutuality in doctor–patient relationships. To the degree this is so for physicians in general, it supports an argument for a broad humanistic reform of the formal and informal medical education curricula that goes beyond teaching specific caring protocols, such as how to deliver bad news. It

also might suggest that those interested in fostering broad orientations toward altruism, integrity, respect, and compassion (Cavanaugh, 2002; Markakis, Beckman, Suchman, & Frankel, 2000) should specifically consider strategies shown to promote holistic development. Indeed, longitudinal evidence suggests that medical education may not now effectively support the development of moral judgment as measured by DIT (George, 1997; George & Skeel, 2003) or the MJI (Self, Schrader, Baldwin, & Wolinsky, 1993). Patenaude, Niyonsenga, and Fafard (2003) and Helkama et al. (2003) have even found decline in the first year of medical school on the written version of the MJI. Similarly, Lind (1998) has found that medical students regressed on his measure of moral judgment competence, whereas other university students showed gains. These null or negative findings for medical education are striking given the strong linear association between education and moral reasoning across most other settings, including graduate school (Rest et al., 1999). At the same time, Bebeau (2002) has noted five invention studies in medical education targeted toward fostering moral reasoning that have yielded evidence for gains. Because these relatively short-term interventions are specifically targeted toward increasing moral reasoning or moral discourse, Self and Olivarez's (1996) finding of sustained moral reasoning gains over four years adds credibility. The task of more fully infusing holistic developmental goals into the packed curriculum and established culture of medical schools may also require nurturing a broader professional identity, for example, one that embraces a team-oriented mutuality that reaches across the diverse role boundaries of teacher, student, physician, and allied health professional.

Accounting and Development

A key ethical concept in accounting and auditing is independence of judgment from subjective bias that might flow from personal vested interests. Ponemon and Gabhart (1990) suggested that auditors at different levels of moral reasoning use this concept differently. For example, at the preconventional level the auditor may be inclined to use independence as a way of maximizing self-interest, which would only include general conformity to the rule so as not to get caught. At the conventional level, conformity to the rule is more ingrained as a way to maintain relationships in terms of referent group norms. Within conventional morality, interpersonal normative morality is based on norms of a local group (stage 3), whereas the norms of social system morality are understood from the perspective of a generalized member of society (stage 4).

Studies of Accounting and Development

Ponemon and Gabhart (1994) reviewed research on the relationship of moral reasoning with accounting and auditing. Some studies they cited as behavioral do not qualify as performance for this review (Arnold & Ponemon, 1991; Ponemon, 1993b; Ponemon & Gabhart, 1990, 1993). Perhaps most relevant are several studies that found those holding the most advanced positions in the field had lower moral reasoning scores, including one by Ponemon (1990) that used the MJI, $r(51) = -.47$. Although Shaub (1994) only found a low negative relationship that did not approach statistical significance using the DIT, Ponemon (1992b) found a strong negative correlation between position level (from staff entry to firm partner) and DIT moral reasoning, $r(179) = -.60$, for a representative sample of U.S. accountants. Provocatively, the pattern of moral reasoning preferences suggested that auditors with more advanced positions in a firm increasingly preferred morality based on interpersonal norms (stage 3) over morality based on concern for the social system (stage 4). Ponemon's (1992b) longitudinal findings from a focused study of an accounting firm revealed a complicated pattern. On one hand, entry-level accountants who made early exits from the firm had lower DIT moral reasoning scores. On the other hand, those in the firm who were promoted to manager also had lower scores. He interpreted the findings as a socialization effect, whereby firm managers tend to promote those who have similar moral reasoning. Indeed, 23 managers' ratings of the promotability of about 30 staff members were related to how similar the manager's moral reasoning was to that of his or her staff (average $r = .24$).

Of course, supervisor ratings and promotion are typically considered to be evidence of the quality of performance, even though they include idiosyncratic biases (Scullen et al., 2000). Thus, those with higher moral reasoning might not be promoted because they extend moral considerations beyond what is generally recognized as effective in comparison with the efficiency of simply following the norms established by the accounting firm. Ponemon (1992b) acknowledged that "by virtue of firm profitability and legal liability concerns, individuals with lower ethical reasoning capacities may be better able to deal with business issues" (p. 252). Still, the societal and postconventional moral perspective raises the question of effective for whom?

Ponemon (1992a) unobtrusively investigated the phenomena of underreporting billable time, whereby auditors make themselves look better to management by appearing to have achieved an amount of work in less time. This may or may not be encouraged by management but is also considered dysfunctional in the profession and would generally be a violation of official firm policy and written standards. Using one-way mirrors to determine the actual amount of time 88 staff-level auditors took to complete a training case, Ponemon found that lower moral reasoning was related to underreporting time. Of course, this was a training case, so underreporting would not be addressed by policy. This study replicates the typical positive and linear relationship between moral judgment and ethical action in other contexts (see reviews by Blasi, 1980; Thoma, 1994), rather than the weaker evidence for a curvilinear relationship in a business context (Bay & Greenberg, 2001; Ponemon, 1993a).

Comments on Accounting

The reviewed studies generally measured DIT moral reasoning. If career position level is taken as evidence of performance, then the conclusion would seem to be that conventional moral reasoning is more effective than higher postconventional moral reasoning in auditing and accounting. Simple conformity to company norms and rules might be related to effectiveness, whereas taking principled stands or evoking societal implications may be counterproductive. However, the emergence of unethical norms may be a concern. The case for effectiveness of moral development beyond adherence to local group norms has a strong claim at the societal level, because independent and unbiased judgment is required by the assumptions of commerce. The auditing profession may need a substantial percentage of auditors developmentally inclined to take at least the social system perspective that defines stage 4 moral judgment. Moreover, the counterproductiveness of taking a principled stand in favor of all stakeholders only seems obvious when the stand is imagined to be rigidly taken and perhaps frequently made. Accounting tends to be associated with conventional interests in Holland's (1985) theory of occupational types, but even so, growth in moral reasoning can be fostered in the context of a liberal education (McNeel, 1994; Ponemon & Glazer, 1990). A key emerging strategy in accounting education is to actively encourage identification with the profession and its ideals rather than with just a particular firm (Pricewaterhouse-Coopers, 2003).

Teaching, Counseling, Nursing, and Development

Both teaching and counseling are professions that focus on the development of others. Like nursing, they also include a caring dimension. White (1985) has found among nurses that ego development positively correlated with nurturance as measured on personality inventories. Holistic development may also be related to a range of interpersonal abilities that support effective teaching and counseling. These include positive expectations for the capacities of others to improve, understanding an individual's frame of reference, establishing mutuality and rapport, diagnosing an individual's unique needs, and adjusting strategies to an individual. In a study of 51 residence hall advisors, Carlozzi, Gaa, and Liberman (1983) found a positive relationship between ego development and empathy, which was measured via recognition of emotions presented on videotape. Borders (1989) found counseling students at lower ego levels had more negative thoughts about their clients, as well as themselves. Follow-up qualitative observations suggested that self-aware counselors felt more frustration and anger at clients, sometimes suggesting the client was even responsible for "making me look bad" (p. 166). In contrast, conscientious counselors wondered whether they were judgmental in the sessions, and individualistic counselors were objective about the session. One counselor wondered about her strong verbal response in the session and whether it was "coming from my need or [the client's] need" (p. 167). For the field of teaching, Chang (1994) has reviewed a number of published and unpublished studies that investigated its distinct moral dimension. As would be expected, teachers with more sophisticated moral reasoning held a more humanistic and democratic view of classroom management, accommodating different viewpoints about social-conventional issues. They were also more likely to view curriculum as something that could be adjusted to the individual student. These internal responses and humanistic orientations suggest ways that holistic development may support teaching and counseling.

Studies of Teaching, Counseling, and Nursing Performance and Development

Duckett and Ryden (1994) found that DIT moral reasoning was related to faculty ratings of the clinical performance of 48 nursing students. These findings are reminiscent of how moral reasoning was related to the clinical performance of physicians and physical therapists. However, Duckett and Ryden's study also included the ACT, a widely used measure of academic readiness for college. The ACT correlated with clinical performance (.42) almost as well as the DIT did (.58) but did not enter the stepwise regression equation. If the ACT had been forced into the equation, it very well may have eliminated the significant relation of moral reasoning to clinical performance. In other words, the correlation of moral reasoning with overall clinical performance may only represent their shared relationship with cognitive ability.

Miller (1981) provided an important critical review of educational research on the interaction between conceptual level and environmental structure in cognitive systems theory (also see Holloway & Wampold, 1986). On one hand, higher conceptual complexity is generally considered to provide interpersonal coping resources for promoting development. On the other hand, a higher conceptual level is primarily important when engaging relatively unstructured environments. D. E. Hunt's (1971) matching model further suggests that those at a high conceptual level might become discouraged in highly structured environments. Rathbone's unpublished study of 20 teachers is particularly informative of the relationship of both the teacher's and student's conceptual level to interdependent mutuality (described by D. E. Hunt, 1971; Miller, 1981). Both higher and lower conceptual level teachers taught less interdependently with lower conceptual level students, but higher conceptual level teachers were also twice as likely to teach interdependently with either kind of student population (also see D. E. Hunt & Joyce, 1967; Murphy & Brown, 1970). Miller concluded his 1981 review with qualified support for the matching model because major research challenges had not been met, but also suggested that there is reasonable support for the relationship of conceptual level to "differences in teaching style" such as empathy, reflective exploration, and flexibility (p. 70).

At least two of the published studies on teaching styles that Miller cited used observational measures of performance. Harvey, White, Prather, Alter, and Hoffmeister (1966) found that teachers at a higher conceptual level expressed greater warmth, were more flexible in meeting the interests and needs of the children, encouraged individual responsibility and creativity, and were less rule-oriented and punitive. Harvey, Prather, White, and Hoffmeister (1968) found that teachers at a higher conceptual level were more resourceful and less dictatorial and punitive. Their students were correspondingly more involved in classroom activities.

A number of studies that were outside the scope of Miller's review or that were conducted since then examine the relationship of holistic development to some form of observed performance as a teacher or counselor. Of 12 additional studies that we found, 10 of them studied the performance of students as preservice teachers or counselors. Their sample sizes range from 24 to 83 (average $n = 51$), sometimes limiting their power to detect substantive relationships. Five studies examined the relationship of development to overall ratings of teacher effectiveness. Reiman (2001) found moral reasoning was related to overall teaching effectiveness, $r(48) = .15$, but the other four studies did not (Bergem, 1986; Cartwright & Simpson, 1990; McNergney & Satterstrom, 1984; Thoma & Rest, 1987). However, two of these (Cartwright & Simpson, 1990; Thoma & Rest, 1987) found a significant or marginally significant relationship with DIT U scores, indicating that student teachers who prioritized moral judgments in hypothetical action choices may be rated as more effective. One found that an Eriksonian measure of ego identity correlated with student teaching performance, even though the PCM did not (McNergney & Satterstrom, 1984).

Studies that looked at particular aspects of teaching performance seem to be more supportive of a relationship to holistic development. For example, some form of interactional mutuality in teaching may be undergirded by holistic development. Maccallum (1993) interviewed 24 high school teachers about 4 hypothetical school discipline incidents, including the response they would make. Teachers with more

sophisticated DIT moral reasoning were more likely to coordinate the points of view of the teacher and students in their response to the incident. However, intentions to take action in a hypothetical situation may not have fidelity with actual performance. Walter and Stivers (1977) studied the performance of 80 student teachers using multiple observation instruments. Student teachers with low identity diffusion and high identity resolution accepted more learner ideas in their classroom teaching and asked higher level questions of their students.

Studies in counseling have generally supported the conclusion that a counselor's holistic development is related to communication of empathy to clients. Bowman and Reeves (1987) found that DIT moral reasoning was related to supervisor ratings of empathy demonstrated by students leading counseling sessions that were required to complete a practicum, $r(34) = .36$. Bowman and Allen (1988) replicated this finding for 20 counseling students selected for either high or low DIT scores. Strohmer, Biggs, Haase, and Purcell (1983) similarly found that PCM cognitive complexity related to ratings of empathy demonstrated in student role-playing responses to videotaped vignettes of clients. In one of two studies, Borders and Fong (1989) found that SCT ego level was related to structured ratings of students' pretraining counseling skills as demonstrated in counseling sessions but not to their growth in counseling skills, that is, when pretraining counseling skills were statistically removed. In the other study, they did not find any relationships between students' SCT ego level and structured ratings of therapist's interactive warmth, negative attitudes, and therapeutic exploration. However, Borders and Fong (1989) also reported on an unpublished study by Zielinski that found a relationship of ego level to both "their pretraining ability to communicate empathetic understanding and their post-training gains in ability to discriminate empathy" (p. 72).

Comments on Teaching, Counseling, and Nursing

Research findings seem to be generally consistent with the proposition that holistic development fosters teachers' interpersonal mutuality in interactions with students (see Reiman & Thies-Sprinthall, 1998) and fosters counselors' communication of empathetic understanding of clients. Thus, holistic development seems likely to support the capacity to build on what others bring to a situation. Such a capacity is one key to effective teaching, counseling, and nursing. In addition, the capacity to draw out others is likely to encourage holistic development in those cared for. Although the reviewed studies do not take into account the covariation of cognitive and holistic development, holistic development arguably has a stronger theoretical connection to communicating an empathetic understanding and collaborative interaction than does cognition, which somewhat mitigates the concern that the relationship to holistic development is piggybacking on cognitive ability.

PARENTING AND DEVELOPMENT

The tasks of parenting have some similarity to those of the helping professions. Azar (2003) emphasizes that parenthood is a relational task that "requires flexible and appropriate expectancies about the role and active capacities to learn 'in the moment' and modify one's thinking, affect, and behavior" (p. 392). Flexibility is particularly necessary because the growing child is constantly changing. The parent–child relationship is enduring and is often considered from a family system perspective, where each family member contributes to and is constrained by the pattern of interactions in the family.

Studies of Parenting Performance and Development

Hauser et al. (1984) investigated SCT ego development and family interactions in a sample of 61 upper- to upper-middle-class families with adolescents. About half of the adolescents were from a psychiatric population with thought disorders. Parents' ego development was correlated with their engaging in a range of speech acts that enabled rather than constrained the adolescent's participation in the interaction, including both cognitive enabling (e.g., problem solving, $r = .26$) and affective enabling ($r = .36$). These relationships remained after controlling for the child's age and psychiatric status. Conversely, parents' ego development was negatively correlated with speech acts that constrained the adolescent's participation, though this association was less robust. Adolescent ego development was similarly correlated with the parents' enabling speech acts.

Bell and Bell (1983) developed a causal model for 70 middle-class families with adolescent daughters that tested the potential effects of parental SCT ego development on a variety of individual and family-level variables. Based on their theoretical understanding, they modeled three layers of mediators between parental ego development and daughter ego development. Some of these mediators were direct measures of parental speech acts coded from an audiotaped discussion with their daughters. In particular, each parent was rated for the amount of affective support of the daughter and the degree of direct response to the daughter in the interaction (validation of daughter). Mother's ego development was directly and positively related to her support of her daughter, whereas other direct relationships between parental ego level and behaviors were not statistically significant. Osofsky and Hunt (1972) similarly found that PCM scores correlated with mother's warmth during a teaching task with a simulated child, $r(40) = .40$.

Also of interest in the Bell and Bell study is a behavioral construct coded at the level of the family's interpersonal dynamic, labeled accurate interpersonal perception. It was indicated by (a) family members taking responsibility for their own actions, feelings, and thoughts in the interaction; (b) a closed atmosphere expressed as an inhibiting overconcern with each other (negative); and (c) covert conflict (negative). Both mother's and father's ego level were directly related to accurate interpersonal perception. We have focused on direct paths from ego development because we have questions about the overall quality of the model specifications. Neither goodness of fit indices nor path coefficients are presented, and some of the findings that include complex negative mediational paths are counterintuitive. Nonetheless, it is worth noting that accurate interpersonal perception in family interactions positively mediated the reproduction of parental ego development in the daughter. In contrast to the implications of the Minnesota Twins Study, there was no direct relationship between parental ego development and daughter ego development.

Walker and Taylor (1991) examined MJI moral development and interactional patterns in 63 families with elementary and middle school–aged children. Parental moral development was unrelated to six categories of parental verbal maneuvers in discussions, including eliciting/re-presenting another's reasoning, affectively supporting another, and showing hostility.

These findings held whether the parental verbal maneuvers were considered individually or grouped into clusters. Although parental moral development was not directly related to performance in the discussion, some configural relationships shed light on how moral development itself may be reproduced in interactions across generations. Neither parent MJI scores nor differences in parent–child moral reasoning, which was scored in a discussion of a dilemma the child brought forward, predicted two-year longitudinal growth. Instead, parental supportive interactions that also socratically represented the child's reasoning in his or her dilemma—while also arguing at a relatively high level of moral reasoning—predicted the child's moral growth. Walker, Hennig, and Krettenauer (2000) replicated this kind of generational reproduction of development in a four-year longitudinal study of 58 families.

Pratt, Hunsberger, Pancer, Roth, and Santolupo (1993) coded interviews of the parents of 28 fifth-grade children for the degree to which they took more than one perspective on an issue and whether these multiple considerations were integrated into a framework. This measure of integrative complexity correlated .39 with ratings of parental support and responsiveness to the child's needs in a homework session. An overall rating of the quality of the homework session, which was linked to the fifth-grader's improvement in long-division, $r = .61$, remained correlated with integrative complexity, $r = .42$, when parental intelligence (WAIS-R math subtest) was controlled.

Comments on Parenting

With the exception of the Walker and Taylor (1991) study, the evidence suggests that holistic development may be related to dynamically open family discussions and emotional support of the children in them. There is also a consistent replication of the reproduction of moral and ego development from parent to child via some kind of open interaction that draws out the perspective of the child about his or her issues. The possibility that children who are most ready to develop are the one's who elicit their parents' openness to their participation in discussion cannot be ruled out, and indeed the Hauser et al. (1984) study provides evidence for this. But, the Pratt et al. (1993) study suggests parental holistic development supports responsive facilitation of a child's learning. Moreover, the relation of parental ego development to the quality of the family's interactive dynamics also suggests that more developed parents are better able to draw out a child's holistic development.

CIVIC AND CREATIVE PERFORMANCE AND DEVELOPMENT

Creative and civic contributions seem intimately connected with holistic ideals. Holistic developmental achievements such as self-authorship and communicating appreciation of both mutuality and individuality can indeed be considered creative or civic contributions. Democratic participation (Putnam, 1995) and socially responsible work of high quality (Gardner, Csikszentmihalyi, & Damon, 2001) are more prototypical civic contributions that might draw on mutuality and self-authorship. A number of studies suggest that a sense of moral responsibility increases with higher stages of MJI moral judgment (Kohlberg, 1984). Erikson's concept of generativity explicitly emphasizes actions by adults toward the welfare of future generations, even though scoring is often based on concern for their future. Although McAdams, Ruetzel, and Foley (1986) did not find concern for generativity related to SCT ego level ($n = 50$), Bradley and Marcia (1998) found a weak relationship (e.g., $r = .20$, $p < .06$). Pratt, Norris, Arnold, and Filyer (1999) also found a small relationship between the MJI and generativity, $r = .22$.

Studies of Civic and Creative Performance

Reviews have suggested that stages of moral judgment are moderately correlated with moral action, about .30 (see Blasi, 1980; Thoma, 1994; Thoma & Rest, 1986). The magnitude of the relationship between moral judgment and action may be reduced by a number of measurement and construct complications. Relative to action, stage of moral development is a very global construct. Blasi (1980) has pointed out that the participant's specific moral interpretation of a situation might easily differ from what the theorist imagines. Also, moral failure may result from other factors, including lack of ability to handle stress (Rest et al., 1999).

Activism is potentially a form of moral civic participation. In a study of 102 college students, Laird

(2003) found that pro-life and pro-choice abortion activists had higher DIT scores than other kinds of club members or noninvolved students, replicating the findings by Haan, Smith, and Block (1968) for the free speech movement. Deemer (reported in Rest, 1986) found that civic responsibility—which included active civic participation at the high end of the scale—was positively related to DIT scores in 100 young adults.

Colby and Damon (1992) found that 23 exemplars of moral commitment had MJI scores well distributed across stages 3 to 5, although only 2 were scored stage 3. Qualitative analyses linked moral commitment to establishing a moral identity. Such an identity implies ego development to a least stage 4, conscientiousness, where individuals organize their sense of self around long-term goals and self-evaluated standards (see Blasi, 1993), unless stage 4 capacities are instead scaffolded by interpersonal relationships or develop as a narrow contextual strand. Although the structural capacity to commit to ideals seems to make possible the centrality of a moral concern for others, the structure of ego development remains distinct from moral identity, at least through the most common stages of adult development (Rogers, 2002).

Vaillant (1993) reported on three longitudinal samples: (1) the almost half-century Grant Study of 248 Harvard men initiated in 1938 by Arlie Bock and Clark Heath, (2) the 35-year study of the Core City sample of 456 socioeconomically disadvantaged males initiated by Sheldon and Eleanor Glueck, and (3) the 45-year Terman study of gifted women with a focus on a subsample of 40 women. Independently rated defense maturity correlated with ratings of job success (r from .34 to .53), job employment (r from .39 to .51), and Eriksonian psychosocial maturity (r from .44 to .66). The interview-based ratings of psychosocial maturity seem to have included actions toward caring for future generations or consolidating cultural achievements. Years of education, IQ, and parental social class did not account for the associations, but there remains the possibility that ratings of defense maturity were influenced by the raters' implicit theory of maturity in relation to job success, employment, and generativity. Reporting on the Grant Study, Vaillant (1977) found that mature defense mechanisms were also related to active public service outside the job.

Vaillant and Vaillant (1990) also reported on the creative accomplishments of the subsample of Terman women. Those with more creative accomplishments (e.g., writing a book) were more than five times as likely to use the mature defense mechanisms of altruism, humor, or sublimation as major defenses. In a larger sample of 107 men with promise at age 55, Vaillant and McCullough (1987) found that SCT ego development correlated with inclusion in *Who's Who in America*, r (106) = .25, by age 65. Also, those who were rated as creative at age 19 had higher SCT scores at age 55. These findings could not be attributed to differences in parental social class, intelligence, or income, as ego development was not correlated with these variables. Helson and Wink (1987) found a similar relationship for women. A woman's ego development at middle age was predicted by faculty nomination of her as creative 20 years earlier (r = .38).

Comments on Civic and Creative Performance

Structural moral development appears to support moral action. Structurally related but distinct moral identity may also be a key factor in establishing consistent moral action. Holistic development appears to be related to broader constructs of civic participation and creativity, though the direction of the relationship is unknown. Surprisingly, we found no investigations of holistic development in relation to the compelling civic task of fostering civil discourse in the public sphere, where a range of skills and dispositions are required to address and mediate differences.

PERSONALITY DEVELOPMENT AND PERFORMANCE

Loevinger (1998a) has suggested that factor analytic descriptions of personality are in principle complementary to stage type theories. However, conscientiousness in the so-called big five personality factor structure, she also argued, conflates the distinction between conformity and conscientiousness that is at the heart of adult ego development in her theory. Indeed, Westenberg and Block (1993) have found that a distinct personality dimension of conformity could be distinguished and that it had the appropriate quadratic relationship to SCT-measured ego development, peaking in strength at the conformity stage of the

SCT. Thus, conscientiousness as derived in the big five personality factor structure is insensitive to whether individuals are diligent because they are acting out of a conformative need to belong or instead conscientious in a broader meaning of the term, such that they are carrying out long-term ideals that are central to who they are. To an external observer, the two may be difficult to distinguish under most circumstances. Indeed, it is possible that some employers prefer the combination of unquestioning group loyalty and diligence over conscientiousness grounded in self-evaluated standards, which would be more difficult to foster, control, and distinguish.

Of the big five personality factors, Conscientiousness is one that has been most consistently related to workplace performance (see Hogan & Holland, 2003) and it has predictive validity beyond measures of cognitive ability, job knowledge, and experience (Kickul & Neuman, 2000; Schmidt & Hunter, 1998; Van Scotter & Motowidlo, 1996). From the perspective of holistic development, this finding suggests the advantage of workers having advanced beyond the egocentric motivation of the zero-sum game that is characteristic of the self-protective stage to at least the group-centeredness of the conformist stage. To move beyond this limited conclusion, it is useful to propose that another big five factor, Openness to Experience, might be considered a viable measure of relatively advanced ego development, which would provide a stronger link to the emerging big five literature in the field of personnel selection.

Openness to Experience as Surrogate for Advanced Development

Hy and Loevinger (1996) suggested that embracing open-mindedness begins to emerge for some at the conscientious stage, but is more characteristic of the next individualistic stage, which is also characterized by greater complexity in the conception of interpersonal interactions and a deep sense of individuality in self and others. McCrae and Costa (1980) selected 240 men between the ages of 35 and 80 in a way that ensured a wide range of ego development. They found that a personality measure of Openness to Experience correlated with the SCT (.23). The monotonic and roughly linear relationship was higher when verbal fluency was controlled (.31). The relationship

remained statistically significant when age and intelligence were controlled. In addition, SCT protocols were scored as *open* or *closed* for 90 men who had extreme scores on the openness to experience measure, yielding a substantial correlation (.66). Hogansen and Lanning (2001) scored 213 SCT protocols from college students for the big five personality characteristics and also found that openness on the SCT was linearly correlated (.43) with SCT ego scores. Einstein and Lanning (1998) found a smaller relationship between the SCT and inventory measures of openness, for 240 women ($r = .24$) and 110 men ($r = .17$).

Studies of Openness and Performance

The speculation that Openness to Experience is a worthwhile (even if flawed) indicator of holistic development cannot be considered established. A particular concern is whether measurement by personality questionnaires captures the crucial integrative aspect of holistic development. Nonetheless, the potential gain in connecting to a vast and systematic literature on performance in the workplace makes the assumption useful.

Openness in Cross-Field Meta-Analyses

Several meta-analyses have investigated the relationship between the big five personality factors and workplace performance, estimating validity correlations that correct for measurement error in the constructs. These meta-analyses include estimates of the generalizability of relationships across or within job types and according to the kind of performance. In the studies meta-analytically reviewed, supervisor ratings were the most typical way of measuring performance. One limitation is that the meta-analyses do not generally track the level of discretion the workers have in their performance, but we can also assume that contextual performance is not narrowly prescribed.

A meta-analysis by Tett, Jackson, and Rothstein (1991) investigated 10 independent samples that included an openness measure. Openness correlated (.27) with overall workplace performance, but the confidence interval also included zero. In a contemporaneous meta-analysis, Barrick and Mount (1991) investigated 69 independent samples that included an openness measure. They found that openness was not related to workplace performance, but was instead, as predicted, correlated (.25) with training performance. Based on these and other reviews, Salgado (1997) meta-analyzed a separate set of 18 mostly European studies where he predicted and also found that openness was primarily related to training performance (.17). Openness was not related to supervisor performance ratings, but did have a very small generalizable correlation (.07) with a set of personnel indicators such as accidents, wages, and absenteeism.

Following Van Scotter and Motowidlo (1996), Hurtz and Donovan (2000) examined the relationship of openness with measures of contextual performance (job dedication and interpersonal facilitation), as well as with task performance. Their meta-analysis included 35 studies using an openness measure that was explicitly designed in the big five framework. In the estimates made across all jobs, openness was neither correlated with contextual nor task performance. But previous findings of a generalizable correlation with training performance were confirmed (.14). More profession specific analyses also found that openness contributed overall to customer service job performance (.17), but not to performance in sales, management, and skilled/semi-skilled occupations. In a smaller set of studies, Mount, Barrick, and Stewart (1998) found somewhat more consistent relationships between openness and supervisor ratings of contextual performance. Meta-analysis of four studies of team-related jobs affirmed a relationship to overall job performance (.16). Meta-analysis of six dyadic service jobs found a similar relationship (.17). In the dyadic service jobs, openness also predicted more specific ratings of the quality of interactions with others (.12).

Hogan and Holland (2003) generally found much stronger meta-analytical relationships between performance and each of the big five personality constructs. Their meta-analysis covered 43 independent samples using the 7-factor Hogan Personality Inventory (HPI). They suggested openness mapped onto two HPI factors they call Intellectance and School Success. However, intellectance/openness had stronger cross-study correlations with big five openness (.33 to .69) than did School Success (.05 to .35), so we report only findings from intellectance/openness. Hogan and Holland found that intellectance/openness correlated with *getting ahead* task performance criteria (.12) but not with *getting along* contextual performance criteria (.03). They specified getting ahead as behavior that yields results and advances the individual in the group and the group with its competition. Examples of performance criteria included works with energy, values productivity, and shows concern with quality. More strikingly, intellectance/openness correlated (.34) with performance criteria that subject matter experts felt were most closely associated with intellectance/openness. Examples of such performance criteria include achieving quality with information, analyzing finances/operations, and displaying good judgment. Intellectance/openness also correlated substantially (.23) with performance criteria that were classified as likely to be related to the HPI Ambition factor, such as exhibits leadership, demonstrates effectiveness, and generates new monthly accounts.

In sum, the meta-analyses have not consistently supported a broadly generalizable relationship between openness and a global category of contextual performance across workforce occupations and positions. Nonetheless, openness may be related to the quality of interactions in customer service, team-oriented, and dyadic interpersonal jobs, as well as leadership and dedication to quality performance.

Leadership Studies and Openness to Experience

Judge and Bono (2000) argued that transformational leadership in particular draws on two aspects of openness: creativity and embracing change. They found openness correlated with subordinates' ratings of transformational leadership on the MLQ, but this effect was not significant when other big five factors were controlled. At the same time, openness was the only scale that predicted subordinate ratings on another measure of leadership effectiveness with the big five and other variables controlled. In a subsequent meta-analytical review of the relationship of openness with leadership across 37 samples, Judge, Bono, Ilies, and Gerhardt (2002) found that openness indeed correlated with leadership (corrected $r = .24$). The relationship held in both business (.23) and student (.28) settings, but not in government and military ones (.06). At the same time, over 90% of the correlations were positive, and a subsequent study by McCormack and Mellor (2002) did find that openness predicted ratings by superiors of senior military leaders even with the other big five factors controlled.

Studies of Openness Controlling for Cognitive Ability

Some studies have addressed the additional question of whether openness contributes incremental validity beyond cognitive capacity in predicting performance. Kickul and Neuman (2000) studied leadership of 320 college students in the context of a leaderless task-oriented group. Group members' ratings of leadership behaviors were used to identify emergent leaders in the group, and the group itself was scored for how well it prioritized items needed in the task, which was based on a survival scenario. Discriminant analysis found that openness, extraversion, and cognitive ability each predicted emergent leaders. The team's performance on the ranking task, however, was unrelated to the emergent leader's openness.

Spector, Schneider, Vance, and Hezlett (2000) investigated openness in relation to the assessment center performance of 429 workers, the vast majority of whom were in managerial or executive positions. Openness correlated with a number of tasks, including performance in a leaderless group (.19). When cognitive ability and three other big five factors were included in the multiple regressions, openness had incremental validity in predicting ratings on two separate tasks that involved giving feedback to others. Lievens, Harris, Van Keer, and Bisqueret (2003) investigated openness in relation to the assessment center performance of 166 European managers and subsequent 18-month training performance of 78 managers in a Japanese context. Openness correlated with training performance (uncorrected $r = .31$), and controlling for cognitive ability did not significantly reduce this relationship (beta = .32). Although openness did not correlate with ratings of teamwork, communication, adaptability, and cross-cultural awareness drawn from various assessments, it did negatively correlate with self-discipline ratings (−.23). The lack of a relationship to adaptability ratings is somewhat surprising. Perhaps it reflects difficulty raters have in distinguishing adaptability required by dynamic change in ongoing tasks rather than just adaptability to a novel task. LePine and colleagues (2000) experimentally demonstrated that openness was related to effectiveness on a cognitive decision-making task only when parameters changed in the ongoing task, not during the initial learning, which suggests that openness is important when learning requires unlearning as well. Openness had incremental

validity over cognitive ability in predicting performance adaptability. Chan and Schmitt (2002) found that openness was related to supervisors' ratings of task performance (.21), job dedication (.17), and interpersonal facilitation (.21) with cognitive ability, job experience, and other big five personality factors controlled.

Holistic Development and Openness Across the Life Span

How much, when, and why adult personality changes, as reflected in the big five, is somewhat controversial, but some findings are relatively clear. Trait rankings relative to one's peers generally become more stable with age (Roberts & DelVecchio, 2000). In terms of mean change, meta-analytical reviews of both cross-sectional and longitudinal research have generally suggested a very slight decrease in Openness to Experience as adults age (Helson, Kwan, John, & Jones, 2002; McCrae et al., 1999). Findings are often similar for studies that use instruments more specifically designed to measure adult holistic development. Cohn (1998) provided a meta-analytical scatterplot of 252 sample means of ego development by age that demonstrated a plateau in ego development near the self-aware stage at about 20 years of age (also see Hy & Loevinger, 1996). We are not aware of a similarly comprehensive analysis on the relationship between age and moral development on the MJI. Pratt, Diessner, Pratt, Hunsberger, and Pancer (1996) cite three cross-sectional studies that are consistent with their finding of no four-year longitudinal change in a sample of 23 middle-age and 27 older adults. Based on their review of seven studies with somewhat inconsistent findings and their own findings from a four-year longitudinal sample (n about 30, ages 5–72), Armon and Dawson (1997) suggested that moral development generally continues to rise diminishingly until middle age, with education controlled, and then levels off or declines.

SOURCES OF CONTINUED HOLISTIC DEVELOPMENT

We are not aware of any longitudinal studies that broadly represent typical levels of adult holistic development beyond the college years. The general cross-sectional finding of a plateau sometime in adulthood might result from contentment with the rewards of a conventional and sometimes conforming life or a societal press toward conventionality and conformity. The plateau may also reflect a dynamic stability whereby adults beyond college generally select environments that reinforce their views (see Alwin, Cohen, & Newcomb, 1991). Many adults may in effect miss out on experiences that would challenge their overall meaning-making structure.

At the same time, specific populations may show continued development when supportive challenges are sought or encountered. Kohn and Schooler demonstrated that the substantive complexity of work supported self-directedness independent of cognitive ability. Armon and Dawson found that education predicted moral development independent of age, which is consistent with other research (see Colby & Kohlberg, 1987). Pratt et al. (1996) found that self-reported health and supportive guidance from others predicted moral development, with age and education controlled. The Alverno Longitudinal Study in particular demonstrated continued holistic development independent of differences in cognitive development, at least through middle age (Mentkowski & Associates, 2000).

We found that women in young adulthood versus middle age developed similarly on the battery of holistic development instruments. Moreover, the mean effect sizes for the five-year period after college (SCT = .47, MJI = .17, MID = .54) generally compared favorably with those during the college years (SCT = −.18, MJI = .31, and MID = .35), with the exception of the DIT (.03 after versus .80 during). Causal modeling of growth in moral reasoning during college linked it to progress in the ability-based curriculum (beta = .18), as well as to critical thinking at entrance to college (beta = .23). After college, a broader integration of self was mediated by breadth of alumna activities and was unrelated to critical thinking ($n = 170$). The mediating construct of breadth of activities was measured via a 12-item index that included self-reported volunteer work, reading, self-reflection, discussion of current events, cultural activities, participation in politics, friendships, and continuing/graduate education. Integration of self was found to be both a lagged cause of breadth of alumna activities (beta = .40) and a reciprocal effect of it (beta = .38). This latter finding suggests that active engagement after college in a broad set of arenas may be related to continued holistic growth. Interest-

ingly, an index of self-reported breadth of preparation in the college's ability-based curriculum had no direct effect on alumna growth in integration of self. Instead, breadth of alumna activities also mediated the effect of breadth of preparation on alumna growth in integration of self. Growth in DIT moral reasoning was *not* moderated by breadth of activities, but in another longitudinal study, Deemer found that young adult growth in DIT moral reasoning was mediated by a conceptually similar composite measure of broad activities (reported in Rest, 1986). Overall, the Alverno causal models suggest that a broad performance-based learning program and breadth of sustained activities can support continued holistic growth in adulthood. Given that these women were predominantly the children of parents who did not complete a college degree, holistic development does not seem limited to the most privileged families.

CONCLUSIONS OF THE REVIEW

We reviewed evidence related to the broad claim that holistic development of self-authorship is critical to effective performance across a broad range of sectors and settings in contemporary society. The longitudinal studies modeling both cognitive and holistic development in relation to workplace performance yielded equivocal findings. Yet the pattern of correlational and causal modeling findings across studies suggests important relationships to particular kinds of performance. Holistic development is sometimes correlated with participative, collaborative, or transformational leadership. Some findings further suggest that executives who have achieved what Loevinger calls the individualistic stage of ego development are better able to lead transformationally, perhaps because they are able to consistently exhibit respectful mutuality and openness to learning. The meta-analytical studies are somewhat inconsistent about the nature of a relationship between openness and workplace performance, but also suggest that leadership and training performance are supported by openness to learning.

Beyond transformational leadership and dynamic adaptation to change, why is there not broader support for the call for the self-authored employee? Self-authorship as a developmental mode of being supports an individual's capacity to contribute to collective inquiry into goals, but this is only one kind of contribution to the workplace and its criticality may be conditional. First, it is likely that relatively few organizations yet actually operate as learning organizations. Not only may more transformational leadership be required from chief executives, but a critical mass of self-authoring employees may also be necessary. Employers may need to foster the development of a greater percentage of their employees to achieve mutuality and dynamic openness as typical modes of interaction, rather than reactiveness and defensiveness. Second, organizations may function effectively enough without meeting the idealized picture of a learning organization. Organizations may be able to act strategically and adapt flexibly to changing circumstances without requiring that the needed developmental capacities become common in workers across the organization. Effective leaders may draw out contributions from employees that they would not otherwise produce and, then, strategically guide and adjust the goals for inquiry accordingly. Future research might focus on whether fields with relatively rapid change and more dispersed leadership show broader relationships between self-authorship and performance.

Holistic development has been consistently related to clinical performance. The study of resident physicians by Sheehan et al. (1985) is particularly compelling because it specifically suggests that ego development may be a causal antecedent of mutuality and sensitivity to ethical issues in the patient encounter. With this kind of humanistic performance criterion, the consequences of holistic development seem less likely to be confused with the unmeasured consequences of cognitive development, which could easily happen for other criteria such as overall clinical performance or transformational leadership. Likewise, holistic development seems to be related to increased empathy and mutuality in teaching, counseling, and parenting. These kinds of relationships are consistent with the theoretical expectation that holistic development includes increased empathy, recognition of individual differences, and respect for others (see Belenky, Clinchy, Goldberger, & Tarule, 1986; Hy & Loevinger, 1996; Josselson, 1998). Given the popular charge that measures such as the SCT and the MJI favor separation and individuation rather than the relational aspects of holistic development (e.g., Broughton & Zahaykevich, 1988; Gilligan, 1982), it seems ironic that their strongest links to performance include communicating empathetic caring and exhibiting mutuality in interactions. Perhaps it has been easy to confuse self-authorship, deciding *for* oneself, with separation, deciding *by* oneself (Kegan, 1994).

Our focus has been on holistic development as a potential causal antecedent of multidimensional performance. But if such performance is represented as persisting over time, it may reciprocally affect holistic development, even though development is typically a broader and generally more stable construct. Indeed, the two longitudinal studies that statistically modeled the relationship of performance with both holistic and cognitive development found evidence suggesting the causal power of performance settings. For example, the Alverno Longitudinal Study found that the breadth of an alumna's activities mediated holistic growth, and Kohn and Schooler (1982, 1983) found that the substantive complexity of work shaped the self-directedness of workers. Although most research does not help us untangle causal direction, it often seems likely to be bidirectional. In particular, interactive mutuality and broad activities, such as civic participation and creative work, may be as much a cause of holistic development as an effect of it.

AN EDUCATIONAL MODEL LINKING ADULT DEVELOPMENT WITH PERFORMANCE

So far, we have limited ourselves to a critical review of psychometric evidence linking multidimensional performance and holistic development. We still need to draw forward implications from this evidence for our broader educational model of the person and for the design of college curricula. To do so, we will touch on findings from the confidential, open-ended longitudinal perspectives interviews that were also part of the Alverno Longitudinal Study (Mentkowski & Associates, 2000). But first, we need to further describe our educational model of the person and how it is connected to its educational context and the wider range of sources of evidence.

For the purposes of this review, we began with the structural part of our model that distinguishes development, reasoning, performance, and self-reflection as domains of growth in the person (figure 22.1). In *Learning That Lasts*, Mentkowski and Associates (2000) identified three transformative learning cycles that integrate the four domains of growth of the

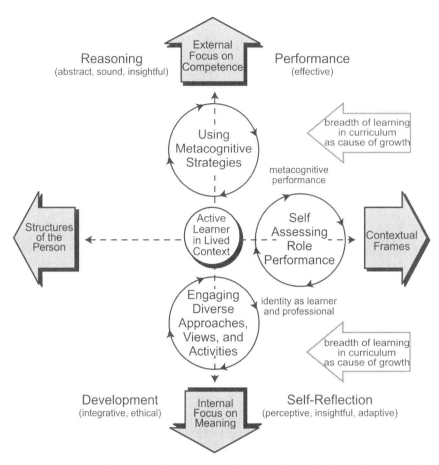

FIGURE 22.2 Transformative learning cycles integrating domains of growth. From Mentkowski & Associates. Copyright © 2000, Jossey-Bass. Reprinted by permission of John Wiley & Sons, Inc.

person. The cycles are: (1) using meta-cognitive strategies; (2) self-assessing role performance; and (3) engaging diverse approaches, views, and activities (see figure 22.2). These transformative learning cycles not only represent further articulation of learning achievements within the model of the person but also specify learning processes that dynamically build on the structure of the model. Cycles two and three in particular suggest how the relationship between holistic development and performance may be mediated.

The second transformative learning cycle, self-assessing role performance, meta-cognitively connects performance with self-reflection. The learner's internal dialogue is about "what I can do across settings and how I can improve." The experience of Alverno faculty is that most students need to be taught how to effectively self-assess their abilities in relation to criteria (Alverno College Faculty, 2000).

Educators often see the importance of developing self assessment to support independent, lifelong learning. We found that self-assessment was related to effective alumna performance when alumnae took a balanced view of their performance and abstracted their abilities beyond the immediate situation (Mentkowski & Associates, 2000; Rogers & Mentkowski, 2004). We concluded that (a) self-assessment of abilities supports transformative learning when it (b) sparks deeper reflective learning that (c) motivationally connects to envisioning role performance. With practice, the learning cycle becomes self-sustaining as individuals gain the capacity to (d) meta-cognitively monitor their performance and make adjustments in their ongoing action. These components of the transformative learning cycle were directly suggested by abilities in the alumna factor Balanced Self-Assessment and Acting from Values.

The third transformative learning cycle, *engaging diverse approaches, views, and activities*, connects self-reflection with holistic development (see figure 22.2). The learner's internal dialogue is about "who I am and who I should become." Causal modeling suggested that engaging in a broad range of activities kick-starts this cycle. In-depth, longitudinal interviews of the students and alumnae about their learning and growth further suggested that engaging discussions of diverse views and trying out diverse approaches to learning led to independent learning and to valuing multiple perspectives (Mentkowski, Much, Kleinman, & Reisetter Hart, 1998). In *Learning That Lasts*, we proposed that (a) engaging diverse approaches, views, and activities supports (b) independent learning, (c) holistic developmental restructuring, (d) appreciation of multiple perspectives, and (e) breadth of learning. This transformative learning cycle resonates with how openness to experience connects to learning in the workplace, and with the conclusions of other researchers (e.g., Joyce & Showers, 1995).

We concluded that this cycle may also synergistically interlink with the self-assessing role performance cycle when an individual consolidates his or her identity (Mentkowski & Associates, 2000). In the context of the Alverno ability-based curriculum (Alverno College Faculty, 1976/1992), we found examples of women integrating identity elements such as "learner," "well-rounded person," "effective performer," and "collaborator" into a broader identity that defined the kind of professional they aspired to be. This particular kind of identity consolidation reflects the integration of a professional and liberal arts education. It may also be an aspect of the developmental restructuring of the whole person. Of all of the holistic developmental measures, it was after all, only the Perry-based MID career essay that correlated with all four of the alumna ability factors.

However, our present review of the literature linking holistic development with mutuality in interaction suggests a theoretical alternative to how the transformative learning cycles may interlink and integrate holistic development and performance. The appreciation for multiple perspectives that Mentkowski and Associates (2000) observed may go deeper toward an appreciation of mutuality. This conclusion is consistent with how the holistic developmental measures tended to correlate with Collaborative Organizational Thinking and Action. So we now propose that when an adult gains a developmental appreciation of multiple perspectives and mutuality, this appreciation directly influences how they envision and carry out role performance. Such appreciation of mutuality may include respect for the autonomy of others. Empathy, the caring cousin of mutuality, also seems to be fostered by a developmental growth that unites an appreciation for individuality with mutuality. Nonetheless, our own research did not find robust correlations between holistic development and the ability factor on which empathy weakly loaded, Developing Others and Perspective Taking.

The first transformative learning cycle, which connects reasoning and performance, reflects the integration of knowing and doing. Fostering and assessing this integration is a central focus of current educational reform in higher education (Ewell, 2002). The adult learner's internal dialogue is concerned with "what I know and how I can do this." Extensive experience thinking about and performing in an area supports (a) automatization of pattern recognition enabling an individual to (b) think in performance. But learners also must (c) actively use reflective spaces to think more deeply about frameworks of knowledge in relation to underlying patterns observed in performance to (d) effectively restructure their knowledge. Through breadth of experience in using diverse frameworks, adult learners can develop the capacity to (e) meta-cognitively select and flexibly use frameworks for constructing performance. Highly effective performers coordinate their meta-cognitive selection of strategies (a moment in cycle 1) with their ongoing meta-cognitive monitoring of their role performance (a moment in cycle 2). Thus, the three transformative learning cycles form a dynamic chain with the self-assessing role performance cycle mediating an indirect link of the other two that can sustain self-directed learning across the four domains. On the competence side of the model (see figure 22.2), a chain link is formed when the individual is able to coordinate elements of meta-cognitive performance. On the model's meaning side, a chain link is formed when the individual consolidates an identity as a learner and professional (see figure 22.2).

IMPLICATIONS

Our review suggests that multidimensional performance and holistic development are sometimes mutually reinforcing domains of growth, even if distinctively different, and that they can more generally be compatible aims. There is evidence that broadening roles in certain ways supports adult holistic development. In particular, breadth of experience across meaningful settings, productive creativity, and the substantive complexity of multidimensional performance at work facilitate holistic development. Not only are broadened roles and the entailed holistic development intrinsically good for the individual worker, they are vital grounds for his or her contribution to civil society. Professional roles in particular invite a civic rationale for holistic development because of their intrinsic connection with the public interest. In professional fields, the public good and the professional's personal interests are not only negotiated in everyday performance but also in the general self-regulating discourse, norms, and codes that establish the field's legitimacy (Gardner et al., 2001; McGuire, 1993). Professional fields are also defined by the practitioners' specialized expertise and skills, but this aspect of professional performance, whether based on declarative or tacit knowledge, is unlikely by itself to be related to adult holistic development.

Where an individual's holistic development supports more effective performance, the case for taking up the challenge of nurturing self-direction, mutuality, individuality, and breadth of perspective in the workplace becomes more robust. A strong case can be made for fostering the holistic development of professionals such as physicians, counselors, and teachers, whose roles directly engage the welfare of the whole personhood of another. The evidence suggests that holistic development of the professional supports empathy and mutuality in interaction, and that these humanistic performance characteristics are themselves linked to effective care. For example, a physician who takes time to collaboratively explore a patient's perspective on alternative treatments may elicit commitment toward carrying out an agreed-on treatment. When professions address the welfare of the whole person, one implication is that the humanistic aspect of the professional role needs to be preserved in the relationship with the client. For example, as changes in delivery of primary medical care are mandated toward the abbreviated 15-minute doctors' visit, special attention needs to be given to how mutuality is preserved (e.g., through team support and physician discretion).

Parenting, likewise involves care for the whole person. Generative care for the child is both intimate and long term. Apparently holistic development reproduces itself across generations, from parent to child and from teacher to learner, through mutuality and empathy. Beyond just becoming more effective facilitators of learning from homework, parents who develop holistically are likely to become better partners with schools in the larger task of preparing the next generation of citizens. To these ends, parents might be encouraged to actively broaden their own horizons and activities for the sake of their children and society. So programs that encourage parental involvement might include activities that broaden both parents and children.

Transformative and participative leadership is another area where multidimensional performance and holistic development are synergistic. For such leaders, influence is consistently based on an appreciative engagement with the perspectives and personhood of others, which may indeed be dependent on advanced meaning-making structures. Fostering holistic development needs to be a crucial part of leadership development programs, but this is not enough. A transformational leader also articulates a vision that creates a sense of collective effectiveness by connecting the perspectives and strivings of individuals to broader exigencies. Thus, transformational leadership requires additional sophisticated capacities, such as conceptual ability, persuasive influence, and tacit knowledge that can be acquired independent of holistic development, even though mutuality shapes how they are expressed.

When contributors primarily use abilities that are largely independent of holistic development, some educators, employers, parents, and civic leaders may see fostering the holistic development of others as a distraction from performance goals. But we have found little evidence for negative relationships between individual differences in these domains, which suggests that they can generally be pursued together without diminishing either. Some concerned citizens may also believe that prosocial dispositions and abilities, such as empathy, may be more efficiently supported by external norms and established procedures than by holistic development. This is certainly plausible, even though a conformist level of individual development may also create ethical fragilities when both internalization of norms and external surveillance are low. But more important, the proper stewardship of such prosocial norms and practices cannot be left safely aside from the developmental tasks of fostering individual integrity and broadened perspectives.

Fostering adult holistic development can also seem insurmountable even when there is agreement within a company, school, foundation, or religious institution that it is needed. The meaning-making structures of others are often hidden from view, develop slowly, and are generally immune to mere rational persuasion. This overstates the developmental challenge however. For example, employers can foster holistic development not only through transformational leadership but also by encouraging employees to broaden their lives through meaningful civic, family, personal, and educational activities. Educators can evoke independent learning through coaching and empathy, as well as through strategies that encourage breadth in learning, discussion of diverse views, and openness to participation in new, diverse, and challenging activities.

Educators who are in colleges and universities may see teaching and assessing for performance as the bigger challenge. It need not, however, mean an unwelcome narrowing of the curriculum. For example, Mentkowski and Associates (2000) found that breadth of learning at graduation from college had a direct effect on collaborative organizational thinking and action in the workplace five years later (beta = .27), as well as on integration of self. The common connection of performance and development to breadth in preparation is reflected by the two parallel right to left arrows in figure 22.2. These arrows symbolize how it is possible to integrate performance expectations with liberal learning. Fostering multidimensional performance in higher education generally requires explicitly defining student learning outcomes so that performance expectations are integrated with the content of each discipline. Assessment of such learning outcomes is best when it is progressive, involves both learner and teacher, and leaves room for active interpretation (Alverno College Faculty, 1979/1994). By making student learning outcomes explicit but also open and expansive, educators can collectively teach and assess for them over time, and students can meta-cognitively take hold of their learning by using these performance expectations to self-assess their abilities and construct a vision of how to perform, processes that they can carry with them after college (Mentkowski & Associates, 2000).

For the individual adult, consolidating one's identity in a broad field of action—so that it matters what kind of learner, parent, or professional one is—establishes an actionable link between one's level of holistic development and role performance. Fostering identity development in adults may seem to make even more demands on educators and employers. But further integration of meaningful identity, including moral identity, is fostered by the same kind of broadening activities, such as volunteer work and civic participation, that support holistic development (Colby, Ehrlich, Beaumont, & Stephens, 2003).

For us, the four domains of growth and transformative learning cycles evocatively organize the enduring aspects of adult educational outcomes and suggest paths to achieving them. Ours is not the only pluralistic model of adult outcomes that educators and workplace trainers might use to broadly explore their educational vision and practices (e.g., Ackerman & Heggestad, 1997; Boyatzis, Cowen, Kolb, & Associates, 1995; Senge, 1990). Beyond such models, what is most needed are ways for encouraging dialogue about them within communities of educators and across sectors of society. For educators, Mentkowski and Associates (2000) set forth an educational theory of learning that lasts that is represented not only by a model of the person (see figure 22.2) but also by a set of learning and action principles derived from formal research, collaborative inquiry across campus and wider consortia of institutions, review of literature and practice, and insights from educating a widely diverse student body. That work articulates ways that a community of educators may comparatively inquire into their own learning principles and educational assumptions.

This chapter has been about how individual differences in performance and development jointly relate to work, family, and citizenship, core endeavors within society. Although we have focused on quantitative evidence, we also have intended to expand both moral and practical vision, rather than limit either. We believe that appreciative and informed dialogue across sectors of society about assumptions and sources of evidence can integrate the wisdom of diverse practices and foster enduring partnerships. In these societal dialogues, judgments of effectiveness must ultimately address assumptions about moral and community purposes, even as deliberation on moral purpose must eventually be concerned with effectiveness. Herein lies the intrinsic value of integrating holistic development and multidimensional performance in higher education, the workplace, and civic society. Collective hope for transcending what now prevails, or seems achievable, can arise when moral imagination becomes further integrated with the wisdom of inquiry and practice.

References

Ackerman, P. L., & Heggestad, E. D. (1997). Intelligence, personality, and interests: Evidence for overlapping traits. *Psychological Bulletin*, 121(2), 219–245.

Adamson, T. E., Baldwin, D. C. Jr., Sheehan, T. J., & Oppenberg, A. A. (1997). Characteristics of surgeons with high and low malpractice claims rates. *Western Journal of Medicine*, 166, 37–44.

Alverno College Faculty. (1976/1992). *Liberal learning at Alverno College*. Milwaukee, WI: Alverno College Institute. (Revised 1981, 1985, 1989, and 1992.)

Alverno College Faculty. (1979/1994). *Student assessment-as-learning at Alverno College*. Milwaukee, WI: Alverno College Institute. (Revised 1985 and 1994)

Alverno College Faculty. (2000). *Self assessment at Alverno College*. (G. Loacker, Ed.). Milwaukee, WI: Alverno College Institute.

Alwin, D. F., Cohen, R. L., & Newcomb, T. M. (1991). *Political attitudes over the life span: The Bennington women after fifty years*. Madison: University of Wisconsin Press.

Armon, C. (1984). Ideals of the good life and moral judgment: Ethical reasoning across the lifespan. In M. L. Commons, F. A. Richards, & C. Armon (Eds.), *Beyond formal operations: Late adolescent and adult cognitive development* (pp. 357–381). New York: Praeger.

Armon, C., & Dawson, T. L. (1997). Developmental trajectories in moral reasoning across the life span. *Journal of Moral Education*, 26, 433–453.

Armon, C., & Dawson, T. L. (2003). The good life: A longitudinal study of adult value reasoning. In J. Demick & C. Andreoletti (Eds.), *Handbook of adult development* (pp. 271–300). New York: Plenum Press.

Arnold, D. F. Sr., & Ponemon, L. A. (1991). Internal auditors' perceptions of whistle-blowing and the influence of moral reasoning: An experiment. *Auditing: A Journal of Practice and Theory*, 10, 1–15.

Azar, S. T. (2003). Adult development and parenthood: A social-cognitive perspective. In J. Demick & C. Andreoletti (Eds.), *Handbook of adult development* (pp. 391–415). New York: Kluwer Academic.

Barrick, M. R., & Mount, M. K. (1991). The big five personality dimensions and job performance: A meta-analysis. *Personnel Psychology*, 44, 1–26.

Bartone, P., Bullis, R. C., Lewis, P., Forsythe, G. B., & Snook, S. (2001). *Psychological development and leader performance in West Point cadets*. Paper presented at the annual meeting of the American Education Research Association, Seattle, WA.

Bartunek, J. M., Gordon, J. R., & Weathersby, R. P. (1983). Developing "complicated" understanding in administrators. *Academy of Management Review*, 8, 273–284.

Bass, B. M. (1998). *Transformational leadership: Industrial, military, and educational impact*. Hillsdale, NJ: Lawrence Erlbaum.

Bass, B. M., & Avolio, B. J. (1995). *MLQ Multifactor Leadership Questionnaire for research: Permission set*. Palo Alto, CA: Mind Garden.

Bay, D. D., & Greenberg, R. R. (2001). The relationship of the DIT and behavior: A replication. *Issues in Accounting Education*, 16, 367–380.

Bebeau, M. (2002). The Defining Issues Test and the four component model: Contributions to professional education. *Journal of Moral Education*, 31, 271–295.

Belenky, M. F., Clinchy, B. M., Goldberger, N. R., & Tarule, J. M. (1986). *Women's ways of knowing: The development of self, voice, and mind*. New York: Basic Books.

Bell, D. C., & Bell, L. G. (1983). Parental validation and support in the development of adolescent daughters. In H. D. Grotevant & C. R. Cooper (Eds.), *Adolescent development in the family* (pp. 27–42). San Francisco: Jossey-Bass.

Ben-Ur, T., & Rogers, G. (1994, June). *Measuring alumna career advancement: An approach based on educational expectations*. Paper presented at the annual meeting of the Association for Institutional Research, New Orleans.

Bergem, T. (1986). Teachers' thinking and behavior: An empirical study of the role of social sensitivity and moral reasoning in the teaching performance of student teachers. *Scandinavian Journal of Educational Research*, 30, 193–203.

Blasi, A. (1980). Bridging moral cognition and moral action: A critical review of the literature. *Psychological Bulletin*, 88, 1–45.

Blasi, A. (1993). The development of identity: Some implications for moral functioning. In G. G. Noam & T. E. Wren (Eds.), *The moral self* (pp. 99–122). Cambridge, MA: MIT Press.

Blasi, A. (1998). Loevinger's theory of ego development and its relationship to the cognitive-developmental approach. In P. M. Westenberg, A. Blasi, & L. D. Cohn (Eds.), *Personality development: Theoretical, empirical, and clinical investigations of Loevinger's conception of ego development* (pp. 13–25). Mahwah, NJ: Lawrence Erlbaum.

Borders, L. D. (1989). Developmental cognitions of first practicum supervisees. *Journal of Counseling Psychology*, 36, 163–169.

Borders, L. D., & Fong, M. L. (1989). Ego development and counseling ability during training. *Counselor Education and Supervision*, 29, 71–83.

Borman, W. C., & Motowidlo, S. J. (1993). Expanding the criterion domain to include elements of contextual performance. In N. Schmitt, W. C. Borman, &

Associates (Eds.), *Personnel selection in organizations* (pp. 71–98). San Francisco: Jossey-Bass.

Bowman, J. T., & Allen, B. R. (1988). Moral development and counselor trainee empathy. *Counseling and Values, 32,* 144–146.

Bowman, J. T., & Reeves, T. G. (1987). Moral development and empathy in counseling. *Counselor Education and Supervision, 26,* 293–298.

Boyatzis, R. E. (1982). *The competent manager: A model for effective performance.* New York: Wiley.

Boyatzis, R. E., Cowen, S. S., Kolb, D. A., & Associates. (1995). *Innovation in professional education: Steps on a journey from teaching to learning.* San Francisco: Jossey-Bass.

Bradley, C. L., & Marcia, J. E. (1998). Generativity–stagnation: A five-category model. *Journal of Personality, 66,* 39–64.

Broughton, J. M., & Zahaykevich, M. K. (1988). Ego and ideology: A critical review of Loevinger's theory. In D. K. Lapsley & F. C. Power (Eds.), *Self, ego, and identity: Integrative approaches* (pp. 179–208). New York: Springer-Verlag.

Campion, M. A., Campion, J. E., & Hudson, J. P. Jr. (1994). Structured interviewing: A note on incremental validity and alternative question types. *Journal of Applied Psychology, 79,* 998–1002.

Carlozzi, A. F., Gaa, J. P., & Liberman, D. B. (1983). Empathy and ego development. *Journal of Counseling Psychology, 30,* 113–116.

Cartwright, C. C., & Simpson, T. L. (1990). The relationship of moral judgment development and teaching effectiveness of student teachers. *Education, 111,* 139–144.

Cavanaugh, S. H. (2002). Professional caring in the curriculum. In G. R. Norman, C. P. M. van der Vleuten, & D. I. Newble (Eds.), *International handbook of research in medical education: Part two* (pp. 981–996). Norwell, MA: Kluwer Academic.

Chan, D., & Schmitt, N. (2002). Situational judgment and job performance. *Human Performance, 15,* 233–254.

Chang, F.-Y. (1994). School teachers' moral reasoning. In J. R. Rest & D. Narváez (Eds.), *Moral development in the professions: Psychology and applied ethics* (pp. 71–84). Hillsdale, NJ: Lawrence Erlbaum.

Cohn, L. D. (1998). Age trends in personality development: A quantitative review. In P. M. Westenberg, A. Blasi, & L. D. Cohn (Eds.), *Personality development: Theoretical, empirical, and clinical investigations of Loevinger's conception of ego development* (pp. 133–143). Mahwah, NJ: Lawrence Erlbaum.

Colby, A., & Damon, W. (1992). *Some do care: Contemporary lives of moral commitment.* New York: Free Press.

Colby, A., Ehrlich, T., Beaumont, E., & Stephens, J. (2003). *Educating citizens: Preparing America's undergraduates for lives of moral and civic responsibility.* San Francisco: Jossey-Bass.

Colby, A., & Kohlberg, L. (in collaboration with Abrahami, A., Gibbs, J., Higgins, A., Kauffman, K., et al.). (1987). *The measurement of moral judgment: Vol. 1. Theoretical foundations and research validation.* New York: Cambridge University Press.

Commons, M. L., Krause, S. R., Fayer, G. A., & Meaney, M. (1993). Atmosphere and stage development in the workplace. In J. Demick & P. M. Miller, *Development in the workplace* (pp. 199–218). Hillsdale, NJ: Lawrence Erlbaum.

Commons, M. L., & Richards, F. A. (with Ruf, F. J., Armstrong-Roche, M., & Bretzius, S.). (1984). A general model of stage theory. In M. L. Commons, F. A. Richards, & C. Armon (Eds.), *Beyond formal operations: Late adolescent and adult cognitive development* (pp. 120–140). New York: Praeger.

Conway, J. M. (1999). Distinguishing contextual performance from task performance for managerial jobs. *Journal of Applied Psychology, 84,* 3–13.

Cushing, A. (2002). Assessment of non-cognitive factors. In G. R. Norman, C. P. M. van der Vleuten, & D. I. Newble (Eds.), *International handbook of research in medical education: Part two* (pp. 711–755). Norwell, MA: Kluwer Academic.

Dawson, T. L. (2002). A comparison of three developmental stage scoring systems. *Journal of Applied Measurement, 3,* 146–189.

DeBack, V., & Mentkowski, M. (1986). Does the baccalaureate make a difference?: Differentiating nurse performance by education and experience. *Journal of Nursing Education, 25,* 275–285.

Demetriou, A. (2002). Tracing psychology's invisible giant and its visible guards. In R. J. Sternberg & E. L. Grigorenko, *The general factor of intelligence: How general is it?* (pp. 3–18). Mahwah, NJ: Lawrence Erlbaum.

de Vries, B., & Walker, L. J. (1986). Moral reasoning and attitudes toward capital punishment. *Developmental Psychology, 22,* 509–513.

Dixon, R. A., & Baltes, P. B. (1986). Toward life-span research on the functions and pragmatics of intelligence. In R. J. Sternberg & R. K. Wagner (Eds.), *Practical intelligence: Nature and origins of competence in the everyday world* (pp. 203–235). New York: Cambridge University Press.

Duckett, L. J., & Ryden, M. B. (1994). Education for ethical nursing practice. In J. R. Rest & D. Narváez (Eds.), *Moral development in the professions: Psychology and applied ethics* (pp. 51–70). Hillsdale, NJ: Lawrence Erlbaum.

Duval, S., & Wicklund, R. A. (1972). *A theory of objective self awareness.* New York: Academic Press.

Einstein, D., & Lanning, K. (1998). Shame, guilt, ego development, and the five-factor model of personality. *Journal of Personality, 66,* 555–582.

Erikson, E. H. (1969). *Gandhi's truth: On the origins of militant nonviolence.* New York: Norton.

Ewell, P. T. (2002). An emerging scholarship: A brief history of assessment. In T. W. Banta & Associates,

Building a scholarship of assessment (pp. 3–25). San Francisco: Jossey-Bass.

Fiedler, F. E. (2002). The curious role of cognitive resources in leadership. In R. E. Riggio, S. E. Murphy, & F. J. Pirozzolo (Eds.), *Multiple intelligences and leadership* (pp. 91–104). Mahwah, NJ: Lawrence Erlbaum.

Fisher, D., Merron, K., & Torbert, W. R. (1987). Human development and managerial effectiveness. *Group and Organization Studies, 12,* 257–273.

Fisher, D., & Torbert, W. R. (1995). *Personal and organizational transformations: The true challenge of continual quality improvement.* London: McGraw-Hill.

Fromm, E. (1947). *Man for himself: An inquiry into the psychology of ethics.* New York: Fawcett.

Gardner, H., Csikszentmihalyi, M., & Damon, W. (2001). *Good work: When excellence and ethics meet.* New York: Basic Books.

George, J. H. (1997). Moral development during surgical residency training. In A. J. J. A. Scherpbier, C. P. M. van der Vleuten, J. J. Rethans, & A. F. W. van der Steeg (Eds.), *Advances in medical education* (pp. 747–748). Dordrecht, Netherlands: Kluwer Academic.

George, J. H., & Skeel, J. (2003, April). *Moral problems in residency training.* Paper presented at the annual meeting of the American Educational Research Association, Chicago.

Gilligan, C. (1982). *In a different voice: Psychological theory and women's development.* Cambridge, MA: Harvard University Press.

Goldhaber, D. E. (2000). *Theories of human development: Integrative perspectives.* Mountain View, CA: Mayfield.

Haan, N., Smith, M. B., & Block, J. (1968). Moral reasoning of young adults: Political-social behavior, family background, and personality correlates. *Journal of Personality and Social Psychology, 10,* 183–201.

Hart, D., & Chmiel, S. (1992). Influence of defense mechanisms on moral judgment development: A longitudinal study. *Developmental Psychology, 28,* 722–730.

Harvey, O. J., Hunt, D. E., & Schroder, H. M. (1961). *Conceptual systems and personality organization.* New York: Wiley.

Harvey, O. J., Prather, M., White, B. J., & Hoffmeister, J. K. (1968). Teachers' beliefs, classroom atmosphere and student behavior. *American Educational Research Journal, 5,* 151–166.

Harvey, O. J., White, B. J., Prather, M. S., Alter, R. D., & Hoffmeister, J. K. (1966). Teachers' belief systems and preschool atmospheres. *Journal of Educational Psychology, 57,* 373–381.

Hauser, S. T., Powers, S. I., Noam, G. G., Jacobson, A. M., Weiss, B., & Follansbee, D. J. (1984). Familial contexts of adolescent ego development. *Child Development, 55,* 195–213.

Helkama, K., Uutela, A., Pohjanheimo, E., Salminen, S., Koponen, A., & Rantanen-Väntsi, L. (2003). Moral reasoning and values in medical school: A longitudinal study in Finland. *Scandinavian Journal of Educational Research, 47,* 399–411.

Helson, R., Kwan, V. S. Y., John, O. P., & Jones, C. (2002). The growing evidence for personality change in adulthood: Findings from research with personality inventories. *Journal of Research in Personality, 36,* 287–306.

Helson, R., & Wink, P. (1987). Two conceptions of maturity examined in the findings of a longitudinal study. *Journal of Personality and Social Psychology, 53,* 531–541.

Hofer, B. K., & Pintrich, P. R. (1997). The development of epistemological theories: Beliefs about knowledge and knowing and their relation to learning. *Review of Educational Research 67,* 88–140.

Hofer, B. K., & Pintrich, P. R. (Eds.). (2002). *Personal epistemology: The psychology of beliefs about knowledge and knowing.* Mahwah, NJ: Lawrence Erlbaum.

Hogan, J., & Holland, B. (2003). Using theory to evaluate personality and job-performance relations: A socioanalytic perspective. *Journal of Applied Psychology, 88,* 100–112.

Hogansen, J., & Lanning, K. (2001). Five factors in Sentence Completion Test categories: Toward rapprochement between trait and maturational approaches to personality. *Journal of Research in Personality, 35,* 449–462.

Holland, J. L. (1985). *Making vocational choices: A theory of careers.* Englewood Cliffs, NJ: Prentice Hall.

Holloway, E. L., & Wampold, B. E. (1986). Relation between conceptual level and counseling-related tasks: A meta-analysis. *Journal of Counseling Psychology, 33,* 310–319.

Huffcutt, A. I., Roth, P. L., & McDaniel, M. A. (1996). A meta-analytic investigation of cognitive ability in employment interview evaluations: Moderating characteristics and implications for incremental validity. *Journal of Applied Psychology, 81,* 459–473.

Huffcutt, A. I., Weekley, J. A., Wiesner, W. H., Degroot, T. G., & Jones, C. (2001). Comparison of situational and behavior description interview questions for higher-level positions. *Personnel Psychology, 54,* 619–644.

Hunt, D. E. (1971). *Matching models in education: The coordination of teaching methods with student characteristics.* Ontario: Ontario Institute for Studies in Education.

Hunt, D. E., & Joyce, B. R. (1967). Teacher trainee personality and initial teaching style. *American Educational Research Journal, 4,* 253–260.

Hunt, E. (1995). *Will we be smart enough? A cognitive analysis of the coming workforce.* New York: Russell Sage.

Hurtz, G. M., & Donovan, J. J. (2000). Personality and job performance: The big five revisited. *Journal of Applied Psychology, 85,* 869–879.

Hy, L. X., & Loevinger, J. (1996). *Measuring ego development* (2nd ed.). Mahwah, NJ: Lawrence Erlbaum.

James, W. (1890/1962). *Psychology: Briefer course.* New York: Collier Books. (Original work published 1890)

Johnson, J. W. (2001). The relative importance of task and contextual performance dimensions to supervisor judgments of overall performance. *Journal of Applied Psychology, 86,* 984–996.

Josephson, J. S. (1988). Feminine orientation as a mediator of moral judgment. *Dissertation Abstracts International, 50,* 751.

Josselson, R. (1998) On becoming the same age as one's mother: Ego development and the growth of subject-subject relationship. In P. M. Westenberg, A. Blasi, & L. D. Cohn (Eds.), *Personality development: Theoretical, empirical, and clinical investigations of Loevinger's conception of ego development* (pp. 237–249). Mahwah, NJ: Lawrence Erlbaum.

Joyce, B., & Showers, B. (1995). *Student achievement through staff development: Fundamentals of school renewal* (2nd ed.). White Plains, NY: Longman.

Judge, T. A., & Bono, J. E. (2000). Five-factor model of personality and transformational leadership. *Journal of Applied Psychology, 85,* 751–765.

Judge, T. A., Bono, J. E., Ilies, R., & Gerhardt, M. W. (2002). Personality and leadership: A qualitative and quantitative review. *Journal of Applied Psychology, 87,* 765–780.

Kegan, R. (1994). *In over our heads: The mental demands of modern life.* Cambridge, MA: Harvard University Press.

Kickul, J., & Neuman, G. (2000). Emergent leadership behaviors: The function of personality and cognitive ability in determining teamwork performance and KSAs. *Journal of Business and Psychology, 15,* 27–51.

King, P. M., & Kitchener, K. S. (1994). *Developing reflective judgment: Understanding and promoting intellectual growth and critical thinking in adolescents and adults.* San Francisco: Jossey-Bass.

King, P. M., Kitchener, K. S., Wood, P. K., & Davison, M. L. (1989). Relationships across developmental domains: A longitudinal study of intellectual, moral, and ego development. In M. L. Commons, J. D. Sinnott, F. A. Richards, & C. Armon (Eds.), *Adult development: Vol. 1. Comparisons and applications of developmental models* (pp. 57–72). New York: Praeger.

Klemp, G. O. Jr. (2001). Competence in context: Identifying core skills for the future. In J. Raven & J. Stephenson (Eds.), *Competence in the learning society* (pp. 129–147). New York: Peter Lang.

Klemp, G. O. Jr., & McClelland, D. C. (1986). What characterizes intelligent functioning among senior managers? In R. J. Sternberg & R. K. Wagner (Eds.), *Practical intelligence: Nature and origins of competence in the everyday world* (pp. 31–50). New York: Cambridge University Press.

Knefelkamp, L., & Widick, C. (1982). *The measure of intellectual development.* College Park: University of Maryland, College Park, Center for Applications of Developmental Instruction.

Kohlberg, L. (1984). *Essays on moral development: Vol. 2. The psychology of moral development.* San Francisco: Harper & Row.

Kohn, M. L., & Schooler, C. (1982). Job conditions and personality: A longitudinal assessment of their reciprocal effects. *American Journal of Sociology, 87,* 1257–1286.

Kohn, M. L., & Schooler, C. (in collaboration with Miller, J., Miller, K. A., Schoenbach, C., & Schoenberg, R.). (1983). *Work and personality: An inquiry into the impact of social stratification.* Norwood, NJ: Ablex.

Labouvie Vief, G., Chiodo, L. M., Goguen, L. A., Diehl, M., & Orwoll, L. (1995). Representations of self across the life span. *Psychology and Aging, 10,* 404–415.

Labouvie-Vief, G., & Diehl, M. (2000). Cognitive complexity and cognitive-affective integration: Related or separate domains of adult development? *Psychology and Aging, 15,* 490–504.

Laird, P. G. (2003). Bridging the divide: The role of perceived control in mediating reasoning and activism. *Journal of Moral Education, 32,* 35–49.

Laske, O. E. (2003). Executive development as adult development. In J. Demick & C. Andreoletti (Eds.), *Handbook of adult development* (pp. 565–584). New York: Kluwer Academic.

Lave, J., & Wenger, E. (1991). *Situated learning: Legitimate peripheral participation.* New York: Cambridge University Press.

LePine, J. A., Colquitt, J. A., & Erez, A. (2000). Adaptability to changing task contexts: Effects of general cognitive ability, conscientiousness, and openness to experience. *Personnel Psychology, 53,* 563–593.

Lievens, F., Harris, M. M., Van Keer, E., & Bisqueret, C. (2003). Predicting cross-cultural training performance: The validity of personality, cognitive ability, and dimensions measured by an assessment center and a behavior description interview. *Journal of Applied Psychology, 88,* 476–489.

Lind, G. (1998). Moral regression in medical students and their learning environment [Electronic version]. *Revista Brasileira de Educacao Médica 24,* 24–33. Retrieved July 23, 2003, from http://www.uni-konstanz.de/ag-moral/b-liste.htm#Education.

Loevinger, J. (1987). *Paradigms of personality.* New York: Freeman.

Loevinger, J. (1998a). The place of the WUSCT for ego development in personality measurement. In J. Loevinger (Ed.), *Technical foundations for measuring ego development: The Washington University Sentence Completion Test* (pp. 77–80). Mahwah, NJ: Lawrence Erlbaum.

Loevinger, J. (1998b). Reliability and validity of the SCT. In J. Loevinger (Ed.), *Technical foundations for measuring ego development: The Washington University Sentence Completion Test* (pp. 29–39). Mahwah, NJ: Lawrence Erlbaum.

Loevinger, J., & Wessler, R. (1970). *Measuring ego development: Vol. 1. Construction and use of a sentence completion test*. San Francisco: Jossey-Bass.

Loevinger, J., Wessler, R., & Redmore, C. (1970). *Measuring ego development: Vol. 2. Scoring manual for women and girls*. San Francisco: Jossey-Bass.

Maccallum, J. A. (1993). Teacher reasoning and moral judgement in the context of student discipline situations. *Journal of Moral Education, 22*, 3–17.

Markakis, K. M., Beckman, H. B., Suchman, A. L., & Frankel, R. M. (2000). The path to professionalism: Cultivating humanistic values and attitudes in residency training. *Academic Medicine, 75*, 141–150.

McAdams, D. P. (1998) Ego, trait, identity. In P. M. Westenberg, A. Blasi, & L. D. Cohn (Eds.), *Personality development: Theoretical, empirical, and clinical investigations of Loevinger's conception of ego development* (pp. 27–38). Mahwah, NJ: Lawrence Erlbaum.

McAdams, D. P., Ruetzel, K., & Foley, J. M. (1986). Complexity and generativity at mid-life: Relations among social motives, ego development, and adults' plans for the future. *Journal of Personality and Social Psychology, 50*, 800–807.

McClelland, D. C. (1961). *The achieving society*. Princeton, NJ: Van Nostrand. (Reissued with a new preface, New York: Irvington, 1976.)

McClelland, D. C. (1978). *Behavioral Event Interview*. Boston: McBer.

McClelland, D. C. (1985). How motives, skills, and values determine what people do. *American Psychologist, 40*, 812–825.

McClelland, D. C. (1987). *Human motivation*. New York: Cambridge University Press.

McCormack, L., & Mellor, D. (2002). The role of personality in leadership: An application of the five-factor model in the Australian military. *Military Psychology, 14*, 179–197.

McCrae, R. R., & Costa, P. T. Jr. (1980). Openness to experience and ego level in Loevinger's Sentence Completion Test: Dispositional contributions to developmental models of personality. *Journal of Personality and Social Psychology, 39*, 1179–1190.

McCrae, R. R., Costa, P. T. Jr., de Lima, M. P., Simões, A., Ostendorf, F., Angleitner, A., et al. (1999). Age differences in personality across the adult life span: Parallels in five cultures. *Developmental Psychology, 35*, 466–477.

McDaniel, M. A., Whetzel, D. L., Schmidt, F. L, & Maurer, S. D. (1994). The validity of employment interviews: A comprehensive review and meta-analysis. *Journal of Applied Psychology, 79*, 599–616.

McGuire, C. H. (1993). Sociocultural changes affecting professions and professionals. In L. Curry, J. F. Wergin, & Associates, *Educating professionals: Responding to new expectations for competence and accountability* (pp. 3–16). San Francisco: Jossey-Bass.

McNeel, S. P. (1994). College teaching and student moral development. In J. R. Rest & D. Narváez (Eds.), *Moral development in the professions: Psychology and applied ethics* (pp. 27–49). Hillsdale, NJ: Lawrence Erlbaum.

McNergney, R., & Satterstrom, L. (1984). Teacher characteristics and teacher performance. *Contemporary Educational Psychology, 9*, 19–24.

Mentkowski, M. (1988). Paths to integrity: Educating for personal growth and professional performance. In S. Srivastva & Associates, *Executive integrity: The search for high human values in organizational life* (pp. 89–121). San Francisco: Jossey-Bass.

Mentkowski, M., & Associates. (2000). *Learning that lasts: Integrating learning, development, and performance in college and beyond*. San Francisco: Jossey-Bass.

Mentkowski, M., Moeser, M., & Strait, M. (1983). *Using the Perry scheme of intellectual and ethical development as a college outcomes measure: A process and criteria for judging student performance* (vols. 1 and 2). Milwaukee, WI: Alverno Productions.

Mentkowski, M., Much, N., Kleinman, L., & Reisetter Hart, J. (1998). *Student and alumna learning in college and beyond: Perspectives from longitudinal interviews*. Milwaukee, Wis.: Alverno College Institute.

Merron, K., Fisher, D., & Torbert, W. R. (1987). Meaning making and management action. *Group and Organization Studies, 12*, 274–286.

Miller, A. (1981). Conceptual matching models and interactional research in education. *Review of Educational Research, 51*, 33–84.

Miller, J., Schooler, C., Kohn, M. L., & Miller, K. A. (1983). Women and work: The psychological effects of occupational conditions. In M. L. Kohn & C. Schooler, *Work and personality: An inquiry into the impact of social stratification* (pp. 195–216). Norwood, NJ: Ablex.

Motowidlo, S. J., Borman, W. C., & Schmit, M. J. (1997). A theory of individual differences in task and contextual performance. *Human Performance, 10*, 71–83.

Motowidlo, S. J., & Van Scotter, J. R. (1994). Evidence that task performance should be distinguished from contextual performance. *Journal of Applied Psychology, 79*, 475–480.

Mount, M. K., Barrick, M. R., & Stewart, G. L. (1998). Five-factor model of personality and performance in jobs involving interpersonal interactions. *Human Performance, 11*, 145–165.

Murphy, P. D., & Brown, M. M. (1970). Conceptual systems and teaching styles. *American Educational Research Journal, 7*, 529–540.

Newman, D. L., Tellegen, A., & Bouchard, T. J. Jr. (1998). Individual differences in adult ego development: Sources of influence in twins reared apart. *Journal of Personality and Social Psychology, 74*, 985–995.

Noam, G. G. (1993). "Normative vulnerabilities" of self and their transformations in moral action. In

G. G. Noam & T. E. Wren (Eds.), *The moral self* (pp. 209–238). Cambridge, MA: MIT Press.

Osofsky, J. D., & Hunt, D. E. (1972). Personality correlates of parental teaching behavior. *Journal of Genetic Psychology, 121,* 3–10.

Patenaude, J., Niyonsenga, T., & Fafard, D. (2003). Changes in students' moral development during medical school: A cohort study. *Canadian Medical Association Journal, 168,* 840–844.

Pepper, S. C. (1970). *World hypotheses: A study in evidence.* Berkeley: University of California Press.

Perry, W. G. Jr. (1970). *Forms of intellectual and ethical development in the college years: A scheme.* New York: Holt, Rinehart & Winston.

Ponemon, L. A. (1990). Ethical judgments in accounting: A cognitive-developmental perspective. *Critical Perspectives on Accounting, 1,* 191–215.

Ponemon, L. A. (1992a). Auditor underreporting of time and moral reasoning: An experimental lab study. *Contemporary Accounting Research, 9,* 171–189.

Ponemon, L. A. (1992b). Ethical reasoning and selection-socialization in accounting. *Accounting, Organizations and Society, 17,* 239–258.

Ponemon, L. A. (1993a). Can ethics be taught in accounting? *Journal of Accounting Education, 11,* 185–209.

Ponemon, L. A. (1993b). The influence of ethical reasoning on auditors' perceptions of management's competence and integrity. *Advances in Accounting, 11,* 1–29.

Ponemon, L. A., & Gabhart, D. R. L. (1990). Auditor independence judgments: A cognitive-developmental model and experimental evidence. *Contemporary Accounting Research, 7,* 227–251.

Ponemon, L. A., & Gabhart, D. R. L. (1993). *Ethical reasoning in accounting and auditing.* Vancouver: Canadian General Accountants' Research Foundation.

Ponemon, L. A., & Gabhart, D. R. L. (1994). Ethical reasoning research in the accounting and auditing professions. In J. R. Rest & D. Narváez (Eds.), *Moral development in the professions: Psychology and applied ethics* (pp. 101–119). Hillsdale, NJ: Lawrence Erlbaum.

Ponemon, L. A., & Glazer, A. (1990). Accounting education and ethical development: The influence of liberal learning on students and alumni in accounting practice. *Issues in Accounting Education, 5,* 21–34.

Pratt, M. W., Diessner, R., Pratt, A., Hunsberger, B., & Pancer, S. M. (1996). Moral and social reasoning and perspective taking in later life: A longitudinal study. *Psychology and Aging, 11,* 66–73.

Pratt, M. W., Hunsberger, B., Pancer, S. M., Roth, D., & Santolupo, S. (1993). Thinking about parenting: Reasoning about developmental issues across the life span. *Developmental Psychology, 29,* 585–595.

Pratt, M. W., Norris, J. E., Arnold, M. L., & Filyer, R. (1999). Generativity and moral development as predictors of value-socialization narratives for young persons across the adult life span: From lessons learned to stories shared. *Psychology and Aging, 14,* 414–426.

Pressley, M., Borkowski, J. G., & Schneider, W. (1987). Cognitive strategies: Good strategy users coordinate metacognition and knowledge. In R. Vasta (Ed.), *Annals of child development* (Vol. 4, pp. 89–129). Greenwich, CT: JAI.

PricewaterhouseCoopers. (2003). *Educating for the public trust: The PricewaterhouseCoopers position on accounting education.* New York: PricewaterhouseCoopers.

Putnam, R. D. (1995). Bowling alone: America's declining social capital. *Journal of Democracy, 6,* 65–78.

Reiman, A. J. (2001, April). *A four-year longitudinal study of principled judgment reasoning in teacher education students.* Paper presented at the annual meeting of the American Education Research Association, Seattle, WA.

Reiman, A. J., & Thies-Sprinthall, L. (1998). *Mentoring and supervision for teacher development.* New York: Longman.

Renner, J., Fuller, R., Lochhead, J., John, J., Tomlinson-Keasey, G., & Campbell, T. (1976). *Test of cognitive development.* Norman: University of Oklahoma Press.

Rest, J. R. (1979). *Revised manual for the Defining Issues Test: An objective test of moral judgment development.* Minneapolis: Minnesota Moral Research Projects.

Rest, J. R. (1986). *Moral development: Advances in research and theory.* New York: Praeger.

Rest, J., Narváez, D., Bebeau, M. J., & Thoma, S. J. (1999). *Postconventional moral thinking: A neo-Kohlbergian approach.* Mahwah, NJ: Lawrence Erlbaum.

Roberts, B. W., & DelVecchio, W. F. (2000). The rank-order consistency of personality traits from childhood to old age: A quantitative review of longitudinal studies. *Psychological Bulletin, 126,* 3–25.

Rogers, G. (1999, April). Learning through curriculum abilities: College learning at work. In M. Eraut (Chair), *Professional learning in the workplace.* Paper presented in a symposium at the annual meeting of the American Educational Research Association, Montreal. Milwaukee, WI: Alverno College Institute.

Rogers, G. (2002). Rethinking moral growth in college and beyond. *Journal of Moral Education, 31,* 325–338.

Rogers, G., & Mentkowski, M. (2004). Abilities that distinguish the effectiveness of five-year alumna performance across work, family, and civic roles: A higher education validation. *Higher Education Research and Development, 23*(3), 347–374.

Rogers, G., Mentkowski, M., Reisetter Hart, J., & Schwan Minik, K. (2001, April). *Disentangling related domains of moral, cognitive, and ego development.* Paper presented at the annual meeting of the American Educational Research Association, Seattle, WA.

Rooke, D., & Torbert, W. R. (1998). Organizational transformation as a function of CEO's developmental stage. *Organizational Development Journal, 16,* 11–28.

Russ-Eft, D., & Brennan, K. (2001). Leadership competencies: A study of leaders at every level in an organization. In J. Raven & J. Stephenson (Eds.), *Competence in the learning society* (pp. 79–91). New York: Peter Lang.

Salgado, J. F. (1997). The five factor model of personality and job performance in the European community. *Journal of Applied Psychology, 82,* 30–43.

Samson, G. E., Graue, M. E., Weinstein, T., & Walberg, H. J. (1984). Academic and occupational performance: A quantitative synthesis. *American Educational Research Journal, 21,* 311–321.

Sanders, C. E., Lubinski, D., & Persson Benbow, C. (1995). Does the Defining Issues Test measure psychological phenomena distinct from verbal ability? An examination of Lykken's query. *Journal of Personality and Social Psychology, 69,* 498–504.

Schmidt, F. L., & Hunter, J. E. (1998). The validity and utility of selection methods in personnel psychology: Practical and theoretical implications of 85 years of research findings. *Psychological Bulletin, 124,* 262–274.

Schommer, M. (1998). The role of adults' beliefs about knowledge in school, work, and everyday life. In M. C. Smith & T. Pourchot, *Adult learning and development: Perspectives from educational psychology* (pp. 127–143). Mahwah, NJ: Lawrence Erlbaum.

Schön, D. A. (1983). *The reflective practitioner: How professionals think in action.* New York: Basic Books.

Schön, D. A. (1987). *Educating the reflective practitioner: Toward a new design for teaching and learning in the professions.* San Francisco: Jossey-Bass.

Schroder, H. M., Driver, M. J., & Streufert, S. (1967). *Human information processing: Individuals and groups functioning in complex social situations.* New York: Holt, Rinehart & Winston.

Scullen, S. E., Mount, M. K., & Goff, M. (2000). Understanding the latent structure of job performance ratings. *Journal of Applied Psychology, 85,* 956–970.

Self, D. J., & Olivarez, M. (1996). Retention of moral reasoning skills over the four years of medical education. *Teaching and Learning in Medicine, 8,* 195–199.

Self, D. J., Schrader, D. E., Baldwin, D. C. Jr., & Wolinsky, F. D. (1993). The moral development of medical students: A pilot study of the possible influence of medical education. *Medical Education, 27,* 26–34.

Senge, P. M. (1990). *The fifth discipline: The art and practice of the learning organization.* New York: Doubleday/Currency.

Shaub, M. K. (1994). An analysis of the association of traditional demographic variables with the moral reasoning of auditing students and auditors. *Journal of Accounting Education, 12,* 1–26.

Sheehan, T. J., Candee, D., Willms, J., Donnelly, J. C., & Husted, S. D. R. (1985). Structural equation models of moral reasoning and physician performance. *Evaluation and the Health Professions, 8,* 379–400.

Sheehan, T. J., Husted, S. D. R., Candee, D., Cook, C. D., & Bargen, M. (1980). Moral judgment as a predictor of clinical performance. *Evaluation and the Health Professions, 3,* 393–404.

Sisola, S. W. (2000). Moral reasoning as a predictor of clinical practice: The development of physical therapy students across the professional curriculum. *Journal of Physical Therapy Education, 14,* 26–34.

Skoe, E. E. A., & von der Lippe, A. L. (2002). Ego development and the ethics of care and justice: The relations among them revisited. *Journal of Personality, 70,* 485–508.

Smith, C. P. (Ed.) (with Atkinson, J. W., McClelland, D. C., & Veroff, J.). (1992). *Motivation and personality: Handbook of thematic content analysis.* New York: Cambridge University Press.

Spector, P. E., Schneider, J. R., Vance, C. A., & Hezlett, S. A. (2000). The relation of cognitive ability and personality traits to assessment center performance. *Journal of Applied Social Psychology, 30,* 1474–1491.

Spencer, L. M. Jr., & Spencer, S. M. (1993). *Competence at work: Models for superior performance.* New York: Wiley.

Sternberg, R. J. (2002). Successful intelligence: A new approach to leadership. In R. E. Riggio, S. E. Murphy, & F. J. Pirozzolo (Eds.), *Multiple intelligences and leadership* (pp. 9–28). Mahwah, NJ: Lawrence Erlbaum.

Sternberg, R. J., Forsythe, G. B., Hedlund, J., Horvath, J. A., Wagner, R. K., Williams, W. M., et al. (2000). *Practical intelligence in everyday life.* New York: Cambridge University Press.

Sternberg, R. J., & Hedlund, J. (2002). Practical intelligence, g, and work psychology. *Human Performance, 15,* 143–160.

Stewart, D. W., Sprinthall, N., & Siemienska, R. (1997). Ethical reasoning in a time of revolution: A study of local officials in Poland. *Public Administration Review, 57,* 445–453.

Strohmer, D. C., Biggs, D. A., Haase, R. F., & Purcell, M. J. (1983). Training counselors to work with disabled clients: Cognitive and affective components. *Counselor Education and Supervision, 23,* 132–141.

Suedfeld, P., & Coren, S. (1992). Cognitive correlates of conceptual complexity. *Personality and Individual Differences, 13,* 1193–1199.

Sullivan, E. V., McCullough, G., & Stager, M. (1970). A developmental study of the relationship between conceptual, ego, and moral development. *Child Development, 41,* 399–411.

Tett, R. P., Jackson, D. N., & Rothstein, M. (1991). Personality measures as predictors of job performance: A meta-analytic review. *Personnel Psychology, 44,* 703–742.

Thoma, S. (1994). Moral judgments and moral action. In J. R. Rest & D. Narváez (Eds.), *Moral development in the professions: Psychology and applied ethics* (pp. 199–211). Hillsdale, NJ: Lawrence Erlbaum.

Thoma, S. J., & Rest, J. (1987). Moral sensitivity and judgment in the development and performance of student teachers. *Moral Education Forum, 12,* 15–20.

Thoma, S. J., & Rest, J. (with Barnett, R.). (1986). Moral judgment, behavior, decision making, and attitudes. In J. R. Rest (Ed.), *Moral development: Advances in research and theory* (pp. 133–175). New York: Praeger.

Turner, N., Barling, J., Epitropaki, O., Butcher, V., & Milner, C. (2002). Transformational leadership and moral reasoning. *Journal of Applied Psychology, 87,* 304–311.

Vaillant, G. E. (1977). *Adaptation to life.* Boston: Little, Brown.

Vaillant, G. E. (1993). *The wisdom of the ego.* Cambridge, MA: Harvard University Press.

Vaillant, G. E., & McCullough, L. (1987). The Washington University Sentence Completion Test compared with other measures of adult ego development. *American Journal of Psychiatry, 144,* 1189–1194.

Vaillant, G. E., & Vaillant, C. O. (1990). Determinants and consequences of creativity in a cohort of gifted women. *Psychology of Women Quarterly, 14,* 607–616.

Van Scotter, J. R., & Motowidlo, S. J. (1996). Interpersonal facilitation and job dedication as separate facets of contextual performance. *Journal of Applied Psychology, 81,* 525–531.

Viswesvaran, C., & Ones, D. S. (2002). Agreements and disagreements on the role of general mental ability (GMA) in industrial, work, and organizational psychology. *Human Performance, 15,* 211–231.

Wagner, R. K., & Sternberg, R. J. (1990). Street smarts. In K. E. Clark & M. B. Clark (Eds.), *Measures of leadership* (pp. 493–504). West Orange, NJ: Leadership Library of America.

Walker, L. J., Hennig, K. H., & Krettenauer, T. (2000). Parent and peer contexts for children's moral reasoning development. *Child Development, 71,* 1033–1048.

Walker, L. J., & Taylor, J. H. (1991). Family interactions and the development of moral reasoning. *Child Development, 62,* 264–283.

Walter, S. A., & Stivers, E. (1977). The relation of student teachers' classroom behavior and Eriksonian ego identity. *Journal of Teacher Education, 28,* 47–50.

Watson, G., & Glaser, E. M. (1964). *Critical Thinking Appraisal* (Manual for Forms YM and ZM). Orlando, FL: Harcourt Brace.

Werner, H. (1957). The concept of development from a comparative and organismic point of view. In D. B. Harris (Ed.), *The concept of development: An issue in the study of human behavior* (pp. 125–148). Minneapolis: University of Minnesota Press.

Westenberg, P. M., & Block, J. (1993). Ego development and individual differences in personality. *Journal of Personality and Social Psychology, 65,* 792–800.

White, M. S. (1985). Ego development in adult women. *Journal of Personality, 53,* 561–574.

Author Index

Subject Index